# CHRONOLOGICAL HISTORY OF U.S. FOREIGN RELATIONS

# CHRONOLOGICAL HISTORY OF U.S. FOREIGN RELATIONS

## Volume II
## 1932–1988

by Lester H. Brune

Richard Dean Burns, Consulting Editor

Routledge
Taylor & Francis Group

NEW YORK AND LONDON

**Editorial Staff:**
Laura Kathleen Smid, *Project Editor*
Jeanne Shu, *Senior Production Editor*
Edward Cone, *Copyeditor*
Cynthia Crippen and Melanie Belkin, *Indexers*
Dennis Teston, *Production Director*
Jennifer Crisp, *Cover Designer*
Indiana University Graphic Services, *Cartographer*
Kate Aker, *Director of Development*
Sylvia K. Miller, *Publishing Director, Reference*

Published in 2003 by
Routledge
29 West 35th Street
New York, NY 10001
www.routledge-ny.com

Published in Great Britain by
Routledge
11 New Fetter Lane
London EC4P 4EE
www.routledge.co.uk

10  9  8  7  6  5  4  3  2  1

Library of Congress Cataloging-in-Publication Data

Brune, Lester H.
    [Chronological history of United States foreign relations]
    Chronological history of U.S. foreign relations / by Lester H. Brune ; Richard
Dean Burns, consulting editor.
        p. cm.
    Rev. ed. of: Chronological history of United States foreign relations. New York :
Garland, 1985–1991.
    Includes bibliographical references and index.
    Contents: v. 1. 1607–1932 – v. 2. 1933–1988 – v. 3. 1989–2000.
    ISBN 0-415-93914-3 (set : alk. paper) – ISBN 0-415-93915-1 (vol. 1 : alk. paper) –
ISBN 0-415-93916-X (vol. 2 : alk. paper) – ISBN 0-415-93917-8 (vol. 3 : alk. paper)
    1. United States—Foreign relations—Chronology. I. Burns, Richard Dean. II. Title.

E183.7 .B745 2002
327.73′002′02—dc21
                                                                          2002023693

Printed on acid-free, 250-year-life paper
Manufactured in the United States of America

# Contents

# XII.  FRANKLIN D. ROOSEVELT AND WORLD WAR II
## *The Failure of Neutrality*

# 1933

### January 30, 1933

***Adolf Hitler, leader of the Nazi Party, is appointed Chancellor of the German government.***

In Germany, the Great Depression posed grave dangers for the fledgling Weimar Republic's government. Both the National Socialist (NAZI) Party and the Communist Party attacked the republic's policies as well as each other. Republican leaders attempted to fulfill the cooperative policies represented by the League of Nations and other international conferences of the 1920s. The radical left and reactionary right groups advocated abandonment of the Treaty of Versailles and blamed all the subsequent shattering consequences on the Allies' unjust punishment of Germany since 1919.

When the economic collapse in America ended the illusion of German prosperity, which had been based on U.S. loans, the plight of the republic multiplied. During the Reichstag (Parliamentary) elections of September 14, 1930, the National Socialists emerged as a major party, increasing their previous 12 seats to 107. On the left, the Socialists retained their 143 seats. The moderate center parties, the mainstay of the republic, lost nearly 100 seats. In presidential elections on March 13, 1932, Hitler received 11,300,000 votes, the Communist Ernst Thalmann, 4,983,341, and President Paul von Hindenburg 18,651,497 votes but fell short of a majority. Hindenburg was eventually reelected after a runoff election on April 10—Hindenburg's majority over Hitler was 6 million out of 36 million votes.

The loss of Reichstag votes in 1930 handicapped the center coalition government. On July 31, 1932, new Reichstag elections made the moderates' situa-tion even more precarious as they became a minority in the legislature. The Nazis held 230 seats, while the Socialists and Communists had 222 seats, but neither would join a coalition ministry. A second Reichstag election on November 24 resulted in a similar deadlock with no group able to form a viable coalition. On December 2, General Kurt von Schleicher tried but failed to form a center-left coalition cabinet.

On January 28, Schleicher resigned and President von Hindenburg offered Adolf Hitler the opportunity to form a center-right coalition. Hitler agreed, provided he was made chancellor. Hindenburg accepted and named Hitler to head a ministry on January 30, which joined the Nazis with the Nationalist Party. Hitler's coalition required a few Center Party votes to receive a majority, and when the Center Party leader, Ludwig Kass, rejected Hitler's demands, the Reichstag dissolved. Chancellor Hitler called new elections in which he controlled key lines of authority in Germany's government.

For the results, see March 5, 1933.

### February 22, 1933

***Oliveira Salazar becomes the Fascist dictator of Portugal, creating a new constitution with himself as president, a cabinet responsible to him alone, and a two-chamber legislature resembling Italy's corporate assembly under Mussolini.***

Throughout the 1920s, Portugal's politics consisted of a struggle between liberal republican forces and military dictatorships. On August 27, 1928, Salazar became minister of finance. In this post, he became a dominant figure by solving Portugal's financial problems through strict economic action and a tight budget. After becoming premier on July 5, 1932, Salazar moved to reorganize the government to legally grant

Thousands of books are tossed into a huge bonfire as Germans give the Nazi salute during a wave of book-burnings throughout the nation during 1933. National Archives

himself full power, a task accomplished on February 22, 1933, when a new constitution was promulgated by Salazar.

### February 24, 1933

***The League of Nations assembly adopts the Lytton report on the Mukden incident of 1931. Japan denounces the League, walks out of the assembly, and quits the League on May 27, 1933.***

Following its establishment by the league on December 10, 1931, the Commission to Investigate the Manchurian Affair was organized under the chairmanship of the earl of Lytton. After visiting Manchuria and obtaining evidence from Chinese and Japanese officials, Lytton presented his report to the league on October 2, 1932. At Japan's request, the league provided time to study the 139-page report and

established a Committee of Nineteen to deal with any future league action.

Although the Lytton Report was conciliatory, the Japanese rejected it. The report laid blame for the Mukden incident on both sides but did not believe Japan's response was self-defense. Nor, said the report, did the creation of Manchukuo come from a "genuine and spontaneous independence movement." It recommended the establishment of an autonomous Manchurian government under Chinese sovereignty. It also recognized Japan's economic interests in the area and believed these should be protected.

In Japan, growing ultranationalist sentiment opposed the compromises implied in the Lytton Report. The cabinet of Premier Wakatsuki was divided on what action to take and resigned in December. The new cabinet of Premier Inukai accepted the Japanese conquest of Manchuria but opposed any further army expansion in China. The cabinet rejected the recommendation that Japan leave Manchuria. When the Assembly of the League of Nations approved the Lytton Report, the Japanese, who had denounced the report, walked out of the Assembly.

Japan's decision to quit the League of Nations was taken following the assassination of Premier Inukai on May 15, 1932. Inukai was the second moderate premier to be killed in two years by a nationalistic fanatic, and his death marked the shift to power of the ultra-right wing nationalist-militarist group in Japan.

### March 4, 1933

**Cordell Hull is commissioned as Secretary of State by President Roosevelt.**

Hull held the high respect of Democratic Party regulars, having served as a Tennessee congressman (1907–1921 and 1923–1931) and senator (1931–1933) for 23 years. Roosevelt chose Hull largely because he was well known as an economic internationalist who opposed protective tariffs and desired reciprocal agreements. Hull guided the State Department until November 30, 1944, longer than any previous secretary of state.

### March 5, 1933

***The Reichstag elections give the Nazis a 288-seat vote but the outlawed Communist Party obtains only 81 seats.***

The election campaign during February led to further street violence between Nazis and Communists. On February 27, a fire destroyed part of the Reichstag building and Hitler denounced the incident as a Communist plot. On the basis of this incident, President Hindenburg issued emergency decrees to suspend free speech and the free press. Nazi storm troops were now free to intimidate the opposition Communists and anyone else with impunity.

The resulting election gave the Nazis 288 seats, the Nationalists 52. The Socialist-Communist seats fell from 222 the previous November to 201. With some Catholic Center votes, the Nazi-Nationalist coalition outlawed the Communist Party and on March 23, 1933, voted dictatorial powers to Hitler until April 1, 1937. A Nazi "legal" revolution occurred during the next two years. The Nazi Party became the only party on July 14, 1933, and Germany became a nation

(the Third Reich) rather than a federal state on January 30, 1934. Judicial, racial, religious, economic, and military legislation gave Hitler and his party complete control of Germany.

### March 18, 1933

**The United States agrees to cooperate with a League of Nations commission to avert war between Peru and Colombia over Leticia.**

Because of a border dispute between Peru and Colombia, the Peruvian army invaded and occupied the village of Leticia on September 1, 1933. At first, the Lima government agreed to withdraw its army, but it changed its policy, and by March 1933 a large-scale war appeared imminent. The League of Nations Advisory Commission offered to mediate the issue, and after Peru agreed, the league's secretary-general asked the United States to cooperate because he did not wish to infringe on the Monroe Doctrine. Secretary Hull and Roosevelt agreed to participate in the league's commission of mediation although not as a voting member.

The league's mediation averted the conflict. The commissioners, including the nonvoting U.S. delegate, went to Leticia and supervised the withdrawal of troops by both nations. A final settlement was made under league auspices on November 2, 1934.

### April 19, 1933

**The United States officially abandons the gold standard.**

This action caused a decline in the dollar value abroad and increased the price of commodities, silver, and stocks on the U.S. exchanges.

### May 29, 1933

**Standard Oil of California (SOCAL) receives oil rights in Saudi Arabia without the need for State Department assistance.**

SOCAL obtained oil concessions from King Ibn Saud because of two favorable circumstances. First, the British treaty of 1927 with Saudi Arabia canceled Britain's right to veto the Saudis' oil concessions included in the Anglo-Arabian Treaty of 1915. Second, an American philanthropist, Charles Crane, had a genuine interest in Arabian culture and gained the friendship of King Ibn Saud, who distrusted the British.

Under Crane's guidance, the king invited Karl S. Twitchell to conduct a geological survey of Arabia that assessed Saudi Arabia's oil reserves. Twitchell and Crane favored SOCAL's proposal for an oil concession and encouraged SOCAL to apply for a grant in 1932.

On May 29, the king chose SOCAL's oil bid in preference to an offer from Britain's Iraq Petroleum Company. To handle its Saudi concession, SOCAL established a subsidiary, the California-Arabian Standard Oil Company, which began oil production just before World War II interfered with its further output.

## May 31, 1933

### *The T'ang-ku truce ends the conflict between China and Japan that began on the night of September 18–19, 1931.*

By March 1933, Japanese forces occupied all of Jehol Province just north of the Great Wall. In April, they advanced south of the wall into China. At this juncture, Tokyo agreed to sign a truce with China by which Chinese troops would evacuate the Tientsin area. The neutralization of the area between Tientsin and Peking would be eventually occupied by Japan in 1937 as its first move toward the conquest of China.

## July 3, 1933

### President Roosevelt disrupts the London Economic Conference by repudiating all temporary currency stabilization proposals.

The London conference met to resolve the chaos of international economic difficulties. Factors that caused the crisis included America's rejection of the Lausanne Conference of 1932 proposal to repudiate all war debts; the default by most Europeans on their December 15, 1932, war debt payments; Great Britain's leaving the gold standard; Roosevelt's calling of a U.S. bank holiday on March 5 to stop bank failures. The London Conference hoped to create a degree of fiscal certainty to offer businessmen and investors a more optimistic future.

Exactly where the new U.S. president stood on these issues did not become clear until July 3. As early as November 22, 1932, the president-elect met with President Hoover to discuss the problems of debts, reparations, and disarmament, but Roosevelt

hesitated to commit himself. He desired to retain the full support of Congress and the nation when he assumed office on March 4, 1933. In subsequent talks before his inauguration, Roosevelt indicated that an international conference would be acceptable, but he did not make it clear whether or not the war debts problem would be negotiable along with other economic problems. Evidently Roosevelt desired to improve the U.S. economy by short-term nationalistic economic measures while seeking better world economic cooperation through long-term international action. In 1933, however, these two goals came into conflict.

Shortly before meeting with British Prime Minister Ramsay MacDonald and French Premier Édouard Herriot on April 21, Roosevelt urged action in Congress to give him authority to devalue the dollar (see April 19, 1933). Roosevelt's action angered and confused the European leaders, but the president calmed their anxiety by discussing proposals for a truce on tariff competition and the possibility of relief for their June 15 debt payments. The three national leaders agreed to convene an economic conference in London on June 12, before the due date for the debt payments. Herriot and MacDonald could not, however, agree with Roosevelt's proposal to wait until each nation settled its domestic economic problems before trying to stabilize international problems. The British and French wanted a temporary stabilization of the dollar value as a basic necessity for their economic reconstruction.

Indeed, while debts and reparations appeared to be the primary question during the London Conference, which began on June 12, the most critical question was international currency value because this directly affected every specific economic issue. The resolution of the U.S. banking crisis by passage of the Glass-Steagall Act and the Emergency Banking Relief Act in March–April 1933 strengthened the dollar on the world currency exchange but weakened the European currencies. Between May and July 1933, the dollar value relative to the British pound sterling increased from $4.02 to a high of $4.40, fluctuating on the speculative market between $4.15 and $4.30.

During the first week of the London Conference, Roosevelt appointed three special negotiators to discuss currency stabilization with Britain and France. As a result of these tripartite meetings, James P. Warburg, Oliver W. Sprague, and George L.

Harrison, the U.S. negotiators, recommended on June 16 that Roosevelt agree to stabilize the dollar at about $4 to the pound sterling and not to inflate the dollar further. The president rejected their proposal, a decision that presaged Roosevelt's statement of July 3, which, because it was made publicly and in definite terms, destroyed the London Conference's chance for success.

In mid-June, however, Roosevelt had not yet closed the door on the stabilization of the dollar. Rumors of stabilization encouraged speculators to increase the dollar value, which reached $4.18 on June 12. The president, therefore, could not accept the $4 proposal of the tripartite committee, and its sessions ceased to be effective after June 17.

On June 21, Roosevelt dispatched Raymond Moley, one of his chief economic advisers, to London to convince the Europeans to accept the American terms. Moley and Roosevelt appeared to have agreed that controlling a limited fluctuation of the dollar value between $4.15 and $4.25 to the pound sterling should satisfy the Europeans. Thus, Moley's arrival in London on June 28 raised hopes that an agreement would result from the London Conference.

On July 3, however, Roosevelt's message to Secretary of State Hull, who headed the U.S. conference delegation, withdrew the limited stabilization compromise that Moley had presented and asserted the president's commitment to national recovery preceding an international currency stabilization. By July the president realized that America's recovery would not come as fast as he had expected in March; in addition, he sensed that the majority of Congress placed American recovery ahead of international, especially European, recovery. Americans generally still failed to comprehend that their economic status correlated closely with international economic health, some blaming European debt defaults and European lassitude for the American problems.

Thus, the July 3 note to Hull stated that the president could not agree to the recent suggestion by Moley that the U.S. Federal Reserve Board should cooperate in limiting the dollar currency fluctuations at about $4.15. The sound internal economy of the nation was, the president said, "a greater factor in its well being than the price of its currency in changing terms of other nations." The concept of stable currencies was, Roosevelt stated, an "old fetish of so-called international bankers." In contrast, he said, stabiliza-

tion could be attained only after the majority of nations balanced their budgets and achieved economic health.

The European delegates at London were astounded by the president's July 3 message. Since April 21, MacDonald and Herriot had believed Roosevelt was ready to reach some compromise on currency values, debts, and other financial matters. It was evident on July 3 that the president's request for general, not specific, cooperation at the London Conference was designed to promote U.S. recovery, if necessary at the expense of Europe's general recovery. Indeed, Roosevelt's peculiarly American attitude about international cooperation had been succinctly stated in his instructions to Moley before Moley left for London on June 21. The president declared: "If other nations will go along and work in our direction, as they said they would . . . then we can cooperate. If they won't, then there's nothing to cooperate about."

To avoid a complete display of disunity between England, France, and America, Roosevelt urged Secretary Hull to keep the conference alive for a while by proposing that the nations work together to raise their domestic prices. In spite of the Europeans' desire to end the conference, Hull kept the sessions going for three weeks, until July 27. No agreements were made, however. Roosevelt's concept of the U.S. national interest prevented a cooperative effort at an international economic settlement in 1933.

### July 15, 1933

*The Four-Power Pact attempts to align Europe's four big powers to maintain peace.*

A favorite idea of Italian leader Benito Mussolini, this pact was signed by Italy, Germany, France, and England. Mussolini disliked the influence of the small nations in the League of Nations and proposed this pact to unite the larger nations to dominate the league. In practice, this agreement had no significance.

### August 12, 1933

**General Machado leaves Cuba: U.S. Ambassador Sumner Welles earns "warm congratulations" from President Roosevelt.**

On May 1, 1933, Welles was sent as ambassador to Cuba with instructions to mediate an end to the civil

Sumner Welles, U.S. Ambassador to Cuba, with President Roosevelt. Franklin D. Roosevelt Library

disorders that opposed the military dictatorship of President Gerardo Machado. The uprising against Machado had begun in 1929. Machado generally suppressed it in 1930, but underground resistance continued, especially among university students and liberal intellectuals in Cuba. Both sides used terroristic tactics, inflicting injuries and death on many innocent Cubans. In addition, the Cuban economy suffered because the Smoot-Hawley Tariff of 1930 levied high duties on sugar, disrupting sales of the export product that yielded 85% of Cuba's income.

Throughout four years of Cuban disorders, President Hoover and Secretary Stimson remained aloof, stating that their noninterventionist policy prohibited becoming involved in another nation's domestic affairs. Although the Platt Amendment permitted U.S. intervention in Cuba, Hoover and Stimson claimed no Americans, only Cubans, were suffering, and that the Cubans must settle their own problems.

In 1933, Roosevelt and Secretary of State Hull also preferred not to intervene in Cuba, but they believed something should be done to end the mounting disorders in the nearby island. They agreed to send, as U.S. ambassador, Sumner Welles to Havana with instructions to negotiate a trade treaty that would ease Cuba's devastating economic condition; to urge Machado to stop his terrorist methods; and to negotiate a truce between the two factions that would allow free elections. Welles had been a State Department troubleshooter in both Santo Domingo and Honduras during the 1920s and believed he could end the Cuban problems.

Between May and August, Welles realized that Machado would not cooperate in accomplishing his objectives. Therefore, Welles contacted Cuban army officials and undertook confidential discussions with the secretary of war, General Alberto Herrera. Although Welles's precise role is not documented, he apparently encouraged army officers to oust

Machado. On August 12, 1933, Machado took a "leave of absence" and fled Cuba by airplane. Before Machado left, however, Welles approved the commissioning of General Cárlos Manuel de Céspedes as Cuba's secretary of state, the officer in line for constitutional succession to the presidency when Machado "retired." Because Céspedes's rule followed constitutional provisions, it was an "orderly" change of government not likely to raise questions about recognition.

Although Welles received Roosevelt's and Secretary Hull's "warm congratulations" for maneuvering Machado's overthrow, their praise proved to be premature. Welles, of course, was ecstatic in describing Céspedes's government as a "new deal for Cuba" and one that "commands" the confidence of the Cuban people. Time, however, has a cynical way of turning on a politician's words. In a second "bloodless" coup, Cárlos Céspedes's rule ended in less than one month.

See September 5, 1933.

## September 5, 1933

### A Cuban coup d'état overthrows Cárlos Céspedes, bringing to power a regime that Roosevelt refuses to recognize.

Following the U.S. optimism that greeted Machado's departure from Cuba on August 12, 1933, Roosevelt's "good neighbor" policy experienced a severe test that eventually tarnished it when the man whom Ambassador Welles supported was overthrown on September 5.

Céspedes's overthrow was led by a group of army sergeants directed by Sergeant Fulgencio BATISTA. Cuba's noncommissioned officers had joined with university students and liberal intellectuals in the belief that General Machado's regime had implicated all the army's generals in the terroristic suppression between 1929 and 1933. Although Batista and his army colleagues shared few ideas with the liberals and students, they united on September 5 in the successful overthrow of Céspedes and the military junta that had backed his government.

When the leaders of the coup established a civilian junta and installed Ramón Grau San Martín as provisional president, Roosevelt accepted the disappointed Welles's opinion that Grau's government should not be recognized. According to Welles, Grau's supporters were radicals and Communists who lacked the sup-

port of the Cuban people. Although Welles's poor judgment about the Céspedes regime should have cautioned Roosevelt about his evaluation of Cuban support, the president did not recognize the new government. This action handicapped Grau's efforts to reform Cuba and became a major factor in his subsequent loss of power to Batista's military faction.

Subsequently, Roosevelt tried a dual policy to give the impression he was a "good neighbor" helping developments in Cuba. He conducted discussions with representatives of Argentina, Brazil, Chile, and Mexico, emphasizing to them that the United States wished to avoid intervention in Cuba even though the situation was dangerous. On the same day, September 6, he sent 20 to 30 ships to Cuban waters to "protect" Americans from disorders. While Welles maneuvered against Grau's government, he was backed not only by Roosevelt but by the American warships in Havana and Santiago harbors.

For the consequences of indirect U.S. intervention, see January 15, 1934.

## October 14, 1933

### Germany withdraws from the Geneva Disarmament Conference and the League of Nations.

Although the Five-Power Declaration of December 11, 1932, brought Germany back to the Geneva Disarmament Conference in February, the divergence between German and French demands increased after the Nazis gained power in Germany on January 30, 1933. Although there were intermittent full and subcommittee sessions of the conference during the next eight months, the German withdrawal on October 14 appeared to William DODD, the American Ambassador to Germany, to have been a premeditated act connected with Hitler's having gained full power in Germany by September.

President Roosevelt named Norman Davis to head the U.S. delegation at the Geneva Conference, but the only commitment the president seemed politically able to make was to support Ramsay MacDonald's March 16 proposal to combine a partial reduction of all armies by half a million with an agreement of the powers to consult if an aggressor attacked another nation. In a speech on May 16, Roosevelt went one step further to placate France by agreeing that the United States would relinquish its traditional neutral rights and refrain from any activity that might damage the attempt of a collective action to punish an aggressor. Of course, Roosevelt made this offer in the context of a disarmament reduction's having been agreed to by the European states. The Germans prevented an agreement on MacDonald's plan, demanding their right to begin rearming because the other European nations had failed to take steps to disarm during the decade and a half since the 1919 peace treaties.

During the last weeks leading to Germany's withdrawal from both the conference and the League of Nations, Norman Davis realized the discussions were fruitless. All that he and Roosevelt could do was to put the United States on record as being concerned about the need for European disarmament. The failure of this conference, which had been in preparation since 1926 and was publicized as the real hope for peace in Europe, resulted in an increased sense of American isolation. The national hatreds among European states seemed impossible to resolve. Thus, the U.S. public thought the Europeans should be left to suffer for their irrational national shortcomings.

See March 5, 1933.

### November 17, 1933

**President Roosevelt and the Soviet Union's foreign minister sign an agreement to normalize relations between the United States and the USSR.**

Following the Bolshevik Revolution of November 1917, the United States refused to recognize the Soviet government. In 1933, however, Roosevelt discerned that American public opinion no longer strongly opposed recognition of the Communist regime. Some businessmen believed diplomatic relations would stimulate trade with the Soviets, and some internationalists thought U.S.-Soviet diplomacy might restrain Japanese ventures in Manchuria. In April 1933, Roosevelt urged Senator Claude Swanson to promote a national discussion about the benefits of recognition.

Roosevelt's principal concerns in Soviet relations were the opposition of religious groups who disapproved of recognition of the atheist Communist government and American nationalists who disliked the propaganda and possible subversive activity of the Communist Party under the direction of the Third Communist International (Comintern). To forestall criticism, Roosevelt met in October with Father Edmund A. Walsh of Georgetown University, the nation's leading Roman Catholic spokesman against Soviet recognition. Roosevelt persuaded Walsh to trust his ability as "a good horse dealer" to require the Soviets to grant Americans religious rights in the USSR and to obtain guarantees against Communist subversive activity in America. Walsh's backing assisted the president.

Having secured some acceptance from public leaders, Roosevelt arranged through Boris Skvirsky, Moscow's trade representative in New York, to issue an invitation to the Soviet Union to send a representative to discuss American-Soviet relations. Because Soviet leader Joseph Stalin now desired cooperation against the rising threat of fascism, the Soviets responded positively and appointed their foreign minister, Maxim LITVINOV, to go to Washington for talks.

Litvinov's negotiations took place from November 8 to 16, 1933. In his formal discussions at the State Department, Litvinov initially showed little interest in meeting American conditions for recognition. On November 10, however, he began direct discussions with the president, and agreements were reached that resulted in the normalization of Soviet-American relations. The Soviets agreed to extend religious freedom to U.S. citizens in the Soviet Union and to negotiate an agreement to provide fair trials for Americans accused of crime there. The Soviet government also agreed not to engage in subversive activities, although the wording of this clause did not include the action of the Communist Party as distinct from the government. Finally, details regarding Soviet debts and U.S. financial claims were delegated to future discussions, the Soviets agreeing to pay between $75 million and $150 million in claims. The debt issue raised less suspicion than it had previously because most major European nations had defaulted on their U.S. debts after 1931.

Although the 1933 agreements restored U.S.-Soviet diplomatic recognition, the trade and international stability that advocates of recognition predicted did not materialize. No immediate consequences may be attributed to recognition; however, it later permitted the "strange alliance" of 1941 to 1945 to proceed without difficulty after Hitler invaded the USSR in June 1941.

### December 26, 1933

**The United States agrees to a nonintervention pact during the Seventh Pan-American Conference at Montevideo.**

Although the Hoover administration had taken steps toward initiating a "good neighbor" policy in the Western Hemisphere, President Roosevelt more strongly endorsed a cooperative policy with Latin American nations. Both in his March 4 inaugural address and during a speech on April 12, 1933, to the board of the Pan-American Union, the president expressed his determination to be a good neighbor and respect the rights of other nations.

Consequently, when the State Department prepared for the Montevideo Conference during October 1933, Roosevelt and Secretary of State Hull, who headed the U.S. delegation to the Uruguay meeting, agreed to focus on promoting Pan-American cooperation. Although Hull experienced anti-Yankee posters and demonstrations as soon as he arrived at Montevideo, he was determined to overcome their animosity.

On December 26, Hull cast the American vote favoring a convention on the rights and duties of states. Article 8 of this agreement included a clause stating: "No state has the right to intervene in the internal or external affairs of another state." Hull accepted this pact with the reservation that a state may "protect lives and property where government has broken down and anarchy exists." He urged the signatories to codify a clear definition of nonintervention in the 1933 treaty and announced that Roosevelt's administration would not intervene in another state's affairs. Somewhat ironically, Hull made this statement at the same time the U.S. warships in Havana harbor protected indirect American political interference in Cuba. Many U.S. critics in Latin America did not overlook this anomaly.

# 1934

### January 15, 1934

**Indirect American intervention in Cuba results in President Grau's resignation: a regime controlled by Batista gains power and U.S. recognition.**

Owing largely to the influence of U.S. Ambassador Sumner Welles, the Roosevelt administration refused to recognize the provisional presidency of Ramón Grau San Martín, who created a civilian junta follow-ing Cépedes's overthrow on September 5, 1933. Without U.S. recognition, Grau could not arrange a trade agreement with the United States or obtain help in reforming the Cuban economy.

By November, Grau's regime became disgusted with Welles's political maneuvering in Cuba and asked Roosevelt to recall the ambassador. Welles had earned the antagonism of most Cuban newspapers and become the symbol of U.S. interference in Cuba. Because Secretary Hull was attending the Inter-American Conference at Montevideo, Welles and Roosevelt decided to keep Cuba's request for Welles's recall secret and to wait several weeks before Welles returned to Washington as assistant secretary of state. On November 24, Roosevelt issued a news release that expressed his confidence in Welles but indicated that the ambassador would be replaced in December by Jefferson Caffery. This did not mean there would be a policy change, Roosevelt asserted, because Caffery's appointment would not bring recognition to Grau's regime. Roosevelt argued that Grau did not have the support of the Cuban people.

Welles returned to Cuba and remained until December 13, hoping he could obtain Grau's resignation on behalf of a candidate approved by himself. On December 12, Welles reported to Washington that he expected Grau to resign and Cárlos Mendieta to become provisional president. To arrange this, Welles held discussions with Colonel (formerly Sergeant) Batista urging the new chief of staff of the Cuban army to withdraw his support from Grau. At the last minute, however, Welles's plans fell through. Grau remained in office for another month, and Welles could not return to the State Department with the prestigious victory he had hoped for: the fall of Grau San Martín.

But Welles had paved the way for the change in Cuba's government on January 15. When Caffery arrived in Cuba, Grau's followers hoped the new ambassador would be conciliatory, providing an opening for Grau's recognition and U.S. economic aid. Caffery disappointed them, however. Having participated in the Welles-Roosevelt decisions on Cuba during November, Caffery knew that the success of his job required the resignation of Grau. More important, Colonel Batista, too, realized that his success depended on U.S. backing that, above all, required a stronger law-and-order regime in Havana.

In early January, Batista informed Grau that the army could no longer support the existing government. Consequently, Grau resigned on January 15 and Cárlos Mendieta, head of the Nationalist Party and the person whom Welles had approved for the job in December, became president of Cuba. Mendieta was the first of a series of presidents who fronted for Batista, who controlled affairs in Cuba. In 1940, a Cuban convention prepared a new constitution organized on the lines of a fascist corporate state. On July 14, 1940, Batista assumed direct control over Cuba, a position he held until December 31, 1958.

In January 1934, Roosevelt moved quickly to grant Mendieta the recognition he withheld from Grau. With Welles's support (Hull returned from Uruguay on January 21), Roosevelt decided on January 18 to recognize the new government soon after Mendieta officially became provisional president. Roosevelt concluded that the Mendieta government would bring order to Cuba and had the support of the Cuban people. How Mendieta's positive qualities were determined so quickly remains a mystery, other than that Mendieta had the approval of Welles in Washington and Batista in Havana. On January 24, the United States recognized Mendieta's government.

For U.S. support of the new regime, see May 29, 1934.

### January 30, 1934

**Congress passes the Gold Reserve Act, ending Roosevelt's experiment with devaluation as a method to increase commodity prices in America's favor.**

During the fall of 1933, Professors George Warren, Irving Fisher, and James Harvey Rogers persuaded the president to purchase gold at rates higher than the world market prices as a means for increasing the price of gold and reducing the dollar's value. Therefore, on October 19, Roosevelt ordered the Reconstruction Finance Corporation to purchase newly mined gold because, the president said, "The United States must take firmly in its own hands the control of the gold value of our dollar" in order to gain "the continued recovery of our commodity prices."

Foreign nations strongly opposed Roosevelt's action. The governor of the Bank of England claimed, "The whole world will be put into bankruptcy." This complaint was not accurate, but neither were the expectations of Roosevelt and his three economics professors. Commodity prices did not rise. The

United States had profited from the devaluation, however, by adding dollars to monetary circulation. The president added these gains to a monetary stabilization fund that could limit British fluctuations of the pound sterling in international exchanges.

Roosevelt also asked Congress on January 15 to pass a Gold Reserve Act. This act permitted the president to stabilize the dollar at 50 to 60% of its former value. On January 31, the day after Congress approved the Gold Reserve Act, Roosevelt fixed the dollar at 59.06% of its pre-1933 gold value. The effect of this act permitted the Treasury to print about $4 additional for each ounce of gold.

### February 2, 1934

**President Roosevelt establishes the Export-Import Bank to encourage overseas commerce.**

Acting under provisions of the Reconstruction Finance Corporation and the National Recovery Act, the president established the Export-Import Bank. It was to finance foreign trade with short-term credits for exporting agricultural commodities; with longer-term credits for U.S. firms exporting industrial manufacturing; and with loans to U.S. exporters where foreign governments did not provide sufficient exchange credit to meet their dollar obligations. Originally two banks were set up: one for trade credits to the Soviet Union, the other for credit facilities with Cuba and other foreign nations. In 1936, these two banks were merged.

### March 24, 1934

**The Tydings-McDuffie Act provides independence to the Philippine Islands in 1946.**

In 1932, Congress passed legislation over President Hoover's veto that granted independence to the Philippines. In October 1933, the Philippine legislature rejected this bill because it excluded Philippine products and labor from the United States. To rectify this criticism, Congress passed the Tydings-McDuffie Act of 1934, which provided for establishing the Philippines as a self-governing commonwealth by 1936. After 10 years under this government and U.S. supervision, the Philippines would receive full independence on July 4, 1946. The Philippine legislature ratified the bill on May 1, 1934.

### March 27, 1934

## The Vinson Naval Parity Act authorizes a U.S. navy program to reach treaty strength.

President Roosevelt designed the Vinson Act as part of the New Deal unemployment relief program. Sometimes referred to as the Vinson-Trammel Act, this bill authorized construction of warships to treaty limits.

In 1928, with the completion of the two aircraft carriers USS *Lexington* and USS *Saratoga,* the U.S. navy nearly achieved its 1922 Five-Power Treaty strength of 5:5:3. The Hoover administration, partly owing to the Depression, had drastically cut the navy's budget for the next four years; these cuts reduced ship construction below treaty limits. In 1933, Roosevelt set aside $238 million of public works funds (PWA) for the construction of 32 ships that totaled 120,000 tons. Not until the Vinson Act of 1938 did Congress authorize a navy program designed to reach treaty strength in five years. To attain this goal, 100 warships and 1,000 aircraft would be built. But Congress did not allocate sufficient funds for the program, and until 1938 the navy was able only to replace obsolete ships.

Although some scholars view the Vinson Act as a hard-line policy against Japan, a policy to achieve the treaty strength of 1922 was insufficient to carry out the U.S. navy's Orange War Plan against Japan. A treaty-size navy was only defensive. A navy designed to oppose Japan required a U.S. fleet capable of offensive action in the western Pacific near Japan's home islands, a navy whose size exceeded the 1922 treaties.

### April 12, 1934

## Nye munitions investigations are approved: the senate establishes a committee to investigate arms manufacturers and the sale of munitions as a cause of war.

Advocates of peace and disarmament between 1919 and 1933 generated several studies about the causes of war that connected arms manufacturers, the so-called merchants of death, to the cause of warfare. Allegedly, these arms salesmen published extensive propaganda to stimulate international hatred and antagonisms, which then caused various governments to purchase their products and, some suspected, bore some responsibility for the outbreak of World War I.

An isolationist senator from North Dakota, Gerald P. Nye, used these allegations to request a Senate investigation of the activity of arms manufacturers before, during, and after 1914. The Senate approved the resolution and Nye became chairman of the investigation committee. Hearings before the committee began in September 1934, and received extensive publicity drawn from the witnesses' testimony and the charges of Nye and other committee members. The large profits of the munitions industry were conclusively shown; however, the ability of these war profiteers to exert covert pressure on governments to declare war could not be demonstrated. Nevertheless, many Americans believed there was a connection between armament manufacturers and governments that, in oversimplified fashion, resulted in war.

The Nye investigations were one influence in the growing isolationist sentiment in the United States at the time when the fascist and militaristic powers became aggressive in Europe and the Far East. The Neutrality Acts passed between 1935 and 1937 resulted in part as a consequence of this committee's allegations.

See August 31, 1935.

### April 13, 1934

## The Johnson Debt Default Act prohibits loans to governments that defaulted on their debts to the United States.

President Roosevelt decided to support Senator Hiram Johnson's loan default act because the major European powers, especially Great Britain, offered what seemed to them as ridiculous terms to settle the debt issue. During the fall of 1933, England said it would pay $460 million to settle all its debts of $8 billion, a sum Roosevelt rejected. On December 15, France defaulted for the third successive time, while England and Italy made only token payments.

Therefore, Roosevelt agreed to support Johnson's bill provided the senator dropped the clause referring to debts of private citizens. Roosevelt was willing to make the U.S. government directly responsible only for default on government bonds and loans. Johnson accepted this change, and the bill passed Congress on April 4. The president signed it on April 13.

The default bill did not produce its intended results. The European nations did not pay their debts or agree to negotiate better terms for cancellation. Furthermore, during the early days of World War II in Europe, Roosevelt had another obstacle to overcome before he could lend money to Great Britain to buy arms in America.

### April 24, 1934

**The United States and Mexico sign a claims convention ending a point of disagreement existing since 1923.**

On August 31, 1923, Mexico had agreed to arbitrate the settlement of indemnity claims incurred between Mexico and America since the claims convention of 1868. A special claims commission worked on the claims cases from 1924 to 1932 but could not reach agreement except on 2 of 3,617 claims. In total, Americans held a half billion dollars of claims, the Mexicans held a quarter billion dollars. Many of these claims were exaggerated, however, as Roosevelt's new ambassador to Mexico, Jonathan DANIELS, discovered. One claim was by an American inventor who demanded $42 million for anticipated profits on a patent used in Mexico; another was by a group of Mexicans claiming title to a sizable amount of land in Los Angeles.

Ambassador Daniels determined that the "good neighbor" policy required a sympathetic settlement with Mexico. He found that Mexico's foreign minister, Puig Casauranc, was willing to reach a compromise but that old-time bureaucrats of the State Department were slow to adjust the issue with Mexico. Daniels decided to seek a lump sum payment based on the proportion of claim awards that six European nations had settled with Mexico in recent years. The Europeans had scaled down 382 million pesos of claims to about 10 million pesos. The percentage varied from country to country, but the foreign returns averaged 2.65%. On this basis, Daniels and Puig agreed on the amount of 2.65% for memorialized claims accepted previously by any claims commission and 1.25% for unmemorialized claims of dubious authenticity. Mexico would pay these claims in 15 years (the Europeans used 30 years) and in dollars (the Europeans used pesos).

Between February and April 1934, Daniels's main obstacle was the Washington bureaucracy in charge of the Mexican claims. These officials argued for another 0.5% payment. Puig refused this concept, and negotiations nearly ended. Finally, Daniels held discussions by phone with the State Department and gained its

reluctant agreement on the originally proposed percentages. The convention with Mexico was signed on April 24, 1934.

### April 28, 1934

**Secretary of State Hull protests the "Amau statement" of a Japanese foreign office spokesman. Soon after, Hull rejects a Japanese suggestion for a spheres-of-influence arrangement in the Pacific Ocean.**

On April 17, 1934, Eiji Amau, a Japanese foreign office spokesman, told a press conference in Tokyo that Japan's geographic position and world mission gave it a duty "to keep peace and order in East Asia." For this reason, the Japanese objected to joint operations by outside groups such as the League of Nations in China.

Amau's statement alarmed both London and Washington because it appeared to be a new statement of Japanese policy. In Tokyo, U.S. Ambassador

Cordell Hull, Secretary of State. National Archives

Joseph C. Grew learned from Foreign Minister Hirota that Amau gave reporters the wrong impression. Hirota said Japan observed the Nine-Power Treaty of 1922 and would not interfere with the bona fide trade of other nations.

Nevertheless, Hull believed Hirota's explanation was vague, and he protested to the Japanese Foreign Office on April 28. Japan, Hull wrote, had multilateral treaties with other nations regarding China and could not assert its will in areas where others had legitimate interests. Great Britain joined Hull in filing a similar protest to Tokyo. As a follow-up to the Amau statement, Hull disclosed his rejection of "realistic" balance-of-power politics with Japan. In May 1934, Hull spoke with the Japanese ambassador at Washington, Hiroshi Saito, who suggested that the United States and Japan might consider the formal recognition of their mutual interests in the Pacific Ocean. His concept envisioned that America would accept Japan's sphere of influence in the western Pacific and Japan would recognize American interests in defined areas of the eastern Pacific. Hull objected to the concept, lecturing Saito on the obligations of international behavior among "highly civilized countries." In addition, Hull said, any special agreement with Japan was contrary to American traditions opposing political alliances.

Generally, Hull's protest to the Amau statement and his conversation with Saito indicated the Roosevelt administration's opposition to Japan's recent actions in Manchuria, although in 1934, Secretary Hull played down American differences with Japan. From 1934 to 1937, Roosevelt hoped to avoid provocation of Japan.

### May 29, 1934

**The United States abrogates the Platt Amendment, ending the limits on Cuban sovereignty but retaining Guantánamo naval base.**

Although the Roosevelt administration had fulfilled only the nonmilitary parts of the "good neighbor" test in Cuba between May 1933 and January 1934, the abrogation of the Platt Amendment became another indication of the U.S. desire to avoid direct intervention in Latin America. However, Sumner Welles's interference in Cuban politics between May and December 1933, and Roosevelt's refusal to recognize the Grau regime between September 1933 and January 1934, revealed an equally effective American capacity to influence Latin American affairs without the use of the army or marines. Only certain scholars and Latin American nationalists noted the indirect interference with the failings of the "good neighbor."

Following the rise to power of the Mendieta-Batista junta in 1934, the Roosevelt administration demonstrated its ability to provide positive assistance to a "friendly" regime in Cuba. In February, the State Department undertook trade negotiations with Cuba that reduced the tariff on sugar and expanded U.S.-Cuban trade. In March, Roosevelt approved a $4 million loan to help Cuba revive its ailing economy. In June, when "conditions of domestic violence" indicated that some Cubans disliked the new regime, Roosevelt limited arms sales to Cuba except to the Mendieta government or those it authorized.

Most dramatic and publicized, however, was the treaty abrogating the Platt Amendment, by which the United States had assumed the right to intervene in Cuban affairs following the Spanish-American War of 1898. The treaty ending the Platt Amendment was signed by Hull, the Cuban ambassador, and, at his special request, Sumner Welles. By this treaty, the United States retained Guantánamo naval base until it might be surrendered by mutual consent in the future. The U.S. Senate ratified the Cuban treaty on June 9, 1934.

### June 12, 1934

**The Reciprocal Trade Agreements Act of 1934 is signed into law, approving the president's authority to negotiate the reduction of tariffs and other trade barriers.**

One of Secretary of State Hull's favorite programs, and the one issue on which Roosevelt gave Hull full support, was the belief in the need for all nations to end their discriminatory trade barriers.

Although Roosevelt informed Hull during the spring of 1933 that he wanted to postpone the Reciprocal Trade Act until 1934, the president appointed an Executive Committee on Commercial Policy on November 11, 1933, and the process of drafting a trade bill began. The committee included Francis B. SAYRE of the State Department as chairman, representatives from the departments of the Treasury, Commerce, and Agriculture; the Tariff Commission; the Agricultural Adjustment Act

Commission; and the National Recovery Act administrator.

The bill was offered to Congress on March 2, 1934, and after the necessary committee hearings was passed by the House on March 29 and the Senate on June 4. As approved with three amendments added by Congress, the Reciprocal Trade Agreements Act provided:

1. Congress delegated power to the president to raise or lower tariffs by 50% or to freeze existing agreements made with separate nations. The delegation of the power to permit the president to make executive agreements on trade relieved the president of having to present each agreement to the U.S. Senate for the two-thirds ratification vote required of a treaty. This would expedite the conclusion of new trade agreements.
2. The State Department would negotiate bilateral trade agreements with separate nations by amending the circumstances existing under the Smoot-Hawley Tariff Act of 1930. As Hull pointed out, however, the most-favored-nation clauses of existing treaties would generally apply any reductions on a product to the same product in existing treaties with all other nations.
3. In addition to tariff reductions, new trade agreements could be made regarding trade quotas, prohibitions, exchange controls, barter agreements, and other trade provisions.
4. A Senate amendment required public hearings to be held on an agreement before it was signed by the president.
5. Cuba's preferred trade status was retained.
6. The president's authority was initially limited to three years but could be extended.

### June 19, 1934

**Congress passes a Silver Purchase Act that benefits U.S. silver producers but destroys China's silver monetary standard.**

Senator Key Pittman of Nevada, who was chairman of the Senate Foreign Relations Committee, had long sought to have the government buy silver until its price reached one-third the value of gold. The congressional approval of this measure resulted in the presidential order of August 9 to the Treasury to buy all U.S. silver at 50 cents an ounce and all newly minted silver at 64.64 cents. The Treasury would pay for these purchases with silver certificates at the rate of $1.29 an ounce. A 50% profits tax precluded a windfall for silver speculators.

The Silver Purchase Act aided U.S. silver producers but disrupted China's monetary system during a difficult political and economic period for the Nationalist Chinese government. The increased silver price produced an increased market in China for American products but drained off China's silver reserves. China's silver exports increased sevenfold, and by November 3, 1935, China had to go off the silver standard.

China appealed to Washington for help in solving its problem, but Roosevelt initially refused to consider the silver purchase as the real cause of China's problem. Not until the Chinese abandoned the silver standard in November did Roosevelt approve some aid. At China's request, the United States bought 173 million ounces of silver on November 13. China agreed to use the funds to stabilize its currency, not to add to its military power against Japan. The Chinese economic situation was partly repaired, but the Japanese had been antagonized by Roosevelt's somewhat erratic behavior toward China.

### July 16, 1934

**The State Department presents a vigorous, lengthy aide-mémoire to the German government, complaining of German debt payment policies to Americans since May 1933.**

Although the State Department received frequent complaints about the persecution of Jews and treatment of American citizens in Germany in 1933–1934, these were considered internal German matters that the United States could orally protest to Nazi officials but for which they could not strongly object. Regarding Hitler's policy on the payment of U.S. debts on loans, however, Secretary of State Hull indicated his outrage in talks with German representatives in Washington and urged the U.S. ambassador to Berlin, William Dodd, to protest strongly to Germany.

The German-American debt disagreement occurred in May 1933 but grew larger by July 1934. On May 8, president of the German Reichsbank, Hjalmar Schacht, followed visits with Hull and President Roosevelt by making the surprise announcement that the German government would cease payments on its external debts, including $2 billion held by Americans. Hull objected strongly, and during the London Economic Conference in July, Schacht agreed to modify his May 8 declaration. Between August 1933 and June 1934, the Germans again made unilateral alterations in their debt policy. The Germans announced that the American debts would be paid 50% in cash, 50% in script redeemable at the German Reichsbank for 75% of the value. The remaining 25% of the script value would subsidize German exports. According to Secretary of State Hull, this partial devaluation of U.S. bonds also allowed the Germans to repurchase the bonds at depreciated market prices.

In Berlin, Ambassador Dodd had presented several ineffective protests to German Foreign Minister Konstantin von Neurath, leading the State Department to file a final, more vigorous protest on July 16, 1934. Dodd, a former University of Chicago history professor with a dislike for "Wall Street" bankers, had not offered effective protests on the debt issue, even though he intensely disliked Hitler's government. Therefore, Hull instructed him to present the entire text of the July 16 memorandum to von Neurath. As a result, the Germans knew of Hull's displeasure even though they assumed no responsibility to change the partial repudiation policy. From the Nazi view, because the Western Allied powers had defaulted on their debts, anything Germany did to repay American bondholders was sufficient.

### July 25, 1934

*A Nazi putsch in Vienna fails; Italy and Yugoslavia aid Austria.*

A band of Nazis seized the radio station in Vienna and announced the resignation of Chancellor Engelburt DOLLFUSS. The Nazis then invaded the chancellery and unintentionally killed Dollfuss, who had established a Fascist dictatorship in Austria during 1933. Dollfuss had destroyed the Socialist opposition by political raids on February 11–15, 1934. However, he also rejected the proposed dominance of the Nazis, who wished to merge with Germany. His anti-Nazi policy caused the coup attempt on July 25. Because Italy and Yugoslavia supported the Austrians, Hitler decided in 1934 not to take over this "German territory."

One result of the putsch of 1934 was Mussolini's temporary willingness to work with France and England against German expansion. Not until 1936 did Hitler and Mussolini agree to work together.

See October 25, 1936.

### October 9, 1934

*King Alexander of Yugoslavia and French Foreign Minister Louis Barthou are assassinated.*

King Alexander and Barthou were in Marseilles following a European tour during which they tried to build an alliance system against Nazi Germany. The assassin was a Macedonian revolutionary who opposed the Yugoslav state that included Croatia and Macedonia. Because the revolutionists' headquarters were in Hungary, a crisis arose in which war was narrowly averted between Yugoslavia and Hungary.

### December 23, 1934

**The American Gulf Oil Company joins the Anglo-Persian Company in obtaining oil concessions in Kuwait.**

In 1931, the Gulf Oil Company requested State Department assistance in gaining Great Britain's approval to apply for oil rights in Kuwait. Gulf had purchased concession rights from the Eastern and General Syndicate in 1925, but the British Colonial Office refused to approve Gulf's application. Under a treaty of 1899, the Sheikh of Kuwait agreed to reject any application unless Great Britain approved.

Secretary of State Stimson protested to the British government, and after two years of discussion, London offered to commend both Gulf and the British-owned Anglo-Persian Company to the sheikh. Because Kuwait's government declined to award two concessions, Gulf and Anglo-Persian agreed to form the Kuwait Oil Company as an equally owned corporation to apply for the concession. Following the formation of this company, the sheikh awarded it the oil rights on December 23, 1934. The company began oil drilling operations in 1936.

### December 29, 1934

**Japan gives the necessary two-year's notice that it will terminate the Washington Naval Limitation Treaty of 1922, effective December 31, 1936.**

Throughout 1934, American, British, and Japanese delegates had informal discussions preparatory to the anticipated naval limitation conference of 1935. The London Treaty of 1930 expired at the end of 1936, and a change in the limits was being considered.

Throughout the discussions of 1934, Japan insisted on gaining naval parity with Britain and America. After Japan's agreement to the London Treaty of 1930, two political assassinations resulted, and the ultranationalist factions that gained power in Tokyo in 1931 would countenance nothing except parity. Great Britain wanted, as during the 1920s, to increase the number of light cruisers in contrast to the American desire for more heavy cruisers. The U.S. delegates were firmly controlled by Roosevelt, however, and the president preferred to continue the existing treaty limits or to reduce the current naval allocations.

By the end of 1934, the forthcoming London Conference appeared to be doomed. Each of the three nations refused to compromise. While Britain was ready to consider a Japanese increase of ratios in exchange for more cruisers, the United States rejected both suggestions. As a result, Japan's announcement on December 29 surprised neither President Roosevelt nor Prime Minister Ramsay MacDonald. They decided nevertheless to proceed with the London Conference, although it was delayed until December 9, 1935, to search for a solution that would permit further limits on naval ships.

See January 15, 1936.

# 1935

### January 7, 1935

*France and Italy sign an agreement regarding north Africa.*

France agreed to concessions with Mussolini regarding Italian rights both in Tunisia and Ethiopia. The French Foreign Office hoped this would promote Italy's goodwill against Germany.

### January 13, 1935

*A plebiscite in the Saar Basin approves reunion with Germany.*

In accordance with the Treaty of Versailles, the League of Nations conducted this plebiscite in the Saar. Ninety percent of the people voted to join Germany in preference to union with France or their continued

administration by the League of Nations. On March 1, the Saar became part of the German Reich.

### January 29, 1935

*The U.S. Senate fails to obtain a two-thirds vote and denies U.S. membership in the World Court.*

Although the Senate had rejected membership in the World Court when Presidents Harding, Coolidge, and Hoover recommended approval, President Roosevelt and Secretary Hull believed there was vast support for it in the Senate in 1934. Subsequently, the State Department prepared a draft treaty for U.S. membership and Senator Joseph T. Robinson of Arkansas offered a resolution for approval on January 16, 1935. A careful Senate poll indicated that more than two-thirds of the senators approved membership.

Over one weekend, however, anti–World Court spokesmen protested sufficiently to change the votes of several senators. The Hearst newspaper chain opposed the court vehemently. On the radio, Father Charles Coughlin, a popular, right-wing Detroit priest, urged his listeners to write letters opposing the court to senators. Between Friday, January 25, when the Senate vote was delayed to Tuesday, January 29, Senate opposition grew from 10 to 36 members. Hearst lobbyists and messengers who carted wheelbarrows of telegrams from Coughlin's audience startled the politicians into shifting their votes. The resolution failed on January 29 by a vote of 52 to 36, 7 votes short of the necessary two-thirds.

Roosevelt was angered by the defeat of the World Court. Historian Robert Dallek contends this experience made Roosevelt and the State Department especially sensitive to isolationist sentiment during the next several years.

### February 2, 1935

*A commercial agreement with Brazil is the first under the Reciprocal Trade Act of 1934.*

Although a special and preferential pact was concluded with Cuba on August 24, 1934, the Brazilian agreement was the first one fully to apply the provisions of the Reciprocal Agreements Act.

Following passage of the new trade bill on June 12, 1934, the president set up a Committee on Trade Agreements headed by Assistant Secretary of State Sayre, who worked with the Trade Agreements

Division of the State Department to prepare tentative rate schedules on a country-by-country basis and to negotiate tariff relations with each nation.

The basic principles that Sayre and the Trade Agreements Division followed are listed here:

1. An item should be negotiated with the nation that was America's chief supplier of the product being lowered in rates.
2. As far as possible, the commodity should be non-competitive with a domestic product.
3. The other nation must also reduce its quota restrictions on the product.

In negotiating the Brazilian agreement, the principal opposition in America was from the manganese lobby. This opposition delayed the signing of the agreement, but eventually that lobby's interests were satisfied and the agreement was signed on February 2. The experience with Brazil caused Secretary Hull to realize that the State Department would have to work slowly and cautiously to guarantee that the basic approach of tariff reductions would not be jeopardized. Nevertheless, by the end of 1936, agreements had been signed with 14 countries: Brazil, Belgium, Haiti, Sweden, Colombia, Canada, Honduras, Netherlands, Switzerland, Nicaragua, Guatemala, France, Finland, and Costa Rica.

The most difficult negotiations on trade reciprocity were with Great Britain. The British agreement was not concluded until January 6, 1939. According to some observers, the shock of the Munich crisis with Hitler during September and October 1938 persuaded the British to make concessions to U.S. treaty demands. By that time, Congress had extended the trade agreement act on March 1, 1937, for another three years.

## March 16, 1935

### *Hitler denounces the disarmament clauses of the Versailles Treaty, announcing that the German army will be increased to 36 divisions.*

According to the German Foreign Office, the Western powers had failed to disarm as provided by the 1919 Versailles Peace Treaty. This failure to act justified German rearmament.

Although France, Italy, and Great Britain protested Hitler's action, they did little else. On April 11, at the Stresa Conference, the three powers organized a common front to oppose Germany, but the agreement proved largely ineffective.

## March 23, 1935

### *Under pressure from Japan, the Soviet Union sells its interests in the Chinese Eastern Railway to Manchukuo.*

This railway had been under constant dispute between Japan and the Soviet Union because it gave the Soviets a direct route between Irkutsk and Vladivostok. After the USSR renounced other czarist treaties with China on May 31, 1924, it retained joint management with China of the railroad through Manchuria. By the act of March 23, the Soviets yielded their control to Japan's puppet government in Manchukuo.

## May 2, 1935

### *France and the USSR form an alliance in case of unprovoked aggression.*

Following Germany's rearmament decree on March 16, France and the Soviet Union undertook discussions to develop a defensive alliance by which an attack on one would result in a two-front war for Germany. Stalin was now promoting anti-Fascist, popular-front movements outside the Soviet Union and was eager to sign. In France, however, the political divisions between right-wing and left-wing groups deepened because of this projected alliance. The rightist conservatives in France denounced any form of agreement with the Communists. This division in French politics persistently weakened French foreign policy between 1935 and 1940 as the struggle between protofascists and socialists caused the deterioration of the centrist advocates of the Third Republic.

## May 16, 1935

### *The Soviet Union and Czechoslovakia conclude an alliance by which Moscow would aid Prague in case of an attack on the Czechoslovaks provided France also acted.*

During the years preceding the Munich crisis of September 1938, the Soviet Union repeatedly sought united action with France and England in opposing Nazi German expansion. The "appeasement" policy followed by London and Paris was anti-Communist, however. Chamberlain, Daladier, and others considered the Soviets a greater menace than the Germans.

See September 29, 1938.

### June 14, 1935

*The Chaco War ends between Bolivia and Paraguay.*

This war broke out in 1932 after four years of peace attempts failed. A truce was finally reached through the mediation efforts of the United States and five South American governments, which also provided for peace talks to be held at Buenos Aires. The peace conferees finally agreed on July 21, 1938, to submit the dispute to arbitration by the presidents of six American countries. The arbitrators awarded most of the Chaco territory to Paraguay but gave Bolivia an outlet to the sea by way of the Paraguay River.

See December 6, 1928.

### June 18, 1935

*Great Britain and Germany sign a naval agreement.*

Hitler suggested the idea of a naval pact because he hoped to gain approval for a general buildup of Germany's armed forces. He promised not to expand the German navy beyond 35% of the British navy, except for submarines. Hitler agreed to a 45% limit on submarines but claimed the right to build to parity, an option Germany exercised in December 1938. The treaty did not significantly affect the rate of German naval construction in 1935–1939; however, Hitler did succeed in gaining the unilateral termination of the naval clauses of the Versailles Treaty.

The French were understandably quite angry over the episode; however, their previous obstructionist demands during disarmament negotiations lessened sympathy for their complaints among other diplomats. The British navy, of course, was still dominant among European powers.

### August 2, 1935

*The British parliament approves the Government of India Act.*

This legislation provided a greater degree of political independence for India. Eleven provincial governments obtained legislatures with appointed governors and received wide local autonomy. A central legisla-

ture was established at Delhi, but the British governor-general retained control of India's national defense and foreign affairs.

### August 31, 1935

*The First Neutrality Act: Congress authorizes the president to embargo arms impartially to belligerents and to forbid U.S. citizens to travel on belligerent ships except at their own risk.*

Since 1933 there had been discussions, but no congressional action, on proposed arms embargoes. In May 1933, President Roosevelt asked Congress for authority to place an embargo on arms destined for an aggressor nation. This resolution had been amended by the Senate Foreign Relations Committee to apply an embargo to both or all warring parties, which would penalize the victim. As a result, the State Department withdrew support from the resolution and it never passed.

This incident indicated, however, a distinct divergence of opinions. President Roosevelt and Secretary Hull wanted the president to have discretionary authority to help the victim nation and to punish the aggressor. Senator Key PITTMAN of Nevada, the chairman of the Senate Foreign Relations Committee, disagreed and persistently advocated that the United States help neither nation because this was the only effective way to remain neutral and not become involved in war.

By the spring of 1935, at least three factors resulted in new congressional bills to embargo armaments. First, the Geneva Disarmament Conference had failed and Germany had taken steps to rebuild its navy and army while both Japan and Italy pursued aggressive actions. Second, the Italian demands escalated against Ethiopia and by August 1935 had reached the crisis proportions that led to war in October. American isolationists wanted to remain out of the conflict in Ethiopia. Third, recent publications regarding America's economic and neutrality violations between 1914 and 1917 caused many Americans to believe that the United States needed new laws to stay away from Europe's perennial problems. Chief among these publications were newspaper reports of the Nye Committee hearings and a popular book published in April 1934, Walter Mills's *The Road to War,* which described how loans to the Allies and the use of neutrality favored England and gradually brought America into the war against

Germany. Other studies suggested other reasons why the United States became involved in Europe in 1917 and implied that America could avoid war only by strictly impartial neutrality.

In the context of the failure of disarmament in Europe, the rising aggressive behavior of the Axis powers, especially in Ethiopia in 1935, and the general atmosphere promoting a need to avoid the mistakes of the period 1914 to 1917, the neutrality resolution of 1935 became the first of a series of congressional bills seeking to keep America neutral and isolated. These three factors also favored Senator Pittman's desire to treat all belligerents the same, even though President Roosevelt preferred discretionary power to identify and embargo arms only to aggressor nations.

In July 1935, after several congressmen introduced bills to embargo arms to belligerents, the State Department drafted a bill for Congress that granted the president the discretionary power he desired. Senator Pittman disliked this bill and the Senate Foreign Relations Committee rejected both it and a second draft that would have limited the embargo to an Italian-Ethiopian war. Because the Senate committee wanted an impartial arms embargo, Roosevelt tried to block all arms and neutrality acts until the next session of Congress, but he failed. In mid-August, all signs indicated that Italy would attack Ethiopia in the near future. Thus, the mood of Congress was to pass some type of neutrality act. On August 20, a group of isolationist senators led by Nye and Arthur Vandenberg began a filibuster, vowing to block several domestic New Deal bills until a mandatory neutrality law was passed. The president relented and supported Senator Pittman, who offered an impartial arms embargo limited to six months. Pittman presented his bill on August 20. By August 24, it passed both houses of Congress, and on August 31 the president signed it.

The August 31 act required a mandatory embargo on "arms, ammunition and implements of war" to all belligerents. The president would define "implements of war" and determine when the embargo would begin. The president had discretionary power to withhold protection from Americans traveling on belligerent ships. The law also prohibited U.S. ships from carrying munitions to belligerents and established a Munitions Control Board to regulate arms shipments. The bill was valid for six months on the assumption that permanent legislation would be made at the next session of Congress (see April 12, 1934).

## October 3, 1935

### *The Italian invasion of Ethiopia begins.*

Difficulties between Ethiopia and Italy began on December 5, 1934, when an Ethiopian-Somaliland border clash occurred between troops of the two nations. Soon after, France recognized Italian concessions in Africa. Attempts by the League of Nations and Great Britain to limit Italy's action against Ethiopia did not succeed. The Italian military, in particular, wished to avenge its defeat at the Battle of Adua in 1896 and to annex all of Ethiopia.

On October 7, the League of Nations declared that Italy was the aggressor, but attempts to use sanctions against Italy failed. The nations disagreed on using oil sanctions. In addition, Hitler used the war crisis to send German troops into the Rhineland in March 1936. The German action posed a more serious situation to Europeans and diverted attention from Ethiopia. On May 5, 1936, Italy proclaimed the annexation of Ethiopia.

See January 7, 1935.

## October 5, 1935

### President Roosevelt proclaims an arms embargo in the Italian-Ethiopian War, the first of several U.S. actions opposing Italy's aggression.

Although Italy attacked Ethiopia without a declaration of war, Roosevelt issued the embargo proclamation before the League of Nations acted on October 7, 1935. Applying the Neutrality Act of August 31, Roosevelt embargoed munitions to both belligerents, even though Italy was the clear aggressor. His proclamation also warned Americans who dealt with either belligerent that they did so at their own risk.

Between October 5 and November 15, the United States took other actions to protect its neutrality. On October 6, Roosevelt warned Americans not to travel on belligerent ships, a warning applying to Italian vessels because Ethiopia had none. On October 30, the president appealed to Americans to forgo commercial or other profits to be made from warring nations. On November 15, Secretary Hull enlarged this "moral embargo" of October 30, urging Americans to halt exports for "war purposes" of such materials as oil, copper, trucks, tractors, scrap steel, and scrap iron. Although not technically "implements of war," Hull said, the sale of these products violated the spirit of neutrality. Prewar sales could be carried out but any increased sales of these commodities would not be "morally" correct.

Unfortunately, neither U.S. action nor the League of Nations sanctions prevented Italy's superior strength from defeating Ethiopia.

See June 20, 1936.

### October 11, 1935

*The League of Nations imposes sanctions on Italy as the aggressor against Ethiopia.*

Following the Italian invasion of Ethiopia on October 3, the league Council declared Italy had "resorted to war in disregard of her obligations under Article XII of the League covenant." On October 7, the council declared that Italy was the aggressor nation and that the 51 members of the assembly would be justified in imposing sanctions on Italy after October 11.

The action of October 11 was not implemented until November 18, when the league applied sanctions. They prohibited the importation of Italian goods and embargoed arms, loans, and raw materials. Significantly, the embargo did not include oil, the product that might have injured Italy the most. In addition, because of French-British objections, the League of Nations did not establish a naval blockade of Italy or close the Suez Canal to Italian ships. These measures would have forced Italy to end the war quickly. The failure of league members to block Italy's aggression indicated once again the ineffectiveness of collective security during the 1930s.

# 1936

### January 15, 1936

**Japan withdraws from the London Naval Conference because the United States and Britain refuse to recognize its right to naval parity.**

Following Japan's December 29, 1934, announcement that it would terminate the Washington Naval Treaty limits in two years, preparations for the London Naval Conference of 1935 went slowly because the United States and Britain disagreed on how best to handle Japan. Great Britain had increasingly turned its attention to European problems. Therefore, London

agreed to follow Washington's lead on the naval treaty with Japan. Roosevelt believed that if he could make Japan the nation that renounced naval disarmament, the American defense and foreign policy program would be assisted. In addition, Roosevelt would become the champion of disarmament and one who reluctantly requested an expansion of the U.S. navy program.

When the London Conference opened on December 9, 1935, the chief of the U.S. delegation, Norman Davis, presented Roosevelt's plan for a 10-year renewal of the Washington Treaty and a 20% reduction in each country's overall naval tonnage. Japan, of course, would never accept those concepts. Tokyo's delegate, Ambassador to the U.S. Hiroshi Saito, proposed parity for Japan with Britain and America and the elimination of all aircraft carriers and battleships.

The conference breakdown came on January 15, 1936. Japan denounced its treatment as an inferior power by the existing treaties. Then Saito and his fellow delegates left London. Because Japan had previously announced that its termination of existing limits would be in effect on December 31, 1936, the two remaining naval powers met with a French representative. Before concluding the London Conference, France, Britain, and America signed a naval treaty on March 25, 1936. The three-power agreement committed the United States and Britain to maintaining parity in their fleets' size and type. The three nations also agreed to exchange information on their fleets and to retain their treaty limits in line with whatever increase Japan made in its fleet.

One significant consequence of the Japanese action was the U.S. congressional agreement to appropriate funds for naval construction.

### February 29, 1936

**The Second Neutrality Act: A congressional joint resolution extends the act of August 31, 1935, with three amendments and one significant change in wording.**

On the day the Neutrality Act of 1935 was scheduled to expire, Congress renewed the basic law with the following changes:

1. The law was extended to May 1, 1937.
2. Loans to belligerents were forbidden in accordance with a State Department request.

3. The president was directed to extend the arms embargo to any new belligerent entering the war. This change indicated a desire to extend the action to any collective action taken against a belligerent.

4. The president could exempt from an arms embargo any American republic at war with a non-American state, provided the American republic was not cooperating with a non-American state.

5. An inadvertent change in wording stated that "whenever the President shall find that there exists a state of war." This phrase replaced the original, which said the president would institute the embargo "upon the outbreak or during the progress of war."

Although the new law did not add clauses to include commodities other than "arms, ammunition or other implements of war," Roosevelt asked the nation to respect the "moral embargo" requested in the Italian-Ethiopian War.

See October 5, 1935.

### March 2, 1936

**The United States and Panama sign a treaty abolishing the U.S. protectorate of Panama.**

Intended to continue fostering "good neighbor" relations, the 1936 Panama treaty limited the U.S. purposes in Panama to the "effectual maintenance, operation, sanitation and protection of the Canal and its auxiliary works." The United States also promised to strictly control the commissary business available to American . military personnel in the Canal Zone at low prices.

Panama ratified the treaty on December 24, 1936. The U.S. Senate delayed ratification, however. Concern about the relationship of the canal's security to America's continental defense prompted some senators to demand clarification of Article X, which required consultation between the two governments in the event of threats of aggression. The Senate wanted assurances that if necessary, the United States could act first and consult afterward. When this was clarified, the Senate ratified the treaty on July 25, 1939.

In addition to agreeing not to intervene in Panamanian affairs, the United States increased its annual payments to Panama and pledged to provide for mutual defense of the Canal Zone.

### March 7, 1936

*Germany denounces the Locarno Pacts of 1925 and moves soldiers into the Rhineland.*

Because of French protests against Hitler's occupation of the Rhineland, war between Germany and France appeared imminent. Although Great Britain and Italy joined France in protests, they would not invoke sanctions or consider other actions against Hitler. Italy was involved in Ethiopia; the British Conservative government of Stanley Baldwin was unwilling to undertake military action.

### May 5, 1936

*The Italian army occupies Addis Ababa, and Mussolini proclaims the conquest of Ethiopia.*

The Italian victory resulted in the collapse of the League of Nations policy toward collective security. Ethiopia was abandoned and the league's economic sanctions against Italy failed to be implemented effectively.

### June 4, 1936

**Treasury Secretary Morgenthau issues countervailing customs duties on a list of imports subsidized by the German government.**

In what Secretary of State Hull described as Morgenthau's "personal war against Germany," the Secretary of the Treasury levied special duties on German imports that the Nazi government had been subsidizing. The Tariff Act of 1930 permitted the Treasury Department to do this. With the approval of President Roosevelt and the attorney general, Morgenthau issued the duty list on June 4.

Inspite of Hull's disagreement, Morgenthau succeeded. At first, Reichsbank President Hjalmar Schacht protested the new duties. But when the United States stood firm, Germany backed down and removed all the subsidies it had granted to German companies for such exports. By September, the United States removed the special duties. Morgenthau could boast that he had checked "Germany's career of economic conquest."

## June 5, 1936

*In France, the left-wing Popular-Front coalition of Léon Blum gains control of the ministry.*

The parliamentary elections of May 3 had given the Socialists and Radical Socialists a majority in the Chamber of Deputies. The Communist Party did not join the ministry but cooperated with the Popular Front. The Blum government tried to install an extensive program of economic and social reforms that caused financial difficulties for the government and led many French to gravitate to the political right.

## June 20, 1936

**The United States ends its embargo following the Italian conquest of Ethiopia: America applies the Nonrecognition Doctrine to Italian-controlled Ethiopia.**

Although President Roosevelt had considered stronger measures against Italy between October 5, when he proclaimed the arms embargo on both belligerents, and December 1935, the unwillingness of England and France to agree to stronger League of Nations measures and the opposition of isolationists such as Senator Hiram Johnson led the president to drop any such plans. Although some observers believed that Washington's willingness to replace European oil losses resulting from an Italian embargo would have encouraged the league states to sanction oil, the uncertainty of league action and the opposition of Johnson kept the United States from such a commitment. Johnson told Roosevelt he must do nothing that might imply that the United States was supporting the League of Nations or Great Britain because his colleagues opposed any hint of such cooperation.

With ineffective international opposition, Italy captured Addis Ababa and took control of Ethiopia on May 5, 1936. When the war was finished, Roosevelt announced on June 20 that the arms embargo, as well as the moral embargo on Italy, no longer applied. About the same time, Secretary of State Hull declared the United States would not recognize the Italian conquest of Ethiopia, just as Secretary Stimson had not recognized Japan's occupation of Manchuria in 1931–1932. America's official correspondence would be addressed only to the King of Italy, not to Italy's preferred title of King of Italy and Emperor of Ethiopia.

See October 11, 1935.

## July 17, 1936

*The Spanish civil war begins as insurgents led by General Francisco Franco and other army chiefs revolt in Spanish Morocco.*

The Spanish republic, established on December 9, 1931, experienced difficulties with separatist movements in Catalonia and with political disputes between republican and socialist left-wing factions. In addition, the army and the Roman Catholic Church opposed the anticlerical legislation affecting education and the property of religious orders. During October 1934, the Catholic Popular Action Party gained positions in the cabinet of Prime Minister Alejandro Lerroux and blocked his attempts in 1935 to solve Spanish problems.

To offset the growth of the Catholic Party and other right-wing groups, the left united in a Popular Front; forced the Lerroux cabinet to call new elections; and on February 16 won a decisive victory over the Conservative, Republican, Catholic, and Monarchist Parties.

The Popular Front victory precipitated General Franco's decision to rally the rightists against the republic. Clerics and army and air force leaders joined Franco, who appealed to the German and Italian fascists for aid. Thus, "volunteers" from Germany and Italy joined the insurgents, and soon the Soviet Union aided the Republican government with military equipment and advisers. After German air raids destroyed Guernica on April 26, 1937, President Roosevelt considered applying an embargo on Berlin and Rome but could not because the Spanish government refused to declare war on Germany or Italy.

After considerable and often bitter fighting, the civil war ended in a victory for Franco's forces on March 28, 1939.

## August 9, 1936

*French Premier Léon Blum follows British advice and calls for a meeting of all European nations to adopt nonintervention policies in the Spanish civil war.*

As the leader of the French Popular Front government of left-wing liberal and Socialist parties in France, Blum's first reaction to the fascist civil war against the Spanish republic was to aid the loyalist republicans in Madrid. Great Britain's Conservative Party ministry did not support this policy, and Foreign Secretary Anthony Eden warned Blum that if

Germany attacked France over the Spanish issue, England would not aid the French.

At Britain's suggestion, Blum called for a general European conference to adopt a nonintervention policy in Spain. Also on August 9, Blum suspended all French war exports to Spain.

For the International Non-Intervention Committee, see October 8, 1936.

### August 11, 1936

**Secretary of State Hull announces a "moral embargo" against both belligerents in the Spanish civil war.**

Following General Franco's Fascist-inspired attack on the Loyalist Republican government of Spain on July 17, 1936, Britain and France urged a general European neutrality in the civil war. Secretary Hull and President Roosevelt found this course of action acceptable, and on August 11, Hull publicly announced the American desire not to assist either side in the war.

Although the Neutrality Act of 1936 did not apply to a civil war, Hull stated he hoped all Americans would apply the spirit of that law to the Spanish conflict. The United States, he said, would "scrupulously refrain from any interference whatsoever in the unfortunate Spanish situation." Despite Hull's statement, many American Roman Catholics favored Franco's effort to overthrow the government.

During the fall of 1936, the Spanish crisis had not yet acquired the ideological dimensions that appeared clearly during the spring of 1937. While some rumors of German and Italian aid to Franco surfaced in August and September, no overt evidence had appeared. Britain and France organized a collective neutrality system in Europe. The policy of neutrality also served Roosevelt well during the presidential campaign of 1936. Although domestic issues predominated in the election, Roosevelt's neutrality in Spain pleased both the isolationists and the European-oriented internationalists during the fall and winter of 1936.

See October 8, 1936, and January 8, 1937.

### August 19, 1936

**The Moscow show trial of old Bolsheviks opens.**

In January 1935, Grigori Zinoviev, Lev Kamenev, and several other old Bolsheviks from the 1917 Revolution were tried for treason in secret sessions and sentenced to prison. In reality, these men had sided with Leon Trotsky against Stalin's rise to power during the 1920's. Trotsky had fled the country while the others appeared to reconcile themselves to Stalin's rule.

Continuing to be suspicious of anyone who differed with him, Stalin decided to stage public "show-trials" in 1936, beginning with those found guilty in 1935. At the second trials, Zinoviev, Kamenev, and fourteen other old Bolsheviks were accused of plotting with enemy countries against Stalin's regime. The sixteen men were convicted and immediately executed. Additional show trials were held between August 1936 and May 1938, during which other Soviet political and military leaders who earned Stalin's distrust were executed after being convicted of treason or of trying to restore bourgeois capitalism. The most important old Bolshevik executed in 1938 was Nikolai I. Bukarin, who opposed Stalin's forced collectivization of the Soviet Union's peasant population in 1929. Details of these events are in Robert Conquest's *The Great Terror: A Reassessment* (1990).

### August 27, 1936

**Egypt and Great Britain conclude a treaty giving Egypt greater local autonomy.**

According to this agreement, the only British forces in Egypt would be in the Suez Canal zone. Egypt would be independent and join the League of Nations, as well as be able to move troops into the Sudan. Finally, Britain and Egypt formed a 20-year alliance that would be reexamined at the end of that period.

### September 25, 1936

**The United States, Great Britain, and France agree to cooperate in maintaining currency stabilization.**

For over a year, British and French representatives had suggested to the U.S. State and Treasury Departments that they desired to cooperate in stabilizing the value of the dollar, franc, and pound. Since the London Economic Conference of 1933, Roosevelt and Secretary of the Treasury Morgenthau had rejected such cooperation. By June 1936, Morgenthau had convinced Roosevelt that currency stability would aid U.S. trade programs. As a result, Morgenthau conducted talks with Britain's Chancellor of the Exchequer Neville Chamberlain during the summer of 1936. France joined the discussions, and on September 25 the three nations exchanged statements agreeing to cooperate in stabilizing the value ratios of their currencies. Belgium, Switzerland, and Holland joined this cooperative effort by the end of 1936.

### October 8, 1936

**At the International Non-Intervention Committee meeting, the USSR objects to Fascist violations of the agreements, but Britain and France do not act.**

The accusations made by the Soviet delegate at the London nonintervention conference illustrate the duplicity of Germany, Italy, and the Soviet Union in proclaiming nonintervention in Spain while at the same time providing aid to either Franco's Nationalist forces or the Loyalist Republican. The first meeting of the Non-Intervention Committee that Léon Blum proposed on August 9, 1936, was held in London on September 9. Subsequently, throughout the civil war the Non-Intervention Committee gave the appearance of advocating no aid to either belligerent, although each of the 24 nations working on the Non-Intervention Committee provided varying degrees of aid to either the Fascist or Republican cause. The historian Hugh Thomas describes the committee's existence after September 9 as moving "from equivocation to hypoc-

risy and humiliation" but enduring until Franco's Fascist forces triumphed.

The Non-Intervention Committee served each nation's interest in different ways. For the British, the Conservative ministry appeared to be acting impartially while following covert practices that aided Franco's forces of "law and order." For France, the Popular Front government placated its liberal and left wings by providing small amounts of secret aid to the republic but appearing to be impartial. For Germany and Italy, their larger amount of aid to Franco was masked sufficiently to greatly assist Franco while the Spanish republicans received little aid, even though they represented the legitimate Spanish government. The Soviet Union provided some help to the Spanish republic but was generally dismayed by the Fascist aid to Franco. The Soviets stayed on the committee to retain British-French goodwill.

On October 15, following its complaint at the committee session about fascist intervention, the Soviet Union rapidly increased its military aid to the Loyalists. The smaller nations that joined the Non-Intervention Committee simply followed the five larger powers: some aided the fascists; some aided the republicans in Spain.

In retrospect, the Non-Intervention Committee's duplicity assisted Franco's forces more than the Loyalists. But it did provide a curious method for avoiding direct confrontations and, thus, a general

Francisco Franco and Adolf Hitler. National Archives

European war. In this respect, the French-British policy was a progenitor of appeasement. In each European country, the general public feared the communist revolutionary threat represented by the Spanish republic more than the Nazi-fascist ideology represented by Franco. The possible continuation of a liberal republican government in Spain was sacrificed to Franco's fascist dictatorship, determining Spain's authoritarian society for the next 40 years.

See May 13, 1938.

## October 25, 1936

### The Berlin-Rome anti-Comintern Pact is formed.

Hitler and Count Ciano of Italy signed an agreement to cooperate in seeking revision of the World War I peace treaties. In 1934–1935, Mussolini had often consulted with England and France because Italy's interests in the Danube region had differed from Hitler's. These conflicts were overlooked in 1936, and the two Fascist dictators agreed to work together against both democratic governments and communism. In November, Japan negotiated with Germany and Italy to join the Axis alliance.

Both Britain and France were deceived by the anti-Comintern rhetoric of the Axis powers. As Italian Foreign Minister Count Galeazzo CIANO asserted, the anti-Comintern pact was "unmistakably anti-British" in Europe, the Mediterranean, and the Far East, not anticommunist. For fascists, of course, anticommunism included the center liberal republican and democratic parties as well as the Soviet Union. During the 1930s, however, many who favored parliamentary government in England and France held an exaggerated fear of communism that led them to embrace the "law and order" speeches of the extreme right. Lacking sufficient devotion to the basic concepts of human rights, the centrists were weak apostles of democracy for whom the watchword slogan was "better Hitler than Stalin." Americans were not immune to this disease. Sumner Welles's opposition to the Cuban regime of Grau San Martín showed similar difficulties.

See September 5, 1933, January 15, 1934, and November 25, 1936.

## November 3, 1936

### Roosevelt wins an overwhelming victory in the presidential contest.

The election campaign was a bitter contest because the Republicans vigorously condemned the New Deal. The Republican nominee was Alfred LANDON of Kansas, and the Republican platform charged that Roosevelt had usurped great power, passed unconstitutional laws, and displaced free enterprise. The Republicans attacked no specific New Deal laws except for the decrease in personal and corporate income taxes.

At their Philadelphia convention, the Democrats renominated Roosevelt. The president's acceptance speech attacked "economic royalists" who created despotisms cloaked in legality. The party platform stood on the four-year record that had ended the severest aspects of the 1929–1933 depression.

On November 3, as one pundit said, nobody was for Roosevelt but the people. Although 80% of the press opposed the president, predictions of a close election did not materialize. Roosevelt won the biggest electoral majority since Monroe in 1820: Landon, 8, Roosevelt, 523. The Democratic majority in the Senate was 77-19; in the House, 328-107.

## November 18, 1936

### Germany and Italy recognize Franco's insurgent government in Spain.

Although they joined the London Non-Intervention Committee on September 9, 1936, Hitler and Mussolini supported General Franco with arms, technical experts, and some troops. On October 1, Franco named himself head of the Spanish state. To aid Franco overtly in blockading the Loyalist supply routes, Germany and Italy formally recognized his regime on November 18.

Although Britain's Conservative government's policy preferred Franco, London withheld recognition to retain the cooperation of French Premiers Léon Blum and Edouard Daladier until their Popular Front governments fell on October 4, 1938.

## November 25, 1936

*Germany and Japan sign an anti-Comintern pact.*

Ostensibly, the pact between Hitler's Nazi government and Japan's military-dominated government emphasized their agreement to oppose communism as identified by the Moscow-dominated Communist Third International (Comintern). Of course, to these ultranationalists "communists" included liberal democrats, socialists, and other center and left-of-center groups.

Japan and Italy also negotiated an agreement, completed on November 6, 1937, which joined the three extreme rightist governments as ideological and political allies.

## December 23, 1936

**Conclusion of a special Pan-American peace conference at Buenos Aires.**

The conference delegates drew up a common neutrality policy in the event of a war in the Americas and established principles of consultation if the peace of the hemisphere should be threatened.

Because the next regular meeting of the Inter-American Conference was not scheduled until 1938, President Roosevelt suggested in 1935 that a special meeting be held on maintaining peace in the Western Hemisphere. The Italian-Ethiopian War and the increased aggressiveness of Germany and Italy, not only in Europe but also in Latin American trade, caused the president to believe a peace conference in

The Good Neighbor policy in practice: President Roosevelt rides with President Justo of Argentina through the streets of Buenos Aires. Franklin D. Roosevelt Library

the Americas would be beneficial. After sounding out representatives of the American republics, Secretary Hull agreed to call a conference. On January 30, 1936, Roosevelt proposed a meeting to be held at Buenos Aires to determine how peace in the Americas "may best be safeguarded."

To emphasize the importance of the meeting, President Roosevelt went by ship to Argentina and addressed the opening-day session of the meeting. Contrasting the peace of the Western Hemisphere with the rise of violence in Europe, the president urged the delegates to effect a united front for peace so that the American republics would consult together "for our mutual safety and our mutual good."

Before adjourning on December 23, the conference made a series of agreements, the most important being those listed below:

1. A Convention for the Maintenance, Preservation, and Reestablishment of Peace that provided for consultation not only in case of the threat of war between American nations but if a war outside America menaced the peace of the Western Hemisphere.
2. A Declaration of Principles of Inter-American Solidarity and Cooperation that "continentalized" the Monroe Doctrine; that is, the American nations would consult whenever an "act susceptible of disturbing the peace of America should be threatened or committed."
3. An Additional Protocol Relative to Non-Intervention stating that the signatories "declare inadmissible the intervention of any one of them, directly or indirectly, and for whatever reason, in the internal or external affairs of any other of the parties." When the United States accepted and ratified this agreement without the reservations of the 1933 Montevideo meeting, it committed itself to a nonintervention policy.

# 1937

### January 8, 1937

**President Roosevelt signs congressional legislation that specifically applies the Impartial Neutrality Embargo to the Spanish civil war.**

From August 11 to December 28, America's "moral embargo" against the shipment of arms to either side in Spain had been generally effective. On December 26, however, the first organized group of 26 American volunteers left New York for Spain. Because these and later U.S. volunteers, all of whom fought for the Loyalist Republicans, officially volunteered when they reached France, the U.S. government could not prosecute them. After January 11, 1937, the passport office stamped all passports as "Not Valid for Spain," but after reaching France, passports became unnecessary for the volunteers.

On December 28, the moral embargo was circumvented by Robert Cruse, who applied for a license to ship $2,775,000 worth of aircraft engines to the Spanish government. Cruse received his license because the State Department had no legal means to reject it. Subsequently, Cruse's cargo left New York the day before the congressional embargo was passed on January 8. Carried on board the Spanish ship *Mar Cantabrico,* the cargo was captured by the Spanish nationalists in the Bay of Biscay and was used by the Fascists rather than the Republican forces in Spain.

Cruse's license application prompted President Roosevelt to urge Congress to make such sales illegal as soon as it reassembled on January 6, 1937. The law as passed on January 6 and signed by the president on January 8 embargoed all sales of arms, ammunition, and implements of war to Spain. Neither belligerent could obtain U.S. arms.

Roosevelt's principal reason for requesting the arms embargo appears to have been his desire to align his policy to what he perceived to be the British-French policy. Whether or not Roosevelt or other Americans understood the role that British Conservatives and France were using in Europe is not certain. Although the U.S. consul at Seville made frequent reports to the State Department on the large amount of German and Italian matériel and the "volunteers" entering Spain, the president may have been too concerned with domestic problems to have noticed.

Whatever the reason for Roosevelt's decision to act "impartially" in Spain, the net result of the U.S. embargo was, as in the case of the British-French embargoes, favorable to the Spanish Fascists. Realizing this, Franco announced in January that the president acted as a "true gentleman" in approving the Embargo Act. The Germans also praised Roosevelt. Increasingly, however, U.S. liberals, Socialists, and Communists condemned the embargo and supplied volunteers to assist the Spanish Republicans.

See October 8, 1936.

### January 30, 1937

*Stalin's purge of the Communist Party extends into military ranks.*

Although the trials and executions of "Old Bolsheviks" whom Stalin distrusted began in 1935, he extended the purges for "treason" to military commanders in 1937. From January 23 to 30, Stalin ordered the execution of 13 more assumed political competitors, the most prominent being Yuri Pyatakov and Karl Radek.

Yet in light of their effect on Soviet fortunes in World War II, Stalin's most crucial purges were of military leaders that began on June 11, 1937. As Robert Conquest reports, the arrest of military officers in May came as a surprise when they were announced. To justify their trials, the Communist Party organ *Pravda* reported on June 15 that a Stalin spokesman said these commanders had "admitted their treacherousness, wreckings, and espionage." *Pravda* did not mention that their interrogators had tortured them.

Among the seven top-ranking military officials executed on June 12, the most prominent were Marshal M. N. Tukhachevsky, the deputy people's commissar of defense, and Yan Gamarnik, the first deputy commissar of defense. As Conquest explains, the "assault on the army" probably derived from a German plot to "betray" Tukhachevsky and cripple the Red Army. Apparently, the Nazi intelligence agency leaked false information to Czech President Edvard Beneš, who passed the report to Stalin. The German head of intelligence, Reinhard Heydrich, engineered the plot by forging a "dossier" of 23 documents. Next, a German agent contacted an official of the Soviet embassy, showing him 2 pages of the dossier and asking payment for the other 30 pages. Moscow quickly responded and bought the dossier for one-half million marks that turned out to be counterfeit. By mid-May, Stalin had the entire document, and between May 20 and 31, he ordered the arrest of the seven military leaders, including Tukhachevsky. Additional army purges followed over the next two years.

Although at least 1 million Soviet citizens were swept away during Stalin's purges of the 1930s, the army executions between May 1937 and September 1938 left the USSR with grave deficiencies in military experience when Germany invaded in 1941. Conquest indicates that the one military area where the Germans were "immensely superior" in 1941 was the quality of command and staff officers. By 1940, at least 428 of the top-level Soviet officer corps had been executed plus many others, perhaps 43,000, who were dismissed from their offices. Robert Conquest's *The Great Terror: A Reassessment* (1990) provides an informed discussion of Stalin's purges.

### May 1, 1937

**The Third Neutrality Act: This act renewed the act of 1936 but added several amendments including "cash and carry" provisions.**

Although continuing the mandatory and impartial arms embargo provisions of the 1936 act, the 1937 act had no time limit and contained three new clauses. These additions:

1. extended the mandatory embargo to civil strife whenever the president should find arms exports "would threaten or endanger the peace of the United States";
2. stated U.S. citizens could not travel on belligerent ships except at their own risk;
3. provided "cash and carry" sales of other goods and empowered the president to forbid the export of commodities other than arms in U.S. ships. The belligerent nation purchasing these goods must use its own ships and have title transferred to the foreign government or agency before leaving the United States. In brief, non-arms commodities had to be paid for in cash, their title transferred from the U.S. seller to the foreign buyer, and the product carried away in foreign ships. Roosevelt liked this provision because in the event of war, England and France were the European nations most likely to benefit from U.S. purchases.

### May 28, 1937

*Chamberlain becomes British prime minister; his appeasement policy toward Germany.*

Since 1934, Stanley Baldwin's Conservative ministry was uncertain about proper policies toward Germany and Italy. When Neville Chamberlain became prime minister on May 28, he followed his prior desire to negotiate peace with Hitler and Mussolini, even if concessions were essential.

As F. S. Northedge's *The Troubled Giant* explains, Chamberlain did not invent "appeasement" but carried it to its logical conclusions, showing that in a violent world the assumptions of many British politicians were "out of place."

Chamberlain's beliefs did not differ from those of the bulk of British public opinion that thought war was the worst evil and should be avoided at almost any cost. He thought peace depended on understanding between the Great Powers, especially Britain and Germany. He had slight respect for France's unstable government and almost no respect for Italy. He abhorred Soviet communism and thought its ongoing purges weakened the Soviet state. As for the United States, he thought isolationism meant Britain could "count on nothing from the Americans but words." With Britain and Germany as the effective powers, Chamberlain believed Britain must remove the injustices of the 1919 Versailles Treaty and the mistrust in the minds of English and Germans. He supposed the appeasement policy could build confidence by making concessions to Hitler.

In 1937, Chamberlain's specific proposals for negotiating with Germany appeared in a memorandum of April 2. Declassified records in Ian Colvin's *The Chamberlain Cabinet* list four items for Britain and France to discuss with Germany. These were making treaties of nonaggression for Western Europe to replace the mutual guarantees signed at Locarno (see October 16, 1925); measures by Germany to respect the territorial integrity of states in Central and eastern Europe; Germany's return as a member of the League of Nations; an international arms limitation agreement.

Chamberlain's first step toward negotiations was on November 17, 1937, when Edward Wood, Lord Halifax went to Germany and talked with Hitler and other officials. On his return, Halifax told the cabinet that Germany appeared to have no "policy of immediate adventure" but was not yet ready to join the League of Nations.

See September 29, 1938.

### July 7, 1937

*An incident between Chinese and Japanese troops at the Marco Polo bridge near Peking soon develops into an undeclared war.*

Although Japan's war plans in 1937 were based on a conflict with the Soviet Union in Manchuria or Mongolia, Tokyo had nearly 7,000 troops in its "legation guard" in Peking and vicinity, many more than any other power. During 1935 and 1936, Japan had negotiated with China to gain Peking's recognition of the Japanese-supported state of Manchukuo, but the Chinese nationalists would not—and could not if they wished to retain their nationalist political base—recognize these Japanese "rights." Consequently, there was frequent friction between Chinese and Japanese forces in the Peking region, and on July 7, Japanese troops on maneuvers near the Marco Polo bridge, 13 kilometers outside Peking, clashed with Chinese troops.

Exactly what happened on July 7 is a mystery. The Chinese claimed the Japanese demanded entrance to the city of Wanping to search for a missing soldier. When the Chinese refused, the Japanese fired artillery that killed or wounded 200 Chinese in Wanping. The Japanese contended that soldiers from China's 29th Army fired on Japanese troops without provocation. When the Japanese asked for negotiations to settle the dispute, the Chinese would not withdraw their troops, and further attacks began on both sides. The incident probably was not planned, but it sparked a larger conflict during the next six weeks. Tokyo ordered an attack on Nanking and, following its conquest in December, attempts to localize the war ended. Fighting continued although war was not declared.

### July 16, 1937

**Secretary of State Hull informs the press that the United States must wait to decide on a policy toward the Chinese-Japanese conflict. The powers hope to localize the war, and Hull issues a peace circular to all nations urging them to adopt and practice the U.S. principles of international good conduct.**

When the "China incident" began on July 7, 1937, the United States and other Western powers hoped to resolve the crisis quickly. Both China and Japan expressed a willingness to seek peace terms, but during the next six months no mediation was accepted. The war in China gained a momentum that did not cease until 1945.

The United States had two principal decisions to make. First, would Japan be held to its obligations under the Nine-Power Pact of 1922? If so, what could be done to require it to follow that treaty? Second, should Roosevelt proclaim the Neutrality

Act of May 1, 1937, to be in effect? Because neither side had declared war, there was a rationale for withholding the neutrality decree, which would harm China more than Japan.

During the summer of 1937, Roosevelt and Hull chose to wait and see what developed in China. As Hull told newsmen on July 16, to invoke the Nine-Power Pact while both sides protested peaceful desires would make the concluding of peace more difficult. Therefore, Hull hoped to mobilize world opinion to bring moral pressure to bear on both Peking and Tokyo. He communicated a message to all governments, urging self-restraint, abstinence from the use of force, peaceful negotiations, sanctity of treaties, promotion of stability among nations, reduction of arms, and the use of orderly processes to resolve international problems.

On September 14, the president issued a decree that stopped government ships from carrying armaments to either China or Japan and warned private shippers that they carried arms at their own risk. Four days later, however, the watchful-waiting policy still applied. A State Department news release said that Hull and Roosevelt were acting on a 24-hour basis toward the Sino-Japanese conflict.

## October 5, 1937

**Roosevelt's "Quarantine Speech": The president states that when there is international lawlessness, the Americas too could be attacked; the international community must join "in a quarantine of the patients" to keep lawlessness from spreading.**

Roosevelt's Chicago speech of October 5 attempted to counteract the isolationist trend in America because both Roosevelt and Secretary of State Hull agreed that American inaction indirectly encouraged the three Axis powers to increase their aggressive acts.

By early September, Hull believed Japan had clearly decided on full-scale war in China. Violent fighting began in the area of Shanghai in August, and Japan declared a blockade of the Chinese coast. Following a bombing in which Chinese planes mistakenly killed 1,700 civilians, including 2 Americans, Roosevelt sent 1,200 U.S. Marines to Shanghai on August 17 to protect U.S. lives and property. Finally, speeches by Premier Konoye and Foreign Minister Hirota on September 5 indicated Japan's commitment to the Chinese war.

At the League of Nations, China appealed for aid, and a special subcommittee investigated the events in

This terrified baby was the only survivor at Shanghai's South Station after a Japanese bombing on August 28, 1937. National Archives

China since July 7. A U.S. delegate, Minister to Switzerland Leland Harrison, joined the subcommittee as a nonvoting member. Harrison kept Hull informed on the committee's progress. Hull refused, however, to make a commitment to Britain or France with regard to Japan. The United States would take parallel action with the league or other powers with whom the United States agreed but could make no advance multilateral commitments of any kind.

The "Quarantine Speech" was Roosevelt's attempt to alert the American people against complete isolation from external conflicts and to highlight the need for nonbelligerent cooperation to punish aggression so disorder would not spread. After describing the recent "reign of terror and international lawlessness," the president stated that the "very foundations of civilization are seriously threatened." To prevent the "spread of this international anarchy," he warned, "peace-loving nations must make a concerted effort" against aggressors. The opposition might be a "quarantine" of the "epidemic of world lawlessness" in order to secure "the health of the community against the spread of the disease." Because America hates war, "America actively engages in the search for peace."

Although historians using the Roosevelt archives realize the president had no specific idea in mind at this time and wished only to search for peace, contemporaries in Europe and America read many hopes or fears into the speech. European leaders who sought U.S. backing for positive action against Germany, Italy, and Japan interpreted the speech as a sign that Roosevelt would approve sanctions against Japan and other aggressors. American noninterventionists recoiled in horror and denunciation of Roosevelt's speech, envisioning it as a collective security action that would lead the nation to war. In Secretary Hull's view, the speech failed of its intention because isolationist editors and politicians attacked the administration's desire to promote greater international cooperation.

Dorothy Borg has compiled a summary of the variety of U.S. opinion after the Quarantine Speech that shows greater support for Roosevelt than he, Hull, and others in Washington perceived. Most editors, religious groups, labor groups, and others favored action short of war to counteract the aggressors. Borg believes the administration was too sensitive to the Hearst press, business newspapers such as the *Wall Street Journal,* and vociferous isolationist senators such as Borah, Vandenberg, and Hiram

Johnson. Nevertheless, the negative perceptions of the speech registered by Secretary Hull and others caused the administration to proceed more cautiously during the next two years. The president's policies seemed often to follow, rather than lead, public opinion in foreign affairs from 1937 to 1941.

### October 6, 1937

***The League of Nations assembly condemns Japan for violating the Nine-Power and Paris Peace Pacts, calling on all nations to give moral support to China.***

The League of Nations acted on recommendations of a special subcommittee on the Sino-Japanese dispute. This group reported on October 5 that Japan's action was not justified by the Marco Polo Bridge incident of July 7, 1937. The League of Nations Assembly also suggested that the signatory members of the Nine-Power Treaty of 1922 should consult regarding the Japanese violations.

In the United States, isolationists believed that the assembly's condemnation of Japan voted the day after Roosevelt's "Quarantine Speech" demonstrated the president's intention to tie U.S. policy to that of other nations. There is no documentary evidence to prove this critical assertion except the State Department's reports from Leland Harrison on the progress of the league subcommittee.

See November 24, 1937.

### October 27, 1937

***Mexico's President Cárdenas decrees a land reform compensation scheme in the Yaqui valley because the United States refuses an offered compromise.***

The land reform measures undertaken on a gradual basis by the Mexican government during the 1920s increased more rapidly after 1934 under President Cárdenas. While 8 million hectares (20 million acres) of land were distributed from 1917 to 1933, Cárdenas distributed nearly 20 million hectares during his six years in office. Because the Mexican government agreed to compensate both foreign and native landowners for the expropriation, issuance of Mexican land bonds or other long-term obligations had to be devised to pay the former owners.

On April 24, 1934, a U.S.-Mexican claims treaty had set up a General Claims Commission to determine proper claims payments, but it allowed the land claims questions to be settled by appointed experts from the State Department and Mexico's Foreign Office. For nearly a year these experts held discussions but could not agree on a settlement. On February 1, 1936, the land compensation claims were returned to be considered by the General Claims Commission. At dispute was Mexico's desire to make one lump sum payment for all land claims. The U.S. delegates refused this approach, demanding that land reform must stop until Mexico could pay for the land as each section was expropriated. The U.S. position was not acceptable to Mexico because it would require lengthy delays before Mexico could pay directly for the land.

Shortly after the earlier land claims negotiations failed and went back to the General Claims group, Cárdenas inaugurated a land reform program in the Yaqui valley of northwest Mexico. The Yaqui land had a special status in Mexico. During Dictator Díaz's last years of office, a group of about 50 U.S. citizens received sizable tracts of unimproved land in the Yaqui River area. The Americans used extensive irrigation methods to develop prosperous winter wheat and rice farms.

In 1936, Mexican natives petitioned Cárdenas to expropriate the irrigated lands, and the Mexican government began steps to fulfill their requests. The president understood the views of the U.S. farmers as well as his own people and took special interest in the Yaqui settlement. After visiting the region, Cárdenas told Ambassador Daniels that U.S. owners had profited from their investment but he would permit them to keep a share of their land.

Throughout 1937, negotiations for a just settlement took place but were fruitless. Finally, on October 27, Cárdenas instituted the guidelines he would follow for the Yaqui valley. Each American farmer could keep 100 hectares (250 acres) of land with water rights. For their loss, they would receive nonirrigated land near the unfinished Angostura Dam. When the dam was completed in 1939, the owners would have sufficient water rights to sell the land in small parcels and make a profit. Cárdenas said that negotiation on his proposal was useless. The Yaqui farmers made out well from this pact because after 1939, the land near the new dam had an excellent selling price.

The other land claims of Americans in Mexico became part of the oil expropriation settlement of November 19, 1941.

**November 24, 1937**

### The Brussels conference of the Nine-Power signatories ends with a weak appeal to China and Japan to cease hostilities.

Acting in accordance with the League of Nations Assembly resolution of October 6, 1937, Belgium invited all nations that had accepted the 1922 Nine-Power Treaty plus Germany, China, and the Soviet Union to attend a meeting to consult on the Sino-Japanese conflict. The treaty signatories included the United States, Great Britain, France, Italy, Japan, Bolivia, Mexico, Denmark, Norway, and Sweden.

The conference appeared to be doomed from the outset. State Department delegate Jay Pierrepont Moffat wrote on November 1 that "even before we meet people are discussing ways to end" the conference. Although preconference discussions indicated nothing would result, Roosevelt told Norman Davis, chief of the U.S. delegation, to prolong it as long as possible to obtain a good effect on public opinion. Germany refused to attend the meeting, and Italy came only to defend Japan. The Japanese denounced the sessions, rejecting the conference's necessity, claiming its members had already condemned Japan, and asserting that the Japanese fought China only in self-defense.

The disarray among the democracies caused the conference to fail. It probably should not have convened at all because the democratic "peace-loving" powers were unwilling to take any action. Roosevelt and Hull willingly sent U.S. delegates to the meetings, but Britain and France did not want to be associated with the calling of the sessions or with being the leader in any decision—they wanted the United States to provide leadership. On November 17, Hull sent the U.S. delegation a list of items for a final conference report but informed Davis not to "assume a position of special leadership in regard thereto." Roosevelt and Hull wanted to pressure but not provoke Japan. Their emphasis in 1937 appeared to be to "not provoke."

The U.S. State Department had generally acted since 1920 on the assumption that the United States had no interests in China worth a war. This dictum continued to apply in 1937 because oral protests against Japan had always been permitted while any threat to support the statements with action was avoided.

The Brussels report of November 24 asked China and Japan to cease hostilities and consult about ending the fighting. No threats or possible sanctions were mentioned. If Japan persisted in aggression, the report said, the Nine-Power signatories would consult again about further action. There was, however, no follow-up to the Brussels Conference.

### December 12, 1937

**The U.S. gunboat *Panay* is sunk by Japanese airplanes; a British ship, HMS *Ladybird*, is fired upon on the same day.**

The *Panay* had sailed up the Yangtze River to Nanking in November 1937 to assist Ambassador Nelson JOHNSON in evacuating the embassy and fleeing to Hankow to escape the approaching Japanese army. On December 9, the *Panay*'s officers saw Japan's shells hitting nearby and they moved the boat 28 miles above the city to avoid danger to the few embassy officials already on board. The *Panay* also convoyed three Standard Oil Company tankers.

During the day of December 12, Ambassador Johnson heard that HMS *Ladybird* had been fired on by the Japanese, killing one seaman and wounding seven others. About midnight, Johnson learned that the Japanese had sunk the *Panay* as well as the three tankers, but he received no details. About the same time, Ambassador Grew in Tokyo received Foreign Minister Hirota, who told Grew that Japanese planes following the Chinese army had mistakenly attacked the *Panay*. Hirota apologized, saying poor visibility led the Japanese to believe the ships were Chinese. The same thing, he told Grew, had happened to the British ship *Ladybird*.

Not until December 15 did eyewitnesses of the attack on the *Panay* tell their stories in Shanghai. Their reports were uniformly similar and contradicted Japan's official version.

1. There was no poor visibility when the four ships were attacked.
2. All ships had U.S. flags and other markings to distinguish them. In addition, U.S. authorities had kept the Japanese informed of the *Panay*'s movement on December 9.
3. Although the first Japanese planes bombed from considerable height, six planes dive-bombed the ships and machine-gunned the area for 20 minutes.
4. When the *Panay* sank, the survivors fled to the tall reeds in the marshland near shore. As Japanese planes searched and machine-gunned the area,

the survivors hid until dark, when they went ashore to a nearby Chinese village for aid.
5. During the attack, 2 Americans died and 30 were wounded.

American public opinion was surprisingly moderate in light of the Japanese attack. Moreover, news reports in Shanghai concerned testimony from the *Panay*'s survivors and accounts of the Japanese atrocities in Nanking when they captured the city. Desiring to avoid war or at least not to fight over an incident in the Far East, many American editors blamed the United States for having ships and citizens in China and urged all Americans to evacuate the war zones. In this atmosphere the Roosevelt administration accepted Japan's apologies. Japan promised to pay indemnities and agreed to investigate and punish the guilty parties. Although Secretary of State Hull did not believe Tokyo's account of the raid, he accepted its apology on December 24 and took no further action.

During the *Panay* crisis, the British government offered to make its protests about the *Ladybird* attack a joint venture with possible punitive action against Japan. Roosevelt and Hull rejected these British advances and followed an independent course of protest to Tokyo. Nevertheless, to prepare for better future coordination of U.S.-British naval action, Roosevelt decided to send a naval liaison person to London.

See December 23, 1937.

### December 23, 1937

**President Roosevelt orders Captain Royal E. Ingersoll of the navy's War Plans Division to London to conduct staff talks with British naval officers.**

Although not directly involved in the policy to be followed in the *Panay* crisis of December 12, 1937, Ingersoll's appointment reflected Roosevelt's growing concern for the revision of the U.S. navy's Orange War Plan, which were based on an offensive war in the western Pacific Ocean. During the winter of 1936–1937, the president had reviewed the Orange Plan, which had been the navy's persistent war strategy since 1921. On January 9, 1937, Roosevelt requested new war plans but received only a lengthy, detailed report that repeated the old Orange Plan. The Navy

War Plans Division apparently could discern no change in U.S. policy since 1922.

Neither the State Department nor President Roosevelt gave the Far East the highest priority in their world strategy. Both were more concerned with European events. On November 10, soon after his "Quarantine Speech," Roosevelt asked Chief of Naval Operations Admiral William D. Leahy to prepare new war plans contingent upon Western Hemispheric defense and a two-ocean war against the Axis powers, with Great Britain as an ally.

It was not easy to persuade the navy to change its old Orange Plan, which required a large, offensive navy. Roosevelt seems to have hoped that direct contact between the British and Ingersoll of the Navy War Plans Division would broaden the naval officer's perspective from antagonism toward Britain to cooperation.

Roosevelt's naval ideas matched his 1938 navy appropriations request to Congress as well. The president sought a two-ocean navy bill during the early months of 1938. Ingersoll's mission to London became the first in a series of cooperative talks between British and U.S. navy, army, and air force officers.

See May 17, 1938. For the change in war plans from Orange as number one priority of the Joint Board of the Army and Navy to the five contingencies of the Rainbow War Plans, see May 11, 1939.

# 1 9 3 8 _____

## January 10, 1938

### The Ludlow Resolution requiring a national referendum to declare war fails in a close vote by the House of Representatives.

Representative Louis Ludlow of Indiana tried on several occasions between 1935 and 1937 to have the House approve a resolution that would require a nationwide vote before war could be declared. Following the *Panay* crisis of December 12, 1937, many congressmen and news editors joined to approve Ludlow's proposal as the best way to stay out of war. Therefore, when Congress convened in January, Ludlow again introduced his bill.

Probably only President Roosevelt's ardent opposition to the Ludlow concept prevented the House from passing the measure. The president wrote a special letter to House Speaker William B. Bankhead, which asserted that Ludlow's bill would "cripple any President in his conduct of foreign relations," encouraging foreign nations to "violate American rights with impunity." The House voted to return Ludlow's bill to committee by 209 to 188.

## March 13, 1938

### *Germany invades and annexes Austria.*

One of Adolf Hitler's objectives was to annex German-speaking Austria and make it an integral part of the Third Reich. Following the aborted Nazi putsch in Vienna on July 25, 1934, Hitler realized he must obtain Italy's support before moving forcefully against Austria. Following the assassination of the Fascist dictator Dollfuss on July 25, 1934, Kurt SCHUSCHNIGG gained control in Vienna but followed his predecessor's anti-Nazi program.

On July 11, 1936, Schuschnigg and Hitler agreed to stop their feud and Germany would recognize Austria's independence. This agreement pleased Mussolini, who formed an Axis alliance with Hitler on October 25, 1936. Schuschnigg, however, interpreted the pact as a proclamation of Austrian independence and, in conflict with Hitler's wishes, announced he would decide the right to restore the Habsburg throne. Schuschnigg also began discussions for an alliance with Czechoslovakia, which became a second point of conflict between Hitler and Austria.

Early in 1938, however, Hitler moved to end Schuschnigg's independent policies. During a February 12 meeting with the Austrian chancellor, Hitler persuaded Schuschnigg to grant amnesty to Nazi prisoners and to admit Nazis to his Austrian Fatherland Front Party. Soon after, Schuschnigg's attempts to break free from the Nazi position resulted in Nazi riots in Austria. Hitler demanded Schuschnigg's capitulation, and Schuschnigg resigned on March 11. The next day, Hitler's army crossed the border and without any Austrian resistance occupied Vienna. On March 13, Arthur Seyss-Inquart, a Nazi who was Austria's minister of the

Adolf Hitler accepts the ovation of the Reichstag in Berlin after announcing the ''peaceful'' acquisition of Austria. National Archives

interior, proclaimed union with Germany, and on March 14, Hitler took possession of Vienna.

### March 18, 1938

**Mexico's President Lázaro Cárdenas announces that his government will expropriate properties of the American and British oil companies.**

Cárdenas's expropriation decree did not stem from Article 27 subsoil clauses of the constitution of 1917, which had troubled U.S. oilmen during the 1920s, or the Morrow-Calles agreement of 1927. The March 18, 1938, decree grew out of a labor dispute that had been ongoing since 1936 between the oil companies and the Syndicate of Petroleum Workers. The union based their demands on Article 123 of the constitution, which contained labor rights for workers.

The petroleum workers' union had organized an industrywide union that on November 3, 1936, made extensive wage and fringe benefit demands on the oil companies, threatening an industrywide strike. When the companies refused to consider what they considered exorbitant demands, President Cárdenas called for a 120-day "cooling off" period to avoid the strike and permit further negotiations. These discussions did not succeed, and on May 28, 1937, a nationwide oil industry strike began.

Ten days after the strike began, the petroleum workers' union applied its labor rights under Article 123 of Mexico's constitution, requesting proceedings by the Federal Board of Conciliation and Arbitration. This procedure included the appointment of a commission of experts to study the case and required the commission to audit the companies' records as a method for deciding the companies' ability to pay the workers' demands. Although the U.S. companies protested the procedures (they never had to submit their open books in U.S. labor proceedings), they had to comply or forfeit their properties automatically. Meanwhile, the workers returned to work while the conciliation board pursued its investigation.

The U.S. companies appealed to the State Department for aid. Secretary Hull asserted that until Mexico treated them unjustly, the State Department could not intervene. The companies were told to use the Mexican legal process to the greatest possible extent.

On December 18, 1937, the Mexican Board of Conciliation and Arbitration handed down its ruling. Based on the report of the commission of experts and rebuttals by both the oil companies and the petroleum workers' union, the board generally followed the findings of the experts' commission that was initially released on August 3, 1937. The report favored most of the union demands. These included an 8-hour day, a 40-hour week, plus vacation, health, and pension benefits. It also recommended a minimum wage for oil workers of 5.40 pesos ($1.50) per day, whereas the company offered a daily minimum wage of 2 pesos ($0.56). The experts' report also claimed that the oil companies' interests opposed the Mexican national interest, describing ways by which the oil companies evaded paying full taxes on their Mexican income by selling oil to a foreign subsidiary at a price lower than market prices.

The oil companies, who were represented by their leading spokesman, Thomas R. Armstrong of Jersey Standard, strongly objected to Mexico's ruling. They convinced Secretary of State Hull that they were unfairly treated because the Mexican government sided with the labor unions. Nevertheless, at Hull's urging they appealed the ruling to the Mexican Supreme Court. President Cárdenas agreed to suspend the wage decision of the conciliation board until the court issued its ruling.

On February 28, the Mexican Supreme Court ruled that the conciliation board ruling was correct and within the legal guidelines of the constitution of 1917. The U.S. oilmen opposed the court decision, contending that, as they had always suspected, Mexico wanted to confiscate their property by economic strangulation. Contrary to the finding of the experts' audit of their books, the companies claimed the labor ruling would destroy their industry.

Because British oil interests controlled two-thirds of the foreign oil production in Mexico and they preferred to negotiate a compromise, the U.S. companies agreed to see what could be done. When the Board of Conciliation ruled on March 15 that the oil companies were guilty of *rebeldia* (defiance) against their decision, the British and American oil representatives met with President Cárdenas. Cárdenas was willing to compromise with the companies on all other points of

the December 1937 labor award if they agreed to a wage increase to 96 cents an hour, an annual cost of 26 million pesos. Cárdenas offered to give his promise to guarantee agreement on the other labor terms, but the oil spokesman told him, "That is hardly sufficient."

On March 18, Cárdenas responded to the oil companies' adamant stand. He applied the Expropriation Act, which the law called for against companies that defied the conciliation board's and the Supreme Court's rulings. Because the "paralysis of the oil industry is imminent" and damage would be suffered by the "general economy of the country," Mexico asserted its sovereign right to compel respect for the nation's legal process. The property of the oil companies was irrevocably expropriated by Mexico.

See January 11, 1928, on origins. For the outcome of the dispute resulting from Cárdenas's decree, see March 27, 1938, and November 19, 1941.

### March 27, 1938

**The U.S. Treasury Department halts its special purchases of Mexican silver, a measure the State Department urged to pressure Mexico to change its oil policy.**

During the fall of 1937, when the dispute between the oil companies and the petroleum workers was under conciliation procedures, a Mexican economic mission under Eduardo Suarez visited Washington seeking financial aid because of the depression and the oil companies' October decision to remove their surplus funds from Mexico. The Mexican peso's value had fallen on the world exchange market, and the Mexicans wanted the United States to purchase Mexican silver to keep its value higher.

Although some Washington officials wanted Secretary of the Treasury Morgenthau to deny the Mexican request in retaliation for the oil dispute, Morgenthau preferred to separate the two questions. He wanted to support Cárdenas in order to avoid any possibility that Mexico would have to seek aid from Germany, Italy, or Japan. Therefore, Morgenthau received President Roosevelt's approval to make special Mexican silver purchases. The Treasury Department agreed to monthly purchases of Mexican silver and to the immediate purchase of 35 million ounces of silver on deposit in America. Subsequently in January and February, the U.S. Treasury purchased Mexican silver.

Following the announcement on March 18 that Mexico would expropriate the oil properties, the State Department asked Morgenthau to suspend the silver purchases. The Treasury Department agreed, and on March 27, 1938, the special monthly purchases ended. This action did not seriously hurt Mexico because Morgenthau did not strictly enforce the act. The Treasury Department continued to buy all Mexican silver on the open spot market, and U.S. silver purchases remained high. One reason that Morgenthau's actions were not strongly opposed in the United States was that most of the silver came from the mines of the American Smelting and Refining Company, the largest U.S. mining interest in Mexico. These U.S. investors would suffer more than Mexico from the March 27 suspension of silver purchases; but Morgenthau's lenient enforcement permitted the U.S. silver investors to continue to profit.

See March 18, 1938.

### March 28, 1938

#### *The Japanese install a reformed government of the Republic of China at Nanking.*

Following the capture of Nanking on December 13, 1937, Tokyo followed the method it used earlier in Manchukuo by establishing a Chinese government with whom it could conduct business on an "official" basis. Subsequently Japan's armies became successful at controlling most of China's larger cities, but the rural areas remained under the control of Chinese guerrillas both from the Chinese Nationalist and Communist factions.

### April 4, 1938

#### Roosevelt approves Secretary of State Hull's recommendation to establish a liaison committee representing the Departments of State and War and the Navy.

The president and Hull had become aware of the lack of coordination between State Department foreign policy decisions and the activity and policy-making of U.S. army and navy officials. In an attempt to repair this deficiency, a Standing Liaison Committee was set up in the spring of 1938 to coordinate diplomatic and military relations. The committee members were Undersecretary of State Sumner Welles, the Chief of Naval Operations (first Admiral Leahy; later, Admiral Stark), and Army Chief of Staff General Marshall.

(This committee was the first step toward the National Security Agency, created after World War II.)

In the years before the Pearl Harbor attack, the committee did not fulfill its original purpose. Its principal achievements between 1938 and 1941 were to coordinate cooperation of the military and diplomats in Latin American relations. The duties Hull foresaw for the committee devolved to the president's War Council in 1941.

The War Council was never an official group. President Roosevelt, who obviously intended to be personally involved in making major foreign policy decisions, would meet informally with the secretaries of war, navy, and state. By the fall of 1941, as problems with Japan increased, these officials met on call of the president to coordinate diplomatic and military activity.

### April 16, 1938

#### *An Anglo-Italian Treaty on the Mediterranean resolves problems between those two nations.*

Great Britain recognized Italian rule over Ethiopia while Italy agreed to respect Spanish territory and to withdraw its "volunteers" at the end of the Spanish civil war. The two nations agreed to maintain the status quo in the Red Sea.

### May 13, 1938

#### The Senate Foreign Relations Committee blocks Senator Nye's resolution to extend cash-and-carry provisions for arms to Spain's loyalist government.

The threatened defeat of the Spanish Republicans by Franco's troops and the terrorist attacks by German and Italian aircraft on Spanish cities led many Americans to advocate some action against the Fascist forces in Spain. By 1938 there were many examples of German and Italian military units fighting with Franco's armies. The bombing of Guernica on April 26, 1937, became the most dramatic evidence of the new terror from the sky. Waves of German planes bombed and strafed the city for three hours, killing 1,654 people and wounding 889 in an indiscriminate attack on the civilian population.

Although many Roman Catholic groups in America, led by Cardinal Mundelein of Chicago, supported Franco, many liberal groups pressured Roosevelt to aid the Republicans. Nye's resolution of

May 3 authorized the president to end the Spanish arms embargo of January 8, 1937, and permit the Spanish Loyalists to obtain arms on the "cash and carry" basis of the Third Neutrality Act of May 1, 1937.

President Roosevelt wanted to consider ways to aid the anti-Fascist forces, but he agreed with Secretary of State Hull that Nye's resolution was not suitable. Subsequently, Hull sent the Senate Foreign Relations Committee a message on May 12 opposing the Nye Resolution. Hull argued that there was danger in Europe that the Spanish war could become a wider international conflict. Therefore, he said, he feared the complications likely to arise from "a reversal of our policy of strict neutrality." The committee concurred, rejecting Nye's proposal by a vote of 17 to 1.

In November 1938, there were renewed attempts to remove the Spanish embargo in favor of the Republicans in Barcelona. Again, Hull contended that only Congress could repeal the arms legislation, and prospects for such action were nil. By the winter of 1938–1939, the Spanish embargo became part of the larger Roosevelt attempt to change the entire Neutrality Act of 1937.

See March 28, 1939.

### May 17, 1938

**A naval construction bill increasing the U.S. navy by 20% is approved by Congress.**

Because the Vinson Bill of 1934 had completed its objective of replacing obsolete warships, the second Vinson bill, in 1938, authorized a total of 18 battleships that would be 20% above the treaty limits of 1922. The 1938 naval bill was promoted as a navy to provide defenses for the two oceans on either side of the United States. The size of this force was not, however, deemed sufficient to provide a U.S. presence in the western Pacific as the Navy's Orange War Plan intended. The president had, nevertheless, begun to persuade the navy to revise the Orange Plan.

See May 11, 1939.

### May 20, 1938

*The first Czech crisis ends when England and France strongly back the Czech government against the demands of the Nazi Konrad Henlein.*

Acting in conjunction with Henlein, the leader of the Sudeten German Party in the Sudeten region of Czechoslovakia, Hitler, on February 20, 1938, promised to protect all German minorities outside the Reich. This fostered a clash between Henlein's demand for autonomy for the German Sudetens and the determination of Czech Premier Milan Hodža to reject outside interference in Czechoslovakia. The Czechs refused to grant concessions to Henlein as suggested by France and England, but Hodža retained their support. On May 20, Henlein agreed to negotiate with Hodža and the crisis temporarily ended. By September, a further crisis developed.

See September 29, 1938.

### August 10, 1938

*Following nearly four weeks of fighting at Changkufeng Hill, Japanese and Soviet forces arrange a truce that reasserts the status quo.*

The fighting took place on the borders of Siberia, Manchukuo, and Korea. This was one of several border incidents between Japan and the Soviet Union that recurred until the signing of the Soviet-Japanese neutrality pact of April 13, 1941.

Soviet military prowess demonstrated in these clashes persuaded Japanese army officers that they did not have the modern weapons to successfully wage a full-scale war against the Soviet Union.

### September 27, 1938

**President Roosevelt appeals to Hitler to negotiate the Czechoslovak crisis.**

A second Czech crisis regarding the German-inhabited Sudetenland began on September 12 when Hitler told a Nazi Party congress that the "tortured and oppressed" Germans in the Sudetenland must be freed. Konrad Henlein, the Sudeten German leader, declared that union with Germany was the only solution to his followers' problem, inspiring anti-Czech demonstrations in the area.

During the May crisis, President Roosevelt and Secretary Hull had remained aloof from the dispute. Between June and September, however, Roosevelt privately urged Britain and France to take a strong stand against Hitler's demands. He could not and would not back these efforts, however. Although Roosevelt realized that the United States had become a vital factor in world decisions, his political concerns with noninterventionist sentiments kept him from committing the United States.

As the crisis grew in September and Hitler gave the Czechs an ultimatum to meet his demands by October 1, Roosevelt sent appeals for peace to the European powers. On September 26, he sent a plea to Prague, Berlin, London, and Paris, urging the governments not to break off negotiations and to find a constructive settlement. Hitler rejected the U.S. appeal, but on September 27 the president made a second attempt. First, he asked Mussolini to assist in persuading Hitler to continue to negotiate. Later that day, he made a direct appeal to Hitler to find a peaceful solution to the problem. The president suggested that a conference of all nations be called to deal not only with the Sudeten issue but also with "correlated" questions.

Significantly, Roosevelt's September 27 appeal to Hitler for a wider international conference included a caveat reflecting the president's concern about isolationist criticism. The president's note said that the United States was not willing to pass judgment on the merits of Hitler's demands and that America could not accept any responsibility in the negotiations.

Although some commentators in 1938 and later believed the president's appeal of September 27 influenced the calling of the Munich Conference of September 29, the U.S. notes had little or no influence on Hitler or Prime Minister Chamberlain. Behind the scenes in Europe, French and British officials had informed Hitler that if he agreed to another meeting, they would accept most of his demands. Hitler attended the Munich sessions to obtain his demands without going to war.

For the first Czech crisis, see May 20, 1938.

## September 29, 1938

### *The Munich Conference solves the Czech crisis because France and England "appease" Hitler: The Appeasement Policy.*

After Hitler's September 12 speech demanded self-determination for Germans in Czechoslovakia's Sudetenland, a European war seemed imminent. On September 15, British Prime Minister Chamberlain met Hitler at Berchtesgaden, where Hitler demanded the annexation of the Sudetenland, which had been given to the Czechs by the Treaty of Versailles for security reasons. Hitler said the Germans would risk war if necessary to obtain these "just" demands of self-determination.

Although French Premier Daladier and the Soviets wanted to strongly oppose Hitler, Chamberlain convinced the Czechs to offer Hitler all areas where one-half of the population was German in exchange for guarantees of their less defensible borders. On September 22, Chamberlain again met with Hitler at Godesberg, but Hitler refused the Czech compromise, saying he would identify what Czech territory belonged to the Third Reich and hold plebiscites only in areas with large German minorities. If Czechoslovakia did not meet these demands by October 1, German armies would occupy "German territory."

War appeared certain after the Godesberg meeting, with the Czech armies mobilizing and German armies preparing for war on the frontiers of France and Czechoslovakia. Yet Chamberlain believed he could avert a war by using Mussolini's "good offices." Subsequently, on September 29, Mussolini joined Hitler, Daladier, and Chamberlain at Munich to decide the fate of Czechoslovakia.

At Munich, Hitler received almost everything he demanded. The Czechs would evacuate areas designated by Hitler. An international commission would determine what areas of Czechoslovakia should be given to Germany, Poland, or Hungary, because the latter two governments also sought "justice" for their people. Britain and France would guarantee the new Czech frontier.

When the international commission completed its work on November 28, Czechoslovakia was reduced in size, making it unable to defend itself if Hitler chose to invade. The final basic results of the Munich Conference were as follows:

1. Without any plebiscites, Germany acquired 10,000 square miles with a population of 3,500,000 of whom 700,000 were Czech.
2. Poland gained 400 square miles (Cieszyn region) with 240,000 inhabitants, fewer than 100,000 of whom were Polish.
3. Hungary received 5,000 square miles and 1,000,000 people.

Chamberlain's policy of appeasement reached its apogee after he returned from Munich. The British public lauded Chamberlain's statement that he brought "peace in our time." British preparations for war ended. Gas-mask drills stopped in London. Chamberlain urged British trade and industrial leaders to visit Germany and make trade agreements.

The final results of the Munich Conference turned Chamberlain's term "appeasement" into a derogatory expression for diplomacy, whereas Chamberlain saw appeasement as a positive way to peacefully settle disputes. In order to understand appeasement as a diplomatic way to compromise, the particular circumstances of 1938 must be understood. The most critical circumstance of the interwar years was the belief of many people in Europe and America that the terms of the Treaty of Versailles should be revised because the Allies had dealt too harshly with Germany in 1919. Chamberlain believed revising these terms would be a just and sufficient way to satisfy Hitler's demands. Like many Europeans and Americans, Chamberlain also thought Soviet communism was a greater menace than fascism and that war between Germany and England would be devastating.

The second circumstance influencing Chamberlain was Britain's failure to prepare for war as rapidly as Hitler. Following World War I, Britain and other democracies including the United States chose to reduce their armed forces and formulate international disarmament treaties to limit every nation's armed forces. Some arms limitation treaties were signed, but when the fascist dictators denounced the treaties, Britain and other democracies did not rearm to match the fascists' arms buildup. As Gaines Post Jr.'s 1993 *Dilemmas of Appeasement* indicates, Chamberlain's diplomatic efforts with Hitler were difficult, if not impossible, because British decisions to rearm fell short. When Stanley Baldwin's cabinet discussed rearmament in 1934–1935, they agreed that British commercial and trade enterprises could not afford large expenditures on armaments. Instead, they opted for a gradual, less costly arms buildup. They assumed Germany would not be ready for war until 1942 and divided the budget equally among Britain's army, navy, and air force. As a result, Hitler knew Germany's armed forces, especially aircraft, were superior to those of Britain and France after 1937. France, of course, relied on its Maginot Line, which proved inadequate to defend against German attack. Regarding the air force in 1938, Britain had only 48 long-range bombers compared with Germany's 800.

Despite Britain's gradual rearmament plans when Chamberlain became prime minister in 1938, he resolved to make sufficient concessions to Germany to persuade Hitler that war was a senseless method to settle boundary disputes.

See March 31, 1939.

### October 4, 1938

*The end of France's left-wing Popular Front ministry.*

From June 5, 1936, to October 4, 1938, Léon Blum and Édouard Daladier had kept together a coalition of left-of-center Popular Front parties. The French Senate could not overthrow the ministry, but the conservatives and extreme rightists in the Senate effectively blocked the leftists from making significant economic or social changes.

The Munich Conference broke up the Popular Front. The Socialists disapproved of the agreement with Hitler, and the Communist Party, which voted with but never joined the ministry, now withdrew its support. Daladier obtained center and right-of-center support in the Chamber of Deputies and continued as premier until March 20, 1940.

### October 6, 1938

*Czechoslovakia is weakened further as Slovak leaders receive the full autonomy they demand; on October 8, Ruthenia gains full autonomy as Carpatho-Ukraine.*

### October 11, 1938

**President Roosevelt calls for a $300 million defense buildup emphasizing the need for 20,000 airplanes.**

Fears and trepidations about a European war and possible aerial bombing that arose before and after the September 29, 1938, Munich Conference led the president to announce plans for a large defense buildup in the 1939 budget. He dramatized his concerns in October and November by proposing an airplane production goal of 20,000 per year. These aircraft would defend the Western Hemisphere from potential attacks. According to some analysts, Germany was becoming capable of building a 2,000-plane bomber force that could cross the 3,300 miles between West Africa near Dakar and the Americas.

Roosevelt's 20,000-plane production schedule did not represent the war plans developed at that time by the Joint Board of the Army and Navy. The president's plan did, however, give U.S. air power proponents their first sign that Roosevelt was aware of aviation's potential in a future war. While U.S. army leaders persuaded Roosevelt to cut his airplane request back to 6,000 planes in January 1939, so that other parts of the army could be funded as a "balanced force," the Army Air Corps had discovered a new champion. By 1941, the president would order greater autonomy for the Air Force, with plans for offensive bomber capabilities on July 3, 1941.

See May 11, 1939.

### November 3, 1938

**Japan's Premier, Prince Konoye, announces Japan's "new order" in East Asia.**

Prior to November 3, Tokyo had persistently assured the U.S. State Department that it never intended to violate U.S. open door rights in China and that the "China incident" was atypical. On November 3, Konoye informed all other nations that they should revise their policies to adjust to the fact that Japan was overseer of a new, stable order in East Asia. The prosperity of this region would be based on mutual aid under the coordination of policies by Japan, Manchukuo, and China. As Foreign Minister Hachiro Arita later explained to Secretary Hull, Japan had freed itself from the Nine-Power Treaty and other bygone documents. Thus, former policies in East Asia were no longer applicable.

The United States protested Japan's methods of changing treaties. On December 30, 1938, U.S. Ambassador Joseph Grew told Arita that changes due to conditions were valid but should be made by the orderly methods of negotiation and agreement, not by fiat.

### November 8, 1938

**The midterm elections for Congress are significant because Republicans and conservative Democrats make gains.**

Roosevelt blundered in 1938 by speaking out against those Democratic candidates who opposed New Deal reforms. Although the Democrats continued to hold over two-thirds of the Senate seats and a majority in the House, the Republicans won 81 House seats and 8 senatorial posts. Especially in the House, conservative Democrats and Republicans could block Roosevelt's legislation if they chose to cooperate.

### November 15, 1938

**Reacting to Germany's attacks on Jews, President Roosevelt recalls U.S. Ambassador Wilson, leaving neither government with full diplomatic representation until the end of World War II.**

Early in November, a Polish Jewish refugee assassinated a German embassy official in Paris. To avenge

Benito Mussolini (left) and Adolf Hitler (right), leaders of the Rome-Berlin Axis in the 1930s

this incident, German Nazi Party personnel began assaults on Jews in Germany. They looted synagogues, burned Jewish property, and forbade Jews such ordinary civil liberties as attending school and driving a car. The German government levied a fine of 1 billion marks on the Jewish community, and there was a determined effort to drive all Jews out of Germany.

The anti-Semitic ideology of the German Nazis had been evident since April 1, 1933, when a national boycott of Jewish businesses began. Jewish lawyers and doctors were barred from practice, and many Jewish businesses were liquidated. On September 15, 1935, the NUREMBERG LAWS deprived Jews of citizenship and forbade their intermarriage with other "races." When Austria was annexed, these laws were extended to that region as well.

The Nazi attacks on November 15, 1938 (Kristallnacht) were the first violent, terroristic depredations against the German Jews. As a result, Jewish immigration increased rapidly from already large proportions between 1933 and 1938. Because the Nazis would not permit the émigrés to take money or property with them, Jewish immigration became difficult because other nations were reluctant to admit immigrants with no sponsor, job opportunities, or money to help them adjust. An international refugee committee was set up in western Europe, but it experienced problems because other nations were still reluctant to admit the propertyless Jews. In addition, British policy in Palestine required that they limit Jewish immigration because of Arab opposition.

On November 15, Roosevelt expressed the American outrage over Nazi actions by recalling U.S. Ambassador Hugh Wilson from Berlin. Announcing this action, the president stated in a press release: "I myself could scarcely believe that such things could occur in a twentieth century civilization." The German response to Roosevelt's action was to call Ambassador Hans Dieckhoff back to Berlin.

See May 17, 1939.

### November 17, 1938

**Great Britain, Canada, and the United States sign a Reciprocal Trade Agreements pact.**

Secretary of State Hull considered the conclusion of this commercial treaty especially significant because Great Britain took the first step away from its imperial preference tariff system. Since the passage of the 1934 U.S. Reciprocal Trade Act, Hull had looked forward to getting London to accept principles of reciprocal, mutually beneficial trade adjustments.

Hull had enlisted the support of William Lyon MacKenzie King, Prime Minister of Canada, in his trade pact, but King had not yet convinced London to make the necessary trade-offs in lowering tariffs. Until October 25, 1938, the British had not offered any concessions. Once they did, the conclusion of a reciprocal trade pact did not take long. Generally, the United States agreed to concessions on textiles, Britain agreed to concessions on agricultural commodities and products. The tripartite agreement was signed on November 17, 1938.

### December 14, 1938

**President Roosevelt announces a $25 million loan to China.**

As Japanese attacks on China intensified in 1938, Roosevelt and Secretary of the Treasury Morgenthau sought some means to assist the Chinese. Because war had not been declared nor the U.S. neutrality acts invoked, Morgenthau recommended a $25 million loan based on the Chinese delivery of tung oil during the next three years. Although Secretary of State Hull warned that the loan would create further Japanese antagonism, the Chinese government accepted the loan terms and Roosevelt announced the transaction on December 14.

### December 24, 1938

**The Lima Declaration of the Eighth Conference of American States asserts that the American governments will defend against all foreign intervention.**

The Lima Declaration of intent, as distinct from a treaty, pledged the 21 nations at the Inter-Americas Conference to unite and consult together in case of an outside threat to any of them. This agreement essentially provided for the unity of the Americas, which had been described at the Buenos Aires Conference on December 23, 1936.

President Roosevelt had begun to prepare a national defense program for the Western Hemisphere, and the Lima declaration supported this concept.

# 1 9 3 9

### January 23, 1939

**News is received in Washington that a French military officer was injured when an American Douglas bomber crashed in California.**

The French officer was Captain Paul Chemidlin, a participant in a French war mission that sought orders for U.S. military equipment. News of the bomber crash incensed isolationist senators such as Arthur Vandenberg and William Borah because it provided evidence for their belief that Roosevelt was cooperating with France and England by giving them advanced U.S. military secrets. These senators and newspaper editors who supported them asserted that Roosevelt was edging the country closer to war through secret alliances.

Under the cash and carry provisions of the U.S. neutrality laws, Jean Monnet of France, a personal friend of U.S. Ambassador to France William Bullitt, arrived in America as early as March 1938, seeking U.S. aircraft to bolster France's defense. Subsequently, Roosevelt skirted the edges of the Neutrality Acts by attempting to meet French aviation needs. Despite opposition from Army Chief of Staff General Marshall and Secretary of War Woodring, the president and Secretary of the Treasury Morgenthau expedited French aviation and other war purchases. Although France fell to the Germans in June 1940, before a substantial number of U.S. planes they had ordered reached Europe, the French had invested over $13 million in the U.S. aircraft industry in 1939. This investment greatly assisted the rapid buildup of U.S. aircraft production capacities.

In 1939, however, news of the Douglas bomber crash caused severe criticism of Roosevelt. It became one factor in Roosevelt's unwillingness to encourage Congress to repeal the arms embargo clauses of the neutrality laws, which, in fact, Congress refused to do in early 1939.

### March 9, 1939

**President Vargas of Brazil and the United States conclude a series of agreements to aid Brazil's economic growth: The Hull-Aranha Agreements.**

Since becoming President of Brazil on October 26, 1930, Getúlio Vargas had sponsored a right-of-center political program that successfully fought off both Communist and Fascist movements. In November 1935, a Communist uprising in Pernambuco state and Rio de Janeiro forced Vargas to use martial law and to prepare a new constitution, which on November 10, 1937, gave him dictatorial powers that he said were not Fascist. To prove this claim, Vargas on March 11, 1938, suppressed a Nazi-inspired "green shirt" (*Integralista*) revolt. He also appealed to the United States to provide economic aid.

Brazil needed economic assistance because the decline in coffee prices during the 1930s prevented Brazilian payments on foreign loans, a situation Vargas wished to resolve. In November 1937, Brazil had defaulted on its loans, and in 1938 Vargas froze all foreign balances because the state had insufficient exchange funds. When Foreign Minister Oswaldo ARANHA came to Washington in January 1939 to negotiate with Secretary Hull, coffee prices were 7.5 cents per pound. They had been 21.7 cents in 1929 and 9.8 cents in 1937. Thus, Brazil needed U.S. aid to enable Vargas to cope with the country's economic problems.

Although the March 9 U.S. aid package helped Brazil, it was not sufficient to satisfy the shortfall of the Brazilian budget. Brazil agreed to renew payments on its foreign loans on July 1, 1939. In return, the United States arranged an Export-Import Bank loan of $19.2 million and agreed to help Brazil purchase ships and railway equipment from the Lloyd Brasileiri Shipping Company. Hull also agreed to ask Congress for $50 million in gold to establish a Brazil Central Reserve Bank, but the U.S. Congress never approved this request.

One long-term result of the March 9 agreement was the exchange of military plans and assistance to enhance the Western Hemispheric defense against the Axis powers. General George C. Marshall visited Brazil for discussions with its military leaders. When Marshall returned to the United States in April 1939, Brazil's army chief of staff, Pedro Aurelio de Goıs Monteiro, came with him aboard the USS *Nashville*.

From this military exchange, the United States received permission to build air and naval bases in northeastern Brazil. The United States provided Brazil's army with technological and financial aid as well as surplus U.S. weapons. Thus, on the eve of the European war, the buildup of U.S. defenses in the Western Hemisphere was underway.

## March 15, 1939

### Germany takes control over all non-German areas of Czechoslovakia. Hungary occupies the Carpatho-Ukraine section of Czechoslovakia.

Following the creation of the autonomous regions of Slovakia and Carpatho-Ukraine on October 6 and 8, 1938, pro-Fascist leaders in those areas appealed to Hitler for support. On March 15, Hitler fulfilled these requests. He declared a German protectorship over Bohemia and Moravia, as well as Slovakia. The Nazi aggressor had moved beyond his claim for justice to minorities and advocated Germany's need for lebensraum, literally "living space."

On February 24, Hungary joined the anti-Comintern pact and was rewarded on March 15. Although Hungarian forces had to fight local resistance, they completed the conquest of the Carpatho-Ukraine on March 15.

## March 17, 1939

### Secretary of State Hull states that the United States will not recognize Hitler's conquest of Czechoslovakia.

The secretary condemned Germany's aggressive action on occupying the state it had promised to guarantee during the Munich Conference of September 29, 1938. Hull declared the United States would continue to recognize the Czech minister to Washington as the rightful representative of the Czechoslovak people.

## March 28, 1939

### The Spanish civil war ends when Madrid surrenders to General Franco's forces.

The final struggle that began in Spain on July 18, 1938, had been bitter and bloody as Franco's insurgents received considerable assistance from Germany and Italy, who had recognized his government on November 18, 1936.

Madrid was under siege from November 6, 1936, to March 28, 1939. The Loyalist Republican government had fled from Madrid to Valencia, and later to Barcelona. Franco's capture of Barcelona on January 26, 1939, effectively ended Loyalist resistance. Madrid held out, however, because General José Miaja sought lenient terms, but Franco demanded unconditional surrender. Following a Communist uprising in

Madrid that Miaja defeated in March, the defenders of the city decided to surrender to Franco with no conditions.

## March 31, 1939

### British and French pledges to aid Poland in the event of aggression end the British appeasement policy.

On March 15, Chamberlain's appeasement of Hitler ended with Germany's conquest of Czechoslovakia. Now, Hitler demanded that Poland cede the free city of Danzig to Germany and construct a railway and highway across Pomorze (the Polish corridor) to the Baltic Sea. In return, Germany would guarantee Poland's frontiers and sign a nonaggression pact. Warsaw rejected these demands and, on appeal to Paris and London, obtained the British-French pledges of March 31 that expanded into a mutual assistance treaty on April 6.

The British decision meant Chamberlain's appeasement policy fell apart. Chamberlain had taken Hitler's demands at face value, believing his territorial objectives were limited to recovering German land lost through the 1919 Versailles Treaty. Hitler's aim, of course, was to conquer Europe.

Chamberlain was not the only mistaken politician in 1939. During the interwar years, Poland never discovered how to unify and strengthen its government. From 1926 until his death on May 12, 1935, Marshal Józef Piłsudski was a military dictator who could not establish a unified state because of opposition. In 1935, Poland abolished its democratic system, but the miltary leaders could not effectively end the opposition of the Socialist and Peasant parties or the Ukrainian nationalists. On March 1, 1937, Colonel Adam Koc's Camp of National Unity secured greater support. Koc's program emphasized anticommunism, army control, land reform, Polanization of minorities such as the Ukrainians, and violent anti-Semitism. Koc was overthrown on January 11, 1938, by General Stanislaus Skwarczynski, whose policies loosened government control of society. In 1939, the Polish army exaggerated its ability to defend the nation. Poland's nationalists despised the Russians, whom they defeated briefly in 1920 (see August 10, 1920), a war resulting in disputed territory until 1939.

Between March and August 1939, France and Britain promised to protect Poland even though there was no practical way for their armed forces to save Poland's ineffective army.

See August 23, 1939.

### April 3, 1939

### The United States recognizes General Franco's government in Spain.

A final offensive by Franco's forces between December 1938 and February 1939 had devastated the Loyalist armies in Catalonia and central Spain. Following the fall of Madrid on April 3, President Roosevelt recognized Franco's government. He had withdrawn the arms embargo from Spain on April 1 because the Fascist Nationalist victory was certain. France and

General Franco is victorious. National Archives

Great Britain had recognized the Franco regime on February 27, 1939.

During the summer and fall of 1938, when a stalemate appeared to have developed in Spain, Roosevelt considered various means for aiding the Spanish Republicans. Following the Munich Conference of September 1938, Roosevelt proposed using the Vatican offices to obtain a three-man commission to mediate the Spanish conflict. This idea was not carried out, but an attempt to relieve starvation conditions of the besieged cities of Barcelona and Madrid was undertaken. The president appointed a Committee for Impartial Civilian Relief in Spain that cooperated with the Red Cross and the American Friends Service Committee to deliver surplus U.S. wheat to the Spanish people. Because this relief principally benefited the Loyalists, American Catholics opposed the committee work. Consequently, the committee provided some assistance to Spain but raised only $50,000 in a fund drive aimed at collecting $500,000.

In his January 4, 1939, state-of-the-union message, Roosevelt spoke sharply against the indifference to lawlessness that resulted in the overthrow of democracies and encouraged aggressors. Yet the president's attempt to have Congress consider a revision of the Neutrality Acts to aid Spain was not successful. The Senate Foreign Relations Committee began a review of the neutrality legislation, but on January 19 the committee suspended all consideration of these bills because of the avalanche of telegrams it received from pro-Loyalist and pro-Franco supporters in America. The suspension of the committee's work on neutrality revision influenced not only the Spanish situation but also Roosevelt's desire to change U.S. neutrality laws generally in the wake of Hitler's aggression in Czechoslovakia between September 1938 and his takeover of that state on March 15, 1939.

Before accepting the fate of the fallen Spanish republic, Roosevelt realized that the democratic powers including America had made a grave mistake in their Spanish policy. He told his cabinet on January 27 that the United States should have simply forbidden the shipping of munitions in U.S. ships. Then Loyalist Spain could have obtained other vessels to carry what was needed "to fight for her life and the lives of some of the rest of us as well, as events will very likely prove." But also, as events proved, neither Congress nor the American public had learned this lesson between 1937 and 1939. The spirit of isolationism refused to die in the United States during the late 1930s. Congress remained reluctant to provide firm backing for the democratic forces in western Europe.

### April 7, 1939

*Italy invades and conquers Albania.*

King Zog of Albania fled to Greece, and an Italian-dominated government was established in Albania.

### April 13, 1939

*Britain and France guarantee Greek independence following Italy's conquest of Albania.*

Since 1919, Greece came increasingly under the control of the military. By 1923, King George II had become a puppet of the military. Political disputes in 1924 led George II to resign, and the proclamation of a republic on May 1 raised Admiral Paul Kondouriottis to power as provisional president. The republic lasted less than a year before first General Theodoros Pangalos (June 25, 1925) and later General Geórgios Kondílis ruled as dictators. This political chaos continued until August 4, 1936, when General Ioannis METAXAS established a dictatorship that rigorously suppressed all opponents. On April 13 he received British-French protection from the Italian threat.

### April 15, 1939

**Roosevelt orders the U.S. fleet to return to its regular station at Pearl Harbor.**

The naval fleet had been on maneuvers in the Caribbean and at the New York World's Fair during the winter and early spring of 1938–1939. After Japan occupied the Spratly Islands and Hainan in February and March 1939, the president ordered the fleet back to its Pacific base as a symbol of U.S. displeasure with Tokyo.

Japan had made further advances down the entire coast of China by early 1939. It captured Canton on October 21 and Hankow on October 25, 1938. Chiang Kai-shek's government moved to the city of Chungking on October 25 and made Chungking the wartime capital. Because the island of Hainan was located off the southwest coast of China, it could be a vital base on the sea lanes from Japan to Singapore.

### April 15, 1939

**President Roosevelt appeals to Hitler and Mussolini to guarantee peace by pledging that they will not attack any of 31 listed nations for the next ten years.**

Alarmed by Hitler's aggression in Czechoslovakia during March 1939 and Italy's conquest of Albania on April 7, President Roosevelt sent a personal communication to the two dictators to proscribe further aggression. Indicating that one African and three European nations had lost their independence recently, Roosevelt listed 31 nations for which he asked a German and Italian pledge of security. Once peace was assured, the president said, the United States would join other nations to negotiate disarmament and the expansion of trade.

As Roosevelt and Hull expected, the dictators' reaction to the message demonstrated their aggressive ambitions. Neither dictator replied directly to the president. Mussolini's comments disclosed his personal reaction as part of an exchange with the Nazi German leader Hermann GÖRING, who was visiting Rome. The two Fascists thought Roosevelt suffered either the side effects of infantile paralysis or "an incipient mental disease." In a speech on April 20, Mussolini flippantly showed his contempt for Roosevelt.

Hitler replied to Roosevelt in a major Reichstag speech on April 28. Using deadpan sarcasm, he delivered a humorous response that had the delegates laughing. Most tellingly, however, Hitler rehearsed all the American isolationist reasons why the president should stay home and mind his own business. He denied Germany wanted to go to war, saying all the Germans desired was to correct the unjust deeds inflicted on Germany in 1919. This, he said, was no more than American intervention in neighboring states of Latin America and other parts of the world. In ending his harangue, Hitler stated that he had canvassed each of the governments listed by Roosevelt and none of them feared a German attack (Hitler's listing of the states pointedly omitted Poland). If any of these nations requested Hitler's assurances, Germany would gladly give them.

In April 1939, the humor of the dictators pleased isolationists in the United States, who accepted their word that they intended no future aggression and that Roosevelt should tend to his own hemispheric problems. As Senator Hiram Johnson, California's foremost isolationist, asserted: "Roosevelt put his chin out and got a resounding whack. I have reached the conclusion," Johnson said, "that there will be no war. . . . Roosevelt wants to fight for little things."

## April 28, 1939

### Hitler denounces the Anglo-German Naval Pact of 1935.

## May 11, 1939

### The Joint Board of the Army and Navy approves the five contingency strategies of Rainbow War Plans, replacing the outmoded primacy of the Orange War Plan against Japan.

Since 1937, President Roosevelt had been seeking to change the Joint Board's emphasis on Orange War Plan for a war against Japan. Although the Joint Board had other contingency war plans, including a Red War Plan against England and a Black War Plan against Germany, its most probable enemy since 1919 had been Japan. While this accorded with Alfred Mahan's Pacific dominance strategy, it never agreed with the State Department's belief that, except for the Western Hemisphere, Europe was the most vital region for the United States.

In November 1937, Roosevelt made it clear that he preferred a strategy for a two-ocean navy with a war in Europe against the Axis as most likely. Subsequently, between February 1938, when Captain Royal Ingersoll returned from discussions with England, and March 11, the Navy and Army War Plans Divisions and finally the Joint Board considered new strategies that became the basis for five Rainbow Plans between 1939 and May 1941.

The Rainbow Plans contingencies designed the following basic estimates:

1. *Rainbow One*—The defense of the Western Hemisphere without any allies was a given factor for all the Rainbow Plans. This was largely a coastal defense plan that concentrated U.S. forces north of 10′ latitude south in the Atlantic and east of longitude 180′ in the Pacific. The Pacific Ocean defense line extended from the Aleutians through Hawaii to the Panama Canal.
2. *Rainbow Two*—The conjecture was that the United States with England and France as allies would fight the Axis alliance. America's European allies would defend in the Atlantic; the United States would mount offensive action in the Pacific. The cooperation of U.S. allies would be crucial in the Atlantic to give America the predominant role in the Pacific.
3. *Rainbow Three*—This was essentially the old Orange War Plan based on a U.S. war against Japan with no allies. The United States would take offensive action against Japan in the western Pacific. This plan did not become operative between 1939 and December 7, 1941.
4. *Rainbow Four*—This concept predicted the worst possible situation for the United States: defending the Western Hemisphere against an Axis alliance that had defeated both France and England. The United States would have full responsibility for a two-ocean war. Rainbow Four became operative when France fell to the Germans in June 1940. Roosevelt, however, amended it by assuming that England would be assisted in surviving against Germany.
5. *Rainbow Five*—This plan assumed an alliance with England against the Axis powers. Europe and "Germany First" were given top priority. In the Pacific, defense would be emphasized, including U.S. responsibility for Southeast Asia between the Philippines and Singapore. This became the basic plan in 1941.

See December 12, 1937; see January 27, 1941, for ABC-1.

## May 17, 1939

### Following the failure of a Jewish-Arab conference on Palestine, Great Britain publishes its proposal for an independent Palestine.

Since the British armies had occupied Jerusalem on December 9, 1917, and undertaken the League of Nations–mandated control of Palestine on April 25, 1920, the Arab-Jewish problem had created considerable difficulties for England. Part of the trouble could be traced back to British duplicity during World War I, when the British made contradictory promises in the Sykes-Picot Agreement of May 9, 1916, and the Balfour Declaration of November 2, 1917. As the influx of Zionist-inspired Jews sought a homeland in Palestine, the Arab inhabitants protested and began attacks on the Jews as early as May 1, 1921. As these attacks increased, the incoming Jews organized to retaliate, and Jewish riots and protests replicated Arab activity by 1932. In 1936, the Arab High Commission united Arabs in a virtual war against Jews, forcing Great Britain to search for a compromise acceptable to both sides.

Between 1936 and 1939, British attempts at compromise failed. A partition plan (Peel Commission Report) of July 8, 1937, seemed sensible to outsiders and was approved by the League of Nations Assembly. Although the World Zionist Congress accepted partition, Jewish non-Zionist groups rejected the Peel plan. So did the Pan-Arab Congress on September 8, 1937.

In February 1939, Britain held a Palestine Conference in London with Jews and Palestinian Arabs, but the conference ended on March 17 with no solution. Therefore, on May 17, the British announced a plan that Britain's Parliament approved on May 23, 1939. The proposal indicated that over a 10-year period, Arabs and Jews would have to share in a Palestinian government while it made a transition to independence. Jewish emigration for the next five years would be 75,000; it would then cease unless the Arabs agreed to a new plan.

The British plan failed to solve the disputes in Palestine. Both Jews and Arabs rejected the proposal, and the British could not implement it. The issue remained to be solved after World War II.

## June 28, 1939

**The first regularly scheduled commercial transatlantic flight is made between New York and Lisbon by Pan-American world airways.**

## July 18, 1939

**Roosevelt's attempt to revise the Neutrality Acts ends following the failure of a White House conference between the President and Senate leaders of both parties.**

Since his state-of-the-union message to Congress on January 4, 1939, the president had endeavored to obtain some type of revision or the repeal of the U.S. Neutrality Acts. His January speech had been directed toward General Franco's impending victory over the Spanish Republicans. In the January message, Roosevelt deplored the threats of aggression in the world that destroyed other democratic governments. He advocated some methods "short of war" by which America would warn dictators of U.S. opposition to their military actions. The Neutrality Acts, he said,

had aided the aggressors and damaged the victims. Therefore, these laws needed to be revised or repealed.

During the months from January to July, isolationist strength especially on the Senate Foreign Relations Committee prevented any significant action by Congress. Although Czechoslovakia and Albania fell and Hitler demanded concessions from Poland, the efforts of Hull and Roosevelt to obtain congressional unity on change in the Neutrality Acts did not succeed.

There were many proposals to revise the neutrality laws, but the only bill approved was a weak House of Representatives measure. On June 29, this House bill passed by a vote of 200-188. The resolution, presented to the House by Representative Solomon Bloom's Committee on Foreign Affairs, repealed the arms embargo and gave the president discretionary power to say when, where, and how the law would apply. Before the bill passed, however, Representative John M. Vorys of Ohio added an amendment that virtually killed the bill's effect by embargoing "arms and ammunition" but not "implements of war." According to Vorys, "implements" were airplanes and items with potential civilian use. He referred especially to the president's desire to sell aircraft to France and England. Roosevelt believed the House measure as passed did more harm than good. He wrote to a friend: "I honestly believe that the [House] vote last night was a stimulus to war and that if the vote had been different it would have been a definite encouragement to peace."

The Senate did not pass even a weak measure in the effort to revise the Neutrality Acts. On July 11, the Senate Foreign Relations Committee rejected Senator Key Pittman's "Peace Bill" by a vote of 12-11. Although this committee action virtually killed any neutrality resolution, the president sought to have the full Senate override the committee recommendation. On July 14, Secretary Hull sent a message to Congress urging it to join with the chief executive in promoting peace. Hull's message reviewed the problems and results of neutrality laws, stressing that world peace required U.S. cooperation as an effective voice in influencing the course of action.

To further assure congressional action, Roosevelt called a meeting at the White House of senators from both parties on July 18. The president told them of problems developing in Europe, and Secretary Hull offered to let them read the confidential dispatches that the State Department had regarding the imminent outbreak of war. The isolationist senators were firm, however. They opposed the repeal of the arms embargo and did not believe war was likely in the near future. Senator Borah refused to examine Hull's reports from Europe and made the most memorable remark of the meeting: "No one can foretell what may happen. But my feeling and belief is that we are not going to have a war. Germany isn't ready for it." On September 1, 1939, Borah's words became famous for their inaccuracy.

### July 24, 1939

***Britain approves the Craigie-Arita Declaration, which recognizes Japan's new status as "enforcer" of law and order in China.***

Japanese aggression continued in 1939 as Japan's forces occupied Hainan Island and the Spratly Islands in February and March. In June, the Japanese sought to pressure the English into vacating Tientsin and the foreign settlements in Shanghai so that Japan's "new order in East Asia" could obtain firmer control of China.

Because Chamberlain feared Hitler's demands in Europe more than Japan's ventures in China, the British ambassador to Tokyo, Sir Robert Craigie, negotiated an agreement with Japan's foreign minister, Hachiro Arita. In their understanding, the British recognized that Japan's army was responsible for security in the Chinese areas it occupied. Britain's consular officers would not impede measures taken by Japanese military authorities in China. Accepting the reality of the situation, Britain retreated from its former strong position in central China and retained Hong Kong as its economic center. U.S. Secretary of State Hull opposed the Craigie-Arita decision and immediately proceeded to abrogate America's 1911 treaty with Japan.

See July 26, 1939.

### July 26, 1939

**The United States gives the required six months' notice that it will terminate its commercial treaty of 1911 with Japan on January 1, 1940.**

Although isolationists in Congress blocked Neutrality Act changes during the spring of 1939, they were willing to consider an arms embargo to combat Japan's aggression in East Asia. During these discussions the question arose as to whether an arms embargo on Japan would violate the commercial treaty of 1911. On July 18, Senator Vandenberg, a leading Republican isolationist, introduced a resolution to abrogate the 1911 treaty.

Roosevelt and Hull took immediate action that would preempt Vandenberg's resolution. They also claimed that the Senate action might not be completed before Congress adjourned. As a result, Roosevelt declared on July 26 that the United States would end its commercial treaty on January 26, 1940.

### August 23, 1939

***A Nazi-Soviet pact is signed at Moscow by which each nation agrees not to attack the other and to be neutral if the other is attacked by a third power.***

The signing of the German-Soviet pact resulted from six months of a complex negotiating game between Germany and Russia and Russia and England, including France. These talks began after Germany annexed all of Czechoslovakia and began making demands for Poland to turn over territory where Germans lived. The unsuccessful talks between England, France and Russia began on April 18 when Soviet Foreign Minister Maxim Litvinoff proposed a Three-Power Alliance to counteract Nazi demands. Litvinoff's offer looked good on the surface but Prime Minister Chamberlain backed off because the proposal failed to clarify Russia's relations with Poland and included clauses requiring assurances that if war began neither of the three parties would accept peace talks unless all parties agreed. In July, the new Soviet Foreign Minister Vyacheslav Molotov proposed talks on military assistance and on August 11 the British-French military mission reached Moscow. Their talks got nowhere, stumbling on Poland's refusal to have Soviet troops cross their territory. While his delegates talked with Molotov, Chamberlain held secret discussion about a non-aggression pact with a German official, Helmut Wohlstat. Thus, by early August, all four powers were involved in divergent negotiations when Germany made demands on Romania as well as Poland. At the same time, Chamberlain learned the Soviets had negotiated with Hitler since July 26.

In the context of these six months of discussions, Chamberlain's main concern was the assurances France and Britain gave to protect Poland from a German attack. The British could find no

Soviet Foreign Minister Vyacheslav Mikhailovich Molotov signs the German-Soviet Non-aggression Pact; Joachim von Ribbentrop and Josef Stalin stand behind him. National Archives

satisfactory way to employ Russian forces in the defense of Poland whose government insisted Soviet troops could not enter their territory to engage the German army and air force. Poland's Foreign Minister Colonel Joszef Beck opposed any concessions to the Soviet Unions and Chamberlain readily agreed. Chamberlain said "I very much agree with him [Beck], for I regard Russia as a very unreliable friend with an enormous irritative power on others." By August, Chamberlain tried to persuade Beck to negotiate with Germany regarding Hitler's demands for Danzig-Polish corridor along the

Vistula River. On August 21, an announcement that a Nazi-Soviet non-aggression pact would be signed ended the possibility of Beck's talking with Hitler.

The final Nazi-Soviet pact was signed on August 23 (actually August 24 at 1 A.M.). In addition to a non-aggression pact, a secret Nazi-Soviet protocol partitioned Poland and divided the four Baltic states. Poland was divided along lines defined by the Pisia, Narew, Vistula and San rivers. In the Baltic, Russia would control Finland, Estonia and Latvia; Germany would control Lithuania. In southeast Europe, Russia could control Bessarabia. With a Soviet agreement finalized, Hitler made final preparations to attack Poland.

See September 1, 1939.

### August 25, 1939

**President Roosevelt notifies Hitler that Poland is willing to negotiate, asking Germany to accept peaceful means to avert war. Roosevelt does not expect Hitler to agree, but wishes to make Germany's aggression clear to the U.S. people.**

Because a European war seemed certain at any moment after the August 23 Nazi-Soviet Pact, Roosevelt had immediately sent a message on the same day to King Victor Emmanuel of Italy to assert his influence for peace. On the 24th, he appealed to Hitler and President Ignace Moscicki of Poland, offering to act as mediator in the process of arbitration or conciliation of the dispute. Moscicki agreed; Hitler never responded.

On August 25, Roosevelt asked Hitler to accept the Polish mediation offer. The president told his advisers he wanted to "put the bee on Germany which nobody had done in 1914." It is necessary, he said, "that history should not record that the first act of aggression of a military character was brought about by Poland." As expected, the Nazi leader ignored the president's second appeal. German preparations were already well underway for the attack on Poland.

### September 1, 1939

*Nazi Germany's armies launch an invasion of Poland.*

Hitler informed his generals to prepare for war on August 22, the day German Foreign Minister Joachim von Ribbentrop left for Moscow. The Germans did not believe England and France would intervene because Hitler would provide good "reasons" to justify war, "whether plausible or not." "The victor," Hitler told his generals, will not be asked "whether he told the truth or not. In starting and making war it is not right, but victory, that matters."

The alleged reason for Germany's invasion was that Poland had not fulfilled Hitler's March demands to have Danzig unite with Germany's East Prussia and allow the Germans to build a railway and highway across the Polish corridor (see March 31, 1939). Although Ian Colvin's *The Chamberlain Cabinet* explains Chamberlain's last-minute attempts until August 31 to resolve the Polish issues, it was not possible to meet Hitler's many demands, the last of which on September 30 was a list of 16 items regarding Poland. As some of Chamberlain's cabinet suspected, Hitler was probably stalling to complete Germany's preparations to launch the attack on Poland. World War II began in Europe when the German armies made their blitzkrieg attack on September 1.

See September 3, 1939.

### September 3, 1939

*British and French ultimatums to Germany on September 2 having been rejected, the two Western powers declare war on Germany.*

For a brief period after Hitler's attack on Poland, England and France hoped the Germans might localize the conflict and negotiate. Hitler had tried to prevent British-French intervention, sending false signs from August 25 to 30 that he was ready to negotiate regarding Poland and blaming Poland's Colonel Beck for not agreeing to the proper atmosphere for discussion. Minister of Economics Hermann Göring sent a Swedish businessman, Birger Dahlerus, to London to see if a Munich-type conference could be undertaken on the basis that Chamberlain would make a prior commitment to support Hitler's demands.

Because of these prewar diversions, England and France took 48 hours to seek a final peaceful diplomatic solution with Hitler. It did not succeed and London and Paris declared war on September 3. The British and French had finally concluded that Hitler's ambitions exceeded the revision of Versailles and they must resort to "balance-of-power" politics to maintain their own security.

### September 4, 1939

**Secretary of State Hull meets with British Ambassador Lord Lothian to arrange to minimize U.S.-British conflicts about neutral rights.**

During the next year, a variety of disputes arose about British action against neutral American ships, U.S. mail, and cables. These matters never became more

Cartoon shows the Axis leaders carving up the world. ``Fruits of Aggression'' filmstrip. National Archives

than irritations, however, because Hull and Lothian equally desired to avoid the antagonisms that developed between 1914 and 1917.

### September 5, 1939

**President Roosevelt announces U.S. neutrality in the European war, applying the Neutrality Acts, which embargoed arms to all belligerents.**

The declaration of war by France and England left Roosevelt no choice but to issue a neutrality decree. Roosevelt did not, however, ask Americans to be neutral in thought as well as deed as Woodrow Wilson had in 1914. In addition, the president began preparations to call a special session of Congress to revise the U.S. neutrality legislation.

See November 4, 1939.

### September 17, 1939

*Soviet forces invade eastern Poland, occupying areas Hitler had designated for the USSR in the secret protocol of the August 23 Nazi-Soviet Pact.*

Soon after occupying eastern Poland, Stalin forced the Baltic states of Estonia, Latvia, and Lithuania to permit the Red Army to establish military bases on their territory. Soon after, 20,000 Soviet soldiers entered these states and the USSR absorbed these small countries.

Although the original Nazi-Soviet Pact gave Lithuania to Germany, a new agreement was concluded on September 28. Stalin proposed to give Germany additional Polish territory as far east as the Bug River (east from the Narew River). In return, the Soviet Union occupied Lithuania.

### October 3, 1939

**The foreign ministers of the Pan-American states meet at Panama and adopt a general declaration of continental neutrality that Pan-Americanizes Roosevelt's neutrality policy.**

The Declaration of Panama provided for the neutral solidarity of the New World republics, slanting the neutrality in favor of the Western democracies as much as Roosevelt's revised Fourth Neutrality Act of November 4, 1939, would allow. The declaration said the American nations would prohibit their inhabitants from engaging in activity affecting neutrality, would recognize the transfer of a merchant vessel flag to another American republic, and would exclude belligerent submarines from their territorial waters in a large war zone surrounding the Western Hemisphere.

Some observers criticized the legal implications of the large, 300-mile-wide security zone that the Panama Declaration drew up for security reasons. They were bothered more by the practical than the legal dimensions of the decree. Because this zone exceeded the normal coastal limits recognized by international law, it could not be "legally" binding unless the belligerent powers accepted it. They did not; in fact, both the British and the French rejected this security zone.

### October 11, 1939

**Albert Einstein and other scientists inform President Roosevelt that an atomic bomb could possibly be developed.**

Einstein's letter was inspired by the atomic scientist Leo SZILARD, who, unlike Einstein, was involved in nuclear fission research. Einstein's letter warned that Germany seemed to be moving to control uranium supplies that were used in nuclear fission. From the suggestion of this message, Roosevelt eventually organized the top-secret Manhattan Project, which produced the world's first atomic weapon in 1945.

See August 13, 1942.

### November 4, 1939

**Roosevelt signs Fourth Revised Neutrality Act that ends the arms embargo and permits cash and carry sales of arms.**

On September 13, the president called a special session of Congress to revise U.S. neutrality legislation. The meetings began on September 21, and, in spite of strong isolationist opposition, Congress amended the neutrality laws in about five weeks.

During the period of debate, Roosevelt's theme was that a cash and carry program would allow France and England to purchase arms in the United States and keep America out of war by preventing the German conquest of those two Western European democracies. The president argued that the United States would not be severely threatened unless Germany defeated England and France. While he avoided specifically stating that America should

directly help the Western democracies, the cash and carry arms sales program would obviously benefit England and France because the British navy controlled the Atlantic Ocean. The cash and carry provisions would permit the Allies to purchase all types of goods but would keep U.S. ships out of the war zones.

To support neutrality revision, Roosevelt encouraged bipartisan backing. Leading Republicans such as Henry Stimson, Frank Knox, who owned the *Chicago Daily News,* and Alfred Landon, the 1936 Republican presidential candidate, spoke in favor of neutrality revision.

Nevertheless, Senate isolationists continued to oppose any changes in the neutrality laws and accused the president of seeking to enhance his personal power to involve America in Europe's war. Senators Borah, Nye, and Vandenberg employed a national radio campaign to promote a mail-in response by all who opposed any chance of involving the country in war.

The mood in Congress had changed, however, since the July defeat of Roosevelt's attempt to revise the Neutrality Acts. On October 27, the Senate approved a revision of the neutrality legislation by a vote of 63 to 30; the House adopted its measure on November 2 by a vote of 243 to 18; a conference bill to settle the final wording of the law passed on November 3.

On November 4, Roosevelt signed the new bill, issued a proclamation lifting the arms embargo, and defined the combat areas where U.S. ships and citizens were excluded. The combat zone included only the waters adjacent to the British Isles and France and the North and Baltic Seas. A major handicap of this revision was to prohibit U.S. ships with cargo other than arms from entering British and French ports. All purchases by the Europeans would be cash and carry.

In addition, the act of November 4 continued all the provisions of the Neutrality Act of 1937 except the change of the arms embargo that permitted arms to be sold on a cash and carry basis. The United States did not return to the defense of its neutral rights, which it had followed from 1914 to 1917 and prior to 1935. U.S. ships could not carry freight or passengers to belligerent ports; U.S. ships could not be armed; American citizens could not travel on belligerent ships; loans to belligerents were prohibited except for short-term, 90-day credits. These provisions of the 1939 Neutrality Act restricted aid that America might have given to the European democracies.

### November 29, 1939

#### Roosevelt's attempt to mediate between the USSR and Finland fails. Soviet planes and troops attack Finland.

Early in October 1939, Moscow demanded military bases in Finland similar to agreements given by the governments of Estonia, Latvia, and Lithuania on September 28. But Finland refused and asked Washington to assist in persuading the Soviets to withdraw their unreasonable requirements. On October 11, Roosevelt sent a telegram to Mikhail KALININ, president of the Soviet Union, asking that country to limit its demands on Finnish independence.

The October 11 message, as well as a similar appeal by Roosevelt on November 29, was rebuffed by the USSR. On November 29, the Soviet army invaded Finland to impose the USSR's demands but met stiff resistance from Finnish forces.

Because the Soviet Union did not officially declare war on Finland, Roosevelt and Hull acted as they had in the Sino-Japanese conflict of 1937. They called for a "moral embargo" on airplane sales to the Soviets but did not apply the Neutrality Acts. Finland would have suffered from the neutrality laws more than the USSR. In addition, diplomatic relations were maintained in Moscow because the Roosevelt administration believed that sooner or later the Soviets would forsake their Nazi pact and join the Western Allies.

During the winter of 1939–1940, the restrictions of neutrality prevented Roosevelt from aiding Finland, much as he desired. Although the president arranged an Export-Import Bank loan of $10 million, the funds could not be used for arms. Finnish Ambassador Hjalmar Procopé desired $60 million that could be used to buy arms and planes.

In January 1940, Senator Prentiss M. Brown of Michigan presented a Senate bill to provide Finland an unrestricted loan. Although the United States had great sympathy for the gallant Finnish defenders, isolationists opposed this measure as another example of Roosevelt's desire for "dictatorial power." Therefore, the president did not strongly support Brown's resolution. On March 2, 1940, a congressional act raised the capital of the Export-Import Bank to $200 million

but limited any one loan to $20 million, which could not be used for armaments.

See March 12, 1940.

### December 24, 1939

#### President Roosevelt appoints a personal representative to the Vatican.

During the fall of 1939, President Roosevelt, Secretary Hull, and others in the State Department discussed the value of having a U.S. representative at the Vatican who could obtain data regarding such issues as the Jewish problem and internal affairs in Spain, Italy, and Germany. Inquiries through U.S. Ambassador William Phillips in Rome indicated that Pope Pius XII would look favorably on such an arrangement. Thus, on Christmas Eve, Roosevelt made public a letter he had written to the pope regarding world peace, and at the same time he announced that Myron C. TAYLOR had been appointed as the president's personal representative to the Vatican.

# 1940

### January 17, 1940

#### President Roosevelt holds an interdepartmental conference to expedite aircraft sales to France and England.

Although French and British orders for U.S. munitions did not materialize as rapidly as Roosevelt had expected during the fall of 1939, by January 1 France ordered 2,095 airplanes and 7,372 aircraft engines; Britain ordered 1,450 airplanes. During December, however, Britain and France had projected that the aircraft order for 1940 would reach 10,000 planes and 20,000 engines, provided they could get the best type available such as the fighter P-40.

In the War, Navy, and State Departments, British and French orders and their desire for the most improved aircraft models caused dissension. Secretary of War Woodring and several high military leaders opposed giving these countries the latest U.S. planes and wanted U.S. needs to be filled before offering them to France and Britain. But the president agreed with Louis Johnson, the assistant secretary of war, who headed the industrial mobilization office. Johnson believed the Allied orders enabled U.S. aircraft manufacturers to expand rapidly and, in the long term, would assist U.S. defense preparations.

Although the president attempted to conciliate Woodring and the army generals at the January 17 meeting, he urged them to expedite the Allied orders, which were needed immediately. It was finally agreed that a percentage of all aircraft could be sold to France and Britain, and that these would be the improved models because those were the models that U.S. industries had to gear up to manufacture.

The conference of January 17 did not resolve all conflicts between Louis Johnson and Secretary Woodring. In March 1940, Roosevelt learned that Army Air Force General Arnold and Woodring refused to let the Allies have secret devices necessary to the planes they had ordered. Roosevelt believed this was nonsense. He instructed Arnold to stop resisting aid to France and Britain and told all three men that their leaks of information to Republicans and isolationists must cease. He told Woodring to accept his views or resign. He told Arnold that any uncooperative officers would be sent to "exile" at Guam. Temporarily, Woodring and Arnold accepted Roosevelt's lead, not challenging him again until June 1940, after the fall of France.

### January 26, 1940

**The United States officially ends its 1911 commercial treaty with Japan.**

The American intention to end the commercial arrangements had been made in July 1939 to meet the necessary six-month notice before termination.

In Tokyo, Foreign Minister Nomura asked Ambassador Grew if a new treaty would be negotiated. Following Hull's advice in December 1939, Grew told Nomura that at present U.S. trade with Japan was on a 24-hour basis and would depend on Japan's further violation of U.S. rights in East Asia. Thus, no U.S. treaty negotiations were begun.

### March 12, 1940

*Finland accepts Soviet peace terms, retaining independence but surrendering territory and making economic and military concessions to Moscow.*

### March 28, 1940

**The conclusion of Sumner Welles's mission to Europe to explore the chances for peace.**

Although the trip was opposed by Secretary of State Hull, on February 9 Roosevelt dispatched Undersecretary of State Welles to Rome, Berlin, Paris, and London, where he explored the possibilities of peace and gained information on conditions in Europe. Since September, neither the Axis powers nor the Western democracies had pursued active military campaigns during this six-month period that came to be known as the "phony war." Exactly what purpose Roosevelt intended for Welles is unclear. Welles said he was told to offer guarantees of disarmament, security, and trade if the four powers would attend a conference to resolve their difficulties. Since Poland had been quickly overrun by German and Soviet troops, the fate of that country could not be considered, but other issues could be identified and resolved to bring peace.

Therefore, Welles interviewed the head of each government in the cities he visited. The mission accomplished nothing. There was, said Welles, no chance for peace based on territorial or economic changes. Each belligerent wanted to enhance its own future security; a practical plan acceptable to all four nations did not seem possible.

### April 9, 1940

*Germany invades Norway with sea and airborne troops. At the same time, German troops occupy Denmark with little Danish resistance.*

Although Norway offered some resistance and Anglo-French forces landed in southern Norway on April 16, Hitler rapidly reinforced the German army, and by April 30, effective Allied resistance ended. The English and French withdrew, and after June 10 only underground activity against Germany remained in Norway.

### May 10, 1940

*Without warning, Germany attacks the Netherlands, Belgium, and Luxemburg. Two days later the Germans attack France, crossing the Meuse river at Sedan.*

### May 10, 1940

*Winston Churchill becomes Britain's prime minister, replacing Neville Chamberlain.*

Churchill headed a coalition cabinet that included both Conservative and Labour Party members. Churchill's rhetoric and dogged persistence rallied the British to resist the Fascist forces and symbolized his nation's determination to defeat its enemies. Churchill had previously established correspondence with President Roosevelt, and the Anglo-Saxon leaders generally cooperated well throughout the war years.

### May 16, 1940

**President Roosevelt asks Congress for $1.18 billion in additional defense appropriations.**

Germany's renewed aggression during April and May led the president to request funds to meet the nation's defense needs. Although Roosevelt had reduced the army budget request in January 1940, he now told Congress that the United States needed to expand its ground forces. In addition, he asked for funding to build the nation's aircraft production up to 50,000 planes per year. He told Congress that planes flying as fast as 300 miles an hour eliminated the oceans as "adequate defensive barriers" to the Americas. Within two weeks, Congress approved more than Roosevelt requested, voting $1.3 billion for defense purposes.

By May 31, Roosevelt requested another increased defense funding bill. Within one month, Congress voted another $1.7 billion, expanded the regular army from 280,000 to 375,000 men, and authorized the president to call the National Guard into service. Hitler's rapid victories in western Europe startled the American public and motivated Congress to act quickly to repair the strength of the armed forces, which had been neglected since the end of World War I.

### May 28, 1940

**Congress approves legislation permitting the president to release army and navy stock to Latin American countries to assist western hemispheric defense.**

For over a year, the War, Navy, and State Departments had requested congressional approval to permit them to supply Latin American countries with ammunition, coast defense and antiaircraft equipment, and warships. The House passed the legislation early in 1940, but the proposal was delayed by various Senate committees until May 28. Passage of this act permitted U.S. naval and military officials to send essential equipment other than the outdated and obsolete surplus materials previously sent to the South Americans.

### June 3, 1940

**Seeking a method to defend America by extended aid to Britain and France, Roosevelt discovers a technique to get "surplus" U.S. equipment to the allies.**

On May 22, Roosevelt had ordered the sale of World War I equipment to the Allies, although the Neutrality Act of 1939 did not permit the U.S. government to do this. Both French Premier Reynaud and British Prime Minister Churchill urged the president to send whatever he could because the Germans' swift victories had not been anticipated.

On June 3, Roosevelt's legal advisers ruled that the government could sell "surplus" military supplies to private parties who could resell them to England and France. In three weeks, the first shipment reached England: 500,000 rifles, 80,000 machine guns, 900 75 mm field guns, and 130 million rounds of ammunition.

### June 10, 1940

**Roosevelt's speech at the University of Virginia (Charlottesville) denounces both isolationists and Italy, and indicates the United States must aid England and France.**

The president said isolationists dreamed that America could be "a lone island in a world dominated by force." Such delusions, he said, would create a "nightmare" for people "handcuffed, hungry, and fed through the bars" by "unpitying masters of other continents." Only an Allied victory, he said, could prevent such imprisonment.

Regarding Italy, the president had appealed on two occasions for Mussolini to strive for peace and to limit the war. Now, on June 10, news came of Italy's attack on France. In Roosevelt's descriptive words, "the hand that held the dagger has struck it into the back of its neighbor."

Finally, the president asserted, in unity America must pursue two objectives: one, to "extend to the opponents of force the material resources of this nation"; and two, to speed U.S. defense preparations so that "the Americas may have equipment and training to the task of any emergency and every defense."

The president's message abandoned any pretense of neutrality. The United States unofficially became a nonbelligerent aiding England and France.

### June 17, 1940

*France surrenders, asking Germany for an armistice.*

The Nazi blitzkrieg moved swiftly through the Low Countries and deep into northern France by May 21, outflanking France's defensive works, the Maginot Line. The Belgian armies surrendered on May 26 and, left in an exposed condition, the British expeditionary force of 250,000 men staged a hasty and gallant retreat by sea at Dunkirk on May 28, leaving most of their equipment behind.

On June 20, Italy declared war against France and Great Britain and invaded southern France. The Italian "stab in the back" served Mussolini's moment of glory but was not essential to the Germans. After evacuating Paris without a fight on June 13, the French government of Paul Reynaud resigned. Marshal Philippe PÉTAIN became premier and asked the Germans for an armistice on June 17.

A Frenchman weeps as German soldiers march into Paris on June 14, 1940. National Archives

The French signed the German armistice demands at Compiègne on June 22. French forces were disarmed and three-fifths of France came completely under German control. The Pétain administration set up headquarters at Vichy on July 2. In London on June 23, General Charles DE GAULLE, heading a French National Committee, pledged to continue French resistance to Germany.

On June 24, Pétain's government and Italy signed an armistice.

### June 18, 1940

**Congress approves the Pittman-Bloom resolution, which opposes the transfer of territory in the western hemisphere from one non-American power to another non-American power.**

The German conquest of western European nations with colonies in the Americas such as the Netherlands, Denmark, and France concerned the State Department. Thus, Secretary Hull drafted a resolution that was sent to the Foreign Relations Committee on June 3. The bill was approved unanimously by the Senate on June 17, and by a vote of 380-8 in the House on June 18.

### June 19, 1940

**Roosevelt appoints two pro-allied Republicans to his cabinet: Henry Stimson as Secretary of War and Frank Knox as Secretary of the Navy.**

By these two appointments, the president not only established a bipartisan consensus for aid to the British but also replaced two isolationist cabinet members. Secretary of War Harry Woodring had especially irritated the president by opposing sales of "surplus" goods to England, claiming the old equipment was useful for training the U.S. army.

Both Stimson and Knox were prominent Republican leaders. Stimson had been secretary of war under William H. Taft and secretary of state under Herbert Hoover. Knox was the Republicans' vice presidential candidate in 1936.

## June 27, 1940

**Roosevelt requires the Joint Board of the Army and Navy to operate contingency plans under Rainbow Four War Plans revised to assume British survival through the winter of 1940–1941.**

The German conquest of France caused the Joint Board of the Army and Navy to shift its contingency war preparations from Rainbow TWO to Rainbow FOUR. Rainbow Two plans assumed a British-French alliance to control the Atlantic while the United States defended in the Pacific. Rainbow Four was a worst-case plan: the United States against the victorious Axis powers with no allies. Under Rainbow Four, all U.S. preparations had to focus on immediate American defense preparations.

Roosevelt disliked the implications of Rainbow Four; consequently, he accepted Prime Minister Churchill's promise that Great Britain would survive regardless of the sacrifice. In order to give Britain a priority in available arms and aircraft, Roosevelt rejected the opinion of Army Chief of Staff Marshall and Chief of Naval Operations Harold Stark, that sending war matériel to Britain was assistance to a lost cause. Roosevelt wanted one-half of all U.S. aircraft and munitions production available for Britain.

Of course, the commander in Chief won the dispute. On June 27, Rainbow Four was amended to reflect the president's desire to aid England. Although the Joint Board did not fully accept Roosevelt's "Germany First" strategy until December 1940, Roosevelt virtually adopted it on June 27, 1940.

See May 11, 1939, and November 12, 1940.

## June 28, 1940

**The Alien Registration Act (Smith Act) attempts to check subversive activity in the United States.**

This act governed the admission and deportation of aliens, and required all aliens to be fingerprinted. The act made it unlawful to teach or advocate the overthrow of the U.S. government by force or violence or to organize or become a member of any group advancing such doctrines.

When the Cold War began after 1945, 11 U.S. Communist Party members were convicted and imprisoned under the Smith Act. In the 1957 *Yates v. U.S.* decision, the Supreme Court reversed the conviction because they were tried for their ideas not for using force or violence.

## July 3, 1940

*The British navy arrives at Oran to take over French ships. The French crews resist and the British sink or capture the major portion of the French fleet anchored off Algeria's coast.*

## July 14, 1940

**Britain's secret agent in New York—"Intrepid"—informs British intelligence that Colonel William J. Donovan has been chosen as President Roosevelt's personal representative.**

"Intrepid" was Sir William Stephenson, a British intelligence officer and friend of Churchill, who set up a headquarters in New York for British secret communications and deciphering activity. Stephenson and his colleagues had stolen the Germans' secret coding machine, Enigma, on August 22, 1939, and learned how to break the German code Ultra. The first successes of Enigma were to discover German plans that led to Britain's successful withdrawal at Dunkirk in May 1940. The interception of German messages corresponded with the events preceding Dunkirk. When these were made known to Roosevelt, the president was sufficiently impressed to appoint Colonel Donovan as his liaison with Stephenson. Later Donovan headed the U.S. Office of Strategic Services (OSS), working closely with Stephenson until 1945. Details about Ultra may be found in Ronald Lewis's *Ultra Goes to War* (1978).

## July 15, 1940

**The Democratic Convention at Chicago nominates President Roosevelt for an unprecedented third term.**

The Democratic platform continued, however, to reflect an isolationist attitude, stating that the United States "will not participate in foreign wars" or send U.S. armed forces to "fight in foreign lands outside the Americas, except in case of attack." Although Secretary of State Hull disliked this statement, Roosevelt told him "there would be no change in our foreign policy."

On June 28 the Republican Convention nominated a presidential candidate, Wendell Willkie, whose foreign policy views were similar to those of Roosevelt. Willkie opposed participation in "foreign wars" but advocated aid to Britain, strong U.S. defenses, and hemispheric cooperation.

## July 20, 1940

### A naval construction bill for $4 billion is signed by President Roosevelt.

This bill, combined with a bill passed on June 14, 1940, authorized the construction of a "two-ocean navy" capable of defensive action in one ocean and freedom of action in the other. More than 1,325,000 tons of naval construction were authorized by these two bills, providing for 250 warships. The new fleet included 7 battleships, 6 battle cruisers, 19 carriers, 60 cruisers, 150 destroyers, and 140 submarines.

## July 25–26, 1940

### President Roosevelt limits but then qualifies U.S. exports of oil and scrap metal to Japan.

The president faced a difficult decision regarding Japanese policy during the summer of 1940. Following the Allied losses in western Europe between April and June 1940, the status of the Far East became less certain. Great Britain wanted the United States either to appease Japan or take strong action such as economic sanctions. In Washington, Morgenthau and Stimson urged sanctions while Sumner Welles and Hull feared that economic pressure would lead Japan to take over the oil supplies of the Dutch East Indies islands that British forces had occupied after the Netherlands fell to the Germans.

Roosevelt's desire to avoid a Japanese war but to take some action against Tokyo's continued conquest of southern China became a middle-course policy lacking the clarity of the other extremes. Consequently, when Secretary of the Treasury Morgenthau asked the president to forbid the export of petroleum, petroleum products, and scrap metal to Japan, Roosevelt agreed and signed a bill to that effect on July 25.

Upon hearing of the Treasury Department order, Hull and Undersecretary of State Welles objected. As written, the order seemed to embargo all U.S. oil and scrap metal shipments to Japan. During a cabinet meeting that day, Roosevelt told Welles and Morgenthau to write a proper order indicating that the United States was not embargoing these products. With Welles's help, Morgenthau issued a revised order on July 26 that narrowly restricted the embargo to aviation motor fuel and high-grade smelting scrap. The State Department interpreted the July 26 order more liberally in Japan's favor. By interpreting aviation fuel to mean high-octane aviation fuel, Japan could still obtain middle-octane fuel needed for its airplanes.

On September 24, however, Roosevelt established an embargo of scrap iron and steel to all countries outside the Western Hemisphere except Great Britain.

## July 30, 1940

### A special Pan-American conference at Havana agrees on a method to prevent the transfer of non-American territory to another non-American power.

While urging Congress to approve the Pittman-Bloom "no-transfer" resolution on June 18, Secretary Hull also invited the Pan-American nations to a meeting in Havana to obtain their cooperation in keeping German control from extending to possessions of the European nations conquered by the Nazis.

There had been frequent reports of German activity in the Western Hemisphere, and several events appeared to confirm those suspicions. On July 7, the Argentine police uncovered plans for an insurrection to establish a Nazi base. Ten days later, the Nacista Party of Chile failed in an effort to overthrow Chile's left-of-center Popular Front government. In addition, Hull feared that Vichy France's control of Martinique, Guadeloupe, and other Caribbean islands might bring German influence into the Western Hemisphere.

At the Havana Conference, which convened on July 21, Argentina's attitude became the chief stumbling block to approval of the U.S. resolution on "no-transfer." The Argentines exported many commodities to Germany and Italy and did not wish to offend these nations. In addition, since 1833 Argentina had claimed the right to take the Falkland Islands from Britain and advocated that, perhaps, the American republics should individually occupy European possessions in the Western Hemisphere.

Eventually, however, Secretary Hull sent a personal appeal to Argentina's President Roberto Ortiz, who had strongly supported the 1938 Declaration of Lima. Ortiz responded positively and Argentina ceased its opposition to the U.S. resolution while reserving the right not to ratify the Havana pact. The Havana agreement not only opposed the transfer of non-American territory but set up a committee to administer any European territory attacked or under threat of being transferred. A collective trusteeship of the signatory American states would take over such territory pending its return to the original power once the war ended in Europe.

See June 18, 1940.

## August 8, 1940

### *The Battle of Britain begins as German aircraft launch attacks on British airfields and vital industries.*

Between August 8 and November 10, 1940, German bombing raids attacked British targets on a frequent but irregular basis. British casualties became as high as 600 per day in September. Finally, after an intensive attack that destroyed the industrial city of Coventry on November 10, German attacks became more sporadic. British defensive efforts caused the loss of 2,375 German airplanes at the cost of 800 British planes.

British bombers retaliated against Germany to some degree. Beginning on August 15, the Royal Air Force raided Berlin, Essen, and other German cities. Britain's air attacks never matched the size of Germany's in 1940, but they helped the morale of British citizens who valiantly endured the German attacks.

## August 16, 1940

### To assist the Latin American nations in their economic problems, Roosevelt appoints Nelson A. Rockefeller as coordinator of Commercial and Cultural relations among the American republics.

During the Havana Conference, the United States had little time to consider the economic problems and the methods for financing the defense projects of Latin American states. Therefore, on August 16 Roosevelt created an American republics office under the Advisory Commission to the Council of National Defense. Rockefeller would centralize U.S. efforts to relieve the Pan-American nations of their economic

concerns. Roosevelt also aided Rockefeller in securing Export-Import Bank funds for the South American nations.

See July 30, 1940.

## August 18, 1940

### President Roosevelt and Canada's Prime Minister MacKenzie King announce the creation of a permanent Joint Board of Defense: The Ogdensburg Agreement.

Although Canada was a belligerent at war against Germany, Roosevelt readily agreed that American defenses required close collaboration with Canada. Meeting in the president's railway car near Ogdensburg, New York, the two leaders adopted a plan for the joint defense of their nations. As announced on August 18, the agreement established a Joint Board of Defense consisting of four or five representatives of each nation. The board would consider the defense of the northern half of the Western Hemisphere from possible attacks by sea, air, or land.

The Joint Board of Defense began meetings on August 24 and provided close cooperation between Canada and the United States throughout World War II.

## September 3, 1940

### Great Britain and America announce a destroyer-for-bases defense agreement.

In this agreement, President Roosevelt transferred 50 overage U.S. destroyers to England, and Prime Minister Churchill gave the United States the right to a 99-year lease on naval and air bases in Newfoundland, Bermuda, the Bahamas, Jamaica, St. Lucia, Trinidad, Antigua, and British Guiana. This arrangement originated from Churchill's June 18 request for destroyers that the British needed to defend convoys from German and Italian submarine attacks.

Roosevelt did not oppose the idea but required time to make certain that the destroyer deal did not meet with strong political opposition in America. In August, Roosevelt offered Churchill the bases-destroyer barter plan, and after some discussion, the British agreed. Roosevelt then sought congressional and public support in America. On several occasions in August, Roosevelt commented on the defense advantages to America of having bases away from

The first air raid on London, September 7, 1940. The dock area is aflame and St. Paul's stands in the background. National Archives.

the North American continent. When the response from various groups in America appeared congenial, the president continued to work out the details of the plan, and on September 3, Washington and London announced the joint approval of the proposal. Although the deal was arranged without congressional sanction, the U.S. public generally approved of the exchange. In substance, however, this agreement moved America and Britain to even closer cooperation.

### September 16, 1940

**Roosevelt signs the Selective Service and Training Act as passed by Congress: the first peacetime program of compulsory military service for the United States.**

This act provided for the registration of all men between 21 and 35 years of age. As chosen in a draft

lottery, the army would train 1,200,000 troops and 800,000 reserves for one year.

On October 1, registration began and listed 16,400,000 men. The first draft numbers were selected on October 29.

Passing this legislation presented some difficulty because of protests by isolationist senators such as Nye and Wheeler. On August 2, 1940, Roosevelt informally and reluctantly expressed his approval of the legislation. On August 17, Republican presidential candidate Willkie also approved the measure. The bill passed both houses of Congress on September 14.

### September 27, 1940

***Japan signs a tripartite pact with Italy and Germany, making the Anti-Comintern Pact a political and military alliance.***

Japan had been uncertain about its alliance with Rome and Berlin because it could not comprehend the Nazi-

Soviet Pact of August 23, 1939, as reflecting only Hitler's temporary policy. But by July 27, 1940, the Konoye government pledged itself to take stronger measures to assure Japan's dominance in East Asia. It decided to end the China Incident successfully and force concessions from Britain in Shanghai and Burma, from the French in Indochina, and from the Dutch in the Dutch East Indies. In August and September, the British withdrew from Shanghai, having previously agreed to close the Burma Road as a supply route for Chiang Kai-shek's Chinese government. In addition, France agreed to recognize Japan's predominant rights in Indochina, while the Dutch undertook negotiations to supply Japan with oil for five years.

In the context of these Japanese policies toward Southeast Asia, the Japanese wanted German and Italian aid against the United States. Thus, the major part of the Axis military pact of September 27 was the three-power agreement to help one another if any were attacked by a power not currently involved in either the European or Sino-Japanese fighting. Obviously, this other power was the United States, which strongly objected to Japan's aggressive action in south and Southeast Asia.

### October 8, 1940

***German troops occupy Romania, beginning a Balkan campaign by the Axis powers. Italy invades Greece on October 28.***

In the Balkans, only Greece offered stiff resistance to the Italian and German armies, holding out with British aid until April 23, 1941. Hungary joined the Axis alliance on November 20, Romania on November 23, Bulgaria on March 1, 1941, and Yugoslavia on March 25. Yet in Yugoslavia, a political coup on March 28 denied the Axis alliance and announced a neutral policy. As a result, German troops moved into Yugoslavia, and the opposition resorted to guerrilla warfare.

### November 5, 1940

**Roosevelt wins the presidential election with a decisive margin over Willkie.**

Although the character of Roosevelt's continued economic reform program was a factor in the 1940 elec-

tion, the issue of war or peace became a vital element of the campaign by October 1940. Willkie's claim that Roosevelt would lead the nation to war won the Republicans many ethnic votes. On October 30 at Boston, Roosevelt made unqualified assurances of his desire for peace. His famous words at Boston were: "I have said this before, but I shall say it again and again and again: Your boys are not going to be sent into any foreign wars."

Later, Roosevelt's critics complained of the deceit in the president's words, "be sent into any foreign wars." Post-election polls showed, however, that the threat of war caused some to vote for Roosevelt as the best leader in case of war (11%); only 2% favored Willkie because he would keep the nation out of war.

Although Willkie won 5 million more votes than Landon had in 1936, he won in only 10 states. The electoral count in 1940 was Roosevelt, 449; Willkie, 82.

### November 12, 1940

**The "Germany First" grand strategy is recommended by Chief of Naval Operations Harold Stark.**

Since 1937, the U.S. navy had been reluctant to divorce itself from the "Japan First" strategy of its traditional Orange War Plan. Although President Roosevelt's influence had established a "Germany First" strategy under an amended Rainbow Four plan on June 27, 1940, CNO Stark and other naval officers continued to focus on the Pacific Ocean for their principal war effort. On November 12, Admiral Stark prepared an extensive analysis of global war strategy that assumed Plan D (Dog) was the best assumption for U.S. policy. Plan D had three essential principles of action: preserving the integrity of the Western Hemisphere; preparing offensive action in the Atlantic to save Britain from Germany; and avoiding war with Japan by making U.S. proposals so specific that Japan would accept them or, if it attacked, using defensive action in the Pacific.

On November 12, Stark presented his recommendations to the Joint Board, General Marshall, Secretary of State Hull, and the president. The other officials ratified Stark's study and it became the basis for discussions with Great Britain and Canada in 1941.

See January 27, 1941.

### December 29, 1940

**President Roosevelt's "Fireside Chat" over national radio networks emphasizes the Axis powers' threat to America and urges an American production buildup to be the "great arsenal of democracy."**

During the fall of 1940, Great Britain experienced financial problems in attempting to continue its purchases of war supplies in America. On December 9, Winston Churchill sent a personal appeal to Roosevelt, outlining Britain's need for more war matériel and ships, as well as requesting elimination of the cash requirements to pay for these materials. Although the potential for a German invasion of the British Isles had diminished, England needed funds and arms to continue the struggle, and had asked Roosevelt to find "ways and means" to continue the flow of supplies to Britain.

By December 12, Roosevelt had conceived the lend-lease program to aid Britain, but he decided to prepare the way for the favorable U.S. reception of this program. After Roosevelt mentioned lend-lease during a December 17 press conference, he explained to reporters: "Suppose my neighbor's home catches fire, and I have a length of hose four or five hundred feet away. If he can take my garden hose and connect it up with his hydrant, I may help him to put out his fire." The president added, "I don't say to him before that operation, 'Neighbor, my garden hose cost me $15; you have to pay me $15 for it.' What is the transaction that goes on? I don't want $15—I want my garden hose back after the fire is over."

On December 20, the president began lend-lease by establishing the Office of Production Management under William D. KNUDSEN to coordinate defense production and to speed all aid "short of war" to Great Britain and other anti-Axis nations.

In this context, Roosevelt's speech of December 29 further stimulated American opinion to provide aid to the democracies. Emphasizing that events abroad affected America, Roosevelt said that democracy and the United States faced their most serious challenge since Jamestown was founded in 1607. If Great Britain fell, the president said, all the world would be threatened by Fascist militarism. To meet this threat, the United States would send all possible aid to opponents of aggression. There would be less

Cartoon of the "Three Horsemen" of the Axis Alliance draws parallel between them and the Bible's Four Horsemen of the Apocalypse, three of which were War, Famine, and Death. National Archives

likelihood of the country's facing war if the United States supported other nations than if it waited for others to be defeated. While any course of action was risky, providing aid to the people of Europe fighting aggression would save America from the agony of war. "We," he said, "must be the great arsenal of democracy. For us this is an emergency as serious as war itself."

Roosevelt's speech proved one of his most popular and effective. Of those who heard the speech, a Gallup poll showed that 80% supported and only 12% opposed aid to Britain. Moreover, the same poll found that 76% of the public heard the speech, the largest number recorded for a presidential speech since 1933.

See January 6, 1941.

# 1941

### January 6, 1941

**The President's State-of-the-Union message informs the nation of his proposal for a lend-lease program and enunciates the "four freedoms."**

Having prepared the way for a lend-lease bill during his December 29, 1940, speech, the president in his annual message to Congress indicated his intention to send Congress a bill to support peoples resisting aggression. This, he said, was the best means to keep "war from our Hemisphere" and to oppose aggressors. Indicating the common objectives of the democratic powers in their fight against totalitarian fascism, Roosevelt declared that victory over the aggressors would mean a world "founded upon four essential human freedoms"—the freedom of speech, of religion, from want, and from fear.

For passage of the Lend-Lease Act, see March 11, 1941.

### January 27, 1941

**High-ranking military officers of the United States, Britain, and Canada convene meetings in Washington to coordinate contingency war plans.**

These staff talks were meant to coordinate American, British, and Canadian activity in the Atlantic and Pacific Oceans. American and British cooperative discussion had been informally pursued since December 23, 1937, when Captain Ingersoll was sent to London by the president. During the summer of 1940, American officers visited London to observe firsthand British experiences in the Battle of Britain.

The meetings from January 27 to March 29 were conducted in secret. The British officers arrived as members of a British purchasing mission. By March 29, the staff officers formulated ABC-1, a coordinated war plan that emphasized a strategy to defeat Germany first, an analysis similar to Admiral Stark's Plan D of November 12, 1940. Although President Roosevelt did not technically approve ABC-1, it was the basis for Rainbow Five war plan of the U.S. Joint Board of the Army and Navy and of a November 1941 revision of Rainbow Five drawn up to reflect Japan's aggression in Southeast Asia during the summer of 1941.

According to ABC-1 (and Rainbow Five), war with Japan should be delayed or avoided as long as possible. If Japan attacked, the U.S. fleet would fight defensively in the Pacific until German defeat was certain. Any American offensive action in the Pacific would be designed to weaken Japan's economy or protect Singapore, the strategic point Churchill considered vital to the British Commonwealth.

### March 5, 1941

**A U.S. agreement with Panama permits the United States to extend air defenses for the canal beyond the canal zone.**

Roosevelt and the Republic of Panama informally agreed that the threat of war in Europe required additional air bases to protect the canal for the duration of the war crisis. This agreement became the basis for a formal treaty signed with Panama on May 18, 1942.

### March 11, 1941

**Congress approves the Lend-Lease Act.**

On January 10, Democratic leaders introduced H.R. 1776 as the Lend-Lease Bill, entitled "An Act to Further Promote the Defense of the United States, and for Other Purposes." The legislation authorized the president to "sell, transfer title to, exchange, lease, lend, or otherwise dispose of . . . any defense article" to countries whose defense was deemed "vital to the defense of the United States." The president would decide if repayment would be "in kind or property, or any other direct or indirect benefit" he thought satisfactory.

Although the Lend-Lease Bill had safe majorities in both houses of Congress, isolationists attacked the measure and required several amendments, none of which seriously hurt the measure. The most extreme isolationist assertion about the proposal was a remark by Senator Burton Wheeler, who called the act the "New Deal's Triple A foreign policy; it will plow under every fourth American boy." The amendments that Roosevelt agreed to placed a time limit on his authority, required periodic reports and consultation with the army and navy on defense equipment, and prevented use of the U.S. navy to transfer lend-lease goods.

On March 11, the amended bill passed the Senate by a vote of 60 to 31; the House by 317 to 17. The initial Lend-Lease Bill authorized expenditures of $7 billion. From 1941 to 1945, lend-lease aid amounted to $50,226,845,387.

The Lend-Lease Act plus extraordinary expenses for the U.S. armed forces required a vast increase in U.S. production from 1941 to 1945. In 1942, the Senate established a Committee to Investigate the National Defense Program to uncover waste and greed that slowed wartime production. Harry S. Truman headed the investigation because he heard rumors of fraud in the construction of new army camps after the 1940 Selective Service Act was approved.

The Truman committee uncovered political kickbacks and graft in the camp construction as well as in many other production programs. An unusual example of the Truman committee work was to give government funds to the Reynolds Aluminum Company to expand its production and compete with ALCOA (Aluminum Company of America), whose monopoly of aluminum production slowed down aircraft production until aluminum prices were increased after 1940. In May 1943, *Time* magazine featured Truman in a cover story regarding the Senate Investigation Committee. Truman's role in wartime production investigations was one reason Roosevelt chose Truman as his 1944 vice presidential nominee.

See September 16, 1940.

### April 3, 1941

*German troops commanded by General Rommel reinforce the Italians in Libya and begin a counterattack to defeat the British.*

The fighting in North Africa began on September 13, 1940, when Italian armies invaded Egypt from Libya. By December 8, a British offensive drove the Italians out of Egypt and captured Tobruk. In addition, British imperial forces defeated the Italians in Somaliland and Ethiopia, liberating Addis Ababa on April 6, 1941.

To regain the offensive, Hitler sent General Erwin Rommel to North Africa with a German army. Rommel's ability and the dispatch of 60,000 British troops to assist Greece forced the British to retreat in Libya, returning to the Egyptian frontier on May 29, 1941.

### April 9, 1941

**The United States and Denmark make an agreement that provides rights for U.S. defense bases in Greenland.**

Secretary of State Hull and Danish Minister Henrik de Kauffmann signed this pact, which effectively permitted the U.S. occupation of Greenland for the duration of the war. Greenland had normally been considered part of the Western Hemisphere, and following the German conquest of Denmark, both England and the United States feared that the Germans might occupy that large Atlantic island.

Although the Nazi-controlled government in Copenhagen rejected this agreement and recalled Kauffmann from his post, the United States did not recognize the recall and continued to accept Kauffmann as the representative of the Danish people.

### April 11, 1941

**Roosevelt informs Churchill that the U.S. Navy will patrol a U.S. security zone including Greenland and the Azores Islands.**

In accordance with the Lend-Lease Act, Roosevelt began to aid British convoys in what became known as the "BATTLE OF THE ATLANTIC" or the "UNDECLARED WAR." With America committed to offer $7 billion of goods to the Allies (mostly to Britain), the British ships required aid to assure their safety. German submarine war had previously sunk 688,000 gross tons between September 3, 1939, and April 9, 1940, and another 2,314,000 gross tons by March 17, 1941.

Initially, U.S. escorts of British ships had been considered the best method, but for political reasons Roosevelt decided the air and navy patrol of a security zone would involve less risk and would be acceptable to the majority of Americans. To patrol this zone, Roosevelt eventually brought 25% of the Pacific fleet to the Atlantic. But he decided not to publicly acknowledge this move. He and Hull desired to retain the naval base at Pearl Harbor as a continuing symbol of U.S. concern for Japanese aggression.

### April 13, 1941

*Japan and the Soviet Union sign a mutual non-aggression pact.*

Until the conclusion of this neutrality pact between Tokyo and the USSR, Roosevelt and Hull considered the possibility that Japan would move north against the Soviets rather than south against Singapore and the Dutch East Indies. Hitler, however, encouraged Tokyo to move to attack Singapore. By obtaining Soviet neutrality in the north, the Japanese could begin action in Indochina during June and July 1941.

### April 15, 1941

**President Roosevelt issues an executive order authorizing reserve officers and enlisted men to join General Chennault's American volunteer group ("Flying Tigers") in China.**

Although General of the Army Air Force Arnold opposed Claire Chennault's attempt to recruit army reserve pilots to fly for the Chinese, Roosevelt and Secretary of the Treasury Morgenthau backed Chennault's suggestion. The Chinese had bought P-40 fighter planes and needed pilots and mechanics to fly and maintain them.

Following the president's approval, Chennault's followers recruited about one hundred men, who left for China on July 10, 1941. A second contingent left in November 1941. These volunteers became famous as the "flying tigers" because of the emblem painted on the nose of their planes. Throughout the war, Chennault's pilots bombed, strafed, harassed, and shot down Japanese aircraft, but contrary to Chennault's expectation, these planes were not sufficient to make up for Chinese military shortcomings.

### April 27, 1941

**American, British, and Dutch naval officers conclude high-level staff planning sessions at Singapore.**

These sessions at Singapore were announced publicly when they began on April 21. Roosevelt hoped they

A Chinese soldier guards American P-40 fighter planes at an airfield in China. The shark-face is the emblem of the "Flying Tigers."
National Archives

would provide a symbol of American concern for potential Japanese action in Southeast Asia. British naval officers sought American assistance in defending that region because the Royal Navy had been largely shifted to the Atlantic and Mediterranean regions. In coordination with ABC-1 war plans formulated at Washington between January 27 and March 29, the Singapore conference prepared ABCD-1 as coordinated efforts to defend the region between Singapore, the Dutch East Indies, and Australia. One consequence of this and other discussions was Roosevelt's decision on July 26 to reinforce the Philippine Islands as a defensive base.

See July 26, 1941.

## May 6, 1941

### President Roosevelt indicates that China is eligible for lend-lease assistance.

This executive action inaugurated a direct U.S. aid program to the Chinese Nationalist government of Chiang Kai-shek. Over the next five years, Chiang's government received $1.5 billion from America. China received only about 3% of the total lend-lease aid given during World War II, because Anglo-American war plans gave China a low military priority and because Japan's occupation of China's coastline required all goods to be airlifted to China's interior from India or Burma. Most lend-lease aid went to Great Britain and the Soviet Union to fight against Germany. U.S. forces did the largest share of the fighting that defeated Japan in the Pacific theater of war.

## May 12, 1941

### Discussions between Secretary of State Hull and Japan's Ambassador Kichisaburo Nomura reach a complicated misunderstanding.

Following Nomura's arrival as ambassador in February 1941, Hull undertook frequent meetings with him to explore possible solutions to U.S.-Japanese disputes in East Asia. The talks were inspired in part by a White House visit of two Roman Catholic clerics on January 23. Bishop James E. Walsh and Father James M. Drought of the Catholic Mission Society of Maryknoll had been in Tokyo and met Japanese Foreign Minister Yosuke MATSUOKA. They gave Roosevelt a memorandum containing their understanding of a Japanese offer to settle disagree-

ments with Washington. Although Hull and Roosevelt were skeptical, they pursued any possible avenue to peace as long as no U.S. principles were sacrificed.

Nomura told Hull he did not know about the Drought-Walsh talks with Matsuoka, but this gap was soon filled when two other Japanese emissaries arrived in Washington: Tadao Wikawa, a banker, and Colonel Hideo Iwakuro, an army spokesman. They knew Drought and Walsh, and the four men collaborated in drawing up a proposal for a U.S.-Japanese agreement that Iwakuro and Drought composed and sent to Hull on April 9.

Many points in the April 9 memorandum appeared acceptable to Hull, but those regarding China's status were not. Because these latter points could be negotiated, Hull met Nomura on April 14 and 16, telling the ambassador that if Tokyo officially offered the Iwakuro-Drought memo, it could be the basis of negotiation. Hull also enumerated four basic U.S. principles that Japan had to respect: (1) territorial integrity, (2) noninterference in another country, (3) equality of commercial opportunity, and (4) changes in the status quo to be made only by peaceful means.

Nomura sent the April 9 Iwakuro-Drought draft to Tokyo, together with Hull's four principles and his statements about the April 9 draft. Nomura's message became garbled in the transpacific communications. Because Foreign Minister Matsuoka never recognized Wikawa and Iwakuro as official representatives or as Nomura's "associates," Tokyo's officials believed the April 9 draft originated with Hull. Many sections of the proposal favored Japan. Therefore, the Japanese Foreign Office accepted it as a basis of discussion, adding other requirements to benefit Tokyo.

Hull not only did not originate the proposal, he generally disliked it. The important parts of the April 9 proposal were as follows:

1. Japan would join the Axis in the war only if a nation not presently at war should aggressively attack Germany or Italy. Japan would decide who was aggressive.
2. The United States would request that Chiang Kai-shek negotiate with Japan on the following basis:

   (a) Japan would gradually withdraw its troops;
   (b) no territorial acquisitions except that Japan would possess Manchukuo (Manchuria);
   (c) no indemnities;

(d) return to the "open door" as the United States and Japan would interpret;

(e) Chiang to form a coalition with the Nanking government of Japan's puppet Governor Wang Ching-wei;

(f) economic cooperation between China and Japan;

(g) a joint Chinese-Japanese defense against communism.

3. If Chiang Kai-shek refused to negotiate, the United States would discontinue aid to China.

4. The United States would resume normal trade with Japan and would assist Tokyo in obtaining oil, rubber, tin, and nickel.

Acting under the misunderstanding that the April 9 proposal was Hull's, Tokyo enlarged the demands that were already unsatisfactory to Hull. In the "Confidential Memorandum" given to Hull on May 12, Tokyo accepted the proposed basis for the Chinese peace talks. However, Matsuoka altered other parts of the April 9 proposal as follows:

1. Japan joined the Axis to prevent other nations (i.e., America) from joining the European war. The United States must agree not to take aggressive measures or assist one nation against another in Europe. Furthermore, the United States and Japan would act "speedily to restore peace in Europe."

2. The United States should sign a secret protocol or make a pledge to stop aid to Chiang if he did not negotiate.

3. In addition to normal trade, the Philippines' independence should be guaranteed by the United States and Japan.

4. The United States should end discrimination against Japanese immigration.

Because Hull believed the April 9 memo was Japan's first proposal (not Hull's, as Tokyo thought), the secretary of state thought Japan had enlarged its earlier requests. To the contrary, when Hull offered a response to Nomura on May 16, Tokyo thought the United States was demanding more concessions than on April 19.

In responding to the May 12 memo, Hull's note to Nomura on May 16 included the following points:

1. Hitler, not the United States or Great Britain, was the aggressor in Europe. Other nations reacted in self-defense. Hitler must withdraw from his conquests and stop aggression, not the anti-Fascist nations.

2. The U.S. attitude toward Europe was self-defense. Japan must declare that its Axis alliance did not affect its negotiations on the Far East.

3. Japanese and Chinese peace talks should be on the basis of friendship, respect for sovereignty, a scheduled Japanese withdrawal, equal commercial opportunity, and negotiations about Manchuria's future.

4. There could be no provisions for the United States to halt its aid to China.

As historian Robert J. C. Butow's detailed study of the early Hull-Nomura talks indicates, this original misconception of proposals between Hull and Tokyo continually plagued the 1941 negotiations. The efforts of Father Drought and his colleagues were well intended but did not bring salutary results.

To continue the talks, Hull accepted the May 12 Japanese memo as the basis of discussion, hoping to persuade Nomura to modify his country's extreme demands. There were other conversations between Hull and Nomura on June 15 and June 21. Hull received new suggestions from Nomura and offered the U.S. objections to the continued unacceptable demands of Tokyo. At this juncture, Japanese aggression in Indochina caused President Roosevelt to take firm action against Japan.

See July 26, 1941.

### May 27, 1941

### President Roosevelt announces an unlimited national emergency.

In proclaiming this emergency, Roosevelt made an address to Congress that described the threat to the Western Hemisphere resulting from the German occupation of French possessions in Africa, which reached to Dakar on the western extremity of Africa across from Brazil. The Battle of the Atlantic, he said, required a victory for the British fleet. To assist, the United States needed to build more ships and to help Britain cut its losses from German submarine attacks.

Roosevelt's speech did not outline specific measures to meet the emergency. Yet the positive public reaction to the speech enabled the president to take some action in June. On June 14, he froze all German and Italian assets in the United States, and on June 16 he ordered all German and Italian consulates to be closed.

### June 22, 1941

*Germany launches an invasion of the Soviet Union.*

The German attack did not surprise Washington. Earlier, England and the United States had learned about the German preparations and warned Soviet leader Stalin of the Nazi German plans. As soon as the war began on the eastern front, Winston Churchill, who had since 1917 been an ardent anti-communist, welcomed the Soviets as a British ally. In Churchill's view, "any man or state who fights on against Nazidom will have our aid." Within two days, Roosevelt agreed.

The German invasion of the USSR penetrated along a 2,000-mile front from Finland (which had allied with the Axis) to Romania. The Germans over-ran the Ukraine and reached Leningrad by early September. Nazi armies reached the outskirts of Moscow before the Soviets undertook a counter-offensive in December 1941.

See June 23, 1941.

### June 23, 1941

**President Roosevelt announces the United States will aid the Soviet Union's war against Germany. He does not yet offer lend-lease aid to the Soviets.**

Following the announcement of the 1939 Nazi-Soviet Pact, U.S. relations with the Soviet Union had cooled considerably. When the Soviets attacked Poland and Finland, the United States requested a moral embargo on airplane and aviation supplies to the aggressor and tried to prevent all war exports to the USSR. The Neutrality Act had not been invoked, because Roosevelt wished to aid Finland and not push the Soviets further into Germany's alliance.

Friendlier American overtures to the Soviet Union began after Japan signed the Tripartite Pact with the Axis on September 27, 1940. Undersecretary of State Welles began regular conversations with Soviet Ambassador Constantin Oumansky between September 1940 and the spring of 1941, but he had no success in wooing the Soviets from the German alliance.

Prior to the German attack on June 22, the State Department seemed reluctant to assist the Soviets against the Nazis. But the attack caused a fast change

German troops attack Russia.
National Archives

in Hull's views. He immediately told Roosevelt and Welles, "We must give Russia all aid to the hilt." Subsequently, Welles told a press conference on June 23 that aid to the USSR in some form would be vital to the defense of America. Welles reported that the president said, "Hitler's armies are today the chief dangers of the Americas."

Between July and November, U.S. aid to the Soviet Union was minimal. The president was seeking additional lend-lease aid for Britain and did not wish to bring the Soviet situation into the political arena in Congress. The additional lend-lease funds passed Congress on October 28, 1941, and on November 6, Roosevelt ordered a credit of $1 billion for Soviet aid, informing the lend-lease administrator that the USSR's defense was "vital to the defense of the United States." The United States and the Soviet Union signed a master lend-lease agreement on June 11, 1942.

### July 3, 1941

**Roosevelt reorganizes the Army Air Force to give it greater autonomy and an air war plans division.**

Since October 11, 1938, President Roosevelt had shown interest in aerial bombing operations. To give greater effect to this in 1941, he worked with Army Chief of Staff General George MARSHALL to organize the Army Air Forces under General Henry H. ARNOLD as commanding general with an Air Staff similar to the Army General Staff. Lieutenant Colonel Harold L. GEORGE was selected to head the Air War Plans Division, and by September, Air War Plan-1 had been prepared, giving the air force's bombers four tasks: a Western Hemispheric air defense, an air offensive against Germany, tactical air operations for an invasion of Europe, and other air operations to defeat the Axis powers.

### July 7, 1941

**The President announces that U.S. Marines have landed in and occupied Iceland.**

In 1940, the British occupied Iceland after the fall of Denmark. In March 1941, reports of German air and submarine activity in the area alarmed Churchill and Roosevelt. A U.S. destroyer sent to the area had become involved in an incident with a German U-boat.

As a result of this incident, Roosevelt's White House adviser Harry HOPKINS and Undersecretary of State Sumner Welles spoke with Iceland's prime minister. On July 1, Iceland accepted U.S. protection and the landing of the marines began on July 6. Because these marines had to be supplied, the U.S. navy convoyed vessels into Icelandic waters with British and Canadian ships joining these convoys for protection.

### July 26, 1941

**Roosevelt freezes Japanese assets and requires licenses for oil shipments to Japan following Japan's occupation of Indochina. The same day he increases the defenses of the Philippine Islands by naming General MacArthur as Commander of Joint U.S.-Philippine defense units and ordering U.S. aircraft to those islands.**

Japan's aggressive moves in Southeast Asia in June and July 1941 nearly resulted in a complete break in U.S. relations with Tokyo. Because American crypt-analysts had broken the Japanese diplomatic code in the spring of 1941, Hull and Roosevelt learned about Japan's planned action in Indochina, but because of Nomura's negotiations in Washington, they hoped Tokyo would delay such acts. The Japanese did not.

On July 2, Japan's cabinet decided to move into Indochina toward Singapore and the East Indies. On July 18, the Japanese demanded that France permit them to occupy eight air and two naval bases in southern Indochina. On July 24, they began moving their armed forces into these bases. The previous day, Undersecretary of State Welles warned Tokyo not to advance its forces into threatening positions against the British and Dutch in Southeast Asia, but Ambassador Nomura could not change the decisions made in Tokyo.

Desiring to delay a break in Japanese relations but to act more forcefully to pressure Tokyo, Roosevelt took two actions between July 24 and 26, 1941. First, to placate Japan, he offered to neutralize Southeast Asia and guarantee equal access to all resources of the region (that is, Dutch East Indies oil) if Japan withdrew from Indochina. At the same time, he announced that Japan's assets in the United States would be frozen and more severe trade restrictions would be applied. Oil and gasoline might still be shipped to Japan, but an export license would be required before such shipments took place.

Actually, Roosevelt's licensing order became a de facto oil embargo on Japan between August and December 7, 1941. The president's policy was applied vigorously by the government agencies processing the license applications. Secretary of State Hull drew up ambiguous licensing guidelines. As a result, the agents reviewing oil license applications found a reason to reject all of them. When Roosevelt learned about the de facto oil embargo in September, he let it stand rather than show weakness to Tokyo.

The decision on July 26 to increase the defense capacity of the Philippine Islands was a significant change in traditional U.S. policy. From 1922 to 1935, the Nine-Power Pact prevented the construction of fortifications in the Philippines. After 1935, U.S. war plans continued to assume that the Philippines could not be defended. When the Joint Board of the Army and Navy prepared Rainbow Five War Plans in May 1941, it included these prior decisions on the Philippines.

In July, however, Germany's attack on the Soviet Union relieved the Nazi threat to the British Isles, while Japan's aggression in Southeast Asia threatened the British and Dutch. Moreover, Britain had urged the U.S. Joint Board to provide some tangible assistance to the British Commonwealth defenses in the South Pacific. By reinforcing the Philippines, the United States could aid Britain and, perhaps, deter further Japanese aggression. Strong defenses in the Philippines, once established, would block the sea route between Japan and the East Indies.

The attempt to build the Philippine defense was twofold. First, General Douglas MacArthur was recalled to active duty as the commander of American and Philippine army units. MacArthur had helped the Philippine army to be organized during the mid-1930s and was most sympathetic to the concept of strongly defending that area. Second, at the suggestion of Air Force General Arnold, Roosevelt ordered four groups of long-range B-17 bombers to be sent to the Philippines as fast as possible. These bombers, once established at Philippine bases, might sink Japanese ships or bomb Japan's bases in Formosa.

After the war plans were changed to defend the Philippines, military estimates indicated that eight months would be the minimum time required before the Philippines would be adequately prepared. When Japan attacked on December 7, 1941, MacArthur had

only a few of the coastal defense preparations completed. The air force preparations had barely begun. One group of B-17s arrived in September 1941; another group was en route and had reached Hawaii on December 7.

In a continued attempt to delay further Japanese aggression, Secretary Hull had renewed his negotiations with Nomura on August 6. Hull preferred not to continue these talks because of Tokyo's duplicity in acting aggressively at the same time that Hull and Nomura negotiated between May and June 21. He agreed to try again because, as he remarked, "From now on our major objective with regard to Japan was to give ourselves more time to prepare our defenses."

## August 12, 1941

### Secret meetings between Roosevelt and Churchill, during which the Atlantic Charter is prepared, come to an end.

Since December 1940, Roosevelt had sought an occasion to meet with Prime Minister Churchill to dramatize for U.S. and world opinion the principles at stake in the fight against the Nazi Germans. Arrangements were made in July, and on August 9, 1941, British naval ships brought Churchill to Placentia Bay off Newfoundland, where the two leaders held their first meeting on board the president's ship, *Augusta*, a heavy cruiser. The major U.S. participants in the talks were General Marshall and Admiral Stark, Undersecretary of State Welles, Lend-Lease Administrator W. Averell Harriman, and the White House adviser Harry Hopkins.

In addition to the Atlantic Charter, the Roosevelt-Churchill meeting resulted in the president's commitment to a larger U.S. navy role in the Atlantic. Churchill pleaded with Roosevelt to obtain a declaration of war from Congress. The president refused because he feared a congressional debate on the issue would seriously divide the nation. To offset Churchill's pleas, Roosevelt agreed to occupy the Azores islands and to escort British convoys. The Azores project was dropped in September by mutual agreement between Churchill and Roosevelt. The naval escort was undertaken almost immediately.

The Atlantic Charter was the historic document formulated by Roosevelt and Churchill between August 9 and 12. The charter was a joint declaration of principles issued by Washington and London on August 14. It was not an alliance but became the basis for Allied war objectives after December 7, 1941. The important points in the charter are listed here:

1. Both nations renounced the desire for territorial or other aggrandizement at the expense of other peoples.
2. The people concerned must decide territorial changes for themselves.
3. People have a right to choose their own government.
4. With due respect to existing obligations (i.e., Britain's Commonwealth preference duties), trade restrictions would be eased and equal access given to raw materials.
5. Cooperation would aid the economic security of all peoples of the world.
6. There must be freedom from want and fear.
7. There must be freedom of the seas.
8. There would be disarmament of aggressors after the war, pending creation of a permanent peace structure.

By September 15, 1941, the Soviet Union and 14 other non-Axis nations had endorsed the Atlantic Charter.

See September 6, 1941.

### August 12, 1941

**With only a one-vote difference, the House of Representatives approves legislation to extend the duty of Selective Service draftees for another 18 months.**

The House vote was 203 to 202. The Senate had approved the measure by a vote of 46 to 30, with 21 senators not voting.

Congressional opposition to an amended Selective Service measure built up in June, when Roosevelt approved a War Department recommendation to extend the service of army draftees and National Guardsmen for the duration of the emergency and to have Congress eliminate the Selective Service Act provision that limited the number of draf-

President Roosevelt and British Prime Minister Winston Churchill meet at sea. The Atlantic Charter is formulated. National Archives

tees to 900,000 and prevented them from serving outside the Western Hemisphere.

On July 21, Roosevelt sent a strongly worded message to Congress, saying: "We ... cannot afford to speculate with the security of America." If the extension were rejected, he said, our "small" army would disintegrate in two months. "The responsibility rests solely with Congress." Roosevelt had already agreed to drop the amendments regarding the use of draftees outside the hemisphere and increasing the size of the army. Yet, as the House vote indicated, the nation was divided on this issue. A public-opinion poll at that time indicated that only 51% of the nation favored the extension of U.S. military service.

## August 17, 1941

**Roosevelt and Hull meet with Ambassador Nomura to warn Japan against any further aggression in east Asia.**

The August 17 meeting resulted from a decision by Roosevelt and Churchill at the Atlantic Conference to warn Japan that future Japanese "encroachments" in the southwest Pacific "might lead to an American-Japanese war." Before informing Nomura of this warning, however, the State Department deleted "war" and added that the United States might "take any and all steps" to safeguard its legitimate rights. In addition, Roosevelt told Nomura that this statement was simply an informal informational memo, not a formal warning.

During the August 17 meeting, Nomura proposed that Roosevelt consider a possible meeting with Premier Konoye in order that the two leaders could resolve all outstanding disputes. The president agreed to consider this suggestion, and on August 28, Hull told Nomura that a high-level meeting could take place if there were a prior agreement in principle on what points would be ratified by the leaders. Any high-level meeting that was inconclusive, Hull said, would do more harm than good. Nomura accepted this suggestion, and the possible Konoye-Roosevelt meeting highlighted U.S.-Japanese discussions in September and October 1941.

See October 16, 1941.

## August 25, 1941

**British and Soviet forces begin the occupation of Iran.**

In a fashion similar to the British-Russian agreement before World War I, Soviet forces took over Azerbaijan and provinces in the north of Iran; the British occupied the southern region and protected the Persian Gulf.

## September 6, 1941

**President Roosevelt announces his "shoot-on-sight" orders to U.S. Naval patrols in the Atlantic defensive zones.**

Although it was not publicly known on September 6, Roosevelt had promised Churchill at the Atlantic Conference (see August 12, 1941) to escort British convoys in waters as far east as Iceland and the Azores and to attack any U-boat showing itself. These escort duties began on September 1, and on September 4, a U.S. destroyer, the *Greer,* was shot at by a German submarine. On September 6, Roosevelt referred to the attack on the *Greer* in announcing to the nation that, henceforth, American naval vessels "will no longer wait until Axis submarines lurking under the water ... strike their deadly blow first." "We have sought no shooting war with Hitler," Roosevelt said. "We do not seek it now. ... But when you see a rattlesnake poised to strike, you do not wait until he has struck before you crush him." Roosevelt realized, he told the national radio audience, that he took a grave step and he had thought and prayed about it. But, he asserted, "In the protection of your Nation and mine it cannot be avoided."

The president's announcement of a virtual "undeclared war" on German ships had been revealed in a misleading fashion. He had not accurately described the circumstances of the attack on the *Greer* or revealed that the *Greer* instigated the attack by cooperating with British aircraft in seeking to destroy the U-boat.

Because newsman in Washington heard rumors about the *Greer* incident that differed from Roosevelt's implied version of the German attack, the Senate Naval Affairs Committee prepared hearings on the incident. By early October, opposition senators revealed a letter from Admiral Stark dated September 20, 1941, that described the *Greer* incident in a different fashion than the president's words had done.

Stark's memorandum to Senator David I. Walsh of the Senate Naval Affairs Committee described the attack as follows: (1) a British airplane spotted the German sub and informed the captain of the *Greer,* which was on escort duty in Icelandic waters. The plane and the U.S. destroyer chased the sub for three hours and the plane dropped four depth charges; (2) the sub fired a torpedo at the *Greer,* which crossed about 100 yards astern; (3) the *Greer* dropped 8 depth charges and the sub fired another torpedo; (4) the *Greer* lost the sub but after a two-hour search discovered it again and dropped 11 more depth charges; (5) after another three-hour search, the *Greer* proceeded to Iceland.

The October news reports of Stark's letter did not result in a cry of outrage in the United States. Although historian Charles Beard and other revisionist writers criticized Roosevelt for his deviousness, the U.S. public in October 1941 apparently wished to punish Germany as much as possible without going to war. Historian Robert Dallek argues that Roosevelt's deviousness was in a "good cause," and contends that the public was not critical of the president because Americans did not want to have to choose between war and no action. Opinion polls indicated 70% of the public wanted to stay out of war, but 70% also wanted to do everything possible to defeat Hitler. Yet, Roosevelt was setting a precedent, used by later presidents, to manipulate public opinion for what he believed to be a "good cause."

### October 16, 1941

**Premier Konoye resigns; General Tojo becomes premier two days later. Discussions about a Roosevelt-Konoye summit conference end.**

Although the prospects for a Konoye-Roosevelt meeting were never good, the end of Konoye's cabinet and the rise of General Hideki Tojo as premier signified the victory of Japan's military hard-liners. On September 6, Japan's Imperial Conference had come the closest ever to seeking a compromise with Britain and America. The Imperial Conference agreed to use diplomatic means to secure certain minimum demands from London and Washington. Although

Japan would agree not to use Indochina as a base of operations to the south and would suspend military activity in the Far East, the Japanese would not leave occupied areas or permit interference in China. The United States rejected Japan's demands because their acceptance would concede Japan's right to establish its Greater East Asian Co-Prosperity Sphere by stationing troops in China.

In September and early October both Hull in Washington and Grew in Tokyo searched for a method to obtain agreement. Nevertheless, on October 2, Hull's note to Nomura indicated that basic disagreements precluded a Roosevelt-Konoye meeting. Neither Konoye nor the less moderate members of the Japanese Imperial Conference would accept terms that included the withdrawal of Japanese forces from any area they had seized by force. On October 12, Tojo, Japan's minister of war, rejected any withdrawal even as a point of principle on which details might have been worked out at a future date.

Tojo now insisted that Konoye stop all discussions of a meeting with Roosevelt. To effect this, Tojo proposed that Konoye's cabinet resign and a new ministry be formed. Konoye complied by resigning on October 16. Two days later Tojo formed a new government. Although Tojo agreed to continue talks with America and sent Saburo Kurusu to aid Nomura in Washington, an Imperial Conference of November 5 adopted a more restricted timetable for concluding discussions with the United States.

See November 26, 1941.

### October 17, 1941

**Eleven U.S. seamen die when a German submarine attacks the destroyer *Kearny*.**

As in the case of the *Greer*, the *Kearny* was fired on by a German submarine in Icelandic waters. The Germans fired three torpedoes, with one hitting the ship's starboard side near the forward fire room. The destroyer was knocked out of action and went to its port in Iceland for repairs.

Although the Navy Department announced the attack and Secretary of State Hull denounced the Germans for an act of piracy, Roosevelt did not refer to the attack until he made a Navy Day Address on October 27, 1941. Roosevelt's speech failed to explain the circumstance surrounding the German firing on the *Kearny*. Secretary of the Navy

The damaged USS *Kearny* (left) is towed into an Icelandic port.
National Archives

Frank Knox explained these details on October 29: "We have wished to avoid shooting. But the shooting has started. And history has recorded who has fired the first shot. . . . America has been attacked."

In contrast to Roosevelt's words, Secretary Knox issued a report on October 29 that said the *Kearny* had gone to the aid of a convoy of merchant ships under attack by German submarines. Knox continued: "On arriving at the scene of the attack the USS *Kearny* dropped depth bombs when she sighted a merchant ship under attack by a submarine. Some time afterward three torpedo tracks were observed approaching the USS *Kearny*." One of the three torpedoes hit the U.S. destroyer. Thus, while the convoy of ships was under attack, the *Kearny* attacked the German submarine first.

For further comments on Roosevelt's incomplete statements about such attacks, see September 6, 1941.

### October 30, 1941

**A U.S. destroyer, *Reuben James*, is attacked and sunk by a German submarine; 115 Americans die.**

The USS *Reuben James* was on convoy escort duty near Iceland when the German submarine attacked. The incident aided Roosevelt in convincing some congressmen that the U.S. neutrality laws should be repealed.

### November 5, 1941

**Japan's Imperial Conference makes the decision that will lead to war. If Washington has not agreed to compromise by November 25, Japan will launch military action in southeast Asia and Hawaii.**

Outside the Japanese political groups, more extreme military factions pushed for a firm solution to the dispute with America. On November 2, a Liaison Conference of extremist Japanese civilian and military officials sent recommendations to the Imperial Conference that the latter group adopted on November 5. Although previous writers have tended to consider Hirohito a figurehead, Herbert B. Bix's *Hirohito and the Making of Japan* (2000) demonstrates that the emperor took an active role in plotting Japan's aggressive undertakings, including the 1941 plans to attack Pearl Harbor and invade the Philippines and Southeast Asia.

As explained in Lester H. Brune's article "Considerations of Force in Cordell Hull's Diplomacy, July 26 to November 26, 1941" (*Diplomatic History*, Fall 1978), the Imperial Conference set demands for the United States to accept (Plan A) to avoid war. If Washington refused Plan A, the second proposal (Plan B) would be presented as an ultimatum for the U.S. to respond to favorably by November 26. On November 7, Ambassador Nomura gave Hull part of the Plan A proposal for peace in East Asia, setting the stage for a final showdown to determine if war would begin or the U.S. would compromise with Japanese demands.

See November 26, 1941.

### November 6, 1941

#### Roosevelt identifies the Soviet Union as being eligible for lend-lease.

On June 23, when the president announced that the United States would aid the Soviet Union in its war with Nazi Germany, he did not indicate what that aid would be and hesitated to apply the Lend-Lease Act. On June 24, he released $39 million of frozen Russian assets and the next day decided not to invoke the Neutrality Act, which would have prohibited U.S. ships from carrying supplies to the Soviet Union. Then on July 23, he sent $22 million of war matériel to the USSR.

The president's most significant decision in July was to send his close adviser Harry Hopkins to Moscow. Hopkins talked with Stalin late in July and returned to report to Roosevelt just before the Atlantic Conference of August 9. Hopkins said Stalin was confident that the Soviet armies would eventually triumph, although a long war was expected. Stalin wanted the United States to send antiaircraft guns, aluminum for planes, 50-caliber machine guns, and 30-caliber rifles. Both Roosevelt and Churchill agreed that they should provide all possible aid to the Soviets.

Washington planners worked on a Victory Program during the summer of 1941 to increase U.S. production that would supply Britain, the Soviets and the U.S. armed forces. In September, Lend-Lease Administrator Harriman visited Moscow with Britain's Lord Beaverbrook to discuss Stalin's military needs. Because the Soviets had 280 army divisions (2 million men) engaging over 3 million German and other Axis-power troops, the eastern front was crucial to the Allied effort.

Prior to the announcement of lend-lease aid to the Soviet Union, Roosevelt undertook methods to convince possible American opponents of the Soviets to accept such aid. He encouraged American Catholics to accept Soviet aid as a necessity and obtained a petition of 100 Protestants who supported help for the USSR. Nevertheless, little opposition appeared to the idea of providing lend-lease to the Soviet ally. After Congress approved a $6 billion additional lend-lease funding on October 24, the president allocated part of it for the Soviets. His decision was formalized on November 6, when he declared that assistance for the Soviet Union under the Lend-Lease Act was approved because its fight was "vital to the defense of the United States."

Harry Hopkins, President Roosevelt's special envoy, visits Moscow regarding Lend-Lease aid. Franklin D. Roosevelt Library

## November 17, 1941

**The President signs legislation that effectively repeals the neutrality laws passed between 1935 and 1939.**

The restricted portions of the neutrality laws were section 2, excluding U.S. ships from belligerent ports; section 3, excluding ships from combat areas; and section 6, forbidding the arming of U.S. merchant ships. Planning to repeal each section separately, Roosevelt asked Congress to repeal section 6 on October 6, 1941. When the Senate Foreign Relations Committee recommended changes on October 25, it added sections 2 and 3, which Secretary Hull told them needed to be abolished eventually.

By the time Congress voted on the bill in November, German submarines had damaged the destroyer *Kearny*, which the president said had been Germany's first shots at America. The Senate passed the bill easily on November 7, but the House vote was close. Largely on a partisan vote, the House approved the repeal of sections 2, 3, and 6 by a vote of 212 to 194. The president signed the measure on November 17.

See October 17, 1941.

## November 19, 1941

**The United States and Mexico announce the settlement of an oil and agrarian expropriation compensation agreement.**

Following Mexico's decision on March 18, 1938, to expropriate American and British oil companies' property, President Cárdenas asserted his desire to compensate the oil companies. Until 1941, however, the oil companies avoided serious negotiations of the settlement because they hoped to pressure Mexico into abrogating the expropriation act. The company's attempts failed in part because of the desire of President Roosevelt and U.S. Ambassador to Mexico Josephus Daniels to deal sympathetically with Mexico and to make the Good Neighbor Policy work.

Daniels played a central role in averting strong State Department pressure in cooperating with the oil companies. Daniels was an old-time Democratic progressive. As President Woodrow Wilson's secretary of the navy, Daniels knew firsthand about the 1913 conflict between Mexican nationalists seeking a better life for their people and the attempt of leaders such as Huerta to return to the Díaz policy of benefiting foreign investors in Mexico. Consequently, Daniels took a strong stand against State Department bureaucrats who supported the oil companies' viewpoint and knew little of the Mexican populace's backing for Cárdenas's policies. Even Secretary of State Hull succumbed to the oil lobbyist contention that Cárdenas was a Communist who wished to create a Mexican Soviet as part of Moscow's world revolution.

Daniels ignored the oil lobbyists' propaganda and backed Mexican leaders seeking a legal but Mexican solution to the issue. Thus, while Hull catered to the oil companies by forbidding the U.S. navy to purchase Mexican oil between 1938 and 1942, Daniels, with Roosevelt's approval, urged the oil companies to negotiate a settlement with Mexico. When the oil company operators sent Donald Richberg to discuss a settlement between March 1939 and January 1940, they required Richberg to present such large demands that Mexico could not accept them.

Two events finally led the oil companies and Hull to begin serious negotiations with Mexico. First, Harry Sinclair's oil company sent Patrick Hurley to Mexico to conclude a separate settlement. Formerly secretary of war under Hoover, Hurley achieved a Mexican settlement in January 1940 by which Sinclair Oil Company received nearly $14 million. Second, the oilmen's hope that the conservative candidate, General Juan Andreu Almazan, for Mexico's presidency would win the election of 1940 or stage a counterrevolution such as General Franco had done in Spain did not materialize. In the July 7, 1940, elections, Almazan lost to General Manuel Ávila Camacho, who was Cárdenas's choice to succeed him. Although Almazan's followers predicted a revolution because of a "corrupt election," no uprising occurred. Later, Almazan claimed the oil companies did not give him the $200,000 they promised, but historians have found no evidence to corroborate the general's assertion.

Both Roosevelt and Daniels hailed Ávila Camacho's victory and Sinclair's independent agreement. Thus, in 1941 serious negotiations began in Washington. The principal dispute was over the value of the U.S. oil properties to be compensated. The oil companies demanded payment for their investment, improvements, and, most significantly, the existing subsoil oil to which they claimed title. Their estimated value was $450 to $500 million. Mexico claimed the companies should be paid for investments and improvements less depreciation. As Hull and his advisers examined the record, they found that the oilmen greatly exaggerated their claims. U.S. tax records of Jersey Standard, the largest U.S. holder, and a U.S. Interior Department study both indicated that the estimated property value was between $13.5 and $20 million.

Secretary Hull reached an agreement that satisfied him in September 1941. The oilmen objected, however, continuing to claim compensation for subsoil rights. When Jersey Standard again rejected Hull's agreement on November 13, Daniels and Roosevelt intervened to convince Hull that he should sign the agreement without the oil companies' approval. Hull obliged and on November 19, he and Mexican Ambassador Castillo Najera signed an exchange of notes outlining the agreement.

The agreement finalized both the oil and the agrarian claims of the United States. Mexico promised to pay a total of $40 million over a 14-year period to settle all oil and agrarian claims. Each government appointed an expert to determine the amount owed to U.S. oil companies. Mexico made an immediate down payment of $9 million. The United States agreed to spend up to $40 million to stabilize the Mexican peso by purchasing 6 million ounces of Mexican silver a month. The U.S. Export-Import Bank loaned Mexico $30 million for road construction, in particular for Mexico's section of the Pan-American Highway.

The U.S. oilmen were bitter and initially rejected the settlement. Yet after some hesitation, they cooperated in supplying data for the U.S. expert, Morris L. Cooke, to reach an exact estimate of their oil values without subsoil rights. Cooke, too, found that the oilmen's estimated values were nowhere near $400 million. On April 18, 1942, Cooke and the Mexican expert, Manuela J. Zevada, issued their report that the oil properties' value was $23,995,991 plus interest since 1938 of $5 million. Jersey Standard's holdings were $18,391,641, a figure corresponding to that made by State Department geologists. These oil estimates did not, of course, include the anticipated future oil profits that the oil companies had included in their valuation.

**November 26, 1941**

### Roosevelt and Hull decide not to seek a modus vivendi with Japan but reaffirm that Japan must accept American principles to secure peace in east Asia.

On November 7, Japan's Ambassador Nomura gave Secretary Hull one part of Japan's Plan A; the remainder was presented to Hull on November 10. Japan's demands were to apply "open door" principles all over the world but it would withdraw from China only after peace was firmly established in the Far East, a process that might take 25 years according to Nomura. Hull rejected these demands and talks broke down regarding Japan's Plan A proposal.

On November 7, Ambassador Nomura gave Hull a portion of Japan's Plan A proposal for peace in East Asia; the remainder of the proposal was communicated to Hull and Roosevelt on November 10. Plan A proposed Japanese requests that were less satisfactory than those of May 12, 1941. Japan wanted the open door principles to apply all over the world. Japan would withdraw from China after peace was firmly established. This might take 25 years, Nomura stated. Nomura's aide, Kurusu, brought no new proposals as Hull had hoped. Consequently, Plan A could not be accepted by the United States. On November 18, it was obvious that Hull's talks with Nomura and Kurusu could not proceed on the basis of Plan A.

On November 20, Nomura presented Plan B to Hull. Essentially, Plan B proposed a modus vivendi. Both sides would cease armed advances in Southeast Asia and the South Pacific, and commercial relations would be restored on the basis existing before July 26, 1941. America would supply oil to Japan and obtain Dutch cooperation in the East Indies. Finally, the United States was to stop aiding Chiang Kai-shek's government in China.

As Hull and his staff began considering a response to Plan B, an ominous warning arrived in the decoded messages of the Japanese Foreign Office. Exactly how much it meant to Hull at that time is uncertain, but Nomura and Kurusu must have realized the implication of Tokyo's note. As translated by America's "Magic" cryptanalysis, Tokyo's secret instructions to Nomura extended to November 29 the deadline for U.S. acceptance of Plan B. This extension was final, however. "This time we mean it that the deadline absolutely cannot be changed. After that, things are automatically going to happen." Tokyo had continued its preparations for war against Britain, the East Indies, and the United States. After November 29, the momentum of those preparations could not be canceled.

In the State Department, U.S. officials first agreed on seeking the 90-day modus vivendi. American army and navy officers believed 90 days' time would just about complete preparations for defending the Philippines (see July 26, 1941). If the United States offered Japan some "chicken feed" concessions for three months, Hull believed Nomura might accept them.

But the modus vivendi was not approved by some U.S. allies. Between November 20 and 26, Hull consulted with other diplomats concerned with Southeast Asia. The Netherlands agreed to the modus vivendi but Britain, Australia, and China did not. Churchill approved part of the concept, but Chiang Kai-shek vigorously opposed it.

On November 26, Hull and Roosevelt made a final decision on Plan B, deciding not to offer a 90-day or any other modus vivendi. On November 25, Hull and Roosevelt met with Army Chief of Staff General Marshall, Chief of Naval Operations Admiral Stark, and Secretaries of War and the Navy, Stimson and Knox. This war council approved the modus vivendi for 90 days as the best way to enable the Philippine defenses to be completed. Although Secretary of State Hull cautioned them that Japan might not agree, he accepted the decision until sometime early the next day.

In a final conversation with Roosevelt on the morning of November 26, Hull opposed the modus vivendi, largely on the basis of two reports he received that morning. First, Winston Churchill wired Hull to complain of the modus vivendi and asserted that China was getting a "very thin diet." Second, Hull received a military report indicating Japanese troop movement in the area of Thailand and Burma, while five Japanese army divisions had steamed south out of Shanghai. Roosevelt also "blew up" at the news of Japan's clandestine activity in Southeast Asia, which anticipated Japanese aggression in that region.

Hull's reports added to Roosevelt's dismay and the two agreed to drop the modus vivendi without again consulting the Navy or War Departments. Hull recommended a hard line that would reassert America's basic principles.

Following the conversation with Roosevelt, Hull met in his office at 4:45 P.M. with Ambassador Nomura and his aide, Kurusu. He told them that if Tokyo accepted U.S. principles, financial cooperation could be worked out immediately. Proposal B was rejected by Hull and the modus vivendi of 90 days was not mentioned.

In addition to stating the principles that the United States wanted Japan to accept, Hull's November 26 note listed 10 points that Tokyo should approve. These points stated the maximum demands of the United States, including Japan's withdrawal from China and Indochina, recognition of the Nationalist government of China at Chungking (Chiang Kai-shek's government), and the abolition of extraterritorial rights of all powers in China. In return, the United States would conclude a new commercial treaty with Japan and cooperate in stabilizing the values of the dollar and the Japanese yen.

Because Hull must have known that Nomura could not accept most of the 10 points, the November 26 memo was referred to by some writers as an ultimatum. It was not. Only Tokyo's deadline, which Hull knew of only through the secret decoding of Japan's code, made rejection of Plan B the last significant discussion between Hull and Nomura. The Japanese representatives told Hull they were not prepared to respond to his notice. They asked for a delay while they consulted their home government.

See December 6 and December 7, 1941.


## November 27, 1941

### A war warning is sent to all commanders of the Asiatic and Pacific fleets and to General MacArthur in the Philippines.

The Roosevelt-Hull decision of November 26 to drop the modus vivendi and affirm U.S. principles led Washington officials to believe that Japan would attack in the near future. When he told Secretary of War Stimson of the decision on the morning of November 27, Hull said: "I have washed my hands of it and it is now in the hands of you and Knox—the Army and the Navy." Although the military leaders, General Marshall and Admiral Stark, asked Roosevelt to reconsider the November 26 decision, it was too late.

Therefore, although a war warning had been sent to all Pacific commanders on November 24, Stimson,

Knox, Marshall, and Stark decided to send another, more direct warning on November 27. This message said:

> This dispatch is to be considered a war warning. Negotiations with Japan ... have ceased and aggressive move by Japan is expected within the next few days. The number and equipment of Japanese troops and organization of naval task forces indicates an amphibious expedition against either the Philippines, Thailand or Kra Peninsula or possibly Borneo.

## December 1, 1941

### The Emperor and Privy Council of Japan approve war with the United States and Britain.

The Liaison Committee of the Imperial Conference met on December 1 and recommended war against the United States. The committee told Hirohito all steps of the November 5 Plans A and B ended because the United States rejected Japan's demands. As Herbert Bix's *Hirohito and the Making of Japan* (2000) shows, Hirohito played a major role in supporting Japan's aggression and readily approved the Liaison Committee's recommendation to carry out the previous war preparations.

See December 7, 1941.

## December 6, 1941

### President Roosevelt appeals to the Japanese emperor to maintain peace with the United States by withdrawing Japanese troops from southeast Asia.

Roosevelt's appeal was a last-ditch attempt to prevent an imminent Japanese attack against Singapore, Burma, and the Dutch East Indies. Following news of the Japanese troop buildup in Southeast Asia since November 26, Roosevelt requested an explanation from Tokyo and discussed possible U.S.-British action in the event of such an attack. Japan had responded to Roosevelt's inquiry by saying the troops were responding to Chinese activities on the frontier of Indochina and Burma.

At the same time, the president's conversations with British Ambassador Lord Halifax indicated that he wished to take parallel, but not united, action with Britain in their protests to Japan. He also implied to Halifax that if Japan attacked British and Dutch territory in Southeast Asia, the United States would help

Britain, possibly by air attacks from the Philippines or a naval blockade of Japan.

On December 6 as Japanese troop ships entered the Gulf of Siam, the president sent his peace message to Emperor Hirohito. Roosevelt said the only certain means to maintain peace and to dispel the "dark clouds" of war was for Japan to withdraw its troops from Southeast Asia. The reply Roosevelt awaited came the next day, not from the emperor but at Pearl Harbor.

## December 7, 1941

### Japanese planes attack U.S. military installations in and around Pearl Harbor at 7:55 A.M. (1:55 P.M. in Washington). Japan's representatives are delayed and do not arrive to inform Hull of the declaration of war until 2:05 P.M.

Soon after November 29, Japan's final preparations for attacks on Southeast Asia, the Philippine Islands, and Pearl Harbor received imperial approval to go forward. News of preliminary Japanese troop movements in Southeast Asia reached Washington on November 26, and Japan's forces were expected to attack there. The Japanese air and naval attacks on Hawaii by a specially trained carrier fleet had not been expected. As proposed by Admiral Isoroku Yamamoto, Japan planned to cripple U.S. naval forces for at least six months while it gained control of Southeast Asia and consolidated it into the Greater East Asian Empire. This was Japan's biggest mistake. Not only did the attack not cripple the fleet because U.S. aircraft carriers were at sea that morning, but the attack rallied the U.S. populace to become nearly unanimous in its determination to win the war. Although Roosevelt had indicated he would help Britain if its bases in Southeast Asia were attacked, the president would have had difficulty getting congressional consent to declare war based on Japan's attacks on Malaya, Thailand, and the Dutch East Indies. Certainly he would not have received the strong backing of the U.S. people that resulted from the direct Japanese attack on Hawaii and the Philippine Islands.

At Pearl Harbor, the Japanese attack lasted from 7:55 to 9:45 A.M. All eight U.S. battleships in port were either sunk (the *Arizona, California,* and *Utah*); grounded (*Nevada*); capsized (*Oklahoma*); or damaged (*Pennsylvania, West Virginia,* and

U.S. aircraft are surprised on the ground at the Naval Air Station at Pearl Harbor. National Archives

*Tennessee*). A total of 19 U.S. ships were sunk or disabled. In addition, 177 U.S. planes were destroyed and 2,335 soldiers and sailors and 68 civilians were killed.

Americans often overlook Japan's simultaneous attacks on December 7–8 in the Philippines and against British forces in Hong Kong and Malaya. Because of the international dateline, these attacks were on December 8 but occurred the same day as the Pearl Harbor raid. The first unofficial word of the Japanese attack in Hawaii reached the Philippines at 3:00 A.M. General MacArthur received confirmation of this at 3:55 A.M. Although MacArthur's staff began meetings at 5:00 A.M., Japan made a successful "surprise" attack on Clark Field at 12:35 P.M. Japan's bombing and strafing attack continued until 1:37 P.M., reducing the U.S. Far Eastern Air Force by 50%. Of 35 B-17s, 18 were destroyed at Clark Field. Also destroyed were 53 pursuit planes and 25 aircraft of other types. The airfield was extensively damaged and 80 servicemen were killed.

Blame for the Clark Field disaster belongs to MacArthur and Air Force Major General Lewis H. Brereton, although MacArthur's hesitancy in permitting an immediate air attack on Formosa gives him a larger share of blame. At 5 A.M. Brereton went to MacArthur's headquarters to request permission for an air offensive against Formosa. Because MacArthur was in conference, his chief of staff, Major General Richard K. Sutherland, told Brereton to prepare for an attack but not to launch it until MacArthur approved. At 10:10 A.M. Sutherland told Brereton that MacArthur approved a reconnaissance mission to Formosa. At 11 A.M. Sutherland called Clark Field and approved a bombing mission.

Events at Clark Field between 5 A.M. and 11 A.M. complicated matters. At dawn, Japanese planes bombed the Philippine ports at Davao in Mindanao and Aparri on Luzon. At 8:30 Brereton ordered all B-17s to become airborne because Japanese planes had been reported north of Clark Field. Brereton again requested that Sutherland give him authority to attack Formosa. When MacArthur's approval came at 10:10 for a reconnaissance flight, Brereton recalled the B-17s to Clark Field to be refueled and readied for an afternoon attack on Formosa. At 12:35, while the pilots were being briefed or at lunch and the bombers were being checked and fueled for their long flights, Japanese bombers and fighters attacked Clark Field. Brereton had not provided air cover for the planes, which were bunched together in preparation for the bombing mission. Exactly why MacArthur delayed ordering the attack on Formosa has never been clarified. Three and a half hours passed between Brereton's first request and the time the B-17s went aloft at 8:30; between 8:30 and 10:10, the B-17s could have been sent but were wasting fuel while airborne as an evasive measure. In Washington, news of Japan's attack on Pearl Harbor was a surprise because the first attacks were expected to begin in Southeast Asia or, perhaps, the Philippines. On December 6, reports of Japanese ships in the Gulf of Siam and the Indochina area had inspired Roosevelt's last-minute appeal to Emperor Hirohito. At 9:30 on the evening of December 6, Roosevelt received the decoded "Magic" translations of 13 out of 14 parts of Japan's response to Hull's November 26 demands to Nomura and Kurusu. On reading the "Magic" reports, Roosevelt realized they meant war but conjectured that the attacks would be in Southeast Asia. The 14th part of the Japanese message did not come through and was not decoded until Sunday morning. This message told Nomura to meet at 1 P.M. with Hull and to announce the break in relations with the United States. The message did not say where and when the attack would be, nor did it tell Nomura to declare war.

Although the "Magic" decoding gave Hull advance notice that Nomura planned to announce the break in relations, the secretary of state did not learn about the Japanese attack on Pearl Harbor until 2:05 P.M. Nomura had called to delay his 1 P.M. appointment with Hull because the clerks in the Japanese embassy had not yet translated and prepared the official notes to break relations with the United States. Nomura apparently did not know the full significance of making his appointment at 1 P.M.

Thus, almost at the same time (2:05) that Roosevelt called Hull to inform him of the attack on Pearl Harbor, Nomura and Kurusu arrived in Hull's outer office. Hull did not receive the Japanese until 2:20 P.M. Hull then read the Japanese response to his November 26 message. The Japanese had denounced all of Hull's requests and told Hull that Tokyo had to break diplomatic relations with America. After read-

ing Japan's note, Hull told the Japanese that "In all my fifty years of public service I have never seen a document that was more crowded with infamous falsehoods and distortions." He dismissed the Japanese from his office without giving them an opportunity to respond.

## December 8, 1941

### Congress formally declares war on Japan.

President Roosevelt's message to Congress asking for war on December 8 emphasized Japan's treachery in the way in which it launched the war. His famous opening words were: "Yesterday, December 7, 1941—a day which will live in infamy—the United States was suddenly and deliberately attacked by naval and air forces of the Empire of Japan." Congress promptly voted for war with only one dissenting vote—that of Jeannette Rankin, who had also voted against war in 1917. Japan's attack united U.S. politicians as nothing else could have, except a similar attack by the Germans. On December 8, Roosevelt did not ask for a declaration of war against Germany and Italy, waiting instead until they declared war.

## December 10, 1941

### Japanese forces make amphibious landings to attack the Philippine islands.

Although Japanese air raids on the Philippines began soon after the attack on Pearl Harbor, their forces did not land until two days later. General MacArthur and his defense forces held out on Luzon Island longer than many expected. Manila fell on January 2, 1942, but the defenders retired to Bataan peninsula while MacArthur established headquarters on the island of Corregidor in Manila Bay. Although MacArthur left Bataan on March 17 to go to Australia as commander of Allied forces in the southwest Pacific, Filipinos and Americans under General Jonathan A. WAINWRIGHT held out on Corregidor until their surrender on May 6, 1942.

In December, 1941, Japanese forces also occupied Guam (December 13), Wake Island (December 22), and Hong Kong (December 25).

# 1942

The lone dissenting vote was cast by Jeannette Rankin, Congresswoman from Montana, who had also voted against the declaration of war in 1917. National Archives

### December 11, 1941

**Germany and Italy declare war on the United States.**

Acting under their agreements as Axis allies of Japan, Rome and Berlin declared war. In response the same day, the U.S. Congress issued a declaration of war against Germany and Italy.

### January 1, 1942

**The United Nations declaration is signed at Washington by 26 nations fighting the Axis powers.**

By this declaration the 26 nations affirmed the Atlantic Charter, pledged not to make a separate peace with their common enemies, and agreed to use all of their military and economic resources to defeat the Axis. The four major powers signing were Great Britain, the Soviet Union, China, and the United States. By the spring of 1945, 47 nations had signed the Declaration of the United Nations.

Unlike its position in World War I, when the United States was an "associated power" rather than an ally, this declaration was a virtual alliance made without Senate approval. Roosevelt's legal advisers checked the documents to be certain the language was a declaration and not a treaty.

### January 14, 1942

**Washington (Arcadia) Conference: Winston Churchill concludes a visit to Washington in which, since December 22, he and Roosevelt had been planning cooperative Anglo-American groups to fight the war.**

During this series of sessions, the president and prime minister set up an Anglo-American Combined Chiefs of Staff to conduct the war. Then, soon after, they established the Combined Boards for Raw Materials, Munitions Assignments, Shipping Adjustments, Production and Resources, and Food. Together these boards and the Combined Chiefs formed a Supreme War Council, but they did not include representatives of China or the Soviet Union. The latter two had been considered for membership, but Roosevelt and Churchill decided that their inclusion caused too many problems.

Strategy for the conduct of the war was also discussed by Churchill and Roosevelt. Basically, ABC-1 became the grand strategy for the conduct of the war. Germany and the defeat of the Axis powers in Europe received first priority of the Anglo-American alliance. Second priority went to defensive action against Japan in the Pacific until Germany's defeat was assured. Some offensive action would be permitted in the Pacific, provided it did not damage the Allied plans for Europe. Finally, third priority was given to the China-Burma-India theater (CBI). Because the basic strategy was that eventually sea power would conquer the chain of islands leading toward Japan, the China theater would entail defensive holding action unless Chiang Kai-shek could be persuaded to prepare and mount a large land-offensive action employing Chinese forces. The story of Chiang's lack of desire to undertake such an action is a separate matter.

During the January meetings, Roosevelt and Churchill also considered the matter of a second front in Europe, deciding that an Allied landing in North Africa would cut German expansion in western Africa and assist the British campaigns in Libya. Before the conference ended, however, Roosevelt agreed to table the question of a North African attack because General Marshall opposed it. In addition, the British army in Libya suffered reversals. Thus, for the time being the African venture was laid aside for future reconsideration.

See February 9, 1942.

### January 28, 1942

**At the Rio de Janeiro Conference of American Foreign Ministers, 21 American republics vote to recommend that their governments break relations with the Axis powers.**

For the United States the important action it desired at the Rio meeting of foreign ministers from January 15 to 28, 1942, was to have each republic break relations if not declare war against the Axis powers. In this respect, Undersecretary of State Welles, who headed the U.S. delegation, had yielded a significant point to Argentina's delegate by changing the conference resolution from "declaring" to read "recommending" that each government should break relations. Secretary of State Hull strongly admonished Welles for giving in to Argentina, but the consequences of the wording probably did not change the circumstances much. Argentina did not sever relations until January 26, 1944, but the pro-Fascist government of President Castillo would not have acted otherwise, regardless of the word used. Chile was the

only other government at the Rio conference that did not immediately sever relations, waiting until January 20, 1943, to do so.

Other decisions made at the Rio Conference included condemning Japan for the Pearl Harbor attack; endorsing the Atlantic Charter; creating an inter-American defense board; severing commercial and financial relations with the Axis nations.

### February 2, 1942

**The affair of St. Pierre and Miquelon ends with the islands occupied by the free French but with Secretary of State Hull ready to resign.**

This issue arose in December 1941, when General de Gaulle proposed that the Free French replace the Vichy government's administration of these islands situated off the coast of Newfoundland. Without obtaining permission from the United States and Canada, whose governments preferred to keep the situation as it existed in the islands, General de Gaulle ordered Admiral Émile Muselier to occupy the islands on December 24 "without saying anything to the foreigners [Canada and America]." Secretary Hull feared this act would damage U.S. relations with the Vichy government, but Roosevelt would not back the secretary and Winston Churchill thought it a minor issue. Consequently, the Free French stayed in control, and on February 2 Hull decided not to contest the matter. Hull considered resigning but Norman Davis, a member of Hull's advisory committee, persuaded him not to do so over this issue. However, Hull resented de Gaulle's high-handed action and subsequently continued to be suspicious of him and his policies.

### February 4, 1942

**Secretary of State Hull and Roosevelt reject Soviet demands for recognition of the USSR's western boundary as being that which the Soviets occupied when Hitler attacked them in June 1941.**

The Soviets told Britain's foreign secretary, Anthony Eden, during a visit late in December 1941 that they wanted their legitimate western boundary line to be that of June 1941. This recognition would have included Soviet possession of Estonia, Latvia, Lithuania, part of eastern Poland, and Bessarabia in

Romania. Eden referred this issue to Churchill and Roosevelt in January 1942, but the Anglo-American leaders rejected Stalin's request as violating the Atlantic Charter.

Because Stalin continued to pursue his request to Eden and to the U.S. ambassador at London, John G. WINANT, Hull sent the president an extended memorandum dealing with this issue on February 4, 1942. Hull indicated that Stalin's demand for a boundary settlement generated mutual suspicions because the small nations that signed the United Nations Declaration would be alarmed. He told Roosevelt that Stalin's test of our "good faith" should not be an agreement to accept new boundaries but to provide the promised military supplies to the Soviet Union.

Roosevelt agreed with Hull and inaugurated a general "boundary policy" for the United States— all boundary questions should wait until the war ended. During the next several months, Churchill nearly agreed to give in to Stalin, but Roosevelt and Hull prevented this.

See May 26, 1942.

### February 9, 1942

**President Roosevelt meets with General Stilwell, who is being sent to China as Chief of Staff to Chiang Kai-shek. Roosevelt attempts to bolster China's importance as much as possible.**

During the January meetings between Churchill and Roosevelt, the Allied leaders endeavored to agree on China's precise role in the war effort against Japan. Churchill thought the president overestimated the importance of China's contribution, finding that Roosevelt adopted "a wholly unreal standard of values" regarding China. The president, however, appreciated the fact that U.S. public opinion had,

Generalissimo and Madame Chiang Kai-shek and Lt. General Joseph W. Stillwell, Commanding General of China. National Archives

for some curious reason, made China its favorite ally. Roosevelt had to placate this "curious" attitude of Americans toward the Chinese. According to a 1942 public opinion poll, 80 to 86% of Americans believed China could be depended on to cooperate with the United States during and after the war.

On January 5, with Churchill's reluctant consent, Roosevelt offered and Chiang accepted the post of supreme commander of the China theater of war. This title implied more than it meant. Chiang had requested a joint Far East command with headquarters at Chungking, and although the British rejected this concept, they agreed to the title offered Chiang because it gave him control only of Allied forces in China. A separate Southwest Pacific Command under Supreme Commander General Sir Archibald WAVELL was established for south and Southeast Asia. Equally significant was that China was not included on the Combined Chiefs of Staff of the Anglo-American command.

On February 9, Roosevelt met with General Joseph W. STILWELL, who had been selected to go to Chungking to serve as chief of staff to Generalissimo Chiang Kai-shek and as commander of U.S. forces in China, Burma, and India. Both Roosevelt and General Marshall had difficulty telling Stilwell exactly what his responsibilities would be in China. Officially, Stilwell was to "increase the effectiveness" of U.S. aid to China and "to improve the combat efficiency of the Chinese army." He was to accept any staff or command position "tendered" to him by Chiang.

The basic problem for Roosevelt to convey to Stilwell was that while Chiang Kai-shek had visions of China's and Chiang's vast importance to the Allied war effort, the president and Churchill gave the China theater a low priority in terms of strategic need and, therefore, of the men, matériel, and war equipment to be supplied to China. The United States decided to emphasize its aviation effort in China and to maintain and improve air transport service to Chungking. With respect to the latter, the president agreed to replace the Burma Road transport link to China, which Japanese forces had captured, with an air route from India across the Himalayan Mountains to China.

Because American aid to China had low priority, Roosevelt hoped to keep Chiang happy by emphasizing China's status as one of the Big Four powers and the long-term gains China would receive by continuing to fight Japan. Although Churchill found these views of the president "strangely out of proportion,"

Roosevelt substituted the rhetoric about Chiang Kai-shek's importance for the practical assistance Chiang desired. Like Churchill, Stilwell was not impressed by the president's banter. "Just a lot of wind," Stilwell wrote after his talk with Roosevelt on February 9.

Over the next three years, Stilwell repaid the scorn of Chiang's dissatisfaction because he confronted the Chinese daily with the reality of their low strategic priority. Roosevelt appeared to be China's friend, but his words belied the fact that the president and Churchill could not and did not believe they should give Chiang all the men, equipment, and monetary aid the latter wished.

See June 29, 1942.

## February 19, 1942

### Japanese Americans living on the West Coast can be relocated by the War Department under an order authorized by President Roosevelt.

Following Japan's attack on Pearl Harbor and Japanese victories in the southwest and central Pacific, the long-standing racial antagonism against Asians in the western United States aroused false reports about Japanese espionage and sabotage. As Peter Irons's *Justice at War* (1983) explains, the mass hysteria was widespread, with both Canada and most Latin American countries adopting expulsion laws against Japanese residents similar to Roosevelt's order.

In documents withheld from the public, Roosevelt's order to exclude persons from restricted military areas was based on a report from the army's West Coast Commander General John L. DeWitt. Admittedly, DeWitt could not justify his recommendation as "military necessity" but on the grounds that Japanese Americans were members of an "enemy race" whose loyalty was suspect. Yet, Roosevelt represented his order as being a "military necessity" to defend against possible sabotage or espionage.

After Roosevelt issued the executive order on February 19, he signed congressional legislation in March to enforce his orders with criminal penalties for those who failed to cooperate. As a result of the legislation, 110,000 Japanese-Americans in the western states were forcibly relocated from their homes, causing many to lose most of their belongings and property. They were sent to internment camps where many remained until their release in 1945 or

An American citizen of Japanese ancestry awaits relocation.
Library of Congress

1946. Meanwhile, the Japanese living in the Hawaiian Islands were not relocated although forced to obey a strict curfew, because of inadequate shipping and the need for their labor.

Of those interned, about 25,000 were released after a loyalty screening and signing an agreement to stay away from their West Coast homes. Ironically, more than 1,000 young men volunteered for military service in Europe, where they suffered many casualties but also earned more medals for their segregated unit than any other army combat brigade.

The U.S. Supreme Court upheld the congressional law in two test cases in 1943. In 1945, after upholding the case of Fred Korematsu, the Supreme Court granted a writ of habeas corpus on a petition of a camp resident and held that Congress had not authorized the continued detention of Japanese Americans cleared as loyal by camp officials.

In 1980, Congress established a Commission on War Relocation and Internment of Civilians to investigate the consequences of the 1943 legislation. In 1983, the Supreme Court vacated the Korematsu conviction that the court had reaffirmed in 1945. Finally, in an effort to end the controversy over the internment program, Congress passed the Civil Liberties Act on August 10, 1988, to redress the wrong done during World War II. The 1988 legislation provided that all internees or their heirs should be paid $20,000 for the suffering and loss of property after 1942. The 1988 legislation did not appropriate funds for these payments, but subsequent appropriations provided for the payments which were completed in 1993. Details of the 1988 law may be found in Leslie T. Hatamiya's *Righting a Wrong* (1993).

For a glimpse at the long-standing anti-Japanese attitude in the western states, see November 2, 1920, and May 15, 1924.

## April 17, 1942

### The United States recalls Ambassador Leahy from the French Vichy government to protest Germany's pressure to reinstate Pierre Laval as French Premier.

Prior to Marshal Pétain's resignation as premier on April 15, the State Department informed the Vichy government that if Laval returned to power the United States would "discontinue its existing relation of confidence." Therefore, when Laval assumed office, Washington recalled Ambassador William Leahy. U.S. Secretary of State Cordell Hull despised Laval as a Nazi collaborator, describing him as "one of the most sinister figures of my time."

The United States retained diplomatic relations with France, and the U.S. chargé d'affaires acted ad interim as the U.S. representative. Secretary Hull desired to retain relations with Vichy because U.S. consuls remained in southern (unoccupied) France and North Africa. The U.S. agents distributed supplies of petroleum and food in North Africa and, under the direction of Robert D. MURPHY, served as sources of information with anti-German groups among the French. After the decision of June 1942 to invade North Africa, these U.S. agents provided more direct assistance to the American effort.

See November 8, 1942.

## April 18, 1942

### American army planes bomb Tokyo and other Japanese cities, a project urged by President Roosevelt to raise the nation's morale after Japan's many victories in the western Pacific.

One of President Roosevelt's major concerns during the spring of 1942 was to counteract U.S. critics who

A B-52 takes off from the deck of the USS *Hornet* to undertake the first air raid on Japan. National Archives

wanted some action to offset Japan's victories in the Pacific. As the president noted, many of the same isolationists who deplored or opposed defense preparations before December 7, 1941, now expected miracles to be performed.

Many of Roosevelt's critics advocated an all-out effort against Japan, in contrast to the "Germany first" strategy agreed to with the British. The fall of Singapore on February 15 led some leading U.S. Anglophobe newspapers to renounce the British as fighting only "to the last American."

Disdaining this opposition, Roosevelt made a radio speech on Washington's birthday to recall the hard times at Valley Forge during the early days of the Revolutionary War. He warned the American people not to listen to those who would "divide and conquer" the members of the United Nations by destroying "our confidence in our own allies." Britain, the USSR, and China, he said, have endured in the war longer than the Americans, and we, too, must adopt their "conquering spirit" and the spirit of Washington to resist the enemy.

Roosevelt knew, however, that tangible evidence such as the bombing of Tokyo would help build U.S. morale. Therefore, he encouraged a suggestion for 16 B-25 bombers to fly from an aircraft carrier to bomb Japan. With less than one month's training in flying a bomber from a carrier deck, Colonel James H. DOOLITTLE led a squadron of 16 planes to attack Japan. Although all the planes dropped their bombs and escaped Japan's antiaircraft guns, none of the planes made it to their destined Chinese airfields. All the B-25s crash-landed or were abandoned when they ran out of fuel. Nevertheless, only 5 of the 80 crew members died in the attack. The raid was praised in America and Colonel (later General) Doolittle became a war hero.

On the United Nations, see January 1, 1942.

## May 7, 1942

### Battle of the Coral Sea repels a Japanese force headed for New Caledonia and New Hebrides, stopping Japanese advances toward Australia.

Because Japanese planes bombed and sunk British naval vessels near Singapore on December 10, only two American carrier task forces remained to combat the Japanese fleet in the western Pacific. The first engagement between the U.S. and Japanese naval fleets was in the Coral Sea northeast of Australia. Forewarned by the United States secret Communications Intelligence (COMINT) that deciphered Japanese military codes, U.S. Naval Commander Admiral Chester Nimitz located the Japanese fleet in the Coral Sea. In the resulting Battle of the Coral Sea, aircraft from two U.S. carrier task forces defeated Japanese aircraft carrier planes. The Battle of the Coral Sea was not only the first Japanese defeat in the Pacific War but also was the first battle fought entirely by aircraft from opposing aircraft carriers.

## May 20, 1942

### The President reverses an executive order of April 13 that gives the Board of Economic Warfare (BEW) the power to negotiate economic matters with foreign governments.

Vice President Henry A. WALLACE, who chaired the Board of Economic Warfare, had convinced the president that the BEW required authority to deal with export and import controls of commodities other than weapons and munitions. On April 13, the president issued an order giving Wallace this authority in spite of the protests of Undersecretary of State Welles, who said the order interfered with State Department jurisdiction over trade relations.

Late in April, Secretary Hull returned from a sick leave and immediately urged the president to rescind the new power of the BEW. He told Roosevelt that Wallace misled him by saying that the secretary of state did not disapprove of the order of April 13. Wallace admitted his lack of candor and Roosevelt drew up a new order on May 20, placing all BEW actions and agents under the State Department and

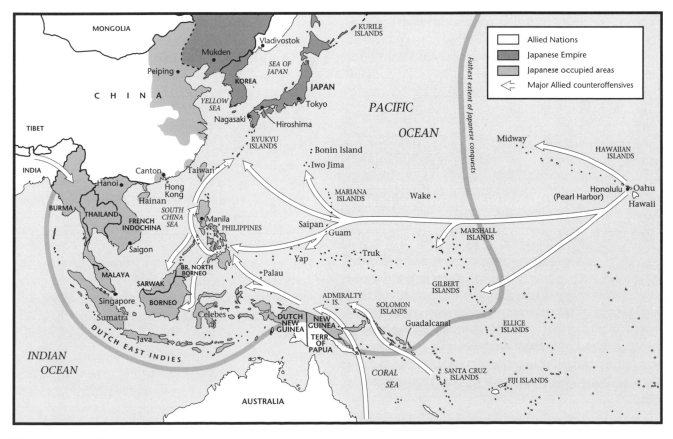

World War II: Pacific theater

foreign diplomatic offices. Nevertheless, Wallace often interfered in diplomatic matters during the next three years.

### May 26, 1942

**England and the Soviet Union sign a 20-year alliance treaty that does not mention the Soviets' western boundary, an omission due to U.S. opposition.**

Between January and May 1942, Anthony Eden and Soviet Commissar for Foreign Affairs Vyacheslav MOLOTOV negotiated a formal treaty of alliance. The principal issue in the discussions was Molotov's insistence that England recognize the USSR's western borders as of June 22, 1941. Secretary of State Hull and President Roosevelt objected strongly to the Soviet demand, and the result was the initial dispute between the Big Three allies.

On March 7, 1942, Churchill cabled Roosevelt that he wanted to accept the Soviets' border request. In the "deadly struggle" with the Germans, Churchill said, we cannot "deny Russia the frontiers she occupied when Germany attacked her." Although Roosevelt searched for some compromise, Hull opposed the Soviet position and Roosevelt eventually agreed with the secretary. The United States informed the British that any boundary agreement would be a "terrible blow" to the "whole cause of the United Nations." In addition, Roosevelt asked the Soviets to send Molotov to Washington to discuss a second front.

Consequently, Eden asked Molotov to accept an alliance with England that did not mention boundaries. Although Molotov had not changed Soviet policy, he agreed. The Anglo-Soviet treaty of May 26 was signed on the basis that neither nation sought "territorial aggrandizement" in the war. From the Soviet view, of course, the boundary of June 22, 1941, did not mean that "territorial aggrandizement" by the Soviets between 1939 and 1941 was included.

See February 4, 1942, and June 1, 1942.

### June 1, 1942

**Roosevelt promises the Soviet Union there will be a second front in Europe by the end of 1942.**

During April 1942, when Britain and the Soviet Union discussed an alliance and the Soviets' future bound-aries, Roosevelt heard about and accepted a U.S. army plan to make coastal raids on Europe by August 1942, preceding a major assault in France by April 1, 1943. To entice the Soviets to forgo their boundary issues in favor of the advantages of a second front against Germany, Roosevelt asked Stalin on April 20 to send Foreign Minister Molotov to America to discuss a second front. Although Churchill and British officers opposed the plan to invade France in 1942, they permitted Roosevelt to explore the possibility of a second front with the USSR.

On May 29, Molotov arrived in Washington to discuss with the president and U.S. military leaders future supplies to the Soviet Union and a second front. Stalin greatly desired the new front as the best means to relieve German military activity on the eastern front. On June 1, Roosevelt, Hopkins, Marshall, and the new CNO, Admiral Ernest S. King, met with Molotov to discuss a second front. Marshall and his aide, General Dwight D. EISENHOWER, had, in April 1942, planned attacks on western Europe. They calculated that the Western allies could begin diversionary air and coastal raids on Europe beginning in August 1942, so that by April 1, 1943, 48 divisions and 5,800 planes would be ready to invade the Continent. On this basis, the president told Molotov to inform Stalin "that we expect the formation of a second front this year." Marshall told the president to qualify this statement because there were many difficulties to overcome. Therefore, the president said the attack would be "sometime in 1942."

Nevertheless, Churchill and the British continued to oppose a cross-channel invasion in 1942 because they feared it might fail. To assuage Roosevelt, the prime minister decided to emphasize the significance of a North African attack as a better preliminary attack on German troops.

See May 26, 1942, and July 27, 1942.

### June 6, 1942

**Battle of Midway ends Japan's advance in the Central Pacific Ocean with a major naval defeat.**

This naval and air battle prevented Japan from seizing Midway Island and eliminated the threat to Hawaii. Japan lost four aircraft carriers and 275 planes and their trained air crews, shifting the balance of naval power in the Pacific to the United States. The U.S. navy lost one carrier and one destroyer in the battle.

This battle is considered the "turning point" in the Pacific war, assuring that Japan could not prevail.

## June 13, 1942

### The Office of Strategic Services (OSS) is established.

By executive order, President Roosevelt created the OSS for intelligence operations abroad and the analysis of strategic information. William J. DONOVAN became the director of the OSS.

## June 29, 1942

### Chiang Kai-shek complains to Roosevelt and threatens to "liquidate" the Chinese theater of war against Japan.

Tensions and personality conflicts between General Stilwell and Chiang Kai-shek heightened soon after the miserable performance of Chinese troops in the Burma campaign of April 1942.

When Stilwell arrived in China in February 1942, he found that Chiang blamed the British command in India and General Wavell for China's difficulties. When Chiang first offered up to 80,000 Chinese troops to Wavell, he had refused. Wavell disliked Chiang's demand that the Chinese should operate in a selected area as an independent unit. Wavell also preferred to rely on British Commonwealth forces from India and Australia to defend Burma. Only through Stilwell's mediation and Australia's reluctance to send forces to Burma did Wavell agree that China should supply three divisions under Stilwell's command in Burma.

The Burma campaign was a disaster. Although American newspapers printed uncritical accounts of Chiang's gallant forces fighting the Japanese in Burma, Generals Wavell and Stilwell knew the Chinese had not performed well. The Chinese did not move when and where they were ordered. In addition, officers to whom Stilwell gave orders appealed to Chiang or acted as they thought Chiang desired. At other times they simply objected to what Stilwell asked them to do. In his diary, Stilwell complained, "I can't shoot them; I can't relieve them." This situation, combined with poor British attitudes and inept-

ness and swift moves by the efficient Japanese, led to the closing of the Burma Road when Lashio fell to Japan on April 29, 1942.

Historian Herbert Feis says of the Burma defeat: "What a trail of harm this debacle left behind." Cut off from their main supply route, Chiang's government became isolated in its mountain capital of Chungking. Chiang could not or would not act aggressively to improve his situation. He blamed everyone except himself for his problems: the small amount of U.S. lend-lease aid, British opposition, and Stilwell, who had "rashly risked" China's armies in Burma. Stilwell blamed Chiang and his inept and corrupt military affiliates for China's problems because their weakness demoralized the entire Chinese army.

Against this background, Chiang presented a formal ultimatum to Washington on June 29. He made three demands: the United States should send three divisions to Burma to reopen the Burma Road; the United States should begin operating 500 combat planes in China by August; and the United States should deliver 5,000 tons of supplies per month over the main route from India to China. If these demands were not fulfilled, the generalissimo said, there would be a "liquidation" of the Chinese war against Japan.

Although Roosevelt never fulfilled Chiang's demands, the Chungking government depended too much on the United States to do more than threaten or act independently. Roosevelt told Chiang that he had to consider the problems of the Middle East and the Pacific as well as China. He agreed to send Lauchlin Currie as a personal representative to Chungking. Finally, although no U.S. divisions could be spared for Burma, the Tenth American Air Force of 265 planes would be built to full capacity for use in China by October 11. In addition, Roosevelt hoped to be able to fly 5,000 tons of supplies per month from India by 1943.

Stilwell recognized that Roosevelt's promised aid was not much more than China already had from the United States. Ever able to provide a cryptic and descriptive summation, Stilwell wrote to his wife: "Peanut [his name for Chiang] and I are on a raft, with one sandwich between us, and the rescue ship is heading away from the scene."

## July 1, 1942

**A formal lend-lease agreement between the Soviet Union and the United States goes into effect.**

This agreement was formally approved when Molotov visited Washington on May 29–June 1, 1942. The pact provided that materials received from the United States would not be transferred by the Soviets to other parties and that at the end of the war any materials still available would be returned to the United States.

## July 27, 1942

**An Anglo-American decision to invade North Africa in the fall of 1942 ("TORCH") is seen by President Roosevelt as a "turning point" in the war.**

Since April 1942, American and British leaders had discussed the question of where a second-front attack on German forces could best be implemented in 1942. Initially, General Marshall and U.S. army leaders preferred to work immediately for a cross-channel invasion of France in 1943. Churchill and his advisers recommended action against either Norway or North Africa, preferring to delay the attack on France to make certain that once begun, the cross-channel landings would be followed through to the defeat of Germany. These matters were fully explored in meetings in Washington between June 18 and 27, but no conclusion was finalized.

On July 18, General Marshall and Admiral King visited London for staff talks with Churchill and the British Chiefs of Staff. The British convinced Marshall that an attack on France (coded "SLEDGEHAMMER") could not succeed. Marshall referred the issue to Roosevelt for a decision. Because the president wanted some type of ground operations against Germany in 1942, he opted for an invasion of North Africa as soon as possible. The British concurred, and as preparations began for this TORCH operation, Roosevelt cabled Churchill that he believed TORCH would be a "turning point" in defeating the Axis, for "we are on our way shoulder to shoulder."

For the Soviet Union's reaction to TORCH, see August 15, 1942. Also see November 8, 1942.

## August 7, 1942

**U.S. forces in the Pacific make their first major offensive attack at Guadalcanal in the Solomon Islands.**

Action in Guadalcanal lasted until February 9, 1943, when the Japanese withdrew. Although Allied war strategy called for defensive action only in the Pacific, the entreaties of Admiral King and General MacArthur caused the president to send more men and aircraft to assist in the attack on Guadalcanal, undermining the Europe-first strategy. By the end of 1942, 9 of 17 U.S. army divisions and 19 of 66 air groups sent overseas went to the Pacific.

## August 13, 1942

**The Manhattan Project to develop the atomic bomb is to be commanded by General Leslie R. Groves.**

Under Groves's direction, construction began by the end of 1942 on the three basic installations of the Manhattan District: the Oak Ridge, Tennessee, U-235 separation plant; the Los Alamos, New Mexico, bomb development laboratory; and the Hanford, Washington, plutonium production works.

At the University of Chicago, scientists on the Argonne Project succeeded in effecting the first self-sustaining nuclear reactor on December 2, 1942.

## August 15, 1942

**The First Moscow Conference ends: Churchill informs Stalin that the second front will be in North Africa, not Europe.**

At Churchill's request, Stalin invited the prime minister to visit Moscow to discuss the two major issues facing the Soviets and the Western Allies: the second front and the difficulties of Allied convoys bringing supplies to the Soviet Union through Archangel. At Churchill's meetings with Stalin, W. Averell Harriman, the lend-lease administrator, represented Roosevelt.

After describing the British air force plans for large bombing attacks on Germany, the prime minister informed Stalin that the second front would be North Africa, not western Europe. Using his charm and enthusiasm on Stalin, Churchill said Anglo-

American strategy depicted Germany as a giant crocodile. By going through North Africa and into southern Europe, Churchill said, the Allies would attack
both the "soft underbelly" and the hard snoot of
Hitler's empire. Stalin was intrigued at first but later
turned surly when he realized that few German divisions would be diverted by the North African campaign. Hitler would shift large numbers of his forces
from the eastern front only if France were attacked
directly. Thus, the second-front dispute with Stalin
continued.

Regarding the supply routes to the Soviet Union,
Stalin showed greater concern about his country's
need for more war matériel. In mid-July, German
submarines sank 23 out of 34 merchant ships being
convoyed to Archangel. The Allied losses in the North
Atlantic reached 400,000 tons in one week, more than
twice the Allies' weekly construction ability. As a
result, the northern convoys to the USSR were suspended for the summer because the long daylight
hours in the area of the North Cape of Norway
made them easy targets. To supplement the convoy,
the Allies made plans for a trans-Caucasian air transport service that they hoped to begin in October.

Following the Moscow sessions, Roosevelt and
Churchill also decided to try some smaller convoys,
and 10 ships were sent to Archangel in October.
Meanwhile, German army attacks were penetrating
deep into southern Russia. Stalin needed planes in
particular to help launch his counteroffensive against
the Germans, which would begin in November 1942.

### November 8, 1942

### The invasion of north Africa by an Anglo-American force commanded by General Dwight D. Eisenhower.

The Allied troops made amphibious landings in
French Morocco and Algeria. Aided by Admiral
Jean-François Darlan of the French Vichy government, Allied forces overran the French garrison and
an armistice was signed on November 11.

One consequence of this invasion was the German
occupation of all parts of France on November 11,
1942. This action caused many French in North
Africa to end their former allegiance to the French
Vichy government.

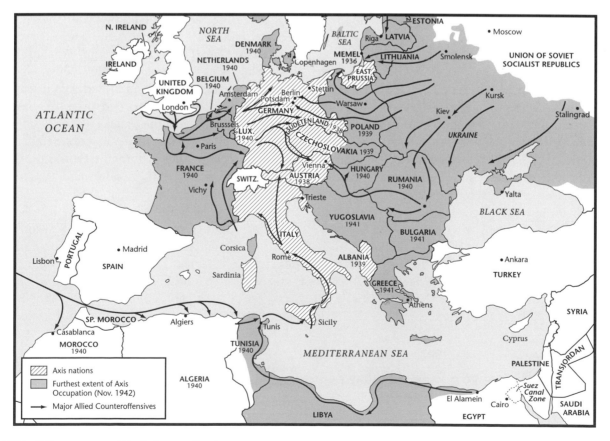

World War II: European and North African theater

Nevertheless, the so-called Darlan Deal caused extensive criticism in Britain and America because Admiral Darlan had been a Vichy collaborator with the Germans. When the North Africa campaign was planned, Robert Murphy, the U.S. representative in North Africa, recommended that Eisenhower bring General Henri Honoré Giraud with him. Giraud, it was hoped, would obtain the cooperation of French officers in North Africa because he was a veteran of both wars and had escaped from a German war camp. When Eisenhower and Giraud reached North Africa, however, Eisenhower discovered that French officers loyal to Marshal Pétain considered both Giraud and General de Gaulle to be disloyal traitors who violated their oaths to the French army.

Luckily, Eisenhower and Murphy learned on November 14 that Admiral Darlan was in Algiers to visit a critically ill son. Although Darlan had continued to work with the Vichy government, he had let Murphy know in October that he could be persuaded to join the Allied cause. In October, Murphy had ignored this suggestion, but when Giraud failed to obtain support from the French officials, Murphy and General Mark Clark visited Darlan, who agreed to stop French resistance in Algeria and Morocco and to cooperate with the Allies. Believing this would save American lives and enable the conquest of these two African states to be easily concluded, Eisenhower agreed to let Darlan take political charge in Algeria and Roosevelt accepted this action.

Although Darlan's compliance achieved excellent military results, General de Gaulle's Free French headquarters in London objected vigorously, loosing a propaganda barrage against Darlan's deal as a "nullification of the United Nations." Until Darlan's assassination on December 24 by a French monarchist, Roosevelt and Secretary Hull, who backed Murphy's proposals, suffered extensive criticism even though Roosevelt on December 16 persuaded Darlan to end Vichy's discriminatory laws against the Jews and other French personnel. By this time, the French in North Africa had turned strongly against Vichy because the Germans had occupied all of France.

### November 19, 1942

#### The Soviet counteroffensive against Germany begins at Stalingrad.

German armies drove deeply into the southern part of the Soviet Union during the summer of 1942, captur-ing Sevastopol on July 1, Rostov on July 24, and beginning the siege of Stalingrad on September 13. On September 21, the Soviets began thrusts against the German lines, first to the northeast, later to the southeast of Stalingrad. On November 19, a full-scale offensive began against Germany. The Soviets' successes temporarily ended Germany's offensive activity on the southern front. At Stalingrad, the Soviet pincer movements surrounded and cut off 22 German army divisions, and 80,000 Germans capitulated on February 2, 1943.

The Soviet victory at Stalingrad is generally considered the turning point in the European theater—after this Hitler had no chance of prevailing.

# 1943

### January 11, 1943

#### Extraterritoriality rights in China are ended by treaties signed between China and the United States in Washington and by China and Britain in Chungking.

For some time Secretary Hull had been aware of the need to end the extraterritorial "unequal treaties" forced on China after the Opium War of 1839–1842. Shortly before Japan invaded China in 1937, Washington and London had undertaken discussions to join in parallel action to end these treaties. The Japanese war delayed these talks until 1942, when the British and Americans again considered action to abolish these treaties with their wartime ally China.

On October 10, 1942, London and Washington simultaneously announced that they were offering treaties to the Nationalist government of China to end these extraterritoriality rights, and negotiations began in November 1942. Because China's principal desire since 1919 had been to be treated on an equal basis with other powers, a clause indicating this was included in the treaty. On January 11, treaties were signed between both China and the United States and China and Britain. Both extraterritoriality and the special privileges granted after the Boxer Rebellion were abolished. The British treaty also ended its special concessions in Tientsin and Canton. Only the immigration issue remained as a disturbing part of U.S.-Chinese historic relations.

See December 17, 1943.

### January 24, 1943

**The Casablanca Conference results in two significant decisions: the plan to invade Sicily and Italy and an agreement on requiring the Axis to surrender unconditionally.**

Roosevelt and Churchill began plans for their meeting at Casablanca in December, even though Stalin said he could not attend. Roosevelt wanted to plan campaigns for 1943 and to get Churchill's agreement for unconditional surrender.

The 1943 campaign issue arose because of basic disagreements between U.S. and British military leaders. General Marshall and his staff preferred giving full attention to the cross-channel attack. American military doctrine centered on the concentration of forces to attack the major enemy fortress at its strongest and most destructive point. This would defeat the enemy quickly and decisively, and in Europe the best way to achieve this goal was to attack through Cherbourg, France, to Berlin. Yet Roosevelt saw immediate advantages in the British plan to hit the soft underbelly of southern Europe, especially Italy and southern France.

Because pre-conference discussions indicated the president's preference, Marshall went to Casablanca to obtain Britain's commitment to build up the Allied base in England for a 1944 assault on western France. Marshall received these commitments at Casablanca, and the British also accepted a combined planning staff for the 1944 assault. In 1943, however, the Allied attacks would be on Sicily and Italy.

In the Pacific, Admiral King and the U.S. Joint Chiefs received some support for following up their Guadalcanal victory by additional attacks on Japanese-held islands. But these operations were limited because they were not to endanger the plans for the continued action against Germany in 1943–1944.

Regarding unconditional surrender, Roosevelt had begun to discuss such a policy as early as May 1942. Saying he desired to avoid Wilson's "mistake" in 1918, Roosevelt also wanted not only to disarm the Axis nations but also to compel them to abandon their Fascist philosophy. Significantly, Roosevelt did not discuss this policy with the Joint Chiefs of Staff. He had discussed it with Secretary of State Hull, who opposed the announcement of unconditional surrender. Hull, like later critics of the policy, contended that such a public announcement would end the possibility of any flexibility in later decisions and would force Germans and Japanese who disliked the Fascists to fight for their nations' honor rather than the overthrow of their distasteful military dictators.

On this issue, however, Roosevelt developed a closed mind. Telling Averell Harriman that Secretary Hull had "rigid ideas" and was stubborn, Roosevelt

At Casablanca, Roosevelt and Churchill meet with General Giraud (left of Roosevelt) and General de Gaulle (left of Churchill), unfriendly rivals for leadership of the Free French forces. National Archives

did not permit Hull to come to Casablanca. The president's excuse was Hull's implication in the "Darlan Deal" in North Africa (see November 8, 1942).

At Casablanca the unconditional surrender decision was discussed but not made part of the official final communiqué by Churchill and Roosevelt. Exactly why is not clear. The only dispute about the doctrine had been whether or not to include Italy in the statement because there were signs that an Italian group hoped to overthrow Mussolini and appeal to the Western powers for an armistice. Later, on January 24, Roosevelt made an oral declaration to newsmen that he and the prime minister had agreed to demand the unconditional surrender of Germany, Italy, and Japan as the only way to assure future peace in the world. Although Roosevelt and Churchill claimed the statement of January 24 was a spontaneous act by the president, historic records do not substantiate this account. Churchill did not want to include Italy in the formula, which probably led the two leaders to avoid further debate on that question by agreement on an oral statement.

One final aspect of the Casablanca Conference was the attempt to get General de Gaulle to agree with the United States and Britain on plans for France's future role. Initially, de Gaulle refused to come to Casablanca. When he finally came on January 12, he generally complained about such incidentals as being surrounded by American bayonets on French territory. De Gaulle had refused to accept Giraud as the head of the North African government following Darlan's assassination, but he consented to be photographed with Giraud for the sake of Allied unity. Generally, de Gaulle proved objectionable to Roosevelt because he claimed authority with no semblance of democratic backing in France. Churchill, however, had become committed to the Free French leader, who came to symbolize for the British the better side of France's fighting ability. On the last day of the conference and without Churchill's knowledge, the president signed the Anfa agreements, which bound the United States to support Giraud in uniting French opponents of Germany. Churchill later insisted that de Gaulle must be included in these agreements.

## March 8, 1943

### Roosevelt again appears to yield to Chiang Kai-shek's demands as a condition for keeping China in the war.

During the winter of 1942–1943, Britain, China, and the United States argued over a campaign in Burma and General Chennault's plan for a strong air offensive against Japan. Although Generals Marshall and Stilwell believed that effective aid to building up ground forces against Japan could be obtained by opening the Burma Road, the British and Chiang—although for different reasons—were reluctant to pursue a war in the jungles of Burma and supported the air attacks advocated by Chennault.

In February 1943, General Arnold visited Chungking, where Chiang presented conditions for the United States to meet in order that China would remain in the war. First, Chiang wanted Chennault to head an independent air force for China to lead attacks on Japan. Between March and May 1943, Roosevelt agreed to assist intensive air operations in China, although Chennault remained under Stilwell's jurisdiction. But this decision was not finalized until April 1943, when Chennault and Stilwell visited Washington to argue their case. In addition, the Burma campaign would be delayed although Chiang agreed to work with the British on a future battle to liberate Burma. This decision was backed by Roosevelt and accepted by Churchill on May 25, 1943, during the Trident Conference. Finally, Roosevelt agreed to send about 500 aircraft to China by November and to increase the air transport supplies to Chiang from India to 10,000 tons per month.

Although Roosevelt seems to have realized that Chiang's forces were corrupt and inefficient because all U.S. and British estimates agreed on this, he told Churchill that he had to placate Chiang for political reasons. Madame Chiang Kai-shek had "invaded" Washington and New York society and exuded a pro-Chinese propaganda that made her the most popular hero in America since Charles Lindbergh in 1927. Churchill could not fathom this mysterious American attraction for Madame Chiang and the Chinese, but after witnessing the emotional attachment of pro-

Chinese U.S. politicians and the pro-Chiang publicity of the *Time-Life* magazine chain of Henry Luce, the prime minister was politically astute enough to appreciate the president's problem. Thus, when Roosevelt spoke to Congress of Chiang as a great democratic leader of China, Churchill and others knew the president's rhetoric was to drum up backing for U.S. ventures overseas. Because Roosevelt seemed to support Chiang, his rhetoric aided Madame Chiang and the China lobby in creating an unrealistic evaluation of the Chinese Nationalists that would later cause vast problems for General Marshall and President Truman in 1945.

Some of Roosevelt's backing of Chiang also lay in the strategic hope that during the postwar era a strong China would become a counterweight to the Soviet Union in Asia. This was a geopolitically astute perception, but Roosevelt refused to force Chiang to adopt any measures that would strengthen his army and gain the support of the Chinese people. Because Roosevelt attached no strings to Chinese aid requiring reforms such as Stilwell recommended, he did nothing to guide the Nationalist government out of its "warlord" mentality.

See May 25, 1943.

### April 27, 1943

### *The Soviet Union suspends relations with Poland's government-in-exile; dispute over Katyn massacres.*

In April 1943, Germany announced it had discovered a mass grave containing at least 10,000 Polish officers in the Katyn Forest, near the Soviet city of Smolensk. The Germans claimed Soviet forces had massacred these officers in the spring of 1940. Although Winston Churchill cautioned the leader of the Polish government-in-exile in London, General Władysław Sikorski, to beware of German attempts to sow discord among the allies, Sikorski asked the International Red Cross to investigate the incident. Stalin denied that request on April 18.

Poland's request for an investigation became the official reason Stalin broke relations with the London exile government that the Soviets had recognized in June 1941. Probably, Stalin was looking for an excuse to break with Sikorski because he sponsored Communists in the Union of Polish Patriots, who were exiled in the USSR. The 1943 Allied split over Poland continued in determining Poland's postwar status. (See October 18, 1944.)

Regarding the massacres, post-Cold War documents confirmed Germany's allegations that Soviet soldiers killed the Polish officers. Soviet documents declassified in 1992 revealed that Stalin ordered the massacre of about 20,000 Poles in the Katyn Forest. On October 14, 1992, Soviet Politburo records and other documents from March 1940 showed Stalin was directly responsible for the massacres. For these reports, see the *New York Times* for October 15 and 16, 1992.

### May 13, 1943

### *The north Africa campaign ends when 250,000 Axis troops surrender in Cape Bon, Tunisia.*

As U.S. forces under General Eisenhower moved into Morocco, Algiers, and Oran after November 8, 1942, British troops in the east forced General Rommel's armies to retreat from Egypt. British forces under General Bernard L. Montgomery launched an offensive from El Alamein on October 23, expelling the German armies from Egypt by November 12. As Rommel's armies retreated, the British regained Tobruk on November 13 and advanced across Libya to occupy Tripoli on January 24, 1943. On March 19, U.S. forces captured El Guettar and joined with British forces in Tunisia on April 7 near Gafsa. The final U.S.-British action in Tunisia defeated German troops at Tunis and Bizerte before the Axis forces surrendered at Cape Bon on May 13.

### May 22, 1943

### **Moscow announces the dissolution of the Third International (Comintern).**

Since 1933, the United States had repeatedly asked the Soviet Union to abandon the subversive activity of the Comintern. Stalin officially did so on May 22. Although this was a gesture of friendship to the United States, the Soviets did not end their attempts to influence the activity of communist parties throughout the world, including the Communist Party of the United States, which Earl Browder led in 1943.

### May 25, 1943

**The Trident Conference ends: Roosevelt, Churchill, and their advisers conclude a series of strategic meetings in Washington.**

In addition to decisions about the China-Burma theater, the Trident Conference worked out further plans for an Allied attack on Sicily and a buildup of forces for the 1944 cross-channel attack. Although British military leaders continued to push for greater efforts in the Mediterranean, General Marshall secured further commitments for the Allies to prepare for the cross-channel attack. The invasion of Sicily in 1943 and perhaps of Italy would be designed as preludes to the major attack on western France. It was also agreed that the full-scale attack on France (ROUNDUP) would be ready by May 1, 1944. A final decision approved an Italian invasion after the Sicilian attack ended.

See March 8, 1943.

### June 3, 1943

**The Food and Agricultural Organization of the United Nations is established at a meeting in Hot Springs, Virginia.**

### July 10, 1943

**Anglo-American forces launch an invasion of Sicily—Operation Husky.**

British, Canadian, and U.S. forces invaded Sicily under the command of General Dwight D. Eisenhower. Over 2,000 vessels conveyed 160,000 men to land along Sicily's southern coast. The allied forces occupied half of Sicily when Palermo fell on July 24. The capture of Sicily, which provided the necessary springboard to the invasion of Italy, was completed by August 17.

### July 25, 1943

***The resignation of Premier Mussolini and his cabinet is announced by King Victor Emmanuel III of Italy.***

Mussolini was replaced by Marshal Pietro Badoglio, who dissolved the Fascist Party on July 28. After German troops rescued him from a prison in Rome on September 12, Mussolini proclaimed a Fascist Republic in Italian areas under German control.

Badoglio's government surrendered to Eisenhower on September 3 and declared war on Germany on October 13.

### August 24, 1943

**The conclusion of the First Quebec Conference (Quadrant) of Roosevelt, Churchill, and their military advisers.**

These meetings from August 11 to 24 confirmed and finalized military decisions made or begun at the Trident Conference, which ended on May 25. The Normandy invasion (OVERLORD) was reaffirmed for May 1, 1944, and supplemental landings in southern France were added (ANVIA, later DRAGON). An attempt to step up military operations in Burma was agreed to, and Lord Louis MOUNTBATTEN was named supreme commander in Southeast Asia.

A decision was also made at Trident to drop the British plans for an Allied attack through the Balkans into central Europe. The Joint Chiefs of Staff opposed this project so strongly that Roosevelt backed them against the British. Although Churchill argued that a Balkan attack would have postwar political advantages against the Soviet Union, General Marshall believed that if the Allied forces became bogged down in the mountainous areas of southeastern Europe, the Soviet armies would capture all of Germany and the Rhineland. Thus, with the president's support, the invasion of the Balkans was not undertaken.

Finally at Quebec, Roosevelt agreed to the full exchange with Britain of U.S. data on atomic energy. In 1942, U.S. and British scientists undertook a joint research effort on the atomic bomb. By 1943, however, U.S. facilities under the Manhattan Project worked on development and manufacturing of the weapon and restricted the exchange of this data. Churchill wanted full cooperation on the project, and to keep the prime minister happy, Roosevelt agreed to resume the unrestricted exchange of data. In a document signed on August 19, the British and Americans agreed not to use these data against each other or communicate them to third parties. Because the United States had the basic production role, the U.S. president had the power to determine what postwar commercial advantages Britain might receive.

Anthony Eden, British Foreign Secretary; President Franklin Roosevelt; Princess Alice (wife of the Governor General of Canada); and Winston Churchill, seated, left to right. National Archives

## September 3, 1943

**The Italian campaign begins when British forces attack from Sicily across the straits of Messina. On September 9, American forces make amphibious landings at Salerno.**

The day before the major Allied operations against Italy began (September 8), the surrender of Italy's government under General Badoglio was announced. Although there was some German resistance in the southern part of Italy, the initial Allied landings were comparatively easy. Salerno was captured by September 18, and by October 14, the Allies crossed the Volturno River north of Naples.

On September 10, German forces took Rome. After Mussolini escaped on September 12 and proclaimed a Fascist republic, German-dominated forces made the central and northern Italian campaign very difficult for the Allies.

## September 10, 1943

**The Allies establish a military-political commission for negotiating with German allies because Stalin dislikes the Anglo-American settlement with Italy without Soviet involvement.**

When British and U.S. authorities began talks with the new Italian ministry of Badoglio in July 1943, Stalin complained that the Soviet Union was not represented on the negotiating team. The Western powers agreed to keep Stalin informed of their discussions, but in August Stalin insisted on forming a special commission to negotiate with "Governments disassociating themselves from Germany."

On September 10, Churchill and Roosevelt agreed to establish a commission at Algiers to deal with Axis negotiations except those with Germany and Japan. But Roosevelt instructed General Eisenhower that the

Men of the 370th Infantry Regiment move through the remains of Prato, Italy, toward the mountain ahead. National Archives

commission was subordinate to the Allied commander in chief. Although Stalin protested, Roosevelt stood firm.

The president understood at this time that the occupation of Italy would set a precedent because it was the first "liberated" European state. He realized the Italian decision would justify Stalin's unilateral action in the Eastern European nations that would be liberated by the Soviet armies. In Italy, however, Roosevelt preferred to minimize the Soviet role, and this set that precedent. When the Red Army took over Romania in early 1944, both Secretary of State Hull and the Joint Chiefs of Staff assumed the Soviets would insist on prime responsibility there. To reach agreement on a policy of liberation, the foreign ministers of the United States, Britain, and the Soviet Union met in Moscow.

See October 13 and 30, 1943.

## September 25, 1943

### Undersecretary of State Welles resigns owing to long-standing difficulties with Secretary of State Hull.

Roosevelt disliked losing Welles because they were close friends and the president got along with Welles better than with anyone else at the State Department. That relationship often led Hull to believe Welles usurped his authority. In addition, by the summer of 1943 Washington circles buzzed about Welles's alleged homosexual activity. Thus, when Hull told Roosevelt that the president would have to choose between the two, the president realized that Welles had become a political liability and accepted his resignation.

## October 13, 1943

### Britain and the United States recognize Badoglio's government in Italy.

General Badoglio replaced Mussolini as premier of Italy on July 25 and soon contacted the Western Allies about surrender terms. Although the British favored recognizing a monarchy under King Victor Emmanuel II, the Americans hesitated to do this, preferring a more liberal government in Italy. The issue was not yet settled on September 3 when Badoglio agreed to the military terms of Italy's surrender.

Somewhat reluctantly, and because Churchill said the only alternatives in Italy were a monarchy, fascism, or communism, Roosevelt agreed to accept Badoglio's regime if he declared war on Germany and expressed his interest in holding democratic elections in the future. On October 13, Badoglio fulfilled these conditions and Roosevelt and Churchill recognized the Italian government.

## October 30, 1943

### The Moscow Conference of Foreign Ministers ends.

Sessions in Moscow between October 19 and 30 were the first three-power meetings of the war. The participants were Secretary of State Hull, Foreign Minister Anthony Eden, and Foreign Minister V. M. Molotov, with their military advisers. The important decisions at this conference were as follows:

1. The Soviet Union was assured that plans for a second front in western Europe were underway.
2. Stalin refused to renew Soviet relations with the Polish government-in-exile in London, which he had ended on April 27, 1943.
3. A European Advisory Commission was created to formulate a postwar policy for Germany. An Advisory Council for Italy was also set up.

4. Stalin promised to enter the war against Japan as soon as Germany was defeated. This was an informal oral commitment made to Secretary Hull.

5. The Four-Nation Declaration stated that a general international organization to maintain peace and security was a necessity. The Four-Nation Declaration was signed for China by the Chinese ambassador to Moscow, Foo Ping-sheung.

6. The Declaration of German Atrocities stated that German war criminals would be apprehended and sent for trial to countries where their crimes had been committed. The Allied governments would jointly punish the "major criminals."

7. Not approved was Secretary Hull's proposal of a "declaration against colonialism." Molotov approved this idea but the British prevented its passage.

8. Austria's annexation by Germany on March 15, 1938 was declared null and void. Although Austria held responsibility for participating in the war on the side of Germany, the final war settlement would consider Austria's contribution to its own liberation.

### November 5, 1943

**The Senate approves the Connally resolution, which favors an international peace organization after World War II; previously (September 21) the house had approved a similar resolution of J. William Fulbright.**

Early in 1943 a group of senators began a bipartisan movement to commit the United States to a postwar international peacekeeping organization. On September 21, the House adopted the Fulbright Resolution to create international machinery with power adequate to establish and maintain a just and lasting peace. The resolution of Senator Tom Connally was worded similarly and approved by the Senate. The Connally Resolution said any treaty to carry out the bill would require a two-thirds Senate vote. It passed the Senate by 85-5.

### November 7, 1943

**_Soviet forces recapture Kiev in the Ukraine._**

Following Soviet successes at Stalingrad on February 2, 1943, the Germans launched a counterattack on July 5, but they made few advances. The Soviet armies repelled them and undertook a new offensive in August that recaptured Smolensk on September 25 and won Kiev by November 7.

The capture of Kiev opened the path toward Polish territory, which the Red Army entered on January 3, 1944.

### November 9, 1943

**The United Nations Relief and Rehabilitation Administration (UNRRA) is established by a meeting of 44 nations in Washington.**

UNRRA would provide aid to liberated populations of Europe and the Far East. Former New York Governor Herbert H. Lehman was named as the first director general of UNRRA.

### November 26, 1943

**The First Cairo Conference results in British and American agreements on China and the far east.**

At Roosevelt's insistence American and British military advisers met with Churchill, Chiang Kai-shek, and China's military leaders. Beginning with a November 22 session on a possible Burmese invasion plan, the delegates considered East Asia's future. While Chiang agreed with the U.S. army that there should be an attack against Japan in Burma, the British could not commit any amphibious troops to attack across the Bay of Bengal. As a result, the Burmese attack was delayed for another year.

Roosevelt particularly pleased Madame and Generalissimo Chiang by agreeing to strip Japan of all its Pacific possessions. Formosa, Manchuria, and all areas taken from China would be returned. In turn, Chiang agreed that the Soviets would receive all of Sakhalin and the Kurile Islands, as well as the use of Darien as a free port. The USSR would cooperate with Chiang in China and agree not to impair China's territorial integrity. In addition, Roosevelt promoted the idea that China was one of the Big Four powers that would have a vital role in Asia after the war. The three powers also made a final agreement that Korea should "in due course become free and independent," a statement Korean exiles denounced for including "in due course" and "not immediately."

After the sessions ended in Cairo on November 26, Roosevelt and Churchill went to Tehran for discussion with Stalin and Soviet military experts. During informal sessions at Tehran, Roosevelt and

Chiang Kai-shek, president of China, and Madame Chiang meet with President Roosevelt. National Archives

Churchill obtained Stalin's oral affirmation of the territorial changes agreed to with Chiang Kai-shek at Cairo.

See December 1, 1943.

### December 1, 1943

### The Big Three Conference ends at Tehran, Iran.

For the first time, Roosevelt, Churchill, and Stalin met to discuss a variety of strategic war issues and postwar plans. Regarding the military situation, the three leaders discussed the coordination of Soviet attacks on Germany with the D day landings in France in 1944. Once again, Stalin agreed to enter the war against Japan as soon as Germany was defeated.

Three key postwar matters were discussed but not finalized at Tehran. First, Roosevelt tried to convince Stalin to use American methods to insure the future security of the Soviet Union in Eastern Europe. Rather than simply annexing the Baltic states or Poland, Roosevelt urged Stalin to use "referendums" and to allow for "self-determination." Churchill indicated that since England had gone to war in 1939 to protect Poland, the British were particularly concerned about the future of Poland. Churchill wanted Stalin to recognize the London Polish government or to give it a vital role in Poland's future government. Neither Roosevelt nor Churchill was concerned about the exact borders of Poland, for these could be adjusted.

They desired, however, that some semblance of self-determination be used in all areas liberated by the Big Four powers.

Regarding Poland's government, Stalin expressed his willingness to grant some representation to the London exiles. He wanted them first to accept the Curzon Line as Poland's eastern border, to renounce Nazism, and to sever all connections with German agents in Poland. They should also give support to the Communist partisans fighting underground in Poland. No final decisions on Poland were made, however.

A variety of ideas was considered by the Big Three concerning postwar Germany. Roosevelt suggested dividing Germany into three parts for political purposes. Churchill conjectured that Prussia, Bavaria, and other states could be separated while Austria and other sections should be formed into a Danubian Confederation. These and other ideas were given to the European Advisory Commission for detailed consideration on Germany.

Finally, Roosevelt requested that the other two leaders join the United States and China in sponsoring an international peace organization after the war. Although Churchill and Stalin both preferred regional peace blocs, the president argued that these seemed to be too much like spheres-of-influence pacts. Stalin eventually agreed that some sort of world organization should be established after the war.

Joseph Stalin (left) with Franklin Roosevelt and Winston Churchill at the Tehran Conference. National Archives

### December 6, 1943

#### The Second Cairo Conference concludes.

Following the Tehran Conference, Roosevelt and Churchill returned to Cairo for further discussions between their military chiefs and with İsmet İnönü, president of Turkey. Great Britain reaffirmed its alliance with Turkey, and the "firm friendship" between Turkey, the United States, and the Soviet Union was recognized. The most significant military decision at the Cairo Conference was the appointment of Dwight D. Eisenhower as commander of allied forces for the invasion of western Europe.

In personal conversations with Churchill at Cairo, the president indicated his suspicions about Stalin's keeping his word regarding intervention in China or in the postwar peace organization. The president also believed that realistic solutions to European problems would be difficult because of the American public's insistence on idealistic standards with other nations.

### December 17, 1943

#### The immigration law excluding Chinese from immigrating to the United States is abrogated.

In 1943, a New York group headed by Richard Walsh, editor of *Asia and the Americans,* formed a Citizens Committee to Repeal Exclusion. Subsequently, several repeal bills were introduced in Congress, and by September House Speaker Sam Rayburn informed the State Department that a bill being considered by the Immigration Committee appeared likely to be approved. Both the president and Undersecretary of State Edward Stettinius for the State Department sent letters recommending this act. As a result, both the House (October 21) and the Senate (November 26) passed the repeal bill, which the president signed on December 17.

The bill applied only to Chinese, not all Asians as the Oriental Exclusion Bill had stated. In addition to repealing Chinese exclusion, the law admitted Chinese under the quota basis of the general Immigration Law.

The quota for Chinese immigrants was 105 per year. The bill also permitted Chinese to become naturalized American citizens.

### December 21, 1943

**General Stilwell begins a campaign to open a road from Ledo through northern Burma to China.**

At the Cairo Conference, the south Burma campaign was canceled. Nevertheless, General Stilwell opened the campaign from Ledo, India, because he wanted a supply road to China's Yunnan Province, and he wished to demonstrate that the Chinese soldiers he trained in India were good fighters. In addition to assistance from the Chinese under Stilwell, the Ledo Campaign was aided by American airborne troops known as Merrill's Marauders, named after General Frank Merrill, and British airborne troops under General Orde Wingate.

Throughout the winter of 1943–1944, Stilwell tried to persuade Chiang Kai-shek to use the Chinese forces in Yunnan to attack from the east toward Ledo, but Chiang refused. Finally, on April 3, 1944, President Roosevelt made a strong appeal to Chiang to use the Yunnan forces that the United States had armed and trained. Chiang finally yielded, and on May 10 the Yunnan Chinese army of 40,000 began an attack across the Salween River into northern Burma.

Nevertheless, the 1944 Burma campaign to open the Ledo Road was extremely long and difficult. The Japanese brought in reinforcements and fought fiercely. The monsoon rains from May to October complicated the struggle and brought disease to Merrill's Marauders. U.S. supplies through Ledo had a 15,000-mile journey to reach the 31,000 U.S. forces along the route. Finally, the Japanese in China began an offensive toward Chungking during the spring of 1944 and frightened Chiang into reducing aid to the Yunnan forces in Burma. The Ledo Road was not opened until January 26, 1945, when the Yunnan forces linked up with Stilwell's forces from India.

See November 26, 1943.

# 1944 _____

### January 11, 1944

**An extensive air bombing campaign begins against Germany.**

Although there had been Allied air raids against the European continent from England since 1939, the 1944 effort had the objective of preparing the way for the Allied attack with amphibious forces against Germany. The air action accelerated, reaching its peak in May 1944—one notable air attack was made by 800 U.S. planes against Berlin on March 6, 1944.

Air Force General Arnold called the week of February 20–26, 1944, "probably the most decisive of the war." During that week, Allied bombers inflicted severe damage on German installations, including the machine plants in Essen and Schweinfurt.

The Anglo-American bombing of Germany intensified from 1943 until the end of the war in May 1945, as the Allies gained air control over the Luftwaffe

American soldiers survey the Eiffel Tower during the liberation of France. National Archives.

(German air force). Most analysis of the bombing effort indicates that the strategic objectives of the air attacks were not met. Until the Allied armies invaded Germany early in 1945, the bombings did not materially reduce Germany's productive capacity, nor did they break the morale of Germany's civilians. Attacks on German cities caused great damage but did not affect production. By the end of 1944 and in early 1945, the Allied raids became "terrorist," hitting anything on the ground whether it was a target or not. The smallest villages became a "military objective."

See February 14, 1945.

### January 16, 1944

**A report from Henry Morgenthau on the Nazi murder of Jews leads Roosevelt to establish a War Refugee Board.**

Reports since 1942 had indicated that the German Nazis had become committed to a policy of total destruction of the European Jews. Governments of the Western powers engaged in the war effort against Germany had found no effective method to rescue or aid the various Jewish populations. On January 16, Secretary of the Treasury Morgenthau prepared a report on the "Acquiescence of this Government in the Murder of the Jews," which charged that the State Department procrastinated in helping to rescue European Jews.

As a result of this report, Roosevelt created a special agency, the War Refugee Board, to assist the immediate rescue of Jews or other minorities threatened with extermination. Consisting of the secretaries of state, Treasury, and war, this board helped Jews in Europe secure visas and funds to emigrate to safety in North Africa, Italy, and America. To avoid immigration quotas, it set up an Emergency Rescue Shelter in the United States as a temporary haven.

### January 22, 1944

**In Italy, landings at Anzio beachhead near Rome begin an assault against fortified German positions in central Italy.**

The Italian fighting was difficult because of the mountainous terrain and the key German defenses at the Gustave Line. Cassino was overrun on May 18, and on June 4, Rome was liberated by the U.S. Fifth Army.

The Italian campaign did have a salutary effect on preparations for the June attack on Normandy. The Germans committed nearly 39 divisions to Italy, which subtracted from Hitler's strength in France and eastern Europe.

### March 26, 1944

**As Soviet troops begin to invade Romania, Churchill obtains Stalin's assent to give Britain primary responsibility for Greece.**

The Soviet Union's successful drive through the Ukraine after the capture of Kiev brought the Soviet army to the borders of Romania by late March. In Greece, Communist-inspired uprisings began, causing Great Britain to be concerned about its traditional control in the Aegean and Mediterranean Seas. As a result, Churchill proposed and Stalin agreed that while the Soviets would have responsibility in Romania, Britain could have the same in Greece.

When Churchill asked Roosevelt to accept this, the president hesitated to give approval because he feared that Americans would understand such an arrangement as a "sphere of influence." Nevertheless, Roosevelt agreed to try it for three months, after which the matter could be reviewed. The Stalin-Churchill agreement became the first of several attempts to reach a settlement on eastern Europe's future.

See November 6, 1943.

### June 2, 1944

**The French provisional government-in-exile is formed in French Algiers.**

This government developed as a joint venture of Giraud and de Gaulle, who had compromised their differences on May 31, 1943, by forming the French Committee of National Liberation. On June 2, the French provisional government proposed its full support in the war against the Axis powers. On October 23, 1944, the United States, Great Britain, and the Soviet Union recognized this government.

See January 24, 1943, on the Casablanca Conference.

### June 6, 1944

## D Day: Operation Overlord begins an Allied invasion 60 miles wide along the Normandy coast of western France.

At 00.16 hours (British time), a Horsa glider crash-landed fifty meters from the bridge crossing the Caen Canal in France. Men from the British 6th Airborne Division left the glider, setting off to throw grenades into the nearby German machine-gun pillbox beside the bridge. A German sentry saw one paratrooper coming toward him and fired a flare into the air before being killed by British Lieutenant Den Brotheridge, who fired a sten gun at him. These were the first shots fired by 176,000 British, American, Canadians, Free French, Polish, Norwegian and other nationalities during the next twenty-four hours by the Allied Expeditionary Force that invaded Normandy to drive out the German armies. As Stephen E. Ambrose's *D-Day June 6, 1944* (1994) explains, the first day of the Overlord Invasion Plan launched 1,000 invasion craft, 600 war-ships, and 11,000 airplanes to transport Allied forces to invade France. The large-scale landings succeeded, and by June 27 Cherbourg was captured. By July 2, the Allies had landed 1 million troops plus 566,648 tons of supplies and 171,532 vehicles. By August 10, Normandy was secured and the Allied armies advanced into France, liberating Paris on August 25, Belgium on September 4, and Luxembourg on September 11.

### June 12, 1944

## Germany launches V-1 pilotless aircraft to bomb southern England.

These jet-propelled aircraft were launched from special sites in France and Belgium, most of them targeted on London. Later, on September 7, the Germans fired 3,400-mile V-2 rockets at London. These attacks were terror-type raids because rocket developments

The invasion of Normandy. After the beaches were secured, the channel waters were crowded with ships and landing craft bringing in men and supplies. Barrage balloons were used to protect the ships from low-flying aircraft. National Archives

had not yet advanced sufficiently to have a substantial effect on the war.

## June 21, 1944

**Vice President Wallace visits China to assist the formation of a coalition Chinese government of Communists and Nationalists.**

Throughout the war against Japan, Chiang Kai-shek had preserved his armies by avoiding conflict with the Japanese in order to blockade the Chinese Communist forces in northern China and to have troops to fight the Communists after the United States and Great Britain defeated Japan. Nearly 500,000 Nationalist forces were in constant deployment to block any Communist advances.

In 1944, Roosevelt and his advisers decided to strive for a Nationalist-Communist Party coalition government so that all China's efforts could be directed against the Japanese enemy. When neither Stilwell nor U.S. Ambassador Clarence Gauss could persuade Chiang to talk with the Communists, Roosevelt sent Vice President Henry Wallace to China to obtain Chiang's cooperation.

Wallace received only a few small concessions from Chiang. He allowed U.S. observers to visit Communist-controlled areas and accepted Roosevelt's offer to attempt a mediation with Moscow. Chiang would not open discussions with Communist leader Mao Tse-tung and strongly opposed cooperation with the Chinese Communists. According to Chiang, Mao was both subject to the "orders of the Third International" and "more communistic than the Russian Communists." Too many Americans, he said, were fooled by the Communists. The United States could best remain aloof and cool toward Mao's bandits.

Chiang told Wallace he agreed with Roosevelt's efforts to gain better relations for the Nationalists with Moscow. He wanted to reach an understanding with the Soviet Union that would cut off aid to Mao. He also asked the vice president to get rid of Ambassador Gauss and General Stilwell and asked the president to appoint a personal representative so that Chiang could deal directly with Roosevelt.

For the results of Chiang's requests, see October 21, 1944.

## June 22, 1944

**The United States severs diplomatic relations with Argentina and urges other American republics to do likewise.**

Following Argentina's failure to uphold the Declaration of the Rio Conference, Secretary of State Hull became increasingly upset with the pro-Fascist sympathies of Argentina. First, Argentine President Castillo and, after February 15, 1944, the new, Perón-backed President Edelmiro Farrell, refused to take effective action against the Axis, although Argentina broke relations with Germany on January 26, 1944.

When Farrell's government did not implement its announced January 1944 break with the Axis, Hull decided to pressure the government to change its policy. Therefore, on June 22, 1944, Hull recalled U.S. Ambassador Norman Armour from Buenos Aires and sent memos to Britain and other Latin American republics to do the same. Britain and all but three of the other American republics did so, virtually isolating Argentina from hemispheric politics. Later Hull froze Argentina's assets in the United States and called for a boycott of Argentina's products. Great Britain's refusal to join the boycott caused this action to fail. Many Americans believed Secretary Hull was being too harsh with Argentina. After Hull resigned in November 1944, steps were taken to repair U.S. relations with Argentina.

See January 28, 1942.

## July 11, 1944

**Roosevelt recognizes General de Gaulle's French Committee on National Liberation as the temporary de facto authority for France.**

From the outset, Roosevelt and Secretary Hull had disliked the arrogance of de Gaulle's claim to represent the French people. At the Casablanca Conference in January 1943, de Gaulle reluctantly agreed to become a copresident with General Giraud in North Africa. In November 1943, however, de Gaulle forced Giraud off the National Committee to give himself sole authority. On November 11, 1943, he dismissed Lebanese demands for independence by suspending the Lebanese constitution, imprisoning Lebanon's ministers, and abolishing Lebanon's parliament.

In early 1944, de Gaulle refused to cooperate with the Allied invasion of France unless the Allies recognized his provisional government as indispensable for success. Roosevelt rejected this concept, arguing that the French people, not de Gaulle, needed to determine their future. Consequently, de Gaulle refused to endorse Allied military francs as legitimate currency or to broadcast his support for the invasion on June 6, 1944. He sent only a few liaison officers to join the invaders on D day.

In June, however, Roosevelt decided to compromise with de Gaulle because of military necessity. He hoped the French general would obtain greater assistance from the French resistance and would aid in the southern invasion of France in August 1944. Thus, he invited de Gaulle to visit Washington, where a recognition agreement was approved. On July 11, Roosevelt announced that the United States recognized the French Committee of National Liberation as France's political authority. Recognition was conditional because de Gaulle agreed that Eisenhower held complete military authority and that the French people retained the right to choose their own government.

### July 22, 1944

### The United Nations Monetary and Financial Conference ends at Bretton Woods, New Hampshire.

The Bretton Woods Conference achieved cooperative agreements by 44 nations to stabilize their national currencies and stimulate world trade. The principal results of the conference were as follows:

1. establishment of the International Monetary Fund (IMF) of $8.8 billion to be used to stabilize national currency exchanges. The United States contributed about 25% of this fund;
2. creation of the International Bank for Reconstruction and Development. Capitalized at $9.1 billion, this bank made loans to nations for postwar economic reconstruction. The United States supplied 35% of these funds.

Significantly, the Soviets refused to be part of these financial arrangements by which, they believed, capitalists sought to continue to control the world economy.

### August 1, 1944

### Polish Home Army in Warsaw attacks the German occupation troops while the Soviets refuse assistance.

The Warsaw uprising broke out at the order of the Polish Home Army headquarters. The Home Army (Armia Krajowa) was an underground organization operating in German-occupied territory and a legal successor of the Polish Army, which was part of the Polish Armed Forces in the country. In association with the Polish government-in-exile based in London, the Home Army's commander-in-chief was General Tadeusz Komorwski. When the Home Army was established its military goal was to liberate Warsaw, save the city from destruction, and protect its inhabitants from mass extermination by the Germans. It also hoped to demonstrate its power by assisting the Soviet Army, whose advanced patrols were only six miles from Warsaw on August 1. In addition, on July 29 the Lublin Committee for National Liberation, whose Polish communist leaders were in Moscow, broadcast a signal for the underground to begin an insurrection to aid the Red Army's liberation of Warsaw. But when the German army halted the Soviet army on the east bank of the Vistula River, the Red Army did not advance toward Warsaw. While the Red Army stalled, Stalin condemned the uprising and prevented American and British air forces from trying to help the Home Army. The Polish Home Army had to fight against at least 20,000 well armed German soldiers whose ranks increased to 50,000 after the insurrection began.

In Moscow, Stalin told Mikolajczyk the Soviets would aid the insurgents, but later he refused to help the Home Army. Stalin wanted to abolish the Home Army because of its affiliation with the anti-communist Polish government-in-exile in London. The Poles, Churchill, and Roosevelt pleaded with Stalin to airlift armaments and supplies to the Home Army, but Stalin refused, saying the insurgents acted recklessly and without his authorization. After repeated requests for aid to the Home Army, Stalin permitted one flight of 104 U.S. airplanes to drop supplies to Warsaw. When these supplies ran out, Stalin refused to allow another airlift of supplies requested by the British and Americans.

By October 4, 1944, the Germans had suppressed the Warsaw uprising. During the uprising, 20,000 insurgents and 150,000 civilians were killed and

25,000 injured. About 16,000 were taken as prisoners-of-war and, despite Soviet protests, were granted the full status of regular soldiers of the Allied forces. As for the Germans, 10,000 were killed and about 9,000 severely wounded.

The Soviet army liberated a ruined Warsaw on January 17, 1945. As a result of the uprising, any hope of creating an anti-Soviet regime in Poland vanished in the immediate post-war years; however, a lingering animosity would ultimately spark other uprisings against domination by the Soviet Union.

### August 15, 1944

**Allied forces land in southern France, launching another invasion against the German occupiers.**

This attack, Operation DRAGOON, was made on the coast between Nice and Marseilles. After securing a beachhead, the U.S. Seventh Army and French First Army continued an offensive up the Rhône River valley.

### September 10, 1944

**Ambassador to the Soviet Union Averell Harriman reports that Moscow has become uncooperative in the past two months.**

Harriman sent a message to President Roosevelt through Harry Hopkins, indicating his concern that relations with the Soviets "have taken a startling turn" since July. The Soviets had become indifferent to U.S. requests and to discussion of vital problems. Specific American requests had been ignored, such as those for air shuttles by U.S. aircraft between Britain and the USSR to bomb or make air reconnaissance of Germany; for the transport of trucks through the Soviet Union to China; to allow U.S. air officers to appraise their bombing raids on Ploesti in Romania; and to plan for later aid against Japan.

The Soviets, Harriman contended, were now "unbending" toward Poland and acted as a "bully" where their interests were involved. Harriman told Roosevelt he would like to return home to report more precisely on these matters. The United States, he said, must be "firm but friendly" and should use a "*quid pro quo* attitude" in discussions with the Soviets.

An American convoy passes through a bombed-out French town after French "liberation." National Archives

### September 12, 1944

**U.S. forces begin the invasion of Germany near Trier.**

This advance force was the first to reach German territory. The first large German city captured by the Allies was Aachen on October 21. The Germans had built secure defenses, known as Westwall, which offered strong resistance to the Allies.

### September 16, 1944

**At the Second Quebec Conference, Roosevelt and Churchill make final plans for victory over Germany and Japan.**

The chief topic of the conference was the German issue. The Anglo-American leaders decided to create occupation zones in Germany. In addition, the Morgenthau plan for Germany was tentatively accepted. This plan wanted to reduce Germany to an agrarian economy by destroying its industrial and war-making capacity and assuring its future weakness in the postwar world.

This decision on Germany did not last long, however. Following the conference, Britain changed its mind about the Morgenthau plan because it wanted industrial reparations from Germany. In addition, reports of the concept in U.S. newspapers forced

Roosevelt to reconsider his approval of the plan. By September 29, the president told journalists that "no one wants to make Germany a wholly agricultural nation again." Privately, he said that Morgenthau had "pulled a boner."

To some degree, the Morgenthau plan had been a reaction to a State Department postwar-planning document and a War Department report that were considered to be "soft" on Germany. Roosevelt told Secretary of War Stimson on August 24 that he had the impression "Germany is to be restored just as much as the Netherlands or Belgium." The president believed the German people had to realize they were a defeated nation, and Morgenthau's plan seemed to clarify this.

By October 1944, Roosevelt had been embarrassed by the severity of Morgenthau's plan. The president still wanted to be "tough with Germany," yet later, at the Yalta Conference of February 1945, the president took a firm stand in trying to limit German reparations for the war. U.S. officials needed some time to determine whether they preferred to repress or rehabilitate postwar Germany.

### October 7, 1944

**The Dumbarton Oaks Conference prepares a basic draft for the United Nations organization.**

Representatives of the United States, Great Britain, the Soviet Union, and China met to draw up plans for the postwar international organization that had been agreed on at the Moscow and Tehran Conference of 1943.

Held in a suburban area of Washington, D.C., the conference agreed on the form of a General Assembly and a Secretariat for the United Nations. It could not decide on the veto issue for the Security Council. This and other questions were considered at Yalta by the Big Three in February 1945. The Dumbarton Oaks draft was finalized at the San Francisco Conference, which convened on April 25, 1945.

### October 18, 1944

**The Second Moscow Conference ends. During the sessions Churchill and Stalin decide on east European "spheres of influence" with which Roosevelt later concurs.**

With Ambassador Averell Harriman representing President Roosevelt, Churchill and Stalin finalized details regarding postwar Eastern Europe. During the first conference session on October 9, Churchill and Stalin agreed on spheres of influence, with the Soviets having 90 percent influence in Romania, 75 percent in Bulgaria, and equal influence with Britain in Yugoslavia and Hungary. The British and Americans would have 90 percent influence in Greece.

Churchill was especially concerned about the civil war in Yugoslavia, where Chetnik guerrillas loyal to King Peter II of Yugoslavia vied for control with the Communist Partisans led by Tito (Josip Broz). Britain had backed the Chetniks until February 1944, when Churchill realized the Chetniks' General Dragoljub Mihailovič collaborated with the Germans. Churchill shifted support to Tito but his decision came too late to receive Tito's blessing. By advocating the unity of all South Slavs rather than devotion to the Serb royal family of Peter II, Tito gained widespread popular backing and triumphed against both the Germans and the Chetniks with little outside military support from Moscow or the Western powers.

Tito solidified his authority in September 1944 when he received Stalin's promise to withdraw the Red Army from Yugoslavia as soon as it helped the Partisans liberate Belgrade from the Germans. On October 20, three weeks after liberating Belgrade, Soviet forces left Yugoslavia. Tito's guerrillas could concentrate on eliminating the remaining Germans, the Chetnik collaborators, and the Nazi-backed Croatian Ustaša, whose members had committed many atrocities against other South Slavs, Jews, and Muslims from 1941 to 1944. By May 15, 1945, Tito controlled Yugoslavia. Mihailovič was captured, convicted of collaboration, and executed in July 1946.

### October 20, 1944

**The Philippine campaign begins as General MacArthur's forces invade Leyte.**

Throughout 1943 and early 1944, preparations leading to the return to the Philippines required a series of Allied campaigns such as landings at the islands of Arawe and New Britain in the Solomon Islands in December 1943, and the Admiralty Islands and Dutch New Guinea during the spring of 1944. The naval and air battle of the Philippine Sea on June

General Douglas MacArthur. National Archives

19–20 sank 3 Japanese carriers and 200 planes, as well as crippling several battleships and cruisers. Later, on October 23–25, the Battle of Leyte Gulf was the last great naval action of the war. It decisively destroyed Japan's sea power and gave the United States control of the Philippine waters. The land battle for the Philippines continued for four months.

See February 5, 1945.

### October 21, 1944

**General Stilwell leaves China after being recalled at Chiang Kai-shek's insistence. Chiang successfully resists Roosevelt's attempt to get Chinese forces to unite in a campaign against the Japanese.**

As a result of Vice President Wallace's visit with Chiang, President Roosevelt decided in July to make a strong demand that Chiang undertake a vigorous campaign against Japan, which he had delayed since 1941. Roosevelt lost the struggle, however. By October 21, Chiang's ability to avoid Roosevelt's demands that China engage Japanese troops demonstrated how a military ruler of a lesser, dependent nation can ignore

with impunity the requests of a greater power. The outcome of Chiang's persistent refusal to engage Japanese forces in China is that military historians will never know how the Pacific war would have ended if the Chinese had fought against Japan with the determination that the Americans did in their Pacific campaigns.

In July 1944, Roosevelt initially tried to pressure Chiang into accepting conditions that might have resulted in an effective Chinese offensive against Japan. Telling Chiang that the "future of Asia is at stake," Roosevelt proposed drastic measures to stem Japanese advances in China and to save both American and Chinese interests. Roosevelt wanted General Stilwell to command all Chinese resources in China, including the Communist armies. He also told Chiang that "air power alone cannot stop" Japan, a tactic for which Chiang and General Chennault had been contending since 1942 with no apparent results. Both of these measures reversed Roosevelt's earlier policy of placating Chiang by avoiding any strings on U.S. aid to obtain a more effective Chinese military effort.

Although in theory Roosevelt held all the cards to make Chiang comply and fight Japan actively, Chiang had survived since 1927 under great odds and he survived again. Initially Chiang wrote Roosevelt that he agreed in principle with all his requests. However, it would take "preparatory time" to effect a change of command to General Stilwell. On July 13, the president walked into Chiang's "time trap." Seeing only a difference in timing between immediate and "preparatory," Roosevelt urged "speed" on Chiang and in August accepted Chiang's request to send a personal representative to China. The president sent Patrick Hurley and Donald Nelson to persuade Chiang to comply. Before Hurley and Nelson arrived at Chungking on September 7, Chiang informed Roosevelt that certain limits would have to be placed on the changes the president proposed in July. These limits, if accepted, would have the practical effects of nullifying Roosevelt's intentions. Chiang's requests were that (1) the Communist forces must accept the Nationalist government of Chiang; (2) clearer relations must be defined between Chiang and Stilwell; (3) the Chinese Nationalists must control all lend-lease aid; (4) Stilwell would command only those Chinese forces *already* fighting Japan. In particular, the first and fourth of these demands would preclude both a settlement with the Communists and Stilwell's effective uniting of all Chinese troops to fight the foreign enemy. For Chiang, Mao was the major enemy, not Japan. As Stilwell wrote to General Marshall, Chiang simply did not want to risk a fight with Japan. He wanted the United States to defeat the Japanese so he could retain all his strength to fight the Chinese Communist Party. Ironically, Henry Luce's *Time* and *Life* magazines edited Theodore White's accurate reporting on Chiang's unwillingness to fight Japan, so Americans who read these popular magazines believed that Chiang had been a democratic freedom fighter against Japan since 1937.

President Roosevelt knew that Luce's pro-Chiang publications were not correct, but he found no method to counteract these stories. Roosevelt himself subscribed to Chiang's administration as the only political group the United States could accept in China. If Roosevelt forced Chiang to comply or caused his replacement by another Chinese leader, he feared the U.S. public would not understand.

On September 16, Roosevelt made one final effort to convince Chiang to take stronger action against Japan. In a message that General Stilwell believed had "a firecracker in every sentence," Roosevelt told Chiang that the United States was faced with losses both in Burma and in eastern China. He feared that China would be lost if Chiang did not act immediately. He concluded that it appeared evident that all "our efforts to save China are to be lost by further delays."

Chiang did not accept Roosevelt's analysis or demands for action. Smugly content to compromise with Japan by living in Chungking while the Japanese controlled all China's major cities and strategic areas, Chiang could wait for the United States to defeat Japan with American lives. Then Chiang could control China. The Chinese leader won the battle with Roosevelt. However, he lost the long-term struggle with Mao because he failed to deal with the corruption and moral decay that rotted his armies as they remained at ease for almost 10 years. Moreover, Chiang had lost his claim to being a "nationalist" and appeared to be just another war lord.

Rather than respond directly to the president's September 16 message, Chiang demanded Stilwell's recall. Chiang told Roosevelt that the only way the centralized command Roosevelt desired could be

effective would be if the American commander was acceptable to Chiang; Stilwell was not. Furthermore, Chiang said, Roosevelt could question the supreme commander on China's right to request the recall of Stilwell, in whom Chiang held no confidence.

Roosevelt gave in. Having learned from the Soviet Union in September and October that it planned to invade Manchuria to fight Japan as soon as the war in Europe ended, Roosevelt decided that a campaign by the Chinese would be unnecessary. This decision meant Roosevelt would not have to face the domestic political risk of attempting Chiang Kai-shek's overthrow.

On October 21, Roosevelt recalled Stilwell, who left for India immediately. On October 28, Major General Albert L. Wedemeyer replaced Stilwell as commander of U.S. forces in China. Roosevelt also withdrew his July suggestion that all Chinese forces unite under one command. Henceforth, Roosevelt did not expect to have any effective Nationalist army operations against Japan. The president's policy in China shifted toward finding a method to have Moscow cooperate in preventing a civil war in China between Mao and Chiang (see June 21, 1944).

## November 7, 1944

### Roosevelt is elected President for a fourth term.

The Republican National Convention nominated Thomas E. DEWEY, governor of New York, on June 27. At Chicago on July 20, the Democrats selected President Roosevelt for reelection. Both parties backed U.S. participation in a postwar international organization and agreed in September not to debate the merits of various forms of organization. Roosevelt's age (62) and ability to survive another four years became a major campaign issue. Roosevelt frequently looked gaunt during the campaign, but he also made some notable campaign speeches recalling the fighting, reformist days of the 1936 campaign.

While the popular vote results were the closest since the Wilson-Hughes campaign of 1916, Roosevelt won a huge electoral victory, 432 to 99. In the popular vote, he won by 3.6 million.

**November 30, 1944**

## Edward R. Stettinius Jr. replaces Cordell Hull as Secretary of State.

Secretary Hull had held the secretaryship longer than any other person, having served since March 1933. Hull's illness made it increasingly difficult for him to continue to serve, so he resigned.

Roosevelt selected Stettinius as secretary because he had served usefully as undersecretary of state. The president wanted an uncontroversial person who would encourage bipartisan support for a sound post-war foreign policy. Stettinius agreed later to serve President Truman until the end of the San Francisco Conference, resigning on July 2, 1945, to become a representative to the United Nations Organization.

# Global Relations in the Nuclear Age

## XIII. ORIGINS OF THE COLD WAR

*Yalta, Potsdam, and the atomic bomb*
*Truman Doctrine, Marshall Plan, and NATO*
*The Korean War*

# 1 9 4 5

### January 21, 1945

**Western front: Allied armies restore the lines that the Germans disrupted during the Battle of the Bulge.**

Between December 16 and 26, 1944, a German counteroffensive dislodged Allied armies near the Ardennes Forest. A portion of the Allied lines gave way as German tanks tried to strike toward Antwerp. Although the German offensive was checked on December 26, the Allies required nearly four weeks to regain the territory they had lost. The Battle of the Bulge cost 77,000 U.S. casualties with 8,000 deaths. In addition, 21,000 men were captured. The Germans sacrificed 600 tanks and over 100,000 men in the offensive.

### January 23, 1945

***Eastern front: A Soviet offensive completes the "liberation" of Poland.***

Beginning on January 12 from the eastern outskirts of Warsaw, the Red Army captured Warsaw on January 17 and carried forward to the Oder River by January 23. There the Soviets regrouped preparatory to an assault on Germany and Berlin.

### February 5, 1945

**U.S. forces begin the invasion of Luzon.**

On this day, General MacArthur achieved his promise to return to the Philippines, from which he had fled in 1942. Manila was liberated on February 23, 1945.

### February 11, 1945

**Yalta conference concludes, having been in session since February 4.**

This summit conference of the Big Three—Winston CHURCHILL, Joseph STALIN, and Franklin D. ROOSEVELT—planned for the postwar status of Europe and for establishing the United Nations. The important conference decisions are listed below:

1. EASTERN EUROPE: The spheres of influence of the USSR and Great Britain remained as agreed to at the Moscow Conference of October 18, 1944.

However, a DECLARATION ON LIBERATED EUROPE asserted the "right of all peoples to choose the form of government under which they will live."

2. POLAND: The Soviet-backed Polish provisional government (LUBLIN GOVERNMENT) was accepted, but Stalin agreed to expand its personnel to include "democratic leaders" both from Poland itself and from the Polish government-in-exile in London.

Stalin, Roosevelt, and Churchill—the ''Big Three''—at Yalta. National Archives

It was agreed that, with a few digressions, the Curzon Line of 1919 would be Poland's eastern boundary. This line gave the Soviet Union Vilna and other territory gained by Poland in the Treaty of Riga (March 18, 1921) ending the Russo-Polish War of 1920. To compensate Poland, the western Polish border was extended to the Oder-Neisse line at the expense of Germany.

3. GERMANY: To give "future peace and security" in Europe, Germany would be required to disarm, be demilitarized, and be dismembered. Germany would be divided into three zones for occupation purposes, with a fourth zone given to France from portions of the British and American zones. Stalin did not recognize France as a fourth "big power," but Churchill and Roosevelt wished to reward the French.

The Big Three also agreed that Germany should pay REPARATIONS, a proposal strongly advocated by Stalin. Specific details on reparations would be prepared by an Allied Reparations Commission consisting of representatives of each of the Big Three powers. Although Churchill objected, a special clause of the Yalta agreements stated that the commission should consider as one proposal that reparations would be $20 billion, with 50% to go to the Soviet Union.

4. THE FAR EAST: The Soviet Union agreed to declare war on Japan within two or three months after Germany surrendered. In return for fighting Japan, Moscow would "regain rights" lost in the 1904–1905 Russo-Japanese War: rights to the southern part of SAKHALIN ISLAND, Port Darien and Port Arthur in China, the MANCHURIAN RAILWAY, and to the KURILE ISLANDS.

To confirm these Soviet rights, Stalin would make a TREATY OF FRIENDSHIP AND ALLIANCE with CHIANG Kai-shek's Nationalist government and gain Chiang's concurrent approval of the YALTA agreements.

5. UNITED NATIONS: Stalin's wish to give separate membership in the United Nations to the Soviet republics of Byelorussia and the Ukraine was approved; the argument used was that this was similar to separate membership for nations in the British Commonwealth.

The veto power of the Big Five (Britain, China, France, the Soviet Union, and the United States) in the Security Council was also discussed. The agreement was that substantive action could be vetoed but that discussion of a topic could not be prevented by veto. Thus, topics involving the Big Five could be discussed and might assist the peaceful settlement of a dispute.

James F. Byrnes, who attended the conference and was the first senior official to return to Washington, became the administration's spokesman and the "authority" on what took place at Yalta. What official Washington, the media, and the public did not know was that Roosevelt had kept Byrnes out of the most sensitive negotiations, and thus he was ignorant of most of the crucial decisions reached at Yalta.

### February 14, 1945

#### U.S. and British air forces bomb Dresden: A review of Allied bombing strategies.

The bombing of Dresden on the night of February 14 caused widespread damage that led to exaggerated reports of the bombing of culturally important cities. The bombing raid of February 14 plus two later raids in March killed some 35,000 persons, according to research by David Irving in 1966. In 1945, exaggerated reports estimated deaths at between 135,000 and 250,000.

Dresden's notoriety arose because of a briefing officer's statement at Eisenhower's headquarters, which was reported by the AP, that "Allied air commanders have made the long-awaited decision to adopt deliberate terror bombing of the great German population centers as a ruthless expedient to hasten Hitler's doom." Army Air Force headquarters in Washington immediately warned Eisenhower's air staff "of the nation-wide serious effect on the Air Forces as we have steadily preached the gospel of precision bombing against military and industrial targets." SHAEF (Supreme Headquarters, Allied Expeditionary Forces) officers responded with a statement that there had been "no change in the American policy of precision bombing directed at military targets."

The RAF had been long engaged in area bombing directed at civilian populations, but the U.S. official directive had remained anchored to precision bombing. For policy to be effective, the bombardier had to see the target to engage in precision bombing; but weather conditions over Germany largely precluded visual sightings. Consequently, the American bombers had been engaged in radar-directed bombing, or "blind bombing," on roughly three-fourths of their missions by the end of 1944—actions that differed only semantically from the RAF's area bombing strategy. See Michael S. Sherry, *The Rise of American Air Power: The Creation of Armageddon* (1987) and for the British side, Noble Franklin, *The Bombing Offensive Against Germany* (1965).

The civilian death toll from aerial bombing in World War II is most difficult to ascertain. British losses have been estimated at about 60,000, German losses put at some 500,000, and Japanese at about 325,000. One should be forewarned, however, that actual figures of deaths and injuries as a result of aerial attacks are impossible to reconstruct, given the resulting chaos—under such circumstances survival became the highest priority and record keeping a very much lower one.

### March 9–10, 1945

#### Mass firebomb air raid on Tokyo is made by 334 Army Air Force B-29s flying from bases in the Marianas.

After U.S. forces captured Saipan on June 15, 1944, the island's air fields became the main location for the U.S. 20th Air Force's B-29s to stage raids on Japan after October 24. Because the Saipan-Tokyo route was a dangerous 14-hour mission flown in daylight precision-bombing at 32,000 feet that passed through Japan's and Iwo Jima's antiaircraft fire, U.S. pilots experienced a heavy casualty rate.

Despite the heavy casualties, the B-29 missions destroyed over one-fourth of Tokyo's buildings and over 1 million persons became homeless from a firestorm that consumed 15.8 square miles. Though figures on casualties vary greatly, 90,000 to 100,000 killed

Typical military photograph taken after an attack on Tokyo. Americans could rarely assess the damage their bombers did to Japan because their view was obscured by smoke. National Archives

are generally accepted estimates. See Richard B. Frank, *Downfall: The End of the Imperial Japanese Empire* (1999), p. 18. Frequent air raids continued and by June, more than 3,100,000 Japanese were homeless in Tokyo.

The frequently cited estimates of some 325,000 civilians killed in Japan as a result of Allied air raids— including Hiroshima and Nagasaki—are most probably quite low. Moreover, these figures probably do not include other nationals residing in Japan, especially Korean laborers.

### March 17, 1945

**U.S. Marines complete the Conquest of Iwo Jima en route to Okinawa.**

After bitter fighting that began on February 19, U.S. Marines raised the flag on Mount Suribachi on February 23 before completing the conquest of the island on March 17. After Iwo Jima's capture, Air Force General Curtis LeMay adopted his new B-29 tactics using low-level flights at 5,000 feet with planes carrying more bombs after removing the plane's rear turret guns and ammunition.

Following victory at Iwo Jima, U.S. forces began an attack on Okinawa that lasted until June 21. Okinawa's capture brought U.S. Air Force bases within 325 miles of Japanese cities. This gave LeMay's air force complete dominance over Japan's air space in July 1945.

### April 4, 1945

**The Berne incident: The United States and Britain do not allow the Soviets to participate in discussions about the German surrender of northern Italy.**

As in the case of the Anglo-American talks with Badoglio's representatives (see September 10, 1943), the United States and Britain had undertaken discussion with Germany's General Karl Wolff to surrender his Italian forces. Wolff came to Berne, Switzerland, early in March 1945 to discuss surrender terms, and Roosevelt told the Joint Chiefs of Staff to handle the meeting as a military matter even though it contained political implications.

When Stalin protested on March 15, Ambassador Harriman told him that his delegates could sit as observers during the formal negotiations but that the Berne talks with Wolff were only preliminary dis-

cussions. On March 29, Stalin again protested, claiming that the Germans had shifted three divisions from Italy to the Soviet front. He believed the Anglo-Americans were plotting with Germany to let the Western Allies take over Germany while the Germans increased their fight against the USSR. On April 4, Roosevelt responded to Stalin's accusations by saying that they were "vile misrepresentations of my actions" and were bitterly resented.

The increased antagonism between the Soviets and the Western powers indicated that the "strange alliance" of World War II had rapidly deteriorated between September 1944 and April 1945. The Berne incident ended because the German surrender in Italy became part of the Anglo-American effort to cooperate with Stalin in the German surrender during April-May 1945. The Western powers desired to work with Moscow in defeating Germany and assuring four-power Allied control in Germany and Berlin as agreed to at Yalta.

In accordance with Eisenhower's decision, U.S. forces reached the Elbe River on April 11, and Soviet forces began fighting their way into Berlin on April 20, where they met strong German resistance until May 1. U.S. and Soviet armies joined at Torgau on the Elbe on April 25, 1945.

### April 7, 1945

**General Eisenhower informs General Marshall that while it is militarily unsound to "make Berlin a major objective," he would adjust plans if the combined Chiefs of Staff gave him a directive to place political considerations first. The Chiefs do not respond.**

During the early months of 1945, U.S. and British officials disagreed about a "race to Berlin" to prevent the Soviets from "liberating" the city. Although Churchill thought there was a psychological value in capturing Berlin, President Roosevelt and the U.S. Joint Chiefs of Staff claimed psychological values should not override military considerations in destroying Germany's army.

Britain's General Montgomery wanted his army of British and Canadian forces to move across the Rhine River and to "race" across northern Germany to Berlin. Montgomery's armies were slow to cross the Rhine, not arriving until March 24, while American forces crossed the Rhine at Remagen on March 8. Meanwhile, the Soviet Union's mechanized forces

American and Russian soldiers meet in Germany. Such friendly meetings are soon to become rare, as mutual suspicion deepens. National Archives

Harry S. Truman is sworn in as the 32d president. National Archives

spearheading the Red Army were 35 miles from Berlin on February 20.

Because Generals Eisenhower and Marshall had opposed a race to Berlin, their decision to move toward the Elbe River through Leipzig and Dresden was mandated by Montgomery's delay. Eisenhower wanted a demarcation line to join the Red Army and to avoid exposing his flanks to attacks by German troops. Thus, Eisenhower and Stalin agreed to make the dividing line at the Elbe-Mulde Rivers.

### April 12, 1945

#### President Franklin D. Roosevelt dies and Harry S. Truman is sworn in as the 32d president.

Roosevelt died of a cerebral hemorrhage at Warm Springs, Georgia. President Truman had seldom been consulted by Roosevelt about foreign policy decisions. Although there were indications shortly before his death that Roosevelt had become convinced of the need for a stronger stand toward Stalin, Truman came to symbolize the idea of "standing up" to the Soviet Union.

### April 21, 1945

#### The Soviet Union and Poland sign a 20-year mutual assistance pact.

Stalin signed this treaty with the Polish provisional government that the Soviets had established under the Lublin Polish leaders. They had not enlarged the government to include members of the London exile government, as Stalin had promised at Yalta. Later, at the San Francisco Conference, which opened on April 25, the Soviets nearly destroyed the conference's work by attempting to have their Polish government represented.

### April 25, 1945

#### The San Francisco Conference on the United Nations convenes.

During the early weeks of the conference, the seating of the Polish delegation and the veto procedure in the Security Council caused much debate.

See June 6 and June 26, 1945.

### May 1, 1945

#### *Adolf Hitler dies in a Berlin bunker.*

Hitler's death by suicide on April 30 was announced in Berlin by Admiral Karl Doenitz on May 1st. On April 28, Benito Mussolini had been captured and executed by Italian anti-Fascists in a village near Lake Como, Italy.

### May 7, 1945

#### Germany's unconditional surrender is signed by Field Marshal Alfred Jodl at 2:41 A.M. French time.

President Truman and Winston Churchill announced the end of the war in Europe on May 8.

### May 11, 1945

**President Truman orders an end to unconditional aid to the Soviet Union and cuts back the Soviets' lend-lease aid, limiting such aid to their military needs for war against Japan.**

Leo CROWLEY, the head of the Foreign Economic Administration, interpreted Truman's orders strictly so that ships bound for the USSR were recalled and prior orders being completed were halted immediately. When he discovered this practice, Truman rescinded Crowley's action on May 12, but not before the Soviet Union complained about this unilateral action.

Actually, Truman's policy on cutbacks in lend-lease as soon as the war ended hurt the British and French more than the Soviets. Truman knew that some leading congressmen wished to stop lend-lease early so that this aid would not be for postwar reconstruction.

### May 14, 1945

**The Democratic Republic of Austria is established with socialist Karl Renner as chancellor.**

Austria was still occupied and divided into four zones, but the Four Powers agreed to recognize the republic within its 1937 frontiers. Attempts by the Big Four to make a final peace treaty with AUSTRIA were unsuccessful until 1955.

### June 5, 1945

**The European Advisory Commission decides on the division of Germany and Berlin.**

Consisting of representatives of Britain, France, the USSR, and the United States, the European Advisory Commission had been studying the best means of dividing Germany for postwar occupation. Because of decisions by the Big Three at the Tehran and Yalta Conferences, France received a portion of the U.S. and British zones but none of the Soviet zone. As agreed on June 5, the Soviets controlled the east zone, Great Britain the north, and the United States and France divided the southern zone of Germany. Berlin was also divided into four parts under the administration of a four-power military command.

Berlin was surrounded entirely by the Soviet eastern zone.

### June 6, 1945

**Harry Hopkins reports from Moscow that Stalin has compromised on the U.N. veto and Polish questions.**

President Truman sent Hopkins to Moscow to confer on issues that were handicapping decisions at the San Francisco Conference. Truman selected Hopkins for this job because, as Roosevelt's former confidant, Hopkins wanted to obtain Soviet cooperation.

Regarding Poland, Hopkins stated the U.S. viewpoint, which accepted the concept of having a government in Poland friendly to the Soviets. The U.S. public had been outraged by Stalin's unilateral recognition of Poland's provisional government. Some of the London Polish government members, Hopkins said, should be accommodated by the Soviets as Polish officials.

After explaining that Soviet security required a nonhostile government in Poland, Stalin agreed that the present Warsaw regime could be enlarged by adding four or five members of other friendly Polish groups to the 18- or 20-member Polish cabinet. Although the London exiles did not like this compromise, Hopkins accepted it and Truman concurred. Truman hoped Stalin would later accept free elections in Poland.

Stalin also agreed to the UN Security Council proposal that any member of the Big Five powers could veto substantive issues but could not veto discussion of any item to be put on the agenda of the council.

### June 21, 1945

**U.S. forces withdraw from parts of East Germany in the Soviet zone, parts of Czechoslovakia, and most of Austria.**

Truman ordered the withdrawal in compliance with the Yalta agreement. The Soviet Union also followed the Yalta pact by permitting American and British troops to move into their Berlin zones on July 4, 1945, and French troops to enter their Berlin zone on August 12, 1945.

Winston Churchill had, since April, urged Truman not to withdraw unless the Soviets met certain requirements regarding Allied aims in eastern

Europe. Truman rejected this advice, although he delayed the withdrawal by about six weeks.

### June 26, 1945

**The United Nations charter is signed by delegates of 50 nations meeting in San Francisco.**

The charter had been unanimously approved on June 25. During the convention, the principal disputes were about Polish representation; the admission of Argentina's delegation because Argentina had not declared war on Germany and Japan until March 27, 1945; and voting procedures in the Security Council.

The United Nations organization consisted of four groups: (1) a General Assembly in which all member nations were represented and had one vote; (2) a Security Council to supervise military and political matters and to approve any substantive action by the United Nations, with veto power for the Big Five (China, France, Great Britain, the United States, and the USSR); (3) an Economic and Social Council; and (4) an International Court of Justice. The United Nations would be administered by a secretary-general elected by the General Assembly.

On July 28, the U.S. Senate ratified the United Nations Charter by a vote of 89 to 2 after six days of debate.

### July 3, 1945

**James F. Byrnes becomes Secretary of State.**

Although Byrnes had little diplomatic experience, he had served in both houses of Congress, on the Supreme Court, and as director of the Office of War Mobilization and Reconversion. However, he had been close to Roosevelt on foreign policy issues as early as 1940, when he managed such legislation as the repeal of the arms embargo, the draft, and lend-lease for the administration. According to historian Robert Messer, the Yalta conference "marked Byrne's first direct involvement in high-level international politics." That meeting "was a formative experience in Byrnes's approach to the conduct of summit diplomacy. It also provided him with a new public image as an expert on wartime foreign policy and a new unofficial role as Roosevelt's 'elder statesman'."

James F. Byrnes. National Archives

Although Truman chose him to be secretary of state because Byrnes "knew what went on at Yalta," in actuality, Byrnes had been absent when most of the crucial decisions were made. Only much later did Truman come to this realization.

### July 16, 1945

**Truman, Churchill, and Stalin begin discussions at Potsdam, near Berlin.**

The Potsdam Conference lasted until August 2, having been interrupted for two days because of British elections, during which Clement Attlee's Labour Party won control of Parliament from Churchill's Conservative Party, with Attlee replacing Churchill at Potsdam on July 28. Although the principal concern of the conference was to implement decisions made at the Yalta Conference of February 1945, Truman also dealt with the July 16 news he received about the successful U.S. test of an atomic bomb. On July 21, Truman received a full report of the test,

Stalin, Truman, and Churchill at Potsdam. Churchill would be replaced by Clement Atlee before the meeting ended. National Archives

showing the bomb's destructive power equaled that of 10,000 to 20,000 tons of TNT.

He shared the information with Churchill, Attlee, and Stalin. Because of the successful test, Truman decided to use or threaten to use the bomb against Japan in order to shorten the war in the Far East and, perhaps, prevent Stalin's Red Army from entering Manchuria to defeat Japanese forces.

See February 11, 1945, and August 2, 1945.

## July 16, 1945

### An atomic bomb is successfully exploded at Alamagordo, New Mexico.

Until this experiment, scientists working on the MANHATTAN PROJECT did not know for certain that their efforts would succeed.

Anticipating the success of the A-BOMB, discussions about using it had begun on May 9, 1945, when an Interim Committee was charged with advising the president on the use of the atomic weapon. The committee consisted of men who wanted the bomb to be used to end the war: Secretary of War Henry Stimson (chairman); George L. Harrison, deputy secretary of war; Vannevar Bush, director of the Office of Scientific Research and Development; Karl T.

Compton of the Manhattan Project; Navy Undersecretary Ralph Bard; Assistant Secretary of State Will Clayton; and James Byrnes, who would formally replace Stettinius after the end of the San Francisco Conference.

On June 16, the Interim Committee reported that there was no "acceptable alternative to direct military use of the bomb." The bomb should be used against Japan as soon as it was operational. A war plant or military installation in Japan should be the target, but Japan should not be warned in advance of the A-bomb.

Some of the scientists involved in the Manhattan Project disagreed with the Interim Committee. Seven members of the University of Chicago group, headed by James O. Franck, proposed holding a public demonstration of the bomb in a deserted place, followed by a warning to Japan to surrender or suffer the consequences of an A-bomb attack. The Interim Committee opposed such a test because if the bomb failed it would render future threats meaningless.

On June 18, Truman met with his War Council (the Joint Chiefs of Staff and the secretaries of war and the navy) to consider future actions against Japan. The A-bomb was mentioned but only briefly, because the test had not yet been made in New Mexico. The

Joint Chiefs presented plans for Operation Olympic, an invasion of the Japanese island of Kyushu on November 1, 1945; and for Operation Coronet, an invasion of Honshu, on or about March 1, 1946. General Marshall believed the invasion would cause at least 250,000 U.S. deaths plus a million Japanese deaths. This invasion was preferred, however, to an offensive against Japan in China and Manchuria.

Truman ordered plans for the invasion of Kyushu to proceed but delayed a decision on the Honshu invasion. These plans were again reviewed on July 16, when Truman had to consider the use of the A-bomb against Japan.

### July 24, 1945

**Truman orders use of the atomic bomb on any of four possible military targets in Japan.**

The identified targets were in the cities of HIROSHIMA, KOKURA, NIIGATA, and NAGASAKI. The precise target would be determined by weather conditions permitting a daylight visual-bombing attack.

### July 26, 1945

**The United States and Great Britain, in concurrence with China, issue an ultimatum to Japan, asking for an unconditional surrender and warning that rejection will lead to the use of vast, destructive force against Japan.**

While at Potsdam, President Truman agreed with Churchill to send Japan an ultimatum to surrender. After obtaining the concurrence of Chiang Kai-shek, the so-called Potsdam Proclamation was released to newspaper and radio reporters.

The proclamation said Japan must choose between being "controlled by those self-willed militaristic advisers" who brought Japan to the "threshold of annihilation" or following the "path of reason" and surrender. It called on the "Government of Japan to proclaim now the unconditional surrender of all the Japanese armed forces," with the alternative being Japan's "prompt and utter destruction."

The proclamation did not mention the existence of the atomic weapon or the possibility of a compromise by which the emperor might remain as Japan's ruler. Truman and Churchill signed the proclamation with the notation that Chiang Kai-shek approved by radio. Stalin did not sign because the Soviets had not yet declared war on Japan.

On July 27, Japanese officials received the proclamation's message by radio, not through diplomatic sources or a neutral country. Japan's military leaders thought the message was "absurd," and on July 28, Prime Minister Susuki told a Tokyo press conference that the proclamation was of no importance and should be "ignored" (*mokusatsu*).

While the prime minister was holding the press conference, American airplanes were dropping 27 million leaflets over Japanese cities. The leaflets explained the ultimatum and listed 11 Japanese cities of which 4 might be destroyed from the air if Japan failed to surrender.

During the same period from July 25 to 28, Japan's ambassador to Moscow asked the Soviet Union to mediate with the Allies to end the war if the Allies would approve concessions to an unconditional surrender such as allowing Japan's emperor to remain in power. Soviet Foreign Minister Molotov delayed his country's response by asking the ambassador to put his ideas in writing. Although the Japanese terms for mediation were neither precise nor clearly known to Japan's ambassador to Moscow, Molotov's delay allowed Soviet troops to move toward Manchuria before declaring war on Japan. Details about these activities are in Charles L. Mee Jr.'s *Meeting at Potsdam* (1975) and Herbert Bix's *Hirohito and the Making of Modern Japan* (2000).

### August 2, 1945

**The Potsdam Conference adjourns.**

Truman apparently believed, according to Robert Messer's *The End of an Alliance*, "that Stalin was an honest man with whom he could deal and who like 'any smart political boss' would keep his word and deliver what he had promised to those other politicians who depended upon that promise."

The Big Three talks considered the details of the German occupation and other European problems. The principal decisions were as follows:

1. *German reparations*—The Soviet Union dropped the $20 billion proposal made at Yalta, agreeing to base reparations on useful materials in the eastern zone and capital equipment available in the three western zones of Germany.
2. *Transfer of Germans*—More than 6.5 million Germans would be transferred to Germany

World War II: Occupation zones in Germany and Austria

from previously disputed territory in Hungary, Czechoslovakia, and Poland.

3. *War crimes*—It was agreed to try leading Nazis for war crimes; an International Military Tribunal was to be set up soon after the conference ended.

4. *German economy*—Proposals accepted would convert the German economy to a principally agricultural one. Powerful industrial cartels would be abolished, and only nonmilitary products would be manufactured by German industry.

5. *Other peace treaties*—A Council of Foreign Ministers representing each of the Big Five powers was directed to prepare peace treaties for Austria, Hungary, Bulgaria, Romania, and Finland. Once Germany regained a central government, the council would draft a peace treaty for Germany.

Truman was reluctant to discuss Stalin's previously pledged willingness to declare war on Japan. According to Messer, "the impact of the successful atomic test the day before the Potsdam conference began makes clear that ... Truman and Byrnes were anxious to keep the Russians out of the war with Japan as much as possible."

## August 6, 1945

### The first atomic bomb used in the war is dropped on Hiroshima, Japan.

Flying from an airfield on Tinian Island, a U.S. air force plane, named ENOLA GAY for pilot PAUL TIBBETS's mother, dropped a uranium nuclear bomb code-named "Little Boy" at 8:16 A.M. Some of the initial consequences for Hiroshima, a city with 320,000 inhabitants at the time, were 130,000 killed or seriously injured; 64,521 buildings destroyed; 70,000 water-main breaks; 52 of 55 hospitals and clinics destroyed; 180 of 200 doctors and 1,654 of 1,780 nurses killed or injured. In addition, 12 U.S. navy pilots were killed while in Hiroshima's prison, although the U.S. government has never admitted this. See Committee for the Compilation of Materials on Damage Caused by the Atomic Bombs in Hiroshima and Nagasaki, *Hiroshima and Nagasaki:*

Hiroshima after the destruction caused by the atomic bomb. National Archives

*The Physical, Medical, and Social Effects of the Atomic Bombings* (1981).

The bomb had a yield of 13 kilotons, equal to the explosive power of 13,000 tons of TNT. The largest conventional bomb used in World War II yielded the power of 10 tons of TNT.

## August 8, 1945

### The Soviet Union declares war on Japan; Soviet armies invade Manchuria.

In keeping with its pledge made at Yalta, the Soviet Union declared war on Japan 30 days after the war ended in Europe.

## August 9, 1945

### The second atomic bomb is dropped on Nagasaki.

Although scheduled originally to be dropped on August 11 if Japan had not surrendered, "Fat Boy," a plutonium bomb, was dropped within 75 hours of the first bomb because of predictions of bad weather over Japan on August 10 and 11. Although the plutonium bomb was more powerful than "Little Boy," damage and casualties were less extensive because of Nagasaki's terrain; approximately 100,000 were killed or seriously wounded.

After World War II, Truman's decision to drop atomic bombs on Japan became controversial. In 1995, on the 50th anniversary of the end of the war, an extensive dispute arose regarding the Smithsonian Institution's exhibition regarding the decision to use the bomb. One faction approved Truman's decision as preventing the deaths of many American soldiers who might have had to invade Japan's home islands; the opponents of the decision cited various counterfactual methods Truman could have used to force Japan's surrender.

## August 14, 1945

### China and the USSR sign a treaty of friendship and alliance.

Stalin recognized Chiang Kai-shek's Nationalist regime as the central government of China. Chiang accepted the Yalta Conference decisions that gave the Soviets the 30-year control of the Manchurian Railway, the use of Darien, and the right to join with China in the exclusive use of Port Arthur as a naval base.

## August 15, 1945

### Japan surrenders "unconditionally" if Hirohito may retain his throne.

After ignoring the Allies' ultimatum of July 26, Japan's leaders did not meet again until August 9, after the United States dropped the second atomic bomb, on Nagasaki. Even at this late date, Japan's military officers wanted to fight on, despite reports that their defense installations were not prepared to defend against an Allied invasion of their home islands. During the meeting between the military commanders

Japanese delegates sign formal surrender documents aboard the USS *Missouri*. National Archives

U.S. occupation forces began to land in Japan on August 26. On September 2, 1945, Japanese delegates signed the formal surrender terms with General Douglas MacArthur on board the USS *Missouri* in Tokyo Bay.

For details of these events, see Bix's article and John Dower's *Embracing Defeat* (2000).

## August 21, 1945

### Lend-lease aid is terminated by the United States.

From its beginning in March 1941 until its final orders were filled in September 1946, lend-lease aid amounted to $50.6 billion, minus reverse lend-lease of $7.8 billion received by the United States from its allies.

## September 2, 1945

### *In Hanoi, Ho Chi Minh proclaims the independence of Vietnam.*

Following the Japanese surrender, Ho Chi Minh and his Viet Minh forces entered Hanoi to replace the Japanese and proclaim his nation's independence from France as well as Japan.

The Viet Minh (Vietnamese Independence League) was a national coalition organization formed in May 1941 to attract all Vietnamese patriots to fight the occupation by Japan as well as the French. It was based on the Indochinese Communist Party, largely because the French had suppressed all the moderate nationalist groups during the 1930s while the smaller Communist group went underground. By 1945, however, the Viet Minh included nationalists from various political groups who had united against France and Japan.

During World War II, the Viet Minh aided Americans on missions against the Japanese in Indochina. They rescued downed pilots, committed sabotage at Japanese military bases, and gave intelligence information to the U.S. Office of Strategic Services (OSS). Many OSS officers admired the Viet Minh's capabilities, urging them to seek U.S. support in their independence struggle.

Perhaps it is not surprising, therefore, that when Ho Chi Minh declared Vietnam's independence in 1945, his decree began: "All men are created equal. They are endowed by their creator with certain

and Prime Minister Susuki Kantaro's cabinet, the military sought at least three concessions from the United States, while Susuki simply wished to retain Japan's imperial authority and the symbolic "national entity" (*kokutai*).

Although historical analysis about the war's end focuses on President Truman's decision to use atomic weapons, Herbert Bix's *Diplomatic History* article (Vol. 19, Spring 1995) argues that the Pacific war was prolonged because of the unrealistic and incompetent actions of Japan's highest leaders, especially Hirohito. Bix demonstrates that on various occasions Hirohito could have ended the war before August 1945. One such instance was the emperor's insistence on fighting the Battle of Okinawa in April 1945. In February, Japan's political and military leaders considered seeking peace negotiations to end the war following reports that the Soviet Union might declare war on Japan by May 1945. In this context of Japan's certain defeat, Hirohito rejected a proposal to negotiate peace terms because he wanted "one more military gain" to restore Japan's war status. Again on July 27, Hirohito "ignored" the Allies' Potsdam ultimatum and did not agree to surrender until early in the morning of August 10, when Susuki proposed that Japan seek one concession of retaining the emperor's authority. The United States accepted this concession, making it impossible to know what would have happened if Truman had insisted on total unconditional surrender rather than accept Japan's surrender in terms of accomplishing the Potsdam declaration.

inalienable rights, among these are life, liberty, and the pursuit of happiness."

Within four weeks, however, the Viet Minh's hopes turned sour. Although President Roosevelt had once spoken on behalf of the end to French colonial power in Indochina, British forces "liberated" that area and brought French colonial officials with them. The French regained Saigon in September and moved to end Vietnamese independence. President Truman ignored Ho Chi Minh's appeals for assistance. Even the exiled Vietnamese Communist leaders in Paris and Moscow counseled Ho to compromise with France.

See November 23, 1946.

### September 9, 1945

*Japan signs capitulation terms with the nationalist government of China at Nanking and with the British at Singapore (September 12).*

China regained control of Inner Mongolia, Manchuria, Formosa, and Hainan Island. The British reoccupied Hong Kong as agreed at Potsdam in July 1945.

### October 20, 1945

**The Council of Foreign Ministers adjourns its first meeting in London.**

Meeting in London, Council meetings began in mid-September, but the talks scheduled to draft a peace treaty for Italy never materialized. When the sessions convened, Soviet Foreign Minister Molotov diverted the agenda to discuss Romania, Bulgaria, and Japan. Molotov's first question to U.S. Secretary of State Byrnes and British Foreign Minister Bevin was why they would not recognize the Romanian government of Petru Groza. Romania's King Michael had been forced by the Soviets to install Groza on March 2. King Michael headed Romania's government after the Soviet army occupied Bucharest in August 1944, but in 1945 the Soviets wanted Groza, a Communist, to be premier.

Secretary Byrnes told Molotov the United States and Britain refused to recognize Romania's new government because Groza was not democratically elected under terms of the Yalta agreement's Declaration of Liberated Europe. Molotov rejected Byrnes's explanation, claiming Groza's government

was a "friendly" neighbor while the former premier was hostile to the Soviet Union. Similarly, Byrnes and Molotov disagreed about Bulgaria's new government, installed by Soviet officials but not recognized by Britain and the United States.

Finally, on September 23, Molotov wanted to discuss having a Control Council for Japan. In his memoirs, Byrnes believed Molotov's proposal on Japan "broke the back of the London Conference" because he not only wanted to devise a new method to replace General MacArthur's authority in Japan but to exclude China and France from discussions on the various peace treaties. Molotov's tactics seemed intended to delay and disrupt the completion of final peace treaties while the Soviets created puppet governments in territory occupied by the Red Army. Although the London sessions officially continued until October 20, Byrnes planned to call for a December meeting in Moscow, where, he believed, Stalin would make compromises Molotov rejected.

See February 11, 1945, and December 26, 1945.

### October 21, 1945

**Left-wing parties win the French elections for a constituent assembly.**

In the elections for 441 seats, the Communists won 152 seats; the Socialists 151, and the Moderates (Mouvement Républicain Populaire—MRP), 138. Nevertheless, on November 16, 1945, General Charles de Gaulle was elected as president of the provisional government.

### November 15, 1945

**The United States, Canada, and Britain agree on an atomic energy control plan to support in the United Nations.**

As Truman remarked in the fall of 1945, the control of atomic weapons would become humankind's major problem. Neither he, Secretary Byrnes, nor others had any precedent on which to proceed. Therefore, a variety of proposals had appeared from advocates of ideas ranging from the free exchange of all secrets with the Soviet Union to U.S. use of the bomb to compel all nations to adopt American policies. Neither of these extremes held the serious attention of American leaders who searched for a means to prevent a nuclear arms race and promote peaceful uses of atomic power.

On November 15, President Truman, British Prime Minister Clement Attlee, and Canadian Prime Minister MacKenzie King agreed on a basic step-by-step proposal to be established under the auspices of a United Nations Atomic Energy Commission. Vannevar BUSH of the Office of Scientific Research had suggested the steps in the proposal:

1. extending the international exchange of all scientific information as a first test of the USSR's good intentions;
2. establishing a UN Committee of Inspection to inspect science laboratories of all nations engaged in atomic research. This would be done on a gradual basis so that the United States would not have to disclose any "secrets" immediately;
3. stockpiling by all nations capable of atomic fission of such materials, which would be used only for peaceful purposes; the Committee of Inspection would oversee their use.

The UN commission would also work to eliminate atomic weapons and to provide safeguards for nations that cooperated with the UN commission. Each stage of the commission's work would be completed only when the confidence of the world had been secured to proceed to the next step.

Once this plan was announced in November 1945, its supporters and critics began to analyze it. Washington's interest in establishing international control, however, decreased as suspicions between the Western nations and the Soviet Union grew after August 1945.

### November 27, 1945

**Patrick J. Hurley resigns as U.S. Ambassador to China. His efforts to mediate between Chiang Kai-shek and Mao Tse-tung fail.**

In announcing his resignation, Hurley leveled charges against State Department officers and Truman's China policy, which provided ammunition for attacks during the next decade on Truman, the Democratic Party, the U.S. Foreign Service, and the State Department. Hurley blamed the failure of his efforts and Chiang's weakness on "career diplomats in the Embassy at Chungking and Far Eastern Division of the State Department." These officials, he asserted, did not implement the "principles of the Atlantic Charter" but supported both Chinese Communists and "British imperialists" against Chiang Kai-shek.

Zhou Enlai, Mao Tse-tung (leader of Communists in China), and Patrick Hurley. National Archives

President Roosevelt had sent Hurley to China on August 18, 1944. As the president's special representative, Hurley was charged with resolving the lengthy dispute between U.S. General Stilwell and Chiang Kai-shek and establishing unity between the Chinese Nationalist and Communist forces so that they would fight the Japanese. Hurley interpreted his mission as maintaining the Nationalist government by supporting Chiang.

Hurley's year in China caused much controversy. He oversaw the removal of General Stilwell; replaced Clarence Gauss as ambassador to China on December 12, 1944; demanded the removal of two career Foreign Service China experts, George Atcheson and John Service, because they disputed his analysis of Chinese developments; and became a friend and admirer of Chiang Kai-shek.

In addition, visiting Moscow on his way to China in August 1944, he became convinced that the Soviet Union differed with Mao Tse-tung's regime and would cooperate with the Nationalist government. Finally, as an old-time Irish-Anglophobe, Hurley was equally convinced that Winston Churchill had usurped Roosevelt's anticolonial policy because he wanted Hong Kong returned and planned to restore Anglo-French control in East Asia. Thus, he blamed U.S. diplomats both for aiding Mao's Communist growth and for supporting British attempts to renew their imperial regime in Asia.

Because he accepted Moscow's good faith and Chiang's power, Hurley lauded the August 1945 pact between China and the Soviet Union. He also was pleased that Truman extended lend-lease aid to Chiang for six months after the war's end and that the U.S. navy aided Chiang by carrying Nationalist troops to northern China. Thus, on September 26, 1945, Hurley returned home ready to resign because he believed everything was calm in China.

During the next month, the State Department kept Hurley informed of the deteriorating relations between the two Chinese factions. Truman and Secretary Byrnes urged him to return to Chungking. Contrary to Hurley's expectation, the Soviet Union did not keep its promises to cooperate with Chiang. The Soviets helped the Communists gain control in Manchuria and refused to allow Nationalist troops to disembark from U.S. ships at Dairen or other ports near Manchuria. Hurley also learned that the truce arrangements between Mao and Chiang had been postponed, and the two sides were as far apart as ever by November 1945. Finally, Hurley was dismayed to discover that against his advice, both George Atcheson and John Service had been posted to Tokyo as consultants on General MacArthur's staff.

Russell Buhite, Hurley's biographer, is not certain what prompted Hurley's actions in November 1945. First, he agreed to return to China but later surprised both Byrnes and Truman by calling a press conference to announce his resignation. Moreover, Buhite cannot explain why Hurley, in his resignation and his testimony to the Senate Foreign Relations Committee, blamed China's problems on the Foreign Service and the State Department rather than on the Soviet Union's failure to cooperate and the intransigent policies of both Mao and Chiang. Hurley's Senate testimony exaggerated the blame of career officers who disagreed with him or "favored" the British and Chinese Communists.

Subsequent to Hurley's charges, Secretary of State Byrnes defended Service and Atcheson, stating that these experts had to be free to give their honest judgments on policy. They were not, Byrnes said, disloyal to Hurley, but their long years of experience in China

gave them different perspectives. Byrnes's support for the Foreign Service officers in 1946 contrasts with the treatment accorded to these experts during the McCarthy era from 1950 to 1954.

### November 27, 1945

### The Marshall mission to China begins.

Immediately after learning of Patrick Hurley's resignation, President Truman called George Marshall, asking him to act as the president's personal representative to China. Truman, Marshall, and Secretary of State Byrnes agreed on December 9, 1945, that U.S. policy was (1) to seek a united and democratic China, and (2) to retain Chinese sovereignty over Manchuria. To do this, Marshall would seek a truce between Mao and Chiang in north China and assist the Nationalist government in replacing the Japanese and Soviet troops that had evacuated northern China.

Marshall's most perplexing problem was how to mediate between the two Chinese groups while the United States continued to support Chiang Kai-shek. He was told that he should pressure Chiang as much as possible, but that the United States would not cease support of the Nationalists. This, of course, made real pressure impossible and, as under Stilwell, Chiang thought he could do as he wished by appealing either to the White House or to the friends of the China-Chiang lobby in Congress.

Although Marshall secured a temporary truce in February 1946, by the summer of 1946 he realized that neither Mao nor Chiang wanted a genuine truce. Chiang wanted to control all Manchuria and seemed successful in June 1946. A new truce from June 7 to 30 was broken by the Communists, and by July 1, 1946, all-out civil war began.

See October 10, 1946.

### December 3, 1945

### General Groves claims the "real atomic secret" is the U.S. monopoly of uranium.

In 1945, most Americans believed the Manhattan Project's "secret" in developing the atomic bomb was the scientific and technological knowledge of U.S. scientists that the Soviet Union lacked. On December 3, General Leslie Groves told the Combined Policy Committee and representatives of the Truman administration that the "real secret" of the U.S. success was obtaining a monopoly of high-grade uranium—Groves did not make this alleged "secret" public until 1954.

Because Groves knew Soviet scientists had the ability to build an atomic weapon, he decided in 1943 to secure U.S. control of the supply of fissionable materials, uranium and thorium. At the 1943 Quebec Conference, the Combined Policy Committee was established to obtain British and Canadian cooperation and enlist aid from the Belgian government-in-exile in London because the Belgian Congo had large deposits of uranium. On December 3, 1945, Groves reported that the United States and its allies controlled 97 percent of the world's high-grade uranium and 35 percent of low-grade deposits, which were more expensive to use for a nuclear weapon. Most of the other 65 percent was in neutral Sweden and the British dominions, although the USSR and South American nations had some low-grade material. According to his calculations on uranium supplies, Groves believed the Soviets would need at least 20 years to build an atomic weapon.

Unfortunately, Groves's calculation was mistaken about a monopoly of uranium. If he had told his "secret" to U.S. scientists such as James Conant or Vannevar Bush, Groves could have learned controlling uranium would not prohibit the Soviets from making an atomic bomb. In 1944, Conant told Secretary of War Henry Stimson that a monopoly of materials was impractical because the supply of heavy hydrogen is "essentially unlimited." In addition, U.S. scientists knew the Soviets could obtain high-grade uranium in East Germany's province of Saxony, liberated by Soviet troops in early 1945; later they would learn of the huge newly discovered deposits in the Urals. In contrast to Groves, Conant and other U.S. scientists predicted the Soviets would have an atomic bomb in four or five years.

As Greg Herken's *The Winning Weapon* (1980) explains, Groves's "secret" created a myth about the U.S. monopoly of scientific and technological superiority that presumed the Soviet Union could not make atomic weapons without Western spies providing all the information. This myth of U.S. scientific superiority promoted Senator Joseph McCarthy's spy allegations after 1950. Soviet documents declassified during the 1990s revealed that by 1945 spies such as Klaus Fuchs and Theodore Hall had provided information from the Manhattan Project to help Soviet

scientists build a bomb by 1949, the time predicted by Conant and Bush.

See September 23, 1949.

## December 13, 1945

### *France and Britain agree to evacuate Syria and grant independence.*

French and British forces sought to reoccupy Syria and Lebanon in May 1945. After six months of rioting and uprisings in Syria, the two Western powers agreed to leave Syria by August 31, 1946.

## December 20, 1945

### The Truman administration backs legislation for civilian control of America's atomic energy.

Although General Leslie Groves and others desired military control of atomic developments, Senator Brien McMahon's bill provided for civilian control. The MCMAHON BILL passed Congress and became law on August 1, 1946. This law also limited Anglo-American nuclear cooperation, which became an issue between the two nations.

## December 26, 1945

### At Moscow, Byrnes and Stalin agree on eastern Europe and Japan.

Following the breakdown of the London Conference of October 20, 1945, Secretary of State Byrnes called for a second foreign ministers' meeting in Moscow, where he hoped Stalin would be easier to deal with than Molotov regarding the status of Romania and Bulgaria. Byrnes persuaded Britain's Foreign Minister Ernest Bevin to attend the Moscow session that began on December 16. Byrnes met with Bevin and Molotov for several days before obtaining the compromises he sought in a session with Stalin on December 23. Regarding Eastern Europe, Stalin agreed to have Bulgaria add opposition leaders to its government and to send a three-power commission to Romania and advise Romanian leaders to add two opposition members to their cabinet. Stalin's concessions did not weaken Soviet control of those two countries, but the agreement justified U.S. diplomatic recognition in order to conclude peace treaties with Bulgaria and Romania.

Civilians receive their first meal in some time at a Red Cross center in Lucca, Italy. National Archives

In other Moscow agreements, Stalin accepted a Western Allies proposal for creating a UN Atomic Energy Commission, while Byrnes approved the formation of an Allied Council to consult with General MacArthur about Japan's occupation, although MacArthur did not have to take the Council's advice. Each of these agreements proved to be irrelevant: the Soviets kept control of Eastern Europe and the United States controlled Japanese developments.

See November 15, 1945; on the UN Atomic Energy plan, see June 14, 1946.

# 1 9 4 6 _____

### January 1, 1946

### Japan's Emperor Hirohito appears to disclaim his divinity, misleading the Western powers.

Although the Tokyo International Military Tribunal granted immunity to Emperor Hirohito from a trial or testifying in cases on Japanese war criminals, General MacArthur's staff suggested the emperor should issue a statement to disclaim his divinity. MacArthur's staff prepared a draft of the emperor's statement, but before the emperor spoke on January 1, Japanese leaders translated the statement into terms and wording they preferred.

As explained in John Dower's *Embracing Defeat* (1999), the Japanese revised Hirohito's message to emphasize a reference to the Meji's Charter Oath of 1868 and bury a sentence on his divinity in the lengthy text. Both U.S. and British officials lauded this single divinity statement, taking it out of a context most Japanese understood as a call for a "new Japan" to unite in recovering from defeat and rebuilding a greater Japan. Dower notes that Hirohito descended only "partway from heaven," because in Japanese eyes the emperor's words were not a renunciation of divinity. At best, Hirohito desired "imperial democracy."

Under MacArthur's leadership in November 1946, Japan was required to adopt a constitution prepared by MacArthur's staff. MacArthur also issued decrees for other reforms such as restoring civil liberties, dissolving the secret police, and liberalizing education. During the same time, MacArthur's administration was unable to break up Japan's financial and industrial cartels, known as *zaibatsu*, or develop independent labor unions. His land reforms were dubious because they created small farms unsuited for the use of modern agricultural mechanization. Although Japan's leaders praised MacArthur's administration, Japan's prewar conservatives retained a strong hold on the government.

### January 10, 1946

### First session of the United Nations opens in London.

### January 19, 1946

### U.N. Security Council hears its first complaint.

Soon after the United Nations held its first meeting on January 10, the U.N. Security Council received a complaint from Iran. The Iranian government contended that the Soviet Union interfered in its internal affairs by refusing to leave territory it occupied in northern Iran during World War II.

For the result of Iran's complaint, see April 3, 1946.

### January 27, 1946

### In the U.S. zone of Germany, local elections are held.

The Christian Democratic Party won the greatest number of local offices; the Social Democrats ranked second. Soon after, similar elections in the British and French zones were also won by the Christian Democrats. The Christian Democrats were a middle of-the-road party whose principal strength was with business interests and Roman Catholics. The Social

Democrats were a slightly left-of-center, evolutionary Socialist party.

The Soviet Union conducted elections in its zone on April 21, 1946. In East Germany, the Social Democrats merged with the Communist Party to form the Socialist Unity Party (SED), the party that dominated subsequent elections in East Germany.

### February 3, 1946

#### Soviet spy ring in Canada is disclosed on Drew Pearson's radio program.

Two weeks later, Canada arrested 22 men accused of spying. According to Prime Minister MacKenzie King, the Canadian authorities moved earlier than their investigation of the spies required, because of Pearson's report.

A wave of SPY SCANDALS and accusations began in the United States as a result of these actions. Soon after, Washington columnist Frank McNaughton said a "confidential source" claimed that the Canadian spies sought data on U.S. atomic secrets and that a Soviet spy ring also operated in the United States. This second ring, McNaughton reported, had not been broken by the FBI, because certain "State Department men" believed it "would upset our relations with Russia."

McNaughton's source was later found to be General Leslie Groves, head of the Manhattan Project. Groves and the army were then involved in a dispute with Senator Brien McMahon over the issue of civilian or military control of U.S. atomic energy policy. Thus, the spy accusations led Congress to amend prior McMahon legislation so that the military could defend against "spies."

Notably, at this time the American public believed there existed some single secret of the atomic bomb that only spies could communicate to the Soviets. Atomic scientists and experts such as Groves knew this was not the case—the basic scientific information has appeared in scientific journals during the 1920s and 1930s. The only "secrets" were who had supplies of uranium and what were the precise technological methods used in the United States to efficiently enrich uranium as the source of atomic power. Groves incorrectly believed he had secured a monopoly of uranium supplies for America.

When the Canadian government issued its report on the spy cases in the summer of 1946, it indicated the Soviets obtained little from their spy ring. The alleged master spy, British physicist Alan Nunn May, gave them samples of enriched uranium ore that General Groves had presented to Canadian scientists in 1944. As Groves later admitted, May had only general knowledge about the atomic bomb and the Soviets did not gain details about building this bomb.

Nevertheless, Soviet spy stories and allegations became recurrent in America after February 1946. This "scare" influenced Congress and the public to refuse to share nuclear "secrets" with allies, as well as to accept a larger degree of military control over atomic energy.

### February 9, 1946

#### A speech by Joseph Stalin is "the declaration of World War III," in the words of Supreme Court Justice William Douglas.

In a speech aimed to bolster domestic morale, Stalin asserted that capitalistic developments led inevitably to war, and he called on the Soviet people to sacrifice as they had during the 1930s to rebuild the USSR.

### February 24, 1946

#### Colonel Juan D. Perón is elected president of Argentina.

As the leading military official in Argentina, Juan Perón had effective control of Argentina during most of World War II, when Argentina remained neutral, and, later, when it became a haven for Fascist and Nazi sympathizers including Adolf Eichmann, a Nazi war criminal who escaped from Germany. When Perón decided to run for the presidency, the U.S. State Department issued a "Blue Book," based on captured German documents, which accused Perón of collaboration with the Nazis.

The U.S. report was inspired by former U.S. Ambassador to Argentina Sprulle BRADEN, who had an intense dislike for Perón and had often spoken against him while he was ambassador in Buenos Aires. The attempt to damage Perón backfired. Perón accused the United States of intervention in his country's internal affairs, and he won the election with no difficulty.

### March 4, 1946

**The United States, Britain, and France issue an unusual appeal, asking the Spanish people to overthrow Franco's Fascist regime.**

Partly because of President Truman's intense dislike for General Franco's government, the United States joined Paris and London in this appeal. The three Western powers searched for some means to give Spain a democratic, anti-Communist administration.

Spain had been excluded from the United Nations at the San Francisco Conference. Later, on December 11, 1946, the UN General Assembly voted to prohibit Spain from participation in any UN activities and urged its members to sever diplomatic relations with Madrid. The appeal of March 4 did not succeed. Franco's hold on the Spanish government was far too great for outsiders to overthrow him by verbal appeals.

### March 5, 1946

**Winston Churchill delivers his "iron curtain" speech at Fulton, Missouri.**

Churchill's speech delineated the growing chasm between the Soviet regions of Eastern Europe and the Western "free states." President Truman evidently knew in advance of Churchill's intent. Not only did Churchill contend that "police states" ruled Eastern Europe, he also emphasized that the Soviets desired "the indefinite expansion of their power and doctrines." The Anglo-Americans, he said, must work with the aid of atomic weapons to create unity in Europe to protect the free nations.

### March 6, 1946

***The French foreign office seeks peace in Indochina by the accords of March 6.***

Vietnam, Laos, and Cambodia were recognized as "free," but not independent, states in the FRENCH UNION. These accords proved to be only a temporary armistice.

### April 3, 1946

**Iran's crisis is resolved when the Soviet Union agrees to withdraw its armed forces.**

The Soviet Union had delayed the withdrawal of its troops that were scheduled to leave Iran by March 2, 1946. During World War II, Britain and the Soviet Union agreed to protect Tehran from the Germans by occupying Iran, with British forces in the south, Soviet troops in the north. After Germany surrendered, Britain and the Soviets agreed to withdraw from Iran by early 1946. The British withdrew before the end of 1945, but in November 1945 Soviet forces helped rebels in Azerbaijan seize power to establish the Autonomous Republic of Azerbaijan. The Soviets also helped Kurdistan rebels establish an independent Kurdish People's Republic. On November 28, Tehran sent two army battalions to regain control of Azerbaijan, but Soviet troops blocked the army from gaining control over the province. At the same time, Moscow sought oil concessions from Iran similar to those Britain held in southern Iran.

In response to these Soviet actions, the United States and Britain supported Iran's January 19 appeal to the UN Security Council to investigate Soviet interference in Iran's northwestern provinces. The Council directed Iran to negotiate and in February Iran's Prime Minister Ahmad Quavam went to Moscow to discuss the situation with Stalin and Foreign Minister Molotov.

The Soviet Union again refused to withdraw its troops on the established deadline of March 2, 1946. On March 5, U.S. Secretary of State Byrnes sent a telegram to Moscow calling for the Soviets' immediate withdrawal from Iran. Although Quavam continued negotiating in Moscow, the United States now received reports from its Azerbaijan consulate that the Red Army was moving forces toward Turkey, Iraq, and Tehran. The Soviets had not replied to his March 5 note, but Byrnes dispatched a second note asking about Soviet troop maneuvers. The Soviet leaders continued their silence until March 15, when the Soviet news agency Tass absolutely denied the allegation that the troops were moving toward Tehran, Turkey, or Iraq.

Byrnes advised Iran to request another Security Council investigation that Tehran submitted on March 25. After Tass announced on April 3 that Soviet forces would leave Iran in six weeks, the Soviet Security Council delegate, Andrey Gromyko, argued that the Council should not consider Iran's problem, but the Council voted to keep the matter on the agenda. One week later, Iran and the Soviets agreed on an oil concession and the Soviet troop withdrawal in May. Under the oil agreement, the Soviets would receive a 51% share of an Iranian-Soviet Oil

Company, but Iran's parliament rejected the oil treaty and the Soviets received no oil concession. In terms of U.S. policy, Byrnes's relatively tough stance against the Soviets signaled that the Truman administration would no longer be conciliatory toward the Soviet Union.

## April 14, 1946

**Chinese civil war is renewed only three months (since January 10) after General Marshall thought a truce had been reached.**

The conflict arose in Manchuria because the Soviet troop withdrawal was timed to benefit a takeover by the Chinese Communists. Chiang Kai-shek objected to this procedure and fighting broke out between the Nationalists and Mao's forces. Marshall reestablished a truce from May 12 to June 30, but all-out civil war began again in July.

## April 20, 1946

**U.S.-Soviet discussions regarding a U.S. loan to the USSR conclude with no results.**

Stalin referred to a possible loan on January 23, 1946, in a discussion with U.S. Ambassador Averell Harriman. He alluded to the recent British loan and wondered if the United States would consider such a Soviet request.

After the Iranian crisis abated in April 1946, the United States agreed on discussions with the Soviets about a loan. The negotiations collapsed, however, because Stalin rejected the Americans' desire to link talks about the loan with agreements on trade with the Balkans and various peace treaties.

The U.S. refusal to negotiate a loan for the Soviets was one of many factors indicating less cooperative policies between the two governments after April 1945.

## May 3, 1946

**The head of the American military government in Germany, General Lucius D. Clay, announces that the Soviet Union can move no more reparations material out of the three western zones of Germany.**

Disagreement on Germany increased in 1946 after the Soviet Union refused Secretary of State Byrnes's offer to permit German reunification if it agreed to be demilitarized. In March, the Soviets changed their reparations policy in East Germany. Rather than continue to remove machinery to the USSR, the Communists decided to use East German labor and resources to produce goods for shipment to the Soviet Union. Coupled with Clay's announcement of May 3, Soviet-American decisions made it impossible to negotiate a treaty for a united Germany.

## May 25, 1946

*The Kingdom of Transjordan is proclaimed under King Emir Abdullah.*

Great Britain relinquished its protectorship and recognized the independence of Transjordan on May 25, 1946. The nation was renamed HASHEMITE KINGDOM OF JORDAN on June 2, 1949.

## June 2, 1946

*In a plebiscite, Italians vote for a republic, rejecting the restoration of a monarchy.*

## June 3, 1946

**Japanese war crime trials begin in Tokyo under American jurisdiction.**

The Potsdam Proclamation said "stern justice shall be meted out to all war criminals, including those who have visited cruelties upon our prisoners" (see July 26, 1945). Accordingly, when the war ended thousands of Japanese ranging from former Prime Minister Hideki Tojo to POW guards were tried for war crimes. An egregious exception for these war crime trials was the refusal of General MacArthur and others to indict and try Japan's Emperor Hirohito for war crimes. At the time, U.S. leaders believed the emperor had been an innocent bystander against "gangster militarists" such as Tojo. Hirohito's lack of innocence was disclosed in Herbert P. Bix's *Hirohito and the Making of Modern Japan* (2000).

In Tokyo's lengthy trials, from May 3, 1946, to November 12, 1948, an 11-judge International Military Tribunal chaired by Australia's Sir William Webb tried 28 high-ranking Japanese accused of crimes against humanity or crimes against peace referred to as "Class A crimes." In particular, the 28 men were held responsible for planning and carrying out Japan's war in the Far East from 1937 to 1945. During the Tokyo trials, the judges dropped 45 of the

55 counts of the indictments against the accused Japanese. When the trials ended in November 1948, a majority of the judges sentenced 7 of the accused to be executed, 16 to life in prison, 1 to 20 years in prison, and 1 to 7 years. Two Japanese died during the trial, while one was excused for mental incompetence. Nineteen other Japanese wartime leaders remained in Tokyo's Sugamo prison but were never tried, being released in December 1948 for alleged "lack of evidence." In part, their release was because by 1948, the United States and its allies preferred to make Japan an ally against the threat of expansion in Asia attempted by the Soviet Union and Chinese Communists. Although critics called the Tokyo trials "victors' justice" or "racism," Tim Maga's *Judgment at Tokyo* (2001) argues that "evil should never go unpunished" and both prosecutors and defense teams acted properly.

In addition to the Tokyo trials, the United States, Australia, Britain, France, the Netherlands, India, China, and the Soviet Union established 50 local tribunals. Of four U.S. tribunals the most controversial ended in the convictions of Japanese General Masaharu Homma and General Tomoyuki Yamashita. As described by William Manchester's *American Caesar* (1978), General MacArthur played a special role in their trials conducted by U.S. military officers answerable to MacArthur. The tribunal was in Manila, where Japanese troops had massacred thousands of Filipino men, women, and children in 1941–1942. In an atmosphere where revenge was sought, the court-martial judges accepted heresy evidence as proof of a crime and seldom permitted witnesses to be cross-examined. Under these circumstances, there was no surprise when Homma and Yamashita were found guilty and sentenced to death. Both generals appealed to the U.S. Supreme Court, but a majority ruled it had no jurisdiction to hear the Japanese appeal. In February and March, MacArthur reviewed each case but ordered their execution carried out in the spring of 1946. Although critics of the Manila trial called it a "kangaroo court," General MacArthur claimed Homma and Yamashita's failure to accord POWs, civilian internees, and noncombatants the protection they were entitled to was a "blot upon the military profession" and a "memory of shame and dishonor."

The seven other allied nations set up tribunals in various Far East and Pacific Island locations. Excepting the Soviet Union, these tribunals tried 5,700 individuals including 173 Taiwanese and 148 Koreans. During these trials 948 received death sentences, of which 50 were commuted after appeals; 1,018 were acquitted; 2,944 received prison sentences; and 279 were never brought to trial for various reasons. Regarding the Soviet Union, the Red Army held secret trials in Manchuria and Korea. It is estimated that 3,000 were summarily executed including 12 Japanese doctors from Manchuria's Unit 731 that conducted lethal medical experiments on prisoners of war. Details about these Japanese trials are in John Dower's *Embracing Defeat* (1999).

## June 14, 1946

### Bernard Baruch presents to the United Nations the American Plan (Baruch Plan) for the international control of atomic energy.

In accepting this plan, President Truman opted for a "hard-line" policy on international control. The United States would agree to disclosing its atomic program and disarmament *after* safeguard and inspection procedures had been adopted that would protect U.S. national security. Previously, the Dean Acheson–David Lilienthal plan would have permitted partial disclosure of information as a good faith gesture prior to acceptance by all nations (including the Soviet Union) of inspection agreements.

The key parts of the Baruch Plan are listed below:

1. Punishment—Penalties for violating the control agreements would be made in the UN Security Council by action that would allow NO VETO by one of the Big Five powers.
2. Scientific disclosures—These would initially be provided in published data only. If any nation desired some data, its request would be approved and filled only if national security was not impaired by its release.
3. Inspection—Mutual inspection of any nation's atomic facilities would be permitted and agreed to before detailed disclosure took place.

The Soviet UN delegate, Andrey Gromyko, wanted prior agreement on disclosure and disarmament, with inspection and controls to come later. His views diverged from Baruch's to such a degree that international control was not possible.

See December 31, 1946.

Bernard Baruch. National Archives

### July 1, 1946

**The United States tests atomic bombs near Bikini Atoll in the South Pacific.**

These July tests used an advanced Nagasaki-type implosion device. Their purpose was to demonstrate the bomb's use in naval warfare, an experiment advocated by the Navy Department.

Directed by Vice Admiral William H. Blandy, two tests resulted from the project code-named CROSSROADS. On July 1, bomb "Able" was dropped from an airplane and landed two miles from its target, a flotilla of 75 obsolete (mothballed) or captured enemy ships of World War II vintage. The results were unimpressive. The bomb exploded in shallow water, sinking few of the ships but making most of them radioactive. On July 25, the second bomb, "Baker," was suspended in 90 feet of water and exploded electrically. It caused spectacular damage in destroying the naval vessels and reinforcing the U.S. navy's desire to have a larger role in nuclear development.

### July 4, 1946

**The Philippine Islands are granted independence by the United States.**

The Philippines created a republic, having elected MANUEL A. ROXAS, head of the Liberal Party, as president on April 23. The U.S. congress also passed the REHABILITATION ACT and the BELL ACT to assist in the economic development of the islands. In return for this aid, a national referendum in the Philippines on March 11, 1947, passed a constitutional amendment to allow U.S. citizens to exploit the island's national resources on a basis of equality with the Filipinos.

One problem that arose in 1946 was a dispute between peasant farmers and landlords who had fled to urban areas during the war. In late 1945, the landlords returned to the villages and demanded that the peasants pay back rent for the three years of the Japanese occupation, enforcing their demands by using local police or mercenary soldiers. Many of the peasants had joined guerrilla forces as part of the resistance movement against the Japanese occupation. Having retained their weapons, many of the peasants decided to use them to resist the landlords and organize a National Peasant Union (PMK—Pambansang Kaisahan ng mga Magbubukid). They also joined a Democratic Alliance Party in cooperation with labor unions, an alliance that elected six members to the Philippine Parliament in 1946.

In the parliament, the majority party refused to seat the six Democratic Alliance members on charges they used terrorist methods during the election campaign. This legislative action incited PMK members to organize a rebellion and to change its name to the People's Liberation Army (Huk—Hukbong Mapagpalata ng Bayan). In 1950, the Philippine Communist Party (PKP) joined the Huks, calling themselves the military army of the revolutionary movement. Although most Huks knew nothing about communism but simply wanted to own their farmland, the Philippine government referred to all Huks as communists.

The conflict between the government and the Huks took place primarily in Central Luzon with the warfare peaking between 1949 and 1951 before subsiding. By the time President Elpidio Quirino adopted a reform program in 1951, emphasizing agricultural policy to conciliate the peasants, many peasants had abandoned the rebellion or had been

U.S. atomic test near Bikini
Atoll in the central Pacific.
National Archives

imprisoned by Philippine forces trained by the United States military. Some Huk and PKP organizations degenerated into individuals who committed murder or robbed banks, but the Huk rebellion ended by 1952.

### July 15, 1946

**Truman signs legislation granting Great Britain credits of $3.75 billion.**

After the cutoff of lend-lease aid in August 1945, the British government experienced increased difficulty in financing the rebuilding of its economy. At Truman's request, Congress approved credits to the British to assist them in purchasing American goods.

### August 1, 1946

**The McMahon Bill on atomic energy is signed into law by President Truman.**

Against McMahon's wishes, the committee's bill had transformed his desire for civilian control into a U.S. military veto on decisions by civilians on the Atomic Energy Commission (AEC). In addition, the bill emphasized restrictions on atomic energy information. The bill even restricted information that the United States could share with Britain and Canada

as it had done during World War II. Finally, the War Department retained control of two essential duties: responsibility for stockpiling uranium and thorium and for monitoring foreign progress on the atomic bomb.

The revised McMahon Bill gave the military a large measure of control over the AEC and fit the "hard-line" nature of the Baruch Plan for control of atomic energy.

### August 1, 1946

**The Fulbright Act to finance foreign study becomes law.**

By act of Congress, U.S. surplus property in foreign countries would be sold and the funds used in that nation to finance scholarships for research and academic exchanges of faculty members.

### August 15, 1946

**A dispute between the Soviet Union and Turkey prompts President Truman to approve a memo stating that the United States would resist any Soviet aggression against Turkey.**

The Soviet Union raised once again a long-held Russian desire to share control of the Straits of the Dardanelles and to establish a naval base in Turkey.

The Turkish government and the United States opposed both of these objectives.

In the Treaty of Unkiar-Iskelessi (1833), the czar succeeded in forcing the Turks to close the straits to non-Russian warships, thereby rendering the Black Sea a virtual *mare clausum*, a closed sea. This was highly unpopular with the Western powers, especially Britain, who were concerned with control of the Mediterranean Sea. The Treaty of Lausanne (1923) demilitarized the straits; however, it was the Montreux Convention (1936), which gave Turkey the right to fortify the straits and to monitor the passage of warships, that the Soviets wanted to modify. As tensions mounted, the British and Americans resisted the Soviet demand to have ready access to the Mediterranean; at the same time the British and Americans wanted the right to send their naval vessels into the Black Sea. This was yet another early Cold War dispute.

See March 12, 1947.

### September 1, 1946

**A Greek plebiscite votes 69% in favor of restoring the monarch, King George II.**

After British forces liberated Greece on October 13, 1944, a civil war broke out between leftist factions (including the EAM Communists) and the Royalist Popular Party. The British arranged a truce on January 11, 1945, with a regency government under Archbishop Damaskinos.

Political instability continued, however, and no leader appeared who could mediate between republicans, royalists, and left-wing parties. The civil war resumed in 1946, with the EAM gaining covert aid from Albania, Yugoslavia, and Bulgaria. The September election of George II took place during the guerrilla struggle, with the left-wing parties boycotting the election.

### September 20, 1946

**Wallace resigns after Truman objects to his critical Madison Square Garden speech.**

In a September 12 speech, Secretary of Commerce and former Vice President Henry A. Wallace sharply criticized the president's "hard-line" against the Soviets and called instead for cooperation with the former ally. This incident disclosed disagreement within Franklin Roosevelt's New Deal coalition about Truman's postwar policies. Harold Ickes and Henry Morgenthau Jr., two of Roosevelt's stalwarts, joined Wallace, who had been Roosevelt's vice president from 1941 to 1945, in opposition to Truman's unwillingness to emphasize international cooperation as the means to peace.

### October 1, 1946

**The Nuremberg War Crimes tribunal announces its decisions.**

The first trials of the International Military Tribunal at Nuremberg were held for the leading Nazi German war criminals between November 14, 1945, and September 30, 1946. During the trial, four judges and four alternates, with one of each from the United States, Britain, France, and the Soviet Union, heard the evidence from American prosecutors Robert Jackson and Telford Taylor. Only 21 major Nazi leaders were tried at Nuremberg because Gustav Krupp's trial was suspended due to his senility, while Adolf Hitler, Heinrich Himmler, Joseph Goebbels, and Robert Ley committed suicide. Of the 21 standing trial, three were acquitted and seven received prison sentences for ten years or more, including Rudolf Hess, who was sentenced for life and incarcerated in Berlin's Spandau prison. Ten defendants were sentenced to execution but Hermann Goering committed suicide while in prison awaiting execution.

In addition to these trials, war crime trials were held in each of the four zones of Germany by the United Nations War Crimes Commission (UNWCC) and by individual nations where such crimes were committed, including those by new governments of former enemy countries in Eastern and central Europe. Tribunals of the Western allies pronounced a total of 1,800 death sentences of which only 500 were carried out. In the Soviet zone, Moscow reported on January 1, 1947, that 14,240 suspects were tried for war crimes with 142 acquitted and 138 sentenced to death; critics said the Soviet data were unreliable. Details about the European trials are in Telford Taylor's *The Anatomy of the Nuremberg Trials* (1992) and in Arieh J. Kochavi's *Prelude to Nuremberg* (1998).

Regarding the trials of war criminals, evidence shows that Anglo-American military officials and intelligence agencies allowed some alleged war criminals to escape through secret "ratlines" to obtain information about the Soviet Union or to recruit spies and create anti-Communist "guerrilla" groups to destabilize Communist governments. Under the U.S. Freedom of Information Act, considerable data were declassified during the 1980s, much of which is described in Christopher Simpson's *Blowback* (1988); also see Stephen Dorril, *MI6: Inside the Covert World of Her Majesty's Secret Intelligence Service* (2000).

### October 10, 1946

**Ambassador George Marshall's mission to China is at an impasse after Chiang Kai-shek violates a promise and captures Kalgan.**

Marshall instructed Chiang not to continue his offensive by capturing Kalgan because the Chinese Communists had agreed to negotiations if the Nationalist army stopped its offensive. In addition, Marshall warned Chiang that the front lines of his armies had been overextended, giving the Communist armies a tactical advantage of supply and attack if the civil war continued. To strengthen his warning, Marshall told Chiang that the United States would cut its economic aid and withdraw the U.S. Marines stationed in China unless Chiang stopped outside Kalgan and accepted peace talks with Mao. Kalgan was the most important city in communist control south of the Great Wall of China. Therefore, Mao claimed the Nationalists' conquest of Kalgan would end the possibility of a peaceful solution to the conflict.

Since the renewal of fighting in June 1946, Marshall had continued efforts to secure negotiations between the Nationalist and Communist leaders. Meanwhile, Chiang's armies had been well supplied by the United States, and the U.S. navy had moved Nationalist troops to strategic places. As a result, the Nationalist offensive had great success between July and October.

Although he originally promised Marshall he would stop his offensive and not capture Kalgan, Chiang changed his mind early in October and announced an offensive against Kalgan. Consequently, Marshall believed his mission's attempt to end the civil war through mediation was no longer possible. He wrote to President Truman that his recall would be appropriate. Both Marshall and the U.S. ambassador to China, J. Leighton

Stuart, believed that Marshall could no longer be impartial between the two warring factions in China.

Despite Marshall's forebodings in October, he remained in China because other methods to achieve a truce seemed possible. Not until December 28 did President Truman and Marshall finally agree that the peace mission was doomed to failure. On January 3, Truman formally recalled Marshall to Washington.

### November 5, 1946

**The Republican Party gains control of both houses of Congress in national elections.**

This was the first national Republican Party victory since 1930. Although President Truman had previously sought bipartisan support for his international policies, the results of this election necessitated even closer cooperation between the president and the opposing party for the next two years.

### November 10, 1946

*France's Fourth Republic begins with elections for the National Assembly.*

After a referendum on May 5 rejected the first draft constitution, a second constituent assembly revised the document and the electorate adopted it on October 13. The new constitution closely resembled that of the Third Republic.

The Assembly election resulted in a deadlock between the Communists, with 186 seats, and the MOUVEMENT RÉPUBLICAIN POPULAIRE (MRP), with 166 delegates. Consequently, the Socialists, with 103 seats, formed a coalition cabinet under Leon Blum. As in the Third Republic, the coalition government in France found it difficult to formulate stable policy, and French political divisions continued to plague the nation.

### November 19, 1946

*Romanian elections confirm the government set up by the Soviet Union.*

After Soviet forces occupied Bucharest on August 31, 1944, they gave the Communist's National Democratic Front (NDF) control of the government. On January 7, 1946, the three-power commission established by the Foreign Ministers Council led the NDF to give several opposition party members cabinet posts.

Despite this change, the NDF restricted the publicity of opposition groups during the general election campaign and non-Communists experienced violent attacks and threats before the November election. Although the United States and Britain protested the lack of democratic elections in Romania, they could do nothing but object to such Communist tactics in Eastern Europe. On July 28, 1947, the NDF forced opposition members to resign from the cabinet and officially dissolved the largest opposition party, the National Peasants Party.

See December 12, 1946.

### November 23, 1946

*French forces bombard the port of Haiphong in Vietnam, an event leading to renewal of Vietnam's war of independence.*

The March 6, 1946, accords had led to further discussions between Ho Chi Minh and the French Colonial Office, but an agreement was never reached that would give a permanent basis for Vietnam as part of the FRENCH UNION.

The French attack on Haiphong resulted from disagreements between French customs officers and the Viet Minh commanders. On December 19, 1946, Vietnamese guerrillas attacked French troops in Hanoi and war began again. The French were determined to retain their position in Indochina.

### December 2, 1946

**The United States and Great Britain agree to provide an economic fusion of their German zones.**

This fusion, known as BIZONIA, hoped to strengthen West Germany's economy. The Anglo-American governments invited France and the Soviet Union to join them, but they refused.

As early as September 6, Secretary of State James Byrnes had announced in Stuttgart that the United States would follow a more lenient policy toward Germany and desired to unify the German economy.

### December 12, 1946

**Peace treaties are completed with the smaller Axis allies of World War II.**

Beginning in Paris on April 25, 1946, a series of conferences among foreign ministers of 21 nations that fought the Axis prepared drafts of these treaties. On December 12, at a meeting in New York City, the treaties were finalized for Italy, Romania, Hungary, Bulgaria, and Finland. The treaties were signed on February 10, 1947.

The U.S. role in obtaining a relatively lenient peace treaty for Italy is of interest. Discussions on the terms of the Italian treaty had begun during the Council of Foreign Ministers meeting in April 1946. By that time, Italy was treated by the United States and Britain as a friendly power more than a former enemy. Therefore, the Anglo-Americans persuaded the USSR to cut its reparations demands from $300 million to $100 million, which could be paid from Italian assets in the Balkans or Italian goods over a period of years. Together with the claims of small countries against Italy, the total Italian reparations payment was $360 million in the treaty of December 12.

On the Italian colonies and the Italy-Yugoslav border there was greater dispute. According to Foreign Minister Molotov, the Soviets held rights to Italian colonies in Africa because the Soviet navy needed bases in the area. The British and Americans opposed this claim and it was decided to leave the colonial issue until after a peace treaty was made.

On the border issue, the old problem of Trieste and Dalmatia appeared once again. In April, the Soviets agreed to accept less territory for Yugoslavia, but Marshal Tito objected and, during the December sessions in Paris, Molotov insisted on changes in the Italian border. Finally, the delegates agreed that the April 1946 territorial border favoring Italy would stand but Italy would pay another $35 million of reparations to Yugoslavia. The peace treaty with Italy was signed with only the colonial issue remaining to be settled.

See February 10, 1947.

### December 31, 1946

**The U.N. Security Council votes to accept the Baruch Plan for control of atomic energy.**

The U.N. Atomic Energy Committee had debated the Baruch proposal since July. A Soviet plan offered by Foreign Minister Andrey Gromyko had been rejected on July 24. Baruch believed that with effort the committee's approval could overcome Soviet efforts to delay his plan. Despite criticism from such opponents as Henry Wallace, Baruch refused to compromise on his plan's basic terms.

By mid-December, Truman, Secretary Byrnes, and Baruch decided to force a U.N. vote by the year's end. Thus, on December 31, Baruch called for a vote. Ten nations approved; the Soviet Union and Poland abstained.

In effect, the Baruch Plan left the United States insisting on a rigid, exclusive monopoly of atomic power—until the Soviets developed their own bomb. No effective international control of nuclear power was attained.

# 1947

### January 8, 1947

## George C. Marshall becomes Secretary of State.

Secretary Byrnes resigned from office because he was tired and in poor health; moreover, his relationship with Truman had deteriorated. The president had decided in January 1946 that he was going to assume more direction of U.S. foreign policy and that the old Truman-Byrnes partnership was going to change.

George C. Marshall, Secretary of State. National Archives

General Marshall had just returned from China, and the president had long desired to appoint him as secretary. Although he was a military man, Marshall's aura of integrity made him a readily acceptable choice. Marshall served as secretary until January 20, 1949.

### January 19, 1947

## *Elections in Poland are won by Socialist Premier Eduard Osobka-Morawski's party, which wins 394 seats to 28 seats for the Peasant Party.*

Deputy Premier Stanisław MIKOŁAJCZYK's Peasant Party suffered from repressive measures by the government. This election ended the provisional government that OSOBKA-MORAWSKI's former Lublin government dominated. Mikołajczyk, who had represented the London exile government, was soon subject to intense criticism. He fled to exile in London on October 24, 1947.

Both Great Britain and the United States charged that the January 19 elections violated the Yalta agreement for "free and honest" elections, but their protests were unavailing as the Communists, with Soviet backing, gained control of Poland's government.

### January 29, 1947

## The United States abandons mediation efforts in China.

In his final report on the Chinese mission, George Marshall said compromise failed because reactionaries in the Kuomintang of Chiang Kai-shek as well as extremists in the Communist Party of China did not want peace. U.S. aid continued to Chiang Kai-shek, reaching over $2 billion between August 1945 and December 31, 1947.

### February 10, 1947

## Peace treaties are signed in Paris with states associated with Germany in World War II.

Italy lost four border areas to France, its Adriatic islands and Venezia Giulia to Yugoslavia, and the Dodecanese Islands to Greece. Trieste became a Free Territory, although boundary disputes continued between Italy and Yugoslavia.

Italy and Austria also had persistent boundary disputes in the Tyrol. By a 1946 agreement between the two countries, the Italians regained South Tyrol as the autonomous province of Trentino-Alto-Adige (formerly Bolzano). Italy agreed to adopt both German and Italian as official languages in the region. Problems continued, however, between the German and Italian population.

In Eastern Europe, Romania lost Bessarabia and northern Bukovina to the USSR but regained Transylvania for its realm. Hungary regained its 1930 borders except for a few minor changes favoring Czechoslovakia. Bulgaria retained South Dobruja; Finland lost the port of Petsamo to the Soviet Union.

### March 10–April 24, 1947

**The Big Four foreign ministers continue to disagree on Germany.**

The Soviets wanted $10 billion in reparations, which conflicted with the British and American desire to make West Germany self-supporting.

The Council of Foreign Ministers met in London later in 1947 (November 25–December 15) to consider the German treaty but, again, could not resolve their differences.

### March 12, 1947

**The Truman Doctrine is initiated by the president in a speech to Congress.**

The immediate occasion for the doctrine was a request to Congress for $400 million in aid to GREECE and TURKEY. Both countries experienced either internal or external Communist threats, which the Truman administration evaluated as evidence of a Soviet plot to expand Soviet control wherever possible.

During the winter of 1946–1947, economic problems in Great Britain caused Prime Minister Attlee's government to decide that the expenses of British naval power in the Mediterranean and economic aid for the Greek government could no longer be met by London. During 1946, the U.S. navy had gradually enlarged its Mediterranean fleet by adding the battleship *Missouri* and the aircraft carrier *Franklin D. Roosevelt*.

In January 1947, the British government informed the White House that it had no choice but to withdraw from the Aegean-Mediterranean region and appealed to the United States to take over in its place. Truman, Marshall, and Dean Acheson, then Undersecretary of State, consulted with congressional leaders including Senator Arthur Vandenberg, the ranking Republican on the Foreign Relations Committee, and with bipartisan political support, the president proposed to seek congressional aid for Greece and Turkey.

Acting on suggestions by some advisers to "scare the hell out of the American people," Truman did the job in this speech. To justify economic and military aid to Greece and Turkey, the president envisioned a struggle between the "free world" and the tyrannical world of communism. Only America, he said, could defend the free world against "attempted subjugation by armed minorities or by outside pressure." Employing a version of an old ploy used to circumvent close scrutiny—the "domino theory"—first suggested by Undersecretary of State Acheson during a White House session with congressmen, Truman claimed that if Greece fell, Turkey would fall, and "confusion and disorder might well spread throughout the entire Middle East."

Truman's rhetoric won the support of Congress, and his doctrine became the guideline for U.S. subsequent global commitments. Although the doctrine was originally planned only for Europe and the Mediterranean, Truman's critics used the implications of his speech to charge him with failure to apply his beliefs in Asia and other parts of the world when Communists threatened.

On May 27, Truman signed the congressional bill providing economic and military aid to Greece and Turkey.

See August 15 and September 1, 1946.

### April 2, 1947

**The U.N. Security Council awards former Japanese islands in the Pacific to the United States under a trusteeship.**

The United States had occupied these islands during World War II, and President Truman had bluntly said the United States would retain them regardless of the U.N. action. These small but strategic islands were the Marianas, Marshalls, and Carolines.

### May 3, 1947

*Japan's new constitution goes into effect.*

The constitution, written largely by U.S. occupation personnel and sounding much like an American political statement, recognized the sovereignty of the people, making the emperor only a symbolic figure. It also protected individual rights and provided large measures of local self-government. The central government would consist of a two-house parliament (DIET) and a ministry whose term of office required majority approval of the Diet.

Article 9 was designed to prevent a renewal of Japanese militarism. It stated, in part:

> Aspiring sincerely to an international peace based on justice and order, the Japanese people forever renounce war as a sovereign right of the nation and the threat or use of force as means of settling international disputes. In order to accomplish the aim of the preceding . . ., land, sea, and air forces, as well as other war potential, will never be maintained.

In the April 1947 elections a right-wing majority gained control of the upper house of councillors, while the Social Democratic Party won the greatest plurality of seats in the House of Representatives. On May 23, the Socialist leader Tetsu KATAYAMA formed a coalition government approved by the Diet.

### May 5, 1947

#### The State Department policy-planning staff is established with George Kennan as director.

The planning group's purpose was to assure long-range policy planning, to provide a framework for planning, and to guide current policy decisions and operations. George Kennan was the logical candidate to head this post, having been the author on the "Long Telegram" in February 1946 that gave the rationale for a policy to contain Soviet expansion that began with the Truman Doctrine. Kennan had served the State Department as a Soviet expert since 1929 and headed the Soviet desk at the State Department in 1937. In 1944, he was the minister-counselor in Moscow and became acquainted with U.S. Ambassador Averell Harriman. In this position, he sent the "Long Telegram" to Washington describing the Soviet Union's desire to expand communism throughout the world by subverting local governments. Because of his detailed 800-page telegram regarding Soviet policy, the State Department brought Kennan to Washington in April 1947 to promote Soviet containment by assisting other nations in solving their economic problems, beginning with the

Truman Doctrine for Greece and Turkey and the Marshall Plan for Europe.

As Joseph M. Siracusa's *Into the Dark House* (1998) explains, Kennan's "Long Telegram" was inspired in part by his British counterpart, Frank Roberts, at Moscow. Both Roberts and Kennan believed the Soviets were hostile toward Western powers, and Anglo-American cooperation was the best way to contain Soviet expansion in Europe and elsewhere.

Kennan's ideas regarding U.S. policy became well known through his "Mr. X" article, "The Sources of Soviet Conduct," in the July 1947 issue of *Foreign Affairs*.

See March 12, 1947.

### June 5, 1947

#### Secretary of State Marshall proposes economic aid to enable European nations to rehabilitate their economies.

Two years after the German surrender, the nations of Western Europe continued to suffer from the destruction of their industry and the economic dislocation of war. Although the United States had provided refugee relief and some loans to Britain and France since 1945, the standard of living of these and other European nations had not recovered from the war. As a result, the local Communist and left-wing political parties were gaining parliamentary seats, especially in France and Italy.

At the time when Truman offered aid to Greece and Turkey in March 1947, a committee of the State-War-Navy Coordinating Committee prepared estimates of European needs and presented a report to Marshall and Undersecretary of State Dean Acheson in the middle of April. It was soon decided that Marshall should propose an aid program for Europe in a Harvard University commencement address on June 5.

Marshall told the Harvard audience that the United States would do whatever was necessary to assist in "the return of normal economic health . . . without which there could be no political stability." The United States wished to fight "hunger, poverty, desperation and chaos." He asked the Europeans to indicate their desire to cooperate with America. If they would draft a program of their needs, the United States would help them.

See June 27, 1947.

## June 25, 1947

### The Soviets veto a U.N. report that foreign neighbors are interfering in the Greek civil war.

Responding to a request of the Greek government, a U.N. Commission investigated the charges of foreign intervention in the Greek civil war. The Greek Communist rebels, the report said, received aid from Albania, Bulgaria, and Yugoslavia. In a vote on the report, the Security Council rejected the commission's action because of a Soviet veto. The official vote had been nine for and two against.

## June 27, 1947

### Foreign ministers of the three major European powers meet to consider Secretary Marshall's aid proposal.

Immediately after Marshall's Harvard University speech, British Foreign Minister Ernest BEVIN rushed to arrange a British-French-Soviet meeting in Paris and began talks with Georges BIDAULT of France. Although Bevin and Bidault hoped the Soviets would not attend, they did. Foreign Minister Molotov arrived in Paris on June 27, with 140 "technical advisers."

During the formal talks, Bevin and Bidault united in preventing Molotov from using delay tactics or seeking a "blank check" from America. Following a session on July 2, there was a clear break with the Soviets. Molotov would not budge from his views; Bevin and Bidault told him they would proceed without him.

On July 3, the British and French governments invited all European states to meet in Paris on July 12 to draw up a coordinated plan for the U.S. government to describe their economic needs. The Soviets still could have attended but did not. Because the United States told Moscow it would have to share information on its financial condition as did all other participants, Stalin refused to participate. If Stalin had joined, Truman and Marshall would have had greater problems in getting Congress to accept the Marshall Plan.

For the results of the Paris meeting, see September 22, 1947.

## July 26, 1947

### National Security Act creates a unified organization of the U.S. Armed Forces.

Although suggestions for a united organization of the nation's defense program had recurred since the 1920s, the serious study of such a plan did not begin until April 1944, when a House Select Committee on Postwar Military Policy held hearings on a War Department unification plan. Additional studies continued throughout 1945, with the War Department generally favoring consolidation of the armed forces and the Navy Department generally preferring closer interservice coordination. The army plan was prepared by General J. LAWTON COLLINS; the navy plan appeared in the EBERSTADT COMMITTEE REPORT of September 1945.

Eventually, on December 19, 1945, President Truman sent a message to Congress on military reorganization, indicating that he favored consolidation of the armed forces. As a result, throughout 1946 there was extensive debate and a number of congressional hearings on military organization. Truman's consolidation view prevailed, however, and the 1947 legislation reflected his ideas, as modified to secure the support of army, navy, and air force leaders.

The 1947 act established the army, navy, and air force as equal departments with civilian administrators, supervised by a single, civilian Secretary of Defense. The act also reorganized the various agencies and departments of government concerned with national security.

Three groups separated from the military were established by Title I of the 1947 act: the National Security Council, Central Intelligence Agency, and National Security Resources Board.

The National Security Council (NSC) would coordinate the foreign and military policies of the nation and advise the president on integrating those policies. Its members were the president; the secretaries of defense, state, army, navy, and air force; the chairman of the Resources Board; and other government officers the president might designate.

The Central Intelligence Agency (CIA) was under the NSC. It would coordinate the intelligence-gathering activity of all government departments, evaluate the data obtained, and report its findings to officials with a "need to know."

The National Security Resources Board (NSRB) would coordinate all military, civilian, and industrial capacities of the nation needed for an emergency mobilization. Chaired by a civilian, the board drew its members from government departments and agencies designated by the president.

Title II of the 1947 act established the National Military Establishment (NME), led by a civilian Secretary of Defense with cabinet status. The NME, which on August 10, 1949, was renamed Department of Defense, consisted of the Departments of the Army, Navy, and Air Force; the Joint Chiefs of Staff; the War Council; the Munitions Board; and the Research and Development Board.

The secretary of defense had authority over all parts of the NME. He was directed to eliminate unnecessary duplication or overlapping in defense procurement, supply, transport, health, research, and storage; and to coordinate the budget preparation of parts of the NME.

Within the NME (Defense Department) the Joint Chiefs held a prominent role. They formulated strategy, issued military directives, and recommended defense policy to the NSC and president. James Forrestal became the secretary of defense on September 17, 1947.

## August 15, 1947

### *India and Pakistan gain independence from Great Britain.*

After Britain decided to give India self-government, religious differences in the subcontinent had to be resolved. This was accomplished in 1947 by partitioning the country between Hindus and Muslims. As a result, the British Parliament approved an Indian Independence Bill on July 5, 1947. The legislation left India in a large middle section of the subcontinent, separating by some 1,000 miles the East and West parts of Pakistan.

On August 15, the Dominion of Pakistan established a government under Prime Minister Liaqat Ali Khan and Governor-General Mohammed Ali Jinnah. India was led by Prime Minister Motilal Nehru and Governor-General Lord Mountbatten. In 1948, the men who led the independence movement both died: Mohandas Gandhi being assassinated on January 30 and Jinnah dying of natural causes on September 11.

## September 2, 1947

### Western hemispheric nations sign an inter-American Mutual Assistance Treaty.

Known as the Rio Pact, the Mutual Assistance Treaty was designed to counteract any aggressor's attack in a defense zone extending from Greenland to Argentina. The treaty became the forerunner of the Organization of American States.

The Rio Pact appeared to anticipate Chile's problems with Communists. On October 21, 1947, Chile broke diplomatic relations with the Soviet Union following the arrest of 200 Communists who had led a series of labor strikes in Chile.

See May 2, 1948.

## September 19, 1947

### General Albert Wedemeyer reports to Truman on his visit to China.

The president sent Wedemeyer to China on July 9 to conduct a fact-finding mission on events since Marshall's mission ended in December 1946. In particular, Truman wanted to know if Chiang Kai-shek had instituted any of the reforms Marshall recommended. Since 1946, the U.S. Marines had evacuated China and a limited arms embargo was used to pressure Chiang to change. Nevertheless, the marines left 6,000 tons of ammunition for Chiang as they departed.

Truman wanted data because the China lobby and Chiang's friends in Congress had become vocal critics of Truman's China policy. They demanded that the Nationalist Chinese be given whatever Chiang wanted.

Wedemeyer's visit ended on August 24, and he took several weeks to write his analysis. Much like Marshall, Wedemeyer believed both sides in the civil war shared blame for the disunity. Nevertheless, he recommended that the United States provide greater military aid if Chiang agreed to "sweeping changes" in his administration and army.

Truman and Marshall disliked Wedemeyer's emphasis on greater aid because Chiang had had 20 years to reform the government and vitalize the army, and had continually failed to do so. Because of their dissatisfaction, Truman sought to keep Wedemeyer's report secret. In doing so, however, he caused greater suspicion among his critics and the general public. Only after the China lobby had successfully depicted

Chiang as a loyal warrior whose aid was unceremoniously cut by Truman did the administration, in August 1949, issue a full explanation of all reports on China.

We cannot know whether providing better information at an early date would have avoided the increasingly bitter and partisan criticism regarding the China problem, which greatly influenced U.S. policy after 1949.

### September 22, 1947

#### Sixteen European nations report to the United States on their needs under the Marshall Plan.

The delegates who convened at Paris on July 12 set up an interim Committee of European Economic Cooperation (CEEC) to prepare a report for the United States. The CEEC estimated that the 16 European nations would need between $16.4 and $22.4 billion over the next four years. Truman presented his request to Congress for funding the CEEC program on December 17, 1947.

### October 5, 1947

#### The Communist Information Bureau (COMINFORM) is created in a conference at Warsaw.

While officially designed to coordinate the activities of Europe's Communist parties, Western observers believed COMINFORM replaced the Comintern as the mechanism for Kremlin control of all local Communist organizations.

### October 30, 1947

#### The General Agreement on Tariffs and Trade (GATT) is signed.

Following six months of negotiations in Geneva, 23 nations approved an effort to lower trade barriers. The GATT had three essential features: a multilateral schedule of tariff concessions; a code of principles governing imports and exports; and periodic meetings that provided an international forum for discussing trade problems. Tariffs were first negotiated on a bilateral basis before there were multinational discussions to form a schedule of tariff concessions.

The commerce of these 23 nations comprised three-fourths of the world's trade. The countries were Australia, Belgium, Brazil, Netherlands, Luxembourg, Canada, Chile, Republic of China, Cuba, Czechoslovakia, France, India, Pakistan, Ceylon, Burma, Lebanon, Syria, New Zealand, Norway, South Africa, United Kingdom, Southern Rhodesia, and United States.

The 1947 Geneva Conference resulted in significant lowering of tariff barriers among the participating nations. About 54% of U.S. dutiable imports were affected by the Geneva reductions. The average of reductions was 18.9%, a sum that was calculated on the lower levels that the United States had previously negotiated in bilateral agreements under the Reciprocity Act of 1934.

### November 14, 1947

#### The U.N. General Assembly votes to recognize Korea's independence.

In September 1945, the United States and the Soviet Union agreed to divide their occupation forces in Korea at the 38th parallel. Later, at the December 1945 Moscow Conference, delegates of the Soviet Union and the United States agreed to form a provisional government for Korea, but this agreement was never enforced. Thus, in September, the United States had referred the issue of the future status of Korea to the United Nations because it could not agree with the Soviet Union on the establishment of a provisional government for all Korea. A U.N. study recommended plans for the withdrawal of both U.S. and Soviet forces and the creation of a Korean government, a proposal approved on November 14, 1947.

### November 29, 1947

#### The U.N. General Assembly approves a partition plan to divide Palestine between Arabs and Jews.

During World War II (May 1942), the Conference of American Zionists had rejected the British plan of 1939 to give Palestine independence under joint administration. In August 1945, President Truman asked Britain to allow at least 100,000 displaced Jews into Palestine after the World Zionist Congress demanded that 1 million Jews be admitted. Although an Anglo-American committee advised on August 29, 1946, against the partition of Palestine, Zionists rejected any state without full Jewish autonomy.

By early 1947, the British announced they would withdraw from Palestine as they had from Greece. On April 2, the British referred the Palestinian problem to the United Nations. A U.N. commission studied the issue and on November 29 recommended that Palestine be divided into Arab and Jewish states. Jerusalem would be under a U.N. Trusteeship. The Jews accepted the U.N. plan but the Arab League rejected it.

On December 17, the Council of the Arab League announced it would use force to stop partition and began raids on Jewish communities in Palestine. A Jewish terrorist group, Irgun ('Stern Gang'), retaliated by guerrilla attacks on Arabs.

### December 17, 1947

**Congress passes the Foreign Aid Act of 1947.**

This act provided $540 million of interim relief to France, Italy, Austria, and China. The legislation was designed to carry the European nations through the winter, pending final enactment of Marshall Plan aid in 1948.

China was added to the list of those receiving aid because of the pro-China views of such leading Republicans as Senators Vandenberg and Styles Bridges. While Marshall, the Joint Chiefs of Staff, and Truman believed aid to China was a poor risk expense, the China lobby vociferously complained that Chiang Kai-shek should be aided as well as Europe.

President Truman also requested funds for the European Recovery Program (Marshall Plan). On March 31, 1948, Congress authorized $5.3 billion for this program. Truman appointed Paul G. Hoffman as chief of the European Cooperation Administration on April 6.

### December 17, 1947

**The Truman administration plans to control exports to Communist states: NSC-17.**

The National Security Council prepared a report titled "Control of Exports to the USSR and Eastern Europe" that described one means of conducting the Cold War by economic action. NSC-17 recommended limited shipment of all goods that were "critically short" in America or would "contribute to Soviet military potential." This policy was based on a recommenda-

tion of the Commerce Department, approved by the State Department.

To operate as quietly as possible and avoid breaking existing commercial treaties with Eastern European nations, Secretary of Commerce Averell Harriman suggested an "R" export-control procedure. The "R" procedure named all Europe as a "recovery area." To assist economic recovery, America would issue export licenses for commodities to Europe, granting a license to an area found to have the "greatest need."

This "R" policy, but not its purpose, was announced by the Commerce Department in a press release of January 15, 1948. As described publicly, goods were not embargoed to any nation; they were simply sent where they were most needed. The Department of Commerce, of course, would decide what nation had the "greatest need."

# 1948

### January 21, 1948

**The State Department publishes captured German documents on the 1939 Nazi-Soviet pact.**

These documents on the temporary alliance of Hitler's Germany with Stalin's USSR seemed to reinforce the growing U.S. belief that German Nazi totalitarianism and Soviet Communist totalitarianism were synonymous. Although Secretary of State Marshall denied it, some American reporters believed the publication of these documents in 1948 supported the U.S. desire to implicate Stalin in using the same tactics that Hitler employed in seeking world domination. Because the documents showed only the Berlin events and Soviet dispatches to Germany, the impression grew that Stalin sought the alliance with Germany in 1939 because Germany and the USSR shared political goals. Therefore, Americans such as President Truman could assert that there was no difference between the totalitarianism of Nazi Germany and the Communist Soviet Union.

Although this analysis had some validity in terms of the Soviet Union's methods of deceit and ruthlessness during the purges of the 1930s, it blurred the ideological distinctions between communism and fascism. Marxian theory adhered to humanistic goals that the Soviet Union failed to implement; the Nazis' antihumanistic and destructive ideology had been vigorously carried out by Hitler by aggression and an attempt to exterminate the Jewish and other peoples. In addition, this analysis considered Soviet armies in Eastern Europe as aggressors, whereas, in fact, they had liberated Eastern European nations from Nazi conquest, just as the Anglo-American offensive had liberated Western Europe.

### January 27, 1948

**Truman signs legislation finalizing the U.S. Information and Education Exchange Act of 1948.**

Under the law, America would prepare and distribute information to promote understanding between the people of the United States and other peoples of the world.

### February 2, 1948

**The United States and Italy sign a Treaty of Friendship, Commerce, and Navigation.**

### February 4, 1948

*Ceylon (present-day Sri Lanka) becomes a self-governing dominion in the British Commonwealth.*

Foreign Minister Jan Masaryk in happier times. National Archives

### February 25, 1948

*A Communist coup is carried out in Czechoslovakia.*

In the 1946 elections for a constituent assembly, the Communists won 114 of 300 seats, gaining a plurality that permitted the Communist Klement Gottwald to form a coalition government. Next, Gottwald threatened a coup unless President Edvard Beneš agreed to a predominantly Communist ministry. The Communists then proceeded to purge the country of anti-Communist groups; one instance of this plan included the mysterious death of Foreign Minister Jan MASARYK, who reportedly committed suicide by falling from his office window. New elections on May 30 had only a single list of Communist candidates, which assured that party's victory.

On June 7, President Beneš resigned and Gottwald became president of the Communist government.

### March 4, 1948

*Argentina and Chile agree to defend jointly their rights in Antarctica and the Falkland (Malvinas) Islands against the British.*

### March 17, 1948

*The Brussels Treaty is signed as a step toward European cooperation.*

The 50-year defensive alliance was approved by delegates of Great Britain, France, Belgium, the Netherlands, and Luxembourg. They also pledged cooperation in economic, social, and military affairs.

The Brussels Treaty broadened a previous French-British defensive alliance against Germany into a pact to coordinate military policies of the five nations against any power that might attack one of them. It was clearly directed against the Soviet Union and ended the traditional neutrality policy of the Benelux nations. It also indicated that both Great Britain under the Labour Party government and France, whose centrist parties had placated the French Communists previously, had become alarmed at Stalin's policies in Europe. France and Britain therefore began a united Western European action to indicate their willingness to confront the Soviet Union if necessary.

### March 20, 1948

**The Soviet delegate walks out of the Allied Control Council, charging that the three Western powers seek to undermine the four-power control of Berlin.**

Early in 1948, previous rifts between the Soviet delegate to the Four-Power Control Council for Germany, Vasily D. Sokolovsky, and the three Western delegates escalated because Sokolovsky vigorously denounced the Allied moves to unify their three zones of West Germany. The Soviet Union hoped to use its veto power in the Control Council to block the Allies' actions, but the three Allied nations were determined not to be deadlocked by the Soviets.

Subsequently, the conflicts at the Four-Power Control Council meetings became what historian Herbert Feis called "brawls." The Western delegates, led by General Lucius Clay of the United States, strongly argued with Sokolovsky and protested Soviet actions in East Germany that violated the Control Council decisions.

Finally, on March 20, the Four-Power Council's sessions broke up and were never again conducted. The final split took place when the Soviets asked the council to consider an attack by Poland and Yugoslavia against Western policy in West Germany. Clay refused, saying those complaints contained false and distorted information. Sokolovsky read a long statement to repeat all of the USSR's charges against the Western powers in Germany. Then the Soviet, who was the March council chairman, adjourned the meeting and left. No new meeting date was set and General Clay decided not to ask the Soviets for another session.

See June 24, 1948.

### March 28, 1948

**The charter of the International Trade Organization (ITO) is finalized at the Havana World Conference on Trade and Employment.**

Sixty nations participated in this conference sponsored by the United Nations, convened on November 21, 1947. The ITO developed from a suggestion made by the United States in December 1945. Its purpose was to create an organization for consultation on trade issues and to formulate a fair practices code for international commerce.

### April 6, 1948

*Finland and the Soviet Union sign a military assistance agreement.*

Earlier in 1948 (February and March), the Soviets also signed treaties of friendship and military assistance with Romania, Hungary, and Bulgaria.

### April 16, 1948

**Sixteen European nations form the Organization for European Economic Cooperation (OEEC).**

This agreement provided for the non-Communist European nations to work together in using U.S. aid under the European Recovery Program (the Marshall Plan).

### May 2, 1948

**The Organization of American States (OAS) is established at Bogotá, Colombia.**

Following up on the Rio Pact of August 1947, the Ninth International Conference of American Republics formed the OAS as an anti-Communist pact for the Western Hemisphere. During the conference deliberations at Bogotá, the meetings had to be suspended for several days because of a local Communist-led revolt that severely damaged the city and took hundreds of lives.

The OAS formed a hemispheric defense council and established a process by which sessions of the defense council would be called in case of aggression against any member nation. It also adopted an anti-Communist resolution at Bogotá.

Not all was harmonious in the Western Hemisphere, however. Many of the Latin American delegates wanted the United States to provide a "little Marshall Plan" to solve their economic problems. President Truman disappointed them by offering only half a billion dollars of Export-Import Bank funds.

### May 7, 1948

***The Congress of Europe meets at the Hague to discuss plans for establishing a European union.***

The honorary chairman was Winston Churchill. This meeting brought to life the dreams of European statesmen, such as the Frenchman Jean MONNET, who sought to create a political plan for the gradual unification of Europe.

### May 14, 1948

***The state of Israel is proclaimed under a provisional government headed by David Ben-Gurion.***

After the British mandate ended and British troops withdrew, the U.N. partition plan went into effect; however, fighting between Arabs and Jews broke out almost immediately. Both the United States and the Soviet Union recognized Israel by May 16, 1948.

### June 1, 1948

**Six-Power agreement defines West Germany's status.**

By 1948, the Western Allies believed Germany would be divided for the foreseeable future and decided the Western section's status should be determined. Following extensive discussions, the United States, Britain, France, Belgium, Luxembourg, and the Netherlands signed a Six-Power agreement. The agreement's main points were that (1) the Ruhr would be under international control; (2) West Germany could join the European Recovery Program; (3) the three Western zones of Germany would be integrated; (4) a constitution would be drafted for a Federal Republic of West Germany.

### June 11, 1948

**The Vandenberg Resolution is approved by the U.S. Senate.**

Sponsored by Republican Senator Arthur H. VANDENBERG, this resolution affirmed U.S. support for regional security pacts such as the Brussels Pact. This resolution was meant to support the State Department's efforts to negotiate U.S. membership in a European defense pact.

Senate approval of the Vandenberg Resolution marked a significant point in the final shifting of U.S. foreign policy from isolationism to international responsibility. As Herbert Feis remarked, Hitler did not change the Republican Party's isolationism; Stalin did. Beginning on April 11, Senator Vandenberg worked with Undersecretary of State Robert Lovett in drafting a resolution that would commit America to the collective defense of Western Europe against any acts of aggression.

On May 19, Vandenberg introduced his resolution as recommended by the Senate Foreign Relations Committee. As approved by the Senate on June 11, the resolution gave Senate favor to any "regional and other collective security arrangements for individual and collective self-defense." The Senate approved the resolution by a vote of 64 to 4.

See April 4, 1949.

### June 24, 1948

**The Soviets begin the Berlin Blockade. The United States launches an airlift.**

Dismayed by the success of the French, British, and Americans in uniting their zones of Germany, the Soviets retaliated by shutting down all land, rail, and water traffic through their zone to Berlin. Apparently they hoped the Western Allies would abandon Berlin and permit it to become the capital city to rally Germans to communism.

After the Soviets sidetracked two trains sent from West Germany to test the blockade, President Truman determined, with British support, to stay in West Berlin and use an airlift to supply the 2.5 million Berliners in their respective zones. The Western Allies also hurt the Soviet–East German economy by a counterblockade of their zone.

The airlift, code-named Operation Vittles, continued to supply West Berlin for over a year. Up to 4,500

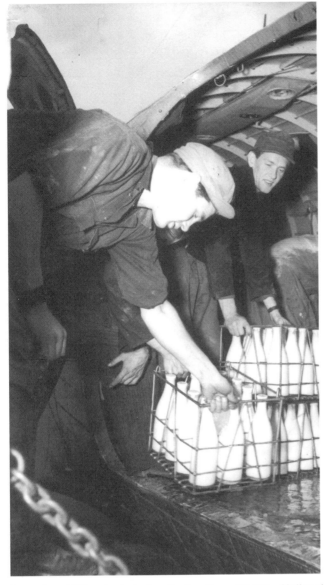

Operation Vittles included milk for the children. National Archives

tons of supplies, including coal, were flown in each day. Although at times these planes encountered Soviet fighter planes, no incident took place. The Soviets did not want a war and finally agreed in 1949 to end the blockade.

Truman's challenge to Moscow gave the United States and its allies much support in Europe, and the blockade backfired against the Soviets. The incident also seemed to demonstrate the validity of the president's "get tough" policy toward communism.

See May 11, 1949.

### June 28, 1948

**Truman orders 60 B-29 bombers sent to British bases and a smaller number to German bases.**

Although this action had been under consideration for some time, the Berlin blockade underscored the need for U.S. bombers at advance European bases as part of the Forward Strategy of defending Europe.

Some news sources implied that these bombers were "atomic-capable," but, in fact, the B-29s sent to Europe had not been modified to carry the atomic bombs available at the time.

### June 28, 1948

***Stalin expels Yugoslavia from the COMINFORM for ideological errors and hostility to the Soviet Union.***

Marshal TITO (Josip BROZ), the wartime resistance leader who was elected to rule Yugoslavia on November 11, 1945, rejected the charges and separated his nation from Soviet control.

During the next 12 months, efforts to heal the breach between Moscow and Belgrade failed.

See September 27, 1949.

### July 30, 1948

**Whittaker Chambers and Elizabeth Bentley tell the House Un-American Activities Committee (HUAC) that Communists infiltrated the State Department in the 1930s.**

Chambers and Bentley were self-confessed former Communist Party members whose testimony became the highlight of the HUAC hearings in the late 1940s. Bentley, called the Red Queen by the press, informed the FBI of some 14 Americans who had spied or were spying for the Soviets, including Assistant Secretary of the Treasury Harry Dexter White, OSS Executive Assistant Duncan C. Lee, and Roosevelt's former aide Lauchlin Currie.

Chambers soon identified Alger Hiss, who had worked in several executive departments after 1933, including the State Department in 1944, as a Communist Party agent. Hiss denied Chambers's testimony, and the long-lived Hiss-Chambers Affair began, an affair that would, among other things, propel Richard Nixon into the national limelight when Nixon backed Chambers.

### August 18, 1948

**A Soviet-dominated conference on navigation of the Danube river ends the Danube Convention as signed by seven Communist nations.**

The Conference on the Danube opened on July 30, 1948, at Belgrade, after Moscow's refusal to delay the sessions until December. The three Western powers reluctantly attended, arguing Austria could have no official role because the Austrian peace treaty was pending. The seven Communist states represented were the USSR, Bulgaria, Czechoslovakia, Hungary, Romania, Yugoslavia, and the Ukraine.

Rather than negotiate a new treaty to supersede the Convention of 1921, the Soviets insisted, and their allies agreed, on using the Soviet draft treaty as the basis for debate and voting. The three Western powers claimed the Soviet draft violated the free navigation of the river by giving the Soviets a "monopoly control" of the Danube. The Western powers offered amendments to the draft but were consistently outvoted by 7 to 3.

The agreement signed on August 18 was essentially a Soviet convention. It passed 7 to 1, with the United States voting no. France and Britain believed that abstaining was the best method for objecting to the "railroading" tactics used by the USSR's Andrey Vishinsky. At the final session, the French delegation spoke harshly of the convention, which "one power issued and a docile majority" accepted.

Following the sessions, France, Great Britain, and the United States issued statements that rejected the document as "Soviet imperialism," and claimed that the nonriparian nations that used the Danube but were not invited to the meeting retained the rights of the 1921 Convention. Austria's delegate stated he could not accept the convention because Austria had not had a vote at the conference.

### October 29, 1948

*In a military coup in Peru, General Manuel Odría overthrows President José Luis Bustamente's government.*

The new government outlawed both Peru's Communist Party and the peasant-worker–supported APRA party.

### November 2, 1948

**Harry S. Truman is reelected president, winning a surprise victory over Thomas E. Dewey.**

Truman received 303 electoral votes to Dewey's 189. The Democrats also gained control of both houses of Congress.

The election campaign included a bitter foreign policy struggle between the Democrats and Henry Wallace's Progressive Party. Wallace blamed Truman for the Cold War against the USSR because he stopped Roosevelt's cooperative policies with the Soviet Union.

Yet despite the defection of Wallace and left-wing New Dealers as well as the right-wing DIXIECRATS, whose candidate was Strom Thurmond, Truman and the Democratic Party center defeated Dewey, Wallace, and Thurmond.

### November 12, 1948

**The Japanese War Crime trials end.**

The Military Tribunal sentenced General Hideki Tojo and 6 other Japanese leaders to death for major war

Henry A. Wallace, one of Truman's challengers. National Archives

crimes; 16 others received sentences of life imprisonment.

## November 20, 1948

### The U.S. Consul General and staff at Mukden, China, are confined to the consulate by the Chinese Communists, beginning a year of "hostage"-style confinement.

Mukden, Manchuria, became the first urban center with foreign diplomatic representation to be captured by Mao Tse-tung's Communist armies. The Communists gained control of the city on October 31 and initially seemed willing to discuss trade agreements with the American, English, and French consuls in Mukden.

On November 14, a problem arose because the three foreign consuls were requested to turn their radio transmitters over to the government within 48 hours. The French and British had no independent transmitters and the U.S. consul, Angus J. WARD, refused to do so until he could receive permission from Washington. He offered, however, to stop transmitting radio messages.

Ward's offer was rejected by the Communists without further consultation. On November 20, Communist soldiers cordoned off the office and residence compounds of the U.S. consulate. The Chinese officials informed Ward that no one could leave the compound or communicate with the outside. The troops cut the consulate's telephone and electrical lines and shut off the water supply. Ward's radio transmitters and generators were also seized. During the next 30 hours, the guards gave the 22 persons only one bucket of water and no food. Although the consulate's electricity was restored in December, Ward did not get to communicate with the outside world until June 7, 1949. The plight of the 22 "hostages" continued for more than a year, causing President Truman to consider military measures to free the "prisoners."

See November 24, 1949.

## December 9–10, 1948

### The U.N. General Assembly adopts a human rights declaration and a genocide convention.

The Universal Declaration of Human Rights was approved at a U.N. General Assembly meeting in Paris. A U.N. commission headed by Eleanor Roosevelt, wife of President Franklin D. Roosevelt, prepared the declaration. The December 10 declaration was a nonbinding statement of principles that would be supplemented by an International Covenant on Human Rights to be drafted by Mrs. Roosevelt's commission. Because the commission members disagreed about its contents, it adjourned in 1953 without an agreement. A second human rights committee was formed and in 1966 presented a covenant divided into two parts; one, an International Covenant of Civil and Political Rights, the other a Covenant on Economic, Social, and Cultural Rights. Although Mrs. Roosevelt traveled the world until her death to promote peace and human rights, as of 2000 the U.S. Senate had ratified only the Covenant on Civil and Political Rights. Conservative congressional leaders claim the Covenant on Economic, Social, and Cultural rights conflicts with the U.S. Constitution.

The Convention on the Prevention and Punishment of Genocide approved by the General Assembly was an international response to the Holocaust committed by the Germans during World War II. Although President Truman sought ratification of the Genocide Convention, the U.S. Senate delayed ratification using constitutional arguments, although a majority of the Senate wanted to protect racial and segregation laws and avoid the scrutiny of U.N. officials. The 1940s were an era in the United States when African Americans often were not allowed to vote and when lynchings were not uncommon in some Southern states. Consequently, the Senate did not ratify the Genocide Convention until 1986, after adding several reservations such as giving the U.S. Constitution precedence over the International Court of Justice. On October 10, 1988, Congress finally passed legislation making genocide a crime and levied fines and imprisonment for anyone convicted of such crimes.

For details on human rights, see Natalie H. Kaufman's *Human Rights Treaties and the Senate: A History of Opposition* (1990) and the excellent philosophical analysis of human rights by eminent scholars from around the world in United Nations Educational, Scientific and Cultural Organization's (UNESCO) volume *Human Rights* (1949). On the Genocide Convention, see Lawrence Leblanc's *The United States and the Genocide Convention* (1991).

# 1949

## January 20, 1949

### President Truman's second inaugural address proposes the Point Four program.

The Point Four program was intended to aid economically underdeveloped areas. Although Point Four received much publicity, the Truman administration did not give it much attention. Congress finally authorized funds for Point Four in May 1950, but appropriations were meager—far below the formulas used in the Marshall Plan.

During Truman's address to Congress, his other three points were encouraging European recovery, fully supporting the United Nations, and pledging aid to those nations defending themselves against Communism. These three points were not new; Point Four was injected into Truman's speech for dramatic effect.

## January 21, 1949

### Dean Acheson replaces George Marshall as Secretary of State.

Acheson had been undersecretary of state from 1945 to 1947, resigning in the spring of 1947 to return to private legal practice. Nevertheless, when Marshall's health required him to resign in December 1948, Truman immediately asked Acheson to become secretary, and the appointment was announced on January 7, 1949.

False charges were raised in the Senate confirmation hearings regarding Acheson's conduct. The unproven allegations came from former U.S. Ambassador to Poland Arthur Lane Bliss and a former State Department associate, Adolf Berle. Bliss charged in his book *I Saw Poland Betrayed* (1948) that Acheson appeased the Soviet Union by giving loans and credits to the Polish government from 1945 to 1947. Berle had told the House Un-American Affairs Committee in August 1948 that Alger Hiss was one of the "Acheson-group" in the State Department that had a "pro-Russian point of view." This latter charge was disproven by Acheson during the Senate hearings in January 1949. It was not Alger Hiss but his brother, Donald, who had worked with Acheson. This testimony did not, however, receive the widespread attention that Berle's charges had in 1948. Later these same

false accusations about Acheson were rehashed by Senator Joseph McCarthy.

Acheson's nomination as secretary was endorsed by a wide variety of people who knew and had worked with him, including Herbert Hoover and John Foster Dulles. Senator Vandenberg, the leading Republican on the Senate Foreign Relations Committee, also supported Acheson, knowing that far from being "soft" on communism, Acheson had strongly urged measures to combat the Soviet Union between 1945 and 1947.

## April 4, 1949

### The North Atlantic Treaty Organization (NATO) is chartered by 12 nations, including the United States.

NATO evolved from the 1948 Brussels Treaty, in which Britain, France, Belgium, the Netherlands, and Luxembourg pledged economic and military cooperation (see March 17, 1948). NATO's charter members included the five members of the Brussels pact plus the United States, Canada, Italy, Portugal, Denmark, Iceland, and Norway.

The ratification of the North Atlantic Treaty by the U.S. Senate on July 21, 1949 (a vote of 82 to 13) committed the United States to a peacetime political-military alliance with Europe for the first time since the abrogation of the French Alliance in 1800.

The treaty signatories agreed to consult together if anyone's security were threatened. Article 5 was a key clause, because it stated: "an armed attack against one or more of them ... shall be considered an attack against them all." Thus, they would join together with whatever action was necessary, "including the use of armed force," to restore the security of the North Atlantic area.

The clause "such action as it deems necessary" limited the pledges of each nation and made the alliance uncertain. The United States believed that the clause was essential because the U.S. constitution required congressional approval to go to war. But other signatories could also use this clause to limit their military commitment.

The NATO charter was more than a military alliance because it permitted continuous cooperation in political, economic, and other nonmilitary fields. Cooperation among the NATO allies was through the treaty organization. Each member sent delegates to the NATO Council, which could "meet promptly at any time." The Council appointed a secretary-general and various committees to assist in its work. Committees included such groups as Defense Planning Committee, Nuclear Defense Affairs Committee, Economic Affairs Committee, and others. A Military Committee had special responsibilities for guidance and recommendations on military matters.

All members ratified the NATO charter, which became effective on August 24, 1949. On September 28, the U.S. Congress approved the Mutual Defense Assistance Program, providing military aid to NATO.

### May 8, 1949

#### *The Federal Republic of Germany (FRG) is formed at Bonn.*

The Germans adopted the Basic Laws of the Federal Republic in meetings at Bonn. On August 14, 1949, elections to the Bundestag (parliament) resulted in a victory for Konrad ADENAUER's Christian Democratic Party, which won a plurality of 31% of the vote, compared with the Social Democrats' 29.2%. Theodore HEUSS became president of the republic and Adenauer became Chancellor.

### May 11, 1949

#### The Berlin blockade ends with a four-power accord on the city.

As early as January 30, 1949, Stalin told an American journalist, Kingsbury Smith, that he would be willing to end the blockade. Yet serious discussions on an agreement to end the crisis did not begin until April. Moscow realized the blockade had not been successful—it had drawn the Western powers closer together rather than dividing them. Finally, Western countermeasures had inflicted considerable damage on the economic life of East Germany and the other Soviet satellites of Eastern Europe.

On May 5, the four powers announced in Berlin that accords had been achieved to end the Soviet blockade as well as the Western nations' countermeasures since the summer of 1948.

The U.S. airlift continued to send supplies to West Berlin until September 30. During the airlift—from July 24, 1948, to September 30, 1949—the Western Allies flew 277,264 flights to Berlin. When the airlift reached its peak between February and June 1949, an average of one plane landed in Berlin every two minutes; 7,000 to 8,000 tons of food and fuel were carried each day.

### May 12, 1949

#### The Far Eastern commission announces the termination of reparations to aid Japan's economic recovery.

The 11-nation Far Eastern Commission had been established in Washington in 1945 to oversee the Allied Control Council in Tokyo. By 1947, the commission began to change its policy from punishing the Japanese to strengthening them as much as possible.

A few of the planes that participated in the airlift. National Archives

The initial change in policy took place in 1948 when the Allies stopped dissolving the *zaibatsu*—the economic empires of 10 Japanese families that controlled 75% of Japan's financial, industrial, and commercial business. In March 1948, George Kennan visited with General MacArthur in Tokyo to explain the necessity for promoting the interests of those upper-class Japanese who were friends of America. This required not economic reform but recovery. American business and banking officials also visited Tokyo to emphasize the same thing to MacArthur.

MacArthur quickly got the message. Previous decrees for the dissolution of 325 Japanese corporations under *zaibatsu* control ended after only nine had been broken up. MacArthur also had the Japanese government alter its labor laws to deny government workers the right to strike or to engage in collective bargaining. In June 1950, MacArthur purged 23 leaders of the Japanese Communist Party and other radical leaders.

The May 12, 1949, order to end the removal of Japanese goods as reparations effectively ended all reparations for Japan. Reparations based on industrial equipment had stopped in 1948. The policy after 1948 was to build a strong Japan as a U.S. ally because China's collapse appeared certain in 1949.

### May 15, 1949

*Communists gain control of the Hungarian government.*

In the first postwar elections on November 3, 1945, the anti-Communist SMALLHOLDERS PARTY won an absolute majority and Ferenc Nagy became premier. With Soviet backing, however, the Communists began a gradual purge of the Smallholders' leaders, accusing them of conspiracy. By early 1949, the Communists' NATIONAL INDEPENDENCE front had purged Nagy and other Smallholders. Jószef Cardinal MINDSZENTY had been sentenced to life in prison but fled to asylum in the U.S. embassy, where he became a symbol of anti-Communist resistance.

On May 15, 1949, a general election resulted in a complete Communist victory, with Istvan DOBI as premier and the real Communist boss, Mátyás RÁKOSI, as deputy premier.

### May 17, 1949

*The British House of Commons adopts the Ireland Bill, giving full independence to Ireland but affirming that Northern Ireland is within the United Kingdom.*

The issue of the partition of Ireland had been disputed since 1945, when Northern Ireland voted for partition and the British government supported its wishes.

On December 21, 1948, the Irish parliament passed and President Sean T. O'KELLY signed the Republic of Ireland bill. On February 10, Northern Ireland again voted for union with Great Britain. The British reorganized both the Ireland Bill and the partition on May 17, 1949.

### June 14, 1949

*The French government returns the Emperor Bao Dai to rule Vietnam.*

In the Élysée Agreement of March 8, 1949, French President Vincent AURIOL and BAO DAI agreed on the establishment of the independent State of Vietnam within the French Union. Paris continued to control matters of finance, trade, defense, foreign affairs, and internal security in Vietnam but agreed to reorganize the southern province of Cochin China as part of a United Vietnam.

Because Ho Chi Minh's forces continued to fight French forces, Paris hoped Bao Dai would provide a political solution to the war by symbolizing Vietnamese independence under French authority.

Bao had few followers in Vietnam and further alienated himself by taking the title emperor as well as chief of state. Bao said the people could prepare a constitution in the future, after order was restored.

### July 16, 1949

*Chiang Kai-shek prepares retreat to Formosa.*

Chiang formed a reorganized supreme council of the NATIONALISTS. When the civil war renewed in 1946, Chiang's forces seemed to make notable advances, but throughout 1948, his corrupt and ineffective officers were not able to gain popular support, which was rallying to the Communists. On January 21, 1949, Chiang resigned as president and retreated to the southwest while Vice President Li Tsung-jen tried to persuade Mao to negotiate a truce. By July, Communist victory appeared certain.

Thus, Chiang prepared to move to Formosa, claiming his followers would reconquer the mainland of China in the future.

See October 1, 1949.

### August 5, 1949

#### To explain U.S. policy relating to Chiang Kai-shek's "loss of China," the State Department issues a white paper.

Consisting of 1,054 pages of documents and a lengthy introduction by Secretary of State ACHESON, the volume's thesis was that the "loss of China" "was beyond the control of the government of the United States." The consequences of the Chinese civil war resulted from "internal Chinese forces" and the inadequate policies of Chiang Kai-shek.

The white paper marked a break in the bipartisan foreign policy fostered by Senator Vandenberg and the Roosevelt-Truman administrations. Many conservative Republicans followed an "Asia-first" policy based strongly on support of Chiang Kai-shek's policies as rationalized by the so-called China lobby, whose leading proponent was the charming Madame Chiang.

The Republican China bloc claimed the white paper was a "whitewash of a wishful, do-nothing policy" that placed all of Asia in danger of Soviet conquest. Their emphasis was on Moscow's monolithic control of all Communists and envisioned Mao's victory as a Soviet triumph. This limited vision ignored what should have been obvious—that all nationalists, including Mao, would object to domination by another outside power. What was little understood at the time was that Mao was strongly suspicious of all Soviet moves.

Others reacted differently to the white paper. Walter Lippmann, a well-known columnist, said the white paper failed to explain "Chiang's stronghold in American policy" for so long. John K. Fairbank, an expert on Chinese history who taught at Harvard, declared the volume was a frank admission that the United States "made the wrong approach to the problem of revolution in Asia."

Nevertheless, the strongly partisan debate over the "loss of China" stimulated the rise of McCarthyism and rabid anti-Communism throughout the 1950s and, for some Americans, for the rest of the century.

### August 10, 1949

#### The Department of Defense is established.

President Truman signed congressional legislation that renamed the national military establishment the Department of Defense. This act gave broader and more definite powers to the secretary of defense than had existed under the old War Department.

### August 22, 1949

#### The first use of atomic weapons by U.S. forces is sanctioned in a recommendation of the Joint Chiefs of Staff (JCS).

Approved two weeks later by the National Security Council (NSC-57), the "first use" principle became part of a NATO defense plan integrating the use of atomic weapons into the war plan. Although the contingency war plan hoped the American nuclear umbrella would deter a Soviet attack on Western Europe, the plan permitted use of the atomic bomb if the Soviets invaded. This JCS plan both promoted and required the May 1949 JCS request for additional funds to expand the production of atomic bombs.

From a strategic viewpoint, the JCS action backed the air force air-atomic methods, and rejected the navy's carrier plane attack method. The Air Force plan code-named OFF TACKLE was prepared during the summer of 1949. It proposed that aircraft, particularly the new B-36, would carry atomic bombs against the Soviet Union, the bomber being the nation's primary weapon. The U.S. navy advocated that "supercarriers" capable of launching planes with atomic bombs should be the first line of U.S. defense.

During the fall of 1949, the navy was losing the status it had enjoyed before 1941. The JCS war plan denigrated the navy carrier-attack program, and Secretary of Defense Louis Johnson stopped construction of the supercarrier, the USS *United States,* which Johnson claimed was too costly.

In October 1949, U.S. navy officers, led by Chief of Naval Operations Admiral Louis Denfeld, staged a last-ditch "admirals revolt" to protest against Johnson and the JCS plan. Taking their case to Congress, high-ranking naval leaders testified in opposition to the "air-atomic" strategy at hearings of the House Armed Services Committee. The navy claimed air force bombers would not be able to penetrate Soviet defenses sufficiently. They also pointed out that if the bombers got through, the air force doctrine of saturation bombing would, as in World War II, not only fail to cause the victims to surrender but would create in them a stronger "will to survive and resist." By using carrier-based bombers, the navy proposed to hit only military targets and Soviet forces to defeat the enemy.

The October "admirals revolt" lost. Both Truman and Secretary of Defense Johnson favored the air-atomic strategy, and the coming of the H-Bomb between 1950 and 1952 seemed to them to confirm that view. Soon after the conclusion of the October hearings, Truman removed Denfeld and other participants in the revolt from their high-level positions.

## September 2, 1949

### *The United Nations Commission on Korea announces that mediation has failed.*

Since the United States referred the Korean problem to the United Nations in September 1947, the commission had sought some means to unify the country and hold national elections. The commission was not, however, permitted by the Communists to operate north of 38° latitude. In 1948, the Republic of Korea was set up in South Korea (August 15), and the Korean People's Democratic Republic in North Korea (September 9).

In respect of the U.N. Commission findings, both the Soviet Union (by December 25, 1948) and the United States (by June 29, 1949) withdrew their occupation forces. Nevertheless, the U.N. Commission could not persuade Kim Il SUNG, the North's leader, and Syngman RHEE, the South's president, to work together to try to reach a satisfactory compromise.

## September 15, 1949

### *The Reciprocal Trade Agreements Act is extended for two years.*

This act renewed the Hull program of 1934, although Hull's original hope of lowering tariffs had been damaged since 1945 because the Republican Congress inserted "escape" clauses to allow certain American producers to get higher tariffs and to set an export control program designed to discriminate against the Communist bloc but that could also be used in trade with the "free" world.

## September 23, 1949

### A White House press release announces that the Soviet Union has detonated an atomic bomb.

The Soviets' successful explosion occurred on August 29, 1949. On September 9, Atomic Energy Commission (AEC) monitors detected excessive radioactivity coming from central Asia, and on September 14, samples of rainwater clouds confirmed this. U.S. intelligence estimated the samples were one month old and that the Soviets used a Nagasaki-type plutonium bomb.

President Truman learned of this success on September 12. He and General Groves doubted the accuracy of the data; however, Groves believed that there was a nuclear accident in the Soviet Union. The intelligence data was certain and Truman released the information on August 23. Soviet documents declassified in the 1990s disclose that the Soviets' 1949 bomb was an exact copy of the U.S. bomb tested in July 1945. For information on data given the Soviet Union by Klaus Fuchs and Theodore Hall, see Christopher Andrews *The Sword and the Shield: The Mitrokhin Archive* (1999).

## September 27, 1949

### *The USSR repudiates its 1945 Treaty of Friendship with Yugoslavia.*

This announcement from Moscow resulted from a lengthy dispute with Yugoslavia's ruler, Marshal TITO. While Tito claimed to follow Communist doctrine, he was a Yugoslav nationalist who rejected Moscow's attempt to centrally control all Communist parties. This intraparty split persisted and "TITOISM" became synonymous with Nationalistic communists who followed policies in the best interests of their own nations and were often anti-Soviet.

## October 1, 1949

### *Mao Tse-tung proclaims the creation of the People's Republic of China.*

Mao became head of the Central People's Administrative Council.

Chiang Kai-shek continued to claim to be the legitimate head of the Chinese government as he

Mao Tse-tung. National Archives

and his Nationalist followers moved their government to the island of Formosa.

## October 7, 1949

### *The Soviet zone of Germany is established as the German Democratic Republic (GDR).*

The Communist Party dominated the new government, with Wilhelm PIECK as president and Otto GROTEWOHL as minister president.

## November 18, 1949

### The Soviet Union and other Communist delegates challenge the right of China's nationalist government to represent China in the United Nations and on the Security Council.

The issue of China's status was first considered by the Security Council in September 1949, when the Nationalist government charged that the USSR had interfered in Chinese affairs, and asked the United Nations to condemn Communist China and recommend that no U.N. member assist Mao's regime in Peking. This caused the People's Republic to inform the secretary-general that the Nationalists had no right to continue to represent the Chinese people in the United Nations. The Nationalist Chinese retained their U.N. membership until October 25, 1971.

France, Great Britain, and other nations had recognized the new Chinese government, but the United States had not. America continued to recognize the Chinese government on Formosa until, as Acheson stated on October 12, the new Peking government "met traditional American conditions." The United States did not finally recognize the People's Republic of China until 1979.

## November 24, 1949

### The U.S. consul at Mukden and 21 others are released after a year's confinement.

Angus Ward, the U.S. consul at Mukden, Manchuria, had been held incommunicado by the Chinese Communists since November 20, 1948. During that time, the U.S. State Department possessed little knowledge of the exact situation at Mukden, although U.S. diplomats in other Chinese cities hoped the problem would be resolved as soon as the civil war ended in China. Mukden had been the first city with foreign consulates captured by the Communists. The advances of Mao's armies had proceeded rapidly during the next nine months, and on October 1, they controlled all China.

During this time, the U.S. State Department and President Truman considered a variety of measures to free Ward and the other 21 persons held at the Mukden consulate. On April 26, Secretary Acheson instructed Oliver CLUBB, the U.S. consul general in Peking, to inform the Communist government that unless it removed the arbitrary restrictions on the Mukden consulate, the United States would close the Mukden office and withdraw its staff. Mao's government did not respond, and on May 17, Acheson notified Clubb that the Mukden consulate should be closed.

Somehow, Acheson's May 17 order to close the Mukden consulate was delivered to Ward on June 7. On June 10, Ward sent a telegram to Clubb in Peking, saying he was trying to evacuate his staff. Ward's hopes proved to be premature. On June 19, the Chinese Communist press reported that its Mukden consulate had been discovered to contain a major U.S. spy operation against the Chinese people. Both Ward in Mukden and the U.S. embassy in Nanking refuted the spy charges. Nevertheless, Ward's plan to evacuate the consulate at Mukden was delayed by the Communist authorities.

Ward's continued detention led President Truman to consider harsher measures in October 1949, when two events raised questions in Washington. First, on October 1, China's Foreign Office asked all foreign representatives in China to recognize the Communist government. Concerned about the status of its crown colony of Hong Kong, Great Britain wanted to recognize the new regime as soon as possible. Concerned about its war in Indochina, France preferred to delay recognition. The United States believed it could not establish relations with Mao's regime until the Ward affair was settled. These considerations prompted the U.S. State Department to begin a diplomatic "offensive," asking all foreign representatives to withhold recognition until Ward was released. China, Acheson said, must demonstrate it could protect diplomatic officials.

The second event in October seemed to be the more serious. On October 24, Ward and four members of his staff were arrested by the Communists for allegedly directing a mob that attacked a Chinese worker. As Ward later explained, the trumped-up assault charges resulted from his attempt to escort from the consulate a Chinese messenger, Ji YUTTENG, who had been fired from the consulate staff. Because Ji refused to leave, there was a scuffle in which Ji and his brother were injured.

Ward's arrest caused an angry reaction in America, where Truman's administration was already under attack for not adequately supporting Chiang Kai-shek. As a result, between October 31 and November 18, Truman explored the possibility of either a blockade of China or military action to liberate Ward and his staff. The Joint Chiefs of Staff and General Omar Bradley, its chairman, advised Truman that military action would be difficult and might lead to a global war. A blockade, they advised, would not be effective. Secretary Acheson's diplomatic offensive seemed to be the best option. At a news conference on November 16, Acheson stated that the United States could not consider recognition until the Americans at Mukden were released.

China's desire for diplomatic recognition by foreign governments may have been the reason that the Mukden affair suddenly ended on November 24. The precise reasons for China's action on November 20, 1948, and on November 24, 1949, are not known. On the latter date, Ward called Clubb in Peking, reporting that he and his four codefendants had been found guilty of the charges against them. They were to be deported, however, in lieu of imprisonment. Within a month, on December 12, Ward and the others who had been confined at Mukden left China on the liner *Lakeland Victory*.

Why the Mukden incident arose is not certain. The best evaluation seems to be that of William N. Stokes, who, as the vice consul at Mukden, had been confined with Ward. Stokes believed that because Mao's civil-war propaganda had denounced the United States and other Western powers for aiding Chiang Kai-shek, and because Mukden was the first contact that Communist authorities and troops had with Western representatives, the hostility of Mao's armies to the West caused the Mukden affair. A year later, the Chinese Communists desired Western recognition; hence the change in China's attitude at Mukden on November 24, 1949.

One consequence of the Mukden affair may have been the U.S. nonrecognition of the People's Republic of China for the next 30 years. Indications are that in 1948–1949, the United States was ready to join the British in accepting the new Chinese government. The Mukden crisis delayed recognition by Washington. Furthermore, the arrest of Ward in October 1949 further inflamed U.S. feelings against China, making it difficult for Truman to grant recognition.

## December 1, 1949

### The U.N. General Assembly adopts a U.S.-British–sponsored "Essentials of Peace" resolution.

The "Essentials of Peace" proposal was the U.S.-British answer to a Soviet-sponsored U.N. resolution against the North Atlantic Treaty Alliance. On September 29, the General Assembly agreed to consider a USSR resolution titled "Condemnation of the preparations for a new war and conclusion of a five-power pact for the strengthening of peace." Without specifically citing the Atlantic pact, the Soviets claimed that the Anglo-American bloc followed an aggressive policy to isolate the Soviets from European politics. They stated this was contrary to the U.N. Charter and that the Big Five powers should handle basic issues of world peace.

The U.S. delegation decided to submit the "Essentials of Peace" resolution as a substitute motion that eventually passed the General Assembly on December 1 by a vote of 53 to 5. The "peace" resolution affirmed the principles of the U.N. Charter and asked all members to cooperate to ease world tensions. The key clause stated the U.S.-British contention that peace was endangered by the Soviet Union's frequent use of the veto power in the Security Council. This clause called on the five powers to show cooperation and "to exercise restraint in the use of the veto" so that the Security Council could act effectively to maintain peace.

### December 27, 1949

#### Indonesia is granted sovereignty by the Netherlands.

Since the Japanese evacuation of the East Indies in 1945, the Republic of Indonesia, which declared independence on August 17, and the Netherlands, which desired to reclaim its colonial ownership, had clashed in war and endeavored to negotiate. After intermittent periods of war, the Netherlands, on the urging of the United States, agreed to a settlement concluded with the aid of the United Nations Good Offices Committee. The Indonesian leader in the independence movement was Achmed SUKARNO.

### December 28, 1949

#### National Security Council document NSC 48/1 indicates southeast Asia is a vital area for the United States.

This document, which was classified secret until the *Pentagon Papers* were published in 1971, indicates that important personnel of the State and Defense Departments, probably Paul Nitze and Dean Acheson, believed even before the Korean War that U.S. interests in Indochina needed to be protected from communism.

NSC 48/1 read in part:

> The extension of communist authority in China represents a grievous political defeat for us. If southeast Asia also is swept by communism we shall have suffered a major political rout the repercussions of which will be felt throughout the rest of the world.

Thus, Mao's victory in China caused the NSC to believe Indochina was the next objective of communism. Notably, no one in the NSC seems to have realized the historic tradition of fierce antagonism between China and Vietnam, a fact on which all academic scholars of Vietnam agreed.

# 1950

### January 12, 1950

#### Secretary of State Acheson describes a "perimeter strategy" for east Asia.

Speaking at the National Press Club, Secretary of State Dean Acheson explained how the U.S. Asian strategy was to control large land areas, such as China, by controlling the surrounding sea perimeter extending in a crescent shape from India to Japan. Acheson described this strategy to persuade Congress to pass the Korean Aid Bill for 1949–1950, to answer Republican complaints that Truman did not do enough to help the Chinese Nationalists, and, above all, to sow seeds of distrust between Mao and Stalin.

Acheson said he did not expect a Chinese-Soviet alliance to last long because Mao did not want Moscow to dominate China. Unlike Eastern Europe, Soviet troops did not occupy China after World War II. Knowing that Mao was in the Moscow meetings with Stalin, Acheson argued that China would find the United States its best friend in keeping the country independent. Acheson's remarks sought to divide Mao and Stalin, declaring that the Soviets were acting to annex parts of China by a "process that is complete in outer Mongolia ... [and] nearly complete in Manchuria," as well as repeating the U.S. hands-off policy for Taiwan. The secretary also recognized U.S. responsibility for economic aid to Korea, Taiwan, and Japan but believed the greatest U.S. threat was a Chinese attack west of the perimeter. (Congress passed the aid bill on February 10.) He also indicated the Communists would use "subversion and penetration" to influence Asia, tactics that would be difficult for the Western Powers to deal with because of anticolonial movements in Asia.

Although January 1950 news reports hardly mentioned the Korean parts of Acheson's speech, after the Korean War began on June 27, Republican opponents such as Senator Joseph McCarthy claimed Acheson's speech gave the Communists a "green light" to attack South Korea. In contrast to McCarthy's claim, Bruce

Cummins's analysis in *The Origins of the Korean War* (1990) demonstrates Acheson assumed the United States must defend both Korea and Japan but hoped to disrupt Chinese-Soviet relations. Those interested in the consequences of Acheson's speech should also consult *Uncertain Partners: Stalin, Mao and the Korean War* (1993), by Sergei N. Goncharov, John W. Lewis, and Xue Litai, especially the translation of the Chinese Xinhua Agency dispatch of January 20 criticizing Acheson's speech as "shameless slander."

On the Soviet-China alliance see February 14, 1950.

### January 13, 1950

**Soviet delegate Jacob Malik walks out of a Security Council session, beginning a seven-month Soviet boycott of U.N. meetings.**

Moscow's decision to walk out of the Security Council followed the failure of a motion to expel the Chinese Nationalists from the United Nations. The vote was 6 to 3 against the motion (Great Britain and Norway abstained). Although the Soviets appeared adamantly in favor of the Peking government, U.N. observers such as British delegate Sir Alexander Colgan believed the Soviet Union preferred to impede admission of Mao's government to the United Nations to more effectively dominate the People's Republic. By preventing further debate on the China issue after the first vote, Moscow's boycott kept China out of the United Nations.

The boycott continued until August 1, 1950.

### January 21, 1950

**Alger Hiss is convicted of perjury on two counts of false testimony before a grand jury of New York state.**

Hiss was convicted for two statements he made to the grand jury: (1) he had not turned over any secret, confidential, or restricted documents to Whittaker Chambers in 1938, and (2) he definitely said he had not seen Chambers after January 1, 1937, whereas he had seen and conversed with Chambers in February and March 1938.

Hiss had been an active New Dealer who worked for the Nye Investigation Committee in the early 1930s and for the State Department. During World War II, he helped plan the foundation of the United Nations and in this capacity was present at the Yalta Conference of February 1945.

Chambers first called attention to Hiss in 1948, during hearings of the House Un-American Activities Committee, where, as an ex-Communist, Chambers became a star witness. Chambers claimed he had known Hiss from 1934 to 1938 as a member of a special underground group in the U.S. Communist Party.

Before HUAC and later the grand jury, Hiss denied having been a member of such a Communist group. He also denied having given Chambers any confidential State Department data. The chief interrogator of Hiss during the HUAC hearings was Congressman Richard Nixon.

Two trials became necessary to convict Hiss. In the first trial, the jury could not reach a verdict (July 8, 1949). The second trial began on November 17, 1949; the jury found him guilty on both counts on January 21.

The precise nature of Hiss's trial and conviction was generally lost on the public, who conceived of Hiss as a Communist spy whose influence aided the Soviet Union during and after World War II. When friends of Hiss, such as Dean Acheson, refused to believe Chambers's testimony and accepted the evidence that contradicted Chambers, the critics of Truman and Acheson alleged that this was further evidence of Communist infiltration of the State Department.

The U.S. Supreme Court rejected Hiss's petition to review the conviction, and he went to prison from March 22, 1950, until November 1954. Hiss continued to profess his innocence, but post–Cold War revelations from Soviet archives of its military intelligence group, the GRU, confirm that Hiss spied for the Soviets at various times after 1934. Details about his espionage are given in six books reviewed by Thomas Powers in the May 11, 2000, issue of the *New York Review of Books*.

See "Verona" files, July 11, 1995.

### January 24, 1950

**British atomic physicist Klaus Fuchs confesses to being a Soviet spy.**

Fuchs was a division chief of theoretical physics in the British atomic program at Harwell. He confessed to giving the Soviets data about American activity at Oak Ridge, Tennessee, and Los Alamos, New Mexico. On March 1, 1950, English courts convicted him of espionage, sentencing him to 14 years in prison. Fuchs's confession led to charges against Harry Gold and, subsequently, Julius and Ethel Rosenberg.

### January 31, 1950

**The decision to hasten development of the hydrogen bomb is announced by President Truman.**

This decision ended intensive debate within the administration about building the superbomb. David Lilienthal and George Kennan wanted the United States to renounce the first use of any atomic bomb and to actively seek international control. Advocates of the H-bomb included General Omar Bradley, the chairman of the Joint Chiefs, and the physicist Edward Teller.

Surprised by news of the Soviet atomic test in 1949 and believing in the unqualified threat of the Soviets' desire to expand, President Truman gave little thought to abandoning the development of the H-bomb. Clearly, by 1950 the H-bomb had come to be seen as a winning, therefore necessary, weapon for America to possess.

### February 7, 1950

**The United States recognizes Bao Dai's government of Vietnam.**

At the same time, the United States recognized the governments of VIETNAM, LAOS, and CAMBODIA as "associated states within the French union."

Laos had been made a free state in the French Union in 1946 under King Norodom SIHANOUK. In the fall of 1949, France gave de jure independence to Cambodia but, as in the case of Vietnam, controlled its defense, foreign affairs, and internal security.

Bao Dai's government had been established with French help in 1949, with the hope that Bao could gain a following to counteract Vietminh influence in Vietnam.

See June 14, 1949.

### February 9, 1950

**Senator Joseph McCarthy charges that many Communist spies have infiltrated the State Department.**

McCarthy's first accusations came during a speech at Wheeling, West Virginia, when he said 205 Communists held high, influential positions in the

Senator Joseph McCarthy. Harry S. Truman Library

State Department. He continued to make such charges in other speeches, giving the number of spies variously as 57, 81, 205, or 11.

Apparently McCarthy's charges were intended to help his 1950 senatorial campaign in Wisconsin, but they also became a simple way for friends of Chiang Kai-shek's government to blame the Chinese Nationalist loss on "reds" in the State Department who had allegedly "sold China down the river."

Regardless of how vague, incorrect, or false, McCarthy's charges found a receptive audience—an audience conceived in Truman's March 1947 "scare the hell out of them" speech and nourished with the evidence of Soviet expansion in "East Europe and China," and the Soviet explosion of an atomic bomb in 1949.

The years from 1950 to 1954 may be called the ERA OF MCCARTHYISM to denote the near-hysterical anti-Communist emotions affecting large segments of U.S. society and foreign policy. Politicians feared to deny or denounce the Wisconsin senator, lest they be accused of being "soft" on communism. Even President Truman and Dean Acheson, in spite of their efforts to initiate America's anti-Communist containment program, fell victim to McCarthyism. Their denials of McCarthy's charges were often not accepted by many Americans.

## February 14, 1950

### *Stalin-Mao talks end with an alliance and the Soviets recognizing Ho Chi Minh's regime.*

Talks between Chinese and Soviet leaders began in December 1949. Following lengthy discussions about various issues, Stalin and Mao signed a 30-year treaty. Stalin wanted a Chinese alliance to divert U.S. attention to Far Eastern struggles for hegemony and give him sufficient time to rebuild powerful forces to challenge Western Europe. Mao's principle desire was to get Stalin to recognize Ho Chi Minh's Communist rebellion against the French in Vietnam and a $300 million Soviet loan for China's military purposes. The Soviet Union's recognition of Ho Chi Minh's regime on January 30 paved the way for the final treaty between China and the USSR on February 14. Details of the making of the alliance are in *Uncertain Partners* (1993), cited under January 12, 1950.

## April 14, 1950

### NSC-68 is presented to the National Security Council.

Drafted by Paul H. Nitze, director of the State Department's Planning Staff, NSC-68 was a secret document depicting the Soviets as aggressively seeking to conquer the world. To counteract the Communists, NSC-68 advocated a greatly enlarged U.S. and European military force, as well as a diplomatic and psychological offensive to roll back previous Soviet expansion. Nitze's document argued that the United States could afford a large buildup of conventional forces without new taxes or crippling inflation if it shifted some production to nonconsumer goods. Conventional forces would make the United States less dependent on nuclear forces if the Soviets attacked, as NSC-68 predicted they might be prepared to do in 1954. In addition, while a U.S. nuclear arsenal would deter the Soviets from using nuclear weapons, the large conventional forces would be more available against Soviet "piecemeal aggression" and limited wars with other countries.

When the Korean War broke out in June 1950, President Truman had reviewed but not approved the defense costs envisioned by NSC-68. Whether or not Congress would have agreed to such a huge defense buildup became an academic question because the war required a defense increase for all branches of the armed forces.

Both before and after NSC-68 was declassified on February 27, 1975, the document has been criticized by many U.S. policy analysts for militarizing foreign policy, upsetting the economy, and being developed for one moment in history. Instead it influenced more than 30 years of U.S. policy.

## June 5, 1950

### President Truman signs his third foreign aid bill, granting nearly $3 billion for the European Recovery Plan and the Point Four Program.

Following Secretary of State George Marshall's June 1947 call for the U.S. to assist Europe's economic recovery, President Truman asked Congress for several types of foreign aid programs. In December 1947, Congress approved funds for interim aid to European countries. Next, on March 31, 1948, Congress approved the basic economic aid for the European Recovery Program known as the Marshall Plan. Truman's third request for foreign economic aid was passed by Congress on June 5, 1950, allowing $3 billion to be used for the Marshall Plan as well as the Point Four Program. Further economic aid for Europe continued until 1952. Michael L. Hogan's *The Marshall Plan* (1987) provides complete details for the U.S. financial aid programs.

## June 25, 1950

### North Korean forces attack South Korea.

Because a U.N. commission was present in South Korea, North Korea was readily identified as the aggressor in crossing the 38th parallel. In the Security Council, the Soviet boycott facilitated action because the USSR could not veto council measures. Consequently, after North Korea rejected a Security Council order to withdraw, President Truman ordered U.S. forces in Japan to support South Korean forces (June 26). The next day, the Security Council asked U.N. members to assist South Korea in defeating the aggressor (June 27). On June 30, Truman ordered U.S. ground troops into the fighting in South Korea, and on July 7, the Security Council agreed that U.N. troops would fight under a commander designated by the United States. President Truman appointed General Douglas MacArthur as

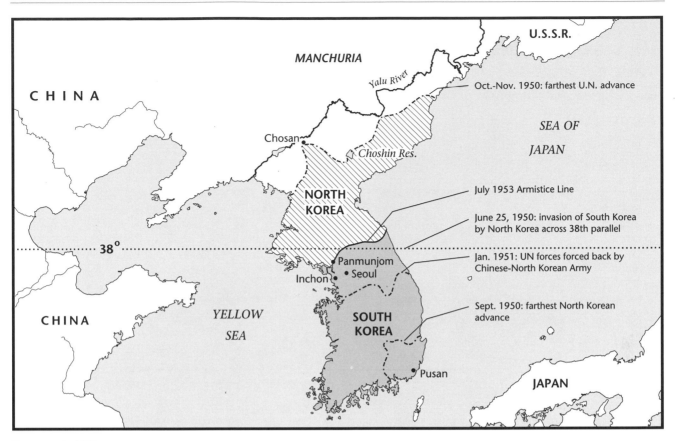

Korea, early 1950s.

the commanding general of United Nations forces in KOREA.

Despite his U.N. designation, MacArthur took orders from Washington, not from the United Nations. Truman and the State Department favored the concept of a unified war effort, but they acted unilaterally in directing military and diplomatic policies in Korea. Sixteen nations sent troops to assist in Korea, with the United States providing 50% of the ground force (South Korea provided most of the other 50%), 86% of the naval power, and 93% of the air power.

After 1980, documents from Soviet and mainland Chinese files revealed more about North Korea's decision to invade South Korea. Although in 1950, President Truman asserted the invasion was part of Stalin's expansion of communism, recent documents show that Kim Il Sung initiated plans to unify Korea while Stalin and Mao Tse-tung were finally persuaded to help North Korea. Kim told Stalin that Communist guerrillas would rise up in South Korea and enable Kim's forces to unify Korea before the United States could respond. Kim was wrong. Not only was Moscow

caught off-guard because it was boycotting sessions of the United Nations and had no delegate to veto UN Security Council action but by mid-July, Kim's forces were stalled at Pusan by U.S. soldiers who arrived to help South Korea.

Strength of the UNC Ground Forces in Korea

A-1

| Date | Total | United States[a] | Republic of Korea[b] | Other United Nations[c] |
|---|---|---|---|---|
| 30 June 1951 | 554,577 | 253,250 | 273,266 | 28,061 |
| 30 June 1952 | 678,051 | 265,864 | 376,418 | 35,769 |
| 31 July 1953 | 932,539 | 302,483 | 590,911 | 39,14S |

[a] Includes marine and navy personnel under operational control of U.S. army.
[b] Includes KATUSA, ROK marines under operational control of U.S. army, and civilian trainees.
[c] See Appendix A-2 for distribution by country.
*Source*: Comptroller of the Army Summary, ROK and U.N. Ground Forces Strength in Korea, Oct. 7, 1954. OCMH Files. From Walter G. Hermes, *Truce Tent and Fighting Front* (Washington, D.C.: Office of the Chief of Military History, USA, 1966), p. 513.

A-2: Other United Nations

| Country | 30 June 1951 | 30 June 1952 | 31 July 1963 |
|---|---|---|---|
| Total | 28,061 | 35,769 | 39,145 |
| British Commonwealth | 15,723 | 21,429 | 24,085 |
| United Kingdom | 8,278 | 13,043 | 14,198 |
| Australia | 912 | 1,844 | 2,282 |
| Canada | 5,403 | 5,155 | 6,146 |
| New Zealand | 797 | 1,111 | 1,389 |
| India[a] | 333 | 276 | 70 |
| Turkey | 4,602 | 4,878 | 5,455 |
| Belgium[b] | 602 | 623 | 944 |
| Colombia | 1,050 | 1,007 | 1,068 |
| Ethiopia | 1,153 | 1,094 | 1,271 |
| France | 738 | 1,185 | 1,119 |
| Greece | 1,027 | 899 | 1,263 |
| Netherlands | 725 | 565 | 819 |
| Philippines | 1,143 | 1,494 | 1,496 |
| Thailand | 1,057 | 2,274 | 1,294 |
| Italy [a] | 0 | 64 | 72 |
| Norway[a] | 79 | 109 | 105 |
| Sweden[a] | 162 | 148 | 154 |

[a] Contribution consisted of noncombat medical units only.
[b] Luxembourg detachment of approximately 44 men.
*Source:* Comptroller of the Army, Summary, ROK and U.N. Ground Forces Strength in Korea, Oct 7, 1954. OCMH files.
From Walter G. Hermes, *Truce Tent and Fighting Front* (Washington, D.C.: Office of the Chief of Military History, USA, 1966), p. 513.

In brief, Stalin was not attempting to expand in East Asia; his main concern was Europe, where in 1948 the Soviet Union lost control of Yugoslavia while NATO was organized to defend Western Europe from any Moscow-inspired aggression.

See January 13, 1950.

### July 20, 1950

**Senator McCarthy's charges that Communists have infiltrated the State Department are found to be untrue by a special Senate subcommittee chaired by Senator Millard Tydings.**

McCarthy did not stop his speeches, however, but continued to level accusations against the Truman administration. Soon after the committee report, McCarthy named Owen LATTIMORE as the "top Russian espionage agent" in the United States. Lattimore was a professor at Johns Hopkins University who frequently served as a consultant to the State Department on affairs of China and Mongolia. When asked to verify his charges against Lattimore, McCarthy said President Truman kept his evidence locked up in the loyalty files. The Tydings Committee then conducted an investigation that cleared Lattimore of McCarthy's charges.

Nevertheless, the Tydings Committee received less attention than Senator McCarthy. Fear and suspicion came to infect many avenues of American life, an emotional atmosphere suited to the irrational accusations of the senator, not to reasoned efforts at response from his critics.

### August 30, 1950

**The United States and the Philippines sign a mutual assistance pact.**

This treaty extended and implemented legislation of 1946. Its three major clauses were (1) a Trading Act to continue free trade until 1954 before a gradual imposition of U.S. tariffs; (2) a Rehabilitation Act to give economic aid to the Philippines; and (3) a military assistance act, which included U.S. bases in the Philippines as well as equipment for the Filipino armed forces.

## September 15, 1950

### A daring attack at Inchon by MacArthur's forces finally halts North Korea's offensive by outflanking the invaders and trapping North Korean forces in a pincer movement.

The first American units to arrive in Korea from Japan were lacking adequate firepower, far from combat-ready, and far too few. Consequently, the initial phase of operations was disastrous as the North Koreans had the added advantage of surprise and planning. The Republic of Korea (ROK) and U.S. forces were unable to stem the North's offensive and were ultimately driven back to the so-called Pusan perimeter.

The U.N. September offensive soon drove the North Koreans back across the 38th parallel—the border between South and North—raising new questions: (1) Should North Korea be liberated from Communist control? (2) Should the U.N. objective be only to contain North Korea at the 38th parallel?

See October 7, 1950, and April 10–11, 1951.

## September 23, 1950

### Congress adopts the McCarran Internal Security Bill over President Truman's veto.

This law required members of the COMMUNIST PARTY and Communist front organizations to register with the attorney general. Indirectly, such registration would self-incriminate a person because the Smith Act of 1940 made it a crime to belong to any group advocating the violent overthrow of the government.

The McCarran Act also allowed deportation of aliens who were Communists and gave the government broad jurisdiction to detain persons in time of war.

Truman vetoed the bill on September 20, arguing that it was a confused measure and would not work properly. But the nation's hysterical anti-Communist mood persuaded most politicians to support the bill. In the House, whose members faced an election in November, the president's veto was overridden after only one hour of discussion. In the Senate, Hubert Humphrey and Paul Douglas conducted a 22-hour filibuster but failed to convince their colleagues to uphold Truman's veto.

General Douglas MacArthur aboard the USS *Mount McKinley* watching the Inchon assault. National Archives

### October 7, 1950

**A U.N. General Assembly resolution agrees that the objective in Korea is to "ensure conditions of stability throughout Korea," and calls for a "unified, independent and democratic government of Korea."**

Both in the Truman administration and at the United Nations, controversy had developed about the waging of the Korean War. Some leaders wished to be lenient to Kim Il Sung's government and simply return to the status quo ante bellum. Others, including Truman, wished to move across the 38th parallel, overthrow Kim's government, and stage "free elections" for a united Korea. The October 7 U.N. resolution was somewhat ambiguous but appeared to favor unification of Korea. At least, Truman first interpreted it in this fashion.

### October 15, 1950

**President Truman and General MacArthur meet at Wake Island.**

Since July 1950, Truman and MacArthur had disagreed about using Chiang Kai-shek's forces against either North Korea or mainland China. MacArthur especially irritated the president by sending a message to the Veterans of Foreign Wars convention, in which he called the efforts to restrain Chiang's forces an "appeasement" of communism.

At Wake Island, Truman reviewed U.S. policy for MacArthur, including the desire to protect Formosa but not to use Nationalist armed forces against the People's Republic of China.

### November 1, 1950

**An assassination attempt is made against President Truman by two Puerto Rican nationalists.**

The attempt on Truman's life occurred outside Blair House in Washington, D.C., where the president lived while parts of the White House were being renovated. Truman's Secret Service killed one of the assassins, Griselio Torresola. The second, Oscar Collazo, killed a Secret Service agent, a crime for which Collazo was arrested, tried, and sentenced to death. Truman, however, commuted his sentence to life imprisonment.

The two Puerto Ricans were members of a minority radical group that advocated complete independence for their homeland. There was, in fact, a division among Puerto Ricans regarding their future status. Many desired to retain their special commonwealth status with the United States; others wished to get statehood; and finally, the most radical elements desired full independence. In the years after World War II, the radicals often committed terrorist acts in the United States to dramatize their program. The attempt on Truman's life was one such act.

### November 3, 1950

**A "uniting for peace" resolution is passed by the U.N. General Assembly.**

This action gave the assembly the right to recommend collective security measures to U.N. members if the use of the veto in the Security Council prevented U.N. action. In effect, this resolution weakened the Big Powers' veto, not only for the Soviets but also for the United States. At the time, however, the U.S. delegation believed it had sufficient influence to control the votes of the assembly and that some method for collective action was needed to bypass the USSR's frequent use of the veto power.

### November 4, 1950

**The United Nations rescinds a 1946 resolution condemning Spain's Fascist government.**

This action reversed not only past U.N. policy but also U.S. policy. In 1945, the United States, Britain, and France opposed Spain's membership in the United Nations, and in 1946 they appealed to the Spanish people to end Francisco Franco's dictatorship.

By 1950, U.S. efforts to unite all non-Communists against the Soviet Union caused a shift in policy. This first became evident when Congress approved $62.5 million in Marshall Plan loans to Spain on September 6, 1950.

The U.N. action on November 4, 1950, prepared the way for Spain's admission to the Western anti-Communist camp. It removed a U.N. resolution of December 11, 1946, that had excluded Spain from all U.N. activity. Several Latin American countries sponsored the resolution to rescind previous action against Spain. The action permitted Spain to participate in special agencies of the United Nations; full U.N. membership for Spain was approved on October 14, 1955.

See March 4, 1946.

## November 7, 1950

### Congressional elections reduce the Democratic majority in both houses of Congress.

Senator McCarthy's activity played a role in this election, with his proponents helping Republicans to win at least three Senate seats: John M. Butler defeated McCarthy's nemesis, Millard Tydings of Maryland; Everett Dirksen won over Majority Leader Scott Lucas of Illinois; and Richard Nixon defeated Helen Gahagan Douglas in California. Altogether, the Democrats lost 5 Senate seats and 28 House seats.

## November 26, 1950

### Chinese Communist forces launch a massive counteroffensive against U.N. troops in the Yalu river valley.

After the United Nations passed a resolution on October 7 to unify Korea, China denounced the U.N. decision. As Chen Jian's research in the 1990s disclosed, China began preparing to help North Korea in July 1950 because Mao Tse-tung wanted to drive all U.S. forces out of the Korean peninsula to expand the Communist revolution in East Asia. In early September, North Korea's armies nearly achieved this objective, but on September 15 U.S. forces launched an invasion at Inchon and captured Seoul. In October, U.N. forces crossed the 38th parallel and some reached the Yalu River on China's border before

U.S. forces pull back from the Chosin Reservoir after the Chinese forces intervene. National Archives

Chinese "volunteers" joined North Korea in a counteroffensive. On November 24, General MacArthur ordered an "end-the-war by Christmas" offensive that failed because it inspired an offensive by massive numbers of Chinese troops. The "surprise" Chinese intervention required U.N. forces to retreat below the 38th parallel. The Communist armies again captured Seoul on January 4, 1951. U.S. and South Korean forces did not reoccupy Seoul until March 14, 1951.

See April 10, 1951.

## November 28, 1950

### *The Colombo Plan is approved by British Commonwealth Parliament.*

For six years, this program would provide £8 billion of economic aid to India, Pakistan, Ceylon, Sarawak, and Borneo, based on British currency that was devalued in 1948 from $4.03 to $2.80 per pound, the Colombo Plan cost Britain a total of 14.4 billion over six years, or 2.6 billion each year.

## December 18, 1950

### Brussels conference of NATO's foreign ministers approves plans for the defense of Western Europe.

The next day, the ministers named General Dwight D. Eisenhower as supreme commander of the North Atlantic forces. The foreign ministers' action finalized NATO plans that had been under preparation since October 1949. The military plan's important sections were as follows: (1) the United States had responsibility to use atomic weapons if necessary to defend NATO nations; (2) a "Forward Strategy" provided for the defense of Germany as far east as possible; (3) sea control would be the duty of the U.S., British, and French fleets; and (4) Western European aircraft would have defensive and short-range bombing responsibilities. To increase NATO's forces, the United States proposed forming 10 divisions of German troops as part of the defense effort.

Adoption of the plan raised two vital questions: (1) How would the NATO ground forces be increased? and (2) How would Germany be rearmed? The first question caused problems in America because congressional critics opposed Truman's plan to send from four to six U.S. divisions to augment NATO forces. The second question raised problems in France because French opinion opposed the rearmament of Germany.

On September 9, 1950, Truman had announced that America would send four new divisions to Europe. In Congress, opponents of this Europe plan challenged Truman's decision. Such spokesmen as former President Herbert HOOVER, Senator Robert TAFT, and Senator Kenneth WHERRY disliked the European orientation of this policy. Generally, they desired greater American activity in the Pacific region, arguing that Europe could defend itself.

Other Republicans backed Truman, however. After New York's Republican Governor Thomas DEWEY and General EISENHOWER defended Truman's program, the Senate passed a series of resolutions on April 4, 1951, which accepted Truman's NATO policy. The Senate agreed that the four U.S. army divisions could go to Europe but requested that the president consult with Congress before sending additional troops.

In contrast to the American difficulty, the German rearmament question caused a lengthier dispute because of French opposition. In October, the French National Assembly adopted Prime Minister René PLEVEN's plan to include German troops in NATO only at the lowest (regiment) level, under a European political authority. Generally, however, the NATO foreign ministers disliked the PLEVEN PLAN. At the December 1950 meeting no satisfactory solution could be found. The foreign ministers finally accepted German troop participation, in principle, but left the details of the plan for later discussion.

See January 15, 1951.

## December 23, 1950

**The United States, France, and the associated states of Indochina (Vietnam, Laos, and Cambodia) sign a mutual defense agreement for military aid in combating Communist forces under Ho Chi Minh.**

This agreement finalized prior American agreements on May 8, 1950, to give aid to France for use in Indochina and to send 35 U.S. military advisers there.

Although Washington wanted the funds for Indochina to go directly to Saigon, the French insisted that all aid go through the Paris office of the French Union. By December 1950, the United States committed $50 million for arms, ammunition, naval vessels, military vehicles, and aircraft.

## December 28, 1950

**O. Edward Clubb, a high-ranking U.S. foreign service officer and expert on China, is ordered to answer allegations before the State Department's Loyalty Security Board (LSB).**

A foreign service officer since 1928, Clubb served principally as a consul in China. He had closed the U.S. consular office in Peking on April 12, 1950, when he returned to Washington to become director of the Office of Chinese Affairs of the State Department.

The allegations made against Clubb on December 28 were anonymous and largely indefinite. Such charges as "viewed some aspects of Communism favorably, 1932–1934" or "friendly toward the USSR and Communism, 1935–1937" made up all but one of the charges. The one specific allegation was that he "delivered a sealed envelope to the office of the editor of the *New Masses* ... for transmittal to Grace HUTCHINS," a reputed Communist. This event took place in 1932. Later, Clubb learned that Whittaker Chambers, an editor of *New Masses* in 1933, was the accuser and that the "sealed envelope" was his letter of introduction to Walt CAMERON, the 1932 editor of *New Masses.*

Following many lengthy interrogations, Clubb received clearance from the LSB on February 8, 1952. He decided, however, to retire from the Foreign Service, dismayed at the shabby treatment accorded someone who had worked for the government for over 20 years.

Clubb's experience was repeated frequently enough to demoralize the professional, objective foreign service officers. Clubb and others had committed the offense of expertly analyzing the events where they served even when their superiors and political appointees in Washington wanted to hear reports that confirmed their prejudices in favor of Chiang Kai-shek. In addition to Clubb, other State Department experts on China who suffered similar rebuffs were John Carter Vincent, John S. Service, and John Paton Davies.

The demoralizing conditions in the State Department was examined by a special State Department Committee on Personnel. In 1954, this committee reported to Secretary of State John Foster

Dulles: "The morale of the [Foreign] Service today stands in need of repair."

# 1951

### January 5, 1951

## A "great debate" begins on Truman's policies in Europe and Korea.

When the Senate convened in January, Republican Senator Robert A. Taft (Ohio) presented a speech that revived a policy of isolationism opposing Truman's commitment to NATO and his limit on the war in Korea to regain the 38th parallel for South Korea. Rather than having America cooperate with NATO or the United Nations, Taft wanted to return to policies some politicians preferred before the Pearl Harbor attack of 1941; that is, a policy under which the the United States would unilaterally decide when and how to intervene abroad. Taft claimed "Truman's War" in Korea was unconstitutional because Congress did not declare war and that Truman made a serious mistake in December 1951 by appointing Dwight D. Eisenhower as commander of NATO forces in Europe, a decision that entangled America in Europe's quarrels.

Taft's ideas were strongly endorsed by former President Herbert Hoover and Republican Senator Kenneth Wherry (Nebraska) among others. Taft's January 5 speech opened a series of Senate debates and congressional hearings that culminated in a Senate hearing on Truman's dismissal of General Douglas MacArthur as commander of U.N. force in Korea.

See April 10, 1951.

### February 26, 1951

## The 22d Amendment to the U.S. Constitution is ratified.

This amendment limited the President of the United States to serving not more than two terms of office. If a vice president became president to serve for more than two years of his predecessor's term, he could have only one other four-year term of office. The amendment did not apply to the incumbent President Truman.

### April 5, 1951

## Julius and Ethel Rosenberg are sentenced to death, having been convicted of conspiring with others to transmit secret information on atomic fission to the Soviet Union.

The Rosenbergs had been arrested in July 1950 as a result of the confession of British spy Klaus FUCHS. His testimony led first to the arrest of Harry GOLD and David GREENGLASS, who implicated the Rosenbergs and Morton SOBELL. The Rosenbergs were the Soviet contacts for Greenglass, who worked at the Los Alamos project.

The Rosenbergs persistently claimed their innocence. They were not accused of any specific overt act of espionage but of conspiracy to transfer secret materials. The U.S. press as well as the court treated the conspirators as traitors. The trial judge, Irving Kaufman, declared: "All our democratic institutions are . . . involved in this great conflict. . . . The punishment to be meted out in this case must therefore serve the maximum interest for the preservation of our society against these traitors in our midst."

The government's case depended largely on the confessions of David Greenglass and Harry Gold. Judge Kaufman also allowed wide latitude for the prosecutor to question the Rosenbergs about their political beliefs. This enabled the government to convince the jury that their motivation to spy depended on their Communist sympathies.

After their conviction, the Rosenberg case followed normal appeal procedures for the next two years. After the Supreme Court rejected a further review, the possibility arose that President Eisenhower would commute the death sentence, provided the Rosenbergs confessed. They did not because they said they were innocent and they could not confess a lie. Consequently, they were electrocuted at Sing Sing Prison, New York, on June 19, 1953. Subsequent evidence from the files of the KGB (Soviet secret police) supported the government's charges.

The coconspirators in the Rosenberg case received prison terms. Morton Sobell and Harry Gold each were given 30-year sentences; David Greenglass was sentenced to 15 years.

The political overtones and uncertain evidence in the Rosenberg case and execution led later to a number of dramatizations. These included a documentary film, *The Unquiet Death of Julius and Ethel Rosenberg*; a play, Donald Freed's *Inquest*; and three novels:

Robert Coover's *The Public Burning*; E.L. Doctorow's *The Book of Daniel*; and Helen Yglesias's *How She Died*.

### April 10–11, 1951

#### President Truman dismisses General MacArthur from all his command positions.

Truman signed the order late in the evening of April 10 to relieve the general for insubordination, announcing the decision in a White House press release at 1 A.M. on April 11, 1951. Although Truman's "firing" of the popular general brought criticism from conservatives, Republicans, and Asia-firsters, the president had the unanimous backing of the Joint Chiefs of Staff, who realized that MacArthur had frequently undermined Truman's policy and had failed to follow proper procedures in the past six months.

The dispute between the general and the president centered on the administration's decision to limit the Korean War to fulfill specific political objectives as the best means of national security policy in the nuclear age. MacArthur preferred to continue the traditional American military policies of permitting the armed forces to take whatever action was necessary to win a "total victory" over the enemy. Thus, the Truman-MacArthur controversy represented a major conflict in policy perceptions prevalent in America during the last half of the 20th century.

One policy recognized that wars in the Third World were, at best, fought for limited political objectives and that containment of Communist expansion was a major goal of U.S. policy. The second attempted to attain a total triumph not just over a political foe but also over an ideologically different way of life that appeared to threaten capitalist democracy.

Specifically, in 1950–1951 the Truman-MacArthur conflict translated into the methods for fighting in Korea after the Chinese intervened in November 1950. MacArthur claimed military restrictions had prevented him from responding effectively to the Chinese attack. He had been directed to use only Korean forces north of the 38th parallel and, even worse, was instructed not to conduct air raids along the Manchurian border. In December, MacArthur publicly objected to these restrictions, telling newsmen that the limits imposed from Washington were "an enormous handicap, without precedent in military history." He could not retaliate effectively against the Chinese.

Initially, Truman sought to silence MacArthur by issuing directives that required that all public statements first be cleared with the White House. MacArthur remained quiet only until February 1951. By that time the opposing Korean forces had

Lieutenant General Matthew Ridgeway, Major General Doyle Hickey, and General MacArthur, just before MacArthur was replaced by Ridgeway as Commander in Chief of the U.N. forces in Korea. National Archives

fought to stabilized positions near the 38th parallel. Then, on February 6, a news "leak" from MacArthur's headquarters disclosed the general's impatience with the restrictions on his activities. He wanted to bomb the Manchurian sanctuaries containing Chinese supplies and to defeat communism not just in Korea but throughout the Orient—a total victory over communism.

In contrast, Truman, in consultation with allies from the United Nations, decided after the Chinese intervention that neither an atomic war nor a Soviet attack on Western Europe would be risked over Korea. The prevailing decision was to contain the Communists in Asia at the 38th parallel. MacArthur opposed this policy, claiming it was an "appeasement" of communism.

Until March, Truman continued to be patient with the general. On March 20, he and the Joint Chiefs agreed to approach North Korea and China to seek a truce in Korea that would restore the 38th parallel. MacArthur responded to this effort by issuing a statement on March 24 in which he offered a military settlement to the Communist commanders. He added a thinly veiled threat, however, that if they refused a truce, the United Nations might extend military operations to coastal areas and interior bases of China.

MacArthur's uncalled for statement convinced Truman to find the right time to dismiss the general. The general's statement undermined the negotiating proposals being laid out. Furthermore, the general went further, sending a letter to the House minority leader and a MacArthur favorite, Republican Joseph W. Martin. The letter of April 5, which Martin read to Congress, reiterated the general's former proposals: to end limits on military operations, to use Chiang Kai-shek's forces in Korea, and to recognize that Asia, not Europe, was the place to defeat the Communist threat.

The letter to Martin was not the cause but the occasion for Truman to remove MacArthur. After consulting with the State Department and the Joint Chiefs of Staff and receiving their unanimous agreement that the general should be dismissed, Truman signed the orders on April 10, appointing General Matthew Ridgeway to replace MacArthur.

The large public outpouring of sympathy for MacArthur on his return to the United States and his speech to a joint session of Congress on April 19 symbolized the split in American understanding of the differences between limited and total war in the nuclear age. Unable to comprehend or uncaring about the implications of a total war against Communist China and, perhaps, the USSR, American demonstrators and many news editors issued startling accusations against the president. The state legislatures of Illinois, Michigan, Florida, and California passed resolutions condemning Truman. Senator Richard Nixon called the dismissal "rank appeasement," asking the Senate to insist on MacArthur's reinstatement and to censure the president. The most extreme criticism came, of course, from Senator McCarthy, who said the president was a "son of a bitch who ought to be impeached."

On May 3, a Senate investigating committee began hearings on the reasons for MacArthur's dismissal, hearing 13 witnesses and recording 3,691 pages of testimony in 42 days. At its finish, the report generally concurred with Truman. General Marshall's statement to the committee summarizes the essence of the group's conclusions. According to Marshall, it was not new for a military commander to be required to act in disagreement with the directives given to him. "What is new and what has brought about the necessity for General MacArthur's removal," he stated, "is the wholly unprecedented situation of a local theater commander *publicly expressing* his displeasure and his disagreement with the foreign and military policy of the United States" (italics added). In such a case, Marshall concluded, "there was no other recourse but to relieve him."

For Truman, not just policy but principle was involved: the principle that the U.S. Constitution guaranteed the superiority of the president, a civil and elected official, over military officers.

In 1951, MacArthur was replaced and, after a brief effort to seek the Republican presidential nomination in 1952, he "faded away." The Senate did not seek to impeach, censure, or override the president. A truce with North Korea was delayed for over two years. The political objective of containment at the 38th parallel was sustained over the concept of total war. Yet the supporters of MacArthur and his attitudes lingered on into future decades.

## May 2, 1951

### *The West German Federal Republic becomes a full member of the Council of Europe.*

This was one step toward the American objective of rearming the Germans and integrating them into the

NATO forces, a process that France remained reluctant to approve.

## May 2, 1951

### *Iran's Majlis (parliament) and senate vote to nationalize Iran's oil industry.*

This action followed an Iranian effort in 1950 to secure a larger share of the oil profits from the British-controlled Anglo-Iranian Oil Company. On April 29, an extremist nationalist leader, Mohammed Mossadegh, was named premier, and he quickly pushed the oil nationalization decree through both legislative bodies.

The British objected to the decree, appealing to the International Court of Justice to require Iran to arbitrate the dispute. Mossadegh refused to recognize the court's jurisdiction and an impasse ensued. For the next two years, Britain and Iran engaged in a diplomatic conflict. Britain demanded compensation for its oil holdings; Iran objected because it claimed the right to abrogate the 1933 oil concession treaty between the two countries.

See August 19, 1953.

## May 4, 1951

### The United States and Iceland agree on a treaty to use Iceland's defense facilities for NATO forces.

## May 18, 1951

### *The U.N. General Assembly approves an arms embargo against Communist China.*

This action followed an assembly declaration on February 1, 1950, that Communist China was an aggressor in the Korean War.

## June 19, 1951

### The U.S. draft of men for military service is extended to July 1, 1955.

President Truman signed legislation lowering the draft age to $18\frac{1}{2}$ years and authorized universal military training (UMT) for all American young men at some unspecified future date. For several years Truman had requested UMT but Congress opposed it. Although this bill approved UMT in principle,

Congress did not provide the necessary funds to make it effective.

## July 8, 1951

### Truce negotiations begin in Korea.

Arrangements for the talks originated on June 23, 1951, when Soviet Ambassador to the U.N. Jacob A. Malik called for cease-fire and armistice talks. Truman announced that the United States was ready for such discussions, and by July 8 talks began at KAESONG. In August, the negotiations stopped, first over U.S. objections to Communist violation of agreed regulations and later because the Communists claimed U.N. planes bombed Kaesong.

On October 8, talks began again at PANMUNJOM near the 38th parallel, where they continued over the next two years. During this time, heavy fighting by both sides frequently interrupted the discussions. Each time, however, the talks began again. During 1952, the principal issue became the repatriation of prisoners of war. After reports that nearly half of the 130,000 prisoners held by the United Nations did not wish to return to Communist tyranny, the North Koreans and Chinese refused to accept such claims and insisted on the full exchange of all prisoners.

Not until the election of President Eisenhower in 1952 did the truce negotiations move toward a successful cease-fire in Korea. Meanwhile, a stalemate

Eisenhower eating with U.S. officers in Korea shortly before his inauguration. National Archives

continued during which negotiating and fighting occurred at different times.

See July 26–27, 1953.

## July 20, 1951

### *King Abdullah of Jordan is assassinated in Jerusalem.*

Abdullah incurred the wrath of many Arabs by proclaiming on December 1, 1948, that he was sovereign and that Jordan would unite all Arab Palestinians.

Abdullah's immediate successor was Emir TALAL, but on August 11, 1952, the parliament declared Talal unfit to rule either due to mental instability or because he opposed British policy in Palestine. Parliament named Abdullah's 17-year-old son, Prince Hussein, as king, a position Hussein assumed on his 18th birthday.

## August 30, 1951

### The United States and the Philippines sign a treaty of mutual defense.

An armed attack on either of the parties in the Pacific would be dangerous "to its own peace and safety", and each party would act against the common danger "in accordance with its own constitutional processes."

## September 1, 1951

### The Anzus Tripartite Security Treaty is signed.

This was a mutual assistance agreement between Australia, New Zealand, and the United States. It was the product of persistent Australian efforts, according to historian Joseph Siracusa, "despite the misgivings of the State Department and with the firm resolve of the Joint Chiefs to keep contacts with the Australians and New Zealanders on defense matters as superficial as possible." See his *America's Australia, Australia's America* (1997).

## September 6, 1951

### A U.S.-Portuguese pact integrates the militarily strategic Azores into NATO's defense structure.

## September 8, 1951

### A peace treaty is signed by the United States and Japan at San Francisco.

The treaty, stimulated by the ongoing Korean War, had been negotiated by John Foster Dulles, a special consultant to U.S. Secretary of State Acheson, and Premier Shigeru YOSHIDA of Japan. At the treaty conference, the Soviet Union objected to the proceedings and its delegate boycotted the final session, refusing to sign the treaty.

Premier Yoshida signs treaty as John Foster Dulles and Secretary of State Dean Acheson look on. National Archives

Because of the relative leniency of the final treaty and the Anglo-American desire to make Japan a strong ally in East Asia, the treaty is referred to as "the Treaty of Reconciliation." Japan's Diet ratified the treaty on November 18, 1951, the U.S. Senate on March 20, 1952.

### September 8, 1951

#### Japan and the United States sign a mutual security treaty.

At the same time as the peace treaty was negotiated, a Mutual Security Treaty was also developed guaranteeing the U.S. presence in Japan. Under the terms of the treaty, U.S. troops and naval and air bases would remain in Japan indefinitely. Japan would not permit any other nation to have bases or military authority within its boundaries without American consent.

### September 20, 1951

#### Greece and Turkey become NATO members.

A meeting of the NATO Council in Ottawa, Canada, recommended the admission of these two states. The formal admission took place in Lisbon on February 20, 1952.

### October 16, 1951

#### Liaqat Al Khan, the Prime Minister of Pakistan, is assassinated.

He was replaced by Kwaja NAZIMUDDIN.

### October 19, 1951

#### The war between Germany and the United States ends formally.

President Truman signed a joint congressional resolution declaring an end to the conflict of 1941–1945. Earlier, on July 9, 1951, Great Britain and France signed a formal agreement with Germany that ended the war for them.

On September 10, the foreign ministers of Great Britain, France, and the United States agreed to replace the West German occupation statute and to use West German troops in a European army.

### October 25, 1951

#### Winston Churchill and the Conservative Party win the British elections.

Churchill replaced Attlee's Socialist government, which had been in power since July 1945. Anthony Eden became minister of foreign affairs.

### October 27, 1951

#### Egypt abrogates the Anglo-Egyptian Treaty of 1936.

Under the 1936 treaty, the last vestiges of British protectorship, including control of the SUEZ CANAL to 1956, had been approved. Thus, by 1956, the British would no longer have a political protectorship over Egypt.

### November 14, 1951

#### An aid agreement is signed by the United States and Yugoslavia.

By this pact, the United States supplied military equipment, materials, and services to the armed forces of Tito's Communist government. The objective of this agreement was to sustain the breach between Tito and Stalin.

See September 27, 1949.

### December 31, 1951

#### Marshall Plan aid ends; the Mutual Security Agency replaces the OEEC.

Not all of Western Europe's economic problems were solved by the Marshall Plan, but most nations had recovered sufficiently from World War II to permit the restoration of an economic pattern resembling that of the prewar era. Moreover, the new Mutual Security Program provided $7.428 billion for economic, military, and technical aid to Europe.

# 1952

### January 5, 1952

#### India and the United States sign a five-year "Point Four" agreement.

Each country would contribute equal funds to develop the Indian economy. Later, on March 1, 1952, Prime Minister Jawaharlal Nehru's Congress

Party won India's first national elections under the federal republican constitution adopted on November 26, 1949.

Although Nehru agreed to this program of economic aid, he refused to accept any political agreements tied to it because he desired to follow a strictly neutral policy between the United States and the Soviet Union.

### January 11, 1952

**The U.N. General Assembly creates a 12-nation disarmament commission to work to regulate, limit, and achieve a "balanced reduction" of armed forces and armaments.**

The commission consisted of the 11 Security Council members and Canada. Frequent disarmament discussion resulted from this commission, but no significant agreements resulted from its work during the next 10 years.

U.S. policy, as stated early in the commission discussions, was not to accept any disarmament or other limitations on military affairs without strict international control and inspection mechanisms to prevent cheating. This position was staunchly promoted by those who counted on Soviet refusal to accept inspections, thus preventing significant arms control or disarmament agreements. It also was taken without extensive examination of its implications.

When the USSR did agree to the U.S. demand for strict inspection during the 1988 INF negotiations, Frances Fitzgerald, *Way Out There in the Blue* (2000) reports that a quandary resulted in Washington:

> On the one hand, the hard-liners—this time in the Congress—insisted on intrusive inspections; on the other hand, the [Joint] Chiefs [of Staff] and the U.S. intelligence agencies did not want the Soviets snooping around U.S. defense plants. "Verification," [Secretary of Defense] Carlucci said, "has proved to be more complex than we thought it would be. The flip side of the coin is its application to us. The more we think about it, the more difficult it becomes."

### February 2, 1952

***Great Britain announces it has successfully exploded an atomic bomb at tests in the Monte Bello islands near Australia.***

### February 6, 1952

***George VI of England dies; Elizabeth II becomes Queen of the United Kingdom.***

### March 10, 1952

***In Cuba General Fulgencio Batista overthrows President Prio Socarras and makes himself Chief of State and Premier.***

Socarras had been elected president for a four-year term on June 1, 1948, but proved to be an ineffective leader.

Batista had been military ruler of Cuba from 1933 to 1944, when he permitted elections to be held while he retired from politics. During the next eight years, however, the predominant AUTENTICO Party failed to carry out necessary reforms and increased corruption and economic instability. Therefore, just before elections were to be held in 1952, Batista again took control, he said, to save Cuba from economic chaos and left-wing radicals who opposed the existing regime.

### April 28, 1952

**General Matthew B. Ridgeway replaces Eisenhower as Supreme Allied Commander in Europe.**

Eisenhower resigned on April 12 to campaign for the Republican nomination for president.

In Korea, General Mark W. Clark replaced Ridgeway as the U.N. Far Eastern commander.

### May 26, 1952

**West Germany's internal independence is agreed to by Britain, France, and the United States.**

In four so-called peace conventions signed at Bonn, West Germany, the three Allies ended their occupation of Germany and gave West Germany virtually complete sovereignty.

### May 27, 1952

**The European Defense Community (EDC) is created to unify western European defense plans and to bind West Germany to this defense.**

In meetings at Paris, a series of documents were signed: (1) the EDC charter signed by France, West

Germany, Italy, Belgium, the Netherlands, and Luxembourg; (2) an EDC treaty with Britain to join together if any nation were attacked; (3) a NATO protocol with West Germany to extend NATO guarantees to that nation; and (4) a declaration in which Britain and the United States agreed to regard a threat to the EDC as a threat to their own security. The U.S. Senate ratified the NATO protocol on July 1, 1952.

See August 30, 1954.

### June 23, 1952

#### *Tunisian nationalists reject a French offer for greater autonomy.*

In Tunisia, the local national leaders wanted greater home rule as a step to full independence. Since February 8, 1951, when Paris first agreed to provide some autonomy for Tunisia within the French Union, the two parties had disagreed about continued French interference in local matters. Late in 1951, Tunisia took the issue to the United Nations, but on January 14, 1952, the Security Council denied the appeal to force the French to give home rule.

Subsequently, riots, violence, and near warfare took place between Tunisians and French forces. On June 23, the French presented new terms of autonomy for Tunisia, but nationalist leaders claimed Paris retained too much authority. Trouble continued in Tunisia, therefore, for the next 18 months.

### June 26, 1952

#### The McCarran-Walter Immigration and Nationality Act is passed by Congress over President Truman's veto.

This act permitted naturalization of Asians and set a quota for their further admission. Truman objected, however, to the clauses that provided for the exclusion and deportation of aliens and the control of U.S. citizens abroad.

### July 1, 1952

#### *The Schuman Plan for integrating Western Europe's coal and steel industries goes into effect.*

This plan was proposed on May 9, 1950, by French Foreign Minister ROBERT SCHUMAN. On April 18, 1951, six nations agreed to establish a single market for coal and steel, an agreement that now became effective. The six nations were France, West Germany, Italy, Belgium, the Netherlands, and Luxembourg.

The Schuman Plan became known as the European Coal and Steel Community (ECSC).

### July 23, 1952

#### *King Farouk of Egypt is overthrown in a coup d'état led by Major General Mohammed Naguib Bey.*

The coup culminated nearly a decade of dispute between the nationalist WAFD PARTY and the monarch, whose main asset was his protection by the British government. The WAFD Party gained control of Egypt's legislature and in 1951 acted to abrogate the Anglo-Egyptian Treaty of 1936.

Early in 1952, disputes between the British and the WAFD intensified, leading on January 18 to a clash between guerrilla forces and the British at Port Said. Subsequently, the WAFD leaders decided to eliminate King Farouk so that they could better control the administrative apparatus of the government. On July 23, Farouk offered little opposition, preferring to flee to exile in France. The WAFD Party under Naguib gained full control in Cairo.

King Farouk. National Archives

### October 20, 1952

*Britain sends troops to Kenya to suppress the fanatic Mau-Mau sect.*

### November 1, 1952

**The United States announces the success of the first thermonuclear (hydrogen) bomb.**

The new H-bomb yielded a force of 14 megatons (14 million tons of TNT). It was exploded on ENEWETAK (old spelling, Eniwetok), an atoll in the Marshall Islands.

### November 5, 1952

**Dwight D. Eisenhower is elected president, defeating the Democratic Party nominee, Adlai Stevenson, former governor of Illinois.**

The Republican Party also gained a slight majority in both houses of Congress.

General Eisenhower's nomination by the Republicans was a victory for the liberal and progressive faction of the party, which included such leaders as Governor Thomas Dewey, Earl Warren, and Nelson Rockefeller. This group hoped that Eisenhower would firmly establish control of the party for the "modern" progressive faction. They would eventually be disappointed, even though Eisenhower served two terms of office. The conservative Old Guard Republicans continued to have great strength in the Senate and House.

Eisenhower's nomination caused bitterness among proponents of Senator Robert Taft, such as Senators Everett Dirksen of Illinois and William Knowland of California.

To placate the conservatives, Eisenhower chose Richard Nixon as his running mate. Yet the philosophical differences between the liberal and conservative Republicans were not healed by the 1952 presidential victory. Especially in foreign affairs, the Old Guard preferred an Asia-first policy and a neo-isolationist, go-it-alone international policy. In contrast, Eisenhower believed Europe deserved first priority in U.S. national security and realized the value of NATO and other U.S. allies in world affairs.

Among the Democrats, the nomination of Stevenson had revived hopes for the continuation of a liberal foreign and domestic program such as Roosevelt's New Deal and Truman's Fair Deal. Truman did not seek the nomination because he believed in the idea of two terms for a president and felt he would follow the 22nd Amendment, even though he was exempt from it. Also his wife, Bess, had become disenchanted with Washington, D.C., and wanted the family to return to Independence, Missouri, where she was now spending most of her time.

Stevenson carried the liberal banner in satisfactory fashion, but General Eisenhower's popularity was too great to overcome in 1952 or, later, in 1956.

# XIV.  STRUGGLES IN THE COLD WAR

*European Security*
*Suez Crisis*
*Castro in Cuba*
*The Vietnam Escalation*

# 1 9 5 3

### January 20, 1953

**President Dwight D. Eisenhower is inaugurated as the 34th president of the United States.**

He appointed John Foster Dulles as secretary of state and Charles Wilson, former president of General Motors Corporation, as secretary of defense.

Dulles was eminently qualified to serve as secretary of state. He had been an adviser to President Wilson during the Paris Peace Conference and a member of the Reparations Commission in 1919. During World War II, he became an internationalist interested in urging Republicans to act in a bipartisan fashion in foreign policy. He had been a delegate to the San Francisco Conference on the United Nations in 1945 and served as a special representative of President Truman to negotiate the Japanese Peace Treaty of 1951.

He served as secretary from January 21, 1953, until illness forced him to resign on April 22, 1959. He died on May 24, 1959.

### March 5, 1953

**Joseph Stalin dies and is interred in the Lenin Mausoleum on Red Square.**

Outside the USSR, two related questions arose after his death. Did Stalin die a natural death? Would his successors adopt new policies?

In the six months prior to his death, Stalin had taken steps to assure a continued hard-line policy. At the 19th Communist Party Congress in October 1953,

he declared that Soviet economic programs must stress heavy industry and agricultural collectivization. He also asserted that tight party controls should be adopted against capitalist aggression, which could be expected at any time.

Joseph Stalin speaking with M. Vyacheslav Molotov, Soviet vice premier, who became foreign minister (1953–1956) after Stalin's death. National Archives

Stalin's continued hard line contrasted with recent statements of some Politburo members. Georgy MALENKOV had urged stress on consumer products and cooperation with Western powers. Stalin seemed to disagree. Stalin seemed to be ready for another party purge. In October, he added 14 members to the Politburo and renamed it the PRESIDIUM of the Central Committee. More threateningly, on January 13, 1953, *Pravda* newspaper reported a "Doctor's Plot," and a group of nine doctors serving in the Kremlin was arrested, accused of assassinating the Soviet Union's chief, propagandist, Andrey Zhadanov, in 1948 and of trying to kill several Red Army generals. By February, rumors in Moscow threatened party members such as Malenkov, M. Vyacheslav MOLOTOV, and Anastas MIKOYAN.

Soviet historian Dmitri Volkogonov's *Autopsy for an Empire* provides a detailed account of Stalin's last days. Volkogonov begins with the dictator's signs of weakness "almost beyond his strength" during his October 1953 speech to the 19th Congress of the Communist Party of the Soviet Union. Soon after, Stalin suffered a number of falling spells, twice falling down stairs. Although he had stopped smoking because of high blood pressure, Stalin continued drinking wine and, despite his doctor's advice, took hot steam baths. On March 1, Stalin's close comrades left his dacha at 4:00 A.M. after a night of feasting. During the day, Stalin never left his bedroom after noon as was usual. By 11:00 P.M. on March 1, his bodyguard and housekeeper entered his room and found him unconscious. At 7:00 A.M. March 2, Lavrenty Beria, head of the secret police, brought a physician who found Stalin in a coma, breathing irregularly and having damage to his cerebral blood vessels. The doctor kept a log of Stalin's symptoms until his death at 9:50 A.M. on March 5. By that time, the Soviet Presidium of the Central Committee met to select Malenkov as chairman of the council and General Secretary of the Communist Party. On the Presidium with Malenkov were Beria, Molotov, Nikolay Bulganin, and Lazar Kaganovich as first deputy chairmen. During the next year, there was a power struggle in the Soviet hierarchy. On March 20, 1953, Nikita Khrushchev succeeded Malenkov as first secretary of the Party. Beria, who was feared by the others for the power he had accumulated, was expelled from his government and party posts on July 10 and executed on December 23, 1953. The power struggle did not end until February 8, 1955, when Malenkov was forced to resign, making Khrushchev the general secretary of the Communist Party and Bulganin chairman of the Presidium.

Both Bulganin and Khrushchev spoke of "collective leadership." They also relaxed the tight controls Stalin had imposed both at home and abroad. In economics, they placed more investment in consumer goods such as textiles and housing, and allowed farmers to grow vegetables in private plots and sell them in the market. Internationally, they mixed claims of military buildups with speeches on "peaceful coexistence." This period, which came to be known as the thaw in Cold War relations, lasted from 1954 to 1960.

## March 27, 1953

### The U.S. Senate confirms the nomination of Charles Bohlen as ambassador to the Soviet Union in spite of Senator McCarthy's attempts to prevent it.

This incident was the first effort of the Eisenhower administration to stand firm against McCarthy's intemperate charges against a government official.

Bohlen's appointment as ambassador had been supported because of his excellent qualifications and Eisenhower's personal acquaintance with him in Paris. McCarthy and his followers charged that Bohlen was a security risk. They claimed that as an assistant secretary of state and interpreter at the 1945 Yalta Conference, he had a role in those decisions. McCarthyites claimed that Roosevelt sold out Chiang Kai-shek at Yalta.

The Senate hearings gave Bohlen an opportunity to clarify the record on the Yalta agreements. He pointed out that Chiang in 1945 greatly appreciated being able to have a pact signed with Stalin to accept his regime. Only the later violations of the Yalta agreements by Stalin caused difficulty, not the Yalta agreements themselves.

During the Senate debate on Bohlen, McCarthy went too far in his charges. After reviewing Bohlen's personnel and FBI files, both Senator Robert Taft and Senator William Knowland, two Republican conservatives who had previously backed McCarthy, reported that they accepted Bohlen's nomination. McCarthy sought to challenge the report of Taft and Knowland and was seriously rebuffed. Secretary of State Dulles and President Eisenhower expressed support for Bohlen and the Senate voted approval, 74 to 13.

Senator McCarthy's fanatic efforts continued for another 18 months before the Senate voted to condemn his method.

See December 2, 1954.

### April 16, 1953

**President Eisenhower is cautious in reacting to the new Soviet leadership's desire for relaxation of the Cold War.**

Eisenhower declared that better relations with the United States would be possible if Moscow first demonstrated its policy by actions such as "free elections in Korea"; approving U.N. control and inspection of "disarmament agreements"; restoring "free choice" in Eastern European nations; and giving similar evidence of policy changes.

In contrast, Winston Churchill on May 11 desired more appreciation of the new Soviet rulers. He suggested a summit conference "on the highest level" to prepare an agenda of problems to resolve. He indicated that President Eisenhower should not, perhaps, expect too much at one time.

Generally, the continued strong anti-Communist feelings in America prevented Washington from responding more positively to Soviet overtures for an easing of tension.

### June 16, 1953

*Soviet tanks and troops are sent in to quell an uprising of workers in East Germany.*

In May, the Soviet Union had abolished its control commission in East Germany and relaxed controls on protests. But it demanded an increase in production for the same wages. Marching in Stalinallee on June 16, workers protested the low wages. Strikes soon spread throughout East Germany until Soviet tanks rolled into Berlin, Dresden, Leipzig, and other cities to smash the demonstrations. The Soviet assault killed 125 people and a thousand more were arrested.

To placate the workers, the Communist government instituted a 10-point reform plan on June 22. This plan increased wages, improved living conditions, ended travel restrictions between East and West Berlin, and announced that martial law would end on July 11.

The United States and its Western allies avoided military intervention in East Germany but employed psychological methods to weaken the Communist government and demonstrate that West Germans benefited by cooperating with the Western powers. In addition to using the Radio in the American Sector (RAIS) of Berlin to inform Germans of the many strikes, riots, and protest movements in the socialist state, the Eisenhower administration devised a program to help feed East Germans. Between July and September 1953, over 75% of the East German population went to West Berlin to get U.S. food packages. By the end of 1953, the East German government had tightened its controls over East Germans to prevent them from obtaining food packages in West Berlin. The U.S. program also solidified support among West Germans for the Federal Republic and its chancellor, Konrad Adenauer.

### July 10–14, 1953

**The U.S. Secretary of State confers in Washington with the French and British foreign ministers.**

Their final communiqué invited the Soviets to meet and discuss German unity and an Austrian peace treaty. They also warned the Soviet and North Korean Communists that the Korean War would

Families of returning POWs waving and greeting as the ship docks at Fort Mason, California. National Archives

reopen if there were truce violations or other Communist aggression in Asia.

### July 26–27, 1953

## An armistice agreement is signed and becomes effective in Korea.

The armistice agreement came slowly despite Eisenhower's visit to Korea on December 14 to seek an end to the war. Not until March 30, when the Chinese suggested letting the prisoner-of-war issue be decided by an international authority, was progress made.

An important historical issue regarding the armistice was whether or not the Eisenhower administration issued an ultimatum on May 22 demanding that Chinese officials make concessions to complete the armistice or risk the U.S. dropping an atomic bomb on China. In 1956, Secretary of State Dulles claimed an ultimatum was delivered to China, but documents declassified 30 years later gave no evidence to support his claim. Perhaps Dulles exaggerated the events of

## Battle Casualties[1]

### Korean and Chinese

|  | Killed | Wounded | POW | Total |
|---|---|---|---|---|
| South Korea[2] | 47,000 | 183,000 | 8,656 | 238,656 |
| North Korea[3] | — | — | 110,723 | 630,723 |
| China[4] | — | — | 21,374 | 381,374 |

### United States

|  | Total | Army | Navy | USMC | Air Force |
|---|---|---|---|---|---|
| Total Casualties | 142,091 | 109,958 | 2,087 | 28,205 | 1,841 |
| Deaths | 33,629 | 279,704 | 458 | 4,267 | 1,200 |
| Killed in action | 23,300 | 19,334 | 279 | 3,308 | 379 |
| Wounded in action | 105,785 | 79,526 | 1,599 | 24,281 | 379 |
| Died | 2,501 | 1,930 | 23 | 537 | 11 |
| Other | 103,284 | 77,596 | 1,576 | 23,744 | 368 |
| Missing in action | 5,866 | 4,442 | 174 | 391 | 859 |
| Died | 5,127 | 3,778 | 152 | 391 | 806 |
| Returned | 715 | 664 | 13 | 0 | 38 |
| Captured or interned | 7,140 | 6,656 | 35 | 225 | 224 |
| Died | 2,701 | 2,662 | 4 | 31 | 4 |
| Returned | 4,418 | 3,973 | 31 | 194 | 220 |
| Refused repatriation | 21 | 21 | 0 | 0 | 0 |

### United Nations (other than United States)

|  | Killed | Wounded | Missing/POW | Total |
|---|---|---|---|---|
| Australia | 261 | 1,034 | 37 | 1,332 |
| Britain | 686 | 2,498 | 1,102 | 4,286 |
| Canada | 294 | 1,202 | 47 | 1,543 |
| New Zealand | 22 | 79 | 1 | 102 |
| Others | 1,931 | 6,484 | 1,582 | 9,997 |
| Total | 3,194 | 11,297 | 2,769 | 17,260 |

1. D. Rees, *Korea: The Limited War* (1964).
2. There were roughly 1 million South Korean civilian casualties,
3. There were roughly 1 million North Korean civilian casualties, and the figure for total casualties includes estimates of dead and wounded.
4. Figure for total casualties includes estimates of both dead and wounded.
*Source*: James T. Matray, *Historical Dictionary of the Korean War* (Westport, Conn. Greenwood, 1991), p. 553.

1953 to explain why U.S. policies of "massive retaliation" and "brinkmanship" could be valuable.

On June 18, Syngman Rhee, president of South Korea, opposed the agreement because it kept Korea divided into two segments and tried to sabotage the negotiations by releasing 27,000 Chinese and North Korean prisoners. Rhee's attempt to stop the talks failed and an armistice was reached in July.

Yet the armistice did not result in a peace treaty or Korean unity. Further negotiations continued on a sporadic basis but without success. The United States assisted South Korea by giving Seoul over $6 billion in the next decade and stationing American troops south of the 38th parallel. But the negotiations for permanent peace would become stalemated.

See January 12, 1954.

## August 8, 1953

**The Union of Soviet Socialist Republics successfully explodes a hydrogen thermonuclear device.**

Premier Malenkov announced the successful test in a speech to the Supreme Soviet in which he emphasized that the Soviet Union was ready to ease tension and seek peace if Western Europe would agree. But he emphasized that the USSR now also had the power to prevent aggressive war by the capitalists.

## August 19, 1953

**Premier Mossadegh's government is overthrown by a coup in Iran. Mohammad Reza Pahlavi regains control as shah.**

Mossadegh was elected Iran's prime minister on April 19, 1951, having become Iran's most outspoken politician seeking more oil profits from Iran than the 20 percent the British had provided in the 1930s. In 1948, Iranian officials began negotiating with the Anglo-Iranian Oil officers to obtain a 50-50 split in the profits, but the British officials refused. Owing to Britain's intransigence, Mossadegh's National Front Party gained a majority in parliament and passed legislation to nationalize the oil wells and take 100 percent of the profits. As Iran's prime minister, Mossadegh offered to negotiate with the British while shutting down the oil production in Iran in the summer of 1951.

Rather than allow Iran to nationalize its oil production, the British government planned clandestine operations to overthrow Mossadegh, obtaining assistance from the U.S. Central Intelligence Agency (CIA). Although President Truman rejected the British request for CIA help, President Eisenhower approved CIA assistance in early 1953. Secretary of State John Foster Dulles believed the Tudeh Communist Party was at work in Iran, although Mossadegh's National Front Party primarily enrolled middle-class Iranian's who sought more money to modernize Iran's economy. Iran's Tudeh Communist Party had been damaged after Stalin backed down and left northern Iran in 1946.

Initially in 1952, the British saw little chance to overthrow Mossadegh because of his popularity, but in March 1953 Iran's Army General Fazollah Zahedi asked CIA agents in Tehran's embassy to support the army's efforts to topple Mossadegh. The CIA approved $1 million to bring down the prime minister, sending both Donald Wilber and Kermit Roosevelt to plan and direct operations. In addition, U.S. General H. Norman Schwarzkopf, father of the general who led U.N. forces in the Gulf War (1990–1991), went to Iran because he had become a friend of Mohammad Reza Pahlavi, the Shah of Iran during a tour of duty in Tehran during World War II.

To overthrow Mossadegh, the CIA and British intelligence agents spread propaganda opposing the prime minister and paid Iranians to stage protests against the National Front Party. In part, these efforts succeeded because Iran's lack of any oil income since 1951 had impoverished many Iranians and caused disputes among National Front Party members. Mossadegh tried to solidify his power by dissolving parliament and holding a referendum to approve his action. Although on August 4 Mossadegh announced that 99 percent of the voters approved, many moderates in Mossadegh's party boycotted the referendum. Finally, on August 13, Roosevelt and Schwarzkopf persuaded the shah to dismiss Mossadegh and make General Zahedi prime minister. On August 19, General Zahedi's troops arrested Mossadegh and Zahedi took office. Details about the CIA's role in Iran can be found in a *New York Times* article on April 16, 2000, that is based on a CIA history of the "Overthrow of Mossadegh of Iran," written in 1954 by Donald N. Wilber, who planned CIA Operation TP-Ajax.

See March 27, 1946, and October 21, 1954.

## September 15, 1953

*Communist China announces that the Soviet Union has agreed to provide massive economic aid to help it build its heavy industry.*

The agreement permitted China to carry out the Five-Year Plan begun in January 1953, but did not specify funds in addition to the $300 million, five-year loan agreed to by Moscow in 1950. In 1954, however, Khrushchev visited Peking and approved a second loan of $130 million.

## September 21, 1953

**Andrey Vishinsky, the Soviet delegate to the United Nations, offers the General Assembly a proposal to reduce all armed forces of the great powers by one-third and to ban the use of atomic weapons.**

The proposal became the basis for the U.N. Disarmament Commission to ask a five-power subcommittee (United States, USSR, Great Britain, France, Canada) to consider the question of an inspection system, a means to prevent surprise attacks, and a nuclear test ban. The subcommittee met from May 13 to June 22, 1954, but achieved no results.

## September 26, 1953

**The United States and Spain agree that the United States may establish air and naval bases in Spain in return for $250 million of economic and military aid.**

This action culminated more than four years of effort by conservative Senators Pat McCarran, Robert Taft, and Owen Brewster working with Spanish head of State Francisco Franco to involve Spain in the free world's battle against Communism. On August 25, 1953, Spain awarded McCarran the Special Medal of the Grand Cross for his devotion to the country. Truman despised Franco but allowed negotiations because U.S. military officers advised him that forward bomber bases were essential to deter the Soviet Union. The agreement was not made, however, until Eisenhower and Dulles accepted the idea of "working with a Fascist."

## October 30, 1953

**President Eisenhower's "new look" policy is described in NSC-162.**

The Eisenhower administration wanted to continue Truman's CONTAINMENT POLICY but developed a new national security plan to replace NSC-68 and its revised defense plan of 1952 (NSC-141). Eisenhower believed the Truman methods failed to provide for a balanced federal budget and were not adaptable to a "long-haul" defense program designed to outlast communism and demonstrate capitalism's superiority.

Showing his concern for budgetary matters, Eisenhower appointed Secretary of the Treasury George Humphrey to the NSC, where he could comment on the fiscal significance of defense plans.

To relate fiscal, foreign, and defense policies, Eisenhower's plan emphasized the primary U.S. effort in maintaining a sufficient nuclear strike force to hit the Soviet Union if a crisis necessitated a nuclear attack. Although in 1953 news reports of Eisenhower's "new look" emphasized "massive retaliation," the president intended to combine a retaliatory air force capability with negotiations to cooperate with the Soviet Union in reducing the risk of a nuclear war that no one could win. In line with the Joint Chiefs of Staffs' desire for a clear decision to use nuclear weapons if needed, Eisenhower opted to build a strong strategic air force while offering to negotiate with Soviet leaders. To seek negotiations, Eisenhower proposed an "atoms for peace" plan in December 1953 and an "open skies" plan in 1955. See December 18, 1953, and July 18, 1955.

To reduce expenditures on U.S. conventional forces, Eisenhower wanted the various U.S. allies to provide armed forces for their own defense. Overall, Eisenhower's new look policy would avoid the $74 billion envisioned in the 1952 fiscal year budget and stabilize defense expenses at between $38 and $40 billion per year.

The particular cuts in the army and navy budgets became clear in February 1954, when Secretary of Defense Wilson told a congressional committee that the army would be decreased from 20 to 17 divisions; the navy would modestly reduce its ships; and the air force would seek 137 wings, not 143. The major defense increase would be $1 billion over 1954 "for continental air defense."

The following tables indicate the shift in defense emphasis involved in the new look policy. They also explain why the army and navy eventually sought aid from Congress and the public to oppose Eisenhower's new look, which met its fiscal and military priority goals by cuts in army and navy budgets and personnel.

Manpower Proposals

|  | December 1953 | October 1954 | June 1955 |
|---|---|---|---|
| Army | 1,500,000 | 1,500,000 | 1,000,000 |
| Navy/Marines | 1,000,000 | 920,000 | 870,000 |
| Air Force | 950,000 | 960,000 | 970,000 |

Defense Budget ($ billion)

| Fiscal | Year 1954 | Fiscal Year 1955 |
|---|---|---|
| Army | $12.9 | $8.8 |
| Navy/Marines | 11.2 | 9.7 |
| Air Force | 15.6 | 16.4 |

### October 30, 1953

**The United States and Japan agree that Japan may enlarge its self-defense forces to protect itself from aggression.**

The Eisenhower administration's effort here were in line with its "new look" policy of both reducing U.S. costs for Japan's defense and enabling local forces to protect themselves from aggression.

### November 21, 1953

**Conflict between Italy and Yugoslavia is averted when both nations agree to a conference proposed by the foreign ministers of the United States, France, and Great Britain.**

The Italian-Yugoslav dispute arose over the disposition of the city of Trieste, which had been pending since 1945. On October 8, the British and U.S. governments announced they would end their occupation of Trieste by giving Italy the city of Trieste and Yugoslavia almost all the surrounding rural areas.

Yugoslav leader Marshal Tito opposed this plan and threatened to march troops into the Italian Zone. The conflict caused the United States, France, and Great Britain to ask the two contending nations to a meeting on the problem. On October 5, 1954, the dispute was resolved according to terms that divided the area between Italy and Yugoslavia.

### December 8, 1953

**President Eisenhower proposes an atoms-for-peace plan to the United Nations.**

Speaking before the U.N. General Assembly, Eisenhower suggested that all nations should pool their fissionable nuclear material to use for peaceful industrial purposes.

The U.S. delegation presented the U.S. atoms-for-peace plan to the United Nations on September 23, 1954. Specifically, the United States suggested that an agency be established for promoting the beneficial uses of atomic energy. The General Assembly unanimously endorsed this plan on December 4, 1954.

# 1954

### January 12, 1954

**Secretary of State John Foster Dulles delivers a speech outlining the "massive retaliation" defense policy of Eisenhower's "new look" program.**

Dulles emphasized that the United States would respond to Communist aggression by building "a great capacity to retaliate" instantly "by means and at places of our choosing."

Although Dulles's speech cited the "new look's" desire to have local defense forces and to prefer to stress the deterrent aspects of the policy, news accounts and critics oversimplified the complex purposes of Eisenhower's concepts and emphasized "massive retaliation" as the whole focus of the new look.

### January 25, 1954

**A big-four foreign ministers conference begins in Berlin, discusses but fails to agree on treaties for Germany and Austria.**

An important by-product of the conference was an agreement to hold a Geneva conference on far eastern problems of Korea and Indochina and to invite Communist China to attend.

Secretary of State Dulles reluctantly agreed to a Chinese presence at Geneva. He did so after Anthony Eden offered a compromise by which all countries

Secretary of State John Foster Dulles. National Archives

representing the U.N. command in Korea would be present on one side, with the delegates of the Soviet Union, Communist China, and North Korea on the other side. But Dulles made it clear, that this did not mean U.S. diplomatic recognition of the Peking government.

See April 26, 1954.

### January 26, 1954

**THE U.S. Senate ratifies a mutual security treaty with South Korea.**

The United States would assist South Korea if it were attacked, but would not assist any attempt by Seoul to unite Korea by force.

### February 25–26, 1954

**The Senate rejects various versions of the Bricker Amendment as well as other proposals to limit the treaty-making powers of the president.**

Senator John Bricker of Ohio, one of a group of conservative Republicans who claimed that the presidential decisions of Franklin Roosevelt and Harry Truman had caused problems for the nation, proposed that executive agreements by the president as well as all treaties must be ratified by both houses of congress and every state. If ratified as a constitutional amendment, Bricker's proposal would have drastically curtailed the executive conduct of foreign affairs, and both Eisenhower and Dulles opposed it. Yet in the Senate, the amendment lost by only one vote.

### March 1, 1954

**The United States successfully tests a hydrogen bomb dropped from an airplane at Bikini Atoll in the Pacific.**

The 15-megaton (15 million tons of TNT) bomb unleashed a heavy amount of radioactive debris. Radioactive particles drifting for over 100 miles landed on and caused illness for the crew of a Japanese fishing boat, *Lucky Dragon* (FUKURYU MARU). This incident revived anti-American feeling in Japan, especially after the boat's radio operator, AIKICHI NAGAKUBO, died of radiation sickness on September 23, 1954.

### March 14, 1954

**Vietminh forces attack 10,000 French soldiers at Dien Bien Phu.**

The Vietminh attack was exactly what French General Henri Navarre had hoped for in November 1953, when he concentrated his forces at the small northern, rural outpost of Dien Bien Phu. The "Navarre plan" wanted to entice the Vietminh's General Vo NGUYEN GIAP from his protracted war guerrilla tactics so that he would engage the French in a conventional battle where Navarre's crack legionnaires could decisively beat the Communists.

Navarre's plan backfired because like many French and, later, American military officers, he underestimated the Vietnamese. The Vietminh fought aggressively and Giap used his artillery in superior fashion to besiege Dien Bien Phu. Monsoon rains also handicapped the French, because they could not adequately resupply their forces.

By March 22, a decisive Communist victory appeared possible, causing Paris to appeal for help to Washington. General Paul Ely came to Washington to seek U.S. air support. The French wanted aircraft from the USS *Boxer* and USS *Essex* to help their besieged forces.

In Washington, Ely's request precipitated a lengthy consideration of whether the United States should intervene in this French colonial war.

### April 4–5, 1954

**President Eisenhower decides not to send immediate assistance to the French besieged at Dien Bien Phu.**

When General Ely first arrived in Washington, rumors in the press suggested that the United States would intervene. Thorough consideration and a desire for Allied and congressional backing caused the president to refuse France such aid.

On March 24, the president stated that the defeat of communism in Southeast Asia was critical to U.S. interests. He and Dulles agreed, however, with a military study (the Erskine Report) prepared in March 1954 that recommended the United States act only in coordination with Great Britain and France. Eisenhower also asked Dulles to consult with congressional leaders to gain their support.

Neither Britain nor France wanted a joint action with the United States. The British were unwilling to aid French colonialism; the French did not want to internationalize the war because Paris wished to retain control over the solution to Indochina's rebellion.

When Secretary of State Dulles and Admiral Arthur D. Radford, chairman of the JCS, met with congressional leaders, they also refused cooperation. The congressmen asked how many of the JCS supported action, learning that only Radford did. General Matthew Ridgeway and others opposed this action. In addition, the congressmen agreed that a multinational force to assist France would be best.

Although Vice President Richard Nixon urged action despite the lack of support, Eisenhower preferred a united approach and the backing of Congress. Therefore, on April 5, he avoided U.S. action on the terms sought by General Ely.

From early April to June 17, Dulles and Eisenhower searched for some other formula to gain "united action" with allies to help the French. The president wrote to Churchill, who rejected his request for British action. Later, Dulles flew to London to try to convince Churchill and Anthony Eden that the Communists should not be permitted to win Indochina. But Dulles could not convince them that

Vietnam was a critical world region. Yet until June 17, when a new French premier, who was committed to secure "peace" in Indochina, took office, Dulles believed that there should be some means to secure French control in Indochina.

See June 4, 1954.

### April 26, 1954

**The Geneva Conference on Korea and Indochina begins.**

As agreed at the Berlin Conference (January–February 1954), the delegations included the Soviet Union, North Korea, Communist China, France, Great Britain, the United States, and 13 other non-Communist nations that had contributed to the U.N. forces in the Korean War.

During the first month, the delegates argued the question of Korea. By June 15, no solution was in sight and the 16 non-Communist delegates issued a statement that further talks "would serve no useful purpose." They blamed the three Communist states for rejecting the principle of Korean independence and unity through free elections.

Several compromises were achieved on the Indochina issue.

See under July 20, 1954.

### May 19, 1954

**The United States and Pakistan sign a mutual defense pact by which Washington helps to arm Pakistan against Communism.**

Secretary of State John Foster Dulles was willing to provide a similar pact for INDIA but Prime Minister NEHRU preferred to remain neutral in the Cold War. India bitterly opposed U.S. aid to Pakistan because of the frequent threats of war between these neighboring nations. Nehru believed Pakistan's arms would be used against India, not the Soviet Union.

Although the Pakistan alliance became part of the Baghdad Pact, the Eisenhower administration never shipped any armaments to Pakistan because of a military coup abolishing Pakistan's republic. But subsequent administrations did send arms to the Pakistanis.

See October 7, 1958.

Chinese delegates at Geneva are led by Prime Minister Chou Enlai (third from left), who meets with his negotiating team. National Archives

### June 1, 1954

**The Personal Security Board of the Atomic Energy Commission unanimously finds Dr. J. Robert Oppenheimer is "loyal" in handling atomic secrets. Nevertheless, it votes 2 to 1 not to reinstate him as a government consultant on atomic energy.**

Although Oppenheimer was one of America's most renowned physicists and had directed the Los Alamos laboratory in producing the atomic bomb in 1945, he had been criticized for opposing the H-BOMB development in 1949, joining many scientists who desired international controls on nuclear weapons.

The Oppenheimer case of 1954 indicated Senator McCarthy's influence on American life. Later, Thomas E. Murray, an AEC member who voted not to reinstate Oppenheimer, admitted his vote was cast in the "exigencies of the moment," the "moment" being McCarthyism.

According to John E. Haynes and Harvey Klehr's *Venona* (1999), the secret Venona files released in 1995 indicate that although Oppenheimer was not "an active Soviet source," he had strong ties to the U.S. Communist Party until 1941. After becoming head of the Manhattan project in 1943, he only gave "security officials enough information to bring about a neutralization of the [spy] problem but not enough

to expose associates to retribution for what they might have already done" (page 330).

### June 4, 1954

***French Premier Joseph Laniel and Vietnamese Emperor Bao Dai sign treaties granting Vietnam "complete independence" in "free association" with France.***

Since February 1953, Paris had negotiated an arrangement to transfer defense and security affairs to the government in Saigon. The agreement on June 4 stopped just short of recognizing complete Vietnamese independence, which France was still reluctant to grant. The Emperor Bao Dai remained as head of state.

### June 9, 1954

**A left-wing government in Guatemala is overthrown with assistance from the U.S. Central Intelligence Agency (CIA).**

Since 1944, Guatemala's political leaders had talked about land reform as a means of resolving social unrest in rural areas. Until the 1951 election of Colonel Jacobo Arbenz GUZMÁN, the reformers had accomplished little. ARBENZ decided that real reform required the takeover of the United Fruit Company, an American company that profited from Guatemala's banana plantations. In 1953, Arbenz's government confiscated 225,000 acres of United Fruit's 300,000 acres of land.

The U.S. State Department protested on behalf of United Fruit, demanding compensation for the property. Arbenz claimed Guatemala could not afford the payment expected by United Fruit and argued that Guatemala's land belonged to its people.

Secretary of State Dulles believed Arbenz was a Communist and must be acted against. In March 1954, Dulles took the issue to the Tenth Inter-American Conference session at Caracas, Venezuela. Without specifying Guatemala, Dulles persuaded the conferees to adopt a declaration that communism was "incompatible with the concept of American freedom," and nations should act to "eradicate and prevent subversive activities." The vote was 17 to 1: Guatemala voted no; Mexico and Argentina abstained; Costa Rica was absent.

In January 1954, Arbenz told reporters the military aid the CIA gave to dictators in Nicaragua, Honduras, and El Salvador amounted to an "international plot" to overthrow Guatemala's government. Arbenz's remarks appeared to be correct. On January 29 rebels led by Colonel Carlos Castillo Armas launched an attack that reached Guatemala's capital city on June 18. Although Arbenz received armaments from Czechoslovakia, his army was no match for the rebels. To oversee Arbenz's ouster in June, Secretary of State Dulles sent John Peurifoy as ambassador to Guatemala. At Peurifoy's direction, Armas headed the military junta that took over Guatemala. Based on declassified documents, Nick Cullather's 1999 book *Secret History: The CIA's Classified Account of Its Operations in Guatemala 1952–1954* provides the story of the CIA's role in the overthrow of Arbenz.

## June 12, 1954

**The French National Assembly votes no confidence in George Bidault's ministry; on June 17, the assembly approves Pierre Mendès-France as head of a new ministerial coalition.**

Bidault's government fell as a result of criticism of his Indochinese policies. Mendès-France promised to solve the problem and vowed to resign if an "honor-

able peace" had not been concluded in Indochina by July 20, 1954.

## June 15, 1954

**Ngo Dinh Diem replaces Buu Loc as Premier of the French-Recognized Vietnamese government.**

Diem, whose rule greatly influenced both Vietnam and the United States from 1954 until his assassination in November 1963, was born in Vietnam of a Mandarin family. During the 1930s, he favored moderate reform to obtain some local government from the French, but by 1933 he abandoned the possibility of cooperating with the French and retired from active politics. In 1948, Diem refused to accept the French terms that Bao Dai had agreed to when he became head of state. Diem spent the early years of the 1950s in the United States at Maryknoll seminaries. There he gained many influential friends including Supreme Court Justice William O. Douglas, Francis Cardinal Spellman, and Senators Mike Mansfield and John F. Kennedy. Thus, when Bao Dai selected Diem as premier in 1954, he chose someone acceptable to the United States.

Although Bao Dai appointed Diem on June 15, he did not announce the new ministry until July 5, 1954.

## July 20, 1954

**The Geneva Conference approves a settlement of the Indochinese war.**

In May, the conferees had become deadlocked on the status of the governments of Laos and Cambodia. On May 31, the delegates approved a British proposal to invite both sides in each Indochinese state to hold cease-fire talks at Geneva. The United States opposed negotiating with the Communists and, while never completely abandoning the conference, became generally less active in cooperating in or leading the decision-making process. Dulles never returned to the conference, sending Walter Bedell Smith as the U.S. representative.

The final Geneva agreements provided for the cessation of hostilities in each of the three Indochinese states (July 20) and for a Final Declaration of the Geneva delegations (July 21). Together, the agreements recognized Laos and Cambodia as independent nations and temporarily divided Vietnam into two parts separated by a demi-

The Geneva conference.
National Archives

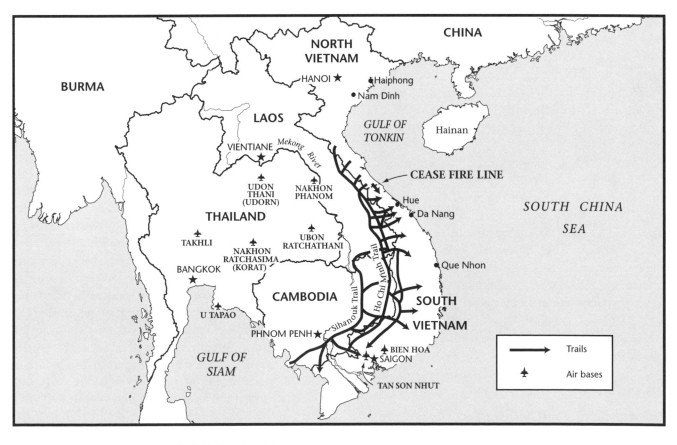

Cambodia, Laos, and Vietnam, 1954. National Archives

Casualties of First Indochina War

| French Forces* | |
| --- | --- |
| Killed in action, dead (noncombat) or missing | 92,797 |
| Wounded | 76,369 |
| Evacuated for medical reasons | 48,673 |

| Vietminh/Civilian | |
| --- | --- |
| Estimates vary from 45,000 to 1,000,000 | |

*These include French, Foreign Legion, African, and Indochinese.
*Source*: Douglas Pike, *Viet Cong* (Cambridge, Mass.: MIT Press, 1966), p. 49.

litarized zone (DMZ) at the 17th parallel. An election in 1956 would unify and decide on a future government of Vietnam.

In Vietnam, each side's forces would regroup on its side of the DMZ. The Viet Minh government of Ho Chi Minh controlled the north with its capital at Hanoi; the Vietnamese Nationalist government of Bao Dai controlled the south from Saigon. French forces could remain in the south but no new forces were to be introduced or rotated by either side. No new military equipment could be added, but replacement of destroyed, damaged, or worn equipment was allowed. Refugees from either side would be able to move freely to the north or south, according to their wishes. Finally, an International Control Commission with representatives from India, Poland, and Canada would supervise the cease-fire accords and the election procedures.

The United States announced it could not accept the conference declaration, but it agreed not to use force or threats to disturb the accords. Furthermore, the United States would view a violation of the accords as a threat to international peace.

Speaking for the Nationalist Vietnamese government at Saigon, Tran Van Do informed the final conference session that his government had reservations about the Geneva accords but would not use force or threats to resist the cease-fire. He said his government would support "every effort to reestablish a real and lasting peace in Vietnam."

## July 23, 1954

**Chinese Communist fighter pilots shoot down a Cathay-Pacific Airways commercial airliner. Later, the Chinese government apologizes to**

**Great Britain, owner of the airline, and agrees to pay compensation. Ten passengers die in the crash; eight survive.**

The Cathay-Pacific plane was shot down in the South China Sea near Hainan Island. Following a strong protest by Prime Minister Churchill, the Chinese government admitted its pilots had mistaken the plane for a Chinese Nationalist airplane. Mao's government apologized and offered to compensate the victims' families and the British airline.

## August 30, 1954

**The French National Assembly rejects the European Defense Community (EDC) treaty.**

The EDC plan had been agreed to on May 27, 1952, but conflicts over French foreign policy in Indochina and Europe prevented the French assembly from voting on the EDC until 1954.

The French veto compelled the NATO allies to seek another method for attaining a united European defense plan. U.S. Secretary of State John Foster DULLES was determined to have German troops in the NATO defense structure. French intransigence was the only factor preventing this.

## September 8, 1954

**The Southeast Asia Treaty Organization (SEATO) is formed at Manila to protect the region from outside attack or "any state or territory hereafter designated."**

The designated states were Cambodia, Laos, and Vietnam. If any state were threatened by subversion or aggression, the signatory states would consult on appropriate action. The members of SEATO were the United States, France, Great Britain, Australia, New Zealand, Thailand, Pakistan, and the Philippines.

In hearings on the SEATO treaty, Senator Alexander Wiley asked Secretary Dulles if agreeing "to counter subversive activity" is not different from agreeing to resist armed attack. Dulles acknowledged that it was different because it involved a Communist threat within a foreign country. Significantly, Dulles added: "We are confronted by an unfortunate fact—most of the countries of the world do not share our view that Communist control of any government anywhere is in itself a danger and a threat." In fact, France, Britain, and most U.S. allies would not accept the unusual U.S. concept expressed by Dulles, that

America must fear any nation with a Communist government. This reflected America's myth that all Communists received orders from Moscow as part of the universal Communist threat to capitalism.

See October 23, 1954.

### October 21, 1954

**American oil companies secure a share in Iran's oil concessions as a result of a State Department deal with Britain and the Iranian government.**

On August 19, 1953, the Iranian nationalist leader Mossadegh was ousted with U.S. aid on behalf of Mohammad Reza Pahlavi. Because the shah did not wish to retain exclusive British ownership of Iranian oil, President Eisenhower's adviser on petroleum, Herbert Hoover Jr., undertook negotiations to form an international consortium to take over the Anglo-Iranian oil concessions. Basically, Hoover and the Eisenhower administration conceived of this as a Cold War necessity to keep Soviet interests out of Iran.

Hoover had to convince not only the British but also the U.S. oil companies that the Iranian consortium was in everyone's best interests. Although long-range studies of U.S. oil requirements anticipated an excess of demand relative to production during the next 20 years, there was an oil glut on the world market in 1953, and the U.S. companies did not want Iranian oil competing in the U.S. market. Hoover, however, gained assurances from the U.S. Justice Department that joint ownership by five American companies would not violate the antitrust laws, and Jersey Standard, Mobil, Gulf, California Standard, and the Texas Company agreed to participate in the consortium.

By October 21, the oil consortium arranged by Hoover concluded a pact with the shah's government that the Iranian Majlis (parliament) ratified. The National Iranian Oil Company was set up. For this company, Iranian oil would be extracted, refined, and marketed by the international oil consortium. Iran received 50% of the profits, and the other 50% were divided by the consortium members as follows: Anglo-Iranian Company, 40%; Royal Dutch Shell, 14%; French Petroleum Company, 6%; and each of the five American companies, 5% for a total 40% U.S. shares. The consortium was named Iranian Oil Exploration and Producing Company.

See December 23, 1973.

### October 23, 1954

**A letter from President Eisenhower offers aid to Ngo Dinh Diem.**

This letter and the SEATO alliance formed the basic "commitment" for U.S. aid to South Vietnam, the region of Vietnam below the 17th parallel established by the Geneva cease-fire agreement.

In his letter, Eisenhower limited aid in accordance with the "new look," which expected Diem to establish satisfactory local defense capabilities. In sum, Eisenhower agreed:

1. to provide a "humanitarian effort" for assisting refugees from the north;
2. to give aid for the "welfare and stability of Diem's government," provided Diem gave "assurances as to the standards of performance" his government would maintain;
3. to provide aid to help Vietnam develop and maintain "a strong, viable state, capable of resisting attempted subversion or aggression through military means";
4. to expect Diem's government to begin "needed reforms" that would establish an independent Vietnam "with a strong government" that would be respected "at home and abroad."

Eisenhower's letter had one other significant consequence: U.S. economic aid began to go directly to Diem's government in Saigon, not through French officials in Paris, as it had since 1950. French Premier Mendès-France thought Washington had agreed to continue sending aid through Paris, a belief that resulted in increased friction between the French and U.S. governments in 1954 and 1955.

See also the French veto of the EDC, August 30, 1954.

### November 2, 1954

**Congressional elections return control of both houses to the Democratic Party by a majority of one in the Senate and 29 in the House.**

This change did not affect Eisenhower's foreign policy at first because the Democratic congressmen held positions closer to the president than many

Republicans, such as Senator William Knowland of California. After 1957, however, Senate Democratic leader Lyndon Johnson attacked Eisenhower's "new look" reduction in conventional forces and his "peaceful coexistence" discussions with Premier Khrushchev.

### November 23, 1954

#### A Communist Chinese military court convicts 13 American airmen of spying and sentences them to long prison terms.

The airmen had disappeared while flying missions during the Korean War. In response to the court's action, the United States protested both to Peking through the British embassy and to the United Nations.

On December 10, the U.N. General Assembly voted 47-5 to condemn China's treatment of the airmen and instructed U.N. Secretary-General Dag HAMMARSKJÖLD to confer with the Chinese. On December 17, after meeting with Hammarskjöld, China's Premier Chou En-lai agreed to release the airmen.

### December 1, 1954

#### The United States and Nationalist China sign a mutual defense pact.

This treaty authorized the United States to disperse its naval forces around Formosa and the Pescadores to protect those island groups. Notably, U.S. protection did not include offshore islands such as Quemoy and Matsu. In addition, the Nationalists stipulated that they would not use their armed forces except in a joint agreement with the United States, a clause to prevent Chiang Kai-shek from unilaterally invading China's mainland. Yet, Dulles feared Chiang did not take the stipulation seriously because he constantly talked about invading China as a "supreme" Nationalist mission.

The U.S.-Nationalist treaty was negotiated following an August 11 declaration by Chinese Foreign Minister Chou En-lai that "the liberation of Taiwan is a glorious, historic mission of the Chinese people." Taiwan, he said, must be freed from the "traitorous Chiang Kai-shek group." When a journalist asked Eisenhower about Chou's statement, the president said "an invasion would have to run over the

Seventh Fleet," which had been stationed in the Formosa Straits since 1950.

When China began intermittently to bombard the offshore islands in August 1954, the United States began negotiating the security treaty finalized on December 2.

See January 25, 1955.

### December 2, 1954

#### A U.S. Senate resolution condemns the conduct of Senator Joseph McCarthy by a vote of 67-22.

This action, together with the Democrats regaining a majority in Congress and removing McCarthy from his chairmanship of the Senate Internal Security Committee, ended the worst aspect of McCarthyism. The vote followed an extensive public hearing that was one of the first congressional actions to be televised nationwide.

Nevertheless, the fears, suspicions, and myths concerning Soviet spies continued to influence attitudes of intense anticommunism among Americans, even those who disliked McCarthy's extreme methods.

# 1955

### January 25, 1955

#### Congress authorizes Eisenhower to use American armed forces to defend Formosa and the Pescadores.

The congressional resolution to defend Formosa resulted from a crisis that developed between 1953 and 1955. Although Truman provided Formosa with U.S. navy support, the Nationalist Chinese engaged in hit-and-run attacks and bombing raids against the Chinese mainland. Eisenhower appeared to alter Truman's policy in a February 2, 1953, speech to Congress by saying the Korean War made it illogical to protect China's mainland from Nationalist Chinese attacks. Eisenhower said the United States had no aggressive designs on the People's Republic of China, but critics claimed Eisenhower "unleashed" the Nationalists to attack China's mainland in any way they desired.

Following the president's 1953 speech, the Nationalist government began persistent raids on China's coastline and built up its armed forces on

Quemoy, Matsu, and Tachen—islands located a few miles from China's mainland. As a result of these Nationalist provocations, the Chinese Communists began bombarding the offshore islands in 1954.

On January 1, 1955, the People's Republic of China escalated its attacks on the offshore islands by intensifying its shelling and constructing jet airfields along the coastline opposite Formosa. On January 10, about 100 mainland planes raided Tachen, located 200 miles from Formosa, while 40,000 Chinese troops captured Ichiang, an island seven miles from Tachen.

These Chinese attacks led Eisenhower to order U.S. navy ships to prepare to convoy Nationalists from Tachen and draw up a January 24 message to Congress giving the president permission to fight the Chinese Communists if necessary. The president told Congress the United Nations would ultimately decide Formosa's status, but the critical situation required congressional authority for using U.S. armed forces to protect Formosa and "such related positions and territories required to assure the defense of Formosa." As Stephen E. Ambrose's *Eisenhower the President* (1984) indicates, Eisenhower did not specify Quemoy and Matsu as part of the defense area. Chiang Kai-shek wanted assurances to protect those two islands, but Eisenhower preferred to "confuse" the situation on Quemoy and Matsu, making any decision dependent on circumstances if the Chinese Communists tried to seize those islands.

On January 28, Congress approved the resolution Eisenhower requested. The House approved it on January 24 by a vote of 410 to 3; the Senate held hearings on the resolution before approving it on January 28 by 83 to 3. The Senate gave further support to the president by ratifying the SEATO treaty on February 1 and the Mutual Security Treaty with Nationalist China on February 9.

In February, the U.N. Security Council discussed Formosa but abandoned its efforts to get a cease-fire in the Formosa Straits because China's Foreign Minister Chou En-lai rejected an invitation to attend the UNSC meeting. In light of China's continued bombardment of the offshore islands, Eisenhower and his staff considered having U.S. forces occupy Quemoy and Matsu or using tactical nuclear weapons against the Chinese forces located opposite Formosa. Eisenhower delayed making either choice, and his caution was rewarded when Chou En-lai offered a conciliatory proposal in April. Speaking to an African-Asian Conference in Bandung, Indonesia,

Chou said he was willing to negotiate with the United States because "the Chinese people are friendly to the American people" and do not want a war. Chou wanted to "relax tensions in the Far East" and especially "relaxing tensions in Taiwan"—the name China preferred to Formosa.

In response to Chou's offer, Secretary of State John Foster Dulles finally agreed to negotiate if there were a cease-fire in the Formosa Straits. Chou agreed and in May 1955, China not only ended the bombardment but released 11 U.S. airmen captured during the Korean War; they had been convicted of espionage and given prison terms by a Chinese court on November 22, 1954. In August 1955 negotiations began in Warsaw, Poland, between the Chinese ambassador to Poland and the U.S. ambassador to Czechoslovakia. The negotiations were unsuccessful because China regarded the issue of Formosa as an internal Chinese affair not subject to international or United Nations interference.

By 1956, the Formosa issue calmed before being renewed in 1958.

See September 8 and December 1 and 2, 1954; see also March 23, 1955.

## February 5, 1955

### *The French National Assembly votes "no confidence" in the ministry of Mendès-France.*

This ministry had arranged the Geneva declarations of July 1954 but ran into difficulty by seeking a compromise with the rebellion in Algeria. Algerian Muslims had started a nationalist uprising in mid-1954 and Mendès-France sought to resolve the problems by compromise. Conservatives in the French National Assembly opposed the suggested reforms in Algeria. They wanted to use the army to regain French glory and defeat the rebels.

The overthrow of Mendès-France's cabinet resulted in two years of political instability that eventually led to General de Gaulle's return to power in 1958.

## February 12, 1955

### The U.S. army agrees with France to take charge of training the army of the Vietnamese national government.

Under this arrangement, General Paul Ely announced that French forces would cease training operations but

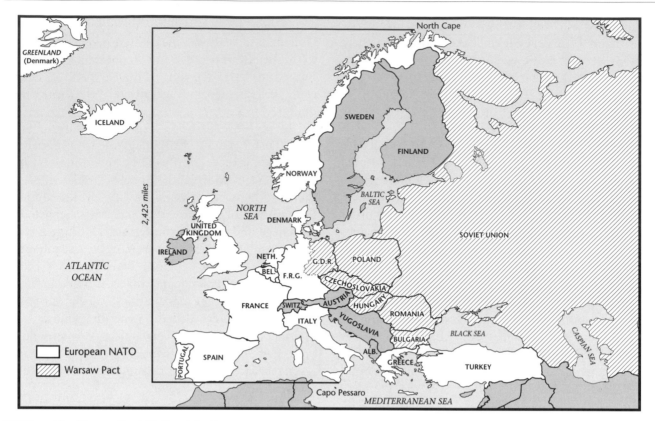

NATO and the Warsaw Pact. National Archives

would continue defensive activity in the northern provinces near the DMZ prior to their final withdrawal in 1956. American General John O'Daniel commanded the training mission in Vietnam after February 12.

This agreement was a vital step toward the United States replacing France as the Western power in Vietnam. U.S. military experts believed that the French had not allowed sufficient independence for Vietnam's officers and that they themselves could more ably prepare Diem's army to fight communism.

### February 18, 1955

#### *The Baghdad Pact creates a defensive alliance between Turkey and Iraq.*

Soon after, Great Britain, Iran, and Pakistan joined the alliance. The United States gave wholehearted support to the pact but never joined it. After 1956, the United States provided economic aid for the pact's members. In 1957, following the Suez crisis with Egypt, the United States met with the Military Committee of the Baghdad Pact and provided weapons for the pact's members.

### March 23, 1955

#### President Eisenhower seeks to clarify Dulles's "massive retaliation" assertions by declaring that the United States would not use nuclear weapons in a "police action."

Actually, Eisenhower's comments at a news conference on March 23 were not intended to "clarify" but to confuse the journalists. The question that had been asked was whether or not the president would use atomic weapons to defend Chinese offshore islands under Chiang Kai-shek's control. On March 12 and 15, Secretary of State Dulles had spoken of the United States using tactical nuclear weapons against Chinese airfields and troops near Quemoy and Matsu. On March 16, Eisenhower told a reporter that the tactical weapons Dulles referred to could be used for "strictly military targets and for strictly military purposes." The president hoped this statement would warn Peking of the dangers of the Quemoy-Matsu crisis.

In the context of these previous statements, a war scare developed in America. Hawks wanted war on mainland China; doves feared that all-out nuclear war with the Soviet Union would result. Thus on March 23, the president withdrew slightly from his March 16 remarks. He told the press that he could not predict how war would occur or what would result. Eisenhower said it would depend on the circumstances at the time the decision was made. There would be no automatic nuclear attack by the United States in the manner that some Americans interpreted as "massive retaliation."

For the Quemoy-Matsu crisis, see January 25, 1955.

## April 18–24, 1955

### *Bandung Conference of Asian-African nations agrees to promote the self-determination of all nations.*

Twenty-nine Asian and African nations attended. This conference was a milestone along the way to the liberation of many former colonial nations from Western European control between 1955 and 1960. Because anticolonialists often used Marxian terminology to explain "the imperialist-capitalist" use of colonies to exploit nations of Asia and Africa, many Americans associated these statements with Moscow's rhetoric, assuming that such conferences as that at Bandung were in fact Communist plots for "national liberation."

Such analysis disclosed how far away some Americans had moved from their anticolonial heritage of 1776, as renewed by Woodrow Wilson and Franklin D. Roosevelt in the 20th century. Prior to the Cold War, America had been a champion of self-determination and the end of European colonial empires.

## May 2, 1955

### *Diem centralizes his political power in Saigon by defeating local sects with whom French officials had compromised by bribery.*

Three large non-Communist sects in the Saigon area had gained much local influence from 1946 to 1954, because France paid them to fight the Vietminh and gave them much local control. These three were Cao Dai, Hoa Hao, and Binh Xuyen. Cao Dai was a religious sect with 2 million members, located northwest of Saigon. Hoa Hao was also a religious

sect with an army that controlled the Mekong River delta region. The strongest sect was the Binh Xuyen, a criminal-style organization that controlled Saigon's gambling, prostitution, drugs, and a police force of 8,000.

Using tactics of divide-and-conquer, Diem gained control over these sects and other smaller ones by the summer of 1955. Between March 21 and May 2, virtual civil war took place in Saigon, as Diem fought the Binh Xuyen and drove them from the city.

Diem's success against the sects increased his prestige. On May 1, he gained control of Vietnam's army from Bao Dai, and on May 5, a political congress in Saigon urged that all Bao Dai's powers be given to Premier Diem, pending the formation of a new government.

## May 7, 1955

### The Western European Union (WEU) is organized to provide a defensive alliance that would include West German forces.

After the French National Assembly rejected the EDC in August 1954, British Foreign Secretary Anthony Eden proposed that a Western European Union, including German forces, four divisions of British troops, and U.S. forces in Europe, be coordinated into a Western European defense program. German Chancellor Konrad Adenauer cooperated by agreeing that West Germany would not "have recourse to force" as a means of uniting Germany.

Eden's plan was officially drawn up and signed by the foreign ministers of Belgium, Britain, France, West Germany, Italy, Luxembourg, and the Netherlands on October 23, 1954. The plan provided for ending the occupation of West Germany and admitting West Germany to NATO.

Under French Premier Mendès-France's guidance, the WEU pact was approved by the French National Assembly on December 24, 1954. Thus, on May 7, concluding formalities organized the WEU, whose members were France, Great Britain, West Germany, Italy, Belgium, Luxembourg, and the Netherlands. The West German Federal Republic joined NATO on May 9, 1955, just two days after gaining sovereign status with the implementation of the Paris treaties (WEU) of October 23, 1954.

## May 14, 1955

### *The Warsaw Pact Defense Alliance is formed by European Communist nations.*

The Warsaw Pact was the Soviet Union's answer to U.S. integration of West German troops into NATO. Eight Eastern European nations signed the pact. Early in January 1956, the East German army became part of the Warsaw Pact forces under Soviet Marshal Ivan S. KONEV.

## May 15, 1955

### The big four powers agree to an Austrian peace treaty.

The foreign ministers of Britain, France, the Soviet Union, and the United States accepted peace terms, agreeing to withdraw all foreign forces from Austria by December 31, 1955.

Unlike Germany, Austria would be a neutral nation much like Switzerland, a decision more palatable to Americans. Following the Austrian agreement, Eisenhower announced he would participate in the July 1955 summit conference at Geneva.

## June 25, 1955

### Soviet foreign minister Molotov apologizes to the United States for the Soviets' shooting down a U.S. navy plane on June 24, offering to pay part of the damages.

The Soviet apology for this incident was unusual because it was contrary to Soviet practice. Both in 1953 and in 1954, the Soviets rejected U.S. protests and claims for damage. On July 29, 1953, the Soviets shot down a B-50 flying near the Siberian coast. On September 6, 1954, a U.S. navy P2V-5 was downed near Siberia. In neither instance did the Soviets respond to U.S. protests, except to claim that the planes had violated Soviet air space.

On June 24, another P2V-5 on patrol in the Bering Sea was shot down by Soviet jet fighter pilots. The plane crash-landed on St. Lawrence Island, injuring seven members of the crew.

The next day, Molotov wrote to the United States, expressing the USSR's regrets for the incident and offering to pay 50% of the damages. Molotov insisted that the American plane was over Soviet air space. He

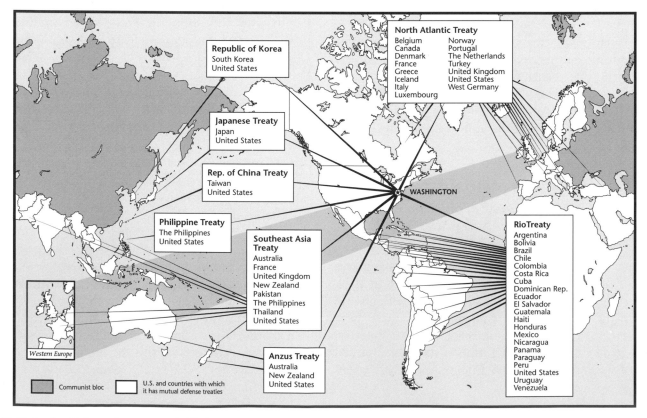

U.S. Collective Defense Arrangement, 1955

Secretary of State Dulles reports to President Eisenhower after returning from Europe, where he signed the Austrian treaty. National Archives

stated, however, that the cloudy sky made errors possible on both sides.

Later, on July 18, the USSR proposed that some method be found to prevent such incidents in the future.

In Washington, President Eisenhower was willing to accept the Soviet response. Secretary Dulles believed that the Soviets should be made to pay a greater compensation, but the State Department did not pursue this matter.

### July 18–23, 1955

**President Dwight Eisenhower, British Prime Minister Anthony Eden, French Premier Edgar Faure, and Soviet Premier Nikolay Bulganin attend the big four summit conference at Geneva.**

The conference discussed the reunification of Germany, European security, and disarmament. The talks stalled, however, on the German issue. The United States wanted Germany to be free to join NATO if it wished; Moscow wanted all foreign forces out of Germany and a neutral country.

During the conference, Eisenhower gained favorable world reaction with an "open skies" proposal. This plan would permit U.S. and Soviet reconnaissance aircraft to photograph each nation's territory to ensure against a surprise attack. In addition, each nation would exchange plans on military facilities.

Although the U.N. General Assembly eventually supported this plan, the Soviet Union refused to permit such verification tactics.

See December 16, 1955.

### July 22, 1955

**A rearmament bill is enacted by the West German parliament.**

The bill authorized the enlistment of 6,000 officers as the nucleus of a 500,000-man army. Compulsory military service was enacted, to become effective July 25, 1956.

### July 27, 1955

**Bulgarian fighter planes shoot down an El Al (Israeli) airliner; 58 passengers are killed.**

The El Al Constellation airliner was en route from London to Israel and strayed off course, flying over Bulgarian territory. Bulgaria admitted on August 3, following its investigation of the incident, that its fighter pilots were "too hasty" in shooting down the aircraft. They pledged to punish the pilots and take steps to prevent a recurrence of the incident. They also agreed to pay compensation to families of the victims and to share in paying for the destroyed plane.

During the fall session of the U.N. General Assembly, member nations approved a resolution on

December 6 that asked all governments to avoid attacks on civilian aircraft that violated their international borders.

For a similar incident of the destruction of a commercial airliner, see July 23, 1954.

### September 13, 1955

*The Soviet Union establishes diplomatic relations with West Germany.*

Soviet recognition of West Germany came one week before the USSR conferred sovereignty on a separate East Germany on September 20. The Soviets also gave East Germany the control of civilian traffic between West Germany and West Berlin.

### September 16, 1955

*An Argentine military junta ousts President Juan Perón.*

On September 23, General Eduardo LONARDI became provisional president but was replaced on November 13 by General Pedro ARAMBURU.

Perón had experienced increased public dissatisfaction after his 1955 effort to deprive the Roman Catholic Church of its tax-exempt status and to abolish teaching of the Catholic religion in all schools. On June 16, the Pope Pius XII excommunicated Perón, while the Argentine navy and air force seized several towns and bombed Buenos Aires. Perón's efforts at compromise with his opponents failed. Consequently, antagonism against him built up in the armed forces and led to the coup d'état of September 16, 1955.

### October 11, 1955

*Canada signs an agreement with the Soviet Union granting most-favored-nation trade privileges and cooperation in Arctic research.*

Canada's Minister for External Affairs, Lester Pearson, negotiated the treaty for Canada.

### October 26, 1955

**Ngo Dinh Diem gains complete control of the South Vietnamese government, proclaiming a republic with himself as the first president.**

Since May 2, Diem had persistently prevented attempts by the French and Bao Dai to unseat him. With U.S. support, Diem rejected French plans to

A group of children join a campaign rally for Ngo Dinh Diem. National Archives

reorganize the government under Bao, and on October 18 he refused to resign as premier when ordered to by Bao Dai.

To gain power, Diem organized a referendum on October 23 that overwhelmingly voted for Diem against Bao Dai. This "election" permitted Diem to proclaim a republic, end Bao Dai's emperorship, and announce that elections for a national legislature would follow in the near future.

### November 8, 1955

**President Eisenhower and Secretary of Defense Wilson give intermediate range missiles (IRBM) equal priority with intercontinental (ICBM) missiles.**

Within the U.S. air force during the early 1950s, internal disputes had slowed the development of both ICBMs and IRBMs. On September 8, 1954, a new ICBM organizational arrangement gave this missile the highest priority for development, ending the air force's inclination to emphasize bomber delivery systems.

In the fall of 1954, the president appointed James Killian to head a committee to review the entire missile program. In February 1955, Killian's group recommended that the IRBMs were "of utmost importance to national security" and should be made operational as early as possible.

To effect the IRBM development, Secretary Wilson established a Ballistic Missiles Committee to oversee missile advances. A separate directive by Wilson told the committee to assign the IRBMs equal priority with the procurement of ICBMs. The IRBM would have a range of 1,500 to 2,000 miles. Although the air force first interpreted the November directive as making the IRBM "second" to the ICBM, this decision was corrected in January 1956. IRBM development required bases in Europe from which they could hit Soviet targets.

See December 19, 1957.

### November 18, 1955

*Soviet Premier Bulganin and Khrushchev, First Secretary of the Communist Party's Central Committee, visit India, Burma, and Afghanistan to promote friendship for the Soviet Union among third world nations.*

### December 14, 1955

*Sixteen nations are admitted to the United Nations.*

They were Albania, Austria, Bulgaria, Cambodia, Ceylon, Finland, Hungary, Ireland, Italy, Jordan, Laos, Libya, Nepal, Portugal, Romania, and Spain.

### December 16, 1955

*Eisenhower's "open skies" plan is approved by the U.N. General Assembly.*

The U.N. action scored some public opinion points for the United States, but the Soviet Union opposed this or any other means for intrusive verification of its military installations.

# 1956

### January 1, 1956

*The Sudan gains complete independence from both Great Britain and Egypt.*

Since 1948, the question of the Sudan's future had been disputed. The Sudan had been a part of the British protectorate of Egypt since 1898, but the Sudanese desired independence from Egypt as well as England. In 1952, the Egyptians rejected Britain's proposal for limited self-government for the Sudan

under Egypt's control. After the overthrow of King Farouk in 1952, the Egyptians agreed to a referendum in the Sudan on whether it wished to be part of Egypt. The Sudanese voted for complete independence, which was arranged to become effective on January 1, 1956.

### January 19, 1956

*The U.N. Security Council unanimously votes to censure Israel for a December 11, 1955, attack on Syria.*

This attack was the most serious of several border engagements between Israeli and Egyptian-Syrian forces during 1955. The 1955 raids occurred in the Gaza Strip near the Sinai Desert and in the Lake Galilee region of the Israeli-Syrian border.

Following the U.N. vote, the United States asserted on February 17 that it would suspend all arms shipments to both Israel and the Arab nations. On April 9, the State Department said it fully supported the U.N. efforts to secure peace in the Middle East. An Israeli-Egyptian cease-fire, arranged by U.N. Secretary-General Hammarskjöld, became effective in April.

### January 28, 1956

*President Eisenhower rejects a friendship proposal by Soviet Premier Bulganin.*

As part of a so-called peace offensive, Premier Bulganin wrote to Eisenhower early in January to propose a 20-year treaty of friendship and economic, cultural, and scientific cooperation. He called the president an outstanding leader and recalled that only during the Russian Civil War of 1918–1920 had the two nations clashed. The two nations had no territorial or interest conflicts. Therefore, Soviet-U.S. cooperation would be based on "vital and long-term interests of both parties."

Because Washington was astounded and uncertain how to receive Bulganin's note and the accompanying treaty draft, Eisenhower replied in polite but evasive terms. He thought Moscow should first cooperate on German unity or aerial inspection.

Consequently, correspondence between Bulganin and the president continued until the Suez and Hungarian crises of October 1956. Exactly why the Soviets made this suggestion is not known. Adam Ulam, a U.S. Sovietologist, believes the Soviets either wished to frighten China into compliance with Soviet terms or Moscow was trying to interest Washington in a treaty against mainland China. These were the early days of the Sino-Soviet split, during which Peking demanded nuclear capabilities and additional heavy industry from their wary Soviet allies.

### February 14, 1956

*Speaking before the 20th Communist Party Congress, Khrushchev criticizes Stalin's crimes against the party and the nation.*

This de-Stalinization speech blamed Stalin for unnecessary party purges and terrorist tactics. Clearly, however, Krushchev blamed Stalin, not the Communist system, for the faults in Soviet policy since 1928. He justified the central party controls and overall objectives of the Soviet government in domestic affairs. Khrushchev's speech enhanced his power and assisted his shift of emphasis to consumer goods and worker incentives as a means to bolster the Soviet economy. The speech's greatest effects, however, were in the Eastern European satellite nations, where Khrushchev's message implied that Communist leaders could use a variety of methods of communism, not just Stalin's. Khrushchev also recognized this change by seeking to heal the breach with Yugoslavia's Tito, whom, he said, Stalin had mistreated (see September 27, 1949).

In international affairs, he proposed a policy of "peaceful coexistence" with capitalist nations while the Soviet Union enhanced its consumer economy.

### March 2, 1956

*France and Spain agree to establish an independent Morocco.*

In 1954, the Arab League's political and religious leaders called for Morocco's independence. This proposal led to outbursts of violence by rebel Muslims seeking separation from French and Spanish control. At the end of 1955, France agreed to recognize a sultan for Morocco who was approved by the Arab League. This enabled Morocco to form a representative cabinet led by Premier M'barek Bekhai. On March 2, 1956, Premier Bekhai and French Foreign Minister Christian Pineau signed a protocol on Moroccan independence.

On April 4, Spain's government declared the termination of its protectorate over northern Morocco and recognized Morocco's independence in a protocol signed by Morocco's Premier and the Spanish foreign minister on April 7, 1956.

Only the international city of Tangiers and southern Morocco remained outside the control of Morocco. After World War II, the United States, Great Britain, France and the Soviet Union had established an international administration for Tangier. On October 20, 1956, a conference of representatives from these four countries plus Spain, Morocco, and Algeria agreed to abolish the international control of Tangiers. Next on April 1, 1958, Spain gave independence to southern Morocco, creating the Kingdom of Morocco.

### April 17, 1956

*The Soviet Union announces it has dissolved the Cominform.*

Since its inception in 1947 as a replacement for the Comintern, the single achievement of the Cominform was the expulsion of Tito and Yugoslavia from the world Communist movement. For this reason, Khrushchev hoped to reconcile Tito to renew his world socialist affiliation by abolishing the Cominform. Tito was not seduced by Khrushchev's ploy. Although the Yugoslav leader conducted negotiations with Moscow, Tito retained and strengthened his role as a neutralist between the two superpowers.

### April 23, 1956

*Khrushchev, while visiting England, announces the Soviet Union will arm guided missiles with H-bombs; he claims Soviet leadership in nuclear weapons.*

### May 9, 1956

**Dulles refuses to supply arms to Israel, claiming that this could lead to a Mideast arms competition with the USSR because the Arab states sought military aid from the Soviets.**

As a crisis seemed imminent in the Middle East because of the demands of Nasser of Egypt and incidents along the Arab-Israeli borders, Dulles hoped to avoid providing U.S. arms for Arabs or Israelis. He denied export licenses for arms to Israel and all Arab states except Iraq and Saudi Arabia. At the same time, however, Dulles encouraged Canada and France to sell F-86 aircraft and French Mystères to Israel. Although the Israeli leaders accepted this tactic, they had already begun preparations with France to undertake preemptive action in the Sinai-Suez area.

See January 19, 1956, and October 29, 1956.

## May 21, 1956

### An U.S. H-bomb dropped from an airplane is detonated at Bikini Atoll.

In a series of nuclear tests code-named Redwing, a B-52 dropped the bomb that exploded at a height of from 10,000 to 15,000 feet. Although Japan complained about the nuclear fallout, U.S. experts said the radioactive debris was slight compared with the 1954 tests.

## June 20, 1956

### Yugoslavia's President Tito concludes a three-week visit to Moscow.

This visit symbolized Khrushchev's promise to improve relations with Tito.

Later in the year (September 19), Khrushchev visited Belgrade. The talks did not go well, however, and on February 19, 1957, Khrushchev said that because Tito rejected the Soviet proposals, Yugoslavia would not get further economic aid from the USSR. In subsequent years, relations between Khrushchev and Tito varied widely as each leader was suspicious of the other's intentions.

## June 28, 1956

### Riots break out in Poznan, Poland, as workers demonstrate for better economic and social conditions.

This was the initial Polish reaction to Khrushchev's de-Stalinization speech. Tensions continued in the USSR throughout 1956, but Władysław Gomułka, who became first Secretary of the Polish Communist Party on October 21, carefully steered Warsaw's policy to gain concessions from Khrushchev without antagonizing the Soviet leader; see November 18, 1956.

## July 1, 1956

### The first three West German divisions join the NATO command.

Germany was committed eventually to provide 12 divisions to NATO.

## July 17, 1956

### Soviet Premier Bulganin and East German Premier Otto Grotewohl declare that the unification of Germany should be worked out by East-West German agreements, not by the four powers that occupied Germany in 1945.

## July 19, 1956

### Dulles cancels the U.S. offer to aid Egypt in constructing the Aswân High dam.

Although in December 1955, the United States, Great Britain, and the World Bank jointly offered funds to Egypt for its dam project on the Nile, President Nasser persistently refused to discuss details of the loan with Washington. Instead, Nasser undertook policies to upset the calm in Ethiopia, Uganda, and the Sudan. He also arranged arms purchases with Communist countries and held talks with the Soviets and Communist Chinese.

On July 19, Egyptian Ambassador to the United States Ahmed Hussein arrived back from Cairo and immediately told Dulles he wanted to finalize the Aswân Dam loan. Negotiations were unnecessary, he said, for if the United States did not guarantee the loan, "the Soviet Union would do so."

Dulles rejected Hussein's abrupt "blackmail" demand. The United States, the secretary said, had assumed Egypt did not want the loan because it had rejected offers to negotiate the arrangement. Conditions in the Middle East needed to improve, Dulles observed, before a loan could be concluded.

Commentators in July 1956 showed surprise that Dulles had abruptly withdrawn the loan. Actually, Dulles had previously discussed the loan with the British and tentatively agreed to withdraw or not renew the offer to Egypt. In addition, Dulles indicated to Hussein that if Egypt desired, further talks on the loan could be undertaken. Nasser chose to accept the Soviet loan.

### July 26, 1956

**Egypt nationalizes the Suez Canal Company.**

Acting in response to Secretary of State Dulles's refusal to fund the Aswân High Dam and because Egypt received only about $2 million as its share of the canal's annual $31 million in profits, Egypt's President Gamal Abdel NASSER announced that, while Egypt would repay investors for their loss, his government would henceforth control and operate the Suez Canal. The British had withdrawn the last of their troops from Suez on June 13, 1956, making it difficult for them to protest as effectively as previously.

Nasser was especially chagrined at the U.S. withdrawal of financial support to construct the Aswân Dam, a project Egypt believed would benefit its economy and help modernize the nation. Dulles and British Prime Minister Anthony Eden had promised to back the Aswân project in December 1955. In February 1956, Eugene Black, president of the World Bank, agreed to provide $200 million for the dam.

Between February and July, Dulles and Eisenhower changed their minds. Owing largely to criticism from Congress, Dulles decided Nasser was too close to his Communist friends to deserve a loan. Dulles underestimated Moscow, because he believed the Soviets would not aid Egypt's costly project. More important, during this presidential election year, Dulles feared opposition from pro-Israeli groups; China lobbyists who disliked Nasser's recognition of mainland China in May 1956; and ardent anti-Communists who objected to Egypt's purchase of arms from Eastern European countries.

Therefore, in spite of prior promises, Dulles announced the withdrawal of U.S. aid for the dam on July 19, 1956, at the very time when Egypt's Ambassador returned to Washington to notify Dulles that Nasser was prepared to accept the terms of the loan.

Within a week, Nasser declared Egypt would take over the Universal Suez Canal Company. Profits from the canal, he claimed, would help build the dam. Nasser's action caused extreme concern in London and Paris, giving rise to the Suez crisis.

See October 23, 1958, and October 29–November 6, 1956.

### October 19, 1956

*The Soviet Union and Japan issue a declaration ending their 11-year state of war.*

Because the two nations could not settle the issue of the KURILE ISLANDS, it went unresolved.

### October 23, 1956

*The Hungarian uprising begins; Soviet forces gain control by November 4.*

Hungarians staged an uprising against Moscow's control that had been established after World War II. In Hungary, dissenters urged government reforms similar to those advocated by Soviet leader Nikita Khrushchev in denouncing Stalinism (see February 14, 1956). As disclosed by declassified Soviet records after 1985, Moscow detected unrest in Budapest in July 1956. Khrushchev expected to end these disputes among Hungary's Communist leaders by having Ernö Gerö replace the notorious Mátyás Rákosi as prime minister on July 18. Khrushchev miscalculated because the real sources of Hungarian opposition to Stalinism were young unskilled workers, university students, and Hungary's soldiers, including a few military officers. These factions agreed on rejecting the economic and political system imposed by Stalin in 1945.

On October 23, the initial rebellion was sparked at the local police station in the village of Drebecen. Although János Kádár, Hungary's Communist Party leader, claimed uprisings were confined to Budapest and other large cities, Hungary's rural areas staged protests prepared by 2,100 workers councils having 28,000 members. Between October 23 and November 4, several hundred thousands of rural inhabitants participated in demonstrations against the regime. In fact, the last rebel stronghold was on the small island of Csepel in Budapest, where Soviet troops did not get control until November 14, 1956.

In Budapest on October 23, the demonstrations drew larger crowds in the afternoon before Gerö asked the Soviets to deploy armed forces to suppress the protestors. Moscow responded by sending 1,130 tanks, 380 armored personnel carriers, and 185 air defense weapons to Budapest on October 24. Their arrival proved counterproductive because without infantry units the tanks and armored vehicles were easy targets to be blown apart by the grenades and Molotov cocktails used by the protestors. Moreover, Hungary's state security police and army refused to support the Soviet forces, some soldiers joining the rebels during the next four days.

In addition to sending Soviet tanks and armored vehicles, Khrushchev again sought to satisfy the rebels by changing Hungary's political leaders. Gerö was replaced as prime minister by Imre Nagy, a Hungarian Communist known to advocate reforms similar to Khrushchev's. Moscow officials also agreed to let Nagy appoint members of opposition parties to government ministries, creating a multiparty coalition government.

On October 28, Nagy agreed with two Soviet representatives in Budapest, Mikhail Suslov and Anastas Mikoyan, to call a cease-fire and remove all Soviet army units from Budapest. The truce calmed the demonstrations in Hungary, but on October 30 Khrushchev became enraged when he learned that Nagy had appointed enough non-socialists to the multiparty coalition to threaten Communist control of Hungary.

Fearing Nagy's action would upset not only Soviet control in Hungary but also in Poland, where de-Stalinization was being debated, Khrushchev decided to send Soviet infantry, tanks, and armored vehicles to put down Hungary's rebellion. On November 1, the Soviet army began deploying throughout Hungary, and on November 4, 60,000 Soviet soldiers entered Budapest to quash the rebellion. The same day, János Kádár, Hungary's Communist Party Chief, replaced Nagy. Soviet power was quickly restored.

After Kádár took charge, Nagy took refuge in the Yugoslav embassy, but later, while on a bus leaving Budapest, he was arrested by Soviet troops under Kádár's orders. Following a show trial in 1958, Nagy was executed. For many Hungarians, Nagy became a national hero, although Soviet documents declassified in 1989 indicate Nagy was an informer for Stalin's secret service during the 1930s and 1940s. In June 1989, Hungarians celebrated the careers of Nagy and other leaders in Budapest's Hero's Square. Details of the declassified Soviet records on 1956 are in the Spring 1995 *Bulletin* of the Cold War International History Project.

See November 18, 1956.

## October 26, 1956

### Diem promulgates a new constitution for South Vietnam.

Early in 1956, Diem's cabinet approved the appointment of an assembly to draw up a constitution. The assembly's recommendation was completed and signed by Diem on October 26.

Establishment of the new government occurred during the period when, according to the Geneva agreements, an election was to take place to unite Vietnam and choose a government that would end the division of the nation. Diem refused to work with the International Control Commission regarding elections, and, despite Hanoi's protests, elections never took place. The United States approved Diem's decision because it was obvious from American intelligence reports that in a "free election," Ho Chi Minh and the Vietminh would win.

In this manner, Diem and the United States bypassed the Geneva Conference's attempt to provide self-determination for all Vietnamese to decide on their future government and national unity.

## October 29–November 6, 1956

### The Suez crisis erupts when Israeli, British, and French forces attack Egypt.

The attack on Suez was one of several Israeli-Egyptian engagements during the years since Israel became a nation in 1948. Britain and France joined the attack in an attempt to regain some control of the Suez Canal following Egypt's nationalization decree of July 26, 1956. Israel had an interest in the canal's status because Egypt had denied Israeli ships the use of the canal, a situation Israel wished to abolish. London and Paris wanted to be certain Cairo never denied them use of the canal because Western European nations depended on oil supplies going through Suez.

After Nasser's nationalization decree, England and France rushed naval units and paratroopers into the region between Cyprus and Suez, threatening to use force if Nasser did not accept joint control plans for the canal.

Compromise efforts had failed between July and October. Secretary of State Dulles proposed the formation of a Suez Canal User's Association (SCUA) to operate the canal, but Nasser refused.

Next, the U.N. Security Council worked out a compromise for an international canal agency. On October 13, the Soviet Union vetoed the plan, even though it appeared Egypt would accept it.

As compromise talks went on, French, British, and Israeli representatives held secret military talks. On October 24, at Sèvres, near Paris, the three nations agreed to a secret joint attack on Suez.

As planned at Sèvres, Israeli troops first launched a raid in the Sinai Desert on October 29. London and Paris sent cease-fire requests to Cairo and Tel Aviv that, as expected, Nasser rejected. On October 31, Anglo-French planes bombed Cairo, Egyptian air bases, and the canal. On November 2, British naval forces and paratroopers occupied Port Said, making Egyptian forces retreat to west of the Canal Zone.

U.N. action to halt the crisis was initially ineffective. The British and French vetoed an October 31 Security Council resolution to "refrain from the use of force." On November 2, a U.N. General Assembly resolution called for a cease-fire and mutual troop withdrawal, but included no method of implementation. Therefore, on November 4, Lester Pearson of Canada proposed that a U.N. emergency force supervise the cease-fire.

Pearson's proposal passed the General Assembly by a vote of 57-0 with 19 abstentions. At 12:15 A.M. on November 5, the assembly authorized General E. L. M. BURNS of Canada to recruit and lead an international force to Suez, with the force to exclude troops from any permanent Security Council members.

On November 6, the Soviet Union supported Egypt when Khrushchev threatened to send Soviet forces to stop the aggressors if a cease-fire did not occur immediately.

Eisenhower and Dulles (who had emergency cancer surgery on November 3) opposed the British-French-Israeli attacks from the outset. They sought to use the United Nations and backed Pearson's attempt to intervene through the assembly. On November 6, Eisenhower decided to apply greater pressure on Britain and France. The United States applied financial pressure by selling British pounds on the currency exchange to damage British currency rates and cutting off oil supplies from Latin America to Europe. Before the end of the day, the fighting in Suez had stopped because the British, French, and Israelis accepted the cease-fire and the intervention of the U.N. supervisory force.

The U.N. supervisory force still had to overcome obstacles before the Suez situation reached peaceful terms.

See June 13, 1957.

## November 6, 1956

**The Republican ticket of Eisenhower and Nixon wins the presidential election, Eisenhower receiving 57% of the vote. The Democrats retain control of both houses of Congress.**

Regarding foreign policy, commentators thought Eisenhower best expressed two major points about which most liberals and conservatives agreed in 1956: (1) the underdeveloped nations, not Europe, were becoming the central area of conflict in the Cold War; and (2) the United States must find a means to keep the "neutrals" and new developing nations tied to U.S. interests or they would become "virtual allies" of the Soviet Union.

## November 18, 1956

*Poland and the Soviet Union agree to compromise and avoid violence.*

In order to avoid the violence taking place in Hungary, Nikita Khrushchev and Poland's Władysław Gomułka made a modus vivendi where by Poland received greater leeway in following its own road to a socialist economic system. Gomułka agreed to maintain Poland's membership in the Warsaw Pact and be a loyal ally of the Soviet government. Informally, this agreement was made on November 18, ending years of problems between Poland and the Soviet Union. (Notably, Stalin had imprisoned Gomułka in 1951 because he advocated "Titoist" policies that permitted Yugoslavia to have its own form of socialist system.)

The Polish-Soviet problems had intensified in June 1956 when Poznan protesters demonstrated against an increase in food prices and hard-line practices of Polish Stalinists. During the demonstrations, Soviet troops fired on and killed 53 people and wounded hundreds more.

To rectify these problems in Poznan and elsewhere, Communists leaders of the Polish Worker's Party (PUWP) debated whether they should retain Stalinist policies or accept proposals of Gomułka to introduce reforms in line with Khrushchev's February speech that de-Stalinized the Soviet Union. Although Gomułka's program called for the eviction of Soviet officers in command of the Polish army, Khrushchev accepted the request to return those Russian officers to the Soviet Union.

Members of the PUWP Plenum at its eighth official meeting on October 19 agreed to remove Soviet General Konstantin K. Rokossovsky, the Soviet commander of the Polish army, from PUWP membership and his seat on the Politburo. The Plenum took this action despite Rokossovsky's threat to use violence against Gomułka and his followers. Amid this crisis, Khrushchev and a delegation of Soviet officials visited Warsaw to clarify the situation. The Soviet leaders talked with Gomułka and the PUWP's current leader, Edward Ochab, about their ideas on the crisis and then flew back to Moscow. Khrushchev met with the Soviet Presidium on October 24, persuading them to accept Gomułka as the first secretary of the PUWP and bring home Rokossovsky and most other Soviet generals in charge of the Polish army.

Later in the day of October 24, Gomułka gave a "victory" speech during a Warsaw rally of at least 300,000 Poles. He said he would lead the Polish way to socialism but also called for an end to all anti-Soviet demonstrations because, he said, Poland needed friendly ties with its Soviet neighbor and the Warsaw Treaty alliance. After Gomułka released Polish Primate Stefan Cardinal Wyszyński from army custody on October 29, he proceeded to finalize the agreement with the Soviet Union signed on November 18. New details about Polish-Soviet relations in 1956 have been found in documents declassified from Russian and Eastern European Archives that appeared in the *Bulletin* of the Cold War International History Project for the Spring issue of 1995.

See February 14, and June 28, 1956.

# 1957

### January 5, 1957

**The Eisenhower Doctrine is presented in an address to Congress.**

The President asked Congress to authorize the use of U.S. armed forces if there were Communist aggression in the Middle East. Congress approved the resolution on March 5, 1957. The congressional resolution stated that a nation must *request assistance* from the United States.

The doctrine was seldom used, however, because U.S. forces could not check the growth of Soviet diplomatic influence in the Middle East, and Arab nations hesitated to request aid because the United States supported Israel.

### February 8, 1957

**Saudi Arabia renews the U.S. lease on the Dhahran air base in exchange for American arms.**

The agreement was announced after King Saud visited Washington for 10 days.

President Eisenhower addresses Congress. Library of Congress

### March 6, 1957

*The British Gold Coast Colony becomes the independent state of Ghana.*

In accordance with a 1956 plebiscite, TOGOLAND united with Ghana. GHANA retained membership in the British Commonwealth.

### March 13, 1957

*Jordan gains independence when Great Britain terminates the 1948 alliance and agrees to withdraw its armed forces within six months.*

King HUSSEIN I, who became monarch of Jordan on May 2, 1953, also acted vigorously to purge his national army of Egyptian and Syrian sympathizers.

Although the United States sympathized with Hussein's actions and later sent arms to aid him, Hussein refused to make any commitments to America and claimed to seek a neutral policy in the Cold War.

### March 24, 1957

*British and U.S. leaders meet at Bermuda to repair strained relations resulting from the Suez crisis.*

Great Britain was represented by Prime Minister HAROLD MACMILLAN, who replaced Eden following the failure of the latter's Suez policy in 1956. President Eisenhower and Macmillan discussed the improvement of British defenses. The British explained their need to cut the number of their troops in NATO from 75,000 to 50,000 (accepted by the WEU on March 19), and Eisenhower agreed to supply Britain with intermediate-range guided missiles.

### March 25, 1957

*The European Common Market is agreed to in the Treaty of Rome.*

France, West Germany, Italy, Belgium, Luxembourg, and the Netherlands were the charter members.

### April 25, 1957

*The Eisenhower Doctrine is applied to help King Hussein of Jordan against the threat of "international Communism."*

Although historians disagree on whether or not the Eisenhower Doctrine applied to the Jordanian crisis, the president ordered the U.S. Sixth Fleet to the eastern Mediterranean, and Secretary Dulles advised that this action was designed to protect Jordan from Syrian and Egyptian pressure. Both Syria and Egypt received Soviet aid, causing Dulles to link them with Moscow's clandestine activity supposedly to promote communism.

On March 13, 1957, Great Britain had agreed with King Hussein to end its treaty of alliance of 1948 and to withdraw British troops in six months. Hussein also lost Britain's financial subsidies, and although Saudi Arabia helped to replace those funds, Hussein had financial problems that Egypt's President Nasser hoped to exploit by forcing Jordan to join Syria and Egypt in forming a United Arab Republic. Hussein opposed the efforts of Syria and Egypt, and President Chamoun of Lebanon asked the United States to act on behalf of Jordan. Partly because of Eisenhower's show of force in the Mediterranean, Hussein maintained power in Jordan and the United States offered him a grant of $10 million.

See September 5, 1957.

### May 1, 1957

*The United States agrees to provide aid to Poland in the form of $95 million worth of commodities and mining machinery.*

The Eisenhower administration began considering possible economic aid to Poland on April 12, 1957, when Secretary of State Christian Herter told a Cabinet meeting that Poland had requested financial assistance. Herter indicated that the State Department believed Poland's Premier Gomułka wanted to avoid becoming a "Moscow tool." In addition, Eisenhower reported a meeting he had with Polish exile leaders in America who favored American assistance to Poland. All cabinet members agreed and legislation was prepared for Congress to approve. On June 7, 1957, Eisenhower signed legislation that approved loans and other financial aid to Poland. Using Public Law 480 of July 10, 1954, the United States sent surplus American food products to be sold for Polish currency in addition to $48.9 million loans for other American commodities and mining machinery.

## May 15, 1957

*Great Britain successfully explodes a hydrogen bomb at Christmas Island.*

## May 30, 1957

*President Batista of Cuba orders the army to intensify its fight against Fidel Castro's rebels in Oriente Province.*

After gaining power in "rigged election" to defeat President Sacarras (see March 10, 1952), Fulgencio Batista established a dictatorship characterized by corruption, repression, and internal dissent. To overthrow Batista, Fidel Castro organized a rebellion by promising free elections, social reform, new schools and economic justice. The Eisenhower administration's response was to deny armaments to both sides, despite the fact that Castro's promises made him popular among many Americans. Although Castro claimed the United States continued arming Batista, the White House denied Castro's claim, saying the U.S. did not send arms to either side.

During the next 20 months, Castro's rebels in the July 26th movement steadily drove Batista's forces back toward Havana. In the U.S., the main issue was whether or not Castro was a Communist. Probably, no one knew or could predict whose side Castro favored until he accepted aid from the Soviet Union and announced he was a Communist in December 1961.

See December 28, 1958.

## June 12, 1957

*The Chinese Communists indicate they are relaxing their severe restrictions on the populace.*

Despite the U.S.-Chinese impasse over Formosa, China's leaders appeared ready to seek friendly relations between the people of China and the people of the United States. During the Bandung Conference (see April 18, 1955), China's Foreign Minister, Chou En-lai, announced that his government did not want

war with the United States and that China was willing to "discuss the question of relaxing tensions in the Far East." Also, in domestic affairs, China's leaders undertook a greater liberalization; perhaps to follow the lead of the Soviet Union's First Secretary Khrushchev's "de-Stalinization" movement.

In accordance with the apparent relaxation, the Chinese Communist press reported on two of Mao Tse-tung's recent speeches in which Mao explained that the government had to liquidate 800,000 Chinese between 1949 and 1954 because of the "contradictions" between these deviationists and the government. Mao hoped there would be freer expression in the future, declaring "Let a hundred flowers bloom, let a hundred schools of thought contend."

Although China's leaders offered conciliatory moves toward the United States, Secretary of State John Foster Dulles rejected their overtures. Some members of Congress and some editorial writers urged the Eisenhower administration to change U.S. policy toward China, but Dulles and Eisenhower stood firm. When 15 American news reporters were offered visas to visit China, Dulles said that he believed China's talk of greater democracy was an aberration and that the U.S. travel ban levied during the Korean War remained in place. The State Department would not validate passports for the newsmen to visit the People's Republic of China. Although some newsmen visited China without valid passports, Dulles's views proved correct. China's experiment with "more democracy" brought internal problems and Mao restored his dictatorial power. In addition, China backed Ho Chi Minh's Communists in their struggle to defeat South Vietnam after 1959.

## June 13, 1957

*The after effects of the Suez crisis of October 1956 are finally resolved when Egypt approves terms for all nations to use the canal.*

After the November 6 cease-fire, Britain and France delayed withdrawing their forces until December 22, 1956 to assume negotiations for use of the canal. Israel refused to withdraw from the GAZA STRIP and AQUABA until Washington agreed to support Israel's free passage through the Gulf of Aquaba (February 11, 1957), and U.N. forces agreed to build a mined fence and to patrol the Gaza border (March 29, 1957). Finally, Israel demanded that terms for the use of the Suez Canal include permission for its ships to navigate the canal. Terms satisfying France and England were approved by Egypt on June 13.

### June 18, 1957

**The U.S. Senate approves the Atoms-for-Peace Treaty.**

This treaty evolved from President Eisenhower's December 1953 proposal through the United Nations where 80 nations had joined in forming the International Atomic Energy Agency, a group including the Soviet Union. The treaty provided for the sharing of fissionable materials for peaceful uses.

### June 30, 1957

**The International Geophysical Year (IGY) begins.**

Scientists from 64 countries cooperated in an intensive study of physical geographic phenomena during an 18-month period.

President Eisenhower signs the International Atomic Energy Agency agreement. Herbert Hoover Library

### July 26, 1957

*A military junta in Colombia assumes control of the government, announcing there will be elections on May 4, 1958.*

The coup against General Rojas PINILLA arose because Rojas violated the constitution in seeking reelection as president on May 8, 1957. Student riots followed and the Roman Catholic Church accused Rojas of murder in suppressing the students. Rojas resigned on May 10, but demonstrations continued in Colombia until the junta agreed to fix new election dates for 1958. On May 4, 1958, Alberto Illeras CAMARGO was elected president.

### August 26, 1957

*The Soviet Union announces it successfully test-fired the first intercontinental ballistic missile, a weapon capable of carrying a nuclear warhead to targets in the United States.*

### September 5, 1957

**President Eisenhower announces plans to airlift arms to Jordan and to assist Lebanon, Turkey, and Iraq against Communist plots from Syria: The Syrian crisis of 1957.**

Tensions increased between Washington and Damascus during the summer of 1957, and the United States concluded that a "takeover by the Communists would soon be completed" in Damascus. A Syrian agreement with the Soviets provided Damascus with $500 million of assistance and military aid. On August 13, Syria charged three American embassy officials with plotting to overthrow President Shukuri al-Kuwatly and forced them to leave the country.

Joined by diplomats from Turkey, Lebanon, Iraq, Israel, Jordan, and Saudi Arabia, the Eisenhower administration became convinced that Moscow wanted Communists to take power in Syria. Eisenhower reaffirmed his Middle East doctrine and took action to prevent Soviet subversion. With assurances of help from the United States, forces of Turkey, Iraq, Jordan, and Lebanon massed around Syria's borders. U.S. air forces were sent to a base in Adana, Turkey, and the Strategic Air Command was placed on alert. The U.S. Sixth Fleet proceeded to the eastern Mediterranean.

Whether or not Eisenhower overreacted to the Syrian situation is not certain. Following the preparations in territory surrounding Syria, the United Nations undertook to calm the affair. Of the nations that sent forces to Syria's borders, only Turkey desired to intervene. Arguments in the United Nations thoroughly aired charges and countercharges, but mediation efforts were rejected. Finally, King Saud informed Washington that the crisis was not serious. By October 31, the dispute faded. Moscow had gained influence in Syria but no Communist takeover was attempted in Damascus.

### October 5, 1957

**Sputnik *becomes the first artificial earth satellite.***

The Soviet Union fired *Sputnik* into an earth orbit by which it circled the world at 18,000 miles per hour. A second satellite, *Sputnik II*, was launched on November 3, carrying a live dog aboard for experimental purposes.

### October 23–25, 1957

**British Prime Minister Macmillan visits Washington to discuss the consequences of the USSR's *Sputnik* launching.**

Following the October 17–20 visit of Queen Elizabeth II to Washington, this session helped to reestablish the "special relationship" between England and America that had become part of U.S. policy since 1941.

### October 26, 1957

***Political troubles in Guatemala follow the assassination of President Castillo Armas (July 26) and the election (October 20) of Miguel Ortiz Passarelli.***

On October 26, a military junta annulled the election and installed Guillermo Flores AVENDANO as interim president. On March 2, 1958, General Miguel Ydiguras FUENTES was elected and installed as president for six years.

### November 7, 1957

**The Gaither Report is presented to the National Security Council.**

In the summer of 1957, President Eisenhower asked a group of private citizens chaired by H. Rowen Gaither to study U.S. defense security for

the country's survival in the atomic age. The final Gaither report went beyond the president's original intent to report on the possibility of bomb shelters for civil defense. Instead, the committee reported on the entire U.S. defense posture. The Gaither Committee claimed the U.S. strategic air force was highly vulnerable to Soviet Intercontinental Ballistic Missiles (ICBMs), leaving the American population critically at risk. It advocated a buildup of U.S. strategic offensive weapons by diversifying missile bases and increasing U.S. forces for conventional war.

The Gaither report also advocated a program to build fallout shelters to protect Americans from nuclear attack. Although Eisenhower rejected shelters as wasteful unless they were blast proof, Democratic Party candidates publicized the need for fallout shelters during the 1958 election, a proposal inspiring some Americans to build backyard shelters during the next decade. The concept of shelters was revived under the Reagan administration.

See March 31, 1982.

### November 7, 1957

**Eisenhower begins a series of "confidence" speeches to reassure the nation that U.S. defenses are excellent and capable of countering any Soviet threat.**

The launching of SPUTNIK by the Soviets in October and the rise of critics of the "new look" policies in Congress, the army, and the navy caused Eisenhower to better inform the public about U.S. force capabilities and the value of his "long-haul" defense policy related to sustaining a prosperous U.S. economy.

Between October 1957 and the end of his second term of office, Eisenhower's massive-retaliation policy with a cost-effective defense program was disputed by former Army Chief of Staff Maxwell Taylor; Senators Lyndon Johnson, John F. Kennedy, and Stuart Symington; and academic commentators Henry Kissinger and Herman Kahn. These and others argued that the United States needed "flexible response" forces, which required a large army and navy as well as strategic and tactical nuclear forces and would necessitate a huge defense budget, far beyond the budget needs Eisenhower believed necessary.

By 1960, the "new look" critics also raised the issue of a "missile gap," which asserted that the

Soviet Union would soon gain superiority over America in missiles. Eisenhower denied the missile-gap theory, but the accusation continued to be pressed by John F. Kennedy and his supporters through the election of 1960. Later, early in 1961, Kennedy's secretary of defense would admit that Eisenhower had been correct; *there was no missile gap.*

Nevertheless, in Congress and among many persons concerned about U.S. defense, both the "flexible response" policy and the "missile gap" were concepts that opposed Eisenhower's "long-haul," economy-concerned, "new look" program.

See October 30, 1953, and December 17, 1957.

### November 7, 1957

***Speaking on the 40th anniversary of the 1917 revolution in Moscow, Mao Tse-Tung provides an overt indication of the divisions between Peking and Moscow that eventually lead to the Sino-Soviet split.***

Mao stated that the international situation was at a turning point because "There are two winds in the world today: the East wind and the West wind." In addition, he said: "I think the characteristic of the situation today is the East wind prevailing over the West wind." Mao was urging strong, committed Communist backing for revolution in the former Asian and African colonies as they struggled to free themselves from Western control. He believed the Chinese victory in 1949 demonstrated the proper tactics to use in the emerging nations and criticized Soviet leader Khrushchev for his program of "peaceful coexistence" with capitalism.

Four months earlier on July 22, Mao showed anger in a conversation with Soviet Ambassador Pavel Judin, complaining about the Soviet Union's "unequal" treatment of China. The Soviets' attitude toward China, Mao said, "can be described as father and son or between cats and mice," rather than as brotherly relations. Mao, of course, wanted China to be the leader of international communism.

On July 31, 1958, Khrushchev flew to Beijing to resolve his differences with Mao, who rejected Khrushchev's overtures for better relations. As a result, Chinese-Soviet differences increased during and after 1958. Mao introduced the policy known as the Great Leap Forward to collectivize Chinese landholdings and extend China's influence in Third World countries, while Khrushchev continued the Soviet emphasis on heavy industry to improve the Soviet economy, giving little attention to the Third World until 1960.

Details regarding the Chinese-Soviet split became available in 1997 when declassified materials from Russia and China revealed new information on the years after 1953. Articles by Vladislav Zubok and Chen Jian summarize the new data in the Cold War International History Project's *Bulletin* for March 1998.

During 1958, the differences became more emphatic. Mao began the Great Leap Forward in China, a program forcing collectivization of land into communes and indoctrinating peasants with Communist ideas. The Soviets insisted on heavy industry first, and preferred to seek mass support from the people as only a secondary part of their branch of communism.

Mao was also striving to devise Communist programs for China that would be aided but not controlled by the Soviet Union.

### November 14, 1957

***East and West Germany sign a $260 million trade agreement for 1958.***

### November 15, 1957

***Portugal extends the U.S.-Azores Island defense pact to 1962.***

The original pact was made in 1951.

### December 5, 1957

***President Sukarno of Indonesia expels all Dutch nationals.***

Throughout the previous three years, Sukarno's government had had political problems with the Netherlands; with rebels in parts of his country such as Sulawesi (the Celebes) and Borneo; and with competing political groups in Jakarta.

To help resolve the economic costs of these continuing problems, Sukarno had repudiated $1 billion of debts to the Netherlands (August 4, 1956) and received a loan from the Soviet Union of $100 million (September 15, 1956).

The immediate 1957 dispute with the Netherlands focused on the continued occupation of West New Guinea by the Dutch. On October

28, 1957, Sukarno threatened to seize West New Guinea if the United Nations failed to resolve the issue. Finally, in December, Sukarno's government organized a 24-hour strike against Dutch business to oppose Dutch rule in West New Guinea. Sukarno also issued a decree to expel all Dutch nationals from Indonesia. As Indonesia's problems continued, the United States was concerned about the Soviet Union gaining control in Indonesia through its loans to Sukarno and the influence of Indonesia's Communist Party as part of Sukarno's ministry.

### December 17, 1957

## The first successful test of America's Intercontinental Ballistic Missile, Atlas.

The air force program for the ICBM began on July 27, 1955. On November 28, 1958, the Series B-ATLAS missile performed a full-range test of 5,506 nautical miles.

The American intermediate range missile, THOR, had its first successful flight on September 20, 1957.

### December 19, 1957

## NATO members conclude their Paris meeting.

The session indicated the European concern about recent Soviet technological developments. A major issue among the delegates centered on the American desire for missile bases in Europe and the Europeans' desire for the United States to pursue disarmament talks. The issue resulted in compromise; the Europeans agreed to accept U.S. intermediate-range missile bases, and the United States said it would discuss any "reasonable proposal" for "comprehensive and controlled disarmament." This dual-related issue constantly reappeared at NATO meetings during future sessions.

In 1957, NATO described the deployment of IRBMs as a temporary measure to deter the Soviets until American ICBMs became operational from U.S. bases. NATO also indicated that missile deployment was subject to American agreement with the countries where missiles were based. Only Great Britain, Italy, and Turkey accepted the U.S. offer to permit missile bases on their soil.

A large part of the difficulty in persuading NATO allies to accept U.S. missile bases was the American desire to keep monopoly control of atomic weapons. As an anonymous French general told a reporter in November 1957, the risk of the absolute weapon was too grave to allow "a single one of the allies the monopoly of a retaliation which in the hour of danger, could be neutralized by the enemy or by the opposition of its own press or public opinion." Although Eisenhower wanted to cooperate further with the allies in nuclear plans and control, Congress and the Joint Committee on Atomic Energy would not permit him to share U.S. "secrets." The U.S. distrust of Europeans as indicated by this unwillingness to share responsibility for nuclear decisions became a persistent point of dispute in NATO.

Eventually under the December 1957 NATO agreement, the United States placed IRBMs in England, Italy, and Turkey—60 Thor missiles in England, 30 Jupiters in Italy, and 15 Jupiters in Turkey. The Turkish Jupiters became a significant problem during the 1962 October missile crisis.

Warsaw Pact members were also concerned about NATO's missile plans. Late in 1957, Poland's Foreign Minister Adam Rapacki had proposed the creation of a nuclear-free zone covering Poland, Czechoslovakia, and the two Germanys. In the zone, atomic, hydrogen, and rocket weapons would be neither manufactured nor deployed. As Adam Ulam's *The Rivals* (1971) suggests, the Rapacki plan was probably written in Moscow, enabling Khrushchev to approve it on March 3, 1958. The United States and NATO rejected the plan because it had "no methods for balanced and equitable limitations of military capabilities" in central Europe. This meant that Warsaw Pact members could assemble larger conventional armed forces in central Europe. In contrast to the potential large Communist forces, NATO faced opposition in West Germany regarding the conscription of a large German army.

See October 28, 1962.

# 1958

### January 23, 1958

*In Venezuela, President Pérez Jiménez is overthrown by a military junta led by Admiral Wolfgang Larrazabal.*

Jiménez had been named provisional president by the National Assembly on January 9, 1954, after several years of political conflict. He was empowered to rule until "constitutional government is reestablished." The new constitution required three years to prepare, but after its approval Jiménez canceled the elections scheduled for December 15, 1957. Subsequently, a revolt broke out against Jiménez on December 31, leading to the military takeover on January 23.

At the time of Vice President Richard Nixon's visit in May, 1958 Venezuela's political difficulties were still in transition, with future political control under dispute. A new constitution was adopted later in 1958, and on December 7, Rómulo BETANCOURT was elected president, taking office on February 13, 1959.

Also see April 28–May 14, 1958.

### January 27, 1958

**The United States and the Soviet Union sign a cultural exchange agreement.**

This pact provided for visits by educators, technicians, sports teams, and musicians on a mutual interchange basis.

### January 31, 1958

**The first U.S. earth satellite, *Explorer I*, is placed in orbit by a modified Jupiter-C rocket.**

This began a series of experiments in the next two years with U.S. earth satellites known as *Explorer*, *Vanguard*, *Discoverer*, *Tiros*, *Nimbus*, and *Essa*.

### February 1, 1958

*The United Arab Republic (UAR) is formed by Egypt's President Nasser and Syrian President Shukri Al-Kuwatly.*

Nasser apparently hoped other Arab nations would join the UAR, meeting the Arab world's most important need: Arab unity. Nasser's dream was not realized, however. Only YEMEN agreed to associate itself

First U.S. satellite is launched, four months after the Russian *Sputnik*. National Archives

with the UAR (March 8, 1958). By September 29, 1961, the UAR broke up when Syria withdrew from the pact.

### February 22, 1958

**The United States agrees to supply England with 60 Thor intermediate-range missiles capable of carrying atomic warheads.**

This was an essential follow-up to the October 1957 meeting between Macmillan and Eisenhower, which reviewed the effect of *Sputnik* on Western defense capabilities.

### February 22, 1958

*Arturo Frondizi is elected president of Argentina, taking office on May 1, 1958.*

After the overthrow of Perón in 1955, a provisional government ruled, first under Lonardi, but then, following a November 13, 1955, coup, under General Pedro Aramburu.

In 1957, a constituent assembly voted to restore the constitution of 1853. Frondizi was selected under this constitution.

### March 27, 1958

#### The United States announces a space flight program is headed for the moon.

Secretary of Defense Neil McElroy reported the president's approval for a program to explore space to "obtain useful data concerning the moon, and to provide a close look at the moon." Officially, the exploratory Pioneer-Ranger programs would be part of the U.S. contribution to the International Geophysical Year.

Although John F. Kennedy later publicized the "race to the moon" featuring a human landing, the Pioneer-Ranger program, which started in 1958, provided essential data on moon-landing sites. It also proposed to counter the Soviet *Sputnik* feat of October 1957 promoting U.S. space technology.

Unfortunately, the Pioneer program's initial rocket launchings failed on August 17, October 11, November 8, and December 6, 1958. Pioneer 4 made a successful fly by the moon on March 3, 1959. On January 2, 1959, the Soviets beat the United States by successfully flying *Luna 1* by the moon; and on September 12, 1959, the Soviet's *Luna 2* impacted on the moon.

Not until July 28, 1964, did a U.S. moon shot begin to surpass the Soviets' achievements. Ranger 7, using television, returned the first high-resolution pictures of lunar mares, which was the basic objective of the Ranger program as a prelude to the manned Apollo flights. The first clear Soviet pictures were transmitted from the moon on July 18, 1965, with the flight of *Zond 7*.

### March 27, 1958

#### Nikita Khrushchev becomes premier as well as head of the Party in the Soviet Union.

In replacing Bulganin as premier, Khrushchev demonstrated he had gained firm control of the central party organization. According to Western Soviet watchers, Khrushchev had nearly lost his position in June 1957. The Communist Party Presidium sought to dismiss him in favor of Bulganin and old Stalinists

such as Molotov, Malenkov, and Kaganovich. By appealing to the whole Central Committee, Khrushchev saved his power because the Central Committee reversed the Presidium decision. This enabled Khrushchev to remove Molotov and his other opponents and, in March 1958, to get rid of Bulganin as well.

### April 28–May 14, 1958

#### Vice President Nixon encounters intense anti-American feelings while touring Latin America.

In some cities, mobs hurled eggs and stones at Nixon. On May 13 in Caracas, mobs attacked his limousine, nearly overturning the car before the vice president escaped.

These events awakened some Americans to the fact that U.S. assistance went to other parts of the world but neglected its neighbors' economic problems. Between 1945 and 1960, for example, the United States gave three times more aid to the Benelux countries than to all 20 Latin American countries combined. U.S. private capital investment continued, but these funds increased the imbalance of the Latin American economies because they unduly profited citizens of the United States.

Nixon's experience led the Eisenhower administration to reconsider its Latin American policy. In December 1959, the Inter-American Development Bank was established with $1 billion to channel low-interest development loans to Latin American nations. In September 1960, a meeting at Bogotá made long-range economic aid plans designed to benefit Latin America's economic growth.

### May 31, 1958

#### De Gaulle heads an emergency government and begins to organize a new French constitution.

Since the National Assembly's "no confidence" vote in Mendès-France's cabinet in February 1955, France had experienced a succession of coalition governments that failed to resolve the nation's economic problems or the rebellion in Algeria. The assembly's reform bill on January 31 was rejected by Algeria's nationalists, and full-scale civil war threatened to begin.

On May 31, 1958, President René Coty named de Gaulle as premier, and on June 1, the assembly voted him emergency powers by 329-244.

On September 28, 1958, the Constitution of the FIFTH REPUBLIC was approved, and following elections (November 23 and 30), de Gaulle became president of the Fifth Republic.

### June 13, 1958

**Six nations agree to discuss technical problems of nuclear test detection at Geneva.**

The participants at Geneva were the United States, Great Britain, the Soviet Union, France, Poland, and Czechoslovakia.

Two months later a panel of scientific experts concurred in a report that it was technically feasible to build a system to detect violations of a nuclear test ban.

### July 10, 1958

*Cambodian Prince Norodom Sihanouk grants recognition to the Chinese Communist regime.*

Sihanouk's action indicated his desire to be neutral in the Cold War between communism and capitalism by following other neutralists who de facto recognized Mao Tse-tung's government.

The recognition of China was one of Prince Sihanouk's earliest acts after gaining control of the Cambodian government. On March 23, 1958, his Communist-Socialist Party won all 61 seats in the National Assembly. While the prince now ruled as prime minister, his father, Norodom SURAMARIT, was king. On June 5, 1960, on the death of his father, Prince Sihanouk became chief of state after a nationwide referendum voted approval.

Prince Sihanouk was not a Communist, although his party's name confused most Americans. His main goal was to keep Cambodia independent by following a neutralist foreign policy.

### July 14, 1958

*In Iraq, an army coup led by General Abdul Karim Al-Kassem assassinates King Faisal II and proclaims a republic.*

Soon after, the new government met with representatives of the UNITED ARAB REPUBLIC to announce that the UAR and IRAQ "stood together as one nation."

Premier Prince Norodum Sihanouk. National Archives

### July 15, 1958

**American forces intervene in Lebanon as 1,400 U.S. marines land on the beaches near Beirut.**

Lebanon's President Camille CHAMOUN requested U.S. help because he feared possible intervention by President Nasser's United Arab Republic (Egypt and Syria).

Lebanon's political system had for some time hinged on cooperation of the three competing religious factions—Christians, Muslims, and Druze. This precarious triad was disrupted in 1958 as street fights and riots advocated a new political alignment. Christian Lebanese such as President Chamoun believed that the UAR had incited the Muslim population to oppose the existing regime. On June 6, Lebanon's Foreign Minister Charles Malik asked the U.N. Security Council to halt the aggression of the UAR. On June 11, U.S. observers were sent to Beirut. As Arab pressure grew, President Chamoun feared a civil war. He asked Eisenhower for assistance.

James Thaber, whose son is in the Army, learns of President Eisenhower's decision to send U.S. troops to Lebanon. National Archives

Washington responded quickly. On July 15, U.S. forces landed but met no resistance. They remained until October 25, after a political compromise was again renewed in Beirut. The Lebanese parliament chose General Faud Chehab as president and approved a cabinet of four Christians, four Muslims, and one Druze. Meanwhile, Lebanon's neighboring Arab nations promised not to interfere in the country's internal affairs.

Eisenhower demonstrated that the United States could intervene in the Middle East with its Sixth Naval Fleet if necessary. Critics charged that the president acted in haste and that Dulles incorrectly blamed the Communists for difficulties in Lebanon and the Middle East in general.

### July 26, 1958

**Romania announces the withdrawal of all Soviet occupation forces.**

This did not end Soviet influence in Bucharest but gave the Romanians more political latitude without the disrupting riots that occurred in Hungary and Poland.

### August 3, 1958

**The USS *Nautilus*, America's first nuclear-powered submarine, completes an undersea crossing of the North Pole.**

### August 13, 1958

**President Eisenhower outlines a new U.S. policy toward the Middle East that recognizes Arab nationalism and ends the tendency to view the area in Cold War terms.**

On August 13, Eisenhower's speech at the United Nations suggested a new attitude toward the Middle East. Rather than simply to link aid to the Arab states in return for a commitment to anticommunism as the Eisenhower Doctrine implied, the president recognized "positive neutralism" as a factor in the Middle East.

As a consequence of his new approach, Eisenhower agreed to send wheat to Egypt in 1959 and to deal evenhandedly with Arabs and Israelis. Some historians discount the concept that Eisenhower began this new approach, attributing it instead to President Kennedy.

### August 23, 1958

**Chinese Communists again bombard the offshore islands of Quemoy and Matsu.**

A crisis in the Formosa Straits that ended in 1955 (see January 28, 1955) was renewed when the Chinese again bombarded Quemoy and Matsu on August 23. The Eisenhower administration believed tension in the Formosa Straits had ended on February 5, 1958, when the U.S. navy's Seventh Fleet evacuated the Nationalist Chinese from Tachen Island.

When the bombardment began again, American commentators assumed Mao Tse-tung had returned to a hard-line policy, enlisting a threat against Formosa to force the United States to threaten or bomb China so Moscow would have to aid China's Communists. Such speculation influenced Eisenhower's advisers, although post–Cold War documents from China and the Soviet Union reveal this speculation was not correct. According to declassified documents, Mao sought to demonstrate

China's support for anti-imperialist uprisings in the Middle East, where the United States sent forces to Lebanon and Iraqi rebels assassinated King Faisal II, whom British "imperialists" controlled previously. Because Mao also wanted to avoid war with the United States, he ordered the Chinese military to do everything possible to avoid hitting American ships.

Whatever China's rationale, Eisenhower ordered the Seventh Fleet to escort Nationalist troops and supplies to Quemoy and Matsu. He also reinforced the fleet by sending an aircraft carrier and four destroyers to the Formosa Straits. In addition, Secretary Dulles announced U.S. forces would aid the Nationalist Chinese in defending Quemoy and Matsu. On September 15, ambassadors from the United States and the People's Republic of China renewed negotiations in Warsaw, Poland. While these talks continued, the Chinese reduced their bombardment of Quemoy and Matsu.

See July 14 and 15, and October 23, 1958.

### August 26, 1958

#### President Eisenhower begins a 12-day visit to Germany, France, and Britain.

The goodwill visit was designed to reassure American allies of the U.S. desire and ability to protect Western Europe. Since the Geneva Conference of 1955, Britain and France complained that Washington did not understand their economic and defense problems. Dulles often used little tact with the Europeans; Eisenhower, it was hoped, would be more capable of gaining continued support and goodwill in the NATO organization and its member nations.

### September 2, 1958

#### Eisenhower signs the National Defense Education Act.

Enacted largely in reaction to the fear of Soviet leadership in science and technology, this bill provided loans to college students, grants for science and foreign-language instruction, and graduate school fellowships for students preparing to teach.

### September 28, 1958

#### *France establishes the French community for its overseas territories.*

Each former colonial state could join the community, vote for complete independence from France, or remain as an overseas territory of France. Only FRENCH SOMALILAND chose to remain a territory. Other former French colonies opted for independence or very loose ties to the French community. These included Guinea, Senegal, Mauritania, Dahomey, Upper Volta, Niger, Mali, Chad, Togo, Ivory Coast, Cameroon, Congo (Brazzaville), Gabon, Malagasy Republic, and the Central African Republic.

### October 7, 1958

#### *A coup in Pakistan annuls the republican constitution of 1956, leading to military control by General Mohammed Ayub Khan on October 30, 1958.*

### October 23, 1958

#### *The Soviet Union agrees to loan Egypt $100 million toward building the Aswân High Dam.*

Construction was scheduled to start on January 1, 1959.

### October 23, 1958

#### Quemoy-Matsu crisis ends after Chiang renounces use of force against mainland China.

The U.S. negotiations with China were stalemated in Warsaw, Poland, because Chinese Nationalists persisted in staging raids on the mainland. To end the crisis, Secretary of States Dulles visited Chiang Kai-shek from October 20 to 22 and persuaded him to change his policy of trying to regain control of China's mainland. Dulles claimed that it perpetuated a potential crisis that, if resulting in war, would be a disaster for the United States and the entire world.

Dulles often talked about a "two-China" policy as the way to permit Chiang to govern Formosa without threatening to retake China's mainland. On October 23, Dulles and Chiang agreed to neutralize Quemoy and Matsu with a reduced number of Nationalist troops and stop commando raids along China's coastline. Dulles announced the United States would continue to recognize Chiang's government and Chiang said the Nationalists would not use force to recapture control of the mainland. The Dulles-Chiang announcements ended the 1958 crisis and Mao stopped shelling the offshore islands.

The cease-fire ended the crisis but did not settle all problems in the Formosan Straits. On October 31, the U.S. State Department revealed that the Nationalists could attack China if there were a large-scale uprising on the mainland. On October 7, 1959, Undersecretary of State Douglas Dillon stated Mao would risk "total" war if China attacked the offshore islands.

See August 23, 1958.

### October 31, 1958

**Conference on a nuclear test ban opens at Geneva between delegates of the United States, Britain, and the Soviet Union.**

During the 1950s, the testing of nuclear weapons caused radioactive particles to travel around the world's atmosphere, and some scientists deplored the present and future hazards of such radioactive rain.

In March, the USSR, Britain, and the United States each announced unilaterally that it would suspend nuclear tests, reserving the right to renew tests if other nations did so.

The October 1958 sessions opened with optimism, but no agreements were reached during the next two years. The discussions did provide a foundation for more successful talks in the 1960s.

See August 5, 1963.

### November 4, 1958

**The Democrats enlarge their control of Congress in national elections; their Senate majority becomes 64 to 34; the House majority, 283 to 153.**

### November 10, 1958

**Khrushchev demands that Western forces leave West Berlin, making it a "free city."**

On November 10, First Secretary Khrushchev during a Soviet-Polish friendship dinner in Moscow demanded that the Western allies leave Berlin. He claimed the Western powers used West Berlin to launch aggressive maneuvers against the German Democratic Republic and other socialist countries including Poland. He also said the impending atomic armament of West Germany by NATO would make the Berlin situation worse if it were not corrected.

On November 27, Khrushchev gave the Western nations details of his demands based on the argument that previous Berlin agreements were nullified by NATO's rearming West Germany. He gave the Western powers six months to negotiate a final peace treaty for Germany that would make West Berlin a free, demilitarized city. Immediately, the United States and its Western allies denounced Khrushchev's ultimatum.

On December 14, the Western allies met to assert their rights and duties in Berlin. The allies agreed that negotiations on Berlin must be made in the broader context of German unity and European security. Eventually, Khrushchev agreed to negotiate on Germany. Details of Khrushchev's personal role on sending the 1958 ultimatum is explained in Hope Harrison's article in the Cold War International History *Bulletin* for Fall 1994.

### December 14, 1958

**The U.S., British, and French foreign ministers reassert their rights and duties in Berlin.**

On November 27, Soviet Premier Khrushchev asserted that the four-power occupation of Berlin should end and the city should be demilitarized. The foreign ministers of the three Western powers rejected the Soviet demand but requested talks with the USSR on Berlin in the context of German unity and European security (December 31).

### December 28, 1958

**A State Department memo on Cuba outlines the need to remove Batista for a centrist party proponent.**

In 1958, the struggle between the Batista government and Fidel Castro's rebels in Cuba began to cause difficulties for the Batista government. Batista's repression and corruption led the State Department to prefer that he resign in favor of a moderate leader, but no method to achieve this could be found. Although some U.S. writers such as Jules Dubois of the *Chicago Tribune* liked Castro's reform proposals,

U.S. diplomats disliked his anti-Americanism and left-wing associates. The report of December 28 indicated that there were Communists in Castro's camp but that the rebels did not appear to be dominated by them.

Thus, the report principally outlined the U.S. dilemma: how to get a moderate reform leader in Cuba. Some Latin American nations assisted in the search for a moderate to replace Batista, but no solution was found. By early January, Castro gained power.

See January 1, 1959.

# 1 9 5 9

### January 1, 1959

**Cuban President Batista resigns after Fidel Castro's forces capture Santa Clara (December 31, 1958).**

Castro's forces marched on Santiago and Havana, giving him control of all Cuba by January 3.

### January 3, 1959

**Alaska becomes the 49th state after Eisenhower signs final documents of approval.**

### January 19, 1959

**The United States rejects a Soviet request to lower U.S.-Soviet trade barriers.**

This request came during a two-week Washington visit by Soviet First Deputy Premier Anastas I. MIKOYAN.

### January 27–February 5, 1959

**At the 21st Communist Party Congress, Khrushchev clarifies several of his ideas on "peaceful coexistence."**

Two basic parts of Khrushchev's strategy for "peaceful coexistence" with capitalism were (1) a declaration that war between socialist and capitalist states was not inevitable. In Khrushchev's view, the Soviets were young and would grow in strength; the Western capitalists were old, becoming weaker, and would collapse as wars of national liberation damaged their imperial-based economies. (2) A proposal to construct an atom-free zone in the Far East and the entire Pacific Ocean. This would preserve the continuance of two real superpowers, preventing China and Japan from developing nuclear weapons. The Soviet premier warned that without such an agreement, his country would continue to mass-produce ICBMs, which gave it the lead in nuclear weapons.

The 21st Congress also disclosed new rifts in Moscow's relations with Tito's Yugoslavia. The Soviets declared their united opposition to Tito's revisionist methods.

### February 19–20, 1959

**President Eisenhower and Mexican President Adolfo López Mateos confer at Acapulco.**

They agreed on construction of the Diablo Dam to enhance U.S.-Mexican economic collaboration.

### March 2, 1959

**Serious anti-American riots begin in Bolivia.**

Although there were reports of at least 14 anti-American demonstrations in Latin American nations during 1959, the most serious was in La Paz, Bolivia. It resulted when *Time* magazine's Latin American edition published the story that a U.S. embassy officer in Bolivia had said that the way to solve Bolivia's economic problems was for "her neighbors to divide up the country and the problems."

For three days, rioters in La Paz and other cities shouted anti-Yankee slogans, attacked U.S.-owned buildings, and burned American flags. American citizens had to be gathered together for protection by police, and the State Department considered evacuating all Americans.

The riots finally ended. To calm things, Secretary Christian Herter informed the Bolivian ambassador that he could not believe the reported statement was correct. *Time* would not retract its report but printed a story that said the "jest" was a quip that both Bolivians and foreigners had repeated for many years.

Together with Vice President Nixon's experiences during his Latin American tour of April 27 to May 15, 1958, the Bolivian riots indicated strained U.S. relations in Latin America.

## March 5, 1959

### The United States signs bilateral defense pacts with Iran, Pakistan, and Turkey.

The death of King Faisal of Iraq during the military coup that brought General Abdul Karin al-Kassem to power in Iraq led to Iraq's proposed withdrawal from the Baghdad Pact, which was formalized on March 24, 1959. To replace this alliance the United States undertook separate treaties with the states along the southern border of the Soviet Union. Soon after forming the alliance with Turkey, the United States obtained permission to establish Intermediate-Range Ballistic Missile bases in Turkey.

After the Baghdad Pact ended, the alliance, without Iraq, was re-created as the Central Treaty Organization (CENTO). The United States did not join the pact but supported its objectives.

## March 31, 1959

### *Communist China completes its takeover of Tibet.*

Fighting between Communists and Tibetans began on March 13, 1959, following Chinese infiltration of this small Himalayan country. The Chinese had always claimed sovereignty over Tibet and began actively to seek control in 1956, when they concluded a treaty with Nepal (September 24, 1956), which surrendered Nepalese rights to the area in recognition of Chinese sovereignty.

The Tibetans stood little chance against Chinese forces, and on March 28, 1959, China's Premier CHOU EN-LAI declared the Tibetan government of the Dalai Lama dissolved, so that a new government for the Tibetan autonomous region could be organized. The Communists gained full control when the Dalai Lama fled to India on March 31.

## April 15, 1959

### Fidel Castro visits Washington, where he declares his regime is "humanistic" but not Communist.

Nevertheless, talks with the Americans about his desired reforms soon caused U.S. opposition. Castro wanted national control over the Cuban economy, which heretofore was manipulated by Americans who owned 80% of Cuba's utilities, 40% of its sugar, and 90% of the mining wealth. Washington

also controlled how much Cuban sugar could enter the U.S. market.

Although Castro's arbitrary arrests and executions of his opponents in January and February alarmed some of his U.S. supporters, his April visit generally left many believing he was a moderate.

During a three-week period, Castro had executed 250 Cubans and many others had been threatened with imprisonment. The United States, however, had sent a new ambassador to Havana, Philip Bonsal, on January 19 and recognized Castro's government. In addition, Castro's demand for U.S. to retain its economic and sugar quotas, as well as his promise to pay for any expropriated property in Cuba, again projected a moderate image during April 1959.

See June 4, 1959.

## April 22, 1959

### Christian A. Herter replaces John Foster Dulles as Secretary of State.

Dulles had been suffering from cancer for several years, having had emergency surgery in November 1956, during the height of the Suez crisis. Dulles died on May 24, 1959.

Herter was highly qualified to be secretary of state. He had served on the U.S. Peace Commission at Paris in 1918–1919 and as Herbert Hoover's personal assistant in the Commerce Department to 1924. He was elected a representative from Massachusetts in Congress from 1943 to 1953 and was on the House Select Committee for the Marshall Plan. Prior to becoming secretary, he served as undersecretary of state from 1957 to 1959. He served as secretary until January 20, 1961.

## May 11, 1959

### Western foreign ministers fail to solve the Berlin problems with the Soviet Union.

After Khrushchev issued an ultimatum on Berlin, the Western foreign ministers rejected Khrushchev's demands as a violation of the 1945 Potsdam Agreement but wanted to avoid a confrontation with the Soviet leader. In March 1959, British Foreign Minister Harold Macmillan visited Moscow, where Khrushchev agreed to cancel the ultimatum provided a summit meeting would discuss the German situation. President Eisenhower agreed a summit could be held provided preliminary talks by foreign ministers showed positive results.

Foreign ministers talks began in Geneva on May 11 but in three months achieved no beneficial results. Because of the deadlock on Germany, Eisenhower invited Khrushchev to visit the United States to discuss the German problem.

See November 10, 1958, and September 15, 1959.

## May 24, 1959

### *A five-year Anglo Soviet trade agreement is signed in Moscow.*

Unlike the United States, Great Britain and most Western European governments welcomed Khrushchev's détente and peaceful coexistence overtures, especially hoping to get new markets for their products. Thus, while Washington rejected trade agreements, European nations pursued negotiations with Moscow.

See January 19, 1959.

## June 4, 1959

### Castro's agrarian reform decree becomes a sign of his more radical intentions.

The Cubans had approved land reform legislation on May 17 that Castro put into operation on June 4. The law abolished all large sugar plantations and decreed that sugar mill operators could not own sugar-growing operations. Both foreign and Cuban landowners were affected. They would be paid by Cuban bonds over a 20-year period at $4\frac{1}{2}\%$ interest. Proceeds from the bonds had to be reinvested in Cuba and could not be converted into dollars. Finally, Castro asserted that the property value would be based on the most recent tax assessment values of the property.

Obviously, property owners protested. On July 12, the U.S. State Department objected to the method of valuation and bond payment and said the action amounted to confiscation, not expropriation, of property. Castro rejected all protests and told television audiences in Cuba that anyone opposing land reform was a traitor. By August 1959, many of Castro's moderate backers began to flee to the United States.

## June 29, 1959

### The St. Lawrence seaway opens officially to link the Great Lakes and the Atlantic Ocean.

Canada and the United States shared the cost of rebuilding the St. Lawrence seaway. Although the Canadians made plans for the project in the 1940s, the U.S. Congress did not authorize seaway funds until May 1953. When completed, the project deepened the seaway and built necessary canals and locks to enable larger ships to use the waterway.

Queen Elizabeth II and President Eisenhower attended the official opening on June 29. During the first year, the volume of cargo on the new seaway increased from 13 million tons in 1959 to 21 million tons in 1960, beginning the annual increase of shipping in subsequent years.

## July 8, 1959

### The United States announces that 200 U.S. planes will be moved from France to West Germany and Great Britain.

French President Charles de Gaulle disagreed with Washington's European defense plans and advocated France's "separate" role in NATO defenses, in preference to an integrated role.

On March 14, U.S.-French defense talks ended in dispute because de Gaulle refused to place one-third of France's Mediterranean fleet under NATO, as previously arranged. De Gaulle believed French "grandeur" required a separate French nuclear force. He also argued that the United States would not use its nuclear forces to defend Europe and, therefore, France needed its own nuclear weapons to deter the Soviet Union.

## July 24, 1959

### "Kitchen debate" between Vice President Nixon and Premier Khrushchev takes place.

Nixon made a goodwill visit to the Soviet Union at the time that an American national exhibit opened in Moscow. He and the Soviet premier attended the opening together and visited a model of an American home on display. As they surveyed the technology of a U.S. kitchen, they began an impromptu argument on the virtues of communism and capitalism that the news media highlighted.

President Eisenhower with Queen Elizabeth on their way to dedicate the St. Lawrence Seaway. Dwight D. Eisenhower Library

### August 19, 1959

**The Central Treaty Organization (CENTO) replaces the Baghdad Pact.**

Because Iraq withdrew from the Baghdad Pact on March 24, CENTO was formed to continue the defensive alliance of Turkey, Iran, Pakistan, and Great Britain. As in the case of the Baghdad Pact, the United States supported but did not join the alliance. America's bilateral defense pacts served the same purpose in the Middle East.

See March 5, 1959.

### August 21, 1959

**Hawaii becomes the 50th U.S. state.**

### September 15, 1959

**Khrushchev tours the United States and meets with Eisenhower at Camp David.**

The Soviet leader visited Washington, the United Nations, Iowa, Los Angeles, and Hollywood's 20th Century-Fox movie studio for the filming of *Can-* *Can.* His request to visit Disneyland was turned down because his security could not be guaranteed.

During his Iowa visit, Khrushchev went to the farm of Roswell Garst, who had visited the USSR earlier to acquaint the Soviets with U.S. seed corn growing and pig-raising techniques. On Garst's farm in Coon Rapids, as elsewhere during his visit, Khrushchev made a hit with many Americans because of his humor and display of common sense.

On the final three days of his visit, Khrushchev met with President Eisenhower at his Camp David retreat. Their meeting appeared to end cordially and the two leaders agreed to discuss further such pending issues as Germany, Berlin's status, and a nuclear test ban. Over the winter, reporters talked about "the spirit of Camp David" as defining better relations between Moscow and Washington.

The Camp David meetings did not accomplish anything specific but served to diffuse the 1959 tensions over Germany. Khrushchev dropped his previous time limit on negotiations regarding Germany, and Eisenhower agreed to a summit meeting in 1960 without the necessity for successful lower-level agreements preceding the summit.

See December 19, 1959.

Premier Khrushchev tours an Iowa farm. National Archives

Adenauer. Their most important decision was to invite Soviet Premier Khrushchev to a summit meeting in Paris. After Khrushchev accepted the invitation, the meeting was set for May 16, 1960.

On December 22, following the Paris meeting, Eisenhower's goodwill trip took him to Italy, Turkey, Pakistan, Afghanistan, India, Iran, Greece, Tunisia, Spain, and Morocco. Despite the tiring journey, Eisenhower ended 1959 by visiting many places where millions of people turned out to welcome him as the world's most respected and beloved leader and peacemaker.

# 1960

### January 19, 1960

### The U.S.-Japanese Treaty of Mutual Security (1951) is renewed.

The treaty renewal caused leftist riots in Japan in an effort to prevent the treaty's ratification by the Japanese House of Representatives. Japan's Premier Nobusuke KISHI and his Liberal Democratic cabinet held firm, however, and the treaty was ratified on June 19, 1960. The treaty continued to permit American military bases on Japanese soil, which was the principal clause detested by the critics of Kishi's government.

See June 12–21, 1960.

### December 1, 1959

### The United States, the USSR, and 10 other nations approve a treaty to reserve the Antarctic for scientific and peaceful purposes.

### December 19, 1959

### Eisenhower's goodwill tour begins with a Paris meeting of NATO leaders.

The first stop on President Eisenhower's 22,370 mile journey to three continents was Paris for a meeting with French President de Gaulle, British Prime Minister Macmillan, and West German Chancellor

### January 28, 1960

### *Burma and mainland China sign a 10-year nonaggression treaty.*

### February 13, 1960

### *Cuba and the USSR sign an economic pact.*

The Soviets agreed to buy 5 million tons of Cuban sugar and to give Castro $100 million of Soviet trade credits.

The Soviet-Cuban agreement was offered by Anastas MIKOYAN, deputy premier of the Soviet Union, who visited Cuba in February. In addition to the credits and sugar purchase, the Soviets would provide technical assistance to build factories in Cuba.

### February 13, 1960

*France explodes its first atomic bomb in the Sahara region of Algeria.*

This successful test fulfilled President de Gaulle's desire to create an independent French nuclear capability.

### March 7, 1960

**The United States renews diplomatic relations with Bulgaria after a nine-year disruption.**

U.S. Minister Edward Page Jr. arrived in Sofia on March 7.

### April 25, 1960

**Khrushchev again raises the Berlin issue, asserting that a separate peace treaty with East Germany would end allied rights in Berlin. Eisenhower replies that western troops would not evacuate West Berlin.**

Throughout 1959, several attempts to resolve the Berlin issue failed. Most notable was the foreign ministers conference at Geneva between May 11 and August 5, 1959, which discussed the issues of Berlin, German reunification, and the guarantee of free elections.

In October at Camp David, there was hope that the Khrushchev-Eisenhower sessions had established a timetable to resolve the Berlin issue. Now, on the eve of the Geneva conference of May 1960, Khrushchev again threatened to settle the question unilaterally.

### April 27, 1960

**South Korean President Syngman Rhee's resignation leads to a military junta.**

On March 15, 1960, Rhee won an unopposed reelection for a fourth term of office. During the elections, protestors criticized Rhee's repressive measures, and in March demonstrators claimed Rhee's Liberal Party rigged elections to the National Assembly. Larger protests began after police fired on rioters, killing 127 people. On April 27, Rhee resigned from office because of the protests.

On July 29, new assembly elections resulted in a victory for Chang Myron's Democratic Party. Because many if South Koreas military leaders opposed Chang's attempts to negotiate a unity proposal with

President Syngman Rhee resigns. National Archives

North Korea's Kim Il Sung, a junta led by Major Park Chung Hee overthrew the Second Republic on May 16, 1961. The United States opposed the military regime and urged Park to restore civilian government. To comply, Park arranged elections for October 15, 1961. After designating himself a civilian, Park restricted campaigns by opponents and won a plurality of the votes before declaring himself president of South Korea.

Park's program for South Korea was to build the country's economy and eventually "win a victory over communism" by taking control of North Korea. He did not change this policy until 1971, when President Nixon announced he would visit China. For details of Korea's governments and unification efforts, see In K. Hwang's essay "Korea's Unification Struggle" in Lester H. Brune (ed.), *The Korean War* (1996).

### May 3, 1960

*The "outer seven" economic group forms the European free trade association (EFTA).*

Nations surrounding the COMMON MARKET NATIONS had signed the STOCKHOLM TREATY in 1959, to cooperate in trade as a means of counteracting Common Market policy. The Free Trade group included Great

Britain, Sweden, Norway, Denmark, Switzerland, Austria, and Portugal.

### May 5, 1960

#### Khrushchev announces a U.S. spy plane has been shot down over the Soviet Union.

The Soviet downing of the U-2, a high-flying reconnaissance aircraft, resulted in a controversy between Moscow and Washington on the eve of the Paris summit. Following Krushchev's announcement, the U.S. Department of State denied it was a spy plane, saying a weather plane flew off course from its base in Turkey or Iran. To rebut the States Department, Khrushchev produced films from the U-2, saying its pilot, Gary Francis Powers, was captured after parachuting to safety. Powers failed to push the destruct mechanism designed to demolish the U-2.

After Khrushchev's disclosure, President Eisenhower stepped in, telling reporters he accepted responsibility for the incident but hoped Khrushchev would not use the affair to disrupt the positive results expected at the forthcoming Paris summit.

Later, the United States disclosed that the U-2 flights began in 1956 when aviation and photo technology made them feasible. These flights provided Eisenhower with specific data on Soviet military technology and showed that some so-called missile experts were mistaken in claiming that a "missile gap" had made for an inferior American defense. Eisenhower kept the U-2 reports secret to prevent the Soviets from learning about new U.S. intelligence breakthroughs. Declassified U-2 photos were released in 1975.

From 1957 to 1960, Eisenhower's critics, including John F. Kennedy and Lyndon B. Johnson, created an atmosphere of distrust about the U.S. defense system. Although Eisenhower frequently denied that there was a missile gap, reputable journalists rebuked the president and accepted the Gaither Report or the claims of U.S. General Maxwell Taylor, who opposed Eisenhower's "new look" policy, or of Henry Kissinger, a political scientist at the time. If the president had released the U-2 data, he would have proven there was no missile gap.

See May 16, 1960, and February 6, 1961.

### May 16, 1960

#### The Paris Summit Conference is aborted because Eisenhower refuses to apologize to Khrushchev for the U-2 flights.

Eisenhower was willing to cancel future flights but refused to apologize. Khrushchev walked out of the conference, blaming the United States for preventing peaceful solutions to world problems. Although British Prime Minister Harold Macmillan tried to heal the differences between Eisenhower and Khrushchev, he could not persuade the Soviet leader to compromise and stay at the conference.

After the Geneva Conference of 1955, summit sessions became highly publicized and open to television cameras and newsmen. As a result, the Great Power leaders could not negotiate on the give-and-take basis that was possible behind closed doors. At the 1960 Paris session, Khrushchev used the news media to berate the president and to claim great powers for the Soviet Union. Diplomatic maneuvering became difficult or impossible in the public glare of the media. Summits of world leaders became, of necessity, sessions to ratify previously accepted treaties, not to engage in negotiations—a matter not often understood by journalists and their public.

### May 27, 1960

#### *A military coup in Turkey ousts Premier Adnan Menderes.*

The overthrow was led by Lieutenant General Jemal GURSEL, who established a junta known as the TURKISH NATIONAL UNION and promised eventually to organize free elections. The new regime announced its continued support for NATO and Turkey's U.S. treaties.

### June 5, 1960

#### Prince Norodom Sihanouk wins control of Cambodia in a national referendum.

Prince Sihanouk had been elected premier of Cambodia on April 7, 1957, as a member of the People's Socialist Communist Party. Following the death of King Norodom Sumarit on April 3, the prince resigned his office and appealed to the nation for acceptance of his control of the country without a new monarch. The referendum of June 5 provided Sihanouk with this authority.

Sihanouk wanted his country to be neutral in the U.S.-Communist dispute in Southeast Asia, which disturbed many Americans who disliked Sihanouk's having some Communist Party members in his government.

### June 12–21, 1960

**President Eisenhower makes a goodwill tour of the Far East, visiting the Philippines, Formosa (Taiwan), Okinawa, and Korea.**

The Far East tour caused difficulty regarding relations with JAPAN. Eisenhower had scheduled a visit to Tokyo, but anti-American riots escalated to such a degree that he canceled his Japanese visit. The rioting focused on the January 1960 renewal of the U.S.-Japanese alliance in terms that left-wing critics in Japan claimed were not favorable to their nation. Eisenhower's visit was planned for the week the treaty ratification was being debated in Japan's House of Representatives, a time when the left-wing parties staged their most violent demonstrations. As a result, Premier Kishi recommended that the president not visit Tokyo at that time.

### June 27, 1960

**Communist bloc countries withdraw from talks by the 10-power Committee on Disarmament meetings in Geneva.**

The meeting had begun optimistically on March 15, 1960, but Khrushchev stopped Soviet participation after the U-2 incident damaged his "peaceful coexistence" concepts and indicated the United States knew of the Soviet weakness in ICBM despite the premier's public claims of superiority.

### June 30, 1960

***Belgium grants the Congo Republic full independence under President Joseph Kasavubu and Premier Patrice Lumumba.***

The Belgians decided in 1959, after nationalist demonstrators in the Belgian Congo demanded independence, to give their colony freedom as soon as possible. Elections took place in the Congo on December 20, 1959, and the elected

Congo assembly demanded immediate, unconditional independence.

Within two weeks of the separation, the new Congo government faced dissident groups that wanted tribal or provincial separation from the central government. The most serious uprising occurred in KATANGA PROVINCE, where dissidents led by Moise TSHOMBE proclaimed independence for the province. Tshombe was backed by European and American copper and cobalt mining interests that desired to keep control of these vital resources and their investments.

Because of these problems, Lumumba asked for U.N. help, and on July 14 the Security Council voted to send a U.N. force to replace Belgian troops and attempt to secure peace among the contending factions. U.N. forces and negotiators led by Secretary-General Dag Hammarskjöld began a four-year effort to mediate amid the contending Congolese factions and to secure an orderly government. While working at this effort, Hammarskjöld perished in an airplane crash in the Congo on September 18, 1961.

### July 1, 1960

**The Soviets shoot down an American plane over the Barents sea, claiming it violated Soviet borders.**

The plane was a reconnaissance bomber (RB-47) that the United States contended was on an IGY mission to collect data on electromagnetic activity in Arctic waters. NATO ships and planes had searched the area for two days, giving it up for lost on June 3.

Finally, on July 11, Moscow announced that a Soviet fighter plane shot down the RB-47 as it flew over Soviet territorial waters, heading for Archangel. The Soviets captured the two American airmen who survived out of a crew of six. Moscow said the two rescued men confessed to being on a spy mission.

The United States reported that when it last radioed to a Norwegian air force base, the RB-47 was 300 miles outside Soviet territory. Washington asked for an impartial U.N. investigation of the incident and for return of the rescued pilots. A U.N. Security Council resolution to conduct an inquiry was vetoed on July 26 by the Soviet Union. The USSR also vetoed a proposal to let Red Cross workers see the two rescued airmen.

### July 6, 1960

#### Congress approves and Eisenhower levies cuts in Cuba's sugar quota. Castro retaliates by nationalizing all U.S. property in Cuba.

On March 15, 1960, President Eisenhower asked Congress to renew the Cuban sugar quota, which had given special prices to Cuba since 1934. He also asked Congress to include authority for the president to change the quota if it was in the national interest. Congress passed this quota law, which Eisenhower signed on July 6, 1960. The only change Congress made in Eisenhower's March request was to permit the president to fix but not increase the sugar quota until April 1, 1961.

After signing the law, the president immediately cut Cuba's 1960 quota by 95%, from 700,000 tons to 39,752 tons. While this action constituted economic intervention in Cuba, Congress approved the law because Castro's connections with the USSR had become apparent since February 13, 1960.

As soon as Eisenhower announced the sugar cut, Castro retaliated by issuing the Nationalization Law, which applied exclusively to Americans. This law ordered the seizure of all U.S. property without compensation. The United States protested this law on July 16, but there was no response from Havana.

As tensions increased between the United States and Cuba, Khrushchev added to the difficulties. On July 9, the Soviet leader pledged Russia's fullest support of Cuba. Soviet rockets, Khrushchev said, could "figuratively speaking support the Cubans in case of Pentagon aggression."

### July 20, 1960

#### A polaris missile is launched from a submerged submarine.

This success gave the U.S. navy a new role in nuclear weapons. The United States gained a new form of deterrent power because the submarines were mobile and difficult to detect by the Soviet Union.

### August 1, 1960

#### *The breakup of the French community begins when the Republic of Dahomey declares independence.*

President de Gaulle had established the French Community on September 28, 1958, as a means of compromising the nationalism of the former French colonies with some degree of French control and trade. Nationalists in most of these areas eventually preferred independence. On April 27, Togo, which had been a U.N. trust territory under French rule, became independent. Dahomey's declaration to be free of the French Community began an exodus of other states. Former French colonies to gain independence were Niger (August 3), Upper Volta (August 5), Ivory Coast (August 7), Chad (August 11), Central African Republic (August 13), Gabon (August 17), Senegal (August 20), Sudan, Mali (September 23), and Mauritania (November 28).

### August 9, 1960

#### In Laos, a coup led by Kong Le returns Souvanna Phouma to power and results in U.S.-Soviet tensions.

After the Geneva Accords of 1954 gave Laos independence, international conflict increased over the failure of this state to achieve political order. The Geneva agreements called for the regrouping of all Communist Pathet Lao (left-wing nationalists) in the two northern provinces of Laos. In 1957, the neutralist Premier Souvanna Phouma compromised with the Communists and brought his half-brother, who was a Communist, into the cabinet.

The compromise failed because Communist election gains in 1958 threatened a left-wing takeover. As a result, civil war began as the extreme right- and left-wing groups fought. Disliking the turn of events, Premier Souvanna resigned on July 23, 1958. Pro-Western ruler Phoui Sanaikone took charge of the government. In October 1958, Phoui promised to bring economic and political reforms to Laos, and the United States provided about $25 million of aid to Laos for 1959.

During 1959, Phoui complained that Communist guerrilla war had begun in Laos and appealed to the United Nations to stop the invasion of North Vietnamese. On September 7, the U.N. Security Council sent a subcommittee to make an "inquiry" in Laos, and in October the subcommittee reported that the North Vietnamese had sent arms and supplies to Laos but that it could not clearly establish whether North Vietnamese troops crossed the border.

The U.N. report led to the resignation of Phoui in December 1959; Kou Abhay then became provisional head of the government. Elections were con-

Premier Souvanna Phouma (left) meets with Mao Tsetung in 1956. National Archives

ducted in April 1960, but they were rigged to favor the government, and the Pathet Lao protested. As a result, guerrilla war increased, and on August 9 a coup overthrew Abhay, installing Tiao Somsanith as head of the new regime. The power behind Tiao was a young army captain, KONG LE. Soon after the government ended its fight against the Communists and brought the neutralist Souvanna Phouma back to office, the coup resulted in a dilemma for the United States because there were now three factors in Laos: the neutral Souvanna Phouma controlled the government but lost control of the army because the pro-Western Phoumi Nosavan headed a conservative group that refused to cooperate with Souvanna. The third faction was the Soviet-supported Pathet Lao. By the end of Eisenhower's term of office in January 1961, no solution to the Laos imbroglio had been reached.

See January 17, 1961.

### August 12, 1960

#### Eisenhower administration supports United Nations peacekeeping mission to keep the Congo united.

Following anti-European riots in Léopoldville, the capital of the Belgium Congo, the Belgium government allowed Congolese nationals to hold elections in May 1960. The elections made Joseph Kasavubu president of the Congo and Patrice Lumumba Prime Minister of the Central government. Subsequently, on June 30, 1960, the Belgium Congo became the independent Congo Republic, later named the Republic of Zaire.

Independence Day was barely celebrated before soldiers in the Congo army, known as the Force Publique, mutinied against their Belgian officers, requiring Belgium to send paratroopers to rescue the officers. About the same time, Moise Tshombe, who in May 1960 was elected governor of Katanga, declared independence for Katanga as a separate state. Tshombe was assisted by the Belgian government, with whom he made a deal to continue mining Katanga's natural resources for sale to Belgian merchants.

In late July, Prime Minister Lumumba requested armaments and financial aid from the United States to help his government regain control of Katanga. When the United States rejected his request, Lumumba turned to the Soviet Union, which quickly airlifted food and weapons to the Léopoldville government. In addition, the United Nations Security Council [UNSC] agreed to send U.N. peacekeepers to help maintain the unity of the Congo. The Eisenhower administration favored the UNSC action, concerned that Katanga's uranium, a substance needed to make nuclear weapons, might be sold to the Soviet Union.

On August 18, Under Secretary of State C. Douglas Dillon told the National Security Council (NSC) that the Soviet Union and Lumumba demanded the U.N. peacekeepers leave the Congo. As Stephen E. Ambrose's *Eisenhower: The President* (1984) explains, Eisenhower decided that rather than have U.N. peacekeepers leave someone must "get rid of that man [Lumumba]." On August 25, the CIA's watchdog Committee 5412 met to discuss what action should be taken against Lumumba. The next day, CIA Director Allen Dulles cabled the CIA agent in Léopoldville that the removal of Lumumba was an "urgent" matter.

On September 5, Congo's President Kasavubu dismissed Lumumba as premier. Lumumba was captured—perhaps with CIA help—and placed in the custody of the U.N. peacekeepers. On September 12, the Congo's Army led by Colonel Joseph Mobutu arrested Lumumba, who was executed either by the army or by "hostile tribesmen."

See September 18, 1961.

### August 16, 1960

*Cyprus becomes an independent republic.*

This government was arranged as a compromise between Greek and Turkish factions after many years of negotiation to end British control of the island. On February 19, 1959, the compromise was designed to give each ethnic group a proportionate share of seats in the National Assembly: 70% for Greeks, 30% for Turks. Some British forces remained at two military enclaves to safeguard the agreement.

On December 15, 1960, GREEK ARCHBISHOP MARKARIOS was elected president; FAZIL FUTCHUK, a Turk, became vice president.

### August 28, 1960

**The San José declaration of the OAS condemns intervention "by any extracontinental power," an indirect warning against Soviet interference in Cuba.**

The United States asked for a special OAS meeting in July 1960, following Soviet Premier Khrushchev's threat to support Cuba with rockets. Khrushchev also told the State Department that the Monroe Doctrine had "outlived its time." During the conference sessions, Secretary of State Herter wanted the group to condemn Castro for violating principles of the inter-American system. The other delegates refused to specify Cuba as a guilty party, preferring to issue a declaration that reaffirmed American "solidarity and security" and opposed intervention by an outside power.

### September 8, 1960

**East Germany institutes a permanent restriction on travel by West Germans to East Berlin.**

West Germans would be required to obtain a police pass to enter East Berlin. The Allies protested this violation of the Four-Power Pact on Berlin.

### September 10, 1960

**The Organization of Petroleum Exporting Countries (OPEC) is formed in Baghdad.**

This group was formed by Sheikh Abdullah Tariki, the minister of petroleum of Saudi Arabia. The original members were Iraq, Iran, Kuwait, Saudi Arabia, and Venezuela. These nations agreed to demand stable oil prices from oil companies.

The impetus to form OPEC occurred when Standard Oil of New Jersey unilaterally cut posted oil prices in 1960, drastically reducing Saudi Arabia's oil revenues. To enable OPEC to function, they set up a secretariat at Geneva with a budget of £150,000.

### September 20, 1960

**At the 1960 session of the U.N. General Assembly, Khrushchev, Tito, and Fidel Castro head their nations' delegations.**

Before the session concluded, the Soviet premier displayed amazing methods of debate. Khrushchev used the United Nations as a forum to woo the support of Third World nations for Soviet policy. Sixteen nations, mostly from Asia and Africa, joined the United Nations during this 15th session of the General Assembly. U.N. membership by October 1960 totaled 98 nations, of which the Asian-African bloc numbered 44.

Khrushchev's September 24 speech at the United Nations attacked Secretary-General Dag Hammarskjöld's policy in the Congo as pro-colonial. He demanded Hammarskjöld's ouster and replacing the secretary-general with a three-man (TROIKA) executive. Both of these proposals were defeated by the assembly.

On October 12, the chairman of the General Assembly, Frederick H. Boland of Ireland, had to suspend the assembly's session because of Khrushchev's outburst. Khrushchev had argued strongly for a resolution to end all colonialism. The Philippine delegate, Lorenzo Sumulong, responded by contending that the resolution should include Soviet imperial control of Eastern Europe. Khrushchev interrupted Sumulong, calling him a U.S. "lackey." As Boland tried to bring order, breaking his gavel in the process, Khrushchev remarked, laughingly, on the weakness of the United Nations. The Soviet premier then took off his shoe and banged it on his desk to protest Sumulong's speech. Chaos erupted before Boland finally adjourned the meeting.

### October 1, 1960

**For the first time since 1903, the U.S. and Panamanian flags are flown together over the canal zone.**

Although the Panamanian flag issue was not the only question about which Panamanians had complained, it symbolized Panama's desire for national respect. Thus, President Eisenhower's decision on September 17 to permit both flags to fly together also symbolized Eisenhower's attempt to relieve some of the difficulties between the United States and Panama.

In February 1955, Eisenhower had agreed to a treaty with Panama regarding U.S. commissary practices and increasing Canal Zone annuities from $430,000 to $1,930,000. By 1957, however, Congress had not appropriated funds for the 1955 treaty, and when Panama objected, Eisenhower persuaded Congress to act by providing funds and averting a crisis.

Nevertheless, demonstrations for Panamanian sovereignty and nationalism continued sporadically. On November 3, 1957, anti-American demonstrators in Panama destroyed much U.S. property and burned the American flag. Although Secretary of State Herter wished to compromise the flag issue with Panama, the U.S. Congress showed its nationalism on February 2, 1960, when the House of Representatives passed a resolution by a vote of 380 to 12, declaring that Panama's flag could not fly in the Canal Zone unless a treaty specifically approved this action.

The Senate did not act on this resolution, and in the fall of 1960, Eisenhower, Herter, and U.S. Ambassador to Panama Joseph S. Farland all agreed that the president should permit the Panamanian flag to be flown. Soon after Congress adjourned in September, Eisenhower issued a statement that approved the flying of both flags over the zone beginning on October 1, 1960.

On April 19, 1960, Eisenhower issued a nine-point program to improve wages and living conditions of the unskilled and semiskilled Panamanian workers in the Canal Zone. He also sought to improve schools and set up apprentice programs for training Panamanians. Americans living in the zone—the "Zonians"—vociferously opposed Eisenhower's program because it threatened their special way of life. Yet Eisenhower's reforms only began to help improve the life of the average Panamanian citizen.

### October 19, 1960

**The U.S. embargoes all exports to Cuba except medicines and certain food products.**

The embargo was intended to put further pressure on Fidel Castro to moderate his anti-American policies.

The next day, Eisenhower recalled the U.S. ambassador to Cuba, Philip Bonsal. Castro had refused to talk with the ambassador since a brief conversation on September 3, 1959. Since January 1, 1959, the United States had requested negotiations with Cuba on 9 formal and 16 informal occasions. Only once, on February 22, 1960, did the Cuban government respond, and then it offered absurd conditions for undertaking negotiations.

### November 8, 1960

**John F. Kennedy defeats Richard M. Nixon in the presidential race.**

Although the election was close, the Democratic Party enlarged its majority in both the House (260 to 172) and the Senate (65 to 35). Kennedy's victory margin was 114,000 votes out of 68.3 million ballots.

During the campaign, neither candidate offered unique foreign policy programs. Both emphasized the importance of the newly developing nations. On defense policy, Kennedy continued to be critical of Eisenhower's alleged complacency toward the USSR and the "loss" of Cuba, and advocated Maxwell Taylor's "flexible response" program for a vigorous

John F. Kennedy. National Archives

defense budget increase. Nixon never provided a firm response to the criticisms of Eisenhower's program.

### November 11–12, 1960

**In Saigon, President Diem regains power after an army paratroop brigade temporarily ousts him from office.**

The paratroop uprising reflected opposition to Diem's policies in the military and among other non-Communist politicians in South Vietnam. In addition to the unsuccessful plot of the paratroopers, 18 old-time non-Communist politicians showed their displeasure with Diem in August 1960 by issuing the so-called Caravelle Manifesto.

The Caravelle group urged Diem to reevaluate his policies by recognizing that not all his critics were Communists. They asked that he hold free elections, end censorship, and stop political repression by releasing political prisoners who filled the jails "to the rafters." They asked Diem to secure dedicated civil servants, end army factionalism, and stop exploiting farmers and workers. They concluded by saying they were not seeking to overthrow Diem but

to appeal to his reason by telling him "hard truths" that those close to him were afraid to report.

Diem reacted like a tyrant, claiming he saw no difference between the Caravelle group and Communists. Therefore, he arrested and imprisoned the 18 signatories of the petition.

Diem eliminated these political reformers easily, but during the next three years, he discovered that eliminating dissent in the army and among Buddhist religious leaders was much more complicated.

By 1960, Diem's publicity had made him as popular in America as he was disliked in South Vietnam. The American Friends of Vietnam had been formed in 1955, and its letterhead cited Senator John F. Kennedy as a founding member. By 1960, the U.S. media called Diem the "tough little miracle man," and *Newsweek*'s Ernest Lindley exclaimed that he was "one of the ablest free Asian leaders." In 1960, both Diem and Chiang Kai-shek won Freedom Foundation awards from a Valley Forge–based organization.

See also December 5, 1960.

### November 19, 1960

**The United States and Canada join 18 members of the OEEC to form the Organization for Economic Co-operation and Development (OECD).**

The purpose of the OECD was to expand trade and economic cooperation and to aid underdeveloped states to expand their economy.

### December 5, 1960

**The U.S. Ambassador to South Vietnam, Elbridge Durbrow, issues a final critical report on Diem's policies.**

After serving four years in Saigon, Ambassador Durbrow had grown increasingly disillusioned with Diem. He said there was only weak domestic support for Diem and blamed many of the problems on corruption in the officer class and the influence of Diem's family members who held high office, especially Ngo Dinh Nhu, Diem's brother, and Madame Nhu. Durbrow wanted Diem replaced if he did not initiate economic reform, broaden the non-Communist base of his cabinet, and eliminate corrupt army and government leaders.

While Durbrow's report indicated the internal causes of South Vietnamese opposition to Diem,

they were not implemented because Kennedy replaced Durbrow with a European expert, Frederick E. Nolting Jr.

### December 5, 1960

*Clearer signs of the Sino-Soviet split are evident at a Moscow meeting of world Communist Parties.*

At the end of the meeting (November 7–December 5, 1960) 81 parties signed a COMMUNIST MANIFESTO that pledged Communist victory by peaceful means and affirmed the Soviet leadership of all Communist parties.

The Chinese Communists' objections to these views reflected the prevailing arguments on policy between Peking and Moscow, which had increased during 1960. On May 14, 1960, Mao Tse-tung published an interview in which he taunted the Soviets for permitting U-2s to spy on them and for believing they could work cooperatively with Western imperialists.

In June, Khrushchev sent letters to a Communist meeting in Romania. The letters attacked Chinese views on Communist policy and blamed Mao for being a revisionist. Khrushchev said the Chinese were madmen and "left adventurists" desiring to unleash a nuclear war.

The November-December sessions in Moscow failed to heal the division between China and the Soviet Union. However, the only country joining China in criticizing Khrushchev was Albania.

### December 20, 1960

*The National Liberation Front (NLF) is created in South Vietnam.*

The NLF said it represented all Vietnamese peoples south of the 17th parallel in their fight against Diem's tyranny.

The formation of the NLF indicated attempts by the South Vietnamese to overthrow Diem's government. After securing control of Saigon in 1955, Diem did not display equal skill in bringing economic reform and political prestige to his government. He failed to carry out land reform for the peasants and increasingly suppressed all who dissented from his policies.

In 1958, the first anti-Diem organizations appeared in the south. The rural groups used sabotage and attacks on village chiefs or informers who were loyal to Diem. As resistance grew in the country, Diem used greater repression, until by 1960 those opposing him decided to organize as the NLF to coordinate their attacks on Saigon and Diem's officials.

# 1961

### January 3, 1961

**The United States severs diplomatic relations with Cuba.**

While the United States recalled Ambassador Bonsal from Havana on October 20, 1960, Castro had assigned no ambassador to Washington since he took office in 1959.

On January 2, 1961, Castro charged that the U.S. embassy in Havana was a center for counterrevolutionaries. He ordered that the embassy staff be reduced from 36 to 11 persons in 48 hours. This convinced President Eisenhower to break diplomatic relations with Cuba.

### January 4, 1961

**Castro's claim that the United States is preparing an invasion is ignored by the U.N. Security Council.**

On October 18, 1960, Cuba first asked the U.N. General Assembly to investigate U.S. plans to invade it. The assembly refused to act. Later, on January 4, 1961, Castro petitioned the U.N. Security Council to prevent U.S. intervention in Cuba. Again, Castro's charges were rebuffed.

On March 17, 1960, President Eisenhower had secretly ordered the Central Intelligence Agency (CIA) to train Cuban exiles for possible guerrilla operations against Castro. By the end of 1960, nearly 1,200 men were being trained by the CIA, most of them in Guatemala. While very few Americans knew about this force, it was an "open" secret elsewhere.

### January 6, 1961

*Soviet Premier Khrushchev asserts that his government will support wars of national liberation.*

Addressing a Communist Party meeting in Moscow, the Soviet leader reiterated his desire for peaceful coexistence with the Western world. The only exception, he stated, was Soviet backing for "just" wars of

Leaders of Communist nations view the celebration of the 46th anniversary of the Soviet Union (November 7, 1961). Left to right: Ho Chi Minh, president of North Vietnam; Soviet premier Nikita Khrushchev; Janos Kadar, Hungarian Communist Party leader; Soviet president Leonid Brezhnev. National Archives

liberation from capitalist imperialism. Khrushchev's speech reflected the era of the end of Western colonialism, which had accelerated after Ghana gained independence in 1957. National uprisings against foreign control had become one of the major causes of conflict throughout the world. This had the greatest impact on British, French, and U.S. policies because they were the powers whose trade and financial policies had become global since the 18th century. When Khrushchev spoke of national liberation, he did not include the many national minorities in the Soviet Union.

### January 17, 1961

**Eisenhower's "farewell address" warns Americans of the dangerous power of the American military-industrial complex.**

During debate on Eisenhower's "new look" policy, the president had become acutely frustrated with the "conjunction of an immense military establishment and a large arms industry" whose "total influence" was felt throughout the nation. Americans, Eisenhower warned, "must guard against the acquisition of unwarranted influence, whether sought or unsought, by the military-industrial complex." Because of this connection, "the potential for the disastrous use of misplaced power exists and will persist."

### January 19, 1961

**The Laotian problem is reviewed for President-Elect Kennedy and his incoming cabinet members.**

Following the return to power of Laotian General Kong Le, the Eisenhower administration opposed Premier Souvanna Phouma's neutralist coalition government that included members of the Pathet Lao communists. In October 1960, Eisenhower sent

Assistant Secretary of State J. Graham Parsons to Vientiane, the capital of Laos, to demand that Souvanna Phouma renounce the Pathet Lao and abandon his neutralist coalition. Eisenhower believed such a coalition would come under the complete control of communists. After Souvanna refused, Eisenhower decided to divert U.S. economic and military assistance through the U.S. Central Intelligence Agency to Phoumi Nosavan, who denounced neutralism and resigned as Minister of Defense in the coalition. This action forced the genuine neutralists in Souvanna's Cabinet to cooperate with the Pathet Lao. By December 1960, the Kong Le-Pathet Lao forces defeated Phoumi Nosavan's forces, driving them out of the region surrounding Vientiane. On December 4, the Soviet Union airlifted military supplies to the Pathet Lao troops, who begin an offensive against Phoumi Nosavan's army.

As a result, President Eisenhower and Secretary of State Herter's review of the Laos situation was that the U.S. was in dangerous trouble in Laos. The new Kennedy administration inherited support for a pro-Western but weak government of Phoumi Nosavan and members of clans who recognized Prince Boun Oum as monarch of Laos. In addition, on January 2, 1962, U.S. delegates to a SEATO meeting requested that the group intervene with a military force to support the pro-Western government, but neither Britain nor France would approve a Laotian intervention. Eisenhower did not want to intervene unilaterally or negotiate with neutralists in Laos, but he sent six U.S. fighter-bombers to assist Phoumi Nosavan's forces. Although Eisenhower thought that saving a pro-Western Laos was the key to the entire region of Southeast Asia, he offered no satisfactory solution to Kennedy and Rusk.

See May 3, 1961.

### January 20, 1961

**President John F. Kennedy's inaugural address calls on the nation to renew its commitment to extend freedom throughout the world.**

In his inaugural address, the president called on the American people to defend freedom in this hour of need. He asserted:

> Let every nation know, whether it wishes us well or ill, that we shall pay any price, bear any burden, meet any hardship, support any friend, oppose

any foe, in order to assure the survival and success of liberty. This much we pledge, and more.

### January 21, 1961

**Dean Rusk is commissioned as Secretary of State under President John F. Kennedy.**

Although Rusk was well qualified to be secretary, President Kennedy desired to be the dominant force in foreign affairs, selecting Rusk as a person who would be loyal and hardworking but not try to capture the headlines. During World War II, Rusk served as a deputy chief of staff in the China-Burma-India theater. Between 1945 and 1952, he held several positions in the State Department, achieving the post of assistant secretary for Far Eastern Affairs in 1950–1951. From 1952 to 1961 he was president of the Rockefeller Foundation. Rusk was secretary throughout the administrations of Kennedy and Johnson, leaving office on January 20, 1969.

### February 6, 1961

**The missile gap is a myth. Secretary of Defense McNamara tells journalists that the "missile-gap" criticism levied against the Eisenhower administration has no foundation in fact.**

Between 1957 and 1961, the widespread criticism of Eisenhower's "new look" policy had been based partly on the incorrect claim that Eisenhower's nuclear sufficiency program to build 200 ICBMs to protect America would create Soviet superiority in nuclear weapons during the early 1960s.

Eisenhower insisted that there was no missile gap, but this theory became so popular that both Republican and Democratic politicians assumed its validity. It was used effectively by Kennedy to assert that Eisenhower's foreign programs had been weak and ineffective. It also was part of Maxwell Taylor's plan to build up the army's counterinsurgency forces to win brushfire wars under the protection of a superior nuclear force umbrella.

Soon after McNamara took over the Defense Department, he saw evidence that Eisenhower's denials of a missile gap were based in fact. In a background briefing, McNamara admitted that there was no missile gap. Nevertheless, neither the Kennedy administration nor the news media played up the fact that the claims of a missile gap had been false.

McNamara and Kennedy wanted to build a superior nuclear force whether or not there was a missile gap. As Richard Aliano has noted, Kennedy wanted a missile gap in reverse, with the gap being on the Soviet side. Therefore the rapid buildup of ICBMs became one part of the large defense expenditures Kennedy promoted for all branches of the armed forces after 1961. In nuclear weapons, by 1967 the United States had increased ICBMs from 200 to 1,000. In addition, the United States had 41 Polaris submarines with 656 missile launchers and 600 long-range bombers for nuclear attack. By 1967, however, the Soviets had responded to the U.S. nuclear race by matching the U.S. nuclear arsenal. Kennedy thus succeeded in stimulating the arms race.

See November 7, 1957.

### February 28, 1961

**Secretary Rusk informs the Senate Foreign Relations Committee that Kennedy, like Eisenhower, supports U.N. action in the Congo.**

Since the Congo dispute first went to the U.N. Security Council during the summer of 1960, the United States had voted with most nations in backing the U.N. peacekeeping mission there and U.N. Secretary-General Dag Hammarskjöld's policy which recognized the Léopoldville government against both the pro-Belgian faction in Katanga and the Soviet-backed forces led by Antonio Gizenga, who had replaced Patrice Lumumba after his execution.

The only problem for the United States was the support given to Tshombe and the rebels in Katanga, whose independence was urged by such conservatives as Senator Barry Goldwater and news editor William F. Buckley. The opponents of the U.N. position increased during the summer of 1961 when the United Nations attempted to use force to defeat Katanga.

See August 12, 1960, and September 18, 1961.

### March 1, 1961

**President Kennedy issues an executive order creating the Peace Corps.**

The Peace Corps was set up to train Americans to go to underdeveloped nations that requested U.S. assistance and to provide teaching and technical services. The idea had been suggested by Hubert Humphrey during the Democratic primaries and was seized

President Kennedy with Peace Corps volunteers.
John F. Kennedy Library

upon by Kennedy. Ideally, the corps would allow Americans and citizens of other nations to work side by side to promote both economic development and the democratic way of life. Kennedy believed the Cold War could be won in Third World nations by demonstrating U.S. virtues on a person-to-person basis.

Kennedy saw the Peace Corps as an important Cold War weapon. He argued that many technicians from the Soviet Union and China "spend their lives abroad in the service of world communism." Young Americans dedicated to freedom, he said, "are fully capable of overcoming the efforts of Mr. Khrushchev's missionaries who are dedicated to undermining that freedom."

### March 13, 1961

**President Kennedy announces the Alliance for Progress to aid Latin America.**

This program, Kennedy said, would extend previous aid of the Eisenhower administration by committing the United States to a 10-year program of $20 billion. Details of the program would be finalized at an Inter-American Conference in Punta del Este, Uruguay, in August.

See August 17, 1961.

### April 17, 1961

**In the U.S.-backed Bay of Pigs invasion, Cuban rebels fail to topple Castro's regime.**

The Eisenhower administration began plans for guerrilla operations in Cuba on March 17, 1960. After the 1960 presidential election, the CIA appraised Kennedy of these plans. Although Secretary Rusk opposed the guerrilla operations, CIA Director Allen Dulles and U.S. Chairman of the Joint Chiefs of Staff General Lyman Lemnitzer assured Kennedy the plans would succeed even though a March 3 CIA report indicated only 25 percent of the Cuban population opposed Castro. Kennedy agreed that planning should continue, but by April 5, the Cuban operation changed from a guerrilla infiltration to an invasion, with Cuban exiles landing near the Zapata swamps at the Bay of Pigs to join Cuban rebels in the mountain area.

From its first hours on April 15, the CIA plans became a fiasco. Of eight B-26 bombers supposed to destroy Cuba's air force, one crashed in the ocean, a second unexpectedly landed in Key West, Florida, and air raids by six B-26s failed to knock out all of Cuba's

planes. Castro's remaining two bombers, four fighter planes, and several T-33 trainer aircraft supported 20,000 Cuban troops with tanks and artillery that quickly surrounded the 1,200 exile rebels who landed at the Zapata swamps on April 17. Although President Kennedy canceled a second B-26 bombing raid on April 26, he acted too late to stop the exiles' invasion effort.

In addition to embarrassing the Kennedy administration, the Bay of Pigs incident damaged U.S. relations with the United Nations Security Council and the Organization of American States. At the United Nations, Ambassador Adlai Stevenson had unknowingly denied the story of U.S. involvement in the rebels' invasion because he had not been fully briefed on the secret operation. America's unilateral operation reaped a harvest of ill will around the world and probably influenced Kennedy's decision to make future attempts to overthrow Castro.

Nearly 40 years later, on April 26, 2000, Maxwell Taylor's secret report on the Bay of Pigs operation was declassified. Taylor disclosed the CIA learned on April 9 that the Soviet Union knew the exact time and day of the amphibious landing but the agency still carried out the planned invasion. As a result, Castro's soldiers repelled the attack in fewer than 72 hours, killing 200 rebels and capturing 1,197 others. The Taylor report did not say who the spy was, but in *Cassidy's Run* author David Wise believes a Mexican, Gilbert López y Rivas, was involved.

The Taylor report was declassified after Peter Kornbluh of the National Security Archives obtained it through resort to the Freedom of Information Act. Kornbluh also requested the release of a four-volume history of the Bay of Pigs operation written by CIA historian Jack B. Pfeiffer, but the CIA continued to withhold that classified study, saying it was still under review.

For release of captives, see December 24, 1962.

### May 3, 1961

**A cease-fire is achieved in Laos soon after the United States threatens military intervention.**

Less noticed than the Cuban Bay of Pigs incident of April 1961 was the fact that the United States seriously considered war in Laos if the Communist advances continued in that state. U.S. support for the rightist regime of Phoumi and Oum in Laos resulted in its growing unpopularity and the strengthening of

President Kennedy briefs the media on the Laotian crisis.
National Archives

Communist and neutralist unity. By March 1961, the Communist drive in Laos left Phoumi's forces in disarray, causing Kennedy and Rusk to seek some means to obtain a neutral, non-Communist state in Laos.

On March 23, Kennedy ordered U.S. forces to move to areas near Laos. The aircraft carrier *Midway* was sent to the Gulf of Siam, a marine unit to Thailand, and forces on Okinawa were placed on alert. At the same time, Secretary Rusk attended a SEATO meeting in Bangkok to obtain support for U.S. military action if necessary.

At Bangkok, Rusk added a clear global dimension to the Truman Doctrine, telling the SEATO delegates that U.S. assistance to "freedom-loving nations" had "no geographical barriers." The French and British, however, did not desire military action in Laos; they did not consider the area to be of vital interest. Nevertheless, Rusk persuaded SEATO delegates to endorse a resolution declaring SEATO's resolve not to "acquiesce" in any takeover of Laos or Vietnam and to keep developments in those countries under review.

While Rusk and Kennedy prepared for possible unilateral military intervention in Laos, British Prime Minister Harold Macmillan arranged for a cease-fire in Laos and a conference at Geneva. Soviet Premier Khrushchev also favored a conference, and

on May 3 a cease-fire was announced in Laos. The Geneva meetings began on May 16 but did not reach agreement until 1962.

See July 23, 1962.

### May 5, 1961

**A NATO council meeting at Oslo discloses European concern for a greater role in NATO defense operations.**

Europeans did not look favorably on Kennedy's shift from the Eisenhower-Dulles "massive retaliation" to a "flexible response" strategy. The Kennedy program to use conventional forces wherever necessary, and to build a superior nuclear force that might or might not be used, seemed to French President de Gaulle and other European leaders to be a design to keep America aloof from the interests of European powers. In addition, the Europeans had grown less dependent on the United States and asked for some degree of control over nuclear weapons and the NATO forces in Europe.

At the Oslo meeting, Secretary Rusk indicated that America would steadfastly support Europe. He could not, however, offer an end to U.S. monopolistic control of the alliance's strategic nuclear weapons. In addition, by asserting that all areas of the world were important and would be defended, Rusk by definition lowered Europe's former rating as the first U.S. priority.

Rusk offered the Europeans five Polaris submarines as part of the NATO command. But he insisted that Americans must command the subs and control nuclear missiles. The Europeans wanted more. They wanted a respected position in the NATO command and spoke of a multilateral defense force (MDF) that would include nuclear weapons under European control. The United States was not willing to relinquish its control of the NATO forces, especially the nuclear forces.

### May 25, 1961

**President Kennedy launches a "moon race" to beat the Soviet Union in landing the first man on the moon.**

Kennedy had asked Vice President Johnson on April 20 to study U.S. space capabilities and determine if the United States had a chance of beating the Soviet Union in the moon race or some other dramatic space program. This feat, Kennedy believed, would reassert U.S. technical superiority over the Soviets.

Johnson, as chairman of the Space Council, conducted a study and reported that the Soviets had larger boosters for a possible moon flight. With a strong U.S. effort, however, the Space Council believed the United States could accomplish a moon mission by 1966 or 1967.

On May 25, Kennedy told Congress that it was time for the United States to organize a "great new American enterprise" and "take a clearly leading role in space achievement." He committed the nation to achieve the goal, "before the decade is out, of landing a man on the moon and returning him safely to earth." This launched the Apollo program, which was successful on July 20, 1969.

### May 30, 1961

*General Rafael Trujillo, the real power in the Dominican Republic, is assassinated.*

Trujillo had directly or indirectly ruled the Dominican Republic since the 1930s. President Joaquin Balaguer, who had fronted for Trujillo since 1960, had difficulty in keeping political order in his nation as opposition groups initiated strikes and demonstrations against his government. To resolve the problems, Balaguer formed a National Civil Union on December 19, 1961, and promised to conduct elections for a constituent assembly in August and to hold general elections by December 1962.

See December 20, 1962.

### June 3–4, 1961

**Kennedy and Khrushchev hold a summit conference in Vienna.**

This meeting was designed to resolve the Berlin issue. On February 17, Premier Khrushchev informed the West German government that West Berlin should become a "free city." In addition, he wished to conclude a final German peace treaty. If not, Khrushchev said, he would sign a separate pact with East Germany.

The Vienna meetings did not settle either the German or the pending Laotian problem. Khrushchev stated he would act unilaterally with East Germany on a German peace treaty if none were achieved by December 1961. If the West interfered, there would be war. Kennedy countered by warning the Soviets that the United States would

President Kennedy and Premier Nikita Khrushchev at the Vienna Summit. John F. Kennedy Library

fight to keep access routes to Berlin. The Soviet Union must not take unilateral action.

Regarding Laos, both leaders expressed their desire for a neutral Laotian state. Khrushchev said, however, that the Pathet Lao would eventually win. Kennedy expressed the American determination to protect Laos. Thus, on both Laos and Germany the two leaders defended a strong position to maintain their status in those areas. As Kennedy told the U.S. public on his return, the Vienna visit was "a very sober two days."

### July 25, 1961

**President Kennedy delivers a speech strongly backing the importance of Berlin as vital to America.**

Because Khrushchev had indicated at Vienna that the Soviets would unilaterally act in Berlin and East Germany by December 1961, Kennedy decided to assert explicit American rights and duties in Berlin.

He refused to negotiate access to Berlin or the U.S. military presence in that city. The president also placed National Reserve troops on duty and announced a 25% increase in U.S. military power.

Kennedy declared the U.S. position on Berlin without prior consultation with American allies, which Rusk had recommended. The president's attitude toward U.S. allies was to avoid reliance on them. Unlike Eisenhower, who strongly emphasized close cooperation with the NATO allies, Kennedy and Johnson believed the United States must act as it believed necessary. In July 1961, Prime Minister Macmillan approved Kennedy's action; President de Gaulle and Chancellor Adenauer were troubled by its bellicose overtones.

### August 13, 1961

#### The Soviets begin construction of the Berlin wall, dividing East and West Berlin.

One of the Soviets' principal concerns in Berlin was the drain of East Germany's educated and technical elite resulting from the flow of exiles to West Germany through the city. After the Vienna Conference of June 1961, this flow increased to 30,000 in July and 4,000 on August 12.

On August 13, East German police erected barriers to separate East and West Berlin. Because Kennedy had never argued for direct access to East Berlin, he and Secretary Rusk protested the barriers

The Berlin Wall with East German soldiers on patrol. Lester Brune

but did not take military action to stop the wall's construction, although some critics argued that Kennedy should have challenged the Soviets with U.S. soldiers. But Kennedy emphasized the wall as a symbol of the Communists' failure to provide adequately for their own people. During the next year, East Germany replaced the original barbed wire barricade with a more elaborate concrete wall and machine-gun nests to prevent East Germans from fleeing to the West.

See October 28, 1961.

### August 17, 1961

#### The Alliance for Progress charter is signed at the Inter-American Conference in Punta del Este.

This meeting finalized a U.S. agreement that all Latin American nations except Cuba had signed. Over 10 years the United States would provide $20 billion for a public and private investment program in Latin America. There would also be another $300 million annual investment from private capital in the United States. The Latin American governments pledged $80 billion of investments over 10 years. In addition, they pledged to enact land, tax, and other socioeconomic reforms in their nations.

Unfortunately, the Alliance for Progress did not function as well as expected. Brazil, Argentina, and Mexico did not want close scrutiny of their programs. Thus, many Latin American governments did not enact the necessary reforms. Although some benefits resulted from the program, orderly, stable, and improved political and economic conditions did not occur in Latin America in the next decade.

### September 18, 1961

#### U.N. Secretary-General Hammarskjöld is killed in a plane crash while seeking a truce in the Congo.

At the time of Hammarskjöld's death, he and Secretary of State Rusk disagreed about the use of U.N. forces against Tshombe's regime in Katanga. The Congo dispute had narrowed to a struggle between Cyrille ADOULA, who was elected premier of the Léopoldville government backed by the United Nations, and Tshombe's state, backed by some European nations, South Africa, and Southern Rhodesia, as well as many U.S. conservatives.

Rusk backed U.N. support for Adoula as the moderate candidate in the Congo but objected to Hammarskjöld's use of U.N. forces against Tshombe. Rusk desired negotiations between Tshombe and Adoula to solve their dispute.

On September 20, two days after Hammarskjöld died in a plane crash in the Congo, the opposing Congolese leaders agreed to a cease-fire. The truce did not end successfully, however. By November 11, Kennedy agreed to Rusk's recommendation to allow the United Nations to use force if necessary against Katanga.

See January 18, 1962.

### September 21, 1961

**Soviet Foreign Minister Andrey Gromyko agrees to delay the USSR's December deadline for settlement of the German issue.**

The United States was greatly disturbed by Khrushchev's threat on June 3, 1961, to act unilaterally on a German peace treaty. Therefore, in September Secretary Rusk and Gromyko discussed the dangerous implications of the situation. During a series of three discussions, Gromyko indicated that the Soviet deadline could be delayed if negotiations began. Rusk agreed to talk, suggesting that a four-power agreement could guarantee Western access to Berlin. In addition, Rusk said that if the German problem were settled, arms limitations in central Europe might be discussed.

The September talks did not end but did relieve East-West tensions over Germany. Although French President de Gaulle and some U.S. critics, such as Harvard Professor Henry Kissinger, believed Rusk's "weakness" bordered on "appeasement," it had not. Rusk had not committed any nation to arms limits but had obtained a delay in the Soviet deadline on Germany. Rusk's talks, combined with Kennedy's frequent assertions of U.S. support for West Berlin, ended the Berlin crisis of 1961. Further talks on Berlin and Germany continued, but Khrushchev's ultimatum no longer added to the tense atmosphere.

### October 28, 1961

**The Berlin crisis ends after the Soviets agree West Berlin military need not show identification.**

When East Berlin officials began building the wall in August, President Kennedy took a cautious approach to determine what action to follow. His caution became a compromise two months later. On October 22, Allen Lightner and his wife drove their Volkswagen bearing U.S. license plates to the Friedrichstrasse crossing point—later called Checkpoint Charlie—but East German border guards stopped them from entering. Lightner called General Lucius Clay, the U.S. military authority in Berlin, who sent a jeep with armed soldiers to escort Lightner's car into East Berlin to see a theater performance. For the next five days, more U.S. soldiers in uniform went through the checkpoint without identifying themselves. On October 27, the crisis escalated with U.S. and Soviet tanks facing each other at Checkpoint Charlie.

The next day, the crisis ended after Kennedy and Khrushchev agreed Western civilians would not cross the border but American, British, and French soldiers in uniform would not be stopped from entering East Berlin. Of course, East Germans continued building the wall separating East and West Berlin.

### November 22, 1961

**President Kennedy approves the "first phase of Vietnam program," which broadens the U.S. commitment to Vietnam by adding U.S. "combat support" troops.**

Although in April 1961 President Kennedy had added 100 advisers to the U.S. contingent and thereby exceeded the number permitted by the Geneva Accords of 1954, his first critical decision on Vietnam was made on November 22. This decision was largely based on a report by General Maxwell Taylor and Walter W. Rostow, who visited Saigon in October 1961. Taylor, who had been the leading critic of Eisenhower's "new look" policy in the late 1950s, became Kennedy's principal military adviser. Rostow was a White House adviser to the president. These two men discounted the 1960 report of Ambassador to Saigon Elbridge Durbrow, which severely criticized Premier Diem of South Vietnam. Taylor and Rostow thought Diem had "extraordinary stability, stubbornness and guts." They recommended a "limited partnership" with Diem.

The November 22 "First Phase..." was based on the Taylor-Rostow recommendations, which were changed to provide fewer combat troops and to delete the objective to "save South Vietnam."

Kennedy ordered a gradually increased number of "combat support" troops to Vietnam. General Taylor, who expected a few highly qualified "Green Berets" to deal easily with "brushfire wars," did not believe many troops would be needed, but he was uncertain just how many because estimates varied from 8,000 to 25,000. In December 1961, 400 men in two helicopter companies with 33 H-21 aircraft reached Saigon. By November 1963, Kennedy had ordered 16,263 "combat support" troops to Vietnam; combat support, according to the White House, meant they would not fire until fired on but would accompany South Vietnamese army patrols.

In addition to these forces, the November 22 plan called for a Strategic Hamlet Program. Based on British counterinsurgency plans used in Malaya, the "Hamlets" were fortified villages for the rural populace to occupy while the Communists were driven out of their home region. Then the peasants could return home in peace. In South Vietnam, unfortunately, the disastrous program was headed by Diem's unpopular and corrupt brother and sister-in-law, Ngo Dinh Nhu and Madame Nhu.

### December 2, 1961

**Fidel Castro announces that he is a Marxist-Leninist.**

Although conservative Americans had suspected throughout the 1950s that Castro was a Communist, the Cuban leader had previously shaded his reform efforts in Cuba with promises of election and compensation for nationalized property. Now, Castro had become dependent on the Soviet Union for economic aid. On December 2, he called for the formation of a united Cuban party to bring communism to Cuba.

# 1962

### January 18, 1962

**Secretary Rusk informs the Senate Foreign Relations Committee that the United States must support Cyrille Adoula and the United Nations in the Congo as the best anticommunist measure.**

Following Secretary-General Hammarskjöld's death on September 18, 1961, a truce was arranged between Tshombe of Katanga and Adoula of the central Congolese government. The truce was not sustained, however, and by November 11, Rusk and Kennedy agreed to allow the United Nations to use whatever force was necessary to persuade Tshombe to negotiate. Tshombe and Adoula agreed on December 21 to end Katanga's secession. Tshombe was slated to have a role in the Léopoldville government.

On January 18, Rusk explained that the United States would continue to back the U.N. program as the best solution to keep the integrity of the Congo and to defeat Communist efforts. Those who backed Tshombe, Rusk said, followed a policy that would weaken Adoula's government and allow the Soviets to defeat both the moderate Adoula and the conservative Tshombe.

In a meeting at the abandoned Belgian airbase at Kitonia, Tshombe violated the December 21 Kitonia agreement. Therefore, the United Nations was required to apply force to restore Katanga to the control of the Léopoldville government.

See December 17, 1962.

### January 31, 1962

**Cuba is excluded from the Inter-American sphere.**

At the end of a 10-day meeting at Punta del Este, Uruguay, the American foreign ministers approved by a two-thirds vote a resolution excluding Cuba from the Inter-American system. Brazil, Argentina, Chile, Ecuador, and Mexico abstained in the vote.

### February 10, 1962

**The USSR and the United States exchange "spies."**

Gary Francis Powers, who piloted the U-2 that crashed in the Soviet Union in 1960, was released in exchange for the U.S. release of Colonel Rudolf Abel, a

Soviet spy who had been convicted of espionage in 1957.

## February 20, 1962

### Lieutenant Colonel John H. Glenn Jr. is the first U.S. astronaut to orbit the earth.

On his flight Glenn circled the earth three times before landing in the Pacific Ocean, where U.S. naval vessels picked him up.

A Soviet citizen had been the first to orbit the earth. On April 12, 1961, Major Yuri A. Gagarin in spaceship *Vostok I* circled the earth for 108 minutes at a maximum altitude of 203 miles.

## March 28, 1962

### *Military leaders in Argentina overthrow President Arturo Frondizi.*

In 1958, Frondizi had become Argentina's first elected president in 12 years. The military junta named José Maria Guido as president. On July 24, Guido banned both the rightist Perónist Party and the Communist

John Glenn with his space capsule. National Archives

Party, and provided government control over the internal affairs of all parties.

## April 8, 1962

### *French voters approve de Gaulle's plan to grant independence to Algeria.*

Since 1955, the Algerian nationalist rebellion had cost the French many lives and much money. De Gaulle finally agreed to make peace with the rebels and grant them independence. Although right-wing Algerian insurgents rejected the proposal, a campaign to eliminate their forces succeeded during the next year.

## April 25, 1962

### By exploding a nuclear device at Christmas Island, the U.S. responds to the Soviets' resumption of nuclear tests in 1961.

On August 31, 1961, Moscow announced the Soviets were renewing nuclear testing, ending the informal 1958 agreements of Khrushchev and Eisenhower that had ended such tests. Soon after, the USSR conducted a series of nuclear tests.

Following a thorough review of the situation, President Kennedy announced on March 2, 1962, that the United States would resume its tests in April unless an effective test ban agreement was reached with the Soviet Union during the interim. In announcing his decision, Kennedy stated that the United States needed to check the effectiveness of high-altitude explosions to counter gains made by the Soviet Union during its 1961 test series. He said no "superbombs" would be detonated and that radiation fallout would be minimized.

The president's decision divided public opinion in America and in other "free world" nations. At home, the White House admitted that the telegrams it received were divided evenly between those in favor and those opposed to the tests. There were large peace and antinuclear demonstrations in New York and other American cities as well as in London and, especially, Japan. The Japanese government warned Washington that it would seek compensation for possible damages to its citizens.

Nevertheless, after Khrushchev spurned a special message from Kennedy and British Prime Minister Macmillan that urged him to accept an effective test ban, Kennedy authorized the tests to begin on April 24. The tests in the region of Christmas Island and, later, Johnson Island and Nevada were conducted between April 25 and November 4, 1963. The tests' time schedule was extended from July to November because the explosions of high-altitude bombs failed on several occasions. Eventually, a total of 36 bombs were exploded by the United States during 1962.

On September 2, the Atomic Energy Commission and the Defense Department admitted that the high-altitude test of July 9 had increased space radiation more than anticipated. In particular, the radiation in the earth's Van Allen belt was extended lower in the atmosphere, where it would remain for at least five years. U.S. scientists disagreed on the effect of radiation in food on Americans. Increased levels of iodine were found in milk taken from cows in parts of the Middle West. Some scientists thought the dosage was approaching dangerous levels. There was no agreement on exactly what level was "dangerous."

On February 2, 1963, Kennedy threatened another series of U.S. nuclear tests if the USSR did not agree to an effective test ban treaty. Discussions had been held between diplomats in London, Moscow, and Washington during the fall and winter of 1962–1963. These talks eventually succeeded.

### June 25, 1962

**In Accra, Ghana, a "world without the bomb" conference begins.**

More than 100 delegates, including those from the United States and the Soviet Union, attended this meeting. During the seven-day conference, the delegates recommended that the United Nations train disarmament inspection teams and called on African states to disarm throughout their continent. The group also recommended the admission of mainland China to the United Nations.

### July 4, 1962

**Kennedy informs the European allies of the United States that they can have nuclear weapons as soon as they achieve political unity.**

Kennedy's message of July 4 responded to the European desire for a multilateral nuclear defense force for NATO. It did not, however, provide the answer French President de Gaulle and other Europeans desired.

### May 26, 1962

**The Netherlands accepts a U.S. plan to settle the West New Guinea dispute with Indonesia.**

A dispute over the possession of West New Guinea had resulted in war between the Netherlands and Indonesia. The United States proposed to end the struggle by mediation on ownership while the United Nations administered the territory and arranged a plebiscite to permit the Papuan inhabitants to decide their future.

After the Dutch accepted the American plan, U.N. Secretary-General U. Thant obtained a cease-fire, and on May 29, the two nations began discussions. Subsequently, on July 31, Indonesia and the Netherlands agreed to transfer West New Guinea (renamed West Irian) to the United Nations on October 1, with the United Nations to transfer it to Indonesia on May 1, 1963. Within six years, Indonesia was to hold a plebiscite of self-determination for the Papuan natives of the area. Kennedy and Rusk hoped this process would keep Indonesian President Sukarno from appealing to the Soviet Union for aid.

Undersecretary of State George Ball. National Archives

Kennedy's speech was a plan by George Ball, the undersecretary of state to whom Rusk delegated European problems. Ball's dream was an integrated Europe, allied with America and generally conducive to U.S. leadership. Because European unity was, at best, in the future, Kennedy's agreement to give Europeans a greater role in a European defense force had no immediate impact. It did not satisfy President de Gaulle or other Europeans.

### July 19, 1962

**To deter overly ambitious generals in Latin America, Kennedy suspends diplomatic relations with, and economic aid to, Peru following a military coup on July 18.**

The military junta displeased the United States by suspending all constitutional rights. To act quickly against the regime, Kennedy immediately cut off U.S. benefits to Peru. Only after the junta agreed to return to constitutional practices did Kennedy renew assistance to Peru on August 17, 1962.

In 1963, the Kennedy administration made similar agreements with right-wing military groups that had usurped the governments of Argentina, Guatemala, and the Dominican Republic. The military leaders in these states all claimed to support anti-Communist positions. The Alliance for Progress of 1961 had not brought democratic regimes to power in Latin America.

### July 23, 1962

**The Geneva conference on Laos agrees to guarantee the independence and neutrality of that state.**

The Geneva Conference had convened on May 16, 1961, as a means of avoiding large-scale U.S. intervention in Laos. Over the next 14 months, the delegates met to gain an effective cease-fire and to form a neutral government acceptable to the three competing factions in Laos. Throughout the year, full-scale war threatened to disrupt the conference, but eventually the three rival princes of Laos reached a settlement. The three rivals were the neutralist Souvanna Phouma, the U.S.-backed rightist Boun Oum, and the leftist Communist-supported Souphanouvong.

By May 1962, Pathet Lao military actions in Laos had advanced over 100 miles. President Kennedy protested these movements and, on May 12, again ordered U.S. naval ships and marines to the Gulf of Siam, and 2,000 U.S. soldiers to Thailand. As a result, the Communist advances stopped and the three Laotian princes again met to negotiate.

In June, the Laotian leaders announced that a 19-member coalition government had been formed under the neutralist Souvanna Phouma. King Savang Vathana installed this ministry on June 22, and political calm returned to Laos. On July 23, delegates at the 14-nation conference in Geneva recognized the Souvanna coalition government. They also signed an agreement to withdraw all foreign troops and guarantee the neutrality of Laos.

See May 3, 1961.

### August 18, 1962

*Venezuela asks the U.N. General Assembly to investigate its boundary with British Guiana.*

Although Venezuela had accepted the arbitration of its boundary with the British in 1899, Caracas claimed that later evidence in the reports of one of its legal advisers of 1899, Severo Mallet-Prevost, showed the arbitration tribunal had not been just but had made a political deal in favor of the British. Therefore, Venezuela continued to press its claims of 1896 against the British.

Although the General Assembly referred the issue to a Special Political Committee, it was not resolved. Venezuela wanted the border settled before the British granted independence to the state of Guyana. Because Guyana's independence was scheduled for 1966, the British insisted that Venezuela form a mixed commission to arbitrate the boundary with Guyana. The mixed commission was established on February 17, 1966, but Venezuela and independent Guyana could not agree on a new boundary settlement. The agreement of 1899 remained operative, although Venezuela continued to adhere to its previous land claims east of the Orinoco River into the territory of Guyana.

See February 20, 1895, and October 1, 1899.

### October 11, 1962

**The Trade Expansion Act of 1962 becomes law—the Kennedy round in American trade policy.**

By 1961, many U.S. international financial experts realized that the United States needed new legislation to give the president greater authority in dealing with foreign tariff and trade policy. The success of the European Common Market after 1957 required special attention. In addition, the U.S. balance of international payments had turned adverse since 1958. During the three-year period 1958–1960, the United States lost $4.7 billion in gold to foreign payments. In contrast, the European Economic Community (EEC) had collectively increased its gold reserves by over $6.5 billion. Because of these conditions, the United States hoped to regain an increase in its exports by obtaining lower trade barriers with Europe and other parts of the world.

The 1962 Trade Expansion Act was designed to gain multilateral reductions for U.S. exports to Europe and Japan. After four years of negotiation among the major GATT members, a protocol signed on June 30, 1967, provided for significant tariff reductions. The United States gained a 35% reduction in nonagricultural exports. While the agricultural agreement varied, the new tariffs favored U.S. exports in all cases excepting Denmark. The United States gained especially favorable reduction from Japan and the United Kingdom.

### October 20, 1962

*China and India begin large-scale fighting in a disputed border area.*

Although Indian border police and Chinese forces had clashed on October 26, 1960, the Chinese-India issue had confined itself to skirmishes before October 1962. India claimed that China unlawfully occupied 12,000 square miles of its territory and demanded its return.

During the three weeks after October 20, Chinese forces made successful incursions into Indian territory. On October 31, India's Premier Nehru asked the United States for aid, and in November, Kennedy sent transport planes and crews to transport Indian troops. The U.S. aid was not necessary. On November 21, Beijing announced that the Chinese would withdraw to their 1957 borders and the fighting ended.

In the United States, the India-China war affected U.S. evaluations of the Sino-Soviet split and China's relations with the West. Although Dean Rusk, Undersecretary of State Chester Bowles, and other U.S. leaders wanted to negotiate with China to take advantage of its poor relations with Moscow, President Kennedy disagreed. He had, in fact, made an agreement with Chiang Kai-shek in 1961 to con-

tinue U.S. support in the United Nations for the Formosan government. Kennedy's Cold War perceptions of Asian affairs prevented him from comprehending the potential significance of the Sino-Soviet split.

### October 22, 1962

**Kennedy informs the nation that there are Soviet-built missile sites in Cuba. He announces a naval quarantine on all missile equipment being shipped to Cuba and calls on Soviet Premier Khrushchev to remove these weapons.**

The Executive Committee of the National Security Council (NSC), which President Kennedy ordered to examine alternative responses to the presence of Soviet missile sites in Cuba, had met regularly from October 16 to October 21. The committee included McGeorge Bundy and Secretary Rusk from the State Department; Secretary of Defense McNamara; CIA Director John McCone; Attorney General Robert Kennedy; and others. In addition, Vice President Johnson, U.N. Ambassador Adlai Stevenson, and the president met with the committee on occasions.

After considering a variety of alternative responses to the Soviets, the Executive Committee, the full NSC, and the president agreed to begin action against the Soviets with a naval blockade of Cuba, escalating subsequent actions only if necessary. Other alternatives considered included such suggestions as an invasion or air strike of Cuba, secret negotiations with Cuba, appeals to the United Nations, and doing nothing. By October 19, the consensus favored a blockade because it could be effective but would leave the decision up to Khrushchev of acting as an aggressor to break the blockade. It also left later alternatives for U.S. action if it failed.

On Sunday, October 21, the full NSC decided to act as follows:

1. The president was to inform the public of the Soviet missiles on October 22 over national television.
2. The naval quarantine was to be announced on television.
3. An appeal for support from the OAS and the United Nations was to be made on Tuesday.
4. Khrushchev was to be asked to remove all missiles from Cuba.

Meeting of the Executive Committee (ExCom) of the National Security Council during the missile crisis. John F. Kennedy Library

5. Dean Acheson and David Bruce would be sent to tell de Gaulle and Macmillan, respectively, of Kennedy's speech in advance.

On Monday, these plans went into operation beginning with Acheson's early-morning flight to London to inform Ambassador Bruce and to Paris to visit de Gaulle. At 5 P.M., Kennedy met with congressional leaders to explain his decision. At 7 P.M., the president outlined his quarantine plans to the U.S. public, explaining that the United States found definite evidence of missile sites in Cuba, although there were no nuclear warheads as yet. Finally, he told the audience that his plan was a difficult and dangerous effort, "But the greatest danger of all would be to do nothing." Kennedy explained that the course chosen was most in keeping with the American character, to seek to avoid war but not to submit or surrender. He concluded: "Our goal is not the victory of might, but the vindication of right—not peace at the expense of freedom, but both peace and freedom, here in this hemisphere, and, we hope, around the world."

The next day, Secretary Rusk obtained approval from the OAS to quarantine Cuba and take measures, including force if necessary, to end the crisis. All OAS members but Uruguay approved the quarantine decision. Brazil, Mexico, and Bolivia abstained from the section authorizing the use of force. At the same time, Adlai Stevenson indicted the Soviet Union for its aggressive action in Cuba. Because of the Soviet veto power, no action was sought in the U.N. Security Council.

The U.S. quarantine went into effect on October 24. A naval task force of 19 ships set up a picket line in the Atlantic, 500 miles from Cuba.

See October 28, 1962.

### October 23, 1962

**President Kennedy signs a $3.9 billion foreign aid bill.**

This bill included clauses that forbade aid to 18 Communist nations and to any nation that shipped arms to Cuba.

### October 28, 1962

**An exchange of personal letters between President Kennedy and Premier Khrushchev ends the Cuban missile crisis. Previously, on October 24, Soviet ships did not try to break through the naval blockade.**

The days from October 24 to 27 were especially critical as Kennedy and his advisers waited to learn what the Soviet ships en route to Cuba would do once they reached the U.S. naval blockade. On October 23, U.S. reconnaissance planes spotted 25 Soviet ships in the Atlantic, most of which seemed to be headed for Cuba. Early on the morning of October 24, the first Soviet vessels approached the quarantine line but, until the last moment, the Americans did not know what to expect.

On October 23, Khrushchev sent two divergent messages about his intentions. In a formal letter to President Kennedy the Soviet leader denounced the

INSPECTION OF SOVIET SHIP VOLGOLES
9 NOVEMBER 1962

President Kennedy's quarantine policy in operation. National Archives

blockade as an act of piracy, bringing the world to the brink of nuclear war. He declared that Soviet ships on their way to Cuba would defy the U.S. blockade. At about the same time, he wrote a note to Bertrand Russell, the British philosopher and pacifist, who had appealed to Khrushchev to avoid war. The Soviet Premier told Russell that he was not reckless, it was the Americans who had acted aggressively. Khrushchev understood the disaster that nuclear war would bring. Therefore, he said, he was ready to make a special effort to avoid war. If the United States agreed, he would consider a top-level meeting to settle the Cuban crisis.

Consequently, as Soviet ships neared the U.S. blockade on October 24, the Americans did not know which orders Khrushchev had given to them, the peaceful or the bellicose one. About 10 A.M. two Soviet ships neared the blockade point. Then the U.S. naval observers radioed that a Soviet submarine was between the Soviet ships and the American ships. The captain of the U.S. carrier *Essex* was ordered to signal the sub to surface. More tension built at the White House. Then, at 10:25 a preliminary message arrived:

the Soviet ships appeared to be stopping. By 10:32, navy reports confirmed that 20 Soviet ships in the area of the blockade line had stopped or were turning to head back to Europe. The quarantine had not been challenged.

Kennedy now sought to arrange the removal of the Soviet missile sites from Cuba. To achieve this goal, two steps were taken on October 25 and 27.

First, the navy was told to let the Soviet ship *Bucharest* pass the blockade because visual sighting indicated it carried no cargo connected with missiles. The ship *Marcula*, however, was stopped and searched. After a two-hour search found no missile equipment, the *Marcula* was allowed to proceed to Cuba. This process was followed with all Soviet ships that had not turned away from their sea route to Cuba.

Second, Kennedy considered the two recent notes from Premier Khrushchev, each of which suggested a settlement. The first, received on October 26, was a personal letter to Kennedy in which the Soviet leader offered to remove the missiles from Cuba if Kennedy gave assurances that the United

States would not invade the island. The second, received on October 27, was a more formal message in which Khrushchev offered to dismantle the Soviet missiles in Cuba if the United States dismantled missile bases in Turkey. Although the Turkish bases were obsolete, Kennedy did not want to swap them under pressure from Moscow. In light of the second note, the Joint Chiefs of Staff recommended that an air strike or an invasion of Cuba would be necessary. Kennedy opposed this step for the moment.

Important information about the October 27 meeting was disclosed during the 1989 Moscow conference of participants in the 1962 missile crisis. During the Moscow conference, Theodore Sorenson confessed he edited Robert Kennedy's diary of the crisis published as *Thirteen Days* by deleting the section showing the president's brother had told Soviet Ambassador Dobrynin the United States would remove its missiles from Turkey as Khrushchev had requested. Dobrynin agreed the Soviets would keep the Turkish missile removal secret because NATO members had not been told about this decision. Of course, the secrecy about Kennedy's concession favored the U.S. president's image of "his finest hour," but it helped avoid a nuclear confrontation. On the basis of Kennedy's pledge not to invade Cuba but to remove the Turkish missiles, Khrushchev accepted the concessions, and on October 28 at nine o'clock, Moscow radio broadcast Khrushchev's willingness to remove the Cuban missiles.

Fidel Castro was angry with Khrushchev because he thought Moscow would be justified in initiating a nuclear attack on the United States. Thus, Castro refused to let U.N. inspectors observe the dismantling of the Soviet missiles. Moscow agreed to let U.S. naval officers visually inspect the removal, with Soviet crews pulling back the tarpaulins to show the missiles aboard Soviet ships on the way home.

Because Castro refused to have on-site U.N. inspections, Kennedy weakened his no-invasion pledge. In a December 14 letter to Khrushchev, Kennedy stated Cuba would not be invaded "while matters take their present favorable course." As Raymond Garthoff explains, in 1970 President Richard Nixon made a definite pledge not to invade Cuba.

See September 25, 1970.

## December 17, 1962

### Kennedy and the National Security Council agree to give military aid to the United Nations to fight Katanga.

During the summer of 1962, Moishe Tshombe violated the Kitonia agreement with Cyrille Adoula's Congo government by refusing to forward tax funds from the secessionist province of Katanga and continued to act independently. Tshombe was supported by the Belgian mining company that paid for his mercenary soldiers.

In October 1962, U.N. Secretary-General U. Thant wanted to place an economic boycott on Katanga. He agreed, however, to try to negotiate again so that the U.S. November elections would end before forceful action began against Tshombe. By December, fighting began between Tshombe and Adoula's forces, and U. Thant decided the United Nations had to take action. Although American opponents of Adoula opposed U.S. military assistance against Tshombe, the National Security Council and President Kennedy agreed on December 17 to provide airlift operations and military equipment to aid the U.N. forces when they invaded Katanga. U.N. troops attacked in January, and on January 15 Tshombe again ended his secession. On June 14, Tshombe fled to exile and the crisis in the Congo finally ended. This was a victory for the Léopoldville government with U.S. and U.N. backing.

## December 20, 1962

### Juan D. Bosch is elected president of the Dominican Republic.

During 1962, a council of state under Rafael Bonnelly had weathered at least two coup attempts before finally holding elections. On December 20, Bosch won the election, taking office on February 27, 1963. His rule lasted only seven months. On September 25, 1963, a group of military leaders overthrew him.

## December 21, 1962

### President Kennedy agrees to replace the British Skybolt project with U.S. Polaris missiles.

The U.S. military supported by Secretary of Defense Robert McNamara objected to giving the Europeans independent nuclear capabilities and did not want to let them share control of U.S. nuclear weapons in

Europe. Consequently, in the fall of 1962, McNamara unilaterally canceled the Skybolt missile program, which would have given Great Britain independent intermediate-range missiles. Secretary Rusk warned McNamara that the cancellation would provide problems for the British government, but McNamara agreed to settle it with Britain's defense minister, Peter Thorneycroft.

This issue arose, however, at the Nassau meeting between Kennedy and Macmillan, because McNamara had not been direct with the British regarding his decision to cancel the Skybolt program. As a result, Macmillan was unwilling to accept the cancellation and strongly objected. Therefore, Kennedy offered to give Britain Polaris missiles *without* nuclear warheads and also agreed to do the same for France. If Britain and France built submarines and warheads for the missiles, they would have to assign the vessels to the NATO forces and not be independent. Macmillan did not like these restrictions but accepted them because he at least had something to soften the blow to British pride.

But U.S.-British relations did not improve because the British felt Americans did not trust them as an ally.

See May 22, 1963.

### December 24, 1962

#### Cuba returns 1,113 Cuban rebels captured in April 1961.

Castro agreed to exchange his "Bay of Pigs" captives for $53 million worth of food and medicine.

# 1963

### January 29, 1963

#### France vetoes Great Britain's application to join the European Economic Community (Common Market).

Urged by the United States, England reluctantly began discussions in 1962 with France and other EEC members for admission to the Common Market. The British application was approved by all members except France. President de Gaulle opposed Britain's entry into the European economic partnership.

In 1961, the U.S expected Britain's application to be approved and the Kennedy administration decided to alter the U.S. Reciprocal Trade Act rather than simply extend it. Thus, Kennedy persuaded Congress to approve a new trade act giving the president more power to bargain with the EEC and help reduce the U.S. trade deficit. The French veto of British membership made the Kennedy Round of tariff negotiations more difficult to complete and continued America's unfavorable trade balance. Details of Kennedy's trade policy are in William S. Borden's article in Thomas Paterson (ed.), *Kennedy's Quest for Victory* (1989).

See March 25, 1968, and October 11, 1962.

### May 8, 1963

#### Buddhist leaders in South Vietnam organize demonstrations protesting Diem's repressive policies.

Between 1961 and 1963, Diem had not enacted any significant reforms but increased his repressive measures because he envisioned every opponent as a "Communist" enemy. Until 1963, the Buddhists had patiently avoided public demonstrations of their dislike for Diem's terrorization of peasants and discriminated against Buddhists.

Diem's methods against the Buddhists reached the breaking point in May 1963, when he forbade them to fly their religious banners in celebrating the Buddha's birthday on May 8. Buddhist leaders at the religious center in Hue defied Diem by carrying their banners and rallying the people to demonstrate against him.

Diem moved to stop the Buddhists. South Vietnamese army units used armored vehicles to break up the crowds. The soldiers opened fire and 9 people were killed, 14 wounded.

Buddhist leaders endeavored to negotiate a solution with Diem but he refused. As a result, U.S. news reports of Buddhist opposition showed clearly for the first time that Diem's problem was not simply the threat of communism but his failure to gain the support of his own people. Buddhist protests continued throughout 1963 and were widely reported on American television.

One photograph that became famous for its dramatic effect showed a young Buddhist monk aflame on a busy Saigon street. The monk had poured gasoline over himself and lit a match to his yellow saffron robes to show his disdain for Diem. When Diem's sister-in-law, Madame Nhu, ridiculed these events as "barbecues," her support in the United States dropped drastically.

### May 12, 1963

*Pakistan and China sign a territorial agreement.*

By this treaty, China ceded 750 square miles of land to Pakistan. This treaty fostered good relations between the two countries, both of whom had disputes with India. On August 29, Pakistan signed an agreement with China to provide scheduled air service to Beijing. This was the first Western agreement for air service to the People's Republic of China.

### May 22, 1963

**NATO's Foreign Ministers Council forms a 10-nation multilateral nuclear striking force.**

The United States had urged the creation of this multinational force as a symbol of its willingness to cooperate with European defense plans. French President de Gaulle did not approve the plan and on June 21 began withdrawing many French naval ships from the NATO Fleet Command.

### May 25, 1963

*The Organization of African Unity is chartered.*

At Addis Ababa, Ethiopia, 30 leaders of African states formed a regional bloc to work together for their economic well-being. On August 5, delegates of 32 African countries formed an African development bank with a capitalization of $250 million.

### June 14, 1963

*The Chinese Communist Party indicts Moscow for "revisionist" domestic policies and says it plans to split with any Communist Party supporting the Soviet Union.*

Since the Communist Party meetings in Moscow on December 5, 1960, signs of Sino-Soviet division had appeared more frequently. Each side urged other national Communist groups to back its views on foreign and domestic policy. The Beijing declaration of June 14 was a bellicose statement demonstrating the split between Mao and the Soviet leadership. In foreign policy, the Chinese rejected the idea of "peaceful coexistence" and seemed more willing to risk nuclear

war. By early 1964, Beijing began recognizing pro-Chinese factions in various nations as the legitimate Communist party in opposition to the Soviet faction.

### June 20, 1963

**The United States and the Soviet Union agree to create a communications "Hot Line" to reduce the risk of accidental war.**

Following the Cuban missile crisis of 1962, the White House proposed a direct emergency communication with the Kremlin as a method of averting any misunderstanding that might lead to war. The Soviet Union accepted this idea on April 5 and on June 20, 1963, formal arrangements were agreed to establish this instant teletype communication system. This agreement was enhanced in 1971.

See September 30, 1971.

### June 26, 1963

**President Kennedy visits West Berlin, promising to defend free Berlin from Communist encroachment.**

Kennedy's speech in Berlin enthralled West Germans as he concluded his defense of freedom with the words, "Ich bin ein Berliner!" (which translates as "I am a jelly-filled donut!"). While a "Berliner" had its colloquial meaning, the German audience appreciated Kennedy's sentiment.

### July 11, 1963

*A military coup in Ecuador overthrows President Carlos Arosemena.*

The government came under the control of a four-man junta headed by Captain Ramón Castro Jijon. The junta outlawed the Communist Party and promised to wipe out Fidel Castro's terrorist guerrillas who had infiltrated Ecuador. The United States recognized the new regime on July 31, 1963.

### July 31, 1963

**Although the CIA estimates that China's policies are not aggressive, President Kennedy and Secretary Rusk believe otherwise: results of a National Security Council meeting.**

Following the Cuban missile crisis of 1962, the president and Rusk spoke about Soviet compliant policies and China's "blatant aggression" in India and elsewhere. Their concern led to a special NSC session on July 31, 1963.

At the meeting, the CIA presented a special estimate of the Chinese situation that discounted Chinese military ambition against India, indicating as others had before that India, not China, had been the aggressor in October 1962. The CIA also dismissed the view that China was acting aggressively in Southeast Asia or elsewhere. The Beijing government spoke often of support for anti-imperial wars but showed respect for U.S. power and still feared the Soviet Union.

Nevertheless, Kennedy, who had always disliked mainland China, continued to back Chiang Kai-shek and deplored Mao's aggressive talk against America. Although Rusk was less opposed to Beijing than Kennedy, he accepted the president's views. Later attempts by Kennedy's apologists to argue that the president was planning to change his China policy have not been well documented.

## July 31, 1963

### The United States abstains in a U.N. Security Council vote on a resolution to stop all arms shipments to Portugal's colonial government of Angola.

Native uprisings against Portuguese rule began in Angola in 1961. As a result, on January 30, 1962, the U.N. General Assembly voted 99-2 to urge Portugal to stop its repressive measures against the "people of Angola." Because the Angola rebel leader Holden ROBERTS had become "friendly" in accepting aid from the Soviet Union and later (January 3, 1964) from China, the United States, Britain, and France faced a dilemma. They wanted Portugal to grant independence to Angola but did not like Roberts's policies. As a result, the three Western powers abstained on a Soviet-sponsored resolution to stop all arms going to Portugal's colonial government.

## August 5, 1963

### A limited nuclear test ban treaty is signed by Britain, the Soviet Union, and the United States.

Three-power talks on a test ban began in Moscow on July 15. The representatives were Soviet Foreign Minister Gromyko, U.S. Undersecretary of State Harriman, and British Minister for Science Viscount Hailsham. The three powers signed the treaty on August 5. When it became effective on October 10, over 100 nations had agreed to it.

The treaty prohibited tests in space, the atmosphere, and underwater. It did not, however, eliminate underground tests. Negotiations seeking to prohibit underground tests continued to be pursued, usually not enthusiastically by the United States, which argued that they could not always be detected. A U.S.-USSR Threshold Test Ban was agreed to in 1974.

See October 31, 1958, and July 3, 1974.

## September 25, 1963

### Dominican President Juan Bosch is overthrown by a right-wing group headed by General Elias Wessin y Wessin and Donald Reid Cabral.

Bosch's election as president of the liberal reform government had been personally approved by President Kennedy in 1962. Therefore, Kennedy cut off aid to the new military junta and tried to pressure it to conduct new elections. In December 1963, President Johnson agreed to recognize Reid's government and renewed its economic assistance.

See April 28, 1965.

## October 19, 1963

*Sir Alec Douglas-Home becomes Prime Minister of England following the retirement of Harold Macmillan.*

## November 1–2, 1963

### A military coup in Saigon overthrows and kills Ngo Dinh Diem.

The increased domestic pressure against Diem that corresponded to the Buddhist protests resulted in several plots by South Vietnamese military generals against Diem. As early as August, U.S. Ambassador to Saigon Henry Cabot Lodge heard of these plots and asked Secretary of State Rusk how to react. Lodge recommended that he give assurances to any anti-Communist groups who opposed Diem.

The White House was not certain how to respond because President Kennedy had to deal with conflicting opinions. General Maxwell Taylor and Walt Rostow of the National Security Council clung to their 1961 plan, urging that the U.S. strategic hamlet and combat-support missions be continued, claiming they would succeed by 1964 or 1965. They blamed

U.S. advisers assist
Vietnamese troop leaders.
National Archives

Diem's younger brother and chief political adviser, Ngo Dinh Nhu, along with Nhu's wife, not Diem, for Saigon's problems. Two senior U.S. diplomats who had spent much time in Vietnam disagreed. Joseph Mendenhall and Rufus Phillips, who headed the hamlet-assistance program, reported that Diem seldom followed U.S. advice and that the Nhus had corrupted the purposes of the hamlet program. In addition, Phillips said, the Nhus gave Taylor and Rostow falsified reports of the pacification program, which made their military evaluations incorrect. Marine General Victor Krulak was enraged by Phillips's charges but neither he nor Taylor would investigate Phillips's data. Phillips's reports showed that the Vietcong (South Vietnamese Communists) had captured 50 hamlets in recent weeks in the southern delta region near Saigon. The Vietcong controlled 80% of Long An province in the south.

Krulak and Taylor preferred to base their reports on the northern provinces because they argued that Diem's problem was the invasion of North Vietnam along the 17th parallel. Phillips told them they should look at the heavily populated southern delta area, where local Communists as well as non-Communists opposed Diem. The dispute, which became a classic between U.S. military and civilian advisers, had begun. The U.S. military saw the war as a Communist invasion from the north; most U.S. civilian advisers saw the domestic economic problems of South Vietnam as the basic threat to the Saigon regime.

Kennedy preferred the military viewpoint. As he told Chet Huntley during an NBC interview on September 9, China instigated the problems in Vietnam and if South Vietnam fell, the Chinese could capture all Indochina and Malaya. He told Huntley, "the war in the future in Southeast Asia was China and the communists." Neither Kennedy nor Johnson wanted to be accused of another "China cop-out," as Truman had been in 1949. As David Halberstam observes in his ironically titled *The Best and the Brightest,* seldom has so much Washington talent been so misguided by its incorrect assessment of circumstances.

Nevertheless, in the fall of 1963 the White House estimates shifted enough to enable Ambassador Lodge to inform the plotters in Saigon that the United States would accept a new government. McNamara and Taylor visited Saigon in September and on their return indicated that while there was "great progress" in U.S. military action, Diem was not popular. The United States, they told Kennedy, should "work with the Diem regime but not support it."

This curious recommendation enabled Secretary Rusk to inform Lodge on October 6 that the United States would accept a new government led by General Duong Van Minh (Big Minh). Subsequently, on the night of November 1–2, 1963, General Minh and his allies staged an attack on the presidential palace, where they captured Diem and the Nhus. Diem tried to rally his loyal troops in Saigon, but outside of his personal guards he had no loyal troops. The assassination of Diem and his brother and sister-in-law does not appear to have been planned by Big Minh. The United States expected they would be exiled. Allegedly, a long-time enemy of Diem led the armored unit that captured the three family leaders. He had them shot before they reached Big Minh's headquarters.

See May 8, 1963.

### November 22, 1963

**President Kennedy is assassinated in Dallas, Texas, and Vice President Lyndon B. Johnson is sworn in as president.**

### December 12, 1963

*Kenya, a former British colony, becomes independent.*

Just two days earlier, Zanzibar became independent. Internal political problems in Kenya did not end, however. On January 24, there was a troop mutiny. President Jomo Kenyata asked British forces to restore order.

Zanzibar and Tanganyika also experienced problems because of an uprising on January 20 at Dar es Salaam. On January 25, the British restored order. Eventually Zanzibar became part of Tanzania, formery Tanganyika, under Jules Nyerere's presidency on October 29, 1964.

### December 26, 1963

**Secretary McNamara informs the president that political conditions in Saigon are unstable.**

The coup against Diem on November 1, 1963, did not solve South Vietnam's political problems. Big Minh's new regime soon came under attack from opposing military groups. Following a visit to Vietnam in December, the secretary of defense presented a gloomy report to Johnson. Present trends, he wrote,

Vice President Lyndon Johnson, Jacqueline Kennedy, and President Kennedy at a Fort Worth, Texas, breakfast. John F. Kennedy Library

"will lead to neutralization at best and more likely to a communist controlled state." The new government was "indecisive and drifting." The internal reform program lacked leadership. Vietcong progress had been great.

McNamara's recommendation was ominous. The United States must watch the situation but prepare "for more forceful moves if the situation does not show early signs of improving."

For more on South Vietnam's continuing political problems, see January 27, 1965.

# 1964

### January 1, 1964

*The Federation of Rhodesia and Nyasaland is dissolved. Three separate states are formed: Nyasaland, Northern Rhodesia, and Southern Rhodesia.*

On October 23, 1953, Great Britain had overseen the establishment of the federation of these three states within the British Commonwealth. Black African majorities within the federation opposed it because they were not effectively represented, and on February 21, 1961, the British revised the federation constitution to address this complaint. The new system did not satisfy black Africans. Although blacks outnumbered whites in the federation by 26 to 1, the electoral rolls gave whites a 10 to 1 superiority of votes.

Between October 1962 and January 1, 1964, Great Britain had to negotiate a settlement that evolved separate status for each of the three states. Both Nyasaland and Northern Rhodesia set up legislatures with black African majorities. In Southern Rhodesia, however, a white majority gained control and Great Britain opposed its request for independence.

Consequently, after the federation was dissolved on January 1, 1964, Northern Rhodesia was renamed Zambia and became independent, with Kenneth Kaunda as prime minister. Nyasaland (later renamed Malawi) was an independent nation with Hastings Banda as prime minister.

Southern Rhodesia's all-white government presented greater problems to the British. On April 13, a radical right government gained control under Ian D. Smith. On April 16, Smith banished, without trial, four black African leaders including Joshua Nkomo.

The first of a series of riots and demonstrations by black Africans was suppressed by Smith's government.

### January 27, 1964

*France grants recognition to the People's Republic of China.*

### February 11, 1964

*Fighting begins on Cyprus between Greeks and Turks.*

This struggle to dominate the island of Cyprus continued throughout 1964 and tensions between Greece and Turkey lasted for over a decade.

### February 21, 1964

*A crisis with Cuba ends when Castro again turns on the water supply to Guantánamo naval base.*

This crisis began on February 2 when the U.S. Coast Guard arrested four Cuban fishing boats in U.S. waters off the Florida Keys. Thirty-six fishermen were turned over to Florida authorities for legal disposition; two fishermen requested political asylum in the United States. Two of the Cuban captains admitted that they had been selected for this "historic venture" as a means of testing "U.S. reactions."

Cuba protested to the United States through Swiss Ambassador Emil Stadelhofer and also complained to the U.N. Security Council. On February 6, Cuba's foreign minister, Raul Roa, sent word that Cuba was cutting off the water to the U.S. naval base at Guantánamo. It would be turned on only when the fishermen were released.

The U.S. navy had contingency plans to supply water at the base on a limited basis, and these were put into effect. In addition, Johnson and the navy agreed immediately to take steps to make Guantánamo self-sufficient by obtaining a permanent water supply and ending the employment of Cubans on the base.

On February 21, the Florida court dropped charges against the Cuban crews but fined the four captains $500 each. All the men were released and Cuba immediately turned on the water to Guantánamo.

Johnson proceeded to carry out the plan to make the base self-sufficient. The 2,000 Cuban employees at the base were released from work, and on April 1 construction of a desalination plant began at Guantánamo. This water processor was completed in December 1964, and the U.S. base was then self-sufficient.

## March 31, 1964

### *In Brazil, military leaders overthrow President João Goulart.*

Goulart had undertaken reforms in line with Kennedy's Alliance for Progress. These changes included distributing federal land to landless peasants, doubling the minimum wage, and expropriating land adjacent to federal highways. Conservatives opposed these reforms, leading to the revolt that sent Goulart into exile. On April 11, Army Chief of Staff General Humberto Castelo Branco was selected to replace Goulart as president.

## April 3, 1964

### A crisis with Panama ends when President Johnson agrees to "review every issue" with Panama, and diplomatic relations resume.

President Eisenhower's September 17, 1960, agreement to permit Panama's flag to fly with the American flag in the Canal Zone had satisfied a symbolic, but not the substantive, complaint of Panamanians regarding their rights in the Canal Zone. On October 1, 1961, President Robert Chiari formally asked the United States to revise the Panama Canal Treaty to provide just rights for Panamanians. The Kennedy administration ignored this request, and the growing discontent led to large-scale riots in Panama beginning on January 7, 1964. Panama broke relations with the United States and demanded a new canal treaty.

The OAS council set up a 17-member committee to find a solution to the U.S.-Panamanian dispute. While its efforts failed, the committee succeeded in obtaining President Johnson's agreement to review all issues in the treaty relations. With this understanding, President Chiari agreed to renew diplomatic relations with the United States.

Although U.S. and Panamanian election-year politics prevented a decision during 1964, a new treaty was formalized in 1965.

See September 24, 1965.

## April 20, 1964

### President Johnson announces that he and Soviet Premier Khrushchev have agreed to reduce the production of U-235 for nuclear weapons.

President Johnson had sought some means to curb the arms race, and in his January 8 state-of-the-union message he announced that the United States was cutting its production of enriched uranium 235 by 25% and was closing several nonessential nuclear military installations.

Between February 22 and April 20, Johnson corresponded with Premier Khrushchev to determine if he would take parallel action in further reducing the Soviet output of U-235, which was used to produce hydrogen bombs. Just as Johnson reached New York to deliver his address of April 20 to the annual Associated Press luncheon, he received a message from Moscow that Khrushchev had agreed on parallel action to reduce U-235 production and to allocate more fissionable material for peaceful uses.

Johnson imparted this information to the public in his speech of April 20. He believed that small steps such as this would lead to limits on nuclear weapons and to the decline of the threat of a nuclear holocaust.

## April 22, 1964

### *Romania's Communist Party insists on the independence of all communist nations and parties.*

The Romanians desired greater freedom from Moscow's interference and began economic negotiations with the United States, France, and other nations. The Romanian Communist Party agreed, however, to support Moscow in its ideological dispute with China.

## April 28, 1964

### *President de Gaulle announces that French naval staff officers will no longer serve under NATO commands.*

Since 1962, de Gaulle had begun to disassociate his nation from NATO organizations. President Kennedy had rejected his suggestion of a pact by which Paris, London, and Washington would jointly oversee Western affairs. Thereafter, de Gaulle began an independent foreign policy program. On January 14, 1963, he rejected a NATO proposal for a multilateral defense force. On January 28, 1964, he signed a five-year trade agreement with the Soviet Union.

### July 10, 1964

**The former Katanga secessionist, Moise Tshombe, becomes premier of the Congo. The United States assists the Congo in ending the rebellion.**

In March 1964, Undersecretary of State for Political Affairs Averell Harriman recommended that President Johnson provide planes and pilots to assist the Congolese in putting down rebels, some of whom were aided by the Chinese Communists. Harriman wanted to support the Government of National Reconciliation groups headed by Cyrille Adoula. Therefore, Johnson sent planes to "train" the Congolese. Soon after, exiled Cubans recruited by the CIA were flying U.S. aircraft against the Congolese rebels.

As the rebel raids increased, Adoula resigned on June 30, leaving the National Reconciliation Party leaderless. Then on July 10, Tshombe—who had fled the region on June 14, 1963—returned from exile and took over as prime minister in the coalition government. Because Tshombe's former secessionist plots made him unacceptable to other black African leaders, only the United States and Belgium helped him against the rebels.

### August 7, 1964

**Congress passes the Tonkin Gulf Resolution authorizing the president to take "all necessary measures to repel any armed attack" in Southeast Asia.**

Although the congressional Tonkin Gulf Resolution resulted from North Vietnamese gunboat attacks on U.S. destroyers off the coast of Vietnam, Congress did not investigate nor did President Johnson accurately report the developments in the United States of secret plans during 1964 that led to the North Vietnamese attack. (Later, in 1966, the Senate did investigate the Tonkin Gulf incident.)

On February 1, 1964, Johnson authorized the use of military Plan 34a for covert action against North Vietnam designed to pressure Hanoi to withdraw from South Vietnamese territory. Plan 34a provided a variety of sabotage and psychological and intelli-gence-gathering operations against North Vietnam. These included U-2 flights to gather intelligence on targets; assisting South Vietnamese commando raids on North Vietnam to destroy railways, bridges, and coastal defense installations; air raids by U.S. fighter-bombers disguised as Laotian air force planes; and destroyer patrols in the Gulf of Tonkin to collect data on Communist radar and coast defenses. Although the Pentagon later claimed the destroyer patrols and commando raids just happened to occur on the nights when the North Vietnamese attacked the American destroyers, Hanoi could not be expected to disassociate the two types of U.S. interference on its coastline and assumed the commandos and the destroyers worked together.

These covert operations are the only explanation for the small North Vietnamese PT boat attacks on the larger destroyers. On August 2, the commander of the USS *Maddox* fired on a group of torpedo boats that, he said, launched their missiles at his ship. Whatever torpedoes were fired were off target, but the U.S. ships and planes from the carrier *Ticonderoga* damaged two PT boats and destroyed a third. On August 4, sonar on U.S. destroyers detected a "sea ablaze with hostile torpedoes" and the U.S. destroyers *Maddox* and *Turner Joy* fired against the "hostile torpedoes." This alleged second attack was mistakenly reported to Washington. Defense Secretary McNamara asked destroyer officers if there was a second attack but received the reply there was a "slight possibility" it had not taken place. By that time on August 5, Senate hearings on the Tonkin Gulf Resolution were underway on the assumption there was an August 4 incident. Later, U.S. navy pilot James B. Stockdale stated that on August 4 there were "no boats, no boat wakes, no ricochets off boats, no boat impacts, no torpedo wakes—nothing but the black sea and American firepower." This information is from Marilyn B. Young's *The Vietnam Wars* (1991).

President Johnson saw the naval incidents on August 2 and 4 as the opportunity to change U.S. Indochina strategy. At 11:30 P.M. on August 4, Johnson went before a nationwide TV audience, inter-rupting all programs to announce the "unprovoked" attack by Communist boats on the U.S. destroyers in the Tonkin Gulf. Communist subversion in South Vietnam "has now been joined by open aggression on the high seas against the United States of America." The president announced he would act with restraint with a simple reprisal raid on North

Vietnam, but he urged Congress to give him greater authority to repel future attacks.

Earlier on May 23, McGeorge Bundy, Special Assistant to the President for National Security, had prepared a resolution for Johnson to obtain such authority from Congress. The president provided this draft to the House and Senate for action. Congress acted quickly. Although Senator Wayne Morse wanted an extended investigation before voting, Senator J. William Fulbright, chairman of the Senate Foreign Relations Committee, refused. The committee supported Fulbright, and with little debate Congress passed the resolution. The House vote was 416 to 0; the Senate vote, 88 to 2.

The Tonkin Gulf Resolution was the closest Congress ever came to a declaration of war in Vietnam. The resolution declared that Southeast Asia was "vital to the national interest and world peace"; therefore, it gave the president the right to "take all necessary steps, including the use of armed forces" to aid any member or protocol state (South Vietnam) of SEATO to defend the region from communism. Only the impending presidential campaign of 1964 prevented Johnson from immediately taking steps to escalate the war in 1964.

Johnson did, however, authorize reprisal raids against North Vietnam. On August 4, within six hours of the reported Tonkin Gulf incident, the Joint Chiefs selected targets and the National Security Council supported the reprisal raids on North Vietnam. Two and a half hours later, planes from the carriers *Ticonderoga* and *Constellation* attacked North Vietnam. Their targets were four torpedo boat bases and an oil storage depot that held 10% of Hanoi's petroleum supply. Following this attack, Johnson ordered U.S. bombers to be deployed in the southwest Pacific pending orders for future raids on Vietnam.

See January 28, 1966, and June 22, 1970.

### October 14, 1964

*Soviet Premier Khrushchev is ousted by Kosygin and Brezhnev.*

An intraparty struggle had arisen in Moscow between 1962 and 1964. To counter his opposition, Khrushchev tried a new method of open deliberations of the Central Committee before hundreds of "plain folk." The attempt to silence the opposition did not succeed because it threatened to undermine the power of the Presidium (formerly the Politburo) and the Central Committee of the Communist Party. After the Presidium members Leonid Brezhnev and Alexsei Kosygin persuaded all members of the Presidium to remove Khrushchev as chairman, the Central Party Committee joined the anti-reform members who opposed Khrushchev. Khrushchev retired to his dacha near Moscow and wrote his memoirs, which were published in the West as *Khrushchev Remembers* (1970).

### October 15, 1964

*James Harold Wilson becomes British Prime Minister following a Labour Party victory with a majority of four seats over the Conservatives, led by Douglas-Home.*

### November 3, 1964

**Lyndon Johnson wins a landslide victory over Barry Goldwater.**

The election of 1964 was the first in which the Republican candidate directly challenged the Cold War consensus policies of containment and the socio-economic programs begun under the New Deal. In domestic affairs, Goldwater opposed such basics as agricultural subsidies and social security. Abroad, he wanted "total victory" over communism, not containment, and made many Americans fear he might launch a nuclear war. Whether or not he actually said, as alleged, that the United States should "lob a nuclear bomb into the men's room at the Kremlin," both his avid followers and his opponents believed he did.

Against Goldwater, Johnson became a symbol of restraint and progress. Even during the Tonkin Gulf crisis, Johnson's single reprisal raid did not accurately indicate the more bellicose secret plans that he had prepared for use in 1965 if necessary. Therefore, Johnson said as little as possible about Vietnam or other foreign issues.

The 1964 election was the apogee of Johnson's political career. He won the greatest popular vote (43 million to 27 million), and the greatest percentage (61.1%) in recent American history. If Southern whites had not deserted Johnson on the civil rights issue, the victory would have been even larger. The electoral college vote was Johnson 486, Goldwater 52.

Texas pep rally for GOP presidential candidate, Senator Barry Goldwater. National Archives

# 1965

### January 27, 1965

#### The U.S. Defense Department reports on South Vietnam's continued political deterioration.

When interfering in Third World conflicts, American political leaders had consistently failed to develop realistic policies to deal with the governments they supported and with the more vigorous and focused leadership of left-wing rebels and Communists. In most cases, the United States found itself supporting a wealthy, entrenched governing elite who adamantly opposed land reform and other badly needed socioeconomic reforms in such areas as corruption, education, public health, and economic opportunities. American "aid" often never reached the people it was supposed to help.

The "rebels" had little difficulty in finding issues that appealed to the exploited and oppressed and that provided them with a strong popular base. The U.S. fear of "communism" had little meaning to those being exploited by corrupt, often brutal, authoritarian governments.

By the end of 1964, Maxwell Taylor, who became the U.S. ambassador to South Vietnam in June 1964, discovered that the South Vietnamese did not want Americans to interfere in their domestic affairs; they only wanted the United States to fight for them.

Reports by Taylor and on January 27, 1965, a summary analysis of the Vietnamese situation by John T. McNaughton (an assistant to McNamara) described the difficulties of the internal political conflicts of 1964 during which Taylor's advice was seldom heeded by the Vietnamese. In January 1964, Big Minh was overthrown by General Nguyen Khanh. In August, a coup against Khanh by General Lan Van Phat aborted and gave power to a triumvirate of Nguyen Cao Ky, Nguyen Chanh Thi, and Nguyen Van Thieu. These three younger officers tried to please Taylor by forming a High National Council. On December 20, however, General Khanh eliminated the National Council and joined Thi and Ky in a new military junta. With the military, religious, and social factions creating chaos in Saigon, the South Vietnamese army could not function effectively.

Because a new government seemed incapable of improvement, Taylor and McNaughton said the war would be won only if the United States controlled it. A vital step to Americanize the war was taken in 1965.

### February 6–7, 1965

#### Johnson orders reprisal air raids after Communists attack U.S. troops at Pleiku.

Plans to escalate the U.S. role in Vietnam began on September 9, 1964, when President Johnson told the principal advisers in the National Security Council to prepare to improve the defenses of South Vietnam. As a result, the NSC principals held lengthy reviews before recommending two options for Johnson, after dropping a third Option C to steadily escalate air raids on North Vietnam. On December 1, Johnson approved Option A to increase counterinsurgency operations against the Vietcong and prepare for reprisal air raids if there were further Communist provocations such as the raid on Bien Hoa on November 1, 1964.

The December 1 decisions were critical but often misunderstood because they were based on a theory of war for limited political objectives. The U.S. Joint Chiefs of Staff urged Johnson to permit the military to use all necessary action short of nuclear war to "save" South Vietnam from communism. Johnson's aim was to fight the war for the political purpose of containing communism at the 17th parallel and thus protect South Vietnam and other Southeast Asian non-Communist nations. Thus political objectives shaped military operations, a strategy not traditionally used by the U.S. military until the 1950–1953 Korean War, when President Truman and General MacArthur disagreed on the political objectives of limited war.

The Pleiku attack of February 6 launched Option A reprisal air attacks. At Pleiku, the Vietcong killed nine U.S. soldiers and severely wounded 76 more. They also destroyed 6 airplanes and 16 helicopters. Following a brief session of the NSC, Johnson ordered Option A reprisals, code named Fleming Dart II. Two air raids by jets from a navy aircraft carrier hit North Vietnamese barracks at Dong Hui and a communications center at Vinh Linh.

The White House announced the reprisals as a response to Vietcong raids at Pleiku and two other southern villages, thereby linking "their" war with "our" war—an attack on U.S. facilities in South Vietnam.

Johnson also told General Westmoreland, the U.S commander in Vietnam, that the reprisals were not the same as the Option C attacks on North Vietnam. Neverthess, Option C gradually escalated air raids on North Vietnam combined with peace negotiations in March. More details on U.S. planning are in the *Gravel Edition of the Pentagon Papers* (1975).

See March 19, 1965.

### March 19, 1965

#### "Rolling Thunder," sustained U.S. bomber attacks, begin against North Vietnam.

President Johnson ordered Option C of his "slow squeeze" tactics to begin against North Vietnam on March 19. Except for specific periods when the president halted these raids to consider possible cease-fire agreements, the Rolling Thunder air attacks continued from March 19, 1965 to March 31, 1968.

The first bombing pause came between May 10 and 18, soon after the initial attacks inspired many international leaders to seek negotiations that would alleviate the conflict in Vietnam. Great Britain and the Soviet Union proposed to reconvene the 1965 Geneva Conference. Neither this effort nor others were successful during the next three years.

In operation, the Rolling Thunder attacks took place at least two or three times each week. Johnson and McNamara controlled the dates and target selection for the raids. Although this control dismayed the U.S. military, Johnson wanted to retain political authority in deciding whether to increase or decrease targets as well as when attacks took place. Nevertheless, the quantity of Rolling Thunder attacks against North Vietnam was astonishing. During a three-year period, 309,996 U.S. bombing raids dropped 408,599 tons of bombs on North Vietnam, most of these in the area between Hanoi and the 17th parallel. Generally, the area around Hanoi, the port of Haiphong, and the Chinese border were avoided. By 1967, Johnson gradually eased this restriction, enumerating new targets such as rail yards or oil installations near Hanoi and Haiphong.

On April 6, 1965, Johnson also sent combat troops to Vietnam, although this was not announced to the public until July 1965.

See July 28, 1965.

A B-52 bomber drops its
750-pound bombs on a
South Vietnamese target.
National Archives

### March 24, 1965

#### American objectives in Vietnam are given a quantitative formulation by John T. McNaughton.

The assistant secretary of international affairs in the Defense Department, McNaughton prepared a memo that justified the U.S. bombing campaign against North Vietnam. This memo stated that U.S. aims in Vietnam were:

70%—to avoid a humiliating defeat (to our reputation as guarantor).
20%—to keep Vietnamese (and adjacent) territory from Chinese hands.
10%—to permit the people of South Vietnam a better, freer way of life.
Also—to emerge from crisis without unacceptable taint from methods used.
NOT—to "help a friend," although it would be hard to stay if South Vietnamese leaders asked them to leave.

Except for the statement of percentages, the speeches of President Johnson, Rusk, and McNamara from 1965 to 1968 appeared to verify McNaughton's listing. McNaughton's memo was secret and confidential, not reaching the U.S. public until the publication of the *Pentagon Papers* in 1971.

### March 24, 1965

#### Protests against the Vietnam War are made during a "teach-in" at the University of Michigan, beginning a new method of dissent.

Although there were a few war dissenters before March 1965, the criticism against the Johnson administration's White Paper of January 1965 that explained North Vietnam's aggression, the Pleiku reprisal raids of February, and the first Rolling Thunder bombings of March, inspired the start of a slow but growing public opposition to the Vietnam War.

Significant dissent arose on college campuses where professors trained in international studies, foreign policy, and Asian or Vietnamese culture opposed the administration's methods. The teach-ins became a means to disseminate information about an area of the world that few Americans knew and about which there were misconceptions based on myth or misinformation. The teach-ins lasted from two hours to all day and night. Some were conducted as debates for and against Johnson's policies; others were informative or were held to explain why U.S. policies erred. Some were argued by moderate dissenters who wanted better U.S. global strategy; others, by radical opponents who described the horrific results of napalm bombs and B-52 raids on helpless South Vietnamese.

The dissenters were aided because Johnson talked about paying for "guns and butter" programs, but the war on poverty was the only low-budget war in American history. In 1965, the Great Society's Office of Economic Opportunity (OEO) received $800 million; the Defense Department obtained $56.6 billion including $5.8 billion for the Vietnam War. In 1966, the OEO received an increase to $1.5 billion; the Defense Department jumped to $72 billion.

Antiwar demonstrations spread across the nation. In 1966 and 1967, Los Angeles, Chicago, Newark, and Detroit had antiwar demonstrations that turned into major riots because Johnson failed to win either the Vietnam War or the War on Poverty. Details on the economic and social consequences of the war are in Anthony Campagna's *The Economic Consequences of the Vietnam War* (1990).

The growth of dissent was indicated in public opinion polls. When Rolling Thunder began in 1965, 50% of the public supported Johnson's Vietnam policy; by December 1965, this had risen to 65%. During 1965, the president's acceptance rate by the public stabilized at 54%. In 1967, his popularity steadily declined. Only 44% agreed with the war program, and a smaller percentage, 23%, thought he was doing a good job as president. By early 1968, Johnson, a devotee of opinion polls, watched the support for the war effort collapse even more.

See March 31, 1968; for other factors in dissent against the war, see October 14, 1965, and January 28, 1966.

### April 7, 1965

**President Johnson emphasizes that America must protect the freedom of the Vietnamese.**

In a speech at Johns Hopkins University, President Johnson sought to counteract the first signs of dissent on his Vietnam policy by describing America's idealistic role in fighting in Vietnam. The United States had a "promise" to keep in Vietnam and must show our allies they can depend on us. In addition, China and North Vietnam were allegedly stepping up their attacks on the "brave people of South Vietnam," and only America could slow this Communist aggression.

Johnson ended his speech with dramatic but ironic words—ironic because he had just introduced the Rolling Thunder bombing campaign in Vietnam. Johnson said at Johns Hopkins that the American people have a very old dream "of a world where disputes are settled by law and reason." They also have a dream "of an end to war." We must make these so, he said, concluding:

> Every night before I turn out my lights to sleep, I ask myself this question: Have I done everything that I can do to unite this country? Have I done everything I can do to help unite the world, to try to bring hope to all the peoples of the world?
> This generation of the world must choose: destroy or build, kill or aid, hate or understand.
> We can do all these on a scale never dreamed of before.
> We will choose life. And so doing will prevail over the enemies within man, and over the natural enemies of all mankind.

### April 28, 1965

**In violation of the OAS charter, President Johnson sends U.S. Marines to intervene in the Dominican Republic, claiming there is a threat of communism.**

Dominican politics had been in flux since May 30, 1961, when Trujillo was assassinated. Juan Bosch had been elected president in 1962 but was overthrown in a coup on September 25, 1963. During 1964, there was frequent unrest in the Dominican Republic when the possibility of another military coup appeared possible. President Reid was not popular. U.S. Ambassador W. Tapley Bennett backed Reid, but a CIA poll showed only 5% of the people favored Reid.

A revolt began on April 24, led by officers who favored the return of Bosch. Secretary of State Rusk disliked Bosch and wanted to prevent his accession to power. Rusk thought Bosch had been ineffective in 1962 and that he was under Communist influence. Neither Rusk nor Johnson wanted another Cuba in the Caribbean. When a CIA-sponsored poll said the Communists supported Bosch, Rusk became convinced that he should not gain control.

Honduran soldiers, first of an inter-American peace force, arrive in the Dominican Republic. National Archives

As a result, when General Wessin counterattacked against Bosch supporters on April 26, Johnson encouraged the general, asking him only to act moderately against the rebels. Wessin failed, however, and when the U.S. embassy called for marines to save the country from communism, Johnson responded quickly to Wessin's request for aid because the government could not protect U.S. lives.

On April 28, 500 marines landed; soon after, 20,000 more soldiers arrived. Johnson gave the U.S. public lurid details of the Communist threat, saying the United States acted on behalf of humanity. His action saved Wessin's counterrevolution from the victory of Bosch's rebels.

The United States never proved that there was a Communist threat in the Dominican Republic. There was danger to Americans in the country because of conflict, but until U.S. forces arrived, Bosch had hoped to get U.S. support because Kennedy had helped him in 1962. In early May, Johnson sent John Barlow Martin to Dominica to check on Communist influence. Martin reported that one rebel, Colonel Francisco Caamano Deno, was a potential Castro because he had a Communist adviser. This inspired Rusk and Johnson to further action to back the loyalists in the island republic.

Somewhat ironically, by May 21, Rusk told the Senate Foreign Relations Committee that the danger of communism had vanished. The administration, he said, could accept either Bosch or his leading opponent, Joaquin Balaguer. Also by mid-May, Rusk had referred the intervention to the OAS Council. The OAS agreed to send a multinational force to oversee the return of stability to the Dominican Republic. Later, in June 1966, the OAS held elections and Balaguer won. The fear of Castro and communism had led Johnson to overreact in April 1965.

### June 12, 1965

***General Thieu and Marshal Ky gain control of the South Vietnamese government, appearing to give unity to South Vietnam.***

Following the political choas in Saigon from December 1964 to June 12, 1965, the government achieved a semblance of order after Thieu and Ky replaced Prime Minister Phan Huy Quat. Thieu became chief of state; Ky became prime minister.

In reality, the Ky-Thieu government created a decentralized order by dividing up the political spoils of South Vietnam with four other generals. The so-called National Leadership Committee that made up the six-man junta set up four corps areas. General Thi held the First Corps area, Vinh Loc the Second, Bao Tri the Third, and Dang Van Quang the Fourth. Each general was in complete charge of his corps area, awarding military and civilian posts to the highest bidder, friends, or relatives. These posts were profitable for the generals—reports were that a province chief's job cost three million piatres plus a 10% kickback each month. Ky was the head of the baronies because his charismatic personality suited the U.S. newsmen, TV cameras, and visiting politicians. Thieu was in the shadows but was the brains behind the junta, and he eventually gained complete power. As David Halberstam and other reporters have documented, in their corps areas the generals' basic motives were personal power and profit. They conserved their troops for personal use, letting the Americans do the fighting as much as possible.

Outwardly, however, Ky and Thieu created an image of government in charge that looked good compared with the era of frequent political changes between November 1963 and June 1965.

See January 25, 1965.

### July 28, 1965

**President Johnson announces he is sending more American forces to Vietnam but tries to explain this as a "restrained" response.**

Because of recent "leaks" to the press in Washington about number of American troops going to South

Members of a Royal Australian Air Force (RAAF) unit arrive at Tan Son Nhut airport. National Archives

Vietnam, President Johnson held a press conference to explain his decisions. On June 8, Robert McClosky of the State Department told reporters that U.S. forces would "fight alongside Viet forces when and if necessary." Although the State Department clarified McClosky's statement on June 9 by saying there had been "no recent change in mission" of U.S. forces, Secretary McNamara on June 16 acknowledged that U.S. combat troops would "act as was necessary" to cope with the enemy.

President Johnson was enraged by the news headlines of June 9 and 17 generated by McClosky's and McNamara's statements. As the *Pentagon Papers* of 1971 indicated, Johnson had specifically instructed everyone on April 1 that the role of U.S. troops should not be reported as a "sudden change in policy." On April 1, the Third Stage of the slow squeeze had been secretly approved. By this decision, 20,000 American troops were ordered to Vietnam, and there was a policy change in the role of U.S. forces. Kennedy's "combat support" role ended. American officers and their troops would assume direct control over actions against the Vietcong and North Vietnamese forces south of the 17th parallel.

Johnson wanted this decision to appear not as a change but as action consistent with Kennedy's commitments. Thus, NSAM-328 of April 6 (whose contents had been approved on April 1) stated:

> The President desires that . . . premature publicity be avoided by all possible precautions. . . . The President's desire is that these movements and changes should be understood as being gradual and wholly consistent with existing policy.

American troop increases had been in limited increments before July 28. Two Marine Battalion Landing Teams of 3,500 men each arrived at Danang on March 8, and by mid-June 75,000 U.S. troops were in South Vietnam. Moreover, the April 1 policy called for forces to come from Australia, South Korea, New Zealand, and the Philippines. At Ambassador Taylor's request, the government of South Vietnam asked other nations for assistance. One Australian battalion arrived in June 1965. Because Britain and France opposed the U.S. operations, SEATO never sanctioned Johnson's "war" in Vietnam.

U.S. air operations south of the 17th parallel were also ordered on April 1. These included both tactical and strategic aircraft operations. General Westmoreland had charge of the fighter and bomber planes assigned to South Vietnam. These planes substituted for ground artillery by bombing and strafing enemy-held areas. They also dropped napalm firebombs and chemical defoliants to burn out or kill vegetation in jungle areas under Communist control. These attacks caused civilian protests both in South Vietnam and the United States because they indiscriminately damaged combatant and noncombatant areas, but the U.S. air force claimed they served a useful purpose. By the end of 1965, the air force had stationed 500 aircraft and 21,000 men at eight major air bases in South Vietnam.

The air force's saturation bombing by B-52s in the south was code-named Arc Light. Beginning in June 1965, B-52s flew area bombing missions from Guam. These area destructive capabilities coming from high-altitude flights gave an extra dimension of fear to both Vietcong and others in the south because the people seldom saw the high-flying planes.

Although the April 1–6 decisions involved the Americanization of the war in South Vietnam, Johnson and his advisers were not certain what terms to use in news releases to the U.S. public.

When the marines landed in March, their mission was described as a "security force" for the U.S. bases at Danang. General Westmoreland's reports called these operations "active counterinsurgency" to give ambiguity to the missions. McClosky on June 8 used the term "fight alongside."

On July 28, the president announced that another 50,000 U.S. troops would be sent to South Vietnam (the *Pentagon Papers* showed the figures approved by July 1965 to be 125,000). This increase, the president said, was minimal and nonprovocative because of the large number of North Vietnamese units fighting in the south. The Communists' spring offensive had made large advances during June 1965, and South Vietnam needed greater assistance. When a reporter asked the president if the troop increase implied less reliance on South Vietnam's troops, Johnson assured him: "It does not imply any change in policy whatsoever."

Johnson's attempt to deceive the newsmen failed. Too many reports of the U.S. "search and destroy" missions in South Vietnam contradicted the president's words. The July 28 press conference caused many reporters to realize that the president had purposely misled them. A "credibility gap" grew larger and larger between the president and the Washington press corps after 1965, further serving the groundswell of popular dissent between 1965 and 1968.

At various times after July 1965, the number of U.S. ground troops increased in South Vietnam as the war became Americanized. By December 1965, there were 267,500 U.S. ground combat troops in South Vietnam; in December 1966, 385,300; in December 1967, 449,800. The peak number of U.S. ground troops in Vietnam occurred in April 1969, when there were 543,400 U.S. military forces in Vietnam.

## September 24, 1965

### The United States and Panama sign a new canal agreement.

Negotiations to change the U.S. treaty with Panama began in 1964 following a series of riots in Panama (see April 3, 1964). During the next year, the United States and Panama agreed to a treaty that granted Panama sovereignty over the Canal Zone, provided economic aid to Panama, and allowed U.S. bases to protect the canal.

## October 3, 1965

### A new immigration act replaces the quota system of 1921.

As passed by Congress and signed by President Johnson, this law set overall immigration limits, including 120,000 from the Western Hemisphere and 170,000 from the rest of the world. Generally, however, it allowed 20,000 immigrants from most nations on a first-come, first-served basis.

## October 14, 1965

### The Department of Defense announces the largest draft call since the Korean War.

One consequence of the escalation of U.S. ground forces in Vietnam was the call for more draftees aged 18 to 35. Although the Defense Department preferred to call up trained military reserves or the National Guard, Johnson opposed this method of enlarging the armed forces. The president believed calling reserves and the National Guard was tantamount to a national crisis that would require a declaration of war. He did not want to engage Congress in that debate, preferring to act under the Gulf of Tonkin Resolution permitting him to "take all necessary measures to repel any armed attack against the forces of the United States and to prevent further aggression."

The call-up of more young men from college or their first job opportunity was not popular. During the two days after the Defense Department's October 14 draft call, antidraft demonstrations broke out on college campuses and in all major U.S. cities. Some young men burned their draft cards to symbolize their determination not to go to Vietnam. The "burn your draft card" campaign became so extensive that Congress passed legislation in 1966 to punish such acts with a $5,000 fine and up to five years in prison.

Antidraft tactics varied during the next decade. Counseling centers were set up to advise young men on how to fake physical and mental tests in order to fail the army's physical examination. Two Roman Catholic priests, Daniel and Phillip Berrigan, led a group of draft resisters in a raid on the Baltimore Selective Service offices to destroy draft files by pouring ox blood on the records. Some young men avoided the draft by going into exile in Canada or Europe. Nearly 40,000 men deserted from the U.S. army in 1968.

Returning war veterans also questioned the war and the draft. On May 8, 1966, the author Lloyd Shearer published an article in *Parade* magazine based on interviews with 88 wounded soldiers at U.S. hospitals. Eighty of the soldiers "declared flatly" that the "South Vietnamese could not be trusted." One said, "maybe the Vietnamese like us, but after spending 10 months there, I can tell you—they sure do a great job hiding it." These men, said Shearer, fought because the president said they should but they were confused about U.S. war objectives and could not understand why most Vietnamese disliked Americans.

*Parade* was a widely read Sunday supplement magazine, and these reports could not help raising questions about Johnson's policy in Vietnam.

### November 20, 1965

***In the last of three resolutions against Southern Rhodesia, the U.N. Security Council orders an oil embargo.***

Because a series of negotiations between Great Britain and Rhodesia in 1963–1964 had failed to reach a compromise to provide an integrated government for Rhodesia, Ian SMITH, the white supremacist president of Rhodesia, had unilaterally declared independence from Britain on November 11, 1965.

On November 13, the first Security Council resolution condemned Rhodesia for its action. The second resolution, on November 17, ordered Britain to put down the Rhodesian rebellion. Finally, on November 20, an oil embargo was voted against Rhodesia. Smith defied each of these actions. Because the Rhodesians refused to negotiate, the Security Council voted economic sanctions against Rhodesia on December 16, 1965.

### November 25, 1965

***Two years of political difficulties end in the Congo as General Mobutu becomes President.***

Maneuvering in the Congo between Moise Tshombe on the right and a left-wing rebel group that took over Stanleyville on August 5, 1964, placed the Congo in political disorder again. The Stanleyville group was put down, and on October 13, 1965, General Kasabuvu removed Tshombe as prime minister of the Léopoldville government. Finally, on November 25, Mobutu overthrew Kasabuvu and order came to the Congo for the first time since June 1960.

On June 30, 1966, Léopoldville was renamed Kinshasa.

### December 7, 1965

***The United States and India sign an agricultural aid treaty in which India also agrees to give agricultural modernization more attention.***

India had experienced severe food shortages in 1964–1965. President Johnson was willing to help but urged Secretary of Agriculture Orville Freeman to link future U.S. food shipments to India's readiness to emphasize food progress as well as industrial advance.

Meeting in Rome with India's minister of food and agriculture, Chidambaro Subramaniam, Freeman worked out an agreement based on Johnson's position. In its next Five-Year Plan, India agreed to give greater attention to supplying more food for itself. In turn, the United States agreed to make necessary wheat shipments to meet India's requirements. The India Treaty became the basis for Johnson's Food for Peace program.

In spite of India's new efforts, the United States had once again to provide India with food in April and December 1966. Johnson limited this aid because he claimed other nations should also respond to India's needs.

See January 15, 1967, and November 12, 1966.

### December 27, 1965

***President Johnson agrees to make the Christmas bombing pause longer in the Rolling Thunder attacks with a widespread diplomatic attempt to achieve peace.***

Since early November, Secretary of Defense McNamara had favored a bombing pause to permit North Vietnam a chance to react positively to the escalated U.S. air and ground action in Vietnam during the past nine months. Both the Joint Chiefs of Staff and Secretary Rusk opposed McNamara's request. In early December, however, Soviet Ambassador Anatoly Dobrynin indicated that the USSR would help obtain an agreement if there was a bombing pause. This convinced Rusk that a bombing pause would succeed or, at least, demonstrate to the

American public that Johnson had tried everything possible to seek peace.

With the backing of both the secretary of state and the secretary of defense, Johnson concurred. On December 24, the United States and South Vietnam had agreed to call a Christmas halt to aggressive action. Therefore, on December 27, Johnson simply extended this pause to permit the State Department to examine a peaceful solution.

In spite of a large-scale and much publicized U.S. diplomatic effort to use the pause to gain negotiations on Vietnam, the pause failed. Between December 27 and January 31, 1966, U.S. diplomats visited Rome, Belgrade, Warsaw, Paris, and London to seek aid in gaining a settlement. Rusk believed the most hopeful effort was a mission from Hungary, Poland, and the Soviet Union that visited Hanoi to try and convince Ho Chi Minh to seek a settlement. This mission failed.

On January 28, Radio Hanoi broadcast Ho Chi Minh's message that America's "so-called search for peace" was "deceitful" and "hypocritical." He insisted that the United States first pull out of Vietnam and recognize the Communist National Liberation Front as the legitimate representative of the people of South Vietnam. On January 31, Johnson ordered the resumption of Rolling Thunder's bombing raids on North Vietnam.

# 1966

### January 17, 1966

### The United States loses a hydrogen bomb in an air collision over Spain.

A U.S. plane carrying four unarmed H-bombs crashed near Palomares, Spain. The consequences were less harmful than expected, although several bombs ruptured sufficiently to poison nearby farmland.

### January 19, 1966

*Indira Gandhi is chosen as Prime Minister of India following the sudden death of Lal Bahadur Shastri on January 11.*

### January 28, 1966

### The Senate Fulbright Committee hearings on Vietnam open in Washington.

Senator J. William Fulbright had been a close friend of President Johnson and had led Senate action in quickly passing the Tonkin Gulf Resolution in August 1964. Fulbright had believed Johnson when the president told him that the resolution was limited and was designed only to steal ground from Senator Goldwater's criticism.

During 1965, Fulbright realized that the president had misled him. Gradually, the senator turned against Johnson and the escalation of the war. Joining with other Democratic Party members on the Senate Foreign Relations Committee, Fulbright began hearings on the Vietnam War on January 28, 1966, during which they would hear both sides of the question. But the hearings provided the television audience and news media with the opportunity to hear and propagate the views of the conflict's major opponents such

Senator J. William Fulbright. Library of Congress

as George Kennan and Lieutenant General James Gavin. In doing so, Fulbright's hearings added to the growing dissent against Johnson's policies in Vietnam.

During the Senate hearings between January 28 and February 18, 1966, Secretary Rusk explained how the war resulted from North Vietnam's "invasion" of South Vietnam and contended that the United States had to keep its pledge to help Saigon. Maxwell Taylor and others also defended Johnson's policy, but their version of the war had already been frequently aired on national television.

More significant was the opportunity for the ideas of Kennan and Gavin to reach a large audience. Kennan believed the war was foolish and not vital to the United States. Gavin argued that different tactics were required to minimize the U.S. role and maximize the role of South Vietnam. Finally, Robert Kennedy testified in favor of new policies in Vietnam. Kennedy thought a coalition with the Communists might be better than with the corrupt regime in Saigon. The Senate hearings helped to turn the liberal "egghead" wing of the Democratic Party against the war.

### February 6, 1966

**France withdraws its troops from NATO and requests NATO to move its headquarters from French soil.**

French President de Gaulle had been hostile toward the United States since 1962 because Washington refused to grant the French a more equitable position in their partnership. In particular de Gaulle disliked the multilateral (MLF) NATO force proposed by George Ball and urged by the United States on its European allies from 1963 to 1966. Having previously withdrawn French naval forces from NATO, de Gaulle now extended French independence by withdrawing all French forces from the organization. In addition, at France's request, NATO headquarters were moved from Paris to Brussels. Soon after, the idea of the MLF was dropped by the United States.

### February 8, 1966

**President Johnson is optimistic at the conclusion of meetings in Hawaii with South Vietnamese leaders Ky and Thieu.**

Between June 12, 1965 and early 1966, the political alliance Ky and Thieu established on June 12, 1965,

seemed to keep political order. Johnson was pleased and on January 31, 1966, invited the two leaders to meet with him in Honolulu.

Ky knew all the right words to satisfy Johnson. Their regime was defeating the enemy, pacifying the countryside, stabilizing the economy, and building democracy. Ky told Johnson that any government may launch a program for a better society, "but such a program cannot be carried forward for long if it is not administered by a really democratic government, one which is put into office by the people themselves and which has the confidence of the people."

At the conclusion of the Honolulu meeting on February 8, the Declaration of Honolulu was issued. In the first part of the decree, the Vietnamese government stated its goals, which included:

1. defeating the Vietcong and those "illegally fighting with them";
2. eradicating social injustice among our people;
3. maintaining a viable economy to build a "better material life for our people";
4. building "true democracy for our land and for our people," including a constitution in a "few months."

The United States promised to support the goals and programs stated by the Vietnamese.

See September 11, 1966.

### February 24, 1966

*Kwame Nkrumah, the Ghanaian dictator who had aligned with the USSR, is overthrown in an army coup led by General J. A. Ankrah.*

### May 14, 1966

**The Ky government attacks Danang and Hue following recent outbreaks of Buddhist-led uprisings.**

The Buddhist riots of 1966, which in many respects reenacted those of 1963, had been precipitated by Prime Minister Ky's attempt to remove General Thi as commander of the First Corps area. With strong support from the Buddhists and the Dai Viet organization of Southern Vietnamese Nationalists, Thi had become independent of Saigon's control. When Ky sought to remove Thi, Buddhists led by Thich Tri Quang, a Buddhist monk, began protests on March 10, 1966. Students, trade unionists, and the Dai Viet aided the Buddhists. A nun and eight young Buddhist bonzes set themselves aflame to protest against Ky's government. The U.S. consulate at Hue was burned.

On May 14, Ky ordered South Vietnamese troops to quell the uprising. Paratroopers landed at Danang airport but were repelled. Next, loyal Vietnamese marines and infantry besieged Hue, provoking Buddhist hunger strikes throughout South Vietnam in sympathy with Hue. By June 8, however, Ky's forces occupied Hue and Danang. Ky alienated the Buddhist leaders by banning their religious processions and all political acts. Many of the leaders in Hue and Danang were imprisoned or exiled. In his memoirs, President Johnson said he "always believed" Thi Quang and his followers were either pro-Communist or their movement was "deeply penetrated" by Hanoi's agents.

### June 29, 1966

**Rolling Thunder's first attack on "Pol" targets begins although Secretary McNamara and others had opposed them.**

Since September 2, 1965, the air force and Joint Chiefs had urged Johnson to permit the bombing of POL (petroleum, oil, lubricants) targets near Hanoi as well as the aerial mining of North Vietnam's seaports. Secretary McNamara opposed these targets because of the increased risk of war with China or the Soviet Union. Moreover, he claimed, the POL storage areas contained only 10% of North Vietnam's needs and their loss would not seriously damage the economy. The JCS favored all efforts to remove the president's restraints on their targets and strongly believed the POL and seaport mines would help the war effort.

Johnson decided in May 1966 not to mine the seaports but to permit the attacks on POL targets. His final orders were delayed, however; first, because British Prime Minister Harold Wilson asked Johnson to reconsider, and later, in June, because Canada sent an official representative to Hanoi to discuss possible peace terms with Ho Chi Minh. After Ambassador Chester Ronning's mission failed, Johnson ordered the POL attacks, which began on June 29.

See November 11, 1966.

### August 18, 1966

**The cultural revolution begins in China.**

The complete Chinese title of Mao's policy from 1966 to the early 1970s was the "great revolution to estab-

lish a propertyless class culture." Edgar Snow described Mao's version of this in his book *The Long Revolution* (1972), which was based on interviews with the chairman of the Chinese Communist Party.

According to Snow, Mao realized by the mid-1960s that the Beijing Party Committee led by Liu Shao-chi was making Mao a cult figure to decrease his power. This group had been strongly influenced by the Soviet apparatus of party controls and bureaucratic prerogatives. As a result, Mao secured supporters in Shanghai as well as the backing of the army under Lin Piao. They organized the masses and the Red Guards to overthrow Liu Shao-chi.

In practice, the cultural revolution emphasized agriculture and the village tradition. It sought to train village youths at the university so they could return to their homes and boost village production and culture. In this sense, it was a conflict between the modernization tendencies of the city, technology, and expertise versus the traditional Chinese village and communal life around which Mao had rallied the Communist Party from 1930 to 1949.

### September 6, 1966

**Prime Minister Verwoerd of South Africa is assassinated.**

Despite this killing, the white supremacist leadership of South Africa was undisturbed. B. J. Vorster became prime minister on September 13, 1966.

### September 11, 1966

**Elections in South Vietnam select delegates for a constituent assembly.**

These elections were set up by the Ky-Thieu government to fulfill a long-sought desire of U.S. advisers to have a "free" election to prepare a constitution for South Vietnam. The election went well; more than two-thirds of the South's adults registered to vote and 81% of those registered voted, electing 117 delegates who represented all political factions except the Buddhists, who boycotted the election. Neither U.S. reporters nor European observers found any significant fraud at the ballot box.

Between October 1966 and March 1967, the assembly delegates met to prepare a constitution. There was much dissension over the type of government to be established. A document was finally drawn up on March 19, 1967, the day before Ky and Thieu met with President Johnson at Guam.

## October 25, 1966

### The Manila Conference is attended by President Johnson and representatives of nations contributing troops to the Vietnam War.

At the invitation of President Marcos of the Philippines, President Johnson met in Manila with General Thieu and Prime Minister Ky of South Vietnam; President Park Chung Hee of South Korea; and Prime Ministers Harold Holt of Australia, Keith Holyoake of New Zealand, and Thanom Kittikachorn of Thailand.

Following a two-day review of the military and nonmilitary situation in Vietnam, the delegates issued three statements:

1. *Goal of freedom.* The seven nations at Manila declared their unity in seeking freedom for Vietnam and other Asian Pacific areas.
2. *Allies seek no permanent bases in Vietnam.* In this statement, South Vietnam asserted it would ask the seven nations to leave Vietnam when peace was restored. The seven allies declared they were in Vietnam only to aid the victim of aggression.

They would withdraw within six months after peace was restored. (Soviet Foreign Minister Andrey Gromyko told Johnson on October 10 that a specific statement on withdrawal would aid peace arrangements. Therefore, Johnson said, the second statement of the Manila Conference clarified Gromyko's suggestion.)
3. *Declaration of peace and progress in Asia and the Pacific.* The seven allies said their objectives were to oppose aggression, poverty, illiteracy, and disease. They would search for peace, reconciliation, and economic, social, and cultural cooperation in Asia.

## November 1, 1966

### Albania's Communist Party breaks with Moscow and allies with China as the "true" Communist Party.

## November 11, 1966

### President Johnson compromises between proposals of Secretary McNamara and the JCS on activity in Vietnam.

Following the inauguration of POL bombing raids on June 29, Secretary McNamara's aides watched the results closely while a group of leading scientists pre-

President Johnson meets with U.S. troops in Vietnam.
National Archives

pared a report, code-named JASON, that suggested new tactics to be used against North Vietnam. Between August 29 and October 15, 1966, the stream of reports from JASON, the CIA, and the Defense Intelligence Agency all concluded that the POL bombings had no critical effect on North Vietnam. On September 4, 1966, the commander in chief for the Pacific had redirected the air force from a POL emphasis to targets causing "attrition on men, supplies and equipment" in North Vietnam.

The conflict over war priorities between Secretary McNamara and the Joint Chiefs focused on new recommendations in October 1966. McNamara's JASON group recommended the construction of an electronic anti-infiltration barrier across the 17th parallel of Vietnam. In addition, McNamara recommended stabilization of the air war or a bombing pause, and the addition of 40,000 combat troops. The JCS disagreed with the secretary, urging an escalation of attacks against the North and requesting an added 150,000 men with the call-up of military reserve units.

Johnson's orders of November 11 sought a middle ground between McNamara and the JCS. He agreed to add 70,000 troops but rejected the call-up of military reserves. At the same time, he rejected the electronic barrier, agreeing with the JCS that it could not work. Finally, Johnson agreed to stabilize the Rolling Thunder attacks. The bombing stabilization was coordinated with an effort by Prime Minister Harold Wilson to persuade Moscow and Hanoi to reconvene the 1954 Geneva talks on Vietnam.

See February 14, 1967.

## November 12, 1966

### President Johnson signs the Food for Peace Act of 1966.

On December 7, 1965, the United States and India signed an agreement to encourage India to modernize its agriculture. President Johnson liked this concept and on February 10, 1966, recommended that Congress approve a program for the United States to assist other nations in agricultural progress by offering U.S. know-how on irrigation, pesticides, and farm equipment to less developed nations. Congress adopted this program and the president signed the bill into law on November 12.

## November 13, 1966

### Israel launches a large-scale reprisal attack on Jordan. The United States later votes to censure Israel in the United Nations.

During 1965–1966, tensions increased on the Syrian-Israeli border as Syria's new radical government under Premier Salah el-Bitar sent Arab guerrillas across the border, causing the Israelis to retaliate. In addition, a Palestinian group, al-Fatah, operated from bases in Lebanon and Jordan to raid Israel. On August 15, Syria and Israel had a serious conflict at Lake Tiberias using planes, tanks, and patrol boats.

On November 13, Israel launched extensive reprisal attacks on the Jordanian towns of al-Samu, Jimba, and Khirbet Karkoy. Jordan appealed to the United Nations, where the Security Council voted to censure Israel. President Johnson also sent military aid to bolster the army of Jordan's King Hussein. Jordan had generally been pro-Western in its policies, but the increase of Palestinian refugees and the al-Fatah Party made it difficult for Hussein to restrain these guerrilla raids on Israel.

# 1 9 6 7

## January 15, 1967

### President Johnson sends Eugene Rostow on a world mission to persuade other nations to help alleviate India's food problems.

Although the United States had supplied wheat shipments to India on various occasions after 1947, including the U.S.-India agreement of December 7, 1965, Johnson believed nations other than the United States should develop responsibility to assist India.

When India appealed to the president for wheat in March 1966, he sent a small amount but decided to restrict the shipments to the "must" requirements, while encouraging India to ask other nations for aid. To emphasize his point, Johnson held up some shipments of wheat between August and December 1966. Some observers criticized him for this policy but Johnson persisted.

By mid-December, Australia and Canada each provided 150,000 tons of wheat for India; other nations did not. The French, in particular, irritated Johnson because they offered only to sell 200,000 tons at the "usual commercial terms."

To get his message more directly to other nations, Johnson asked George Woods, president of the World Bank, to talk with other nations about aid to India. On January 15, he sent Eugene Rostow, the undersecretary of state, on a round-the-world mission to solicit greater assistance. Eventually in 1967, other governments helped India including Canada, Australia, the Soviet Union, Britain, France, West Germany, Japan, Belgium, Austria, and the Scandinavian countries. With this additional aid India obtained nearly 10 million tons of wheat in 1967. During 1965 and 1966, the United States alone had sent 8 million tons and 6 million tons, respectively.

This aid from 1965 to 1967 and India's new agricultural program—the "green revolution"—increased food supplies considerably after 1967. Unfortunately, India's subsequent large population increase outran its food increase in Malthusian fashion.

### January 26, 1967

**Secretary of Defense McNamara informs a senate committee of U.S. nuclear strategy: the concept of mutual assured destruction (MAD) is evolved.**

On January 26, McNamara's testimony before the Senate Armed Services Committee was made public. He indicated that the Soviets had "faster-than-expected" built up their ICBM force and deployed an antiballistic-missile defense (ABM) around Moscow. Although the secretary stated that the United States would presently have superiority by three times in the number of ICBMs until the early 1970s, the Soviets were catching up and their ABM program represented a new menace the United States should meet.

McNamara said the U.S. nuclear strategy needed two basic capabilities:

1. *'Assured destruction'* as a deterrent. To absorb a surprise first strike and be able to inflict an "unacceptable degree of damage" on any combination of aggressors;
2. *'Damage limitation'* ability to restrict destruction of the U.S. population and industry. This required a build up of America's ABM missiles—the Nike-X program.

Secretary of Defense Robert McNamara. National Archives

Together these strategic goals would achieve a state of mutual assured destruction (MAD) that would be a strong deterrent against the use of nuclear weapons. "U.S. fatalities from a Soviet first strike could total about 120 million; even after absorbing that attack, we could inflict on the Soviet Union more than 120 million fatalities." With an American ABM system, the increase in the Soviet ICBM system would give it a second-strike ability to kill some 120 million Americans.

Because both sides would spend money—the United States on ABMs; the Soviets on ICBMs—it seemed in both nations' interests that negotiation should permit each to save money. Thus, McNamara wanted to talk with Moscow about an ABM limitation. Meanwhile, he urged that the Nike-X program be continued until an agreement was reached.

## January 27, 1967

### The United States, the Soviet Union, and 58 other countries sign the Outer Space Treaty.

This treaty embodied a variety of potential outer space contingencies that the signatories agreed to follow including the following: no nation can claim sovereignty over a celestial body such as the moon or planets; outer space will not be used for military purposes; astronauts or equipment forced to land on foreign territory will be returned; the launching country is liable for damage by its rockets, satellites, or space vehicles. The most notable of the clauses in this treaty was the agreement to prohibit weapons of war in outer space.

This treaty formalized a resolution of October 1963 in which the U.N. General Assembly called on all nations to avoid placing nuclear weapons in orbit around the earth. At that time, both the United States and the USSR independently declared that they would abide by the U.N. resolution. On April 25, 1967, the U.S. Senate ratified the treaty unanimously.

## February 14, 1967

### In Mexico City, 14 Latin American nations sign the Treaty of Tlatelolco: A treaty calling for denuclearization.

The Cuban missile crisis of October 1962 provided the catalyst for the Latin American Nuclear-Free Zone (NFZ) initiative. Costa Rica had presented the idea of a NFZ to the Council of the Organization of American States in 1958 and Brazil joined Bolivia, Chile, and Ecuador in introducing a similar proposal to the U.N. General Assembly in November 1962. Mexico, however, took the lead in the subsequent protracted negotiations between 1964 and 1967. By 1969, 11 nations had ratified the treaty, and by 1992 there were 23 full parties to the agreement.

## February 14, 1967

### British Prime Minister Wilson's attempt to reconvene the Geneva Conference on Vietnam is not successful.

During the fall and winter of 1966–1967, Wilson and U.S. President Johnson agreed that Washington would stabilize its bombing activity while the prime minister persuaded Soviet Premier Alexsey Kosygin to invite participants in the 1954 Geneva talks to reconvene and resolve the Vietnam War. In addition, other tactics were used to seek negotiations with Hanoi.

Initially, in October and November, Ambassador Lodge and Janusz Lewandowski, the Polish delegate on the International Control Commission, conducted talks to arrange meetings in Warsaw between U.S. and North Vietnamese delegates. On December 6, 1966, U.S. delegates waited in Warsaw but the North Vietnamese never showed up, saying they refused because the United States had bombed targets near Hanoi on December 4.

On February 8, 1967, Johnson wrote a personal letter to Ho Chi Minh and also ordered a halt to the bombing as part of a Tet holidays general truce arrangement. The North Vietnamese never responded to Johnson's request for direct talks with Ho Chi Minh.

Throughout this period, Harold Wilson contacted Kosygin, inviting him to London for discussion of various matters including Vietnam. The Soviet premier agreed and visited London early in February 1967. Wilson's plans did not succeed. Johnson wanted Hanoi to stop sending supplies to the South before a bombing halt; Ho Chi Minh demanded that the bombing stop while there was only a partial cessation of supplies reaching the South. Wilson blamed Johnson for requiring too much in order to achieve peace, growing dismayed by the president's intransigence. Subsequently, there was a diplomatic misunderstanding between London and Washington about Johnson's minimum requirements.

Johnson extended the Tet truce until February 13, but Wilson and Kosygin could find no grounds for an agreement between Hanoi and Washington. On February 14, Johnson ordered the renewal of the bombing of North Vietnam.

## February 22, 1967

### President Johnson escalates the Vietnamese air war.

After the Tet truce failed on February 14, 1967, Johnson decided to take more vigorous action against North Vietnam. Thus, on February 22, he approved the JCS plan for the aerial mining of North Vietnam's waterways (except Haiphong Harbor) and authorized Rolling Thunder attacks on the Thai Nguyen Iron and Steel Works near Hanoi.

The USS *Kitty Hawk*, with A-4 Skyhawks on its deck, on "Yankee Station" in the Gulf of Tonkin. National Archives

The aerial mining began on February 27, 1967; the attack on the iron-steel complex was made on March 10, 1967.

### March 20, 1967

**At Guam, President Johnson learns about South Vietnam's new constitution and discusses nonmilitary problems with Ky and Thieu.**

At their first meeting on March 20, Johnson received a copy of the Vietnamese constitution that had been finalized by the constituent assembly the night before in Saigon. The document was patterned on the U.S. government, having a president, Senate, and House of Representatives. Ky told Johnson there would be a "popularly chosen government" selected later in the year. Most of the Guam sessions were spent discussing Vietnam's economy and such matters as inflation, black markets, corruption, land reform, and food supplies. Johnson said he would send former Tennessee Valley Authority (TVA) Chief David E. Lilienthal to aid the Vietnamese economists and planners.

The only military matter discussed was the need for regular South Vietnamese army units to make a greater effort to provide security for the hamlets and villages that U.S.-directed pacification teams helped to rid of Communist guerrilla units. Whether President Johnson and his advisers realized the full implication of this shortcoming is not clear. This involved the relationship between South Vietnamese army leaders and the local populace, which was seldom a beneficent relationship. It also related to the manner in which the generals of the four corps areas elected to use, or not use, the army forces at their command. This is where corruption thrived and the local populace suffered. Consequently, villagers resented the South Vietnamese soldiers and many joined the Vietcong.

As General Westmoreland told President Johnson in 1967, the Communists continued successfully to recruit southerners to their ranks, enabling the Vietcong to replace their losses faster than the U.S. attrition tactics killed the Vietcong. There is no evidence that Johnson ever asked: How could this be if democracy was progressing so well?

### April 21, 1967

**A military coup in Greece overthrows the king. Konstantinos Kollias becomes prime minister of Greece.**

The king of Greece, Constantine, went into exile in Rome on December 14, 1967.

### May 19, 1967

**McNamara recommends that military escalation of the Vietnam War cease and greater attention be given to the political and economic problems of South Vietnam.**

McNamara's lengthy memo of May 19 reflected the growing division between the JCS and the Defense Department on the methods to be used in South Vietnam. The split between the civilian and military groups in the U.S. defense establishment was an argument not between hawks and doves but about the proper strategic goods and methods to be used in Vietnam. Both groups wanted to defeat the insurgents and protect South Vietnam. They divided on the war's limitations, as correlated with America's specific objectives in Vietnam.

In 1967, McNamara believed the air attacks on the North had not been effective. He did believe, however, that the basic U.S. goal in the South was attained because America had prevented the fall of South Vietnam to communism. Now, McNamara contended, the United States should continue to protect the South militarily but attention must be given to the precise means for gaining a strong, viable government in Saigon that could win the "hearts and minds" of the South Vietnamese. Until this objective was achieved that nation would always be threatened by revolution. Military solutions could not achieve this goal because political problems required different methods.

The JCS solidly opposed McNamara, never fully understanding the Clausewitzian principle of war for political ends. The U.S. armed forces wanted more planes, troops, and military authority to force North Vietnam to permit the creation of an independent non-Communist South Vietnam. The military wanted more bombing targets and another 100,000 men during the spring of 1967.

Thus by May 1967, the conflicting objectives and methods in South Vietnam intensified friction between McNamara and the JCS. Although McNamara was supported by McGeorge Bundy, William Bundy, the CIA's senior analysts, and the Pentagon's Systems Analysis Team, the president deferred to the military, making the secretary's position difficult.

McNamara's May 19 memo intended to provide a detailed argument favoring the program of the civilians in the Defense Department. Using data prepared by Alain Enthoven's computer systems office, the memo showed that each troop escalation yielded fewer results. Assuming the "body-kill" counts were accurate, 100,000 added soldiers would kill 431 enemies each week, a rate that would require 10 years to gain complete surrender. Errors of assumption in the system would, the report said, make the time longer.

Computer data also showed that the Rolling Thunder attacks achieved few results. The air raids on POL targets, Hanoi, and communication links to China had cost heavy losses of men and matériel but yielded no long-term results. In addition, the North Vietnamese will to survive increased as bombing attacks increased. Thus, more bombs would be counterproductive in forcing Hanoi to surrender.

On the positive side, McNamara wanted to step up the pacification program in South Vietnam. Counterinsurgency, he said, meant building a viable economy and government, not laying waste to the country. The army's attrition tactics were exactly those that could not win in the South. If there were a ceiling on U.S. troop additions, Westmoreland and the U.S. military would have to use forces more efficiently as well as strive to pacify South Vietnam. If American troops were used passively, the government and army of South Vietnam could have a greater role in maintaining their own security. Perhaps the South Vietnamese army could learn to be as effective as the South Korean forces, which had been known for their fighting ability since 1953.

Finally, McNamara argued that stabilizing U.S. troop levels would bring an economic benefit to South Vietnam. Inflation in South Vietnam was 20% during the first quarter of 1967, and those figures seemed ready to increase. The unstable economy handicapped Thieu's government, the secretary said.

Therefore, for economic, political, and military reasons, the May 19 program proposed new approaches to this war. First, it asked for 30,000 more troops that would become the maximum for U.S. combat forces. Second, it proposed concentrating all air attacks between the 17th and 20th parallels to interdict troops and supplies entering the South. Finally, and crucially, McNamara wanted a broadly based representative government set up in Saigon, committed to economic and social reforms to win the people's loyalty. This political phase of the war had to be won while the limited U.S. troops prevented a Communist victory. These methods would secure

South Vietnam's peace and contain communism north of the 17th parallel.

McNamara's memo of May 19 was considered a bureaucratic declaration of war by the JCS and Westmoreland. To counterattack the civilians, the JCS turned to their main supporters: the president, Congress, and especially the Preparedness Subcommittee of the Senate Armed Forces Committee.

See August 25, 1967.

---

**May 23, 1967**

**President Johnson charges that Egypt's blockade of the Gulf of Aqaba violates international law; he reaffirms Eisenhower's 1957 commitment to keep the Strait of Tiran open to Aqaba.**

A Middle East crisis had been brewing for nearly a year. On November 13, 1966, the Israelis made a large reprisal raid on Jordan. On April 7, 1967, the Syrians and Israelis had a border skirmish. Subsequently, Damascus urged Egypt's Nasser to assist it against their common enemy.

To show his solidarity with Syria, Nasser asked the U.N. forces to leave Sharm el Sheikh at the mouth of the Gulf of Aqaba. The multinational U.N. force had been in the Sinai area since 1956 as part of the agreement that ended the Suez crisis. U.N. Secretary-General U. Thant decided to withdraw and Egyptian troops entered the area. At the same time Nasser warned Israel that if it attacked Syria, Egypt would enter the conflict. To further pressure Israel, Nasser announced on May 22 that Israeli ships could no longer pass through the Strait of Tiran leading to the Israeli port of Aqaba.

In Washington on May 22, Johnson asked both Israel and Egypt to maintain the peace. To emphasize the U.S. concern, Johnson received a message from Eisenhower on his commitment to Israel regarding the Gulf of Aqaba. After this meeting, Johnson declared that the United States had been pledged to keep the port of Aqaba open. Egypt, he said, must cease its illegal blockade.

Johnson took two other steps to avert a conflict. On May 31, the United States asked the U.N. Security Council to appeal to all parties in the Middle East to use diplomacy to resolve the dispute. Both the Arabs and the Soviet Union opposed this resolution.

When the United Nations could not act, Johnson accepted the British suggestion that a multilateral naval force assemble and move through the Strait of Tiran. When other nations doubted the value of this tactic, the United States and Britain sought to obtain a pledge from Egypt to permit all neutral flags to carry goods to Israel at Aqaba. Egypt refused, but so did Israel. Tel Aviv's government wanted its right to free passage without strings. Israel agreed, however, to give the United States two weeks to work out a settlement. War seemed imminent, sooner or later.

See June 5, 1967.

---

**May 30, 1967**

*Civil war begins in Nigeria as Biafra, the eastern region of the nation, proclaims independence under Lt. Col. Odomegwu Ojukwa.*

The war ended on January 15, 1970, when Biafran rebels agreed to surrender.

---

**June 5, 1967**

*Israeli forces launch air attacks on airfields in Egypt, Iraq, Syria, and Jordan; then Israeli infantry attacks on three fronts: the Six-Day War.*

Although President Johnson was still attempting to organize a multinational naval force to keep the port of Aqaba open and to persuade the United Nations to approve a resolution on the right of innocent passage in the Strait of Tiran, the Israeli cabinet on June 3 secretly voted for war and launched its attack on June 5.

The Israeli campaign was highly successful. In three days, the Israelis overran the Gaza Strip and most of the Sinai peninsula, including Sharm el Sheik. In the east, they captured the west bank of the Jordan River and the part of Jerusalem that Israel had not taken over in the 1949 war. In the northeast, they occupied the strategic Golan Heights on the Syrian border. Having accomplished its objectives, Israel agreed to a cease-fire on June 11.

See June 6, 1967.

## June 5, 1967

**Soviet Premier Alexsey Kosygin calls President Johnson regarding the Middle East War: The first use of the hot line in a crisis.**

At 7:57 A.M., Secretary of Defense Robert McNamara called Johnson to inform him that the hot line was being activated for a call from Moscow. This special line had been installed on August 30, 1963, but was previously used only for tests and to exchange New Year's greetings.

On June 5, trouble arose because the communications line from the Pentagon to the Situation Room of the White House failed to operate. McNamara had to find a technician to repair this defect while Chairman Kosygin waited on the Kremlin end.

Fortunately, the line was repaired so that Kosygin and Johnson could agree to work for a cease-fire. Johnson was to exert influence on Israel; Kosygin, on Syria and Egypt. Thus, both leaders agreed on the necessity to settle the dispute.

In addition, Johnson informed Kosygin that the Egyptian charge that a U.S. carrier aircraft helped Israel was not true. Because the Soviet navy had intelligence-gathering ships in the eastern Mediterranean, Kosygin knew that Egypt's claims were false. Johnson asked the Soviet chairman to explain this to Cairo.

## June 6, 1967

**The U.N. Security Council passes Resolution 234, demanding a cease-fire in the Middle Eastern War.**

Although Egypt and Jordan agreed immediately to the cease-fire, Syria and Israel did not. Finally, on June 9, Syria accepted a cease-fire and the United States had to pressure Israel to do likewise. Tel Aviv agreed to do so on June 11, and the six-day war ended in victories for Israel. The postwar details now had to be dealt with in the United Nations because Resolution 234 did not state what the boundaries would be following the cease-fire.

During the final efforts to get Israel and Syria to accept a cease-fire on June 9–11, Johnson and Kosygin again used the hot line to keep one another appraised of developments. Both Israel and Syria were prepared to accept the cease-fire, but their mutual mistrust prevented either from quickly agreeing to an effective halt in the fighting. At 3 a.m. on June 10, the cease-fire

seemed to have been accepted. It was not fully implemented, however, until June 11.

## June 8, 1967

**An Israeli gunboat mistakenly torpedoes an American naval communications ship, *The Liberty*. Using the Moscow "hot line," Johnson tells Kosygin that U.S. carrier planes were flying only to investigate the incident.**

*The Liberty* was in international waters when torpedoed by an Israeli ship. This occurred early in the morning, but not until 11 A.M. did the Israelis report that their gunboat had attacked in error and offer their apologies.

To avoid confusion when the incident was first announced, Johnson phoned Kosygin to tell him why U.S. carrier planes were present off the Sinai coast. Earlier, on June 5, Egypt had falsely charged that U.S. carrier planes had participated in the attacks on Arab airfields. Johnson wanted the Soviets to know exactly what U.S. aircraft were doing on June 8.

## June 9, 1967

**Arab oil ministers declare an oil embargo against Britain and France for assisting Israel in the Six-Day War.**

This was the first political oil boycott by the Arab oil states. The boycott was short-lived, ending immediately after Israel defeated Egypt, Syria, and Jordan between June 6 and 11, 1967. But it indicated a possible future boycott of more serious consequences in case of political problems in the Middle East. Western Europe was dependent on the Middle East for 20% of its oil needs.

## June 17, 1967

**China explodes its first hydrogen bomb.**

## June 25, 1967

**President Johnson and Premier Kosygin conclude meetings at Glassboro, New Jersey, with no specific results.**

The Glassboro meetings took place because the Soviet leader visited the United Nations to support the Arab cause in discussions following the Six-Day War of June 5–11, 1967. Desiring to arrange future talks on nuclear arms limitations, Johnson asked Kosygin to visit the White House. The Soviets did not wish to go to Washington because such a visit might be misconstrued by the Arabs. Therefore, Johnson arranged for the use of the home of the president of Glassboro State College in New Jersey.

The sessions lasted for two days, with many warm feelings exchanged but no specific agreements. Johnson wanted to set dates for disarmament talks; Kosygin wanted the United States to qualify some of its strong support for Israel and to compromise on Middle Eastern problems. Thus, except for the fact that the two leaders learned to better appreciate each other's positions, the Glassboro meeting accomplished little.

### August 25, 1967

**The Senate Armed Forces Committee supports the JCS, strongly opposes McNamara's ideas, and blames Johnson for not using the "unanimous weight of professional military judgment."**

Following a June 1, 1967, rebuttal of Secretary McNamara's May 19 report, the Joint Chiefs, led by Chief of Staff General Earle G. WHEELER and U.S. Commander, Pacific Vice Admiral U.S.C. Sharp Jr., contacted their friend Senator John Stennis, who chaired the Senate Armed Services Committee. Stennis arranged secret committee hearings between August 9 to 25 to review the military aspects of the Vietnam War.

Wheeler and Sharp presented the JCS views on the war. They admitted the air war was not effective but blamed this on Johnson's bombing restrictions. They wanted the air targets enlarged and to be permitted to make the U.S. air presence felt over Hanoi and Haiphong. They gave the subcommittee a list of 57 targets that should be bombed in North Vietnam.

Although McNamara testified on behalf of his proposals, the Stennis report was a foregone conclusion. The senators could not comprehend Enthoven's computer analysis or differentiate between attrition and counterinsurgency strategy. As usual, the Armed Services Committee gave the military what they wanted. The Stennis Report, which came after the hearings ended on August 25, reflected that attitude. It urged Johnson to end his restriction on troops and bombing targets. Most surprising, it attacked the president, their fellow Democrat, for not following the

opinion and recommendations of military experts. Because Johnson cherished the support of the generals and the Senate, the president and Secretary McNamara had reached the parting of the ways.

See November 2, 1967, and November 28, 1967.

### September 3, 1967

**The South Vietnamese presidential election is won by the Thieu-Ky slate, although the election is not well conducted.**

Unlike the 1966 election for the constituent assembly, the election for control of the government was managed by Ky and Thieu to keep the "delicate balance" that the military junta had established during the summer of 1965. The constituent assembly had designated 12 candidates for the presidency, one for each political faction in the assembly. Only Ky and Thieu seemed capable of winning, but a problem developed because both wished to be president. South Vietnam's military commanders met to resolve the conflict, persuading Ky to be a vice presidential candidate, while Thieu became their presidential nominee.

The campaign and election were considered by most observers in South Vietnam to be a farce. Two of the 12 assembly nominees could not run: one, because he advocated a neutrality agreement with North Vietnam; the other, Big Minh, was in exile. An effort to get the eight civilian candidates to unite against Ky and Thieu did not succeed.

Thus, Thieu's victory on September 3 was no surprise. The surprise was his campaign manager's ineptness in stuffing the ballot boxes. In Saigon, where U.S. observers congregated, Ky and Thieu ran poorly. As a result, their advocates stuffed thousands of ballots into the boxes after the polls closed. Following the election, the eight losing candidates accused Thieu of fraud and tried to invalidate the vote. Before 1967 ended, however, Thieu retaliated by imprisoning 20 of his leading political, religious, and labor opponents. Any political opponents who refused to accept Thieu's presidency suffered a similar fate after 1967.

Despite the fraudulent election, Thieu provided a semblance of political order in South Vietnam, and order was what Johnson preferred. Political calm and a lack of coups d'état in Saigon had become equated with a politically sound government. Thieu's system did not, however, encourage the South Vietnamese to vigorously support anticommunism as a way of life. Rather, it spawned apathy, immorality, and corruption in South Vietnam—which answered the question often asked by U.S. reporters: "Why don't our Vietnamese fight as well as the Communist Vietnamese?"

### September 29, 1967

**President Johnson says the United States will stop bombing North Vietnam when the Communists accept "productive discussions" for peace: the San Antonio formula.**

During the summer of 1967, demonstrations to stop the U.S. bombing intensified in the United States and Europe, eventually culminating in the protest of 500,000 in Washington, D.C., on October 21.

In a speech to the National Legislative Conference on September 29, Johnson publicly announced a proposal which he had privately agreed to with French intermediaries during August 1967. In July, two Frenchmen, Herbert Marcovich, a scientist, and Raymond Aubrac, who knew Ho Chi Minh, returned from Hanoi with news that Hanoi would negotiate as soon as the U.S. bombing ended. The Frenchmen contacted Henry Kissinger, then a Harvard professor and adviser to the governor of New York, Nelson Rockefeller, asking him to find out if Washington would accept Hanoi's offer. Johnson agreed that the United States would halt the bombing if "productive discussions" followed and if North Vietnam agreed not to build up its forces and supplies during the truce. To persuade Hanoi that the French delegates were authentic representatives, Johnson informed Kissinger that the two men could inform Hanoi that the United States was reducing its bombing in the Hanoi area as a signal of Washington's intent.

The effort of the two Frenchmen failed. On August 24, Johnson learned that Hanoi would not renew visas for Marcovich and Aubrac. Later, Hanoi's delegation at Paris informed the two Frenchmen that there could be no negotiations until the United States stopped bombing and removed its forces from Vietnam.

Subsequently, Johnson decided to announce publicly the formula that he had previously given to the two Frenchmen, although he did not mention the French effort during the San Antonio speech. While observers in September thought Johnson had made a new proposal, it was one that Hanoi had already rejected.

### October 9, 1967

*Reports from Bolivia are that Che Guevara has been killed by Bolivian troops.*

Che, who symbolized the radical, Castro-type of Communist reform for Latin America, had been leading guerrillas in Bolivia against the government when he was reported to have been killed. While the initial stories of Che's death appeared dubious, they were later confirmed.

### October 12, 1967

**Rusk says America's vital interest in Vietnam is due to the danger of the Chinese acquiring nuclear weapons.**

Rusk had previously told the journalists that the United States was in Vietnam to "defend our vital national interests." Because the Johnson administration often used this term but never defined it, Jon Finney of the *New York Times* asked Rusk what the United States had at stake in Vietnam.

Rusk referred to the future threat of China, saying Beijing had nominated itself as an enemy by proclaiming a "militant doctrine of the world revolution." Beijing had inspired the Vietnamese to engage in the war against the South.

Rusk's words surprised many U.S. commentators. Most leading Far Eastern scholars in academies and in the Far East Section of the State Department did not see China as a menace. Beijing's leaders always passionately denounced the Western powers, but Mao Tsetung usually acted with caution.

Rusk appeared to be intentionally raising the specter of the Chinese threat. However, if China were truly the enemy, then wasting U.S. resources in Vietnam would appear to be nonsense. The United States should have been planning responses to the Chinese threat, not Hanoi. Rusk seemed therefore simply to be repeating the anti-Chinese rhetoric that had been popular among the Right in the United States since 1949.

### November 2, 1967

**Johnson confers with the "wise men" regarding McNamara and the Vietnam War strategy.**

President Johnson assembled this group of advisers for a White House meeting because he faced

McNamara's opposition to his plan to escalate the war. Following the Stennis Report of August 25, 1967, Johnson decided in October to increase U.S. forces by 45,000, compared with McNamara's recommendation for 30,000 and the JCS's desire for 100,000. More important, Johnson rejected the secretary of defense's proposal to place a ceiling on future force increases. He also ordered Rolling Thunder to target 52 of the 57 targets listed by the JCS for the Stennis Committee.

On October 31, McNamara discussed his opposition to the JCS with Johnson and prepared a memo that essentially summarized the arguments and proposals made on May 19, 1967. McNamara recommended a troop ceiling and suggested a cut in bombing raids coupled with a truce appeal to Hanoi. Finally, he asked for a study of military operations to reduce U.S. casualties and to persuade South Vietnam's army to assume more responsibility for self-defense.

The "wise men" met with Johnson to discuss McNamara's recommendations and future policy in Vietnam. The group included Dean Acheson, George Ball, Maxwell Taylor, and McGeorge Bundy. These advisers believed the war was going well and thought the gradual escalation should continue. They could not accept McNamara's proposal to cut Rolling Thunder because they believed North Vietnam should be ready to surrender soon.

In addition to the wise men, Johnson asked the next Secretary of Defense Clark Clifford and the Associate Justice of the Supreme Court Abe Fortas to comment on the secretary's proposal. They both agreed with Johnson. Significantly, however, none of these men was briefed by McNamara, by Enthoven's systems analysis studies, or by any explanation of the difference between the attrition strategy and counterinsurgency efforts that McNamara made. On the basis of these talks with other advisers, Johnson agreed to have McNamara resign.

See May 19, August 25, and November 28, 1967.

### November 17, 1967

*The U.N. Security Council recommends sanctions against Portugal until it grants independence to its overseas colonies.*

### November 22, 1967

**U.N. Security Council resolution 242 states terms for a long-term solution to the Six-Day War of June 5, 1967.**

From June 11 to November, a variety of proposals to settle the Middle East crisis had been debated in the United Nations. Because the cease-fire agreement did not establish boundaries, the Soviet Union and the Arab nations wanted Israel to withdraw to its borders of June 4, 1967, evacuating the strategic military areas Israeli forces won during the fighting. Backed by the United States, Israel refused to withdraw without long-term security guarantees.

U.N. Resolution 242 was based on suggestions by President Johnson and offered a peace favorable to all parties. It provided for free navigation of international waterways, justice for refugees (i.e., Palestinians), recognition of the sovereignty of all states with secure borders, and withdrawal of Israel from all occupied territories. This resolution, interpreted as an entity by the United States and Israel, reestablished close "special relations" between the two countries The Arab world was critical of the Americans for fully backing Israel against them in the Middle East.

### November 26, 1967

*The People's Republic of South Yemen is proclaimed.*

On November 5, President Sallal of Yemen was deposed and a three-man presidential committee formed. The radical left group had gained power and adopted a Communist style of government, aided by the Soviet Union.

### November 28, 1967

**McNamara resigns but agrees to stay until Clark Clifford can replace him on March 1, 1968.**

Between May 19, when the secretary outlined his detailed recommendations for action in Vietnam, and October 31, when he stated his opposition to the Joint Chiefs, relations between the president and the secretary grew increasingly tense. After meeting with the "wise men" and others in November, Johnson decided to replace the secretary. As Johnson later confessed to his biographer, Doris Kearns (later Doris Kearns Godwin), he once thought McNamara had

Clark Clifford, right, with
Walt W. Rostow. Lyndon
Baines Johnson Library

become a loyal friend. In November, however, the president realized the secretary was too much of a Kennedy man who imbibed Robert Kennedy's dissenting ideas.

On November 28, McNamara tendered his resignation to Johnson, who arranged for him to become the head of the World Bank. Johnson's concern about dropping McNamara continued to haunt him, however. In his memoirs, Johnson says he decided on December 18, 1967, to write himself a special memorandum giving his personal views on McNamara's October 31 proposals. The memo is reproduced in the appendix to Johnson's *The Vantage Point* (1971). While it responds to the secretary's proposals, the memo is notable as evidence that Johnson lacked the imagination necessary to visualize the strategic implications of McNamara's counterinsurgency ideas compared with the military's strategy of attrition.

For McNamara's October 31 views, see
November 2, 1967.

### November 30, 1967

**Senator Eugene McCarthy announces he will be a "peace candidate," seeking the Democratic presidential nomination in 1968.**

Although Senator McCarthy of Minnesota agreed with Senator Fulbright's opposition to Johnson's pol-icy in Vietnam, he had been reluctant to campaign against the president. In November, however, Allard Lowenstein, who headed a group of student dissenters, persuaded McCarthy to run because he could expect 7 million college students to assist in the campaign. Although McCarthy's "children's crusade" enlisted many young people, the senator's amateur politicians were not well organized. McCarthy played one significant role in U.S. politics, however, in the New Hampshire primary.

See March 12, 1968.

### December 1, 1967

***France vetoes the admission of Great Britain into the European Economic Community (Common Market).***

Prior to the British application for Common Market membership on May 11, the question of joining was a controversial political issue in England. France objected to the membership because it wanted Great Britain to end its British Commonwealth trade agreements before being admitted. For the second time, France opposed British membership in Europe's common market (see January 29, 1963).

# 1 9 6 8 _____

### January 16, 1968

*The United Kingdom withdraws its forces from the Persian Gulf and the far east.*

The British government was retreating further from its previous imperial commitments east of Suez, a not unusual decision inasmuch as its east coast African colonies had gained their independence between 1958 and 1967.

### January 23, 1968

**North Korea seizes the USS *Pueblo*, a navy electronic spy ship, in international waters.**

During the night of January 22–23, a North Korean submarine chaser and three patrol boats challenged the *Pueblo* and boarded the U.S. ship with an armed party. North Korea claimed the *Pueblo* was seven miles offshore. According to the *Pueblo*'s commander, the ship was $15\frac{1}{2}$ nautical miles from shore, outside North Korea's 12-mile limit. During the foray, one American was killed and four injured. As a surveillance ship, the *Pueblo* was virtually unarmed and unprotected.

North Korea also took 82 Americans captive. To obtain their release, President Johnson used diplomatic channels. Other U.S. methods were considered by the National Security Council but appeared too risky to the lives of the captives. Although Johnson sent 350 airplanes to bases in South Korea to deter further aggression, he worked through the United Nations, the Kremlin, and other nations to finally obtain the captives' release. It took 11 months to gain the freedom of the *Pueblo*'s officers and crew.

### January 26, 1968

**General Westmoreland's year-end report for 1967 emphasizes the desperation of the Communist enemy in Vietnam.**

Accurately or not, the U.S. commander in Vietnam and the U.S. ambassador to Saigon, Ellsworth Bunker, had been issuing favorable reports. In November 1967, the two leading U.S. figures in South Vietnam had visited Washington to spread the good word about U.S. successes. Before congressional committees and such luncheon groups as the National Press Club, they characterized the Vietnam struggle as near-

ing a victory. According to Westmoreland, the United States would soon "weaken the enemy and strengthen our friends until we have become superfluous." On invitations to the 1967 New Year's Eve party at the embassy in Saigon, the party message read, "Come and see the light at the end of the tunnel," the code words for winning the war.

Just before Westmoreland composed his annual report, the North Vietnamese attacked exactly where the U.S. military preferred, at Khe Sanh on the strategic border between Laos, South Vietnam, and the 17th parallel. Attacking on January 21, the North Vietnamese fought the type of battle favorable to U.S. firepower. In the north, away from urban areas, American forces could exploit their arsenals without concern for endangering the South Vietnamese population.

Thus, Westmoreland's January 26 report reflected an added touch of optimism. He wrote that the enemy was "resorting to desperation tactics" to attain a "military/psychological victory" and had failed in these attempts since October 1967.

From November to January 26, this optimistic news enabled President Johnson to look forward eagerly to the 1968 presidential campaign. However, the euphoria reaped contrary results. Four days after Westmoreland reported, the Communists launched the Tet offensive.

### January 30–31, 1968

**The Tet Offensive begins in South Vietnam.**

In retrospect, the North Vietnamese attack on Khe Sanh on January 20 had been only diversionary. While U.S. forces rushed north to engage the enemy at Khe Sanh, the Communists initiated their Tet offensive farther south. Its initial assaults appeared successful and, thereby, damaged Johnson's credibility for having publicized the recent optimistic reports of U.S. successes.

During the first days of Tet, in its attacks on Saigon the Vietcong hit the U.S. embassy, the Presidential Palace, the South Vietnamese military headquarters, and Saigon's air bases. Although they were supposed to have been subdued, the Vietcong soon appeared to be everywhere. Communist troops overran Vietnam's former capital city and religious centers in Hue and raided 39 provincial capitals and 76 other cities and towns. Unfortunately for North Vietnam's General Giap, the South Vietnamese did

During the Tet offensive, television reports showed the range of fighting to the dismay of many Americans, who had believed that the end of the war was in sight. National Archives

not rise up to join the Communists, as he had believed they would. The southern populace was apathetic to both Communist and American appeals. During Tet, this helped the United States because without their anticipated local support, the Communists had to withdraw or be driven from the cities after February 13.

Giap had miscalculated. Using Mao's doctrine of protracted war, Giap believed the time had come to employ his rural armies to gain control of the urban areas. Tet 1968 was not the time. As a result, the Tet offensive eventually cost the Communists heavily. It made new enemies for Communists in the South, and it caused the loss of 45,000 Communist soldiers and much equipment. Khe Sanh and Hue held out for several weeks until mid-March, but documents captured from Giap's forces showed that Tet failed to meet Giap's basic objectives.

Nevertheless, if Tet proved to be a blow to the Communists, it was also a disaster for the American perspectives on the war. Although the full implications of Tet 1968 may always be controversial, Tet probably paved the way for both

North Vietnam and President Johnson to initiate negotiations.

See January 26, 1968; for the Tet's impact on the United States, see March 25–26 and March 31, 1968.

### March 12, 1968

#### Senator McCarthy nearly defeats President Johnson in the New Hampshire primary.

Senator McCarthy's near victory surprised Johnson and most observers because the "children's crusade" had not been well organized after November 30, 1967. Moreover, Johnson's campaign experts had predicted an easy victory with landslide figures of 70 to 80%. Johnson obtained only 49.5% of the vote to McCarthy's 42.2%. Political pundits interpreted McCarthy's near victory as a blow to the president's Vietnam policy.

### March 16, 1968

#### Senator Robert Kennedy of New York announces he will campaign for the presidential nomination.

In November 1967, some Democratic liberals had urged Kennedy to campaign against Johnson, but he refused. Traditionally, party loyalty ruled that insiders should not challenge an incumbent president, and Kennedy's advisers preferred to wait until 1972. McCarthy's near victory in New Hampshire on March 12 and the disaster that appeared to befall the United States in the Tet offensive of January-February convinced Kennedy that he should challenge the president. Kennedy's candidacy surprised and dismayed Johnson and probably was one factor that influenced the president's decision to withdraw as a nominee on March 31.

### March 25–26, 1968

#### Johnson meets with the "wise men" to decide future policy in Vietnam following the Tet débâcle.

North Vietnam's Tet offensive, Eugene McCarthy's near victory in New Hampshire, and Robert Kennedy's announced candidacy left President Johnson in a quandary. The JCS wanted more troops and more extensive bombing in Vietnam, while a report by the new secretary of defense, Clark Clifford, sought a compromise. Finally, economic

President Johnson's "Wise Men" (left to right, clockwise): Johnson, Secretary Robert McNamara, Secretary Henry Fowler, McGeorge Bundy, Dean Acheson, John Cowles, Arthur Dean, General Omar Bradley, John J. McCloy, Robert Lovett (?), Bill Bundy (?), George Ball, Secretary Dean Rusk. Lyndon Baines Johnson Library, photo by Yoichi Okamoto

problems over taxes and an unfavorable trade balance added to Johnson's problems. To help him decide on a course of action, Clifford persuaded the president to convene the "wise men," his trusted advisers from outside the bureaucracy.

The Tet offensive had been quelled by mid-March, but its psychological effects on the American public had been disastrous. The optimistic reports of Westmoreland and Bunker at the end of 1967 had led Americans to believe Communists were nearly wiped out. Tet demonstrated that Communist fighting capabilities remained substantial. Johnson compounded this problem because two days after the Tet offensive began, he asserted that the U.S. military had prior knowledge of the attacks and would immediately counterattack. His analysis was wrong. For the next 10 days, Communist advances continued and Hue was captured.

Johnson lost the backing of moderates during the Tet offensive. In the newspapers, cartoonists poked fun at the president, depicting him weeping crocodile tears because of destruction in Vietnam. Humorist Art Buchwald wrote a parody of Johnson as General George Custer just before the Little Big Horn massacre; Custer (Johnson) asserted: "We have the Sioux on the run," because the battle "had just turned the corner" and he could see "the light at the end of the tunnel." Of course, the massacre of Custer's men followed.

There were other causes of U.S. disillusionment in Vietnam. A U.S. army major at Ben Tri remarked: "It became necessary to destroy the town to save it." *Life* magazine published the gruesome picture of Saigon's police chief shooting a Vietcong prisoner in cold blood on the street. The president's press secretary claimed that Walter Cronkite, America's most prominent TV news anchorman, had turned against Johnson when he stated "we weren't winning the war," despite Johnson's statements to the contrary. Reportedly Johnson remarked, "Well, if I've lost Cronkite, I've lost Middle America."

Unlike Cronkite, the military officers' reaction to Tet was to seek fewer restraints on their battle tactics. As early as February 3, the JCS asked Johnson to give air force commanders complete authority to select targets. Generals Wheeler and Westmoreland wanted 206,000 additional troops as well as the mobilization of all military reserves.

Wheeler's mobilization request alarmed Johnson. The president knew the difference between a limited containment action and an all-out World War II–type war. He was never prepared to support the latter in South Vietnam because that nation was not that vital to the United States. Thus, as previously, Johnson rejected proposals to call up the National Guard and reserve units. Wheeler's request so disturbed Johnson that he asked Secretary of Defense Designate Clifford to organize a committee to study the problem "from A to Z."

The Clifford Committee's report of March 4 further startled the president. Unlike McNamara, who the president believed had been tainted with Kennedy's influence, Clark Clifford was a longtime Washington friend of Johnson. In November, Clifford had counseled Johnson to follow his own policy, not McNamara's. Yet between November and March, Clifford changed his perspective on Vietnam.

Looking back later, Clifford remembered that his first doubts about U.S. policy in Vietnam had been planted during the summer of 1967. During a trip to Asian nations as, Clifford discovered that none of America's allies shared Washington's great fear of communism in Vietnam. His requests for more troops in Vietnam had largely been shunned by the leaders of Australia, New Zealand, Thailand, the Philippines, and South Korea. Each of them sent token forces to South Vietnam only to placate the United States, not because they feared Hanoi's victory. By March 1968, Clifford altered his Vietnam analysis completely, largely because of the Tet offensive, General Wheeler's request for greater military control, and the findings of the policy review board he headed from February 26 to March 4.

During the review, Clifford became familiar with the civilian-military division inside the Pentagon. He talked with and studied the computer data used by McNamara's advisers—Paul Nitze, Paul C. Warnke, and Alain Enthoven. He began to grasp the political dimensions of South Vietnam's problem, realizing that U.S. military strength could not solve the country's internal problems. At the same time, he heard fully the all-out war opinions of Generals Wheeler and Taylor, and National Security Adviser Walter Rostow as they sought full mobilization of U.S. forces.

The Clifford Committee's report of March 4 represented a compromise, not the new attitudes of its chairman. Because it was a composite of the civilian and military proposals, the March 4 report simply made Johnson less certain of how to proceed. While Johnson pondered the report and observed the final defeat of the Communist Tet offensive, he experienced a new crisis during mid-March—an economic one.

Johnson's attempted guns-and-butter economy began to come unhinged by early 1968. In 1967, the president sought an income tax surcharge to finance his programs, but the Democratic leaders in Congress rejected the tax. In January 1968, Johnson again asked Congress for a 10% tax surcharge. This time Southern Democrats, led by Wilbur Mills of the House Committee on Ways and Means, preferred to spend more on the war but less on Johnson's social programs as the best method to cut the budget deficits.

In March, the tax conflict became complicated by the rapid decline in the value of the dollar on the gold market. The U.S. international trade balance had been experiencing trouble since the 1960s. The Kennedy Round of trade and tariff reforms tried to band-aid the problem, but by 1967 the imbalance became more acute. During the last quarter of 1967, U.S. trade imbalances were $7 billion and this trend continued into 1968. The Tet offensive caused a flurry of international speculation, and during the first 10 weeks of 1968, the dollar's value declined on the gold market by $327 million.

To stem the gold dollar decline in March, the United States and its European allies arranged temporary relief by buying dollars to raise their value artificially. Because other "free world" currencies were pegged to the dollar, U.S. economic shortfalls affected the currency and budget of many countries. The instability of the dollar was temporarily rectified in March, but the international financial community informed the United States that it must correct its budget and tax problem. Both the "Great Escalation" and the Great Society were jeopardized by financial problems in 1968.

Johnson's call upon the wise men to meet on March 25 came at a difficult time militarily, diplomatically, economically, and with regard to domestic dissent. Clifford had urged Johnson to consider a bombing halt and negotiations; the wise men, he said, could focus on this issue as the central problem requiring an answer.

Clifford handled the wise men's March meeting discreetly. For their first meeting on March 25, Clifford gave Johnson's advisers a briefing at the State Department. During this session, Clifford familiarized them with detailed computer data prepared by Nitze, Enthoven, and Warnke, as well as with the military proposals of Wheeler and Westmoreland. Their data were updated to reflect the Tet offensive information.

As a result of the March 25 briefing, Johnson's White House meeting with the advisers took a divergent turn on March 26. During a breakfast session, the advisers heard an up-to-date report on Tet by General

Wheeler, who had just flown in from Saigon at 6 A.M. Wheeler was optimistic. Tet had damaged the Communist forces. The South Vietnamese army had fought "commendably." Although Wheeler avoided mentioning his request for full mobilization, which he knew Johnson disliked, he asked for only 13,000 troops to aid the pacification effort. Johnson had already agreed to send an additional 30,000 combat troops.

Following Wheeler's report, General Taylor spoke strongly in favor of escalation of the bombing targets and of providing more combat troops for Vietnam. But Taylor stood almost alone. Most of the wise men told Johnson that a new counterinsurgency strategy was necessary. The military, they believed, had prevented the fall of South Vietnam. Now the United States should stabilize its combat role by emphasizing internal reform in that country. In addition, they said, the political divisions and dissent at home were serious disturbances of national harmony. Although each adviser emphasized different concepts, the same men who backed the military attrition strategy in November now supported the Pentagon civilians who stressed counterinsurgency.

Johnson was distraught. Someone, he said, "had poisoned the well." The men whose opinions Johnson most respected had changed their views, but Johnson could not believe that Tet alone had done this. Clifford later remarked: "The meeting with the Wise Men served the purpose that I hoped it would. It really shook the president."

At first, Johnson was angry. He asked to hear the briefing that the wise men received at the State Department on March 25. He learned they had been fully informed of both the civilian and the military perspectives in the Pentagon. He also learned that his good friend Clark Clifford agreed not with Wheeler but with McNamara.

Johnson was resilient, however. His long political experience permitted him to change his policy.

See October 11, 1962, and March 31, 1968.

### March 31, 1968

**Johnson announces dramatic changes: a bombing halt, a request for North Vietnam to negotiate, his withdrawal as a 1968 presidential candidate.**

Sometime after the "wise men's" meeting of March 25–26, the president decided to salvage what fame he

might as a statesman. Although he never admitted any past errors nor directly proposed the counterinsurgency strategy desired by McNamara and Clifford, he changed the terms of U.S. involvement in Vietnam between March 31, 1968, and January 1969. The change began with a television address on March 31.

The most dramatic part of Johnson's address came last, his decision not to run for reelection. Exactly when Johnson decided not to be a nominee is not certain. In his memoirs, the president said he had decided early after 1964 but waited for the right moment to announce it. Various sources indicate he mentioned retirement between 1965 and 1968. On March 31, Johnson believed his decision to retire would be a special signal of his sincerity in seeking negotiations with Hanoi. The proposal to talk would not be seen as a political tactic.

The other two announcements on March 31 were vital to developments in Vietnam, demonstrating that Johnson had not wavered since 1965 in his determination to fight a limited war there. First, he announced that U.S. aircraft and naval ships would no longer attack North Vietnam except in the "area of the demilitarized zone," that is, between the 17th and 20th parallels. He called on Ho Chi Minh to "respond positively and favorably" by agreeing to negotiate.

Second, the president announced the moderate increase of U.S. troop strength in South Vietnam. This moderate increase (30,000) would protect South Vietnam. Our first priority, Johnson said, would be to improve South Vietnam's ability to defend itself militarily and politically. Although he did not specify this, his statement reflected the counterinsurgency policy that the civilians in the Defense Department had been advocating.

Without saying so, Johnson ended the policy of escalation that governed the years 1965–1968. He privately rejected the JCS's full mobilization plan and retained presidential control of the war to attain political objectives. His subsequent activity in striving to open negotiations with Hanoi indicated both his presidential control and his desire to make certain that North Vietnam did not perceive his March 31 speech as a sign of weakness.

See May 13, 1968.

## April 4, 1968

### Martin Luther King Jr. is assassinated in Memphis, Tennessee.

Dr. King had become the symbol and leading spokesman for the broad moderate group of liberal Americans who sought social justice. Because the Vietnam War siphoned funding from Johnson's social programs and the army drafted a disproportionate number of black youth, King had dissented from Johnson's war policy. His assassination left more radical black American leaders to vie to replace King and his nonviolent methods.

On June 8, 1968, Britain's Scotland Yard arrested James Earl Ray in response to a U.S. request for Ray's extradition for the murder of King. An escaped convict, Ray waived extradition hearings and returned to the United States for questioning. Ray confessed to the crime and was sentenced to life in prison. Later, he recanted his confession, but the courts found no sufficient reason for changing the verdict. He died in prison.

## May 13, 1968

### U.S. and North Vietnamese delegates open discussions in Paris to talk about negotiations.

Although on April 4 North Vietnamese officials denounced Johnson's speech of March 31 as an imperialist plot, they secretly contacted the United States to indicate their willingness to talk. They wanted the United States to stop all bombing and other acts of war, but Johnson refused. Finally, the two sides agreed to talk about conditions for beginning talks. They held their first session at Paris on May 13.

W. Averell Harriman represented the United States at Paris; Xuan Thuy represented North Vietnam. Neither the Vietcong nor the Saigon regime had direct representation.

See October 31, 1968.

## June 5, 1968

### Robert F. Kennedy is assassinated on the day of his presidential primary victory in California.

Kennedy was shot by the Palestinian extremist Sirhan B. Sirhan, who opposed Kennedy's pro-Israel views. Kennedy had become the leading contender for the Democratic presidential nomination. His death left Vice President Hubert Humphrey as the likely nominee.

## June 24, 1968

### Federal troops and police disperse demonstrators in the poor people's campaign.

In order to dissent against Johnson's guns-and-butter policy, which sacrificed the butter, demonstrators moved into Washington to deliver their protest to Congress. Coming just after a series of riots in April that resulted from Martin Luther King's assassination, the poor people's campaign dismayed the president. The "poor people" built a shantytown called Resurrection City on the mall near the Capitol, from which they moved out each day to protest before Congress and at the White House gates. Finally, Johnson and the Washington, D.C., city fathers decided to abolish Resurrection City. They removed the people from the mall and destroyed the shanty homes on June 24. At one time, 50,000 individuals participated in the "poor people's" protest.

## July 1, 1968

### Nuclear Non-Proliferation Treaty signed; United States and Soviet Union discuss nuclear arms limitations.

After negotiations since 1963, the Nuclear Non-Proliferation Treaty (NPT) was signed in the White House by the United States, USSR and Britain and 50 other countries. Later, France and China, two other nuclear powers, also signed the treaty. The major nuclear powers promised to work for nuclear arms control and disarmament; the nonnuclear nations pledged not to obtain nuclear weapons from any nuclear power. In addition, the nuclear powers agreed to assist nonnuclear weapons countries in obtaining nuclear power for peaceful purposes. The U.S. Senate ratified the treaty on March 13, 1969. Details on NPT history are in George Bunn's *Extending the Non-Proliferation Treaty*, a 1994 publication of the American Society of International Law.

Regarding the U.S.-Soviet talks about nuclear arms limitations, President Johnson met with Soviet leader Alexsey Kosygin from June 22 to 25, 1961, to discuss possible negotiations on antiballistic missile systems (ABM), as well as intercontinental ballistic missiles (ICBM). Kosygin, who had been in New York for a UN meeting on the Middle East, was initially uncertain about possible negotiations. Yet on June 30 Kosygin sent Johnson a message that a Soviet broadcast on July 1 would announce that U.S.-Soviet negotiations on arms limitations would be held in the near future. Thus, the same day Johnson signed the NPT, he announced future negotiations on both ABM and ICBM limitations.

On August 19, Ambassador to the United States Anatoly Dobrynin informed Secretary of State Dean Rusk that arms limitation talks could begin on October 15, 1968, and President Johnson could announce his trip to Moscow to inaugurate the arms talks. Unfortunately, Johnson never made the trip. On August 20 at 8:00 A.M., Dobrynin informed Johnson that Warsaw Pact nations, including the USSR, had accepted a Czechoslovak "invitation" to end a "conspiracy" against the Czech "social order." Although Dobrynin's message concluded that the Czech events should not prevent Johnson's October visit nor damage U.S.-Soviet relations, Johnson disagreed. Secretary Rusk informed Dobrynin that the president could not visit Moscow because of Warsaw Pact members' intervention in Czechoslovakia.

The ABM and ICBM limitation negotiations were delayed until Richard Nixon became president. See November 17, 1969.

See August 20, 1968.

## July 1, 1968

### President Thieu accepts responsibility for the conduct of the American CIA's Operation Phoenix to eliminate the Vietcong's leadership infrastructure (VCI).

This project had been designed by the CIA as a means to reduce Vietcong operational ability after the United States had withdrawn its troops. Thieu's officials would arrest and punish captured Vietcong who directed the insurgency efforts in South Vietnam. About 50 U.S. civilian CIA advisers and 600 U.S. military men assisted Thieu's government.

The clandestine Phoenix operations used strong-arm methods to eliminate the Vietcong. Paid informants were recruited, normal search and arrest procedures were avoided, and torture was used to interrogate suspects. There was a large number of killings in the process (see the table at the end of this entry). Other Vietcong suspects were imprisoned or "rallied" to support the Saigon government.

In 1970 information on Phoenix was leaked to American journalists, and the morality of its methods became controversial. Although the White House–CIA view was that the Vietcong were terrorists who deserved their fate, the critics charged that Phoenix methods were not only wrong but also punished or "neutralized" many innocent people. Reporters uncovered a number of gruesome stories of assassination and misinformation that caused persons to be killed because of a grudge or of homes broken into at night. Robert Komer's 1971 study of Phoenix concluded that although 20,000 Vietcong leaders were allegedly killed or otherwise neutralized, the project was a "largely ineffective effort."

Phoenix Operations Against Vietcong, 1968–1971

| Year | Captured | Rallied to Thieu | Killed | Total | % Killed |
|---|---|---|---|---|---|
| 1968 | 11,288 | 2,229 | 2,559 | 15,776 | 16 |
| 1969 | 8,575 | 4,832 | 6,187 | 19,534 | 32 |
| | Sentenced* | | | | |
| 1970 | 6,405 | 7,745 | 8,191 | 22,341 | 37 |
| 1971 (May) | 2,770 | 2,911 | 3,650 | 9,331 | 39 |

*Source*: U.S. House of Representatives, Committee on Government Operations, U.S. Assistance Program in Vietnam, Hearing, 92d Congress, 1st Session, July 15–August 2, 1971, p. 83.
*After January 1970, all Vietcong sentenced to jail were considered "neutralized."

Vietcong/North Vietnamese Assassinations and Abductions, 1957–1972

| Year | Assassinated | Abducted |
|---|---|---|
| 1957–60 | 1,700* | 2,000* |
| 1961 | 1,300* | 1,318 |
| 1962 | 1,118 | 1,118 |
| 1963 | 827 | 1,596 |
| 1964 | 516 | 1,525 |
| 1965 | 305 | 1,730 |
| 1966 | 1,732 | 3,810 |
| 1967 | 3,707 | 5,357 |
| 1968 | 5,389 | 8,759 |
| 1969 | 6,202 | 6,289 |
| 1970 | 5,951 | 6,872 |
| 1971 | 3,573 | 5,006 |
| 1972 | 4,405 | 13,119 |
| Totals | 36,725 | 58,499 |

*Source*: Douglas Pike, *The Viet-Cong Strategy of Terror* (Saigon, 1970), p. 82; Guenter Lewy, *America in Vietnam* (New York: Oxford University Press, 1978), p. 454.
*estimated

## August 20, 1968

### Warsaw Pact forces invade Czechoslovakia: The Brezhnev Doctrine

Although Moscow accepted Alexander Dubček as Czechoslovakia's leader early in 1968, the Soviet Presidium became alarmed by Dubček's reforms during what became known as the "Prague Spring." These reforms included the ending of Communist censorship, the abolishing of the secret police, and the relieving of restrictions on non-Communist political parties. According to Stephen F. Cohen's *Rethinking the Soviet Experience* (1985), Dubcek's "socialism with a human face" resembled Khrushchev's reform program after 1956. In 1964, Leonid Brezhnev and Alexsey Kosygin ousted Khrushchev, abandoned his reforms, and adopted conservative practices including "the preeminent symbol of the past, Stalin himself."

Between 1992 and 1998, the Cold War History Project's *Bulletins* published documents declassified from Communist archives in the Soviet Union, East Germany, Poland, and Ukraine. These documents indicated that Communist leaders in those countries feared Dubček's reforms would spill over into their nations. In addition, reports from hard line Communists in Czechoslovakia alerted Soviet leadership regarding Dubček's "dangerous" reforms. Because the Soviets had few military bases in Czechoslovakia, Brezhnev wanted to place more troops and Soviet controlled nuclear weapons on Czech territory. Previously, Dubček had refused a "temporary deployment" of Soviet forces as part of the Warsaw Pact strategy.

After Dubček rejected several of Brezhnev's offers to compromise, the Soviet leaders decided to invade with 300,000 Soviet and Warsaw Pact troops, excepting Romania. When they invaded on August 20, Warsaw Pact forces easily overcame the Czech defenders. According to the declassified documents, the invading communist forces killed 100 armed Czechoslovakian citizens and seriously wounded 335. In addition, 433 unarmed Czechoslovak civilians were killed, although they were unarmed in opposing the invaders. Warsaw Pact forces experienced only one death from combat, while another 19 were killed in traffic accidents or by "friendly fire."

In addition to delaying the arms limitation talks with the United States, the Soviet invasion heralded the Brezhnev Doctrine, under which the Soviet Union arrogated to itself the right to intervene militarily against any Warsaw Pact socialist state. Between 1968 and 1991, 75,000 to 80,000 Soviet troops remained on Czech soil. In early 1969, Dubcek resigned as Chairman of the Czechoslovakian Communist Party and was replaced by Gustav Husak.

## August 28, 1968

### The Democratic Party convention nominates Hubert Humphrey for president while police fight demonstrators in downtown Chicago.

While the Democratic Party divided seriously on foreign policy during the convention, 11,900 Chicago police, 7,500 members of the Illinois National Guard, and about 1,000 FBI and Secret Service agents tried to protect the delegates and the city from radical groups. For several days before and during the convention, police had tried to subdue and disperse the Students for a Democratic Society (SDS), the Youth International Party (YIPPES), and other dissident groups that made Chicago a focal point of protest against the war in Vietnam.

The protests climaxed on August 28, the same day Humphrey was nominated for president. In Grant Park and at the Michigan Avenue Hilton Hotel, demonstrators and police clashed with tear gas, clubs, rocks, and waterbags dropped from hotel windows. Television scenes of the riots were interspersed with Humphrey's nomination scenes at Convention Hall. The rioters were kept away from the convention by a mile-square chain link fence topped by barbed wire. Convention delegates were screened by an electronic pass system.

Inside the convention from August 26 to 28, the groups opposing Johnson's Vietnam policy lost their attempt to have an antiwar plank agreed upon by the delegates, but they issued a minority statement. The official platform backed Johnson's policy, opposing a complete bombing halt and promising a Vietnam government chosen by "free election." The minority groups advocated the unconditional end of the war, halting all bombing, and forming a coalition government in Saigon that would include the Vietcong. Although the minority was led by Senator George McGovern and Senator Edward Kennedy, they did not support another person for president.

Right-wing Democrats did run another candidate in the Dixiecrat style of 1948. Governor George

Wallace of Alabama formed the American Independent Party.

See November 5, 1968.

### October 5–6, 1968

*Violence begins in Northern Ireland with riots in Londonderry by Catholics demanding civil rights from the Protestant government.*

Although the government of Northern Ireland instituted some reforms on November 22, tensions increased. The provisional Irish Republican Army of the Catholics began fighting the Protestants under the Rev. Ian Paisley on November 30. These riots and virtual civil war continued into 1969.

See July 20, 1982.

### October 9, 1968

*Peru nationalizes the International Petroleum Corporation, a subsidiary of Exxon.*

Peru expropriated the property of Exxon and filed a claim against the U.S. oil company for $690 million in past excess profits.

U.S. relations with Peru had been deteriorating throughout 1968. On May 16, the State Department suspended economic aid to Peru after that government spent $20 million to purchase military jet planes from France. Washington claimed that its military aid legislation required a cutoff of aid if a developing nation used funds to purchase military equipment.

Anti-American rioting began in Peru during the period from June to September, ending in the overthrow of President Belaunde's government by a military junta headed by General Juan Alvardo Velasco. The new regime decreed the nationalization of the International Petroleum Corporation.

### October 31, 1968

*The United States and North Vietnam agree to conduct formal negotiations for peace; President Johnson halts all bombing in North Vietnam; Hanoi agrees to stop rocket attacks and raids on cities in South Vietnam.*

From May 13 to October 30, Johnson's personal representative Averell Harriman and North Vietnamese diplomat Xuan Thuy pursued a joint process of formal and secret talks to try to arrange a cease-fire and the beginning of formal truce agreements.

Unofficially, these talks were opposed by the Joint Chiefs of Staff (JCS) in Washington and Thieu's government in Saigon, both of whom thought that discussions and any bombing restrictions benefited Hanoi. President Johnson tended to support the JCS view that Thieu had to be satisfied and grow stronger. Harriman and the Democratic presidential nominee, Hubert Humphrey, wanted a more complete turnaround in U.S. policy, hoping for a return to the divided Vietnam of 1954. They believed the first steps in this process were to stop the bombing, start negotiations, and move to a complete cease-fire in Vietnam.

Until October 15 Johnson would not accept any concession in addition to those he had made on March 31. The talks had become stymied by October, indicating that Johnson would not end his administration on a positive note unless he agreed to halt the bombing. To accomplish this, Harriman got Hanoi to agree that Thieu's government could have a direct role in the peace negotiations while the National Liberation Front represented the Vietcong.

Having arranged this compromise, Johnson reported on October 31 that all bombing would cease in North Vietnam; that is, the bombing from the 17th to the 20th parallel, which had continued after March 31. The president announced that peace talks would begin, involving four parties but with two sides in negotiations: the United States/South Vietnam as one side; the NFL/Hanoi as the second. On the negative side, there was no cease-fire or truce. Negotiations would proceed while fighting continued, except for the restrictions against Rolling Thunder's bombing of the North and Hanoi's attacks on South Vietnam's cities.

In line with these agreements, Johnson ordered the bombing halt that North Vietnam required before the peace talks would begin. South Vietnam's President Thieu had privately agreed to participate in the talks after Hanoi promised to respect the demilitarized zone (DMZ) and not attack South Vietnamese cities. Yet the peace talks never took place. Two days after the bombing halt began on October 31, Thieu announced the South Vietnamese would not take part in the talks because they could not sit down with the Vietcong.

Thieu's reasons for refusing to participate quickly became controversial. Nixon claimed the bombing halt was negotiated for political reasons to help Humphrey's candidacy. In fact, Nixon had his campaign manager contact Anna Chan Chennault, the Chinese widow of the wartime hero General Claire Chennault, to tell President Thieu that Nixon would "see that Vietnam gets better treatment from me than under the Democrats." Democratic candidate Humphrey had told Thieu prolonged U.S. aid was "not in the cards.'

Although historians such as Stephen Ambrose's *Nixon: The Triumph of a Politician* (1989) offered much evidence of Nixon's deceptive practice in persuading Thieu to reject peace talks, Anthony Summers's *The Arrogance of Power: The Secret World of Richard Nixon* (2000) finds the smoking-gun evidence that Nixon secretly sabotaged the peace talks then kept the fighting going for five more years, with more than 20,000 Americans and about 1 million Vietnamese being killed during that period. In 1969, Nixon renewed negotiations with the North Vietnamese.

See May 14, 1969.

**November 5, 1968**

### Richard Nixon is elected president.

Nixon had won an easy Republican nomination for president, winning many primaries by cultivating a new image of maturity after his political loss to Kennedy in 1960 and the California governorship in 1962. The split in the Democratic Party over foreign policy caused many liberal Democrats to boycott the election. In addition, George Wallace's party cost Humphrey votes in the South. Although Humphrey broke with Johnson on Vietnam in October, his late surge in public opinion polls came too late for a victory.

In the November 5 ballot, Nixon's popular vote was 31,785,148; Humphrey's was 31,274,503; Wallace received 9,901,151. The electoral college vote was Nixon, 301; Humphrey, 191; Wallace, 46. The Democratic Party retained control of Congress.

See August 28, 1968.

# XV.   DÉTENTE OR COLD WAR?

*Nixon Doctrine*
*Vietnam Truce*
*Problems in Asia, Africa, and Latin America*
*Crises in Iran and Afghanistan*

# 1 9 6 9

### January 20, 1969

**Nixon's inaugural address indicates his desire to change U.S. policy to more "realistic" diplomacy, although the implication of his words and prior writing on foreign policy do not clearly define this for his audience.**

Although Nixon had explained some of his foreign policy views in an October 1967 article for the quarterly *Foreign Affairs,* his inaugural address and his selection of Henry Kissinger as National Security Adviser led a wider group of persons with international interests to realize that a major new approach to U.S. foreign relations was to be attempted.

Nixon's inaugural speech outlined some of the attitudes of the power politics that the Nixon Doctrine later asserted more definitely. Thus, the president stated: "After a period of confrontation, we are entering an era of negotiation.... We seek an open world—open to ideas, open to the exchange of goods and people—a world in which no people, great or small, will live in angry isolation.... We cannot expect to make everyone our friend, but we can try to make no one our enemy.... [But] let us leave no doubt that we will be as strong as we need to be for as long as we need to be."

### January 21, 1969

**William Pierce Rogers is commissioned as Secretary of State in President Nixon's cabinet.**

Rogers had much experience in Washington, having served as President Eisenhower's attorney general from 1957 to 1961. Nixon selected Rogers not for his foreign policy expertise but for his talents at handling Congress and the press. President Nixon wished to control foreign policy himself, selecting Henry Kissinger as his National Security Adviser to centralize international policy-making in the White House.

Kissinger was a former Harvard professor of international relations and had served as Nelson Rockefeller's foreign policy adviser. He agreed with Nixon's basic policy views on balance-of-power diplomacy, being a scholar of the two leading 19th-century power balance diplomats, Prince Metternich of Austria and Otto von Bismarck of Germany (see January 20, 1969).

Kissinger and Nixon moved immediately on January 20 to give the White House direct access to American ambassadors abroad. He and Nixon drafted messages to the ambassadors and personal letters to 15 leaders of foreign governments, including the Soviet Union's Leonid Brezhnev. Kissinger obtained Rogers's consent to address the ambassadors. The messages to the heads of state were delivered to their Washington embassies by NSC aides. Subsequently, Nixon and Kissinger consulted Rogers only when he could be useful. In decision making, the State Department was generally bypassed.

William P. Rogers. Richard M. Nixon Library.

### February 23, 1969

**Nixon emphasizes his desire to consult more with America's European allies as he leaves on a one-week visit to European nations.**

When the president embarked on his European trip on February 23 he told dignitaries at Andrews Air Force Base that he believed progress in settling world affairs made it "necessary to consult with our friends." The grave problems he wished to discuss with other leaders included Vietnam, the Mideast, monetary affairs, and others.

Nixon's itinerary included Brussels, where he visited King Baudouin and the NATO Council; London, to renew assurance of the Anglo-American "special relation'; Bonn and West Berlin; four days with de Gaulle in Paris; and Rome and Vatican City to meet Italian leaders and Pope Paul VI. Nixon returned to the United States on March 2, having launched his term of office with a gesture he hoped would gain better U.S. relations with Europe.

### March 2, 1969

*Soviet and Chinese troops clash on the border at the Ussuri River.*

This was one of several border skirmishes in 1969–1970 that indicated the nadir of the Sino-Soviet split.

### March 11, 1969

*Golda Meir becomes Prime Minister of Israel.*

The Russian-born, American-raised Meir had moved to Tel Aviv with her husband in 1921. There, she had joined the Ben Gurion Mapai Party, becoming Israel's foreign minister and Secretary General of the party before assuming the position of Prime Minister after the death of Levi Eshkol.

### March 14, 1969

**Nixon requests the approval of Congress for the "safeguard" antiballistic missile (ABM) system.**

Early in March, Kissinger's NSC staff completed NSSM-3, a study of the U.S. military posture regarding the strategic arms limitation talks (SALT), which President Johnson had wanted to begin with the Soviet Union prior to the invasion of Czechoslovakia. Relying on NSSM-3, Nixon decided to seek ABM funding to buy time prior to the SALT negotiations and to gain a bargaining chip against the USSR's ABM defenses under construction around Moscow.

As a result, on March 14 Nixon announced he would ask Congress for a Safeguard ABM system to replace President Johnson's plans for a "thin line" ABM Sentinel system allegedly for defense from a Chinese nuclear attack. Because Secretary of State Rusk and President Johnson had attempted to solicit better relations with Moscow in 1967–1968, they had announced that the Chinese "menace" required the Sentinel ABM defense.

Nixon's Safeguard ABMs would begin their deployment around two Minuteman ICBM sites in North Dakota, increasing further deployments as warranted by Soviet responses. By defending America's second-strike capability at the Minuteman bases, Nixon said the United States demonstrated it did

President Richard M. Nixon
and National Security
Adviser Henry Kissinger.
National Archives

not have a first-strike nuclear strategy. The second-strike strategy required that U.S. ICBMs be able to survive a Soviet first strike to retaliate in kind. Thus, Nixon argued, the Soviet ABM defense of Moscow was creating a first-strike capacity because the Soviet defenses of their cities protected them from the U.S. second strike aimed at the centers of Soviet population. In reality, the rhetoric of first- and second-strike tactics partly obscured the fact that, as Secretary of Defense McNamara had indicated in 1967, Mutual Assured Destruction (MAD) had given each side sufficient weaponry and warheads to destroy much of the world should a nuclear war begin.

Nevertheless, in the nuclear limitation game that the United States and the USSR played from 1969 to 1979, ABM and other tactical claims and preparations became part of the complex methodology by which the United States and the Soviet Union sought to stabilize their nuclear arms competition.

See August 20, 1968; for the beginning of SALT I negotiations, see November 17, 1969.

### March 18, 1969

#### President Nixon orders the first secret bombing attacks on Cambodia.

President Nixon's secret orders to extend the Vietnam War into neutral Cambodia led to the first in a series of bombings between March 18, 1968, and April 1970. The secrecy of the operations was maintained until 1973, when congressional investigations followed a report on the operation by Major Hal Knight, a radar officer near Saigon, who objected because he thought the falsification of records violated Article 107 of the Military Code of Justice.

Nixon, Kissinger, and other high U.S. officials had conspired to keep information on this extension of the war from Congress and the public. Prince Sihanouk of Cambodia, Soviet, North Vietnamese, and Chinese officials and most Western European leaders knew about it, but not the American public. Nixon did not want to risk the criticism of dissenters at home. Or, as some analysts claim, the secrecy was to demonstrate to Moscow President Nixon's willingness to use American power and to do so secretly to accomplish his goals.

The Cambodian bombings had been recommended for some time by U.S. military officers who contended that Communist "sanctuaries" in eastern Cambodia were the principal base of supplies for North Vietnamese and Vietcong forces in the southern delta area. President Johnson had tried to obtain Prince Sihanouk's permission to eliminate the sanctuaries, but he would not permit the Pentagon to attack without Cambodian approval.

In January 1969, Nixon asked the Joint Chiefs for recommendations on Cambodia, indicating his willingness to violate Cambodian neutrality if necessary. On February 9, General Abrams, the U.S. Commander in Vietnam, recommended "a short-duration, concentrated B-52 attack of up to 60 sorties" to destroy the central headquarters of the Communists (COSVN) in eastern Cambodia. Pentagon intelligence located the headquarters at Base Area 353 in the "fishhook" area of Cambodia, which geographically jutted into South Vietnam northwest of Saigon. Abrams believed that the B-52 attacks would minimize the violation of Cambodian territory to one minute per sortie and that few Cambodian civilians would be killed. The destruction of COSVN, Abrams said, would "have a very significant effect on enemy operations throughout South Vietnam."

President Nixon approved Abrams's proposal but insisted on strict secrecy, objecting to Secretary of Defense Laird's desire to inform congressional leaders. To maintain secrecy, a "dual reporting" system was devised by the Pentagon. The B-52s would leave Guam for Vietnamese targets. Once over South Vietnam, ground radar controllers would redirect the planes to Cambodia without the pilot or navigator realizing the location of the new target. The radar controllers knew, however, and would send two reports to General Abrams, one for the original targets and one for the revised target. Officially, the bombs fell on Vietnam. Major Knight was a radar controller who had first appealed to his superiors to amend the false documents. When they refused to follow through, Knight later appealed to Congress.

General Abrams's February 9 recommendation for a few low-level attacks never accomplished its objective, assuming his assumptions about the sanctuaries were correct. Following the March 18 bombing of Base 353, a U.S. Special Forces team code-named Daniel Boone entered the area to survey the damage. The team of 12 men commanded by Captain Bill Orthman flew helicopters to the area, but after they landed and moved toward the jungle, the enemy attacked. Nine men were killed; three Vietnamese and Orthman were wounded but got back to the helicopter and survived.

Overlooking Abrams's miscalculation, Nixon ordered additional bombings, but the objectives of these attacks were never fulfilled. During the next year there were 3,875 sorties in which the B-52s dropped 108,823 tons of bombs. The Communist bases survived, being relocated farther inland. Only Cambodian civilians suffered from the bombings.

The U.S. incursion into Cambodia in April 1970 led to the complete end of Cambodian neutrality.

See March 18, 1970.

## May 10, 1969

### In Vietnam, Operation Apache Snow indicates the U.S. Army has not adjusted to the use of General Abrams's "area security" strategy.

Although General Abrams, who succeeded Westmoreland as U.S. commander in Vietnam on April 10, 1968, had introduced new strategic methods for the war, Abrams's "area security" plan broke so severely with the U.S. army's traditional attrition warfare that U.S. officers either could not or would not forsake the attrition strategy. As designed by Abrams and approved by President Nixon early in 1969, U.S. and Army of the Republic of Vietnam (ARVN) action would cooperate with the local South Vietnamese People's Self-Defense Forces (PSDF) to clear and secure an area of Vietcong (VC) influence. Because the PSDF had knowledge of local conditions, the United States and ARVN would work closely with them. These would be small-unit actions that would emphasize every effort to avoid devastating the local area and, thus the PSDF could avoid the dislocation and killing of the local people such as occurred from attrition firepower. Together ARVN and PSDF would protect the future security of a region step by step. Thus, Abrams's methods deemphasized "body count" and stressed "local loyalty." The area security plan would counteract the Communist-protracted warfare. It was approved by Nixon because it fit well with his Vietnamization plans.

There was one major problem with the Abrams plan. It radically changed the way U.S. officers were trained to fight. West Point taught big-unit action, firepower, attrition through death and destruction. From the Indian frontier to Korea these methods had won. Thus, U.S. army doctrine eschewed political goals: military goals were ends in themselves. Area security might win the Vietnamese "hearts and minds," but as Major General Julian Ewell wrote in 1969, "I guess I basically feel that the 'hearts and minds' approach can be overdone. In the Delta, the only way to overcome VC [Vietcong] control and terror is by brute force applied against the VC." Another senior officer criticized Abrams's methods more succinctly: "I'll be damned if I'll permit the

United States Army, its institutions, its doctrine, and its tradition to be destroyed just to win this lousy war." As Guenter Lewy's *America in Vietnam* (1978) concludes: "Abrams' campaign plan, for the most part, remained a paper exercise."

About one year after Abrams took command, Operation Apache Snow, including the famous battle of Hamburger Hill, represented U.S. "old-style" heroism and the inability of the United States or its trained ARVN units to accept Abrams's plan. Apache Snow was a big-unit action by the U.S. 101st Airborne Division and the First ARVN Division in the 30-mile-long A Shau valley near the borders of South Vietnam, Laos, and the 17th parallel.

The first day, B-52s, artillery, and naval guns bombarded the valley. The second day, U.S. airborne troops and ARVN helicopters entered the valley and eventually reached Hill 937, where a strong enemy force held out. Lodged on a rugged, densely forested, heavily fortified hill, the Vietcong held out for 10 days. The U.S. Field Commander, Major General Melvin Zais, threw more and more men into battle, where they were "chewed up like meat" on "Hamburger Hill." The U.S. air force flew 272 sorties and dropped 1 million pounds of bombs including napalm. The artillery fired 21,732 rounds at the hill. Finally, fighting bunker to bunker, the U.S. soldiers secured Hill 937. U.S. losses were 56 killed, 420 wounded; the enemy lost 505 troops.

Once Hill 937 was secured, however, it was abandoned. The search-and-destroy operation had killed the enemy. Hill 937 had no political or military value such as Abrams had prescribed. In fact, the U.S. pacification agency reported that Vietcong terrorism increased in formerly "pacified" areas while the battle of Hamburger Hill raged.

Abrams's area security plans collapsed before the search-and-destroy attrition methods. Old army methods still needed to be attuned to new world conditions. American soldiers fought heroically, but their gallant efforts provided no results.

### May 14, 1969

**Nixon offers peace terms unacceptable to North Vietnam.**

Speaking on nationwide television, President Nixon announced a peace plan for Vietnam. His proposal called for a cease-fire, the withdrawal of all American and North Vietnamese troops, an exchange of prisoners of war, and the creation of an international commission to conduct free elections in South Vietnam.

News commentators noted that this proposal had no chance to be accepted by North Vietnam. Its terms would have accomplished what the United States had not achieved during the last five years: the withdrawal of Vietcong forces and an election to divide Vietnam, with Thieu in charge in the South. At best, Nixon's so-called eight-point plan expressed the extreme bargaining position for U.S. truce negotiations at the Paris peace talks.

### June 8, 1969

**President Nixon and President Thieu announce the initial withdrawal of U.S. forces from South Vietnam: the Vietnamization process begins.**

Nixon had approved the initial "Vietnamization" plans on May 14 but waited to announce the decision until after a meeting at Midway Island during which Thieu had little choice but to accept the plan. Significantly, the initial study—NSSM-1—drafted by Kissinger's national security team in January 1969 recommended plans for the gradual U.S. withdrawal from Vietnam. These plans were reviewed and redesigned slightly in NSSM-36 and -37 during April before Nixon accepted them.

Thus, following talks with Thieu and General Creighton ABRAMS, Nixon announced the Vietnamization program on June 8. On Thieu's recommendation, Nixon told reporters that 25,000 U.S. combat troops would be withdrawn as the first step in allowing South Vietnamese forces to take over their nation's self-defense. Thieu and Abrams agreed that with proper training by U.S. officers and with U.S. equipment, the Army of the Republic of Vietnam (ARVN) could protect their country from communism. Training of the Vietnamese had begun under Abrams's orders in 1968, and it showed signs of success.

Nixon did not give a precise timetable for withdrawal of U.S. troops. He said the situation in Vietnam would be reviewed regularly and future withdrawals would be in accord with ARVN's capacity to take charge. Later, in Washington, the president asserted that "no action will be taken" in the Vietnamization process that would "threaten the safety of our troops and the troops of our allies" or "the right of self-determination for the people of

South Vietnam." The initial secret plans of the NSC indicated that the summer of 1972 would be the earliest date when South Vietnam might be able to defend itself.

As Nixon explained to reporters at Guam on July 25, Vietnamization fitted the Nixon policy by which local defense forces would be aided, trained, and equipped to defend themselves. Not stated, but a part of the Nixon-Kissinger strategy, Vietnam was no longer considered a vital interest of the United States in global relations.

## June 15, 1969

### *Georges Pompidou is elected president of France following de Gaulle's resignation.*

French economic problems increased in 1968, causing serious student riots in Paris and the Paris suburb of Nanterre. The Gaullists in parliament held only a one-vote majority, making it difficult to govern efficiently. To strengthen presidential power, President de Gaulle suggested reforms of the French Senate, but in a referendum the majority rejected this by 52.87% on April 28, 1969. De Gaulle resigned and Alain Poher became interim president.

Pompidou was elected president on June 15 with 58% of the vote. The new prime minister was Jacques Chaban-Delmas.

On August 10, Pompidou devalued the franc to solve some of the country's economic difficulties.

## July 15, 1969

### Nixon sends a secret letter to Ho Chi Minh.

Although U.S. negotiations with North Vietnam had been conducted in Paris since January 25, these were public meetings with both South Vietnamese and NLF delegates present, as agreed to in October 1968. Nixon had designated the former Senator from Massachusetts Henry Cabot Lodge to head the U.S. delegation, replacing Averell Harriman and the team Johnson had appointed in May 1968.

Kissinger suggested to Nixon in February that the open Paris sessions could never reach an agreement. But he believed that high-level secret discussions in Paris with a North Vietnamese delegate could achieve success. To do this without Ambassador Lodge's knowledge, Kissinger arranged for Jean Sainteny, a retired French diplomat and friend of Kissinger, to deliver to Xuan Thuy, Hanoi's delegate in Paris, an oral message regarding secret talks as well as a letter from Nixon to Ho Chi Minh.

Following Nixon's world tour and the beginning of Vietnamization in July, the president decided to enact Kissinger's proposal with Sainteny acting as the go-between. Although Ho did not respond to Nixon's letter for over four weeks, he responded immediately to the suggestion for secret talks. The first session began in Paris on August 4, 1969.

## July 20, 1969

### U.S. astronauts make the first moon landing.

Neil A. Armstrong and Edwin E. Aldrin Jr. landed the lunar module *Eagle* on the moon. Armstrong became the first man to walk on the moon's surface. After $21\frac{1}{2}$ hours on the moon, the *Eagle* rejoined *Apollo 11*, which had been orbiting the moon after ejecting *Eagle* for the landing. Astronaut Michael Collins commanded the *Apollo 11*. Live TV broadcasts sent pictures of the landing back to the earth for viewers around the world to watch.

A second U.S. moon landing was made on November 19–20, 1969. Four more moon visits were made by Americans between 1970 and 1972. Only one moon mission experienced difficulty: *Apollo 13*. This mission was aborted but the three astronauts landed safely in the Pacific Ocean on April 17, 1970.

The moon landing program was the consequence of John F. Kennedy's call for a U.S. program to land the first man on the moon.

See May 25, 1961.

## July 25, 1969

### At Guam, Nixon informally tells reporters the policies that will become basic to the Nixon Doctrine regarding Asia and, by implication, other regions of the world.

Unlike the Truman Doctrine, which derived essentially from one presidential speech on March 12, 1947, the Nixon Doctrine was first disclosed casually by the president in July and November 1969, before it was formally defined in a report to Congress during January 1970.

Nixon arrived in Guam as part of a world tour during which he greeted the U.S. astronauts on their return from the first moon flight. During the evening

Nixon joking with *Apollo 11* astronauts aboard the USS *Hornet*, July 24, 1969. Richard M. Nixon Library

of July 25, he met with news reporters for an off-the-record conversation that the White House later made public. In somewhat rambling fashion, Nixon told the reporters that nationalism had changed the world, especially Asia. The United States needed to recognize this fact and, while keeping commitments, let other countries develop in their own fashion. The United States had to avoid policies that made others "so dependent on us that we are dragged into conflicts such as the one that we have in Vietnam."

During later questioning by reporters, Nixon summarized his ideas more precisely. He said the United States in its Asian relations must be quite emphatic on two points: "one, that we will keep our treaty commitments ... for example, with Thailand under SEATO; but, two, that as far as the problems of internal security are concerned, as far as the problems of military defense, except for the threat of a major power involving nuclear weapons, that the United States is going to encourage and has a right to expect that this problem will be increasingly handled by, and the responsibility for it taken by, the Asian nations themselves."

The president also said that the policy of letting Asians protect themselves would be effective only after the Vietnam War ended. Until then, the United States had of necessity to remain in command.

During his subsequent visits to Manila, Djakarta, Bangkok, and Saigon, Nixon made much the same point regarding Asians' eventually assuming control of their own internal and defense needs. On July 31, Nixon flew to India, where relations with the United States were not satisfactory, and continued on to Pakistan and Romania before flying back to Washington.

See August 3, 1969.

## August 3, 1969

### Nixon returns from a world tour that ended with a visit to Romania.

Following a trip to greet the moon astronauts in the Pacific and visit Guam and four capitals of Southeast Asia, Nixon made final stops in India, Pakistan, and Romania. Relations in neutralist India were tense because of that country's close ties with Moscow and its desire for the United States to leave Vietnam. Pro-American Pakistan was more congenial, giving Nixon the nation's highest medal, the Nishan-e-Pakistan.

The visit to Bucharest, Romania, impressed Nixon the most. On August 2, thousands of citizens in this Communist state greeted the president. The Romanian enthusiasm was subtly more anti-Soviet than pro-American because the government of Nicolae Ceauşescu wanted to show the nation's limited independence of the Soviet Union. Both Nixon and Ceaușescu expressed the desire for open contacts with all nations.

Having traveled around the world, Nixon arrived back at Andrews Air Force Base near Washington on the evening of August 3.

See July 25, 1969.

### August 4, 1969

**Kissinger and Xuan Thuy conduct their first secret negotiations in Paris.**

On July 26, Ho Chi Minh sent word to President Nixon that North Vietnam would empower Xuan Thuy to hold high-level secret talks in Paris. Nixon selected Kissinger to represent him, and bypassing Lodge and the State Department, Nixon entrusted the secret arrangements to his old friend Lieutenant General Vernon A. Walters, the U.S. defense attaché at the Paris embassy.

On August 3, Nixon's plane en route from Romania had stopped briefly in London for a presidential visit with Prime Minister Wilson. Kissinger and two of his aides, Anthony Lake and Helmut Sonnenfeldt, left the presidential plane Air Force One and boarded a U.S. military aircraft for Paris. The Americans spent the night at General Walters's Neuilly apartment and Kissinger met publicly with President de Gaulle to brief him on Nixon's recent trips. De Gaulle also agreed to help Kissinger preserve the secrecy of his future talks with Xuan Thuy in Paris.

On the afternoon of August 4, Kissinger and his assistants visited Jean Sainteny's apartment, where they were introduced to Xuan Thuy and his aide. The first talks led to an agreement to hold future secret talks, although no date was set for the next meeting.

### August 13, 1969

**Fighting breaks out on the Sino-Soviet border.**

This border clash was the last in a series of Chinese-Soviet border incidents during 1969, highlighting 1969 as reaching a low point in relations between Moscow and Beijing. Following a clash on March 2 along the Ussuri River border, the two governments exchanged heated accusations intermixed with border engagements. The most serious fighting took place on March 15, June 11, and August 13. Soviet Premier Kosygin stopped in Beijing on September 11 following the funeral of Ho Chi Minh (see September 3, 1969) in Hanoi. Talks to resolve the border problems began on October 19 but were not resolved during the next month.

### September 1, 1969

*In Libya, Colonel Mu'ammar Al-Gadhafi leads a successful coup overthrowing King Idris I.*

A strong pro-Arab, who, some claimed, wanted to replace Nasser as the Arab's leading spokesman, Gadhafi took a hard line against the Western powers and Israel.

### September 3, 1969

**Ho Chi Minh dies, soon after answering Nixon's personal letter on August 25.**

Although Nixon and Kissinger believed Ho's death was good news for the United States because it would leave Hanoi leaderless, they had, as was often true of other Americans, underestimated the North Vietnamese political structure. The North Vietnamese leaders were united in their devotion to expelling the Americans and reuniting Vietnam.

On August 25, Ho had sent his reply to Nixon's letter of July 15, 1969. Ho's response showed the gulf between the perceptions of the two leaders regarding Vietnam. Whereas Nixon believed the United States was rightfully fighting in Vietnam for its Saigon ally, Ho saw the U.S. role as that of direct aggression to preserve imperialism and in violation of the "fundamental rights" of the Vietnamese people. He told Nixon that only if the United States left Vietnam could Vietnamese rights and world peace be secured.

The letters exchanged between Nixon and Ho were released by the State Department for publication on November 4, 1969.

### October 21, 1969

*In West Germany, Willy Brandt becomes chancellor, leading the Social Democratic Party.*

Brandt was an exponent of building better relations with Eastern European countries and the Soviet Union.

### October 21, 1969

**The Shah of Iran visits with President Nixon. The president tells the Shah that Iran should become the dominant power in the Persian Gulf.**

Although the visit to Washington of Reza Shah Pahlavi was largely ceremonial, Nixon stressed to the shah Iran's important role in the Middle East. National Security Council Study NSSM-66 indicated that as Great Britain abdicated more and more power east of Suez, the United States needed allies such as Iran to control the Straits of Hormuz in the Persian Gulf oil region.

In public, Nixon referred to Iran "as one of the strongest, the proudest among all nations of the world." The shah, Nixon said, had made land reforms that were a "revolution in terms of social, economic, and political progress."

### November 17, 1969

**The United States and the Soviet Union begin SALT I negotiations in Helsinki.**

Discussions between Moscow and Washington about limiting offensive and defensive nuclear weapons had been considered but had been delayed since August 20, 1969. Not until October 20 did Ambassador Dobrynin inform Nixon and Kissinger that the Soviets were ready to begin arms discussions. Because the U.S. Senate had finalized the law approving ABM construction on August 6, the United States was also ready to undertake talks. On October 25, the

Nixon with the Shah of Iran.
National Archives

two governments jointly announced that discussions covering offensive and defensive weapons would begin at Helsinki on November 17. All substantive announcements would be made jointly.

The principal issues confronting the SALT I negotiations from the U.S. viewpoint were the ABM, MIRV warheads, and verification. Nixon and Kissinger had agreed that the United States wanted to eliminate the ABM systems if possible. They had sought ABM funding only as a bargaining chip to be given away during the talks. The greatest U.S. concern was to retain leadership in MIRV technology. MIRV warheads—multiple independent reentry vehicles—are clusters of separately targeted nuclear warheads. These MIRVs could be deployed on the Minuteman and U.S. submarine launchers. Considered by technicians to be the biggest breakthrough since the hydrogen bomb, MIRV gave the United States a qualitative advantage over the Soviet Union. Nixon believed the USSR delayed the SALT discussions to perfect its own MIRV system. In fact, there was a dispute within the Nixon administration between Secretary of Defense Melvin Laird, and Richard Helms of the CIA. Laird insisted that the Soviets already had minimum MIRVs available with three separate warheads. Helms's intelligence data indicated it would be 1972 before the Soviets had this capability. Although the Soviets did not gain MIRV technology until 1973, Kissinger assumed Laird was correct and obtained limits on Soviet offensive missiles.

The verification issue was always one of the most problematic for U.S. negotiators. Here again, Laird and Kissinger differed with Helms. The CIA believed that electronic surveillance and telemetry permitted the United States to keep aware of Soviet weapons including such capabilities as MIRV. Kissinger, who apparently disliked Helms personally, argued that Helms and the CIA had a "vested interest" in verification and could not therefore be relied on to judge the requirements of it.

Thus when the SALT talks convened, the principal U.S. concerns were to stop ABM systems, to protect U.S. advantages in MIRV, and to seek the most satisfactory verification methods possible. To conduct the U.S. discussions, Nixon named Special Ambassador Gerard C. Smith, director of the U.S. Arms Control and Disarmament Agency. The first round of talks lasted until December 22, 1969.

## November 21, 1969

**The United States agrees to return Okinawa to Japan as a result of discussions in Washington between President Nixon and Japan's Prime Minister Eisaku Sato.**

During 1969, two issues disturbed relations between Japan and America: Japan's desire to regain Okinawa and the importation of Japanese textiles. As a lawyer for U.S.-owned corporations during the 1960s, Nixon had often visited Tokyo and liked the conservative political-business circles of that country. He was eager therefore to satisfy Japan's major request in 1969, the return of Okinawa. Nixon had convinced the Joint Chiefs of Staff that U.S. planes and nuclear weapons requirements would not be damaged if they later had to be removed from Okinawa. Consultation with Tokyo on these affairs was necessary.

Thus, when Sato reached Washington on November 19, Nixon was prepared to agree on details of the U.S. withdrawal from Okinawa. Sato stated that the U.S. Treaty of Mutual Cooperation would be extended to Okinawa. Thus, U.S.-Japanese consultations on air bases in Okinawa would have the same terms as those in the Japanese home islands. In addition, the prime minister approved the continued use of B-52 bases on Okinawa for action in Indochina, where the United States fought for "self-determination for the people of South Vietnam." The treaty on Okinawa was finalized in April 1970.

The textile issue was not easily resolved. In April, Maurice Stans, the U.S. secretary of commerce, visited Tokyo but failed to reach a textile agreement after he had harshly criticized Japan's efforts. In November 1969, Sato told Nixon he would place self-limits by Japanese on their textiles. Sato's promise was vague, however, and this trade issue was not resolved for two more years.

## November 25, 1969

**Nixon proclaims U.S. ratification of the Nuclear Non-proliferation Treaty and announces that the United States will renounce chemical-biological weapons by having the U.S. Senate ratify the Geneva protocol of 1925.**

The Non-Proliferation Treaty had been signed by the United States on July 1, 1968, but was not ratified by the U.S. Senate until March 1969. In the interim, 108 nations (but not China or France) signed the treaty that Nixon proclaimed for the United States.

On the same day, Nixon committed the United States not to make first use of chemical, incapacitating, or biological weapons. He would submit the 1925 protocol to the Senate because the United States had not previously accepted this pact. Henceforth, said Nixon, America would confine its chemical-biological research to "immunization and safety methods."

In 1975, U.S. Senate investigators found that the CIA had ignored Nixon's 1969 suggestion to destroy its stocks of toxins used in biological warfare. It had retained stocks of cobra venom and Saxitonit, a toxin causing instant death. The 1925 protocol was not ratified until 1975.

*See January 22, 1975.*

### December 8, 1969

**In a press conference, President Nixon refers to the My Lai "massacre" as an isolated incident not representing U.S. policy.**

The My Lai massacre had taken place on March 16, 1969, but had not been reported by U.S. newspapers until November 16. During this action, U.S. troops led by Lieutenant William L. Calley shot 450 unarmed South Vietnam villagers. Although there were other reports of individual atrocities in North Vietnam, My Lai and the Phoenix operations of 1968–1972 became the most notorious illustrations of the type of horrific incidents frequently associated with guerrilla warfare.

During his press conference, Nixon was asked to react to the My Lai report. He said, "We cannot ever condone or use atrocities against civilians" to bring security to Vietnam. He hoped this event would not "smear the decent men that have gone to Vietnam" on a vital mission.

### December 19, 1969

**Secretary of State Rogers explains that his October plan for the Middle East has been rejected by the USSR and Egypt.**

Nixon and Kissinger had decided in March 1969 to have Secretary Rogers conduct discussions with the Soviet Union regarding a solution to the Arab-Israeli quarrels that continued following the Six-Day War of 1967 and U.N. Resolution 242's interpretation. Nixon believed the two superpowers should determine a plan for their client states—Israel and Egypt—that would have to be accepted by them. With Joseph Sisco of the State Department's Near Eastern Division conducting most of the day-to-day negotiations with Soviet Ambassador Dobrynin during the spring and summer of 1969, the so-called Rogers Plan emerged by September and was "signed off on" (approved) by the National Security Council on October 19.

Although the White House never fully supported the Rogers Plan, its principal features were that (1) the Sinai would be demilitarized with Israel's security guaranteed in the Strait of Tiran; (2) after Israel withdrew from the occupied territory, the Arabs and Israelis would negotiate details of peace "in some manner"; and (3) special discussions would settle the issue of the Gaza Strip. The precise definition of where Israel would withdraw was not provided.

When Israel's Prime Minister Golda Meir visited Washington on September 25–26, Nixon did not confide in her about the Rogers Plan or U.S.-Soviet discussions. He told her the White House fully supported Israel but that he had trouble dealing with others in the State Department and the NSC.

After the NSC approved the Rogers Plan on October 19, the secretary held extensive talks with Soviet Foreign Minister Andrey Gromyko in New York. The two worked out an agreement for the approval of Egypt and Israel. By their terms, the territories that Israel would withdraw from were those taken from Egypt in 1967 except for "insubstantial alterations," which was one of Rogers's phrases. In return, Egypt would assure the security of Israeli borders.

The Rogers Plan, as he explained in December, did not survive long. Late in October, after the United States had orally explained the plan to Israel, Tel Aviv announced that the Soviet-American plan called for "direct negotiations" between Israel and Egypt. Egypt's foreign minister, Mahmoud Riad, protested against this phrase. At best, he told Moscow, he would participate only in "indirect talks," which itself was a concession because of strong Arab opposition to talks that would appear to recognize Israel's right to exist as a state.

Although the Rogers plan might have survived if Nixon had fully supported it, he did not. By December, Dobrynin informed Rogers and Sisco that the Soviet Union no longer backed the plan because of Egyptian opposition. Before the speech of December 19, in which Rogers explained the aborting of his proposal, Rogers had neglected to inform Israel of the Soviet notification. Abba Eban, Israel's foreign minister, objected strongly to any effort of outside parties to impose a peace on Israel. As a result, U.S.-Israeli relations were strained by the end of 1969.

# 1 9 7 0

### January 8, 1970

**President Thieu of South Vietnam informs reporters that it would be "impossible and impractical" to withdraw all U.S. troops from Vietnam in 1970.**

Since the announced Vietnamization program of June 8, 1969, there had been extensive speculation in South Vietnam and the United States regarding the time of America's complete withdrawal.

A vital part of Vietnamization was the question of South Vietnam's preparations to take charge of local defense. During the summer of 1968, President Thieu had called a general mobilization in South Vietnam. All army reserves were called up and a draft began of men 18 and 19 years old. In addition, men aged 16–17 and over 38 years could be drafted into Socialized People's Self-Defense Forces (PSDF). By 1972, the ARVN and other regular South Vietnamese forces totaled 516,000, fewer than the American total of 542,000 at its peak in January 1969.

U.S. military advisers expected that a trained and equipped PSDF of nearly 500,000 would add to Saigon's total defense establishment. The critical problem was for the Saigon government to obtain the respect and loyalty of local leaders of the PSDF. Gaining this local loyalty had been a persistent problem for Saigon's dictatorial regime since 1954. Enlarging the PSDF was simple; achieving their allegiance and motivation was a different matter.

### January 20, 1970

**U.S. Ambassador to Poland Walter Stoessel Jr. and China's Chargé d'Affaires Lei Yang conduct talks in Warsaw.**

The U.S. and Chinese representatives had held 133 sessions in Warsaw since 1955, but since 1965 these had dwindled to only one or two a year, with only one in 1968 (January 8). On November 26, 1968, the Chinese chargé had sent Stoessel a note suggesting a formal meeting with a U.S. representative on February 20, 1969. Later, Chinese diplomats said they had read president-elect Nixon's article in the October 1967 issue of *Foreign Affairs* and were impressed by his advocacy of normalizing U.S. relations with China. Although Nixon, through Secretary of State Rusk, agreed to a meeting with the Chinese in Warsaw in February, the session was canceled because a Chinese diplomat in the Netherlands defected to the West and Beijing blamed the United States.

Both Nixon and Kissinger were willing to hold talks with the Chinese and sought in various ways to encourage this during 1969. On May 24, Secretary of State Rogers visited Pakistan and, along with other matters, told Yahya Khan, who had good relations with China, that the United States desired to make diplomatic contact with Beijing. On July 21, the State Department announced that certain professional persons could obtain valid passports for China and that U.S. residents abroad or tourists could buy a limited amount of Communist Chinese goods to bring back with them to America.

Finally, on December 12, Ambassador Stoessel, acting on instructions from Nixon, informally contacted Lei Yang at a Yugoslav reception, telling Lei's interpreter that the United States would like to arrange a meeting. Two days later, Lei sent Stoessel an invitation to visit him at the Chinese embassy on January 20, 1970.

At the January meeting and again at a meeting in the U.S. embassy on February 20, Stoessel and Lei exchanged formal and polite views. Stoessel also suggested that perhaps a "high-level emissary" from America could visit Beijing. No firm agreement resulted from this overture, but Stoessel and Lei decided to hold monthly sessions thereafter.

### February 18, 1970

**The Nixon Doctrine is described in a report to Congress titled "Foreign Policy for the 1970s."**

Although Nixon had informally commented on the principles of his policy during a news conference at Guam on July 25 and in a national TV speech on November 3, 1969, the Nixon Doctrine was not precisely spelled out until his report to Congress of February 18, 1970.

This report identified three basic points of the Nixon Doctrine:

1. The United States would keep all of its commitments to its allies.
2. The allies should provide their own troops for self-defense against communism.
3. The United States would provide a nuclear shield and economic aid for its allies.

Despite the Nixon Doctrine's resemblance to Eisenhower's "new look," Nixon did not offer to decrease U.S. defense expenditures or rely principally on larger U.S. ICBM capabilities. In fact, Nixon was negotiating with the Soviets on ICBM and ABM limitations.

Nixon principally wanted the United States to "participate" but no longer undertake all the defense for its allies. To provide U.S. aid, funds for the Military Assistance Programs increased in 1971 by $2 billion over Johnson's last budget. The United States also increased its sale of arms to its allies. For example, from 1953 to 1973, the U.S. sold Iran $205 billion worth of weapons, a sale helping to offset the balance of payments due to the increase in oil prices during the 1970s. Nevertheless, American allies would, said Nixon, "define the nature of their own security and determine the path of their own progress."

See October 30, 1953, and November 17, 1969.

## March 18, 1970

### *Prince Sihanouk of Cambodia is overthrown by his prime minister, Lon Nol.*

Since becoming leader in Cambodia on June 5, 1960, Sihanouk often irritated U.S. officials because of his desire to remain neutral in both the Cold War and the Vietnam conflict. U.S. claims of Communist sanctuaries in eastern Cambodia were shrugged off by the prince as "illegal" or "under control." Essentially, Prince Sihanouk believed his people would fare best if he kept his nation as aloof as possible from direct involvement in the north-south conflict in Vietnam.

As William Shawcross's *Sideshow* (1979) explains, Sihanouk's policies toward North Vietnam's sanctuaries in Cambodia were unacceptable to Premier Lon Nol and Deputy Premier Sirik Matek. In particular, Matek, a cousin of the king, opposed Sihanouk because in 1941 the French crowned Sihanouk as

King of Cambodia, passing over Matek's family. Thus, while Sihanouk vacationed in France during March 1970, Matek persuaded Lon Nol to seek American support to replace Sihanouk as king. Hoping to obtain U.S. backing, Matek and Lon Nol promoted anti-Vietnamese demonstrations along the border with Vietnam and in front of Phnom Penh's embassy of the Provisional Government of South Vietnam (Vietcong). They not only canceled the trade agreement with North Vietnam, closing the port of Sihanoukville for Hanoi to buy Cambodian products, but also ordered Hanoi to withdraw all its troops from Cambodia in 72 hours. On March 17–18, they completed their coup by arresting Sihanouk's supporters in and near Phnom Penh.

Although President Richard Nixon's decision to begin bombing Cambodia on March 18 undoubtedly influenced Sihanouk's ouster, Shawcross found no evidence that America's Central Intelligence Agency was directly involved in the Cambodian events staged by Matek and Lon Nol. Indeed, if Sihanouk had immediately come home from France on March 18, Shawcross believes his supporters would have rallied to his side because the new government was on shaky ground in opposing North Vietnam as well as Sihanouk. Rather than risk going to Phnom Penh, Sihanouk flew to Beijing and organized resistance against Matek and Lon Nol. While President Nixon recognized Lon Nol's regime, Sihanouk allied with Communists in Cambodia's Khmer Rouge and North Vietnam.

## March 19, 1970

### *Government heads of East and West Germany meet at Erfurt.*

After becoming chancellor of West Germany in October 1969, Willy Brandt announced the policy of *Ostpolitik* aimed at promoting détente with states of Eastern Europe. His initial step was to meet in Erfurt with East Germany's Prime Minister Willi Stoph. Following the March 19 session, delegates from the two German states began negotiations resulting in the signing of a treaty on December 22, 1972. This treaty entailed reciprocal recognition between East and West Germany. Brandt also sought a treaty with Poland.

See December 7, 1970.

## April 30, 1970

**President Nixon tells the U.S. public that American and South Vietnamese forces have made an "incursion" against Communist sanctuaries in Cambodia.**

The U.S.-ARVN attack on Cambodia began on April 29. To his television audience on April 30, Nixon explained that Cambodia had been neutral since 1954, and U.S. policy "had been to scrupulously respect the neutrality of the Cambodian people." Nixon asserted that only North Vietnam "has not respected that neutrality." The Communists, Nixon stated, had large bases in Cambodia for training, weapons, ammunition, air strips, prisoner-of-war compounds, and planning headquarters. Previously the United States had not moved against these bases, Nixon claimed, "because we did not wish to violate the territory of a neutral nation"—here he failed to acknowledge the U.S. bombings that began in Cambodia on March 18, 1969.

Antiwar protestors in New York City use a coffin to represent the deaths in Vietnam. National Archives

Nixon noted that the Communists had recently stepped up their attacks on Cambodia and were encircling the capital city of Phnom Penh. Therefore, the U.S. and South Vietnamese forces had to clean out the Communist bases to secure the freedom of South Vietnam and permit the process of Vietnamization to be successful.

Nixon asked the American people to understand and support his decision. "Free institutions," he said, "are under attack from without and within." America cannot be a "pitiful, helpless giant" in a totalitarian world. "I would rather be a one-term president and do what I believe is right than to be a two-term president at the cost of seeing America become a second-rate power and to see this nation accept its first defeat in its proud 190 year history." America, he concluded, was being tested. If we fail, "all other nations will be on notice that despite its overwhelming power the United States, when a real crisis comes, will be found wanting."

The idea to send 74,000 troops into Cambodia originated in October 1969 when the U.S. Commanding General in Vietnam, General Abrams, and the Joint Chiefs of Staff recommended that ground forces invade both Cambodia and Laos to destroy the Communist bases. By October, Abrams realized that his February 9 bombing proposal had been incorrect. The military-bureaucratic game, however, does not admit mistakes.

Nixon delayed action on the October request until April 1970. By then, many things had changed. The bombing had clearly failed, Sihanouk had been ousted, and in the secret Paris peace negotiations during early 1970, the North Vietnamese had not offered any significant compromises. Nixon did not ally with Lon Nol because the Cambodian leader was as much anti-Vietnamese as he was anti-Communist. In April, Lon Nol had appealed to the United Nations to help Cambodia get rid of both the Communists and the South Vietnamese who operated on the western borders of his state.

Kissinger claims in his memoirs that he obtained approval for the Cambodian "incursion" from Senator John Stennis, chairman of the Senate Armed Forces Committee. He wrote that Stennis like other Southern senators "sometimes lagged behind the moral currents of their time, but on national security and foreign policy they were towers of strength." No other congressmen were told in advance about the April 29–30 decision. Both Secretary of State Rogers and Secretary of Defense Laird cautioned Nixon about the constitutional question involved in ordering a ground attack on neutral Cambodia, but the president ignored their advice.

The Cambodian incursion became a 90-day raid with, at best, limited success. As another "search and destroy" mission, there were some benefits. U.S. forces encountered little resistance in their 21-mile invasion. The tanks, planes, and armored vehicles destroyed small towns such as Snuol and Mimot. At Snuol, the 11th Armored Cavalry Regiment's tanks shelled the village for 24 hours. On occupying the village they found seven dead bodies, one a small Cambodian girl. Elsewhere, U.S. forces captured large caches of rice, arms, and ammunition. In addition, George Herring's *America's Longest War* (1996 edition) indicates that some 2,000 enemy troops were killed, 16,000 acres of jungle were cleared, and 8,000 enemy bunkers were destroyed.

Generally, however, the U.S. objective of destroying significant sanctuaries failed. An August 1970 Defense Department study stated that Communist attacks had been disrupted "to some extent." The incursion had not "substantially reduced NVA capabilities in Cambodia." The Communists lost perhaps 25% of their supplies, but these would be replenished within 75 days or less.

Neither Kissinger nor Nixon agreed with the Pentagon's August report. Kissinger claimed the attacks bought two years' time to carry out Vietnamization. The Communists did not launch another offensive action in Vietnam until 1972. Of course, the Communists may have simply been awaiting a better time to make their next major attack.

As in the case of the secret bombing, Cambodians suffered the most. The Khmer Rouge stepped up its attacks on Lon Nol's forces. Although the Nixon administration gave Phnom Penh $273 million of economic aid and military equipment for an army of 220,000, the new government was unable to sustain itself. During the next decade Cambodia experienced destruction, starvation, and genocide. First the Khmer Rouge under Pol Pot, and later the Vietnamese conquered the ancient kingdom.

## May 4, 1970

### At Kent State University, four students are killed by Ohio National Guardsmen. Ten days later, police at Jackson State college kill two antiwar demonstrators.

A major consequence of Nixon's "incursion" into Cambodia was the greatest outburst of antiwar dissent since the president took office. Demonstrations at colleges and universities began on May 1. In both Ohio and Mississippi, inspired perhaps by Nixon's claim that dissenters were disloyal, national guardsmen and police responded by shooting, and killed six dissenters.

At Kent, Ohio, Governor John Rhodes denounced the demonstrators as "worse than brown shirts and the communist element," ordering 750 guardsmen to the campus after someone set fire to an Army ROTC building. On May 4, Kent State students staged a peaceful assembly to protest the war. For still unclear reasons, a group of guardsmen moved to disperse the crowd, advancing in full battle gear and carrying loaded M-1 rifles. The guardsmen fired at the unarmed students, later asserting there was sniper fire, an unsubstantiated charge. Two young women and two young men died; nine students lay wounded, one permanently paralyzed. An investigation disclosed that the students had no weapons other than a few rocks.

On May 14, a protest at Jackson State College had similar results. Drawn to the campus by reports of rock and bottle throwing, city and state police found a large crowd protesting the Cambodian invasion. For reasons that a later investigation called "completely unwarranted and unjustified," the police fired 150 rounds of ammunition into the assembly and a nearby women's dormitory. Two students were killed, 12 wounded. The President's Commission on Campus Unrest found that a combination of racial animosity and pro-war feelings probably caused the police to open fire.

During the spring of 1970, over 448 colleges experienced some form of protest. At the end of May, 100,000 dissidents marched in Washington. Police used tear gas and made mass arrests to stop the protestors.

## June 9, 1970

**A crisis erupts in Jordan when the Palestinian Liberation Front rebels and holds a group of Americans hostage at Amman's Intercontinental Hotel.**

The crisis in Jordan began as a conflict between the Popular Front for the Liberation of Palestine (PFLP) and King Hussein of Jordan. Hussein was a moderate and usually pro-Western Arab ruler. Because Jordan had become a major haven for Palestinian refugees after the Arab-Israeli war of 1948–1949, Hussein had increasing difficulty preventing the Palestinians in Jordan from conducting raids into Israel. This resulted in Israeli retaliatory attacks on Jordan and disrupted Hussein's society. In 1970, Hussein used the army to prohibit future Palestinian raids. This caused anger among the PFLP as well as the more moderate Palestine Liberation Organization headed by Yasser ARAFAT.

When the Palestinian uprising began on June 9, members of the PFLP took some Americans hostage in the Intercontinental Hotel to express their opposition to U.S. support for Israel. Moreover, some American homes in Jordan were looted and Major Robert P. Perry, an embassy military attaché, was killed by shots fired into his house.

The U.S. ambassador to Amman, Harry L. Odell, reported that it was too dangerous to evacuate U.S. personnel from the airport because of heavy fighting in the city. As a result, the White House undertook contingency discussions to prepare either a paratroop drop at Amman or to ferry Americans by helicopter to aircraft carriers in the Mediterranean Sea.

Fortunately, on June 12, King Hussein responded with force and the guerrillas accepted a truce. The hostages were released and the fighting ended. The uprising indicated a factor in Middle Eastern affairs not previously given much attention: the status of Palestinian refugees who had become organized and were ready to demand the right to a homeland in territory controlled by Israel.

## June 18, 1970

*Edward Heath becomes prime minister of Britain after a Conservative electoral victory.*

## June 22, 1970

**The U.S. Senate terminates the Tonkin Gulf Resolution of 1964. This is one of several congressional attempts to challenge continued U.S. involvement in Southeast Asia.**

Although the Senate repealed the Tonkin Gulf Resolution overwhelmingly, most congressional measures to restrict Nixon's activity were limited or unsuccessful. Included among these actions were the following:

1. May—Senate approved section of Cooper-Church amendment to prohibit funds for Cambodia after July 1, 1970, unless authorized by Congress. President Nixon had promised to have all troops out of Cambodia by July 1.
2. June 10—Senate rejected a proposal authorizing the president to send troops back into Cambodia if necessary to protect Americans in Vietnam.
3. June 23—Senate rejected the "end-the-war" McGovern-Hatfield amendment to ban all funds expended in Vietnam after December 31, 1970, unless Congress declared war.
4. June 29—Senate rejected a proposal to allow Nixon to aid "other nations such as Thailand" in helping Cambodia.
5. June 30—Senate approved Cooper-Church amendment to ban all funds for training Cambodians. This bill was rejected by the House of Representatives on July 7.

Although none of these measures specifically tied the president's hands, they all represented a considerable dissatisfaction in Congress regarding Nixon's policy in Vietnam and Cambodia.

## August 7, 1970

**The United States arranges a cease-fire in the Middle East: Rogers Plan II.**

Throughout the first seven months of 1970, border conflicts between Israel and three of its neighbors—Syria, Jordan, Egypt—had steadily escalated to the status of an undeclared war. In addition, the Soviet Union extended its influence in the region by increasing its arms and missiles in Egypt as well as using Soviet "experts" to fly missions protecting Egypt.

The United States wanted some means to lessen Soviet influence or, as Kissinger told reporters in a "backgrounder" in early July, to expel the Soviets. (A "backgrounder" was a remark that could not be publicly attributed to Kissinger but that, by mid-July 1970, most diplomats knew meant "Kissinger.")

Beginning as border skirmishes in 1969, the conflicts in the Middle East multiplied. On the Golan Heights border of Syria and Israel there often were heavy tank and artillery duels in addition to border raids. Along the Jordanian border, Palestinian raids became frequent until the Hussein-Palestinian dispute of June 9–12 finally reduced the PFLP-PLO raids.

The Egypt-Israeli border became the most serious area, however, for a war of attrition had begun. After the breakdown of the 1969 Rogers Plan, the Soviets rapidly increased their delivery of modern weapons to Egypt. Advanced jet fighter bomber MIG-23s and SAMs (surface-to-air missiles) gave Egypt a new integrated air-defense system. Soviet personnel also manned the SAM-3 batteries, while Soviet pilots flew jets against Israeli invasion planes. At the same time, Israel urged the United States to send Phantom and Skyhawk jets to bolster their defenses. Nixon and Kissinger restricted these deliveries, however, to persuade Moscow to limit arms to the area as a means of moving toward permanent peace arrangements.

Egypt and the Soviet Union had become closer allies after the Israelis launched "deep penetration" air raids against Egypt beginning in January 1970. By February, the Israeli air force controlled Egyptian skies from Alexandria to Aswân, even attacking Cairo-West air base. Reportedly, the Israelis shot down five MIGs flown by Soviets and killed a Soviet general during one air raid.

The Soviets response between February and July was to rapidly deploy more planes and SAM bases in Egypt. Eventually Israeli raids became so risky that during April and May, they curtailed penetration attacks, limiting their air attacks to the Suez area. The situation became so tense that Israel considered large-scale invasion plans to destroy SAM bases along the Suez Canal before they were completed by Egypt and the Soviet Union.

Following the end of the Jordanian crisis on June 12, Nixon, Kissinger, and Rogers agreed to launch a new peace initiative in the Middle East. On June 25,

after prior consultations without agreement by the various parties involved, Rogers announced his cease-fire plan. His hope was to obtain an Egyptian-Jordanian-Israeli cease-fire while the U.N. mediator, Gunnar Jarring, undertook negotiations to implement U.N. Resolution 242 or some other acceptable proposal. Syria was left out of the Rogers proposal because Damascus never accepted in principle 1967's U.N. Resolution 242. The same day he offered his proposal, Rogers announced that the United States would withhold plane shipments to Israel. Privately, Rogers explained to Israeli Ambassador Yitzhak Rabin that if the cease-fire did not work within a short time, U.S. aircraft deliveries would resume.

To pressure Moscow and Cairo to accept the cease-fire, Kissinger and Nixon made tough statements about expelling the Soviets or giving Israel huge new arms supplies. At the same time, Rogers, who was not fully aware of Kissinger's tactics, had qualified these tough statements by, for example, distinguishing between "expelling" the Soviets and "lessening" their influence.

The Soviet Union demonstrated its own "toughness." While considering Rogers Plan II and encouraging Cairo and Amman to accept the plan, Kosygin delayed any commitment while rushing additional SAM-3s to be deployed along the Egyptian side of the Suez Canal. Moscow planned to protect its client by providing more secure air defense if a cease-fire broke down.

By late July, Egypt and Jordan had accepted Rogers's June 25 plan in principle. Israel had to comply before the details could be worked out for a cease-fire arrangement. Before the August 7 cease-fire went into effect, the United States obtained a secret agreement that none of the parties would increase their arms or defense units during the cease-fire. Israel also wanted assurances that the Soviet Union would respect the agreements. Rogers talked with Soviet Ambassador Dobrynin, receiving a commitment from him, but not an absolute one, to respect the cease-fire as well as the arms "standstill" agreements.

Finally, on August 7 the cease-fire went into effect. The situation remained precarious, however, and hardly had the arrangements begun before violations of the agreement took place.

See December 19, 1969.

### September 6, 1970

**The second Jordanian crisis of 1970: the PFLP hijacks three commercial airliners, holding 475 hostages near Amman.**

Although the cease-fire of August 7, 1970, did not settle the difficulties in the Middle East, the Palestinian radicals wanted to prevent any settlement by disturbing the equilibrium of the region. To demonstrate their ability to disrupt the world community, the PFLP organized four skyjackings of airliners on September 6–7, 1970. Three of these succeeded, and the planes and passengers on Trans-World Airways, Swiss Air, and British Overseas Airways were commandeered and flown to an abandoned British airfield 35 miles from Amman, which the PFLP called Revolution Field.

The fourth skyjack attempt, on an El Al (Israeli) plane, failed. Shortly after taking off from London, two Arabs ordered the airplane's crew to fly to Amman. An Israeli security guard aboard the El Al acted quickly. He shot the man and subdued his companion, a woman named Leila Khaled, who was arrested when the plane returned to London.

In Jordan, the PFLP demanded the release of all Palestinian and pro-Palestinian prisoners jailed in Israel, West Germany, Switzerland, and Britain. While the Swiss complied, the United States joined Britain and Israel in rejecting the demands but offering to negotiate. They asked the International Red Cross to contact the PFLP for possible discussions.

Nixon agreed to preparations to intervene in Jordan if necessary. On September 9, he announced that the United States was delivering 18 Phantom jets to Israel. He also sent six C-130 U.S. air force transports to a Turkish base at Incirlik, 350 miles from Amman, where they would be ready to bring out the PFLP hostages. The U.S. Sixth Fleet was ordered to the Israeli-Lebanese coast and 25 U.S. air force Phantom jets were sent to Incirlik.

At Revolution Field near Amman, the Red Cross negotiators achieved a compromise with the PFLP by September 12. Although the Palestinians blew up the three airliners, they took the hostages to a camp near the village of Zerqua preparatory to working out a deal with the Red Cross. Israel agreed to release 450 Arab prisoners it had taken since September 6 and the British agreed to release Khaled. In exchange, the PFLP released all but 55 Jewish passengers. The Jewish passengers were held until September 29,

when the PFLP secured the actual release of the 450 Israeli-held Palestinians.

### September 15, 1970

**King Hussein of Jordan attacks the Palestinian refugee camps to abolish the PFLP and PLO power in Jordan.**

While the last non-Jewish hostages of the PFLP were being released from the camp at Zerqua, King Hussein decided the moment was opportune to eliminate the Palestinian "state-within-a-state" that the PFLP and PLO had created in their refugee camps in Jordan. The Royal Army and tank corps moved to take over the camps, forcing the Palestinians to relocate or go into exile in Syria or Iraq.

Hussein's action was a civil war with international repercussions. Both Syrian and Iraqi forces with Moscow's quiet support moved to their borders in a threatening menace to aid the Palestinians. The Israeli government of Golda Meir preferred a viable Jordanian government under the Hasemite King Hussein and considered the possibility of backing him against the Palestinians and other Arabs. In this context, the United States had to decide on a satisfactory response.

See September 6, 1970, and September 22, 1970.

### September 22, 1970

**At the peak of the crisis over Hussein's fight with the Palestinians, Nixon agrees to protect Israel if it will assist Jordan. Within 48 hours, the tensions abate.**

Because the Soviet Union's client states of Syria and Iraq backed the Palestinian organizations in Jordan as a way to keep the refugees out of their own lands, King Hussein's campaign to eliminate the fedayeen caused widespread international concerns. President Nixon was ready to back Hussein as far as necessary but hoped he would not have to commit American troops to intervene.

Initially, on September 16 and 17, the president publicly warned Moscow that the United States and Israel might intervene if Syria and Iraq attacked Jordan. He talked with Israeli Prime Minister Golda Meir, who was on a scheduled visit to the United States, telling her that the United States favored Hussein but Israel should use restraint as long as possible. He also contacted the Soviet chargé in

Kissinger, Nixon, and Israeli prime minister Golda Meir at a 1974 meeting. National Archives

Washington (Ambassador Dobrynin was on leave) and asked the Soviets to restrain its two Arab associates.

Although the Soviets said they would restrain Syria, they did not or could not. On September 19, 300 Syrian tanks attacked Jordan, bringing a severe world crisis. If Hussein fell, Israel and perhaps the United States would have to move to help Jordan.

Hussein survived, however. On September 20, Hussein asked for Israeli air support to make an all-out offensive against Syria and the Palestinians. The Israelis were reluctant to comply without U.S. guarantees of protection on their southern (Egyptian) border. Nixon and his staff reviewed their options. On September 19, the president had alerted American troops in the United States and Europe, while ordering emergency preparations by airborne battalions at Fort Bragg, Georgia, and in West Germany. Now at Meir's request the president agreed on September 22 to protect Israel from the Soviet Union and Egypt if she helped Hussein maintain his authority in Jordan.

Nixon's commitment brought the United States and the USSR to the brink of war. Fortunately, the crisis stopped. All Hussein needed was enough encouragement to commit his tanks and air force to an all-out war on Syria and the Palestinians. The promises of Israel and America supplied this, and by September 23, Hussein's army turned the Syrians back. Perhaps Moscow, too, had pressured Damascus to stop the attacks.

Consequently, tensions relaxed temporarily in Jordan. Hussein had established his position against the Palestinians. Soon after, however, the PFLP, PLO, and other Palestinian groups moved to reestablish a position of strength in Lebanon.

## September 25, 1970

### An alleged Cuban crisis arises about the possible construction of a Soviet nuclear submarine base at Cienfuegos, Cuba.

While there is some evidence that the Soviets had begun some new type of activity at Cienfuegos during the summer of 1970, exactly what was done is not clear. During July, Admiral E.P. Holmes of the Atlantic Fleet told a congressional committee that the Soviets *might* build a submarine base in Cuba. According to Kissinger, U-2 flights on September 10 showed construction activity that he interpreted to be a nuclear submarine base. He indicated this in a press background briefing on September 16. The article appeared in the *New York Times* on September 25, causing other congressmen to accuse Moscow of deception.

Subsequently, Kissinger claimed a diplomatic triumph for putting pressure on the Soviets to stop their construction. After the *Times* story appeared, Ambassador Dobrynin denied it. Kissinger later claimed he confronted the ambassador with photo evidence and Dobrynin turned "ashen," asking to consult Moscow. On October 5, Dobrynin—followed on October 13 by the TASS news agency in Moscow—denied that the Soviet Union was building a submarine base in Cuba. The "crisis" disappeared as fast as Kissinger had inaugurated it during his September 16 briefing.

In 1989, Raymond Garthoff's *Reflections on the Cuban Missile Crisis* (1989 edition) indicates the crisis ended because President Nixon pledged that the United States would not invade Cuba.

### September 28, 1970

*President Nasser of Egypt dies of a heart attack.*

On September 29, Vice President Anwar Sadat was sworn in as acting president. On October 15, Sadat was elected president.

### October 6, 1970

**President Nixon announces a new peace initiative to North Vietnam that contributes nothing new. It is seen as a political ploy to help Republican congressmen in the November elections.**

Nixon's much publicized "new initiative" called for a cease-fire-in-place in all Indochina, the convocation of an Indochina Peace Conference, and the "immediate and unconditional release of all prisoners of war held by both sides." Hanoi saw no advantages to these proposals and, on October 9, dismissed them as "a maneuver to deceive world opinion." Nixon used the plan as evidence of his desire for peace, asking voters to provide Republican congressmen to support him in his effort.

### October 17, 1970

*Great Britain makes a major oil find in the North Sea.*

### October 24, 1970

**CIA efforts fail to influence the defeat of Salvador Allende as president of Chile.**

As disclosed by the Senate Select Committee on Intelligence Activities in 1975, the CIA had been attempting to prevent the rise to power of left-wing liberal groups in Chile since at least the days of President Kennedy. Alarmed by the rise of Castro in Cuba, Kennedy apparently ordered the CIA in 1962 to use $180,000 to help the conservative Christian Democratic candidate Eduardo Frei Montalvo defeat the Socialist Salvador Allende Gossens. Frei won in 1964 and, perhaps boastfully, a CIA report said that U.S. funds of $3 million made the difference in the election.

Additional funds were continually used in Chile to aid pro-American candidates, but by 1970 Allende's chances of victory appeared to increase. Both the U.S. business community and Ambassador Edward Korry, who backed U.S. business interests, feared that if elected, Allende would nationalize copper mines and other U.S. investments. Thus, in March 1970, the Forty Committee of the NSC, which regulated covert intelligence operations, agreed to spend $135,000 to subsidize "spoiling" operations critical of Allende. In June, an additional $300,000 was authorized by the Forty Committee because Korry flooded the State Department with alarming messages that Allende's victory would be worse than Castro's. In addition to CIA funds, International Telephone and Telegraph and other U.S. business firms spent monies to assist the National Party candidate, Jorge Allessandri.

On September 4, 1970, no candidate won a majority in the Chilean elections. Allende received 36.3%; Allesandri, 35.3%; and a third, left-wing candidate, Radomiro Tomic, received 28.4%. If one put Tomic's left-of-center vote with Allende's, the rightist candidate, Allesandri, clearly seemed likely to lose. In accord with the Chilean constitution, the absence of a majority victory sent the names of the two leading candidates to the Congress to select the president. The ballot would be between Allende and Allesandri.

Although a CIA report in September 1970 found that the United States had "no vital interests within Chile" and the world balance would "not be significantly altered by an Allende regime," it asserted that Allende's victory would be a "psychological setback to the U.S. as well as a definite advance for the Marxist idea." In reality, Allende was not pro-Soviet or a Communist, although many conservative U.S. cold warriors such as Ambassador Korry believed anyone left of center was a Bolshevik working for Moscow. Allende was an advocate of Marxian ideals. In Chile, he was the candidate of Unidad Popular, a coalition of several leftist parties advocating economic nationalism for Chile and broad social reforms. Like many Mexican nationalists between 1911 and 1941, Allende antagonized U.S. business by espousing a program to use Chilean resources to benefit the Chilean people. This constantly translated into a candidate's being an advocate of Soviet Bolshevism when viewed through the prism of U.S. investors.

Therefore on September 8 and 14, the Forty Committee authorized the CIA and Ambassador Korry to use $350,000 of covert funds to bribe moderate Christian Democratic congressmen who had backed Tomic. Their votes for Allesandri in the congressional balloting for president on October 24 would defeat Allende.

On September 15, however, Nixon and Kissinger went one step further, ordering Richard Helms of the CIA to support military factions in Chile who opposed Allende. The CIA had considered backing a military leader in Chile since 1969. The political interference programs of the NSC were called "Track I" and the military coup plans, "Track II." By September 15, Helms had evidently convinced Nixon and Kissinger that an Allende victory was akin to a Communist victory. Because Kissinger was notably lacking in knowledge of Latin America, he could easily be persuaded. Kissinger demonstrated his attitude during a news briefing on September 16. He told reporters that if Chile fell, then Argentina, Peru, and Bolivia would follow. What would happen to the "Organization of American States ... is extremely problematical." These "domino" theories abounded in the United States after 1947.

Nixon's September 15 approval of Track II aid to the Chilean military involved the CIA in a scenario that assured Allende's election. Although the exact connection of the CIA to the plot to kidnap General Rene Schneider is not known, this plan went awry. The Chilean military wanted Schneider out of the way because he was a strong constitutionalist. It was planned that his abduction would be blamed on the Left, giving the Right an excuse to seize power. Unfortunately, Schneider was killed during the kidnap attempt and the right wing was implicated, not the left.

After anti-army protests arose, the Chilean generals showed their loyalty by joining to support the constitutional decision of Congress on October 24. Allende was elected president. The plans of the CIA and the NSC were not laid aside, however.

## November 10, 1970

### General de Gaulle dies in France.

To many of the French de Gaulle had been the symbol of France's pre-1940s glory as a great empire and civilization. He had created the stable Fifth French Republic and was its first president after 1957.

## November 21–22, 1970

### A group of American volunteers stages an unsuccessful attack on a POW camp in North Vietnam.

This raid against a POW camp at Sontay, 23 miles west of Hanoi, was made by volunteer troops from the U.S. army's Special Forces and the air force's Special Operations Force. Reportedly, 70 to 100 Americans were prisoners at Sontay, but when the U.S. helicopters landed, they found the place deserted. The POWs had been moved. Following a brief firefight with North Vietnamese in the area, the U.S. troops boarded their helicopters to return south. The raid was not reported in the United States until November 24.

The POW issue became one of the principal concerns of many Americans as Nixon's Vietnamization program proceeded. The Communists knew this and used the POW exchange as a trump card in all negotiations.

## November 21–22, 1970

### U.S. fighter-bombers from Thailand stage heavy air attacks all over North Vietnam.

Secretary Rogers told Congress that these raids were retaliatory because the North Vietnamese and Vietcong had shelled Saigon and Hue in violation of the October 31, 1968, agreement. Some observers believed these attacks were designed to warn Hanoi because it had recently infiltrated about 200,000 troops into South Vietnam. Others related them to the U.S. attack on the Sontay POW camp on the night of November 21–22.

## December 7, 1970

### Poland and West Germany sign a treaty that recognizes the Oder-Neisse River line as the German-Polish border.

This treaty was signed by Polish Premier Józef Cyrankiewicz and West German Chancellor Willy Brandt. The border had been established as part of the Yalta compromise in 1944–1945 to award Poland with former German territory in the west as compensation for the extension of the Soviet Union's border into former eastern Polish land. Final ratification of this treaty was delayed because it was coupled

The Hoa Lo prison (''Hanoi Hilton''), where 352 POWs were concentrated after the failed raid on Son Tay prison. Ironically, the prison was razed in 1994 and a luxury hotel built on the grounds. National Archives

with the Quadritite Agreement on Berlin by the West German government.

See June 3, 1972.

### December 14, 1970

#### *Riots occur in Gdansk, Poland, as workers protest the government's economic policy.*

Polish workers' complaints against Communist rule had steadily increased in 1970, leading to a large-scale uprising of shipyard workers in Gdansk. In response to these difficulties, the government promised to rectify some of the complaints. On December 24, the Polish Communist Party followed Soviet advice by naming Edward Gierek to replace Władysław Gomułka as first secretary of the Communist Party.

### December 16, 1970

#### *A rebellion begins in Eritrea.*

About 10,000 insurgents threatened to overthrow the government of this East African state. The conflict made the so-called Horn of Africa on the northeast coast a new area of global strategic concern.

### December 28, 1970

#### The United States persuades Israel to resume talks with U.N. mediator Gunnar Jarring.

The Middle East peace talks that resulted from the cease-fire of August 7, 1970, provided for mediation by the United Nations. Israel broke off these discussions on August 27 because it claimed Egypt had violated the cease-fire by basing more Soviet SAM-3s along the Suez Canal. CIA photos verified the Israeli charge and in September and October, the United States passed new legislation to send new weapons to Israel such as the Shrike missile, which could neutralize the SAM-3.

Following the Jordanian events of September and October 1970, U.S. allies urged Washington to try again to keep peace by mediation in the Middle East. Finally, on December 28, under pressure from Washington, the Israeli government agreed to formal discussions with Jarring. The U.N. mediator hoped to shuttle between Israeli and Egyptian delegations to seek a method to solve the Sinai dispute.

# 1971

### January 15, 1971

*Egypt's Aswân High Dam is dedicated.*

The construction of the Aswân Dam was a cooperative project between Egypt and the Soviet Union following the Suez Crisis of 1956. The dam began operations on July 21, 1970, when its final generators were turned on.

On January 15, President Sadat of Egypt and the USSR's President Nikolay Podgorny led dedication ceremonies for the project. Soon thereafter, Moscow and Cairo signed a 15-year friendship pact.

See May 27, 1971.

### January 25, 1971

*In Uganda, a military coup led by General Idi Amin is successful.*

### February 8, 1971

**South Vietnam's invasion of Laos to wipe out communist sanctuaries and the Ho Chi Minh Trail becomes a disaster.**

Since the beginning of Rolling Thunder in 1965, the United States had tried to eliminate the Ho Chi Minh supply route and other North Vietnamese sanctuaries on the border of Laos and the two Vietnams. To permit ground forces to accomplish this task, General Abrams urged the ARVN leaders to plan an operation into Laos. Code-named Lam Son 619 (Total Victory), the ARVN operation, aided by U.S. air strike and helicopters, attacked the Laotian border in a planned five-to-eight-week invasion.

During the first two weeks of battle, the ARVN succeeded. General Abrams reported the ARVN "are fighting ... in a superior way." Nixon bragged to reporters about the qualities of South Vietnam's new army.

Late in February, however, ARVN ran into trouble, first with the Laotian terrain, next with North Vietnamese forces. The Ho Chi Minh trail proved to be a labyrinth of footpaths with crisscrossing single-lane dirt roads meandering through thick jungles. The unguided could not tell where trails began or ended.

The entire complex covered an area 5 miles wide and 100 miles long. It was not possible permanently to disrupt or destroy the so-called trail.

About the time that this maze was discovered, the North Vietnamese had begun to engage in conventional warfare. Tanks aligned in mass formation advanced on the ARVN foot soldiers. Saigon's forces broke off their attack and began a retreat that soon turned into a rout. As TV cameras recorded the scenes, ARVN troops crowded aboard or hung onto the tails and landing gear of U.S. helicopters sent to rescue them. ARVN suffered heavy casualties and lost large quantities of U.S. equipment in the retreat.

This Laotian fiasco not only hurt Nixon's pride but also demoralized the ARVN troops whom their U.S. trainers had been seeking to build into a quality defense force in South Vietnam.

### February 11, 1971

**Eighty nations sign the Seabed Arms Control Treaty, which prohibits nuclear weapons on the ocean floor.**

The U.N. Disarmament Committee in Geneva proposed this pact by which signatories agreed not to place nuclear missile launchers on the bottom of seas or oceans. The United States, the Soviet Union, and Great Britain were the important signees among the 80 nations. France and China refused to sign it.

### February 14, 1971

*Western oil companies and six Persian Gulf oil nations agree to raise prices: The Tehran Agreement.*

The Arab oil states accepted the leadership of Reza Shah Pahlavi of Iran in negotiating with oil companies to increase their demands for control of their oil resources. To do so, the shah threatened an oil embargo, although he tried to separate his politics from the radical anti-Western policies of Libya's al Gadhafi, who had unilaterally forced a 30¢ per barrel oil increase on Libyan oil companies in 1970. According to Tad Szulc's *The Illusion of Peace* (1978), President Nixon let U.S. oil companies work out deals with Libya and other Middle Eastern States, not being concerned until the Tehran Agreement's oil prices affected Americans in May 1971.

By the Tehran Agreement, the Western oil companies accepted an immediate posted oil price increase from $1.80 to $2.15 per barrel for 1971 and an annual 2.5% increase between June 1, 1971, and January 1, 1975. The companies also accepted a 55% income tax. The Western oil companies said the pact increased the stability of the oil supply. They simply added the extra oil costs to their customers' bills in Western Europe and the United States.

As inflationary prices resulted in the Western nations after 1971, the Arab nations and Iran required the oil companies to amend their agreements in 1972 to increase the posted oil prices to offset the decreased value of the dollar. In January 1972, prices increased another 8.94%, and in April 1972 they went up another 7.5%. The shah was a leader in these moves to gain oil revenue and continued to be until his overthrow in 1979.

See November 7, 1973.

### March 16, 1971

**Secretary Rogers proposes a mideast peace plan because the U.N. discussions have broken down. Israel rejects it and another deadlock results.**

Following Israel's agreement to renew mediation on December 28, 1970, UN mediator Gunnar Jarring undertook discussions in Egypt, Jordan, and Israel. Jarring did not handle the affair well. On February 8, he made the unrealistic proposal that Israel withdraw to its 1948 borders and followed this by making the Israeli rejection public. Consequently Israel withdrew from further talks even though Egypt had agreed to extend the truce of August 1970.

In March, Secretary of State Rogers undertook to resolve the dispute. After working quietly to review the situation Rogers offered a plan on March 16. If Israel withdrew to the pre-June 1967 borders, Egypt would guarantee peace in the Sinai and an international force, including U.S. troops, would monitor the region.

Egypt rejected this plan. By March 1971, Prime Minister Golda Meir said Israel "cannot trust Rogers' offer, even if it is proposed in good faith." As a result, another deadlock occurred in the Middle East. Although Rogers visited both Sadat and Meir in May 1970, both sides were inflexible. Meir was especially upset that the United States was again restricting arms sales to Israel while the Soviet Union bolstered its military aid to Egypt.

See May 27, 1971.

### March 24, 1971

**Congress rejects public funding for a supersonic transport plane (SST).**

Extensive debates in the United States at large, as well as in Congress, showed a general uneasiness about the necessity for a superfast airplane. Environmental concerns as well as the technical and economic viability of the project caused its rejection. Not even the nationalistic claim that the Soviets and the western Europeans had developed an SST aroused significant support for the project.

### April 6, 1971

**Ping-Pong Diplomacy: while in Japan, Chinese ping-pong team members invite the U.S. team to China as soon as the Nagoya tournament ends.**

Although the United States and China had been quietly but frequently sounding each other out to renew normal diplomatic relations, Beijing followed an unusual method to indicate its willingness to negotiate with Washington. Prior talks had begun in Warsaw (January 20, 1970) and through contacts by way of Lahore, Pakistan, and Romania. On March 15, 1971, the State Department again signaled Beijing because it completely lifted the travel ban by Americans to China that had been partly raised on July 21, 1970.

The April 6 invitation came from the Chinese ping-pong team, which had participated in an international tournament in Nagoya, Japan. On the last day, Chinese team members invited the Americans to come and play against them in China. Graham B. Steenhoven, president of the U.S. Table Tennis Association, contacted the American ambassador in Tokyo. By telegram, the State Department responded positively.

The American group arrived in Beijing on April 10. It included nine team members, four officials, two wives, and three American journalists. Although the Chinese easily won at ping-pong, the U.S. team had an unusual reception at the Great Hall of the People. Premier Chou En-lai told them: "You have opened a new page in the relations of the Chinese and American people. I am confident that this beginning again of our friendship will certainly meet with majority support of our two peoples." The U.S. team invited

China's ping-pong team to visit the United States, and Chou accepted.

## April 14, 1971

**President Nixon picks up China's "ping-pong" overture, announcing he plans to end restrictions on travel and plans to "create broader opportunities for contacts between the Chinese and American peoples."**

Nixon had eagerly awaited Chou En-lai's indication that better relations were needed. After learning of Chou's favorable speech to the U.S. table tennis team on April 14, he indicated that the NSC recommended and he approved the following actions that did not require legislation or negotiation:

1. to expedite visas for visitors from the People's Republic of China to America;
2. to relax U.S. currency controls on China;
3. to end U.S. restrictions on oil sales to Chinese-owned or chartered ships or aircraft;
4. to allow U.S. vessels to carry Chinese cargo again;
5. to create a list of nonstrategic materials that could soon be exported to China.

## April 16, 1971

**President Nixon explains two vital parts of his Vietnam strategy: (1) To use air power and small U.S. ground forces until peace is made; (2) To have all U.S. POWs released as a condition of withdrawing all U.S. forces.**

On April 16, the president specified this particular part of his plan for Vietnam. Earlier, on April 7, Nixon announced on national television that 100,000 U.S. forces would be brought home between May 1 and December 1. This would leave about 175,000 men in Vietnam in 1975 with only 60,000 to 75,000 in combat units. Thus, Nixon explained to the American Society of Newspaper Editors on April 16 that he hoped after the peace treaty was made to bring all U.S. troops home so that the South's government could defend itself.

Again, as he had more and more in 1970, Nixon stressed the POW issue as one the United States would insist on before it withdrew completely. In his speech of April 16, he made the POW release a sine qua non of final U.S. withdrawal.

## May 3, 1971

**A massive antiwar demonstration in Washington, D.C., leads to the arrest of nearly 12,000 people.**

## May 27, 1971

*Cairo and Moscow announce an Egyptian-Soviet treaty of friendship and cooperation.*

Article 8 of this treaty pledged the Soviet Union to help Egypt in the military field. Since September 1970, Egypt had received 100 MIG-21 fighters and 16 MIG-8 troop-carrying helicopters.

## June 13, 1971

**The *New York Times* begins publishing the texts of secret Vietnam documents: The *Pentagon Papers*.**

The multivolume series of documents known as the *Pentagon Papers* had been compiled by aides of Secretary of Defense McNamara in 1967–1968 as a systematic study of exactly how the United States became involved in Vietnam between 1945 and 1968. In addition to an analytical text, it included copies of secret documents available in Pentagon files that included any circulated from the White House and State Department.

Later, Nixon learned that these documents had been leaked to the *Times* by Daniel ELLSBERG, a former member of Kissinger's NSC staff who went to work in 1969 at the RAND Corporation. At RAND, Ellsberg read and made photocopies of the *Pentagon Papers*, a document available to RAND because it was a "think tank" for the Defense Department. In addition to the *Times* edition, which was a selected version of the papers, the *Pentagon Papers* were later published in a five-volume Senator Michael Gravel edition (1971) and a 12-volume Government Printing Office edition.

Ellsberg's act had future repercussions for Nixon. Concerned about leaks, the president established a 'Plumbers Unit' in the White House that became involved in a variety of clandestine activity during the next two years. Its first project was a covert operation to obtain Ellsberg's file from the office of his psychiatrist, Dr. Lewis J. Fielding, on August 25. This operation was the White House's first authoriza-

802    July 9, 1971

tion of illegal action, which ultimately led to Nixon's resignation in 1974.

## July 9, 1971

### NSC Chairman Kissinger secretly interrupts an around-the-world trip to fly to Beijing from Rawalpindi, Pakistan. In China, Kissinger consults with Foreign Minister Chou En-Lai.

Arrangements for Kissinger's secret trip to Beijing originated late in April 1971. Chou's invitation—by way of Pakistan—for a high-level delegate to visit the Chinese capital had been made and accepted. A specific date for the visit was set in mid-June, and on July 1, Kissinger left on a world tour that took him to Pakistan by July 8. After visiting Saigon, Bangkok, and New Delhi, Kissinger arrived at Rawalpindi, where Pakistan's Foreign Minister Khan Sultan took great pains to assure the secrecy of Kissinger's departure to and return from China.

On the evening of July 8, Kissinger canceled a dinner because of illness, slipping from his room to an automobile that took him back to the airport. The next morning a Secret Service agent disguised as the NSC chairman set out to recover from his illness by resting at Nathia Gali.

Meanwhile, Kissinger flew by Pakistani Airlines to Beijing, where he met on July 9–10 with Chou En-lai. These sessions went splendidly as the personalities of the two officials were compatible. Their discussions included the following points:

1. The United States would recognize that Taiwan was part of China; the issue would be settled by the Chinese themselves. Kissinger accepted this because on April 26, a special U.S. presidential commission recommended that the United States approve the seating of the People's Republic in the United Nations, but without expelling Nationalist China. This commission included fairly conservative Republicans such as Henry Cabot Lodge and Senators Robert A. Taft Jr. and Bourke B. Hickenlooper.
2. Chou indicated that he expected the United States would some day sever relations with the Nationalist government, but he set no date or precondition on this.
3. Kissinger said Nixon could not break with Chiang Kai-shek immediately but hoped for good relations with Beijing anyway.

4. The People's Republic would be accepted in the United Nations, but the precise status of Nationalist China was left unsettled.
5. Kissinger said the United States believed, as Nixon had stated in a speech on July 6, 1971, that mainland China was one of the five great power centers of the world.
6. Chou invited President Nixon to visit China in 1972; Kissinger accepted.
7. Future contact would be through the U.S. and Chinese embassies in Paris.

## July 15, 1971

### President Nixon announces on television that he will visit the People's Republic of China before May 1972.

Kissinger returned to Washington from his Beijing visit on July 13. Following extensive discussions, the president decided to announce the visit on July 15, as Chou and Kissinger had agreed. Nixon relaxed most of the day, then flew to California to make the broadcast from San Clemente. This sequence of events is important because until he reached Los Angeles about 5:30 P.M. California time, he did not notify Secretary of State Rogers so that U.S. allies could be contacted in advance.

When Rogers phoned the State Department, its Asian specialist, Marshall Green, was concerned that Japan must know in advance. He telegraphed Ambassador Armin Meyer in Tokyo but the message arrived too late. Nixon was on television and the Armed Forces radio station while Meyer was having his hair cut. Rogers did call the ambassadors of Japan, Nationalist China, and the USSR in advance. Nationalist Chinese Ambassador James C.H. Shen was shocked, calling Nixon's move a "shabby deal."

Although American allies generally concurred with Nixon, they all felt dismayed by not being consulted, especially the Japanese. Nixon and Kissinger's style, however, was often to work outside the normal diplomatic apparatus and protocol channels of the State Department.

Nevertheless, Nixon surprised many Americans when he announced his proposed visit—he had changed a U.S. policy that dated back to October 1949. He told his audience that the United States sought "friendly relations with all nations." The visit would reduce tensions with China and promote peace "not

Kissinger secretly visits Chou En-lai to prepare for Nixon's visit. National Archives

just for our generation but for future generations on this earth we share together."

## August 9, 1971

### *India and the Soviet Union sign a 10-year treaty of friendship and cooperation.*

Similar to the Soviets' May 27 treaty with Egypt, this pact provided for Soviet military aid to India. Although both nations claimed the pact was to maintain peace in South Asia, the United States and Pakistan believed it aimed at the latter country as a threat of war. They were correct.

See December 3, 1971.

### August 12, 1971

*The Soviet Union and West Germany sign a treaty making the European frontiers established in 1945 "inviolable."*

German Chancellor Willy Brandt negotiated this treaty with Moscow as part of his *Ostpolitik*, aimed at promoting détente. In particular, West Germany recognized the Oder-Neisse border between Poland and Germany.

See December 7, 1970, and June 3, 1972.

### August 15, 1971

**President Nixon announces a "new economic policy." This includes a 10% import tax surcharge that has international consequences.**

The U.S. foreign trade imbalance had been growing since March 1968, and European nations wanted the United States to devalue the dollar in terms of gold to a more realistic ratio. Gold had held at $35 per ounce since 1933. By 1971, the speculative gold exchange no longer valued dollars sufficiently, causing the currency and trade of all nations based on the dollar to suffer.

Following a lengthy meeting of the NSC, the Treasury Department, and others, Nixon decided to take three important actions on August 15:

1. A wage-price freeze was set up for the United States.
2. The convertibility of the dollar to gold was temporarily suspended.
3. There would be a 10% import surcharge. Nixon claimed the surcharge would stabilize the dollar better than devaluation. He announced it would be temporary but did not specify for how long.

The trade surcharge shocked America's allies, who had not been consulted before the announcement by Nixon. In reality, these policies were temporary expedients that delayed a crisis in which the U.S. would be unable to exchange gold for dollars on the international market. Later in 1971, delgates at an international conference discussed arrangements to handle the world's monetary affairs.

See March 25–26, 1968, and December 17, 1971.

### September 3, 1971

**The Quadripartite Agreement on Berlin is signed to solve some of the past tensions in that divided city.**

Ambassadorial-level talks regarding Berlin began among the four powers during February 1970. The talks dragged on until May 14, 1971, when Soviet First Secretary Brezhnev agreed to discuss possible mutual reductions of Warsaw Pact and NATO forces if the West would discuss the confirmation of the postwar European borders.

Following detailed discussions between June and August, the four-power pact was signed in Berlin on September 3. The agreement's main clauses were as follows:

1. Traffic to and from West Berlin would be unimpeded.
2. West Berliners could visit East Berlin and East Germany for up to 30 days per year.
3. East Berliners could enter the West, but their departures were to be controlled by East Germany.
4. The three Western powers agreed that Berlin's western sectors were not a "constituent" part of West Germany and would not be governed by it.
5. Four-power rule was retained in Berlin.

The Berlin accords were ratified by East Berlin and West Germany on December 17, by West Berlin and East Germany on December 20. The Berlin Wall remained in place as a symbol of East Germany's need to keep its people locked in. The force reduction talks did not begin as scheduled in October 1971 because the Soviets would not receive the NATO delegation in Moscow.

The final protocols on the Quadripartite Agreement of 1971 were not ratified until 1972.

See June 3, 1972. Also see West Germany's treaties with the Soviet Union and Poland of August 12, 1971, and December 7, 1970.

### September 5, 1971

**A *New York Times* report indicates the Soviet Union has developed an intercontinental supersonic bomber, the Backfire.**

This was the world's first supersonic bomber. The White House learned of its successful testing in

March 1971. The *Times* article was based on a CIA study, including drawings of the plane. The Pentagon refused officially to discuss the "sensitive" intelligence on the Backfire bomber.

### September 30, 1971

**The United States and the USSR sign two minor agreements to try to avoid an accidental nuclear war.**

These two agreements stated that (1) the nation under nuclear attack would try to ascertain if it were an accidental launch or not. This pact tried to strengthen fail-safe procedures, although no specific actions in case of an attack could be precisely predetermined; (2) the Washington-Moscow hot line was switched to space satellite communications to make it swifter and less vulnerable to disruption in case of an accidental launch.

For more on the hot line, see June 29, 1984.

### October 3, 1971

**President Thieu wins reelection in South Vietnam with 82% of the vote.**

Although Thieu staged the election to please his U.S. advisers, the campaign threatened for a while to become a real contest, with former South Vietnamese politicians Marshal Ky or General Big Minh. In particular, Big Minh ran as an advocate of neutrality and negotiations with Hanoi, a program that, in Paris, Le Duc Tho told Kissinger was a favorable possibility for North Vietnam to consider.

Neither Ky nor Minh remained as a candidate for president until October 3. On August 5, the Supreme Court of the Republic of Vietnam ruled that as a former vice president, Ky could not run for election. Big Minh first tried to get the United States to guarantee a fair election. On April 12, Minh gave the U.S. embassy a document in which Thieu instructed all government and military officers in South Vietnam to ensure his victory. The Americans claimed to be "neutral" in the election, however, and, therefore, unable to interfere. On August 20, Minh withdrew from the race, charging that the election process was corrupt.

With no opposition, Thieu won 82% of the vote. He had learned that the Americans did not like election results favoring him by 94 to 98%; yet even 82% was large for a "democratic" candidate.

By 1971, most observers of Thieu's government either criticized or excused his political methods. Critics said his government had less support than that of Diem in 1963; at least Diem had the Catholic backing that Thieu had lost by 1971. After 1968, Thieu talked about political, economic, and military reform but never took any significant action in these areas.

### October 12, 1971

**Washington and Moscow announce that Nixon will visit the Soviet Union in May 1972.**

While reporters believed the signing of SALT I was near, the president cautioned that this pact might not be achieved by that time. In other respects, the announcement of Nixon's visit was no surprise. Since his July 15 decision to visit China, most observers believed the visit to the USSR would come sooner or later.

### October 15, 1971

**The United States and Japan sign a three-year agreement on textiles.**

Since Nixon's meeting with Prime Minister Sato in November 1969, a better atmosphere for trade negotiations had gradually been created. In March 1971, the Japanese Textile Federation in Washington struck a bargain with Wilbur Mills, chairman of the House Ways and Means Committee, by which they unilaterally agreed to limit their exports. This irritated Nixon, who disliked Mills's action, but it began to solve the U.S. trade deficit with Japan, which reached $3 billion in 1971.

On September 26, 1971, Japan's Emperor Hirohito and his empress visited Alaska and were warmly greeted by the president. This symbolized better relations and helped the two countries reach a trade agreement in October.

### October 25, 1971

**The People's Republic of China is admitted, the nationalist government of Taiwan expelled, from the United Nations.**

Although the U.S. State Department acted as if it wished to have both Chinese governments in the United Nations, Chou En-lai told Kissinger in July that the Beijing regime could not be represented unless Taiwan left the United Nations.

Beginning on August 2, however, Secretary Rogers stated that the United States would support the seating of the mainland regime but oppose Taiwan's expulsion. The United States submitted such a resolution to the U.N. General Assembly on August 20 and solicited votes to support Taiwan. Until September 16, the United States left undisclosed its view of the Chinese seat as one of the Big Five permanent members of the Security Council if Taiwan remained. Then Nixon announced that the United States would vote for Beijing's position on the council because it reflected "realities." After that statement, the United States lost all but a small hard core of followers on the U.N. vote.

The U.N. action on October 25 was essentially a foregone conclusion. In the General Assembly, the U.S. vote to keep the Nationalists as members lost by 59 to 54. Ninety minutes later, an Albanian resolution to admit the People's Republic and expel Nationalist China carried by a vote of 76 to 35. The United States voted for this resolution. Taiwan's delegation, led by Liu Chieh, quietly gathered its papers and left the hall. The Beijing delegation arrived in New York on November 12.

## October 26, 1971

### Henry Kissinger leaves China with news that Nixon's 1972 visit is arranged.

Kissinger made his second visit to Chou En-lai on October 20, realizing that the details of the president's visit could be finalized following the U.N. vote on October 24 or 25. Thus, on the day after the U.N. vote that expelled the Taiwanese government, Beijing was assured that the United States had complied with its July request. Officially, the White House announced on November 29 that Nixon's visit to China would begin on February 21, 1972.

## December 3, 1971

### *War begins between India and Pakistan.*

There had been a buildup of tension between these two old antagonists since 1970 following the outbreak of a rebellion in Bengal, East Pakistan. Because of Pakistani persecution, 5 million refugees fled from Bengal to India, where Prime Minister Indira Gandhi championed their cause. The rebels had proclaimed the independent republic of Bangladesh on

March 26, 1971, causing the Pakistanis to take further measures to suppress the rebellion.

On December 3, Indian troops invaded Bengal and with help from the rebels trapped 90,000 Pakistani troops. In West Pakistan, Indian armies took over land in the disputed areas of Kashmir.

See December 17, 1971.

## December 17, 1971

### The group of ten agree on new international monetary arrangements by which the U.S. dollar is devalued and exchange rates "float."

Because America's major economic partners could no longer accept the 10% surcharge and continued declining value of the dollar—which Nixon permitted in his August 15 "new economic policy"—the United States as one of the leading financial nations had to work out a new exchange program with the European Community, Canada, and Japan.

Negotiations for the December 17 agreement had been conducted at the Portuguese Azores between U.S. delegates and a French group headed by French President Georges Pompidou. Meeting on the Azores island of Tercerira beginning December 13, Nixon and Pompidou reached the basic agreement that was formalized on December 17 in Washington with delegates of the other nations. Nixon in particular had to overrule Secretary of the Treasury John Connally's belief that the United States should strongarm other nations such as Germany and Japan to devalue their currencies. To the contrary, Secretary of Labor George Shultz argued for floating currency rates. Nixon rejected Shultz's proposal in August, but it was accepted during the Azores meeting with Pompidou. Unlike Connally, Shultz had extensive business experience in international trade.

Nixon and Kissinger accepted the floating currency concept and dollar devaluation during the Azores sessions, an idea with which Pompidou agreed. This basic pact was announced as the Azores Pact on December 14 and ratified by the other European nations, Canada, and Japan on December 17. The agreement permitted all national currencies to float on the exchange market within "broader permissible margins" around a devalued dollar. The immediate devaluation of the dollar was from $35 to $38 an ounce of gold. This was a 9% dollar devaluation, compared with Japan's devaluation of the yen by 17%, the

West German mark's change by $13\frac{1}{2}$%, and the British pound and French franc change of $8\frac{1}{2}$%. The United States ended the 10% import surcharge and the non-convertibility of the dollar decreed on August 15. Extensive trade negotiations between the United States and the other nine nations would also begin.

### December 17, 1971

**Pakistan and India agree to a cease-fire, partly owing to U.S. action to prevent a wider war.**

After war broke out on December 3, President Nixon sought a truce through the United Nations and took action that "tilted" toward Pakistan to limit the war. The U.N. resolutions did not gain a truce because the Soviet Union vetoed three attempts to pass them.

Although publicly claiming U.S. neutrality on December 6, Nixon acted in a fashion that prevented a disastrous defeat for Pakistan. He persuaded Jordan and Iran to send obsolete F-5, F-86, and F-104 jets to Pakistan. He also ordered a naval task force led by an aircraft carrier to move from the Pacific to the Bay of Bengal. This act indicated to India and its Soviet ally that the United States might aid Pakistan if necessary.

Whether Nixon would have employed military force is unclear. U.S. public opinion favored the Bengalis as victims of Pakistani persecution. Thus, presidential action would have been difficult to justify. Fortunately, India agreed to a cease-fire in East Pakistan on December 14 and in West Pakistan on December 17. The major result of the war was creation of Bangladesh as an independent nation.

# 1972

### January 22, 1972

*The United Kingdom is accepted as a member of the European Economic Community Common Market.*

Because French President de Gaulle had vetoed the British membership application on December 18, 1967, Prime Minister Heath held discussions with President Pompidou of France on May 21 to agree on terms of Britain's admission. As a result the EEC voted in favor of English membership on June 23, 1971. On October 28, the British Parliament approved the terms of membership, and on January 22, 1972, the EEC formally voted to admit the British. On the same day, Ireland and Denmark also were accepted as members of the Common Market. The membership of these three nations became effective on January 1, 1973.

### January 25, 1972

**To a national television audience, Nixon outlines a plan to end the Vietnam War and discloses Kissinger's secret talks in Paris.**

President Nixon told the public he was presenting a plan for peace to North Vietnam that should "end the war now" because it was "both generous and far-reaching." In reality, the proposal Nixon described was a slightly revised version of a plan offered to Le Duc Tho in Paris on October 11, 1971. The proposal included withdrawal of all U.S. forces within six months of an agreement, new elections in South Vietnam after Thieu's prior resignation, an independent body to conduct elections in which the Communists could run candidates, and a U.S. aid program to help rebuild Vietnam.

To impress his fellow Americans with his willingness to "try to break the deadlock in the negotiations," Nixon informed the public about Kissinger's secret talks in Paris since August 4, 1969. The national security adviser had met 12 times with Le Duc Tho, Xuan Thuy, or both. Nixon reported that until recently, the secret talks had appeared to progress, but the Communists late in 1971 again became reluctant to compromise on any point.

Nixon's speech indicated that, contrary to public impressions, he had been making extra efforts to seek peace. North Vietnam appeared for the first time to have been the party blocking a successful truce arrangement. Nixon's 1972 peace suggestions had been rejected by Hanoi in October 1971. Nevertheless, he had made a fresh proposal and the Communists had not responded seriously to it between October and January.

### January 30, 1972

*Pakistan withdraws from the British Commonwealth after Great Britain recognizes the independence of Bangladesh.*

Although the truce with India of December 1971 virtually assured the independence of Bangladesh, Pakistan refused to recognize the loss of its eastern territory. As a result, London's recognition of the government of Prime Minister Sheikh Mujibur Rahman was opposed by Pakistan. On April 18, 1972, Bangladesh became a member of the British Commonwealth.

### February 17, 1972

**President Nixon leaves for China, making his entire journey a television spectacular.**

From his departure before an honor guard, Vice President Spiro Agnew, members of Congress, and 8,000 well-wishers until his return on February 28, Nixon used the China tour to promote his 1972 presidential campaign. After stopping in Hawaii and Guam, Air Force One reached Peking at 11:40 A.M. on February 21. Nixon and Kissinger went immediately to visit with Chairman Mao Tse-tung. Subsequently, live television reports carried into American homes his visits to the Great Hall of the People, the Great Wall, Hangchow, and Shanghai. On the final day in Shanghai, Nixon and Chou En-lai issued what became known as the Shanghai Communiqué, which described the working relations between Washington and Beijing. The important parts of this message were as follows:

1. On Vietnam, the United States declared that after a truce the U.S. forces would withdraw and permit the peoples of Indochina to "determine their destiny without outside intervention." America, the message incorrectly stated, had always sought "a negotiated solution" to the Vietnam War.
2. The United States said it would retain strong ties with South Korea and Japan.
3. In South Asia, Nixon promised U.S. support for the rights of peoples in India, Pakistan, and elsewhere to "shape their own future in peace, free of military threats, and without having the areas become the subject of great power rivalry."
4. Chou declared China wanted all nations to be treated as free and equal; "it opposes hegemony and power politics of any kind."
5. China supported the "peoples of Vietnam, Laos and Cambodia in their efforts" but said nothing about the U.S. presence in the area.
6. China opposed any Japanese "revival and outward expansion" of "militarism," favoring a "peaceful and neutral Japan."
7. China said it backed Pakistan in its "struggle to preserve ... its independence and sovereignty." This referred indirectly to China's alliance against India.
8. The United States and China agreed to conduct relations on the "principles of respect for the sovereignty and integrity of all states, non-interference in the internal affairs of other states, equality and mutual benefits, and peaceful coexistence."
9. Regarding Taiwan, China stated that it could have no full diplomatic relations with the United States

The Nixons, with interpreters, and Secretary of State William Rogers visit the Great Wall of China, February 24, 1972. National Archives

as long as Washington recognized the Taiwan regime. Without a definite date, Nixon promised the gradual U.S. withdrawal of its forces from Taiwan, agreeing that there is but one China and Taiwan is part of it.

10. China and the United States promised to broaden "people to people" exchanges, bilateral trade, and exchanges in science, technology, sports, and journalism. The two nations would remain in direct contact and establish "liaison missions" in lieu of normal diplomatic representation.

### February 25, 1972

**Secret bombings of North Vietnam are disclosed in a letter to Senator Hughes of the Senate Armed Services committee.**

Similar to the secret Cambodian bombings of 1969–1970, the aggressive U.S. air force attacks on North Vietnam between November 1971 and March 1972 were made public after February 25. Air Force Sergeant Lonni Douglas Franks wrote to Senator Harold E. Hughes to describe these actions and request a public investigation. Subsequent hearings of the Senate committee between June and September 1972 indicated that the Nixon administration had condoned, if not approved, these violations of the 1968 agreement with Hanoi.

The secret bombings of 1971–1972 had been conducted by the Seventh Air Force, commanded by General John D. Lavelle. To justify the attacks, air force personnel filed reports that reconnaissance planes had been attacked and the fighter escorts had retaliated. A second set of reports for General Lavelle would list only the planes and the targets struck by the B-52s. The targets were not the surface-to-air missile (SAM) bases but truck parks, petroleum depots, troop concentrations, and other suitable targets such as Rolling Thunder used before 1968.

General Lavelle explained that he designed the attacks and the report system to impede the pre-invasion buildup of Communist forces. He said "higher authorities" encouraged him to use "protective air strikes" to attack other targets. He considered his method similar to the navy's practice of sending an aircraft as bait over North Vietnam's coast and retaliating after the North's fire had been provoked. General John D. Ryan told the committee that the Defense Department had issued "liberal interpretations" of Communist targets during 1971 and that

by January 1972, the revised regulations justified the targets Lavelle had hit. Thus, the committee tried to locate exactly by whom the changes in guidelines had been ordered. They could not obtain evidence from the Defense Department either to corroborate or to refute that a "higher authority" was responsible. These documents were refused to the committee.

General Lavelle suffered the consequences. He was relieved of command, reduced in rank, and retired from the service. According to the Senate committee report, Lavelle had ordered 28 unauthorized missions with 147 sorties by B-52s in a three-month period of 1971–1972.

### March 13, 1972

*The United Kingdom grants full diplomatic recognition to the People's Republic of China.*

In their agreement with China, the British raised their recognition to the ambassadorial level for the first time since 1950. They also withdrew their consulate from Taiwan. The British were one of many nations granting the mainland government formal recognition during 1972.

### March 30, 1972

**North Vietnam begins offensive action in South Vietnam that lasts until early June.**

Although General Giap began to build up his forces in the fall of 1971 for an attack, President Nixon ignored these reports in favor of more optimistic signs so that planned U.S. withdrawals could continue. Thus, although Ambassador Bunker warned the White House that it underestimated the Communist preparations, the Vietnamization process continued. When the Communists began their 'Easter Offensive' on March 30, only 6,000 U.S. combat troops remained in South Vietnam. As a result, ARVN bore the brunt of the March-June offensive.

Giap's forces attacked on three fronts: across the demilitarized zone and the Laotian border into the northern and central highlands, then, later, after ARVN forces moved north from Saigon, into the southern delta region near Saigon. Using 200 Soviet T-54 tanks and large numbers of 130 mm guns, the Communists overran the outposts north and west of Highways 9 and 13 leading to Hue and An Loc. By April, An Loc and Kontum were besieged and the

Communists had nearly cut the country into two parts.

After Thieu sent ARVN troops north, other Communists attacked the delta regions. Lacking ground forces, General Abrams ordered B-52s from Guam to hit the delta. Previously, the United States had avoided B-52 raids in the populous delta. Now these planes struck in this area, destroying many peasant villages and homes as much as they hurt the Communists. The B-52 attacks and the Vietcong attacks severely damaged America's pacification program in the South. An estimated 365,000 villagers went under Communist control in the delta area during this period.

In June, ARVN counterattacks began to succeed. Parachute drops relieved An Loc although the siege dragged on until September. At Kontum, ARVN's 23rd Division troops moved in and held the city. The tide of battle favored ARVN after June 1. Some ARVN forces did commendably well; others did not hold up, however. The People's Self-Defense Force functioned well in the north but seemed to be demoralized in the delta region.

The military consensus was that U.S. air support was the decisive factor in the successful defenses. Air strikes at An Loc and Kontum allowed the besieged cities to hold fast. In Quang Tri Province air attacks knocked out enemy tanks and 130 mm guns. How ARVN would do without U.S. air cover remained unclear.

### April 4, 1972

**Nixon orders renewed B-52 raids on North Vietnam, the first since 1969. The president believes the large Communist Easter offensive justifies his action.**

Since President Johnson's October 31, 1968, announcement to halt Rolling Thunder, the only U.S. air attacks on North Vietnam had been low-level retaliatory fighter-bomber attacks. After General Giap's large-scale offensive of March 30 began while the United States had only 6,000 troops remaining in the South, Nixon wanted to reaffirm U.S. resolve by responding with a strong attack against the enemy.

The initial B-52 bombing raids were limited to the area from the 17th to the 20th parallel. Nixon decided also to test Moscow's link to Hanoi by additional bombings plus the mining of Haiphong harbor. To enact this maneuver, Nixon sent Henry Kissinger on a special mission to Moscow before the new escalation began.

See April 20 and May 8, 1972. For data on Nixon's secret bombing of North Vietnam, see February 25, 1972.

### April 20, 1972

**National Security Adviser Kissinger begins a secret four-day meeting with Soviet leader Brezhnev to find out the Kremlin's reaction to an escalation of U.S. activity against North Vietnam and to promote new conditions for the peace negotiations in Paris.**

Kissinger's secret mission to Moscow from April 20 to 24 was summit politics in its most dramatic fashion. He and President Nixon kept the mission so secret that Secretary of State Rogers did not know of it, nor did U.S. Ambassador to the Soviet Union Jacob D. Beam until, on the last day, Kissinger called him.

Nixon and Kissinger achieved two objectives during these secret talks. First, they learned that détente with the United States took precedence for Moscow over the events in Vietnam. This resulted because Kissinger told Brezhnev that Nixon believed he had to do two things to punish North Vietnam for the Easter offensive: (1) begin a general bombing of North Vietnam, and (2) mine Haiphong harbor as the strongest U.S. action yet taken against Hanoi. Brezhnev understood this necessity. Although Moscow had protested the B-52 attacks of April 4, he and Kissinger realized this was only a formality. In addition, Brezhnev would not interfere with the U.S. escalation in the north but would continue supplies to Hanoi as best he could.

The crucial question Brezhnev answered was yes, he would receive Nixon on his long-planned visit to Moscow on May 22, 1972. The U.S.-planned escalation would not damage the Soviet Union's reception of Nixon on this historic visit.

The second objective of Kissinger's visit was to gain Brezhnev's backing for a U.S. proposal to break the deadlock in Kissinger's secret peace talks with Le Duc Tho. Because Brezhnev had yielded regarding the bombing escalation as a sign of Soviet interest in détente, Kissinger showed the U.S. desire for big-power détente by yielding on a significant point in the truce talks with Hanoi: the United States would agree to a cease-fire-in-place on the basis of North

Vietnam's troops in the South before the March 30 Easter offensive. This meant that Hanoi could keep 100,000 North Vietnamese in the South after the truce and until a final settlement between North and South Vietnam. Kissinger asked only that Hanoi permit Thieu to remain in power in Saigon from the time of the cease-fire until the final settlement.

Brezhnev realized that Kissinger made a major concession to allow Hanoi's troops to remain in the South. The Thieu matter appeared inconsequential to the Kremlin leaders. Therefore, Brezhnev accepted Kissinger's offer. He immediately dispatched Konstantin KATUSHEV, the Politburo member in charge of allied relations, to Hanoi to deliver Kissinger's new proposal and to arrange a renewal of the secret Paris talks between Kissinger and Le Duc Tho.

Kissinger was elated. On April 24, before leaving Moscow, he called Ambassador Beam and told him that not even the State Department must know about the secret visit. Beam knew because he would be Kissinger's contact point with Brezhnev in working out arrangements for the new truce talks via Katushev. He said the president demanded secrecy to avoid any leaks.

Regarding Nixon's escalated attacks on Hanoi, see
May 8, 1972.

## May 8, 1972

### President Nixon orders the mining of Haiphong Harbor and renews large-scale B-52 attacks on North Vietnam as Linebacker I.

Whereas the April 4 B-52 attacks were limited to the 20th parallel, Linebacker I duplicated many of Rolling Thunder's North Vietnamese targets. Only the 30-mile limit of China's border was restricted. New targets included the Paul Doumer bridge in Hanoi; bridge and rail lines leading to China; fuel dumps; power plants; pipelines to China; and all missile or antiaircraft sites. The B-52 now had TV- and laser-guided bombs for more accuracy and fewer plane losses. Linebacker I continued until October 23, 1972.

The order to mine Haiphong harbor was the most critical escalation ordered by Nixon. The Joint Chiefs had urged the mining of Hanoi's port since 1965, but heretofore the risk of possible war with China or the Soviet Union seemed too great in case one of those nations' ships were hit. Nixon's

détente policy negated the previous risks. His February 1972 visit to China and Kissinger's secret talks in Moscow of April 20–24 guaranteed that those two major powers would not interfere but would accept the closing of the harbor.

Because the secret arrangements made by Nixon with Brezhnev were unknown to the president's critics, Nixon could chuckle at their vociferous denunciation of his announcement that Haiphong harbor would be mined. The dissenters said nuclear war was being risked with the Soviet Union. Not until Nixon arrived in Moscow to begin talks on May 22 did the dissenting pundits concede that President Nixon had pulled off the mining without Soviet opposition.

Soon after May 8, the mining of the sea areas around North Vietnam began. Flying crisscross patterns, U.S. planes laid the mines in the water, setting them to explode at various depths. The aircraft placed over 8,000 mines in the coastal port areas and 3,000 in the inland waterways. Prior to the aerial mining, foreign ships had been given three days' notice to leave the area. The warning was effective. All ships, including Communist-bloc vessels, left the region without serious incident.

Only General Giap and Hanoi's Communists were surprised that neither Beijing nor Moscow did more than issue mild protests to Washington. While U.S. planes completed the mining process late in May, Brezhnev and Nixon wined and dined in Moscow and China's diplomats arranged new trade deals with the United States. Hanoi's Communist Party newspaper, *Nhan Dan,* bitterly complained that Brezhnev's reception of Nixon was like "throwing a life preserver to a drowning pirate."

Nevertheless, the Joint Chiefs' expectation that mining the harbor would seriously hurt Hanoi was another miscalculation. Much of North Vietnam's foreign trade simply went overland. Highways from China to Hanoi became clogged with trucks carrying supplies. New oil pipelines kept fuel plentiful, and a French news correspondent in Hanoi found no evidence of a critical lack of supplies during the summer of 1972. As some observers had previously told the JCS, 90% of North Vietnam's supplies always came overland, making the earlier risk of mining the sea areas unimportant. For hawks in America, however, mining the North Vietnamese port areas had come to symbolize the hard line against the Communists.

## May 22–30, 1972

### Nixon visits Brezhnev in Moscow: he signs the ABM Treaty and SALT I agreement.

President Nixon was the first U.S. president to visit Moscow, although Nixon had visited as vice president (see July 24, 1959). The 1972 visit was part of Nixon's triangular policy to play off the USSR against the Chinese. His visit with President Brezhnev would also allow Nixon to claim credit for the arms control agreement. To complete that agreement, Nixon made concessions to Brezhnev that baffled American nuclear arms control experts who were critical of Nixon's ignorance about essential details of ABM missiles and strategic armaments. Detailed information on the Moscow meeting and agreements is provided in Raymond Garthoff's 1985 book *Détente and Confrontation.*

To summarize the sessions, Nixon and Brezhnev signed two arms control agreements and several agreements for cultural exchanges. First, the two arms control pacts were an Anti-Ballistic Missile Treaty (ABM) and a Strategic Arms Limitation Agreement (SALT I). Both agreements had been prepared during secret talks that began in 1969 (see November 17, 1969). The discussions were completed between March and May 1972 by chief U.S. negotiator Gerard Smith and the Soviet's Vladimir Semenov. Smith was assisted by National Security Adviser Henry Kissinger's visit with Brezhnev in April (see April 20, 1972).

The ABM Treaty limited each side to two ABM sites, separated by no fewer than 1,300 kilometers so that they would not overlap. Later, Nixon and Brezhnev reduced ABM sites from two to one (see July 3, 1974). The limited ABM sites were essential to the SALT I agreement that was based on the concept of mutual assured destruction (MAD). Under MAD, if one side launched a nuclear attack, the other side would retain sufficient nuclear weapons to destroy the aggressor; that is, both sides would suffer nuclear destruction.

Agreement on the ABM Treaty enabled Nixon and Brezhnev to sign the Interim Agreement on Certain Measures with Respect to Strategic Offensive Arms. The term *interim* indicated both sides proposed to continue negotiations for a SALT II treaty while each side restricted its existing launching sites for intercontinental missiles (ICBMs). The SALT I clauses may be summarized as follows: (1) a freeze banned the start of any new ICBM launching sites after July 1, 1972. (2) Existing launching sites could not be moved or replaced by new ones. (3) Small ICBM launchers could not be converted to large ICBM sites. (4) ICBM silos under construction could be completed. (5) Except as otherwise limited, modernization and replacement of strategic missiles and launchers was permitted.

As Garthoff explains, SALT I failed to define small or light and large or heavy ICBM missiles and to limit increases in the size of silos being modernized. U.S. negotiator Smith wanted to resolve these issues but Nixon did not wish to delay news about the signing of an arms control agreement, an event to enhance his campaign for a second term as president.

In the long term, the most critical factor ignored by SALT I was consideration of the development of multiple independent targetable reentry vehicles (MIRVs). MIRV technology permitted each launcher to carry as many as 10 nuclear warheads aimed at ten different targets. The US had already tested and deployed some MIRV launchers, but Soviet MIRVs were from three to five years behind the American program.

Although the Senate ratified the ABM Treaty and Congress approved funds for implementing it under Public Law 92-448, which Nixon signed on November 15, 1972, many Republican politicians later criticized SALT, the ABM Treaty, and Nixon's détente policy. In particular, the Committee on the Present Danger was formed in 1976 to oppose the agreements and détente.

In addition to arms control, Nixon and Brezhnev signed a "Basic Principles of Relations" for both nations to live in peace and security. Other agreements were to improve trade and cultural relations and cooperation in science and technology, including a joint *Apollo-Soyuz* orbital space mission.

See July 15–17, 1975;
March 1, 1976.

## June 3, 1972

### The Quadripartite Agreement on Berlin is fully ratified.

The final exchange of ratifications of the agreement signed on September 3, 1971, awaited the ratification of West Germany's 1970–1971 treaties with the Soviet Union and Poland. These treaties had been delayed by the German Bundestag because the opponents of the treaties wanted to be certain that Germany retained its right to self-determination, to membership in the European Common Market, and to future reunification with East Germany. Those doubts satisfied, the Bundestag ratified the two treaties on May 19. The Soviet Union and Poland ratified the treaties by May 31, 1972. This action cleared the way for the exchange of ratifications on the Berlin pact on June 3. A new relationship had been formalized between the two Germanies and Poland.

See August 12, 1971, and December 7, 1970.

### June 17, 1972

**The Watergate break-in at the Democratic National Headquarters is linked to the Committee to Re-elect the President (CREEP).**

Watergate is an apartment-hotel complex in Washington, D.C. Initially a relatively small incident, Nixon's denials of involvement prevented it from affecting his 1972 campaign. However, further investigation resulted in disclosures that led to his resignation as president in August 1974.

### July 18, 1972

***Egypt's President Sadat expels 20,000 Soviet "advisers."***

Ostensibly, Sadat was upset with Moscow because First Secretary Brezhnev refused to supply him with modern military technology to prepare for war with Israel. The only Soviets Sadat permitted to remain were 200 advisers on SAM missile sites.

### July 19, 1972

**Henry Kissinger and Le Duc Tho renew truce negotiations in Paris that finally lead to a settlement.**

The renewed discussions in Paris came 10 months after Kissinger and Le Duc Tho reached an impasse during a session on September 13, 1971. Kissinger's April 20–24, 1972, talks with Brezhnev opened the door for both to renew negotiations and to find a settlement in the formal and secret discussions that had been held intermittently in Paris since May 1968.

The formal talks in Paris had become a sideshow because of the many secret and separate discussions

Kissinger meets with North Vietnam's Le Duc Tho (right) in Paris. National Archives

that Kissinger held with either Le Duc Tho or Xuan Thuy. They were important as a symbol of four parties negotiating and as the group that would finalize any treaty resulting from the secret talks. The U.S. head of the formal delegation in July 1972 was William Porter. The first head of the delegation, Henry Cabot Lodge, resigned on November 20, 1969. From July 1, 1970, to July 1971, Ambassador to London David Bruce led the U.S. delegation. Finally, Porter took over for Bruce in July 1972.

Kissinger's secret talks had resulted in 12 meetings between August 1969 and September 13, 1971, when the talks became deadlocked. His first discussions with Le Duc Tho were in February 1970. The lengthiest series of secret discussions occurred between May 31 and September 13, 1971. On at least six different trips to Paris in 1971, Kissinger and Le Duc Tho exchanged various proposals, but all talks broke down by September 13. Although Kissinger made another proposal on October 11, 1971, the North Vietnamese refused to meet again until more substantive changes were made by the United States.

The principal deadlock in 1971 resulted from U.S. insistence on two points: (1) mutual withdrawal of all "foreign" troops from South Vietnam because to Kissinger "foreign" included North Vietnamese; and (2) leaving President Thieu in charge in South Vietnam to negotiate a final settlement with the Communists. The second proposal had particularly concerned Hanoi during 1971 because Hanoi did not want the United States to allow Thieu to be reelected again as president of South Vietnam during the October 11 elections.

By July 1972, both Kissinger and North Vietnam had become aware of the need for each side to compromise. Kissinger had outlined a new U.S. position on the cease-fire-in-place when he talked with Brezhnev on April 20, 1972. During a press conference in Paris on May 12, Le Duc Tho indicated his willingness to make a major concession: to permit Saigon to be represented on a three-party "government of broad national concord reflecting the real political situation in South Vietnam." Tho's only qualification was that Thieu could not be chosen by the South Vietnamese as a representative.

Before July, a variety of developments enabled the new discussions to begin. The Communists'

spring offensive, Nixon's retaliatory B-52 strikes, and the successful defense of their territory by the ARVN with U.S. air support were factors causing the North Vietnamese to become more conciliatory when the July 19 meetings began. The most vital reality to North Vietnam, however, was that both Beijing and Moscow urged Hanoi to negotiate a U.S. withdrawal from Vietnam. Hanoi had hoped China and the USSR would reject Nixon's détente overtures unless the United States stopped all military action in Vietnam. By canceling the Moscow summit and halting Chinese-U.S. trade discussions, Hanoi's Communist allies could have pressured Nixon to withdraw more rapidly from Vietnam. This policy had been rejected by the Soviet Union and China, each of which had its reasons for encouraging détente with America.

North Vietnam, therefore, had both military and diplomatic reasons for moving toward a truce. Until U.S. air support was taken away from Saigon, the Communists could not win in Vietnam. Without Soviet or Chinese diplomatic backing, a coalition government in the South would have to precede a definite Communist victory.

For Nixon and Kissinger, the desire to pull out of Vietnam was part of their realistic global strategy and part of the president's 1972 campaign strategy at home. Détente and satisfactory relations with Moscow and Peking required that the United States relinquish its exaggerated concern for the minor issue of Vietnam in its big power relations, that is, to release the U.S. foothold in Southeast Asia that the Chinese disliked. Vietnam, not Taiwan, was the primary obstacle to Nixon and Kissinger's rapprochement with Beijing. At home, the increased dissent against the prolonged war in Vietnam that Nixon had promised to end during the 1968 campaign and the belief that George McGovern was a serious contender for a presidential victory required Nixon to demonstrate that the Vietnamization process was nearly fulfilled. As Nixon's exaggerated concern in planning the Watergate burglary of June 17 demonstrates, the president wanted to avoid all possible risks of defeat in 1972.

On July 19, therefore, Le Duc Tho and Kissinger began what became their final round of discussions for truce arrangements.

For the outcome, see October 26, 1972.

### September 5, 1972

**Palestinian guerrillas take hostages at the Olympic village in Munich.**

On September 5, Black September guerrillas killed two members of Israel's Olympic team and held nine others hostage. The terrorists wanted Israel to release 200 Arab prisoners. When the Israeli government refused, the West German government flew the guerrillas by helicopter to a military airport at Fürstenfeldbruck, telling them that a Lufthansa plane would take them to Egypt.

At the airport, West German police attacked the terrorists. In the battle the nine hostages were killed, along with five Arabs and one German police officer.

### October 26, 1972

**Kissinger announces that "peace is at hand" in Vietnam. The only remaining issues are the American requirement for the precise language needed for an "honorable withdrawal" and to protect President Thieu's government.**

In light of the draft treaty that Kissinger negotiated with Le Duc Tho between July 19 and October 26, Kissinger's remarks to this press conference misled reporters. The real issue delaying the peace process was Nixon's need to convince Thieu to accept the proposals drawn up by Kissinger in Paris.

Although Kissinger tried on August 15 and from October 16 to 22 to gain Thieu's approval, the National Security Adviser did not persuade Thieu to concede. Kissinger had tried to persuade Nixon not to give Thieu veto power over the treaty, but Nixon refused. For political reasons, the president could not risk loud protests from Saigon because the "peace with honor" concept required Thieu's acceptance of any truce.

Nevertheless, the basic framework of the January 1973 truce terms had been worked out by October 16. Briefly summarized, the agreements and the controversial points accepted by Le Duc Tho and Kissinger between July 19 and October 16 were as follows:

1. *Cease-fire-in-place.* The important terms influencing this agreement were that all U.S. troops would withdraw within 60 days of the cease-fire, and all U.S. prisoners of war would be released within 60 days of the cease-fire. Although the agreement did not so specify, omission of withdrawal terms for the North Vietnamese meant that those forces would remain in place in South Vietnam.

2. *"Two-party" National Council of Reconciliation and Concord to implement truce terms and reunify Vietnam.* The original Kissinger plan for a

Nixon policy team: left to right: Richard M. Helms, Henry Kissinger, William P. Rogers, Nixon, Melvin R. Laird, Thomas H. Moorer, Alexander M. Haig. National Archives

Tripartite Commission formed by Thieu's regime, the Provisional Revolutionary Government (formerly the National Liberation Front), and South Vietnamese neutralists was rejected by Thieu. To attempt to satisfy Thieu, Kissinger on October 11 changed the name to "National Council" and referred only to the "two parties" in South Vietnam. Between October 11 and 26, however, Thieu also rejected this proposal. Thieu wanted to be the only government recognized in the South, a position that would have prevented any truce treaty. On October 26, therefore, Thieu had not accepted this idea.

3. *United States to stop bombing first.* The October 16 agreement called for the United States to stop bombing by October 23 so that the treaty could be signed on October 30–31. Linebacker I bombings ceased on October 23, but the treaty was not signed because of Thieu's objections.

4. *Replacement of war matériel.* When the first treaty draft was accepted on October 11, there was no agreement on this. Kissinger wanted loose terminology that would permit the United States to keep Thieu well supplied after the cease-fire; Tho wanted a narrow definition to prevent replacements as much as possible. The North Vietnamese accepted Kissinger's terms on replacement on October 22, 1972.

Because Thieu refused to sign the treaty on October 23 as provided for in the Kissinger-Tho plan of October 11, Hanoi broadcast a report that announced the terms it had agreed to and condemned Washington and Saigon for breaking their promise to sign and disturbing world peace. Beijing and Moscow joined Hanoi's opposition to U.S. actions.

The Communist protests unintentionally helped to smooth over the Nixon-Kissinger problems with Thieu. Thus, at the press conference on October 26, Kissinger could appear to make the Nixon administration the champion of peace but also the champion of the Thieu government's rights. Kissinger's "peace is at hand" statement indicated that only technical details needed to be resolved. One more round of talks with Le Duc Tho should resolve the matter, Kissinger said. At the same time, by requiring Thieu's agreement before signing, Nixon and Kissinger appeared to be defenders of "peace with honor," making certain that the technicalities of the truce would preserve the independence of South Vietnam. In this manner, Nixon's reelection campaign was not damaged but assisted on the eve of U.S. balloting.

## November 7, 1972

### President Nixon is reelected by a large margin.

Following his nomination on July 13 by the Democratic National Convention, George McGovern waged an ineffectual campaign that included the withdrawal of Thomas Eagleton as the vice presidential candidate when his history of psychiatric treatment was revealed. R. Sargent Shriver replaced Eagleton.

The Republicans nominated Richard Nixon and Spiro T. Agnew on August 23. Their platform supported Nixon's foreign policy, advocated welfare reform, and opposed the busing of school children to achieve racial integration. McGovern's platform emphasized the immediate end to the Vietnam War and a guaranteed income for the poor.

The war issue became insignificant after Henry Kissinger's "peace is at hand" statement of October 26.

Nixon won 520 electoral votes to 17 for McGovern, who carried only Massachusetts and Washington, D.C.

## November 9, 1972

### The United States, France, Great Britain, and the Soviet Union agree that both the East German and the West German governments may join the United Nations.

As a follow-up to the Berlin agreement ratified on June 3, 1972, delegates of the four powers met in Berlin to decide on a method for accepting both governments as U.N. members.

This was part of an overall arrangement by which the East and West Germans cooperated to improve their relations as part of détente in central Europe. As early as March 19, 1970, Chancellor Willy Brandt of the Bonn government had visited Erfurt to conduct talks with Prime Minister Willie Stoph of East Germany.

### December 16, 1972

**Kissinger claims the Paris peace talks are at an impasse because of Hanoi's intransigence. The United States may need to renew air attacks.**

Between Kissinger's October 26 "peace is at hand" statement and his December 16 press conference, close observers realized that the differences between the negotiators in Paris were greater than "technical details." After the peace talks were renewed in Paris on November 20, Saigon's demands for 69 changes in the draft treaty and Kissinger's initial attempt to support Saigon nearly brought the negotiations to an end.

Nixon's attempts to placate Thieu to get his agreement had been unsuccessful during November. Nixon demonstrated U.S. support by speeding a rapid increase of military supplies to South Vietnam through Projects Enhance and Enhance Plus, which began on October 14. But the rapid delivery of 70 tanks and 600 helicopters and fighter planes by early December did not persuade Thieu to yield.

Nixon also sent a personal letter to Thieu on November 14 telling him the United States would take "swift and severe retaliatory action" against the Communists if they violated the truce terms. Moreover, he warned Thieu that his best security would be the sympathy of American and world opinion, a benefit that Thieu sacrificed by being an obstacle to the peace process. The South Vietnamese leader held firm; the destiny of all the people of South Vietnam was his to protect, Thieu claimed.

Because Saigon's demands precluded a truce solution, Kissinger asked Le Duc Tho to renew secret and separate discussions on December 4. Kissinger was willing to return to the October draft treaty but he demanded a timetable by which the treaty would be signed on December 22, 1972. Kissinger wanted several changes in the October treaty to placate Thieu, but Le Duc Tho charged that the new concepts were complicated and could not be answered in the 48-hour limit that Kissinger desired. Kissinger became and frustrated. First Thieu, now Le Duc Tho were being difficult.

By December 11, the Kissinger-Tho talks had reached an impasse. The national security adviser returned to Washington on December 13. Kissinger and Nixon agreed that they must vigorously bomb North Vietnam as Kissinger frequently had threatened during the November 1972 negotiations to make their

points. Hanoi was sent a 72-hour ultimatum. It must agree to the issues pending during the December 4–11, 1972, peace talks or it would be bombed again.

At his December 16 press conference Kissinger never mentioned the ultimatum to Hanoi or the problem of Saigon's 69 demands. He emphasized that North Vietnam was responsible for the negotiating problems. Le Duc Tho, he stated, had raised "one frivolous issue after another." Because Hanoi rejected these peace terms, the security adviser feared that the United States might have to renew its bombing raids on the North. On December 18 these attacks began on a larger scale than ever before.

### December 18, 1972

**The United States begins punishng bombing raids on North Vietnam: The "Christmas Bombing" by Linebacker II.**

Nixon and Kissinger decided to make the "Christmas" bombing raids with no outside advice. Although Secretary of Defense Laird wrote the president opposing a military response to the Paris deadlock, neither Laird nor Secretary of State Rogers was brought into the discussion by Nixon and Kissinger. In addition, since the Cambodian incursion of April 1970, Kissinger had lost most of the highly competent NSC staff he recruited in 1969. Those who had resigned included Morton Halperin, Roger Morris, Anthony Lake, and William Watts.

When, as expected, Hanoi rejected Nixon's 72-hour ultimatum, Nixon ordered the Linebacker II attacks to begin on December 18. For these attacks, Nixon released the air force from almost all previous restrictions. The purpose of the bombing was allegedly to cripple daily life in Hanoi and Haiphong, the

Munitions Expended by U.S. Forces in World War II, Korea, and Indochina (thousand metric tons)

|  | Air | Ground | Total | Air/Total % |
|---|---|---|---|---|
| World War II | 1,957 | 3,572 | 5,529 | 35.4 |
| Korea | 634 | 1,913 | 2,547 | 24.8 |
| Indochina* | 6,410 | 6,847 | 13,221 | 48.5 |

*Does not include munitions expended before 1966 and 377,310 tons of air munitions and 162,550 tons of ground munitions expended in 1973.
Source: SIPRI, Anti-Personnel Weapons (London: Taylor & Francis, 1978), p. 46.

two major cities of North Vietnam. Between December 18 and 29, except for Christmas Day, incessant air raids were launched from Guam by 200 B-52s aided by F-4s and F-111s from Thailand and South Vietnam. Using carpet-bombing tactics, every three-plane B-52 mission attacked a target area one and one-half miles long and one-half mile wide. The planes dropped 15,000 tons of bombs on their section of target, and little but rubble remained except for a few houses with roofs or windows remaining. For example, on the night of December 27–28, whether by design or accident, the Khan Thieu residential district of Hanoi was hit. Fortunately, most of the 28,198 people had evacuated that area. After the raid only a few houses still had roofs or windows.

The bombing attacks of December 18–29 were controversial. Critics such as Telford Taylor argue that they hit civilian areas and were largely indiscriminate "terror" attacks. Military authorities emphasize that they targeted only military areas, but that "spillage" caused residences and hospitals to be hit off-target. In addition, Guenter Lewy's analysis shows that the 11-day attack was not as severe as the attacks on Dresden and Tokyo during World War II. In North Vietnam, reported deaths from the raids were 2,200 to 5,000 compared to the 35,000 or more who died at Dresden and the some 87,000 killed in Tokyo raids.

Undoubtedly, the bombings were denounced in America because the public had been told "peace is at hand" and "only technical details" had to be worked out. The U.S. Vietnamization process seemed to be nearly completed and U.S. military advisers in Saigon were optimistic about the capabilities of the troops they had been training since 1968. Given these expectations, the Christmas bombings appeared to be purposeless and vengeful attempts to coerce Hanoi to accept some technicalities in Paris.

The results of the bombings are also controversial. Nixon and Kissinger claim the bombings brought the North Vietnamese delegates back to agree at the bargaining table. Their critics argue that public opposition to the bombing caused Nixon to agree to negotiate again. Somewhat paradoxically, Lewy claims the bombings were not terroristic but did force Le Duc Tho to return to Paris. Bombing critics such as Gareth Porter and Alan Goodman say the bombings were terroristic but were not the reason that negotiations began again.

Whatever the reason, on December 30, President Nixon announced that the bombings above the 20th parallel had stopped and negotiations would begin again in Paris in January. Later, the White House said it acted in response to Hanoi's pleas to stop bombing; the North Vietnamese said they had never broken off the talks, and Kissinger returned to Paris because of world opinion and the "fact" that 34 B-52s had been lost. The U.S. air force acknowledged 15 losses.

Perhaps the greatest effect of the December Linebacker II raids was that Nixon and Thieu lost the sympathy of a majority of U.S. congressmen. A poll of senators on December 20 indicated they opposed the bombing 45 to 19 and favored legislation to end the war 45 to 25. When Congress returned to the Capitol in January, most members were ready to cut off funds for the war, a measure they had previously rejected. World opinion blamed both Thieu and Nixon for the "terror" attacks. None of the NATO nations approved, and Pope Paul VI deplored the "resumption of harsh and massive war action" in Vietnam. Thieu's regime could no longer be seen by most as an unwilling victim or an embattled republic; this new attitude lasted until the fall of Saigon in April 1975.

As one commentator remarked, Kissinger violated one of the principal rules of Bismarck's 19th-century realistic politics: never punish a weaker enemy when his surrender is near.

# 1973

### January 27, 1973

**In Paris, the four delegations in the Vietnam negotiations sign the truce agreements.**

The Paris talks between Kissinger and Le Duc Tho resumed on January 8, 1973. President Nixon wanted a truce before his second inauguration but did not quite achieve that goal. Although the Paris delegates did not initial the draft treaty until January 23, Nixon had ordered an end to all war action by the United States on January 15 because Kissinger informed him the treaty was practically agreed to. The cease-fire in Vietnam officially began at 24:00 Greenwich Mean Time on January 27, 1973.

Actually, two separate treaties were signed in Paris because Thieu's delegation refused to sign a document that specifically mentioned the Provisional Revolutionary Government (PRG). One treaty was signed by two parties, the Democratic Republic of (North) Vietnam (DRV) and the United States. This treaty had the concurrent agreement of the other two parties. The second treaty was a four-party treaty signed by the DRV, the United States, the PRG, and the Republic of South Vietnam.

During the last week of negotiations, Kissinger had yielded most disputed points to North Vietnam although, of course, he never admitted this. The two scholars of the truce process, Allan Goldman and Gareth Porter, agree that the January truce differed in no substantial ways from the October draft.

Despite Thieu's objections, the most critical clauses of the October draft were intact:

1. North Vietnamese troops would remain in place in South Vietnam, but the United States was to withdraw in 60 days.
2. Both sides were to exchange prisoners of war in 60 days, but Saigon's political "detainees" would be handled after the truce.
3. Military equipment could be replaced on a one-to-one basis.
4. An International Control Commission of 1,160 persons would implement the truce terms.
5. The National Council on Reconciliation and Concord would carry out elections and negotiate to reunite Vietnam. In the two-party treaty, both the Provisional Government and Thieu's Republic of Vietnam were included. In the four-party treaty the Council consisted of the "two parties in South Vietnam."
6. Contrary to Thieu's wishes, the 17th parallel was not a boundary between states but remained, as in the 1954 Geneva Treaty, a "provisional and not a political or territorial boundary" until Vietnam was united as one nation.

Nixon had forced Thieu to agree to the treaty. The same day the December bombing began (December 18), Nixon sent Alexander Haig, a member of the National Security Staff, to Saigon to inform Thieu that he must accept the settlement agreed to by Nixon or each party would go his "separate way." Haig had been instructed not to negotiate. Thieu had to decide whether "to continue our alliance" or whether Nixon should "seek a settlement with the enemy which serves United States interests alone."

On January 5, Nixon again put pressure on Thieu. Nixon wrote him that his "best guarantee" for survival was unity with Washington. This, he said, "would be gravely jeopardized if you persist in your present course." Nixon also promised to make certain that the North Vietnamese would not violate the truce terms. This and other personal promises by Nixon held little substance in future years as his actions in the Watergate cover-up would lead to his resignation as president in August 1974.

See October 26, 1972.

**February 9, 1973**

**The United States resumes the bombing of Cambodia, claiming the communists have not respected a cease-fire agreement.**

Between February and August 1973, Nixon and his opponents in Congress argued continually regarding the renewed bombing of Cambodia after the Vietnamese truce went into effect on January 27. The administration contended that North Vietnamese troops and the Khmer Rouge continued fighting in Cambodia and that Lon Nol, the prime minister of Cambodia, requested U.S. aid. Congressional critics such as Senator Stuart SYMINGTON pointed out that in every military appropriations bill since October 1970, a proviso forbade the bombing of Cambodia except to protect Americans in Vietnam. Therefore, the continued bombing after the 1973 Vietnam truce was illegal.

Henry Kissinger endeavored during the final Paris peace talks of 1972–1973 to arrange cease-fires in Laos and Cambodia as well as Vietnam. Le Duc Tho assured him this could be done in Laos because Hanoi had control over the Laotian Communists. The same, Le Duc Tho said, could not be done for Cambodia because the Khmer Rouge were too independent. In fact, the traditional enmity between the Khmer and Vietnamese ethnic groups caused the Cambodians to distrust and disdain all Vietnamese—who reciprocated these feelings. Kissinger, however, was ill informed about Cambodia and apparently did not understand or believe Le Duc Tho's assertion.

On January 23, 1973, during the final discussions in Paris, Kissinger read a unilateral statement saying that Lon Nol would suspend offensive attacks and the United States would stop bombing Cambodia. If the Khmer Rouge and North Vietnamese reciprocated, there would be a de facto cease-fire. If not, the U.S. air force would resume bombing until there was a cease-fire.

Kissinger did not advocate or engage in any talks between the Khmer Rouge and Lon Nol. For Kissinger and other U.S. officials, Cambodia was a "sideshow" to sustaining South Vietnam. Although he urged Lon Nol and the Communists to negotiate, Kissinger never actively fostered this process. Lon Nol would have profited from a cease-fire because the Khmer Rouge were on the verge of victory. Le Duc Tho and Hanoi encouraged the Khmer to stop fighting. The Khmer leaders and, in Beijing exile, Prince Sihanouk believed Hanoi simply wanted to damage the cause of Cambodia so that the Vietnamese could conquer that country at a later date. Therefore, the Khmer ignored Hanoi's requests.

By February 9, the de facto cease-fire had not materialized. Thus, Nixon and Kissinger agreed to renew the bombing of Cambodia. This action would not only support Lon Nol but demonstrate to Hanoi that Nixon was determined to require North Vietnam to fulfill the 1973 truce. Indirectly, therefore, the White House viewed the Cambodian bombing as continuing evidence of its backing of Thieu. Nixon did not, however, ask Congress to repeal its prior legislation against the Cambodian bombing as Symington suggested he should do.

The renewed bombing of Cambodia after February 9 was not a token bombing to indicate dissatisfaction to Hanoi but a large-scale, massive series of bombing attacks by B-52s from Guam and fighter bombers from Thailand. During the 12 months of 1972, B-52s dropped 37,000 tons of bombs on Cambodia. In March 1973, they dropped 24,000; in April 35,000, and in May 36,000 tons. The fighter-bombers had dropped 16,513 tons in 1972. In April 1973, these aircraft dropped 15,000 tons; the figure rose to 19,000 tons in July.

The U.S. bombings of Cambodia in 1973 prevented the fall of Lon Nol's government, but, as in the case of Thieu in Vietnam, U.S. military action weakened rather than strengthened Lon Nol's support among the people. Internally, the Khmer Rouge successes between 1971 and 1973 caused the government of Lon Nol and Prince Sirik Matak to use repressive methods. Consequently, those Cambodians who opposed the Khmer Rouge sought the return of Sihanouk. This tactic never succeeded because Sihanouk increasingly preferred an alliance with the Khmer Rouge against Lon Nol as the best way to regain control of Cambodia. In July 1973, when Kissinger offered to talk with Sihanouk, it was too late. The exiled prince could not risk association with the United States.

For congressional action on the Cambodian bombing, see July 1, 1973.

## February 15, 1973

### Cuba and the United States sign an antihijacking agreement.

The number of incidents in which U.S. aircraft were hijacked and forced to fly to Havana caused difficulty for both nations. By this agreement, each country would try or extradite hijackers who forced aircraft to land in either the United States or Cuba.

## February 21, 1973

### An Israeli fighter plane shoots down a Libyan commercial airliner that had strayed over the Israeli-occupied Sinai Peninsula: 109 are killed.

According to Israel, the Libyan airliner flew over highly sensitive military concentrations in the Sinai. The Libyan pilot acknowledged but ignored Israeli warnings. Later, tape recordings of the conversations between the Libyan pilot and the Cairo, Egypt, control tower indicated that the pilot believed he was over Egyptian territory and that the fighter planes were Egypt's. An Airline Pilots Association investigation, which condemned Israel for its act, stated that the principal problem was that the airline pilot and the fighter pilots had no method for communicating.

There were 113 passengers and crew on the Libyan plane; 109 died in the crash. Most passengers were Libyan and Egyptian because the plane's flight had been from Bengazi to Cairo. Four crew members who died were French. One passenger was American.

On February 24, Israel's Defense Minister Dayan stated that Israel made an error of judgment but that "serious responsibility" for the incident was that of the airline pilot. Israeli Premier Meir expressed regret for the loss of life in the incident. On March 6, Israel announced it would pay $30,000 in compensation to families of the victims of the crash.

Libya's Foreign Minister Min Kikhia denounced the Israeli action as "criminal," claiming the plane lost its way because of communication difficulties and poor weather. A *New York Times* editorial on February 23 criticized the Israeli acts, stating that it was "at best a horrifying blunder . . . an act of callousness that not even the savagery of previous Arab actions can excuse."

Both the Israeli and the U.S. governments expressed the hope that this incident would not interfere with discussions looking toward a peace settlement in the Middle East.

For similar incidents, see July 23, 1954, and July 27, 1955.

### March 1, 1973

*Eight guerrillas of the Palestinian Black September group shoot their way into the Saudi Arabian embassy in the Sudan.*

The guerrillas seized five hostages including the U.S. ambassador, his deputy, and a Belgian chargé d'affaires.

### March 19, 1973

*Talks between the Republic of Vietnam (RVN) and the Provisional Revolutionary Government of Vietnam (PRG) begin at St. Cloud, France.*

The first conference agenda item concerned setting a date for elections to the National Council on Reconciliation and Concord (NCRC). Disagreement occurred immediately. The RVN wanted North Vietnamese troops to withdraw from the South before the election; the PRG wanted all fighting, including frequent skirmishes along the cease-fire line, to stop before elections. The NCRC was never elected. Formal but infrequent meetings continued at St. Cloud until January 25, 1974, when the delegates adjourned because their meetings were superfluous.

### March 21, 1973

**The United States vetoes a U.N. Security Council resolution favoring the restoration of Panamanian sovereignty in the canal zone.**

In order to change the issue of the Panama Canal from a bilateral question with the United States to an international issue, Panama's head of state, General Omar Torrijos, invited the U.N. Security Council to conduct a meeting in Panama between March 15 and March 21. As a result, the council, with strong backing from all Latin American and other developing nations, offered a resolution stating that the United States should restore Panamanian national sovereignty over its entire territory. In the vote, 13 council members approved, Great Britain abstained, and the United States vetoed the resolution.

### March 29, 1973

**The last U.S. soldier leaves Vietnam. All American prisoners of war are returned but the fate of many missing in action is not known.**

By March 29, about 1,000 POWs had returned to the United States, as had the last of the 6,000 combat troops who remained at the end of 1972. More than 2.5 million Americans served in Vietnam between 1961 and 1973. During the conflict, over 50,000 Americans were killed, and 300,000 wounded, and MIAs numbered 2,300.

When the last U.S. soldier left on March 29, the war effectively ended for the United States.

### May 17, 1973

**The Senate Watergate hearings begin, presided over by Senator Sam J. Ervin.**

During the hearings, which lasted until August 7, former White House Counsel John Dean testified that

U.S. POWs/MIAs in Four Wars

| POWs | Total | WWI | WWII | Korean | Vietnam |
|---|---|---|---|---|---|
| Captured/Interned | 142,227 | 4,120 | 130,201 | 7,140 | 766 |
| Died as POW | 17,034 | 147 | 14,072 | 2,701 | 114 |
| Returned to U.S. Control | 125,171 | 3,973 | 116,169 | 4,418 | 651 |
| Missing in Action | 92,693 | 3,350 | 78,773 | 8,177 | 2,338 |

American POWs lift off from Hanoi on their way home. National Archives

President Nixon was full party to the attempted cover-up of his reelection committee's role in the Watergate burglary. Presidential assistant Alexander Butterfield revealed the White House system for tape recording conversations, making the tapes and their content a critical factor in the further investigation of the president's methods of secrecy and duplicity.

### June 16, 1973

**Soviet leader Leonid Brezhnev arrives in the United States for a summit meeting with President Nixon.**

The main achievement of this visit was a pact to prevent nuclear war that Brezhnev and Nixon signed on June 22. The two nations would conduct "urgent conversations" if needed to avert nuclear war between themselves or with a third power. Nixon and Brezhnev also signed agreements on agricultural cooperation, oceanographic research, and cultural exchanges.

### June 30, 1973

**The U.S. Selective Service Act expires.**

On President Nixon's recommendation, Congress did not renew the law providing for drafting of men into

President Nixon and Soviet Premier Leonid Brezhnev. National Archives

the armed forces. For the first time in 25 years, the armed forces became entirely voluntary.

### July 1, 1973

**Congressional legislation prohibits the use of funds to bomb Cambodia or to engage in further military action in Indochina without prior approval of Congress after August 15, 1973.**

The arguments between Nixon and his critics about the renewed bombing of Cambodia on February 9, 1973, added to the president's difficulties with the hearings of Senator Sam Ervin's Watergate committee during the spring of 1973.

The first indication that Congress no longer accepted Nixon's explanation of the Cambodian bombings came on May 10, when the U.S. House of Representatives voted 219-188 in the Supplemental Appropriations Bill to stop funds for bombing Cambodia. This bill also passed the Senate, but Nixon vetoed it on June 26. The House did not have sufficient votes to override the veto.

Because Nixon needed the Supplemental Appropriations Bill, he agreed to compromise, accepting a statement on the Cambodian bombing that permitted it to continue until August 15 so that truce arrangements could be worked out. Although some congressmen objected to the compromise, the majority accepted it as a "realistic" solution. The bill was approved on June 30; Nixon signed it on July 1.

Later, both Nixon and Kissinger claimed the peace talks on Cambodia in 1973 failed because Congress had abrogated the bombing powers of the president on June 30. Kissinger said that "delicate negotiations" for a truce were underway, but he never revealed any details of these transactions. In his book *Sideshow,* which was based on extensive research in documents secured under the Freedom of Information Act as well as interviews with various participants, William Shawcross could find no evidence of such talks. Nevertheless, the U.S. bombing of Cambodia stopped on August 15.

At a farewell press conference in Phnom Penh on September 4, U.S. Ambassador Emory C. Swank said the war in Cambodia after 1970 was Indochina's most "useless war."

### July 12, 1973

**Hearings on Nixon's secret bombing of Cambodia begin after the Senate Armed Services Committee learns that they occurred.**

Major Hal Knight, a radar operator who had handled the "dual bombing" reports on the Cambodian bombings, wrote Senator William Proxmire of Wisconsin in October 1972 about the secret bombing tactics and believed that the American people should know about this. Knight protested the false record system to his commanding officer. His objections first brought him low efficiency ratings and finally the news that he would be discharged. Thus, he asked Senator Proxmire to investigate the bombings.

Proxmire gave Knight's letter to Senator Harold Hughes, on the Senate Armed Forces Committee, and between March 28 and July 1973, Hughes secured versions of the 1969–1970 bombing reports that were the sanitized official reports to which Knight had objected.

On July 12, Hughes searched further into the matter. During committee hearings at which General George Brown testified on his appointment to become air force chief of staff, Hughes asked Brown if the United States had conducted air strikes in Cambodia before May 1970. Requesting that the committee go into secret session, Brown told them that B-52s had bombed Cambodia in 1969–1970. Brown knew because he had been in Saigon as General Abrams's deputy for air operations from August 1968 to August 1970.

Following the hearings on July 12, Brown returned to the Pentagon, reflected on his secret testimony, and decided to send the committee an explanation of the Cambodian raids. The "dual reports," he said, were not technically falsified reports because "they were not intended to deceive those with a security need to know." This admission was hardly sufficient. During July and August, the Senate Armed Services Committee hearings disclosed Nixon's secret orders as well as information on the bombings between March 1969 and April 1970.

See March 18, 1969.

### August 19, 1973

*Greece proclaims a republican government.*

Since the rebellion against King Constantine on April 21, 1967, the provisional leaders had elected a constituent assembly that ended the monarchy and approved a republican form of government. George Papadopoulos was elected president of Greece.

## September 1, 1973

### Libya announces the takeover of 51% of U.S. oil concessions.

During 1960 the discovery of oil reserves in Libya made that nation a major producer of crude oil. Following the overthrow of the king in 1969, the military leaders under al-Gadhafi began to demand an increase in oil prices and new treaty concessions with the West. In 1973, the government unilaterally declared that it must have a 51% share of all oil concessions held by U.S. investors.

## September 11, 1973

### A military coup in Chile overthrows President Allende, who dies. Later, a U.S. Senate investigating committee indicates that Nixon and Kissinger had used CIA operations to destabilize Chile's economy and assist anti-Allende groups.

The military coup against Allende was Chile's first overthrow of a democratic government since 1932, a record unparalleled in recent Latin American history. U.S. authorities had feared that Allende's electoral victory in 1970 was a victory for Communist-inspired takeovers in Latin America. As a result, the CIA used funds to buy anti-Allende votes and to aid opposition candidates. The Nixon administration also suspended negotiations with Chile to roll over its external debt. The United States wanted the debt to include funds covering Chile's expropriation of U.S. property in copper mines and the ITT Company.

By mid-1973, the Chilean economy was in disarray. In June, miners, teachers, physicians, and students went on strike. On June 21, Allende supporters and opponents fought a bloody pitched battle in Santiago. Prior to the September 11 coup, Allende had averted several rebellions by diverse military factions.

In August, shopkeepers, taxi drivers, truck owners, and professional groups staged strikes. Allende had lost the support of the middle classes and his overthrow appeared to be imminent. After General Carlos Gonzáles resigned as defense and army chief on August 23, Allende chose General Augusto Pinochet Ugarte to replace him. Although Pinochet said he was loyal to Allende, his loyalty soon proved shallow.

The occasion for the military coup was Allende's announcement of his intention to seek a national referendum creating a unicameral congress to replace the two-house legislature.

Pinochet now turned against Allende, taking charge of an organization that aimed to overthrow the president. On September 11, army forces took over Moneda Palace. Whether Allende was killed or committed suicide is uncertain; his widow claimed the military murdered him.

Following the coup, the CIA (according to the Senate Select Committee on Intelligence Activities) spent $34,000 to finance a public relations campaign that would give Pinochet a "positive" image and gain support for the new regime. This was difficult because during the next months Pinochet executed many opposition leaders and enforced repressive measures against all dissenters.

See October 24, 1970.

## September 21, 1973

### Henry A. Kissinger is confirmed by the Senate as Secretary of State.

On September 3, Secretary Rogers resigned to return to his law practice. The appointment of Kissinger was no surprise because as assistant to the president for national security affairs, Kissinger had worked closely with Nixon to control U.S. foreign policy. Secretary Rogers had carried out assignments in special areas such as the Middle East, but generally Kissinger's NSC staff superseded most significant diplomatic activity usually carried out by the State Department.

Kissinger's appointment as secretary returned the policy development apparatus to the State Department. Nevertheless, the power he had wielded as head of the NSC allowed later appointees to this post to challenge the role of the Secretary of State.

## October 6, 1973

### An Arab-Israeli conflict breaks out: the Yom Kippur War.

Although throughout September there had been intelligence reports of war preparations by Egypt, Jordan, and Syria, Secretary of State Kissinger misread the signals until the last moment. At 9 P.M. on October

5, Ray Cline of the State Department's Bureau of Intelligence and Research concluded that war would break out soon, but Kissinger continued to rely on his former NSC staffers rather than the State Department. The NSC discounted Cline's report. As a result, the secretary did not accept the imminence of war until he received a telegram from Ambassador to Israel Kenneth Keating on October 6, which reported that Prime Minister Golda Meir expected a Syrian-Egyptian attack that day.

The timing of the secretary's information was vital because not until the last moment did he realize that the Soviet Union was, apparently, not following the expected détente prescription of influencing the Arab states to avoid war. Kissinger contacted Prime Minister Meir and obtained her agreement not to make a preemptive strike. In previous such situations Israeli strategy was to strike first. This time Meir altered tactics and Israel took only defensive action in the Sinai and the Golan Heights when the Egyptian-Syrian attacks began.

At 8 A.M. on October 6, Egyptian forces crossed the Suez Canal into the Sinai, and the Syrians attacked the Golan Heights. King Hussein of Jordan accepted the role of simply mobilizing his army on the Israeli border to provide a threat that required Israel to maintain some defensive units along the Jordan River.

Although Kissinger believed the Israeli army and air force would quickly turn back the Arabs, this did not happen during the first week of the war. Using Soviet-supplied surface-to-air missiles, tanks, and MIG jet fighters, the Egyptian forces broke through the Bar-Lev defense lines in the Sinai and made significant advances between October 6 and 15. In addition, the Soviet Union airlifted huge quantities of arms to Damascus and Cairo. Israel urged Washington to reciprocate by rushing Phantom jets and other military equipment to Tel Aviv, but Nixon and Kissinger were slow to respond.

See October 13, 1973.

### October 10, 1973

#### Vice President Spiro Agnew resigns.

Long the rhetorical champion of law, order, and "good faith," Agnew had been implicated in bribery and accused of income tax evasion. His resignation was part of an arrangement for dropping charges of bribery, conspiracy, and extortion. In return, Agnew

Vice President Spiro Agnew. National Archives

pleaded no contest on the income tax charges and resigned as vice president.

Nixon nominated Gerald Ford for vice president and Congress confirmed him. Constitutional provisions for this unusual process had been provided by the 25th Amendment (ratified in 1967) to the Constitution. Ford was sworn in as vice president on December 6.

### October 13, 1973

#### Nixon authorizes a full-scale airlift of equipment to Israel following a week of delay.

During the first week of the Arab-Israeli war, the United States failed to provide Tel Aviv with military supplies equaling those the Soviets sent to Syria and Egypt. Exactly why there was a delay is controversial. President Nixon was deeply involved in a crisis over the Watergate tapes and Vice President Agnew's resignation. Therefore, most observers believe Secretary of State Kissinger played the leading role—with

Nixon's backing—in the U.S. decisions. Kissinger, however, blamed Secretary of Defense James Schlesinger and his deputy, William Clements, for the delay in aiding Israel.

More probable, however, is the view that Kissinger hoped to make sure Israel realized its dependence on the United States so that it would follow the secretary's plans to obtain a broad settlement between Arabs and Jews in the Middle East. In addition, Kissinger had mistakenly counted on First Secretary Brezhnev's desire to maintain the détente relationship to restrain the Soviet Union's Arab allies. Moscow knew in advance of the impending attack on Israel, and, rather than warn Kissinger, Brezhnev sent large quantities of military supplies to Egypt and Syria during the two weeks before October 6.

Between October 6 and 13, Kissinger chose to seek a cease-fire resolution in the United Nations and to avoid sending Israel the equipment it desired. When talking with Israel's ambassador to the United States, Simcha Dinitz, Kissinger implied that he was willing to send aid to Israel but that the Defense Department's bureaucracy hampered prompt action. On one occasion, Kissinger asked Dinitz if Israel would pick up U.S. equipment in El Al aircraft whose tail emblem of the Star of David would be painted over. On another occasion, he told Dinitz he was seeking charter planes to fly equipment to the Portuguese Azores, from where Israel could transport the equipment to Tel Aviv. Kissinger's "games" were designed to make him appear the champion of Israel even though his objective was to demonstrate that he controlled Israel's fate.

Not until October 13 did Kissinger and Nixon agree to use U.S. military aircraft to rush supplies to Israel. During the first week of the war, Israeli forces had not been able to turn back the Egyptians, and the Soviet Union was rushing around-the-clock airlifts of equipment to Cairo and Damascus. In addition, proposals for a cease-fire had been rejected by Egyptian President Sadat. Finally, Ambassador Dinitz had threatened to go public regarding Washington's delay by appealing to friendly senators and the American Jewish community.

Once the White House approved aid to Israel, the State Department quickly received Portugal's permission to refuel U.S. military planes in the Azores, and the Pentagon worked 24 hours a day to send Phantom jets, tanks, 155 mm shells, and other equipment. Moreover, as soon as Israel knew the United States would replenish its military equipment, its army proceeded with plans for a bold attack across the Suez. This attack began on October 16 and quickly turned the war to Israel's favor.

See October 16, 1973.

### October 16, 1973

**The Arab states begin an oil embargo the same day that Israel launches an offensive across the Suez Canal.**

Although the United States was not informed of the Arab oil embargo until October 17, U.S. oil companies began receiving telegrams on October 16 informing them that oil shipments to the United States, Western Europe, and Japan would soon cease. The Arab states had warned Secretary Kissinger that if necessary, they were prepared to use oil as a weapon on behalf of Syria and Egypt. After the U.S. airlift of supplies began for Israel, the Arab leaders began to apply the embargo. On October 17, the Arabs announced a 10% cut in oil production. On October 18, Abu Dhabi instituted its oil embargo. Libya did likewise on October 19. On October 20 and 21, Saudi Arabia, Kuwait, and Algeria inaugurated oil embargoes.

As plans for the Arab oil embargo proceeded, Israel launched an offensive into Egypt on the night of October 15–16. Using rafts to cross the Suez Canal, Israeli commandos reached Egyptian territory in force on the morning of the 16th and began their attack on Egypt. Led by General Ariel Sharon, the Israelis advanced rapidly. After 72 hours they were within 50 miles of Cairo. At the same time, Israel began a counteroffensive against Syria, soon reaching within artillery range of Damascus. The tide of battle had turned. By October 18, Syria, Egypt, and the Soviet Union desired a cease-fire as quickly as possible.

See October 25, 1973.

### October 20, 1973

**President Nixon fires Archibald Cox, the special Watergate prosecutor: The Saturday night "massacre."**

Nixon's personal difficulties escalated during the summer of 1973 when knowledge of White House taped recordings of Oval Office conversations was disclosed. Nixon sought to withhold the tapes by suggesting that Senator John Stennis should review them and give summaries to the Senate Select Committee and to Circuit Court Judge John Sirica, who was in charge of the Watergate burglary trial. Nixon's counsel also wanted Archibald Cox, the Watergate special prosecutor, to agree to relinquish the right to further subpoenas.

When Cox rejected Nixon's proposals, the president fired him and abolished the special prosecutor's office. Attorney General Elliot Richardson and his deputy, William Ruckleshaus, refused to fire Cox, who was Richardson's appointee, and instead both resigned.

The American public responded with massive protests to Nixon's Saturday night action. Over 250,000 telegrams of opposition reached the White House. Subsequently, the president released the tapes to Judge Sirica and appointed a new special prosecutor, Leon Jaworski.

### October 25, 1973

### A cease-fire is finally achieved in the Arab-Israeli War: Nixon puts the U.S. military on alert.

Within 48 hours after General Sharon's forces attacked Egypt on October 16, President Sadat and the Soviet Union's leaders realized that an early cease-fire was needed. On October 18, Ambassador Dobrynin gave Kissinger a copy of a Soviet proposal for a cease-fire and total withdrawal of Israel from all occupied Arab lands, including the Old City of Jerusalem. This proposal was quickly rejected by the secretary of state.

Kissinger agreed to fly to Moscow, however, where he could work in consultation with Brezhnev in solving the Middle East crisis. Arriving in Moscow on October 20, the day that Nixon fired Archibald Cox as the Watergate special prosecutor, Kissinger worked out a cease-fire proposal with Brezhnev that the United Nations passed on October 22 (Resolution 338). The cease-fire was soon violated because Egypt's Third Army Corps tried to break free of the Israeli army's encirclement. The Egyptian action and the arrival of more Soviet equipment in Cairo permitted Israel to tighten its grip on the Egyptians, preparatory to a possible complete decimation of Egypt's forces.

Thus, another crisis occurred between October 22 and 25. A second cease-fire was approved on October 23, but it also failed on October 23. Blaming Israel for the violations, Brezhnev sent a personal message to Nixon that Ambassador Dobrynin read to Kissinger at 10 P.M. on October 24. The message seemed ominous. After urging that a joint Soviet-American force go to Egypt to restore peace, Brezhnev concluded:

> I will say it straight, that if you find it impossible to act together with us in this matter, we should be faced with the necessity urgently to consider the question of taking appropriate steps unilaterally. Israel cannot be allowed to get away with the violations.

About this same time, U.S. intelligence reported that seven Soviet airborne divisions had been alerted in the USSR and Hungary and that additional Soviet ships had entered the Mediterranean Sea, where the Soviets now had 85 ships. Although the accuracy of these reports was uncertain, Kissinger and Nixon assumed the worst, i.e., that the Soviet Union was ready for unilateral action in the Middle East.

Considering there was a "high probability" of Soviet action, Nixon took military and diplomatic action between 11:30 P.M. and 1:30 A.M. on October 24–25. He ordered a global alert of most U.S. forces. There are five degrees of U.S. alerts ranging from Defense Condition (Def Con) 5, the lowest form, to Def Con 1, which means war. At 1:30 A.M. Def Con 3 went into effect for all U.S. army, air force, and naval stations, while Def Con 2 applied to the U.S. Mediterranean fleet.

At the same time, Nixon dispatched an answer to Brezhnev. He said Israel had not "brazenly" violated the cease-fire, asserting there was no need for a U.S.-Soviet force in the region. The United States could not permit unilateral Soviet action. "Instead," he said, "non-veto and non-nuclear powers should comprise the peace force sent to the Middle East by the United Nations."

One flap of the Kissinger process on October 24–25 was his failure to consult with any NATO allies until the U.S. alert was underway. The British ambassador was piqued and reportedly told the secretary: "Why tell us, Henry? Tell your friends—the Russians." Other NATO allies were equally distressed, particularly because Nixon and Kissinger had frequently treated them in such cavalier fashion. If there was a genuine Soviet threat as on October 25 as Kissinger later argued, the NATO allies might have to bear the brunt of Soviet action.

Indeed, many observers thought Nixon conjured the Soviet threat and the alert to divert attention from

Watergate and to show his decisiveness in dealing with Moscow. In such a context, there was no "probable" threat and no need for an alert. Nixon's letter to Brezhnev would have sufficed.

Whatever the circumstances that resulted in the effective cease-fire, it was achieved on October 25. U.N. Security Council Resolution 340 was passed 14-0 and accepted by the belligerents. The resolution provided for a cease-fire, a small-powers U.N. force to patrol the problem areas, and an international conference to finalize an armistice. The cease-fire became effective on October 26. The U.S. Defense Department ended its alert as quickly as it had called it.

Whether or not the alert was connected to Watergate, on October 26 Nixon implied in a news conference that it should be. In his usual rambling style, the president claimed the Soviets miscalculated because of Watergate. Nevertheless, he said, the Soviet leaders knew how Nixon had acted in Cambodia and in the mining of Haiphong Harbor in 1972. Thus, he argued on October 25, Brezhnev knew he had to yield when Nixon ordered the alert on October 24.

See December 21, 1973.

### November 7, 1973

**Nixon informs the nation that it must change its consumption of oil and gas to achieve oil independence by 1980.**

The Arab oil embargo, which began on October 16, had reduced the U.S. oil supply by 13%, which would reach 17% during the winter of 1973–1974, Nixon told the nation in a television address. Americans, he said, must conserve oil by reducing airplane flights, reducing home heating to 65° or 68°, and reducing automobile speed (50 to 55 miles an hour maximum).

On November 8, Nixon asked Congress for legislation to provide $10 billion for Project Independence, so that the United States could become self-sufficient in oil and therefore better able to conduct its foreign policy.

In addition to oil shortages, the Arab oil embargo led to large increases in oil prices. Iran did not join the embargo, but the shah more than doubled the price of Iranian oil. Other OPEC countries such as Venezuela and Nigeria followed the shah's lead. These increases continued after the oil embargo ended in 1974, placing a new burden on America's already unfavorable balance of trade.

See December 23, 1973.

### November 7, 1973

**Both houses of Congress override Nixon's veto of the War Powers Act.**

For some time, opponents of the U.S. war in Vietnam had sought legislation to limit presidential authority to involve the United States in war without the approval of Congress or a declaration of war. President Truman, they said, set the precedent in acting against North Korea in June 1950; but the Vietnam conflict clearly indicated what they deemed to be the excessive power of the executive to act without the concurrence of the legislative branch.

The bill approved on November 7 began its legislative enactment on July 18, when the House passed the bill. This act required the president to report to Congress within 48 hours after he committed U.S. troops to hostilities anywhere in the world. The president would have 60 days to gain congressional approval for the commitment. If he did not do so, the hostile action by the United States would have to stop. Congress retained power to act on its own to support ordering the commitment before 60 days passed.

Because the Senate version of this bill differed in details, it did not get through a conference committee to be approved until October 12. On October 24, President Nixon vetoed the bill. His veto did not hold, however. On November 7, the House overrode the veto by a vote of 284-135 (barely two-thirds); the Senate overrode the veto by 75-18.

### November 25, 1973

*In a bloodless coup, Greek President George Papadopoulos is overthrown.*

A military government was set up under General Phaidon Gizikis. On August 19, 1973, Greece had become a republic under President Papadopoulos.

### November 30, 1973

**Defense Secretary Schlesinger announces that the Pentagon will seek new weapons programs to preserve the "essential equivalency" of U.S. nuclear power systems relative to the Soviets.**

The Middle East crisis and the Soviet violation of its détente pledges during the fall of 1973 prompted the Department of Defense to believe that the second round of the Strategic Arms Limitation Talks (SALT II) would not succeed. Therefore, as reinsurance, the United States had to equal or exceed the Soviet missile systems.

From this perspective, Schlesinger announced that the Pentagon desired the following:

1. a larger ICBM weapon because Soviet ICBM weapons now had MIRV capabilities;
2. a mobile land-based missile system;
3. MIRV missiles for all existing U.S. missiles;
4. an accelerated production of ballistic missile submarines.

By the term "essential equivalency," Schlesinger indicated he wanted U.S. weapons to be equal or superior to the USSR's in every nuclear category—land-based, manned bombers, and submarines.

Opponents of this new concept, including the NSC staff, calculated nuclear parity in terms of the overall equivalency of missiles possessed by the Soviet Union and the United States. Schlesinger's concept became popular with U.S. politicians who opposed détente and talked of Soviet superiority in land-based ICBMs—the one category of ballistic missiles that the Soviets possessed in greater numbers than the United States. For this group the mobile land-based MX missile system became the weapon essential for U.S. defenses between 1974 and the early 1980s.

### December 13, 1973

**The Vienna Conference to reduce conventional forces in Central Europe adjourns with no progress.**

The Vienna Conference of 19 nations opened on October 30. Its purpose was to achieve a mutual balanced-force reduction of conventional forces between NATO and Warsaw Pact nations. After a month and a half of sessions, no agreements could be reached. On December 17, an article in the Soviet Communist Party newspaper *Pravda* claimed that the Vienna conferees had developed more distrust because the NATO representatives proposed an alteration in existing force levels that would benefit the Western European nations.

### December 20, 1973

**Secretary Kissinger meets in Paris with North Vietnam's Le Duc Tho.**

This session, which proved to be Kissinger's final meeting with Le Duc Tho, achieved no results. Kissinger urged that Vietnam pull its forces out of Cambodia but Tho refused.

Following the session, the State Department sent a circular letter to all U.S. diplomatic posts summarizing North Vietnam's frequent violations of the January 1973 truce. The message concluded: "while we cannot predict their decision, the Communists clearly have a viable option to launch another major offensive [in Vietnam]."

### December 21, 1973

**The conference on the Middle East convenes in Geneva. For the first time Arab and Israeli officials exchange views in the same room.**

Following the October 25 cease-fire agreement, Secretary Kissinger became the key figure in bringing together representatives of Israel, Egypt, and Jordan. On November 7, Kissinger met Egypt's President Sadat in Cairo. The meetings led to full-scale U.S.-Egyptian diplomatic relations as well as Sadat's agreement that Egypt would negotiate with Israel. Kissinger also visited Damascus, where he persuaded Syria's President Hafiz al-Assad to offer a list of Israeli prisoners held by Syria. This gesture enabled Israel to justify the Geneva talks even though Syria refused to attend the December 21 sessions.

The formal Geneva sessions lasted only two days. With Kissinger and Soviet Foreign Minister Gromyko as observers, Egypt and Israel agreed that their military officers would meet on December 26 to settle the military problem along the Egyptian-Israeli borders of the Suez Canal. This was the beginning of a series of talks that returned those borders to their place as of October 5, 1973.

### December 23, 1973

*The Shah of Iran announces increased oil prices.*

Rumors had begun circulating in October 1973 that Iran and other nations that had not joined the Arab oil boycott after October 16, 1973, would increase their crude oil prices. On December 23, the Iranian government announced that its oil prices would increase from $5.10 to $11.65 per barrel. Other non-Arab members of OPEC (Nigeria and Venezuela) also adopted the $11.65 price. Thus, U.S. oil shortages since November were now matched by the doubling of the price of available oil.

The shah had initially increased Iran's oil prices on October 16 when the Arab boycott began. At that time, he unilaterally announced an increase in Iranian oil from about $3 to $5.10 per barrel. Thus the December 23 decree was Iran's second increase in three months in 1973.

# 1974

### January 18, 1974

**The Israeli and Egyptian Chiefs of Staff disengage their armies in the Sinai. Following five days of shuttle diplomacy. Secretary Kissinger obtains an agreement between Egypt and Israel.**

After the Geneva Conference of December 21–22, Israeli and Egyptian officials began discussions on December 26. When in early January the peace process became stymied, Secretary Kissinger undertook a series of trips between Jerusalem and Aswân, where Sadat spent the winter months, to achieve a peace formula. The final agreement grew out of a proposal by Israeli Defense Minister Moshe Dayan. It was based on the following five zones in the Suez area:

1. an Egyptian zone 10 miles east of Suez in the Sinai with limited forces to patrol the area (about 7,000 men);
2. a U.N. buffer zone patrolled by a small-power U.N. force;
3. an Israeli zone in the Sinai;
4. two zones on each side of the Sinai in which no SAM missiles would be allowed for either Egypt or Israel;
5. the west bank of the canal, from which Israel would withdraw all forces.

In secret agreements, Kissinger gave Israel a memorandum saying that Egypt would clear the Suez Canal, rebuild cities, and resume peacetime activities along the canal. The United States also agreed to "make every effort to be fully responsive on a continuing and long-term basis to Israel's military equipment requirements." Sadat also agreed that Israel's non-military barges could use the Suez Canal. Finally, both nations permitted the United States to conduct aerial surveillance over the disengaged area.

On January 18, Israeli and Egyptian troops began withdrawal according to the zonal plan.

### February 7, 1974

**Secretary Kissinger visits Panama, where he signs a statement of principles for negotiations on the canal issue.**

Following the U.S. veto of the U.N. Security Council resolution on Panama on March 21, 1973, Secretary Kissinger decided to provide for a more conciliatory U.S. policy in Latin America. Consequently, in September 1973, he appointed Ambassador at Large Ellsworth Bunker to renew discussions on the canal with Panama. Previous negotiations begun with Panama in 1964 had resulted in draft treaties rejected by Panama. Talks broke off in 1971 and were not seriously undertaken again until Bunker's appointment in 1974.

Bunker's discussions with Juan Antonio TACK, Panama's minister of foreign affairs, resulted in a Statement of Principles signed by Tack and Kissinger on February 7, 1974. These principles are summarized below:

1. A new treaty will replace the 1903 treaty.
2. The United States will abandon the 1903 concept of "perpetuity" so that a fixed termination date can be negotiated. This was the most critical U.S. concession.
3. The treaty will provide for terminating U.S. jurisdiction in the future.
4. The new treaty shall return all canal territory to Panama but will provide for American transit and defense of the canal.
5. Panama shall have an equal share of the canal's benefits.
6. The new treaty will permit Panama to join in the canal's administration.
7. Panama and the United States will jointly protect and defend the canal.
8. The United States and Panama will agree on joint studies to enlarge the canal's capacity for new, larger ships.

Detailed negotiations to prepare the process for implementing these eight points would be continued between U.S. and Panamanian officials until a treaty was attained.

See September 7, 1977.

## February 11, 1974

**A Washington conference to unify the western powers on an oil consumer action program is unsuccessful.**

On January 9, President Nixon invited the foreign ministers of Canada, West Germany, France, Italy, Japan, the Netherlands, Norway, and Great Britain to meet on February 11. The meeting's purpose was to unite the industrialized nations on a policy regarding oil supplies and prices. The nine nations could not agree, however, and disputes among them caused some bitterness, especially between the United States and European nations such as France, which preferred to arrange an independent deal with the Arab nations. Thus, the conference did not succeed.

## February 13, 1974

*The Soviet Union deports and revokes the citizenship of Aleksandr Solzhenitsyn, a Nobel prize–winning author and dissident.*

Solzhenitsyn was sent to West Germany. Later he moved to the United States, where he continued to strongly criticize the Soviet government.

## February 27, 1974

*An army coup in Ethiopia forces the government to resign.*

Led by radical Marxists, the new leaders of Ethiopia gained complete control of the country on June 29, deposing Emperor Haile Selassie on September 12, 1974.

## February 28, 1974

**The United States and Egypt resume full diplomatic relations.**

Diplomatic relations between the two nations had ended during the Six-Day War in June 1967. On November 7, 1973, Secretary Kissinger and Egypt's President Sadat agreed to reopen their respective embassies and consular offices. This process was officially begun on February 28, 1974.

## February 28, 1974

*Britain's general elections give no party a majority. On March 4, Labour Party leader Harold Wilson forms a minority government.*

Both the Conservative and Labour Parties failed to gain 51% of the seats in Parliament. Between February 28 and March 4, Conservative Prime Minister Heath tried to gain sufficient Liberal Party votes to gain a majority. The Liberals rejected Heath's proposal, leading to Harold Wilson's decision to create a minority Labour government, which gained sufficient votes to be installed on March 4.

## March 1, 1974

**A federal grand jury indicts seven key White House and CREEP officials for various felonies.**

The grand jury wanted to indict President Nixon, but Special Prosecutor Leon Jaworski persuaded them not to because of constitutional questions concerning the indictment of a president still in office.

## March 17, 1974

**The Arab oil producers lift their oil embargo.**

The Arab oil embargo had been set up in October 1973 as a form of political pressure against the Western powers that tended to support Israel in wars against Arab nations, in this instance the current war between Israel, Egypt, and Syria.

In a meeting at Tripoli, Libya, on March 5, the majority of Arab countries agreed to lift the embargo. Led by the Saudi Arabian delegation, proponents of lifting the ban argued that the Israeli-Egyptian settlement indicated the crisis had ended. Libya and Syria wanted to retain the embargo but were outvoted. Officially, the end of the embargo was announced on March 17.

## April 25, 1974

*A revolution in Portugal overthrows the dictatorial regime of Premier Marcello Caetano.*

Caetano and his predecessor, dictator Antonio de Oliveira Salazar, had fought for 14 years to keep control of Portugal's colonies of Angola, Mozambique, and Guinea-Bissau. The costly wars exhausted Portugal's economy. In addition, its young army officers had begun to sympathize with the leftist ideas of the colonial nationalists.

One of the revolution's first acts was to suspend the colonial wars and to grant independence to Portugal's imperial possessions, to be effective at the end of 1975. Black rulers, most of whom claimed to be Marxists, would gain control of Portugal's three African states.

### May 18, 1974

*India explodes a nuclear device.*

Using waste from the nuclear power plant's fuel supplied by Canada, India developed the capabilities for producing nuclear weapons. India had been one of several nations that had refused to sign the Nuclear Non-Proliferation Treaty.

### May 31, 1974

**Israel and Syria agree to disengage their armies in the Golan Heights following 32 days of talks with Secretary of State Kissinger, who shuttles between Damascus and Jerusalem.**

Although the Egyptians made peace with Israel on January 18, President Assad of Syria was adamant about his desire to obtain some territory, such as the town of Quneitra from Israel. The Israeli government was not willing to give up any hard-won territory. As a result, these two nations continued a war of attrition both on the ground and in the air in the region surrounding the Golan Heights until May 29. The agreement provided for a U.N.-protected buffer zone between the two states and for limited-forces zones along the immediate boundary of each nation. The Israeli army pulled out of Syrian territory occupied during the war of 1973.

### June 14, 1974

**The United States and Egypt sign a statement of principles of cooperation that contains a clause providing nuclear fuel to Egypt. Several days later, a similar promise is made to Israel.**

On a visit to the Middle East, President Nixon stopped in Egypt to meet with President Sadat. Before Nixon left Cairo on June 14, the two leaders issued a statement on the Principles of Relations and Cooperation Between Egypt and the United States. The controversial clause in this agreement provided U.S. aid in helping Egypt to develop nuclear power reactors and supplying fuel for this capacity. There were protests against this in both Israel and the United States. As Tad Szulc's *The Illusion of Peace* (1978) explains, Israel was concerned that Egypt might use the waste from the power plant to make a nuclear weapon just as India had in May 1974.

Nixon and Kissinger claimed that Egypt would have obtained this technology from the Soviets unless the United States offered it under strict regulations to prevent the Egyptians from using nuclear waste to develop weapons. Nevertheless, as Szulc indicates, the reaction against Nixon's plan became so intense that the United States never fulfilled this agreement with Egypt.

In addition to the statement of principles, later reports alleged that Nixon told Sadat that it was the desire of the United States that Israel return to its pre-1967 boundaries. Reportedly, Nixon and Kissinger made similar statements to President Assad of Syria in a meeting in Damascus on June 15. Whether or not such verbal or written commitments on the Israeli borders were made has not been verified. If so, they were not considered binding on later U.S. presidents but were part of the Nixon-Kissinger plan to appear to operate even-handedly with both Israel and the Arabs.

Meeting on June 17 with Israeli Prime Minister Yitzak Rabin as part of his tour, Nixon agreed that Israel would have access to the same nuclear power fuel and technology as Egypt. In addition, Nixon urged Israel to negotiate with Jordan regarding the West Bank territory of the Jordan River. This was an emotional issue in Israel, however, because many Israelis believed the West Bank should, like Jerusalem, remain under their nation's control. Prime Minister Meir said she could not negotiate this issue with King Hussein without a specific mandate from her people.

On June 17–18, Nixon met with King Hussein and explained the U.S. desire for Jordanian negotiations with Israel. Hussein was willing to conduct such talks but Israel was not. Nixon agreed to continue U.S. military and economic aid to Jordan.

*See May 18, 1974.*

## July 3, 1974

**President Nixon leaves Moscow, having achieved little of significance.**

Nixon's visits to Brussels for NATO talks and to Moscow from June 27 to July 3, 1974, had been designed for no reason except to boost the president's political status. In talks with Brezhnev on SALT II agreements, neither leader had cleared proposals in advance with his military leaders and, therefore, nothing could be accomplished. The ABM agreement of 1972 was amended to permit only one rather than two ABM sites. A Threshold Test Ban Treaty (effective March 31, 1976) was signed prohibiting nuclear weapons tests having a yield exceeding 150 kilotons, thereby extending the 1963 Test Ban prohibitions.

Agreements were signed to cooperate in energy, housing, and artificial heart research. But these pacts did not require a summit meeting. The concept of détente and goodwill was refurbished during the visit, but Nixon's future at home did not benefit, given the Watergate problem.

One incident during Nixon's visit caused him to be criticized on his return home. U.S. television networks covering the visit had prepared reports on Soviet dissidents to transmit to the United States. Just as a report began on Andrey D. Sakharov, the noted physicist and dissenter, the TV screens went black. Soviet technicians had shut off the reports. However, Nixon did not comment on this or urge Brezhnev to do something about Soviet repression of human rights. As George Will, a U.S. columnist, said, perhaps Brezhnev knew Nixon's opinion of the press was not favorable.

See June 20, 1963.

## July 20, 1974

***Turkish forces land on Cyprus to oppose a Greek takeover and protect the Turkish minority. Kissinger fails to avert the Turkish invasion.***

The Turkish attack was in reaction to a military coup d'état by the Greek military junta in Athens that overthrew Archbishop Makarios, who was president of Cyprus.

Although Kissinger knew in advance of the plan of General Dimitrious Ionnides to overthrow Makarios, he did not act to prevent the coup. Once it happened, Kissinger sought unsuccessfully to persuade Turkey not to send armed forces to Cyprus. The United States did arrange for a cease-fire on July 21, after Turkish army units were already in position. Nevertheless, the groundwork was laid for renewed conflict in Cyprus.

See October 18, 1974.

Soviet Premier Brezhnev and President Nixon in Moscow. National Archives

### July 30, 1974

**The House Judiciary Committee votes three articles of impeachment against President Nixon.**

Following an extensive investigation of the Watergate cover-up and other reports of the president's activity since 1969, the House Judiciary Committee found Nixon guilty of three impeachable offenses: obstruction of justice, violation of his oath of office, and defiance of the impeachment process.

Ironically, the president and vice president (Nixon and Agnew) had campaigned for office on a "law and order" platform, and both resigned from office when indicted for illegal behavior. This contributed to a general American disillusionment with politicians during the 1970s, which also had an unfortunate influence on foreign policy as well.

See October 10, 1973, and August 8, 1974.

### August 8, 1974

**President Nixon announces his resignation, effective at noon on August 9, 1974.**

Although the House committee's impeachment votes must have led the president to thoroughly review his situation, Nixon did not refer to them in his letter of resignation. The letter he tendered to Secretary of State Kissinger simply stated that he resigned the office of president. Vice President Gerald R. Ford became president on August 9. He pardoned Nixon unconditionally on September 8.

Once again using the 25th Amendment, Ford nominated Nelson A. Rockefeller for the vice presidency. Congress approved, and on December 19 Rockefeller was sworn in as vice president.

### September 30, 1974

*Several months of political dispute end in Portugal as General Francisco Costa Gomes becomes president.*

A military coup in Lisbon overturned President Caetaro on April 25. General Antonio de Spinola became president with Senhor Adelino de Palma Carolas as prime minister on July 9. Carolas resigned and a new cabinet was created by Colores Vasco Gonçalves. Further difficulties led to Spinola's resignation on September 30.

Gerald R. Ford, Jr. Library of Congress

### October 18, 1974

**President Ford signs legislation threatening to cut off U.S. aid to Turkey.**

Although the Ford administration opposed the congressional threat to stop military and economic aid to Turkey, the movement to do so had begun in August 1974, following the second Turkish attack against Greek control of Cyprus.

The first Turkish troops landed on Cyprus on July 20 following the Greek military overthrow of Cypriot President Makarios. Soon after a cease-fire in Cyprus on July 21, liberal opponents of the Greek military junta in Athens overturned the rule of General Ionnides, bringing back a civilian Greek regime under Konstantinos Karamanlis. Because the liberals continued Greek efforts to dominate the Cypriot government, hoping to make it part of Greece, Turkey broke the cease-fire on August 14, landed reinforcements, and sought to conquer additional territory on Cyprus.

Greeks in Athens and Greek-Americans strongly protested the Turkish invasion and blamed Secretary Kissinger for not restraining Turkey. Pro-Greek lobbyists in Washington persuaded the House of Representatives to pass an amendment to a funding bill for federal departments, cutting off aid to Turkey. The House amendment was vetoed by President Ford on October 14. Because the House could not override the veto, a compromise was reached between Ford and congressional leaders. According to the compromise law, U.S. aid to Turkey would continue until December 10, 1974, provided Turkey did not send additional military equipment to Cyprus.

This October 18 law did not end the crisis in U.S.-Turkish relations. The Cyprus crisis continued, and on February 5, 1975, U.S. aid to Turkey halted. Turkey retaliated by closing down all NATO and U.S. bases on its territory. The U.S. bases had the vital function of monitoring weapons and missile activity in the Soviet Union.

See July 24, 1975.

**November 24, 1974**

**President Ford and Soviet leader Brezhnev place a ceiling on offensive nuclear weapons in a meeting at Vladivostok.**

Since 1972, U.S. and Soviet negotiators had sought some formula to limit strategic nuclear weapons. As late as July 3, when President Nixon left Moscow, the United States wanted to limit the number of Soviet MIRV warheads.

Between July and October, negotiators sought to attain some limit on offensive weapons because both nations already held overkill proportions of such weapons, but for reasons of prestige neither wanted to have a total lower than that of the other. In October, Kissinger visited Moscow to propose a formula granting each side parity in overall offensive warheads. During their sessions the secretary of state

President Ford and Soviet Premier Brezhnev meet at Vladivostok. Gerald R. Ford Library

and Brezhnev reached an agreement that became the basis of the Vladivostok formula. The Soviets agreed not to count the 500 U.S. bombers based in Europe as part of the U.S. strategic arsenal. This was a significant Soviet concession because U.S. aircraft in Europe could reach Soviet territory and, heretofore, Brezhnev had insisted that they be counted in the total of U.S. warhead launchers. On the part of the United States, Kissinger conceded that the USSR could continue to fit its warheads with MIRVs. The United States had been ahead in MIRV weapons, and as part of the overall parity, the Soviets could now build as many MIRV weapons as the United States held.

The Vladivostok formula as signed by Ford and Brezhnev was based on overall nuclear parity for the United States and the USSR. Specifically, the agreement was an aide-mémoire designed to be the basic framework for a SALT II agreement. The agreement included the following:

1. Each nation would have a 2,400 aggregate limit on nuclear delivery vehicles (ICBMs, SLBMs, and heavy bombers).
2. Each nation would have a 1,320 aggregate limit on MIRV systems.
3. No new land-based ICBM launchers would be built.
4. There would be limits on new types of strategic offensive weapons.
5. The new agreement would extend through 1985.

Following the summit, President Ford expected that SALT II might be finalized in 1975. As negotiators began drafting a treaty to suit the Vladivostok formula, however, difficulties arose. The two critical concerns that prevented the conclusion of SALT II in 1975 were (1) how U.S. cruise missiles would be counted, and (2) whether the new Soviet Backfire bomber should be counted as a heavy bomber under SALT II. These questions were not addressed again until 1977, after President Carter had succeeded Ford.

See March 30, 1977.

### December 7, 1974

*Archbishop Makarios returns to Cyprus.*

Between August and November, the new liberal Greek government agreed to restore Makarios as president of Cyprus and the Turkish Cypriot Rauf Denktash as vice president. Makarios immediately began seeking negotiations with Turkey to withdraw its invasion forces from the island.

### December 20, 1974

**Congress refuses to grant the Soviet Union the most-favored-nation trade status, placing restrictions on U.S. trade with the Soviets pending liberalization of their Jewish emigration policy.**

Opponents of détente with the Soviet Union complained that U.S. trade helped Moscow but brought no reciprocal advantages to the United States. They contended that the 1972 grain treaty resulted only in higher costs for U.S. consumers, although U.S. farmers also profited from higher grain prices.

Senator Henry Jackson, an outspoken opponent of détente, proposed that U.S. trade policies be linked with Soviet emigration policy, in particular its limitations on exit visas for Jews desiring to leave the Soviet Union. Thus on December 20, 1974, Congress approved the Trade Reform Bill with amendments that permitted lower tariffs for the Soviet Union only after Moscow eased its emigration restrictions. Both Jackson and Secretary Kissinger thought the Soviets were in sufficient need of U.S. trade to be convinced to increase the number of Jewish emigration visas. Thus, the USSR was not given the most-favored-nation status, an international trade principle that would have given the Soviets the trade benefits awarded to other nations friendly to the United States. In addition, the bill limited Soviet credits through the Export-Import Bank to $300 million, a sum that Secretary Kissinger denounced as "peanuts."

Senator Jackson and Kissinger miscalculated the Soviets' reaction to the U.S. trade amendments. On January 14, 1975, the Soviets rejected the U.S. trade agreement. The Kremlin considered its emigration policy an internal issue. Rather than easing Jewish emigration restrictions, the Soviets tightened them, cutting such visas to 13,200 for 1975, down from 35,000 Jewish visas in 1973. The Jackson amendments were a grave blow to the détente policy of Nixon and Kissinger.

# 1975

### January 8, 1975

**Twenty nations agree in Washington to recycle petrodollars to avoid a global recession.**

Unlike the Washington Conference of February 11, 1974, which failed to deal with the oil problem, the 1975 session was attended by representatives of the developing nations and oil-producing nations as well as the industrial powers. The 20 nations agreed to add a $6 billion oil facility to the International Monetary Fund (IMF) to help consuming nations pay their oil bills and to give interest rate subsidies to 30 poor nations. The $6 billion would be borrowed from oil producers to recycle the assets those nations held as a consequence of the greatly increased oil prices since October 1973.

During a separate session, 10 industrial nations agreed to set up a $25 billion "safety net" fund for emergency use by the "poor" nations. In future meetings, the quota payments for each industrial country would be established. The United States would contribute the greatest single amount, about $7 billion.

### January 8, 1975

***North Vietnam's General Van Tien Dung learns of unexpected successes by his forces in South Vietnam and decides to step up his attacks.***

During 1974, the truce of 1973 had completely broken down in South Vietnam. The disputes at St. Cloud between the conflicting parties ended on January 25, 1974, and the International Control Commission could persuade neither the PRG nor President Thieu to cooperate in settling disputes and the constant skirmishes along the cease-fire line.

Initially, from February 1973 to February 1974, Thieu seized additional territory and extended his control over the South. U.S. analysts estimated in February 1974 that the RVN had seized 15% of the land controlled by the PRG in January 1973, including 779 hamlets and 1 million people. Thieu also tightened his controls in the South, a policy that did not endear him to the people.

During 1974, however, the Communist leaders moved from a passive to an aggressive effort to counteract Thieu's control. Once American forces had

withdrawn and U.S. bombing stopped in Cambodia, Hanoi secured a major advantage because U.S. air support had been Thieu's biggest asset. Although in 1974 Nixon asked Congress to give more money to Saigon, he could offer little evidence to support his views because all reports from Vietnam indicated that both sides violated the truce and that until the fall of 1974, Saigon was the major violator.

Preceding the fall of 1974, Hanoi had built a long-term logistical system for its efforts against Saigon. Where the Ho Chi Minh trail had existed, it built a road eight meters wide through the Truong Mountains. It laid a pipeline into the central highlands of South Vietnam and recruited North Vietnamese to help "unify" the nation. Because these buildups did not appear as confrontational in South Vietnam, they seemed less harmful than Thieu's land grabbing and suppression of all dissenters or "neutralists" in South Vietnam.

Subsequently, while Americans experienced the unusual historic events of Nixon's resignation and Ford's ascension to power, the North Vietnamese undertook small-scale aggressions in the South during the fall of 1974. These probing actions disclosed weak support for Thieu among the local populace and the People's Defense Forces in South Vietnam. On January 8, General Dung learned that all of Phuoc Long Province had fallen under Communist control.

Surprised but pleased, Dung sped his plans for a 1975 offensive. He hoped to make sufficient inroads into the South in 1975 to win a victory in 1976. These plans, which Dung published in a 1976 account of the war, miscalculated the weakness of the Army of the Republic of Vietnam. After Dung began his large-scale offensive on March 1, 1975, ARVN's defense efforts crumbled quickly.

See March 19, 1973, and March 14, 1975.

### January 22, 1975

**President Ford approves the Geneva protocol of 1925 and the 1972 Biological Convention, with U.S. affirmations on the scope of chemical or biological uses under the protocol.**

Unlike the United States, many nations had ratified the 1925 agreement on chemical and biological war weapons. Consequently, several attempts had been made from 1945 to 1975 to obtain U.S. approval. In

1969, the issue arose in the United Nations, leading President Nixon to resubmit the treaty to the Senate.

Between 1969 and 1974, the protocol was not ratified by the Senate because of interpretations about its application to nonlethal chemical herbicides and tear gas. To resolve these questions, President Ford affirmed in 1974 that under the protocol, America would renounce first use of herbicides in war excepting use "applicable to their domestic use" or their riot-control use in "defensive military modes to save lives." Under these guidelines, the Senate ratified the Geneva Protocol on December 16, 1974. President Ford signed the ratification on January 22, 1975.

At the same time that the Senate ratified the Geneva Protocol, it also approved the Convention on the Prohibition of the Development, Production, and Stockpiling of Bacteriological (Biological) and Toxin Weapons and on Their Destruction. This treaty had been signed by the USSR, Great Britain, and the United States on April 10, 1972. Its ratification was delayed by the Senate until the U.S. position on chemical weapons was clarified. Following the guidelines adopted by the Ford administration for the Geneva pact, the Senate ratified the 1972 convention on December 16, 1974; Ford signed it on January 22, 1975.

See November 25, 1969.

### March 14, 1975

*President Thieu of South Vietnam decides to withdraw his forces from the highland areas and concentrate them along the coast leading to Saigon. This becomes a critical decision because ARVN commanders have no precise plans for the retreat that became a rout.*

President Thieu's decision reflected the quick success of the Communist offensive that began on March 1, 1975. After cutting Highways 19 and 21 between the coast and the central highlands, North Vietnamese forces captured Ban Me Thuot and threatened Pleiku and Kontum. Pleiku, the former center of a large U.S. support base, had prospered during the war. The local populace was not secure, however, because General Nguyen Van Toan, whom Thieu appointed in 1972, controlled the heroin trade and ARVN troops had been corrupted by this illegal traffic, as well as by the addiction of a third of the soldiers.

On March 14, after conferring with other ARVN officers, Thieu decided to retreat from Pleiku and Kontum and concentrate the ARVN defenses along the coastal areas. The retreat from the two cities was a disaster. The upper-ranked officers left quickly; the lower-ranked officers had no plans to retreat. Command of the troops disintegrated. Soldiers mutinied, looted, raped, and left Pleiku burning as the Communists arrived. Many ARVN troops had their families with them, and they fled in trucks or wagons, or by backpacking down Highway 19 toward the coast. About 250,000 people fled the highlands.

General Dung followed his advantage as quickly as logistical control allowed. In the north on March 18, Communists captured Quang Tri and moved south. Between March 24 and 28, the Pleiku chaos was repeated at Hue and Danang. At Danang's docks, refugees and troops vied for the last boats to Saigon, while Communist forces shelled the beaches. Between March 1 and March 28, Thieu's forces lost two-thirds of their territory, half of their 1.1 million-man army and local defense forces, and most of the air force. Former U.S. military equipment at Pleiku and Danang fell into Communist hands because the retreating ARVN troops did not take time to destroy it.

See April 29, 1975.

### March 25, 1975

*King Faisal of Saudi Arabia is murdered by his nephew, Prince Faisal.*

The prince was disgruntled with politics in the royal palace. After an examination found him to be mentally sane, the prince was publicly beheaded for his crime in June 1975. The new Saudi ruler was King Khaled, with Prince Fahd exercising the role of prime minister. The new regime did not alter the relatively moderate policy of Saudi Arabia in the Middle East.

### April 5, 1975

*Chiang Kai-Shek dies in Taiwan.*

On April 6, Yen Chin-kar became the president of the Republic of China. Following Chiang's death, his son Chiang Ching-kuo gained primary power in Nationalist China.

## April 12, 1975

### *Muslim and Christian factions fight in Lebanon.*

Open warfare shook the precarious political balance between Muslims and Christians in Lebanon. Phalangist Christian military forces, a private army led by Pierre Gemayel, fought against the Palestinian guerrilla bases that had moved into Lebanon after King Hussein ejected them from Jordan in 1971. Fighting between the Phalangists and Palestinians first took place in May 1973, leading the Syrian army to enter Lebanon in November 1973. Cease-fire arrangements had been attempted but broke down in early April, culminating in the large-scale battle on April 12 in which an estimated 150 Lebanese died.

## April 13, 1975

### *Fighting erupts between Palestinians and Christian militia in Lebanon.*

There had been increased tensions in Lebanon since 1971 because the Palestinian refugees in that state had become aggressive under the leadership of Yasser Arafat of the Palestine Liberation Organization (PLO). The precarious balance between Muslim and Christian political officers became unhinged because the Muslim leaders claimed Christian army officers allowed extremists of the Phalangist militia to use anti-Arab tactics to quiet the Palestinians. Early in 1975, the Muslim leaders demanded the formation of military councils on which they and the Christian officers would jointly make decisions. Lebanon's President Camille Chamoun and the Phalangists rejected these demands.

An incident on April 13 caused large-scale conflict after gunfire was exchanged between Phalangist troops and Palestinian militants. Each side claimed the other fired first when a busload of Palestinians engaged Christian troops in a small-scale battle. Fighting spread to Beirut and other parts of Lebanon, and large-scale rocket and machine gun attacks occurred during the next three days. Attempts to resolve the dispute and reassert the government's authority were not successful. No one knew at the time, but the April 13 incident ignited a conflict that totally despoiled Lebanon during the next 15 years.

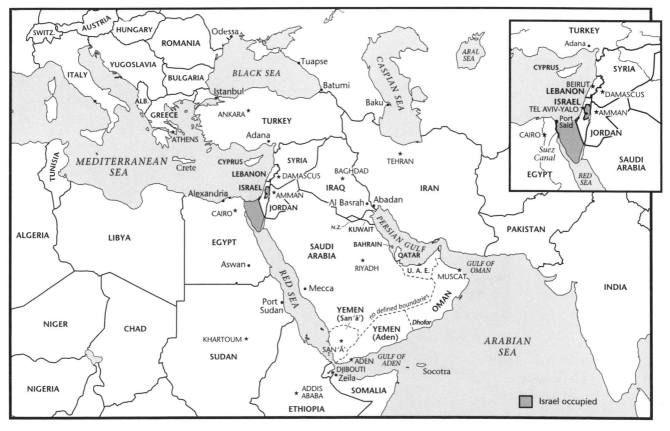

The Middle East, 1975

### April 17, 1975

***Cambodia falls to the forces of the Khmer Rouge as Phnom Penh surrenders after a long siege.***

Former President Lon Nol had left Cambodia for exile on April 1, turning the government over to General Saukham Khoy.

### April 25, 1975

***Portugal conducts its first free election in 50 years.***

After the election, the Ruling High Council became a mixture of non-Communist military officers and Communists. This allowed the non-Communist Council members to press for less radical economic measures.

### April 29, 1975

**The last American "chopper" evacuates the U.S. embassy in Saigon.**

The collapse of the South Vietnamese forces and government of President Thieu came faster than anyone, even the Communists, anticipated. Thieu's apparently trained and well-equipped armies of 1973 crumbled, owing in large measure to the corruption, decay, and self-centeredness of the high-level officer corps that Generals Ky and Thieu created in 1967. While a few ARVN soldiers showed skill and bravery during the final weeks, they could not make up for the general decay of South Vietnam's military and political structure, which the United States had been unable to influence between 1954 and 1973.

Throughout most of March 1975, President Ford and Secretary of State Kissinger worried more about Cambodia than about Saigon. Phnom Penh had been surrounded for some time and the Khmer Rouge tightened its grip on the city early in 1975. Eventually, Phnom Penh fell on April 17 after the United States evacuated the embassy on April 12.

Regarding Vietnam, Washington officials were constantly beguiled by the allegedly successful Vietnamization program of 1968 to 1973. Even after Pleiku fell, the Pentagon expected the "well-trained" ARVN to counterattack as they had during the 1972 Easter Offensive. On March 24, *Time* magazine quoted U.S. military officials as predicting that Saigon would soon establish "battle-field equi-

U.S. navy crewmen carry two of the refugees brought by a VNAF helicopter. National Archives

librium." On March 31, *Time* praised Thieu for his "gritty gamble to evacuate the highlands" and save the "body of South Vietnam." U.S. experts gave Thieu "high marks for his strategy of retreat."

In retrospect, Saigon would have fallen earlier except for the gallant defense of ARVN units at Xuan Loc on Highway 4 near Saigon. On April 28, the RVN National Assembly announced that General Duong Van Minh had replaced President Thieu. Because the North Vietnamese had previously offered to negotiate with a neutralist advocate such as Minh, the assembly hoped Saigon would be spared. But it was too late for negotiations. The communists refused to negotiate with Minh but accepted his surrender on April 30.

The U.S. embassy and its "friends" completed their evacuation late in the evening of April 29. U.S. Ambassador Graham Martin delayed the evacuation to provide exit for pro-American Vietnamese. On April 20, President Ford ordered the immediate departure of U.S. personnel, and until April 29, helicopters relaying refugees to U.S. ships tried to carry all the people they could. American TV cameras relayed the chaotic evacuation scenes back to U.S. firesides. Less influential Vietnamese "friends" climbed the embassy walls and sought to reach a departing helicopter. Finally, the last U.S. helicopter left. Saigon had fallen to the communists, following a "decent interval" of 27 months since the truce of January 1973.

See March 14, 1975.

### May 15, 1975

**The *Mayaguez* incident ends after U.S. marines rescue the ship's crew from Cambodia.**

This incident began on May 12 when President Ford learned that a private U.S. cargo ship, the *Mayaguez,* had been fired on, boarded, and captured by Cambodian patrol boats 55 miles off their coastline in the Gulf of Thailand. Because the United States had no diplomatic relations with the Pol Pot regime in Phnom Penh, Washington found it difficult to learn exactly what Cambodia intended. Two other foreign boats had recently been harassed by Cambodian patrol boats, but there had been no warnings sent to keep ships out of the region.

On Tuesday, May 13, the president ordered 1,000 marines to fly from Okinawa to Utapao air base in Thailand, although the Thai government, which had not been consulted, protested this action. In addition, the aircraft carrier *Coral Sea* and two destroyers were sent to the Gulf of Thailand.

On Wednesday, Ford appealed to U.N. Secretary-General Kurt Waldheim for assistance. At the same time, however, the president and the NSC decided to take military action as soon as possible. Thus, without waiting for the United Nations to act, the United States began an assault against Cambodia on the evening of May 14 (morning of May 15 in Cambodia). While U.S. helicopters carried marines to Koh Tang, the island where the *Mayaguez* had been taken, the destroyer USS *Holt* approached the cargo ship and marines boarded the vessel. They found it was empty. At 11:13 A.M. Cambodian time, a Thai fishing boat approached the destroyer. The fishing boat flew a white flag and carried the 39 *Mayaguez* crew members.

Ralph Wetterhahn's 2001 book *The Mayaguez Incident and the End of the Vietnam War* offers new evidence about the events of May 12 to May 15, 1975. The book shows that the *Mayaguez*'s 40-member crew was never held on Koh Tang island, invaded by the U.S. Marines, but on Rong Sam Len island. In addition, Wetterhahn found that more U.S. servicemen were killed during the operation than the Ford administration admitted, including 23 men killed when a helicopter crashed in Thailand and three Marines who were inadvertently left behind on Koh Tang island, where they were captured and murdered by the Khmer Rouge. The assault may not have been necessary, however, because from 7:07 to 7:26 A.M. (Cambodian time) a Phnom Penh radio message received in Bangkok indicated Cambodia would surrender the *Mayaguez.* The marine assault had begun at 6:20 A.M.

### June 5, 1975

**President Sadat reopens the Suez Canal to international shipping.**

The canal had been closed since the 1967 Six-Day War with Israel. During his discussion with Secretary Kissinger in November 1973, Sadat had agreed to return the Suez operations to normal and to permit nonmilitary Israeli ships to use the canal.

### June 10, 1975

**The Rockefeller commission's report on the CIA finds its overall record good but notes some areas of illegal action that must be remedied.**

Because there were extensive claims of illegal CIA activities, President Ford appointed Vice President Nelson Rockefeller on January 5 to head an investigative commission to review the organization's activity.

Following five months of study, the commission report, entitled "CIA Activities Within the United States," found that the agency overstepped the bounds of legality in some areas. The violations involved errors of judgment, not crimes, in seeking to protect the national security. The areas where the CIA overstepped its bounds included (1) opening the mail of private citizens since 1959; (2) preparing computer files on the names and actions of over 300,000 citizens; (3) experimenting with mind-expanding drugs on unknowing subjects; (4) giving President Nixon secret data on the Kennedys that was used for political purposes; and (5) keeping a Soviet defector in solitary confinement for three years while checking on his credibility.

The commission also uncovered material regarding CIA plots of attempted or actual assassinations of foreign leaders during the Eisenhower and Kennedy administrations. President Ford directed that these data not be made public, but they were turned over to a congressional committee on the intelligence services. The Rockefeller Commission recommended that a joint congressional committee have oversight of intelligence agencies.

The Rockefeller Commission recommended an administrative reorganization of the CIA to prevent a recurrence of what had occurred. It did not propose a fundamental alteration of the CIA's authority as the predominant U.S. agency for intelligence gathering. But critics of the CIA claimed that the Rockefeller Commission did not go far enough and that more serious actions and attitudes of the CIA needed to be corrected.

See November 21, 1975.

### June 26, 1975

*India's Prime Minister Indira Gandhi declares a state of emergency and arrests several hundred political opponents.*

On June 12, the High Court of Allahabad disqualified Gandhi for office for six years on the grounds of corrupt practice in the 1971 election in Uttar Pradesh. Gandhi appealed the ruling and was allowed to stay in office.

On June 26, Gandhi said the emergency decree was necessary to safeguard the country's unity and stability. Her opponents claimed she acted to secure her continuance in power. On November 7, India's Supreme Court invalidated the Allahabad Court ruling against Gandhi.

### July 1, 1975

*Vietnam is united as one nation.*

Following the fall of Saigon on April 29 and the unconditional surrender of the Republic of Vietnam, the effort to unite an independent Vietnam that began in September 1945 became an accomplished fact 30 years later.

### July 11, 1975

*Black nationalist groups in Angola begin to fight for dominance as Portugal proceeds with plans to grant independence.*

In January 1975, Portugal's plans to grant Angola independence by November 11 seemed to be going smoothly because the three nationalist factions said they would cooperate in forming an interim government. During the next four months fighting broke out, becoming more serious by July 11. In Luanda, the capital, the Marxist Popular Front for the Liberation of Angola had gained control. It expelled the Conservative National Front for the Total independence of Angola from the capital. The third group, the National Union for the Total independence of

South Vietnamese refugees
flee from the Communists.
National Archives

Angola, was much smaller and had not yet been involved in the fighting.

Portugal tried to mediate the dispute but had failed. There was a minority of 400,000 white settlers in Angola, but many of these had fled into exile to avoid involvement in the fighting.

### July 15–17, 1975

#### Apollo 18–Soyuz 19: A joint U.S.-Soviet space venture.

As one of President Nixon-First Secretary Brezhnev's détente achievements, a joint space program was agreed upon. This was completed in July 1975. The U.S. and Soviet spacecraft rendezvoused and docked while orbiting the earth, linking the two ships. Their crews exchanged visits and shared meals in space. Prior to the launching of the mission, the astronauts visited the space facilities of each other's nation. The American astronauts were Vance D. Brand, Thomas P. Stafford, and Donald K. Slayton. The Soviet astronauts were Aleksey A. Leonov and Valeriy N. Kubasov.

### July 24, 1975

#### The House of Representatives rejects President Ford's request to lift the arms embargo on Turkey.

Ford requested $185 million in military aid for Turkey to make up for the Turkish aid program that Congress cut off on October 18, 1974, after Turkey used U.S. weapons to invade Cyprus. Ford wanted the aid restored so that the activity of U.S. military installations in Turkey could return to normal. These bases monitored Soviet missile and troop movements.

Arguing that Turkey violated the Foreign Military Assistance Act in using the weapons in Cyprus, House members refused to renew aid to Turkey. In Washington, a large Greek lobby opposed aid to Turkey; the Turks had no similar Turkish-American interest group.

Immediately after the House rejected the aid bill, Turkey halted all activity at 20 U.S. military bases within its borders. At President Ford's urging, the House reconsidered the July 24 vote and on October 2 voted to ease the Turkish embargo. The Senate rejected the change, however. Congress continued the embargo until 1978.

See September 26, 1978.

### August 1, 1975

**Representatives of 35 nations sign the Helsinki agreements that legitimize the Soviet Union's territorial gains in Europe since 1940 and guarantee human rights and the free flow of ideas in both eastern and western Europe.**

After several months of negotiation at Vienna in 1974–1975, the Helsinki document was finalized in a three-day conference on European security. It was called officially the "final act of the conference on security and cooperation in Europe."

A principal part of the agreement confirmed the Eastern European boundaries established by the Red Army in 1945, a reality that President Franklin D. Roosevelt had conceded during World War II. These borders included the Soviets' absorption of the three Baltic states (Estonia, Latvia, and Lithuania); the Soviet takeover of Ruthenia (formerly part of Czechoslovakia) and Bessarabia (formerly Romanian territory); the westward shift of Poland's border, whereby Poland lost territory in the east to the Soviet Unions but gained German territory in the west; Romania's acquisition of Transylvania (formerly Hungarian); and the partition of Germany. This "ersatz peace treaty" declared that the new frontiers were "inviolable." It also stated that borders might be changed by peaceful agreement, a clause West Germany desired in the hope that the two Germanys might one day reunite.

The second part of the Helsinki document was designed to guarantee certain human rights in Europe. All nations subscribed to the concept that they would permit more human freedom and free contacts between their peoples and those of other nations. To evaluate better the "human rights" accords, the security conference agreed to reconvene in June 1977 to assess the situation. The U.S. State Department emphasized the advantages of having the Soviets agree to improve these rights; the Soviets emphasized the Helsinki agreement that recognized the political boundaries existing since 1945.

During the three-day meeting marking the Helsinki Accord, divided into what delegates called Baskets I, II, and III, speeches by Soviet First Secretary Brezhnev and U.S. President Ford showed the divergence of interests of the two superpowers in signing the Helsinki Accords. Brezhnev's address emphasized that under the Accord, states could no longer interfere in the internal affairs of another nation. Although some observers thought the Soviet Union might no longer interfere in the affairs of its Warsaw Pact allies, Brezhnev really meant the United States should not complain about human rights in or the emigration policies of the Soviet Union.

President Ford's message to the Helsinki delegates emphasized the accords as a method to improve the daily life of people living in both Eastern and Western Europe. Ford said, however, that the new agreement would be judged "not by promises made but by promises kept."

### August 29, 1975

**Venezuela nationalizes its oil industry, which had been largely controlled by the Shell, Exxon, and Gulf oil companies.**

On August 29, President Carlos Andrés Pérez signed a bill passed by the Venezuelan Congress that nationalized, with compensation, all foreign-owned oil companies. The companies, which were largely U.S. owned, would receive government bonds according to the net book value of their assets. On October 9, the Venezuelans fixed this compensation to the oil companies at $1 billion.

President Pérez wanted foreigners to remain in the oil industry to provide expertise. Therefore, technical assistance contracts were to be made with the oil companies for the continued operation of the oil wells.

Unlike their response to earlier nationalization projects (for example, that of Mexico during the 1930s), the U.S. companies' and government's response was calm. This was largely due to President Pérez's efforts to retain the friendliness of the oil operators and to the State Department's prior experience with the need to recognize such oil takeovers.

### September 1, 1975

**Egypt and Israel sign an additional agreement on buffer zones in the Sinai, setting up an early-warning system entrusted to the United States.**

The agreement of September 1 was based on the January 18, 1974, Israeli-Egyptian pact. It provided a more sophisticated means of avoiding aggression by Egypt or Israel through the Giddi or Mitla Passes in the Sinai desert. At those locations the two nations would establish surveillance stations. The United

States would erect three watch stations to be operated by 200 U.S. civilian personnel. Electronic sensor fields would be set up at each end of the pass. Any movement of armed forces other than the U.N. Emergency Forces would be reported by the American surveillance teams.

## September 5, 1975

**President Ford escapes an assassination attempt.**

The assassination attempts was made by Lynette Fromm in Sacramento, California. Ford was saved when Secret Service bodyguards pushed the gun aside. Fromm was a follower of Charles Manson, who was serving life imprisonment for the murder of actress Sharon Tate and others in 1969. Seventeen days later (September 23) Sara Jane Moore fired a shot at President Ford but missed. Both Fromm and Moore were tried and convicted of attempts to murder the president and given terms of life in prison, Fromm on December 18, 1975; Moore on January 16, 1976.

## October 2, 1975

**Emperor Hirohito of Japan begins his first state visit to the United States.**

## November 10, 1975

**A U.N. General Assembly resolution condemns Zionism as a form of racism.**

This U.N. action was a strong rebuff to both Israel and the United States, which had fought to prevent its passage. It indicated that the political makeup of the General Assembly had changed considerably since 1945. The United Nations had tripled its membership in 30 years, most of the new nations coming from former imperial and colonial regions previously dominated by the United States and western European countries.

These less developed nations were poor, nondemocratic, nonwhite, and hostile to the U.S. policy that, in the pursuit of "anticommunism," frequently promoted authoritarian and repressive governments. The United States had become identified, in the minds of these nations, with nondemocratic and intrusive

foreign policies. Consequently, they often voted against U.S.-sponsored projects.

See November 5, 1977.

## November 10, 1975

*Angola obtains independence from Portugal.*

Lisbon decided to grant Angola independence even though the three factions seeking power in Luanda would not give the nation a united government. Fighting for control continued.

See January 11, 1976.

## November 20, 1975

*General Franco, Spain's fascist leader, dies. On November 22, King Juan Carlos is sworn in as Spain's ruler.*

## November 21, 1975

**The Church committee of the U.S. Senate reports previous CIA involvement in plots to assassinate foreign leaders.**

Between 1970 and 1974, there were many accusations that the Federal Bureau of Investigation and the Central Intelligence Agency had engaged in illegal covert activity. Because CIA action directly affected U.S. foreign relations, the investigation of its activities particularly affected U.S. diplomacy.

Two committees investigated the CIA during 1975. One, a "blue-ribbon" panel chaired by Vice President Rockefeller, began its investigation on January 5. On June 10, its report indicated that the CIA had exceeded its charter by conducting domestic surveillance of U.S. citizens.

The second, the Senate Investigative Committee, headed by Frank Church, delved into CIA activity abroad. The most sensational findings of the committee were the CIA's involvement in assassination plots. Among nations where the CIA's involvement was identified were Cuba, Zaïre, the Dominican Republic, South Vietnam, and Chile. The methods varied, usually being to encourage or pay parties already willing to carry out an assassination.

Later in December, the Church Committee cleared the CIA of direct responsibility for the overthrow and murder of Chile's Salvador Allende. But the CIA and the Nixon administration had assisted anti-Allende groups in Chile.

### December 5, 1975

**President Ford concludes a five-day visit to China.**

There was no significant agenda for Ford to pursue in his talks with Chinese officials. The tour was largely designed to project a favorable public relations image for the president and to confirm prior U.S.-Chinese friendship. During this visit, Ford and China's leader, Deng Xiaoping, renewed the commitment of their two nations to the Shanghai communiqué of February 1972. Ford also restated orally the U.S. commitment to remain a major power in the Pacific.

# 1976

### January 11, 1976

*The Organization of African Unity deadlocks on the issue of Angola's government.*

The OAU called an emergency meeting to resolve the Angolan issue but adjourned with no results on January 11. Twenty-two African states favored recognition of the Soviet-backed government of the Popular Movement for the Liberation of Angola; 22 other African states opposed this government. The 50-50 split prevented the OAU from acting.

See January 27, 1976.

### January 26, 1976

**The United States vetoes a U.N. Security Council resolution condemning Israel's settlements on the West Bank of the Jordan and calling for an independent Palestinian state.**

During the debate preceding the Security Council vote, U.S. Ambassador Daniel Moynihan strongly objected to a council decision to permit the Palestine Liberation Organization to sit at the council table and participate in the discussions, which began on January 12. The U.S. veto of this decision did not apply to the procedural vote of 11 to 1, which seated the PLO. As a result of this action, Israel refused to be present at the council debate.

The council debate of January 12 followed a series of violent demonstrations by Arabs in the West Bank territory occupied by Israel in June 1967. The Israelis had begun settlements in this area and had conducted midnight searches of Arab homes in the West Bank.

They had also detained many Arabs suspected of causing trouble. Between 1967 and 1975, Israel had set up 55 Jewish settlements in territory occupied in 1967.

On January 26, the Security Council voted on a resolution stating that Israel should withdraw from all Arab territory and calling for an independent Palestinian state. The vote, as on January 12, was 11-1, the U.S. veto preventing the resolution from passing. Great Britain, France, and Italy abstained. Following a similar debate and resolution vote on March 22, the United States cast a veto against condemning Israeli settlement policy in the occupied area.

### January 27, 1976

**Congress rejects President Ford's request for aid to Angola. The House of Representatives concurs with prior Senate action in refusing to provide $28 million for Angola's anti-communist factions.**

Between May and December 1976, reports surfaced of the Ford administration's covert aid of $32 million to support Angolan rebels opposing the Luanda government, which held the dominant position in that African state. According to State Department officials, the Soviets had provided $200 million and 11,000 Cuban troops to support the Popular Movement in Angola. In December 1976, U.S. news reports indicated that the United States had given covert military aid to two Angolan groups opposing the Luanda government: the Bakongo tribal group, which led the National Liberation Front of Angola; and the Ovimbudu tribal group, which formed the Union for the Total Independence of Angola. The White House denied that Americans were recruited to fight in Angola but would not comment on reports that Cuban refugees fought on behalf of the U.S.-backed factions in that country. South Africa also supported the same factions in Angola, but the apartheid policies of the Johannesburg government only served to detract from the arguments that favored the U.S.-backed factions in Angola.

In December, President Ford asked Congress for additional military aid to Angola even though he and Secretary of State Kissinger refused to apply direct pressure on Moscow to stop assisting the Luanda government. The president rejected a proposal to restrict grain shipments to the Soviets, and Secretary of State

Kissinger objected to suggestions that SALT II be halted unless Moscow cooperated in Angola.

Thus, in presenting the case for Angola to Congress, Ford used only rhetoric to imply that the domino theory might lead to the spread of further Communist victories in Africa. Congress rejected these arguments, especially because the United States appeared to be backing the weaker side in Angola. The Bakongo and Ovimbudu tribal groups were not effective and refused to cooperate against the Luanda government. The breadth of congressional opposition to Ford's request is seen in the House vote of 323 to 99. Votes to end aid to Angola were cast by 251 Democrats and 72 Republicans.

See December 1, 1976.

### February 6, 1976

**Lockheed Aircraft Corporation admits bribery payments to officials of Japan, Sweden, the Netherlands, and Italy.**

In hearings of the Senate Subcommittee on Multinational Corporations, Lockheed officials indicated that they had spent about $24.4 million in bribes to assist their business operations in foreign countries. Later disclosures indicated bribes were also made to officials of Colombia, Spain, South Africa, Nigeria, and Turkey.

### March 1, 1976

**President Ford tells newsmen he wants to drop the word *détente* from his political vocabulary.**

Criticism from the right wing of the Republican Party, headed by Ronald Reagan, caused Ford to move away from détente because it was a concept that many Americans seemed unable to comprehend.

President Nixon and his adviser, Henry Kissinger, had never been careful to school the U.S. public in the nuances of power politics and the advantages of reaching mutual agreements with the Soviet Union. Following Nixon's resignation in August 1974, Secretary of State Kissinger endeavored to deliver more speeches throughout the country to clarify his policies with the USSR. From August 20, 1974, to early 1976, he made 16 such speeches. He also sent four of his principal advisers around the nation to conduct town-meeting sessions on foreign policy.

Generally, however, these meetings convinced Kissinger and his aides that there was widespread disagreement with the administration's policies. Although experts on international affairs continued to laud détente and the emphasis on political realities espoused by Kissinger, the U.S. public did not. Nixon's radical change from the moralistic, anti-Communist rhetoric begun under President Truman and carried on by Ronald Reagan and Senator Henry Jackson continued to rouse the anti-Communist pulse of conservative Americans.

By January 1976, many European observers stated they found Kissinger's rhetoric becoming more flamboyant in talking of "domino" Communist victories in Africa. One British editor stated that Kissinger's private comments were "reminiscent of John Foster Dulles" as he talked of dominoes in Europe if the Italian Communists should be elected, leading to Communist governments in Paris, Madrid, and Lisbon as well. Such signs indicated that Kissinger as well as Ford was ready to end détente as a U.S.-Soviet policy whose time had not yet arrived.

### March 11, 1976

**The port of New York Authority bans the landing of the British-French supersonic aircraft Concorde.**

The Concorde's flights from Paris and London to Washington began in April but were delayed in gaining permission to land in New York.

The State of New York had passed legislation barring any planes with excessive noise levels from landing in the state. The Port of New York Authority, which had jurisdiction over Kennedy International Airport, ruled that the Concorde could not land until its noise levels were evaluated elsewhere.

As a consequence, while the Concorde began scheduled flights to Dulles International Airport on May 24, it did not receive this privilege from Kennedy Airport until 1977. During the intervening year and a half, courts in New York continued the ban against the Concorde. The French government protested to the State Department, causing ill will between France and the United States. Eventually, on October 19, 1977, the U.S. Supreme Court ruled that the New York ban was illegal because it conflicted with federal regulations approving the landing of the Concorde in New York. On November 22, the French and British

SST airliners began regular service from Kennedy Airport.

### March 14, 1976

*Egypt ends its 1971 treaty of friendship with the Soviet Union.*

Prime Minister Sadat distrusted the Soviet advisers in Egypt. Soon after, Sadat undertook talks for a treaty with mainland China.

### March 18, 1976

**The United States stops all aid to India.**

The halting of U.S. aid to India resulted because negotiations about economic assistance broke down in February 1976. Washington was upset because Prime Minister Indira Gandhi accused the CIA of trying to undermine her government. The amount of aid involved totaled about $65 million for 1976.

### March 24, 1976

*A military coup in Argentina overthrows President Maria Estella Perón.*

The wife of former President Juan Perón was found guilty of embezzlement by Argentinian courts on October 25 and allowed to go into exile. Following the coup, General Jorge Videla was named president by the military junta.

### March 28, 1976

*Southeast Asian nations form a treaty of friendship and cooperation.*

The nations signing this agreement were the Philippines, Singapore, Malaysia, Thailand, and Indonesia. They formed a new organization: the Association of Southeast Asian Nations (ASEAN).

### April 5, 1976

*James Callaghan replaces Harold Wilson as prime minister of the United Kingdom.*

Wilson announced his retirement on March 16, 1976. On the third ballot at a Labour Party Convention, Callaghan received 176 votes to 137 for Michael Foot.

### April 5, 1976

*Cambodia's Prince Norodom Sihanouk resigns as head of state in favor of Khieu Samphan.*

### May 28, 1976

**The United States and the USSR sign a treaty on nonmilitary nuclear explosions.**

The treaty limited any single underground nuclear test to the equivalent of 150,000 tons of TNT. If any explosion exceeded this limit, the other side had the right to an on-site inspection. In practice, no inspections were anticipated because neither nation planned larger explosion tests.

### June 4, 1976

*The Palestine Liberation Organization (PLO) gains recognition as a member of the International Labor Organization at the World Employment Conference in Geneva.*

Under Yasser Arafat's leadership, the PLO sought greater recognition from various U.N. affiliates such as the ILO. On January 27, 1976, the PLO became a member of the U.N. Conference on Trade and Development. On September 6, it became a member of the Arab League.

### June 16, 1976

**In Lebanon, the U.S. ambassador, Francis E. Meloy Jr., and his economic counselor, Robert O. Waring, are shot and killed.**

The two Americans were shot while en route to a meeting; their bodies were abandoned in a garbage dump. The United States and Great Britain immediately planned to evacuate Americans and British in Lebanon.

For further data on Lebanon's unrest, see April 13, 1975, and November 8, 1976.

### June 30, 1976

*Europe's Communist Parties, after a two-day meeting, declare that each national party is independent and equal to other parties.*

This conference should have ended the myth of a Communist monolith controlled by Moscow. Although the Soviet Union continued to exercise control wherever it had military forces in place,

Communist parties outside the Soviet orbit followed, as they often had previously, their own national attitudes toward Communist methods and local policies. Nevertheless, the conference dramatized the new tactic of non-Soviet parties that emphasized their separate programs for their respective nation's particular needs. This policy soon became known, and condemned, as "Eurocommunism."

### July 4, 1976

**Israeli commandos attack the airport at Entebbe, Uganda, freeing 98 Jewish captives and the crew of a hijacked Air France aircraft.**

Palestinian terrorists intercepted the Air France plane in the air near Athens, forcing the pilot to fly to Entebbe, Uganda, on June 30. The next day, all non-Jewish passengers were released.

The Israeli commandos flew to Entebbe, where they attacked the hangar in which the hostages were held. Three hostages were killed; one was wounded and taken to an Entebbe hospital, where she was allegedly murdered. Generally, the Israeli raid was successful.

### July 20, 1976

**The U.S. spacecraft *Viking* lands on Mars and transmits photographs to Earth.**

On September 3, *Viking 2* landed on Mars.

### August 18, 1976

**At Panmunjom, Korea, North Korean forces attack and kill two U.S. Army officers. The incident ends with a North Korean apology on August 21.**

The North Koreans attacked a U.N. Forces contingent in the Joint Security Area at Panmunjom. The U.N. group was trimming trees in the area to permit two U.N. command posts to see each other, when 30 North Korean soldiers appeared on the scene. They asked the U.N. officials to stop their work, and when they refused, the North Koreans attacked the U.N. forces personally, beating them with ax handles and clubs. The U.N. commanders suffered the worst beatings and died. They were Captain Arthur G. Bonifas and Lieutenant Mark I. Barrett.

U.S. officials in Korea believed the incident was part of North Korea's attempt to publicize tensions between U.S. and Korean troops, hoping the United States would withdraw.

The American reaction was to move up U.S. F-4 and F-111 aircraft from Okinawa and Idaho. The Pentagon also sent the Midway naval task force into the area and raised the region's alert status to Def Con 3: war is likely but not imminent. In addition, on August 21, a U.N. work team under heavy guard went to the Security Defense Area at Panmunjom and cut down the tree that previously was only being trimmed.

On August 21, North Korea's President Kim Il Sung sent an unprecedented message to the Korean U.N. headquarters. Kim expressed his regret at the incident and hoped such incidents could be prevented in the future. The U.N. command believed its response affirmed U.N. rights in the area and successfully calmed the incident.

### September 9, 1976

**Mao Tse-Tung dies; new Party Chairman Hua Guofeng arrests the "gang of four."**

The Chinese Communist Party (CCP) chairman since 1927, Mao led the People's Republic of China since 1949. His death came soon after Chou En-lai died on January 8, 1976. Hua Guofeng replaced Chou as prime minister in January and became Deputy Chairman of the CCP on April 1, following a series of riot in Beijing.

In November 1976, Hua launched attacks on the radical "gang of four" who had led the Cultural Revolution in the 1960s. The gang included Mao's widow, Chiang Ching, who was arrested by Hua along with three other radical CCP members. Joined by Li Hsien-nien as prime minister, Hua directed a modernization program for China in contrast to the "gang of four's" rural program.

See August 18, 1966, and December 15, 1978.

### November 2, 1976

**James Earl "Jimmy" Carter is elected President.**

Running against Gerald Ford, whom the Republicans nominated on August 19, Carter advocated reforms in Washington to cut government costs and emphasized human rights in foreign affairs. Ford's platform upheld the Nixon-Kissinger policies except for deemphasizing détente with the Soviet Union. Ford's prin-

James Earl "Jimmy" Carter. National Archives

cipal opponent before the August convention was Ronald Reagan, whose strong conservative group claimed that Nixon's détente policy had weakened the United States in relation to the Soviet Union. Carter avoided making any definitive statements on détente, and his foreign policies were not clarified prior to the election.

On the November 2 ballot, Carter received 297 electoral votes to Ford's 241. This was the closest election since the Nixon-Kennedy campaign of 1960.

See March 1, 1976.

### November 8, 1976

*Syria occupies Lebanon in a "peacekeeping" role designed to end 19 months of civil war.*

Fighting among PLO, Lebanese Christian, and Lebanese Muslim forces had defied solution for over a year. Between April and August 1976, Syrian forces moved into eastern Lebanon to restore peace, and in October an Arab League plan provided for Syria's temporary occupation until Lebanon restored an orderly government. On November 8, Syrian forces entered western Lebanon and on November 10 occupied Beirut. Lebanon's President Elias Sarkis now had to reorganize a compromise government, hoping to regain the peace that existed before 1975.

### November 15, 1976

**After Vietnam is united the United States vetoes its U.N. membership.**

Following Communist elections in April 1976, Vietnam's two parts were united officially on June 24, 1976. Vietnam applied for membership in the United Nations, but on November 15, the United States vetoed the application. Washington claimed Hanoi was not cooperating in providing information about 395 Americans listed as missing in action (MIA) during the Vietnam War. Representatives of the two countries continued talks in Paris about the MIAs, but the United States was not satisfied about the data Hanoi provided.

See July 20, 1977.

### December 1, 1976

**With the United States abstaining, Angola becomes the 146th member of the United Nations.**

Following the end of U.S. aid to the opponents of the government of President Agestinho Neto of Angola, the triumph of the Luanda regime became certain. By October 1, 1976, Portugal recognized Neto's government as the successor to the former Portuguese colony. On November 10, Neto and Soviet leader Leonid Brezhnev signed a 20-year friendship treaty in Moscow. Nevertheless, when Angola's membership in the United Nations was voted on, the United States decided to abstain rather than veto it because as early as February 21, 1976, the State Department had told Gulf Oil and Boeing Aircraft they could undertake business deals with Neto's government.

See January 27, 1976.

### December 1, 1976

*José López Portillo becomes president of Mexico.*

### December 16, 1976

*OPEC increases oil prices in a meeting at Qatar.*

Although Saudi Arabia and the United Arab Emirates agreed only to a 5% increase, the other 11 OPEC members raised their oil prices by 10%. Saudi Arabia not only announced a smaller price increase but indicated it would increase oil production. Some observers believed that the Saudi oil minister, Sheik Ahmed Zaki Yamani, was indicating to President-elect Carter that he should pressure Israel to be more flexible in solving Middle East problems.

# 1977

### January 20, 1977

**Cyrus Vance is commissioned as Secretary of State.**

Vance was a New York lawyer who had held diplomatic posts in both the Kennedy and the Johnson administrations. Thus, he provided a link with the eastern foreign policy establishment.

As his national security adviser, President Carter selected Zbigniew Brzezinski, a professor of international relations whose views often differed from Henry Kissinger's. Vance and Brzezinski soon began competing to influence Carter and his foreign policy.

### January 26, 1977

**Two young Americans are indicted for selling the Soviet Union data on U.S. space satellite systems used to gather intelligence about Soviet weapons.**

Christopher Boyce and Andrew Daulton Lee of Palos Verdes, California, were indicted by a federal grand jury in Los Angeles on 12 counts of espionage. Lee had been arrested near the Soviet embassy in Mexico City on January 6, 1977. A heroin addict and fugitive from justice in California, Lee had relayed data obtained by Boyce to Soviet agents in Mexico between 1975 and January 1977. Boyce was a $140-a-week clerk at the TRW Defense and Space Systems Group in Redondo Beach, California.

TRW was the Thompson-Ramo-Woolridge Corporation, which since 1959 had worked on U.S. intercontinental missile systems such as Atlas, Titan, Thor, and Minuteman. Since 1960, TRW had experimented with and operated for the Defense Department more than a dozen earth satellite projects

Secretary of State Cyrus Vance and President Carter. Jimmy Carter Library

in order to collect data about Soviet weapons. It also processed and analyzed the data for the Pentagon.

Within five months after going to work for TRW in 1974, Boyce had a security clearance for the highest TRW special project at the Redondo Beach plant: Project Rhyolite. This was a covert electronic surveillance system that monitored activity in the USSR and China. Boyce worked as a clerk in the code room, which linked ground stations placed secretly in Australia with the CIA in Washington. During the next two years, Boyce also had contact with Project Argus, an advanced Rhyolite system. He also handled plans for Project 20,030-Pyramid, a futuristic scheme for TRW space satellite systems.

Following his arrest, Boyce cooperated with U.S. intelligence authorities in attempting to recall all the data he had photographed and given to the Soviets through Lee, but he had not kept a systematic account of the data he copied. At the least, the Soviets gained data to decode the telemetry reports used by the United States. They also changed all their codes for future messages sent from their satellites.

On September 12, 1977, having been found guilty on eight counts of espionage and conspiracy to commit espionage, Boyce was sentenced to 40 years in prison. In a separate trial, Lee was also found guilty of espionage and sentenced to life imprisonment. Boyce's lesser sentence was due to his cooperation. On January 21, 1980, Boyce escaped from Lompoc Prison, California. He was recaptured on August 22, 1981.

The data given to the Soviets by Boyce and Lee seriously handicapped U.S. intelligence-gathering systems for the next several years. Some opponents of SALT II, after it was signed by the United States and the Soviet Union in 1979, claimed that America's verification system of Soviet weapons was in such disarray since 1977 that the United States could not know if SALT I had been violated or if SALT II might be violated by the USSR. Even though Project 20,030-Pyramid was canceled by TRW, knowledge of its future U.S. expectations would assist Soviet intelligence operations in learning to counter the U.S. satellite spy system. Prior to the Lee-Boyce case, U.S. spy satellite operations had been secret. President Carter did not publicly admit their existence until October 1978.

**February 17, 1977**

**President Carter sends a personal letter to Soviet dissident Andrey Sakharov that supports Sakharov's dissenting beliefs.**

In accordance with his 1976 campaign position on U.S. concern for human rights, President Carter issued a number of statements in February 1977 criticizing human rights restrictions in the Soviet bloc. Carter's most dramatic effort was a letter to Soviet physicist Sakharov. Carter told Sakharov he would ask the U.N. Human Rights Commission to investigate the arrest of dissidents in the Soviet Union.

The Soviet government denounced Carter for interfering in their internal affairs, declaring that the United States should first improve human rights in some of the dictatorships it supported in Latin America and Africa.

**March 9, 1977**

**President Carter announces the United States will withdraw about 30,000 troops from South Korea during the next three or four years.**

Carter stated that during the past 25 years, South Korea's ability to defend itself had reached the point where the reduction in U.S. forces was feasible. The decision, he said, did not affect the continuing obligation of the United States to defend South Korea if necessary.

See July 20, 1979.

**March 16, 1977**

**In Lebanon, Kamal Jumblatt, the chieftain of the Druse Muslim sect, is assassinated.**

Although the Syrian occupation of November 1976 was designed to resolve Lebanon's internal problems, it had not done so. Frequent riots and terrorist attacks by Druse, Christian Phalangist militia, and Muslims continued in 1977, and included Jumblatt's assassination. On March 18, 1977, Kamal's only son, Walid Jumblatt, became head of the Druse sect and leader of the Progressive Socialist Party in Lebanon.

## March 24, 1977

**The United States and Cuba inaugurate official talks regarding fishing zones and normalizing relations.**

During the next two months these talks made some progress in instituting new diplomatic ties. In early June, the two nations announced that Cuba would establish an "interest section" in Washington; the United States would do likewise in Havana. Nevertheless, the negotiations were tense, and each side seemed reluctant to go too far in the direction of friendship.

## March 30, 1977

**Secretary of State Vance informs reporters that the Soviets have rejected an arms limitation proposal prepared by the Carter administration.**

According to Vance, who met with reporters in Moscow after sessions with Soviet leader Brezhnev and Foreign Minister Gromyko, the Soviets simply rejected the Carter proposals as inequitable.

Hoping to go beyond the Vladivostok formula of November 1974 to achieve a reduction of nuclear armaments, Vance and Carter suggested two proposals to Brezhnev:

1. to sign a SALT II treaty based on the Vladivostok formula but to defer for the future the controversy over cruise missiles and the Backfire bomber;
2. to proceed with SALT III discussions to obtain a comprehensive proposal for progress in arms control by reducing nuclear weapons. This second proposal would (a) substantially reduce the aggregate number of strategic delivery vehicles; (b) reduce the number of modern large ballistic missile launchers; (c) reduce the MIRV (multiple independently targeted reentry vehicles) missile launchers; and (d) limit the number of ICBM launchers.

According to Vance, the Soviets would not accept these proposals because they did not believe the deal would be to their advantage. Vance stated that he did not think the Soviet decision on arms was connected to Carter's complaints about Moscow's violations of human rights.

## April 10, 1977

**France sends planes and Morocco sends troops to aid Zairean President Mobutu against rebels in Shaba province.**

For some time rebels in Zaire (the former Congo) increased in strength, threatening the regime of President Mobutu. France sent 1,500 Moroccan

The Carter foreign policy team: left to right: National Security Adviser Zbigniew Brzezinski, President Carter, Secretary of State Cyrus Vance. Jimmy Carter Library

troops to bolster the government. The Carter administration hesitated to provide too much aid for Mobutu but authorized $15 million for "nonlethal" equipment in March and April 1977.

### May 17, 1977

*In a significant political change, Israel's Labour Party loses an election after 29 years in office. The new prime minister is Menachem Begin of the Likud Party.*

### May 18, 1977

**The United States, the USSR, and 32 other nations sign a U.N. agreement banning environmental warfare.**

This pact prohibited experiments with or the use of military methods that would alter weather patterns or other environmental phenomena. From 1972 to 1974, the United States conducted a study of "environmental war" that led to a Senate resolution urging the president to negotiate a treaty prohibiting such action. At a Moscow summit on July 3, 1974, President Nixon and Soviet leader Brezhnev approved a draft treaty that each nation submitted to the U.N. Conference of the Committee on Disarmament (CCD) in Geneva on August 21, 1975. This U.S.-Soviet draft became the basis for the treaty signed on May 18, 1977.

### June 3, 1977

**A series of conferences between rich and poor nations (north-south) ends with no significant results.**

For over 18 months, dialogue had been conducted in Paris between 8 industrialized nations including the United States and 19 developing nations. The rich nations wanted to pressure OPEC to cut its oil prices; the poor nations wanted drastic reforms of the world's trade structure to redistribute the world's wealth. The developing nations also requested a moratorium on the $200 billion of debts they had accumulated; the rich nations offered only $1 billion of funding. More North-South talks were scheduled for November 1977 in Geneva.

### June 15, 1977

*The British Commonwealth Conference condemns the regime of Uganda's Idi Amin, having barred him from the conference sessions.*

Since gaining power in Uganda on January 25, 1971, Amin had become notorious for his inhumane treatment of his political and tribal opponents. Efforts to rally world opinion against Amin resulted in the decision of the Commonwealth nations meeting in London from June 8 to June 15 to condemn Amin for his "massive violations of basic human rights."

By the end of 1977, a movement to oust Amin developed. Exiles formed a "Ugandan National Liberation Front," and, helped by neighboring Tanzania, the front succeeded in overthrowing Amin on April 1, 1979.

### June 15, 1977

*Spain conducts its first election in 40 years. Adolfo Suarez's Democratic Center Union receives a majority of seats in Parliament.*

### June 21, 1977

*At a Communist conference in Warsaw, the Soviet delegation condemns Eurocommunism as ideological heresy.*

The Kremlin denounced Eurocommunism, a term that included the willingness of Western Communist parties to renounce revolution and pursue parliamentary methods to gain power. In addition, Eurocommunists such as Santiago Carillo of Spain and Enrico Berlinguer of Italy rejected Moscow's claim to dominance of other Communist parties because the USSR was the world's first socialist country.

See June 30, 1976.

### July 1, 1977

**President Carter cancels production of the controversial B-1 bomber program.**

The president astounded newsmen at a press conference on July 1 by opening the session with the statement that the expensive B-1 program would be ended except for minimal testing developments in the unlikely event "that the cruise missile system had trouble." Carter told the press: "I think that in toto the B-1, a very expensive weapons system conceived in the absence of the cruise missile factor, is not necessary."

Carter's decision was logical, not political, and aroused resentment from members of Congress who hoped the B-1 would provide economic benefits in their district or who believed the United States had to be superior to the USSR in all categories of weapons. The B-1s would cost more than $100 million each. However, they would create 69,000 jobs directly and 122,700 jobs by ripple effect. In contrast to the B-1, the cruise missile was, according to its advocates, cheap, accurate, and powerful, and able to avoid Soviet detection systems after being launched from existing B-52 planes outside the Soviet defense perimeter. As a result, the cruise missiles could penetrate into the Soviet Union more effectively than manned bombers.

### July 8, 1977

**President Carter's request to Congress for the sale to Iran of seven airborne warning and control system (AWACS) planes arouses opposition before its approval.**

Carter's request for the sale of AWACS might have been only a formality except for the Americans who demonstrated outside the White House against the shah of Iran. Both in and out of Congress, there was opposition to the shah's repression of human rights, including his executions of members of opposition groups.

Between July and October, intense congressional opposition sought to ban the sale of the seven AWACS to Iran. Led by Senators Hubert Humphrey and Clifford P. Case, the ban proponents cited not only the shah's repression but also the danger of risking the loss of the "sensitive technology" of the AWACS to Iranian radicals. Nevertheless, with the help of Senate Majority Leader Robert Byrd, Carter convinced Congress on October 8 not to block the sale. On November 9, Iran confirmed that it had purchased seven AWACS from the United States.

Opposition to the shah continued. When the shah was received at the White House on November 15, a large demonstration took place outside the White House gates. The police used tear gas to disperse the demonstrators; some of the gas fumes wafted to the area where President Carter was conducting ceremonies for the shah.

### July 16, 1977

*Libyan and Egyptian forces clash when Egyptian jets bomb and strafe a Libyan air base near Tobruk.*

President Sadat of Egypt and Colonel Gadhafi of Libya had often had acrimonious exchanges. Gadhafi had been verbally attacking Sadat for seeking peace negotiations with Israel. But their enmity nearly erupted in war in mid-July. Following a border raid by Libyan forces in early July, Egypt retaliated by attacking Tobruk. Later, on July 22, Sadat said his forces gave Gadhafi a "lesson he could never forget."

### July 20, 1977

*Vietnam is recommended for U.N. membership by the Security Council.*

Vietnam's membership became certain because the United States announced in May that it would not use its Security Council veto again to prevent Hanoi from joining the United Nations. In May, Hanoi's delegates told U.S. diplomats in Paris they would intensify their search for 795 Americans missing in Vietnam. This number increased to 2,338 after all Pentagon records were released by 1990. By September 30, Hanoi delivered the remains of 22 U.S. servicemen to American representatives. About the same time, the U.N. General Assembly finalized Vietnam's admission to its organization.

### August 8, 1977

*Ethiopia and Somalia engage in full-scale war on the horn of Africa.*

Each side claimed the other began this conflict, but Somalia appeared to be the aggressor. It captured most of the southern third of Ethiopia, which it claimed to be Somalia territory. The Soviet Union had the most to lose in this conflict because Moscow supported Ethiopia's government and had naval facilities at the port of Berbera in Somalia.

See November 13, 1977.

### September 7, 1977

**The United States and Panama sign the treaties on the future operation and defense of the Panama Canal.**

President Carter and the head of the Panamanian government, General Omar Torrijos, signed the trea-

General Torrijos and President Carter shake hands after signing the treaties at the Pan-American Union. At rear, left to right: U.S. negotiators Sol M. Linowitz and Ellsworth Bunker, OAS Secretary General Alejandro Orfila. Jimmy Carter Library

ties in the presence of representatives of 25 other American republics and Canada. The treaties resulted from negotiations begun in 1964 and conducted at various times under Presidents Johnson, Nixon, Ford, and Carter. The key decision permitting successful negotiations had been a statement of eight principles signed by Torrijos and Secretary of State Kissinger on February 7, 1974. The first treaty dealt with the transition of canal ownership over a period of 20 years, to end on December 31, 1999. The second treaty provided for U.S.-Panamanian relations after the Panamanians assumed full jurisdiction over the canal in the year 2000.

The first treaty provided for a Joint Commission of five Americans and four Panamanians gradually to phase out U.S. control of the canal and prepare the way for Panama's operation of it. Until 1999, a Joint U.S.-Panama Defense Commission would regulate the defense of the canal. The second treaty provided for the neutrality of the canal, future canal toll charges, and the joint U.S.-Panamanian defense of the canal. The agreement also provided for a joint study on the feasibility of a new sea-level canal. If this canal were built, terms for its construction would be negotiated.

In addition to the two treaties, the United States pledged outside the treaty to arrange loans of up to $200 million of Export-Import Bank credits to Panama; up to $75 million in AID housing guarantees; and a $20 million Overseas Private Investment Loan Corporation guarantee for Panama. The United States and Panama also agreed that all U.S. civilians employed in the Canal Zone could keep their jobs until retirement.

See June 16, 1978.

### October 17, 1977

*A West German commando unit successfully liberates 87 hostages held by 4 Arab skyjackers at an airfield in Mogadishu, Somalia.*

The Lufthansa aircraft was captured by 4 terrorists on October 13. They demanded the release of 11 terrorists held in Germany and 2 held in Turkey. The German commando unit used stun grenades to attack the plane. All the hostages were freed, although the terrorists had previously killed the plane's pilot. Three of the terrorists were killed; the fourth was wounded.

### November 5, 1977

**The United States withdraws from the International Labor Organization (ILO).**

This U.N. agency had become increasingly politicized by Arab and Communist delegations. In 1974, the ILO voted a resolution to condemn Israel for "racism" in administering Arab territory under its control, and Secretary Kissinger warned the ILO that the United States would withdraw unless the group concerned itself only with labor conditions. President Carter decided to withdraw U.S. membership until the ILO changed its rules and policies.

See also November 10, 1975.

### November 13, 1977

*Somalia expels 6,000 Soviet advisers and breaks diplomatic relations with Cuba.*

Somalia had been a Soviet ally for eight years but was angered by Soviet aid to Ethiopia in the conflict that broke out on August 8, 1977, between the two African neighbors. Somalia obtained aid against Ethiopia from France and the conservative Arab states.

### November 15, 1977

*Prime Minister Begin invites Egypt's President Sadat to visit Israel. Sadat accepts, heralding a new relationship between Egypt and Israel.*

Early in November, Sadat had suggested he would be willing to visit Israel. Nevertheless, Begin's invitation surprised most observers.

After 29 years of enmity Egypt and Israel finally began a search for peaceful relations. On November 19, Sadat flew to Israel, where he talked with Begin. He addressed Israel's Knesset (parliament) on November 20. When Sadat returned to Cairo on November 21, cheering crowds indicated many Egyptians lauded these new peace overtures.

See December 14, 1977.

### December 2, 1977

*Radical Arab leaders meet in Tripoli to unite against Egypt's moves toward peace with Israel.*

Leaders of Libya, Algeria, Iraq, South Yemen, Syria, and the PLO opposed President Sadat's new policy of negotiating with Israel.

On December 5, Egypt expelled the ambassadors of each of these radical Arab states except the one from Iraq.

### December 14, 1977

**A Cairo summit meeting of representatives of the United States, Egypt, and Israel convenes to discuss peace proposals.**

Following his visit to Israel, President Sadat of Egypt offered to negotiate directly with Israel, and Prime Minister Begin agreed (November 27). As a result sessions began in Cairo on December 14 and included U.S. representatives.

Initially, Sadat had hoped to persuade the Soviet Union and the other Arab states to join the talks, but Syria led the Arab radicals in rejecting the Egyptian proposal. Moscow also refused to join a multinational meeting on the Middle East. Therefore, Sadat called for direct Israeli-Egyptian talks with only U.S. representatives involved in the discussions. Although American diplomats preferred a multinational agreement on Middle Eastern problems, President Carter decided to encourage the new initiatives of Begin and Sadat. Nevertheless, both Sadat and Carter continued to seek support for the Cairo talks from moderate Arab leaders in Jordan, Saudi Arabia, and the Persian Gulf states.

See September 17, 1978.

### December 29, 1977

**President Carter arrives in Warsaw, his first stop on a tour to Poland, Iran, India, Saudi Arabia, France, and Belgium.**

Carter made this trip for several reasons:

1. a desire for East-West accords with such Communist nations as Poland, Hungary, and Romania;
2. a desire to improve the image of the shah of Iran in America. The United States depended on the shah as a major ally in the Middle East, although the shah had been severely criticized in the U.S. news media because of his repressive measures against dissenters;
3. a desire to improve relations with India, whose president, Morarji R. Desai, had indicated his desire to end the tensions created with America by Indira Gandhi's policies;
4. a desire to show Saudi Arabia that the United States welcomed its friendship as well as its "friendly" oil policies;
5. a desire to bolster continued good U.S. relations with French President Valéry Giscard d'Estaing;
6. a desire to visit NATO headquarters in Brussels and symbolically reaffirm the American commitment to NATO as the keystone of U.S. alliances.

# 1978

### January 13, 1978

**The United States and Japan sign a trade agreement in an attempt to forestall demands for protectionism by some American business interests.**

Robert STRAUSS, President Carter's trade negotiator, spent six months negotiating this treaty with Japan. At the signing, Strauss described his effort as having "redefined the economic relations between our two great nations." U.S. business interests believed Strauss exaggerated, although Japan had promised some concessions.

To reduce its trade imbalances with the United States, which totaled $8 billion in 1977, Tokyo agreed to decrease its tariffs on 300 imports, liberalize its quotas on agricultural products such as California's citrus fruits, and stimulate a 7% growth rate in Japan's economy (it had been 5.3% in 1977). Strauss admitted that the 1978 agreement was just one step in the direction of Japan's further reduction of tariffs and agricultural quotas. He hoped further Japanese changes would be forthcoming in the future.

### February 26, 1978

*China and Japan sign a $20 billion trade agreement in Shanghai.*

By this pact, Japan would buy over 47 million tons of oil from China and 9 million tons of coal. China would purchase Japanese steel and a variety of other manufactured products.

### February 28, 1978

**The State Department issues a Senate Foreign Relations Committee report that finds the Soviet Union has generally complied with the 1972 SALT I agreements.**

The report on SALT I compliance had been prepared to counteract critics' arguments that Moscow had not fulfilled its agreements with President Nixon.

### March 3, 1978

**The United States and Hungary sign a trade agreement granting each other the most-favored-nation status.**

Paving the way for this trade arrangement with Communist Hungary, the United States had returned to Hungary the Crown of St. Stephen. On January 6, Secretary Vance in elaborate ceremonies delivered the crown to Budapest. The crown was Hungary's symbol of nationhood, having been given to King Stephen I by Pope Sylvester II in the year 1000. At the end of World War II, American troops were given the crown by a Hungarian colonel. It had been stored at Fort Knox, Kentucky, since that time. President Carter stated that he returned the crown to Hungary because it belonged to no regime but to the people of Hungary.

See March 30, 1979

### March 8, 1978

*Somalia withdraws its forces from Ethiopia and seeks a negotiated settlement.*

The withdrawal from Ethiopia's Ogaden Province seemed to make Ethiopia the temporary victor together with its Cuban and Soviet allies. Somalia had invaded Ogaden Province claiming it as its own territory. On March 20, the United States announced it would send $7 million of food aid to Somalia.

See May 16, 1978.

### March 10, 1978

*Palestinian terrorists stage an amphibious attack on Israel's coast near Tel Aviv, killing 33 Israelis.*

The terrorists landed in rubber boats. They hijacked a tourist bus and attacked other vehicles on the highway along the coast. Then they waged a suicide battle against Israeli forces. In the conflict four of the five terrorists were killed in addition to the 33 Israelis; 70 Israelis were wounded.

At the time of the attack, Israel's Prime Minister Begin was in the United States conducting peace talks with President Carter. The two leaders hoped to end the stalled talks between Egypt and Israel. Because of the terrorist attack, Begin rushed home and the peace talks halted.

### March 14, 1978

*Israeli forces attack Palestinian bases in southern Lebanon, retaliating for the March 10 terrorist attack.*

About 20,000 Israeli troops crossed the border into southern Lebanon while their jet aircraft bombed and strafed as far north as Beirut. The Israeli purpose, said Prime Minister Begin, was to occupy a four- to six-mile-wide "security strip" in Lebanon.

On March 19, the U.N. Security Council called for an Israeli withdrawal and established a 4,000-man U.N. interim force to patrol the border area between Lebanon and Israel. Israel announced a cease-fire on March 21 and U.N. troops arrived on March 22. On June 13, Israel completed its withdrawal from Lebanon but turned over the six-mile zone in southern Lebanon to Christian Phalangist militia who were anti-Palestinian. This caused renewed fighting in

Lebanon with the Palestinians and Syrians opposing the Christians.

## March 21, 1978

*Three black leaders in Rhodesia become members of an interim government under the white leader, Ian Smith.*

This so-called Salisbury Agreement, arranged on February 17 by Smith, had been opposed by the United States and other Western powers because it omitted more radical and stronger black Rhodesian leaders. Smith planned to have an election on December 31 to provide for a transition to black majority rule in Rhodesia.

The December elections were delayed, however, until April 20, 1979. U.S. and British efforts to obtain representation for all black factions continued throughout 1978 but were not successful.

See July 30, 1979.

## April 7, 1978

*President Carter announces he has deferred production of the neutron bomb.*

During the summer of 1977, the neutron bomb had become public knowledge when a budget item of the Energy Research and Development Administration included an outlay for an "Enhanced Radiation Warhead." This was the neutron bomb, an antipersonnel device that would damage humans more than buildings. It was an intense radioactive bomb that would be deployed in Europe for use against the tanks of the Warsaw Pact armies.

In 1977, the neutron bomb became controversial. After Congress approved funds for its development, Carter had to decide whether to continue to prepare the weapon for deployment. The bomb's critics claimed that using the bomb would begin an escalation of other nuclear weapons if war should begin.

During a NATO meeting in March 1978, the European powers were divided on use of the neutron bomb. The NATO Council finally voted that the United States should produce the weapon. Its deployment in Europe, however, would be delayed to determine if the Soviet Union would restrain its development of SS-20 missiles aimed against Western Europe.

Evidently, President Carter decided not to produce the bomb unless some European nations first

agreed to deploy it. On March 20, he sent Deputy Secretary of State Warren Christopher to sound out England and West Germany. Neither nation would agree to deploy the bomb at that time. Therefore, Carter decided to delay its production.

On April 19, 1978, the NATO Nuclear Planning Group decided to keep the neutron bomb option open for possible future use. Subsequently, after further discussions with the NATO governments, President Carter decided on October 18 that components of the neutron bomb would be produced by the United States.

## April 20, 1978

*Soviet jet fighter planes force a Korean Boeing 707 jetliner to land near Murmansk: Two passengers are killed.*

A Korean commercial airliner en route from Seoul to Paris flew 1,000 miles off course, crossing into Soviet airspace. Fired on by Soviet planes, the airliner made an emergency landing on a frozen lake south of Murmansk, 390 miles northeast of Leningrad (present-day St. Petersburg). Soviet authorities claimed they forced the Korean plane to land but did not admit shooting at it, as the Korean pilot and his passengers averred. The passengers on the plane were immediately released by the Soviets, but the pilot and navigator were held for questioning until April 29, 1978.

For prior attacks on airliners, see July 23, 1954; July 27, 1955; February 21, 1973.

## April 27, 1978

*Afghan military coup overthrows the Daoud regime: The "April Revolution."*

Although Afghan Communists established the People's Democratic Party of Afghanistan (PDPA) in 1965, King Muhammad Zahir Shah experienced few problems while receiving aid from both the United States and the Soviet Union. The nation's political problems began in 1973 when Muhammad Daoud Khan overthrew the King. Trying to unify competing Afghan political parties, Daoud appointed some PDPA members as government and military officials, especially favoring those from the Parcham faction of the PDPA rather than the Khalq members. In 1975, Daoud formed his own political party after a constituent assembly wrote a constitution to create a

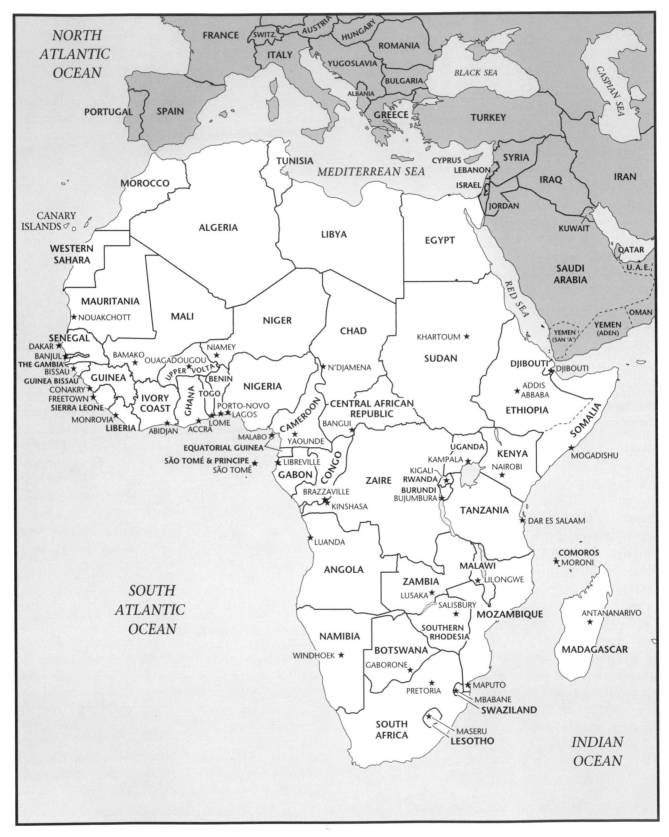

*NORTH ATLANTIC OCEAN*

FRANCE SWITZ. AUSTRIA HUNGARY

ITALY ROMANIA

YUGOSLAVIA

BULGARIA *BLACK SEA*

*CASPIAN SEA*

ALBANIA

PORTUGAL SPAIN GREECE TURKEY

TUNISIA *MEDITERREAN SEA* CYPRUS SYRIA

LEBANON IRAQ IRAN

MOROCCO ISRAEL

JORDAN

CANARY ISLANDS KUWAIT

WESTERN SAHARA ALGERIA LIBYA EGYPT QATAR

U.A.E.

SAUDI ARABIA

*RED SEA* OMAN

MAURITANIA

MALI NIGER CHAD YEMEN (SAN 'A') YEMEN (ADEN)

NOUAKCHOTT

KHARTOUM ★

SENEGAL NIAMEY SUDAN DJIBOUTI DJIBOUTI

DAKAR BAMAKO OUAGADOUGOU

BANJUL ADDIS ABBABA

THE GAMBIA BISSAU UPPER VOLTA BENIN N'DJAMENA

GUINEA BISSAU GUINEA TOGO NIGERIA CENTRAL AFRICAN REPUBLIC ETHIOPIA SOMALIA

CONAKRY GHANA PORTO-NOVO

FREETOWN IVORY COAST LAGOS CAMEROON

SIERRA LEONE COAST LOME BANGUI UGANDA KENYA

MONROVIA ABIDJAN ACCRA YAOUNDE KAMPALA

LIBERIA MALABO NAIROBI MOGADISHU

EQUATORIAL GUINEA LIBREVILLE KIGALI

SÃO TOMÉ & PRINCIPE ZAIRE RWANDA

SÃO TOMÉ GABON CONGO BURUNDI

BRAZZAVILLE BUJUMBURA TANZANIA

KINSHASA DAR ES SALAAM

LUANDA COMOROS MORONI

ANGOLA MALAWI

ZAMBIA LILONGWE

*SOUTH ATLANTIC OCEAN* LUSAKA ANTANANARIVO

SALISBURY MOZAMBIQUE

NAMIBIA SOUTHERN RHODESIA MADAGASCAR

BOTSWANA

WINDHOEK GABORONE MAPUTO

PRETORIA MBABANE

SWAZILAND

SOUTH AFRICA MASERU

LESOTHO *INDIAN OCEAN*

Africa, 1978

one-party state that excluded all parties including the PDPA.

According to Henry S. Bradsher's *Afghan Communism and Soviet Intervention* (1999 ed.), Daoud's centralization of power in Kabul caused opposition groups to form, especially in rural areas where fundamentalist Muslims preferred King Zahir's royal government because it gave local power to villages and cities as well as Islamic mullahs. By 1978, opposition groups grew in strength with the PDPA Parcham and Khalq factions uniting to get rid of Daoud.

On April 23, Afghan police arrested seven Parcham and Khalq political leaders while Daoud declared that an "anti-Islamic" plot had been uncovered. Alarmed by these arrests, Afghan Army Major Muhammad Aslan Watanjar persuaded the air force chief of staff to join in an attack on the palace during a meeting when Daoud was deciding on the fate of the seven PDPA leaders. Watanjar led a force of 60 tanks and 600 men in an attack on Daoud's residence while the air force strafed and fired rockets to disperse 1,800 presidential guardsmen. Because Daoud's loyal generals failed to rally loyal troops, the palace guard surrendered. Watanjar's men entered the palace, where they slaughtered Daoud, his family, and most of his ministers. Later, they also killed members of Daoud's Mohammadzai clan.

Following Daoud's death, PDPA leaders Nur Muhammad Taraki, Hafizullah Amin of the Khalq faction, and Babrak Karmal of the Parcham headed the government. The PDPA unity ended within three months with Amin as prime minister and Taraki as president and PDPA secretary-general forcing Karmal and other Parcham out of their political and military positions. The April revolution failed to satisfy the rural opposition, which increased after Amin instituted Communist methods of land, education, and social reforms to create a secular state. Although Afghanistan and the Soviet Union signed a Friendship Treaty on December 5, 1978, political disorders continued in Afghanistan.

See February 14, 1979.

## May 16, 1978

### *War breaks out again in the Horn of Africa when Ethiopia invades Eritrea.*

Following Somalia's withdrawal from fighting in Ethiopia on March 8, the Ethiopians were aided by the Soviet Union in preparing to regain territory that Ethiopia claimed in Eritrea. By November 29, Ethiopia said it had crushed the Eritreans. Rebels in Eritrea launched guerrilla warfare against Ethiopia.

## May 18, 1978

### The United States, France, and Belgium rush aid to Zaire when a rebellion recurs in Shaba province.

President Mobutu of Zaire claimed that Cuba and the Soviet Union aided the Shaba rebels. President Carter quickly sent $17 million of nonlethal military aid to Zaire. He also ordered U.S. transport planes to shuttle French and Belgian forces to Kolwezi to rescue 3,000 stranded Europeans and Americans. The president disclosed the U.S. action on May 19.

The conflict in Zaire ended quickly. The Belgian and French forces left the area by May 25. The United States charged that Cuba knew about the invasion, permitting the guerrillas to stage their operations in Angola before launching their attack on Zaire.

On June 5, the United States airlifted another 1,500 Moroccan troops to Zaire. By July 29, the last Western forces evacuated Zaire after Zaire and Angola agreed to prevent future guerrilla outbreaks along their borders.

## May 24, 1978

### *The Soviet Union successfully tests a hunter-killer satellite.*

This test followed the USSR's agreement with Secretary of State Vance on April 10 to begin negotiations to suspend the testing of hunter-killer satellites. These earth satellites were capable of finding and blowing up enemy satellites in space. U.S.-Soviet negotiations for a ban on these space weapons began on June 8 at Helsinki with Paul Warnke heading the U.S. delegation.

## June 16, 1978

### The United States and Panama exchange ratification of the two Panama Canal treaties signed on September 7, 1977.

To demonstrate U.S. goodwill toward Panama and its leader, Omar Torrijos, President Carter visited Panama to participate in special ceremonies for the final exchange of ratification of the canal treaties.

Between September 7 and April 1978, the Panama treaties had to overcome intensive opposition from U.S. congressmen prior to Senate ratification. Treaty opponents such as Senator Strom Thurmond and former California Governor Ronald Reagan made some valid and some preposterous claims. Among their valid concerns were issues of how the joint defense measures would function and whether the Panamanian people viewed the treaty as a friendly act. More Americans seemed impressed, however, by critics' comments that had little or no substance. These comments included such statements as "We bought the canal, we paid for it, it is ours," or that the treaty was a victory for communism and would promote victories for our enemies in Latin America.

After the Senate debate on the treaties began in January 1978, President Carter did all he could to insure their ratification. He spoke on television; he enlisted support from Republicans such as Henry Kissinger, former President Ford, and Senate Minority Leader Howard H. Baker Jr.; and he gained the support of all members of the Joint Chiefs of Staff.

On March 16, before the Senate voted on the treaty guaranteeing the canal's neutrality, Carter telephoned 16 unfriendly senators to offer his aid in passing their local-interest legislative bills provided they voted for the Panama treaty. Led by Baker and Senate Majority Leader Robert C. Byrd, a two-thirds majority of the senators approved the treaty by one vote (68) more than necessary. The second and more vital treaty, which replaced the 1903 treaty, did not come to a vote in the Senate until April 18. Again the Senate vote was 68 to 32, barely the two-thirds necessary to ratify it.

Between March 16 and April 18, a serious problem arose because of an amendment introduced by Senator Dennis DeConcini, a Democrat from Arizona. The amendment stated that if necessary, the United States could intervene in Panama to secure the continued operation of the canal after the year 2000. This amendment was opposed by Panama's General Omar Torrijos, and doubts arose as to whether Panama would accept the amendment. In addition, Torrijos circulated a letter among members of the United Nations complaining about the DeConcini reservation.

By April 18, however, pro-treaty senators had added a statement to DeConcini's amendment asserting that the United States would not intervene in Panama's internal affairs. The DeConcini amendment was thereby clarified as applying only to U.S. defense requirements during a war in which Panama was a participant. Torrijos indicated he would accept the revised DeConcini amendment.

Following the compromise on DeConcini's amendment, the Senate's approval was obtained. The final ratifications of the two treaties were exchanged in Panama on June 16, 1978.

## June 29, 1978

### *Vietnam becomes a member of COMECON, the Soviet-Bloc economic alliance.*

COMECON was the Soviet-backed Council for Mutual Economic Assistance. On November 3, 1978, Vietnam and the USSR signed a Treaty of Friendship and Cooperation that further solidified their alliance. The admission of Vietnam to the Soviet economic sphere indicated Moscow's continued interest in hegemony in south and Southeast Asia, a policy the Chinese disliked intensely.

## July 18, 1978

### U.S.-Soviet détente is threatened but finally assured after August 1978.

Tensions in U.S.-Soviet relations intensified during the spring of 1978, climaxing on July 18 when the Soviet Union sentenced Anatoly Sharansky to prison for 13 years. Throughout May and June, President Carter's policy seemed to change because of his complaints against Soviet human rights violations. Unofficial U.S. protests and boycotts began on May 19 when the U.S. Committee of Concerned Scientists protested Yuri Orlov's imprisonment for seven years and delegates of the National Academy of Science canceled their participation in a Moscow scientific symposium. Several U.S. protests also denounced the convictions and imprisonment of other Soviet scientists or Jewish activists. The first official U.S. opposition to these events came on July 10, when President Carter warned the Soviets that Sharansky's imminent trial would undermine détente relations. Previously, Carter appeared ready to confront the Soviets in a June 7 speech at the U.S. Naval Academy, concluding with the words "The Soviet Unions can choose either confrontation or cooperation. The United States is adequately prepared to meet either choice."

Carter's June 7 speech dismayed Secretary of State Cyrus Vance because the president seemed to express the hard-line anti-Soviet views of National Security Adviser Zbigniew Brzezinski. Apparently Carter was unsure about the divergent opinions expressed by Vance and Brzezinski regarding cooperation or confrontation with Moscow.

Following Sharansky's conviction on July 18, Carter confronted Breznev by canceling the sale of a $6.8 million Sperry Univac computer to Soviet news agency TASS. In addition, all sales of U.S. petroleum technology now had to be approved on a case-by-case basis by the Department of Commerce and Brzezinski. The Soviets wanted $1 billion of petroleum equipment but could purchase some of it in Europe.

By mid-August, Carter changed his mind regarding confrontation with the Soviets. The president was angry on April 10 when Secretary of Commerce Juanita Kreps unilaterally approved a Dresser Industries application to sell a $145 million electron-beam welder and drill bits to the Soviets. Soon after, he gradually shelved his human rights emphasis in favor of obtaining the SALT II agreement with President Brezhnev.

In November, Carter reviewed the U.S. trade policy with Kreps and Vance, agreeing to normalize trade relations with Moscow. During the same period, Soviet authorities shifted their policies to permit dissidents to emigrate rather than be arrested and imprisoned. By the end of 1978, 30,000 Jews were allowed to emigrate, twice the average number for the four preceding years. These changes enabled Carter to justify his approval of oil drilling equipment he previously prohibited. On December 4, Secretary Kreps and Secretary of the Treasury David Blumenthal visited Moscow to announce that $65 million of oil equipment was approved for delivery to the Soviet Union. On April 5, 1979, the sale of the Sperry Univac computer was approved.

Details about these 1978 events are covered in Raymond Garthoff's *Détente and Confrontation* (1985).

See June 18, 1979.

## July 18, 1978

### The People's Republic of China closes its borders to ethnic Chinese fleeing from Vietnam.

Trouble began on the Chinese-Vietnamese border after the Socialist Republic of Vietnam expelled 70,000 Chinese on May 24, 1978. In retaliation on June 9, China canceled 70 aid projects in Vietnam and recalled 1,000 Chinese technicians. Between August 8 and 27, 1978, Beijing and Hanoi attempted but failed to reach a settlement on the status of the ethnic Chinese in Vietnam, most of whom had lived in Indochina with their families for many generations.

## July 27, 1978

### The U.N. Security Council approves a peace plan for Namibia (South-West Africa) that appears likely to end a 12-year dispute with South Africa.

Since 1965, the United Nations had sought a way to persuade South Africa to yield control over South-West Africa, which it had secured as a mandate in 1920. The white apartheid government of South Africa refused to do so unless the white minority of Namibia was secured and a moderate, pro–South African government was set up. These conditions were almost impossible to meet because of the rise of black African nationalism.

During 1977–1978, the United States, Canada, West Germany, France, and Great Britain conducted a series of talks with both sides and came up with a plan whereby they put pressure on South Africa to accept by threatening economic sanctions. On March 23, the U.N. Council for Namibia adopted a declaration for sanctions, and on May 3, the U.N. General Assembly did the same. On April 25, South Africa agreed to the five-nation plan. On July 12, the South-West African People's Organization (SWAPO) agreed to the plan. This raised hopes that the problem would be settled.

When the U.N. Security Council met on July 27, the one outstanding question seemed to be South Africa's demand that Walvis Bay—the only seaport in the state—should not be part of Namibia. The Security Council passed Resolution 431, which called for the independence of Namibia "at the earliest possible date." U.N.-supervised elections would decide the future government of the state. The council also passed Resolution 432, making Walvis Bay part of Namibia.

South Africa now decided to oppose the April 23 plan, rejecting Resolution 432. South Africa decided to hold its own internal election for South-West Africa on December 4, action the U.N. Security Council opposed on November 13 (Resolution 439). By the end of the year, the Namibia issue was unresolved, and South Africa asked the United Nations to stop assistance to SWAPO.

**September 17, 1978**

### Egypt and Israel sign two agreements designed to bring peace to the Middle East: The Camp David Accords.

President Sadat's visit to Jerusalem in November 1977 heralded improved prospects for peace in the Middle East. During the first half of 1978, however, these efforts became stalled as the two nations talked with U.S. and other leaders in an attempt to resolve a priori such questions as Israel's settlements in the land occupied on the West Bank and the Gaza Strip in 1967 and the status of the PLO. In addition, the March attack of terrorists against Tel Aviv and Israel's invasion of Lebanon caused further difficulty for the peace process.

Egypt's President Anwar Sadat shakes hands with Israel's Prime Minister Menachem Begin at Camp David. Jimmy Carter Library

During the summer of 1978, several attempts to renew negotiations were unsuccessful or short-lived. On July 5, Egypt offered a six-point plan that Israel rejected. In July, Sadat held meetings in Austria with both Shimon Peres of Israel's Labour Party and Israeli Defense Minister Ezer Weizman. Finally, on July 18–19, the foreign ministers of Egypt, Israel, and the United States met at Leeds Castle in England.

Eventually, President Carter's August 8 invitation to Begin and Sadat to meet on September 5 at Camp David was accepted and proved to be fruitful. After 12 days of intense negotiations with Carter acting as mediator and prodder, Begin and Sadat agreed to sign two documents: "A Framework for Peace in the Middle East" and "A Framework for the Conclusion of a Peace Treaty Between Egypt and Israel." The first treaty sought a solution to the problems involving Israel, Jordan, and the Palestinians and proved to be the more difficult to carry out. The second called for an Israeli-Egyptian peace treaty to be concluded in three months and to provide for subsequent Israeli withdrawal from Egyptian territory in the Sinai.

The treaties signed on September 17 in an atmosphere of hope and euphoria were only guidelines for peace. Negotiations for the Israeli-Egyptian peace treaty as well as agreements signed by Israel with other Arab states were required to carry out both treaties.

See September 23, November 5, and December 14, 1978, and March 26, 1979.

## September 23, 1978

### *The radical Arab states reject the Camp David Accords and break diplomatic and economic relations with Egypt.*

Meeting in Damascus, the Arab Front for Steadfastness and Confrontation strongly denounced Egyptian President Sadat's agreements with Israel. These Arab governments were Syria, Libya, South Yemen, Algeria, and the PLO, which claimed to be the provisional government for Palestinians.

## September 26, 1978

### The three-year-old Turkish arms embargo is lifted when President Carter signs the International Security Assistance Act of 1978.

Although President Ford had opposed the arms embargo in 1974 and 1975, Congress required it after February 5, 1975, because of Turkey's intervention to help the Turkish minority on Cyprus against the Greeks. Subsequent attempts by Presidents Ford and Carter to end the embargo were resisted by Congress, owing largely to the influence of pro-Greek lobbyists in Washington.

Although the Cypriot issue had not been resolved in 1978, the Carter administration persuaded Congress to end the embargo by citing evidence of U.S. military needs in Turkey as well as evidence that Greece prevented a Cypriot solution as much as Turkey did. Although the Senate vote in July 1978 required the certification that Turkey had contributed to settle the Cyprus issue, both Carter and the House voted to approve this limit so that the arms embargo could be ended for Turkey. Carter signed this legislation on September 26, 1978.

## September 30, 1978

### Following eight months of internal troubles in Nicaragua, President Anastasio Somoza accedes to U.S. demands that he accept the international mediation group to settle the disturbances.

Nicaragua's internal problems began on January 24, 1978, when business and labor groups joined the anti-Somoza Sandinista National Liberation Federation (FSLN) in protesting the assassination on January 10 of Nicaragua's leading newspaper *La Prensa*'s anti-Somoza editor, Pedro Chamorro.

For the first time since the beginning of the Sandinista's 45-year struggle against Somoza, a broad spectrum of middle-class bankers and business leaders acted against the Nicaraguan dictator. On August 28, a businessman's strike took place, and fighting broke out between police and strikers. The conflict grew and, on September 13, Somoza declared martial law.

To end the disturbances and investigate reports of Somoza's terrorist methods, Carter sent a special ambassador to Nicaragua, William Jorden. On September 25, Jorden informed Somoza that the United States would cut off its economic aid unless he accepted mediation by the United States, the Dominican Republic, and Guatemala. Somoza agreed to mediation on September 30, but during the next several months he sought to delay any reforms. On December 27, the Organization of American States planned a plebiscite that opposition groups accepted but Somoza rejected on January 18, 1979. Somoza's intransigence eventually led to his exile in 1979.

See July 17, 1979.

### October 1, 1978

**President Carter concedes that the United States has used spy satellites.**

Public knowledge that the United States might have been using satellites in space to gather intelligence first surfaced widely during 1977, when two young Americans were accused of selling spy satellite data to the Soviets. In a speech on October 1, Carter indicated that the United States had covertly used spy satellites for more than a decade. This intelligence gathering, he said, was essential to national security.

See January 26, 1977.

### October 13, 1978

**The House committee investigating bribery by South Korean officials issues a relatively mild report.**

The House had investigated the "Koreagate" scandal for 18 months. In its final report, the committee found that four representatives had received between $1,000 and $4,000 each to use either for personal expenses or political campaigns, although all four denied the charge. Six representatives were found not culpable. The House majority whip, John Brademas, was cleared of wrongdoing but was criticized for accepting a foreign political contribution of $2,950 at the same time he was urging Congress to outlaw such gifts. Speaker of the House Thomas "Tip" O'Neill was cleared of all charges but was chastised for attending lavish parties given by Tongsun Park, the central Korean figure in the investigation.

### October 23, 1978

*The USSR tests a cruiselike missile.*

The cruise missile had been rapidly developed by the United States as a possible substitute for a manned bomber. Until the announcement of this test, the United States had been the only power with cruise technology. The October 23 test indicated that the Soviets had developed such technology and might soon have these weapons in its arsenal.

### November 5, 1978

*The Arab states, excluding Egypt, meet in Damascus to try to unify their ranks against Egypt and Israel.*

During this Arab summit, the most significant result was that the disputes between Iraq and the PLO and between Jordan and the PLO were reconciled. The efforts of the radical Arab states to isolate Egypt completely were not successful, while Egypt and Israel still sought a final peace treaty.

See March 31, 1979.

### November 13, 1978

*Mexico announces that billions of barrels of crude oil should be available in the area around Tampico.*

This oil discovery inaugurated an optimistic development program in Mexico based on the expected income from the Tampico oil wells.

### November 26–27, 1978

*The shah's difficulties reach crisis proportions when a successful 24-hour strike is called by Iranian religious leaders.*

Opposition to Shah Mohammad REZA PAHLAVI grew during 1978—first, riots in Tabriz on February 21; later, when Muslim extremists rioted in 24 cities on May 9. By August 5, a coalition of left extremists, moderates, and conservative Muslims demonstrated against the shah; 16 people were shot by the government's forces.

Although the shah declared martial law on September 7, it was widely ignored. The shah's main religious opponent, the Aytollah Ruholla KHOMEINI, was allowed to return from Iraqi exile in 1976, but was expelled to France on October 4, 1978. As the 24-hour strike of November 26–27 indicated, Khomeini's influence continued.

See January 16, 1979.

### December 3, 1978

*Vietnam launches an invasion of Cambodia.*

There had been reports of fighting between Cambodia and Vietnam since December 1977. On December 3, 1978, Hanoi radio said the Kampuchean (Cambodian) United Front for National Salvation had been formed to overthrow the tyrant Prime Minister Pol Pot, who had gained control after the Khmer Rouge overthrew Lon Nol's government in April 1975. By December 30, Vietnamese forces had joined Cambodian guerrillas in capturing the Cambodian town of Kratie.

Pol Pot earned the enmity of Hanoi because he refused to be subservient to the Vietnamese and had purged Cambodia of all opponents in bloody executions in 1975–1976. By December 1978, the "Communist" states of Vietnam and Cambodia were engaged in war, Vietnam being backed by the Soviet Union, China giving some aid to Cambodia.

### December 14, 1978

**Egypt and Israel are unable to meet their three-month deadline for a peace treaty despite American mediation attempts.**

The September 17 accords provided only a basis for peace; further diplomatic negotiations began at Blair House in Washington on October 12 in an attempt to reach a final agreement. In addition, Secretary of State Vance made frequent visits to Israel and Egypt to seek agreement on sticky points.

In Vance's last attempt at reconciliation from December 10 to 14, he worked out a peace formula with Sadat, but the Begin government continued to reject Egyptian demands for clarity on the timing for Palestinian self-rule in the West Bank and Gaza, and for recognition that Egypt had to consider its defense pacts with other Arab states. Israel rejected the Egyptian demands, saying it could review the Sinai issue and the "target" date, not "fixed" date, for Palestinian self-rule but not those parts regarding Egypt's relations with other Arab nations. Generally the dispute focused on a major flaw in the Camp David accords: there was no definite statement on the linkage between the Egyptian peace treaty and Palestinian self-rule. Cairo claimed they were linked; Begin said not necessarily. President Carter tended to agree with Sadat, thus worsening relations between Israel and America. On November 5, Carter and Vance insisted that linkage of the two agreements was essential. The next day, Israel's cabinet rejected this concept. Thus on December 14 there was an impasse on this issue.

### December 15, 1978

**Washington and Beijing issue joint communiqués announcing the establishment of diplomatic relations and the termination in 12 months of the U.S. Defense Treaty with the Republic of China (Taiwan).**

On national television at 9 P.M., President Carter announced that the United States and the People's Republic of China would establish normal diplomatic relations beginning January 1, 1979. At the same time, in Beijing, China's Premier and Communist Party Chairman Hua Guofeng read a similar statement to news reporters. It was Hua's first press conference.

Although the normalization of U.S.-Chinese relations had been expected since President Nixon visited China in February 1972, the process was slowed because of Watergate, Mao's death, the Vietnam War, and the overthrow of the "Gang of Four" (see September 9, 1976). On May 20–22, National Security Adviser Brzezinski had visited Beijing where he proposed, with the agreement of Deputy Premier Deng Xiaoping, to negotiate the normalization. Subsequently, in secret sessions, the U.S. liaison officer in Beijing, Leonard WOODCOCK, and the Chinese began discussions. In addition, Brzezinski met in Washington with Chinese envoys Han Tsu and Chai Tse-min.

Early in December the negotiations moved quickly to a conclusion. On December 12, Woodcock visited with Deng, who accepted an invitation to visit the United States in 1979. This signaled the Chinese willingness to normalize relations soon, and both sides worked on a communiqué to be issued on December 15. Prior to his television address, Carter briefed U.S. congressional leaders and met with Soviet Ambassador Anatoly Dobrynin to inform him that the U.S.-Chinese decision would not influence U.S. relations with Moscow.

In his message, Carter said normal relations would begin on January 1, with each nation opening an embassy in the other's capital city. Carter indicated that while the United States would give Taiwan the necessary 12 months' notice required to end the 1954 mutual defense treaty, the normalization would not "jeopardize the well-being of the people of Taiwan." The U.S.-Beijing communiqué stated that "there is but one China, and Taiwan is part of China," a belief that Taiwan's government shared. Carter said that while the United States would recognize Beijing as the "sole legal government of China," Beijing had given assurances it would not seek to reunite Taiwan by force. The United States, Carter said, "will maintain cultural, commercial and other unofficial relations with the people of Taiwan." America could also continue to sell Taiwan "selective defensive weaponry" such as interceptor aircraft, antitank weapons, and artillery. Following his speech, Carter told a press conference: "The interests of Taiwan have been adequately protected."

Despite Carter's assurances on Taiwan, there remained a number of strong pro-Taiwan groups in the United States that protested strongly against Carter's move. Arizona Republican Senator Barry Goldwater called the president's action "cowardly." On December 22, Goldwater and 14 other legislators filed suit in U.S. District Court to prevent the termination of the 1954 treaty with Taiwan. Goldwater argued that the Senate had ratified the 1954 treaty; therefore, the president needed Senate approval to end it. Although a district court ruled on October 17, 1979, that the president could not abrogate the 1954 treaty, a Federal Appeals Court reversed the decision on November 30, 1979, upholding the president's action. On December 13, the U.S. Supreme Court upheld the appeals court ruling.

### December 17, 1978

*Meeting at Abu Dhabi, OPEC's delegations set a 14.5% oil price increase to be carried out in stages starting January 1, 1979.*

### December 31, 1978

**The United States and the Philippines sign a five-year agreement for continued U.S. use of Filipino military bases.**

The agreement provided $500 million of U.S. economic and military aid for the Philippines.

# 1979 _____

### January 1, 1979

**The United States and the People's Republic of China resume diplomatic recognition with ceremonies in Beijing and Washington.**

On February 26, the U.S. Senate confirmed Carter's appointment of Leonard Woodcock as ambassador to

Senator Barry Goldwater goes to court to challenge the termination of the 1954 mutual defense pact. Library of Congress

China. Woodcock had been serving as the U.S. liaison officer in Beijing.

### January 7, 1979

*Vietnam and the Kampuchean National United Front conquer Cambodia as Phnom Penh falls.*

The next day, Heng Samrin was named head of the Kampuchean People's Revolutionary Council. On January 15, the appeal of Prince Sihanouk of Cambodia to the U.N. Security Council resulted in a resolution asking Vietnam to withdraw from Cambodia (Kampuchea). The resolution was vetoed by the Soviet Union.

### January 16, 1979

## The Shah of Iran leaves for Aswân. His power in Iran is ended.

Between 1953 and 1973, the United States had come to rely on Reza Shah Pahlavi of Iran as a strong anti-Communist, pro-Western power in the Persian Gulf region. Following the overthrow of the Mossadegh government in 1953, the shah enhanced his power by undertaking to increase Iran's share of its oil revenues. By agreements with British Petroleum and the Consortium of International Oil Companies in 1954, the shah received 40% ownership of the oil corporations. He also created the National Iranian Oil Company (NIOC) to exploit his nation's oil outside the concession areas. The NIOC controlled about 10% of Iran's oil in 1961.

After 1962, the shah combined an attempt to bring economic reforms and modernization to Iran with efforts to obtain larger income from Iran's oil concessions. Joining the newly formed OPEC (September 10, 1960), the shah worked with other oil-producing nations to stabilize their prices and to unify their policies toward the oil companies.

Following the first oil boycott of the West, the shah moved to acquire leadership in the Middle East's oil politics. Appearing as a moderate and non-boycotting leader on whom the United States could depend, the shah persuaded the oil companies to give him 25% of their Iranian concession area in 1967 and

began pressuring the oil companies to give the oil nations greater influence. The shah avoided the radical confrontation style of Libya's Gadhafi. Nevertheless, the February 4, 1971, Teheran Agreement, which the shah and other Persian Gulf countries made with the oil companies, established the dominant position for OPEC in future oil decisions. On March 20, 1973, the shah obtained the St. Moritz agreement from Iran's oil companies. This pact brought all Iranian oil production under NIOC. Thus before the October 1973 Yom Kippur War, Iran was set to lead the OPEC nations in rapidly increasing oil prices to Western nations.

Although the shah led the Middle Eastern states in obtaining greater power for the OPEC nations, neither President Nixon, Secretary Kissinger, nor subsequent U.S. presidents seriously criticized the shah for undermining the economic prosperity of the Western world. By 1973, the shah's anticommunism required U.S. support at almost any cost.

U.S. backing for the shah continued even though his economic modernization program in Iran did not envisage political and social reforms. As Iran's standard of living began to improve, social, economic, political, and religious critics began to demonstrate against the shah's repressive regime. Claiming all opponents were "Communists," the shah organized the SAVAK (secret police), which used torture, imprisonment, exile, and other methods to suppress all his opponents. In addition, Iran's reform program was

President Carter and the Shah of Iran during better days. Jimmy Carter Library

poorly planned and mismanaged, giving his efforts an unsatisfactory domestic structure. Such needs as education, redistribution of wealth, and caring for Iran's minority Kurds and other groups were neglected. The bureaucracy he created to bring reforms became both corrupt and incompetent. By 1977, Iran was experiencing high inflation and economic and social inequities. The shah's absolute rule could not surmount these problems.

In 1977, the shah appointed a new prime minister, Jamshid Amuzegar, who was expected to liberalize the government, end corruption, and establish the human rights desired by President Carter. These measures came too late, opening the way for underground opposition groups to rally public support against the shah. The Ayatollah Khomeini, the Shiite Muslim leader whom the shah exiled to France in 1978, returned to Iran. Khomeini was determined to overthrow the shah because he believed that SAVAK was responsible for the death of his son.

During the summer of 1978, Iranian protests developed into nationwide anti-shah movements led by students, intellectuals, professionals, the middle class, workers, and religious zealots favoring Khomeini. The critics' rallying point became Khomeini, who advocated an Islamic republic under traditional Islamic law. Many leftist-Marxist or moderate republican protesters followed the crowds, reluctant to oppose Khomeini. The shah's decision to exile Khomeini on October 4, 1978, inflamed the masses even more, and his attempts to find ways to appease the opposition did not succeed.

By the end of 1978, Iran experienced much bloodshed, strikes, and an ineffectual government. Throughout 1978, President Carter supported the shah while urging him to establish a civilian government or become a constitutional monarch. In January 1979, the shah looked for more moderate political supporters by turning to the National Front Party, which Mossadegh had established in the 1950s. The shah agreed to give most of his power to the National Front, appointing Shahpur BAKHTIAR as head of a new government. In addition, the shah agreed to leave the country temporarily and not return as an absolute monarch. This arrangement was completed on January 16, and the shah left for a "holiday" abroad. The plan did not succeed. For the outcome see February 1, 1979.

See June 9, 1967.

### January 30, 1979

### China's Deputy Premier Deng Xiaoping begins a visit to Washington.

While visiting the United States, Deng signed scientific and cultural accords. He also made strong remarks against the Soviet Union, from which President Carter had to disassociate the United States.

### February 1, 1979

### *Khomeini arrives in Iran from exile and forms his own provisional government.*

Khomeini rejected the government that the shah had formed in Tehran before his departure on January 16. Moreover, the populace in Tehran clearly favored Khomeini over the shah's appointee, Bakhtiar.

When the ayatollah returned from Paris to Iran on February 1, Bakhtiar asked him to form a government of national unity, but Khomeini refused. On February 5, Khomeini appointed Mehdi Bazargan as prime minister of a provisional government. Bakhtiar resigned on February 11 after army leaders withdrew their support from his regime. Soon after, leftist and religious fanatics in Iran began arresting, imprisoning, and executing persons associated with the shah's regime.

The United States hoped to maintain normal relations with Iran's new government. The U.S. ambassador, William H. Sullivan, met with Bazargan for the first time on February 21. Later, discussions began for American businessmen to operate in Iran and for the United States to provide spare parts for the military equipment it had supplied to the shah. Because of the increased anti-Americanism in Iran, the establishment of normal relations became a slow process, for the new government distrusted the United States. This distrust built into active dislike when America permitted the shah to come to New York in October.

See November 4, 1979.

### February 4, 1979

### Chinese translations into pinyin adopted by Library of Congress and the *New York Times*.

In 1958, pinyin was devised by linguists in the People's Republic of China to simplify the translation of Chinese characters to roman letters. The system was adopted for official translations in 1978 by the People's Republic of China. On January 28, when

China's leader, Deng Xiaoping began a 10-day visit to the United States, Deng's presence made Americans aware of their lack of Chinese translators, partly owing to the failure to adopt pinyin. As a result, the Library of Congress decided in January 1979 to adopt pinyin to catalogue Chinese publications. On February 4, the *New York Times* announced it would begin using pinyin on March 5, 1979.

### February 12, 1979

*Fighting breaks out in Chad between two political groups.*

With the support of France and Nigeria, a cease-fire was arranged and became effective by March 20, 1979.

### February 14, 1979

**The U.S. Ambassador to Afghanistan, Adolph Dubs, is abducted and killed by right-wing Muslim terrorists.**

Although the United States believed the Soviet Union was responsible for Dubs's assassination, later information showed that the events of February 14 were more complicated than at first believed. Dubs was abducted by four members of a dissident Tajik faction that wanted to exchange him for three imprisoned Tajik. U.S. diplomats in Kabul sought to meet the abductors' request but Prime Minister Amin refused to negotiate. As a result, Afghan police supported by Soviet advisers rushed the kidnapers' hideaway, an act that resulted in the deaths of the four abductors as well as Dubs. For details of the event see Henry Bradsher's *Afghan Communism and Soviet Intervention* (1999 ed.), p. 47.

Following Dubs's death, the Soviet Union tried to restore order in Afghanistan by ending the disputes between Amin and President Taraki. Although Amin and Taraki claimed to be nonaligned in international affairs, the number of Soviet military and political advisers steadily increased because of the continued opposition of rural and religious groups. After a major July uprising in the city of Herat, Soviet advisers tried to persuade Amin to end his reform program or be replaced by someone willing to change the socialist reforms to calm the rural opposition. On September 14, Soviet pressure led Taraki's loyalists to try but fail to assassinate Amin. In response on September 16, Amin had Taraki arrested and executed along with four of Taraki's loyalists.

Amin gained complete political power in Kabul, but continuing guerrilla warfare outside the capital grew more severe. In Moscow, Soviet President Brezhnev and the Communist Party Politburo planned stronger measures to assert control in Afghanistan.

See December 28, 1979.

### February 17, 1979

*Chinese forces invade Vietnam along a 480-mile border.*

Although Beijing stated the Chinese incursion was limited and intended to punish Vietnam for its exile of ethnic Chinese and invasion of Cambodia, the Soviet Union threatened China, stating that it would support its Vietnamese ally. On March 5, Chinese Premier Hua Guofeng, announced the withdrawal of Chinese troops because the "punishment" of Vietnam had been completed. The Chinese reported on May 2 that they had lost 20,000 soldiers; Vietnam claims they lost 50,000. The Chinese may have miscalculated the effectiveness of their own forces.

### March 6, 1979

**President Carter orders a U.S. naval task force to the Arabian Sea after fighting begins between the Yemen Arab Republic (YAR) and the Soviet-supported People's Democratic Republic of Yemen (PDRY).**

The northern YAR had frequently exchanged harsh words with the southern PDRY. In 1979, however, intense fighting began along their border, and the YAR asked the Arab League for help. While the league sought to arrange a cease-fire, President Carter sent a naval task force as a show of support. On March 9, the United States delivered $390 million of arms to the YAR. Carter acted to protect security in the region where Soviet support for the PDRY tried to expand, not only into north Yemen but into Ethiopia and Somalia.

Under Arab League auspices, North and South Yemen agreed to a cease-fire on March 30. The two states also agreed to strive for cooperative relations.

## March 12, 1979

### The Central Treaty Organization breaks up when Pakistan withdraws on March 12, Turkey on March 15.

The United States had experienced increasingly poor relations with both Pakistan and Turkey. The latter disliked U.S. policy in the Cypriot crisis during which Congress cut off aid to Turkey. President Carter had criticized Pakistan for its arrest and later execution of former Prime Minister Zultikar Ali Bhutto on April 4. On April 6, the United States cut off all economic and military aid to Pakistan because of reports that the government was acquiring a nuclear weapons capability.

See November 21, 1979.

## March 26, 1979

### Egypt and Israel sign a peace treaty in Washington.

President Carter's persistent pressure on Egyptian President Sadat and Israeli Prime Minister Begin to conclude a peace treaty finally reached fruition on March 13. Following the president's consultations in Cairo and Jerusalem, the Egyptian and Israeli leaders reached agreement on the issues of the West Bank and Gaza Strip. These questions continued to defy solution and had caused negotiations to break down on December 14, 1978. Israel made the issue more difficult by announcing its approval of new Jewish settlements on the West Bank on January 15, 1979. As a result, negotiations in Washington under Secretary Vance's mediation failed on February 23.

The signing of the Camp David Accords. National Archives

Carter's successful diplomatic effort began on March 1–5 when, after meetings in Washington, Prime Minister Begin agreed to a set of U.S. compromises. On March 8, the president flew to Cairo, where President Sadat accepted part of the agreement but desired several changes. On March 10, Carter flew to Jerusalem, where after three days of discussion he convinced Begin to accept terms of compromise with Sadat. That same day, March 13, Carter stopped for $2\frac{1}{2}$ hours in Cairo and gained Sadat's approval before returning to Washington. Before boarding his plane in Cairo, the president indicated to newsmen that if the Israeli cabinet approved, the treaty agreement could be concluded. Formal drafts of the treaty were prepared and ready for Sadat and Begin to sign on March 26 after Israel's cabinet had approved Begin's recommendations.

The important points of the Israeli-Egyptian peace treaty were as follows:

1. Israel would submit to Egypt a detailed timetable to withdraw from the Sinai peninsula. The first stage would be in nine months, and over a three-year period Israel would withdraw all its troops and settlers from the Sinai. The area would generally be demilitarized, permitting Egypt to have only one division of troops there. Egypt could use the two existing airports only for civilian purposes. U.N. troops would remain along the Gulf of Aqaba and the eastern border of the Sinai.
2. One month after Israel made the first withdrawal behind the El Arish-Ras Muhammad line, the two nations would exchange ambassadors and establish normal diplomatic relations.
3. Egypt would end its economic boycott of Israel and grant Israel the right of passage through the Suez Canal. Israel could buy oil from the Sinai fields at nondiscriminatory prices. The United States would guarantee Israel a satisfactory oil supply for 15 years.
4. The two nations would conclude trade and cultural exchange arrangements and open their borders to each other's citizens.
5. Negotiations on Palestinian self-rule on the West Bank and Gaza Strip would be targeted for completion in 12 months. There would then be a 5-year transition period to decide the final status of the West Bank and Gaza. These clauses did not set any deadline for settlement and later proved to be

unworkable. The status of East Jerusalem was not mentioned in the peace treaty.

To help Egypt and Israel conclude their pact, President Carter promised that, with the consent of Congress, the United States would provide about $4.8 billion of aid to the two nations over three years. Egypt and Israel would each get about $2 billion of military aid plus $500 million for economic support. Some observers expected these costs to be higher in the future.

Israel's cabinet formally ratified the treaty on April 1, Egypt on April 10. The two nations exchanged ratifications on April 25. The U.S. Senate approved the military-economic aid package on May 14; the House did so on May 30.

### March 30, 1979

*A western bank consortium announces loans of $300 million to Hungary and $550 million to Poland.*

One consequence of détente was the increased number of loans from Western European and American bankers to Warsaw Pact countries, enabling Eastern European purchases in the West.

### March 31, 1979

*Meeting in Baghdad, the Arab League and PLO approve a complete break in economic and diplomatic relations with Egypt. They move the League's headquarters from Cairo to Tunis.*

On March 27, anticipating the league's decision, Egypt announced it would freeze its relations with Arab League members. On April 8, the PLO Council announced it would intensify its violent attacks on Israel, Egypt, and the United States. On April 23, Saudi Arabia broke diplomatic but not economic ties with Egypt.

### April 10, 1979

**President Carter signs legislation establishing special U.S. ties with Taiwan: the Taiwan Relations Act.**

This legislation established U.S. relations with Taiwan to replace Washington's previous recognition of the Taiwanese government as the Republic of China. Under the 1979 agreement, the two countries' embassies and consulates were replaced by the Taiwan Coordinating Council for North American Affairs in Washington and the American Institute in Taiwan. The agreement permitted the United States to sell defensive arms to Taiwan and continued prior legal and economic relations between the United States and Taiwan.

## May 3, 1979

*In British general elections, Margaret Thatcher, the Conservative Party leader, becomes Britain's first woman Prime Minister.*

## May 14, 1979

**The United States and China sign a trade treaty granting China the most-favored-nation status.**

This treaty was drawn up and signed in Beijing by Commerce Secretary Juanita Kreps and China's Trade Minister Li Qing.

President Carter sent the Chinese Trade Treaty to Congress for approval on October 23, saying he hoped Congress would also grant the Soviet Union the same status. Congress approved the Chinese Trade Treaty on January 24, 1980; it became effective on February 1, 1980. The Soviet Union was not granted most-favored-nation status, however.

## May 22, 1979

*In Canadian elections, the Progressive Conservative Charles J. Clark defeats the Liberal Prime Minister, Pierre Trudeau.*

Clark's party obtained a majority of only six votes. On November 14 and 20, 1979, the Conservatives lost five by-elections, reducing Clark's majority to one.

## May 25, 1979

**Israel returns El Arish to Egypt, the first step in its withdrawal from the Sinai peninsula.**

On May 26, Secretary of State Vance, Israeli Prime Minister Begin, and Egyptian President Sadat met in Beersheba, Israel, to begin talks on an autonomy plan for the Palestinians.

## June 8, 1979

**President Carter approves full-scale development of the MX missile.**

Carter reported on the status of the MX before leaving for the Vienna summit to sign SALT II. The MX was designed to modernize the U.S. ICBM system which, in terms of land-based missiles, lagged behind the new Soviet land-based SS-18s and SS-19s. To make the MX less vulnerable to the Soviet first strike, U.S. plans were to make the MX a mobile force, moving it around on tracks in underground tunnels to varied launch sites in the Southwestern United States. The MX was permitted under SALT II.

On September 7, 1979, Carter announced that the United States would spend $33 billion to deploy 200 MX missiles that would be fully operational in 1989. The mobile MX missiles were never deployed. The Reagan administration continued the MX program but had to change to stationary MX missiles based in hardened silos because no realistic mobile basing system could be devised.

See October 2, 1981.

## June 10, 1979

*Elections for the first European Parliament are completed.*

In direct elections where citizens of the European Union cast 110 million votes, 410 members were elected to form a European Parliament. On July 17, at the first session of the group in Strasbourg, Simone WEIL, a French delegate, was elected president. Although the European Parliament had little political power, it was an additional, symbolic step in the direction of a united Europe.

## June 18, 1979

**At a Vienna summit meeting, President Carter and President Brezhnev sign SALT II, a five-year treaty limiting maximum numbers of ICBMs and long-range bombers.**

SALT II had been negotiated for nearly seven years, having been intended further to restrict strategic missiles that were limited by the United States and the USSR in 1972. The final agreement on SALT II had been announced by Secretary Vance on May 9, although at the Vienna meeting, Presidents Carter and Brezhnev exchanged letters in which the Soviets agreed not to produce and deploy more than 30 Soviet TU-26 (Backfire) bombers in any one year.

Because of earlier domestic criticism about SALT II, President Carter addressed Congress two hours after he returned to Washington from the Vienna meetings. In his speech and in later administration testimony to Congress on SALT II, Carter, Vance, and members of the JCS advocated ratification of SALT by emphasizing the following points:

1. SALT II will help maintain a stable balance of missile forces between the United States and the Soviet Union. According to SALT II each side would have an aggregate of 2,250 missiles and heavy bombers, 1,320 cruise carriers and MIRVed missiles, and 1,200 MIRVed ICBMs. Because the Soviets were above these numbers, they would destroy or dismantle 250 of their systems. While many of those destroyed would be old, they still had the power of America's Minuteman II or Polaris missiles. Without SALT II, the Soviets could keep and add to these 250 missiles or bombers.
2. Verification would continue to be based on U.S. systems, but for the first time there was agreement not to encrypt telemetric information if it impeded compliance with the treaty. In addition, regular data would be exchanged on strategic forces, rules for counting weapons were simplified, and the USSR would ban its SS-16 mobile missile, which was difficult to verify because it could constantly be moved around.
3. Agreement on SALT II would open the way to negotiating further limits under SALT III.
4. Ratification was important to U.S. allies and U.S. leadership. The NATO allies did not want Soviet superiority or the political tensions and pressure stemming from lack of agreement.

For the results of the SALT II ratification process, see January 2, 1980.

### June 28, 1979

**As the refugee problem becomes enormous in Southeast Asia, President Carter doubles the U.S. refugee quota to 14,000 per month for the next year.**

Other nations also had to be enlisted to assist the war refugees fleeing from Cambodia and Vietnam. Thailand became the principal base of operations for refugee programs because people fled there from the neighboring states. By November 18, the Thais had a camp for 200,000 refugees, which proved insufficient. On August 3, a Red Cross committee visited Cambodia, reporting that over 2.25 million Cambodians faced starvation because of the policies of the Pol Pot regime and the Vietnamese invasion. Emergency food relief operations began on August 28.

### July 14, 1979

**Ethiopian forces launch an offensive against Eritrean rebels as war again breaks out in the horn of Africa.**

On August 3, U.S. officials estimated there were 11,000 to 14,000 Cuban troops and 1,000 to 1,200 Soviet military advisers and troops in Ethiopia.

### July 17, 1979

**Following U.S.-sponsored proposals, the Nicaraguan Congress accepts President Somoza's resignation. Congress names President Francisco Urcuyo Malaños to succeed Somoza.**

Between October 1978 and January 1979, attempts by the Organization of American States to mediate Nicaragua's internal problems failed. Consequently, Somoza became increasingly isolated from supporters at home and abroad because businessmen, the middle class, church leaders, and union members joined with the Sandinistas' FSLN group against the president. On June 4, a nationwide strike began and the rebels named a five-man junta to rule, headed by Sergio Ramírez MERCADO.

Between June 21 and 23, the foreign ministers of the OAS met in Washington, adopting a six-point plan proposed by U.S. Secretary of State Vance. The plan set up a peace force and asked for the "immediate replacement" of Somoza's government.

On June 27, U.S. Ambassador William G. Bowdler met in Panama with FSLN leaders and demanded that two more moderates be added to the junta. With Bowdler satisfied that the junta represented many groups, the unified junta named an 18-man cabinet on July 14, asking Nicaragua's Congress to recognize this cabinet and to replace Somoza.

On July 17, Nicaragua's Congress accepted the peace plan. It accepted Somoza's resignation and exile to the Bahamas. On July 19 rebel forces occupied

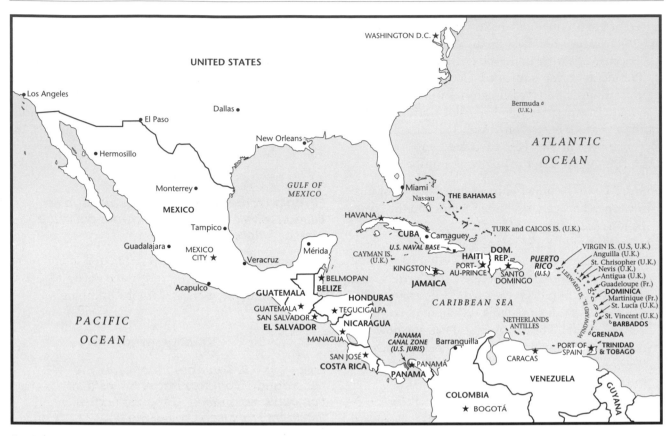

Central America and the Caribbean, 1979

Managua. The next day the junta's cabinet was sworn into office. The Somoza regime had ended.

See April 27, 1980, and September 30, 1978.

## July 20, 1979

### President Carter halts the pullout of U.S. troops from South Korea.

On February 17, 1979, delegates from North and South Korea began meetings to seek cooperation and a process to reunite their nation. After these talks failed, Carter and President Park of South Korea proposed on July 10 that North Korea join them in a three-way discussion on national unity. Premier Kim Il Sung of North Korea rejected this proposal. In addition, the U.N. command at the 38th parallel truce zone reported that North Korea had built new fortifications within 100 yards of the truce border.

As a result of the failure of unity talks and evidence of North Korea's defense buildup, President Carter announced that the United States would delay the withdrawal of American forces from South

Korea until at least 1981. Carter had announced withdrawal plans on March 9, 1977.

## July 20, 1979

### The U.N. Security Council passes a resolution urging Israel to halt construction of West Bank settlements. The United States abstains.

Since January 15, Israel had renewed its policy of approving Jewish settlements in territory occupied during the 1967 war. This issue had not been specifically settled in the March 26, 1979, peace treaty between Egypt and Israel, although the two nations began negotiations on autonomy for the Palestinians on May 26. Prime Minister Begin claimed he had not agreed to stop these settlements even though President Carter opposed them. On September 18, Carter said that Israel's decision of September 16 to permit Israelis to purchase land on the West Bank and Gaza Strip was "contrary to the spirit and intent" of the negotiations between Egypt and Israel. Prime Minister Begin did not agree with the president's assertion.

### July 26, 1979

*Nigeria nationalizes the British Petroleum and Shell oil companies.*

### July 30, 1979

**Congress compromises with the president on a resolution regarding economic sanctions against Rhodesia.**

Since April 24, when a new Rhodesian government was established under Bishop Abel T. MUZOREWA, head of the United African National Congress, some groups in the United States had urged the president to lift U.S. economic sanctions against Rhodesia, officially renamed ZIMBABWE on May 31, 1979.

President Carter was not willing to lift the sanctions because the new regime did not involve the Patriotic Front black factions in the elections of April 17–21. Great Britain, the United States, and other powers contended that the Patriotic Front, headed by Joshua Nkomo and Robert Mugabe, must be included in Muzorewa's government. The Organization of African Unity agreed, asserting in a declaration of July 21 that the Patriotic Front was the legal representative of Zimbabwe.

Both the U.S. Senate (June 13) and the House (June 28) passed resolutions that called for the president to lift the economic sanctions on Zimbabwe. On July 30, however, a Senate-House conference committee agreed to a compromise resolution that required Carter to lift sanctions by November 15, unless he decided it was not in the national interest.

Between August and October 22, British diplomats appointed by Prime Minister Thatcher worked out a compromise agreement to accept the British plan for a cease-fire and the establishment of a new government. Because this process had not been completed by December 3, Secretary of State Vance said that President Carter would lift the sanctions on Zimbabwe one month after the British governor arrived in Salisbury to carry out the transition to a black majority government of all black factions in Zimbabwe.

See March 4, 1980.

### August 1, 1979

**The U.S. Department of Agriculture ends a secret session with Soviet delegates in London by announcing that the United States will sell the USSR an additional 10 million tons of both wheat and corn in the next 14 months.**

This agreement was followed on October 3 by an Agriculture Department announcement that over the next year the USSR would buy a record 25 million metric tons of corn and wheat from the United States. It was also disclosed that Secretary of Defense Harold Brown had banned the sale of advanced computer technology to the Soviets.

### August 6, 1979

**The United States announces it has offered to deploy from 200 to 600 medium-range Pershing II and cruise missiles in NATO countries.**

NATO had been considering the possible deployment of medium-range missiles since January 19, 1979. These nuclear-warhead missiles were to counteract the Soviets deployment of SS-20 missiles aimed at Western Europe. Medium-range weapons were not part of the SALT I or SALT II pacts.

On October 4, the NATO High-Level Group approved deployment of these weapons, and between December 11 and 14, both the NATO defense ministers and the NATO Ministerial Council approved deployment of the missiles.

There were some limitations on these NATO decisions. On December 6, the Dutch parliament rejected the stationing of Pershing II missiles on Dutch territory. West Germany accepted deployment of the Pershing II and cruise missiles on the basis that SALT II would be ratified and there would be new talks with the USSR on reducing nuclear forces in Europe.

On October 6, Soviet President Brezhnev offered to reduce the number of intermediate-range missile deployed in the western part of the Soviet Union and withdraw 20,000 troops and 1,000 tanks from East Germany if NATO would not deploy Pershing II missiles in Germany. Although West German Chancellor

Helmut Schmidt urged NATO to accept Brezhnev's offer, on October 9 President Carter rejected Brezhnev's proposal because he considered it too vague on vital details.

See June 16, 1980, and August 6, 1981

### August 15, 1979

**Andrew Young, the U.S. Ambassador to the United Nations, resigns after admitting he made unauthorized contacts with the PLO.**

During his $2\frac{1}{2}$ years as Carter's appointee to the United Nations, Young generated much goodwill for the United States in contacts with African leaders. Often, however, Young made incautious or impulsive statements. To replace him, Carter appointed Young's deputy at the United Nations, Donald F. McHenry.

### September 4, 1979

**The United States and the Democratic Republic of Germany (east) conclude a consular agreement after two years of negotiations.**

### September 7, 1979

**President Carter asks the Soviet Union to respect America's concern about the Soviet military brigade stationed in Cuba. The president tells a national television audience the brigade poses no threat to the United States.**

Beginning on February 10, there were reports of increased Soviet military activity in Cuba. First the Defense Department confirmed that Cuba had received Soviet submarines and two torpedo boats. On March 28, there were reports that the USSR was building submarine bases in Cuba, and on August 31, the president stated that 2,000 to 3,000 Soviet combat troops had arrived in Cuba.

On October 1, Carter announced the establishment of a new U.S. Caribbean task force to offset Cuban-Soviet activity in that region. The president hoped this show of U.S. strength, plus President Brezhnev's statement that the Soviet forces were not in Cuba for combat purposes, would mollify senators who based their opposition to SALT II on this Soviet action. Carter's October 1 action did not gain any new converts for SALT II, however.

Ambassador Andrew Young with President Carter. Jimmy Carter Library

## September 19, 1979

**The United States undertakes a larger role in the Sinai because the United Nations ended its emergency force in July 1979 and Israel rejected the U.N. Truce Supervisory Organization (UNTSO).**

On July 24, the U.N. Security Council did not renew the emergency force and voted to install the UNTSO to oversee the Sinai situation. The United States and the Soviets had drawn up the UNTSO proposal on July 19 but could not obtain the approval of Israel. Prime Minister Begin objected to the UNTSO because he said unarmed observers could not perform the duties required of a U.N. neutral group. Moreover, the Israelis feared a possible repetition of an early U.N. withdrawal as had happened in June 1967, just before the Arab-Israeli war broke out.

By September 1979, the U.N. forces were nearly withdrawn, necessitating a new plan to oversee the three stages of Israel's withdrawal and the Egyptian occupation of the Sinai. In the trilateral agreement of September 19, the United States agreed to enlarge the duties of its Sinai Security Mission (SSM), which had been set up early in 1976 to operate an early-warning system in the Giddi and Mitla Passes.

As the U.N. emergency force began its withdrawal, the SSM assumed more duties although they were not to begin officially until February 1, 1980. Diplomatic arrangements were not completed until April 14, 1980, however, because the 1979 Trilateral Pact was not approved by the Israeli government until March 25 and by the Egyptians until April 2, 1980. Fortunately, no crisis occurred in the Sinai during the interim period from July 24, 1979 to April 1980.

## September 21, 1979

**Mexico and the United States agree on natural gas prices tied to OPEC oil prices.**

This agreement had been negotiated after much dispute. During the fall of 1977, talks on natural gas prices broke off because the United States rejected Mexico's price requests as excessive. On April 3, 1979, another round of negotiations began, resulting in the agreement of September 21.

## September 27, 1979

**Carter signs legislation to implement the Panama Canal treaties.**

To operate through committees under the two canal treaties that would become effective on October 1, 1979, the president asked Congress in January 1979 to pass the following legislation:

1. creating a Panama Canal Commission;
2. forming new bases for setting canal tolls;
3. arranging joint U.S.-Panamanian committees to carry out the treaties until 1999;
4. making special provisions for U.S. employees in the Canal Zone or for their emigration to the United States;
5. providing necessary funds to carry out the above provisions.

Although opponents of the Panama treaties threatened to defeat the implementing laws, they were not successful. The House and Senate approved the laws and Carter signed them on September 27.

## October 15, 1979

***El Salvador's President Carlos Huberto Romero is overthrown in a bloodless military coup led by Colonels Adolfo Majano and Jaime Gutiérrez.***

There had been fighting between leftist rebels of the Popular Revolutionary Bloc (PRB) and government forces since May 4, when the PRB occupied the French and Costa Rican embassies as well as the San Salvador Cathedral, holding 11 hostages.

Following the coup of October 15, a ruling junta was set up in El Salvador on October 23, promising to solve the political and economic problems of the state. Nevertheless, guerrilla warfare continued in El Salvador. On October 30, a rebel attempt to capture the U.S. embassy in San Salvador was repulsed; the State Department blamed Cuba for backing the rebel attack.

See October 24, 1979.

### October 22, 1979

**Carter announces that the United States will send arms to Morocco to aid King Hasan II against the Polisario guerrillas in the western Sahara.**

The Polisario group had secured aid from Syria, Ethiopia, and Algeria. On December 6, 1979, the Organization of African Unity called on Morocco to withdraw from the Western Sahara, but King Hasan II refused. Through intermittent attacks on Morocco's southern and western borders, the Polisario continued guerrilla war against the government.

### October 24, 1979

**In El Salvador, leftists occupy two ministries and take 130 hostages in protest against the new Junta.**

The Salvadoran leftists disliked the junta led by Majano and Gutiérrez that had gained power on October 15. Dramatizing their refusal to accept the regime, they occupied two ministries in San Salvador, asking for higher wages and an investigation of Salvador's treatment of political prisoners.

On October 30, the leftists also raided the U.S. embassy but could not secure it or gain hostages. Subsequently, on November 6, they ended their occupation of the ministry quarters and released their hostages. The junta promised to increase wages.

### October 26, 1979

**The South Korean intelligence service (KCIA) Chief assassinates President Park, his bodyguard, and four other Korean officials.**

This incident resulted in a year of demonstrations, protests, and internal fighting in Seoul. Not until September 1, 1980, did President Chun Doo Hwan provide some degree of order in South Korean politics.

### November 4, 1979

**The U.S. embassy in Tehran is stormed by Iranian students, who seize 60 hostages and demand the shah's return before they will release them.**

In some respects the crisis in Iran had begun in early October when the State Department accepted pleas from Henry Kissinger and David Rockefeller to admit the former shah of Iran to the United States so that he could undergo treatment for cancer in New York. Iran's government had warned that such a decision would turn the Iranian people against America.

Following the November 4 embassy attack, the United States refused to return the shah to Iran. The Carter administration did not, however, know how to handle the unusual circumstances. Normally, a host country protects foreign diplomats, but the Iranian government would not take action to free the hostages. Rather, Khomeini and his followers supported the demand for the shah's return, using the crisis to rally the nation to oppose the United States and to back Khomeini and the fundamentalist Islamic republic that had been established in a national referendum on April 1, 1979.

Although the United States sought to establish normal relations with the government of Prime Minister Barzargun following the shah's exile in January 1979, dealing with the new government was difficult. The Islamic Revolutionary Council and many of Iran's 60,000 mullahs each seemed to share some small part of the ayatollah's power. Barzargun held little real political power, and on November 5 he resigned as leader of the provisional government. The Revolutionary Council gained full control in Iran.

Subsequently, between November 4 and the end of 1979, various unsuccessful attempts were made to end the U.S. embassy crisis or to negotiate with Iran. The U.N. Security Council agreed unanimously to demand the release of the hostages; the PLO vainly sought to negotiate the hostages' release on November 8; U.N. Secretary-General Kurt Waldheim could not persuade the Iranians to negotiate, and although the International Court of Justice ordered the immediate release of the hostages on December 15, the court could not enforce its ruling. None of these methods worked because Khomeini rejected them as decadent Western policies.

The Iranians made only three concessions during the first 60 days of the crisis. On November 19 and 20 the students released five women and eight black male hostages; on November 22, they freed five non-American hostages. In addition, on December 24, Khomeini permitted three American clergymen, chosen by him, to come to the U.S. embassy and conduct religious services for the American hostages. The crisis continued throughout 1980.

## November 15, 1979

*Israel returns the Mount Sinai region to Egypt two months ahead of schedule.*

Although Prime Minister Begin's government carried out its Sinai withdrawal agreement with Egypt, serious issues arose in the Middle East throughout 1979, because Israel continued to expand Jewish settlements on the West Bank and persistently raided southern Lebanon to attack PLO bases in that area.

The Arab autonomy talks between Egypt and Israel were stalemated. On October 21, Moshe Dayan resigned as Israel's foreign minister because he disagreed with Begin's policy on the West Bank settlements and his arresting of moderate Palestinians in the West Bank. Begin claimed that both Jerusalem and the West Bank were part of Israel's traditional territory—Judea and Samaria. During the Camp David talks of 1978 and the Egyptian Peace Treaty negotiations of early 1979, President Carter avoided demanding definite pledges from Begin on this issue because it would probably have ended the discussions. The Arab autonomy talks between Israel and Egypt had been unable to move Begin and his followers from their prior views on the West Bank territory or Jerusalem.

## November 20, 1979

*At the Grand Mosque in Mecca, guerrilla forces launch an attack forcing Saudi Arabia to close the mosque.*

The Saudis said the attackers were 500 organized guerrillas; other reports said the attack was led by fundamentalist Muslims who opposed the Saudi government. The Saudi army dispersed or arrested the attacking force. The Grand Mosque was reopened on December 16, 1979.

## November 21, 1979

*In Pakistan, the U.S. embassy is partly burned and a U.S. marine guard is killed.*

U.S. relations with Pakistan had deteriorated rapidly in 1978–1979. In addition, Muslim extremists in Pakistan had been inspired by the example of Khomeini in Iran to attack Western institutions, which allegedly corrupted the traditions of Islam. In this atmosphere, the U.S. embassy in Islamabad was attacked by a mob and partly burned. Marine Chief Warrant Officer Bryan Elis and two Pakistani employees were killed in the attack. But Pakistani troops fought the Muslim demonstrators and rescued 100 Americans from the embassy grounds, ending the mob activity.

See March 12, 1979.

## November 29, 1979

**The United States cuts Chile's military and economic aid because the government refuses to extradite three men accused of involvement in the assassination of Orlando Letelier in Washington.**

Letelier had been Chile's foreign minister under Allende and was a critic of President Pinochet's military government before he was assassinated in 1976. On October 1, the Chilean Supreme Court upheld Pinochet's refusal to extradite the Chileans as requested by the United States. President Carter's November 29 action halted a $6.6 million package of military spare parts for Chile. Loans to Chile were also canceled by the Export-Import Bank.

President Carter's decision was based on human rights considerations, although he probably did not know about the CIA continued activity in Chile, even after the 1975 Senate investigation concluded the CIA assisted groups opposed to Allende. As disclosed in a declassified report to Congress on September 18, 2000, the CIA not only helped Augusto Pinochet's dictatorial regime during the 1970s but also used U.S. funds to assist General Manuel Conteras, the head of Chile's infamous secret police (DINA). Conteras had ordered the 1976 car bombing in Washington, D.C., that killed former Chilean foreign minister Orlando Letelier and his American associate Ronnie Karpen Moffit.

In the 2000 report on "CIA Activities in Chile," Congress learned the CIA not only knew about the killing of Letelier but also about DINA's killing of political opponents in other countries, known as Operation Condor. In 2000, Conteras was in a Chilean prison after being convicted of running a torture center where hundreds of Chileans were murdered or simply disappeared. The September 18 report summarizes CIA action but does not include still classified documentary evidence.

See November 21, 1975.

### December 2, 1979

#### Pro-Khomeini groups attack the U.S. embassy in Libya.

This incident in Tripoli was one of several radical Muslim attacks on U.S. property and personnel in 1979. The United States protested to the government of Mu'ammar al-Gadhafi, who had threatened to curtail oil exports to the United States. On December 10, however, Gadhafi ended his threats, saying he had received assurances that the United States would seek to become more neutral toward the Arabs in the Middle East. Thus, U.S. oil producers in Libya could continue their operations.

### December 28, 1979

#### The Soviet invasion of Afghanistan. President Carter calls President Brezhnev to warn of "serious consequences if the Soviets do not withdraw."

Following Ambassador Dubs's assassination (see February 14, 1979), the Afghan government steadily lost ground to mujahideen despite Soviet advisers and military armaments received from Moscow. After Soviet efforts to control Afghan Prime Minister Amin failed in September, the Soviets increased their military forces along the Afghan border and made plans to invade Afghanistan if necessary.

Using documents of the Soviet government declassified in 1995, Odd Arne Wested's essay in the Cold War International History Project's *Bulletin* (Winter 1996/97) describes the steps taken by Moscow's leaders in deciding to intervene in December 1979. Despite opposition from Prime Minister Aleksey Kosygin and other Politburo members, Yuri Andropov of the KGB (secret police) and Defense Minister Dmitri Ustinov convinced an ailing President Brezhnev of the need to intervene. To persuade Brezhnev, Andropov cited the dangers of events in Iran (see November 4, 1979) and the possibility the United States might deploy short-range missiles in Afghanistan just as West Germany agreed to do on December 6 (see August 6, 1979).

On December 12, the Politburo ratified the proposal to intervene. Within six days, Soviet forces were in place on the Afghan border and an operational team arrived at Kabul's airport base. The main operation began at 3:00 P.M. on December 25 with 6,000 airborne troops landing in Kabul, while in western Afghanistan motorized rifle units crossed the border. By December 27, Soviet paratroops and two KGB units attacked Amin's residence. After overcoming the palace guards, the Soviet troops executed Amin and several of his closest aides.

In the United States, the arrival of the airborne units on December 27 prompted President Carter's December 28 call on the hot line telephone to Brezhnev to warn him of the "serious consequences" if the Soviet troops were not withdrawn. Carter also sent Deputy Secretary of State Warren Christopher to Europe for discussions with NATO allies. Christopher learned that most European officials thought Carter had overreacted because the Soviet takeover did not threaten Europe's vital interests.

Carter and National Security Adviser Zbigniew Brzezinski disagreed with the Europeans in believing that Soviet control of Afghanistan confirmed the Soviet desire to expand into a strategic location, a view anticipating the Carter Doctrine. See January 23, 1980.

On December 31, following Brezhnev's statement that the Afghan government requested the Soviet troops to enter their country, Carter told reporters, Brezhnev's explanation was "obviously false." Throughout the 1980s, Soviet leaders continually maintained that Afghanistan asked Moscow to intervene. For example, the Soviet leader Mikhail Gorbachev's *Perestroika* (1987) indicates that Kabul asked 11 times "before we assented."

Undoubtedly Kabul leaders asked several times for small Soviet units, but they never asked for the massive invasion in 1979. In October 1979, a KGB report warned Soviet leader Brezhnev that to send "Soviet troops to Afghanistan means war, and there is no way to win it without exterminating the entire nation." Details about the KGB and other Soviet decisions on this subject are in Henry Bradsher's *Afghan Communism and Soviet Intervention* (1999 ed.).

# 1980

### January 2, 1980

#### President Carter asks the Senate to delay its ratification of SALT II because of the Soviet invasion of Afghanistan.

Although the Senate Foreign Relations Committee voted 9-6 on November 9 to send the SALT II treaty to the full Senate with a recommendation favoring ratification, much opposition to the treaty had developed, especially among Republican Party members. On December 16, a group of 16 senators sent the president a letter requesting him to delay the Senate vote on SALT II until after the presidential elections. Carter did not comply with this request but, following the Soviet action in Kabul on December 27, he asked the Senate to delay voting on SALT II. On June 6, 1980, the State Department announced that SALT II and Afghanistan were "inseparable." Thus, the Senate never voted on the ratification of SALT II.

Upon announcing the decision on SALT II on January 2, the White House indicated that the United States would continue to abide by the SALT I treaty, which had been extended in 1977 after its original expiration date. On May 9, President Carter told the Philadelphia World Affairs Council that he hoped eventually to have SALT II ratified, saying the United States would observe SALT II treaty terms as long as the Soviets did.

### January 3, 1980

**The United States agrees to sell the Republic of China (Taiwan) $280 million of defensive arms.**

This deal did not include the advanced fighter jet planes requested by Taiwan.

### January 4, 1980

**President Carter announces measures against the Soviet Union because of its "invasion" of Afghanistan.**

The détente relationship between the United States and the Soviet Union had grown shaky throughout 1979. Some observers attributed this to the fact that Moscow feared Carter's decision to normalize relations with China in December 1978; others viewed it as due to U.S. concern that the Soviets had violated the détente relationship in Angola, Ethiopia, and, finally, on December 27–28, in Afghanistan. Whatever the reason, Carter's announcement of retaliatory measures against the Soviet Union for invading Afghanistan indicated that a Cold War relationship had developed again between Washington and Moscow, a relationship disturbing to many European statesmen who cherished the results of détente between 1969 and 1979. Asked on New

Year's Eve 1979 whether the Afghanistan affair had changed his perceptions of the Soviets, President Carter candidly asserted: "This action of the Soviets has made a more dramatic change in my own opinion of what the Soviets' ultimate goals are than anything they've done in the previous time I've been in office." On January 4, the president announced that the United States was placing an embargo on sales to the Soviets of advanced technology, grain, and other strategic items. He also said he would seek a Western boycott of the Summer Olympic Games scheduled to be held in Moscow in 1980 if Soviet aggression continued.

On January 2, the president wrote a letter to Senate Majority Leader Robert Byrd, asking the Senate to delay its vote on ratification of SALT II until "Congress and I can assess Soviet actions."

On January 8, Carter took additional measures to implement his hard line toward Moscow. He ordered the withdrawal of the American advanced consular group preparing to establish an office in Kiev and expelled 17 Soviet diplomats planning to open a consulate in New York. He also suspended current high-technology licenses and shipments of such equipment to the Soviet Union.

Carter's continuing reprisals in future weeks include the following actions:

1. On January 18, he ordered curbs on Soviet phosphate ammonia exports. Although on February 3 the White House said there might be future phosphate export licenses, Carter made this embargo indefinite on February 25.
2. On January 21, Carter sent personal messages to 100 foreign government leaders asking them to boycott the Olympics if the Soviets did not leave Afghanistan by February 20.
3. Carter banned the export of all computer spare parts for the Kama River truck plant on January 21.

Carter's embargo actions were strongly criticized by some American politicians. As Senator Edward Kennedy said, "it's going to hurt the American farmer and taxpayer more than the Soviet aggressor." With regard to the embargo's effect on grain prices, the Carter administration pledged to buy up 14.5 million tons of corn, wheat, and soybeans (at a cost of $2.6 billion). On January 7–8, grain trading was suspended for two days to allow prices to stabilize, but then, on January 9, prices dropped as far as regulations permitted. The administration did nothing to assist manufacturers of machinery and technology or their employees.

Carter endeavored to persuade U.S. allies around the world to impose a similar embargo but failed to convince most of them. This enabled the Soviet Union to shop among other nations for replacements and needed commodities, especially corn and wheat. It also caused tension with Japan and the U.S.'s European allies who disagreed with the embargo.

## January 6, 1980

*Indira Gandhi's Congress Party returns to power in India by winning 350 of 542 seats in Parliament.*

## January 9, 1980

*Saudi Arabia executes 63 members of the extremist Aahdi sect, which had attacked the Grand Mosque at Mecca on November 20, 1979.*

In addition to beheading 63 radical Muslims, the Saudis sentenced 19 to prison terms, acquitted 38, and sent 23 women and minors to "reeducation" centers.

## January 14, 1980

*The U.N. General Assembly adopts Resolution ES-612, demanding the immediate and total withdrawal of all foreign forces (Soviet) from Afghanistan.*

The vote of the General Assembly was 104 to 18 with 18 abstaining and 12 absent. Although assembly votes are nonbinding, this vote was the first in which many "nonaligned" nations voted against the Soviet Union. Only Moscow's 18 allies voted against the resolution. Libya and Romania were notably absent when the vote was cast.

## January 23, 1980

**President Carter claims that the Persian Gulf area is a "vital American interest": The Carter Doctrine.**

In his state of the union message to Congress, the president extended U.S. global defense protection to the Arab oil states and the region along the Soviet Union's southern border. Specifically, Carter asserted that "any attempt by any outside force to gain control

of the Persian Gulf region will be regarded as an assault on the vital interests of the United States.... Such an assault will be repelled by use of any means necessary, including military force."

To implement the new U.S. defense perimeter, Carter asked Congress for a 5% increase in the defense budget for 1981, a sum he had resisted as "too much" during 1979. He also indicated that he would ask Congress for authority to register young Americans for selective service, although he added, "I hope that it will not become necessary to impose the draft."

President Carter's message was warmly received by Americans, who had become incensed at the Iranian crisis and appalled at the Soviet intervention in Afghanistan. Thus, during the next several months, Carter continued to display his hard-line anti-Communist stance. On February 11, the United States strengthened its presence in the Persian Gulf and the Indian Ocean by announcing agreements to obtain military facilities in Oman, Kenya, and Somalia. On April 8, Saudi Arabia refused to accept requests for U.S. military facilities but agreed (March 18) to provide financial aid for north Yemen to replace aid formerly received from Moscow. The United States also agreed to provide 60 F-15 fighter planes for the Saudi Arabian defense forces.

Perhaps the most significant U.S. agreement in the Middle East was military cooperation with Egypt. On January 8, Cairo indicated that the United States had tested its Airborne Warning and Control (AWAC) planes by using Egyptian bases as a stopover for flights to Iran. On July 10, the United States and Egypt began a 90-day joint training exercise using American F-4E jet planes, paratroopers, and other forces of the two nations. On November 12, 1980, the United States sent advanced units of its Rapid Deployment Force (RDF) to Egypt for 12 days of joint exercises. The RDF was designed by the U.S. armed forces as a unit that could be quickly sent to any crisis area to counteract enemy (Communist) activity. Thus, the RDF could carry out the Carter Doctrine with conventional forces in the Persian Gulf.

The one aspect of the Carter Doctrine that was questioned the most by some U.S. politicians was the status of U.S.-Pakistani relations. One unidentified senator was quoted as saying: "If Russian troops chase Afghan rebels into Pakistan, do we want American boys up in the Khyber Pass trying to stop them?" U.S. defenses under such contingencies would operate at an extreme logistic disadvantage compared with Soviet home bases. In addition, Pakistan's stability and reliability were questioned. On January 13, Pakistan rejected a U.S. offer of $400 million in economic-military aid as "peanuts." Nevertheless, the United States continued to woo Pakistan, pledging on October 30 to assist that country in case of Soviet attack.

See March 12 and November 21, 1979.

### January 24, 1980

**Congress approves the U.S.-Chinese Trade Act, giving China the most-favored-nation status.**

Although the Carter administration had previously requested the most-favored-nation status for the USSR as well as China, this request no longer applied after the Soviet invasion of Afghanistan in 1979. Therefore, Congress granted Beijing a trade concession that the United States denied to Moscow.

### January 29, 1980

**The day after closing its embassy in Tehran, Canada discloses that it helped six U.S. Embassy employees escape.**

After hiding the six Americans in its embassy for three months, Canada supplied them with forged Canadian diplomatic passports and smuggled them out on commercial air flights on January 26 and 27. Iran denounced the Canadian act and its foreign minister, Sadegh Ghotbzadeh, declared, "sooner or later, somewhere in the world, Canada will pay."

### February 13, 1980

**Carter announces the end of the 27-month U.S. boycott of the International Labor Organization. The United States rejoins the group on February 18, 1980.**

The State Department stated that the ILO had ceased its previous practice of making statements on political and other nonlabor issues, a practice the United States had objected to in 1977.

See November 5, 1977.

### February 17, 1980

*Pierre Trudeau is reelected as Canada's prime minister.*

Trudeau's Liberal Party defeated Joe Clark's Progressive Conservatives, who had won a narrow majority of parliamentary seats in 1979, holding office for less than one year.

### February 19, 1980

**The European Economic Community's Foreign Ministers reject President Carter's request to boycott the 1980 Moscow Olympics. Carter announces the U.S. boycott the next day.**

Although the EEC members issued a resolution calling on the Soviet Union to pull its troops out of Afghanistan, the European ministers did not believe the Olympics should be mixed up with political questions. Without EEC support, President Carter announced on February 20 that the United States would boycott the Olympics in 1980.

The EEC ministers also refused to support the U.S. embargo of high-technology equipment to the Soviet Union. They believed Carter overreacted to Moscow's actions on December 27, and did not consider the Afghan buffer state as "vital to European interests" compared with better relations with the Soviets.

### February 23, 1980

**A U.N. commission of inquiry arrives in Tehran in hopes the hostage crisis may be settled.**

The U.N. Commission was established by the Security Council on January 11 at Iran's request for an inquiry into its demands for the return to Iran of the shah and his wealth. U.N. Secretary-General Kurt Waldheim, believed the U.N. group could settle the hostage crisis by discussions with Khomeini and Iran's foreign minister, Abolhassan Bani-Sadr.

On February 11, Bani-Sadr stated that the hostages could be released if the United States admitted its "crimes" in the last 25 years, pledged noninterference in Iran, and recognized Iran's right to have the shah extradited. The shah had left New York in December 1979 and remained in Panama until March 23, 1980, when he moved to Egypt.

Waldheim's optimism about the commission's work was not justified. Even as the U.N. group traveled to Iran, Bani-Sadr and Khomeini indicated they considered it the commission's duty to investigate the shah's crimes, not to settle the hostage issue. On the day the U.N. panel arrived, Khomeini stated that the fate of the hostages would be decided in April by the Islamic Consultative Assembly. In the light of such statements, the commission's members became demoralized. Following two weeks of interviews in Iran, the U.N. panel left on March 11; Secretary Waldheim admitted that its work had failed and that the commission was "suspended."

### February 27, 1980

**Leftist guerrillas occupy the Dominican Republic's embassy in Bogotá, Colombia, taking 80 hostages including U.S. Ambassador Diego Asencio.**

Two dozen Colombians entered the Dominican embassy during a reception, occupied the building, and held the hostages. The rebels demanded $50 million, publication of a manifesto of their protests, and release of 311 "political" prisoners in Colombia.

The hostages were held in Bogotá until the negotiation of their release on April 27. The Colombian government released nine rebel prisoners and agreed to have observers from the Human Rights Commission of the Organization of American States at the trials of the other prisoners. In addition, the guerrillas at the Dominican embassy were paid $2.5 million and allowed to take a plane to safety in Cuba.

### March 3, 1980

**Carter admits the U.N. vote to censure Israel should have been an abstention.**

The West Bank settlement issue arose on February 10 when the Israeli cabinet agreed Jews could establish a settlement in the Arab town of Hebron. Although Israel delayed a final parliamentary vote on the Hebron settlement, world public opinion opposed the cabinet decision. On February 17, the U.N. Security Council received a resolution but behind the scenes U.S. Ambassador Donald McHenry sought a compromise resolution.

Because President Carter opposed the growth of Jewish settlements in Palestinian land on the West Bank of the Jordan River and in Jerusalem, he told U.S. Ambassador to the United Nations Donald

McHenry to accept any U.N.S.C. resolution that simply said settlements were illegal. In New York, McHenry sought some compromise with other U.N.S.C. members in accordance with Carter's instructions, while at the White House, Carter's foreign policy advisers discussed the proper wording to satisfy Israeli objections to the previously proposed resolution. On March 1, McHenry cast the U.S. vote to approve the resolution, believing Secretary of State Cyrus Vance had approved the wording.

Unfortunately, some unknown State Department bureaucrat erred in transmitting the resolution's wording to McHenry, and when the resolution's official passing was reported, critics objected to the U.S. vote of approval. As the memoirs of National Security Adviser Zbigniew Brzezinski (*Power and Principal*, 1983) and Secretary Vance (*Hard Choices*, 1983) indicate, President Carter was not confused, as some critics thought, but only wanted a simple statement about the illegality of the Jewish settlements under United Nations resolution 242 in 1967. As a result, Carter insisted that Vance retract the U.S. vote by saying there was an internal misunderstanding. Both Brzezinski and Vance opposed Carter's decision to retract the vote, but Vance dutifully did so. Carter's decision was a principal reason Vance resigned as Secretary of State in April 1980.

### March 4, 1980

**Robert Mugabe's party wins the majority of seats in Zimbabwe's election. He becomes premier on March 11.**

After Bishop Abel T. Muzorewa became President of Zimbabwe (formerly Rhodesia) on April 24, 1979 (see July 30, 1979), the United States and the Organization of African Unity insisted that the black Patriotic Front, headed by Robert Mugabe and Joshua Nkomo, be represented in the new government. To accommodate the U.S. and OAS, the British offered the "Lancaster House" proposals that Ian Smith's white government and the Patriotic Front accepted on November 15, 1979. The Soviet Union had assisted the Patriotic Front and Soviet leader Brezhnev cooperated with the British and Americans in the transition to an independent Zimbabwe.

Thus, on March 4, 1980, the British conducted elections for Zimbabwe's Parliament, in which 80 of the 100 seats were allotted to blacks. Of these 80, Mugabe's African National Front won 57 seats and

Nkomo's African National Political Union won 20 seats; the other 3 seats went to smaller parties. Mugabe became Prime Minister of Zimbabwe and assured Rhodesian whites "there is a place for everybody in this country," naming Ian Smith to a cabinet position.

On April 14, President Carter named Robert V. Keeley as ambassador to Zimbabwe and pledged $20 million in economic aid for both 1980 and 1981. On September 25, Zimbabwe joined the United Nations. Mugabe's conciliatory policies during the next year demonstrated that U.S. predictions of a Communist radicalization of Zimbabwe were incorrect.

## March 6, 1980

### El Salvador's junta, acting on U.S. advice, decrees land reforms, nationalizes the banks, and declares a 30-day state of siege.

The Salvador junta led by Colonels Adolfo Arnoldo, Majano Ramos, and Jaime Abdul Gutiérrez had gained power on October 15 with a promise to reform a nation in which previous military leaders ran the state to benefit the wealthy minority. As a U.S. official said, El Salvador was a "classic setting for social and political unrest" because 2% of the population owned 60% of the nation's arable land.

The United States sought to head off further unrest in El Salvador by blocking a right-wing coup on February 23. In February 1980, Washington granted El Salvador $100 million in economic and military aid, asking the junta to make social reforms. Thus, on March 6, the government confiscated 376 estates covering 700,000 acres of land, promising to redistribute it to peasants. The government offered to pay the former landholders in government bonds. The decree on the siege, which banned demonstrations to maintain order while the reforms were carried out, engendered much opposition from both left-wing and right-wing groups in Salvador, the left-wing because the payments for land were not in cash, the right-wing because they wanted to keep large estates.

## March 24, 1980

### *El Salvador's liberal archbishop Oscar Romero is assassinated by right-wing terrorists.*

Rather than ending violence by the left- and right-wing extremists in El Salvador, the junta's March 6 announcement of economic reforms caused greater disturbances. The right wing opposed the land reform as too radical; the Marxists denounced the reforms as too little, while also protesting the 30-day siege.

The slaying of Archbishop Romero led to more violence. During the funeral on March 30, gunfire broke out near the cathedral, causing the 30,000 mourners to panic. More than 30 people were killed. Who began the gunfire was uncertain. Some people blamed Salvadoran armed forces occupying the National Palace near the cathedral; others blamed the leftists, who, the U.S. State Department claimed, had received aid from Cuba.

## March 29, 1980

### Agreement reached on U.S. bases in Turkey as well as on economic and military cooperation.

Following the Cypriot crisis, U.S.-Turkish relations seriously deteriorated. Throughout 1979, however, there was steady improvement owing partly to U.S. concern for the Middle East following the fall of the shah of Iran. Although Turkey rejected a U.S. request on May 15 to permit U-2 flights from Turkish bases as a means for verifying Soviet compliance with the SALT treaties, the renewal of talks between Greek and Turkish Cypriot leaders on May 18 enabled the United States to undertake negotiations to renew U.S. aid to Turkey. Talks began on August 13 that eventually resulted in the five-year agreement signed on March 29, 1980. In that agreement, the United States did not gain Turkish agreement to provide bases for U-2 flights over the USSR. It received one air base, four intelligence-gathering bases, and seven communications centers. Turkey received $450 million per year.

In mid-June 1980, the International Monetary Fund approved a three-year, $1.6 billion loan to

Turkey, the largest in the fund's history. During 1980, Turkey received over $3 billion from sources in NATO, becoming the third-largest recipient of U.S. assistance after Israel and Egypt. A portion of this made up for aid cut off by the United States during the Cypriot crisis.

### April 4–5, 1980

*Over 10,000 Cubans jam Peru's embassy in Havana after Castro announces that all Cubans who enter the embassy peacefully are free to leave Cuba if they obtain foreign entry visas.*

The Peruvian embassy had been harboring 25 Cubans who had crashed a bus through the embassy gates to get past a Cuban guard. Apparently to retaliate against Peru, Castro issued his offer, which permitted any Cubans who wished to emigrate to do so. On April 5, more than 10,000 citizens indicated they wanted to leave Cuba by arriving at the embassy. Castro's action caused difficulty for the Peruvians because they did not want 10,000 Cuban emigres. Lima called on its Andean Pact neighbors to help. Peru also said most of the Cubans wanted to go to the United States. The initial U.S. reaction was that the Latin American countries should take the lead in opening their doors to the refugees.

See May 5, 1980.

### April 7, 1980

**President Carter breaks diplomatic relations with Iran and bans U.S. exports to that country.**

From January to April 7, the United States conducted quiet diplomacy with Iran's President Bani-Sadr, hoping to reach a compromise on the hostage question. Following the failure of U.N. Secretary-General Kurt Waldheim's inquiry group on March 11, Bani-Sadr asked the United States for time until the Iranian Revolutionary Council met so that the government could persuade the militants to turn over the hostages. In this context, Carter believed a tough U.S. stance would hinder Bani-Sadr's efforts.

On April 6, when the Revolutionary Council met, it placed the fate of the hostages in the hands of Khomeini, not the government of Bani-Sadr. Khomeini stated that the militants would continue

to hold the hostages until the Majlis (parliament) met later in the summer.

These circumstances caused Carter to break relations with Iran on April 7. He also imposed an economic boycott and asked the U.S. allies to join in these sanctions. He then proposed legislation to allow Americans who held debt claims against Iran to settle their bills by drawing on the $8 billion of Iran's frozen assets in the United States.

While announcing these measures, the president said the United States "will pursue every—and I repeat—every legal use of [U.S.] power to bring our people home, free and safe." Later, Carter told a group of editors that among his "legal" remedies, he did not "foreclose the option of using military force" or other punitive action.

### April 25, 1980

**A U.S. rescue mission to liberate the American hostages in Iran aborts 250 miles from Tehran because of mechanical problems.**

President Carter ordered the failed clandestine rescue mission, which resulted in the accidental deaths of eight U.S. servicemen.

The U.S. operation had been planned since November as one means of rescue if negotiations failed. Volunteer antiterrorist specialists from U.S. army, navy, and marine units had rehearsed their plan under the leadership of Colonel Charles Beckwith. President Carter did not give the operation a go-ahead until April 16. During the mission, six C-130 transport planes carried a 90-man commando team from an Egyptian base to Iran on Thursday evening, April 24. The transports also carried helicopter fuel, weapons, and communications-jamming equipment. After refueling at a Persian Gulf base, the transports landed in Iran after dark.

To rendezvous with the C-130 transports, eight Sikorsky RH-53 helicopters left the aircraft carrier *Nimitz,* stationed in the Gulf of Oman. Helicopter equipment failure began soon after takeoff because one helicopter had to return to the carrier and a second was forced down during a sandstorm over southern Iran. The remaining six copters flew 600 miles to join the transport planes and commandos at 11:15 P.M. Iranian time. Their rendezvous point was near Tabas in the Dasht-i-Kavir salt desert, 200 miles southeast of Tehran.

The operational plans called for the helicopters to fly the 90-man team north to hide in a mountain area near Tehran. On the night of April 25, trucks driven by U.S. agents already in Iran would carry the team into the city. At a prearranged time the commandos would assault the U.S. compound and Foreign Ministry building to free the hostages. Helicopters would fly into the city and carry the team and hostages to an abandoned airstrip outside Tehran. Finally, two C-141s would fly to the airstrip, pick up the Americans, and carry them to safety in the desert area of Saudi Arabia.

The rescue operation never got beyond the initial salt desert rendezvous point. The landing team first had the unexpected interruption of capturing a busload of Iranians who came on the scene. Next, as the helicopters refueled, one developed a hydraulic problem. The mission plan called for a minimum of six helicopters. With only five remaining, Colonel Beckwith recommended aborting the mission; the president agreed.

As the mission aborted and the C-130s prepared to carry out both the 90-man team and the helicopter crews, another disaster took place. While refueling in the desert darkness, a helicopter collided with a C-130. Ammunition aboard the transport plane exploded, killing eight servicemen. The commandos had to crowd aboard the remaining transport planes. At 4 A.M. the rescue team left behind the dead soldiers, six helicopters, and the wrecked C-130 and flew out to Masirah, a small island near Oman.

One consequence of the raid was that the Iranians scattered the U.S. hostages to various locations outside the U.S. embassy, making a second military rescue operation almost impossible. At home, the disaster caused further embarrassment for the president. Because all branches of the armed services insisted on being represented, preparations for the mission appear to have been compromised. Consequently, the mission seemed to reflect the very indecisiveness of the president about which critics had frequently complained.

### April 27, 1980

*The Nicaraguan junta loses two moderate members who opposed the Sandinista policies.*

Since the overthrow of Somoza on July 17, 1979, there had been frequent disagreements in the mixed mod-

erate-radical junta the United States had sanctioned. The formation of a Sandinist Popular Army on July 28 and the political-economic accords signed with Moscow on March 20, 1980, were the two actions by the Sandinist members of the junta that were most criticized by Americans.

The announcement by the National Council of State that the number of Sandinist members would increase from one-third to a majority resulted in the resignation of the two moderates, Violeta Barios de Chamorro (April 19) and Alfonso Callejas (April 22). De Chamorro resigned for "reasons of health." As the owner of *La Prensa*, the nation's leading independent newspaper, she had been troubled by a Sandinist-organized strike that shut down the paper. Callejas, a businessman, resigned to protest the April 21 decree giving the Sandinists a majority of council votes.

On April 22, the council stated it would appoint other moderates to the junta. On May 19, two moderates, Rafael Rivas and Arturo Cruz, joined the National Council membership. Nevertheless, the new council moved rapidly to undertake radical measures for full Sandinist control of Nicaragua. Having gained a majority of council seats, the Sandinistas proceeded to obtain a firm hold on the nation.

### April 29, 1980

**Edmund Muskie is named Secretary of State following Secretary Vance's resignation in opposition to the aborted hostage rescue attempt.**

Vance had submitted his resignation to President Carter on April 21, three days before the aborted raid against Iran, which the secretary had opposed. But he agreed not to announce his resignation until the raid ended.

Edmund Muskie, a senator from Maine, had made his reputation in domestic, not foreign, affairs. He had been the Democratic vice presidential nominee in 1968 but lost the presidential nomination to McGovern in 1972. Some observers said Muskie was named secretary because, unlike Vance, he would not clash with the more aggressive proposals of National Security Adviser Brzezinski, to whom Carter had turned increasingly after the Afghanistan crisis.

In his first significant speech as secretary, Muskie told the Foreign Policy Association on July 7 that the State Department would place less stress on human rights issues and provide essential economic, social, and military aid to non-Communist nations regardless of their civil rights record.

## May 4, 1980

### Marshal Tito of Yugoslavia dies.

Yugoslavia's 1974 constitution provided that upon Tito's death, the eight-member presidency would replace him. The constitution had created a nine-member presidency that, excepting Tito, had representatives from each of Yugoslavia's six republics and from the two autonomous regions of Vojvodina and Kosovo. The head of the presidency would rotate every May 15, a provision that weakened the federal government's power. This was not a problem as long as Tito was in control as chairman of Yugoslavia's Communist Party. After Tito's death, no leader came forward to assume his powerful role. The eight-member presidency caused the central government to fragment before disintegrating after 1988.

See November 18, 1988.

## May 5, 1980

### President Carter announces the United States will welcome "with an open heart and open arms" all refugees from Cuba.

On April 5, when Fidel Castro dropped all barriers to Cubans wishing to emigrate, the U.S. government had hesitated about the proper response. Washington agreed to take 3,500 of the 10,000 Cubans who went to Peru's embassy in Havana. Peru took 1,000; Venezuela and Spain, 500 each; Costa Rica and Canada, 300; and Ecuador, 200.

On April 21, Castro suspended the airlift of refugees to Costa Rica and opened a ship-to-shore boat shuttle from Muriel, Cuba, to Key West. By May 5, about 30,000 Cubans had reached the United States, whose policy was to admit all Cubans who reached the mainland of the United States. Cuban-Americans attempted to free their relatives and bring them to the United States, but Castro decreed that of the passengers on each boat only one-third could be relatives; one-third would come from the group still at Peru's embassy; and one-third would be Castro's "trash'—political dissidents, criminals, and those the government wished to get rid of, including the mentally ill.

Carter's May 5 declaration meant that all Cuban American relatives might eventually come to Florida. Therefore, the president declared a state of emergency in Florida and set aside $10 million to feed and clothe the refugees.

About this same time, refugees from Haiti began crowding onto boats to reach Florida and be accepted by the United States. Most Haitians, however, were declared economic, not political, refugees, even though it was as much Cuba's poor economy as Castro's dictatorship that caused most Cubans to flee. As a result, lawyers for the Haitians went to court, claiming that their clients had been discriminated against because they were black and had fled a dictatorship that was on good terms with the United States.

See May 14, 1980.

## May 14, 1980

### President Carter qualifies his "open arms" for refugees statement of May 5 and orders limits on airlifts and sealifts to screen out undesirables.

From April 21 to mid-May, 60,000 refugees poured into Key West from Cuba. Many boat owners had overloaded their vessels to obtain more profits from charging each refugee for the transportation. In one instance, an overcrowded boat capsized, drowning 12 persons. Therefore, Carter proposed to Castro that he assist in making the refugee flow orderly and assist in first clearing people leaving Cuba for the United States.

Castro chose to ignore Carter's suggestion and the exodus continued until September 26. Between April 21 and September 26, 125,262 refugees came to the United States from Cuba. Because Cuba did not screen its emigrants, the United States had to establish refugee centers to evaluate the status of each immigrant and assist each in locating work or other support after leaving the refugee center.

## May 16, 1980

### Secretary Muskie meets in Vienna with Soviet Foreign Minister Gromyko in the first high-level U.S.-Soviet meeting in eight months.

Secretary Muskie described the sessions as "introductory." During other meetings at Vienna that included

British and French delegates, Muskie spoke bluntly in asserting that "an act of aggression [i.e., Afghanistan] anywhere threatens security everywhere."

### May 18, 1980

*In response to an American request for European action to oppose Iran's hostage policy, the European economic community leaders place limited sanctions on Iran.*

The economic sanctions voted by the EEC became effective on May 22 and applied to all contracts made with Iran since November 4, 1979. The British government accepted slightly different sanctions on Iran, limiting them to new contracts only, those made after May 22.

### May 26, 1980

*The target day for Egypt and Israel to complete West Bank autonomy talks ends with no results.*

The 1979 Egyptian-Israeli peace treaty had scheduled autonomy talks to resolve the issue of Arab autonomy in lands occupied by Israel in 1967. Eight rounds of talks had been held, but like the ninth-round discussions from February 27 to March 4, 1980, they ended in disagreement. Efforts by President Carter to renew talks were rejected by Egyptian President Sadat on May 15, because Israel's Knesset (parliament) had approved a bill declaring that Jerusalem was the capital of Israel. On May 18, the Israeli cabinet also opposed another round of autonomy talks.

Israel's relations with Egypt and the United States reached a low point during the spring of 1980. On May 2, six Jewish settlers were killed by Palestinian terrorists in Hebron. In retaliation, Israel deported three West Bank Arab officials to Lebanon for inflammatory criticism of Israel. On May 8, the U.N. Security Council voted for the fourth time in three months to censure Israel. The United States abstained from voting on the resolution although the Carter administration disapproved Prime Minister Begin's West Bank settlement policy.

On June 2, 1980, Jewish terrorists placed bombs in Palestinian automobiles; two bombs exploded, maiming two West Bank Arab mayors and an Israeli trying to defuse a third bomb. Other Jewish terrorists threw hand grenades in Hebron, injuring seven Arabs.

Because of these tensions and the continuing Jewish settlement of occupied West Bank territory, the autonomy discussions became impossible.

### May 27, 1980

*The first Chinese head of state to visit Japan in 2,000 years, Hua Guofeng arrives in Tokyo.*

Hua and Japanese Prime Minister Ohira met to discuss trade relations and joint cooperation against the USSR in East Asia.

### May 30, 1980

*West Germany and the Soviet Union sign a treaty on oil and gas exploration and use.*

West German and other European statesmen wished to separate détente in Europe from the U.S.-Soviet tensions that appeared to have ended détente. Thus, the Germans signed the oil–natural gas proposals that were being negotiated with Moscow.

Détente also continued to be pursued in relations between East and West Germany. On April 30, the two German states signed a $282 million transportation agreement to permit road, railway, and water links between West Berlin and West Germany.

### June 16, 1980

**President Carter sends West German Chancellor Helmut Schmidt a letter warning him not to agree with Soviet President Brezhnev on freezing U.S. missile deployments in Europe.**

Apparently the president felt European leaders were acting in concert with Moscow without consulting Washington. On May 19, French President Giscard d'Estaing met with Brezhnev in Warsaw without consulting the United States. Carter did not want Schmidt to do the same, even though the German leader had announced his meeting with Brezhnev as early as January 17, 1980. The publicity given to Carter's letter caused many Europeans to object to the president's interference, especially because Washington had frequently acted without first consulting its European allies.

On June 21, Carter held a meeting with Schmidt prior to the Venice economic summit sessions. The United States was concerned that its alliance with the European nations was drifting. Reportedly, Carter and

Schmidt did not get along personally, and Carter's June 16 letter had upset the German Chancellor. Schmidt wanted to strengthen NATO but disagreed with U.S. proposals to stretch NATO forces into the area of the Persian Gulf. After their talk in Venice, the two leaders' sense of disunity seemed to diminish. Carter stated that Schmidt supported the 1979 NATO decision to deploy missiles in Europe.

Nevertheless, both Schmidt and Giscard d'Estaing of France expressed their disappointment with U.S. policy. From July 7 to 11, 1980, these two leaders met in Bonn to reaffirm the German-French alliance. Their joint communiqué on July 11 urged an independent role for Europe in world affairs. Such a role would not end the American alliance but would separate common European policies from Washington's authority in order to enact programs in the interests of the Western European states.

### June 17, 1980

*Vietnamese forces attack across the Thai border, striking at refugee camps holding Cambodians.*

Following U.S. protests of these attacks, the Vietnamese withdrew. The raid caused the deaths of 24 Thai and 1,000 refugees. As these border incidents continued, the United States gave Thailand $32.5 million of military equipment on July 1. On October 22, the U.N. General Assembly passed a resolution calling for the Vietnamese to pull out of Cambodia. The United Nations continued to recognize the exiled government of Pol Pot as Cambodia's legitimate rulers.

### June 18, 1980

**Following visits in Washington with American officials, Jordan's King Hussein indicates he will join mideast talks with Egypt and Israel if Israel agrees to return the occupied territory.**

Seeking to revive and extend the West Bank autonomy talks, President Carter hoped King Hussein would agree to participate, a maneuver that could end the Israeli-Egyptian deadlock. Hussein refused to join the discussions on autonomy without specific commitments from Israel.

Nevertheless, the United States promised to sell Jordan 100 M-60 tanks with night-vision scopes and laser-range finders. Pro-Israeli groups in Congress opposed these sales, but the State Department said

the arrangement was to prevent a Jordanian arms pact with the Soviet Union.

See May 26, 1980.

### June 19, 1980

**President Carter asks Congress to approve shipments of enriched uranium fuel to India.**

On May 7, the president indicated that the United States had agreed to send India nuclear fuel for its Tarapur plant. Although the U.S. Nuclear Regulatory Commission (NRC) voted against the proposal on May 16, Carter overruled the NRC. The NRC objected because India refused to comply with international regulations on the use of nuclear power and on the development of nuclear weapons. The president favored the agreement to prevent closer ties between India and the Soviet Union.

Congress held extensive debates before agreeing to allow the shipment of 38 tons of uranium fuel. The House had rejected the proposal on September 18, but the Senate removed the objection clauses, and a conference committee agreed to accept Carter's recommendation on September 24, 1980.

### June 22, 1980

*In Japanese elections, the Liberal Democratic Party (LDP) wins a 30-seat majority in the lower house, although its leader, Prime Minister Masayoshi Ohira, died on June 12.*

On June 16, the LDP selected former Agricultural Minister Zenko Suzuki as prime minister. On August 18, Suzuki reaffirmed Japan's commitment to the U.S.-Japanese security treaty.

### June 25, 1980

**Congress approves Carter's request for revival of the selective service system.**

There had been discussions about reviving selective service and universal military training for several years because voluntary enlistments often fell short of armed forces requirements. Therefore, to indicate his continuing concern for the nation's defenses, President Carter asked Congress on February 8 to pass legislation for registering men and women under selective service for possible conscription "to resist further Soviet aggression." On February 26, the administration bill requested $45 million to make registration operative. The Senate approved this bill on the basis of $13.3 million on June 12; the House approved the bill on June 25.

### June 26, 1980

*France successfully tests a neutron bomb.*

This French weapon was experimental. The French government said it would decide in two or three years about whether or not to produce such weapons in quantity and deploy them.

### June 26, 1980

*A U.N. Security Council resolution condemns South Africa's invasion of Angola, asking for its immediate withdrawal.*

On June 13, South Africa said it had raided bases in Angola being used by Namibian rebels for raids into South-West Africa. On June 26, Angola claimed that 3,000 South African troops had occupied its southern towns and killed over 300 civilians. The Security Council backed Angola's demands for South Africa to withdraw. The vote was 12-0; the United States and two other members abstained.

### July 1, 1980

*West German Chancellor Schmidt and Soviet President Brezhnev meet in Moscow to discuss détente.*

Following two days of talks with Soviet officials, the West German leader reported that the Soviets were prepared to negotiate with the United States on intermediate-range missiles to be stationed in Europe. He said he had asked the Soviet leader to pull Soviet troops out of Afghanistan but had received no commitment from Brezhnev. Finally, he said, the Germans and Soviets continued plans for the $13.3 billion natural gas pipeline to be constructed between Siberia and West Germany.

Following the Moscow talks, Schmidt sent West Germany's foreign minister, Hans Dietrich Genscher, to Washington on July 2 to provide details of his conversations to President Carter.

### July 4, 1980

**The Organization of African Unity (OAU) demands that the United States remove its base on Diego Garcia and return the island to Mauritius.**

The U.S. navy had occupied the Indian Ocean island of Diego Garcia during the early 1970s, gradually replacing the British fleet that previously used the island as a strategic naval base. The OAU protest was not acceptable to the United States because Washington believed the base was more vital than ever, owing to the Iranian and Afghanistan incidents of 1979 and the Carter Doctrine.

### July 19, 1980

**As the Olympics open in Moscow, 59 nations join the United States in boycotting the games.**

Among the major nations joining the U.S. boycott were West Germany, China, Japan, Canada, and Kenya.

### July 25, 1980

**The U.S. State Department takes action to oppose the military coup in Bolivia.**

Following a Bolivian election on June 29, Bolivia's armed forces staged their fourth military takeover in 26 months on July 17. The junta, headed by General Luis Garciá Meza Tejada claimed that the Popular Democratic Party, headed by Herman Siles ZUAZO, was Communist. Zuazo gained the largest percentage of votes (38.7%) of any of the 15 presidential candidates. General Meza began a program of arrest, torture, and execution that led the Organization of American States and the Andean Pact presidents to condemn the military regime. On July 25, the State Department announced the U.S. would withdraw its military advisers and economic aid from Bolivia and "strongly" support the OAS condemnation of Bolivia.

### July 27, 1980

*Mohammad Reza Pahlavi dies in Egypt.*

The shah died from cancer and circulatory shock after 18 months of exile and a long illness.

## July 30, 1980

*The Israeli Knesset (parliament) approves legislation making Jerusalem the "united and undivided" capital of Israel.*

Following this decision, Prime Minister Begin said he planned to move his office to East Jerusalem. Israel's action made the autonomy talks with Egypt more difficult because they implied that Israel would not compromise on its occupation of East Jerusalem or on its West Bank settlement policy.

## August 5, 1980

**White House administration aides disclose that Carter approved Presidential Directive 59, providing a new American nuclear strategy that accepts the concept of a "winnable nuclear war."**

While Directive 59 was not made public and Secretary of Defense Harold Brown said on August 10 it was not a "major break with past policies, but an evolutionary development," the implications of the directive were vitally significant to nuclear strategic and operational decisions.

Since November 1975, when Secretary of Defense James Schlesinger resigned after President Ford agreed with Secretary of State Kissinger on the U.S. defense budget for fiscal 1977, scholars of nuclear strategy knew that their dispute reflected the Pentagon's proposals to increase greatly the American military establishment's role by changing from the concept of mutually assured destruction (MAD) to a "counterforce" strategy that envisioned both a limited and a winnable nuclear war.

In explaining Directive 59, Secretary Brown and President Carter insisted that the United States was not seeking a first-strike capacity. Brown said the U.S. strategy was to give the president options to use "countervailing" force, that is, the nuclear capacity to hit Soviet military targets or population centers and to do so at various levels of limited force that could be retaliatory but might be first strike. This selectivity of targets and force levels would permit U.S. and Soviet leaders to play a chesslike game during which each sought to calculate what level of nuclear attack would be sufficient to obtain the surrender of the enemy. Whether called "countervailing" or "counterforce," the strategy of Directive 59 reversed

the strategic concepts that supported nuclear parity, deterrence, and détente.

Since being described as MAD by Secretary of Defense Robert McNamara in 1967, the U.S. nuclear strategy of mutual deterrence as well as the Nixon-Kissinger détente and SALT I and SALT II programs had been based on limiting strategic nuclear arms and U.S. parity with the Soviets. In this context, Directive 59 suggested that the Carter administration had accepted the concept contained in the Republican platform of Ronald Reagan adopted during the July 1980 national convention. This platform called for a "clear capability to destroy [Soviet] military targets." Both this statement and the terminology and rhetoric used by the Republican right wing and by Secretary of Defense Brown confused rather than clarified the strategic substance of the two nuclear strategies: MAD and counterforce."

The counterforce strategy, which Pentagon officials claimed the Soviet military had also adopted, was based on a nuclear scenario totally different from mutual assured destruction. Under the MAD doctrine, each side possessed sufficient nuclear weapons to sustain a first strike and to retaliate against the other nation's population centers in sufficient destructive force to prevent either side from winning a nuclear war—hence, mutual assured destruction prevented war because each side was vulnerable, deterring either party from using such weapons. Nuclear war was considered to be a lose-lose contest.

During the 1970s, hawks in both the Soviet and U.S. military hierarchy began to consider the possibility of a LIMITED nuclear war, in which one side could force the other to surrender before striking back. The basic assumption was that if one power launched a nuclear first strike and knocked out a sufficient number of the enemy's nuclear weapons, the nation attacked might decide not to commit its nuclear weapons in a second strike and risk escalating the conflict to total nuclear war. Or as another scenario suggested, if both nations attacked the nuclear weapons, not the population, centers of each other, the country that sustained the greater damage would surrender to the other power. In either case, there were two presupposed results: (1) the nuclear war would be limited, and (2) one side would surrender, the other side would win; that is, the loser would be forced to follow the winner's orders. Hence, a winnable nuclear war.

Although the counterforce strategy included weapons to conduct first and, perhaps, second strikes against the enemy's nuclear-weapons bases, rather than its population centers, critics of counterforce claimed these assumptions were, like Dr. Strangelove's suicide-superbomb, based on a false premise. In reality, they said, any first strike would soon escalate the war to a global holocaust. Neither side would surrender as long as it held any nuclear retaliatory weapons. The first strike could never knock out all the nuclear warheads of the other side; so if one power dared to risk a nuclear attack, the war would lead to mutual destruction. What U.S. president, the critics said, would hesitate to strike back if his nation were attacked, especially if hesitation meant surrender to communism? Or what Communist leader would surrender as long as he had a few weapons left to unleash?

To the military planners in the Kremlin and the Pentagon, the counterforce strategy meant larger military budgets. For these hawks, MAD and parity resulted in an admittedly stable nuclear budget and their inability to employ their highest-priced and most sophisticated weapons. As a result, the Soviet and U.S. military searched for bigger and better weapons of greater accuracy and larger initial damage to be "certain" to destroy their opponent's "military targets"—weapons that deterrence strategy dictated they would never use.

Even before approving Directive 59, Carter steadily moved in the direction of the new strategy by approving the MX-mobile missile system on September 7, 1979. The MX was one Pentagon answer to the Soviets' large SS-18 and SS-19 intercontinental missiles. The MX bases would be mobile because the U.S. analysts expected that under the limited-war plan, the U.S. missiles would likely be used only on a second-strike basis. Mobility permitted the MX to evade destruction and required the Soviets to target more warheads to be certain to knock out all the MX weapons.

In addition to the MX missiles, the Pentagon developed more powerful and more accurate submarine missiles for its Trident submarines, including advanced Ballistic Reentry Systems for accuracy. The U.S. air force developed the Precision Guided Reentry Vehicle to give the MX great accuracy. This accuracy would provide a greater capability of destroying the weapons of the opponent.

In strategic terms, opponents of SALT II used the counterforce strategy to justify their claims that the Soviet Union was developing new weapons and strategy to endeavor to "win" a nuclear war. On August 5, Carter adopted the nuclear counterforce strategy. In part, the president's decision reflected the hard-line anti-Communist attitude he had adopted after January 4, 1980. Hard-liners in America believed if the Soviets thought they could "win," the United States must reciprocate and believe it could "win" a limited and survivable nuclear war.

As a follow-up to the new strategy, Secretary Brown told an audience at the Naval War College on August 20 that American ICBMs may now be vulnerable to Soviet missiles. Significantly, Brown did not mention the U.S. bomber force and the navy submarine missiles, both of which had missile-launching capacity that the Soviets could not knock out. As Brown's opponents emphasized, the Soviets relied almost completely on ICBMs, while the United States had a triad of excellent nuclear launchers that included submarine missiles, a large manned bomber force, and land-based ICBMs.

Also on August 20, the Pentagon announced it was developing the "stealth aircraft," a bomber invisible to Soviet radar because it would have aerodynamic and technical features enabling it to fly low and evade detection by the Soviet warning system. In both "stealth" and cruise missile technology, the United States had a significant edge on the Soviets.

### August 13, 1980

#### Polish strikes begin a crisis lasting until December 1981.

In addition to earlier smaller strikes in Poland, the large-scale strike of 70,000 workers began on August 13 at the Gdansk shipyard on the Baltic Sea. The Gdansk workers demanded an independent union and the reinstatement of the leader Lech Wałęsa who had been dismissed during 1970 protest demonstrations. In 1970, after Polish leader Gomułka authorized Polish military units to fire on unarmed strikers, killing 45 of them, the Communist Party replaced Gomułka with Edward Gierek.

In March 1980, a few dissidents protested working conditions, but serious turmoil began on July 18 after the government increased meat prices. On August 13, the Gdansk trade union began protests that drew more workers and protesters in other Polish cities during the next several months.

At first, Moscow believed strikers were led by diverse but divided groups of workers. Soviet intelligence reported that Wałęsa's Solidarity trade union was the largest group but was more moderate than the radical Committee for Workers Defense (KOR). In light of these reports, Gierek decided to compromise with an Interfactory Strike Committee representing 21 factories, including the Gdansk shipyard. On August 17, Gierek agreed to increase workers pay and later agreed that workers could form independent unions. Gierek's concessions alarmed Soviet leaders, who decided to replace him with Stanisław Kania as the Polish Communist Party's first secretary.

Kania accepted Gierek's compromises with the unions, enabling Wałęsa's union to form a charter and register officially ·in a Warsaw court as Solidarity. Wałęsa's charter was required to include a clause stating the Polish Communist Party had the "leading role" in union activities. Details on post–Cold War declassified data about Poland's 1980–1981 crisis are in the Cold War International History Project's *Bulletins* for Winter 1995–1996 and Winter 1998.

See December 14, 1970, and December 3, 1980.

### August 20, 1980

**The United States abstains on a U.N. Security Council resolution that censures Israel for annexing east Jerusalem and requests all nations to remove their embassies from Jerusalem.**

Significantly, the council vote demonstrated how Israel's West Bank policy isolated it from all other nations. The resolution vote was 14 in favor, none opposed, the United States abstaining. Soon after the resolution passed, 13 nations that had embassies in Jerusalem announced they would close them and relocate to Tel Aviv.

### August 25, 1980

**Ronald Reagan, the Republican party's presidential candidate, issues a "definitive" statement that he accepts the current unofficial relationship between the United States and Taiwan.**

Candidate Reagan issued the statement following news reports that Chinese officials in Beijing, meeting with Republican vice presidential nominee George Bush, told Bush that Reagan's previous views on Taiwan endangered Chinese-American relations and world peace.

Reagan had long been associated with right-wing Republican groups who supported Taiwan and opposed the recognition of mainland China. Until his statement of August 25, the presidential nominee's current views had not been clarified on the U.S. policy recognizing Beijing's status as China's government, and on the U.S. special legislation on Taiwan.

### August 27, 1980

*South Korean leader Chun Doo Hwan assumes the presidency.*

Following student uprisings in Seoul, Kwangju, and other towns, Chun, who had been made head of the Korean Central Intelligence Agency on April 14, forcefully to suppress the riots, close the universities, and extend martial law throughout South Korea. By August, Chun had solidified his power and conducted an election that guaranteed his victory and selection as president on August 27.

President Carter, who in his early years in office championed human rights, told a *Boston Globe* reporter that Chun "favors complete democracy" but "the Koreans are not ready for that, according to their own judgment."

### August 30, 1980

*The Polish government grants workers the right to strike and form independent unions.*

Attempting to meet some of the workers' demands and end extensive strikes, the Polish government yielded to two principal demands of the workers. These actions led Moscow to become more concerned about Poland's situation. On September 3, the Soviets loaned Poland $100 million in economic aid. They also decided that Edward Gierek should be dismissed as First Secretary of the Polish Communist Party.

By September 22, the unions had prepared a labor charter and registered in a Warsaw court as a united organization known as SOLIDARITY, with Lech Wałęsa as their leader. The Warsaw court legalized the union on October 24 with the provision that it recognize the Communist Party's "leading role" in Poland's unions.

Yet workers were not satisfied. Strike activity was renewed in 200 plants in Czestochowa and other, smaller cities on November 15. As a result, on November 19, under a threat of a national Solidarity strike, Poland's Supreme Court agreed to delete the lower court's wording on "the Communist Party's leading role," inserting the phrase in a separate protocol to the union charter.

Solidarity's demands put more pressure on the Polish government from Moscow where Soviet leaders watched to make certain that the party's compromises with Polish workers did not weaken its leading role in Polish society.

See December 3, 1980.

### September 4, 1980

*Iraq and Iran go to war as an Iraqi Army seizes 90 square miles of territory north of the Shatt Al Arab waterway.*

As the war began, there were immediate attempts by the PLO and the Arab League to mediate the boundary dispute, but to no avail. The United States and the Soviet Union both pledged neutrality in the conflict. The Iran-Iraqi conflict became a lengthy war of attrition with neither side willing to compromise or capable of launching a sustained major offensive to defeat the other.

### September 19, 1980

*Belgium government agrees to deploy 48 U.S. missiles if arms talks between the United States and the Soviets fail.*

### October 2, 1980

*The British Labour Party backs unilateral disarmament to prevent nuclear war.*

This was the first time in 20 years that the leftist faction gained sufficient votes in the Labour Party Convention to pass a resolution for unilateral disarmament. This vote was also a sign of the split developing between moderates and radicals in that party. On November 10, 1980, Michael Foot, a radical Laborite, was named as the British Labour Party Chief.

### October 5, 1980

*In West German elections, Helmut Schmidt's Democratic Coalition wins.*

As a result, Schmidt was reelected as the West German chancellor on November 5, 1980.

### October 13, 1980

*The Marshall Islands and the Federated States of Micronesia accept a "free association" accord with the United States.*

These Pacific islands had been under U.S. trusteeship with the United Nations. They now assumed a semi-independent status. The Federated States included the islands of Truk, Yap, Ponape, and Kosrae. On November 15, 1980, a similar accord was signed by the island Republic of Palau.

### October 17, 1980

*The Soviet Union and the United States begin talks on limiting theater nuclear forces (TNF).*

Although President Brezhnev told the State Department on January 3 that the TNF talks on long-range intermediate missiles in Europe could not be successful, discussions began on October 17, and the first round of discussions ended on November 17. The Soviets wanted the United States and NATO to renounce the December 1979 decision to deploy Pershing II and cruise missiles prior to negotiations. After the United States refused, the talks began but under difficulties that handicapped their success. Although no results were achieved by November 17, NATO's Nuclear

Planning Group met on November 14 and approved the current U.S. nuclear strategy.

See February 26, 1981.

### October 22, 1980

**The United States signs a grain purchase agreement with China.**

According to this grain accord, China would purchase up to nine million tons of grain annually over the next four years. The grain purchase pact helped Carter's presidential campaign because U.S. farmers had complained of price decreases resulting from the Soviet grain embargo imposed by the president in January 1980.

### October 24, 1980

**_Greece rejoins NATO after its parliament approves a compromise agreement on Turkey._**

The Cypriot crisis between Turkey and Greece had led Athens to withdraw its military cooperation with NATO to defend the Aegean Sea area in coordination with Turkey. Stressing the need to strengthen the Western alliance in light of the Iranian and Afghanistan conflicts, the U.S. and Turkish governments made concessions to Greece to obtain its re-entry into NATO. Greece and Turkey still had to negotiate the details of their NATO cooperation in the Aegean.

### November 4, 1980

**Ronald W. Reagan is elected president, winning a clear-cut victory over President Carter.**

Former governor of California and spokesman for conservative groups in the Republican Party, Reagan won the nomination at the national convention in Detroit on July 17. President Carter was nominated by the Democratic Convention in New York on August 14. While Carter ran on his record, Reagan campaigned on a platform emphasizing the renewal of America's preeminent military position against the Soviets and the return to concepts of supply-side economics that would supposedly stimulate business investments, thereby revitalizing the economy.

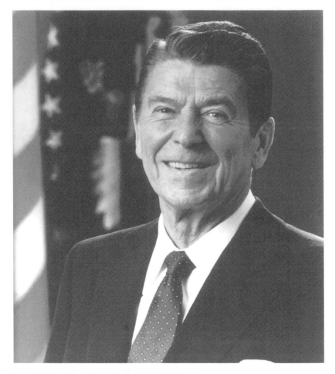

Ronald W. Reagan. National Archives

In the election, Reagan won 489 electoral votes to Carter's 49. The Republicans gained control of the Senate by a six-vote majority; the Democrats retained control of the House with a 57-vote majority.

### November 11, 1980

**Signs of a possible settlement with Iran appear as the United States begins talks in Algeria, whose government agrees to act as an intermediary with Iran.**

The initial indication that Iran might discuss a solution to the hostage crisis came on September 12, 1980, when the Ayatollah Khomeini announced four conditions for the release of the Americans. His terms were to return the shah's wealth, cancel U.S. claims against Iran, unfreeze Iranian assets, and promise future non-interference in Iran. The Carter administration approached Khomeini's announcement cautiously, not wishing to raise unfounded hopes among Americans.

On October 21, after President Bani-Sadr repeated Khomeini's terms, Carter pledged he would unfreeze the assets and end U.S. sanctions. He had agreed to noninterference in Iran on several occasions in the past. Carter also asked Tehran to begin direct negotiations to settle the hostage crisis. Bani-Sadr refused to negotiate directly.

The final steps toward Algeria's offer to act as a go-between were taken on November 2 and 3, when the Iranian Majlis (parliament) approved Khomeini's four terms and the student militants at the U.S. embassy agreed to transfer "responsibility" for the hostages to the government.

The next act was up to the United States. On November 11, Deputy Secretary of State Warren Christopher went to Algiers for a 30-hour talk with Algerian representatives. Christopher explained the U.S. position; the Algerians agreed to convey the details of the U.S. response to Tehran. The process that finally gained the hostages' release had begun.

See January 20, 1981.

## November 28, 1980

**Senator Charles Percy meets with Leonid Brezhnev in Moscow, reporting that the Soviets would like to start SALT III talks as soon as possible.**

Percy, who became the chairman of the Senate Foreign Relations Committee in January 1981, was the first high U.S. official to speak with Brezhnev since Carter signed SALT II in June 1979. During his week in Moscow, Percy talked for about 10 hours with Brezhnev and other officials. They discussed Poland, Afghanistan, and oil, as well as arms limitations. Percy also appeared on Soviet national television. Although the Illinois senator told the Soviets that SALT II was dead regarding Senate ratification, Brezhnev indicated he was ready to begin new talks on another strategic arms treaty.

## December 3, 1980

**President Carter is concerned about Poland owing to rumors of Soviet intervention.**

Although Poland's Supreme Court recognized Solidarity (see August 30, 1980), the Soviet Union closed Poland's borders with East Germany, and on December 1 the Polish Communist Party's Central Committee removed four members from the Politburo, ostensibly in response to orders from Moscow. In this tense atmosphere, U.S. support for Solidarity led President Carter to announce U.S. concern for the "unprecedented" build-up of 55,000 Soviet troops along Poland's borders. On December

12, NATO adopted a U.S. proposal to warn the Soviet Union that invading Poland would end the détente policies adopted in the 1970s.

Meanwhile on December 5, Stanisław Kania, the first secretary of Poland's Communist Party (Polish United Workers Party), met with Warsaw Pact members in Moscow. Although Poland's neighbors in the Warsaw Pact feared the spillover of Solidarity's independence, the allies agreed with Kania's proposal to resolve the crisis by making no more concessions to the "anti-socialist elements" in Polish society and using Polish security forces to "normalize" the situation. By December 12, Kania told union leaders to end the strikes and he would meet with union organizer Lech Wałęsa to discuss the union's future. In addition, Poland's Catholic Church asked dissidents to avoid provocative acts. Kania labeled the Western media reports of recent events a "hysterical campaign" with no factual basis, although Poland's crisis was ongoing. Declassified documents on Poland are in the Cold War International History Project's *Bulletin* (Winter 1998).

See August 13, 1980, and February 9, 1981.

## December 4, 1980

**As right-wing violence increases in El Salvador, the bodies of four U.S. women missionaries are found near San Salvador.**

The bodies found were those of three Roman Catholic nuns and one lay worker. Their van had been ambushed and the women killed. The Carter administration called for the suspension of $25 million in aid to El Salvador and asked for a thorough investigation because Salvadorean security forces were allegedly involved in the murder.

Just six days before, rightist terrorists had attacked a meeting of the Democratic Revolutionary Front at a San Salvador high school. They dragged away 24 persons while 200 members of the National Guard and police stood by. The bodies of the six leftist leaders were dumped outside the city, including those of the front's president, Enrique Alvarez Córdova, and of the Popular Revolutionary Bloc's leader, Juan Chacon.

Carter had been providing only nonlethal aid to El Salvador because of the government's human rights violations. There had been 8,000 political killings in El Salvador during 11 months of 1980. In November, however, a group of right-wing

Salvadoreans had met with President-elect Reagan, reporting afterward that the new administration seemed more receptive to their military aid requests. On January 18, 1981, Carter authorized sending El Salvador $5 million of combat equipment. Reagan followed with another $25 million and 20 military advisers on March 2, 1981.

### December 6, 1980

**Reagan issues a statement backing the Camp David Accords as a continued basis for Middle East peace.**

The U.S. Special Representative for the Middle East, Sol M. Lenowitz, indicated that the president-elect assured him he backed the autonomy talks between Egypt and Israel, although they had not borne fruit in 1980. On December 18, Lenowitz ended a visit to Cairo and Tel Aviv by reading a statement in which both Egyptian President Sadat and Israeli Prime Minister Begin reaffirmed the Camp David accords. On December 27, however, Cairo asked to delay the autonomy talks, which were set to resume on January 13. The Egyptians gave no reason for the delay.

### December 11, 1980

**War between Syria and Jordan is averted after both nations pull their forces back from the border.**

On November 29, Syria reportedly had 35,000 troops ready to invade Jordan because King Hussein conducted an Arab League meeting in Amman that had been boycotted by the radical Arab nations, including Syria. Jordan retaliated by sending 24,000 troops to its border with Syria and, on December 1, asked the United States to rush arms deliveries to Amman.

The crisis ended, however, because King Khalid of Saudi Arabia intervened, calming both Arab states. On December 10, Syrian forces withdrew from the border; the next day, Jordan's forces drew back. Allegedly, Syria feared that Hussein and the Saudis might agree to join Egypt in negotiating with Israel. This fear did not materialize.

### December 16, 1980

**Meeting in Bali, the OPEC nations announce another increase of oil prices to a maximum of $41 per barrel.**

This was the third significant oil price increase in 1980. On January 27, Saudi Arabia and other states had increased prices to $26; on May 14, the price went to $28; and on June 10, it rose to $30 per barrel.

# 1981

### January 3, 1981

**In El Salvador, right-wing assassins kill the head of the government's land reform program and two U.S. agricultural experts.**

Those assassinated were José Rodolfo Vivera and two Americans, Michael P. Hammer and Mark David Pearlman. The three were killed while eating dinner in San Salvador's Sheraton Hotel.

The killing of the land reform head in El Salvador raised questions about the success of the program during the nine months since it began. Thus far only 15% of the land was affected, leaving 85% of the coffee, 75% of the cotton, and 60% of sugarcane production in the hands of a few wealthy families. Most peasants were still landless, while others were members of cooperative groups formed to organize production on the former plantations. Apparently, some co-ops managed well, such as one at San Isidro. Others, such as one at El Penon, had to pay much of its profit in protection money to the local military commander and soldiers who "guarded" the ranch.

Since March 1979, right-wing groups opposing land reform had killed 200 peasant cooperative leaders and five farm institute employees. With the slaying of Vivera, the rightists got rid of the principal architect of the land program.

### January 20, 1981

**The American hostages are freed, leaving Tehran for Algeria just minutes after President Reagan is sworn in as president.**

The use of Algerian officials as intermediaries between Tehran and Washington began on November 11,

President Carter meets the
hostages returning from Iran.
Jimmy Carter Library

1980, and proved successful on January 19, 1981. Initially, it appeared that Khomeini was ready to release the American hostages before Christmas Day, but his demand for $9 billion was rejected by President Carter as "ransom," which the United States would not pay.

On December 30, the U.S. negotiator, Warren Christopher, met with the Algerians and worked out a plan to place $5 billion in an escrow account at the time the hostages were released. Under Carter's instruction, Christopher set a deadline for the offer of January 16, warning that when the new president replaced Carter on January 20, negotiations on the hostages would have to begin anew. President-elect Reagan had given a qualified approval to fulfill any terms worked out by Carter, but he would not give Iran a "blank check." Reagan's reputation as a hard-liner in foreign relations probably led the Iranians to decide to end the discussions with Carter rather than take a chance on the new president.

Subsequently, on January 3, the Algerians gave the U.S. proposal to Tehran. Khomeini accepted Algeria's offer to act as the guarantor of the hostage accord, and on January 14, Iran's Majlis (parliament) approved a bill authorizing the government to conduct binding negotiations with the United States. By January 16, 1981, Iranian officers told Algiers there were no further obstacles to the hostages' release, and the

final details of the financial and legal terms of the accords had to be worked out in Algiers by British and American financial and legal experts. The accords were signed by Christopher on January 19. The next day, the 52 hostages flew from Iran to Algeria, ending 444 days of captivity. They were transferred to U.S. custody and flown to American military hospitals in Wiesbaden, Germany. On January 21, former President Carter flew to Germany and visited with the former captives.

The important terms of the Iranian-American agreements included what experts called the biggest single financial transaction in history. First, $8 billion was assembled in the Bank of England from $11 to $12 billion of the Iranian assets in the United States. Of that total, $5.5 billion was deposited in foreign branches of U.S. banks and $2.5 billion was in gold and securities in the Federal Reserve Bank of New York.

As soon as the hostages were released, Iran received nearly $2.9 billion; U.S. and some foreign banks got $3.6 billion in loan repayments due from Iran. The balance of $1.5 billion went into an escrow account to settle disputes between the Western banks and Iran over loans and interest.

Other financial transactions would follow. Iran would get another $1 to $2 billion from its various U.S. assets. Iranian bank deposits of about $2.2 billion would go to the Bank of England, which would put another $1 billion into the escrow account for other U.S. claims against Iran.

After this complex arrangement resolved the issues of the shah's assets in the United States and U.S. claims against Iran, the other condition set by Iran was comparatively simple to agree on: the U.S. promise not to interfere in Iranian affairs.

## XVI. THE REAGAN YEARS

### *End of the Cold War*

# 1981

### January 20, 1981

**Ronald Wilson Reagan inaugurated president;
Alexander Haig becomes secretary of state.**

The inauguration of President Reagan occurred just
minutes after Iran freed the U.S. hostages it had
held since November 1979. The next day the U.S.
Senate confirmed Alexander M. HAIG, Jr. as secretary of state. A West Point graduate, Haig served in
Vietnam and at the National Security Council before
becoming President Nixon's White House chief of
staff in May 1973 and NATO commander in the fall
of 1974.

   Haig shared President Reagan's belief that Soviet
communism was the source of all global problems. In
his inaugural address, Reagan pledged to renew U.S.
military power and global prestige. His initial budget
called for income tax reductions of 30 percent, cutting
social programs, and rebuilding the nation's military
power to assure superiority over the Soviet Union. In
a speech at West Point on May 27, 1981, Reagan
claimed that the USSR was an "evil empire" that
desired to destroy America.

   See November 4, 1979, and January 20, 1981, for
   details of the hostages' capture and release.

### January 24, 1981

**South Korea ends martial law.**

President Chun Doo Hwan announced the end of
South Korea's martial law that he imposed on May
17, 1980, to end disorders following the assassination
of President Tongsun Park. Chun's decision came just

before he left Korea to visit the United States. At the
White House on February 3, President Reagan praised
the move toward democracy and promised to keep
39,000 U.S. troops in South Korea, an issue of concern
to Seoul because President Carter had suggested withdrawing 30,000 of those troops. On February 25, 1981,

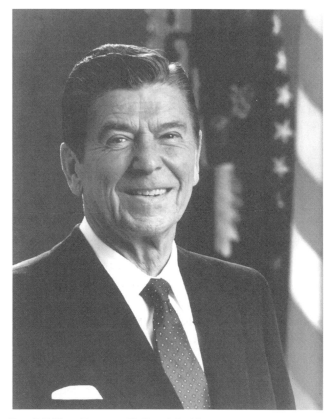

Ronald Wilson Reagan. National Archives

President Chun was reelected to another seven-year term.

See October 26, 1979, and August 27, 1980; see also March 9, 1977.

## January 28, 1981

### Border war between Peru and Ecuador.

Ecuador had claimed an area of Peru near the Amazon River since the 1930s. The two countries had subsequently accepted a border under the Rio Protocol of 1942. However, after productive oil wells were drilled in the area, Ecuador again sought to extend its border and built an armed camp in the disputed area during 1980. When Peru sought to evict those troops, war broke out.

Acting as guarantors of the 1942 protocol, the United States, Argentina, Brazil, and Chile intervened and achieved a cease-fire by February 1. Tension continued between Quito and Lima, and the four powers had to continue to oversee their behavior for another four years.

## January 29, 1981

### The United States is dissatisfied when Japan does not meet U.S. requests to increase its defense budget.

As the U.S. economy experienced hard times during the late 1970s and the 1980s, U.S. presidents looked for larger defense expenditures by its NATO allies and Japan to share the Cold War burdens.

When the Japanese defense minister Joji Omura visited Washington at the end of January 1981, U.S. Secretary of Defense Caspar WEINBERGER informed him that the United States had expected Japan's current budget (approved in Tokyo on January 13) to increased by 11%. Yet it had been increased by only 7.6%, to $12 billion. Because Japan had spent so little on defense since 1945, U.S. defense managers believed immediate expenditures were essential. American strategy envisioned a Japanese defense force able to defend a perimeter of 1,000 miles around the Japanese shores if the Soviet Union attacked.

Both in Washington and upon his return home, Omura resisted demands for a more rapid defense buildup. Subsequently, Japan and the Reagan administration were often at odds over these defense costs, especially after President Reagan undertook a gigantic leap in U.S. military expenditures from 1981 to 1984.

## January 29, 1981

### Philippine President Ferdinand E. Marcos announces he will seek reelection on an April 7 ballot.

Prior to the April election, Marcos endeavored to promote his candidacy. On January 17, 1981, he ended martial law, which had been imposed in 1972, and gave more power back to the National Assembly. He also set up an electoral commission to conduct the election.

Marcos's actions did not satisfy the opposition, however. They complained that the commission would not guarantee an honest election and boycotted the April 7 election. As a result, Marcos easily won another six-year term because 6 million voters joined the boycott.

## February 1, 1981

### Ambassador to El Salvador Robert E. White is replaced because he publicly criticized the Salvadoran government.

Ambassador White had become increasingly dismayed with President José Napoleon Duarte's inept handling of land reform and his failure to control the Salvadoran military from committing atrocities against peasants and the opposition. President Reagan then named a career officer, Frederic Chapin, to be ambassador.

Like the Carter administration since 1979, Reagan's administration conceived of Duarte as a moderate non-Marxist. Duarte spoke like a reform moderate who realized that the rich fought to deny any benefits to the poor, and he advocated giving land to the peasants. But his efforts at land reform were limited. Even worse, rather than controlling the military, he collaborated with the generals who made him president in 1979. Other civilian reformers had resigned from the government to protest the continued personal power of the defense minister, Colonel José Guillermo García, who, in the view of many, used Duarte to hide military crimes and corruption.

Two rebel groups opposed the junta that gained power in 1979: the radical Farabundo Marti National Liberation Front (FMLN), made up of five guerrilla factions; and the Democratic Revolutionary Front (FDR), which coordinated efforts of forty groups ranging from priests and the professional middle class to

Social Democrats and Christian Democrats, including some guerrilla forces.

The FDR's first president was Enrique Alvarez Cordova, a wealthy landowner who resigned as minister of agriculture because the junta was dominated by the military.

In November 1980, Alvarez and five other FDR leaders were assassinated by uniformed soldiers who attacked the Jesuit high school where the leaders met. The successor to Alvarez was Guillermo Manuel Ungo, a lawyer and professor at El Salvador's Catholic University. Because he had been threatened with assassination, Ungo traveled abroad to seek support for the FDR. Ungo claimed to favor socialist democracy but not communism.

In this context, Ambassador White became a critic of El Salvador's military order and of Duarte's inability to control them. Nevertheless, the Reagan administration believed Duarte was the most likely moderate candidate available for El Salvador.

**February 9, 1981**

### Secretary of State Alexander Haig and Secretary of Defense Caspar Weinberger formulate a plan to cooperate in policy formulation.

In national security decisions, increased friction had arisen during the past 20 years between the roles of the Departments of State and Defense and the National Security Council. Hoping to avoid the disparities in policy planning that he experienced during his service in the Nixon administration, Haig obtained President Reagan's permission to clarify the role of the State Department in such undertakings.

Subsequently, on February 9, Haig and Weinberger agreed to give the State Department the leading role in most foreign policy matters, while the Defense Department retained some statutes by working through interagency committees operating out of the Pentagon. In addition, Haig and Weinberger

Left to right: Edwin Meese, Secretary of Defense Caspar Weinberger, President Reagan, Vice President George H. W. Bush, Secretary of State Alexander Haig. Ronald Reagan Library

agreed to schedule frequent meetings to discuss policies.

In particular, this formulation delegated the National Security Council to the lesser role of coordinating preparations of the two departments. The new national security adviser, Richard Allen, accepted the lesser role, but the NSC staff disliked this subordination, and Allen's successor would seek to strengthen its position.

See March 24, 1981; see also January 4, 1982.

## February 9, 1981

### Polish Defense Minister Wojciech Jaruzelski becomes prime minister.

Since August 1980, the Solidarity trade union movement had staged strikes, and protests disrupted Poland, leading to the threat of Soviet military intervention. On January 5, Solidarity leader Lech Wałęsa met with government officials, but they failed to agree on worker's demands such as a five-day workweek.

To end the disorder, JARUZELSKI took the post of Prime Minister after firing Józef Pinkowski and asked the workers, students, and middle-class demonstrators to give him "ninety days of peace" to bring reforms. On February 18, some student groups gained the right to form a union, and some farmers reached accords with the government on farm prices.

See March 30, 1981.

## February 18, 1981

### President Reagan calls for tax cuts, lower welfare costs, and increased defense expenditures.

Pursuing his election campaign messages of an income tax cut, less welfare, and regaining military superiority over the Soviet Union, Reagan proposed to Congress in his state of the union message a 30% income tax cut over three years with rates on high incomes being trimmed the most to stimulate investment. He requested national defense outlays of $181.5 billion, increasing by $35 billion the amount President Carter had sought for fiscal year 1982.

Between May 20 and August 13, Congress approved most of Reagan's request. Taxes were cut by 25% over three years, social programs cut by $36 billion, and military expenses increased by $25 billion to $188 billion for the year.

The national debt reached a landmark during 1981. On September 29, Congress raised the debt ceiling to over $1 trillion—to $1,079,000,000,000. During the next four years this debt doubled to over $2 trillion.

See November 14, 1985.

## February 23, 1981

### The State Department reports that the Soviet Union and Cuba give "massive" aid to rebels in El Salvador.

Release of the State Department report "Communist Interference in El Salvador" launched an extensive U.S. campaign to assist the government of El Salvador in defeating left-wing rebels. The report called the rebellion a "textbook case" of a major Soviet thrust in Central America. On February 22, the White House warned Cuba against sending arms to Salvadoran rebels, declaring a U.S. naval blockade would be used if necessary. Together, these actions implemented a decision President-elect Reagan reportedly had made in December to make El Salvador a testing ground for displaying U.S. willingness to counteract communist aggression. Thus, El Salvador's rebellion became part of the larger East-West struggle.

When the left-wing rebellion in El Salvador began during the 1970s, President Carter had assisted the government while urging it to enact economic, social, and political reforms. When a land-reform campaign began, however, right-wing groups in the army and government became active in limiting or stopping the reformers. In 1980 and early 1981, advocates of reform including a Roman Catholic archbishop, four American missionary nurses, and two agricultural experts were assassinated. President Carter cut off U.S. aid after the murders, but on January 11, 1981, he resumed nonlethal aid after the rebels launched a new offensive against the government. On January 18, Carter released $5 million of military aid to help El Salvador fight the rebels.

Against this background, Reagan decided to scrap Carter's emphasis on political and human rights reforms and to send more military aid to El Salvador. Thus, the State Department report justified Reagan's future aid program to El Salvador.

Although many investigative journalists, including one from the *Wall Street Journal*, argued that the report exaggerated Soviet involvement, the State

Department defended its February 23 report in a subsequent report of June 18, 1981.

See March 6 and 24, 1980; December 4, 1980; and January 3, 1981; for subsequent U.S. aid to El Salvador, see February 1, 1981, and March 2, 1981.

### February 24, 1981

*A right-wing coup fails in Spain.*

For 18 hours beginning February 23, members of the Spanish Civil Guard held hostage 345 deputies of the Spanish Cortes (parliament) while demanding a strong military leader to replace Premier Adolfo Suarez, who had resigned on January 30. The Cortes was in session to select a new ministry. The coup ended after King Juan Carlos ordered the civil guardsmen, under Lt. Col. Antonio Tejero Molina, to surrender. Following the coup, the Cortes elected Leopoldo Calvo Sotels as premier.

### February 25, 1981

**The United States vetoes U.N. human rights report that cites Chile and other U.S. allies for violations.**

President Reagan had appointed Jeane KIRKPATRICK as America's U.N. delegate because he accepted her belief that human rights shortcomings of right-wing "authoritarian" regimes were not as bad as those of a left-wing "totalitarian" government because the former permitted reform toward democracy. This position differed from that of the Carter administration, which argued that all violations were equally bad and advocated the adoption of reforms by U.S. friends as well as foes. The policy change began when Ambassador Kirkpatrick vetoed this UN report.

Chile was one such authoritarian regime that Reagan preferred to assist rather than reform. On July 1, 1981, the President used this rationale to provide development loans to Chile.

Jeane Kirkpatrick, U.S. ambassador to the United Nations, receives a Medal of Freedom from President Reagan (April 22, 1981). Ronald Reagan Library

## February 26, 1981

### President Reagan affirms NATO's 1979 decision to modernize long-range theater nuclear forces parallel with arms control negotiations.

Based on the belief that recently deployed Soviet intermediate-range missiles gave the communists strategic advantages in Europe, the North Atlantic Treaty Organization prepared to deploy Pershing II and cruise missiles while simultaneously conducting arms talks for reducing long-range theater nuclear forces (LRTNF) missiles. The Pershing II and the Soviets' SS-20s both had range estimates of about 5,000 kilometers, a distance so close to the 5,500 kilometers attributed to Intercontinental Ballistic Missiles (ICBM) that the term LRTNF better described them. Missiles with ranges under 5,000 kilometers were also called Intermediate Range Missiles.

The NATO "dual track" agreement had the support of Secretary of State Haig, who advocated close consultation with NATO allies, in contrast with Secretary of Defense Weinberger's desire to act unilaterally and ignore allied viewpoints, as well as to minimize arms control talks. In brief, Haig preferred the détente spirit of the 1970s; Weinberger wished to revive the Republican Party's preference for unilateral action to achieve U.S. military primacy.

Reagan's statement to affirm the NATO dual track was made during a White House meeting with British Prime Minister Margaret Thatcher. According to the *Time* magazine reporter Strobe Talbott, the statement was inserted in the speech by one of Secretary Haig's friends on the National Security Council.

Whatever the circumstances, Reagan's public statement clearly connected his administration with NATO's position that required the early continuance of arms talks with the Soviet Union. On May 20–22, during White House meetings with West German Chancellor Helmut Schmidt, Reagan repeated his support for the dual track. At Schmidt's urging, Reagan said the United States would begin arms talks before the year ended.

For NATO's 1979 decision, see August 6, 1979, and November 18, 1981.

## March 1, 1981

### President Reagan considers sending U.S. armaments to help rebels in Afghanistan.

Although President Carter had previously sent $60 million of arms to the Afghan rebels opposing the Soviet intervention in their country, Reagan's first statement was to "consider sending" aid to the Afghan mujahideen rebels against Babrak Karmal's government, which had been installed by the Soviet army. Reagan's comment responded to Soviet leader Leonid Brezhnev's announcement on February 26 that Soviet troops would stay in Afghanistan until "outside aggression" ended. Brezhnev voiced Moscow's propaganda line that the United States used Afghan rebels to support Western imperialist expansion.

In contrast to "consider sending," both Reagan and Carter sent CIA agents who infiltrated via Pakistan to assist the Afghan guerrillas. In addition to aiding the rebels, the Reagan administration claimed that the Soviet Union used chemical weapons in Afghanistan.

See June 15 and September 13, 1981.

## March 2, 1981

### The Reagan administration increases assistance for El Salvador's fight against left-wing rebels.

Acting according to prior assertions that Communists in Cuba and the Soviet Union were giving massive aid to El Salvador's rebels, the State Department stated that $25 million in military equipment and 20 additional military advisers would be sent to El Salvador. By March 22, there were 56 American advisers in that country.

On March 4, after the Salvadoran right-wing leader Roberto d'Aubuisson boasted that the CIA aided him, Secretary of State Haig warned against a right-wing coup to overthrow President Duarte.

On March 6, following public criticism that he was embroiling the nation in another foreign intervention, President Reagan defended his aid to El Salvador but said it would not be another Vietnam.

See February 23, 1981.

## March 3, 1981

**The State Department announces U.S. adherence to both strategic arms limitation treaties (SALT I and SALT II) provided the Soviet Union adheres.**

The United States and the Soviet Union had ratified SALT I, but following the signing of SALT II in 1978, President Carter withdrew the treaty from Senate consideration after Soviet armies intervened in Afghanistan in 1979.

Coming in the late stages of the Vietnam War, SALT I and the Anti-Ballistic Missile Treaty (ABM) of 1972 had not drawn much public attention. Based on the concept of mutual assured destruction (MAD), in which no one could win a nuclear war, SALT I and the ABM treaty were intended as first steps to further missile limitation.

By the time SALT II was signed by Carter and Brezhnev in 1979, many conservatives in the United States criticized the arms limits as benefiting the communists, while some strategic theorists conjectured that in a carefully calculated nuclear exchange it was possible to "win" a nuclear war. This theory led its advocates to criticize SALT II as favoring the Soviets because presumably they had more advanced missiles with greater accuracy, which carried up to ten separate nuclear warheads apiece. Consequently in 1979, Ronald Reagan and other conservatives had opposed SALT II, even before the Soviets intervened in Afghanistan.

On March 3, however, the Reagan administration decided to abide by the SALT II agreements pending further strategic arms talks with Moscow, provided the USSR did the same.

On SALT I see March 14 and November 17, 1969, and November 24, 1974; on SALT II, see June 18, 1979, and January 2, 1980; and on MAD, see January 26, 1967.

## March 3, 1981

**President Reagan rejects the Law of the Sea Treaty negotiated by a U.N. commission during Carter's presidency.**

At a conference in Geneva during which the United Nations Commission on Law of the Sea hoped to conclude a previously prepared treaty, President Reagan instructed the U.S. delegation to oppose the finalization of the work, saying the new president wished to review the document more thoroughly.

George Taft, a State Department attorney who had worked on the treaty, told congressional committees that Reagan, in particular, wanted guarantees that U.S. companies would have access to seabed mining.

Soon after the Geneva meeting, Taft and George P. Oldrick, who had directed the U.S. delegation under the Carter administration, were replaced by Reagan appointees, and James L. Malone became the delegation head on May 8, 1981. The review that Reagan wanted had allegedly not yet been completed when the U.N. Commission met in August and the Law of the Sea proposals were delayed again.

See December 9, 1981.

## March 4, 1981

**Mozambique expels three American diplomats it accuses of spying; the United States stops food assistance.**

On January 30, 1981, South African armed forces had raided Maputo, the capital of Mozambique, where, they claimed, the African National Congress (ANC) had its headquarters. In Johannesburg, South African forces claimed they had killed many ANC "terrorists" and destroyed the headquarters of the group, which led the black South Africans' struggle for equality and the right of majority rule.

Before cutting food assistance and revoking a $5 million credit line for Mozambique, the U.S. State Department offered an unusual explanation for the spying charge. On March 5, the U.S. said that Cuban agents had tried to force the three diplomats to obtain secret information, and when the ploy failed, Cuba pushed Mozambique into condemning the Americans, a scenario that Mozambique and Cuba denied. The three U.S. diplomats were Frederick Bryce Lundahl, Louis Leon Oliver, and Arthur F. Russel, whose wife, Patricia, was also expelled.

## March 6, 1981

**Before leaving for a Canadian visit, President Reagan asks the Senate to approve a Canadian-U.S. boundary treaty.**

The boundary treaty involved agreeing on the boundary line for the Gulf of Maine. When the Senate voted its approval unanimously on May 2, it added an amendment that left the final boundary settlement to a decision of the International Court of Justice, a condition Canada accepted.

See October 12, 1984.

### March 7, 1981

**Chester A. Bitterman, a U.S. adviser in Colombia, is killed by the left-wing M-19 movement.**

On January 19, Bitterman was abducted from an American language school, the Summer Language Institute, by five hooded gunmen. The M-19 group said Bitterman was a CIA spy who would be released if Colombia expelled the institute, for which Bitterman was an adviser. The leftists thought all U.S. missionaries should leave Colombia, and the institute was funded by the Southern Baptists Foreign Mission Board. The institute refused to close, and following several threats, the M-19 kidnappers executed Bitterman.

### March 9, 1981

**President Reagan rejects a Soviet request for a moratorium on deployment of medium-range missiles in Europe.**

At a session of the 26th Communist Party Congress on February 26, Soviet leader Leonid Brezhnev proposed a ban on future missile deployment in Europe. Brezhnev then wrote letters to the United States and other NATO nations requesting a meeting to accept his missile freeze. President Reagan rejected such a meeting and Secretary of State Haig said a freeze would weaken the deterrent strength of Western Europe.

On March 31, 1981, a NATO Special Consultative Group meeting in Brussels also opposed Brezhnev's request. The NATO communiqué said the USSR had already deployed 222 SS-20 missiles aimed at Western Europe. Therefore, a missile freeze would leave NATO without any means to deter the SS-20s.

### March 16, 1981

**Egypt provides military aid to Chad's rebels in their conflict with Libya.**

Although Chad's President Goukouni Oueddi had agreed on January 11, 1981, to merge his country with Libya, many of Chad's political leaders rejected Libyan President Mu'ammar al-Gadhafi's attempt to annex this former French colony. Egypt, which had many complaints against Libya, agreed to aid the Chadian rebels.

### March 19, 1981

**President Reagan assures the People's Republic of China (PRC) that he will not jeopardize its ties with the United States.**

Because President Reagan had been a staunch supporter of the Republic of China (ROC) on Taiwan prior to his 1980 election, the PRC perceived Reagan's policies with great suspicion. For example, when the Netherlands sold two submarines to the ROC on January 18, Beijing blamed the U.S. government.

To stabilize or improve U.S. relations with the PRC, Secretary of State Haig urged the president to reassure the mainland Chinese. Thus, on March 19, Reagan met with PRC Ambassador Choi Zemin, to whom the president explained his desire for good relations with Beijing.

As a follow-up to this session, former President Gerald Ford visited China on March 23, where he expressed the same desire for good relations to China's leader, Deng Xiaoping. Ford was reported to have recommended that the United States sell armaments to the PRC.

See June 16, 1981.

### March 20, 1981

**Initial meeting of the International Congress of Physicians for Prevention of Nuclear War.**

Because in both superpowers, the United States and the USSR, strategists sometimes talked about a winnable nuclear war, many groups in the early 1980s formulated plans to challenge the idea that any nation could win a nuclear war. Moreover, they hoped to convince their audiences that nuclear armaments were wasteful for all nations.

One such group was made up of physicians headed by Harvard cardiologists Bernard Lown and James Muller, who prepared for this first conference to discuss methods for preventing war. Participants came from Japan, France, Britain, the United States, and the Soviet Union to discuss the medical effects of small atomic warheads dropped on the Japanese cities of Hiroshima and Nagasaki in 1945. These specialists described the effects that thermonuclear war could have on human life and society.

The U.S. experts pointed out that a 20-megaton nuclear warhead was 1,000 times as powerful as the bomb that flattened Hiroshima. If such a warhead were dropped on Boston, the blast would destroy everything in a four-mile radius and fire storms would devastate everything within a ten-mile radius. Of Boston's 3 million metropolitan population, about 2.2 million would be killed, while the survivors would be maimed, burned, or in shock. Moreover, the survivors likely would develop new, virtually incurable ailments from radiation poisoning and contaminated food and water. Perhaps 900 out of 6,000 Boston physicians would survive, but their medical centers would not.

### March 21, 1981

### European antimissile demonstrations annoy the Reagan administration.

A pacifist and antinuclear movement had been growing in Western Europe ever since the NATO decision to follow the dual-track ruling of preparing to deploy Pershing and cruise missiles in Europe. In January and March, large demonstrations took place in many of the cities of Sweden, Norway, Denmark, Holland, and Belgium. In West Germany, plans were underway for an April 4 demonstration in Bonn, which attracted over 15,000 marchers.

On March 21, National Security Adviser Richard V. Allen severely criticized the European protests.

### March 24, 1981

### Vice President George Bush is named to head a crisis-management team.

Although Secretary of State Haig was told by President Reagan that this announcement meant only that Bush would be chairman of the National Security Council in the president's absence, the arrangement was not satisfactory to Haig. The news of the title "head of crisis-management team" appears to have been devised by President Reagan's White House "troika" of Edwin Meese III, Counselor to the President; James Baker III, Chief of Staff; and Michael Deaver, White House Aid, to let Haig know he could not control the White House.

In his memoirs, Secretary Haig claims that his agreement with Defense Secretary Weinberger was

Vice President George H. W. Bush. National Archives

simply to clarify policies, plans, and lines of authority. Edwin Meese and many of Reagan's "California" friends disliked the Pennsylvanian Haig's attitudes and viewed his actions as his quest for increased power.

Although Haig wrote a letter of resignation following the March 24 incident, Reagan reassured him that he should stay in office. Nevertheless, Haig did not fit in with Reagan's White House team and eventually resigned in 1982.

See February 9, 1981, and June 25, 1982.

### March 30, 1981

## Assassination attempt on President Reagan fails.

As Reagan left the Washington Hilton Hotel after giving a speech, twenty-five-year-old John W. Hinckley Jr. fired six shots on the president's party with a .22 caliber gun loaded with explosive bullets called Devastators. One bullet struck the president in the left side, entering his lung without exploding; other shots hit Press Secretary James S. Brady and two law enforcement officers. Brady's head wound left him partially handicapped, and after recovery, he and his wife Sarah became leading spokespersons for gun control legislation. Hinckley was later judged mentally incompetent and sentenced to a mental hospital.

Because of the day's confusion, Secretary of State Alexander Haig committed a political blunder that led to negative press reports. Since Vice President Bush was in Texas, Haig told cabinet officers at a White House meeting that he was "in charge," citing incorrectly the procedures for presidential succession. Haig's claim was also unnecessary because the president recovered after the bullet was removed from his lung during several hours of surgery.

### March 30, 1981

## *Poland's Solidarity trade union cancels a strike because some of its demands are met.*

Since Prime Minister Jaruzelski took office on February 9, 1981, there had been several wildcat strikes and confrontations between police and demonstrators, but Solidarity gave the prime minister time to meet its demands. Reforms came slowly, however; the call for a national strike was designed to speed up a few changes, some of which were met; others were not.

See April 2 and July 20, 1981.

### March 31, 1981

## *Hijacking of an Indonesian aircraft is foiled by Indonesian commandos.*

On March 28, Islamic extremists took over an Indonesian jet headed for Thailand and demanded the release of 20 Indonesian prisoners. This effort failed because commandos attacked the plane, killing four of the five hijackers and freeing all 55 hostages.

### April 1, 1981

## The United States suspends $15 million of aid to Nicaragua.

In contrast to its support of El Salvador's government, the Reagan administration strongly opposed the rise to power of the Sandinista leaders in Nicaragua, claiming they were backed by Cuba and the Soviet Union and that they sent arms to El Salvador's rebels, the Farabundo Marti National Liberation Front (FMLN).

Washington's claim about Soviet-Cuban aid seemed to be verified on April 24, when Nicaragua announced the receipt of 20,000 tons of grain from Moscow, a $100 million loan from Libya, and $64 million of technical aid from Cuba. The Reagan administration believed this was part of a communist plot to dominate Central America.

### April 2, 1981

## The United States gives $70 million of surplus food to Poland.

The new ministry of Wojciech Jaruzelski inherited severe economic problems including insufficient food. On March 1, the government rationed sugar and, on April 1, meat. On April 14, butter and grain were rationed—the first food restrictions since 1945. U.S. food surpluses were sent as relief efforts to feed the Polish people.

Other efforts to help Poland included 11 banks of Western Europe rescheduling $2.37 billion of long-term debt on June 25, and a U.S. loan of $35 million on July 28 to purchase 350,000 tons of corn. Unfortunately, this assistance was not sufficient to solve the Polish problems.

### April 6, 1981

## The State Department proposes the "Zimbabwe formula" to obtain Namibia's (South-West Africa's) statehood.

Assistant Secretary of State for African Affairs Chester A. Crocker and Secretary of State Alexander Haig announced new U.S. policies regarding Namibia's problems. Called the "Zimbabwe formula," it adopted the method that Zimbabwe used when, as Southern Rhodesia, it gained independence from Britain. Crocker wanted the competing parties in

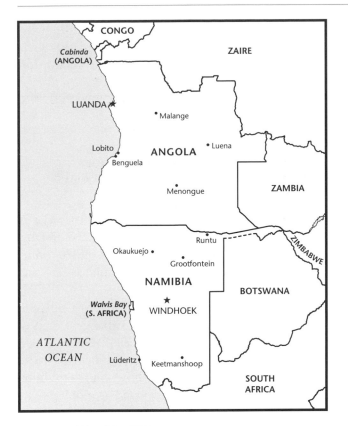

Angola and Namibia, 1981

Neto share power with the anti-Marxist Angolan rebel force headed by Jonas Savimbi, known as UNITA (National Union for Total Independence of Angola).

Crocker's proposal was suspect to black Africans because the Reagan administration appeared to work with white-dominated South Africa.

See July 27, 1978, and June 26, 1980; also see April 16 and April 23, 1981.

## April 12, 1981

### The first American space shuttle, *Columbia*, is launched into orbit at Cape Canaveral.

*Columbia* was a reusable shuttle plane. After making 36 orbits of the earth, *Columbia* landed at Edwards Air Force Base, California. It was piloted by the Air Force Colonel John W. Young and Navy Captain Robert L. Crippen.

On November 12, 1981, *Columbia* was again launched successfully but concluded its flight early because of fuel cell failure.

Namibia to agree on a state charter before holding elections.

This proposal altered plans established by the Carter administration under which U.N. Resolution 431 called for an immediate U.N.-supervised election to give Namibia independence, after which the political factions in that state could decide on a constitution. Carter had worked with a Western European "contact group" to cooperate with the United Nations in these plans. In 1978, a solution seemed near but was disrupted by South African demands.

Increasingly separating the United States from the United Nations formula, the Reagan administration used "constructive disengagement" to obtain South African cooperation. Hence, the proposal for agreement on a charter before elections and before independence from South African control. It was revealed on May 31, 1981, that a Crocker memo of February 7, 1981, circulating in the State Department, indicated that America's Namibian strategy would be linked to the evacuation of Cuban troops from Angola and the requirement that Angola's government of Agastino

## April 16, 1981

### Six black African states condemn Reagan's policies for Africa.

Meeting in Luanda, Angola, representatives from Angola, Botswana, Mozambique, Tanzania, Zambia, and Zimbabwe condemned the Reagan administration's efforts to repeal the Clark Amendment and to forsake the U.N. policy for Namibian independence.

Named for Senator Dick Clark, the Clark Amendment was approved by Congress in 1976 to prevent U.S. aid to any of the competing factions opposing Angola's government. The Reagan administration desired to repeal the amendment so it could renew aid to Jonas Savimbi's UNITA, which opposed the Angolan government.

In addition, the African representatives wanted to use the U.N. formula for supervised elections in Namibia to force South Africa to grant independence. Their opposition to Chester Crocker's "Zimbabwe formula" came just before Crocker's April 23 visit to Angola.

See April 6 and 23, 1981.

## April 23, 1981

**The United States indicates Cuban troops must leave Angola before attempts can be made to secure Namibia's independence from South Africa.**

From April 6 to 23, Assistant Secretary of State Chester Crocker toured Africa to seek support for his "Zimbabwe formula" on Namibia. His last stop was Luanda, Angola, where he told Angola's President Neto that Cuban troops must leave Angola before an effective Namibian solution could result. The Cubans had assisted Neto in gaining independence from Portugal, but now, the United States claimed, they armed and trained Namibian rebels known as SWAPO (South-West African People's Organization), who were led by Sam Nujoma. SWAPO's principal opposition in Namibia was the South African–supported all-white Democratic Turnhalle Alliance led by Dirk Mudge.

Neither Angola nor other black African countries accepted Crocker's proposals, preferring U.N. Resolution 431 for immediate elections and independence. On April 30, 1981, when the U.N. Security Council voted on resolutions to force South Africa to hold elections, the United States, France, and Britain vetoed the proposals.

For details of Crocker's proposal, see April 6, 1981; also see June 27 and August 31, 1981.

## April 24, 1981

**President Reagan ends the U.S. grain embargo against the Soviet Union.**

Following nearly a decade of profitable U.S. grain sales to the USSR, President Carter levied a grain embargo against the Soviet Union on January 4, 1980, to punish Moscow for intervening in Afghanistan. The Soviets, however, found other nations ready to sell grain to them, including some grain previously purchased from the United States. Consequently, the embargo hurt U.S. farm income most of all—a situation President Reagan now hoped to rectify.

By ending the grain embargo, Reagan did not abolish all U.S. Export restrictions on trade with the Soviet Union. There were still restrictions on fishing and high-technology products. In fact, Reagan tried to enforce restrictions on technology more vigorously than previous presidents.

On August 5, U.S. and Soviet negotiators signed an agreement in Vienna that committed the Soviet Union to purchase from 6 million to 8 million tons of grain each year.

See January 8, 1982.

## April 24, 1981

**The Department of Defense announces creation of a Persian Gulf command with a unified rapid-deployment force.**

This announcement by Secretary of Defense Caspar Weinberger established a military structure designed to carry out the "Carter Doctrine" of 1980, which pledged to protect the Persian Gulf as a "vital American interest."

President Carter had sent Airborne Warning and Control System aircraft (AWACS) to Egypt, and on April 21, Reagan proposed to sell five AWACS to Saudi Arabia to help defend its oil fields. Neither Carter nor Reagan clarified how far the United States would go to protect land regions of the Persian Gulf, but both said it was America's responsibility to protect the area from communism.

Because Israel protested the sale of AWACS to Saudi Arabia, serious political problems faced the Reagan administration by September 1981.

See January 23, 1980; see also October 28, 1981.

## April 27, 1981

**Western bankers reschedule Poland's $2.4 billion debt.**

To assist Poland in solving its economic problems without Soviet intervention, banking representatives of the United States and 14 other Western nations revised the terms of Poland's debt repayments—the first time this had been done for a communist nation.

## April 30, 1981

**Retired Army General Edward L. Rowney is appointed as chief U.S. negotiator for the strategic arms talks with the Soviet Union.**

Rowney had been a military representative on the delegation that negotiated SALT II with the Soviet Union. In 1979, after President Carter signed the agreement with Soviet President Leonid Brezhnev, Rowney resigned and lobbied in opposition to ratification of SALT II. This opposition endeared him to the Reagan administration, and after passing over Rowney for Eugene Rostow to head the Arms Control and Disarmament Agency, Reagan appointed him to carry on arms discussions with the Soviet Union. The obvious intent of this maneuver was to retard movement toward any new controls on strategic nuclear armaments.

Rowney would later be replaced by Paul Nitze in a move by the new secretary of state, George Shultz, to gain control of the negotiations.

## May 1, 1981

### Japan agrees to a three-year curb on automobile exports.

Japan's agreement to limit auto exports was made in Tokyo during talks between U.S. Special Trade Representative William Brock and Japan's trade official, Naomiro Amaya. There was growing U.S. congressional sympathy for tariff protection to correct the U.S. TRADE IMBALANCE. To delay such action, Japan accepted limits on auto exports and promised to seek ways to allow more U.S. imports into Japan. One consequence of Japan's action was to permit U.S. automakers to increase prices of their cars.

## May 7, 1981

### Mexico and Nicaragua sign a $200 million aid package.

In defiance of the Reagan administration's opposition to Nicaragua, Mexico agreed to help the Sandinista leader Daniel Ortega Saavedra.

See April 27, 1980.

## May 10, 1981

### Socialist François Mitterrand is elected president of France.

In the second round of the French electoral effort to give one candidate a majority, MITTERRAND won 51.76% of the vote; President Valéry Giscard d'Estang received 48.24%. In the first-round election on April 26, Communist Party leader Georges Marchais had 15.4%. For the first time since 1954, left and left-center parties ruled France. Mitterrand was inaugurated as president on May 22.

## May 13, 1981

### Pope John Paul II is shot and wounded.

Police arrested an escaped Turkish criminal, Mehmet Ali Agca, whose gunshots in Vatican Square wounded the pope and two tourists. The pope recovered; Italy sentenced Agca to life in prison on July 22, 1981.

## May 20, 1981

### The United States votes against a World Health Organization (WHO) proposal to ban food companies from promoting infant formulas in preference to breast feeding.

For several years, medical data collected by the WHO substantiated that the advertising of infant formulas in Third World countries and the United States caused thousands of infant deaths because parents misinterpreted the promotional messages. Consequently, babies did not get the nutrients they required—nutrients best acquired from breast feeding. The two American doctors who worked on these studies at WHO, Stephen Joseph and Eugene N. Babb, favored the WHO proposal to prohibit misleading promotion of baby foods.

The vote on the proposal at the WHO conference was 93 to 3 with 9 abstentions. The United States cast one of the three negative votes and was the only major nation to vote against the proposal. President Reagan's explanation was that regulations on such food companies would set a precedent and cause future WHO regulations to multiply. Joseph and Babb resigned as U.S. delegates in protest against Reagan's order to vote no.

Ernst Lefever, Reagan's nominee for the assistant secretary for human rights, suffered from this decision and lost his nomination.

See June 6, 1981.

## June 6, 1981

### Ernst Lefever's nomination as assistant secretary for human rights is rejected by the Senate Foreign Relations Committee; Lefever withdraws his nomination.

Lefever's stand against President Carter's human rights agenda had made him a dubious choice for this job, but the U.S vote against the World Health

Organization's (WHO) infant formula proposal ended Lefever's chance for Senate approval.

The infant formula issue affected Lefever because the Washington-based Ethics and Public Policy Center, which he headed, was involved with the Nestlé company of Switzerland, the leading manufacturer of baby food. Lefever's center published a study that supported Nestlé's infant formula and opposed the WHO regulation. It was disclosed also that Nestlé's gave Lefever's center a $25,000 grant, a coincidence that seemed to raise serious "ethical questions" for the Ethics Center but one whose validity a Lefever spokesman denied.

Subsequently, the May 20 vote against the WHO regulation seemed to link the Nestlé grant to the Reagan decision. In addition, after Reagan ordered his delegates to vote no, 90% of the White House mail opposed the president's decision.

In the Senate Foreign Relations Committee, Lefever's prior negative views on human rights, added to the WHO incident, led many Republicans as well as Democrats to distance themselves from the director of the Ethics and Public Policy Center. After the Senate Committee recommended the rejection of Lefever's nomination by a vote of 13 to 4, Lefever withdrew his nomination.

### June 7, 1981

*Israeli planes destroy a French-built nuclear reactor near Baghdad, Iraq.*

The government of Israel said that F-15 and F-16 jets had flown from Israel to Iraq to destroy a plant capable of giving Iraq a nuclear bomb. Prime Minister Menachem Begin asserted that the attack was a "morally supreme act of national self-defense."

While Israel was widely criticized for its action, Iraq announced its nuclear program would continue. Because it was building the reactor while fighting a war with Iran, the Iraqi government had assured Iran in October 1980 that the nuclear weapon was intended to attack Israel, not Iran. In other instances, Iraq said the research lab was only for training its scientists. The United States condemned Israel for its action but only mildly rebuked Begin's government. President Reagan held up the delivery of F-15 and F-16 planes to Israel until August 17, 1981. In the U.N. Security Council, U.S. Ambassador Jeane Kirkpatrick voted with the other 14 members to condemn Israel but only after obtaining a resolution that removed the economic sanctions that Iraq wanted against Israel.

### June 15, 1981

**Pakistan receives a $3 billion, five-year military and economic aid package from the United States.**

Although some representatives believed Pakistan should receive no aid because, they alleged, it was building nuclear weapons, the Reagan administration favored the package to assist U.S. interests in the Persian Gulf and to help Afghan rebels who were fighting against Afghanistan's communist-backed government. State Department spokesperson James L. Buckley told Congress that Pakistan had "absolutely assured" him that it was not developing nuclear weapons.

Congress remained dubious, and on October 12, 1981, the Senate voted 57 to 46 to cut off aid to Pakistan or India if either tested a nuclear device.

### June 16, 1981

**Seeking better relations with Mainland China, the United States agrees to sell it arms.**

Since March 19, 1981, the Reagan administration had endeavored to cement relations with the People's Republic of China (PRC). The June 16 decision was made after Secretary of State Haig told reporters that close U.S.-PRC ties were a "strategic imperative" because of the growing Soviet threat. The arms decision on June 16 was made in principle, depending on future military-technological discussions to implement the agreement.

The United States took two other actions in June 1981 that favored China. On June 2, the United States and the PRC agreed on the use of the Export-Import Bank to obtain Chinese credits. On June 4, Washington lifted trade curbs against China.

### June 16, 1981

*Philippine President Ferdinand Marcos is elected to another term of office; the opposition boycotts the election.*

Marcos's election victory showed support of 88% of those voting. Six million of Marcos's opponents boycotted the election, just as they had boycotted the April 7 plebiscite, which changed the constitution to allow Marcos to be reelected for an unlimited number of times.

The United States supported Marcos despite the political tension in the Philippines. At Marcos's inauguration on July 1, Vice President George Bush pledged U.S. assistance.

### June 27, 1981

*Organization of African Unity (OAU) condemns the United States for "collusion" with South Africa.*

The OAU voted unanimously to protest America's Namibian policy because it favored South Africa. In addition, the OAU meeting called for an African peacekeeping force in Chad and obtained a ceasefire in western Africa, where Polisario rebels opposed Morocco's King Hassan II.

> See April 6, 1981; on Chad, see October 30 and November 27, 1981; on Morocco, see October 19, 1981.

### June 29, 1981

*The Central Committee of the Communist Party of the People's Republic of China concludes its sixth plenum session.*

During the three-day meeting, the committee selected Hi Yaobang as party chairman with Zhao Ziyang as his deputy. China's real political leader was Deng Xiaoping, who headed the party's Military Commission.

### June 29, 1981

*Japan resists U.S. pressure to increase its national defense budget.*

Generally, Japanese public opinion opposed spending more for defense purposes, even though Prime Minister Zenko Suzuki told President Reagan on May 8, 1981, that Japan would increase its defense budget (see also January 29, 1981).

Two recent incidents stimulated Japan's opposition to a bigger defense establishment. On April 9, a Japanese freighter sank in the East China Sea after colliding with a U.S. nuclear submarine, killing two Japanese seamen. Second, on May 18, former U.S. Ambassador to Japan Edwin Reischauer disclosed that there was a secret U.S. accord with Japan in 1960 to allow the U.S. navy to carry nuclear arms in and out of Japan. These and other events caused two Japanese cabinet ministers to resign in May 1981 and strengthened Japan's will to resist U.S. proposals for large military budgets.

On June 29, Japan's defense chief, Joji Omura, visited U.S. Secretary of Defense Caspar Weinberger in Washington to inform the United States that Tokyo would not increase national defense spending.

> See March 26–31, 1982.

### June 29, 1981

*The United States agrees to help Egypt purchase two nuclear energy plants.*

Egypt's 1979 peace agreement with Israel and the Persian Gulf–Iranian crisis since 1980 had brought the United States and Egypt to a close partnership. Because Egypt needed sources of energy in addition to the water-powered generators at the Aswân High Dam, Washington agreed to provide $2 billion to enable it to obtain two large atomic reactors and fuel to generate electric power. Nuclear materials made available would serve only peaceful purposes, and the approval process of the International Atomic Energy Agency would follow.

### July 12, 1981

*An Israeli right-wing coalition government is formed by Menachem Begin following inconclusive elections.*

During the July 5 election, BEGIN'S LIKUD PARTY won 48 Knesset seats; the Labor Party won 47 seats. Begin bargained with three small religious parties to obtain 13 votes and a majority of the 160 Knesset members.

### July 12, 1981

*El Salvador's bishop claims his nation's army has recently murdered 28 civilians, but President Reagan rejects the church's request for an investigation.*

Bishop Arturo Rivera y Damos referred to the massacre of 28 peasants found in a crude grave on the banks of the Metayato River, 36 miles from San Salvador. He also blamed the army for the disappearance of 70 other civilians and for an attack on the church in Chalatenango. Rivera y Damos had become acting archbishop following the assassination of Archbishop Oscar Amulfo Romero in 1980.

The Reagan administration's staunch anticommunist position toward the Salvadoran rebels caused it to ignore the Salvadoran Catholic Church leaders' claims against the government as well as their plans for negotiations between rebels and President Duarte. Washington approved Duarte's plans for elections in one or two years in which all who renounced violence could vote.

See March 24, 1980; December 4, 1980; January 3, 1981; and August 27, 1981.

### July 14–20, 1981

*Polish Communist Party session reorganizes leadership and announces a wage freeze and a 110% price increase on most products.*

The party reorganization strengthened the power of Prime Minister Wojciech Jaruzelski by ousting party leader Edward Gierek and six of his associates and by electing 200 Central Committee members by secret ballot.

See December 13, 1981.

### July 20–21, 1981

**Seventh annual economic summit reveals that the Reagan administration's policies diverge from those of Western Europe and Japan.**

Meeting in Ottawa, Canada, the seven major industrial nations focused on high U.S. interest rates of up to 22% and President Reagan's desire to curb technological trade with the Soviet Union. Moreover, while the other six summit nations desired economic aid for Third World countries, Reagan believed Third World problems resulted because those nations needed to be hospitable to private capital investment. Nevertheless, the final summit communiqué papered over the disagreements on policy with promises each leader could adjust to domestic considerations. In addition to the United States, other nations attending the annual summit were Canada, France, West Germany, Great Britain, Italy, and Japan.

### July 29, 1981

*Radicals in Iran consolidate power; President Abolhassan Bani-Sadr is arrested and exiled.*

After BANI-SADR negotiated the release of the U.S. hostages in January 1981, he came under attack by Muslim extremists for yielding too much to

Washington. By March 1981, supporters and opponents of Bani-Sadr conducted street fights in Teheran. Fearing a coup, Bani-Sadr had gone into hiding prior to his arrest. Initially, the government was taken over by a three-man council.

On July 24, Bani-Sadr's Prime Minister Mohammad Ali Rajai was elected president with 80% of the 14 million votes cast. This election was rejected by the Islamic extremists, and on July 29, Rajai and Bani-Sadr fled for asylum to France. Rajai and eight of his followers were killed on August 30 by a bomb thrown into his Paris office.

See October 2, 1981.

### July 30, 1981

**A new U.S. immigration policy is announced regarding Mexican workers.**

The steady, often illegal influx of Mexicans into the southwestern United States seemed to necessitate some American limitation. The Reagan administration's policy, which fined employers of illegal aliens, began a two-year trial to legalize Mexican "guest" workers, and provided a conditional amnesty to illegal aliens.

### August 1, 1981

**Panamanian President Torrijos is killed in a plane crash.**

General Omar TORRIJOS Herrera was best known to Americans as the signer of the 1978 treaties by which the United States would cede control of the Panama Canal to Panama in the year 2000.

Following Torrijos's death, there was a contest for power during which Colonel Manuel Antonio Noriega, chief of military intelligence, won the struggle against the head of the National Guard, Colonel Horencio Florez Aquilas.

See June 16, 1978.

### August 6, 1981

**Neutron bomb production is resumed by President Reagan.**

Reversing President Carter's decision to halt neutron bomb production, Reagan agreed with Secretary of Defense Caspar Weinberger's desire to prepare neutron bombs for European defense purposes. In his announcement, Reagan said the United States does not expect to deploy the bombs in Europe without consulting its European allies. Substantial European opposition to the neutron bomb arose early in 1981 after Weinberger stated on February 3 that he favored their deployment as the best means to counter Soviet tank superiority in Europe. In Holland, the two main political parties opposed deployment of the bomb, and the West German government wanted consultation on the issue with Washington.

See April 7, 1978.

## August 13, 1981

### The United States vetoes a loan of $20 million to Guyana.

Although the U.S. veto was hedged by economic technicalities, it was known that President Reagan wanted Guyana to accept a "free-market" economy before obtaining a loan from the InterAmerican Development Bank. In addition, Great Britain claimed that President Forbes Burnham of Guyana won his 1980 election in a corrupt manner.

Since gaining power with U.S. help in 1968, Burnham had assumed near-dictatorial powers. But worse from the Reagan perspective, Burnham had nationalized 80% of the country's economy. Reagan wanted Guyana to use private loans and denationalize industry. Burnham claimed, in vain, that if he failed, his main opponent, a Marxist, Cheddi B. Jagan, could gain power.

## August 17, 1981

### India purchases 1.51 million tons of wheat from the United States for $293 million.

The significance of this purchase is that it was the first time since 1977 that India needed wheat imports. The green revolution in India and elsewhere had sharply cut that country's need to import U.S. grain for four years.

## August 18, 1981

### Rejecting U.S. claims that it needed military aid, Costa Rica asks for economic assistance.

The U.S. ambassador to the United Nations, Jeane Kirkpatrick, had remarked that Costa Rica needed arms to fight communism, a statement Costa Rica's government denied. Often referred to as Central America's best democracy, Costa Rica opposed U.S.

intervention in the affairs of Nicaragua and El Salvador and did not wish to be involved militarily.

## August 19, 1981

### U.S. navy planes shoot down two Libyan jets in the Gulf of Sidra.

Ever since the United States closed the Libyan mission in Washington on May 6, 1981, there was a continual flurry of charges and countercharges between President Reagan and Libya's Mu'ammar al-Gadhafi. Reagan claimed Libya supported terrorists. On June 2, Assistant Secretary of State for African Affairs Chester CROCKER of the State Department warned Libya that the United States would act if Gadhafi aided rebels in Chad, just south of Libya.

One argument between Washington and Tripoli focused on Gadhafi's claim that the entire Gulf of Sidra belonged to Libya. The United States and other naval powers held that the northern section of the gulf lay within international waters.

While flying in the disputed zone, two U.S. Navy F-14 jets were attacked by two Libyan SU-22s; the Americans shot down the Libyan planes with heat-seeking missiles. Washington denied Libya's claim that one American F-14 was downed and claimed it acted to uphold the concept of internationally accepted waterways. On August 23, Gadhafi admitted that his planes had fired first on the F-14s.

## August 27, 1981

### Salvadoran authorities release the man accused of killing three agricultural advisers in January 1981.

Several weeks after the murder of two American and one Salvadoran agricultural experts, Ricardo Sol Meza, a wealthy landowner, was charged with the crime and put in prison. On August 22, he was released without bail because the judge ruled there was insufficient evidence against him. Originally, a waitress in the café where the men were killed had identified Meza as the gunman, but later she changed her testimony, denying she had seen Meza. One other man suspected of the murder, Hans Christ, was being held as a suspect by U.S. authorities in Miami, Florida. El Salvador had not asked for his extradition.

On the murder of these men, see January 3, 1981.

### August 31, 1981

**The United States vetoes a U.N. condemnation of South Africa's raid on Angola on July 12.**

The South African forces had attacked a SWAPO base 90 miles inside Angola, where they left 114 persons dead. After Angola requested U.N. aid, South Africa argued it pursued SWAPO rebels who attacked South-West Africa. SWAPO was the South-West Africa People's Organization group advocating the independence of Namibia from South Africa.

Following the U.S. veto of Security Council action, the U.N. General Assembly passed a resolution on September 14 that condemned South Africa and singled out the United States for blame in vetoing the Security Council action.

This veto was the Reagan administration's third action in 1981 that favored South Africa. On March 2, the United States voted against a U.N. General Assembly motion to reject the credentials of South Africa's delegation because of its apartheid policies. The motion passed with 112 votes. On March 6, the United States abstained in an assembly vote to place a trade embargo on South Africa.

On two occasions in 1981, black African nations condemned U.S. favor of South Africa.
See April 16 and June 27, 1981; on Namibia's future, see September 24, 1981.

### August 31, 1981

**A bomb at Ramstein air force base, West Germany, destroys property and injures 20 people.**

While the terrorist Baader-Meinhof group of the Red Army faction claimed credit for the bombing, the event symbolized the growing peace movement in West Germany and Europe that opposed U.S. missiles on their territory as well as dependence on the United States for their security.

The Ramstein attack inaugurated a wave of terrorist incidents in West Germany where the Red Army faction had been quiescent for three years. On September 1, seven U.S. cars were set afire at Wiesbaden; on September 15, terrorists fired a grenade launcher but failed to injure the U.S. NATO commander in Heidelberg, General Frederick J. Kroesar; and on September 16, West German authorities defused two bombs at the U.S. base in Frankfurt.

West German officials blamed a minority of 12 to 15 hard-core Red Army radicals and had 30 suspects on their wanted list. They said another 150 associates cooperated with the radicals by giving them supplies and safe houses.

### September 5, 1981

**The United States and the People's Republic of China sign a cultural exchange pact in Beijing.**

This agreement permitted the exchange of students, teachers, and scholars of the arts and sciences, as well as art exhibits and visits by music groups.

### September 13, 1981

**Secretary of State Haig accuses communist nations of using chemical weapons in Southeast Asia and Afghanistan.**

During a visit to West Berlin, Haig made charges that began a lengthy controversy over so-called yellow rain that the Soviet Union allegedly used during conflicts in Asia. A variety of scientific studies of yellow rain resulted, with most scientists finding no sufficient evidence to justify the Reagan administration's claims.
See January 14, 1982.

### September 15, 1981

*Egypt expels the Soviet ambassador, six aides, and 1,000 Soviets accused of subverting the government.*

The Soviet ambassador, Vladimir P. Polyakov, his aides, and the Soviet technicians were ordered to leave Egypt. In retaliation, on September 17, Moscow expelled Egyptian officials.

### September 15, 1981

**U.S. aid package for Pakistan of $3.2 billion includes F-16 aircraft.**

Washington had negotiated with Pakistan for nearly two years in reaching this agreement. Realizing the United States wanted his help in supplying aid to Afghanistan and providing security for the Persian Gulf, Pakistan's President Mohammad Zia UL-HAQ sought the most favorable terms possible. He had rejected offers from President Carter and agreed to the $3 billion deal only if President Reagan wrote that this did not imply a security alliance with Pakistan.

Among congressional leaders, a major issue was the possibility of Pakistan's development of nuclear weapons. The September 15 agreement ignored this issue, but Undersecretary of State James Buckley told the House Foreign Affairs Committee that Pakistan knew a nuclear detonation would end all U.S. aid. In approving the aid package on October 12, the U.S. Senate voted to cut off aid if a nuclear device were tested.

See January 23, 1980.

### September 17, 1981

**Funds for the United Nations Educational, Scientific, and Cultural Organization (UNESCO) are cut by the U.S. House of Representatives.**

The solid House vote indicated most Americans' concern that nations of the Third World dominated committees of the United Nations. This opinion spread after May 17, 1981, when a UNESCO commission on mass communication voted for an International Information Order that permitted Third World countries to censor foreign information about themselves. These countries argued that the news media were a tool of industrial power that discriminated against them by publishing adverse data. Because censorship clashed with American concepts of a free press, UNESCO appeared to violate basic human rights.

### September 23, 1981

**Two American military advisers are wounded by gunshots in Honduras.**

The U.S. advisers were training Honduran military to defend themselves. The Honduran radicals who wounded the Americans stated on September 24 that the shooting and the subsequent bombing of Honduras's parliament building began a drive to rid Honduras of "Yankee imperialists."

### September 24, 1981

**The Western nations contact group prepares a revised plan for granting Namibia independence.**

This group of representatives from the United States and four Western European countries offered a proposal for territory in Southwest Africa under South African control to become the independent state of Namibia. The plan adopted resembled a three-year-old U.N. plan for a timetable to phase out South African control, conduct elections, and establish a Namibian government. The new government would be based on ideas of one person, one vote, the end of all racial discrimination, and a bill of rights.

From October 28 to November 6, representatives of the contact group visited South-West Africa and the two states crucial to resolving the process, South Africa and Angola. They got support for the plan from the South-West African Turnhalle Alliance, a mixed group led by Dirk Mudge, but both South Africa and Angola expressed reservations about supporting the plan.

See April 23, 1981.

### September 25, 1981

*Belize becomes the 156th member of the United Nations.*

Formerly British Honduras, Belize had reached agreement for independence from Great Britain on March 11, 1981. On September 20, it became independent with George C. Price as Prime Minister.

### September 26, 1981

**The Pentagon issues a booklet titled "Soviet Military Power" intended to promote greatly increased U.S. defense expenditures.**

Since taking office in January 1981, Secretary of Defense Caspar Weinberger had argued that the United States had fallen behind the Soviet Union in defense effectiveness and that the United States needed a five-year program to regain the military superiority held during the period from 1945 to 1965. Weinberger wanted $1.7 billion more than President Jimmy Carter proposed for fiscal 1982 and $158 billion more than Carter proposed for the next five years, figures that were understated compared to the cost of the new weapons systems the Pentagon desired in 1981.

To create an alarming vision of Soviet power, the widely criticized Pentagon booklet claimed the Soviets had leadership in army, navy, air force, and missile defenses, omitting data that, critics said, contradicted their exaggerated threat. For example, the text said the Soviets operated 377 submarines, including 180 nuclear-powered subs, compared with 115 U.S. navy submarines, but it only hinted at the U.S. navy's superior technology by saying that the Soviets were "reducing the U.S. lead in virtually every important basic technology."

Generally, the booklet indicated that Soviet ground forces had increased since 1969 by 30 divisions to total 180 divisions and that they fielded 50,000 tanks, 20,000 artillery pieces, 5,200 helicopters, over 3,500 tactical bombers and fighter planes, and 7,000 nuclear warheads. It asserted that the Soviets spent 12% to 14% of their gross national product on defense, compared with America's 7%, but it did not mention that the U.S. GNP was at least twice that of the Soviets. It also left American allied forces out of the picture, ignoring that together the United States, NATO members, Japan, and China spend more on defense than the Soviet Union, the Warsaw Pact countries, Cuba, and Vietnam. Nor did it relate China's threat on the Soviet border to any comparable threat on U.S. borders.

One of President Reagan's largest defense budget items was an attempt to "regain" U.S. naval superiority. In May 1981, U.S. Navy Secretary John F. Lehman Jr. indicated that an offensive-minded "maritime strategy" was the best deterrent to Soviet power. He convinced Reagan to increase the navy from 450 to 600 ships during the 1980s.

Apparently, the Pentagon booklet originated from a briefing that Weinberger gave to NATO defense experts in April 1981. They urged such a document as a means to help them obtain greater defense funding from their national legislatures.

## September 30, 1981

### Haiti and the United States agree that U.S. Coast Guard ships may patrol Haitian waters to stop illegal immigrants.

Arguing that over 60,000 Haitians had fled to the United States since 1972 for economic rather than political reasons, the Reagan administration and Haitian leader Jean Claude (Baby Doc) Duvalier exchanged notes to stop the migration. Most recent Haitian arrivals had been put in U.S. detention camps for deportation because they were not refugees, according to the U.S. policies in effect. Washington had expelled 3,900 of these detainees on January 30, 1981.

Under the new agreement, the first Coast Guard interception occurred on October 25 when a boat with 57 Haitians aboard was returned to Haiti. American civil rights leaders complained because almost all Cuban refugees were admitted freely while Haitians were turned back to a despotic ruler because they were black and Duvalier, unlike Cuba's Fidel Castro, was not communist.

## October 2, 1981

### President Reagan's defense program is announced; it includes both stationary MX missiles in hardened silos and B-1 bombers.

Reagan's announcement caused much debate among defense experts in the U.S. Senate because of past experiences with the MX (Reagan called it the "Peacemaker") and the B-1. President Carter had proposed deployment of the MX in large underground tunnels designed to help the MX survive a first-strike before retaliation under the MAD doctrine (mutual assured destruction). In contrast, Reagan's proposal to put the MX in missile silos seemed to be predicated on a first-strike, or launch-on-warning, American plan because the MX would be more vulnerable to a Soviet first strike than under the Carter plan. And vulnerable missiles could not be second-strike weapons.

As for the B-1 bomber, both its use and its capability had been contested prior to its cancellation by President Carter, who favored the less expensive, more accurate cruise missile, whose flight pattern would be difficult for the Soviets to detect.

In brief, Reagan's program favored the aggressive, offensive nuclear strategy that many of his supporters on the Committee for the Clear and Present Danger sponsored during the 1970s in claiming that a nuclear war could be fought and won with the proper weapons and a good civilian defense. As reported in interviews with Reagan and other members of his administration by Robert Scheer of the *Los Angeles Times*, the new president entered office advocating a nuclear defense that was threatening to those who preferred a U.S. policy of deterrence to avert a nuclear exchange.

For the MX, see June 8, 1979 and August 5, 1980; for the B-1, see July 1, 1977.

## October 2, 1981

*A religious extremist, Muhammad Ali Khamenei, is elected president of Iran.*

This election followed the overthrow on June 21, 1981, of the more moderate Bani-Sadr. Between July and October more than 1,000 moderate government officials were executed. Khamenei was the first clergyman to be elected president, winning 95% of the 16.8 million votes cast.

## October 6, 1981

*Assassination of Egyptian President Anwar-as-Sadat by a Muslim radical; Hosni Mubarak becomes president.*

Ever since the Egyptian republic was established in 1952, Muslim fundamentalists, many of them in the Muslim Brotherhood, advocated an Islamic theocracy resembling a caliphate, a form of government adopted by Islamic states in the seventh and eighth centuries. The Muslim Brotherhood advocated violent means to achieve their goal, and had been declared illegal in Egypt. Continuing as an underground group, the Brotherhood gained strength after President SADAT signed the Camp David accords to make peace with Israel.

Prior to his assassination, Sadat had arrested over 1,000 critics on the night of September 3–4, 1981, and told the Parliament that extremist groups had to be dissolved because they upset the social order. He also deposed the Coptic Pope Shenula III, whose headquarters in Cairo was a source of religious discontent. Subsequently, in a September 9 election, Sadat gained 99.45% of the vote.

Sadat was killed during a military parade in Cairo. Four army gunmen broke ranks before Sadat's reviewing stand, hurling smoke bombs and grenades and firing submachine guns. Sadat and 6 spectators died; 40 others were wounded. One assassin was immediately killed, and three were captured. Other plotters were arrested later, and, on April 15, 1982, five convicted men were executed.

On October 7, Parliament selected Vice President MUBARAK to succeed Sadat, an action confirmed in an October 13 election. Mubarak pledged to honor all of Sadat's treaties and commitments. Subsequently, although unknown to most Western observers, Mubarak kept his pledge regarding Sadat's security and economic programs.

See September 17, 1978

## October 7, 1981

*The President of the Republic of China (ROC) on Taiwan refuses to negotiate unity with Mainland China.*

During 1981, Beijing made several overtures to conduct talks on unity with the ROC, but ROC president Chiang Ching-kuo, claimed to be leader of the real Chinese government. This government had fled to Taiwan in 1949 after the communists defeated the Nationalist forces of Chiang Kai-shek.

## October 19, 1981

*Morocco's fight with Polisario rebels heats up in October.*

Moroccan jet fighters chased rebels into neighboring Mauritania following an unsuccessful rebel attack. Six days earlier, the Polisario used Soviet-made surface-to-air missiles to shoot down two Moroccan planes. With aid from several Middle Eastern states, the Polisario tried to gain independence for the Western Sahara region.

See October 22, 1979.

## October 22–23, 1981

*North-South conference of rich and poor nations achieves nothing of substance.*

Initiated in 1980 by an international development commission headed by West Germany's former Chancellor Willy Brandt, the idea of a dialogue between northern hemispheric industrial nations and southern hemispheric developing nations was intended to provide economic assistance to the poor southern nations. As a preliminary to the October session, the foreign ministers of 14 developing and 8 industrial nations met in August 1981 to form an agenda for its leaders to follow. The agenda identified five basic areas for discussion in October: economic cooperation, trade, food reserves, alternative energy sources, and fiscal-monetary questions.

During the October 22–23 meeting at the Mexican resort of Cancún, the three dominant figures were President Reagan, Prime Minister Margaret Thatcher of Great Britain, and Chancellor Helmut Schmidt of

President Reagan and British Prime Minister Margaret Thatcher. Ronald Reagan Library

West Germany. While the developing nations wanted all international economic issues to be decided by the United Nations, where each nation has one vote regardless of size or wealth, Reagan, Thatcher, and Schmidt rejected this concept. They insisted that key global economic decisions must continue to be made in the three organizations in which developing nations had no voice or vote—the World Bank, the International Monetary Fund, and the General Agreement on Tariffs and Trade organization.

Moreover, the Cancún discussions revealed that the 14 developing nations had different economic interests to protect, making particular agreements hard to reach. At its final session, the 22 delegates agreed that North-South talks should continue, but they could not agree on a future date or agenda for a meeting.

## October 24, 1981

### Large-scale antinuclear rallies take place in Europe.

European groups opposing the U.S. deployment of nuclear weapons in Europe agreed on October 24 as a day to stage demonstrations. In London, 150,000 rallied; in Rome, 100,000 protested; in Paris and Brussels, thousands demonstrated against nuclear weapons. In Bonn, over 250,000 protested the presence of U.S. missiles in Germany.

Peace marches occurred even in Eastern European countries during the fall of 1981. On October 20, protesters in Bulgaria called for a Balkan nuclear-free zone, and on November 12, over 100,000 marchers in Bucharest, Romania, staged an antinuclear protest.

## October 28, 1981

### The U.S. Senate finalizes the approval of the sale of American airborne warning and control system planes (AWACS) to Saudi Arabia.

Since April 21, when President Reagan proposed the sale of five AWACS aircraft to Saudi Arabia, political tension heated up not only between Israel and the Arab states but also between Congress and the White House. Pro-Jewish lobbyists opposed the sale because Israel feared the planes would be used against it by the Arabs. The Reagan administration argued that the AWACS were early-warning planes to assist reconnaissance in the Persian Gulf region and that Saudi Arabia would share its information with the United States.

U.S. law stated that the president's approval of the sale of the radar planes could be stopped if both houses of Congress opposed it. On August 25, Reagan presented the formal request to sell $8.5 billion of planes and equipment to the Saudis, and public debate began. On October 14, the House of Representatives voted 301 to 111 to reject the sale, but Reagan hoped the Republican-controlled Senate would approve it.

In the Senate, the two issues were whether the Unites States would retain some control over the information gathered by the AWACS and whether the Saudis would prohibit their use against Israel. Saudi Arabian officials rejected the concept of joint control, but before the Senate vote, Reagan sent the Senate a letter certifying that the Saudis agreed not to use the planes against Israel. This sufficed to win the votes of some undecided senators and the vote favored the sale by 52 to 48. Since only one house of Congress was required to approve the sale, the House rejection was overruled by this Senate vote.

During the Iran-Contra hearing of 1986–87, a secret protocol of the U.S. sale to Saudi Arabia was revealed. As part of the deal, the Saudi government promised to give money to anticommunist resistance groups when requested by Washington. Later, as part of the Project Democracy covert program, Saudi Arabia gave at least $30 million to help the Nicaraguan rebels.

On Project Democracy's covert side, see January 14, 1983.

### October 30, 1981

*France demands that Libya pull its troops out of Chad.*

Since early 1981 when Libya sought to annex Chad (see March 16, 1981), a civil war developed in Chad between those who favored and those who opposed union with Libya. The French government decided to publicly call for Libya to withdraw, threatening French intervention if necessary. As a follow-up to this warning, the French provided arms to Chad's President Goukouni on November 4, 1981.

By the time French aid arrived, Libyan President Mu'ammar al-Gadhafi decided to pull his troops out of Chad. Civil war continued, however, with rebel groups seeking to overthrow President Goukouni.

See November 27–28, 1981.

### November 10, 1981

*Arab delegations meet in Saudi Arabia as the Gulf Cooperation Council seeks common policy regarding Israel.*

Five nations plus Saudi Arabia, the host country, made up this council: Bahrain, Kuwait, Qatar, Oman, and the United Arab Emirates. This group had just been organized in 1980, and these oil-rich nations (with an estimated one-third of all world oil reserves) wanted to play some role in international decisions regarding the Middle East. Primarily at this session they took the first steps to approve a regional economic market and to establish common defense priorities.

In addition, they approved a Middle East peace plan proposed by Crown Prince Fahd of Saudi Arabia. It demanded a Palestinian state but provided for Israeli security under the Arabs' acceptance of Israel's right to exist. This was one of the first Arab plans for a peace settlement that recognized Israel as a state.

### November 11, 1981

*Antigua and Barbados admitted to the United Nations.*

The two islands joined together and became the 157th member of the United Nations.

### November 14, 1981

*U.S.-Egyptian forces conduct Operation Bright Star military exercises, the biggest U.S. war game in the Middle East since 1945.*

Preparing for a contingency of desert war, over 850 U.S. paratroopers bailed out over Egypt's desert area. Then 4,000 other U.S. military personnel arrived at Cairo West Air Base, transported by C-5A, C-141, and C-130 planes plus trucks, personnel carriers, and 150 mm field guns, some of which also arrived on navy ships. On November 24, six B-52 bombers flew from North Dakota bases, refueled three times in midair, and skimmed across the desert to drop bombs. Principally, these war game results showed the continued inadequacy of America's rapid-deployment forces. Even when planned ahead, many problems arose during the ten-day event.

### November 16, 1981

*Visiting Washington, Venezuelan President Luis Herrera Campins opposes U.S. military intervention in Nicaragua.*

HERRERA's warning resulted from reports about possible U.S. military action against Nicaragua or Cuba, because those countries had aided Salvadoran rebels. Venezuela, Mexico, and other members of the Organization of American States generally opposed

U.S. intervention in Nicaragua. On November 23, Mexico's foreign minister also warned U.S. Secretary of State Haig against acting against Nicaragua.

### November 18, 1981

**President Ronald Reagan calls for the "zero-option" on long-range theater nuclear forces (LRTNF) of the NATO and Warsaw Pact powers.**

Reagan's televised address set the American agenda for the U.S.-Soviet arms control talks set to begin in Geneva on November 30, 1981. The "ZERO-OPTION" meant that NATO would cancel its planned deployment of Pershing II and cruise missiles if the Soviet Union scrapped all its LRTNF—its SS-20, SS-4, and SS-5 theater nuclear missiles.

The zero-option evolved from the German term *null-losen* when the issue of basing intermediate-range missiles appeared between 1975 and 1980. Initially, as the Soviet Union deployed SS-20 missiles targeted at Western Europe, Chancellor Helmut Schmidt of West Germany proposed the introduction of U.S. Pershing II missiles as a countermeasure. Within three years, however, Schmidt and other Western European leaders feared that the deployment of SS-20s in the East and Pershing IIs in the West would make Europe a nuclear battleground between the two superpowers. As a result, Schmidt changed his mind, introducing the phrase *null-losen* to signify eliminating both the SS-20s and the Pershing IIs.

Within the Reagan administration, zero-option had two diverging interpretations. Defense Secretary Caspar Weinberger and others who opposed the arms control agenda believed zero-option was a nonnegotiable U.S. requirement that the Soviets would never accept. Secretary of State Alexander Haig saw the zero-option covering all nuclear weapons with European targets and also as the maximum U.S. demand that, as in normal diplomacy, was flexible and open to negotiations to obtain mutual agreement with Moscow at some lower level.

Tending to support Weinberger, President Reagan accepted the concept that the Soviets had to eliminate all their theater nuclear weapons, not just the SS-20s as Schmidt had proposed. In the context of a nonnegotiable demand, the arms control talks in Geneva seemed to be destined for stalemate.

See February 26, 1981; for European reaction to Reagan's speech, see November 24, 1981.

### November 19, 1981

*West Germany and the Soviet Union reach accord on construction of a pipeline from Siberia to central Germany.*

Designed to help Germany and other Western European countries secure natural gas as an alternative to Middle East oil, this project became solidified on July 24, 1981, when West German banks agreed to a $10 billion loan to the Soviets to finance the pipeline's construction. The political accord finalized the project.

### November 21, 1981

*One hundred mercenaries fail to overthrow the government of the Seychelles islands.*

After the effort failed, 44 mercenaries hijacked an Air India jet, which flew them to Durban, South Africa. Although the South African Supreme Court sentenced 42 of the mercenaries to prison on July 27, 1982, South Africa's government enraged world opinion because it released 34 of the convicts on November 27, 1982.

On July 6, 1982, a Seychelles court sentenced four of the foreign mercenaries to death and a fifth rebel to prison for the coup attempt.

### November 22, 1981

*Andrey Sakharov and wife begin a hunger strike in Moscow, protesting that their stepson cannot join his fiancée in the United States.*

This act by Sakharov, a physicist who was a Nobel Peace laureate, received international attention. It ended on December 8 when Soviet authorities permitted the stepson to leave.

### November 22, 1981

**Greek government announces a schedule to remove U.S. bases.**

Elected to office following successes in the October 18, 1981, Greek vote, Prime Minister Andreas PAPANDREOU of the Panhellenic Socialist Movement challenged the Western European alliances made by his predecessors. Thus, Papandreou set a timetable to remove U.S. naval bases in Piraeus, the port of Athens, and on Crete; to ban U.S. nuclear weapons from Greek soil, and to renegotiate Greece's role in

NATO and the European Economic Community (EEC).

The prime minister contended that NATO gave "unrestrained military aid to Greece's enemy, Turkey," and did not protect the nation's eastern border. He was ready to bargain for concessions from the United States but set the timetable to avoid delay. He also called for a Greek referendum concerning withdrawal from the EEC.

### November 23, 1981

**President Reagan issues National Security Decision Directive (NSDD) 17, which gives the Central Intelligence Agency authority to fund a group rebelling against the government of Nicaragua: origin of the "Contra" movement.**

NSDD 17 was a classified document whose contents were leaked to the *Washington Post* and *New York Times* in February and March 1982. The directive ordered the CIA to "work with foreign governments" to undermine the Sandinista government of Nicaragua.

Reportedly, the CIA had already been working with Argentine military officers who trained Nicaraguan exiles and mercenaries in northern Nicaragua and Honduras. The CIA was given $19 million to assemble and arm 500 contras in addition to 1,000 exiles trained by Argentina.

### November 24, 1981

**West German Chancellor Schmidt tells Soviet President Brezhnev he doubts President Reagan's objectives in seeking the "zero-option."**

Although initial public reaction to Reagan's November 18 speech was favorably received by American editorialists, Schmidt and other European political leaders reacted cautiously because of Reagan's previous harsh rhetoric against the Soviet Union. In addition, Schmidt disliked Reagan's October 16, 1981, statement that a tactical nuclear exchange in Europe would not mean an all-out U.S.-USSR nuclear war. Although Reagan, on October 21, clarified his belief that any threat to Europe was a threat to the United States, Schmidt distrusted the president.

Thus, during a four-day meeting in Bonn with Soviet leader Leonid Brezhnev, Schmidt sympathized with the Soviet desire for arms control, giving qualified support to the zero-option. Like U.S. Secretary of State Alexander Haig, Schmidt saw the zero-option as a starting point of talks because it could not be a final U.S. option for arms control.

See November 18, 1981.

### November 27–28, 1981

*Five African nations assist Chad against Libya.*

Although Libya announced its withdrawal from Chad on November 3, neither the black African leaders nor the French believed that President Gadhafi would give up in Chad. The decision by the African leaders came in response to a meeting of French African leaders on November 4 that asked for African forces to help Chad. France had pledged an active military and economic role to help Chad remain independent.

### November 29, 1981

*In the first Honduran elections since 1971, Roberto Suazo Cordova is chosen president.*

The United States had pressured the Honduran government of General Policarpo Paz García to end his corrupt nine-year reign and permit a free election.

### November 30, 1981

**Geneva missile talks begin between Paul H. Nitze of the United States and Yuli A. Kvitsinsky of the USSR.**

Although President Reagan announced his zero-option on November 18, U.S. delegates had no specific treaty proposal to offer on November 30. The Soviet delegate offered a four-point program for a nuclear-free Europe that Soviet President Brezhnev shared with West German Chancellor Helmut Schmidt on November 24, 1981. The Soviets proposed (1) a moratorium on all 1,000 to 5,500 km–range missiles in Europe; (2) negotiations for reduction of these weapons; (3) reducing to zero all medium-range systems that threatened Europe, meaning British and French as well as U.S. and Soviet missiles; and (4) elimination of all tactical nuclear weapons in Europe with a range of fewer than 1,000 kilometers. In sum, the four points would have eliminated missiles but left Europe subject to the Soviets' superior position in conventional weapons.

Both Reagan's (November 18) and Brezhnev's proposals appeared as political ploys, not genuine attempts at gaining arms control. The first round of talks achieved nothing and adjourned on December 17, 1981.

### December 9, 1981

**At a United Nations Law of the Sea Conference, the U.S. delegation again prevents completion of a treaty.**

To the frustration of delegations from other nations, this third conference still failed to reach an agreement, which many member nations thought had been finished before Ronald Reagan became president.

Striving to satisfy five U.S. business consortia wanting to profit from seabed mining, the Reagan administration did not advocate a laissez-faire attitude as it often did because the consortium managers wanted an international agreement limited to helping them stabilize costs while avoiding conflicting claims to seabed rights.

The Reagan team and its lobbyists wanted to renegotiate two parts of the earlier treaty. One was Article 82, which was based on the concept that the ocean's mineral wealth was a common heritage of humankind and therefore would give royalty payments to Third World countries for minerals mined in ocean areas more than 200 miles from their coastlines. For U.S. businessmen, Article 82 was, wrote William Safire in the *New York Times*, "a great rip off" to benefit the Third World. For the Carter administration and most developed European nations that had supported Article 82, this concept helped Third World powers play catch-up with the industrial nations that had exploited the Third World to obtain raw materials for several hundred years.

The second provision that Reagan's team wanted to change created an international cartel to mine such seabed minerals as copper, nickel, cobalt, and manganese. The United States delegation considered these minerals to be of strategic value; therefore, their extraction was essential to some sort of U.S. control.

Because of the U.S. objections, the Law of the Sea Treaty was not completed at the December U.N. conference.

See March 3, 1981.

### December 10, 1981

**President Reagan bans travel to Libya and asks 1,500 Americans to leave that country.**

Following the August 19 naval incident in the Gulf of Sidra, tensions increased between Tripoli and Washington. On December 3, U.S. law officers claimed that five Libyan terrorists had plotted to assassinate the president, and on November 22, *Newsweek* magazine reported that Libyan death squads had contracted to kill Americans, a charge Libya denied and asked the United Nations to investigate on November 23, 1981. Neither of these charges was ever substantiated.

### December 11, 1981

*Argentine President Roberto Eduardo Viola is overthrown by General Leopoldo Galtiera.*

Sworn in as Argentina's president on March 29, Viola had named General Horacio Tomás Liendo to assume presidential duties after Viola developed heart problems. On December 18, Galtiera's coup removed both Viola and Liendo from power.

### December 11, 1981

*Javier Pérez de Cuellar of Peru is chosen secretary-general of the U.N. security council.*

The selection of Pérez de Cuellar ended a deadlock that began on October 27, 1981. In the dispute, one group favored the reelection of Kurt Waldheim of Austria and a second group, including the People's Republic of China and many Third World nations, preferred the Tanzanian foreign minister, Salim A. Salim. After Waldheim withdrew his candidacy, the two factions compromised by selecting Pérez de Cuellar. The U.N. General Assembly approved the selection on December 15, 1981.

### December 11, 1981

**Organization of Petroleum Exporting Countries (OPEC) ends a bad year by cutting oil prices.**

OPEC's success depended on all members respecting agreements on prices and production. After oil prices reached $41 per barrel in December 1980, some member countries began to renege on OPEC instructions by selling at lower prices, increasing production, or seeking higher prices on their own. The steady decline in world oil demand after 1979 also affected the national income of oil-exporting countries. In April 1981, for example, Mexico cut oil prices when its customers refused to pay a $3 premium. Mexico needed money to pay the large debt it had incurred during the 1970s.

Throughout 1981, OPEC had trouble keeping members in line. On May 26, OPEC agreed to vary prices from $36 to $41 per barrel and to cut production by 10%. But after Libya and Nigeria both cut prices by $2 to $4, OPEC members met in August and deadlocked over prices. On October 29 at Geneva, OPEC approved a price of $34 through 1982, but this did not hold.

By December 11, OPEC unity was in disarray, but members again agreed to cut prices between 20 cents and $1 per barrel. These price cuts were good news to OPEC's customers and to President Reagan's economic program.

## December 11, 1981

### West and East German presidents meet for the first time since 1970.

Chancellor Helmut SCHMIDT's efforts to better West German relations with Eastern Europe seemed to pay off when President Erich HONECKER welcomed Schmidt to East Germany to discuss trade relations.

## December 13, 1981

### Poland's Prime Minister Jaruzelski declares martial law.

Demonstrations, protests, and strikes continued in Poland after Jaruzelski's 90-day "period of peace" ended in May 1981 with no significant economic improvement. On October 13, three Polish cities had wildcat strikes, and 12,000 textile workers walked off the job. On October 20, steelworkers at Katowice occupied the steel mill, where they found a radio station to assist them. The Soviet Union had called for a crackdown against protesters on September 17, but strikes continued in October and November, with 190,000 students striking on November 12.

On December 12, the Solidarity trade union issued a new set of demands for the Polish government to fulfill. The next day Jaruzelski decreed martial law throughout Poland. The decree suspended all civil rights and labor union activity while Polish police arrested many union leaders and brought Solidarity

leader Lech Wałęsa to Warsaw where he could be controlled. On December 30, Jaruzelski sought to demonstrate an interest in improving Poland's economic condition by appointing three groups to plan political, social, and economic reforms. (See December 23, 1981.)

Jaruzelski's reasons for calling martial law became controversial. On December 24, the prime minister said he chose martial law as the lesser of two evils, the alternative being a Soviet invasion. Later, Jaruzelski's statement was challenged by members of Solidarity as well as the Soviet Union. The controversy continued in the post–Cold War era although Jaruzelski's reputation improved after 1981 when he showed concern for the Polish people's preferences. (See July 24, 1986.)

After 1989, opened archives of Poland, the Soviet Union, and other Warsaw Pact members disclosed that Jaruzelski chose martial law even though the Soviet Union refused to intervene despite the prime minister's plea for military assistance. Details about declassified documents and other sources regarding Poland's 1980–81 developments are in the Cold War International History Project's *Bulletin* (Winter 1998), especially Mark Kramer's article and Jaruzelski's response.

See February 9 and March 30, 1981.

## December 14, 1981

### President Reagan reacts to Poland's martial law by suspending all aid to Warsaw and warning of "grave" consequences if repression continues.

Other Western countries also reacted strongly to the Polish repression. On December 16, foreign bankers refused further loans to Poland and insisted on payments and interest of prior loans. While the Soviet Union denied involvement in Poland, Western nations blamed Moscow as much as Jaruzelski for the Polish action.

## December 14, 1981

### Congress retains the Clark Amendment but authorizes $11.4 billion of foreign aid.

The Reagan administration had persistently asked for the repeal of the Clark Amendment, which restricted economic aid to rebels in Angola. The House of Representatives refused to repeal this amendment while the Senate approved. The report of a congressional conference committee accepted the House version of the bill, which retained the Clark Amendment. This amendment prevented the White House from assisting any faction in Angola. Reagan wanted to help the leader of UNITA, Jonas Savimbi.

See April 6 and April 23, 1981.

### December 14, 1981

**Israel annexes the Golan Heights, which it took from Syria in 1967.**

Since the Six-Day War of 1967, Israel had claimed that the Golan Heights was occupied territory. On December 14, the Knesset (parliament) voted to annex the area to Israel.

After Syrian forces entered Lebanon in 1976, tension increased between Israel and Damascus because Syria helped the Palestinians who lived in Lebanon and often staged attacks on Israeli territory.

On April 29, 1981, serious problems arose because Syria moved Soviet-supplied surface-to-air missiles (SAM) into Lebanon to shoot down Israeli planes that bombed and strafed the Palestinian camps. On May 28, 1981, Israeli planes destroyed a Libyan SAM-9 missile located in Damascus. Israel also announced it would assist the Christian Phalangist armies in Lebanon, a group opposing the Palestinians.

President Reagan sent Philip C. Habib as his special envoy to the Middle East on May 5, but after four rounds of talks between Israeli Prime Minister Menachem Begin and Syrian President Hafez Assad (May 13 to 22; June 9 to 25; July 9 to 24; and November 29 to December 11) and several cease-fires that were not respected, the situation remained chaotic.

The annexation of the Golan Heights also increased problems between Israel and the United States. President Reagan announced suspension of an agreement on strategic cooperation signed on November 30, 1981. Prime Minister Begin responded harshly, saying "no power on Earth" would make Israel repeal the annexation and that U.S. conduct in Vietnam gave Washington no moral ability to oppose Israel's bombing of Beirut or a PLO camp.

The annexation was probably done to preempt U.S. demands that Israel withdraw from all territories it occupied in 1967.

See June 5, 1967; see also November 8, 1976.

### December 15, 1981

**Congress approves the largest peacetime military expenditure in the nation's history: $199.7 billion plus construction authorization of $7.1 billion for fiscal 1982.**

Although Congress and the president had argued since July 1981 about budget allocations, the most crucial issue was not congressional support for a military buildup but about how deeply the federal government would cut social spending. President Reagan urged drastic cuts in social programs, while Democrats and many moderate Republicans in Congress resisted large cuts in nonmilitary programs. The dispute prevented passage of spending authorizations by the normal October 1 deadline for the 1982 fiscal year, and Congress and the president had agreed on stopgap spending provisions on October 2 and November 19.

The budget dispute continued into December, and about the time another stopgap bill expired on December 15, Congress and the White House agreed on an omnibus appropriations bill. The military budget included large expenditures in new programs that would require continued large-scale funding in future years. Reagan accepted more social program funding than he desired and blamed Congress for upsetting his plans to balance the budget by 1984.

### December 16, 1981

**U.N. General Assembly resolution calls on El Salvador to negotiate peace with its rebels.**

The United States opposed this resolution but it passed: 68 for, 22 against, and 53 abstaining. The United States argued that Cuba and Nicaragua supplied arms to the rebels, who would stop fighting if these shipments stopped.

### December 17, 1981

**Terrorists abduct the U.S. Commander of NATO forces for southern Europe.**

Brigadier General James L. Dozier was kidnapped from his Verona, Italy, apartment by an Italian terrorist group, the Red Brigade. After 42 days in captivity, Dozier was rescued by Italian national police. The police had rounded up scores of suspects in

December, one of whom gave information leading to the Red Brigade hideout in Padua. Dozier was not hurt and no shots were fired during the police raid.

### December 23, 1981

**President Reagan's economic sanctions punish the Soviet Union for Poland's martial law.**

On December 23, after Poland's Prime Minister Jaruzelski decreed martial law, President Reagan announced restrictions on aviation and fishing imports and curbed loans to Poland. Previously on December 13, Reagan said he wrote to Soviet President Brezhnev, warning him the United States would take action if martial law continued. On December 29, Reagan added more sanctions by stopping future sales of electronic and computer equipment as well as oil and gas machinery including a $90 million sale of pipe-laying tractors essential to the building of a natural gas pipeline from Siberia to central Europe. However, Reagan neither ended U.S. grain purchases nor suspended arms talks scheduled for January 12, 1982.

Although European leaders believed U.S. sanctions would not help Poland, the European Economic Community agreed not to undercut the sanctions.

Documents declassified after 1989 indicate that the CIA had contacts with four Polish officials who gave the Americans secret information about Polish events in 1980–81. In particular, the CIA had reports from Colonel Ryszard Kuklinski, a high-ranking Polish army officer, that the Soviets told Jaruzelski the Red Army would not intervene even though there were many Soviet troops along the Polish border. Thus, the Soviet Union was not primarily to blame for Juruzelski's invocation of martial law. Details about Kuklinski are in the Cold War International History Project's *Bulletin* (Winter 1998) in the article "Jaruzelski, the Soviet Union and the Imposition of Martial Law in Poland: New Light on the Mystery of December 1981," by Mark Kramer.

# 1982

### January 4, 1982

**William P. Clark replaces Richard V. Allen as national security adviser: the NSC role is enlarged.**

Allen had come under public criticism for allegedly receiving cash and gifts from Japanese businessmen seeking access to the White House. In addition, President Reagan's close advisers believed Clark as national security adviser would assume greater authority over foreign policy decisions, a role that Secretary of State Alexander Haig wanted.

Clark had little experience in foreign affairs, having been a California state supreme court judge before Reagan became president. More crucial, as a longtime friend of the president, Clark would report directly to Reagan. Previously, Allen had reported to Edwin Meese, the president's counselor.

### January 8, 1982

**The United States refuses to grant an export license to General Electric Company to sell natural gas pipeline equipment to the Soviet Union.**

Although President Reagan claimed that the restrictions on technology sales to the Soviets was punishment for Moscow's involvement in Poland, the Reagan administration actually hoped to weaken the Soviet economy by preventing the construction and sale of natural gas to Western Europe. In addition, many of Reagan's advisers did not like European leaders' attempts to pursue interests apart from the United States and thus opposed the natural gas project, which West Germany, France, and others had worked out with Moscow.

To further assert the embargo in 1982, Reagan extended the ban to products that relied on the technology developed by General Electric and other U.S. companies. To do so, he tried to prohibit European technical products from being sold to the Soviets if the European industries had used a license from the Americans to employ U.S. technology. The Europeans, of course, objected to this policy.

To placate Washington, the European Economic Community (EEC) voted on March 11 to reduce their 1982 imports from the USSR by $140 million, having first rejected a proposal to reduce imports by $350 million.

See November 19, 1981, and January 18, 1982.

### January 10–11, 1982

**A Haitian coup attempt fails to overthrow President Jean-Claude Duvalier.**

Haitian exiles based in Florida and led by Bernard Sansaricq invaded and took over Tortuga Island until Duvalier's forces chased them away. On January 14, U.S. authorities in Florida arrested Sansaricq for violating U.S. neutrality laws.

### January 11, 1982

**President Reagan's attempt to please two Chinas satisfies neither.**

While the Reagan administration said it recognized China's only government as being the People's Republic (PRC), the president continued to assist the Republic of China on Taiwan (ROC) in order to mollify his right-wing supporters, who insisted that the ROC was the legitimate Chinese government.

On January 11, when Reagan approved the sale of F-5E jet planes to the ROC but refused to approve Taiwan's request for more advanced planes, the president pleased neither side. Senator Jesse Helms (R-N.C.) said the president had assured him that Taiwan would get more sophisticated planes. At the same time, the PRC objected to the sale of any U.S. planes to the ROC and asserted that Sino-American relations faced a severe test over this question.

See August 16, 1982.

### January 14, 1982

**President Reagan proposes a budget item to produce new binary nerve gas weapons, ending the nation's 13-year moratorium on making lethal nerve gas weapons.**

Citing his administration's claim that the Soviet Union was using chemical weapons in Southeast Asia and Afghanistan, the President told Congress that developing binary chemical weapons was essential to deter Soviet use of such weapons.

Defense Secretary Caspar Weinberger later explained that binary nerve gas would be used in Bigeye aerial bombs and in 155 mm artillery shells. Binary gases consist of two chemicals that alone are not lethal but, when mixed together as a bomb descends or as a shell is fired, become lethal on exploding.

In February 1982, Reagan announced U.S. plans to end its 13-year moratorium on chemical weapons by producing binary weapons. Nevertheless, Reagan's proposal ran into serious debate in Congress.

See September 13, 1981, for additional charges that the Soviets used chemical weapons; see also March 8, 1982; August 16, 1982.

### January 18, 1982

**An American military attaché in Paris is killed by Lebanese terrorists.**

Lieutenant Colonel Charles Ray was shot outside his home. In a phone call, the Lebanese Armed Revolutionary Faction claimed responsibility for the attack. Later, on April 10, 1981, Paris police reported that the gun used to kill Ray had also been used in the attempt on Christian A. Chapman's life, the American chargé d'affaires in Paris during November 1981.

### January 19, 1982

**Japan and Western European nations refuse the U.S. request for economic sanctions against Poland and the Soviet Union.**

To punish Poland and the USSR for the repressive measures taken by the Polish government on December 13, 1981, President Reagan asked a meeting of delegates from NATO nations and Japan to adopt similar economic sanctions, especially by embargoing the export of high-technology products to the Soviet Union.

Meeting in Brussels, the United States and its major allies readily agreed that Poland's government should be condemned for decreeing martial law. However, the allies rejected the U.S. request for sanctions. Although only 4% of Western Europe's trade was with Eastern Europe, most of those products were high-technology equipment that required a stable source of customers because of their costly production. European banks also had made many loans to Eastern European countries, which repaid them through trading activity. Consequently, industrialists and bankers in France, West Germany, Italy, and

Great Britain opposed U.S. sanctions as worthless in influencing the Soviets. European leaders pointed out that President Reagan did not stop U.S. grain shipments to the Soviet Union because he did not want to harm U.S. agriculture.

Subsequently, Western European governments continued their economic relations with the communist countries. On January 13, the West German government told West German businessmen that it would not restrict natural gas pipeline materials to the USSR. On January 23, France signed a 25-year agreement to purchase 2,980 billion cubic feet of Siberian natural gas each year. On February 10, French banks agreed to loan the USSR $140 million to purchase French equipment for the pipeline.

See July 22, 1982.

## January 25, 1982

### Polish Prime Minister Wojciech Jaruzelski denounces U.S. economic sanctions and defends martial law.

Jaruzelski said that civil war would have erupted in Poland if he had not used martial law to quell the disturbances. Following his speech, the Polish government took three actions to demonstrate the prime minister's resolve: parliament approved the December 1981 martial law decrees; on January 28, Polish police released a film to "prove" allegations that nine Americans engaged in espionage in Poland; and on February 8, Jaruzelski's cabinet proposed plans to free Poland from economic dependence on the West.

On April 6, Western banks indicated that Poland had paid interest due on its 1981 debt and rescheduled $2.4 billion of 1981 principal that Poland could not pay, a plan that was revised on November 3, 1982, to defer repayment of the $2.4 billion for eight years.

More significantly, on January 31, 1982, to avert troubles for Western bankers President Reagan declared that Poland was not in default on its debts. The United States decided to pay $71 million in interest that Poland owed on loans for American agricultural products.

## January 26, 1982

### Secretary of State Alexander Haig links the renewal of strategic arms talks to the settlement of Poland's crisis.

Although Soviet Foreign Minister Andrey Gromyko told Haig that Polish problems were internal affairs of a third country and thus not appropriate for U.S.-USSR discussions, this negative response did not long delay the strategic arms talks.

Actually, Haig's statement indicated that President Reagan had decided to continue strategic negotiations with the Soviets, a position that hard-line advisers of the president, such as Jeane J. Kirkpatrick, desired. Moreover, Reagan did not use the Polish situation to halt the intermediate theater nuclear weapons negotiations that began their second round in Geneva in January 1982.

See February 2, 1982; see also June 29, 1982.

Reagan's principal reaction to Poland's martial law was economic sanctions, a situation that greatly disturbed U.S.-NATO relations but hardly harmed Moscow.

On U.S. sanctions, see January 19, 1982.

## January 28, 1982

### To obtain more economic aid for El Salvador, President Reagan certifies that El Salvador has improved its human rights record during the past year.

Despite the alleged massacre of civilians by the Salvadoran military and reports of serious human rights abuses, Reagan reported human rights progress in that country, as required by Congress before economic aid could be sent. On January 27, a guerrilla attack on the country's largest air base destroyed four U.S.-supplied helicopters and six other aircraft. This attack indicated to El Salvador's government the need for U.S. aid.

On February 1, 1982, the Defense Department sent $55 million of emergency supplies to El Salvador, and Reagan asked Congress to approve an additional $100 million for 1982.

Some data that contradicted Reagan's certificate of progress in El Salvador included a Roman Catholic Legal Aid Office report that 13,353 noncombatants were killed in 1981 and a Human Rights Commission report that 16,276 died in 1981. Both groups claimed that El Salvador's military groups were responsible for most of the murders.

The U.S. State Department called these death reports insurgent propaganda. Evidence of El Salvador's progress, the department stated, was the arrest in January 1982 of six suspects for the murder of four American missionaries in December 1980. Previously, El Salvador had freed six suspects in this murder case.

See December 4, 1980; see also July 12, 1981.

### January 29, 1982

**France sells Nicaragua arms despite U.S. opposition.**

Criticizing countries (i.e., the United States) that imposed their will on other nations, French Foreign Minister Claude Cheyson said France would not cancel its $15.8 million arms sale to Nicaragua. President Reagan wanted Europeans to embargo arms to Nicaragua and to aid the Contra rebels. France said its sale made Managua less dependent on the Soviet Union.

### January 31, 1982

**India and Pakistan agree to discuss a nonaggression pact.**

Pakistan's Foreign Minister, Agha Shahi, met with Indian Foreign Minister, Chinmoy Gharekhan, in New Delhi, where they accepted the principle of mutual nonaggression, a concept that if made into a treaty would be a landmark between two countries that had often fought each other since gaining independence in 1947. To assist this process, a joint commission was formed to meet regularly on regional problems. Nevertheless, the dispute over Kashmir continued to haunt Indo-Pakistani relations.

### February 2, 1982

*The Syrian army attacks members of the Muslim Brotherhood in Hama, where a bloodbath allegedly occurs.*

As part of their opposition to President Hafiz al-Assad and the ruling Alawite sect of northern Syria, radicals of the Muslim Brotherhood had exploded a car bomb that killed over 100 people in Damascus in December 1981.

To retaliate, the Syrian army on February 2, 1982, sought to arrest some radicals in Hama, a village 120 miles north of Damascus. By February 10, the incident mushroomed into a large-scale fight during which most of the Brotherhood's leaders were killed. Although thousands of others were reported to have been killed, the exact extent of the slaughter was unclear because the Syrian army sealed off the city from all outsiders.

### February 2, 1982

**A draft proposal of President Reagan's "zero-option" arms treaty is presented to Soviet delegates at Geneva.**

The second round of intermediate-range arms talks in Geneva found the United States and the USSR offering different proposals, neither of which was acceptable to the other side.

Reagan's zero-option proposal had not been ready to present during the November 1981 talks but was now offered. The Soviets said it was not acceptable because it did not include the elimination of French and British missiles and therefore would give NATO an advantage over the Soviets.

On February 3, the Soviets proposed that each side cut two-thirds of its medium-range missiles. The United States rejected this idea, arguing that it would leave the Soviets superior in conventional and nuclear weapons in Europe.

See November 30, 1981.

### February 11, 1982

**MX missile-basing debate heats up after the Defense Department says it will deploy the first 40 MX in vacated, nonhardened Minuteman silos.**

Ever since the Reagan administration abandoned President Jimmy Carter's underground basing plan, the Department of Defense seemed uncertain what basing scheme to adopt, a critical matter because it involved the broader strategy of whether the MX would be a second-strike retaliatory weapon or a U.S. first-strike weapon because it could not survive a Soviet attack.

In October 1981, Defense Secretary Caspar Weinberger talked about basing up to 36 MX in obsolete Titan missile silos in Arkansas, Kansas, and Missouri. In January 1982, however, Reagan officials indicated that existing Minuteman silos would be used, a decision announced on February 11. This choice would save $3 billion on rebuilding silos and would avoid the necessity of obtaining the Soviet Union's permission to harden the silos, a condition required by SALT II that, though unratified, both nations treated as being operative.

Critics of the old silo-basing mode immediately challenged the decision. Tom Wicker of the *New York Times* wrote that the use of existing silos would make the MX vulnerable and would be correctly perceived by Moscow as a new U.S. first-strike weapon. By March 19, the Senate Armed Services Committee voted to have Congress block the February 11 plan and deny any MX production funds unless permanent, hardened silos were used.

Following this advice, the Senate committee deleted $2.1 billion from the defense budget for fiscal 1983. The debate on this question had only begun.

See October 2, 1981, and December 21, 1982.

### February 24, 1982

#### The Caribbean Basin Initiative (CBI) is announced by President Reagan.

This proposal was designed to provide nations of the Caribbean Sea and Central America with freer access to the U.S. market, giving them trade concessions not extended to other nations.

### February 26, 1982

#### The United States relaxes its export restrictions on South Africa.

As part of its effort at "positive disengagement" to gain South African concessions in problem regions such as Namibia, President Reagan ended many limits that previous U.S. administrations had placed on South African trade to coerce concessions. For opposite reasons, Reagan ended most trade limits. On

March 11, 1982, Reagan also eased restrictions on South African military officials visiting the United States in search of arms; on November 11, Washington supported an International Monetary Fund loan of $1.1 billion to South Africa.

Many spokespersons in the United States opposed Reagan's actions because they believed such benefits enabled South Africa to continue its apartheid policies at home and its military interference in Namibia (South-West Africa) and Angola.

See December 9, 1982.

### March 4, 1982

#### The Reagan administration has difficulty finding evidence that Cuba and Nicaragua are helping rebels in El Salvador.

With White House mail running 10 to 1 against the president's policies in El Salvador and with over 100 congressmen urging Reagan to seek negotiations, Secretary of State Alexander Haig experienced difficulty in providing the "overwhelming and irrefutable" evidence that he told a congressional committee was available to prove that Salvadoran rebels were aided by Cuba and Nicaragua.

In early March, two administration attempts to offer proof backfired. First, on March 4, after Haig told congressmen that the United States had captured a Nicaraguan officer sent to aid El Salvador's rebels, the captive escaped and obtained safe-conduct from the Mexican embassy. Mexican officials said the man was a 19-year-old university student who was "captured" on his way home to Nicaragua.

On March 7, the State Department suffered more embarrassment when it called a press conference to present a Nicaraguan who would verify the U.S. claims of foreign intervention in El Salvador. Orlando José Tardencillas Espinosa was presented to the reporters, but he refuted the claims that he was supposed to verify. As a guerrilla captured in El Salvador, Espinosa said he was taken to the U.S. embassy and instructed to give evidence that Cubans were aiding the rebels. "They gave me an option," he said; "I could come here or face certain death. All my previous statements about training in Ethiopia and Cuba were false."

The State Department's only remaining option was to say it could not give all evidence because CIA sources would be damaged. Subsequently, William Casey, director of the CIA, gave a classified briefing to 26 "leakproof" former officials who reported his evidence was "very persuasive." CIA photos showed military bases similar to Cuba's, Soviet-type armored tanks, and four airfield runways being lengthened for jet planes. The Nicaraguan government said these were defense preparations resulting from the threat of a U.S. invasion, denying that it aided El Salvador's rebels.

### March 7, 1982

***In Guatemala, General Ángel Anibal Guevara is elected president but is replaced within a month by General Efrain Ríos Montt.***

Some observers believed that the guerrilla conflict was more widespread in Guatemala than in El Salvador. Preceding the election, competing guerrilla groups intensified their attacks while the army used a scorched earth program to eradicate guerrilla hideouts. Within 12 months, Amnesty International reported that at least 13,500 people had been killed in Guatemala.

Even among Guatemalan politicians, there was intense preelection conflict. All four candidates for president were conservatives because the two liberal candidates had been assassinated. There were also charges of fraud in the election won by General Guevara. Finally, on March 23, a three-man army junta took over the government, ousting Guevara. General Ríos MONTT headed the junta. On June 9, 1982, Montt deposed his two partners, suspended the constitution, named himself president, and declared a state of siege.

### March 8, 1982

**The Reagan administration claims Soviet forces have killed at least 3,000 people in Afghanistan with chemical weapons.**

To substantiate this and previous claims that the Soviets used chemical weapons, Deputy Secretary of State Walter J. Stoessel offered evidence of 47 incidents with 3,042 deaths between 1978 and 1981. The data were based on accounts of Afghan defectors, including some who said they had been trained in chemical warfare by Soviet advisers. Stoessel admitted he had no samples of the chemicals or the weapons; nor did he have pictures showing toxic weapon use. He asserted, however, that the victims' physical symp-

toms and the dates of the alleged attacks supported his claims.

Both on March 22 and on December 5, 1982, the State Department issued reports containing circumstantial evidence that Soviet, Laotian, and Vietnamese forces used chemical weapons causing over 10,000 deaths since 1975. These accounts of "yellow rain" chemicals were questioned by many scientists who argued that the incidents and symptoms could have resulted from the same type of herbicides the United States used in Vietnam. They argued that the State Department gave no hard, direct evidence of chemical attacks.

In the 1987 article "Sverdlovsk and Yellow Rain: Two Classes of Soviet Non-compliance," published in volume 11 (Spring 1987) of *International Security*, Professor Elisa D. Harris reviewed all the Reagan administration claims since September 13, 1981, concluding that they were filled with errors and inconsistencies. She believed verification problems caused the difficulties but that those who favored the renewed U.S. production of chemical weapons used the false data to bolster their cause and to undermine the arms control process.

See September 13, 1981.

### March 10, 1982

**The United Nations Human Rights Commission votes to urge Poland to restore fundamental freedoms.**

The United States voted with the 19-vote majority; 13 nations opposed the resolution, and 10 abstained.

On March 2, 1982, Polish Prime Minister Wojciech Jaruzelski met with Soviet President Leonid Brezhnev, informing him that future challenges to communism would be "cut short." Since December 1981, Poland's martial law kept a tight reign on domestic order, with demonstrators being arrested and strikes being prevented or broken.

### March 10, 1982

**The United States embargoes almost all trade with Libya, claiming that it supports terrorists and subversive activities.**

Placing export licensing requirements on all Libyan purchases other than food and medicine, President Reagan also banned all Libyan oil imports and prohibited any high-technology exports to Libya. About 2% of U.S. oil had come from Libya.

U.S. allies in Europe refused to cooperate by levying similar sanctions. They disagreed with Reagan's claim that Libya's leader, Mu'ammar al-Gadhafi, was the chief supporter of terrorists.

### March 14, 1982

**During a major Contra attack in Nicaragua, the U.S.-backed rebels seriously damage bridges on the Negro and Coco Rivers by detonating explosives.**

The Contras had been organizing throughout 1981 with the aid of the CIA and Argentina. This attack was made by the Nicaraguan Democratic Front (FDN), which consisted of many former military members of the dictatorial Somoza government that was overthrown in 1979. The leader of the FDN was Enrique Bermudez Varela, who had been a colonel in Somoza's National Guard and had served as Somoza's defense attaché in Washington in 1977.

The FDN made continuous raids into Nicaragua following this first significant action. Most of the raids were on industrial, transportation, and agricultural targets to weaken the economy. Bermudez hoped to seize the whole eastern Costa de Mosquitos province, a goal he never achieved.

See November 23, 1981.

### March 18, 1982

**In Pusan, South Korea, unknown arsonists burn the American cultural center as anti-Americanism grows.**

Although the extent of anti-Americanism in South Korea was unclear, this attack indicated some extensive opposition. Students at Seoul's National University circulated leaflets calling for the withdrawal of the 40,000 U.S. troops stationed in South Korea. But many Koreans feared such action would cause a war between the two Koreas.

The two students arrested for the fire in Pusan said they opposed U.S. backing of the repressive regime of President Chun Doo Hwan.

### March 24, 1982

*A coup d'état in Bangladesh brings General Muhammad Ershad to power.*

Since gaining independence in 1971, Bangladesh had made some progress under President Ziaur Rahman from 1975 to 1980. The country began to produce more food while parents had fewer children in the overpopulated nation.

From 1980 to 1982, however, political conflict arose. First, Rahman was assassinated, and President Abdus Sattar was elected in May 1981. Military leaders complained, however, that Sattar's civilian leadership brought corruption, and on March 24, a military coup overthrew Sattar. General ERSHAD took over, indicating there could be elections in two years if order were restored.

See December 17, 1971, and January 30, 1972.

### March 26–31, 1982

**Visiting Japan and Korea, Defense Secretary Caspar Weinberger asks Tokyo to increase its defense budget and Seoul to protect civil rights.**

As Japan's economy made it the predominate prosperous nation of the world, Americans increasingly felt Tokyo should undertake a greater share of its defense burden, which the United States had funded since the end of World War II. The Japanese were reluctant to do so, but on August 1, 1982, Prime Minister Zeiko Suzaki announced there would be a $64 billion increase in the military budget over the next five years, a 60% increase.

In South Korea, Weinberger expressed U.S. dissatisfaction with President Chun Doo Hwan's political repression. Early in March 1982, Chun amnestied to 2,863 prisoners, including 287 political prisoners, but he kept all opposition party leaders in jail. Chun's major achievement during his first year in office was securing the Olympic Games for Seoul in 1988.

See June 29, 1981.

### March 28, 1982

**El Salvador's election does not give the moderate Christian Democratic (CD) Party the majority preferred by the United States.**

Although President José Napoleon DUARTE's CD Party received a plurality of 35.4%, the right-wing

National Republican Alliance of Roberto d'Aubuisson and other smaller right-wing groups gained 52.4% of the vote, as well as 36 of the 60 seats in the Constituent Assembly, which was elected to write a new constitution. The CDs had only 24 assembly seats. Because left-wing guerrillas boycotted the election, the 1.5 million votes were considered a large turnout, over which more than 500 foreign observers watched.

Within a month of the election the American-backed CDs lost their leadership posts to d'Aubuisson, an alleged leader of the right-wing death squads, who became president of the Constituent Assembly and named a political nonentity, Alvara Alfredo Magaña, as president of El Salvador. Former U.S. Ambassador to El Salvador Robert E. White called d'Aubuisson a "pathological killer," but the Reagan administration now looked for virtues in d'Aubuisson, who received U.S. economic aid.

See May 20, 1982.

### March 31, 1982

**Deputy Undersecretary of Defense T. K. Jones finally testifies to Congress regarding his extremist survivalist claims during a nuclear war.**

Since January 1982, the Senate Subcommittee on Arms Control of the Foreign Relations Committee had tried to get Jones to appear and describe the extremist claims he made publicly regarding a civil defense scheme to enable most of the population to survive a nuclear war. Jones failed to appear at a scheduled hearing, possibly because his extremist ideas embarrassed the Reagan Defense Department.

In many speeches to right-wing groups and in a January 16 interview with Robert Scheer, published in the *Los Angeles Times*, Jones claimed that if every American had a shovel to dig a hole and then cover himself with three feet of dirt, 98% of the population could survive a nuclear war. Before the committee, Jones claimed the United States should do this or something similar, because the Soviet Union's shovel program would permit the Soviets to initiate a nuclear war as they would be protected. Jones said Scheer misinterpreted his position, although the reporter's book *With Enough Shovels* includes the verbatim interview as tape-recorded by Scheer.

Advocates of a protracted nuclear war, who wanted the United States to be able to survive rather

than fear a nuclear conflict, had been part of the Committee on the Clear and Present Danger, which before the 1980 election supported Reagan's views that the Soviet threat had grown because the USSR violated arms control treaties. While Reagan sought votes from these groups and appointed Jones to office on behalf of those interest groups, Jones did not represent the general thought of the Defense Department.

At the March 31 hearings, Richard N. Perle, the assistant defense secretary for international security, accompanied Jones and told the subcommittee that Jones did not speak for the Defense Department on civil defense methods. Perle said civil defense plans were designed to mitigate the consequences if a limited nuclear strike were made with a week's warning before the attack.

### March 31, 1982

***Vietnam drops General Giap of Vietnam War fame from membership in the Communist Party Politburo.***

General Vo Nguyen Giap had been the communists' chief military planner for the war in Indochina from 1945 to 1975. He was one of six party leaders removed from a leadership role as younger party members gained authority.

### April 1, 1972

**Panama assumes police responsibility in the Canal Zone.**

Acting in accordance with a process worked out by an implementation commission for the 1978 Panama Canal Treaty, Panama's first step was to replace U.S. control of the Canal Zone's police function. Future steps would lead to Panama's gaining complete control by 1999.

See June 16, 1978, and September 27, 1979.

### April 2, 1982

***The Falkland Islands War begins when Argentina invades the British-owned islands.***

The April 2 invasion of the Falkland Islands proper began the conflict between Argentina and Great Britain, even though Argentine commandos had landed on South Georgia Island on March 25, 1982. Control of the Falklands and the South Sandwich

Islands had been contested by Britain and Argentina since the early nineteenth century.

Although London had tried to end its responsibility for the islands for many years, diplomatic efforts failed because the British respected the local Falklanders' opposition to any link with Argentina. When Argentina invaded on April 2, Britain had only 80 Royal Marines on the islands and one Antarctic ship nearby.

Although London ignored Argentina's occupation of South Georgia on March 25, Britain's Prime Minister Margaret Thatcher reacted forcefully after Argentina took over the Falklands and South Sandwich Islands. She ordered a 35-ship task force to the South Atlantic and imposed economic sanctions on Argentina backed by the European Economic Community on April 10.

While U.S. Secretary of State Alexander Haig and U.S. Secretary-General Javier Pérez de Cuellar sought a cease-fire, British naval forces blockaded the islands on April 12. Because diplomacy failed to get Argentina to withdraw, British forces attacked South Georgia Island on April 25 and, by June 14, forced all Argentine forces to surrender on the main Falkland Islands.

Two critical military incidents occurred during the struggle. First, a British submarine sank the Argentine cruiser *General Belgrano* on May 3, killing over 300 seamen; second, on May 4, an Argentine Exocet missile hit the British cruiser HMS *Sheffield*, killing 30 crewmen.

Diplomatic efforts by Haig and Pérez de Cuellar failed because each side presented nonnegotiable terms. Secretary Haig tried shuttle diplomacy between London and Buenos Aires and also asked the Organization of American States (OAS) to help achieve a cease-fire. Neither effort had the desired result, and on April 30, President Reagan announced U.S. support for Great Britain, accused Argentina of "armed aggression," and ordered sanctions against Buenos Aires.

OAS members were initially uncertain about how to react, but after the British responded with force, most Latin American nations supported Argentina. On April 21, against U.S. objections, the OAS voted "to consider collective action against Britain." On April 28, OAS delegates adopted a resolution to support Argentina and urge both sides to withdraw their troops.

On June 14, Argentine forces surrendered, and on June 18, the two sides agreed on the return of 10,000 Argentine prisoners taken by the British. On June 26, the British governor of the Falklands returned to his home. On July 12, Reagan lifted sanctions against Argentina but banned U.S. military sales to that country.

During the next seven years, Britain and Argentina held frequent discussions but could not resolve the issue of sovereignty over the Falkland Islands. In October 1989, the two nations agreed to normalize economic and diplomatic relations while the British retained their 2,500-man garrison in the Falklands.

See January 26, August 19, and December 15, 1832, and January 14, 1839; see also July 30, 1940, and March 4, 1948.

## April 17, 1982

### Queen Elizabeth II proclaims Canada's own constitution.

Although Great Britain had long been willing to let Canada have a constitution to replace the British North America Act of 1867, the event was delayed because Canada's ten provinces could not agree on a document. Finally, Canada's Prime Minister Elliott TRUDEAU decided to implement a new constitution after obtaining agreement from all provinces except French-speaking Quebec. Subsequently, on March 29, 1982, the United Kingdom's Parliament ceded its power to amend any Canadian constitution, an act enabling Queen Elizabeth II to visit Canada and officially grant the Constitutional act for Canada to govern itself.

## April 18, 1982

### Ground Zero Week is launched by antinuclear war advocates in the United States.

To publicize their campaign against what they considered the Cold War mentality of the Reagan administration and promote a freeze on all nuclear weapons as a first step toward general and complete nuclear disarmament, the National Nuclear Freeze Committee designated week of April 18–25 as a nationwide campaign of seminars, lectures, teach-ins, and marches to point up the horrors of nuclear war.

Several events related to nuclear war or disarmament preceded and inspired GROUND ZERO WEEK. Two of the most important were a Senate resolution for an immediate nuclear freeze, sponsored by Senators Edward Kennedy (D-Mass.) and Mark Hatfield (R-Oreg.), and the efforts of former presidential advisers McGeorge Bundy, George F. Kennan, Gerard Smith, and Robert S. McNamara to persuade the United States and its NATO allies to declare a "no first use" of nuclear weapons policy in the event of a European war.

The Kennedy-Hatfield resolution called on the United States to seek agreement with the Soviets on a verifiable means to stop the production and deployment of nuclear weapons. It argued that the Reagan administration's policy of seeking U.S. nuclear superiority to force the Soviets to accept arms reduction was "voodoo arms control, which says you must have more in order to have less."

Opponents of the nuclear freeze, such as Republican leader Robert Michel of Illinois, argued that defending freedom, not the possession of nuclear arms, was the main U.S. issue. Freedom, he said, could be defended only by the deterrent power of U.S. nuclear arms.

The "no first use" declaration sought by Bundy, Kennan, Smith, and McNamara was explained in the spring 1982 issue of *Foreign Affairs* magazine and during a Washington press conference on April 8, 1982. Although NATO had retained the "first use" option for nuclear weapons since its founding in 1949, the four former presidential advisers argued that nuclear fighting could never be limited to Europe once it started, and Europeans doubted that Washington would risk the nuclear destruction of the United States if Soviet tanks attacked West Germany. The strain between the United States and its European allies also fueled European antiwar protests, which preferred some alternative to a nuclear holocaust. Bundy and McNamara had been close advisers to Presidents Kennedy and Johnson; Smith had been President Nixon's chief negotiator for SALT I (1972); Kennan was the State Department official who conceived the containment policy in 1948. These former officials advocated a buildup of NATO's conventional forces as the best means of reducing the risk of Soviet aggression and avoiding the chance of nuclear war. "No first use" signified that NATO would retaliate with nuclear weapons if the Soviets used them, but NATO forces would not initiate the first nuclear strike.

Many advocates of the U.S. freeze movement had less explicit reasons for their support, but all agreed that President Reagan's antagonistic rhetoric toward the Soviet Union and his desire to regain U.S. military superiority increased the danger of nuclear war.

The U.S. antinuclear sentiment probably had its greatest practical impact in Congress, where efforts were successful in limiting the large defense expenditures President Reagan advocated. Thus the Senate Armed Services Committee voted in April 1981 to cut $2.1 billion from funds to deploy 40 MX intercontinental ballistic missiles. The committee wanted to know how the president intended to deploy the missiles because he had abandoned President Carter's plans for a mobile underground base designed as a "second-strike" retaliatory basing-mode.

In contrast to the concerns of Congress, Secretary of State Alexander Haig stated on April 6 that the United States would not renounce the "first use" doctrine or agree to a nuclear freeze at present levels of weapons.

See February 11 and June 12, 1982.

## April 25, 1982

### *Israel withdraws from the Sinai Peninsula, returning the territory to Egypt.*

By completing its withdrawal from the Sinai, Israel fulfilled the terms of the Egyptian-Israeli Treaty of 1979, leaving land it had occupied during the Six-Day War (1967).

After Israel annexed the Golan Heights on December 14, 1981, U.S. diplomats feared Israel would also remain in the Sinai, where some Jewish settlers had to be forcibly evicted. Israel's Prime Minister Menachem Begin contended, however, that the Golan's annexation permitted Israel to forego security interests in the Sinai.

In accordance with prior agreement, a United States Sinai Security Mission had been enlarged to operate an early-warning system in the Giddi and Mitlai passes into the Sinai. This system was coordinated with the U.N.'s multinational peacekeeping force in the Sinai.

Although Israel's withdrawal fulfilled one part of the 1979 Camp David accords, Prime Minister Begin's policy of increasing Jewish settlements in the West

Bank territory made fulfillment of the second part of the accords most difficult. The second part said Israel would grant "autonomy" to Palestinians living in the Israeli-occupied West Bank and Gaza Strip regions. To complicate the issue further, Begin had moved Israel's capital city to Jerusalem in violation of previous U.N. agreements.

From January 12 to 28, Secretary of State Haig visited Cairo and Jerusalem several times but could not gain an agreement on the West Bank–Gaza "autonomy" issue for Palestinians.

See June 5, 1967, March 26 and September 19, 1979, and September 17, 1978; see also May 26 and July 30, 1980.

### April 28, 1982

**The U.N. General Assembly votes to condemn Israel and to rebuke the United States for supporting Israel.**

Israeli Prime Minister Begin's policy of defending the Sinai withdrawal by refusing to give up Israel's "occupied territories" on the West Bank and in Gaza increased antagonism between Jewish settlers in the occupied areas and the Palestinian majority living there. Begin told the Israeli Knesset (parliament) that he would demand Israel's sovereignty over the West Bank and Gaza and would never dismantle Jewish settlements as he had in the Sinai; rather, he would expand and consolidate Jewish settlements in the remaining occupied areas.

During the weeks before the Sinai withdrawal, Israeli soldiers and settlers killed 15 Arabs, as many as they had killed during all of 1981. In March 1982, after Israel removed from office the mayors of three Arab towns, the United States vetoed U.N. Security Council resolutions denouncing Israel's action.

Finally, on April 28, Third World nations favoring the Palestinians proposed resolutions against Begin's policies in the General Assembly, where the United States had no veto power. The assembly vote against Israel and the United States was approved—86 in favor, 20 opposing, and 36 abstaining.

See April 25, 1982.

### April 30, 1982

**The United States votes against the Law of the Sea Treaty after it rejects compromises suggested by other nations at the U.N. conference.**

After changing the Law of the Sea Treaty to guarantee seabed mining rights for private enterprise and to prevent a global cartel from favoring Third World rights to future profits, U.N. conference delegates, who had been meeting since March 8, claimed they had "exhausted all possibilities of agreement" and decided to vote. Although the United States objected to regulations that restricted American business interests from seabed mining, the U.S. delegates said they voted against the treaty because of an amendment that allowed new regulations to be enacted without consulting a state involved in that problem.

The United States did not persuade any nations except Turkey, Venezuela, and Israel to join its opposition, while the Soviet Union, Great Britain, and West Germany abstained. Favoring the treaty were 130 nations, including Japan and France. The treaty was scheduled to be signed officially during a U.N. meeting at Kingston, Jamaica.

See December 9 and 10, 1982.

### May 3, 1982

*Jordanian volunteers go to help Iraq fight Iran.*

Arab support for Iran and Iraq was divided; Jordan and most Arab states backed Iraq either covertly or overtly, while Syria and Libya helped Iran. Jordan's decision to permit volunteers to fight for Iraq was announced the day after U.N. mediator Olaf Palme reported that attempts to end the Iran-Iraq war had failed.

### May 5, 1982

*Hungary becomes the first Warsaw Pact nation to join the International Monetary Fund (IMF).*

Hungarian agriculture and trade had increased remarkably under the liberalized economic program of its communist leaders. During 1982, Budapest's Central European International Bank established good relations with six Western European banks and took steps to switch to free-market trade and investment activities. Hungary had applied for membership in the IMF on November 5, 1981, and by May 5, 1982, its application was approved.

### May 9, 1982

**President Reagan proposes strategic arms reduction talks (START) with the Soviet Union, which would not limit but would cut back on nuclear weapons.**

Addressing graduates at Eureka College, Illinois, the president's alma mater, Reagan emphasized that in strategic arms talks the United States wanted nuclear weapons reductions, not limitations as in the 1970s SALT negotiations. He proposed a ceiling of 850 intercontinental launchers and 5,000 warheads with a sublimit of 2,500 warheads on land-based missiles. Both sides would destroy some existing weapons—the Soviets eliminating more launchers and the United States, more warheads.

From a U.S. perspective, Reagan's START prescription favored the views of the State Department and Secretary Alexander Haig, in opposition to proposals of the Defense Department and Secretary Caspar Weinberger. Using suggestions from Richard Perle, an undersecretary of defense, Weinberger wanted to reduce missile throw weights, which would have required deeper Soviet reductions. The State Department argued that this would be impossible for the Soviets to accept and would cause America's NATO allies to question the sincerity of the proposal.

In part, Reagan's decision was a political response to the growing nuclear freeze movements in the United States and Europe. Several nuclear freeze resolutions were before Congress, and others would be on state ballots during the November 1982 elections.

Although on May 18 Soviet Chairman Leonid Brezhnev criticized Reagan's proposal as a "one-sided" idea that would give the United States nuclear superiority, on May 30 the two powers agreed to begin strategic arms discussions on June 29 at Geneva.

### May 9, 1982

**After a visit to the People's Republic of China (PRC), Vice President George Bush failed to end Beijing's opposition to U.S. arms sales to the Republic of China on Taiwan (ROC).**

Bush, who had been the U.S. ambassador to the PRC under President Nixon, believed he could explain to the Chinese the sale of U.S. F5-E fighter planes to the ROC in January 1982. He did not succeed because Beijing considered Taiwan a province of China, not a separate nation. On June 2, Senator Howard Baker, Jr. (R-Tenn.) visited China and found the Chinese angry about the U.S. arms sales to Taiwan.

The situation became more difficult when President Reagan, on July 16, announced that Taiwan and the United States would cooperate in the production of the F5-E planes. Reagan wanted to retain the political support of right-wing Republicans who favored Taiwan.

See August 16, 1982.

### May 10, 1982

**Hopes for U.S. Nicaraguan peace negotiations fade when Nicaragua signs a five-year, $166.8 million aid agreement with the Soviet Union.**

Talks to improve Washington's relations with Managua seemed possible on April 14, 1982, after Nicaragua accepted U.S. proposals for negotiations. On April 18, Nicaragua requested immediate discussions, but the United States replied it was not yet prepared. Subsequently, the Soviet-Nicaraguan five-year pact confirmed the administration's opinions about the communist threat in Central America, and hopes for talks disappeared.

### May 16, 1982

**Salvador Jorge Blanco is elected president of the Dominican Republic.**

During the 1965 U.S. intervention, Jorge BLANCO helped draft the agreement for U.S. Marines to leave the island. For the next 12 years, however, right-wing leader Joaquín Balaguer ruled before losing an election in 1978 to Antonio Guzmán Fernández, who was a member of Jorge Blanco's Dominican Revolutionary Party.

Before Jorge Blanco's inauguration on August 16, 1982, President Guzmán committed suicide, perhaps because he feared the corruption charges being readied against his regime. In July 1982, the U.S. Senate voted to withhold $100 million in land reform funds because an audit disclosed that over $6 million of previous funds had been siphoned off to private farmers and military commanders.

See April 28, 1965.

## May 20, 1982

### El Salvador suspends its land reform program, alarming the U.S. senate.

After Roberto d'Aubuisson became president of El Salvador's Constituent Assembly on April 22, he moved to eliminate or change the land reforms of former President Duarte. The May 20 action suspended the U.S designed "land-to-the-tiller" program, which would have allowed 85% of sharecropping peasant families to purchase up to 17 acres of the land they worked. Earlier, the assembly had canceled Duarte's program for converting medium-sized farms into cooperatives.

Because d'Aubuisson's had done exactly what U.S. congressional leaders feared, the Republican-controlled Senate Foreign Relations Committee voted to cancel $100 million of the $166 million President Reagan had requested for military aid to El Salvador unless land reform was undertaken. D'Aubuisson said a new program would be enacted, and Senator Christopher Dodd (D-Conn.) called suitable land reform the "linchpin" in defeating guerrillas in El Salvador.

See March 28 and October 23, 1982.

## May 24, 1982

### Expiration of the U.S. Soviet space cooperation agreement of 1972.

The Reagan administration decided not to renew this agreement because relations with the Soviets had cooled during the Carter administration and had not improved since Reagan became president. The 1972 agreement's most dramatic result had been the 1975 Apollo 18–Soyuz 19 flight. Discussion of other joint space flights had ended in the fall of 1977 because the United States believed the scientific and technological return was minimal. More modest levels of cooperation had continued in biology and planetary science, which sent test animals into space as late as 1979. Under a separate agreement another biosatellite mission was set for 1983.

On December 29, 1981, President Reagan had decided not to renew Soviet agreements on space, energy research, and space science and technology as part of the sanctions applied against the Soviet Union when Poland imposed martial law. The energy agreement expired on June 28, 1982; the agreement on science and technology expired on July 8, 1982.

See July 15–17, 1975.

## May 27, 1982

### The United States and Morocco agree that the U.S. air force may use Moroccan air bases during emergencies in Africa and the Middle East.

An agreement for the possible use of Moroccan bases was concluded after King HASSAN II of Morocco visited Washington, D.C. The Moroccan base agreement included radar facilities that were an important part of the rapid-deployment force that the Pentagon was preparing for Middle East contingencies.

## May 29, 1982

### The Department of Defense issues a defense guidance (plan) that explicitly prepares for "protracted nuclear conflict."

During early 1982, President Reagan asked the Joint Chiefs of Staff to revise the Single Integrated Operational Plan (SIOP) for fighting the next war so that the United States would prevail in a nuclear war. While this task was not unusual, the chiefs were uneasy about the enthusiasm that Richard Perle and others in the administration showed for the enhancement of the nuclear war–fighting capacity that assumed a limited nuclear war could be fought and won.

The chairman of the Joint Chiefs of Staff, General David Jones, said in June 1982 that he did not see "much of a chance" for any nuclear war to be limited. To fight protracted nuclear war, the Reagan administration wanted the expensive infrastructure essential to nuclear war fighting, that is, not just superior weapons but also superior C3I—superior command, control, communications, and intelligence facilities—to survive all nuclear attacks.

In addition to this nuclear capacity "beyond deterrence," the 1982 defense guidance called for using economic warfare against the USSR, boosting China's military potential to threaten the Soviets, and developing capacities for guerrilla warfare against Eastern European and other communist targets.

As information about this plan leaked to the press and the public, Americans and Europeans became alarmed. When American leaders talked about fighting and winning a nuclear war, the potential destruction encouraged the promotion of a nuclear freeze as a step to nuclear disarmament.

See August 5, 1980, for more on this issue; on survival, see also March 31, 1982, and June 12 and October 22, 1982.

### June 1, 1982

**The United States declares its willingness to help mainland China develop its nuclear power industry.**

For China's modernization program, nuclear power plants would be an essential source of energy. This announcement sanctioned the desire of U.S. companies to build nuclear power plants in China. Deputy Secretary of State Walter J. Stoessel Jr. also began talks with Chinese representatives about nuclear cooperation.

Not coincidental, perhaps, was the fact that on May 29 and 30, 1982, the *New York Times* reported that recent plans of the Department of Defense proposed "measured military assistance" to China to keep as many Soviet forces as possible tied down on the Soviet-Chinese border. China's development of nuclear power had a direct impact on these plans.

See May 29, 1982.

### June 1, 1982

**As a prelude to President Reagan's upcoming visit to West Germany, terrorists bomb four U.S. military bases in the Federal Republic of Germany.**

The bombing attacks were conducted by a small organization, the Revolutionary Cells Terrorist Group. In contrast, large pro-American rallies were held in Munich and Bonn, where West Germans demon-

strated their appreciation of the U.S. alliance with their country since 1948.

### June 4–6, 1982

**The annual summit of the seven major industrial nations is held at Versailles, France.**

The summit discussions were conducted carefully because the European members did not want to embarass President Reagan, whose large budget deficits were detrimental to the other G-7 nations' economies. Europeans blamed the high interest rates and budget deficit of the United States for their economic recessions.

Although little agreement was reached, the seven leaders agreed to consult closely on their national economic policies.

### June 6, 1982

**American Vietnam veterans obtain some data from Vietnam regarding POWs/MIAs.**

Six veterans and three other Americans made an unofficial visit to Hanoi to seek better relations. After their six-day visit, they obtained a few answers to the major problem that beset relations between the two countries—the belief of many Americans that the Vietnamese held live American prisoners of war or men listed as missing in action.

Hanoi denied having any living POWs/MIAs, but the U.S. delegation received information about four soldiers believed to have been killed and a promise that more American bodies would be returned. On October 14, 1982, Hanoi offered the United States the remains of five Americans and material evidence about three others believed to have been MIAs.

### June 6, 1982

*Israeli forces invade Lebanon seeking to defeat Palestinian armies; a lengthy crisis begins.*

Assisted by Christian armies led by Saad Haddad, a Lebanese army officer, the Israelis conducted eight days of intensive fighting against the forces of Palestinian refugees, Lebanese Muslim forces, and the Syrian army. By June 13, Israeli units reached the outskirts of Beirut, where they linked up with Christian Phalangist armies and captured the Beirut-to-Damascus highway; thereby, the Israelis sealed off men and supplies coming to Beirut from Syria.

Hints of an impending Israeli invasion abounded since December 1981 because Israeli and Palestinian forces raided and counterraided along the south border of Lebanon following Israel's annexation of the Golan Heights. On April 9 the United States expressed concern about the Israeli military buildup along the Lebanese border. On April 16 Lebanon's President Elias Sarkis asked the United States and the USSR to prevent an invasion.

The incident that persuaded Israel's cabinet to launch an invasion was the attempted assassination of Ambassador Shlomo Argov by a Palestinian terrorist in London. Argov survived, although paralyzed, and British police captured the assassin, Hassan Said, and two other Palestinians from the Iraqi-backed Abu Nidal group. Although Israeli intelligence believed that Iraq wanted to provoke Israel to defeat the Syrians (an enemy of Iraq), Prime Minister Begin did not tell Israeli cabinet members about this possibility because Begin and his defense minister wanted to invade Lebanon.

Thus, with cabinet approval, Defense Minister Ariel SHARON launched the attack on Lebanon in Operation Peace for Galilee, a bid to end the threat of the Palestine Liberation Organization (PLO) in Lebanon and to end PLO influence in the West Bank and Gaza, so that compliant Palestinian inhabitants would accede to Israel's annexation of those territories. To achieve this Sharon also planned Operation Big Pines to crush the PLO infrastructure in Beirut and drive them out of Lebanon.

Initially, Sharon's plans went well. The U.N. interim forces, which since 1978 had failed to keep the border peace, did not resist the Israeli attack. By June 8, Israeli armies were beyond the 25-mile security zone of southern Lebanon that Sharon told the Israeli cabinet he wanted to control. Israel's army and air force did not stop, however. On June 9 and 10, Israeli planes wiped out 17 of the 19 surface-to-air missile sites that the Soviet Union had given the Syrians and shattered the Syrian air force by shooting down at least 72 Soviet-built MiG-25 fighter planes. Because Sharon did not want to destroy Syria, all that remained was to capture control of the road outside Beirut leading to Damascus and to link up with the Lebanese Christian forces of General Bashir GEMAYEL on June 13.

Sharon had planned that Gemayel's Lebanese Christian army would wipe out the PLO, but Gemayel did not want to go too far to lose Muslim support toward the creation of a postwar Lebanese government. As a result, Israel's commanders avoided a bloody fight in Beirut's streets by undertaking a heavy bombardment of PLO positions in Beirut and preventing food and munitions from reaching PLO Chairman Yasser Arafat's forces. Subsequently, from June 14 to August 13, Israeli tanks, artillery, and aircraft bombarded West Beirut, the enclave of about 16,000 Palestinians and their supporters.

See March 14, 1978; see also August 21 and September 1, 14, and 18, 1982.

### June 8, 1982

**President Reagan announces Project Democracy in a speech to the British Parliament. The project evolves into two segments—one covert, the other overt.**

Although receiving little attention immediately after President Reagan delivered his speech to members of the British Parliament, Project Democracy became a two-track program designed to fulfill the Reagan administration's attempt to promote democracy in countries where authoritarian regimes existed. Project Democracy became a reality after Congress funded a governmental agency called the National Endowment for Democracy on November 22, 1983. The Endowment's overt projects provided funds to support democratic elections outside the United States. For covert programs, the Reagan administration used Endowment for Democracy funds to oppose Soviet activity in nations such as Nicaragua during the 1980s. (See January 14, 1983.)

As part of his May-June trip to Europe, Reagan was invited by British leaders to speak at the Westminster House of Parliament, following his attendance at the G-7 sessions in Versailles, France. During the G-7 sessions, Reagan had tried to persuade other G-7 representatives to stop their trade credits and commercial activities with Warsaw Pact nations, especially the Soviet Union, but had failed to convince the Europeans to change their commercial activities because they favored increased trade with the Soviet Empire.

In London, President Reagan's speech to Parliament focused primarily on his long-standing opposition to Marxian-Leninism as practiced in the

Soviet Union. Reagan's speech expressed his firm belief that the forces of freedom would inevitably triumph over communism, an ideology that would soon be thrown on "the ash-heaps of history." In conclusion, Reagan said "Let us now begin a major effort to secure the best—a crusade for freedom that would engage the faith and fortitude of the next generation."

Following Reagan's June 8 speech, some commentators called it a valuable statement about democracy's challenge to communist rule; other pundits feared the Reagan administration was ready to take enormous risks designed to "roll back" the Soviet Empire. Yet Reagan's deeds did not fit his words. Reagan had lifted the embargo on grain sales to the Soviet Union imposed by President Carter in 1980 after the Soviet forces invaded Afghanistan. Also, he did little when General Jaruzelski declared martial law in Poland in December 1981. (See December 13, 1981).

See January 14, 1983.

### June 12, 1982

**Largest disarmament rally in American history assembles in New York in favor of a nuclear freeze.**

Around the world, people conducted anti-nuclear weapons demonstrations during the spring and summer of 1982. In New York on June 12, crowds estimated at up to 750,000 rallied to promote disarmament.

This event preceded the convening of a special United Nations Disarmament Conference, where Soviet proposals gained favor while President Reagan's responses brought condemnation from peace advocates in the United States and abroad. During the opening session the Soviet delegates pledged not to be the first to use nuclear weapons, a pledge U.S. planners consistently rejected. In addition to opposing the Soviet pledge as "unverifiable and unenforceable," President Reagan, addressing the conference, denounced the Soviet Union for creating tyranny around the world.

On "no first use," see April 18, 1982.

### June 16, 1982

**The United States supports a Cambodian government-in-exile formed by three competing Cambodian groups.**

Officially renamed KAMPUCHEA in 1975, Cambodia had experienced many deaths under the Communist

leader Pol Pot's government before Vietnamese armies defeated his regime, the Khmer Rouge, in 1978–79. To unify groups fighting to force Vietnam's withdrawal, these rebel groups had joined under Prince Norodom Sihanouk and two of his rivals, former Prime Minister Son Sann and the Khmer Rouge spokesman Khieu Samphan. In 1978, the United States encouraged the unity of these groups against Vietnam.

On October 29, 1982, a resolution of the U.N. General Assembly called on Vietnam to remove its 180,000 troops from Cambodia, but Hanoi ignored the request.

See December 3, 1978; January 7, February 17, and June 28, 1979; and June 17, 1980.

### June 21, 1982

**The U.S. air force forms a Space Command to expand U.S. military operations in space.**

The decision to form a special division for space activity gave the air force an impetus to plan and operate military space missions of its own, as well as in cooperation with the National Aeronautics and Space Administration (NASA). As NASA's shuttle flights developed during the 1980s, there was an increased use of the shuttle for military missions of the Space Command.

### June 24, 1982

*A French astronaut joins the Soviet cosmonauts aboard the Soviet T-G spacecraft.*

French Air Force Colonel Jean-Loup Chrétien became the first astronaut who was neither Soviet nor American. He joined the Soviets in a nine-day space flight.

### June 25, 1982

**George P. Shultz is nominated for Secretary of State to replace Alexander Haig, who resigned effective July 5.**

Although Haig gave no public reasons for resigning, his differences in outlook with the rest of the Reagan administration probably determined his action. Haig often disagreed with Secretary of Defense Caspar Weinberger, who used confrontational tactics against U.S. allies.

The current Middle East activity especially dismayed Haig, who was unable to get the Reagan administration to adapt clear, consistent policies between the State and Defense Departments and the National Security Agency.

### June 29, 1982

### Strategic arms reduction talks (START) begin in Geneva between U.S. and Soviet delegates.

Since President Reagan's speech of May 9, 1982, the U.S. media had dubbed the U.S.-USSR negotiations on intercontinental nuclear weapons as START. These talks paralleled other U.S.-USSR negotiations on intermediate theater nuclear weapons that had begun on November 30, 1981.

The U.S. delegation to START was headed by retired General Edward Rowney, who had represented the Joint Chiefs of Staff at the SALT II talks until he resigned in 1979 because of objections to the Carter administration's "weak" position on the talks. Rowney agreed with President Reagan that the United States had to regain its lost strategic nuclear superiority and generally disliked the arms control approach.

The Soviet delegation was led by Viktor A. Karpov, who had worked on SALT II as the principal deputy to chief negotiator Vladimir Semyonov until the final stages of the talks. Although Karpov had been sent home for awhile to treat his alcoholism, he returned in 1982 to demonstrate the Soviet view that START was a descendent of SALT I and SALT II.

Just as Soviet President Brezhnev's May 18 response to Reagan's START proposal suggested a hard Soviet line to counter the U.S. hard line, the talks opened on June 29 with both sides more focused on propaganda rather than serious negotiations. In response to Reagan's START proposals, the USSR offered reductions in its long-range missile and bomber forces if the United States would end its plans to deploy medium-range missiles in Europe and restrict developments of its cruise missiles. This proposal linked the strategic missile talks with the intermediate-range talks, a proposition the United States did not reject but tried to avoid in 1982 and 1983.

On July 20, the Reagan administration refused to renew talks with the USSR and Great Britain on a comprehensive nuclear test ban. The talks had been become stalemate in 1980 after the Soviet intervention in Afghanistan..

### July 8, 1982

### The Mutual and Balanced Force Reduction (MBFR) talks continue in disagreement in Vienna.

Delegates of the North Atlantic Treaty Organization (NATO) and of the Warsaw Pact countries had been sporadically negotiating reductions in their conventional European forces since 1973. Typical of their discussions was the NATO proposal of July 8 to put a ceiling of 900,000 men on each side, a suggestion that the Warsaw Pact delegates questioned but responded to with no enthusiasm.

Many in the Reagan administration wanted to stall these talks until the U.S. military achieved superiority. This approach added to the distrust of both sides regarding each other's official data on existing forces and possible verification methods. Following the 1982 discussion in Vienna, Richard Starr, the chief U.S. negotiator, resigned and was told by Richard Perle, an assistant secretary of defense, "Congratulations! You have obviously done a good job, because nothing happened." Perle was one of the administration's major opponent of arms control efforts.

### July 12, 1982

### Somalia requests and receives U.S. aid against an alleged Ethiopian invasion.

Border tensions existed between Ethiopia and Somalia since 1977, when Somalia tried to assert its right to the Ogaden desert region in Ethiopia. Ethiopia was aided by the Soviet Union and Cuban soldiers, while the United States began aiding Somalia in March 1978.

In 1982, Somalia said Ethiopia began an invasion on July 1 and 11 days later asked for help to halt Ethiopia's successful assault. Ethiopia argued that it only aided rebels of the Western Somalia Liberation Front, who desired to overthrow the Somali government. The rebels, backed by Ethiopia, also had military equipment from the Soviet Union, South Yemen, East Germany, and Cuba.

The United States airlifted $5.5 million of military aid to Somalia on July 24, although by that time Somalia claimed it had driven the Ethiopians back across the border.

See August 8, 1977, and March 8, 1978.

## July 19, 1982

**David Dodge, the acting president of American University in Beirut, Lebanon, is abducted by an unidentified gunman.**

Although Lebanese police and security forces of the Palestine Liberation Organization searched for Dodge, the reason for his abduction and the identity of his captors remained a mystery.

See July 21, 1983.

## July 20, 1982

*Irish terrorists stage two attacks in London, killing 22.*

The Irish Republican Army (IRA) proclaimed these terrorist attacks were in "self-defense" against British control over Northern Ireland. The IRA exploded bombs in two places: the first near Hyde Park struck a detachment of the Queen's Household Cavalry, killing 16 and injuring 50 soldiers, as well as killing 7 horses; the second bombing, in Regent's Park, blew up a bandstand while the Royal Greenjackets Band were performing, killing 6 and injuring 8 musicians. This was the largest IRA terror attack since 1979.

## July 22, 1982

*France defies President Reagan's embargo on Soviet gas pipeline equipment.*

Although French President François Mitterrand supported the deployment of U.S. missiles in Europe, he agreed with other Western European leaders that the Soviet natural gas pipeline was needed and would not enhance the strategic position of the USSR.

President Ronald Reagan, who on January 8, 1982, prohibited General Electric from selling pipeline technology to the Soviets, had on June 18 formally extended trade sanctions to include foreign subsidiaries or foreign companies licensed to use U.S. technology for their equipment. Not only had France defied Reagan's unilateral action but West Germany, Italy, and Great Britain rejected the president's attempt to control their export products.

See August 26 and November 13, 1982.

## July 23, 1982

**The International Whaling Commission (IWC) votes to prohibit all commercial whaling, starting in 1986.**

The IWC had documented the depletion of whales, and the commission's leaders feared that, without a ban, the world population of whales would be extinguished. A majority of IWC representatives agreed by a vote of 25 to 7. After 1986, the IWC resolution stated that only native subsistence herders, such as North American Eskimo, could kill whales for survival purposes.

On November 8, 1982, five whaling countries filed a protest against the prohibition—Japan, the Soviet Union, Chile, Peru, and Norway. In the United States, conservationists formed the Whale Protector Fund to raise money to enable the IWC to enforce the ban.

## August 7, 1982

*Armenian terrorists kill two American tourists at Ankara, Turkey.*

As revenge for massacres of Armenians by the Ottoman Empire, Armenian terrorists often bombed Turkish buildings or killed Turkish officials.

The indiscriminate terror attack at the Ankara airport resulted in the deaths of two Americans, but the U.S. media did not give it as much publicity as PLO terror attacks received. Later, in August 1982, an Armenian terrorist shot and killed a Turkish military attaché in Ottawa, Canada.

See November 30, 1894; August 26, 1896; and April 20, 1915.

## August 16, 1982

**A Senate-house conference committee opposes funding for nerve gas weapons.**

Following President Reagan's decision to renew the U.S. production of nerve gas weapons, many in Congress opposed this step. While the Republican-controlled Senate voted 49 to 45 on May 14 to approve $54 million for chemical weapons, the House voted on July 22 against such weapon production by 251 to 159.

On August 13, the Senate-House conference committee seeking to rectify budget differences voted to accept such funding, but on August 16 the joint committee removed the funds for nerve gas weapons. The issue of chemical weapons production was pursued again by the Reagan administration and finally passed.

See January 14, 1982, and November 8, 1983.

### August 16, 1982

**The United States and the People's Republic of China (PRC) sign an agreement on their relations with the Republic of China (ROC) on Taiwan.**

To stabilize relations between Beijing and Washington, the Chinese government agreed to use only peaceful means to regain Taiwan; the United States agreed to reduce the present level of its arms aid to the ROC, a decision Taiwan protested.

Friction had arisen early in 1982 after the United States sold aircraft and arms to the ROC because neither Vice President Bush, who visited Beijing from May 5 to May 9, nor Senator Howard Baker (R-Tenn.), who visited from May 30 to June 2, could persuade China of the U.S. position toward Taiwan. Therefore, the two sides decided to make a formal agreement to follow.

### August 17, 1982

**The People's Republic of China rejects Vietnam's request for a cease-fire in their border war.**

The failure of this cease-fire effort resulted in new PRC-Vietnam border skirmishes on September 13, 15, and 18. Border attacks between these two countries had been staged several times since the first in 1979.

See February 17, 1979.

### August 20, 1982

**The United States assists in Mexico's debt problem.**

Like other Latin American nations, Mexico experienced difficulty in repaying its foreign debts, owing in part to the decline of oil prices since 1979. Following talks in New York, Mexico received a 90-day postponement of payment of the principal of its $10 billion debt. U.S. officials also offered a multi-billion dollar plan for future debt repayments, including a $1.85 billion loan from the United States and 11 other industrial nations.

As part of the debt plan, Mexican President PORTILLO nationalized private Mexican banks, imposed foreign-exchange controls, and began a two-tier exchange rate for the peso. On November 10, 1982, Mexico agreed to austere economic measures in order to obtain a $3.84 billion credit from the International Monetary Fund. On December 19, Mexico devalued the peso and eased its restrictions on international monetary exchanges.

### August 21, 1982

**PLO troops begin leaving Lebanon as part of an effort to end Israel's invasion.**

Following Israel's June 6, 1982, invasion of Lebanon, many cease-fire and truce efforts had been undertaken by the United Nations and by Philip Habib, an American diplomat sent by President Reagan. Eventually, between June 27 and August 6, Habib worked out plans for peacekeeping forces from Italy, France, and the United States to come to Lebanon to oversee safe-conduct for Yasser Arafat, chairman of the Palestine Liberation Organization (PLO), and the removal of his military forces from the country. On July 29, the Arab League of foreign ministers approved the plan and made provisions for the future security of the Palestinian refugees who remained in Lebanon. Jordan and Syria would admit a limited number of the PLO soldiers, while others were distributed in various Muslim countries, with Arafat establishing PLO headquarters in Tunisia.

Three hundred French paratroopers arrived in Lebanon on August 20; the Italians sent 400 commandos; the United States sent 800 marines, who arrived in Lebanon on September 27, 1982. During the next two weeks, about 15,000 Palestinians and Syrians left West Beirut for eight Arab countries. Syrian forces left Beirut but did not evacuate eastern Lebanon, where they had been stationed since 1976. Lebanon still faced the problem of organizing a new government; Palestinian refugee families in Lebanon still hoped the PLO would regain its homeland on the West Bank of the Jordan River.

See September 1, 14, and 18, 1982.

**August 26, 1982**

## The United States levies penalties against French companies that export gas pipeline equipment to the Soviet Union.

In accordance with its July 22, 1982, announcement that it would honor technology contracts with Moscow, a French freighter carried three compressors bound for the Soviet Union. In retaliation, the U.S. Commerce Department directed penalties against two French companies that furnished this equipment—the French Dresser subsidiary in Dallas, Texas, and the French-owned Creusot-Loire Company.

Other European nations supported the French against the United States. West Germany urged its companies to continue their Soviet sales, and Britain's John Brown Engineering Company shipped three turbines to the Soviets, on August 31, 1982. On October 5, President Reagan banned exports of U.S. materials to four U.S. subsidiaries in West Germany.

Usually a supporter of Reagan, British Prime Minister Margaret THATCHER telephoned the president to say that 10,000 British jobs were involved in the $182 million Soviet deal for 21 turbines. This factor led Reagan to modify his stand. On September 1, Treasury Secretary Donald Regan said the United States would reduce British sanctions, and President Reagan later announced that the United States would simply prevent violators of the sanctions from buying U.S. oil and gas equipment but not other U.S. products. The United States continued to experience problems on this issue with its NATO allies.

See November 13, 1982.

**September 1, 1982**

## President Reagan proposes the "Jordanian solution" for a Middle East peace settlement.

While the multinational force evacuated PLO troops from Lebanon and peace seemed possible, President Reagan proposed a "fresh start" in resolving the Gaza Strip–West Bank problem of a Palestinian homeland, the root cause of Israel's invasion of Lebanon. The idea of a Jordanian-supervised state was not new, but Reagan realized Israel opposed an independent Palestinian state west of the Jordan River. The president surprised some Jewish leaders, however, by also calling for a freeze on Jewish settlements in the occupied territories and Israel's ultimate withdrawal from Gaza and the West Bank. In fact, Israeli Prime

Minister Menachem Begin and Defense Minister Ariel Sharon hoped the defeat of the PLO in Lebanon would end Jewish problems on the West Bank and lead to Israel's annexation of the occupied territories.

While notable, Reagan's proposals had little effect. Events in Lebanon after September 1, Israel's opposition to the Jordanian solution, and, finally, the announcement on April 11, 1983, by Jordan's King Hussein that he refused to cooperate rendered Reagan's unilateral effort ineffective.

See August 21, 1982; September 14 and 18, and November 26, 1982.

**September 8, 1982**

## A Helsinki Watch group in the Soviet Union disbands because of arrests and deportations.

This group of Soviet dissidents had formed to report on the Soviet Union's fulfillment of the Helsinki Accords. Because Moscow had sent 16 Helsinki Watch members to labor camps or internal exile, only 3 members remained by 1982.

See August 1, 1975.

**September 14, 1982**

## *Lebanese President Bashir Gemayel is assassinated in Beirut.*

A moderate Lebanese Christian leader, Bashir Gemayel had been elected to obtain a compromise political settlement with the Muslims of Lebanon. Gemayel was killed when 440 pounds of explosives blew up a Christian Phalangist branch office in East Beirut. On October 1, Gemayel's Christian Phalangist Party said its security agency had captured Habib Shartourmi, a Lebanese who confessed to the murder. Although Bashir Gemayel's elder brother, Amin Gemayel, was named president on September 20, Lebanon's peace prospects vanished, and conditions became more volatile after Christians attacked two Palestinian refugee camps.

During Bashir Gemayel's brief tenure as president, a rift began between Israel and the Lebanese Christians. Meeting with Gemayel on September 1, after being infuriated by news of President Reagan's peace proposal, Israel's Prime Minister Menachem Begin demanded that Lebanon sign a peace treaty and that the Christian General Saad Haddad be made Lebanon's defense minister. Gemayel refused, saying he would only sign a nonaggression pact and that Haddad would be tried for treason because of his dealings with Israel. In brief, Gemayel wanted Israel's aid but did not want to damage Lebanon's political interest in reconstructing a new Christian-Muslim state; Begin wanted a Lebanon that acted separately from any Arab interest and took orders from Israel.

See September 18, 1982.

### September 17, 1982

*In West Germany, Helmut Schmidt's government collapses when the Free Democrats withdraw support; Helmut Kohl becomes chancellor on October 7.*

Schmidt's Social Democrat–Free Democrat coalition had been in office since 1969. His hold on the Free Democrats, a "classical liberal" group, steadily dwindled after 1980 when his health weakened and West Germany's relations with Eastern European countries became difficult because of the issues surrounding the deployment of U.S. Pershing II missiles in West Germany. In addition, the rise of the Green-Alternative List party created a group that attracted votes from Schmidt's Social Democratic Party (SPD) by emphasizing a mix of pacifist and ecological issues.

On October 7, Helmut KOHL of the Christian Democratic Party became chancellor, having obtained the support of the Free Democratic leader, Hans-Dietrich Genscher, who retained the position of foreign minister under Kohl. On October 29, the SPD selected West Berlin Mayor Hans-Jochen Vogel to replace Schmidt as party leader.

### September 18, 1982

*Lebanese Christians massacre Palestinian refugees in Sabra and Shatila, West Beirut camps under Israeli protection.*

Rumors of unusual fighting in West Beirut were not confirmed until September 18, after U.S. embassy officers and others visited the Palestinian refugee camps of Sabra and Shatila. Later investigations disclosed that the Israeli commander in Beirut, General Amir Drori, permitted Christian Phalangist militia to enter the two Palestinian shantytowns and eliminate 2,000 supposed terrorists who, the Israelis believed, were left behind by the PLO evacuation.

On September 16, Israeli troops moved into West Beirut, where they surrounded and sealed off Sabra and Shatila, opening the way for 1,500 Christian militia to enter. While the Israeli army set off illumination flares to provide light during the night, the Christian troops invaded house after house, often killing entire families, some still in their beds. Workers at two nearby hospitals began to realize that something unusual was happening after wounded civilians began arriving in large numbers.

The Christian attack continued all day Friday with Israeli officers making no effort to intervene and, in some cases, forcing the Palestinians who fled the area to turn back or be shot. The Christians even invaded the hospitals, shooting and killing one medical doctor while he and several nurses carried a white surrender flag. Many nurses were raped and shot before an International Red Cross convoy took over the hospitals early in the day.

On the same day Israeli leaders knew what was happening, but Defense Minister Ariel Sharon said they agreed to let the Christians stay in the camps until Saturday morning, probably so they could "clean up" the mess and hide as many bodies as possible. On Saturday, outsiders found that the Christians had bulldozed earth, sand, and garbage to cover over the Palestinian corpses.

Throughout the world, outrage was expressed against the Lebanese Christians and the Israeli leaders. In Israel, demonstrations against the government's actions forced Prime Minister Begin to establish a commission to examine what happened.

See September 20, 1982, and February 8, 1983.

### September 20, 1982

**The bombing of the U.S. embassy in Beirut kills 23.**

At 11:45 A.M., a van with diplomatic license plates pulled up to an embassy checkpoint, where its driver shot a Lebanese security guard and raced his engine to drive zigzag through three rows of concrete blocks intended to slow down traffic. The British ambassador was visiting the embassy and his British bodyguard fired at the van, causing the driver to fall out the door. The van lurched and hit a parked car. The van's 350 pounds of explosives blew up 30 feet from the embassy building but collapsed it's facade. Apparently, the driver had intended to reach the parking garage beneath the embassy but did not make it.

Among the eight Americans killed were two U.S. military liaison officers—an army officer, Kenneth V. Welch, and a navy officer, Michael Ray Wagner. The pro-Iranian Islamic Holy War group claimed that one of its members was the suicide car bomber.

In the midst of a congressional election, President Reagan played down the consequences of the bombing in Lebanon.

### September 21, 1982

**President Reagan agrees to send U.S. Marines back to Lebanon to join French and Italian forces as a "peacekeeping" team.**

The massacre of Palestinians at Sabra and Shatila brought renewed tension to Lebanon. At Lebanon's request, the United States joined France and Italy in returning their forces that had withdrawn on September 10 after evacuating the PLO armies.

When the multilateral peace forces returned to Lebanon late in September, there was turmoil throughout the nation. After Amin Gemayel took over from his assassinated brother, the government controlled only 20% of the country. Israeli forces remained south of Beirut, Syrian troops were in eastern Lebanon and Sunni and Shiite Muslims were not committed to Gemayel's leadership. In addition, various factions of the Christian Phalangist militia often acted independently.

These political problems changed the peacekeeping mission, which on August 21, had only to evacuate PLO forces. In particular, U.S. leaders gradually enlarged and altered the intent of their initial presence in Lebanon.

See November 1, 1982.

### September 24, 1982

**The United States and other NATO nations withdraw from the International Atomic Energy Conference after Israel is denied a seat.**

Secretary of State George Shultz stated that the United States would leave any U.N. agency that voted to exclude Israel from its deliberations; the United States said it would also withhold payment of $8.5 million assessed for the 1982 operations of the Atomic Energy Agency. Not until May 6, 1983, did the United States rejoin this U.N. group.

### September 26, 1982

**The Atlantic Richfield Oil Company (ARCO) wins a contract to drill for oil off the China coast.**

On February 16, 1982, the People's Republic of China announced that bids would be open for oil exploration and production rights in its offshore waters. U.S. ARCO obtained the right to explore 3,500 square miles of the South China Sea, where experts predicted at least 30 billion barrels of oil could be located. China needed new energy sources to pursue its economic modernization program.

### September 27, 1982

**U.S. Forces land at Beirut.**

U.S. Marines arrived to participate in peacekeeping activities in Beirut.

### September 29, 1982

*Venezuela receives aid in revising its foreign debt structure.*

Decreasing oil prices after 1979 brought economic hardship to Venezuela as well as Mexico. On September 29, Venezuela asked to convert short-term debts with New York banks into long-term obligations of the nation's central bank. On October 10, it had to refinance $35 billion of debts due for payment in April 1983.

For Mexico's debt problems, see August 20, 1982.

### October 2, 1982

**Congress approves a stop-gap spending bill because of disputes with the White House over budget allocations.**

As during the fall of 1981, Congress and President Reagan fought over budget funds because the president desired deeper cuts in social programs and an increase in defense expenditures. In 1982, Republican conservatives proposed a constitutional amendment requiring a balanced budget, even though neither the president nor Congress was ready to provide one.

The House passed a spending bill on September 23 that maintained government activity from October 1 to December 15, later extended by the Senate to December 22. The Senate authorization bill passed on September 30, but the congressional joint committee did not report on reconciling the two bills until October 2, the second day of the 1982 fiscal year. Reagan signed the bill, which permitted spending based on existing programs. Further action on the 1982 spending authorization took place from December 17 to 22, 1982.

### October 8, 1982

*Poland bans all trade unions, including Solidarity.*

Since August 31, 1982, when demonstrators began celebrating the second anniversary of the founding of the Solidarity trade union, there had been numerous clashes between police and antigovernment groups. Banning the unions, Prime Minister Jaruzelski claimed, was the only way to solve the nation's problems. Solidarity strikes continued, however, and on October 11, the government arrested 148 people.

In retaliation for the ban on Solidarity, President Reagan, on October 9, suspended Poland's most-favored-nation trade status, thereby restricting Polish exports to the United States.

See November 20, 1982

### October 21, 1982

**The United States and the European Economic Community (EEC) agree to limit European steel exports.**

For nearly two years, the United States and the EEC had argued and traded threats regarding limits on steel exports to the United States or the end of European subsidies to national steel industries. U.S. steel industry executives claimed that they lost sales because the subsidized European exports allowed cheaper prices for European steel.

During the summer of 1982, the United States and the EEC almost parted company on this issue. The U.S. Commerce Department threatened on June 11, 1982, to levy countervailing duties on steel imports; an EEC offer on July 22 to cut exports by 10% was not accepted by the U.S. steel industry.

In the October 21 agreement, the EEC limited steel exports to about 5% of the U.S. market, a drop of 1.3% from the 1981 level. As a result, U.S. steel companies, which had operated at 40% of capacity, withdrew charges of unfair practices against Europe.

### October 22, 1982

**The National Council of Catholic Bishops proposes a pastoral letter that opposes U.S. nuclear policy.**

Titled "The Challenge of Peace," the Catholic bishops issued a statement that had been in preparation since July 1981 and was revised from an initial draft of June 1982. The October 22 draft stated that "stringent limits must be set on the government's use of nuclear weapons." It opposed the first use of nuclear weapons or any use against civilian targets and any concept that proposed to fight a "protracted nuclear war." Deterrence, the bishops said, is justified only if it is a step on the way to progressive nuclear disarmament. They called for a bilateral verifiable freeze on nuclear weapons and a comprehensive test ban treaty.

Generally, the bishops' action reflected the widespread concern with President Reagan's harsh anticommunist policies and his effort to establish U.S. nuclear superiority. The nuclear freeze movement, which grew in Europe and the United States, led the bishops to issue a statement of the church's moral concern for actions the government took on behalf of its people.

See May 29, 1982.

### October 22, 1982

**The United States and the Marshall Islands conclude an agreement on future relations.**

Located in the South Pacific, the Marshall Islands was one of a group of Pacific islands over which the United States held trusteeship after World War II. The Marshalls and the Micronesia Islands gained semi-independent status in 1980, but disputes continued over U.S. nuclear tests that were conducted at the Kwajalein atoll. Islanders demonstrated against missile and antimissile tests conducted in June 1982 and over the visits of U.S. navy ships that carried nuclear weapons.

The October 22 agreement included clauses for U.S. payment to the Marshalls of at least $1.5 billion during the next 30 years when tests could be permitted. Many islanders were unhappy with the treaty, however, because it did not stop nuclear testing.

On October 1, 1982, the Federated States of Micronesia were given limited independence from the United States, which retained its military rights in the islands.

## October 23, 1982

### The Reagan administration voices concern about right-wing activity in El Salvador.

The particular event that stirred President Reagan to criticize El Salvador was the abduction of five key political opponents of Roberto d'Aubuisson, who, since becoming president of El Salvador's Constituent Assembly in April 1982, had ended land reform and was alleged to support paramilitary groups in killing many opponents.

Previously, U.S. Ambassador Deane R. Hinton had avoided criticism of the right wing. The abduction of the five noncommunist politicians occurred just after a Salvadoran court freed the army officials accused of killing two American land reform experts on January 3, 1981, saying there was "insufficient evidence" to hold them. On November 17, 1982, Washington saw signs of a slight change in El Salvador when a judge ordered the trial of five national guardsmen accused of killing four American missionaries on December 4, 1980.

See May 20, 1982.

## October 28, 1982

### Spain's Socialist Worker's Party wins control of parliament in a landslide election.

The Socialist victory made Felipe Gonzáles MARQUES prime minister. On December 16, Gonzáles informed U.S. Secretary of State Shultz that Spain would remain a loyal U.S. ally but that it was halting the integration of its forces into the North Atlantic Treaty Organization.

## November 1, 1982

### President Reagan expands U.S. peacekeeping duties in Lebanon.

Because negotiations for the withdrawal of Israeli and Syrian forces from Lebanon became stymied, Lebanon's President Amin Gemayel requested further assistance from Washington. On November 1, Reagan agreed to undertake army patrol duties in East Beirut.

During the remainder of 1982, Reagan added other duties to the U.S. mission in Lebanon: on November 29, Reagan doubled the size of U.S. forces; on December 2, he agreed to rebuild the Lebanese army at a cost of $85 million; and on December 5, he extended the U.S. mission into 1983. Observers saw that U.S. forces were no longer a neutral peacekeeper but a force favoring Gemayel's government, a development opposed by the Muslims.

## November 1, 1982

### The Reagan administration states it is supporting covert operations against the Nicaraguan government from Honduran bases.

Following a *Newsweek* magazine report that the U.S. ambassador to Honduras, John D. Negroponte, was in charge of arming and training Nicaraguan exiles to fight the Sandinista regime, the Reagan administration admitted that the CIA assisted these exiles in Honduras. Argentina had helped the Nicaraguan exiles in 1981, but the Falkland Islands War halted aid from Buenos Aires.

According to the White House, U.S. aid was not to overthrow the Nicaraguan government but to "keep it off balance" and halt the flow of military aid through Nicaragua to El Salvador's rebels. Thus, under U.S. auspices, Nicaraguan exiles began border skirmishes and hit-and-run raids from Honduras into Nicaragua.

## November 2, 1982

### In off-year U.S. elections Democrats gain 26 seats in the House of Representatives; Republicans retain their eight-seat Senate majority.

In addition to the congressional elections, voters approved referenda for a U.S.-Soviet nuclear weapons freeze in eight states, 30 cities, and the District of Columbia.

## November 7, 1982

### Turkish voters approve a new constitution and elect General Kenan Evren president.

Turkey's republican government ended temporarily in September 1980 when a military junta overthrew it. On January 1, 1982, General Evren announced a timetable to prepare a new constitution for ratification in November. General elections were planned for 1983.

Although some European countries suspended economic aid to Turkey after the 1980 coup, the United States did not. In January 1982, U.S. Defense

Secretary Caspar Weinberger visited Ankara to promise continued U.S. support for Turkey.

### November 10, 1982

**The Reagan administration indicates Japan has not fulfilled promises to lower trade barriers.**

Although Japan had generally adhered to its March 29, 1982, promise to reduce automobile exports by 1.68 million units, it had not effectively reduced tariffs and other trade barriers on 200 products as promised on May 27, 1982. Japan's continued large trade imbalance with the United States caused many congressmen to propose tariff legislation against Tokyo, a step President Reagan did not desire. On November 10, Reagan did not say what the retaliation might be.

### November 10, 1982

*Soviet President Leonid Brezhnev dies. He is replaced by Yuri A. Andropov on November 12.*

Because Brezhnev had been ill for several years, ANDROPOV, the former head of the secret police (KGB), had already begun to consolidate his power. Vice President George Bush represented the United States at Brezhnev's funeral on November 15.

### November 11, 1982

*Prime Minister Thatcher reveals that a British intelligence officer gave NATO secrets to the Soviet Union.*

Margaret Thatcher indicated that Geoffrey Arthur Prime had pleaded guilty to passing secret data to the Soviets from his post at the Government Communications Headquarters. British officials admitted that the information Prime passed on was of "incalculable harm" to U.S. and NATO security interests. Prime was sent to prison for 35 years.

### November 13, 1982

**President Reagan lifts U.S. sanctions against foreign countries who sell pipeline equipment to the U.S.S.R.**

In applying sanctions against France and Great Britain on August 26 and September 9, Reagan created widespread protest and now had to save face. Britain's Prime Minister Thatcher deserted Reagan and warned that he damaged transatlantic relations in trying to forbid Europeans from shipping pipeline components to the Soviets. In October, Secretary of State George Shultz could not reach a compromise with the Europeans, while at home the Republican minority leader in the House of Representatives, Robert Michel, tried to overturn Reagan's policy because it damaged sales by Caterpillar Tractor Company, which was located in Michel's district.

In withdrawing U.S sanctions against the European companies, Reagan stated that the allies had reached "substantial agreement" on economic strategy toward Moscow. Nevertheless, France, West Germany, and Great Britain all denied any deal with Washington. To further "save face" for Reagan, on December 13 the U.S. Defense Department warned Austria to stop transferring sensitive technology to the Soviets.

On December 14, the United States and France agreed to study economic measures against the Warsaw Pact countries. These talks did not limit either side, but they were conciliatory. While Secretary of State Shultz read a six-point proposal on "realistic" ways to deal with Moscow, French Foreign Minister Claude Cheysson nodded but later said France did not limit its freedom of action on any points.

See January 8 and August 26, 1982.

### November 13, 1982

**The Vietnam War Memorial is dedicated in Washington.**

This monument to 57,939 U.S. soldiers killed or missing in the Vietnam War was intended to help Vietnam veterans receive the respect that they felt had not been previously shown to them.

### November 17, 1982

*West Germany says it has captured its foremost terrorist suspect, Christian Klar of the Red Army Faction.*

The Red Army was the principal terrorist group that had bombed and harassed U.S military installations and personnel in Europe for over ten years. Klar's arrest followed the capture of two of his associates in Frankfurt who possessed coded plans of the terrorists, army depots. Klar was picked up in woods near

Hamburg, where he was digging up an arms cache. Although the Red Army was hurt by the leader's capture, its terrorist activity continued.

### November 17, 1982

**Edwin P. Wilson, a former CIA officer, is convicted of smuggling arms to Libya in 1979.**

This was but the first of several trials Wilson faced from smuggling plastic explosives to Libya and conspiring to kill a Libyan in Egypt. The jury did not believe Wilson's story that he acted on orders of the Central Intelligence Agency and convicted him on seven of the eight counts of aiding Libya's Mu'ammar al-Gadhafi.

### November 18, 1982

*Without consulting its foreign creditors, Argentina substitutes bonds and promissory notes to replace $4.7 billion in cash owed.*

Following the Falkland Islands War, Argentina tried to solve its economic problems by devaluing the peso on May 5 and again on July 5, in addition to other measures to control domestic credit. In October 1982, when Argentina applied for loans to the International Monetary Fund, it was told to impose austerity policies, such as raising prices and cutting wages, methods that conservatives in the Reagan administration said would discipline Third World nations to act more responsibly.

In November, Argentina decided to pursue tactics more suitable to its nation's interests. It defied the foreign bankers, who feared that Argentina's course might be adopted by other nations. This threat enabled Argentina to secure a $1.1 billion loan from New York banks on December 30, 1982.

### November 20, 1982

*Leaders of Poland's Solidarity trade union cancel a December protest after Prime Minister Jaruzelski offers conciliatory terms.*

Although Poland's martial law continued, Jaruzelski decided early in November to work with Solidarity's leaders by releasing Lech Wałęsa from internment on November 14. On November 29, he freed another 327 interned protestors.

There was a step back toward repression when the Polish government prevented Wałęsa from delivering a speech in Gdansk, but conciliation continued after the Polish Council of State decreed that martial law would end on December 31, 1982. On December 23, the government released all but seven Solidarity leaders arrested for violating martial law.

### November 26, 1982

*Palestinian groups backed by Syria announce their opposition to President Reagan's September peace plan.*

Pro-Syrian Palestinian leaders who opposed Yasser Arafat's leadership met in Damascus and condemned Reagan's September 1, 1982, plan because it did not recognize the Palestine Liberation Organization as the "sole and legitimate representative of the Palestinian people."

Unlike the Damascus groups, Arafat did not announce a position on the plan until he talked with King Hussein of Jordan, who had a central role under Reagan's proposal. On December 14, Hussein and Arafat announced that a "special relationship" existed between Jordan and any future Palestinian entity on the West Bank of the Jordan River. On December 20, Hussein visited the United States, where he said the time was not "ripe" for Jordan to help the peace process.

See March 14, 1984.

### December 1, 1982

**Visiting Brazil, President Reagan grants economic concessions to help resolve Brazil's debt problem.**

Like that of Mexico, Argentina, and other Latin American nations, Brazil's foreign debt problem became serious because of high interest rates and a drop in value of the nation's exports, in the case of Brazil, lower world prices for coffee and sugar. Because President Reagan believed Brazil had recently moved toward democratic politics, he offered a package of economic benefits, providing $1.2 billion in short-term loans, waiving import quotas for industrial sugar products, and forgetting previous demands that Brazil abolish export subsidies on products competing with U.S. goods.

Brazil required greater funding, however. On December 29, it accepted stringent austerity measures to obtain $546.5 million as part of a $6 billion loan from the International Monetary Fund.

### December 3, 1982

**The UNESCO Commission on Mass Communications satisfies the desires of U.S. and other Western nations to modify Third World censorship.**

Since 1981, there had been a dispute about news reporting in the United Nations Educational, Scientific, and Cultural Organization (UNESCO). Developing Third World nations wanted to permit their governments to control information given by their media to Western newsmen, claiming that Western reporters held prejudices against their cultures. American delegates to the Communications Commission led other industrialized nations in arguing that government censorship limited free speech. The Reagan administration refused to finance UNESCO media projects but had offered economic aid to help Third World nations develop their own communications networks if they accepted standards of free speech and free press.

To satisfy U.S. desires, the Communications Commission, on December 3, offered changes in prior proposals that allowed censorship. Unfortunately, the changes discussed on December 3 did not prevail very long. On December 10, the U.N. General Assembly adopted a resolution that permitted governments to censor or ban television satellite broadcasts coming from abroad. The United States and Western European delegates opposed this decision, but as in the case of UNESCO, Third World delegates had more votes in the assembly. This was one of several disputes that led the United States to withdraw from UNESCO.

See December 28, 1983.

### December 6–8, 1982

**Pakistan's President Zia visits Washington to resolve issues on military aid and nuclear power.**

Although the Reagan administration was eager to assist Pakistan as a conduit for aid to the Afghan rebels, the military aid had been in dispute for a year because of allegations that Pakistan was developing a nuclear bomb. At the request of Congress, the Central Intelligence Agency made a report in January 1982 that predicted Pakistan would have nuclear weapons by 1985.

President Reagan meets with Pakistan's President Muhammad Zia ul-Haq regarding military aid.
Ronald Reagan Library

On January 26, Pakistan's President Muhammad Zia ul-Haq had denied Pakistan was developing nuclear weapons, but since the International Atomic Energy Agency had accused him as well of similar intentions, Zia visited Washington from December 6 to 8 to speak with Reagan, members of Congress, and Washington newsmen. Zia said Pakistan wanted nuclear energy only for peaceful purposes.

Zia also had to settle misunderstandings about economic and military aid from the United States. The latter agreed that the F-16 planes Pakistan purchased would eventually have the advanced technology on which Zia insisted, and President Reagan confirmed the U.S. commitment to give Pakistan $3.2 billion over five years. Pakistan received its first six F-16 planes on January 15, 1983.

### December 9, 1982

**Nicaragua blames U.S. aid to the Contra rebels for the deaths of 75 children killed when Contras shoot down a helicopter evacuating Nicaraguans from Honduran border villages.**

The helicopter that crashed in northern Nicaragua had been transporting people living in the area where Contras from U.S.-supplied Honduran bases had invaded to burn crops and destroy villages. Nicaragua's pleas for aid against the U.S. threat were partly answered on December 13 when a group of foreign bankers provided Nicaragua with $30 million to help meet payments on its $40 million foreign debt.

### December 9, 1982

*South African forces raid Lesotho to eliminate African National Congress members.*

The Kingdom of Lesotho was invaded by South African troops; 42 people including 30 alleged radicals who sought black independence from white control in South Africa were killed.

In retaliation for the raid, the members of the African National Congress planted a bomb that exploded and damaged a nuclear power plant in South Africa ten days later.

### December 10, 1982

**The United States refuses to sign the Law of the Sea Treaty.**

Since taking office in 1981, President Reagan and his administration had opposed the seabed mining provisions of the Law of the Sea Treaty. Subsequent efforts failed to achieve a compromise on the treaty terms when it was voted on in April 1982.

President Reagan said he firmly objected to the treaty because, in the terms of conservative *New York Times* columnist William Safire, it violated principles of free enterprise. The State Department persuaded Great Britain and West Germany to join the United States in not signing the treaty, but both said they did not rule out adopting it later. On December 30, 1982, Reagan said the United States would not pay $1 million per year of its U.N. assessment, which funded the treaty.

One hundred seventeen nations signed the treaty. Representatives of Third World nations and U.N. Secretary-General Javier Pérez de Cuellar hailed the treaty as promising great benefits. In addition to regulations on seabed mining, the treaty had provisions on territorial waters, free passage, exclusive economic zones, and the use of straits and the continental shelf.

See April 30, 1982.

### December 20, 1982

*In four meetings during 1982, OPEC members cannot agree to raise prices and cut production of oil.*

Throughout 1982, the Organization of Petroleum Exporting Countries officially held the price of oil at $34 per barrel, but on spot markets and in special deals many crude oil sales were at lower prices. OPEC met on March 20, May 21, July 8–10, and December 19–20. In December, the members reaffirmed the $34 price and raised production ceilings but could not agree on each member nation's production quotas.

## December 21, 1982

### President Reagan signs legislation that prohibits using funds to "overthrow" the Nicaraguan government—the first version of the Boland Amendment.

Even though most members of Congress wanted to stop Nicaraguan aid to the rebels in El Salvador, they also opposed the use of American funds to help the Contra rebels in Nicaragua overthrow their government. Led by Edward P. Boland (Dem.-Mass.) the House of Representatives Select Committee on Intelligence approved legislation in July 1982 that prohibited the Central Intelligence Agency (CIA) or the Department of Defense (DOD) from providing military equipment and training to groups whose purpose was "overthrowing the government of Nicaragua." The Senate Select Committee on Intelligence also approved this restriction in August 1982.

The select committee's prohibition remained secret until December 1982 to protect CIA operations, but after Boland read a November 1, 1982, *Newsweek* article about the CIA's expanding the war against Nicaragua, he confronted CIA director William Casey, who admitted that the Contras had grown from 500 to 4,000 men. Deciding to publicize the committee's amendment, Boland read it to the House on December 8, 1982. It was then incorporated into the 1983 Intelligence Authorization Act and approved by the House in a 411-to-0 vote. After Casey told the Senate committee there was no problem with the amendment, the Senate passed the bill, and President Reagan signed it on December 21, 1982. This amendment became part of the $230 billion military appropriation bill, the largest peacetime military legislation ever approved by Congress.

Casey was playing word games with Congress. Although one member of the Senate Select Committee, Daniel Patrick Moynihan (D-N.Y.), told Casey he expected the CIA to conform to the letter and spirit of the law, Casey used the ambiguity of the statement "to overthrow the government" to continue secret aid to the Contras, contending that the Contras' purpose was to harass the government, not overthrow it.

After consulting CIA lawyers, Casey instructed CIA agents to warn Contra leaders against the term "overthrow the government" and to denounce any Contra leader who publicly used those words.

According to Casey, the Contra purpose should be called harassment, destabilization, interdicting arms to El Salvador, or "causing problems" for the Sandinista government.

On the future of the Boland Amendment, see December 9, 1983.

## December 21, 1982

### President Reagan agrees to a compromise on the MX missile.

Since Reagan announced on October 2, 1981, that the MX would be deployed in silos, not in a more protected underground track system, the president and congressional leaders argued over the program for the new U.S. intercontinental ballistic missile system.

At the request of Congress, the U.S. air force on November 4, 1982, had presented plans for a "dense pack" deployment of the MX in Wyoming. The 100 MXs initially would be spaced 1,800 feet apart in Minuteman missile silos hardened to withstand a pressure of 10,000 pounds per square mile. Located within an area 1.5 meters wide and 14 miles long, the air force calculated that the first Soviet missile to explode would result in "fratricide," causing later Soviet missiles to destroy themselves before hitting other MX silos. They estimated that 50 U.S. missiles would survive and be fired as a retaliatory strike on the Soviet Union. Many experts disputed the air force scenario, arguing that the dense pack sacrificed survivability and claiming such deployment made the MX a first-strike weapon, not a retaliatory deterrent.

As the dispute over MX deployment continued, President Reagan made a television speech on November 22 to defend the dense pack deployment as a survivable defensive weapon, which he had renamed "peacemaker." The new MX name never caught on, however; Congress remained convinced that its first-strike potential raised the risk of nuclear war.

Between December 17 and 20, Congress and the White House compromised on MX funding. Congress authorized $2.5 billion for research and development of the missile but eliminated production funds until it could approve a satisfactory basing plan. Reagan also appointed a special committee to study the MX basing problem before funds for production would be provided in 1984.

See February 11, 1982, and April 11, 1983.

# 1983

## January 8, 1983

*The Contadora process begins as foreign ministers of four Latin American nations meet on Panama's Contadora Island to seek a peaceful end to conflicts in El Salvador and Nicaragua.*

The nations sponsoring this peace process were Mexico, Venezuela, Colombia, and Panama. The Contadora Initiative gained great respect during the next several years, as diplomats from the four nations negotiated treaties within Central America to try to demilitarize the region and reconcile warring factions. It rejected President Reagan's view of its troubles as being fomented by the Soviet Union.

## January 12, 1983

**President Reagan's dismissal of Eugene Rostow as arms control director indicates influence of extreme conservatives in the White House.**

Rostow was selected as director of the Arms Control and Disarmament Agency in 1981 because he was perceived as an opponent of all arms control agreements and would prevent Secretary of State Alexander Haig from compromising with Moscow. By the end of 1982, however, Rostow was disliked by Reagan and National Security Adviser William Clark because he treated them like "not-very-bright" law students and was not a member of the president's California team.

In addition, Rostow now favored the desire of Paul Nitze, Reagan's ambassador for long-range theater nuclear force negotiations, for firm but flexible arms control agreements with the Soviets, a position that Reagan's hawkish advisers opposed. Consequently, when Rostow did not resign after the White House withdrew its support for Senate confirmation of Robert T. Grey as Rostow's deputy, Clark and Reagan decided to fire Rostow and appoint a more staunch opponent of arms control, Kenneth Adelman. The nomination of Adelman caused much controversy, and the Senate Foreign Relations Committee recommended his rejection on February 24. Reagan had to lobby hard to gain Senate approval for Adelman on April 14, 1983.

See January 15, 1983.

## January 14, 1983

**President Reagan secretly approves covert action by the National Security Council to promote Project Democracy.**

Project Democracy had been announced by Reagan in a June 8, 1982, speech to the British Parliament. While the project's public side was funded by Congress on November 22, 1983, as the National Endowment for Democracy, its unannounced covert side was placed under the NSC by a document that Congress declassified as part of the Iran-Contra scandal in 1987.

National Security Decision Directive 77 of January 14, 1983, was titled "Management of Public Diplomacy Relative to National Security." It set up several planning groups for "public diplomacy" that would support the growth of democratic institutions by foreign governments and private groups. While

Lt. Col. Oliver North confers with an associate in the Oval office during a meeting concerning Nicaragua. Ronald Reagan Library

some NSC teams planned propaganda to promote anticommunist groups such as the Nicaraguan rebels by planting stories in the press, other groups planned secret action to counter activity by the Soviet Union or its surrogates. Finally, one NSC team sought funds from private individuals or foreign governments to finance U.S. covert activity.

In October 1983, NSC Adviser Robert C. McFarlane appointed Lt. Col. Oliver L. North to head Project Democracy's covert arm. During the 1987 Iran-Contra hearings, Congress learned that taxpayer financing for Project Democracy was partly used by North for aid to the Nicaraguan Contras from 1984 to 1986.

### January 15, 1983

**The *New York Times* publishes the story of the "walk in the woods" missile agreement between Paul Nitze and the Soviet negotiator, Yuli Kvitsinsky.**

According to a news report that the *Time* magazine reporter Strobe Talbott says Arms Control Director Eugene Rostow leaked to the *Times*, during July 1982 in Geneva, Nitze and Kvitsinsky had concluded an informal agreement to limit medium-range missiles, while meeting during a private walk in the woods away from other delegates and "bugging" devices. The two diplomats proposed a package deal by which the Soviets would reduce their SS-20s by two-thirds, giving them 75 SS-20s with 225 warheads; the United States would deploy no Pershing IIs but could deploy 75 Tomahawk cruise missiles with 300 warheads.

When the two negotiators returned to their homes, however, neither the Reagan administration nor the Soviet leadership accepted the proposal. If accepted, the medium-range missile problem would have been resolved, and the deployment of U.S. missiles in Europe would cease. When negotiations began again in Geneva on January 27, 1983, the United States returned to its earlier "zero-option" and the USSR to its earlier plans for a nuclear-free central Europe. These represented hard-line positions for each negotiator.

See January 12, 1983.

### January 17, 1983

*Radical PLO factions reject President Reagan's September 1982 Middle East peace plan, but they disagree on other matters.*

Following PLO leader Yasser Arafat's eviction from Lebanon in August 1982, anti-Arafat PLO groups secured help from Syria and Libya. Eventually, these groups became divided, but at Tripoli, Libya, they agreed in January, 1983 to oppose Reagan's plan for the PLO and the "Jordanian solution" to the West Bank conflict. During January, these factions fought among themselves from their camps in eastern and northern Lebanon, especially in the area of Tripoli, Lebanon.

See June 24, 1983.

### January 19, 1983

**Japanese Prime Minister Yasuhiro Nakasone visits the United States to discuss Japanese trade barriers and possible Japanese rearmament.**

Since occupying the White House, the Reagan administration had made only slight headway in prodding Japan to loosen its trade restrictions and to spend more on defense. Before leaving Tokyo, Nakasone announced on January 13 that he would liberalize import restrictions on automobiles, pharmaceuticals, and other products. In practice, however, most American businesspeople had found that such orders did not effectively permit foreign competition in Japan.

In defense matters, Nakasone promised the president he would increase Japan's military budget and begin to share responsibility with the United States for the surveillance of Soviet planes and ships in the vicinity of the Japanese islands. As part of this promise, on February 8 Nakasone risked public displeasure in Japan by allowing nuclear-powered U.S. aircraft carriers to dock in Japanese harbors.

### January 20, 1983

*French President François Mitterrand and West German Chancellor Helmut Kohl reaffirm support for the Atlantic Alliance.*

Mitterrand and Kohl met in Bonn to celebrate the twentieth anniversary of the French-German

Friendship Treaty. During their meeting, they pledged to continue support of the Atlantic Alliance and warned others (i.e., the Soviet Union) not to try to split the friendship between the United States and Western Europe. Their statement solidified support for NATO's dual-track policy of preparing to deploy Pershing II missiles by the end of 1983 if U.S.-Soviet intermediate-range arms control talks did not succeed. On March 23, 1983, NATO's defense ministers also confirmed the dual-track policy.

### January 20, 1983

*Israeli authorities force professors at West Bank universities to pledge not to support the PLO; 34 faculty who refuse are fired.*

Because the 1982 Israeli invasion of Lebanon did not lessen support for the Palestine Liberation Organization among Arabs living on the West Bank, Israel sought new measures to eliminate PLO influence. One such method was to get rid of teachers who backed the PLO. Like other similar harsh measures, this one did not work but damaged the education of Arab students.

### January 21, 1983

**President Reagan certifies El Salvador's progress in protecting human rights to make that nation eligible for U.S. economic aid.**

For many observers, meeting the congressional requirement that nations receiving U.S. aid be certified by the president as protecting human rights was difficult to judge. An American medical team had recently visited El Salvador and found numerous human rights violations. Other groups concurred that there were violations.

Nevertheless, by certifying that the Salvadorans had made progress, Reagan could ignore contrary findings and send the $60 million in aid that Congress appropriated in 1982. The president made a similar certification on July 20, 1983, to obtain more funding for El Salvador.

For congressional reactions, see November 12, 1983.

### February 1, 1983

**U.S. forces stage "war games" with Honduran forces in Central America—Operation Big Pine. Nicaragua protests.**

U.S. military advisers had begun using Honduras as a supply and training base for the army of El Salvador and for Nicaraguan exiles who raided across the border against Nicaragua's Sandinista government. The 1983 war games involved over 6,000 troops, the largest such exercise ever held in Central America.

Claiming that the exiles entered their country and killed 192 people during January, Nicaragua protested the war games and on March 23, 1983, complained to the United Nations, where it accused Washington of plotting to overthrow the Sandinista government. The Reagan administration ignored Nicaragua's protests and on July 20, 1983, announced new military exercises with Honduras. These 1983 exercises were a culmination of U.S. aid provided to the Nicaraguan rebels through Honduras since 1981. In return for U.S. economic aid of $30 million in 1982, Honduras allowed the United States to train and supply the Nicaraguan rebels. The United States also "loaned" Honduras a fleet of 23 helicopters and other aircraft.

See November 23, 1981, and November 1, 1982.

### February 4, 1983

**U.S. delegates at the U.N. Committee on Disarmament propose a ban on chemical weapons.**

At the Geneva meeting of the U.N. Disarmament Committee, Vice President George Bush announced what the U.S. State Department called a "new initiative in the field" by describing the details for an effective weapons ban. The principal elements of the proposal were the following:

1. Systematic on-site inspection of chemical weapons stocks, production facilities, and plans to destroy stocks.
2. Inspection of the destruction of stock and production facilities.
3. Inspection of facilities for legal chemical production that could be diverted to weapons production.
4. A multilateral complaint mechanism for compliance issues.

The U.S. specifically objected to Soviet "self-inspection" proposals or to suggestions that satellite photography could do the job, because clandestine production could occur without being detected. As was frequently the case, the inspection issue sidetracked progress for four years. The Soviets by the spring of 1987 came to accept the idea of "quick challenge" inspections, while Americans modified their demand for "anywhere, anytime" inspections.

See August 11, 1987.

### February 6, 1983

#### Secretary of State George Shultz concludes a four-day visit to China.

During its first two years, the Reagan administration experienced difficulties with the People's Republic of China because the president had been a staunch opponent of "Red" China throughout his political career. While the most serious issues between the two countries related to U.S. aid to Taiwan (Republic of China) and mainland China's textile exports, other issues developed over minor affairs such as the "refugee status" of tennis star Hu Na and the attempts of nine American soldiers to obtain $41.3 million through U.S. courts to repay them for defaulting 1911 Imperial Chinese Railroad bonds. On February 10, 1983, a U.S. district court ordered China to pay these bondholders.

Shultz's visit did not resolve any problems but clarified U.S. policy by indicating the Reagan administration would not stop its economic and military aid to Taiwan but might gradually reduce Taiwan's military aid if the People's Republic of China maintained friendly relations with America. In response to Shultz's question about China's relations with the Soviet Union, Chinese Communist Party Chairman Deng Xiaoping agreed to cooperate with the United States against Soviet aggression in Cambodia and Afghanistan.

See July 22, 1983, and May 1, 1984.

### February 8, 1983

#### Opening session of the Second Conference on Security and Cooperation in Europe begins in Madrid, Spain.

The most significant outcome of this meeting was an agreement between delegates of the NATO and Warsaw Pact nations to go beyond the 1975 Helsinki Final Act. The Final Act emphasized secure national borders and human rights as confidence-building measures (CBMs). Additional measures to reduce tension required binding, verifiable constraints on military movements or a nonaggression treaty such as the Warsaw Pact nations proposed on January 5, 1983.

At Madrid, 35 European nations plus Canada and the United States agreed to negotiate military CBMs and to meet in Stockholm in 1984 to conclude such measures.

See August 1, 1975; January 17, 1984.

### February 8, 1983

#### *The Israeli commission that investigated the September 1982 massacres at Sabra and Shatila reports that Defense Minister Sharon and three officers were guilty of not fulfilling their duties.*

Chaired by Israel's Supreme Court President Yitzchak Kahan, the commission reported that the Christian Phalangist forces were directly responsible for the slaughters at the PLO refugee camps. However, it continued, high-ranking Israeli officials had general control over the region and their "indirect responsibility cannot be disregarded" since they were responsible for safety and public order. While the report said Prime Minister Begin had not participated in the decision to let the Phalangists enter the camps, Begin heard about the entry and did nothing for two days. Sharon's responsibilities were greater and his "blunders constitute the nonfulfillment of duties."

The Kahan commission suggested that Begin remove Sharon as defense minister and urged the dismissal of the three officers—General Yehosha Saguy, chief of military intelligence; General Amir Drori, the Beirut area commander; and General Amos Yaron, intelligence chief in the Beirut area.

Sharon resigned as defense minister, but Begin appointed him as cabinet minister without portfolio. Sharon was not contrite. He denounced the Kahan report and claimed to be a martyr of insidious American plots to implement the Reagan plan for removing Israel from the West Bank and Gaza. Begin remained as prime minister for five months then resigned on September 12, to be replaced by a new Likud Party leader, Yitzhak Shamir.

## February 10, 1983

*The Soviet Union withdraws from the World Psychiatric Association.*

The Soviet delegates expected to be expelled as the result of an investigation by the association into allegations that Soviet psychiatrists used their professional position for political purposes. Although the issue was not voted upon and many members preferred to maintain contacts with their Soviet counterparts, the Soviet members decided to avoid further criticism. The Cuban and Bulgarian psychiatrists also withdrew.

To critics of Soviet psychiatry, an incident in the spring of 1983 verified their claims of the political use of psychiatry. On May 28, Vladimir Danchev, a Moscow radio announcer, was fired because he criticized Soviet action in Afghanistan. On June 22, 1983, Danchev was committed to a psychiatric hospital for treatment. The Soviet Union remained out of the World Psychiatric Association until September 1989, when the Soviet group was given probationary membership.

## February 16, 1983

**President Reagan confirms that U.S. surveillance planes (AWAC) staged military exercises off the coast of Libya.**

As tensions arose in northern Africa between Libya and three of its neighbors—Egypt, Chad, and the Sudan—the United States showed concern by dispatching AWAC reconnaissance planes and the U.S. aircraft carrier *Nimitz* with its three escort vessels. U.S. intelligence reports said that Libya might try to overthrow Sudan's President Gaafar al-Nimeiry. Other reports indicated a Libyan troop buildup on its southern border.

See June 23, 1983.

## February 18, 1983

**Petroleum price war is stimulated when the British National Oil Corporation cuts prices by $3.00 per barrel to $30.50.**

Throughout 1982, the Organization of Petroleum Exporting Countries (OPEC) had difficulty in maintaining prices at $34.00 per barrel. Now the British action caused Nigeria to cut its price on February 19 to $30.00. (Though Nigeria was an OPEC member and Britain was not, low oil prices had already damaged Nigeria's economy.)

OPEC held an emergency meeting from February 20 to 25 but reached no agreement. On March 14, OPEC negotiators agreed to cut prices to $29 per barrel and to limit their 1983 production to 17.5 million barrels per day, an action OPEC members endorsed on June 18.

## February 25, 1983

**An El Salvador peace commission is formed to urge all social and political sectors to participate in the democratic process to solve their nation's problems.**

President Alvara Magana appointed this peace commission to prepare amnesty laws that might persuade left-wing guerrilla forces to end their opposition to the government. Members of the commission were the bishop of Santiago de Mariá, Rene Revelo; former foreign minister of El Salvador, José Trabanino; and a Populist Party leader, Francisco Quinonez.

The peace commission's creation had been stalled by right-wing members of Roberto d'Aubuisson's National Republican Alliance (ARENA), which formed a coalition in March 1982 to control the Constituent Assembly. President Magana had joined with assembly moderates in January to cut back ARENA's power and demonstrate to the United States that the right wing's notorious death squads might be controlled.

On January 27, eight conservatives had defected from d'Aubuisson's coalition to vote with the Christian Democratic minority to limit ARENA's power. The moderates passed laws preventing ARENA from vetoing assembly decisions that d'Aubuisson disapproved and abolishing d'Aubuisson's right to set the assembly's agenda. Magana's appointment of the peace commission intended to prepare methods for ending the civil war with the guerrillas.

See March 28, 1982.

## March 5, 1983

*The Australian Labor Party gains a parliamentary majority in elections; its leader, Robert Hawke, replaces the Liberal Party's Malcolm Fraser.*

During the election, one of Hawke's principal platforms was to reevaluate the ANZUS Treaty regarding Australia's right to prohibit U.S. Navy ships carrying nuclear weapons from visiting Australian ports under the ANZUS treaty.

## March 6, 1983

*Helmut Kohl's victory in West German elections solidifies his position as chancellor.*

Kohl had succeeded Social Democrat Helmut Schmidt as chancellor in October 1982 and formed a Bundestag (lower house) coalition with the Free Democrats. In the March 6 elections, Kohl's Christian Democrats won 244 seats in the 498-member Bundestag; the Social Democrats won only 193 seats; the Free Democrats and minor parties, 34 seats; and the new left-wing Green-Alternative List, 27 seats. Kohl's CDs and the Free Democrats had sufficient votes to control proceedings in the Bundestag.

## March 8, 1983

*President Reagan tells a convention of Evangelical Christians that the Soviet Union is an "Evil Empire," the "focus of evil in the modern world."*

Among various Christian organizations in the United States, the Evangelicals were recognized as the most conservative, right-wing group whose theology required that born-again Christians hate communism as the Antichrist of the twentieth century. These groups promoted President Reagan's revival of Cold War antagonisms and desired to make the United States militarily superior to the USSR.

Reagan's March 8 speech became known for its most virulent attack on the Soviet Union. It came just after a State Department report of February 14, 1983, contended that there were 4 million forced laborers in the Soviet Union, at least 10,000 of whom were religious or political prisoners. It came the day before the U.S. Defense Department released a booklet, "Soviet Military Power," that, claiming Soviet power was superior, said the United States had "begun to catch up" but was five years away from equality with the USSR. The Defense Department's report was roundly criticized by many informed observers for using questionable data.

## March 10, 1983

*The U.S. redefines the International Law of the Sea Treaty.*

After the Reagan administration rejected the 1982 Law of the Sea Treaty and refused to pay a $1 million U.N. assessment to fund it, the president moved to define the rights of U.S. nationals for exploration of the seabeds.

The administration proclaimed the country had an exclusive zone to use all seabed resources up to 200 miles from U.S. coastlines.

See December 10, 1982.

## March 12, 1983

*The convention of 101 nonaligned Third World nations issues a report that criticizes U.S. policy in Central America and urges economic assistance to Third World nations.*

Meeting in New Delhi, India, the final declarations from this summit moved away from the pro-Soviet statements made during the 1979 sessions in Havana, Cuba. Chaired by Indian Prime Minister Indira GANDHI, the 1983 meeting emphasized the Third World's need for economic aid, urging both Moscow and Washington to stop the nuclear arms race. The group did, however, criticize U.S. policy in Central America and its support of South Africa in delaying independence for Namibia.

## March 21, 1983

*Reports among West Bank Palestinians say hundreds of children die mysteriously.*

While Palestinian newspapers claimed that Israel was poisoning the Arabs, an Israeli investigative report on March 31 said the deaths were due to a "psychological and hysterical epidemic" among the Arab population. These Israeli reports were confirmed on April 25 by an American team from the Center for Disease Control and on May 11 by medical experts of the World Health Organization.

### March 23, 1983

**After President Reagan criticizes the Soviet militarization of Grenada, Grenada's prime minister charges that the United States plans to overthrow his government.**

President Reagan's speech to the National Association of Manufacturers emphasized the U.S. need to counter the Soviet threat in the Caribbean and Central America. He asserted that the Cuban-Soviet alliance was acting aggressively in the Caribbean, and he charged that the two communist nations had financed the building of a 10,000-foot runway on the island of Grenada. Because Grenada had no air force, the president argued, the large airport was evidence of a communist power projection "unrelated to any conceivable threat" to Grenada.

Following the address, several American commentators noted that the airport was part of Grenada's plans to attract tourists, a recommendation of the European Economic Community in 1982 when it granted Grenada $16 million to boost its economy.

The airfield compared to runways on Caribbean islands such as Aruba.

Alarmed at the possibility of a U.S. attack, Prime Minister Maurice Bishop called the small Grenada army to full alert. Bishop's New Jewel Movement had gained control of Grenada's government in 1979 by overthrowing the military dictatorship of Eric Gairy, who fled to the United States, from whence he sought support for a return to power. The March 23 incident was hardly noticed in the United States, until President Reagan ordered an invasion of Grenada.

See October 25, 1983.

### March 23, 1983

**President Reagan calls for a strategic defense initiative (SDI) to permit the United States to defend itself from all Soviet intercontinental ballistic missiles: "star wars."**

Coming fewer than three weeks before a presidential commission on the MX missile reported that the

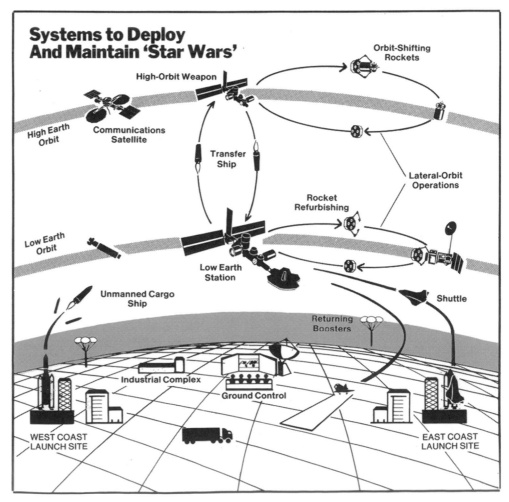

A chart showing how President Reagan's strategic defense system might look. Department of Defense

"window of vulnerability" of U.S. defenses had never existed, President Reagan's speech transformed the 1982 disputes over the MX deployment to disputes over the viability of an SDI that might create what Reagan called a "dome-like protective umbrella to ward off Soviet nuclear warheads." Reagan's dramatic speech added the SDI to subsequent arms negotiations during his presidency.

Originally known as an antiballistic missile defense (ABM), or a ballistic missile defense (BMD) system, the concept of missile protection had been considered since the 1950s. After the 1972 ABM treaty between the United States and the USSR restricted missile defense because it destabilized the practice of MUTUAL ASSURED DESTRUCTION (MAD), slight public attention was given to the issue of missile defenses. Both sides conducted research and development of BMD as permitted by the 1972 treaty. In addition, while the 1972 agreement permitted each side to build one ABM site, the United States did not build its site.

Initial reports about Reagan's SDI decision focused on the role of Edward Teller, a Hungarian-born physicist who had worked on nuclear weapons after World War II and who was a prominent scientist at California's Lawrence Livermore Laboratory. In contrast, the historian Frances Fitzgerald's *Way Out There in the Blue* (2000) examined a variety of these early reports. Fitzgerald concluded that neither the Livermore Laboratory nor the State Department, Defense Department, and Joint Chiefs of Staff knew that President Reagan had tailored his March 23 speech to elicit a favorable response from his television audience. During the day before his 8:00 P.M. speech, Reagan made extensive changes in the draft written by his science adviser, George Keyworth. After deleting several phrases such as "no near-term panaceas," Reagan emphasized why the U.S. arms buildup was necessary. His speech ended with "I call upon the scientific community in this country, who gave us nuclear weapons, to turn their great talents to the cause of mankind and world peace, to give us the means of rendering these weapons impotent and obsolete."

Making nuclear weapons obsolete was precisely what most Americans wanted, especially those who found it difficult to interpret the complexities of nuclear arms control, which included esoteric terms such as SALT I, Anti-Ballistic Missile Treaty' and "nuclear war-fighting." On March 26, Michael

Deaver, the White House deputy chief of staff, told Soviet Ambassador Anatoly Dobrynin that the SDI speech was simply a campaign effort to neutralize the nuclear threat by blunting Democrats who "attacked Reagan as a warmonger." In contrast, Secretary of State George Shultz, Defense Secretary Caspar Weinberger, and Edward Teller disliked Reagan's edited speech but did not express their dissatisfaction to the president.

Nevertheless, Reagan's March 23 speech captured wide public attention, resulting in ongoing scientific disputes about SDI's viability. While SDI had some potential to defend U.S. missiles from a first strike, this moderate concept became blurred by the Reagan administration's bloated claims that it had found a perfect way to defend the country from nuclear attack. Thus, Reagan's SDI proposal preempted the problem of the U.S. making the MX a retaliatory second-strike weapon as proposed by a commission appointed by President Reagan in December 1982 and chaired by Brent Scowcroft to study the MX basing problem. In addition, it gave Reagan another card in the arms control game with the Soviet Union. The Soviets believed SDI was part of Reagan's effort to gain U.S. nuclear superiority beforea first nuclear strike.

On the ABM Treaty from 1967 to 1974, see January 26 and 27, 1967; January 26, 1967; March 14, 1969; November 17, 1969; and July 3, 1974. For the MX, see December 21, 1982, and April 11, 1983.

## March 30, 1983

### New U.S. proposals to limit intermediate-range missiles are proposed in Geneva; the Soviets reject them.

To show America's NATO allies U.S. flexibility in seeking an agreement with the USSR, President Reagan had U.S. delegates propose an interim solution at Geneva on March 29, which he announced publicly on March 30, 1983. The White House also exchanged letters with West German Chancellor Helmut Kohl, British Prime Minister Margaret Thatcher, and other NATO leaders before making the proposal.

The essence of the interim proposal was to begin cutting intermediate-range missiles by reducing Soviet SS-20s to a level of equality with the number of Pershing or cruise missiles NATO would deploy. Next, the Soviets would cut their worldwide deployment of intermediate-range missiles, which numbered 572, and the United States would match that number. Most crucial was that the new U.S. position involved *global* intermediate-range limits of U.S. and Soviet missiles, not just European-based missiles.

On April 2, Soviet Foreign Minister Andrey Gromyko rejected the U.S. proposal because it did not allay Soviet concerns regarding French and British missiles capable of hitting Soviet territory and treated Asian missiles as part of European arms control without involving Chinese missiles. In the Soviet view, any missile capable of reaching the Soviet homeland would have destructive results, whatever its point of origin. The United States had no comparable non-Soviet intermediate-range threat to its home territory. Deployment of the Pershing IIs in Europe was, therefore, what the Soviets desired to prevent.

### March 31, 1983

*Vietnamese forces attack a Kampuchean refugee camp in Thailand, killing 200 civilians and 5 Thai soldiers.*

In the Vietnamese-Cambodian War, Hanoi's forces had driven the Khmer Rouge armies to the border, where an estimated 45,000 Cambodian refugees had crossed into Thailand. Claiming that many of the Khmer Rouge army personnel were among the refugees, the Vietnamese staged this attack into Thailand.

Thailand retaliated by bombarding Vietnamese positions in Cambodia, but more Vietnamese raids were expected. As an ally of Thailand, the United States sent additional military aid to that country on April 4, but there were no further large-scale Vietnamese attacks during 1983.

### April 7, 1983

*After the United States grants asylum to Chinese tennis star Hu Na, the People's Republic of China cancels its sports and cultural exchanges with the United States for 1983.*

During a 1982 Chinese tennis tour in California, Hu Na left her hotel and hid in a friend's house from Chinese authorities. The Chinese protested against her request for political asylum, and for eight months the Reagan administration delayed a decision. Although various U.S. groups supported Hu Na's

request, the State Department did not want to damage relations with China, which were already tense over U.S. arms sales to Taiwan. Beijing would grant her immigration status but refused to concede that Hu Na had fled because of political persecution. Nevertheless, Washington decided to give Hu Na asylum. China retaliated by canceling 19 sports and cultural agreements planned with Americans for 1983.

Despite the disagreements, President Reagan accepted the diplomatic credentials of China's new ambassador, Zhang Wenjin, on April 8, 1982.

### April 9, 1983

**The U.S. space shuttle *Challenger* has its first successful space flight.**

The flight included time for the crew to have a four-hour space walk. One problem was encountered when a giant communications satellite that the shuttle deployed went out of control and had to be stabilized from the ground. The second *Challenger* flight took place on June 18, carrying the nation's first female astronaut, Sally K. Ride.

### April 11, 1983

**A presidential commission on the MX missile offers recommendations.**

The Scowcroft Commission, named after its chairman, Brent Scowcroft, was appointed by President Reagan in accordance with an agreement with Congress on December 17, 1982. Its members were former Secretaries of State Henry Kissinger and Alexander Haig; six former Defense Department secretaries or undersecretaries, including James Schlesinger, Harold Brown, Melvin Laird, Donald Rumsfeld, William Perry, and William Clements; former CIA directors Richard Helms and John McCone; White House insider Thomas Reed; Massachusetts Institute of Technology scientist John Deutch; retired Vice Admiral Levering Smith; and the vice president of the American Federation of Labor, John Lyons.

The commission report denied that the 1970s arms control treaties would create a "window of vulnerability" during the mid-1980s, a claim made by President Reagan during the 1980 presidential election. Nevertheless, because the MX was nearly ready to be deployed, its use should be as a temporary weapon to prevent a Soviet attack.

After deploying the first 100 MX missiles in silos, however, the commission wanted to deploy small Midgetman missiles carrying one warhead each, because they would be mobile and, therefore, better able to survive a first strike and act as a second-strike retaliatory force. The commission indicated that the Midgetman development and deployment would require at least ten years and would cost about $40 billion to $50 billion.

The Scowcroft report convinced Congress to release $625 million for the MX on May 25, 1983. On June 17, the MX had its first successful test launch.

## April 15, 1983

### A Sandinista war hero, Eden Pastora Gómez, announces plans to overthrow the Sandinista junta of Daniel Ortega Saavedra.

Pastora was the legendary Commander Zero, who in August 1978 led the rebel unit that captured the National Palace in Managua, an event leading to the overthrow of the Somoza regime and the Sandinista victory. Pastora served as vice minister of defense in the Sandinista government until April 15, 1982, when he resigned in opposition to Ortega's communist policies. He and Alfonso Robelo Callejas cofounded the Democratic Revolutionary Alliance (ARDE), which opposed Ortega.

Organizing his rebel force, the Sandino Revolutionary Front (FRS), in southern Nicaragua, Pastora announced the start of a war of liberation. The "Contra group" of rebels, which had gained most of Washington's support, was based in northern Nicaragua and Honduras. Called the Nicaraguan Democratic Front, it was headed by Enrique Bermudez. Pastora disapproved of this rebel group because it had too many army officers from the Somoza regime.

See March 14, 1982.

## April 18, 1983

### Terrorists bomb the U.S. embassy in Beirut; 63 persons are killed, including 17 Americans.

A pro-Iranian Muslim faction claimed responsibility for this attack, which was well planned and targeted to alarm not only Americans but also those in Beirut who believed the United States guaranteed their security. About one-half of the Americans killed were CIA agents, including Robert C. Ames, the agency's principal Middle East analyst.

See October 23, 1983.

## April 20, 1983

### Brazilian authorities impound arms headed for Nicaragua aboard a Libyan cargo aircraft.

Planes flying from Libya landed to refuel in Brazil, where customs officials discovered arms that were not on the cargo list. Brazil unloaded the armaments, released the crew, and, on June 8, agreed to return the aircraft to Libya. The United States claimed that the military items came originally from the Soviet Union and, therefore, substantiated U.S. contentions that the Sandinistas were assisted by the Soviets.

## May 3, 1983

### Congress challenges President Reagan's Central American policy.

Disagreeing with the president's emphasis on a military solution to problems in Nicaragua and El Salvador, the House Permanent Select Committee on Intelligence on May 3 approved legislation to ban covert aid to the Nicaraguan rebels. Because the Senate Intelligence Committee wanted to aid the Contras, the two committees compromised by giving $19 million of the $36 million requested. The joint congressional committee also approved $80 million of covert aid to any friendly Central American country willing to help the United States stop Cuban arms shipments to Nicaragua or El Salvador.

To secure the congressional compromise, President Reagan appointed Richard Stone, a former Democratic Senator from Florida, as a special envoy to visit Central America to seek peace negotiations and endorsed the Contadora Group's efforts to obtain peace. Reagan also agreed to appoint a special commission headed by Henry KISSINGER, to study U.S. policy in Latin America, especially focusing on Central America. Secretary of State George Shultz hoped the Kissinger Commission would provide Congress with a positive statement about Reagan's policy in Central America before Congress adjourned in 1983, but the Commission's work was not completed until January 1984.

See March 14, 1982; April 15, 1983; and January 10, 1984.

## May 6, 1983

### U.S. representative returns to International Atomic Energy Agency (IAEA) meeting after Israel's membership is certified.

On September 24, 1982, United States delegate Richard T. Kennedy and several Western European delegates walked out of the IAEA meeting in Vienna after delegates voted 41–39 to expel Israel from the IAEA. African and Arab delegates to the IAEA had joined ranks in voting against Israel, claiming Israel violated IAEA guidelines by refusing to let IAEA inspectors examine all of its nuclear energy facilities, a claim Israel denied.

On October 16, Secretary of State George Shultz commended Kennedy's decision to leave the IAEA meeting, adding the United States was withholding $8.5 million scheduled to be paid to the IAEA during 1982. Shultz also asked Kennedy to form a committee to thoroughly review U.S. membership in the IAEA.

After the reassessment was completed in January 1983, Kennedy reported to Shultz that the IAEA played a key role in international relations by regulating nuclear energy facilities and preventing the proliferation of nuclear weapons in other countries. The report concluded that some IAEA delegates damaged the IAEA's reputation by politicizing meetings such as that held in September 1982. The U.S. should not tolerate those who sought to play politics during IAEA meetings.

After this report was made public, Kennedy met with IAEA Director General Hans Blix on February 22, 1983 and Blix agreed to certify Israel's membership at the next IAEA meeting. On May 6, 1983, Blix's promise was confirmed at the IAEA's general meeting. Following this action, Israeli, American, and all Western European delegates once again attended the IAEA sessions.

## May 10, 1983

### President Reagan cuts Nicaragua's sugar quotas by 90%.

To punish the Sandinistas for what Reagan called "subversion and violence," the United States reduced its sugar imports from Nicaragua to 6,000 short tons from its current annual quota of 56,800 tons. Reagan indicated that this would reduce the Sandinistas' ability to support subversion in El Salvador. Managua's government said the reduction cost it $54 million and

appealed to the Council of the General Agreement on Tariffs and Trade (GATT), claiming that the United States violated its treaty.

See March 13, 1984.

## May 15, 1983

### Japan seeks trade relations with both Koreas, welcoming a North Korean delegation to Tokyo.

As a first step toward better Japanese relations with North Korea, North Korean judges visited Tokyo for an international judicial meeting. Japan made it a ceremonial occasion to impress the North Koreans with their goodwill.

On January 11, 1983, Japan's interest in South Korea was demonstrated when Prime Minister Yasuhiro Nakasone visited Seoul, becoming the first Japanese leader to visit Korea since 1945.

## May 17, 1983

### Lebanon and Israel sign a withdrawal agreement.

Recognizing that the Lebanese war had ended, Israel agreed to withdraw its forces from Lebanon provided that Syrian and Palestinian forces also left. The pact, supported by U.S. Secretary of State George Shultz, restricted Lebanese military deployments along the Israeli border and required Lebanon to name Major Saad Haddad, a "friend to Israel," as deputy commander for antiterrorist intelligence.

The pact had few results. Syria rejected it, refusing to withdraw and closing all land communications between Beirut and eastern Lebanon. Moreover, civil war broke out in Lebanon not only between Palestine Liberation Organization (PLO) and Syrian factions but also among different Lebanese Christian military groups.

See June 24 and August 2, 1983.

## May 27, 1983

### The U.S. State Department removes two moderate diplomats from important positions in Central American affairs.

Thomas Enders, the Assistant Secretary of State for Inter-American Affairs, and Deane Hinton, the U.S.

Ambassador to El Salvador, were replaced respectively on May 27 and June 2, 1983. Secretary of State George Shultz approved their dismissal in an attempt to prevent National Security Adviser William Clark from gaining control over policy making for Central America. In accordance with State Department policy in 1981, Enders and Hinton pursued a dual-track policy of persuading Central America to accept peaceful solutions to their problems. Using the dual-track, Enders proposed negotiations to solve disputes but employed the threat of possible U.S. military action as an incentive to enable diplomacy to resolve problems in El Salvador, Nicaragua, Honduras, and Guatemala.

On October 2, 1982, Enders organized a forum of Central American leaders in San Jose, Costa Rica, to discuss peaceful ways to resolve their mutual problems. Forum members prepared the San Jose Declaration, which called for each Central American country to create and maintain democratic governments based on the people's will as expressed in free and regular elections. The declaration also said each country should prevent the use of its territory to support, supply or train "terrorist or subversive elements" aimed at the overthrow of another government.

According to Secretary Shultz's memoir, the San Jose principals were controversial among the Sandinistas and their supporters but they were also opposed by CIA Director William Casey and "hardliners on the NSC staff," such as William Clark. Subsequently, Clark told President Reagan that Enders must be removed from his State Department position. Clark's opinion gained support from U.S. Ambassador to the United Nations Jeane Kirkpatrick and from Casey, both of whom claimed Enders was "soft on communism." Clark and Kirkpatrick advocated military and CIA action to aid the right-wing government of El Salvador and to send military and financial aid to Nicaragua's Contra rebels, who fought against the left-wing Sandinista government of Nicaragua that gained control in 1979 elections. (See July 17, 1979.)

Hoping to regain control of policy in Central America, Shultz tried to satisfy Clark by replacing Enders with Langhorne Anthony Motley, who was Ambassador to Brazil, and by making Enders Ambassador to Spain. As for Hinton, Clark and Casey claimed that his reports about the murders committed by men affiliated with El Salvador's government demonstrated Hinton's inability to support U.S. policy of assisting the government's campaign to defeat left-wing rebels supported by Cuban and Soviet communists. (See October 23, 1982 and November 12, 1983.) To satisfy Clark, Shultz replaced Hinton with Thomas Pickering, who was ambassador to Nigeria; Hinton became ambassador to Panama.

## May 28, 1983

### Leaders of seven major industrial nations hold annual summit at Williamsburg, Virginia.

This summit meeting of the leaders of the United States, Great Britain, Canada, France, West Germany, Italy, and Japan ended with no concrete results. Under pressure from the other six leaders, President Reagan agreed to some flexibility in arms control discussions with the USSR, and in return, the European leaders would deploy U.S. Pershing II and cruise missiles if no agreement were reached.

On the economic front, the group's final communiqué glossed over the fact that the six U.S. allies blamed high U.S. interest rates and the growing American national debt for their economic problems. The official release simply noted the need to rectify the problem of high interest rates.

## May 30, 1983

### The Philippines and the United States sign an agreement on U.S. military bases in the islands.

To continue using Subic Bay Naval Base and Clark Air Force Base for another five years, the United States would pay the Philippines $900 million—$400 million more than the 1979 agreement required. Because some Philippine groups objected to using the bases for nuclear weapons, the agreement provided for joint consultation regarding base operations, including the stationing of intercontinental missiles.

U.S. ambassador to the Philippines, Michael H. Armacost said the pact put U.S.-Philippine relations back on an "even keel." On June 25, Secretary of State George Shultz visited Manila, where he praised President Ferdinand Marcos for his excellent leadership and reaffirmed U.S. support despite recent demonstrations against the Marcos government.

## June 6, 1983

**Tension increases between Nicaragua and the United States when Managua expels three U.S. diplomats it accuses of plotting to kill Sandinista officials.**

The United States denied Nicaragua's June 6 allegation and retaliated by expelling 21 Nicaraguan consular officials and closing 6 Nicaraguan consulates in the United States. Nevertheless, ambassadorial relations remained intact with both sides finding advantages to retaining official contact.

See May 10, 1983.

## June 17, 1983

**First successful test launch of the MX missile.**

Although Congress and President Reagan still argued over the production and deployment of the MX, it approached its final development stage with a 4,700-mile flight across the Pacific to drop six simulated warheads near Kwajalein Island in the Marshalls.

## June 23, 1983

**Libyan-supported rebels invade northern Chad, seeking to overthrow the government of President Hissen Habré.**

Chad's troubles began on June 7, 1982, after Habré ousted President Goukouni Oueddei, who fled and gained support from Libya. Although on February 28, Libya and Chad tried to resolve the issue of Chadian rebels backed by Libyan leader Mu'ammar al-Gadhafi, the talks failed. On June 23, 3,500 rebel forces crossed from Libya to march against Chad's government. France and the United States backed the Habré government, and by August the rebel threat had dissipated.

See August 23, 1983.

## June 24, 1983

**Syria expels PLO chairman Yasser Arafat because of heavy fighting between two PLO factions in Lebanon.**

After the Palestinian Liberation Organization (PLO) evacuated West Beirut (see August 21, 1982), PLO members who were loyal to ARAFAT remained in eastern and northern Lebanon but began quarreling with pro-Syrian Aalawite Muslims, Sunni Muslims, Iraq Baathist Party members, and Muslim Brotherhood members from Egypt.

On May 22, 1983, Arafat returned to the Baalbek area of eastern Lebanon where he tried to squelch a rebellion of dissident PLO members who received support from Libya's President Mu'ammar al-Gadhafi. After a battle ensued on June 1, Syrian President Hafiz al-Assad expelled Arafat from Lebanese regions controlled by Syrian forces. Arafat was unable to reconcile the PLO factions and on June 21, Arafat's loyalists suffered another defeat from the PLO dissidents, who forced the loyalists to flee to Tunisia.

For other conflicts in Lebanon, see August 2 and December 20, 1983.

## June 24, 1983

**The U.N.-sponsored Afghan peace talks achieve no results.**

The June 24 meeting in Geneva concluded a second round of negotiations between parties involved in the Afghanistan war. The first round, on June 16, 1982, consisted of "proximity" talks conducted by U.N. mediator Diégo Cordovez, an Ecuadoran lawyer. In these "proximity" meetings, Cordovez shuttled between Afghan and Soviet diplomats in one room and Pakistani and U.S. diplomats in another room. This shuttle diplomacy reached no conclusions but determined that the chief problem was finding a method to withdraw foreign troops either before or after a cease-fire and peace agreement.

The Soviet Union had urged the United Nations to supervise these negotiations. After Soviet President Leonid Brezhnev died on November 10, 1982, the new Soviet leader, Yuri Andropov, wanted to end the Afghan conflict while the Soviets still held a strong position in Afghanistan. The Soviets' main problem was finding an Afghan leader willing to accept peace terms through compromise arrangements with Pakistan, the principal supporter of the Afghan rebels. The June 1983 sessions achieved no solutions to the Afghan conflict, which remained unsolved until 1988. Meanwhile, the United States accused the Soviet Union of using chemical weapons in Afghanistan.

See February 21, 1984.

### June 27, 1983

*After Italian elections, Socialist Bettino Craxi forms a five-party coalition government.*

Although Craxi's Socialist Party won only about 10% of the vote, it was the largest of four minority parties and came to power because of irreconcilable differences between Italy's two largest parties—the Christian Democrats and the Communists—which each won about 30% of the vote. During 1982, the Socialists had forced three cabinet changes by leaving the Christian Democrats coalition. Now, Craxi formed his own coalition of Communists, Socialists, and members of other parties.

### June 27, 1983

*The Soviet Soyuz T-9 spacecraft is launched and successfully docks the next day with the orbiting Salyut 7 space station.*

Despite this Soviet success, a Soviet spacecraft exploded during its launch on September 27, 1983. The Soviet cosmonauts were saved because their escape rocket fired safely.

### July 5, 1983

*President Reagan announces measures to protect American specialty steel producers from foreign competition.*

By 1981, when President Reagan appointed William Brock as the United States Trade Representative, America's share of the world's steel production had dropped from 26% in 1960 to 11%. Brock's primary duty was to oversee favorable trade negotiations with foreign countries. Like many Republican conservatives, Brock advocated free trade throughout the world, but as the U.S. Trade Representative he took measures to protect powerful American industries from unfair trade practices of foreign competitors, especially in the steel and automotive industries.

In 1982, Brock obtained an agreement with the European Economic Community (EEC) to limit EEC steel exports (see October 21, 1982) but U.S. steel companies continued to complain about Japan's unfair practices in the production of specialty steel products. On February 25, 1983, Brock rejected the steel manufacturer's complaints against Japanese steel activities. Nevertheless, President Reagan wanted to help the steel industry and asked the U.S.

International Trade Commission (ITC) to examine the status of U.S. tariffs on specialty steel.

The ITC had been established in 1916 as an executive agency to recommend decisions about raising tariffs when U.S. industries were threatened by foreign imports. The commission consisted of two Democrats and two Republicans, plus a neutral member with no direct political party ties. In response to Reagan's request, ITC members voted three to two to recommend the imposition of a 70% tariff on specialty steel imports.

Reagan accepted the ITC recommendation even though his two Republican appointees to the ITC voted against it. Apparently, Brock and Reagan willingly aided the steel industry despite the fact that many conservative Republicans opposed all tariffs and restrictions on trade. These Republicans argued that members of the workers steel unions should take a 70% pay cut to make the steel industry competitive, although no world free trade market existed.

### July 8, 1983

*A Caribbean Community (CARICOM) conference in Trinidad criticizes the United States for delays in granting economic aid promised in Reagan's Caribbean basin initiative; Congress approves part of Reagan's Caribbean request on July 20.*

CARICOM—English-speaking nations in the Caribbean Community—met to discuss ways of ending their economic recession by accelerating their economic integration. They expected to be assisted by Reagan's proposed economic program.

Despite the CARICOM leaders' desire for significant U.S. aid, the House of Representatives voted on July 14 to cut back the funds President Reagan had requested for the Caribbean area. Later on July 19, a Senate-House conference committee approved legislation to give the Caribbean nations duty-free access for certain products sold to the United States.

See November 12, 1983.

### July 15, 1983

*Armenian terrorists explode a bomb at Orly airport, outside Paris. Six are killed including one American.*

The Orly bombing was the second Armenian terrorist attack in two days. On July 14, Armenian nationalists assassinated a Turkish diplomat in Brussels, Belgium. The next day, Armenians set off a bomb in a suitcase at the Turkish Airlines check-in counter at Orly, killing six persons.

These two attacks were followed by another on July 27, when five Armenian terrorists were killed while attempting to take over the Turkish embassy in Lisbon, Portugal.

See July 27, 1983.

### July 21, 1983

*Poland's government ends martial law but expands Prime Minister Wojciech Jaruzelski's power to arrest and detain dissenters.*

The number of demonstrations in Poland had grown after 2,000 protesters marched in Gdansk on March 13 and 14, 1983. The visit of POPE JOHN PAUL II from June 16 to 23 temporarily quieted the country because the pope met with Solidarity leader Lech Wałęsa, as well as with Jaruzelski. Wałęsa received the Nobel Peace Prize on October 5, 1983, because he used nonviolent methods in confronting the government.

Ending martial law on July 21 did not satisfy most members of Solidarity because the Sejm (parliament) also enlarged the police power of the government. On November 22, the Sejm further enhanced Jaruzelski's power and named him chairman of a new National Defense Committee.

### July 21, 1983

**Syria gains the release of David Dodge of the American University of Beirut.**

In June 1982, Iranian Shiite gunmen had abducted Dodge from his presidential office at the American University of Beirut. Dodge was taken to Iran until July 21, 1983, when Syria's President Hafiz al-Assad arranged with Iran's government for Dodge's release. In spite of Assad's help, a wave of American kidnappings in Lebanon began in 1984.

See June 19, 1982, and May 6, 1984.

### July 21, 1983

*A general strike in Brazil follows a government decree imposing more austerity measures to solve the country's economic problems.*

Workers struck because President João Baptista Figueiredo cut their pay raises to 80% of inflation,

the inflation rate being 127%. He also decreed that prices must increase, which lowered Brazil's standard of living. The austerity decrees were required by the International Monetary Fund (IMF), which gave Brazil a loan to service its $90 billion foreign debt. In February 1983, Brazil had devalued its currency by 23% to obtain a $5.4 million loan from the IMF. On September 26, Brazil received a loan of $11 billion to service its debt.

Such measures involved Brazil and other Third World nations in a vicious cycle of debts, loans, political instability, and social unrest because of the austerity decrees.

### July 22, 1983

**China denounces American plans to sell more weapons to Taiwan, claiming a violation of an agreement of August 1982.**

After July 15, when the United States announced the sale to Taiwan of $530 million of military equipment, Beijing protested to U.S. Ambassador Arthur Hummel Jr. These new sales would total $800 million of U.S. armaments to Taiwan in 1983.

Since this exceeded the $600 million of sales in 1982, China asserted it was not the decrease in arms sales to Taiwan that the Reagan administration had agreed to in 1982. The U.S. State Department argued that high inflation rates made the 1983 figure an actual decrease in real value. The dispute further cooled China's relations with the United States during Reagan's first administration.

See August 16, 1982; see also April 7, 1983.

### July 25, 1983

**News is leaked in Washington that large-scale U.S. military exercises off the Atlantic and Pacific coasts of Nicaragua are underway to intimidate the Sandinistas.**

On the eve of a congressional vote on aid to the Nicaraguan rebels, news reports said the U.S navy aircraft carrier *Ranger* had arrived off the Atlantic coast of Nicaragua. This was part of "Big Pine 2," a six-month series of army and navy exercises along both coasts of Central America. Nineteen naval ships and about 4,000 U.S. army and marine forces were deployed.

Although President Reagan played down the news by saying it was simply one of many such exercises, one unidentified Pentagon official stated, "We want to persuade the bad guys in Nicaragua and Cuba that we are positioned to blockade, invade or interdict if they cross a particular threshold." An immediate response to the news was a House of Representatives vote to cut off aid to the U.S.-backed rebels fighting Nicaragua.

See July 28, 1983.

### July 27, 1983

*Armenian gunmen storm the Turkish embassy in Lisbon, Portugal, killing seven people.*

Desiring publicity for the cause of Armenian rebels trying to gain independence from Turkey, five gunmen of the Armenia Revolutionary Army attacked the residence of Turkey's ambassador to Portugal. Before police regained control of the residence, the five gunmen, one hostage, and one policeman were killed.

### July 28, 1983

**The Soviet Union agrees to purchase 9–12 million metric tons of U.S. grain each year for the next five years.**

During the peak of détente in the 1970s, before President Jimmy Carter embargoed grain to the USSR in 1981, the Soviets had purchased about 20 million tons a year. In 1983–84, the Soviets were expected to import 40 million tons and might have bought more U.S. grain than that prescribed in the July 28 agreement.

### July 28, 1983

**The House of Representatives cuts off U.S. covert aid to the Nicaraguan rebels.**

For some time, members of Congress and the American public had the impression that President Reagan was risking war in Central America by pushing military means to overthrow Nicaragua's Sandinista regime. Although the president called a televised news conference on July 26 to dispel such notions about his policy, he did not succeed.

To exemplify the range of public concerns, Republicans Olympia Snowe of Maine and Lynn Martin of Illinois voted with the Democratic majority to prohibit aid to the Contras. Snowe said she was confused about the U.S. role in Nicaragua; Martin feared that Reagan wanted to overthrow the Sandinista government.

Despite the House vote in favor of Massachusetts Democratic Senator Edward Boland's amendment to stop aid to the Contras, the Senate did not concur and some aid went to the Contras.

See December 9, 1983.

### August 2, 1983

*Lebanese factions fight civil war, with the heaviest fighting near Beirut.*

Although it had made an agreement with Israeli troops to leave Lebanon, President Amin Gemayel's government experienced greater problems in restoring the political compromises that had maintained peace in Lebanon before 1975. On July 15, heavy fighting broke out in Beirut between Gemayel's Lebanese army and Muslim Shiites militias. On July 23, Walid Jumblat, the Druze leader, announced the formation of a National Liberation Front among leaders of several Lebanese Muslim groups. An eclectic religious group, predominating in the Shouf Mountains east of Beirut, the Druze had gained control of this region after Israeli troops left on September 4, 1983.

The six factions fighting in early August included three Christian Phalangist groups, at least two PLO Muslim groups, and Jumblat's National Front. By mid-September, U.S. forces in Lebanon undertook the new role of assisting Gemayel's Lebanese army.

See September 13, 1983.

### August 8, 1983

*Guatemalan military coup overthrows President Rios Montt.*

Rios Montt had run into increasing opposition since June 29, when he ordered a "state of alert" that restricted civil rights and freedom of the press. Claiming they wished to restore order, a military group headed by Defense Minister Brigadier General Oscar Humbert Mejia Victores took over the government on August 8.

**August 20, 1983**

**President Reagan ends all controls concerning sales of U.S. gas pipeline equipment to the USSR.**

This action ended a two-year argument between the United States and its Western European allies over supplying the Soviet Union with modern technology to construct a gas pipeline from Siberia to central Europe.

See November 13, 1982.

**August 21, 1983**

**Benigno S. Aquino Jr., a political opponent of Philippine President Marcos, is assassinated just after leaving the airplane that brought him to Manila from self-imposed exile in the United States.**

AQUINO had decided to return from his three-year exile to lead dissenters who advocated new elections. Accompanied by many TV and news reporters, Aquino was the first to leave the plane after landing in Manila. Although body guards escorted him, an airport maintenance worker got close enough to assassinate Aquino before the guards killed the worker.

President Ferdinand MARCOS denied government responsibility for the killing, but large rallies of protestors marched against Marcos, whom they blamed for plotting the murder. To pacify demonstrators, Marcos appointed a commission of inquiry.

See September 29, 1983.

**August 23, 1983**

**The United States withdraws AWAC planes aiding Chad's government after French forces arrive to help fight rebels supported by Libya.**

After rebels based in Libya attacked northern Chad on June 23, 1983, France warned Libya it would send troops if Chad's President Hissen Habré was endangered. The United States gave Chad a $15 million increase in military aid and, on August 3, sent AWAC reconnaissance planes to Sudanese bases to monitor the Libyan-backed rebel movements.

Because Libya bombed Chad's government forces, both the United States and France sent antiaircraft weapons to assist Habré's forces. As soon as 3,000 French troops arrived in August to assist Habré, the rebel advances stopped, and a stalemate developed between the government and the rebels. Thus, the United States decided to withdraw its AWAC from the Sudan.

**August 24, 1983**

**Iran pays $419.5 million of U.S. claims to relieve its debts.**

To meet its U.S. obligations, Iran transferred funds to the U.S. Export-Import Bank from the $1.42 billion escrow account set up when U.S. hostages were released in January 1981. So far, Iran had settled accounts with 20 U.S. banks and repaid nearly all of the $10 billion debt inherited from the shah's government in 1979.

U.S. foreign sales to Iran continued, especially such items as Boeing transport jets and electronic and power plant equipment. During the first six months of 1983, U.S. exporters sold $97 million of goods to Tehran. Iran was expected to earn $20 billion in oil exports during 1983.

**August 26, 1983**

**Soviet President Yuri Andropov offers to "liquidate" the SS-20s withdrawn from Europe as part of an arms agreement.**

Because the United States and its allies feared that Soviet SS-20s could be moved to Asian targets if they were removed from Europe, the United States had talked about making a global agreement on intermediate-range nuclear forces (INF). Desiring to limit present INF discussions to Europe, Andropov stated that the Soviets would destroy any SS-20s that were restricted by arms reductions. This Soviet proposal looked like a breakthrough but was limited because Moscow insisted on counting French and British missiles in any agreement signed with the United States. By counting French and British missiles, Andropov said that the Soviets could retain 162 missiles while destroying 81 missiles if the United States did not deploy Pershing IIs in Europe. Then, a Soviet and NATO balance would be attained, he declared.

Because Washington could not control the use of British and French missiles not under NATO authority, the U.S. negotiators argued that other nations' weapons could not be counted. Hence, the stalemate in the U.S.-Soviet INF talks continued.

See March 30 and November 23, 1983.

### August 28, 1983

*Israeli Prime Minister Menachem Begin announces his resignation.*

The transition to a new cabinet was completed on September 12, when the six parties in the Likud coalition named Yitzhak SHAMIR as prime minister.

### September 1, 1983

**The Soviets shoot down a South Korean passenger plane that strays into Soviet airspace.**

The Soviet Union stated that an unidentified plane had intruded over Soviet territory on an espionage mission. The Korean Air Lines Boeing 747 aircraft was en route from the United States to Seoul, Korea, with 269 passengers, including 61 Americans, when it was shot down. The United States denied the allegation that KAL flight 007 was collecting data about Soviet air defenses but admitted the plane had strayed off course.

President Reagan's reaction was milder than many observers expected. He expressed outrage at the killing of innocent victims and suspended all Soviet commercial aircraft flights to U.S. airports. His words were not matched by other punitive measures such as stopping arms control talks in Geneva or halting U.S. grain sales. While there was increased tension, President Reagan contended that the United States should continue its dialogue with Moscow in a "quest for peace."

This incident resulted partly from the recent Soviet buildup of army, navy, and air force units in eastern Asia. This activity countered Soviet fears of a Chinese attack as well as the recent U.S. plan to obtain naval supremacy. In 1981, President Reagan's secretary of the navy, John Lehman, announced a "maritime strategy" to develop a 600-ship U.S. fleet against the Soviet Union. Lehman's maritime strategy called for an offensive "force projection" against Soviet fleet and coastal targets. This meant preparing several U.S. aircraft carriers and other forces to move into narrow waterways (choke points) surrounding the Soviet Union. One strategic choke point was the Sea of Japan, where five narrow straits leading into the open Pacific Ocean could be easily mined, blockaded, or bombed. This would bottle up the Soviet's Pacific-based fleet at Vladivostok. Combined with the air forces of the United States, South Korea, and Japan,

the maritime strategy could give the United States distinct military advantages in the northwestern Pacific. It also contributed to Soviet suspicions about the off-course flight of KAL-007 as a spy mission.

Thus, when KAL-007 skirted sensitive Soviet military installations between Japan and the Soviet Union, both U.S. and Japanese intelligence monitored the flight. These tapes indicated that the plane strayed hundreds of miles off course for unexplained reasons. Eight Soviet planes tracked the Boeing aircraft for over two hours before ground commanders ordered its fighter planes to fire the air-to-air missile that downed the plane. The Soviets said the KAL pilot did not respond to Soviet warnings or their efforts to make contact. Evidence regarding KAL's penetration of Soviet airspace is inconclusive despite many studies about the event.

On Shultz's reaction to the incident, see September 8, 1983.

### September 8, 1983

**Secretary of State Shultz has a stormy session with Soviet Foreign Minister Andrey Gromyko.**

While denouncing the shooting down of KAL flight 007 by Soviet pilots, President Reagan minimized conflict with Moscow and kept the arms control talks active until the U.S. Pershing IIs were deployed in Europe. Consequently, Secretary Shultz kept an appointment with GROMYKO in Madrid to discuss a Reagan-Andropov summit meeting in 1984.

The deaths of the 269 passengers had infuriated Shultz, however, and his anger showed up in his meeting with Gromyko. The Madrid meeting was one of the most volatile between high-level U.S.-Soviet delegates in some time, making Secretary Shultz more combative and less willing to offer concessions on arms control with the Soviets. On September 26, however, President Reagan offered the Soviets a new intermediate-range nuclear forces (INF) missile proposal during a speech at the United Nations.

### September 8, 1983

**Greece permits four U.S. bases to remain on Greek soil for five years.**

Since taking office on October 18, 1981, Greek Prime Minister Andreas Papandreou had threatened to abolish the U.S. bases because he desired an independent Greek foreign policy. Even while Greece negotiated with Washington on February 24, 1983, Papandreou met with Soviet Prime Minister Nikolay A. Tikhonov and joined the Soviets in calling for a nuclear-free zone and limited armed forces in the Balkans.

Undoubtedly, Papandreou hoped to nudge the U.S. toward better terms for Greece, because on September 8, he signed an agreement concluded by negotiators on July 15, 1983. The pact retained four major U.S. bases in Greece in return for $500 million per year, up from previous funding of $280 million annually. The United States also promised to maintain a balance of military power between Greece and Turkey, the historic rival of Greece even though both countries were NATO members.

### September 9, 1983

#### Four Central American states approve the Contadora objectives for peace.

The Contadora process begun by four Latin American countries Mexico, Colombia, Venezuela, and Panama on January 8, 1983, pursued a variety of proposals to end the Central American wars involving Nicaragua, El Salvador, and U.S.-based rebels in Honduras.

At Cancún, Mexico, on July 17, they urged the Central American states, Cuba, and the United States to renew peace efforts. The Contadora diplomats now decided to spell out possible methods for peacemaking in the September 9 "Document of Objectives." This document favored regional negotiations, democratic pluralism, national compromises to reconcile rebel groups with national governments, a halt to support of paramilitary forces, agreement for arms limitations, withdrawal of all foreign advisers, and methods to verify the agreements concluded.

Although none of the nations involved in Central America's conflicts formally rejected the September 9 proposals, the United States, Nicaragua, and El Salvador failed to take them seriously. Nevertheless, the Contadora nations continued their attempts to bring about peace.

See September 25, 1984.

### September 13, 1983

#### U.S. forces in Lebanon are authorized to use naval gunfire and air strikes to defend themselves; the U.S. role escalates.

The U.S. role in Lebanon escalated because the multilateral peacekeeping force that returned to Lebanon after the massacres at Sabra and Shatila on September 16–18, 1982, had gradually tied itself to the defense of Amir Gemayel's Lebanese government after the civil war began during July and August 1983. On September 1, President Reagan ordered 2,000 marine reinforcements to the eastern Mediterranean, and U.S. naval guns first fired at Druze positions east of Beirut on September 8. Thus, the September 13 order backed earlier naval action and approved future firing.

The U.S. navy became more involved on September 17 and 18 when naval guns bombarded Syrian-controlled regions of Lebanon. French peacekeeping forces entered the fray on September 22, when French combat planes struck rebel camps outside Beirut after rebels shelled French positions in Beirut. During the fighting in Beirut between Christian and Muslim armies, two U.S. Marines and four French soldiers were killed between August 29 and 31, 1983.

See August 2, 1983, and September 18 and 21, 1982.

### September 26, 1983

#### President Reagan offers an INF missile proposal the Soviets reject as deception.

As the November date drew near for deploying U.S Pershing II missiles in Europe, the president demonstrated a willingness to negotiate with the Soviet Union. The U.S. proposal, which U.S. negotiator Paul Nitze offered to the Soviets at Geneva, stated that for any global limitation the Soviets established on intermediate-range missiles, the United States would deploy its intermediate-range nuclear forces (INF) in similar proportions, including those deployed in NATO countries. Thus, while some U.S. missiles would be stationed in Europe, they would decrease in proportion to the Soviets' willingness to decrease their SS-20s in Europe.

The Soviets found nothing substantially new in the U.S. proposal. President Andropov said that Washington talked of flexibility but did not address the real issue of the number of French, British, and U.S. missiles able to strike Soviet territory. The breakdown of the INF talks seemed apparent and in November became a reality.

See November 23, 1983.

### September 29, 1983

#### Congress permits U.S. Marines to remain in Lebanon for another 18 months.

Prior to August 1983, President Reagan avoided invoking the War Powers Act by telling Congress the U.S. forces did not face imminent hostilities. The renewal of large-scale civil war in Lebanon, the killing of two marines on August 29, and Reagan's dispatch of another 2,000 marines on September 1 caused congressional leaders to insist that the president invoke the War Powers Act to obtain congressional consent to keep forces in the eastern Mediterranean. It was clear to most members of Congress that the original U.S. peacekeeping role had changed, a belief reinforced by the September 13 U.S. decision to permit naval bombardment of rebel positions.

Reagan's disdain for the limits that the War Powers Act placed on the executive was countered by his supporters who thought a congressional role avoided the analogy of Lebanon as another Vietnam conflict taking place without legislative approval. Republican congressmen such as Henry Hyde and Robert H. Michel (both R-Ill.) wanted to rid the nation of the self-doubt inherited from the Vietnam experience, while conservative Democratic Senator John Stennis of Mississippi said the American people were concerned about where their "boys" would fight and die. A *New York Times*/CBS poll indicated that two out of three Americans thought Lebanon resembled Vietnam and that Americans disapproved of Reagan's foreign policies by 47% to 38%, with 15% abstaining.

Actually, most Congress members wanted to keep the marines in Lebanon but insisted that Reagan use the War Powers Act. Reagan finally relented, and with little debate the congressional resolution to keep U.S. forces in the eastern Mediterranean passed on September 29.

### September 29, 1983

#### President Reagan cancels a visit to the Philippines.

Officially, Reagan said the Southeast Asia visit planned for November conflicted with changes in congressional schedules for legislative enactments. Reagan assured President Marcos that U.S. friendship toward the Philippines was as "warm and firm" as ever. Nevertheless, most commentators believed Reagan did not want to become involved in Philippine domestic issues arising after Benigno Aquino's assassination.

See August 21, 1983, and October 23, 1984.

### September 30, 1983

#### World financial crisis leaves the World Bank and the International Monetary Fund (IMF) in need of $6 billion; President Reagan offers $3 billion.

A joint meeting of World Bank and IMF members in Washington, D.C., disclosed that their commitments to assist countries with debt problems would exceed their resources by $6 billion before the end of the year. Throughout the year many Third World countries could not meet their debt payments. As a result of the expected shortfall in financial resources, President Reagan asked Congress for an increase of $8.4 billion, including $3 billion in emergency funds, to help the IMF meet its commitments. Congress approved the appropriation on November 18, 1983.

### October 9, 1983

#### *In Rangoon, Burma, a terrorist bomb fails to kill South Korean President Chun Doo Hwan, but 20 persons die.*

On October 10, Burma arrested two North Koreans for the bombing that killed four South Korean cabinet members and 16 other people. The bomb did not hit its intended target, President Chun Doo Hwan.

On November 4, Burma broke diplomatic relations with North Korea, claiming it had proof that the North Korean government was involved in the bombing. On returning to Seoul after the bombing, Chun said "I cannot control the raging anger and

980 October 10, 1983

bitter grief of this tragedy." This feeling was shared by U.S. Secretary of State George Shultz, who had developed close relations with South Korea's Foreign Minister Lee Bum Suh, one of the four cabinet ministers killed in Rangoon.

### October 10, 1983

**Nicaraguan rebels destroy oil and gasoline tanks in Corinto, forcing the evacuation of the city.**

The Contra attack on Corinto, which was designed to damage the nation's economy, had been planned by the U.S. Central Intelligence Agency, a fact President Reagan later admitted. It occurred just one week after an American pilot, whom the Nicaraguans captured after shooting down his plane, described the CIA's involvement in Contra operations.

Although President Reagan claimed the Contra attacks were designed to weaken and harass the Sandinista government, Nicaragua's leader, Daniel Ortega, called on "friendly governments" to help him defend Nicaragua against an impending U.S. invasion.

### October 17, 1983

**Robert C. McFarlane replaces William Clark as national security adviser.**

McFarlane became Reagan's special envoy to the Middle East on July 22, 1983, and he was now elevated to head the National Security Council. Clark became secretary of the interior on October 13, 1983.

### October 22, 1983

**Rumors indicated that President Reagan has secret plans to organize a Jordanian strike force for the Middle East.**

In early October, rumors from Israel indicated that the United States was organizing Jordanian commando teams. While details were not publicized, the Pentagon had been training 8,000 Jordanians during the past 30 months. Their mission would be to move to any Persian Gulf trouble spot to prevent rebellions. Allegedly, the Pentagon provided $220 million, three C-130 transport planes, and sophisticated weapons for the Jordanians.

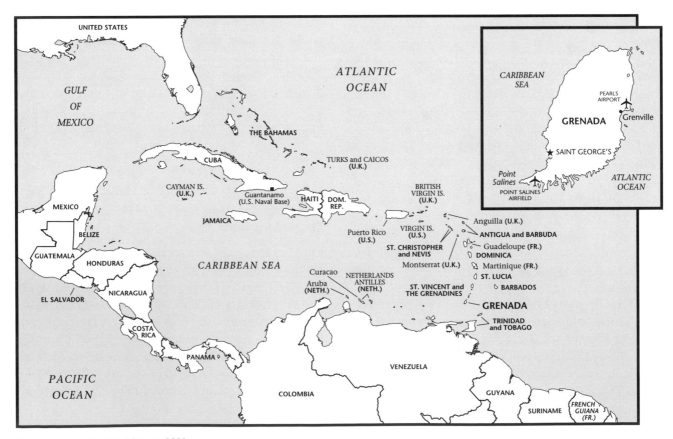

Grenada and the Caribbean, 1983

The Israeli government opposed such plans, and the disclosure ended the idea. Nevertheless, the ploy cast light both on Reagan's desire to involve Jordan deeply in his Middle East peace plans and on the shallow thinking of Reagan's advisers, who thought other Arab states would rely on Jordanians for help. Jordan denied that the plan existed.

On Reagan's peace plan, see September 1, 1982.

## October 23, 1983

### A suicide truck-bomb destroys a U.S. Marine barracks in Beirut, Lebanon, killing 241 marines and naval personnel; a similar attack on a French compound kills 58 French paratroopers.

The U.S. Marine barracks was blown up by the driver of a truck who, at daybreak, smashed his vehicle past two marine sentry posts, through an iron gate, over an 18-inch sewer pipe, through a row of sandbags, and past a second sentry before hitting the building housing the marines with 12,000 pounds of explosives.

This tragedy caused a Pentagon investigation led by retired Admiral L. J. Long. In its report issued on December 28, 1983, the Long Commission asked two basic questions: why was the barracks not suitably protected after the bombing of the U.S. embassy on April 18, 1983? And why was a terrorist attack not anticipated? The central answer was the failure of the Reagan administration to make a clear, definite change in military orders to the marines and the U.S. public as Reagan shifted policy in Lebanon from a "passive" peacekeeping role to the aggressive policy of bombarding Muslim and Syrian positions in defense of President Amin Gemayel's government. The Long Commission said the peacekeeping team could not by itself shore up the Gemayel government and urged President Reagan to reexamine alternative methods of achieving American objectives, including "a more vigorous and demanding approach in pursuing diplomatic alternatives."

Two days before the report, Reagan attempted to minimize its potential negative impact by telling a press conference that the armed forces were not to blame but that the president's office was. The marines' deaths shocked the public and Congress, leading the Reagan administration to withdraw the U.S military from Lebanon as soon as politically feasible.

See February 15, 1984.

## October 24, 1983

### President Reagan says Americans should engage in subversive warfare if it serves the national interest.

During a news conference in which he admitted that the CIA helped Nicaraguan rebels who subverted the Sandinista government, the president asserted: "I do believe in the right of a country, when it believes that its interests are best served, to practice covert activity" that will bring change in a foreign country. Although Reagan did not clarify his precise goals in helping Nicaraguan rebels, the State Department said U.S. policy wanted the Sandinistas to stop their repression.

Most commentators and members of Congress believed Reagan wanted to overthrow the Sandinistas, employing a policy resembling Soviet subversive tactics. This opinion about Reagan's policy spurred congressional leaders to challenge sending U.S. funds to the Contras.

See October 10, 1983.

## October 25, 1983

### Grenada is invaded by U.S. forces with allies from other Caribbean states.

About 6,000 American Army Rangers and marines joined 400 troops from Jamaica, Barbados, and four members of the Organization of Eastern Caribbean States (OECS) to invade Grenada by air, land, and sea. American paratroopers landed on an airfield being built by Cuban workers, while the navy landed marines and allied soldiers on the beaches of Grenada.

Facing only 750 Cuban and Grenadian soldiers on an island with a population of about 110,000, the Americans and their allies had little trouble meeting their military objectives by October 28. The invaders evacuated 599 U.S. citizens who wanted to leave, mostly students at St. George's Medical School. American casualties totaled 18 killed and 116 wounded; the Cubans lost 24, and 59 were wounded; and 45 Grenadians were killed and 337 wounded, including 21 killed when a mental hospital was accidentally bombed.

By November 23, communist representatives on the island were sent home, including all Cubans except one diplomat, 17 Libyans, 15 North Koreans, 49 Soviets, 10 East Germans, and 3 Bulgarians. By December 15, all U.S. combat forces had evacuated the island; few troops remained to train a Grenadian militia and police and to provide medical and logistic support for a new Grenadian government. The new regime was an Advisory Council appointed by Governor General Paul Scoon, who represented Great Britain's Queen Elizabeth as the official head of state of Grenada.

Two major issues arose regarding the U.S. invasion: Why did Washington attack this tiny island? Were the U.S military authorities justified in restricting newsmen seeking to report the war?

The U.S. decision to invade went back to March when Grenada's Prime Minister Maurice BISHOP said he feared a U.S. attack, a baseless but prophetic claim. Because the United States disliked the construction of a 10,000-foot runway on Grenada by Cubans, Prime Minister Bishop visited Washington in June 1983, where he was viewed as a moderate socialist. On his return to Grenada, however, Bishop became involved in disputes with radicals of the New Jewel Movement (NJM) at the NJM Central Committee meetings on July 13–19 and August 26. Bishop was challenged by a pro-Cuban faction led by Bernard Coard, who, on September 14–16, gained control of the Politburo, which made party policy.

Following a visit to Moscow and Havana, Bishop tried to regain control of the NJM, but he lost and was placed under house arrest by the Central Committee. Coard was named prime minister, while real power devolved on General Hudson Austin.

On October 19, a crowd of 1,000 Bishop supporters freed him from house arrest and marched to Fort Rupert, where Bishop took over the central office. Within a few hours, however, Austin's People's Revolutionary Army (PRA) converged on the fort, fired into the crowd, and arrested Bishop and three of his former cabinet members. Austin's men executed these four and two union leaders who were in the fort's courtyard. Austin's Military Council gained control and announced an around-the-clock curfew with orders to the army to shoot violators on sight. Austin also closed the airport for several days.

The diplomatic situation leading to President Reagan's invasion order evolved between October 13 and 20, 1983. As explained by the State Department, an interagency group reviewed the unrest in Grenada and on October 14 asked the Joint Chiefs of Staff to examine its contingency evacuation plans. Following the murder of Bishop on October 19, the interagency group considered using military force, and the next day, several U.S. ships heading for Lebanon were diverted to Grenada. Information about this diversion caused the governments of Cuba and Grenada to inform Washington that Americans would be protected on Grenada and to urge that negotiations precede any attack. The White House ignored these requests.

Also on October 20, the day U.S. ships were diverted, the prime minister of Barbados, J. M. G. Adams, asked Washington to do something about the violence in Grenada. He found a receptive audience, and although Adams could not induce representatives of the larger Caribbean Community to join in any action, he persuaded representatives of the smaller OECS to meet in Barbados on October 21. The OECS asked the United States to help end the violence on Grenada. At the October 21 meeting, Grenada was not represented or heard from, but the six other OECS nations—Antigua and Barbuda, St. Lucia, St. Vincent and the Grenadines, Monserrat, Dominica, and St. Christopher and Nevis—favored U.S. action.

Between October 21 and 24, Prime Minister Adams also obtained support from Jamaica and contacted Grenada's governor general, Sir Paul Scoon, who agreed to ask for U.S. assistance in restoring order. Adams informed the U.S. State Department of Scoon's agreement on October 24, even though Scoon's official appeal did not reach Washington until October 27. Scoon's appeal was a vital part of the U.S. justification for acting under a regional defense agreement.

In fact, President Reagan ordered the Pentagon to invade on October 22. State Department officials said this early order was the reason that the Cuban and Grenadian attempts to prevent the attack were ignored. In addition, Austin's opening of Grenada's airport on October 24 was ignored by the White House. Austin had closed the airport from October 19 to 24, a decision cited as evidence that American students on Grenada could not get out. After evidence of the airport's opening on October 24 became known, Reagan stopped talking about the students' being captive in Grenada.

Immediately following the attack, the Reagan administration offered two basic reasons for invading. Initially, the safety of the medical students and other Americans was emphasized. By October 29, this rationale was dropped and Reagan argued that the U.S. takeover prevented a communist coup with Soviet and Cuban support. U.S. officials found thousands of documents on Grenada that allegedly proved that the New Jewel Movement was directed by Cubans and Soviets. Included in the documents that were deposited in the National Archives were proposals to raise the 600-man Grenadian army to 10,000, secret military agreements and arms purchase plans with East Germany and Czechoslovakia, and a variety of suggestions for making Grenada a Cuban-Soviet satellite. As long as these plans were not compared with the Pentagon contingency plans, the evidence seemed startling. The Reagan administration believed the worst about all communists in 1983 and treated the captured documents as if their plotting would come to pass if the United States had not invaded.

If Reagan's advisers thought the worst of the plans in the document, they also believed the worst of the American media. The Pentagon's success in restricting journalists from reporting the events in Grenada raised serious questions about a free press in a free society. During the first five days of the Grenadian "war," American military officials prevented full news coverage. For two days, no newspeople could go to Grenada, causing Haynes Johnson, a news columnist, to say it was the first war "produced, filmed and reported by the Pentagon." News releases and tapes for television were prepared and given to reporters by American military officers. Thus, information about how real the communist threat was on October 25, how U.S. forces behaved, and what resulted was presented only by Pentagon dispatches. When ABC-TV personnel hired fishing boats to reach Grenada, U.S. naval ships scared them off by dropping buoys in their path or unfurling the big guns of their ships. Vice Admiral Joseph Metcalf II, who had charge of the censorship, threatened reporters: "We'll stop you. We've got the means to do that."

After 48 hours of the war, as fighting nearly ended, Admiral Metcalf allowed journalists to form a 15-reporter pool to visit the island and share the information with journalists not in the pool. Then, for two days, groups of 27 to 47 journalists were taken for two-hour guided tours of Grenada.

Finally, on October 30, President Reagan told the Pentagon to ease up on reporters, and the next day journalists received free access to the island. When more than 200 journalists arrived on October 31, the Cuban fighters were gone, and only cheerful Grenadians welcomed them. Reporters had difficulties getting stories out because the island's radio transmission center had been bombed, and the U.S. military had severed all cable and telephone facilities.

Prominent newsmen and many members of Congress criticized the news restrictions. The American Society of Newspaper Editors wired a protest to Defense Secretary Caspar Weinberger, and a Senate resolution calling for an end to news restrictions passed by a vote of 53 to 18.

Ironically, U.S. delegates to UNESCO opposed press restrictions that Third World governments and the Soviet Union favored. When debate on this issue took place at a UNESCO meeting in Paris during the week of November 7, 1983, the United States threatened to cut UNESCO funds if it imposed press limitations.

See March 23 and December 28, 1983.

## October 28, 1983

### The United States vetoes a U.N. Security Council resolution condemning the Grenada invasion; Britain's Prime Minister Thatcher strongly opposes President Reagan's action.

Many European allies of the United States were dismayed by Reagan's use of force rather than diplomacy against this small island. Chief among Reagan's critics was Britain's Prime Minister Margaret Thatcher, usually one of his strongest supporters. In an interview on January 21, 1984, Thatcher repeated her strong disagreement with the U.S. invasion of Grenada refuting every justification used by the president. She said British citizens on Grenada felt no danger and did not believe Americans were in danger, that the airstrip being built was just like those on at least three other tourist islands, and that the United States could tolerate a communist government on the tiny island, assuming it was communist.

Above all, she believed there must be an overwhelming case to justify using force. All other political channels should precede the use of the military. "In the free world," she said, "we do not pursue our objectives by force, whereas we have always said that the difference was that the Soviets did." Unlike some American "conservatives," the prime minister added, the British conservative tradition recognized the dangers of permitting right-wing extremists to extol military power.

While the United States vetoed a U.N. Security Council resolution denouncing the Grenada invasion, the U.N. General Assembly condemned the United States by a vote of 108 to 9, with 27 abstentions.

## October 30, 1983

*Military rule ends in Argentina when the Civic Union candidate is elected president.*

The election of Raul ALFONSIN ended the dominance of Argentina's Peronist Party as well as its military rulers. Alfonsin's party won 129 seats in the 254-member Chamber of Deputies. The new civilian leaders organized a military commission that recommended trials for military officers who led the 1982 Falkland Islands War and a special investigating commission to learn about the disappearance of 6,000 persons during the eight years of military rule.

## November 1, 1983

**An international scientific conference receives a study that claims a limited nuclear war could cause a "nuclear winter" and the end of human life.**

During a two-day meeting in Washington, D.C., 50 scientists discussed the findings from teams of U.S. and Soviet scientists who reported on studies of "The World after Nuclear War." Both teams concluded that nuclear war would alter the climate of the Northern Hemisphere, causing months of darkness and freezing weather known as "NUCLEAR WINTER."

The U.S. group headed by Richard P. Turco, an atmospheric chemist, included Owen B. Toon, Thomas J. Ackerman, James B. Pollack, and Carl Sagan; the group used the acronym TTAPS from their last names. Based on a detailed computer study, the TTAPS report hypothesized a nuclear war involving 10,400 explosions for a total of 5,000 megatons—less than half of the existing nuclear arsenal, which was 12,000 megatons. The TTAPS results included 1.1 billion persons dead; 1.1 billion seriously wounded but having no medical service; and 100,000 tons (90,700 metric tons) of soot and dust blown into the upper atmosphere for each megaton exploded. Because of the soot and dust, the Northern Hemisphere's normal heat and light would be blocked, allowing only 5% normal sunlight even in mid-July. Noncoastal temperatures would fall to 13 degrees Fahrenheit (minus 25 Celsius) for months. The impact of the climate change would last for several years and carry some soot and dust to the Southern Hemisphere. Surviving plants would be unable to photosynthesize food from light, so the natural food chain would be destroyed. When the darkness ended, the earth would receive high levels of ultraviolet radiation because of the depleted ozone layer around the globe.

Conducting their experiments at the Moscow Academy of Science, the Soviet team offered a more grim report than TTAPS. Using the same 5,000-megaton model as TTAPS, the Soviets found that in 40 days temperatures at Murmansk would drop 100 degrees Fahrenheit; those in the United States would fall 60 degrees Fahrenheit (34 degrees Celsius).

During discussions, none of the scientists found significant points for disagreement. The American ecologist Paul Erlich said that a full-scale nuclear war would leave the Northern Hemisphere uninhabitable, and if it spread south, "we could not preclude the extinction of homo sapiens." The U.S. report was published in brief in *Science* 222 (December 23, 1983, pp. 1283–92). For a list of articles and studies on nuclear winter, see Carl Sagan's letter to the editors of *Foreign Affairs* 65 (Fall 1986: 163–68).

## November 3, 1983

*White South African voters approve a constitution giving Indians and mixed-colored groups limited political rights.*

The 2.7 million white voters of South Africa agreed to give limited political rights to Indians and people of mixed races for the first time in 50 years. The constitution did not affect the black majority population of the nation, but 800,000 Asians and 2.5 million mixed-blood citizens would be able to elect members to a separate third chamber of parliament.

## November 4, 1983

*Terrorist truck-bomb destroys Israeli Army headquarters in Tyre, Lebanon.*

Loaded with explosives, a truck crashed through the entrance to Israeli army headquarters and hit the main building. The bombing killed 60 people—32 Arabs and 28 Israeli military personnel. The suicide driver of the truck was assumed to be a Shiite Muslim.

In retaliation, Israeli jet planes bombed Palestinian positions.

### November 6, 1983

*Turgut Ozal's Independent Motherland Party wins 212 seats in Turkey's 400-member parliament.*

This election ended the rule of the military junta that had taken power during a 1980 coup. Ozal became prime minister of a civilian cabinet on December 13, 1983.

See November 7, 1982.

### November 8, 1983

**Vice President George Bush's vote enables the Senate to approve funds for binary nerve gas weapons; funds are cut ten days later.**

Although on September 15 Congress authorized funds to produce and stockpile nerve gas, the MX missile, and the B-1 bomber, debate on the need for nerve gas continued. On October 31, the Senate Appropriations Committee eliminated the nerve gas funds. However, Vice President Bush's tie-breaking vote restored these funds on November 8.

A joint congressional committee on November 18 eliminated the chemical weapons funds once again because the House delegates also opposed nerve gas. As a result, the appropriated funds for the $249.8 billion defense bill for 1984 did not include nerve gas.

See April 18, 1984.

### November 12, 1983

**Congress votes to limit aid to El Salvador unless the murderers of four American missionaries are convicted.**

The four American nuns had been killed in December 1980. Upon taking office in 1981, the Reagan administration acted with indifference toward the murders even though these deaths aroused great concern among the U.S. public. The U.S. ambassador to El Salvador, Dean Hinton, charged El Salvador's government with a cover-up to protect its military leaders. In April 1981, six former national guardsmen had been arrested as suspects, but they were released on January 10, 1983, owing to insufficient evidence. Similarly, on April 29, 1982, El Salvador released three men who had been indicted for killing land reform agents on January 3, 1981.

The "nun's case" became stalemated until 1983, when Senator Arlen Specter (R-Pa.) visited El Salvador, where local Catholic priests and others persuaded him that the government was protecting high-level military men who ordered the killing. Specter decided not to try to end all U.S. aid to El Salvador but proposed to limit aid until El Salvador convicted the killers. He added an amendment to PL-98-151, an act to continue existing foreign aid bills for 1984, which stated that 30% of the $64.8 million for El Salvador would be withheld until the murderers were convicted.

Specter's amendment had more influence on El Salvador than congressional amendments, which required the president to certify El Salvador's progress in human rights.

See December 4, 1980; November 30, 1983; and May 24, 1984.

### November 15, 1983

**Terrorists murder U.S. Navy Captain George Tsantes and his Greek chauffeur in Athens, Greece.**

Captain Tsantes was killed by two unidentified gunmen while on his way to work. Greek police investigating the attack later reported that Tsantes was shot by the same gun that killed U.S. CIA agent Richard Welch in 1975.

### November 15, 1983

*A Turkish state is set up in northern Cyprus, a measure denounced by the United Nations.*

The Cyprus problem of the 1970s quieted down after Greece and Turkey reached a compromise in 1980. The Turkish minority on Cyprus was angry, however, because no changes had been made in the way the Greek majority treated them. As a result, the Turkish leader Rauf Denktash carried out his previous threats by creating a separate Turkish state in the region—the Turkish Cypriot Republic.

The Greek government protested to the United Nations, where the Security Council, including the U.S. delegate, denounced Denktash's move, asking the Turkish army to disband in northern Cyprus. U.S. relations with Greece and Turkey were disrupted.

See October 24, 1980.

### November 17, 1983

*Retaliating for the October 23 bombing of its Beirut barracks, France sends aircraft to attack pro-Iranian rebels in eastern Lebanon.*

The French jets struck a pro-Iranian Shiite militia base near Baalbek, causing heavy casualties. The French said the retaliatory raid was to discourage fresh terrorist attacks even as unidentified terrorists fired grenades at French positions in Beirut—retaliation for retaliation.

### November 23, 1983

**The Soviet Union walks out of the INF negotiations to protest the U.S. deployment of Pershing IIs and cruise missiles.**

Although negotiations to limit intermediate-range missiles continued on a regular basis during 1983, the Geneva sessions uncovered no grounds for agreement. Although suggestions to renew the "walk-in-the-woods" proposal or interim reductions were sought, none came close to agreement. The United States proposed some global limit on intermediate range nuclear forces (INF), but the Soviets were concerned about counting French and British missiles capable of hitting the USSR. The two sides could not resolve these basic matters.

Despite widespread public protests in Europe against the deployment of Pershing IIs and cruise missiles, the United States began installing cruise missiles in England on November 14 and Pershing IIs in West Germany on November 23. On November 16, the Italian Chamber of Deputies endorsed the NATO deployment of nuclear missiles, and on November 22, the West German Bundestag did the same by a vote of 286 to 226, with one abstention.

As the U.S. deployment of Pershing II and Tomahawk cruise missiles began, the current status of intermediate-range missiles was as follows:

1. Soviet missiles: While its antiquated SS-4 and SS-5 missiles were active, the Soviets had deployed 360 modern solid-fueled SS-20s in the past 6 years, scattered over 38 sites. Of these, about two-thirds are west of the Ural Mountains, aimed at European targets with a range of 3,100 miles. Each is mirved with three 150-kiloton warheads and had reloadable launchers. They could hit West Germany after a 20-minute flight.

2. U.S.-NATO missiles: The United States had 108 Pershing Is in Europe with a range of 500 miles. These would be replaced by the 1,000-mile-range Pershing IIs, which were solid-fueled and carried one 250-kiloton warhead with a terminal guidance system that provided great accuracy. It could not hit Moscow from West Germany but could hit many other parts of the western Soviet Union. Tomahawk cruise missiles would replace manned bombers. These mobile launchers fired four cruise missiles, each having one 200-kiloton warhead. The Tomahawk flew at a slow speed of 500 miles per hour but could fly below radar at 50 to 200 feet above ground on a zigzag course and strike within 10 to 20 yards of its target. NATO planned to deploy 464 Tomahawks in Britain, West Germany, Belgium, Italy, and the Netherlands.

See January 15, March 30, and September 26, 1983; see also December 8, 1983, and November 22, 1984.

### November 28, 1983

**Launching of U.S. space shuttle Columbia includes a European on the six-man crew.**

The Columbia launched a European-built space laboratory that performed scientific experiments before returning to Earth on December 8. The Spacelab's prime contractor, from West Germany, put up half of the $1 billion cost. A physicist from Stuttgart, West Germany, Ulf Merbold, was a crew member. The lab scheduled 71 experiments for its nine-day mission, and most went very well, including the first ever observation of deuterium, a form of hydrogen.

### November 29, 1983

**President Reagan and Israeli Prime Minister Yitzhak Shamir establish a joint committee to coordinate military plans.**

Reagan and Shamir signed this agreement when the Israeli prime minister visited Washington seeking ways to cooperate in supporting the Lebanese government, which was engaged in conflict with Syria as well as with various Muslim and Druze groups. Many moderate Arab nations protested the formation of this joint committee because it pushed the United States almost completely into the Israeli camp. A leading Kuwaiti newspaper, *Al-Qabas*, wrote that Reagan's policy "in blindly tying American strategy to Israel" created resentment among moderate Arab states.

The Arabs had reason to express concern. During November 1983, U.S. news sources disclosed that Reagan had signed the highly classified paper "Middle East National Security Decision Directive 111" on October 29, 1983. This directive emphasized the need for better relations with Israel on Middle East problems. Subsequently, the State Department's undersecretary for political affairs, Lawrence S. Eagleburger, visited Jerusalem to discuss U.S. desires and to plan the meeting of Prime Minister Shamir with President Reagan.

While details of the November 29 agreement were not revealed, the proposed cooperative efforts included joint military exercises, stockpiling U.S. military equipment in Israel for use in the Middle East, sharing intelligence data, planning jointly for military contingencies, and the use of Israeli ports by naval ships of the U.S. Sixth Fleet in the Mediterranean.

## November 30, 1983

**President Reagan vetoes legislation requiring that U.S. aid to El Salvador depends on the president's certifying that El Salvador improved human rights.**

Disdainful of the need to certify human rights progress, the president wished to end this annoyance. He did so one day after the State Department denied a U.S. visa to Roberto D'Aubuisson, president of El Salvador's Constituent Assembly and the notorious head of the right-wing Arena party associated with death-squad killings of guerrillas as well as moderate political and religious leaders. Moreover, on November 25, 1983, the U.S. ambassador to El Salvador, Thomas R. Pickering, condemned the right-wing groups whose actions, he said, threatened to bring a cut off of future U.S. economic and military aid.

Reagan's veto appeared to signal that right-wing violations of human rights did not matter. Senator Claiborne Pell (D-R.I.) denounced Reagan's veto, saying that Congress would not allow U.S. aid to be "poured into a nation that has not demonstrated a will to undertake basic reforms." El Salvador's Human Rights Commission had estimated that 40,000 people had been killed by death squads in the last four years. These reports led Deputy

Secretary of State Kenneth W. Dam to tell a group of Latin American leaders at a Miami, Florida, conference that "the death squads are enemies of democracy every bit as much as the guerrillas."

Congress continued to challenge Reagan's disdain for certifying human rights progress.

See January 4, 1984.

## December 4, 1983

**A day of serious combat between U.S. and Syrian forces in Lebanon.**

After Syrian planes attacked U.S. reconnaissance aircraft on December 3, carrier-based U.S. aircraft raided Syrian positions. Two of 28 American planes were lost with one pilot killed and one captured; Syria said two persons died in the U.S attack. About the same time, eight U.S. Marines were killed by artillery fired from Druze militiamen east of Beirut.

Although the U.S. air raid caused consternation among some parliamentarians in Great Britain and Italy, whose peacekeeping forces in Lebanon seemed to be endangered, the British, Italian, and French foreign officers agreed at a NATO session in Brussels to keep their forces in Lebanon. On December 20, 1983, however, Italy announced plans to reduce its forces, and on January 2, 1984, France indicated it planned to withdraw 482 of its 1,700-man contingent. The United States announced withdrawal plans on February 15, 1984.

## December 6, 1983

**West Germany and the United States agree to replace Nike Hercules antiaircraft missiles with Patriot missiles.**

At a NATO meeting, U.S. Defense Secretary Caspar Weinberger and West German Defense Minister Manfred Worner signed an agreement to spend $3 billion for U.S. Patriot missiles and West German Roland missiles to improve western European defenses against Soviet intermediate-range missiles. Weinberger's spokesperson said the Patriot and Roland missiles used conventional warheads and would replace the U.S. Nike Hercules missiles in Germany that used nuclear warheads. The Patriot-Roland antimissile system would complement U.S. Pershing II offensive missiles, which began to be deployed in Britain and West Germany in November 1983.

### December 8, 1983

**Soviet delegates end the START negotiations and refuse to schedule a date to resume talks.**

As a follow-up to its abandoning the INF negotiations on November 23, Moscow told the American delegates at the Strategic Arms Reduction Talks (START) in Geneva that the recent deployment of U.S. missiles in Western Europe required extensive reconsideration of its START positions. The Soviet delegate refused to set future meeting dates for strategic arms talks.

### December 9, 1983

**President Reagan signs a bill to aid Nicaraguan rebels, which eliminates the Boland Amendment but restricts Contra aid to $24 million for 1984.**

The Boland Amendment, which Congress approved in 1982, seemed obsolete by December 1983 because several incidents indicated that the Nicaraguan rebels could not overthrow the Sandinista government. President Reagan said the Contras' purpose was to stop Sandinista aid to Salvadoran rebels and to persuade the Sandinistas to amnesty the Contras so they could participate in the political processes and not have to resort to violence. Finally, in November 1983, a national intelligence estimate given both to the House's Select Committee on Intelligence and the Senate's Intelligence Committee stated that the Contras could never overthrow the Sandinista government.

Subsequently, Boland (D-Mass.) lost support for the renewal of his amendment but persuaded the House and Senate select committees to agree that $24 million appropriated for Contra aid would be the absolute ceiling spent in 1984 fiscal year. President Reagan signed this legislation as part of the 1984 military authorization bill.

While Boland's prohibition was temporarily ended, the Reagan administration disliked the ceiling placed on aid and looked for other methods to help the Contra rebels.

See December 21, 1982; September 1 and October 12, 1984, as well as November 3, 1986.

### December 11, 1983

*Bangladeshi President Hossain Muhammad Ershad renews martial law to reassert his military authority.*

General Ershad gained power in 1981 by leading a coup against former President Ziaur Rahman. He decided to assert his military authority because opposition riots in November had killed six people and injured hundreds. He looked to the United States for economic aid to improve the nation's agriculture and hoped to impress Washington by announcing that he would conduct elections in 1984 after order was restored.

### December 12, 1983

**Terrorist bomb attacks on the French and U.S. embassies and elsewhere in Kuwait kill 7 and injure 77.**

One terrorist was killed in the bombings, and Kuwait arrested 18 conspirators on December 27, 1983. The terrorists were pro-Iranian Shiites whose release would be sought as the object of various terrorist kidnappings during the next several years. Apparently, the attack occurred in Kuwait because it was the most accessible state in the Persian Gulf and supported Iraq in its war against Iran. Kuwait was ruled by Sunni Muslims, but many Kuwaiti Shiites admired Iran's spiritual leader, the Ayatollah Khomeini.

### December 17, 1983

*Irish terrorists kill five persons during rush hour at Harrods department store in London.*

A car bomb was exploded by members of the Irish Republican Army, although IRA leaders stated the bombing was not authorized. In addition to killing five people, the bomb wounded 77 others.

### December 19, 1983

*Japanese Prime Minister Nakasone forms a coalition cabinet to remain in office because his Liberal Democratic Party lost its parliamentary majority.*

To remain in power after the December 18 election, Yasuhiro Nakasone gained backing from eight independent members of the Japanese Diet. He blamed his party's loss on former Prime Minister Kakuei Tanaka, who was convicted, along with four codefendants, on October 12, 1983, of taking bribes from American Lockheed Corporation. Tanaka was sentenced to four years in jail.

### December 20, 1983

*Greek ships under U.N. flags evacuate 2,000 of Yasser Arafat's Palestinian troops from Tripoli, Lebanon.*

Supported by Syria, Palestinians who rebelled against Yasser Arafat's leadership of the Palestine Liberation Organization (PLO) had chased Arafat's loyalists back toward the Mediterranean seaport of Tripoli, where Arafat set up downtown headquarters on November 17, vowing to fight to the end. On November 23 Arafat agreed to a cease-fire that Saudi Arabian officials had persuaded the PLO rebels to offer if Arafat's troops left Lebanon.

On December 3, U.N. Secretary-General Javier Pérez de Cuellar allowed Greek ships to fly the U.N. flag to evacuate Arafat. Nevertheless, the Greek operation was delayed because Israeli gunboats repeatedly bombarded PLO positions of both Arafat and the PLO rebels. The Israelis preferred to see the PLO rival groups kill each other. Finally on December 19, the United States publicly asked Israel to permit the evacuation. Israel relented, and Arafat's forces left Lebanon by December 20, 1983.

For the conflict's beginning, see June 24, 1983.

### December 22, 1983

**Federal Trade Commission approves plans for General Motors and Toyota Corporation of Japan to produce small cars in California.**

The two corporations had announced plans for their joint venture on February 14, 1983. The Federal Trade Commission decision led to other joint automobile ventures between U.S. and Japanese companies.

### December 22, 1983

**During a visit to Cairo, PLO leader Yasser Arafat strengthens relations with Egypt.**

Mutual interests led Arafat and Egyptian President Hosni Mubarak to patch up political differences that

arose when Egypt made peace with Israel in 1979. The Palestine Liberation Organization needed friends after its 1982 and 1983 débâcle in Lebanon.

Mubarak realized that Israel had backed away from the Camp David agreement by refusing to establish autonomy for West Bank Palestinians. Egypt accordingly suffered strained relations with other Arab states. While Egypt's reconciliation with Arafat surprised some Arab leaders, the course of recent events made such action understandable.

See January 19, 1984.

### December 23, 1983

**Laos returns the bones of several American airmen shot down during the Vietnam War.**

The Laotian government gave U.S. authorities some "bone fragments" identified as those of American soldiers missing in action during the Vietnam War. A team of U.S. experts had visited the crash site of a C-130 aircraft shot down in December 1972, but beyond a survey of the area, the bone fragments were all they found.

### December 24, 1983

*South African forces invade Angola to wipe out Namibian guerrilla bases.*

Although on June 23 the Reagan administration reaffirmed its commitment to a pro–South African policy of "constructive engagement" to speak out against the South African apartheid that oppressed the non-white population and to seek independence for South-West Africa. The "constructive engagement" policy made little headway because it also demanded the withdrawal of Cuban troops from Angola prior to negotiations on Namibia.

The year ended with another South African incursion into Angola, even though on December 15, South Africa said it would withdraw its troops from Angola beginning on January 31, 1984. Johannesburg's pledges were offset by its constant military action in Angola and its takeover of the South-West African government on January 18, 1983.

### December 28, 1983

**The United States announces it will withdraw from UNESCO in 1985, protesting the group's politicization.**

Officially, the United States gave one year's notice of intention to withdraw. In a letter to UNESCO Director General M'Bow, Secretary of State Shultz said the United States was concerned about the "trends in the management, policy and budget of UNESCO," which made the group ineffective.

Among many reasons for the U.S. action was dissatisfaction with UNESCO's commission on mass communication, which advocated restrictions on press access to events in Third World nations. Assistant Secretary of State for International Organization Affairs Gregory Newell broadened the U.S complaint, stating that "UNESCO has extraneously politicized virtually every subject it deals with. It has exhibited hostility toward a free society, especially a free market and a free press, and it has demonstrated unrestrained budgeting expansion."

The United States claimed that UNESCO's high ideals had been forgotten since Third World nations gained a controlling influence over the organization. In 1974, the U.S. Congress suspended UNESCO aid after the U.N. agency excluded Israel from a regional group. Aid was resumed in 1977 after UNESCO readmitted Israel. In 1980, UNESCO made it difficult for American journalists by permitting Third World governments to censor their reports, while refusing to help educate Third World refugees. Finally, Washington disliked the rapid increase of the UNESCO budget from $165.1 million to $374.4 million in the past ten years. The United States paid 25% of this budget but had no effective control over its expenditures. The U.S. withdrawal became effective after December 31, 1984.

### December 28, 1983

**U.S. Defense Department commission blames military commanders for serious errors in Beirut bombing of the marine barracks.**

Both the House Armed Services Committee and a five-member Defense Department commission investigated the Beirut bombing that killed 241 Americans on October 23, 1983. On December 19, the House panel charged marine commanders with "serious errors" that permitted the terrorists to get past U.S. security posts.

The December 28 Defense Department report agreed that the military commanders made serious security and intelligence mistakes. It also suggested that the Reagan administration reconsider the military mission's role in Lebanon and its political options in the Middle East.

# 1984

### January 1, 1984

***Natural gas from the Soviets' trans-Siberian pipeline is delivered to France for the first time.***

Because President Reagan opposed the sale of Western technology to the Soviets, the construction and completion of this link between Soviet Central Asia and Western Europe became a symbol of French and German willingness to override Reagan's anticommunist fervor to benefit their countries' economies. Natural gas from the USSR made Western Europeans less dependent on oil from the Middle East.

See January 8, August 26, and November 13, 1982; see also August 20, 1983.

### January 3, 1984

**Syria releases U.S. navy pilot.**

A leading spokesman for African Americans, the Reverend Jesse Jackson, visited Damascus, Syria, on January 2 and suggested that President Hafiz al-Assad arrange for the release of Lieutenant Robert O. Goodman Jr., a navy pilot whose plane had been shot down during a December 4 raid on Syrian anti-aircraft batteries in eastern Lebanon.

Although President Reagan initially called Jackson's mission to Syria "naive grandstanding," the pilot's release led Reagan to congratulate Jackson and thank President al-Assad. Hopes that Syria's gesture would foster Middle East peace were not justified, however.

Navy Lieutenant Robert O. Goodman, Jr., and the Reverend Jesse Jackson meet with the president. Ronald Reagan Library

### January 4, 1984

**Thirty-three Democrats in the House of Representatives challenge President Reagan's pocket veto of the law requiring reports on El Salvador's progress in human rights.**

On November 30, 1983, the president delayed signing legislation on aid to El Salvador in order to eliminate the requirement of reporting to Congress on human rights. El Salvador's right-wing death squads frequently killed political opponents despite U.S. protests. After the 33 representatives went to court, the U.S. Senate voted on January 26 to join the suit, arguing that the president had acted unconstitutionally. While these representatives went to court, other House members introduced a bill to require the president to certify human rights progress in El Salvador.

See August 29, 1984.

### January 10, 1984

**A bipartisan commission on Central America recommends military aid to El Salvador and denounces Cuba and the Soviet Union for aiding rebels.**

Former Secretary of State Henry Kissinger headed this commission whose report provided data that both proponents and opponents of President Reagan's Central American policy used in debate. The report recommended increased military aid to the Salvadoran government, whose war with left-wing rebels was stalemated. But despite Reagan's wishes, the commission wanted this aid tied to the president's certification of human rights progress in El Salvador.

While devoting less attention to Nicaragua, the report stated that the consolidation of a Marxist-Leninist regime there would pose a constant security threat to Central America. In particular, Nicaragua was a threat because it received arms and military advisers from the Soviet Union, Cuba, and other communist countries, while supplying weapons to left-wing rebels in El Salvador. Although the commission reached no consensus on Reagan's support for the Nicaraguan rebels, it endorsed the Contadora peace efforts for Central America.

On February 3, President Reagan used the commission findings to ask Congress for a five-year $8 billion aid package for Central America. The commission believed the region's problems were due to poverty, injustice, and closed political systems. It advocated reforms that were prevented by the intrusion of outside powers such as Cuba and the Soviet Union, who, it claimed, exploited the people for strategic political advantages. Central Americans themselves should solve their problems.

Generally, the report was not acceptable to many Washington politicians and did not establish the bipartisan support President Reagan desired. Democrats and many Republicans in Congress opposed Reagan's emphasis on military solutions to problems in El Salvador and Nicaragua. Moreover, the American public did not believe, as the commission did, that there was danger of a Soviet takeover in Central America.

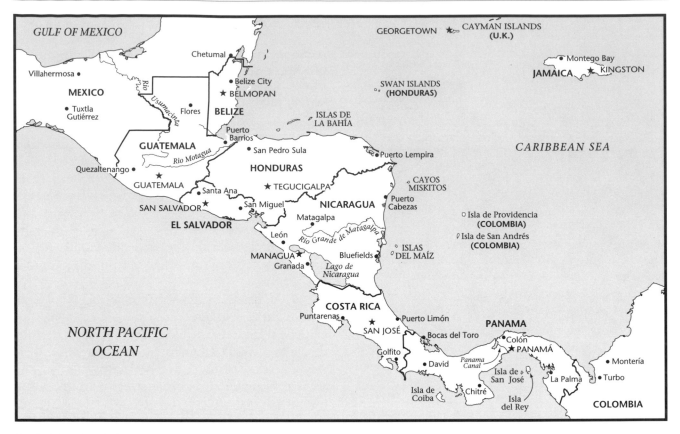

Central America, 1984

The commission members were former Republican Senator Nicholas F. Brady, San Antonio mayor Henry G. Cisneros, former Texas governor Williams Clements, Yale economics professor Carlos F. Dias Alejandro, National Federation of Independent Business President William S. Johnson, A.F.L.-C.I.O. President Lane Kirkland, political scientist Richard M. Scammon, Boston University President John Silber, former Democratic Party Chairman Robert S. Strauss, the medical care Project Hope President William B. Walsh, and Henry Kissinger as chairman.

### January 12, 1984

**During a visit to the United States, Chinese Prime Minister Zhao Ziyang accepts cooperation in trade and scientific exchanges.**

American-Chinese relations had chilled considerably since 1980 because of trade problems and especially because the Reagan administration sent military aid to the Chinese regime on Taiwan. Nevertheless, as part of their triangular relations with the Soviet Union, both China and the United States had common interests in maintaining friendship. China needed U.S. technology and capital investments for its modernization program.

See August 16, 1982; April 7, 1983; and May 1, 1984.

### January 13, 1984

**The European Economic Community (EEC) retaliates for U.S. restrictions on specialty steel imports.**

The EEC action was the latest in a continuing argument over the steel trade between Western Europe and the United States. It was the consequence of the Reagan administration's July 5, 1983, decision to restrict imports of types of European steel that, U.S. steelmakers contended, received government subsidies.

The EEC sanctions led to negotiations that resulted in the lowering of EEC barriers on February 28, 1984. After another round of negotiations, Reagan's trade advisers reached a new compromise with the EEC.

See November 27, 1984.

## January 16, 1984

**President Reagan sets a new tone in U.S.-Soviet relations, offering compromise and flexibility in future arms talks.**

The collapse of all U.S.-Soviet nuclear arms control talks on November 23, 1983, alarmed many of America's European allies and many members of the U.S. Congress. Other commentators saw the advice of the President's wife, Nancy Reagan, at work when her husband began to talk more like a peacemaker than a warmonger on January 16.

Whatever the reasons for his shift, the president's address became the first of several messages that stopped calling the Soviet Union an evil empire and used terms such as "mutual compromise" or making 1984 a "year of opportunity for peace." The president and his advisers argued that the nation's three years of defense expenditures now gave the United States a greater deterrent power so that Moscow would be willing to accept arms control.

Nevertheless, the January 16 speech was made in an atmosphere of tension, not agreement. On January 11, NATO officials accused the Soviets of deploying more SS-20 missiles in Europe, and on January 23, the Reagan administration issued a report alleging that Moscow had violated at least seven arms control agreements. Perhaps Reagan viewed an election year as a time to balance appeals to peace with warnings about the dangers of communism to satisfy both moderate Americans and hawks.

## January 17, 1984

**Conference on Confidence and Security-Building Measures (CBM) opens in Stockholm, Sweden, including delegates from NATO and Warsaw Pact countries.**

Meeting as agreed at the Madrid Conference on Security and Cooperation in September 1983, the sessions began with U.S. Secretary of State George Shultz offering a six-point proposal of NATO member nations regarding the exchange of military data and activities that could reduce East-West tensions. On January 18, Soviet Foreign Minister Andrei Gromyko attacked the Reagan administration for its obsession with military power but listed six alternative proposals on confidence-building measures emphasizing a nuclear-free zone in central Europe. NATO's proposals included exchanging military data annually, notifying about future military exercises and military movements, permitting observation of military activity, providing for inspection of suspected activity, and developing better ways to communicate.

See January 15, 1989.

## January 19, 1984

***Egypt is reinstated to membership in the Organization of Islam. The PLO opposes this.***

This organization was one of two groups that expelled Egypt in 1979 because President Anwar-Sadat signed a peace treaty with Israel; the other group was the Arab League. In granting readmission, the organization said Egypt should accept the group's condemnation of the 1978 Camp David accords. Nevertheless, Egypt was not denied admission when it refused to change its policies to join the group. Egypt's formal admission was ratified on April 2, 1984. Egypt's status was more critical to the Arab League, which tried to unify Arab political programs, but Egypt was not reinstated to that group. Most of the 42 delegates in the Organization of Islam were moderates who disliked the violence advocated by Islamic fundamentalists.

On January 4, 1984, hard-liners in the Palestine Liberation Organization rejected Yasser Arafat's proposal to reconcile with Egypt.

See March 31, 1979.

## January 23, 1984

**U.S. Congress is told that the Soviet Union has violated arms control treaties. Six days later, the USSR protests against U.S. violations.**

In its 50-page report, the Reagan administration described an "expanding pattern of Soviet violations or possible violations" of arms agreements. The two major U.S. charges were the testing of the PL-5 (or SS-X-5) missile, which violated SALT II if it had the ten warheads suspected by U.S. intelligence, and the building of a giant radar station at Abalakova, in the Krasnoyarsk region of central Siberia. This latter discovery was considered more serious because the radar base's inland location violated parts of the 1972 Anti-Ballistic Missile (ABM) Treaty. Other U.S. allegations regarded the Soviet use of chemical weapons and the encoding of missile test signals so that the United States could not verify them. The administration issued a similar report on October 10, 1984.

This report did not escape serious challenge by arms control experts. To these specialists, many of the charges appeared to be contrived or exaggerated to meet the anti–arms control attitude of the administration.

On January 29, the Soviet Union protested U.S. violations, such as conducting nuclear tests above the threshold limit and upgrading radar stations on the Atlantic and Pacific coastlines in violation of the 1972 ABM Treaty.

### January 25, 1984

**Japan increases its military budget by 6.55%, taking another step in defense burden sharing at U.S. request.**

The 1984 budget of Prime Minister Nakasone sought a compromise on defense expenditures that would be large enough to placate Washington but small enough to avoid upsetting those Japanese who thought that the military already received too much funding.

U.S. Secretary of Defense Caspar Weinberger was only partially placated. He welcomed the increase but wanted Tokyo to increase military costs at an "even greater pace in future years." On December 28, 1984, Nakasone again increased Japan's defense expenditures by another 6.9%.

### January 25, 1984

**Defense Secretary Weinberger informs Congress that the "Midgetman" ICBM could be ready for deployment in 1992.**

As a follow-up to the 1983 Scowcroft Report, the Defense Department developed the smaller, single-warhead missile as a successor to the ten-warhead MX missile. Weinberger said the Midgetman system would have 1,000 missiles with each weighing 30,000 pounds and carrying 1,000-pound nuclear warheads up to a range of 6,000 miles. The manned truck to transport the missiles would be reinforced to withstand winds of 600 to 900 miles per hour arising from nearby enemy explosions.

A major problem was to obtain a lightweight guidance system accurate enough to hit a Soviet ICBM silo. The Pentagon estimated that the 1,000 Midgetmen would cost from $65 billion to $75 billion. It requested $715 million in the 1985 budget to

develop the missile, a 50% increase over its 1984 allocation.

See April 11, 1983.

### January 29, 1984

**The Reagan administration completes grants of economic aid to three "authoritarian" governments of Latin America.**

In contrast to President Carter's refusal to aid dictators of the right or the left who violated human rights, the Reagan administration differentiated between "authoritarian" right-wing dictators and totalitarian left-wing rulers because the former were capable of reform, while the latter ruled without hope of possible reform. Reagan had adopted the distinction between Left and Right rulers from U.S. Ambassador to the United Nations Jeane Kirkpatrick's "Dictatorships and Double Standards," *Commentary* (November 1979).

Between January 25 and 29, the United States provided aid to the three "authoritarian" powers in Latin America. On January 25, Chile's military regime restructured its $1.6 billion debt to make repayment easier. On January 27, Brazil obtained foreign loans of $6.5 billion, and the administration lifted U.S. export controls on technology to benefit Brazil's arms industry. Finally, on January 28, the United States sold $2 million worth of helicopter parts to Guatemala after its dictator, General Oscar Mejia Victores, announced that elections could be held on July 1, 1985.

See March 14, 1986.

### February 1, 1984

**Norway expels five Soviet diplomats accused of espionage after it arrests a Norwegian civil servant.**

Norway based its espionage claims on data obtained from Arne Treholt, who spied for the Soviet Union and Iraq. Treholt had access to sensitive data as the chief of information of the Foreign Ministry and a Norwegian delegate to the United Nations. The U.S. Federal Bureau of Investigation assisted the Norwegians on the case for over three years before Treholt was arrested at Oslo's airport on January 21, 1984, on the way to give more information to the Soviet secret police. Allegedly, he also sold classified documents to Iraq for $50,000.

## February 5, 1984

### *Lebanon's government collapses because of Muslim groups fighting Lebanon's army.*

After Israeli troops withdrew from Lebanon, Lebanon's President Amin Gemayel was unable to restore Lebanese Christian relations with the many Muslim factions aided by Syria and Iran, despite help from American forces. Gemayel failed in his attempts to reach compromises with Muslim moderates led by Lebanon's Prime Minister Shafik al-Wazan. Gemayel's government never became strong enough to contend with Lebanon's dissident Muslims, who were backed by Syria's President Hafez Assad and Iran's religious leaders.

On February 5, Lebanon's government collapsed when Prime Minister Shafik and other moderate Muslim cabinet members resigned. Gemayel's problems occurred just as American, French, Italian, and British troops prepared to withdraw. After the Muslim cabinet members left Beirut on February 6, dissident Muslim forces took control of West Beirut. The next day 1,400 U.S. Marines redeployed from the Beirut airport to American naval ships along the Lebanese coast where U.S. naval aircraft and guns could bombard Muslim, Druze, and Syrian military positions.

During the fighting in Lebanon, Gemayel's Christian armies fought against a variety of Muslim groups that included Nabih Berri's Amal Shiites, Syria's Sunni Muslim Alawites, members of Egypt's Muslim Brotherhood, pro-Iranian Islamic Jihad members, Palestinian followers of George Habash's Popular Front for the Liberation of Palestine, members of Naysef Hawatmeh's Democratic Front for the Liberation of Palestine, and Walid Jumblatt's Druze, an eclectic religious group.

Throughout February, Gemayel's Christian army fought these Muslim groups, especially those surrounding Beirut. Although Israeli aircraft and American naval guns assisted the Christians, Gemayel eventually contacted Syrian President Assad to negotiate better relations with the Muslims.

See February 15 and March 5, 1984.

## February 9, 1984

### *Soviet President Yuri Andropov dies; he is replaced by Konstantin U. Chernenko.*

Illness caused Andropov's death at age 69. His funeral on February 14 was attended by most high-ranking world leaders. Vice President George Bush represented the United States.

On February 13, after the Communist Party's Central Committee elected CHERNENKO as general secretary, Mikhail S. Gorbachev, the Politburo member in charge of agriculture, delivered the key speech in closing the plenum of the party's Politburo.

On February 23, Chernenko was made chairman of the USSR Defense Council. On April 11, he was named chairman of the Presidium of the Supreme Soviet. The 72-year-old Chernenko was a protégé of the late President Leonid Brezhnev and in 1982 had advocated internal economic reforms. To some Western observers, he appeared as a compromise candidate between Politburo members who favored military build-ups and those who wanted economic reform.

The April 11 Politburo meeting proved auspicious. Gorbachev, who was the organ's youngest member and a representative of the reform faction, gave the speech nominating Chernenko as president of the Supreme Soviet. Gorbachev's performance signified that he was Chernenko's heir apparent.

## February 15, 1984

### The White House plans to withdraw U.S. forces from Lebanon by March 15, 1984.

As fighting grew between competing Lebanese groups in early 1984, the United States suffered more casualties, and U.S. congressional members became concerned. On January 8, two marines were wounded and one was killed; on January 30 another marine was killed and several were wounded. Subsequently, on February 1 and 2, the Democratic caucus in the House and Senate approved resolutions asking President Reagan to withdraw the U.S. Marines from Lebanon.

After British and Italian forces left the area on February 7, the United States redeployed its marines to ships off the Lebanese coast. Although French troops remained, their government planned to withdraw them in March.

While planning the U.S. withdrawal, the Reagan administration continued to demonstrate American interests in the region. On February 15, U.S. naval planes and ships bombarded areas dangerous to Lebanese President Amin Gemayel. On February 22, Reagan told reporters the marines would not just "bug out and go home" but might return if it served the cause of peace in Lebanon. Peace, however, was a long distance away in Lebanon.

See February 5, 1984.

### February 15, 1984

**Terrorists in Rome assassinate U.S. General Leamon R. Hunt.**

General Leamon R. Hunt, director general of the ten-nation Sinai peacekeeping force, was shot by a group identifying itself as the Fighting Communist Party, a faction linked to the Red Brigade in Italy. The caller said they wanted all "imperialist forces to leave Lebanon."

### February 18, 1984

*China and the Soviet Union sign a $1.2 billion trade agreement, increasing their 1984 trade by 50%.*

This trade deal had been completed in January, but the announcement was delayed owing to Soviet President Yuri Andropov's death. He had sought better relations with the Chinese. China's Deputy Prime Minister Min Wan-li attended Andropov's funeral, after which the deal was jointly announced.

### February 21, 1984

**The United States tells a Geneva arms control meeting that the Soviets had used chemical weapons in Laos, Cambodia, and Afghanistan.**

Although the United States contended that the Soviets had used chemical weapons in Southeast Asia and Afghanistan, many scientific investigators argued that there were other, perhaps better, explanations for the toxic materials causing illness in refugees who fled from the conflicts in those two areas.

During the 1984 Geneva Conference on Disarmament, both the United States and the USSR offered proposals to control chemical weapons. On January 10, Moscow proposed that both Warsaw Pact and NATO members ban chemical weapons. On February 21, the Soviets also offered to permit inspection rights to verify a chemical weapons arms control system. The U.S. proposal was made in April.

See April 18, 1984, and September 9, 1986.

### February 22, 1984

**Secret American talks with the PLO are confirmed by Secretary of State Shultz.**

The *New York Times* had previously reported that the State Department held secret talks with the Palestine Liberation Organization. However, the facts were not confirmed until February 22, 1984, when Shultz informed the Senate Foreign Relations Committee.

Shultz indicated that John Edwin Mroz conducted talks with PLO leader Yasser Arafat over a nine-month period in 1981 and 1982. Shultz declared that the only result of the discussions was to disprove those who said that the cause of peace would be helped if the two sides talked with each other. There had been no positive results.

### March 5, 1984

*Lebanon abrogates its 1983 withdrawal agreement with Israel and seeks compromise with Syria.*

The 1983 Lebanese-Israeli agreement achieved few results because Israel's evacuation of Lebanon depended on a Syrian troop withdrawal (see May 17, 1983). Subsequently, civil war developed between the government of President Amin Gemayel and the Muslim and Druze factions that joined Syria in opposing Gemayel's connections with Israel and the United States. Saudi Arabia's attempt to halt the conflict on September 25, 1983, had failed.

Thus, Gemayel sought peace terms with Syria and began by renouncing the Israeli agreement. On February 16, Gemayel had offered a peace plan to Syria's President Hafiz al-Assad, an offer rejected by Assad. Nevertheless, Gemayel visited Damascus for a two-day meeting with Assad and other Syrian officials. Although Assad denied that he had forced Gemayel to abrogate the Israeli agreement, the president of Lebanon did so on March 5. Gemayel also gained President Assad's influence to arrange a meeting among the rival Lebanese political-military factions.

See February 5 and April 19, 1984.

### March 13, 1984

**The GATT council upholds Nicaragua's contention that the United States violated GATT rules by cutting Nicaragua's sugar quotas.**

The Reagan administration had ordered the cut in Nicaraguan sugar imports to the United States in 1983. This action reduced the quota from 56,800 tons in 1982 to 6,000 tons in 1983. Nicaragua complained to the General Agreement on Tariffs and Trade (GATT) Council in Geneva that it lost $54 million because of Reagan's action.

Drawing on the report of its study panel, the 90-member GATT Council ruled that the United States violated trade rules and should either renew Nicaragua's sugar quota or restrict all foreign sugar suppliers on the same basis. The Reagan administration rejected the GATT ruling, refusing to rescind its action against Nicaragua. Although the United States had been a principal advocate of GATT since its inception, President Reagan's unilateral action overrode the council's effectiveness in pushing for "free trade" principles.

See October 30, 1947.

### March 14, 1984

**Jordan's King Hussein rejects American proposals for talks with Israel, saying Washington is pro-Israel.**

President Reagan wanted King Hussein to represent Palestinian interests and establish a Jordanian protectorship over the West Bank Arab sectors. The U.S. proposal was made in 1982 but Hussein delayed a decision. Apparently, his meeting with Yasser Arafat, chairman of the Palestine Liberation Organization, from February 26 to March 1 persuaded Hussein to join other Arab states in opposing the U.S. plan.

Hussein told a *New York Times* reporter that during election years, U.S. politicians had no principles but succumbed to the "dictates of Israel." He disliked America's refusal to condemn Jewish settlements on the West Bank, believing Israel would never end its West Bank occupation unless the United States cut off

its economic assistance, something the United States would not do. Hussein claimed the United States praised Afghan rebels as freedom fighters but called Palestinian rebels terrorists. The King's remarks anticipated President Reagan's decision on March 21 to cancel the sale of Stinger antiaircraft missiles to help Jordan defend itself from Iran and Syria. King Hussein claimed that the Jewish lobby in the United States told members of Congress that Jordan would use these weapons against Israel.

Under similar circumstances, after the United States refused to sell AWACS to Saudi Arabia, the Saudis purchased a $4 billion air defense system from France on January 16, 1982. King Hussein asked the Soviet Union for help and received it.

See October 28, 1981, and September 1, 1982; see also January 5, 1985.

### March 16, 1984

*Mozambique and South Africa end tensions as both governments stop support for rebels opposing the other.*

By this agreement, Mozambique closed its borders to the African National Congress (ANC), which opposed South Africa's apartheid policies. The ANC headquarters were in Mozambique and had often been attacked by South African forces trying to subdue them. South Africa would no longer raid Mozambique territory if the borders were closed to the ANC. In return, South Africa stopped helping the Mozambique National Resistance guerrillas who received sanctuary in South Africa to fight against the Mozambique government.

On March 24, 1984, Mozambique fulfilled its agreement when its forces raided suspected ANC camps in Maputo, forcing the ANC to relocate. On June 12, 1984, the United States rewarded Mozambique by ending its ban on economic aid and giving that nation $500,000. This action dismayed U.S. critics of South African apartheid.

### March 18, 1984

**U.S. surveillance planes in Egypt monitor trouble between Libya and the Sudan.**

There had been tension between Libya and the Sudan for some time because Sudanese President Gaafar al-Nimeiry accused Libya's Mu'ammar al-Gadhafi of assisting Sudanese rebels fighting against Nimeiry's regime. This tension verged on war after an unidentified plane flew over the Sudanese city of Omdurman and dropped five bombs, killing five people and wounding two others. Libya denied sending the aircraft and claimed that the United States had fabricated the incident to justify sending aid to Egypt and the Sudan in opposing Libya. Egypt had been helping the Sudan to construct a defense network, and the American AWACS supplemented those facilities.

The crisis subsided, however, and by April 19, the AWACS could be withdrawn.

### March 23, 1984

*Japanese Prime Minister Nakasone visits China and offers the Chinese a $2.1 billion industrial development loan.*

Although Chinese-Japanese relations grew friendly after Japan renewed diplomatic relations with Beijing in 1972, Prime Minister Yasuhiro Nakasone promoted economic ties with China and South Korea. He also hoped these two nations would improve their relationship with each other.

In addition to arranging the $2.1 billion low-interest loan for China, Nakasone discussed with his Chinese hosts the future of East Asian relations with the United States and the Soviet Union. China's leader, Deng Xiaoping, indicated that China hoped for better ties with Washington but Deng could not predict improved ties with Moscow.

### March 31, 1984

**In Honduras, the pro-American General Gustavo Alvarez Martínez is exiled to Costa Rica; he is replaced by Air Force General Walter López Reyes.**

Under General Alvarez Martínez, the United States had built Honduran air strips and military bases to train and supply anti-Sandinista rebels to fight in Nicaragua. The United States increased its military aid to Honduras from $9.1 million in 1981 to $41 million in 1984, and its economic aid from $47 million to $108.5 million. After the United States announced on February 9 that its forces in Honduras would double to carry out new military exercises, these plans caused complaints among the Honduran army and air force.

While not anti-American, the new commander of the Honduran armed forces, General López Reyes,

said he would adjust the nation's economy by spending less on defense and more to stimulate export. He also promised full support for the Contadora process to bring peace to Central America.

### April 3, 1984

**Secretary of State George Shultz approves preemptive action against terrorists—the "Shultz Doctrine."**

Believing that terrorist acts in Lebanon had upset U.S. policy and cost American lives, Shultz was eager to have the U.S. government use antiterrorist tactics. In a public address, he stated that the best way to combat terrorism was to retaliate against terrorists or to strike preemptively against groups planning terrorist raids.

In a national security directive of 1982, President Reagan gave the State Department jurisdiction over terrorist activity. Subsequently, in March 1984, Shultz tried to involve the Pentagon and the Central Intelligence Agency in attacking the terrorists. Lt. Colonel Oliver North of the National Security Council staff drafted a plan to kill potential or verified terrorists. Although previous executive orders prohibited U.S. involvement in foreign assassinations, the *Washington Post* reporter Bob Woodward indicated that Colonel North thought it was "time to kill the . . . terrorists by using CIA trained teams of foreign nationals to neutralize them."

Although Shultz probably did not agree with North's extreme remedy, the colonel expressed the attitude of many Americans. Shultz probably intended that the CIA should obtain intelligence to prevent a terrorist attack. In some cases this happened, but tracking every terrorist cell was impossible.

Because the Beirut bombings of the U.S. embassy and U.S. Marine barracks in 1983 had heightened public awareness of the terrorist threat, the "Shultz Doctrine" of preemptive or retaliatory strikes gained much attention in 1984. Following President Reagan's reelection in November 1984, invoking the Shultz Doctrine seemed more likely, leading Defense Secretary Caspar Weinberger to prepare criteria for deploying the U.S. armed forces by limiting circumstances for the State Department to call for military action. American military officers believed the use of clandestine force incited terrorists to retaliate in greater force.

In contrast to the Pentagon's caution, the CIA under William Casey seemed willing to use any methods to achieve its end. Moreover, the National Security Council gained wide authority from President Reagan. Thus, NSC staff members such as Colonel North were anxious to engage in clandestine attacks on those who opposed U.S. policy as well as terrorists.

George Ball became a severe critic of the Shultz Doctrine. A former adviser to President Lyndon Johnson and one of the few in the Johnson White House to oppose the 1965 Vietnam escalation, Ball argued in the *New York Times* on December 16, 1984, that Shultz forgot the basic concepts that American leadership traditionally reflected. Rather than reduce the United States to the lowest level of terrorist behavior, Ball wanted other nations to follow a U.S. leader who sought collective international action against all forms of group or state sponsored terrorism.

See November 28, 1984.

## April 4, 1984

### U.S. complicity in mining Nicaraguan seaports is revealed.

After the Nicaraguan Contra rebels announced on January 8, 1984, that they had mined their nation's seaports, minor news stories appeared of ships being damaged by the mines. On February 25, three Nicaraguan fishing trawlers were hit near the El Bluff port on the Atlantic coast. Next, a Dutch cargo ship and freighters from Panama, Japan, and Liberia were damaged off the Pacific coastal waters near Puerto Corinto and Puerto Sandino. Finally on March 20, a Soviet tanker was struck.

On March 30, Nicaragua appealed to the United Nations, claiming that the United States had been involved in the mining operation. Within a week news leaked that the CIA had helped plan and carry out the mining. When the U.N. Security Council voted to condemn the mining on April 4, the United States vetoed the resolution. The next day, French Foreign Minister Claude Cheysson offered to cooperate with other European countries in sweeping the mines from Nicaraguan ports. France had voted for the Security Council resolution, and although the British delegate abstained in the vote, British Prime Minister Margaret Thatcher strongly protested the mining as a dangerous precedent against trade on the high seas.

On April 7, information leaked by the Reagan administration confirmed the CIA role in mining Nicaragua's harbors. President Reagan approved the operation in December 1983, and the CIA supervised Contra forces, who laid mines along both seacoasts of Nicaragua and in Lake Nicaragua. Since the CIA wanted only to frighten foreign ships entering Nicaraguan ports, its operatives located a Martin Marietta plant that made "firecracker" mines that created mostly noise and splash and would damage but not sink a ship. This detail had been kept secret because the purpose was to cut off trade to Nicaragua or to increase insurance rates for ships using Nicaraguan ports.

News of direct U.S. involvement in the mining operation shocked many members of Congress, America's NATO allies, and other international observers. Although Deputy Secretary of State Kenneth W. Dam called the mining "collective self-defense" to stop Nicaragua's supply of weapons to El Salvador, both the House of Representatives and the Senate passed resolutions on April 10 and 11, respectively, that condemned the Reagan administration's action. In the Senate, 41 Republicans joined the Democrats in approving the resolution. Senator Barry M. Goldwater (R-Ariz.) wrote a critical letter to CIA Director William Casey saying that such action was an "act of war," and was deplorable.

See April 15 and May 20, 1984.

## April 7, 1984

### *Vietnam reports that it repelled a Chinese invasion of 2,000 troops.*

Since the Vietnamese conquest of Cambodia (Kampuchea) in 1979, warfare had sometimes erupted on the Chinese-Vietnamese border. On April 2, 1984, China shelled Vietnamese border forces in retaliation for a Vietnamese attack and later reported killing or wounding 35 Vietnamese alleged to have planted land mines on Chinese soil. Vietnam accused China of attacking on April 6, but stated that China had failed. These incidents may have been a Chinese attempt to bolster the Khmer Rouge forces of Pol Pot in Cambodia. The Khmer armies rallied against Vietnam by gaining supplies from Thailand, where many Cambodians fled as refugees.

The United States was indirectly involved in these Southeast Asian conflicts. The United States sent aid to the Cambodian refugees, and the Reagan administration increased military assistance to Thailand, which included 40 M-8 tanks and some advanced F-16A fighter aircraft. This equipment was supposedly to help Bangkok defend its border areas.

See December 3, 1978, and January 7 and February 17, 1979.

### April 12, 1984

*After capturing four Palestinians who hijacked a bus, Israel's security police are accused of beating two captives to death.*

On April 12, four Palestinians took over a bus with 35 passengers aboard and tried to exchange their captives for Arab prisoners in Israeli jails. Israeli police attacked the bus on April 13, killing two Palestinians and capturing two others. Soon after, investigative journalists reported that the Israeli security police had not only blown up the homes of the four West Bank Palestinians but had beaten the two captives to death.

On April 25, the Israeli Defense Ministry announced that the journalists violated military censorship because they published classified photographs. The ministry did appoint a commission to investigate, however, and on May 23, it verified that the two captives had been beaten to death and said the culprits would be criminally prosecuted.

See June 25, 1986.

### April 13, 1984

**With Congress in recess, President Reagan uses emergency powers to send $32 million of military aid to El Salvador.**

After Congress left for its Easter recess, the president sent helicopters, ammunition, medical equipment, and spare parts to El Salvador. Congress had refused to fund military aid until the Salvadoran election was finalized in May. Reagan took the $32 million from funds appropriated for other countries.

The president said he waited until the recess to avoid a confrontation with Congress, telling his weekly radio audience that he could not turn his back "on this crisis at our doorsteps." He wanted Congress to approve another $62 million for El Salvador when it returned from recess, a request made more difficult because of Reagan's emergency action that, legally, Congress did not have to approve.

Despite Reagan's desire to aid El Salvador and Nicaragua's Contra rebels, many members of Congress and the public disagreed. A Louis Harris poll found on May 17, 1984, that 74% of Americans opposed U.S. aid to El Salvador.

See May 5, 1984.

### April 15, 1984

**Senator Daniel Patrick Moynihan symbolically resigns in protest from the Senate Select Committee on Intelligence because the CIA mined Nicaraguan waters, but rejoins after CIA director William Casey apologizes.**

Moynihan (D-N.Y.) and Senator Barry Goldwater (R-Ariz.) accused the CIA of not informing them of the covert mining of Nicaragua's harbors. Initially, Casey argued that he had told congressional intelligence committees about the mining. Meeting with the Committee on Intelligence, Casey read briefings of March 8 and 13 that mentioned the mining, and Senator Malcolm Wallop (R-Wyo.) contended that these comments made clear the CIA's intentions.

Moynihan disagreed. He said that on March 8 the only reference was the word "mine" in a 27-word sentence. On March 13, the word "mines" appeared once in a 26-word sentence. Casey mentioned this in the midst of other Contra actions and never said the CIA was involved or that Reagan had authorized the mining. On April 26, Casey admitted to the committee that he had not kept the group adequately informed in the timely manner required by legislation.

See April 4, 1984.

### April 15, 1984

**Terrorists kill two American diplomats in Namibia; the U.S. State Department says the attack was random and the car bomb was not aimed at U.S. envoys.**

The two Americans who died were in South-West Africa helping a U.N. team monitor peace efforts between South Africa and the South-West African People's Organization (SWAPO) rebels. The agents, Dennis Keough and Lieutenant Colonel Ken Crabtree, were having their car serviced at a gas station when a bomb exploded inside the station. After investigating, U.S. Ambassador to South Africa Herman Nickel stated that the terrorist bomb had not been aimed specifically at the Americans.

## April 17, 1984

**Nicaragua takes its complaint against the United States for aiding the Contra rebels to the International Court of Justice, whose restraining order is ignored by the United States.**

Nicaragua pursued action against American assistance to the rebels not only in the United Nations but also at the International Court of Justice at The Hague, a body whose opinions the United States had heretofore respected. Nevertheless, on April 8, the Reagan administration stated that it did not recognize the court's jurisdiction over the Nicaraguan issue, calling it a "domestic" issue and a propaganda ploy of the Sandinista regime.

The court disagreed with the U.S. view and, after hearing Nicaragua's case, issued a restraining order on May 10. It declared that the United States should halt its mine blockade of Nicaraguan harbors while the court investigated other allegations of the case. Although the Reagan administration said it had stopped mining operations before May 10, it rejected the court's jurisdiction and said it would do so for the next two years. The U.S. decision led foreign leaders to question the International Court's values relative to other nations.

In 1946, when the U.S. Congress recognized the International Court's authority, it reserved the right to reject the court's involvement in "domestic issues," a term that, as in the Nicaraguan case, could be interpreted broadly. Over two-thirds of the 158 nations that recognized the court refused to grant it full authority over internal issues. For example, in 1970, Canada refused to accept the court's jurisdiction over a U.S. complaint on marine pollution caused by Canadians.

Nevertheless, the American Society of International Lawyers, during a convention in Washington, D.C., adopted a resolution opposing the Reagan administration's position on the Nicaraguan issue. In international law, the blockade of a nation's coast is an act of war, and mining a nation's harbors is a principal means of an effective blockade. During the 1962 Cuban missile crisis, President John F. Kennedy's administration not only did not mine Cuba's harbors, but the U.S navy

patrolled the sea at some distance from Cuba's coast, where it carefully selected ships to inspect for nuclear missile material. Whether Kennedy's tactics were considered by Reagan is not known. Senator Malcolm Wallop (R-Wyo.), who usually backed Reagan's policies, suggested that a better course of action would have been to countersue Nicaragua for supporting El Salvador's rebels.

See October 22, 1962, and April 4, 1984.

## April 17, 1984

*Gunfire from the Libyan embassy in London kills a policewoman and wounds ten persons demonstrating against Libya.*

Following the shooting, British police sealed off the embassy and asked the building's occupants to surrender. Although Libya had allowed members of the Libyan Revolutionary Student Forum to take over the building, it was, legally, Libyan territory that the British protected under international law. In addition, the British acted cautiously to avoid reprisals against their embassy in Libya.

By April 27, the issue ended when Britain broke diplomatic relations with Libya and permitted the embassy occupants to fly home. Later, the British government indicated that Libyan diplomats had asked the British authorities to prevent the anti-Gadhafi demonstrations, but they had refused. Soon after, U.S. intelligence satellites intercepted a telephone message from Libya to its London embassy that ordered the staff not to react "passively" to the demonstrators. This order may have precipitated the machine gun fire that killed the British police officer. Finally, British action was related to a March 8, 1984, bombing of a British nightclub that injured 26 people and was blamed on Libya.

## April 18, 1984

**Vice President Bush proposes a ban on chemical weapons that seems designed to precipitate Soviet objections.**

During March 1984, President Reagan accepted a draft treaty that would prohibit the use of chemical weapons as proposed by Secretary of State George Shultz. On March 30, President Reagan told a press conference that Vice President George Bush would offer this draft treaty during the United Nations

Disarmament Conference to begin on April 18 in Geneva. Reagan said the draft would be a "bold" initiative for a comprehensive ban on chemical weapons. In its April 16 edition, *Time* magazine reported the U.S. proposal was "framed in terms guaranteed to invite Soviet objections" because the treaty required strict verification of each nation's chemical facilities.

Produced by a compromise between the U.S. State and Defense Departments, the plan called for $1.126 billion to finance a chemical weapons buildup, while Bush traveled to Geneva to ask the U.N. Conference on Disarmament to adopt a procedure permitting inspection of all government-owned or -controlled facilities on 24 hours' notice. This terminology exempted privately owned plants from inspection, the very kind the United States used for its production. Because Soviet "government-owned" industry produced all defense material, the U.S. proposal would open Soviet industry to inspection. As expected, the Soviet delegates objected.

President Reagan's attempt to begin production of nerve gas weapons was temporarily blocked by the House of Representatives, which deleted funds for the project on June 1, 1984.

See April 18, 1984.

### April 19, 1984

*While a cease-fire begins, Lebanese President Gemayel and Syrian President Assad arrange shared power for a new Lebanese government and army.*

On March 20, nine Lebanese factions accepted a cease-fire that achieved some security in Beirut because it was supervised by an 1,800-man police contingent deployed along a ten-mile line separating Christian from Muslim Druze forces.

President Amin Gemayel's cooperation with Syrian President Hafiz al-Assad offered hope for peace in Lebanon. Plans proceeded to create a government representing all of the national religious/political factions, a key provision being that Gemayel would give equal power to Muslims in Lebanon. In the pre-1975 government the Christians had a six- to five–member advantage in representation. Thus, Gemayel appointed a Muslim leader, Rashid Karami, as prime minister and pre-

pared to establish an army with members from all religious factions.

See June 23, 1984.

### April 19, 1984

*Egypt and the Soviet Union renew diplomatic relations.*

Diplomatic relations were severed in 1981 by Egyptian President Anwar as-Sadat, who accused the Soviet delegation of subverting his government. Believing relations should be restored, Egyptian President Hosni Mubarak contacted Moscow, and on April 19 both governments announced their agreement. The process was finalized on July 6, when the Soviet Ambassador Aleksandr V. Belonogov reached Cairo and Egypt's Ambassador Salah Bassiouni went to Moscow.

See September 15, 1981.

### April 22, 1984

*Jonas Savimbi takes responsibility for bombing Cuban barracks in Huambo, Angola.*

Savimbi, the head of the National Union for Political Independence of Angola (UNITA), which had been fighting against the government, claimed that over 200 people were killed when a jeep loaded with dynamite was driven into a Cuban military barracks and exploded. Among the dead, he said, were 37 Cuban officers and 2 Soviet army officers. Angola reported that 14 Cubans and 10 Angolans died while 70 persons were injured.

Although the U.S. Central Intelligence Agency rejected Cuban complaints that the United States had assisted the terrorists, the Reagan administration not only assisted Savimbi but also praised him for using the same tactics that the White House had denounced when the U.S. Marine barracks in Lebanon were bombed on October 25, 1983. On March 19, Cuba had offered to withdraw its 25,000 troops from Angola, but the United States and South Africa objected because Cuba wanted the United States and South Africa to stop aiding UNITA.

### May 1, 1984

#### President Reagan concludes a five-day visit to China, where he signs accords on nuclear cooperation and cultural relations.

The Reagan administration wanted to improve relations with China, which had deteriorated badly because the president had dispatched arms to Taiwan and tried to restrict Chinese textile imports. In addition to approving agreements on nuclear cooperation and cultural and scientific exchanges during his visit from April 26 to May 1, Reagan applauded China's desire to reunite peacefully with Taiwan and agreed to send advanced U.S. computer technology to China.

China's leader, Zhao Ziyang, urged Reagan to stop deploying missiles in Western Europe and to negotiate arms control agreements with the USSR. Although Reagan addressed the Chinese people on television, his speech was taped, and when the tape was broadcast, the Chinese had deleted Reagan's anti-Soviet rhetoric and references to the Soviets' shooting down a Korean Air Lines plane in September 1983.

### May 5, 1984

#### José Napoleon Duarte wins the runoff election in El Salvador.

This was a runoff election because no candidate won a majority on March 25. U.S. officials approved of Duarte's victory because the Christian Democratic Party leader was considered the "democratic-moderate," while Roberto d'Aubuisson, the National Republican Party candidate, was known as the power behind the right-wing death squads that terrorized the populace. Although Duarte won 52% of the vote, d'Aubuisson's showing revealed the strength of landowners, the military, and their allies. On February 2, former U.S. Ambassador to El Salvador Robert White told a congressional committee that d'Aubuisson oversaw the assassination of Archbishop Oscar Romero, which was confirmed on March 21 by former Salvadoran intelligence officer Roberto Santivanez.

Because the Christian Democrats lacked a majority in the National Assembly, they formed a coalition cabinet that weakened Duarte's position. During his campaign, Duarte promised what the U.S. Congress wanted to hear—to stop the death squads, to pursue land reform, and to negotiate peace with the rebels. Reports were that the CIA spent $2.1 million to help Duarte's campaign. Duarte espoused the same goals as when he was El Salvador's president from December 1980 to April 1982; he did little then to reform the military or support land reform.

Nevertheless, Duarte's election enabled President Reagan to persuade Congress to continue to provide military aid to El Salvador.

On the assassination of Romero, see March 24, 1980, and June 22 and August 10, 1984.

Chinese Prime Minister Deng Xiaoping entertains President and Mrs. Reagan at the great Hall of the People. Ronald Reagan Library

### May 6, 1984

*Panamanian elections are won by Nicolas Ardito Barletta in a close race against Arnulfo Arias Madrid.*

The close race caused disputes about the vote count and delayed Barletta's taking office officially until October 11, 1984. Arias Madrid had been elected president three previous times but was overthrown each time by the military because he tried to reorganize the corrupt National Defense Forces, through which General Manuel Noriega controlled Panama.

Barletta was Noriega's "front man" but won the election by only 1,713 votes out of 600,000 accepted ballots. During the counting, over 750,000 ballots had been challenged. After the Electoral Commission named Barletta the winner, he visited Washington, D.C., on July 27, where he received praise from the Reagan administration that it later regretted extending.

See February 4, 1988.

### May 6, 1984

**Members of Islamic Holy War in Lebanon kidnap the Reverend Benjamin Thomas Weir, their fifth American victim in 1984.**

In addition to kidnapping four Americans early in 1984, on January 18 gunmen from the Islamic Holy War assassinated Malcolm H. Kerr, president of American University.

Weir had worked in Beirut for nearly 30 years. As with three other American victims, he was held by a pro-Iranian extremist group that wanted the release of Shiite Muslims being held in a Kuwaiti prison for attacking the French and American embassies (see December 12, 1983). Weir was released in 1985.

The three other kidnapped Americans were Frank Reigier, an engineer on the faculty of American University, who was captured on February 10 but freed by Nabih Berri, the leader of the Amal Shiite forces who found the house where Reigier was captive; Jeremy Levine, the Beirut bureau chief of Cable News Network, who disappeared on March 7 but escaped to Syria on February 14, 1985; and William F. Buckley, the Central Intelligence Agency's operative in Beirut, who was abducted on March 16, then interrogated and tortured. His death was disclosed in 1985.

See September 18 and October 12, 1985.

### May 7, 1984

**The Soviet Union refuses to participate in the summer Olympic Games, held at Los Angeles.**

Although claiming there was inadequate security for its athletes, Moscow was disturbed because President Carter had withdrawn Americans from the 1980

President Reagan meets with newly-elected President José Napoleon Duarte of El Salvador. Ronald Reagan Library

Olympics in Moscow and because on March 1, 1984, the United States denied a visa to Oleg Yermishkin, a Soviet Olympic official who, Washington said, was in the Soviet secret police (KGB). The Soviets had denounced this U.S. action but did not announce their withdrawal from the 1984 summer games until they persuaded other communist nations to join the boycott.

Soon after, Bulgaria, East Germany, Czechoslovakia, Vietnam, Laos, and Mongolia refused to participate in the games. The absence of these countries enabled the United States to dominate the 1984 Olympics.

See July 28, 1984.

### May 9, 1984

**Libyan leader Mu'ammar Al-Gadhafi accuses the United States and Britain of attempting to assassinate him.**

Gadhafi complained that a May 8 attack was planned in Washington and London. Twenty gunmen attacked the barracks where Gadhafi usually resided, but they failed to kill the leader because loyal Libyan troops killed 15 of them. On May 13, Gadhafi's security forces captured and killed the alleged leader of the plot, Wajdi Alshwehdi. Gadhafi also used this incident to eliminate other opponents. On June 11, 1984, Amnesty International reported that over 3,000 persons had been arrested and detained and that 7 had been arbitrarily executed by Libyan security forces.

### May 9, 1984

**On a visit to Japan Vice President George Bush urges the Japanese to lower their import restrictions and liberalize their financial markets.**

Bush's visit with Prime Minister Nakasone and other Japanese officials dramatized the persisting U.S. effort to blame Japan for the unfavorable U.S. trade balance and to seek changes in Japanese commercial policy.

On January 30, 1984, Japan signed an agreement to let U.S. telecommunications firms compete with Japanese on an equal basis in its domestic market. On April 21, Tokyo deregulated some of its financial markets so that foreign bankers and investment firms could operate in Japan. Later, on May 29, the two nations agreed to strengthen the yen and create an international Euro-yen market for European currency.

Japan steadily invested more in U.S. corporations. On April 24, 1984, Nippon Kokan bought a 50% share in U.S. Intergroup Steel, a subsidiary of National Steel.

For additional financial cooperation, see September 6, 1984.

### May 10, 1984

**The Danish parliament refuses to deploy U.S. missiles that NATO had assigned; the Dutch delay deployment.**

In Denmark, the antinuclear missile movement was successful in electing its candidates to parliament. Denmark became the first NATO country to reject plans to deploy U.S. intermediate-range missiles as a countermeasure to the Soviet Union's SS-20 missiles.

More serious to NATO plans, the Dutch decided on June 13 to delay their scheduled deployment of 48 cruise missiles. The Dutch parliament voted 79 to 71 to delay deployment for two years, pending a possible arms control agreement between the Soviet Union and the United States.

### May 14, 1984

**Philippine elections enable the New Society Movement of President Ferdinand Marcos to retain control of the National Assembly; opposition leaders claim fraud was used.**

The Laban Party, opponents of President Ferdinand Marcos, decided on February 26 to participate in the elections despite the unsatisfactory manner in which Marcos's commission investigated the assassination of Benigno Aquino, its former leader (see August 21, 1983). Although other parties boycotted the election, the Laban leaders hoped that the National Cultural Movement for Free Elections would prevent fraud at the polls. That group had recruited 150,000 volunteer poll watchers to oversee the election.

In the May 14 vote, Laban increased its assembly representation from 14 to 62, while the Free Elections group claimed that alleged fraud in at least 51 districts should be investigated. If Laban had won those seats, then it would have had a majority in the National Assembly. Rejecting the allegations of fraud, Marcos contended that he had earned a "new mandate" to rule. Marcos did not, however, have the landslide victory he claimed in prior elections.

## May 14, 1984

### President Reagan certifies that Haiti has improved its human rights record and can receive U.S. economic aid.

Although the Haitian dictator Jean-Claude Duvalier promised to guarantee a free press and respect human rights, as soon as an opposition newspaper criticized the government, Duvalier on May 10 banned all opposition activity. Opposition to Duvalier continued, and on May 30, 1984, the U.S. Federal Bureau of Investigation arrested 13 persons in Sidell, Louisiana, for plotting to overthrow Haiti's government.

Nevertheless, the Reagan administration certified that Haiti had improved its performance in protecting human rights and thus was eligible to obtain U.S. aid. American corporations had considerable investments in light industry in Haiti and received the support of Duvalier in keeping Haitian labor cost low.

See February 7, 1986.

## May 15, 1984

### The Senate rejects President Reagan's appointment of Leslie Lenkowsky as deputy director of the U.S. Information Agency (USIA).

Lenkowsky's confirmation failed because he had blacklisted prominent Americans from speaking in the USIA's overseas program. News of the blacklist became public on February 9, 1984, after Lenkowsky admitted to a congressional committee that the Reagan administration had a list of 81 liberals and anti-Reaganites who should not be accepted for the agency speakers program. The *New York Times* published 84 names on March 15, including those of Ralph Nader, David Brinkley, Walter Cronkite, and Coretta Scott King. Although Lenkowsky denied preparing the list, his testimony was refuted by two USIA officials, W. Scott Thomson and John Moshen. Members of Congress objected to the blacklists as restricting free speech and making the USIA program contradictory to American ideals of free expression of opinion.

## May 16, 1984

### Mexico's president warns against using force in Central America and urges support of the Contadora group.

While visiting Washington, President Miguel de la Madrid HURTADO addressed a joint session of Congress to explain that the communist threat was not serious in Central America. Because Mexico led the Contadora effort of Latin American nations seeking a negotiated peace in that region, de la Madrid wanted U.S. policy to give primary attention to that effort, something the Reagan administration had not done.

In addition to asking Congress to support Contadora, de la Madrid said that U.S. budget deficits caused higher interest rates, which lowered standards of living in Mexico and other debtor nations. Every 1% increase in U.S. interest rates, he stated, added $3.5 billion a year to the interest that developing nations paid on their debts.

Because of de la Madrid's criticism, President Reagan gave him a cold reception at the White House. The only agreement they reached was Mexico's promise to end direct export subsidies if the United States showed proof of injury before Mexico levied tariffs to protect key trade items.

## May 20, 1984

### The Arab League condemns Iran for attacking Saudi Arabian and Kuwaiti oil tankers in the Persian Gulf but rejects a U.S. offer of naval protection.

Since early 1984, Iraq had attacked Iranian ships at the Kharq Island Oil Terminal, while Iran retaliated against pro-Iraqi ships in the Persian Gulf. Iraq used five French-made Super Etendard fighter planes to fire at ships carrying Iranian oil; Iran fired at Saudi and Kuwaiti oil tankers. Six ships had been damaged, and the Saudi oil tanker *Al Ahood* remained ablaze for two weeks after an Iraqi missile strike. Iraqi missiles also sank a Greek-owned cargo ship headed for Iran.

As a result, ship insurance rates soared and oil market futures increased their price. Most oil companies stopped using ports in the northern part of the Gulf near Kharq. Although the United States, Western

Europe, and Japan were less dependent on gulf oil than during the 1970s, if Iran closed the Strait of Hormuz, as it threatened to do, then world oil prices would increase by up to 20%.

The United States offered to protect the oil lanes and the Strait of Hormuz if the Arab League provided naval bases in the Gulf. An American battle group headed by the aircraft carrier *Kitty Hawk* was in the Arabian Sea and ready to operate. At this time, however, the Arab League preferred to keep U.S. ships at a distance. In Iran, Speaker of Parliament Hojatolislam Hashemi Rafsanjani stated that Iran would wage holy war "everywhere in the world" if other nations intervened in the Persian Gulf.

See June 5, 1984.

## May 20, 1984

**The Soviet Union announces recent missile deployment in retaliation for U.S. military buildups in Western Europe.**

Over a period of six days, Moscow took steps to counter U.S. military activities. First, on May 14, the Soviets deployed more intermediate-range nuclear missiles in East Germany in response to the U.S. deployment of Pershing IIs in West Germany beginning in November 1983. Second, on May 20, Soviet officials increased the number of nuclear missile submarines patrolling off the coast of the United States.

## May 24, 1984

**Two days after acquitting an army officer of killing three agricultural advisers, a Salvadoran court convicts five national guardsmen for killing four American Catholic nuns.**

These two events in May highlighted the limits on U.S. policy in getting El Salvador to prosecute death squads in its army who committed terrorist acts. On May 22, Salvadoran courts freed the army officer accused of slaying two Americans and one Salvadoran land reform official in January 1981.

On May 24, however, the court sentenced killers of the Catholic nuns to 30 years in prison. The conviction was based on evidence pieced together for the prosecutor by the U.S. Federal Bureau of Investigation. This case was not closed, however, because Salvadoran President José Napoleon Duarte had not followed up on allegations that Defense Minister Carlos Eugenio Vides had "quite possibly" covered up for the leaders who ordered the four women shot.

See January 3, 1981, and December 4, 1980.

## May 27, 1984

**Egyptian President Hosni Mubarak's party wins 391 of 448 parliamentary seats.**

While President MUBARAK's National Democratic Party remained dominant in Egyptian politics, the election indicated the revival of the liberal New Wafd Party, which gained 57 seats in parliament. President Anwar as-Sadat had barred the Wafd from politics in 1978, but on February 12, 1984, an Egyptian court overruled Sadat's order, permitting the New Wafd leaders to campaign. The Wafd organization had led Egypt's independence movement prior to the military coup of 1952.

See February 28, 1922, and July 23, 1952.

## May 30, 1984

**Eden Pastora Gómez, a Nicaraguan rebel leader, is wounded by a bomb, that kills three journalists including one American. Later investigations implicate the CIA in the assassination plot.**

PASTORA had led rebels in the 1979 overthrow of Nicaragua's Somoza regime. After breaking with the Sandinistas in 1982, he formed a rebel group in southern Nicaragua but refused to work with the U.S.-backed northern rebels, the FDN Contras, because their leaders had been national guard officers under the Somoza regime. Initially the United States provided funds for Pastora's ARDE group, but by 1984, the Central Intelligence Agency wanted Pastora to unite with the Contras to end congressional complaints that they were a right-wing military organization, compared with Pastora's more "democratic" group.

Because Pastora refused to join the Contras or be subservient to the CIA, the agency gave him a deadline of May 30, 1984, to change his mind or be cut off from future U.S. funds. According to investigative journalist Leslie Cockburn, the CIA not only enticed another ARDE commander, Alfonso Robelo, to break with Pastora but also plotted to kill Pastora if he refused to join the Contras.

On the day that the CIA deadline ran out, a professional killer from Libya, Amal Galil, disguised as a photojournalist, tried to kill Pastora during his press conference in La Penca, a town on the Costa Rican border. After the La Penca bombing, the ABC News stringer Tony Avirgan and the *New York Times* stringer Martha Honey investigated the bombing. Avirgan described his presence at the bombing: "I was just sitting on a box, actually not very far from where the bomb was planted, drinking a cup of coffee. And I mean its not even nice to think about, but one of the reasons I wasn't killed was because there was another journalist, a good friend [Linda Frazier], who was standing right in front of me and took the major impact of the blast and she was killed." Avirgan's experience led him to join with Honey to investigate the bombing.

Although the U.S. State Department attributed the bombing to a Spanish Basque terror group and claimed that Frazier had planted the bomb, the Avirgan-Honey investigation proved that the State Department had misled reporters in Washington. Their investigation showed that Galil traveled to Costa Rica with the stolen Danish passport of Per Anker Hansen, a freelance photographer. Galil (Hansen) carried a metal photographer's box when the group of journalist went to La Penca on May 30 and placed it near Pastora just before the blast. The next day Galil disappeared from Costa Rica, having been aided by John Hull, an American rancher whose farm was a staging ground for the delivery of CIA weapons to the Contras. Hansen's escape was also planned by Costa Rica's Directorate of Intelligence and Security (DIS).

Pastora himself blamed Lt. Colonel Oliver NORTH of the National Security Council staff, who frequently criticized Pastora as a drug dealer and praised the FDN rebel leaders despite their Somoza connections. In July 1984, after recovering from his wounds, Pastora visited Washington but was told by the U.S. State Department that his rebel group would receive no more economic or military aid from the United States.

See March 14, 1982, and April 15, 1983.

## June 5, 1984

### *Saudi planes shoot down an Iranian plane over the Persian Gulf.*

Defending its interests against Iranian attacks on oil tankers in the gulf, Saudi F-15 fighter planes directed by American AWACS reconnaissance planes attacked an Iranian plane preparing to hit a Kuwaiti tanker near Al Arabiyah in the Persian Gulf. Although the Saudis reported they shot down two Iranian planes, U.S. sources said only one Iranian F-4 fighter was downed.

Trouble in the gulf escalated in early 1984 when Iraq began shooting at ships using Iran's Kharq Island Oil Terminal and Iran began shooting at ships using Kuwaiti or Saudi ports. After the Arab League condemned Iran's action on May 20, President Reagan agreed on May 29 to send the Saudis 400 Stinger antiaircraft missile launchers.

On June 10, both Iran and Iraq told U.N. Secretary-General Javier Pérez de Cuellar that they would stop attacks on civilian targets. They did not end attacks on shipping, however, because both countries sought to use these attacks to win the war they had waged since 1980.

See September 4, 1980; see also May 20 and August 2, 1984.

## June 6, 1984

### The fortieth anniversary of World War II, D-day, is celebrated by President Reagan and other Western leaders.

Veterans of the D-Day, 1944 landing joined President Reagan, Great Britain's Queen Elizabeth, and France's President François Mitterrand to celebrate the event beginning the liberation of Western Europe from the Germans. Mitterrand stated that Nazis are foes of all people but that the German people have been reconciled with their present-day allies. President Reagan paid tribute to the at least 20 million Soviet citizens who died in the war but criticized the Soviet Union for dominating its Eastern European neighbors.

### June 9, 1984

**Leaders of the seven largest industrial democracies end their annual summit meeting in London.**

This annual summit, in which President Reagan and other leaders discussed economic affairs, achieved no significant results. The final communiqué focused on the Third World debt problem and the need to liberalize trade regulations. The European leaders urged President Reagan to cut the U.S. budget deficit and lower interest rates. The president replied that he disliked high interest rates but resisted efforts to raise U.S. taxes to cut the deficit and high interest costs.

### June 10, 1984

**The SDI program claims a significant advance when a homing device intercepts and destroys a mock ballistic missile warhead in midcourse flight.**

Following President Reagan's call to develop the Strategic Defense Initiative (SDI), the Defense Department established an SDI Organization in January 1984 to determine the feasibility of such a program.

Following three tests, which failed for "mechanical reasons," the SDI launched a rocket from Meck Island in the Kwajalein Archipelago, a part of the Marshall Islands, that struck a Minuteman I intercontinental missile launched 30 minutes before from Vanderbilt Air Force Base, California, that was flying 100 miles above the earth. The Defense Department said this experiment showed that the homing guidance system and kinetic energy weapons could destroy enemy missiles by colliding with them at great speed.

The SDI proposed to intercept Soviet missiles or warheads at one of three phases of flight—in the boost phase, where missiles were most vulnerable after being fired; in the midcourse phase, where MIRV warheads separated but were harder to detect; and in the reentry phase, as the warheads returned to the earth's atmosphere heading for their targets. The June 10 test demonstrated how a missile in the midcourse or reentry phase might be hit.

Critics of SDI contended that the June 10 test greatly oversimplified the problems involved in tracking, finding, and striking ten warheads per launcher speeding through space and reentering to hit U.S.

targets. On August 18, 1993 the *New York Times* reported that four former members of the Reagan administration contended the 1984 SDI Homing Overlay Experiment (HOE) test had been rigged to make the test appear that a "bullet hit a bullet in space." The *Times* article led the Pentagon and the General Accounting Office (GAO) to examine these charges. A year later, on July 23, 1999, the *New York Times* reported the investigation showed Pentagon officials installed a small bomb to explode in the dummy warhead when the HOE interceptor flew past. The Pentagon's idea was to deceive the Soviet Union about SDI's capabilities but, of course, it also fooled American news reporters, Congress, and the public.

See March 23, 1983.

### June 20, 1984

**The Nunn Amendment to reduce the number of U.S. troops in Western Europe is defeated.**

A member of the Senate Armed Services Committee, Senator Sam Nunn (D-Gra.) wanted Western Europeans to pay a larger share of their defense costs. The NATO nations, he argued, had agreed in 1978 to increase these expenditures by 3% a year, but most did not do so. Except for the United States, only Canada increased its defense budget (by 5%), and Great Britain increased its by 3% in 1983. In contrast, West Germany's increase was 1.9%, Italy's 1.1%, and France's 0.9%.

The Nunn Amendment required the withdrawal of 30,000 American soldiers from Europe each year that the NATO members failed to fulfill the 3% increase. The United States had assigned 326,414 troops to NATO.

Although Nunn wanted to encourage larger NATO defense expenditures, the NATO leaders were dismayed with the amendment because they had already taken great political risks by deploying American missiles on their territory in 1983. Moreover, the Europeans contended that since 1970 their increase had been 44% (averaging over 3% a year), while Washington's increase was only 27% in 14 years. Their economies, they argued, suffered because of high U.S. interest rates. West German leaders added that their compulsory military service created an essential strategic reserve, while the United States had canceled its draft in 1973.

The Reagan administration lobbied to defeat Nunn's amendment, and Senator William Cohen (R-Me.) proposed a substitute amendment urging the NATO allies to increase their defense contributions but omitting clauses about troop withdrawals. On June 20, the U.S. Senate voted 55 to 41 to defeat the Nunn Amendment but approved Cohen's amendment of the U.S. concern about the burden of sharing NATO defense costs.

### June 22, 1984

**A plot by El Salvador's right wing to kill U.S. Ambassador Thomas R. Pickering is thwarted.**

Reagan administration officials revealed that members of Roberto d'Aubuisson's Arena Party had planned to kill Ambassador Pickering in May 1984. The d'Aubuisson group disliked the CIA's role in helping El Salvador's President José Napoleon Duarte win the election of May 5, 1984. Although d'Aubuisson denied any involvement in the plot, President Reagan sent his roving ambassador General Vernon Walters to El Salvador to warn right-wing Arena leaders of serious consequences if their "death squads" tried to kill Pickering. The plan was aborted (but see June 25, 1984).

President Duarte never fulfilled his preelection promise to investigate the military-connected death squads but did appoint Colonel Rinaldo Golcher to clean up the Treasury Police. Golcher found that intelligence division S-2 of the Treasury Police was linked to a 2,000-man force that had carried out executions and other abuses. One result of Golcher's investigation was the removal of Colonel Nicolas Carranza as head of the Treasury Police. Carranza, who was in the pay of the CIA, was connected to the death squads and implicated d'Aubuisson in the murder of El Salvador's Archbishop Romero in 1980. He was sent to West Germany as a military attaché on May 24, 1984.

### June 23, 1984

**Lebanon's government of national unity establishes a Christian-Muslim army.**

Plans for a unified army had been worked out by the unity government of President Amin Gemayel and Prime Minister Rashid KARAMI with the mediation of Syria's Vice President Abdel Halim Kaddam.

On June 12, Karami formed a coalition cabinet representing Christians, Muslims, and Druze, even though the cease-fire of April 19 had failed to stop violence, which intensified in Beirut the week of June 10, when over 100 people were killed.

To gain an effective unity army, it was essential to impose order among the competing paramilitary factions. To achieve this, the Muslims accepted Maronite Christian General Michel Aoun as army commander, and the Christians abolished decrees giving local commanders control over their army contingents. A Druze leader, Nadim el-Hakin, became the army chief of staff, and a Shiite Muslim became head of the Public Intelligence Directorate. Overall control of the army was under a six-man multireligious council of two Christians, two Muslims, and two Druze.

To integrate army ranks, the two army brigades in Beirut became a mixture of Christians and Muslims: the Muslim Sixth Brigade was augmented by Christians and the Christian Fifth Brigade was augmented by Muslims. On July 4, these brigades replaced the militiamen who since April 19 had policed the Green Line separating East and West Beirut.

Although Prime Minister Karami was optimistic about the new political-military plans, the key issue of Christian rights to power in a nation where 60% of the population was Muslim (40% being Shiite) had not been resolved. The French had provided for Christian power before withdrawing in 1946, but the population majority now favored the Muslims. The Christian minority feared the changes, and in June 1984, two Christian Phalangist groups refused to abandon their militia. In addition, the issue of Israel's withdrawal of troops remained.

See March 5 and April 19, 1984; April 16, 1985.

### June 25, 1984

**The United States and Nicaragua conduct peace talks at Manzanillo, Mexico, the first of a series of nine rounds of talks.**

The Manzanillo talks resulted from Secretary of State George Shultz's surprise visit with Nicaragua's President Daniel Ortega in Managua on June 1, 1984. Shultz stopped there after attending the inauguration of El Salvador's President Duarte. During the discussions on June 25, the United States said it hoped the bilateral talks could coordinate with the Contadora process in obtaining a broad regional agreement. Nicaragua was most interested in preventing U.S. or Contra rebel attacks.

See September 25, 1984.

### June 25, 1984

**El Salvador's Roberto d'Aubuisson visits several U.S. senators who prefer his methods to those of El Salvador's president.**

Although d'Aubuisson was a leader of right-wing death squads and had been implicated in attempts to assassinate Thomas Pickering, the U.S. ambassador to El Salvador, the Reagan administration granted him a visa. A conservative group, the Young Americans for Freedom, sponsored d'Aubuisson's visit, and Senator Jesse Helms (R-N.C.) hosted receptions with about a dozen members of Congress. Helms stated that he admired d'Aubuisson's use of terror to wipe out the rebels in El Salvador, tactics that had caused killings on both sides for the past five years despite extensive U.S. aid.

Because the Reagan administration had denied visas to liberal and left-wing foreigners desiring to visit the United States, many critics believed d'Aubuisson should also have been prevented from entering the country. Although U.S. State Department officials admitted that d'Aubuisson probably knew in advance of the plot against Ambassador Pickering, they claimed he was not directly involved.

See June 22, 1984.

### June 29, 1984

**The Soviet Union seeks negotiations to ban weapons in space but rejects counterproposals by the United States.**

In a formal diplomatic note, the Soviet Union offered to conduct talks on banning space weapons. The Reagan administration stated that space weapons should be part of broader arms control talks. On July 21, the USSR made a second offer, while the United States made two counteroffers on July 24 and July 28. Moscow rejected the suggestions for broader talks and negotiations did not begin.

On July 17, Moscow and Washington did agree to modernize the hot line communications system between the White House and the Kremlin.

See November 22 and December 18, 1984.

### June 29, 1984

**The Reverend Jesse Jackson, a Democratic presidential candidate, returns from Cuba, bringing 22 Americans and 26 Cuban political prisoners freed by Cuban leader Fidel Castro. This leads to Cuban-American talks.**

Soon after Jackson returned, U.S. and Cuban representatives began talks on July 12 in New York City about returning to Cuba the Cuban criminals and mental patients who arrived in the United States during the 1980 boatlift.

See April 4–5 and May 5 and 14, 1980.

### July 17, 1984

**Vietnam returns the remains of eight American sevicemen killed during the war.**

Although on July 11 Secretary of State George Shultz announced that negotiations with Vietnam had been stalemated because Hanoi was not willing to provide data on all the 2,489 American personnel listed as missing, Hanoi returned some of the bones it believed to be Americans' remains. A U.S. military specialist flew to Hanoi, briefly checked the boxes of remains, and shipped them to the Military Identification Center in Hawaii. Identifying the bones was an arduous task, but on July 28, the U.S. army confirmed that one of the eight belonged to Dominic Sansone, who had been killed in 1969.

Because of the POW/MIA attention given to the Vietnam War, on July 2, the U.S. State Department said a total of 2,489 men were unaccounted for in Vietnam, while 8,177 were unaccounted for from the Korean War (1951–53). Richard Nixon precipitated the Vietnam POW issue on April 16, 1971, when he made the return of all American POWs a condition for North Vietnam to fulfill before American troops would leave Vietnam. Nixon's conditions did not mention American troops listed as missing-in-action. His omission became clear in March 1973, when the POWs returned home.

See April 16, 1971, and March 24, 1973.

## July 18, 1984

**The U.S. Drug Enforcement Agency (DEA) claims that Nicaraguan leaders engage in drug smuggling; the Sandinistas deny the charges.**

The DEA filed affidavits in Miami's district court that Nicaragua was directly involved in the cocaine traffic from South America. They arrested six suspects in Miami and charged them with handling cocaine that allegedly came from Colombia through Nicaragua. On July 28, a federal grand jury indicted one Nicaraguan, Frederico Vaughan, and ten others, including three top-level Colombian cocaine traffickers. One Colombian official, Pablo Escobar, was in a photograph released on August 8 that allegedly showed him loading cocaine onto a plane in Nicaragua.

Although DEA evidence implicated Vaughan, an aide to Nicaragua's interior minister, the agency had no firm evidence for its accusations against Interior Minister Tomás Borge or the Defense Minister Humberto Ortega. On August 2, a defector, Antonio Farach, told a Senate committee that Humberto was involved in drugs but could provide no indictable evidence.

## July 21, 1984

**A congressional report says U.S. military forces are not combat ready, a claim denied by the Defense Department.**

The Democratic-controlled House Appropriations Committee issued a report that claimed the U.S. armed forces were less combat ready than they had been before the Reagan administration's large defense buildup. Because most defense spending of the Reagan administration was on elaborate new weapons systems and naval construction, the preparedness of the armed forces for conventional war had been neglected. Several field commanders, the report said, complained of being shortchanged on such essentials as spare parts and communications equipment.

This report caused much controversy, and in August the Pentagon denied the report's findings, declaring that there were sufficient supplies for 30 days of conventional combat. Moreover, it stated that this capacity would double if Congress did not cut future defense funding.

See also August 2 and September 19, 1984.

## July 21, 1984

**The United States praises Poland for granting amnesty but declines to lift U.S. economic sanctions.**

The Reagan administration continued the sanctions placed on Poland when the government declared martial law on December 13, 1981. Although Poland had recently freed 652 political prisoners and 35,000 common criminals, the president wanted evidence that the Polish communists improved their human rights practices before ending the sanctions.

Nevertheless, on August 3, 1984, Reagan lifted the ban on cultural and scientific exchanges with Poland and restored the rights of Poland's airline (LOT) to land in the United States. Agricultural and trade sanctions remained in place.

## July 26, 1984

*The question of Namibia's independence remains unresolved; unsuccessful talks end between South Africa and SWAPO.*

For the second time in 1984, representatives of the South-West African People's Organization (SWAPO) and South Africa discussed proposals for elections that would lead to independence for South-West Africa (Namibia). Discussions on May 11–13 in Lusaka, Zambia, had been fruitless, and a second round of talks in the Cape Verde Islands ended after only a few hours. Unresolved issues included the terms for a cease-fire and how many groups other than SWAPO could have representation in Namibia's political future. In addition, the presence of Cuban forces in Angola helping SWAPO guerrillas displeased South Africa, a linkage SWAPO said was irrelevant to Namibia because the Cubans protected only Angola's government.

## July 28, 1984

**As the Olympic Games begin in Los Angeles, the Soviet Union and 11 of its "friends" do not participate.**

Without the participation of the Soviet Union and East Germany, two major Olympic "powers," the United States had little competition in winning 83 gold medals. The games became a celebration of U.S. nationalism. On August 18, 1984, the 11 nations that joined the Soviet Olympic boycott were invited to Moscow for the Friendship Games.

### August 2, 1984

**A U.S. mine-sweeping team arrives in the Red Sea to clear mines that had damaged 15 ships since July 9, 1984; the Pentagon's response time is slow.**

When Suez Canal traffic slowed because of the mines, the mystery was who laid them. Although an extremist religious group, Islamic Jihad, claimed it had done so, Iran, which sponsored Jihad, said it was not responsible. Iran's opponent, Iraq, also denied any involvement.

Britain and France sent mine-sweeping ships to the Red Sea, and President Reagan acted at the request of Egyptian President Hosni Mubarak by dispatching 200 sailors and four Sea Stallion helicopters to the area. Because the helicopters required ten days to reach the Red Sea, the Pentagon's rapid-deployment capability was questioned. The Defense Department explained that it decided not to use an Egyptian land base and, therefore, the helicopters needed a ship for operations. This required sending 200 sailors to Rota, Spain, to board a refitted marine assault ship, the *Shreveport*, for transportation to the Red Sea. Nevertheless, the response time raised questions about the effectiveness of Reagan's enormous defense buildup since 1981.

See July 21, 1984.

### August 5–6, 1984

**At the U.N. Conference on Population, the United States opposes the funding of abortions.**

This U.N. conference met in Mexico City, in a country where, despite a family planning program, the population had doubled in ten years. In his opening address, Rafael M. Salas, the Filipino who chaired the meeting, predicted an overcrowded world of 10.5 billion people in which scarce resources would drastically lower the quality of life: 42% of children under five would be malnourished; 25% of families would be inadequately housed; and 600 million people would live in poverty.

Although leaders of developing nations realized the need for family planning, the Reagan adminis-

tration not only maintained a U.S. prohibition on aid for abortion but also refused to permit private agencies to receive assistance if they performed or promoted abortions. The chief U.S. delegate, James L. Buckley, said the free-market economy should follow the "natural mechanism for slowing population growth." This late-nineteenth-century Social Darwinistic formula meant, in practice, that poor children would be born to starve and suffer through a short life. Although Buckley did not say so, the "natural mechanism" assumed that the unfit would die.

The final conference report recommended international efforts to improve the status of women, end forced marriages, and delay childbearing in cultures where giving birth was common at an early age.

### August 10, 1984

**A House-Senate committee approves $70 million in military aid to El Salvador.**

Following elections on March 25 in El Salvador, Congress rejected President Reagan's request for aid because a runoff vote was held in May, and El Salvador's policies were uncertain.

In May the moderate Christian Democrat won, and during July, President José Napoleon Duarte visited Washington to gain support from the two leading House Democrats—Majority Leader James Wright of Texas and House Appropriations Committee Chairman Clarence D. Long of Louisiana. On August 8, President Reagan at a press conference, showed infrared film and other intelligence data to "prove" that Nicaragua had sent arms to rebels in El Salvador. Duarte wanted funds either to fight the rebels or to persuade them to negotiate peace.

Although on January 16, 1984, President Reagan reported that death squad killings in El Salvador increased significantly in 1983, on July 13, 1984, the State Department said there were "only" 93 per month in 1984. Some members of Congress feared that Duarte could not control the right wing and gain peace. Consequently, the House-Senate committee allocated only $70 million, not the $117 million of El Salvador military aid that Reagan had requested. The committee also provided $112 million of economic aid.

See May 5 and June 22, 1984.

## August 11, 1984

**Believing the microphone he is using is being tested, President Reagan broadcasts a joke about bombing Moscow.**

Preceding his Saturday radio show, President Reagan thought only a voice check was underway and quipped, "My fellow Americans, I am pleased to tell you I just signed legislation which abolished Russia forever. The bombing begins in five minutes." Because the radio lines were open, many listeners heard the president's words.

America's European allies were embarrassed by the president's black humor; the Soviet media interpreted the comment as typical of Reagan's hostility. But Republican supporters on Reagan's presidential campaign trail applauded lustily whenever Reagan repeated his jest.

For Reagan's "Evil Empire," speech, see March 8, 1983.

## August 13, 1984

**Morocco and Libya sign a treaty that greatly disturbs the United States.**

Although King HASSAN II of Morocco and Libyan leader Mu'ammar AL-GADHAFI had common interests in allying against Algeria, Tunisia, and Mauritania, this treaty surprised the United States. The State Department viewed King Hassan as a special friend and Gadhafi as a dedicated enemy. The agreement was a nonaggression pact between Libya and Morocco, setting up regular meetings on defense preparations.

Because the United States resented Hassan's secret negotiations, the king sent his chief adviser, Redi Guedira, to visit Secretary of State George Shultz. The Moroccans argued that Gadhafi showed moderation by evacuating Libyan forces from Chad in 1983 and believed King Hassan could moderate the Libyan leader's behavior. Hassan thought Reagan exaggerated Libya's threat to peace. Nevertheless, Secretary Shultz told Morocco not to permit U.S. arms to reach Libya.

## August 20, 1984

**Greece withdraws from military exercises with the United States.**

Greek Prime Minister Andreas Papandreou announced that Greek forces would not carry out military exercises with NATO forces set for September 1984 because of Turkish threats to Greek security. The long tradition of Greek-Turkish antagonism caused problems between these two NATO members.

There had been tension between Washington and Athens since July 8, 1984, when the United States blocked the sale of Norwegian planes to Greece. After Papandreou threatened to shut down the Voice of America station in Greece, the United States approved the sale.

The exercise cancellation was one of several anti-American incidents reflecting the Greek public's belief that the United States favored Turkey and dominated Greek policy. Papandreou had denounced U.S. imperialism and defended the Soviet Union as a faithful opponent of capitalism. He claimed in 1983 that the Korean Air Lines flight KAL-007, which the Soviets shot down, was on a CIA spy mission. He angered Washington by freeing a suspected Arab terrorist. Later, in October 1984, he denounced Poland's Solidarity trade union and praised Polish leader Wojciech Jaruzelski for trying to crush them with martial law. Of course, Solidarity was not crushed. Anti-Americanism won Papandreou votes.

Papandreou did, however, renew the treaty permitting U.S. bases to remain in Greece (see September 8, 1983). His close associates said he was not anti-American but that he only boosted both Greek independence from Washington and Greek national self-esteem.

See March 6, 1821; November 30, 1829; April 17, 1897; August 10, 1920; and July 20, 1974; October 18, 1974; July 24, 1975. Also see June 2, 1985.

## August 23–24, 1984

**Colombia's government and two rebel groups agree to fight drug lords.**

To wage war on Colombia's drug lords, two rebel groups agreed to a cease-fire on March 28, 1984. Colombian President Belisario Betancur signed a truce with representatives of the Popular Liberation Army on August 23 and with M-19 rebels on August 24. Only one smaller Cuban-backed communist group, the National Liberation Army, rejected the cease-fire and truce.

Betancur now was ready to fight the cocaine dealers in Colombia. He inaugurated this drug war on May 1, 1984, in a speech urging the people to back a state of siege against the drug lords and not to associate the drug war with the economic and social demands of the rebels. The drug war was to be a long, difficult effort for Colombia and the United States.

### August 25, 1984

#### The Soviet Union successfully tests a new long-range ground-launched cruise missile.

This test report caused Soviet and U.S. spokesmen to ask who had the cruise missile first. TASS, the Soviet news agency, said the cruise missile was a response to Washington's deployment of cruise missiles in Western Europe since November 1983. The U.S. State Department said Moscow had developed cruise missile technology long before the United States deployed its missiles.

On August 28, the Congressional Office of Technological Assessment reported that if cruise missiles could evade radar and other defenses as U.S. experts argued, then their use could make all ICBM land-based missiles vulnerable and obsolete. Praises for the cruise came, of course, from proponents of a weapon whose potential had yet to be proven.

### August 29, 1984

#### A U.S. court of appeals rules against President Reagan's pocket veto of a bill requiring a report on El Salvador's human rights progress.

In November 1983, President Reagan had not signed, and therefore vetoed, congressional legislation that prohibited economic aid to El Salvador unless the president reported that human rights had been improved during the past year. On January 4, 1984, 33 members of Congress, led by Congressman Michael D. Barnes (D-Md.) filed suit to challenge the constitutionality of Reagan's pocket veto.

The appeals court upheld the congressional view, ruling that the president's action was not valid. Subsequently on September 14, Secretary of State George Shultz followed legislative requests by certifying that El Salvador had made progress in curbing human rights violations. That same day, Reagan sent new jet aircraft and helicopters to El Salvador.

### September 1, 1984

#### Nicaraguan soldiers shoot down a rebel helicopter, killing two Americans.

Proving that American citizens were in combat in Nicaragua, this incident took place when three American Cessna planes and one Hughes 500 MD helicopter flew from a CIA-controlled base in Honduras, crossed into Nicaragua, and fired 24 rockets at a military school in the small town of Santa Clara. Nicaraguan antiaircraft guns shot down the helicopter, killing two Americans and one Nicaraguan rebel. The two Cessna planes returned safely to Honduras.

The two Americans were Dana Parker and James P. Powell. Parker was an undercover detective for the Huntsville, Alabama, Police Department and a member of the Twentieth Special Forces Group of the Alabama National Guard. A Huntsville official told the CBS News reporter Leslie Cockburn that Parker was a "paid assassin, who had killed three Cuban government officials." Powell was a pilot from Memphis, Tennessee, who never told his family or friends of his connections. Later, Tom Posey, an Alabama grocer and head of the Civilian Military Assistance group, claimed that the two Americans worked for him.

Evidence from the Iran-Contra hearings of 1986–87 indicated that Lieutenant Colonel Oliver North was in Honduras on August 31 and wanted to postpone the raid because the helicopter was the only one the Contras had. North called the Americans "non-official assistants," but the CIA said they were private mercenaries with no official ties. In reality, they were part of the so-called private group organized by North, an aide to the National Security Council.

The origin of the two Cessna planes also became a political issue. On September 14, Senator Jim Sassor (D-Tenn.) told reporters that the planes belonged to the New York National Guard but were declared "excess" in December 1983 and flown to the Air Force Logistics Command at Andrews Air Force Base in Washington, D.C. In February 1984, the U.S. Air Force gave them to "Project Elephant Herd," which in turn gave them to Summit Aviation, a Delaware company that converted them for military use. Summit Aviation had a reputation for aiding CIA operations. Elephant Herd was an interagency task force of the U.S. military—in this case the Defense Department and the Central

Intelligence Agency. The political question raised by the transfer of the Cessnas was the violation of the December 1983 legislation that restricted funding to the Contras to $24 million.

See January 14 and December 9, 1983.

### September 4, 1984

*Hope for better relations between East and West Germany fades after East German leader Erich Honecker postpones a visit to West Germany.*

Honecker was scheduled to visit Bonn on September 23, but pressure from Moscow apparently caused him to cancel the meeting. Previous events in 1984 had improved relations between the two German states. On January 22, East Germany permitted six citizens who sought asylum in the U.S. embassy in Berlin to go to West Germany. During Soviet President Yuri Andropov's funeral on February 13, West German Chancellor Helmut Kohl met Honecker for the first time.

On July 27, however, Moscow showed dissatisfaction with the German developments. After East and West German negotiators agreed to ease restrictions on their trade and travel, the Soviet Union protested that Bonn was trying to weaken socialism in East Germany. Thus, Honecker's cancellation indicated that the Soviet Union had put a break on changes in East Germany's relations with West Germany.

### September 4, 1984

*Canada's Progressive Conservative Party ousts the Liberal Party, winning 211 of 282 seats in the House of Commons.*

Because of the Liberals' defeat, Brian MULRONEY replaced John N. Turner as Canada's prime minister. Turner had replaced Pierre Trudeau as the Liberal leader on June 18, 1984.

### September 5, 1984

*Prime Minister P.W. Botha is elected as the first executive president under South Africa's new constitution.*

Under the constitution approved on November 3, 1983, the mixed-race "coloreds" elected representatives to a third chamber of parliament, principally made up of South Africans of Indian origin. On

August 28, the National People's Party won 18 of 40 seats in the third house. Despite their enfranchisement, most coloreds were not enthusiastic, and only 20% of those eligible voted.

In addition to a third chamber, the new constitution increased the power of President Botha, who now had authority to veto legislation and to summon or dismiss parliament.

### September 6, 1984

*The first overnight and overseas futures trading opens between Chicago's Mercantile Exchange and Singapore's International Monetary Exchange.*

On August 28, the commodity Futures Trading Commission in Washington, D.C. approved an around-the-clock global market exchange. Initially, the market traded West German marks and Eurodollars. By November 7, it began trading futures on the Japanese yen. Generally, this activity opened avenues for other global stock transactions among New York, London, and Tokyo.

### September 6, 1984

*The United States vetoes a U.N. resolution that demands Israel's withdrawal from Lebanon.*

The Security Council resolution asked Israel to evacuate its armed forces from Lebanon and to lift all restrictions on Lebanese civilians in southern Lebanon. As on prior occasions, the United States appeared as Israel's only friend on the council. On September 6, 1984, President Reagan made a campaign promise to a B'nai B'rith convention, saying he would maintain "unwavering support for Israel." Despite the U.S. veto, Lebanon and Israel negotiated a troop withdrawal on October 31, 1984.

See June 6, 1985.

### September 7, 1984

*The largest debt rescheduling in history occurs when international banks restructure Mexico's $48.5 billion debt.*

Mexico, whose total foreign debt was $95 billion, received a 10- to 14-year extension on its 1990 debt. This reward was for undertaking a domestic austerity program and encouraging exports. Although Latin American countries asked on June 21 that foreign bankers treat them as a group on debt policy, U.S. and other banks insisted on treating each country on a case-by-case basis.

### September 11, 1984

**President Reagan says the Soviet Union can purchase ten million metric tons of U.S. grain.**

Because of an abnormally hot, dry season, the Soviet Union had its worst harvest since 1975. Although Reagan increased the amount of grain the Soviets received, U.S. farmers requested such purchases to relieve their surplus. Between June 29 and October 18, the USSR purchased about 15.2 million metric tons of U.S. corn and wheat.

This was the president's second effort in 1984 to help the Soviets as well as American economic interests. On July 25, he ended the ban on Soviet fishing in U.S. waters imposed by President Jimmy Carter in 1980.

### September 19, 1984

**A General Accounting Office (GAO) investigator tells Congress about defects in the navy's air-to-air missiles.**

Testifying before the House Subcommittee on National Security of the Government Operations Committee, GAO investigator Frank C. Conahan indicated that thousands of the navy's air-to-air missiles were useless because of defects. Up to 33% of the Sparrow and 25% of the Sidewinder missiles were listed in recent navy records as "unserviceable."

In earlier testimony, on September 12 Assistant Defense Secretary Lawrence J. Korb admitted that many air combat missiles could not be used but estimated the number to be about 21%. Korb blamed Congress because it insisted on competitive bidding in defense contracts. As one reporter observed, this was odd because Korb represented an administration that extolled competitive free enterprise. Other defense experts blamed the problem on the military's insistence on technologically complex weapons that were prone to difficult maintenance problems.

See July 21, 1984.

### September 20, 1984

**The U.S. embassy in Beirut is bombed by a pro-Iranian shiite.**

Driving a station wagon loaded with 3,000 pounds of TNT, a Lebanese member of Islamic Jihad hit the U.S. embassy annex northeast of Beirut, where most embassy work took place. Destroying the building's facade, the blast killed 7 Americans and 2 Lebanese, as well as 24 Lebanese waiting in line to apply for visas. Involved in the presidential campaign, President Reagan told reporters that he contemplated no immediate retaliation.

### September 21, 1984

**The Coordinadora group refuses offers to participate in Nicaragua's November elections.**

On March 16, 1984, Nicaragua announced an election for November and revised the law to encourage opposition parties to participate. On July 25, 1984, Arturo Cruz and other Sandinista opponents formed the Coordinadora group and sought negotiations to clarify the election terms for eligibility of participants. The European-based Socialist International mediated these efforts.

On August 22, the attempt to hold an election nearly failed when the Sandinistas said three opposition groups could not participate because they had not registered their candidates. On September 21, Sandinista leader Daniel Ortega gave the opposition until September 30 to meet candidate requirements. When the Coordinadora rejected this proposal, further talks occurred with the Socialist International but did not succeed. As a result, Cruz and his followers boycotted the November 4 elections.

While pro-democracy groups in Nicaragua and the United States wanted Cruz to run, hard-liners among the Contra rebels and the Reagan administration preferred to discredit the elections. These hard-liners won by claiming that since Ortega refused the terms laid out by Cruz, the elections could not be democratic and free.

See November 4, 1984.

## September 23, 1984

### The United States closes its School of the Americas to comply with the 1978 Panama treaty.

For 38 years, the SCHOOL OF THE AMERICAS trained Latin American military officers. Although it was intended to teach these officers respect for democracy as well as military instruction, the school provided better training in killing and clandestine warfare than in inculcating respect for the principle of civilian control of the military as an essential of a democratic society.

## September 24, 1984

### In U.N. speeches, President Reagan urges renewed arms control talks, but Soviet Foreign Minister Gromyko criticizes U.S. policies.

Even compared with his January address, Reagan's U.N. speech had a distinct tone of moderation toward the Soviet Union. He appealed to Moscow to establish "a better working relationship" to "shorten the distance" from the United States on arms control. The president concluded, "We recognize that there is no sane alternative to negotiation on arms control and other issues between our two nations which have the capacity to destroy civilization as we know it."

Although GROMYKO avoided Soviet demands for the withdrawal of U.S. missiles from Europe, he stated that "concrete deeds and not verbal assurances are necessary to the normalization of relations with America." Gromyko thought Reagan's moderation was part of a presidential campaign to calm the fears generated by Reagan's earlier tough stances. Referring to Reagan's previous speeches, Gromyko told the U.N. General Assembly: "all we hear is that strength, strength, and above all strength is the guarantee of international peace. In other words, weapons, weapons, and still more weapons." Thus, Gromyko did not believe that Reagan sincerely sought better relations.

Following the U.N. session, Gromyko met with Secretary of State George Shultz and visited Washington, D.C. President Reagan had never before met with a high-ranking Soviet official. Gromyko also took the unprecedented step of meeting with Walter Mondale, the Democratic candidate in the November 1984 presidential election.

See January 16, 1984.

## September 24, 1984

### The World Bank approves $2 billion for sub-Saharan African nations but has funding problems.

Agreed to by delegates from both developing and developed countries at the World Bank meeting, the $2 billion was emergency aid to relieve the desperate economic conditions of sub-Saharan African nations. During the meeting, the United States opposed a West German plan to give investment funds for African economic reforms. Under President Reagan's guidelines, the U.S. delegates wanted Africans to seek private-sector investment initiatives rather than state-controlled programs.

On September 24, the World Bank delegates approved the West German plan but were unable to find governments willing to pledge the $2 billion. The United States refused to contribute, and Treasury Secretary Donald T. Regan said the Africans should obtain funds from the International Development Association. The World Bank, whose official name was the International Bank for Reconstruction and Development, needed not only the $2 billion of emergency aid but also $9 billion for the regular programs approved on May 24, 1984. At the end of 1984, the World Bank was still searching for $1 billion to fully fund emergency aid to Africa.

## September 25, 1984

### Nicaragua and the United States disagree on the Contadora peace proposals at the sixth round of talks in Manzanillo, Mexico.

Although Nicaragua initially rejected Contadora proposals made on September 7, 1984, the Sandinista delegates offered them as the basis for the sixth round of U.S.-Nicaraguan talks at Manzanillo on September 25. The Contadora proposition was to eliminate all foreign military schools, bases, and advisers as well as military-based political parties in Central America.

The Reagan administration refused to accept the Contadora proposals, stating that the Sandinistas deceived the public by their alleged acceptance. The U.S. State Department wanted the proposals to provide adequate verification methods and to avoid an immediate cut off of all U.S. aid to the Contras and Honduras.

At Manzanillo, the U.S. delegation offered to limit U.S. military exercises in Central America and to agree to a step-by-step phasing out of military forces in the region. However, the Nicaraguan delegates maintained their support for the September 7 Contadora proposals. Thus, the sixth meeting at Manzanillo since June 25, reached no solutions.

See December 10, 1984.

## September 25, 1984

### Hong Kong's future status is agreed on by China and the United Kingdom.

In 1997, Great Britain's 99-year lease on Hong Kong would end, and the territory would revert to the People's Republic of China. For two years, London and Beijing had negotiated the transfer of authority before reaching a settlement. On September 18, the British and Chinese embassies announced a draft agreement that the British cabinet approved on September 21, and British and Chinese representatives signed on September 25. Finally, the British Parliament approved it on December 19, 1984.

The pact allowed the people of Hong Kong to retain "all the rights and freedoms they now have until 2047." It preserved Hong Kong's own convertible currency and its property, trading, and travel rights. The present school system would continue, as would freedom of the press and religion. In A.D. 2000, China would become responsible for defending the territory of Hong Kong.

## September 25, 1984

### By adopting austerity measures, Argentina obtains $1.42 billion in credits from the International Monetary Fund (IMF).

Although Argentina received a $500 million loan on March 30 from the IMF and $350 million on June 29 to meet its foreign debt obligations, its long-term debt-payment problem remained. For Argentina and other debt-burdened nations, the dilemma was how to avoid defaulting on payments and losing future credit opportunity while also stimulating domestic economic growth to raise living standards.

Argentina tried on June 21, 1984, to get other debtor nations to form a united front against the international bankers, but these attempts could not succeed without cooperation from the money lenders. Consequently, as the September 30 deadline for inter-

est and principal payments approached, Argentina accepted an AUSTERITY PROGRAM demanded by the IMF and obtained economic aid to pay its obligations. The austerity program cost the government political loyalty at home because it restricted wage benefits and cut social programs to reduce the budget and cut inflation.

While President Raul Alfonsin struggled to create a democratic nation after ending military control, he faced the opposition of labor unions demanding wage increases, the Peronist Party's political challenge, and angry military cliques.

See October 30, 1983.

## September 28–29, 1984

### Foreign ministers of 12 European and 9 Latin American states support the Contadora effort in Central America.

Western European and Central American leaders met in San José, Costa Rica, to bypass U.S. efforts to isolate Nicaragua from European trade and commerce. U.S. NATO allies opposed President Reagan's enmity toward Nicaragua's government and believed that Central America needed economic aid to improve living standards and solve the region's problems.

Reagan had isolated the U.S. from world opinion when he mined Nicaraguan waters.

See April 4, 1984.

## October 3, 1984

### In two days' time, two Americans, including an FBI agent, are arrested for selling secrets.

On October 1, a naval intelligence analyst, Samuel L. Morison, was arrested for selling secret photos of a Soviet aircraft carrier to the British journal *Jane's Defense Weekly*. Two days later, an FBI agent, Richard W. Miller, was charged with selling secret documents to the Soviet Union, that gave a detailed picture of U.S. intelligence activity. Miller was to receive $65,000 in gold and cash from two Soviet emigrés—Nicolay and Svetlana Ogorodnikov—whom the FBI also arrested. Svetlana Ogorodnikov claimed to be a KGB major in Soviet intelligence, but U.S. authorities claimed she was an amateur spy.

On October 17, 1985, a federal grand jury found Morison guilty of selling secrets, he received only a two-year prison sentence because his lawyers portrayed him as a patriotic American seeking more funds for the U.S. navy by disclosing secret data about Soviet naval power. Miller was convicted on June 19, 1986, and sentenced to life in prison. The Ogorodnikovs pleaded guilty on June 26, 1985; he received an 8-year prison sentence and she, an 18-year sentence.

### October 9, 1984

**Israeli-Prime Minister Shimon Peres accepts President Reagan's offer of U.S. economic aid.**

After becoming prime minister on September 13, PERES visited Washington from October 7 to 10 seeking assistance for a five-year plan to restructure Israel's debt. Israel currently suffered from 800% inflation and was having difficulty in paying foreign debts. Reagan promised to help, and a joint study group was formed to oversee economic affairs. Reagan released immediately all of the $1.2 billion Congress had appropriated and agreed to give $2.6 billion in non-repayable grants for 1985. Israel began austerity measures that included freezing wages and prices and halting the importation of 50 luxury items.

### October 10, 1984

**The Defense Department rules for a journalists' pool to cover U.S. combat operations; journalists gain some changes.**

The Defense Department wanted a pool of reporters to accompany troops during the first stages of combat and share data with the media. There would be no provisions for individual journalists to collect independent information.

Following protests because daily newspapers had no representation in the pool, the Defense Department increased the pool from 6 to 12 persons—one each from TV networks CBS, NBC, ABC, and CNN; two TV crewmen; one photographer; one from a radio network; one each from AP and UPI; one for weekly news magazines; and one for daily newspapers. The secretary of defense made final allocations of reporters to the pool.

### October 12, 1984

**A second Boland Amendment prohibits U.S. government agencies from aiding Nicaragua's Contra rebels.**

For the fiscal year 1985 beginning October 1, the Reagan administration not only failed to obtain the $28 million it sought for the rebels but also was prohibited from sending any type of aid to the Contras. Previously, the BOLAND AMENDMENT of 1982, which banned aid to "overthrow" the Nicaraguan government, was easily ignored by the CIA. In December 1983 all that Congressman Edward Boland (D.-Mass.) could do was limit U.S. aid to $24 million for 1984.

By September 1984, evidence of the CIA's double-dealing with Congress and stories of the Contras' terrorist methods persuaded many Republican members of Congress to join Democrats in opposing President Reagan's policy. Most damaging to the president was the CIA's mining of Nicaraguan waters and evidence that the overthrow of the Sandinistas was the real purpose of the Contras despite Reagan's statements to the contrary.

Initially, the House and Senate deadlocked on ending all Contra aid. On June 25, however, the Senate voted 88 to 1 to separate the Contra aid issue from the 1985 supplemental appropriations bill, and Reagan's request for $20 million for the Contras seemed doomed. In July and August, however, Reagan released intelligence data designed to revive Contra aid. On July 18, a State Department report described Nicaragua's military buildup and support for subversive activity in Central America. On August 2, an alleged Nicaraguan defector told the Senate Subcommittee on Drug Abuse that Nicaraguan officials, including the president's brother, Humberto Ortega, were smuggling drugs. On August 8, Reagan showed a press conference infrared film and other CIA data that allegedly proved that Nicaragua had transferred military equipment to rebels in El Salvador.

On June 18, the U.S. Drug Enforcement Agency (DEA) had firm evidence against only one aide to the Nicaraguan interior minister. During the Iran-Contra hearings of 1986–87, evidence indicated that the Contras and CIA agents condoned drug sales to finance the rebels. According to the Georgetown University professors Robert Parry and Peter Kornbluh in the 1988 issue of *Foreign Policy*, this aspect of the Iran-Contra investigation was not pursued. Although the Iran-Contra disclosures were secret in 1984, there was enough evidence to raise doubts about the Contras among members of Congress. Moreover, most congressional members and the American public seemed immune to Reagan's exaggerated support for the Contra "freedom fighters."

Consequently, after the October 1 deadline for the Continuing Appropriations Resolution passed, Senate members of the joint House-Senate conference committee yielded to Boland's persistent request to cut off Contra funds. Those in Congress who supported Reagan felt the President had not kept them informed of events while his appointees deceived them about the Contra situation, which the recent downing of the Contra helicopter demonstrated. On October 10, the Senate accepted Boland's amendment, and on October 12, Congress approved the bill. The senators' only concession to the president was that the White House could again request Contra funds after February 28, 1985.

In contrast to the 1982 Boland Amendment, the 1984 version applied to any accounting procedure of any government agency, even restricting the "transfer of equipment acquired at no cost." Rather than simply prohibit aid intended to "overthrow the government," as in December 1982, the 1984 Boland Amendment stated:

> No funds available to the Central Intelligence Agency, the Department of Defense, or any other agency or entity of the United States involved in intelligence activities may be obligated or expended for the purpose of which would have the effect of supporting, directly or indirectly, military or paramilitary operations in Nicaragua by any nation, group, organization, movement, or individual.

During floor debate, Boland said the provision meant that "if you are engaged in support of the Contras, you are involved in intelligence activities. So you are covered [by the ban]."

President Reagan signed the law on October 12, 1984, but his legal counselors later argued that the National Security Council (NSC) was not covered by the prohibition. Opponents of this interpretation cited Reagan's Executive Order 12333 of December 4, 1981, which defined the NSC as providing guidance for "all national foreign intelligence, counterintelligence, and special activities."

See December 21, 1982, and December 9, 1983; see also April 4, July 18, and September 1, 1984.

### October 12, 1984

**The U.S.-Canadian boundary dispute over the Gulf of Maine is resolved by the International Court of Justice.**

The court decision ended a 20-year dispute between Canada and the United States. Both nations had agreed to accept the court's decision. As a result, the United States was awarded 66% of the Gulf of Maine and Canada the remainder. The area involved 30,000 square nautical miles of sea including the Georges Bank fishing grounds.

See March 6, 1981.

### October 12, 1984

***Provisional Irish Republican Army terrorists almost assassinate British Prime Minister Margaret Thatcher.***

The terrorists planted a bomb at Brighton's Grand Hotel, where the annual Conservative Party conference was being held. Because most of the British cabinet attended, a successful bombing would have wiped out the British government. The bomb exploded late, however, and government officials were saved. Four persons died in the attack, and 20 were injured. On June 10, 1986 Patrick J. Magee and four codefendants were found guilty of planning the bombing and 16 other bombings in England and were sentenced to life in prison.

### October 15, 1984

**A CIA manual instructs Nicaraguan rebels on assassinating and blackmailing leaders.**

The Associated Press revealed the existence of the CIA manual. Titled "Operaciones sicologicas en Guerra de guerrillas" ("Psychological Operations in Guerrilla Warfare"), this 89-page pamphlet advocated tactics such as the public execution of government officials, arranging the deaths of Sandinista politicians, killing rebel leaders to make them martyrs, blackmailing citizens to work for the rebels, and other forms of terror and sabotage against the Nicaraguan government. Some beneficial methods were also cited, such as helping to harvest crops, teaching peasants to read, and improving village hygiene.

Nevertheless, as one reporter said, it read like a manual for the Vietcong in Vietnam or communist rebels in El Salvador. Because it was prepared by a U.S. agency, it undercut President Reagan's moralistic statements against state-sponsored terrorism as in Libya, Syria, and Iran.

For the United States, the difference was that the press and Congress could challenge the chief executive to stop such activity. The disclosure resulted in four government investigations of the manual and CIA tactics in Central America. In addition to Senate and House investigations, the General Accounting Office investigated the manual, and on October 18, President Reagan ordered an investigation. The president did not, however, heed House Speaker Thomas (Tip) O'Neill's demand to fire CIA director William Casey.

The CIA claimed that the manual helped rebels avoid combat and use persuasion, a claim readers of the manual could not find. It had been prepared by a low-level contract employee of the CIA. The 2,000 copies were published and distributed by a Contra leader, Edgar Chamorro.

On November 10, a CIA investigation said publication of the manual violated no law but recommended penalties to punish six mid-level CIA agents. CIA director Casey said he never reviewed or approved the manual.

### October 15, 1984

*Salvadoran President Duarte meets with rebel leaders, agreeing to form a joint peace commission; there are few results.*

Fulfilling a campaign promise and encouraged by the United States, President José Napoleon DUARTE offered peace talks with the rebels during an October 8, 1984, speech at the United Nations. The rebels accepted and, on October 15, met with Duarte at a Roman Catholic church in La Palma, El Salvador. The rebel leaders were Guillermo Ungo, Rubén Zamora, Ternan Cienfuegos, and Nidia Díaz.

The five men formed a peace commission with four members from each side and a Roman Catholic bishop as mediator. Talks were held from November 30 to December 2 but achieved only a 13-day cease-fire for the Christmas holidays. On October 16,

Roberto d'Aubuisson, El Salvador's right-wing leader, opposed the talks and the peace group.

See June 25, 1984.

### October 17, 1984

*Oil prices are cut by the United Kingdom and Norway; OPEC calls an emergency meeting.*

Britain's National Oil Corporation and Norway's Statoil decreased their crude oil prices from between $1.25 and $1.38 per barrel, depending on the grade of oil, lowering prices to about $30 per barrel. Because Western European demand for oil weakened after natural gas arrived from the Trans-Siberian pipeline (see January 1, 1984), there were some secret oil sales that lowered prices even more prior to October 17. The next day Nigeria, an OPEC member, lowered its price by $2 per barrel. OPEC members met at Geneva on October 29, agreeing to cut oil production by 8% per day to keep prices at $29 per barrel.

### October 19, 1984

*An unarmed American plane crashes in El Salvador, killing four CIA agents.*

The agents were on a surveillance mission that had been cleared by the CIA director, William S. Casey, who had previously informed the Senate Select Committee on Intelligence about the flight. Although the rebels claimed to have shot down the plane, the exact reasons for the crash were unknown—apparently a mechanical failure caused the accident. The CIA's caution in informing the senators spared the Reagan administration some embarrassment.

See April 15, 1984.

### October 23, 1984

*High-ranking Philippine officials are accused of assassinating Benigno Aquino, a political opponent of President Marcos.*

A four-member panel that investigated Aquino's killing stated that the armed forces chief of staff, General Fabian C. Ver, and several other officers had planned the assassination. The panel's chairwoman, Corazon Agrava, issued a minority view that blamed only air force General Luther Custadio and six soldiers. One opposition leader, Salvador Laurel, stated that if Ver was to be blamed then President Ferdinand Marcos must be blamed as well. The panel rejected Marcos's claim that a communist had shot Aquino. Marcos put General Ver on a leave of absence and asked a government ombudsman to determine if charges against any other military men should be taken to a special court.

See August 21, 1983.

## October 28, 1984

### *Israeli terrorist fires an antitank rocket at a crowded Palestinian bus, killing one Arab and wounding ten others.*

This was the most dramatic of a series of Jewish terrorist attacks against Palestinians who lived in the Israeli-occupied territory of the West Bank and the Gaza Strip. Although Israel's Prime Minister Shimon Peres condemned the attack, Palestinian students began demonstrating by throwing stones at Jews on October 29. Because most of the students attended Bethlehem University, the government closed the school from October 30 to November 5 to quiet the students.

Israeli authorities had detained three soldiers for questioning about the attack. On November 3, they arrested Army Private David Ben-Shimol for firing the weapon at the bus. Although Ben-Shimol was imprisoned by Israel, he said the incident was revenge for Jewish casualties caused by the Palestinians.

## October 29, 1984

### *Food relief for widespread Ethiopian famine faces political problems.*

Politics impedes efficient distribution of international food deliveries for Ethiopia while a million people faced starvation. By mid-November, the slow arrival of food became a political controversy. Ethiopia blamed anticommunists in Britain and the United States for delaying the shipments to make Ethiopia's communist regime collapse. The United States blamed Addis Ababa's rulers, citing the government's expenditure of $100 million to celebrate the regime's tenth anniversary and its use of famine to fight rebels in the three provinces where food was most needed—Tigre, Eritrea, and Wollo. Other observers noted that Ethiopia's lack of trucks and adequate roads slowed the shipment of food to the hinterlands.

## October 29, 1984

### *Japanese Prime Minister Yasuhiro Nakasone is elected to a second term as head of the Liberal Democratic Party.*

Although party leaders traditionally retired after one two-year term, the top leaders reelected NAKASONE, who was the favorite of the dominant faction led by former Prime Minister Kakuei Tanaka. Nakasone also broke tradition by appointing two of his party rivals to the cabinet—Shintaro Abe as foreign minister and Noboru Takeshita as finance minister.

## October 30, 1984

### *A Polish priest who favored the Solidarity trade union is murdered by state security forces.*

The body of the Reverend Jerzy Popieluszko, who had been abducted on October 19, was found on October 30. The priest became a martyr to the cause of Solidarity. Eventually, the priest's death came to be blamed not on Polish leader Wojciech Jaruzelski but on hard-liners in the state security network who opposed compromise with Solidarity leaders. Since July, Jaruzelski's policy of amnesty and cooperation with Solidarity had disturbed Polish Stalinists.

After the priest's body was found, Jaruzelski ordered an investigation and suspended a general and two colonels of the Interior Ministry, which controlled the state security office. On February 7, 1985, after a trial, Colonel Adam Pietruszka and Captain Grzegarz Piotrowski received 25-year prison terms. Two police lieutenants, Leszek Pekala and Waldemar Chmielewski, received sentences of 15 years and 14 years, respectively. Piotrowski said his orders came from a very high level. The two policemen said they never intended to kill Popieluszko but only tried to persuade him to stop working for Solidarity.

See July 21, 1984.

## October 31, 1984

### *Indian Prime Minister Indira Gandhi is assassinated by two Sikh bodyguards; her son Rajiv Gandhi replaces her.*

The prime minister was shot and killed just outside her New Delhi home. Gandhi's assassination brought a period of terror when enraged Hindus murdered any Sikhs they could find, while looting and burning their homes. For several years, Gandhi had tried to end conflict with Sikh terrorists, who sought independence for their Punjab province in northern India. On June 6, 1984, Gandhi had tried to suppress the Sikhs by attacking their temple in Amritsar. Her death at their hands made the situation explosive.

Rajiv Gandhi, who became head of the National Congress Party and prime minister, was a former airline pilot but had understudied his mother for three years. On December 28, Congress won 401 of 508 seats in India's parliament.

## November 4, 1984

### Nicaraguan elections give the Sandinista National Liberation Front 63% of the vote—61 of 90 National Assembly seats.

Although the Coordinadora opposition groups boycotted and tried to discredit the election, many foreign observers praised the election and the "national dialogue" that the government conducted with Coordinadora groups ranging from the Marxist-Leninist Party led by an idealistic communist, Domingo Sánchez Salgado, to the Roman Catholic hierarchy. Both the newspaper *La Prensa* and Catholic bishops were allowed to publish reports that criticized Sandinista policies.

While Sandinista Vice President Sergie Ramírez Mercado wanted the elections to reflect a popular consensus, hard-line Sandinistas used threats of a U.S. invasion to propose strong attacks on enemies of the government. Arturo Cruz and other pro-U.S. candidates who boycotted the elections denounced the restrictions that prevented a fair election. Yet, for general world opinion the 1984 Nicaraguan elections legitimatized the rule of Daniel Ortega's Sandinista party.

See September 21, 1984.

## November 6, 1984

### Ronald Reagan is reelected president by a landslide over Walter Mondale.

Although President Reagan's electoral count of 525 votes was the largest total in history, his 60% of the popular vote was less than the 61.1% that Lyndon Johnson won in 1964. Reagan's coattails did not extend to congressional Republicans, who lost two Senate seats and remained a minority in the House. The Republicans picked up 14 seats in the House but

fell short of regaining 26 seats lost in 1982, when Democratic candidates triumphed.

See November 3, 1964.

## November 6, 1984

### The U.S. State Department claims Soviet MiG-21 fighter planes are going to Nicaragua.

The "crisis" began on November 6, when the State Department warned Moscow not to permit fighter planes to reach Nicaragua. Although Nicaragua denied the report, President Reagan sent 25 warships to the area of Puerto Corinto and SR-71 spy planes on reconnaissance flights with unmuffled sonic booms that could be heard throughout Nicaragua's countryside. Normally, the SR-71 flights were secret and muffled, but Reagan wished to make a show of U.S. power for the Sandinistas. The noise also seemed to confirm Ortega's claim that the United States planned to invade Nicaragua. Ortega called up 50,000 Nicaraguan reservists. In addition to the reservists, thousands of Nicaraguan students rallied to defend their nation.

The tension continued for three days until the Soviet freighter, which was allegedly carrying the MiG-21s, arrived at Corinto. The Sandinista government escorted carloads of reporters from Managua to Corinto, where boxes of unassembled helicopter parts—not MiGs—were loaded into military trucks.

In Washington, the State Department tried to explain that an unidentified official had leaked false information, which Secretary of State George Shultz called a "criminal act." Yet the State Department never found and punished anyone. Secretary of Defense Caspar Weinberger said the flow of helicopters and surface-to-air missiles had increased because Nicaragua planned to invade a neighbor. Ortega said the weapons were defensive because Nicaragua would fight hard if the United States attacked.

## November 12, 1984

### Secretary of State George P. Shultz says the United States deplores Chile's declaration of a state of siege.

For the second time in 1984, Chile's President Augusto Pinochet took emergency measures to silence public protests. On March 23, he closed the universities and imposed press censorship because of opposition demonstrations. Pinochet's November 6 measures were more drastic. He imposed a curfew, assumed new arrest and censorship powers, sent the army to raid slum areas, and rounded up the entire male population to screen for suspected terrorists. In Santiago, over 2,000 suspects were singled out as troublemakers or Marxist subversives and sent to exile in villages.

Despite these actions, Chile received a $448 million loan from the International Development Bank on December 12, 1984.

## November 19, 1984

### France informs Washington that its forces will return to Chad if Libya's troops remain.

French forces assisted Chad in 1983 (see June 23 and August 23, 1983), but following negotiations with Libya, the two African countries agreed on September 17, 1984, that Libya's forces would withdraw exactly when the French did. Paris announced that both nations had withdrawn by November 10, but the United States protested that Libya did not withdraw.

On November 15 and 16, French President François Mitterrand and Libyan leader Muʻammar al-Gadhafi secretly discussed the Chad withdrawal. After the meeting, Mitterrand admitted Libyan troops had not left Chad but would soon do so. He informed the United States that French forces would return if Libya did not leave. Mitterrand's willingness to return to Chad restored some credibility for France in the eyes of its former African colonies, which depended on French backing.

## November 20, 1984

### Salvadoran courts halt proceedings against an army officer accused of murdering three land reform experts.

El Salvador's supreme court upheld a May 22, 1984, appeals court ruling that acquitted an army officer in the 1981 murder of two American and one Salvadoran land reform experts.

Although two men convicted of the murder testified that Lieutenant Isidro López Sibrian ordered the killings and supplied weapons for the job, they could not identify Sibrian in a police lineup. Other witnesses disclosed that the police let Sibrian dye his red hair black and shave off his mustache before the lineup.

Both the appeals court and the supreme court ruled against the prosecutor's charge that Sibrian should not have been allowed to change his appearance before the police lineup. On November 29 President Duarte announced that Sibrian had been discharged from the army with no pension.

See January 3, 1981.

## November 22, 1984

### Washington and Moscow announce that new arms talk will begin on January 7, 1985.

The first signs that arms talks, which ended in 1983, when the Soviet delegates walked out, would begin again came on November 7, when President Reagan told a post-election press conference that he wanted progress on an arms control treaty. On November 14, the Soviet Union expressed interest in a broadened series of talks.

The official announcement on November 22 said U.S. Secretary of State Shultz and Soviet Foreign Minister Gromyko would discuss "the entire complex of questions concerning nuclear and space weapons" and set objectives for future talks. The Soviets argued that the discussions were not a return to the status quo of 1983 but totally new talks encompassing all types of nuclear weapons.

See November 23, 1983.

## November 22–29, 1984

### PLO National Council backs Yasser Arafat; King Hussein of Jordan calls for Palestinian self-determination in Israeli-occupied territory.

Meeting in Amman, Jordan, 261 delegates of the Palestine Liberation Council voted for ARAFAT and called for an "escalation of the military struggle against Israel." Since 1969, Arafat had been leader of Fatah, the group with the largest number of members of the Palestine Liberation Organization (PLO). The PLO's 261 delegates outvoted seven other groups on the Palestinian National Council (PNC). The seven groups were the Popular Front for the Liberation of Palestine, the Popular Front for the Liberation of Palestine General Command, the Popular Democratic Front, the Syrian-backed SASQA, the Iraq-backed Arab Liberation Front, and the Libyan-backed Palestine Liberation Front.

During the conference, Jordan's King Hussein asked the PLO to negotiate with Israel on the basis of U.N. Security Council Resolution 242, which stipulated that Israel should withdraw from territories it had occupied. Hussein also called for Arab self-determination in territories occupied by Israeli troops in 1967. The PLO rejected Resolution 242 because it failed to mention a separate Palestinian state.

See November 22, 1967.

### November 24, 1984

**Edgar Chamorro is dismissed as a Contra leader because he criticized U.S. policy.**

The Miami, Florida–based Nicaraguan Democratic Force, which was the exiles' largest anti-Sandinista group, expelled Chamorro because the Central Intelligence Agency disliked his public criticism of their covert operations in Nicaragua. On October 19, Chamorro publicly disputed the White House explanation of the CIA's guerrilla manual as being designed to lessen the guerrillas' harsh attacks on the Nicaraguan population. On October 31, Chamorro elaborated on his CIA connections, saying the CIA had recruited him two years ago to force changes in the Sandinista government.

CIA director William Casey had ordered the Contras to disavow any member who publicly stated that the Contras purpose was to overthrow the government of Nicaragua because such statements antagonized the U.S. Congress. Chamorro was a moderate among Contra leaders because many were former officials of the pre-1979 Somoza government.

See October 15, 1984.

### November 26, 1984

**The International Court of Justice rules it has jurisdiction over Nicaragua's suit against the United States.**

While the World Court ruled 15 to 1 to consider Nicaragua's complaint that U.S. support for the Contra rebels violated international law, the Reagan administration believed a great power could not allow the court to limit its military options, a view contrary to America's traditional championing of the rule of law to settle disputes. In 1980, for example, the United States condemned Iran for ignoring a World Court decision to release U.S. hostages in Tehran.

The Reagan administration acted unilaterally not only at the World Court but also with its vetoes in the U.N. Security Council and at meetings of UNESCO and the Organization of American States. Columbia University law professor Richard N. Gardner said the president isolated the United States from the world forums and its traditional allies regarding the value of international law. To justify the Reagan administration stances, U.S. Ambassador to the United Nations Jeane J. Kirkpatrick argued that World Court justices from communist or Third World countries were not neutral toward the United States.

### November 26, 1984

**The United States and Iraq reestablish diplomatic relations broken in 1967.**

During the Iraq-Iran war, which began in September 1980, the United States gradually sympathized with Iraq. During a Washington visit by Iraqi Foreign Minister Tariq Aziz, these developments led to restoration of relations between Baghdad and Washington by the exchange of ambassadors. Since October 1984, Iraqi President Saddam Hussein performed the difficult task of improving relations with both the United States and the Soviet Union. Moscow also renewed formal diplomatic relations with Baghdad during 1984.

The United States renewed relations with Iraq despite clear evidence that Iraq had used chemical weapons against Iran. A team of U.N. experts reported on March 26, 1984, that there was evidence that Iraq used chemical weapons against Iran. On March 5, a U.S. State Department asserted even more firmly that Iraq had used chemical weapons. At Washington's request, the West German government took steps to stop its chemical industries from exporting chemicals to Iraq.

Nevertheless, Reagan ignored such evidence of Iraq's illegal acts when he decided to recognize that country. Reagan also encouraged European and U.S. business interests and arms dealers to assist Iraq. As a result, Saddam Hussein's armed forces obtained new weapons from many parts of the world, becoming militarily stronger than Iran or any Arab power. In 1987, when an Iraqi missile damaged a U.S. naval ship in the Persian Gulf, Reagan blamed Iran.

See May 17, 1987.

## November 27, 1984

**President Reagan prohibits the importation of European steel pipe or tubing for the remainder of 1984.**

The United States and the European Economic Community (EEC) quarreled over European steel imports to the United States throughout 1984. After the President restricted imports on specialty steel products in 1983, the EEC responded by levying sanctions on U.S. steel products in January 1984. This led to a compromise limiting U.S. imports of steel pipe and tubing, announced on November 20.

U.S. steelmakers opposed the compromise as unfair and pressured the White House to reject it. Reagan yielded by stopping the importation of EEC piping and tubing for the rest of the year until new discussions could begin with the Europeans.

See July 5, 1983; January 13, 1984; and January 10, 1985.

## November 28, 1984

**Defense Secretary Caspar W. Weinberger cites six criteria for using U.S. military force.**

In a speech delivered with President Reagan's approval and the endorsement of the National Security Council, Weinberger enunciated six criteria to be met before the nation would resort to military force, as follows:

1. Do not commit forces unless it is in our vital interest or that of our allies.
2. Forces should be committed only with the "clear intention of winning."
3. There should be clear objectives with forces used to fulfill those objectives.
4. The relationship between forces and objectives must be "continually reassessed and adjusted if necessary."
5. There must be assured support of the "American people and their elected representatives in Congress."
6. "The commitment of U.S. forces to combat should be a last resort."

Weinberger said these criteria evolved from past doubts and debates and should guide the nation's leaders in meeting future national security threats.

## December 3, 1984

**The Union Carbide pesticide plant in Bhopal, India, leaks poisonous gas.**

The accidental leak of carbon monoxide at Bhopal raised general questions about global environmental standards because nations such as India had inadequate codes and understaffed agencies to protect its citizens. The Organization for Economic Cooperation and Development (OECD) considered this issue but could not agree on a solution. President Jimmy Carter had issued an executive order for American companies to meet strict requirements in exporting dangerous substances, but President Reagan canceled the order in 1981. Most experts said the most effective means to assure safety was to enforce corporate liability for harm done by corporate activity. In India, an $850 billion class-action lawsuit was filed against Union Carbide, immediately causing its stock value to fall by 30%.

The Bhopal accident killed over 2,000 people and injured some 50,000 more. It was considered as severe as the Chernobyl accident (see April 26, 1986). Union Carbide contributed $1.83 million to India's emergency relief effort at Bhopal.

## December 4, 1984

**Four Kuwaitis who favor Iran's Shiites hijack a Kuwaiti passenger plane and take it to Teheran, where Iranian police free the hostages after two Americans are killed.**

The Shiites who took over the Kuwaiti Airlines flight held 161 persons hostage. They demanded the release of 17 Shiites whom Kuwait had imprisoned for attacking the U.S. and French embassies on December 12, 1983.

Although the hijackers killed two American hostages to dramatize their demands, Iranian police disguised as a cleaning crew boarded the plane on December 9, arrested the hijackers, and freed the surviving hostages. The two Americans killed were officials of the Agency for International Development—Charles F. Hegna and William J. Stanford.

On December 11, the United States accused Iran of helping the hostages and causing the two American deaths by delaying capture of the hijackers. Two other Americans among the freed hostages denied the U.S. accusation, claiming that Iranian police acted as best they could in the situation. Iran refused to extradite the hijackers to the United States and tried them instead in Tehran.

## December 4, 1984

**In Grenadian elections, the New National Party wins 14 of 15 seats in parliament; Herbert A. Blaize becomes prime minister.**

Blaize was Washington's choice from the outset of the election campaign. American diplomats hinted that the United States would have to reconsider its $50 million aid package if the leftist New Jewel party of Sir Eric Gairy won the election. The new Blaize government needed economic assistance and foreign investment to lower Grenada's 40% unemployment rate.

## December 5, 1984

**Paul H. Nitze is named special arms control adviser to Secretary of State Shultz.**

Larry Speakes, President Reagan's White House spokesman, announced Nitze's appointment, a significant gesture because it indicated the president backed George Shultz's flexible attitude toward arms control talks scheduled to begin with the Soviet Union on January 7, 1985.

Nitze was recognized as more willing to compromise with the Soviet Union than were former Defense Department arms control spokesmen such as Richard Perle. Previously, Nitze's so-called walk-in-the-woods proposals of 1982 had been rejected. Having Nitze as an adviser was unusual, but it gave Shultz a means to bypass the Arms Control and Disarmament Agency, the National Security Council, as well as Perle. Insiders saw this appointment as a victory by Shultz over Defense Secretary Caspar Weinberger, who opposed arms control.

See January 15, 1983.

## December 8, 1984

**The Reagan administration approves a visa for El Salvador's right-wing leader Roberto d'Aubuisson, having refused visas earlier for four Salvadoran human rights leaders.**

Because the Reagan administration had made an issue of denying U.S. visas to "undesirable" political persons, critics protested when d'Aubuisson, an alleged leader of El Salvador's death squads, received a visa in

June 1984 and again in December. This latter visa was particularly criticized because on November 12 the Reagan administration denied visas to four Salvadorans who had been invited to Boston to receive the Robert F. Kennedy Human Rights Award for their work among El Salvador's poor and underprivileged who had suffered at the hands of the "death squads."

It was to D'Aubuisson's advantage that he was the guest of Senator Jesse Helms, (R-N.C). Helms was a leading figure among the right-wing fundamentalists who supported Reagan's presidential campaigns. A view opposed to that of Helms had been expressed on February 2, 1984, by former U.S. Ambassador to El Salvador Robert E. White, who told a congressional committee that d'Aubuisson was involved in the 1980 murder of Archbishop Oscar Arnulfo.

## December 10, 1984

**Nicaragua and the United States conclude a round of talks at Manzanillo, Mexico.**

Since failing to agree on peace procedures during a series of talks after June 25, 1984, Nicaraguan-U.S. delegates continued to disagree at talks on November 19 and on December 10. After returning to Washington, the American delegates recommended a halt to further talks, and on January 18, 1985, the Reagan administration suspended discussions at Manzanillo. Generally, Nicaragua wanted to limit agreements to disarmament, and the United States wanted Nicaragua to accept obligations to democratize the government and be reconciled with its rebel groups. Nicaragua claimed those issues were internal matters not subject to international negotiation.

See also June 25 and September 25, 1984.

## December 13, 1984

**U.S. courts refuse to extradite an Irish Republican Army terrorist, claiming U.S. laws prohibit extradition for political crimes.**

The United Kingdom requested the extradition of Joseph Patrick Thomas Doherty for trial in the killing of a British soldier. Despite frequent U.S. complaints that other nations refused to extradite terrorists for trial, the American federal judge rejected the British request. Doherty escaped from a Belfast, Northern Ireland, prison in 1981 just before his conviction for murdering a British captain during an IRA ambush of a British army patrol in Northern Ireland. Nevertheless, the New York judge called the murder a political act, which was nonextraditable. Judge John E. Sprizzi ruled that although the IRA did not engage in traditional warfare, it had discipline and organization.

In London there were angry reactions. One conservative member of Parliament, Jill Knight, said the United States approved "murder, maiming and terrorism." Many Irish Americans condoned Irish terrorism, contributing money to the IRA.

See October 20, 1986.

### December 14, 1984

**The United States and Cuba agree to exchange persons involved in the 1980 boatlift.**

According to the agreement, Cuba would repatriate 2,746 Cuban criminals and mental patients sent to the United States in 1980; the United States would admit more political refugees and political prisoners, with preference being given to relatives of U.S citizens or of Cubans with permanent resident status in the United States. The agreement did not indicate whether Cuba would prosecute those returned under the agreement. This became an issue in the federal court of Atlanta, Georgia, where the return of excludable immigrants had stopped because of fear that they would be punished by Castro's government.

### December 18, 1984

**A California aerospace worker is arrested for selling Stealth bomber technology to the Soviet Union's Communist Party.**

Thomas Patrick Cavanaugh, a 40-year-old Northrop Corporation engineer, tried to sell the Stealth secrets to pay the heavy debts he owed. Cavanaugh was sentenced to life in prison on May 23, 1985.

### December 18, 1984

**U.S. Defense Department officials report that two U.S. reconnaissance planes provoked a major Soviet response.**

The U.S. reconnaissance planes were from two American aircraft carriers participating in the fleet's naval maneuvers in the Sea of Japan near the main Soviet Far Eastern base at Vladivostok. They provoked a Soviet response of more than 100 aircraft and warships to defend their far eastern bases.

During November 1984, Soviet military maneuvers had disturbed Japanese authorities. After 7 Soviet bombers flew into international airspace near South Korea and Japan, Japan's Defense Agency scrambled 32 jet planes to warn the Soviets, and Tokyo protested to the Soviet Union for violating Japan's airspace.

### December 18, 1984

**Soviet leader Mikhail Gorbachev visits Great Britain, gaining plaudits for advocating arms reductions.**

The 53-year-old Soviet leader, who was considered to be second in command in the Kremlin, won praise from the British public. Even Prime Minister Margaret Thatcher declared, "I like Mr. Gorbachev. We can do business together."

American diplomats were concerned about Britain's favorable reception of Gorbachev's talk about limiting the Strategic Defense Initiative (SDI) program promoted by President Reagan. French President François Mitterrand vigorously opposed Reagan's Strategic Defense Initiative (SDI), referring to it as unnecessary "overarming" and stimulating the militarization of space.

President Reagan frequently stated that the "Star Wars" program was not a negotiating topic with the Soviet Union. On December 29, White House officials said the United States would not limit SDI research but might restrain it if future negotiation limited both offensive and defensive weapons. Since his reelection in November, Reagan and his advisers had debated their future arms control policy.

### December 19, 1984

**The United States reaffirms its decision to withdraw from UNESCO on December 31, 1984.**

As was the case one year earlier when the Reagan administration announced the U.S. withdrawal, the White House said UNESCO's politicization continued because its leadership showed an "endemic hostility" toward a free society, especially to "those that protect a free press, free markets, and above all, individual human rights." Only if UNESCO returned to its original principles would the United States renew its membership.

Although Great Britain joined the United States by leaving UNESCO in 1985, UNESCO's secretary-general, Amadou-Mahtar M'Bow of Senegal, said the loss of U.S. revenue would have no adverse effect on the agency. Before December ended, West Germany and Singapore also left UNESCO.

### December 25, 1984

*Vietnam invades four Khmer Rouge rebel camps near the Thai border.*

During 1984, frequent skirmishes took place between Vietnamese and Khmer Rouge rebel forces along the Thai borderlands. On January 27 and 28, the Khmer captured Siern Reap before withdrawing to Thailand. On April 14, a Vietnamese offensive chased 100,000 Kampuchean (Cambodian) refugees fleeing over the border to Thailand. On December 25 and 26, the Vietnamese raided other Khmer camps, hoping to destroy them before the spring monsoons prevented the use of tanks and trucks to move Vietnam's army. The largest camp hit was at Rithisen, from which 60,000 civilians fled to Thailand.

### December 29, 1984

*OPEC ministers agree to new oil prices but reject production cuts.*

Throughout 1984, the members of the Organization of Petroleum Exporting Countries endeavored to prevent price reductions. At meetings on July 10 and 11 and again on October 29, they maintained existing prices but reduced production quotas after both the United Kingdom and Nigeria cut their prices.

On December 29, OPEC appointed a special panel to monitor member compliance with production and price levels but did not indicate what would be done if members did not comply. OPEC members wanted prices to be about $29 per barrel without reducing production.

See October 17, 1984.

# 1985

### January 2, 1985

**President Reagan and Japanese Prime Minister Nakasone discuss opening Japan's markets to more U.S. goods.**

During a meeting in California, the two leaders reached agreement for high-level efforts to end Japan's obstructions of U.S. imports. As the U.S. trade imbalance reached over $150 billion per year and the U.S. national debt soared from $1 trillion in 1981 to nearly $2 trillion during 1985, the United States needed to export more manufactured goods. At the same time, however, Japanese banking leaders helped the United States finance its debt by placing $50 billion of Japanese overseas investments in U.S. Treasury securities.

See April 9, 1985.

### January 5, 1985

**Jordan buys Soviet antiaircraft weapons and denounces the United States for refusing to sell to it.**

Jordanian army Chief of Staff General Sharif Zaid bin Shaki said this purchase was made because the United States refused to sell weapons to Jordan for its mobile defense force. Jordan obtained Soviet shoulder-fired antiaircraft weapons resembling the Stingers whose sale President Reagan had canceled owing to opposition from Congress and the Israeli lobby.

See March 14, 1984, and November 12, 1985.

### January 8, 1985

**A fifth American hostage is seized by Muslim terrorists in Beirut.**

The Reverend Martin Laurence Jenco, director of Catholic Relief Services in Beirut, was kidnapped by the Islamic Jihad, a radical Shiite group. He was the fifth American captured since March 16, 1984, when William Buckley was taken. Other Americans held by terrorists were the Presbyterian missionary Benjamin Weir, the CNN American bureau chief Jeremy Levin, and a librarian at American University in Beirut, Peter Kilburn, captured on December 3, 1984. On February

Japanese Prime Minister Yasuhiro Nakasone discusses measures to lessen the Japan-U.S. trade imbalance with President Reagan at his ranch. Ronald Reagan Library

14, Levin escaped and the Syrian army returned him to U.S. officials.

Generally, the Reagan administration and the media played down the fate of these hostages. On January 22, 1985, there was a flurry of news reports on the captives after a video tape appeared in which Buckley appealed to Washington to act for their quick release. The kidnappers demanded the release of 17 Shiite Muslims held in Kuwait for terrorist attacks on the U.S. and French embassies in Kuwait. The Reagan administration and Kuwait refused this demand.

Subsequently, in 1985, three other Americans were kidnapped—Terry A. Anderson, an Associated Press reporter, on March 16; David P. Jacobsen, director of the American University Hospital, on May 28; and Thomas M. Sutherland, dean of agriculture at American University, on June 9, 1985. Yet, in September, one hostage was freed.

See also May 6, 1984, and September 18, 1985.

## January 8, 1985

### The United States and the Soviet Union agree to resume arms control negotiations.

Secretary of State George P. Shultz and Soviet Foreign Minister Andrey A. Gromyko concluded two days of talks in Geneva by announcing that their nations would renew negotiations on nuclear weapons, which had broken off in 1983. The new talks would combine discussions on intermediate-range (INF) and intercontinental (ICBM) nuclear weapons, as the United States preferred. As a U.S. concession, the talks would include the arms race in space, an issue prompted by President Reagan's Strategic Defense Initiative (SDI).

In September 1984, Reagan indicated that the United States could accept restrictions on antisatellite tests (ASAT) if the talks included both offensive and defensive weapons. During December 1984, news leaks from Reagan administration officials reported a controversy over the future SDI program. Several officials told reporters that the advanced SDI program might be abandoned if the Soviets made concessions on offensive missiles. On December 22, Reagan's science advisers reported that SDI had been scaled back to the more modest goal of protecting U.S. ICBM missiles. The next day, however, Secretary of Defense Caspar Weinberger denied this report, reaffirming that SDI's objective was to defend the entire nation from enemy nuclear missiles, and it was not a bargaining chip in arms talks.

At present, SDI's only function was to defend the ICBMs by destroying Soviet missiles entering the earth's atmosphere over North America. This made it an antiballistic missile (ABM), which was restricted by the 1972 ABM treaty. Weinberger did not want the ABM question raised with the Soviets, even though major scientific and technological breakthroughs were necessary before SDI could destroy enemy missiles immediately after launching or while in their midcourse trajectory in space.

Gromyko seemed ready to discuss other missiles without agreement on SDI even though, on January 13, he told a television interviewer that an arms agreement depended on U.S. limitations on SDI. Neither Shultz nor Gromyko made statements about ASAT tests.

See November 23, 1983, and February 11, 1985.

### January 10, 1985

**The United States and the European Economic Community set new quotas on European steel tubes and pipes exported to America.**

U.S. Special Trade Representative William Brock negotiated this agreement with representatives of the ten-member European Economic Community (EEC). It ended an embargo that President Reagan had placed on the importation of European steel pipes and tubing. The EEC would limit its U.S. exports to 7.6% of the American steel demand, a percentage that could change only if there were a short supply of U.S.-made steel. The Congressional Budget Office calculated that the restrictions on steel imports would cost American consumers $18 billion per year in products made with more costly American steel.

See November 27, 1984, and November 1, 1985.

### January 11, 1985

**Canada denies reports that U.S. nuclear weapons would deploy in Canada during a war.**

Following a report from U.S experts that nuclear weapons would be based in Canada if war broke out involving the United States, opposition to the plan spread throughout Canada. The Canadian government stated that it had not known about these plans, but opposition parties remained skeptical. At this time, U.S. and Canadian military leaders conducted talks about modernizing the Arctic Circle network of North American radar stations. On January 24, 1985, they agreed to spend $1.2 billion on improving the radar network to detect low-flying aircraft. Some Canadians opposed this action, largely because they feared that the U.S. Strategic Defense Initiative destabilized relations with the Soviet Union and endangered Canadian security.

### January 14, 1985

**Rights of political asylum are challenged when federal prosecutors arrest 16 persons assisting Central American refugees.**

The Reagan administration welcomed refugees fleeing from the Sandinistas in Nicaragua and Fidel Castro's Cuba, but when underground groups in the United States helped refugees fleeing persecution from the governments of Guatemala and El Salvador, which were aided by Washington, the Department of Justice harassed and finally arrested those who provided sanctuary to the refugees.

On January 14, federal officials arrested three nuns, two priests, a Protestant minister, and ten volunteers accused of helping "illegal immigrants" in regions from Arizona to New York. They also arrested 60 aliens as unindicted coconspirators for violating the law. The Reagan administration claimed refugees from Guatemala and El Salvador came to the United States for economic reasons, not from fear of persecution.

On May 1, 1986, the defendants were convicted of smuggling illegal immigrants. The Reverend John Fife, the Presbyterian minister who founded the Sanctuary Movement, received five years in prison; eight others got lesser sentences; all said they would continue their Christian mission.

### January 15, 1985

*Brazil chooses its first civilian president in 21 years.*

Leader of the opposition Democratic Alliance Party, Tancredo de Almeida Neves defeated the Social Democratic candidate, Paulo Salim Maluf. Direct presidential elections were to be conducted in 1988. Neves's term of office was cut short, however, by his death on April 21. Vice President Jose Sarney replaced him.

### January 20, 1985

**Ronald Reagan is sworn in to begin his second term as president.**

President Reagan's second inaugural address focused on his popularity in winning a second term and having overseen two years of economic growth. He proposed to continue America's military buildup against "totalitarian darkness" while hoping to see all nuclear weapons eliminated from the earth, seemingly incompatible goals.

### January 23, 1985

**The 24-hour delay of the *Discovery* space shuttle mission dramatizes its shift to military missions.**

*Discovery*'s military mission had been discussed since December 19, 1984, when a *Washington Post* article used "leaked" information describing the electronic intelligence signals that would come from a satellite carried into space. After Secretary of Defense Caspar Weinberger accused the *Post* of "irresponsible journalism," the *Post* editors replied that all published data came from sources outside the Pentagon and that the *Post* had, in fact, withheld data it found sensitive to the national security.

On January 22 and 23, U.S. army generals in Florida were dismayed when the military mission was delayed by cold weather because military missions should be operable whenever required. More crucial, observers noted that Reagan's "Star Wars" program caused the overall expenditures for space programs to become military missions. Prior to 1982, the National Aeronautics and Space Administration's (NASA) budget had aimed primarily at civilian and scientific projects. Since then the Defense Department spent $12.9 billion on space shuttle projects. NASA had $6.8 billion for projects, of which one-fourth supported Pentagon needs.

### January 24, 1985

**President Reagan denounces Iran's foreign minister for assisting Nicaragua's military buildup.**

When Reagan denounced Iran for assisting Nicaragua, the news media gave little attention because it was directly connected to the "Reagan Doctrine" that President Reagan announced previously regarding subversive warfare to overthrow totalitarian communist regimes in Nicaragua and other Third World countries (see entry for October 24, 1983).

What Reagan did not disclose in October 1983 were plans to secretly use a few members of the National Security Council (NSC) to bypass the State Department and the Central Intelligence Agency. In 1982, this inner circle of the NSC staff undertook secret parts of Reagan's "Project Democracy" to begin private initiatives that would not be reported to Congress as part of the CIA's annual report on its activities.

Secretary of State George Shultz first heard of the secret projects during the Spring of 1985, three months after Reagan denounced Iran's aid to Nicaragua. In mid-April 1985, Shultz learned Israel had informed the White House that Iran wanted American made TOW anti-tank missiles to use in its war against Iraq (see September 4, 1980). Shultz also learned the White House NSC staff had already sent 100 TOW missiles to Iran in exchange for the release of American hostages (see January 8, 1985).

In memoirs published in 1993, Shultz indicates he opposed the White House policy regarding the exchange of arms to Iran for the release of hostages. "In four major battles between mid-1985 and Fall 1986," Shultz writes, "I had fought to stop such a deal and each time I felt—or had been assured that—my view had prevailed. But this snake never died, no matter how many times I hacked at it."

The final story of Reagan's "Project Democracy" for Iran and Nicaragua was not revealed until 1986 (see November 3, 1986 and successive entries).

**January 24, 1985**

***Time* magazine is found not guilty of libel charges filed by Israeli Defense Minister Ariel Sharon regarding the 1982 massacres at Sabra and Shatila.**

The trial decision actually allowed both *Time* and Sharon to claim victory. Although the jury found the February 21, 1983 *Time* story false in saying Sharon had encouraged the Lebanese Phalangists to massacre Palestinians, the jury also ruled that *Time* had not acted with "actual malice."

On the massacres in Lebanon, see September 18, 1982.

**January 26, 1985**

***Pope John Paul II visits Latin America, and denounces "liberation theology," which many Roman Catholic priests advocate.***

The Roman pontiff visited Venezuela, Ecuador, Peru, and Trinidad between January 26 and February 5, 1985. During the visits it became clear that John Paul emphasized hierarchical organization by which the Roman Catholic Church decided what teachings were to be communicated to the faithful. This view had prevailed for centuries until the Second Vatican Council of the 1960s, which viewed the church as "the people of God," with a theology that developed from problems people experienced. The latter view was accepted by Catholic "liberation theologians" such as Friar Leonardo Boff of Brazil and priests and layworkers working to improve the lower classes' economic security.

**January 28, 1985**

***OPEC members cut oil price against objections by Algeria, Libya, Iran, and Gabon.***

Despite outward unity during their Geneva conference, the Organization of Petroleum Exporting Countries remained divided on the key issues of production quotas and crude oil prices. While OPEC's majority, headed by Saudi Arabia's oil minister, Sheik Ahmed Zaki Yamani, wanted prices to remain at $28 per barrel, nations seeking greater oil sales preferred lower prices. Lower prices cut U.S. gasoline costs by seven cents per gallon in early 1985 to $1.24 for regular unleaded gasoline. The low price, however, hurt debtor nations such as Nigeria and non-OPEC

member Mexico, because they received insufficient income to pay their foreign debts.

**February 4, 1985**

**New Zealand bans the U.S. navy destroyer U.S.S. *Buchanan* from its ports unless it carries no nuclear weapons. Australia also opposes U.S. nuclear policy.**

Under the ANZUS Treaty of Mutual Security (Australia–New Zealand–U.S. alliance), U.S. naval ships frequently visited New Zealand's ports during naval exercises in the South Pacific. Recently, however, intense opposition developed in New Zealand and Australia to the potential danger of nuclear weapons. Thus, Washington realized that those nations might close their ports to ships using nuclear weapons, but it had refused to indicate which of its vessels carried those weapons.

On July 14, 1984, New Zealand's Labor Party, headed by Prime Minister David Lange, was elected on a platform that opposed nuclear weapons on New Zealand territory. Consequently, after Lange blocked the U.S. destroyer, the value of the ANZUS alliance became doubtful. On February 26, 1985, the United States canceled naval exercises scheduled with New Zealand and reduced its military and intelligence cooperation with that country. Australia also opposed U.S. nuclear policy. On February 5, it abrogated a pledge to assist tests of U.S. MX missiles; on March 4, it canceled a meeting of the ANZUS Security Council scheduled for July.

**February 7, 1985**

**Because of Chile's human rights violations, the United States abstains from approving a loan to Chile.**

Although the Reagan administration tried quiet diplomacy to persuade Chile's President Augusto Pinochet to make his regime more democratic, the efforts had failed thus far. Washington disapproved of a proposed bank loan because of Chile's human rights violations. The State Department's February report on human rights indicated a deterioration of rights because 58 people died and 515 were injured in violence in Chile during 1984.

### February 8, 1985

**President Reagan names General Vernon Walters to be U.S. ambassador to the United Nations.**

The former ambassador, Jeane J. Kirkpatrick, had resigned on January 30, 1985. The U.S. Senate confirmed Walters on May 16, 1985. Walters shared Kirkpatrick's hard-line views against the Soviet Union but was less independent-minded than his predecessor in expressing extreme prejudices against those with whom he disagreed.

### February 11, 1985

**President Reagan declares that the SDI program will continue even if an offensive arms control agreement is reached with the Soviet Union.**

Although the January 8 communiqué of Secretary of State George Shultz and Soviet Foreign Minister Andrey Gromyko indicated an arms race in space should be avoided, President Reagan defended the need to pursue the Strategic Defense Initiative (SDI) to provide a defense against enemy missiles aimed at the United States.

Reagan contended that space defense should not be confused with nuclear arms control, even though many strategic analysts said that SDI would offset Soviet offensive intercontinental ballistic missiles. In a dubious analogy, Reagan said that SDI resembled gas masks in the 1930s because after the 1925 ban on chemical weapons, nations still prepared for poisonous gas attacks if war were to begin. He did not continue the analogy by saying the masks were superfluous despite all the destruction of World War II.

See January 8, 1985.

### February 11, 1985

**Saudi King Fahd visits Washington but concludes no major agreement.**

Fahd's visit was symbolic as the first visit of a Saudi king since 1971. President Reagan wanted the Saudi ruler to use his influence on Arabs in Egypt, Kuwait, Iraq, Qatar, the United Arab Emirates, and Saudi Arabia making peace with Israel, but Fahd wanted the United States to use its influence to pressure Israel to make concessions on a peace agreement.

General Vernon Walters with President Reagan. Ronald Reagan Library

## February 11, 1985

*Jordanian King Hussein and PLO leader Yasser Arafat agree on principles for peace with Israel.*

Since September 1, 1982, when President Reagan proposed a "Jordanian solution" to settle the Israeli-Palestinian question, Washington had anticipated some clear response from KING HUSSEIN and the Palestine Liberation Organization's Yasser Arafat. The February 11 statement by the two Arab leaders was ambiguous but hopeful. Apparently, Hussein and Arafat would negotiate with Israel on the basis of U.N. resolutions 242 and 338. They would guarantee to prevent violence against Israel in return for land to create a Palestinian state on the West Bank of the Jordan River.

American and Israeli reactions were as expected. When Hussein visited the United States on May 29, 1985, Washington saw possibilities but requested clarifications. Israel's two major parties were divided—the conservative Likud Party refusing to exchange land for peace, the liberal Labor Party wanting to keep the door open for talks.

## February 12, 1985

*In South Korean elections, the New Korea Democratic Party wins 67 seats.*

The elections not only affirmed the leadership of President Chun Doo Hwan but also signaled the rise of Kim Dae Jung's newly formed New Korea Democratic Party.

Kim's party was formed in January 1985 while Kim awaited his return from two years of exile in the United States. When Kim arrived at the airport in Seoul on February 8, he was seized and placed under house arrest despite the presence of 37 Americans who had accompanied him as a protective measure. Although the government prohibited Kim from campaigning, his party won 67 seats while the old Democratic Korea Party lost 46 seats. Kim wanted to unite opponents of Chun Doo Hwan's government.

## February 21, 1985

*The USSR permits the International Atomic Energy Commission (IAEC) to make on-site inspection of its nuclear plants.*

For the first time, the Soviet Union allowed the IAEC to inspect civilian power plants using nuclear reactors. Although some critics indicated the agreement permitted inspection only of older plants and not the most advanced Soviet models, the United States praised the new policy as a step toward opening Soviet society.

## February 25, 1985

**President Reagan calls Nicaraguan rebels "the moral equal of the Founding Fathers."**

In early 1985, Reagan undertook a major public relations campaign to obtain congressional backing for the Contra rebels fighting Nicaragua's Sandinista government. His most exaggerated effort came on February 25, when he told a group of conservative supporters that the Contras were the equivalent of America's Founding Fathers.

Such language left members of Congress skeptical of Reagan's motives and his deficient knowledge of American history in comparing George Washington to the Contra leader, who was a former officer of Nicaragua's dictator Anastasio Somoza's National Guard and who used the guerrilla manual compiled by the CIA. In other speeches during February, Reagan called the Contras "our brothers" and "freedom fighters" like Simón Bolívar. In contrast to his support for the Contras, on February 28 Reagan criticized Nicaragua for sending 100 Cuban advisers home as an attempt to influence the U.S. Congress, not as a step for peace.

See October 15, 1984, and April 24, 1985.

## February 25, 1985

*In elections to Pakistan's National Assembly, center parties make some gains.*

These were the first assembly elections since President Muhammad Zia ul-Haq disbanded the assembly in 1977. On March 10, President Zia reinstated the

1973 constitution but omitted sections regarding personal freedom, judicial powers, and subversion.

During the election, President Zia banned political parties, rallies, and loudspeakers. Nevertheless, despite a boycott by some opponents, nearly 53% of the electorate voted, defeating seven members of Zia's cabinet and many lower-level candidates. Zia said he would permit freer elections in the future. Nevertheless, on August 29, 1985, when Benazir Bhutto, daughter of Zulfikar Ali-Bhutto, former president of Pakistan who was overthrown in 1973, returned to Pakistan from exile in America on August 29, 1985, she was placed under house arrest.

### February 28, 1985

#### Irish terrorists kill nine police officers by firing a barrage at police barracks.

The Irish Republican Army (IRA) began killing Irish Protestants in Belfast on January 15 when a man joy-riding in a car was shot and killed. On February 1, the IRA shot and killed a bus driver, and on May 3, a Royal Ulster Constabulary officer was murdered by an IRA terrorist.

The worst among these IRA attacks took place on February 28, when IRA terrorists fired a barrage of gun rounds at the Constabulary barrack's office in Belfast. The barrage killed nine police officers, making a total of 12 Irish Protestants being killed during the first months of 1985. Because IRA terrorists covered their faces with masks, the culprits were seldom caught and arrested.

### March 1, 1985

#### A Defense Department report says a nuclear war may cause climatic disaster, but this does not affect defense policies.

A 17-page study titled "The Potential Effect of Nuclear War on Climate" was issued by the Pentagon in response to claims about "NUCLEAR WINTER" raised by the astronomer Carl Sagan and other environmentalists. Although admitting climatic disaster was possible, the booklet said the Soviet Union used the concept of "nuclear winter" as propaganda, a veiled implication that some American scientists were "tools" of Moscow. Moreover, the Pentagon claimed that its current nuclear deterrent policy, including the development of a spaced-based defense, was the best means to prevent a nuclear war.

See November 1, 1983.

### March 3, 1985

#### The Pentagon abandons plans for civil defense evacuation of U.S. cities.

Although some Reagan administration advisers in 1981 desired to match the Soviet Union's alleged plans to evacuate cities to survive a "protracted nuclear war," previous funds spent on this were wasted when the Pentagon dropped the Crisis Relocation Plan. Defense Department officials said that congressional budget cuts prevented further expenditures. The "Crisis Relocation Plan" was designed to accelerate the evacuation of America's largest cities prior to a nuclear attack. This was part of a larger Pentagon plan to build blast shelters and concrete underground structures to withstand the impact of a nuclear bomb on. Originally, the Pentagon estimated the cost of real estate and bomb shelters at $10 billion, a large portion of the Department of Defense budget.

See March 31, 1982.

### March 5, 1985

#### In Cambodia (Kampuchea), Vietnam wins a third major victory on Thailand's border.

Supporting its appointed Cambodian government, Vietnam continued fighting against guerrilla forces of the Khmer Rouge in the jungles along the Thai border. On January 8, the Vietnamese captured the main headquarters of the Khmer People's National Liberation Front, forcing them to retreat into Thai refugee camps. On February 15, the Vietnamese took over the Khmer Rouge headquarters camp near Thailand. Finally, on March 5, the Vietnamese overran the headquarters of Cambodian guerrillas who supported the exiled Prince Norodom Sihanouk, causing Thailand to denounce Vietnam for crossing its border, a charge Hanoi denied.

These Vietnamese victories led to U.S. aid to "noncommunist" rebels in Cambodia. President Reagan requested assistance from Congress on April 9, 1985. Subsequently, the foreign aid bill signed on August 8 allocated funds to Cambodian guerrillas.

### March 6, 1985

**An American drug enforcement agent is murdered in Mexico, causing friction between Mexico and the United States.**

On February 7, the U.S. agent Enrique Camarena Salazar and his Mexican pilot were kidnapped in Guadalajara, Mexico, while investigating the involvement of high-level Mexican officials in drug smuggling. One week later, on February 15, the United States ordered a massive manhunt along the border, accusing Mexico of not moving to capture the criminals.

Camarena and his pilot were found dead on March 6, and by March 14, Mexico said it had arrested 13 persons including 3 police officials. The U.S. Drug Enforcement Agency, claiming that high-level Mexican authorities protecting the drug dealers remained at large, continued to investigate the case.

### March 8, 1985

*A car bomb explodes in Beirut, killing 80 people but missing its intended victim, Sheikh Fadlallah, a radical shiite.*

The car bomb exploded a few yards from the home of Sheikh Muhammad Hussein Fadlallah, a Lebanese Shiite militant rumored to have been in charge of the bombing of the U.S. Marine barracks in Beirut in 1983. Because a bomb also exploded on March 4 at a Shiite mosque in the southern Lebanese village of Marakah, killing 11 people, the Lebanese Muslims blamed Israel and the United States, while staging demonstrations in Beirut and threatening to retaliate. To show the flag and prevent retaliation, the Reagan administration dispatched the aircraft carrier *Eisenhower* and an escort cruiser to the coast of Lebanon.

According to *Washington Post* reporter Bob Woodward, part of this tragedy was that the March 8 bombing was an attempt by the U.S. Central Intelligence Agency to kill Fadlallah. Woodward claims that CIA director William Casey had been working with agents of Saudi Arabia to punish Fadlallah for bombing the marine barracks. The Saudis hired a member of Great Britain's Elite Commando Unit to plan the attack. The car filled with explosives came to within 50 yards of Fadlallah's residence but did not injure him. It killed instead 80 Lebanese and wounded 200 others.

Following the failure of the attack, Woodward says, the Saudi government paid Sheikh Fadlallah $2 million not to attack Americans.

See October 23, 1983.

### March 10, 1985

*Soviet leader Konstantin Chernenko dies of heart failure. He is replaced by Mikhail S. Gorbachev the next day.*

President Chernenko had been ill throughout his 13 months as Soviet leader. His state funeral was perfunctory. Only hours after his death Soviet Foreign Minister Andrey A. Gromyko, one of the few surviving Stalinists, nominated Gorbachev as Communist Party General Secretary. To Vice President George Bush, who represented the United States at Chernenko's funeral, and to other foreign dignitaries, Gorbachev indicated that his first priority would be to improve the Soviet economy. He wanted to return to the détente spirit of the early 1970s by having better relations with the United States and Western Europe. Gorbachev also sought to restructure the Soviet economy (perestroika) and to promote more openness (glasnost) in Soviet society.

### March 21, 1985

**Japan voluntarily ceiling increases auto exports to the United States.**

Since 1981, the Reagan administration had attempted to get Japan to limit its automobile exports to the United States. Although Japan agreed to reduce its auto exports in 1982, Tokyo refused to end tariffs and other trade barriers on possible American imports, a principal factor resulting in a large trade imbalance between the United States and Japan (see November 10, 1982).

On March 21, 1985, Japan announced it would voluntarily restrict its auto exports to America. Nevertheless, Japan's new voluntary ceiling on these auto exports was actually a 24.3% increase relative to its auto exports between 1981 and 1984. After American automobile manufacturers condemned Japan's so-called "new ceiling," the United States Senate passed a resolution branding Japan an "unfair trader." Immediately afterward, senators from states where automobiles were manufactured introduced protective tariff legislation against Japanese imports, but the United States Congress did not approve any protective tariff legislation against Japan.

### March 22, 1985

**Reports are leaked that U.S. military planes flew Ethiopian Jews to Israel.**

On January 3, 1985, Israel reported that it had airlifted Jews for five years without permission from Ethiopia's government. Ethiopia denounced this scheme, and Israel agreed on January 5 to stop the airlifts. On March 22, newsmen learned that U.S. aircraft had replaced the Israelis in airlifting Jews. The *Los Angeles Times* reported that the CIA had rescued 10,000 Ethiopian Jews between January 3 and March 20, an operation U.S. Senate leaders approved in a secret letter to President Reagan.

### March 24, 1985

**A Soviet sentry kills an American officer on surveillance in East Germany.**

Major Arthur D. Nicholson Jr. was shot by the sentry near a small town outside Berlin. Nicholson and a companion, Sergeant Jesse G. Schatz, were on a routine reconnaissance mission permitted by the Big-Four power accords with Germany at the end of World War II. The shooting was debated for several months afterward because U.S. and Soviet versions of the event differed. The Soviets said Nicholson was spying in an off-limits zone. When warned by the Soviet guard, Nicholson was said to have fled and was shot. Sergeant Schatz was in a nearby car.

To the contrary, the Americans claimed the two officers were in a car 300 to 500 yards outside a zone whose off-limits status had ended on February 20, 1985. It was not known why the Soviet guard fired three shots at the American car, killing Nicholson. For over one hour, the Soviets did not allow the U.S. major to receive first aid.

Although President Reagan expressed outrage at the shooting, he told reporters that plans for a summit with Soviet leader Mikhail Gorbachev would continue. He declared that such incidents made meetings with Gorbachev even more essential.

### March 29, 1985

*Spain and Portugal are admitted to the European Economic Community (EEC).*

Discussions about the admission of these two countries to the EEC had been underway for six years before agreement was reached on March 29. A treaty formalizing this act was signed on June 12, and their admission became effective on January 1, 1986. With the addition of Spain and Portugal, the EEC had 12 member nations.

### March 31, 1985

*In El Salvador, President Duarte's Christian Democratic Party defeats right-wing parties, gaining 33 of 60 National Assembly seats.*

Although there were charges of corruption in this election, the Salvadoran army backed Duarte's claim that the errors were of little significance. The right-wing party of Roberto d'Aubuisson was the loser, although it retained power in the military. The United States had promoted Duarte's reelection as a sign that El Salvador was more democratic. Duarte said he would try to negotiate peace with his opponents.

### April 2, 1985

**The Defense Department's fourth edition of *Soviet Military Power* accuses the USSR of a large-scale military buildup.**

As in three previous reports during the Reagan administration, the Pentagon warned of the Kremlin's aggressive military expansion. Defense Secretary Caspar Weinberger presented portions of the 143-page report on a satellite television hookup with Western Europe and Japan. Important parts of the report said that the Soviets were ready to deploy SS-24s launched from railroad cars, each carrying 10 nuclear warheads; had launched 2 new Delta-IV class submarines with 16 SS-NA-23 missiles each; had added five divisions to their ground forces; and supplied Nicaragua with 17,000 metric tons of military supplies.

On February 1, 1985, and again on December 23, the Reagan administration issued reports on Soviet violations of arms control agreements. Most knowledgeable observers recognized these reports as propaganda aimed at influencing the American people and

Congress to support the Reagan military buildup and to avoid arms control agreements.

### April 6, 1985

*The government of Sudan is overthrown because of austerity measures imposed by the International Monetary Fund (IMF).*

On June 25, 1984, the government of President Gaafar al-Nimeiry accepted IMF economic requirements to obtain a $90 million loan. Since then, Nimeiry had curbed subsidies on food that increased food prices, limited credit for purchasing imports, and devalued the Sudanese currency. The drought affecting this region and the influx of refugees from Chad and Ethiopia exacerbated public dissatisfaction as expressed in protests and strikes.

As a result, on April 6, Sudan's army conducted a coup d'état and the Defense Minister Abd al-Rahman Siwar al-Dahab took power. U.S. loans to the Sudan were cut off, causing greater problems for the new government. One result of this difficulty was that the Sudan looked to Libya's Mu'ammar al-Gadhafi for help, restoring full diplomatic relations with Libya on April 24. On July 8, the Sudan began receiving military aid from Libya, which made the Reagan administration express "grave concern" for the Sudan's future.

### April 7, 1985

**Soviet leader Mikhail Gorbachev declares a moratorium on deployment of Soviet intermediate-range missiles; the United States objects.**

In an interview with the Communist Party paper *Pravda*, Gorbachev said he wanted to speed up the Geneva arms talks by stopping the deployment of Soviet SS-20s targeted for Europe. Gorbachev's interview was part of a peace offensive that made him popular in Western Europe. He followed it on May 27 by blaming the Reagan administration's Strategic Defense Initiative for making arms control impossible. He also expressed the hope of meeting with President Reagan in the near future.

Though the Reagan administration opposed the moratorium because it would leave Moscow with an eight-to-one advantage over the United States in intermediate-range missiles, the idea of a meeting was acceptable to the president because in March

1985 Reagan had written Gorbachev a letter to suggest talks.

On the SDIs, see February 11, 1985; on the peace offensive, see July 29, 1985.

### April 9, 1985

*Prime Minister Yasuhiro Nakasone urges Japanese consumers to buy more foreign goods.*

During a television address in which he announced liberalized trade regulations to benefit imports of pharmaceuticals and telecommunications equipment, Nakasone asked the Japanese to "Buy American," a request consonant with his agreements with President Reagan but difficult to fulfill because the Japanese were not accustomed to purchasing items that the United States exported.

Twice more in 1985, Nakasone took steps to open Japanese markets to foreign goods. On July 30, he ordered 88 measures to relax restrictions on imports. On October 15, he stimulated domestic demand by providing incentives for housing construction, consumer credits, and public works projects using foreign-made equipment. These measures had no immediate effect on the level of U.S. exports, but Nakasone tried. Changing Japanese consumer habits was another problem.

See January 2, 1985.

### April 11, 1985

*Albanian leader Enver Hoxha dies and is replaced by Ramiz Alia.*

Under Hoxha, Albania became isolated from the rest of the world for over 40 years. An orthodox communist, Hoxha broke with the Soviet Union in 1961 and supported mainland China. The new ruler, Ramiz Alia, continued the policy of isolation; no foreigners were invited to Hoxha's funeral.

### April 11, 1985

**The United States cancels a naval visit to China, denying it promised to send no ships that carried nuclear weapons.**

On January 11, 1985, in response to an invitation from the People's Republic of China, Washington scheduled a naval visit for May 13, 1985. The United States canceled the visit on April 11, the day after Beijing reported a U.S. pledge to send no ships with nuclear weapons.

The U.S. navy was sensitive about identifying which warships carried nuclear weapons. Identification became an issue because U.S. allies such as Japan, New Zealand, and Australia allowed nonnuclear ships to visit their ports but wanted to block those carrying nuclear weapons.

See February 4, 1985.

## April 16, 1985

### Fighting among rival Muslim factions nearly brings down Lebanon's government.

Efforts during 1984 to establish a combined Christian-Muslim government (see June 23, 1984) foundered during 1985 because of divisions among various Muslim groups.

On April 16, Amal Shiite military groups attacked and defeated a combination of Palestinian and Sunni Mourabitoun Muslim forces after heavy fighting. This caused Muslim Prime Minister Rashid Karami and his cabinet to resign. Because Syria backed the coalition of Christian President Amin Gemayel and Karami, Damascus persuaded Karami to stay in office.

Nevertheless, problems continued in Lebanon. The Amal Shiites led by Nabih Berri had become Lebanon's largest religious group, with 1 million followers, compared with the 650,000 Sunni Muslims and 650,000 Christian Maronites. The Shiites were not represented in the Gemayel-Karami coalition.

See June 7 and December 28, 1985.

## April 24, 1985

### The House of Representatives rejects President Reagan's request for aid to the Contras.

Despite the president's public relations promotion of the Contra rebels as "our brothers," whom he likened to America's "Founding Fathers," Congress rejected these efforts. Reagan's claim to have support from Pope John Paul and Latin American leaders in seeking peace in Nicaragua had been denied by the Vatican and the Latin Americans, a ploy that further polarized the president's opposition.

Finally, a secret report to Congress implying that U.S. forces might be used if "other policy alternatives failed" had the negative consequence of justifying the worst fears of Congress that a new "Vietnam" was being readied. For all these reasons, the House voted

against President Reagan's request for $14 million of aid to the Contras. As it turned out, however, Nicaraguan President Daniel Ortega's decision to visit Moscow on April 28 enabled Reagan to get the aid.

See February 25, May 1, and August 8, 1985.

## April 26, 1985

### Warsaw Pact members agree to a 20-year extension of their alliance.

Soviet leader Mikhail Gorbachev presided over the meeting of the communist-bloc powers. During the session, Gorbachev called on Western European nations to restrain their deployment of missiles and to help eliminate the danger of "nuclear extinction" if war should occur.

## May 1, 1985

### President Reagan places a trade embargo on Nicaragua.

Alleging that Nicaragua's policies were an "extraordinary threat" to the nation, Reagan stopped all trade to that country effective May 7, 1985. He also prohibited Nicaraguan aircraft or ships from entering the United States. While this action hurt the Nicaraguan economy, it also helped the Sandinista government obtain economic aid not only from the Soviet Union but also from U.S. allies who disagreed with Reagan's policies.

See November 12, 1985.

## May 2, 1985

### Annual economic summit of seven industrial nations convenes in Bonn. Discussion of trade agreements begins.

Again, as in recent annual summits, this meeting of seven heads of state symbolized their cooperative economic efforts, even though they disagreed on policy details. President Reagan wanted a commitment to schedule a new round of GATT trade liberalization talks, but the French objected and refused to accept a specific date to begin those negotiations. The French said that clarification about a specific agenda needed to precede formal trade talks.

Reagan also failed to get allied support for his Strategic Defense Initiative program. Although West Germany and Italy indicated interest in the proposal, neither the French nor the British would make a commitment as "subcontractors." Reagan had offered to distribute some research projects to U.S. allies to obtain their backing.

See November 28, 1985.

### May 5, 1985

#### President Reagan visits the military cemetery at Bitburg, Germany, arousing a storm of controversy.

Widespread controversy arose on April 11, 1985, when President Reagan's White House spokesman announced Reagan would visit a German cemetery in Bitburg during his European trip in May. In reaction to this announcement, Nathan Perlmutter, the National Director of the Anti-Defamation League of B'nai B'rith told a *Washington Post* reporter "I think this visit to a cemetery of German soldiers is an act of grace because it is good to express friendship to a former enemy. But the asymmetry of doing this while choosing not to visit the graves of that enemy's victims is insensitive, and it not a healing act."

On April 12, the controversy heated up over Bitburg when it was revealed that Bitburg graves included at least 49 graves of members of the Waffen SS, the military arm of the Waffen whose members served as Hitler's bodyguards, committed atrocities against civilians, and ran the concentration camps where millions perished during the Nazi regime.

Secretary of State George Shultz's 1993 memoir provides details about the controversy surrounding the Bitburg visit. He explains how Reagan decided to visit the graves of Holocaust victims at Bergen-Belsen as well as the Bitburg cemetery; Chancellor Helmut Kohl sent messages to Reagan urging him not to cancel the Bitburg visit because it would result in the fall of Kohl's majority in the West German Reichstag; and many U.S. citizens, as well as European leaders such as British Prime Minister Margaret Thatcher and Italian Prime Minister Betino Craxi, reacted negatively to the visit. Shutz also describes Reagan's visit to Bergen-Belsen, where President and Mrs Nancy Reagan walked among the mounds of earth thrown over mass graves, including the grave of Anne Frank.

Before leaving Germany, Reagan also visited the U.S. Air Force Base at Bitburg. Reagan told crowds at the Air Force base that "Some old wounds have been reopened, and that I regret very much because this should be a time of healing." To Holocaust survivors, Reagan said "Your terrible suffering has made you ever vigilant against evil. I promise we will never forget."

### May 9, 1985

#### The United States and Japan plan jointly to build a space station.

This agreement was for the preliminary design of a space station to be built by the United States. Japan would develop plans for a laboratory module and outside work deck for the station at a cost of $22 million. The station would carry six to eight astronauts. On April 16, the U.S. National Aeronautics and Space Administration also signed an agreement with Canada for construction of a solar cell generator for a space platform at a cost of $8.8 million.

### May 20, 1985

#### The U.S. Information Agency begins broadcasting on Radio Marti, sending news programs to Cuban audiences.

At President Reagan's request in 1983, Congress approved the broadcasting of Voice of America programs to Cuba. The radio's opening was delayed because of problems in getting a director and qualified staff. On May 20, Radio Marti began broadcasts to Cuba for $14\frac{1}{2}$ hours per day.

Cuba objected to the invasion of its air and communications space and retaliated in two ways—first, by jamming the broadcasts; second, by suspending a 1984 agreement allowing up to 20,000 Cuban immigrants per year to enter the United States and accepting the return of 2,746 Cuban criminals and mental patients sent to the United States in the 1980 boatlift.

See May 5, 1980.

### May 20, 1985

#### The spy ring of retired naval officer John A. Walker Jr. is broken up after 15 years of selling material to the Soviets.

The WALKER SPY RING was uncovered by the Federal Bureau of Investigation after Walker's wife provided the essential information. Initially, while serving as a navy chief warrant officer aboard a submarine; later, after retiring, Walker led a group of two relatives and a friend who sold Soviet agents classified data on U.S. communications and key-code methods.

On May 20, the FBI arrested Walker for selling classified documents. Two days later, they arrested his son, Seaman Michael Walker, who was aboard the USS *Nimitz*. Subsequently, they arrested a third relative, Navy Lieutenant Commander Arthur J. Walker, and a family friend, retired Chief Petty Officer Jerry A. Whitworth. In court, John A. Walker pleaded guilty and was sentenced to life in prison. He plea-bargained to get his son a 25-year prison term in exchange for giving a complete accounting of the material sold to the Soviets. Arthur Walker was fined $250,000 and sentenced to life in prison for espionage and conspiracy.

See July 24, 1986, on Whitworth's conviction.

### June 1, 1985

*Alan García Pérez is declared president of Peru after his chief opponent withdraws from a runoff election.*

On April 14, Pérez won 46% of the vote to his opponent's 21.3%. On April 25, however, the second-place United Left candidate conceded victory and withdrew from the election.

### June 2, 1985

*Greek Prime Minister Papandreou retains control of Parliament.*

The victory of Andreas Papandreou and the Pan Hellenic Socialist Movement was greater than expected. The Socialists won 45.8% of the vote and 161 seats in the 300-member parliament; the conservative New Democracy won 125 seats; the Communist Party, 13 seats. In 1981, Papandreou stated he would close all U.S. naval bases in Greece but eventually negotiated a new treaty with Washington. The U.S. State Department was upset because Papandreou's anti-American rhetoric led Greek terrorists to bomb a military base near Athens on February 2, 1985, injuring 57 Americans. Privately, Greek officials said Papandreou sought independence from Washington.

See September 8, 1983, and August 20, 1984.

### June 6, 1985

*Israeli troops complete their evacuation of Lebanon, leaving advisers to aid the Lebanese.*

Israel and Lebanon had agreed to a troop withdrawal on October 31, 1984, which Israel's cabinet approved on January 14, 1985. The first stage of withdrawal began on February 16; the last took place on June 6.

The withdrawal was difficult for the Israeli forces because radical Shiites in southern Lebanon attacked them with sniper fire and suicide bombings, causing many Israeli casualties. In addition, on April 2, when Israeli soldiers moved 1,100 Lebanese prisoners of war to Israel, the United States and other nations protested the move for violating the Geneva Convention. On May 20, Israel exchanged the Lebanese prisoners for two Israeli soldiers captured during the 1982 invasion of Lebanon.

### June 7, 1985

*Lebanese Christians seize 24 soldiers of the U.N. peacekeeping force, claiming they helped Muslims.*

Allegedly under the oversight of Israeli troops, most of whom had withdrawn from Lebanon, the South Lebanon Army captured 24 Finnish soldiers who were part of the U.N. force keeping peace among groups on Israel's northern border. Although the Finnish soldiers were released unharmed eight days later, this Christian militia incident was a low point in bringing to light the divisions within the Lebanese government of Christian President Amin Gemayel. On March 24, General Samir Geagea and about 4,000 Christians broke with Gemayel's leadership and fought Muslims and other Christian forces in Beirut and at the southern city of Sidon. In these clashes over 110 persons died before other Christian forces removed Geagea from his command.

After the Israeli forces withdrew during the spring of 1985, competing Muslim armies also fought one another.

See April 16, 1985.

## June 10, 1985

### President Reagan says the United States will abide by SALT II by dismantling a Poseidon submarine.

Although some arms control experts believed the president would exceed the SALT II limits when the U.S. launched a new Trident submarine armed with 24 missiles, Reagan ordered the dismantling of one Poseidon with 16 nuclear missiles to keep the United States under the limit of 1,200 multiple warheads agreed to in 1979.

President Reagan told reporters that this action was designed to encourage restraint in deployment of nuclear weapons and the success of the current Geneva arms talks. He called on the Soviet Union to show restraints and end its violations of previous arms treaties.

On SALT II, see June 18, 1979, and January 2 and 4, 1980.

## June 11, 1985

### Indian Prime Minister Rajiv Gandhi begins a visit to the United States.

Although Washington expected India to continue its neutral stance between the Soviet Union and the United States, Gandhi pleased many American politicians by a speech to the Congress that urged creation of an independent, nonaligned Afghanistan. India, he said, backed U.N. and U.S. efforts to get Soviet troops out of Afghanistan.

## June 11, 1985

### Criticizing poor Soviet economic performance, Mikhail Gorbachev advocates Soviet economic reform.

In a major address, Gorbachev followed up his previous statements, which urged better economic performance (April 8) and action to combat alcoholism (May 16), by claiming that broad changes were needed in the Soviet economy. Revealing to Communist Party officials that the Politburo, the party's ruling organ, had rejected the draft of a five-year plan for 1986–90, Gorbachev said that the Soviet Union needed to renovate existing industry and obtain better consumer products to sell at home and abroad.

He berated economic managers, singling out Soviet steelmakers for manufacturing poor products and squandering their use of metals. On October 15, Gorbachev announced a five-year plan, which the Communist Party Congress reviewed in February 1986.

See February 25, 1986.

## June 11, 1985

### Lebanese Shiite terrorists hijack a Royal Jordanian airplane but release the passengers after their demands are rejected.

After taking over the Jordanian Boeing 727 in Beirut, the hijackers flew to Cyprus, to Sicily, and back to Beirut. They wanted all Palestinian forces to be evacuated from Lebanon. On June 12, after their demands were refused, they released the passengers and crew but blew up the plane.

The next day, Palestinian terrorists commandeered a Lebanese airplane in retaliation for the Shiite attack. They flew the Boeing 707 to Amman, Jordan, where it was released to Jordanian officials.

## June 14, 1985

### Two Lebanese Shiite terrorists hijack a Transworld airlines plane beginning an 18-day hostage crisis in Beirut.

Within 20 minutes after TWA Flight 847 left Athens for Rome, two hijackers took over the plane. Crashing through the locked cockpit door, they ordered the captain to fly to Beirut, then to Algiers, then back to Beirut. At the Beirut airport, they shot a U.S. navy diver, Robert Dean Stethem, whom they had already beaten, dropping his dead body onto the airport tarmac.

On June 15, the terrorists ordered the plane to fly to Algiers again, where women, children, non-Americans, and five flight attendants were released. The hijackers also demanded the release of 76 prisoners held in Israeli jails. On June 16, the plane returned to Beirut, where Shiite Amal militia replaced the two hijackers and the Amal leader, Nabih Berri, negotiated for the hostages' release.

On June 17, the remaining 37 passengers were taken off the plane, leaving aboard only the captain and 2 crew members. The hostages were taken to various houses in Beirut, while 4 infirm persons were released on June 18 and June 26.

Negotiations among Washington, Jerusalem, and Beirut reached no solution until June 30. While President Reagan warned of economic or military reprisals against the Lebanese Amal Shiites, he decided not to use force to free the hostages. At the same time, Reagan wanted to separate the hostages' release from Israel's decision to free Arab prisoners of war so that it technically would not be a negotiated exchange. After terms were accepted on June 30, the hostages were taken by car to Damascus, where Syrian President Hafiz al-Assad had helped gain their release. The hostages then flew to West Germany before returning to Andrews Air Force Base in Washington, D.C., on July 2, 1985.

Unlike President Carter during the Iranian hostage crisis of 1979–81, President Reagan maintained a favorable image in the United States owing partly to his "teflon" methods of shifting blame elsewhere, partly to political skill in conducting business as usual. He condemned the terrorists as barbarians while quietly making concessions and rejecting the use of force.

In May 1989, a West German court sentenced Lebanese-born Muhammad Ali Hammadi to life in prison for the hijacking and Stethem's murder. Hammadi was captured by the West Germans in January 1987 while smuggling explosives through Frankfurt airport. The second hijacker remained at large.

### June 19, 1985

### Salvadoran terrorists kill 13 persons including six Americans at sidewalk cafés.

The attack was aimed at four off-duty U.S. Marine guards who were among the victims. A leftist rebel group attacked three outdoor cafés, firing machine guns at patrons.

One of the ten terrorists was killed immediately. On August 27, El Salvador announced that three suspects in the killings had been arrested. They were members of the Central American Revolutionary Worker's Group, one of five Salvadoran guerrilla organizations.

### June 23, 1985

### Sikh terrorists stage two aircraft bombings, one over the Atlantic, the other at Tokyo airport.

There seemed little doubt that Sikh terrorists from India had planted the bomb that exploded on an Air India plane crossing the Atlantic Ocean to London, killing 329 persons on board. The second bomb exploded in the baggage area of Tokyo International Airport, having been in a suitcase on board a Canadian Pacific Airlines plane that arrived ahead of schedule. On November 6, 1985, the Canadian Royal Mounted Police arrested two Sikh immigrants in Canada, charging them only with possession of illegal explosives, although they were suspects in the bombing incident.

The two June 23 bombings were part of a series of terrorist attacks. In Madrid, Spain, a group called the Organization of the Oppressed bombed a British Airways office, killing 1 woman and wounding 27 others. Two blocks away, two gunmen shot up the office of the Jordanian Air Jordan airline, wounding two people. At Rome's Leonardo da Vinci Airport, a bomb exploding in the baggage area injured 12 people. And in Athens, Greece, a car bomb exploded outside a hotel housing U.S. military officers, but no one was killed.

### July 2, 1985

### Eduard A. Shevardnadze becomes Soviet Foreign Minister, replacing Andrei Gromyko, who becomes president.

At a meeting of the Supreme Soviet, Communist Party First Secretary Mikhail Gorbachev announced that Gromyko would become the president of the Soviet Union, a largely honorific title. By selecting Shevardnadze, who had no experience in foreign affairs, the new Soviet leader could formulate his own international policy that the new foreign minister would carry out. Gromyko had been a leading Soviet figure throughout the 40 years of the Cold War.

## July 4, 1985

*In Zimbabwe's first election, the Zimbabwe African National Union (ZANU) wins 63 of 80 black parliamentary seats.*

Robert MUGABE, head of the ZANU, became prime minister. In addition to the 63 black Africans elected to the National Assembly, the Conservative alliance, headed by Ian D. Smith, won 15 of the 20 seats allocated to whites. Mugabe wanted to scrap the 1980 constitution, which guaranteed the nation's white minority a role in the government, and create a one-party socialist state under ZANU. Mugabe's party did not, however, receive 70% of the parliamentary vote necessary to amend the constitution.

On Rhodesia's becoming Zimbabwe, see July 30, 1979, and March 4, 1980.

## July 7, 1985

**Vietnam returns the remains of 26 Americans.**

At the invitation of Hanoi, a U.S. research group made a three-day mission to Vietnam to discuss evidence of prisoners of war and missing-in-action Americans from the Vietnam War. The group searched a B-52 crash site near Hanoi and were promised the remains of 26 servicemen and "material evidence" on six others, which were delivered in August and taken to the Hawaiian records center for POW-MIAs.

In June, another American team visited Laos to excavate the wreckage of an AC130 gunship shot down in 1973. Its search produced 13 identifiable sets of remains.

The State Department hoped that talks with Hanoi might reveal the whereabouts of the remaining 2,464 Americans unaccounted for since 1975. The Pentagon pointed out, however, that 8,100 Americans were unaccounted for from the Korean War and 78,000 from World War II, even though the United States had access to World War II battlefields and crash sites. Neither of these conflicts had stirred the American public about POW-MIAs as did the Vietnam conflict.

## July 8, 1985

**President Reagan says Iran, Libya, North Korea, Cuba, and Nicaragua sponsor world terrorism.**

Addressing the American Bar Association, Reagan denounced these five nations as outlaw states that undertook a "new international version of Murder, Inc." by sponsoring terror groups that they trained, financed, and directed, especially against the United States. Notably, Syria was no longer on Reagan's list, probably because its president had helped to free the TWA hostages.

See June 14, 1985.

## July 8, 1985

*Canada imposes economic sanctions on South Africa, protesting apartheid.*

Because many Canadians opposed South Africa's racial policies, Canada's minister of external affairs, Joe Clark, took action to limit trade with South Africa. Clark said these were not extreme measures, but additional sanctions might result if South African policy did not change. The government prohibited Canadian firms from processing uranium and asked all companies doing business with South Africa to employ nondiscriminatory personnel policies.

On September 13, Clark announced sanctions that embargoed air traffic to South Africa and called for a voluntary ban on new bank loans and crude oil trade.

To compare with U.S. policy, see July 26, 1985.

## July 10, 1985

**Congress repeals the Clark Amendment, ending restrictions on U.S. aid to Angolan rebels.**

When approved by Congress in 1976, the Clark Amendment opposed the Central Intelligence Agency's secret aid to anticommunist rebels in Angola. On June 11, the Senate repealed the Clark Amendment; the House did so on July 10, 1985. Since becoming president in 1981, Ronald Reagan sought repeal to aid Jonas Savimbi, who headed the National Union of Total Independence for Angola

(UNITA) guerrillas that sought to overthrow the government, which received assistance from Cuba.

Congress approved $30 million for UNITA on August 8, but Reagan withheld half of it while trying to persuade Angola to send Cuban troops home. November talks with Angola failed, and Reagan released all UNITA funds on December 10, 1985.

### July 10, 1985

*China and the Soviet Union double their trade to $14 billion over four years.*

In addition to establishing bartering agreements worth an estimated $14 billion, the Chinese and Soviets also made an economic and technical cooperation agreement by which the USSR would construct seven new factories in China.

### July 10, 1985

*An Israeli court convicts 15 Jewish settlers who committed terrorist acts against Arabs on the West Bank.*

Following a 13-month trial, Israeli courts for the first time convicted Jews of crimes against Arabs. Of the 15 who were tried, 3 were convicted of murder, and 12 others were convicted of attempted murder, possession of illegal weapons, and conspiracy. Many Israeli citizens criticized the decision.

The Likud Party's Foreign Minister Yitzhak Shamir said the convicts were "excellent boys" who made a little mistake and should be pardoned. Israeli President Chaim Herzog said he would consider pardons on a case-by-case basis.

### July 12, 1985

*President Reagan reinstates regulations on the export of military technology.*

The president signed the 1985 Export Administrative Extension Act to carry on a 1979 act that expired in 1983. In 1983–84, Reagan used the International Emergency Economic Powers Act to control exports of U.S. technology. The law relaxed restrictions on high-technology exports to Japan and America's NATO allies. The Commerce Department and the U.S. Customs Agency would draw up guidelines for export controls, which the Defense and Justice Departments would review.

See August 20, 1983.

### July 13, 1985

*African famine victims are aided by $70 million from all-day rock concerts in 152 countries.*

Prompted by a July 5 U.N. report of a food crisis in Africa, "Live Aid" became the publicity title for two rock concerts, one in Philadelphia, the other in London. There were seven other concerts, transmitted to 152 countries by intercontinental satellite communications, that reached an audience of 1.5 million. Even a Soviet rock group was included. In addition, American musicians released a recording titled *We Are the World,* whose sales raised $45 million. The British Band Aid Group recorded *Do They Know It's Christmas,* which raised $11 million.

### July 16, 1985

*Senator Jesse Helms protests Secretary of State Shultz's anticonservative policies.*

During 1985, the right-wing Heritage Foundation and its champion, Senator Jesse HELMS (R-N.C.) claimed President Reagan's administration had stopped its hard-line anticommunist policies because of Secretary of State George Shultz. To publicize this, Helms vowed to block 29 pending State Department appointees unless 6 conservatives were assured of jobs. Shultz was also castigated on July 2 at a Heritage Foundation forum where three former Reagan-appointed ambassadors claimed Shultz was "undermining" Reagan's foreign policy. David Funderbunk, former ambassador to Romania; Charles Lichenstein, former U.N. delegate; and Curtin Winsor Jr., former ambassador to Costa Rica each said Shultz had purged conservative appointees in favor of career Foreign Service personnel.

After delaying a Senate vote on the 29 appointees from June 20 to July 16, Helms talked with Reagan and Shultz, agreeing to permit the Senate vote, which approved all 29. Helms said his wishes had been met, but the incident pointed to a defection of right-wing ideologies during Reagan's second term.

See March 14, 1986.

## July 23, 1985

### Chinese President Li Xiannian signs a nuclear power agreement but criticizes charges against China's population policy.

During his July 23 visit with President Reagan at the White House, Li was most agreeable, and the two leaders announced a pact for nuclear power cooperation, which could involve the sale of U.S. nonmilitary nuclear reactors to China.

Earlier, on July 11, Li spoke harshly against a House of Representatives vote that cut $56 million from a U.N. fund aiding nations to control their rapid population growth. Li said U.S. reports of China's forced abortions and the sterilization of women were "based on fabrications and distortions of Chinese policy." U.S. opposition, he argued, interfered in China's internal affairs. The House of Representatives denied these funds on July 10.

For more on the House action, see September 30, 1985.

## July 23, 1985

### *South and North Korean officials meet for the first time in 40 years to discuss unification.*

This meeting at Panmunjom on the 38th parallel met with little success in fostering unity but provided for the reunion of some Korean families who had not met for 40 years. With planning by the Korean Red Cross on September 20, 1985, 151 North Koreans and 157 South Koreans from various families visited Seoul or Pyongyang for reunions with family members.

## July 26, 1985

### The United States abstains on a U.N. resolution to suspend new investments in South Africa.

France sponsored this resolution in the U.N. Security Council as a reaction to South Africa's imposition of emergency controls on its citizens on July 20, 1985. South Africa argued that black African unrest had caused the deaths of nearly 500 people since August 1984. Its emergency decrees gave police and the army powers to quell the opposition to the regime, including searches at will and detaining people without charge or legal aid.

Although the United States and Great Britain abstained, the resolution passed. On August 1, ten European Economic Community nations, including Spain and Portugal recalled their ambassadors from South Africa to protest the state of emergency. In Washington, President Reagan preferred "quiet diplomacy" toward South Africa rather than sanctions. Nevertheless, the House of Representatives voted 380 to 48 for a "mild" package of economic sanctions, and the Senate was expected to pass it if it could avoid a filibuster by right-wing senator Jesse Helms (R-N.C.).

See September 9, 1985.

## July 29, 1985

### The Soviet Union places a moratorium on nuclear tests until January 1986, to be extended if the United States agrees.

During 1985, Soviet leader Mikhail Gorbachev made various proposals to commit the Reagan administration to arms control so the Soviets could divert more funds to economic development. Reagan called these Soviet proposals "propaganda" and refused to follow suit, saying the nuclear tests were not verifiable.

Gorbachev said ending of nuclear tests would be a "major contribution to consolidating strategic stability and peace on earth." Gorbachev's messages made him popular among many Europeans who lived under the threat of nuclear war between the two superpowers.

On September 10, Gorbachev suggested a chemical-weapons-free-zone in central Europe. Again, the White House said this would have to be verifiable.

See April 7, 1985.

## August 6, 1985

### *West German incidents disclose the presence of East German spies in Bonn.*

On August 6, the disappearance of the secretary of the West German economics minister, Sonja Lueneburg, began a month in which other Bonn officials disappeared or defected to East Germany. Margaret Hoecke, a secretary in West German President Richard von Weizsacker's office, confessed to being a spy. Soon after, two political lobbyists defected to East Germany. On August 14, Bonn's third-ranking intelligence officer, Hans Joachim Tiedge, vanished and turned up in East Germany. Finally, on September 16, a secretary in Chancellor Helmut Kohl's office, Herta Astrid, and her husband defected to the East. Of these, Tiedge's spying was the most serious because he knew West German agents in East Germany and had access to NATO operational data.

### August 8, 1985

**President Reagan signs a foreign aid bill that includes many congressional restrictions on the executive, although the Clark Amendment is abolished.**

This was the first time since 1981 that the foreign aid bill was not simply a continuing resolution of Congress, although those resolutions often contained amendments to restrict U.S. funding for military or nonmilitary purposes.

The 1985 bill authorized $6.26 billion in military aid for 1986 and 1987, the total of $12.77 billion being a 5% increase over 1985; Reagan had requested a 13% increase. The bill limited the president's authority to waive restrictions on arms sales to $750 million per year, with no more than $50 million to one country being waived. Thus, a maximum of 15 countries could receive $50 million per year.

Other highlights of the bill were the following:

1. The United States could not negotiate with the Palestine Liberation Organization.
2. The President need not certify El Salvador's human rights progress.
3. Guatemala received no military aid until it elected a civilian government and ended human rights abuses.
4. Nicaraguan rebels received $27 million in nonmilitary aid, but the CIA could not administer it.
5. The Philippines received $70 million in "nonlethal" equipment but was warned to begin human rights reforms.
6. Increased aid was granted to anticommunist rebels in Afghanistan and Cambodia.
7. The Clark Amendment, which banned aid to Angolan rebels, was repealed.
8. Aid to Libya and any other nation linked to terrorism was prohibited.
9. Aid to Pakistan was barred unless the president certified that it had no nuclear weapons.

### August 8, 1985

**Two Americans are killed by a terrorist bomb at a West German air base.**

The worst bomb explosion at a West German base since 1981 (see August 3, 1981 and June 1, 1982)

occurred at the U.S. military installation—Rhein-Main Air Base. In addition to killing Americans, 20 other persons were injured. The terrorist groups claiming responsibility for the attack were the West German Red Army Faction and the French Direct Action Group. On August 13, German police disclosed that the terrorists had also killed an off-duty American soldier to steal his papers and gain admission to the base.

Other terrorist attacks occurred in West Germany in July and August. On July 10, six British soldiers were injured in a bomb explosion near a British base. On August 15, a terrorist bomb damaged a radio tower at the U.S. Armed Forces radio base.

### August 26, 1985

**President Reagan says South Africa has a "reformist government," provoking complaints against his "racist" views.**

The president made comments in a radio interview that were favorable toward South Africa. Although President P. W. Botha imposed a state of emergency in South Africa on July 20, Reagan said Botha had a "reformist administration." Reagan also used one of Botha's arguments by declaring that the black majority in South Africa was only a combination of ten different tribal African minorities. Reagan also said Botha had ended racial discrimination in public places.

By September 6, the White House explained that the president had been misunderstood. Press Secretary Larry Speakes said Reagan had intended to say that Pretoria and Cape Town had taken some steps to end discrimination in public places. President Reagan issued a statement saying that he "carelessly gave the impression he believed racial segregation was eliminated." South Africa's Archbishop Desmond Tutu later told reporters that the president "is a racist, pure and simple."

See September 9, 1985.

### August 30, 1985

*Poland's Solidarity leader, Lech Wałęsa, calls for new talks with the government to benefit the nation.*

Although Solidarity demonstrations protested Prime Minister Wojciech Jaruzelski's austerity measures on February 13 and May 1, no results were achieved.

Initiating a new approach on the fifth anniversary of Solidarity's founding, Wałęsa issued a 500-page report containing a plan for ending Poland's social and economic difficulties. He urged the government to consult with Solidarity to achieve such a program.

### September 9, 1985

*President Reagan imposes limited trade sanctions on South Africa, prompting the Senate to postpone consideration of a sanctions bill.*

Although President Reagan previously opposed sanctions, he said some action might pressure South Africa to end apartheid. The president's sanctions included restrictions on exports of nuclear technology, a ban on the sale of computers for security agencies, and prohibitions on most U.S. bank loans. These mild measures achieved a compromise with congressional advocates of stronger sanctions.

See July 26, 1985.

### September 10, 1985

*The daughter of El Salvador's president is kidnapped.*

The oldest daughter of President José Napoleon Duarte, Inés Duarte Duran, and a friend were abducted by gunmen who killed one bodyguard and wounded another during the fracas. On September 18, a faction of the Salvadoran rebels, the Pedro Pablo Castillo Front, claimed they held Duran, demanding the release of 34 rebels in exchange for her and her friend. They also asked for the cessation of all military operations against them.

Following extensive discussions, the rebels freed Duran and her friend unharmed on October 24. They also freed captive 23 mayors and other government officials in exchange for the release of 22 political prisoners and safe conduct out of the country for 101 guerrillas disabled in the fighting.

The mayors, like Duarte's daughter, had been kidnapped when the guerrillas changed to new tactics because the American-supplied Salvadoran army was too strong to defeat in a conventional war. Kidnappings and terror attacks would destabilize the country and permit the guerrillas to survive. A longer, more disruptive war seemed to be underway in El Salvador.

### September 12, 1985

*The United Kingdom exposes a major Soviet intelligence network, expelling 25 Soviet agents.*

Great Britain discovered this spy network following the defection of a British-based Soviet agent, Oleg Gordievsky, a veteran of 23 years with the KGB, the Soviet secret police. Following the British expulsion of the Soviets, Moscow expelled 25 British diplomats on September 14. This led to another round of retaliatory expulsions—the British sent six Soviet diplomats home on September 16, and Moscow returned six British on September 18.

Britain revealed that Gordievsky had been a "double agent" with British intelligence for over 20 years. He defected because his activity had been discovered by the KGB.

### September 12, 1985

*The World Court begins hearings on Nicaragua's complaint of U.S. military operations against it. The United States alters its tradition favoring international law.*

Although on January 18 the United States rejected the World Court's invitation to defend itself against Nicaragua's accusations, the court held hearings from September 12 to 20. While the World Court heard evidence such as the March 5 Americans Watch Human Rights report accusing the Contra rebels of atrocities, the most critical testimony against the United States was the report of former Contra leader Edgar Chamorro, who stated that the CIA actively encouraged the rebels to use a terrorist campaign against civilians to turn them against the Sandinista government.

On October 7, the State Department asserted that the United States would not comply with World Court decisions, because the court served "political ends" hostile to the United States. This contention altered traditional U.S. policy to seek and support the rule of law in international affairs. Senator Mark Hatfield (R-Oreg.) criticized the Reagan administration's position, noting that "Khomeini, Qaddafi and all other world-class thugs who thrive on the rule of the jungle will no doubt welcome this decision."

## September 12, 1985

### The Contadora nations propose their "final" peace plan for Central America.

The four major Contadora states of Mexico, Venezuela, Columbia, and Panama had tried since 1983 to obtain peace in Nicaragua, El Salvador, and Guatemala (see January 8, 1983). The present Contadora peace concept proposed removing all foreign military advisers from all states in the region and prohibiting foreign nations from supporting any group trying to overthrow a Central American government. The Contadora members asked each Central American government to respond to their plan by November 21, but Nicaragua rejected the plan on November 11 because it required neither the withdrawal of United States military advisers nor end the enlargement of guerrilla forces in the region. Nicaragua's rejection of the plan required Contadora representatives to meet again on November 19 (see December 18, 1986).

See January 8, 1983.

## September 13, 1985

### The U.S. air force successfully tests an antisatellite missile.

Despite Soviet objections that this test violated nuclear arms treaties, the air force proceeded with it because the White House stated on April 7, 1985, that the antiballistic test did not violate the 1972 ABM treaty. During the test, a missile from an F-15 fighter plane hit and destroyed an orbiting derelict satellite flying 290 miles above the Pacific Ocean. The missile's ability to hit a space satellite was an essential step for continuing to pursue Reagan's Strategic Defense Initiative.

## September 16, 1985

### The Chinese Communist Party (CCP) appoints younger members to replace older Politburo and Central Committee members.

At its annual session in Beijing, the CCP made the most extensive leadership changes since 1949. Ten retiring Politburo members and 64 of 340 Central Committee members were replaced. Earlier, on June 18, Chinese leaders had replaced 9 senior ministers with younger men. During its September 16–22 meeting, the party also approved a four-year economic plan that continued the market-oriented program begun by Chinese leader Deng Xiaoping.

## September 18, 1985

### President Reagan announces the release of an American hostage in Lebanon.

The Reverend Benjamin Weir had been held captive for 16 months. Although Reagan's deal with Iran to exchange hostages for TOW missiles (see September 1, 1984) did not become known to the public until 1986 (see November 3, 1986), Weir was the first of three American hostages to be liberated by this clandestine activity of Reagan's National Security Council members (see November 3, 1986).

At the time of Weir's release, a State Department official insisted "we don't make deals" and attributed Weir's release to Israel's release of 1,035 Palestinians from an Israel prison camp an event connected to the TWA hostage crisis (see June 14, 1985). Weir told President Reagan that his captors were willing to negotiate the release of other American hostages. The Reverend Martin Jenco was released on July 26, 1986, and David Jacobsen on November 2, 1986. For the fate of hostage William Buckley, see October 12, 1985.

See June 14, 1985; on hostage William Buckley, see October 12, 1985.

## September 22, 1985

### The "Plaza Accord" among five industrial nations lowers the dollar's value.

The Group of Five industrial powers met at the Plaza Hotel in New York to conclude three months of negotiations on trade and currency. The agreement said the five nations would intervene in the currency market to devalue the dollar, whose value had risen because of high U.S. interest rates financing the national debt, which reached $2 trillion by the end of 1985.

Secretary of the Treasury James Baker and Federal Reserve Board Chairman Paul Volker represented the United States at the Plaza meeting, having persuaded President Reagan to reverse policies that let the dollar float freely on the currency markets. Baker believed a lower dollar value would lower U.S. export prices and encourage foreign sales of U.S. goods. Representatives of Great Britain, France, West Germany, Japan, and the United States agreed to sell dollars when necessary to drive down the dollar value. The other leaders urged Baker to reduce U.S. budget deficits and interest rates to stabilize currency values.

The day after the accord was announced, the value of the dollar dropped by 5.2%, a record one-day decline. During the next four years, the U.S. trade balance improved but not enough to correct the trade imbalance with Japan. It became cheaper for Japan to invest in U.S business enterprises and to build Japanese assembly plants in the United States while importing Japanese auto parts for its U.S. plants. Before the Plaza Accord, the Japanese yen was 263 per dollar and by 1989 it was 132 yen per dollar. Similar results enhanced the ability of the Germans and the British to invest in America. The alternative would have been to balance the U.S. budget by raising taxes and lower interest paid on the national debt. American politicians, especially Republicans, had avoided this "sacrifice" and campaigned instead on a policy of no new taxes.

See October 7, 1985, and January 19, 1986.

### September 26, 1985

**A top KGB agent defects to the United States—the curious case of Vitaly Yurchenko.**

Assumed to be the fifth-highest officer of the Soviet secret police (KGB), Yurchenko disappeared from his Rome post in early September and was reported to have defected to the United States, where the Central Intelligence Agency secretly debriefed him. On November 4, 1985, Yurchenko unexpectedly appeared for a news conference at the Soviet embassy in Washington. He told reporters the CIA had drugged and abducted him from Italy, bringing him to the United States, where he was held and questioned. He escaped and came to the embassy to return home. The U.S. State Department claimed Yurchenko had willingly defected and given the CIA valuable information. After the Soviets permitted a State Department official to interview Yurchenko privately, the officer said Yurchenko wanted to return home, and he did so on November 6. CIA spokesmen said Yurchenko divulged the names of several Americans who spied for the Soviet Union, and these persons were under investigation. On November 25, 1985, Ronald Pelton, a National Security Agency official, was arrested on the basis of Yurchenko's revelations. On June 5, 1986, Pelton was convicted and sentenced to life in prison.

### September 26, 1985

***The United Kingdom sells Saudi Arabia $4.5 billion of advanced technology aircraft.***

While the Saudis wanted to purchase American-built aircraft, the United States refused under pressure from Jewish lobby groups. Thus, various U.S. allies made sales prohibited to American aircraft companies.

See March 14, 1984.

### September 28, 1985

**The State Department announces a program for U.S. embassies.**

This $5.5 billion five-year program was planned to make American ambassadorial residencies around the world secure from terrorism and to counteract Soviet espionage efforts. On August 21, the State Department reported that its Moscow Embassy staff had discovered that the Soviet Union used a compound called "spy dust" picked up by the shoes or hands of U.S embassy personnel and visitors. The Soviets could then follow the individuals by using ultraviolet light to make their tracks visible.

### September 29, 1985

***Roberto D'Aubuisson resigns as head of El Salvador's right-wing National Republican Alliance.***

Although this announcement ostensibly removed the notorious d'Aubuisson from El Salvador's rightist party, most U.S. observers doubted that the resignation ended his control over the military groups (death squads) that carried out attacks on left-wing radicals in El Salvador.

See June 22, 1984.

### September 30, 1985

**A U.S. federal court stops the release of $10 million for U.N. population control programs.**

This court action resulted from a civil suit filed by two congressmen who opposed giving U.S. funds to the United Nations Fund for Population Assistance. They filed suit against the State Department's Agency for International Development (AID) on the basis of a congressional restriction against funding abortions and sterilizations, which was in the foreign aid bill signed by President Reagan on August 8, 1985.

A congressional amendment restricted such funds, but most observers believed its use was at the discretion of President Reagan. Because both AID and U.N. officials said the $10 million would go to groups other than the Chinese, whose policies the amendment opposed, the Reagan administration had, on September 25, released part of the money Congress authorized. Nevertheless, ardent opponents of abortion opposed any funds for population control and sued in federal court. Judge Louis Oberdorfer ruled that the $10 million could not be spent by AID.

## September 30, 1985

### *Four Soviet diplomats are kidnapped in West Beirut.*

The first Soviet citizens to be abducted in Lebanon, the Islamic Liberation Organization said, would be executed unless Syrian-backed militia stopped attacks on Tripoli. Although one Soviet captive, was found dead in West Beirut on October 2, the other captives were released unharmed. On October 30, 1985, some commentators claimed that strong Soviet threats gained their release. Two more probable factors were that the kidnappers were moderate Sunni (not Shiite) Muslims and Syria produced the hostages because it depended on Soviet arms.

## October 1, 1985

### *Israeli planes bomb PLO headquarters in Tunis and kill over 70 persons.*

Although President Reagan initially called the Israeli raid, in retaliation for three Israelis killed in Cyprus, a "legitimate response," on October 2, he modified his statement, saying it "cannot be condoned" because many innocent persons died in the Tunis air raid.

Tunis had remained neutral in Middle East conflicts, its president, Habib Bourguiba, allowing the Palestinians to come there from Lebanon in 1982 as a humanitarian gesture after other nations had rejected the refugees. Although the U.N. Security Council voted to condemn Israel's attack (the United States abstained), such resolutions did not influence Israel. Following the raid, Shiite radicals in Lebanon stated that a U.S. hostage, William Buckley, had been executed in retaliation.

See August 21, 1982, and October 12, 1985.

## October 1, 1985

### *Mexico's international debt payments are rescheduled.*

Mexico had suffered economic problems well before a severe earthquake struck Mexico City, killing 4,000 and destroying billions of dollars worth of property. On July 24, the Mexican government cut its 1985 budget by $410 billion and devalued the peso by 20% to offset its decreasing revenue because of falling oil prices.

Following the earthquake, many nations rushed aid to victims of the catastrophe, but this did not solve Mexico's long-term debt problem. The international banking community agreed on October 1 to postpone Mexico's payments of $950 million, due in October and November, and to pursue further negotiations on Mexico's debt structuring.

See September 7, 1984.

## October 7, 1985

### *Four Palestinian terrorists hijack the Italian cruise ship* Achille Lauro *in the Mediterranean sea.*

The hijackers held over 400 persons hostage on ship, demanding that 50 Palestinians be released from Israeli jails. After murdering one American passenger, Leon Klinghoffer, the hijackers negotiated with Egyptian authorities before taking the ship to Port Said, where the passengers and crew were set free on October 9. Unaware of the murder of Klinghoffer, the Egyptians had agreed to give the Palestinians safe passage out of Egypt.

See October 10, 1985.

## October 7, 1985

### *Chrysler Auto Corporation and Japan's Mitsubishi plan to build an Illinois car plant.*

This cooperative agreement provided for a $500 million auto plant with Chrysler having a 20% share in the venture. Sixty percent of the automobile parts, including the transmissions, would be imported from Japan. The state of Illinois outbid several other states by offering tax and property incentives.

Nevertheless, as decisions on the Plaza accord had indicated (see September 22, 1985), such joint ventures as Japan made with Chrysler enabled the Japanese to invest cheaply in U.S. enterprises while maintaining high production on auto parts they sent to the United States because of the lower dollar value compared to Japanese currency.

See September 22, 1985.

### October 10, 1985

**U.S. Navy planes intercept an Egyptian airplane carrying the *Achille Lauro* hijackers, forcing it to land in Sicily, where Italian authorities arrest the terrorists.**

On October 7, Egyptian authorities had obtained the release of the 400 passengers on the cruise ship ACHILLE LAURO by promising the four hijackers safe-conduct. The hijackers hoped to fly to Tunisia, where the Palestine Liberation Organization was headquartered. Tunisia refused to admit them, but they boarded an Egyptian commercial aircraft for Tunis.

Soon after the plane left Egyptian territory, President Reagan ordered U.S. fighter planes from the carrier *Saratoga* to intercept the airliner, forcing its pilot to land the Boeing 737 in Sicily. American and Italian troops from a Sicilian base took over the plane, and Italian authorities arrested the four Arabs for murder and kidnapping. Seventeen American *Achille Lauro* passengers were flown from Port Said, Egypt, to Sicily, where they identified the hijackers.

International reactions to Reagan's action were significant. Although Secretary of Defense Caspar Weinberger had cautioned the president to inform Egypt's President Hosni Mubarak of the plan, Reagan did not do so. Reagan's unilateral decision ignored a valuable Middle East ally and humiliated Mubarak. In Cairo, this caused mass student demonstrations against Mubarak and the United States. Mubarak claimed that the PLO had agreed to try the hijackers, and he acted to save the lives of 400 people, but Reagan refused to apologize for his insult to Egypt.

American-Italian relations also soured. Italian authorities were informed of the Sicilian landing at the last moment, and American and Italian troops nearly clashed because of disputes when the plane landed. Soon after, the Italian government released Muhammad Abbas Zaida from custody, an action Washington protested because he was the notorious Abu Abbas, who, the Americans believed, planned the takeover of *Achille Lauro*. Abbas had been on the Egyptian plane with the hijackers, but the Italians said he had no direct connection with the cruise

ship affair. Abbas flew to Yugoslavia, which also rejected a U.S. request for extradition.

Italy's Prime Minister Bettino Craxi also complained about the high-handed U.S. tactics. He said Washington had never asked permission to land its two C-141 troop carriers on Sicily. In addition, he contended that U.S. fighter planes had violated Italian airspace by following the Egyptian airline bringing the arrested hijackers from Sicily to Rome.

On July 19, 1986, 11 of the 15 charged in the hijacking were sentenced to life in prison by a court in Genoa, Italy. The judge also imposed life sentences in absentia on Muhammad Abbas and two associates who planned the hijacking.

See October 17, 1985.

### October 11, 1985

**At the IMF–World Bank conference in South Korea, Secretary of the Treasury James Baker proposes aid to debtor nations.**

The conference of 149 member countries of the International Monetary Fund (IMF) and the World Bank advanced the question of how industrial nations could help Third World countries obtain private investments while developing market-oriented economies.

The Baker Plan proposed establishing a $30 billion fund, in addition to the $50 billion already allocated, over three years to allow debtor countries to develop market policies that would boost domestic savings, investments, and growth. As Baker and other delegates noted, successful Third World countries like South Korea, Singapore, and Taiwan had abandoned government controls, using market policies to attract foreign investment and gain momentum for industrial growth. Baker wanted to promote these practices by inducing Third World nations to abandon the economic controls that most post-colonial countries had adopted in their attempt to become economically independent of Western powers.

See September 30, 1987.

### October 12, 1985

**Lebanon's Islamic Jihad says it executed an American hostage.**

William F. BUCKLEY was the Central Intelligence Agency's agent in Beirut. He had been kidnapped by Islamic Jihad, a pro-Iranian Shiite group (see May 6,

1984 and October 1, 1985). The terrorists said they executed him because Israel used U.S. planes in its raid against Tunis.

Following speculation on Buckley's death, on December 12, 1985, Jack Anderson, a Washington-based investigative columnist, reported that Buckley had been tortured and killed in Lebanon. CIA director William Casey had hoped Iran would release him as part of the Iran arms-for-hostages deal, which was disclosed in 1986.

See May 6, 1984; October 1, 1985; and November 3, 1986.

### October 15, 1985

**Nicaraguan President Daniel Ortega declares a national emergency, blaming the "brutal aggression by North America and its internal allies."**

Ortega suspended, for one year, free expression, public assembly, privacy of mail and home, and the right to strike, claiming that some religious institutions and media outlets were allies of Washington. He was also troubled by workers demonstrating in Managua to obtain their unpaid year-end bonuses.

Ortega had substantial reasons for thinking that Washington continued to help the Contras, even though Congress had restricted military aid to them in 1984 and 1985. On August 8, 1985, President Reagan admitted that a *New York Times* article was correct in stating that National Security Council officials advised the rebels. Neither Reagan nor the *Times* disclosed the full extent of this clandestine aid, until the Iran-Contra scandal surfaced in 1986.

On Contra restrictions, see October 10, 1984; August 8, 1985; and November 3, 1986.

### October 16, 1985

**President Reagan's personal envoy, Paul Laxalt, visits Philippine President Marcos to urge reforms.**

Since the 1983 assassination of Benigno Aquino, the political situation in the Philippines had worsened. As a result, the U.S. foreign aid bill that Reagan signed on August 8 specified Philippine aid only for "nonlethal" equipment and warned that Marcos could lose all aid if his human rights record did not improve.

On September 25, the acquittal of the men accused of killing Aquino stimulated further protests

in Namibia, especially after Marcos reinstated one suspect, General Fabian Ver, as head of the Philippine armed forces.

Senator Laxalt (R-Nev.) told Marcos that Washington was concerned about his future, urging him to respond positively to his opponents.

See August 21, 1983, and November 26, 1985.

### October 17, 1985

**Italian Prime Minister Bettino Craxi resigns because of a dispute growing out of the *Achille Lauro* incident.**

Following the arrest of the hijackers of the Italian cruise ship *Achille Lauro*, Craxi's government allowed Islamic Jihad terrorist Abu Abbas to go free because he was not directly involved in the hijacking of the vessel. The United States protested, claiming to have evidence implicating him as the originator of the plan. Other Italian politicians supported the U.S. argument, in particular, Defense Minister Giovanni Spadolini, who rallied support in the Chamber of Deputies to obtain Craxi's resignation. Italy's political crisis did not last long, however. On October 30, Craxi formed a five-party coalition that urged the Palestine Liberation Organization to pursue peaceful negotiations.

See October 10, 1985.

### October 24, 1985

**President Reagan meets with leaders of allied nations to discuss his Geneva summit preparations.**

Reagan met with the leaders of the United Kingdom, Canada, Italy, West Germany, and Japan. French President François Mitterrand declined an invitation, while leaders of Belgium and the Netherlands were upset not to have been invited. Generally, the Europeans expected little from the first Reagan-Gorbachev meeting but hoped the U.S. president would not cause the summit to fail by pushing his Strategic Defence Initiative (SDI). Recently, National Security Adviser Robert C. McFarlane startled both Bonn and London by remarking that the 1972 Anti-Ballistic Missile Treaty might be abandoned so that the SDI system could be tested and deployed. Europeans saw the SDI as destabilizing the deterrent nuclear policies already in place.

Because Reagan and his advisers were seldom sensitive to the advice of European leaders, most observers doubted that their views were influential. Reagan gave his U.N. speech the same day, and both West German and British officials privately expressed dismay that the president talked tough against the Soviet Union but offered no arms control proposals to seize the peace initiative from Soviet leader Mikhail Gorbachev.

On November 1, 1985, Reagan tried to mollify his European critics by proposing to cut nuclear warheads by 50%, with a ceiling of 4,500. But this plan contained nothing new from prior proposals.

See November 21, 1985.

### October 24, 1985

**President Reagan calls for a "fresh start" in U.S.-Soviet relations while blaming Moscow for conflicts.**

Speaking before the U.N. General Assembly, the president stated his desire to lead peace efforts and end difficulties with the Soviet Union. Nevertheless, Reagan's "fresh start" consisted mostly of old criticisms of Soviet involvement in conflicts in Angola, Afghanistan, and elsewhere, his implication being that the Soviets were untrustworthy.

### October 24, 1985

**A Soviet seaman jumps ship and causes friction in U.S.-Soviet relations before he is returned to the USSR.**

A 22-year-old sailor, Miroslav Medved, precipitated a dispute with the Soviets by jumping into the Mississippi River near New Orleans to escape Soviet control, but then changed his mind about defecting. Initially, on White House orders, American officials and doctors examined Medved, keeping him in a naval facility overnight to make sure he was not ill or drugged. Then the defector signed a statement that he wanted to return to his ship. A U.S. air force psychiatrist who interviewed Medved believed the Soviet ship's captain had indicated to Medved that his parents might be harmed if their son did not return.

Although a U.S. Senate resolution opposed the forced return of political asylum seekers, President Reagan decided that all evidence showed Medved wanted to go home. Reagan told Republican leaders

that he resented the suggestion of Senator Jesse Helms (R-N.C.) that he "threw this guy to the wolves because we're getting ready for Geneva," where Reagan was to meet with Soviet leader Mikhail Gorbachev.

### October 25, 1985

*Argentina imposes a state of siege to combat right-wing terrorists.*

Argentina's President Raul Alfonsin faced economic and political difficulties. The military commission established in 1983 had ordered trials of military officers implicated in the disappearance of 6,000 Argentines (see October 30, 1983), while military cliques opposed the trials (see September 28, 1984). The trial of generals implicated in the murders of opponents had been underway since April 22, stirring up violent protests from pro-military individuals. Inflation and foreign loan payments also hindered Alfonsin's government, and on June 14, he announced wage-price controls, cuts in government spending, and a devalued currency. These austerity measures further dampened Alfonsin's popularity.

The violence of the right was a more serious problem, however, and to bring order to the cities, the president decreed a 60-day state of siege. This worked fairly well, and the strict regulations were rescinded in 45 days—on December 7, 1985.

### October 27, 1985

**A press report indicates the Soviet Union would stop work on its Asian radar base if the United States stopped modernizing radar stations in England and Greenland.**

The *London Times* reported on October 27 that at the Geneva arms talks, the chief Soviet delegate, Yuli Kvitsinsky, offered to stop building the Krasnoyarsk Radar Station, which, the United States claimed, violated the 1972 Anti-Ballistic Missile Treaty because it was an early-warning defense system. Heretofore, the Soviets had denied these charges.

The Soviets wanted the United States to stop modernizing its 20-year-old radar bases at Thule, Greenland, and Fylingdales Moor, England. They said such changes violated the 1972 treaty, a claim that some British politicians accepted.

On October 29, the U.S. State Department expressed doubt that Moscow would forsake its Central Asian facility and announced that the

United States would modernize its bases. It claimed the U.S. bases did not violate the 1972 agreement. The Soviet offer was Gorbachev's attempt to gain favorable public opinion before his November summit meeting with President Reagan.

See October 24, 1985.

### October 30, 1985

#### West Germans operate a mission of the U.S. space shuttle *Challenger*.

The first manned space flight managed by a nation other than the United States or the USSR, this mission lasted from October 30 to November 6 under the control of West German space controllers on behalf of the European Space Agency. In addition to five American astronauts, two Germans and one Dutch physicists were aboard to conduct 76 scientific experiments in a European-built space lab carried in the *Challenger*'s cargo bay. The experiments included manufacture of metal alloys in space and studies of motion sickness. West Germany paid the United States $65 million for the use of *Challenger*.

### November 1, 1985

#### The United States and the European Economic Community reach agreement on steel marketing.

This agreement tried to resolve a perennial issue of the past decade, in which American steel companies tried to restrict European steel imports, claiming that their low prices resulted from subsidies. Under the plan, European steelmakers could increase their market share in ten categories of steel products from 18.5% to 25% of the U.S. market while reducing their share in other steel categories and limiting their sales of steel pipes and tubing to 7.6% of the U.S. market. It became effective on January 1, 1986.

### November 1, 1985

#### The Netherlands says it will deploy U.S. medium-range missiles in 1988.

Rejecting Soviet leader Mikhail Gorbachev's request that it delay voting on U.S. missile deployment, the Dutch parliament approved deployment but delayed it until 1988 to determine whether a U.S.-Soviet treaty might restrict these missiles.

In contrast to the Netherlands' policy, the Belgian parliament on March 20, 1985, had approved deployment of 48 U.S. cruise missiles, and 16 were deployed during March 1985. Italy, Great Britain, and West Germany also deployed cruise or Pershing II missiles after November 1983.

### November 2, 1985

#### *South Africa restricts the news media from covering Antiapartheid protests.*

Although since July 20, 1985, when emergency measures were introduced in South Africa, the United Nations and many European nations protested the limits on civil liberties by P. W. Botha's government, these measures continued. On November 2, South Africa imposed restrictions on television, radio, and news photos of demonstrations against the government. The United States was one of the few that did not react strongly against Botha's actions.

See August 26, 1985, for President Reagan's sympathetic policy toward Botha.

### November 6, 1985

#### *In Bogotá, Colombia, leftist guerrillas invade the Palace of Justice before police counterattack.*

The guerrillas from the M-19 group had fought many battles with the government by kidnapping police or attacking police stations. In addition, police believed M-19 had links with drug traffickers in Colombia. On November 6, the gunmen captured the courthouse, taking supreme court judges and some 300 others as hostages. The M-19 leaders threatened to put Colombia's President Belisario Betancur on trial before his own judges.

Betancur refused to negotiate with the guerrillas, and on November 7 he ordered the army and police to attack Bogotá's central court house, the Palace of Justice, in full force. The building was stormed and an estimated 100 people perished, including nine judges as well as guerrillas, soldiers, police, and civilians. One victim, Andrés Almarales, was the M-19 leader, released from prison under an amnesty in 1984. Colombia's travails continued on November 13 when the Nevado del Ruiz volcano erupted, destroying 14 towns and killing an estimated 25,000 people.

## November 12, 1985

**A congressional resolution prohibits the sale of U.S. arms to Jordan unless it begins negotiations with Israel by March 1, 1986.**

President Reagan informed Congress on September 27 of his intentions to sell Jordan $1.5 billion to $1.9 billion of armaments. On October 23, the Senate approved the sale provided Jordan began peace talks with Israel. On November 12, the House of Representatives approved the Senate action.

King Hussein of Jordan tried to promote negotiations with Israel either through a joint Jordanian-Palestinian arrangement or at an international conference of all parties, including the Soviet Union and the United States. Thus far, however, Hussein had found no method agreeable to both Israel and the Palestine Liberation Organization.

See November 15, 1985.

## November 12, 1985

*The European Economic Community signs an economic cooperation pact with six Central American states including Nicaragua.*

Meeting in Luxembourg, EEC members increased their assistance to Costa Rica, El Salvador, Honduras, Panama, Guatemala, and Nicaragua. A West German proposal to link any nation's part of the $33 million to its observance of human rights was voted down. The Europeans urged all foreign nations to withdraw their troops from Central America and adopt the Contadora peace plan. Just the previous day, Nicaragua had rejected the most recent Contadora plan.

See September 12, 1985.

## November 14, 1985

**The U.S. national debt reaches $2 trillion as President Reagan signs a stopgap finance bill.**

Soon after becoming president in 1981, Ronald Reagan promised to balance the budget by 1984, a promise that his 1981 tax cut and a huge military buildup had doomed to failure. The national debt after 200 years, reached $1 trillion in 1981.

Reagan's distinction was to double the debt in four years, leading Republican conservatives to propose a constitutional amendment to require a balanced budget. Instead, Reagan signed the Gramm-Rudman Bill designed to balance the annual budget by 1991. Meanwhile, the national debt moved toward the $3 trillion mark while annual interest rates on the debt grew larger. The leading nation in purchasing U.S. treasury bills to finance the deficit was Japan.

See December 12, 1985.

## November 15, 1985

*Peace efforts by Israeli Prime Minister Shimon Peres and Jordanian King Hussein are stymied by Israel's right wing.*

Since February 24, 1985, Middle East peace plans seemed possible after Egyptian President Hosni MUBARAK suggested a summit meeting among the United States, Egypt, Israel, and Jordanian-Palestinian representatives. After Israel indicated its willingness, quiet discussions took place, highlighted by Mubarak's visit to the United States from March 9 to 13 and King Hussein's visit with President Reagan on May 29. Following his visit, Hussein stated that the Palestine Liberation Organization would recognize Israel's right to exist even though PLO chairman Yasser Arafat refused to comment on Hussein's statement on June 6.

Although problems arose on August 7 when Israel rejected a list of Palestinian representatives chosen by Arafat to attend preparatory peace talks, these frictions seemed to dissipate after U.S. Assistant Secretary of State Richard W. Murphy visited the Middle East on August 18 to meet with Israeli and Egyptian officials. On October 1, Israel's bombing of Tunis endangered the proposed negotiations, but on October 21, Prime Minister Peres offered to travel to Amman, Jordan, for peace talks. King Hussein welcomed the offer, and on October 28, Israel's Knesset (parliament) approved Peres's peace proposal by a vote of 68 to 10.

In early November, however, hopes faded. On November 10, members of the Israeli right-wing became upset when the *New York Times* reported that Peres had agreed to an international conference on the Middle East to which King Hussein would bring Palestinians acceptable to Israel. The report incensed Israeli Minister of Trade Ariel Sharon, but, more important, that leader of the right-wing bloc publicly criticized Peres, and the Labor-Likud coalition that governed Israel nearly collapsed before Sharon apologized on November 15, 1985.

Nevertheless, this incident showed Israel's shaky support for Peres's peace plan and caused King Hussein to abandon agreements he had made with the Israeli prime minister. On December 11, Hussein joined Syrian President Hafiz al-Assad in calling for a U.N. conference to settle the Middle East crisis. Hussein wanted to end Arab criticism of his talks with Israel.

See February 11 and October 1, 1985.

### November 20, 1985

#### Poland's creditors agree to reschedule debt payments due in 1985.

Known as the Club of Paris, 17 Western nations that had loaned $12 billion to Poland between 1982 and 1984 agreed to reschedule $1.3 billion over a ten-year period with a five-year grace period to assist the Polish economy. After Prime Minister Wojciech Jaruzelski resigned on November 6, 1985, Polish leaders talked about changing its controlled economy to a market economy. Prime Minister Zbigniew Messner told parliament he wanted to link wages to productivity, stimulate individual initiative, and increase investment. Previously, conservative forces in the Communist Party had prevented changes, but Messner and Jaruzelski, who was also Communist Party First Secretary, promised to overcome this problem.

### November 20, 1985

#### Yelena Bonner, wife of Andrey Sakharov, receives permission to visit the United States; ten others get exit visas.

SAKHAROV, a dissident Soviet physicist, and his wife had been sent to internal exile in Gorky in 1980. On several occasions, they had requested visas to visit relatives in the United States or to receive medical treatment for Bonner's glaucoma and heart disease. A report that Bonner had received permission to leave was announced by U.S. Secretary of State George Shultz on October 31, and on November 20, Bonner reported that she could visit the United States in December but not talk with reporters. She reached the United States on December 6, 1985. Following Bonner's return to the Soviet Union in 1986, her children told reporters that photographs brought to the United States by Bonner showing Sakharov in good health had been faked by the Soviet photographer to hide the fact that Sakharov's health had deteriorated from his hunger strikes protesting Soviet policies.

### November 21, 1985

#### The Reagan-Gorbachev summit ends with six minor agreements and good rapport between the two leaders.

At the first U.S.-USSR summit of top leaders since 1979, President Reagan and Communist Party First Secretary Gorbachev signed six bilateral agreements on cultural and scientific exchanges; the opening of consulates in Kiev and New York; air safety in the North Pacific to prevent incidents such as the Korean Air Line destruction in 1983 (see September 1, 1983); the resumption of civil aviation ties; magnetic fusion research; and environmental protection.

Although there were no breakthroughs on arms control or human rights issues, the summit promised future good relations because the two leaders got along well. Reagan and Gorbachev spent five hours in private talks, more than scheduled. These talks were described as frank, cordial, and businesslike, but both leaders later expressed optimism about ensuring peaceful relations—Gorbachev remarking that "the world has become a more secure place" and Reagan informing Congress that the two leaders understood each other better and "that's a key to peace."

Following the sessions on November 21, Reagan flew to Brussels, Belgium, to brief America's North Atlantic Treaty Organization allies on the meetings; Gorbachev went to Prague, Czechoslovakia, for meetings with the USSR's Warsaw Pact members.

One glitch in the summit, the *New York Times* disclosed on November 16, was that Defense Secretary Caspar Weinberger had urged the president to take a tough line on arms control, to make no concessions on the Strategic Defense Initiative, and not to extend SALT II. Reagan learned about the letter while en route to Geneva and told reporters he would have preferred to read it in his office, not in the *New York Times*.

### November 21, 1985

#### U.S. Navy analyst and his wife are charged with spying for Israel.

Jonathan Jay Pollard, a civilian who worked as a counterintelligence specialist in the U.S. navy, was arrested in Washington near the Israeli embassy, where he and his wife were attempting to seek political asylum. Pollard sold intelligence data to Israel; his wife,

Anne L. Henderson-Pollard, was charged with possessing "unauthorized" documents. Pollard admitted selling information to Israel and Pakistan, although officials of both countries denied it.

Israeli Prime Minister Shimon Peres apologized to the United States to the extent that spying did take place. On December 1, Peres agreed to cooperate with a U.S. investigation. According to the *New York Times*, the Israeli government, on December 21, fired Rafael Eita, the Israeli intelligence official involved in the Pollard case, but later promoted him to a high army post. On March 4, 1987, Pollard was sentenced to life in prison and his wife, to five years.

## November 23, 1985

### *After an Egyptian plane is hijacked, Egyptian commandos stage a bloody rescue mission that kills 60 hostages held by terrorists.*

Soon after an Egyptian airliner left Athens airport for Cairo, five terrorists took charge and ordered the pilot to fly to Malta, where they demanded fuel to continue their journey. The Maltese authorities offered fuel only if the 98 hostages were freed. The terrorists refused and began shooting hostages one at a time, throwing their bodies onto the tarmac of the airfield.

Four women and one man had been shot before Egyptian commandos attacked. These forces flew to Malta and stormed the plane to rescue the hostages. Rather than yield, the terrorists fired their weapons and detonated three phosphorous hand grenades, which set the plane on fire. During the fighting, 60 passengers as well as 4 of the 5 terrorists were killed. Three of the five victims thrown on to the tarmac miraculously survived their gunshot wounds. Egypt blamed the attack on Abu Nidal, a Palestinian terrorist supported by Libya leader Mu'ammar al-Gadhafi.

## November 23, 1985

### A former CIA agent, Larry Wu-tai Chin, is arrested on charges of spying for China.

According to charges against China filed by FBI investigators, Chin gave the Chinese highly classified data during the 30-year period that he worked for the Central Intelligence Agency. Chin was convicted on February 15, 1986, but committed suicide on February 21.

## November 26, 1985

### *The Philippines plans national elections for February 7, 1986.*

Reacting to demonstrations in Manila and pressured by the Reagan administration to make reforms, President Ferdinand Marcos asked the National Assembly to change the election date from 1987 to early 1986, and the assembly complied. Observers believed Marcos wanted a quick election to prevent the opposition from organizing, but this did not happen. On December 3, the wife of the assassinated Benigno Aquino announced her candidacy. Corazon Aquino formed an eight-party coalition led by her People's Struggle and the United Nationalist Democratic Organization (UNIDO) of Salvador H. Laurel, who was the vice presidential candidate. Although the Aquino-Laurel coalition nearly collapsed, the two patched up their differences when they agreed to be on the UNIDO Party ticket.

President Marcos also took steps to increase his popularity. On November 11, he resigned as president, effective after the 1986 election. On December 11, he became the presidential nominee of the Philippine's New Society Movement, with a former foreign minister, Arturo M. Tolentino, as the vice presidential nominee.

See February 25, 1986.

## November 28, 1985

### *GATT members agree on multilateral trade liberalization talks in 1986.*

The principal feature of the eighth round of talks since 1947 would be discussions on trade rules to cover services such as insurance, banking, and communications, an agenda desired by the United States. The General Agreement on Tariffs and Trade (GATT) was created in 1947 for capitalist nations to cooperate in lowering trade barriers and to move toward free trade. The last round of negotiations, the so-called Tokyo round, ended in 1979. There were 90 member nations and Mexico applied for membership on November 24, 1985.

See September 15, 1986; for the origins of GATT, see October 30, 1947.

### November 29, 1985

**Six foreign securities companies gain membership on the Tokyo Stock Exchange.**

For the first time in its 107-year history, the Tokyo exchange allowed six foreign firms to join—three American and three British. Each company paid an estimated $5 million for a seat on the exchange beginning in 1986. The three American firms were Merrill Lynch, Goldman, Sachs, and Morgan Stanley.

### December 2, 1985

*European Economic Community member states revise the 1957 Treaty of Rome and agree to remove their final trade barriers by 1992.*

Meeting in Luxembourg from December 2–4, 1985, the 12 EEC nations (including 1986 members-to-be, Spain and Portugal) revised the 1957 treaty to eliminate their remaining trade barriers in 1992. The European countries would then have the economic unity that U.S. states gained after the American Civil War.

### December 4, 1985

**John M. Poindexter replaces Robert C. McFarlane as national security adviser.**

According to White House observers, McFarlane resigned because he found it difficult to "fight over turf" with President Reagan's chief of staff, Donald T. Regan. Poindexter, a navy admiral, was McFarlane's deputy, but his policy views were not known outside official circles.

### December 5, 1985

*Great Britain announces its withdrawal from UNESCO at the end of 1985.*

The British government of Prime Minister Margaret Thatcher followed the lead of the United States, which had abandoned the United Nations Educational, Scientific, and Cultural Organization in 1984. Although in October 1985, UNESCO officials had reformed some of the methods the Reagan administration deemed "hostile" to a free society, neither Great Britain nor the United States thought the changes sufficed.

Admiral John Poindexter. Ronald Reagan Library

### December 5, 1985

**The Organization of American States gives its secretary-general greater power.**

Meeting in Cartagena, Colombia, from December 2 to 5, 1985, the 31 delegates of the OAS revised its original charter to grant more authority to the secretary-general. In particular, the secretary could convene members whenever matters affecting the hemisphere's peace and security needed action.

On other agenda items, the U.S. delegate, Secretary of State George Shultz, prevented the readmission of Cuba and rejected proposals of other OAS members for further peace talks between Shultz and representatives of Nicaragua.

### December 8, 1985

*At a Geneva session, OPEC members abandon their pricing structure; world oil prices drop in the next two days.*

At two prior meetings in 1985 (see January 28), the Organization of Petroleum Exporting Countries reached no agreement on oil prices because Algeria, Libya, and Iran opposed existing production quotas. Consequently, after a two-day session in Geneva,

OPEC members tried to protect their fixed shares of the world market by cutting prices when necessary. This would end OPEC's attempts to regulate production and prices. By December 10, however, after prices fell OPEC members moved to reassert controls. From a high of $39 per barrel in 1979, crude oil prices fell to $19 per barrel in 1985.

See March 24, 1986.

### December 8, 1985

#### The South Asian Association for Regional Cooperation is formed by seven nations.

Concluding a two-day summit of south Asian leaders, this association was created to promote cooperation in agriculture, transportation, and communications. The members were Bangladesh, Bhutan, India, Maldives, Nepal, Pakistan, and Sri Lanka.

### December 8, 1985

#### Guatemalans elect their first civilian president in 15 years.

Marco Cerezo Arevalo, the head of the Christian Democratic Party, won 68% of the vote. A previous election on November 3 had failed to elect a clear winner. Arevalo wanted to promote land reform, better housing, and adequate health care. Despite his landslide victory, the president faced strong opposition from conservative landowners, businessmen, and the military, who opposed reforms. Arevalo hoped the military would keep its promise not to obstruct government programs. His reforms were slow to materialize, and periodic battles between government forces and left-wing guerrillas continued throughout the 1980s.

See October 7, 1987.

### December 10, 1985

#### The Nobel Peace Prize is awarded to the International Physicians for the Prevention of Nuclear War.

Founded in December 1980 by Soviet and American medical doctors concerned about public ignorance of the effects of nuclear war, the physicians group seldom gained much media coverage. It was notable, however, as a joint venture of medical experts from the Soviet Union and the United States. Its cofounders were Dr. Bernard Lown, a cardiologist at Harvard

School of Public Health, and Dr. Yevgeny Chazov, director of the Soviet Union's Cardiological Institute and a member of the Central Committee of the Communist Party.

Just after Lown and Chazov arrived in Norway to receive the award, a newsman disclosed that Chazov had signed a 1973 letter denouncing Soviet physicist Andrey D. Sakharov, who won the Nobel Peace Prize in 1975 for advocating human rights in the USSR. Chazov refused to discuss the 1973 letter, but Lown defended him as an "honest guy" and said the crucial issue was the right of survival against a possible nuclear war. Unfortunately, this incident marred the ceremony, designed to publicize the cooperative efforts of U.S. and Soviet medical doctors trying to prevent the nuclear conflict. The group said it had 135,000 physician members who represented 47 different nations.

### December 12, 1985

#### President Reagan signs the Gramm-Rudman bill trying to end the budget deficit by 1991.

The GRAMM-RUDMAN bill mandated a balanced federal budget during the next five years. President Reagan perceived the law as forcing Congress to cut domestic spending, but Reagan feared Congress would slice military spending or increase taxes. Failure to decrease spending would trigger automatic cuts in all federal programs, with one-half coming from domestic funds, the other half from the military. Congressional concern for a balanced budget developed because the national debt had doubled in four years, reaching $2 trillion in 1985.

See November 14, 1985.

### December 16, 1985

#### Belgian police arrest four terrorists for bombing NATO installations and a U.S. bank.

The Belgian police arrested three men and one woman who belonged to the Communist Combatant Cells, accusing them of committing 27 bombing incidents during the past 14 months. These bombings included the December 4, 1985, attack on a Bank of America branch in Antwerp and the December 6 bombings of NATO installations west of Brussels and at Versailles, France.

## December 18, 1985

### Secretary of State George Shultz visits Eastern Europe.

After attending a North Atlantic Council meeting in Brussels, Belgium, Secretary Shultz went to Berlin to view the Berlin Wall before continuing to the Danube region. Shultz wanted to visit Eastern European leaders to encourage better relations with the United States. President Reagan agreed Shultz should visit leaders of Romania, Hungary, Bulgaria, and Yugoslavia even though hard-line anti-communists in the White House, such as Patrick Buchanan, urged Reagan to avoid all contacts with the Eastern European communists.

Shultz began by flying to Romania, where he visited with Nicolae Ceauşescu. He asked Ceauşescu to stop Romania's discriminatory policies against Jews and German Christians living in Romania and to allow any of these minorities to emigrate if they desired. Ceauşescu made no promises to Shultz on these affairs but agreed to accept Shultz's offer to obtain the most-favored trade status for Romania (see June 2, 1987).

Next, Shultz visited Budapest where he talked with Hungary's communist leader Janos Kadar. Shultz had kind words for Hungary's successful economic reforms but Kadar asked Shultz not to talk in public about how Hungary's policies differed from the Soviet Union's economic policy. Kadar also accepted Shultz's offer to obtain a most-favored nation trade status for Hungary.

In Bulgaria and Yugoslavia, Shultz especially criticized their leaders' willingness to harbor terrorists, a practice Shultz asked them to abolish if they desired better relations with the Western world. During his visit with Yugoslav Foreign Minister Raf Dizdarevic, Shultz strongly condemned Yugoslavia for releasing Muhammad Abbas Zaida (Abu Abbas), whom U.S. authorities blamed for masterminding the attack on the *Achille Lauro* cruise ship (see October 10 and 17, 1985).

Shultz's 1995 memoir *Turmoil and Triumph* describes a press conference in Belgrade during which Dizdarevic told reporters Yugoslavia condemned terrorism but said we "must also view the causes that lead to it," because terrorism can only be eliminated if the causes are ended. Shultz was enraged by Dizdarevic's remarks. Pounding a table with his fist, Shultz asserted: "Hijacking the Italian ship, murdering an American, torturing and holding" other Americans is not justified by any cause. "It is wrong." In his memoir, Shultz says he was more angry with Iraq, whose leader Saddam Hussein had previously assured Washington that Iraq had severed all connections with terrorist groups but allowed Abu Abbas to live in Baghdad after he left Yugoslavia. The United States was supporting Iraq in its war against Iran during the 1980s (see September 4, 1980).
See October 10, 1985.

## December 19, 1985

### President Reagan rejects Mikhail Gorbachev's offer of on-site inspections at nuclear test sites.

The president disclosed that the Soviet leader had offered an inspection system for test sites in a letter of December 5, 1985. Reagan rejected this although U.S. policy had sought on-site inspection for many years. Reagan's only positive comment was to suggest bilateral talks to consider halting nuclear tests. Since 1981, the Reagan administration had opposed test restrictions because the United States had developed advanced nuclear weapons technology.

## December 20, 1985

### The White House announces that lie detector tests will be used on government officials suspected of espionage.

For some time, the Reagan administration had sought methods to end leaks of information that it considered sensitive to national security. On November 1, a presidential order stated that government officials with access to classified data might be required to take a polygraph test. Many persons disliked the general nature of this order, and on December 19, Secretary of State George Shultz opposed it, saying he would resign if he had to be tested.

The December 20 announcement toned down the original directive by limiting tests to people who were suspected of leaking classified data.

## December 27, 1985

### Terrorists attack Israeli airline check-in counters at Rome and Vienna airports, killing 19 and wounding 114.

At nine in the morning, four gunmen armed with AK-47 automatic weapons struck at the El Al Airlines counters in the Rome and Vienna airports. In Rome, four attackers fired at passengers at the El Al, Pan American, and TWA counters. Three of the terrorists were killed, and the other was wounded and captured by Italian police and Israeli security guards.

In Vienna, three terrorists threw hand grenades at the El Al counter and tried to flee in a car. One gunman was killed, and the other two were captured by Austrian police. Although the Palestine Liberation Organization was blamed for these atrocities, its chairman, Yasser Arafat, denied being involved. According to Secretary of State George Shultz's memoir, the Rome and Vienna attacks were carried out by Palestinian terrorists, assisted by Libya's Mu'ammar al-Gadhafi. The Palestinians carried Tunisian passports that records showed were confiscated by Libya. In addition, Gadhafi hailed the airport killings, which included one American girl, as "heroic."

### December 28, 1985

*Meeting in Damascus, rival Lebanese leaders try to end ten years of civil war.*

Syrian President Hafiz al-Assad sought to end Lebanon's internecine conflict by bringing all Christian, Muslim, and Druze leaders together. The efforts appeared successful when Nabih Berri, the Amal Shiite leader, said the warring groups agreed to end their conflicts. The various militias were to disarm during the next 12 months while political problems were being settled. Unfortunately, the pact failed; fighting resumed on January 13.

See July 4, 1986.

# 1986

### January 12, 1986

**Iranians stop and search a U.S. merchant freighter; President Reagan says it may be within international rights.**

An Iranian naval vessel stopped the U.S. freighter *President Taylor* in the Persian Gulf. The *Taylor* was stopped for 45 minutes while Iranian sailors searched for contraband weapons that might be destined for Iraq, with whom Iran was at war. Although the *Taylor*'s captain radioed U.S. naval vessels in the Indian Ocean to ask for help against Iran, the American warships arrived after the Iranians had completed their search. Having found no contraband

aboard the *Taylor*, Iran permitted the *Taylor* to proceed on course toward Iraq with its cargo of wheat and other food supplies.

After the Iran-Iraq war began (see September 4, 1980), Iran's navy stopped and searched hundreds of ships for contraband, a policy permitted under international law that allowed contraband weapons to be confiscated during wartime. Thus, President Reagan did not protest the search of the *Taylor*. Following this incident, the Reagan administration considered future action in the Persian Gulf because the Iran-Iraq war continued. (See May 19, 1987.)

### January 13–14, 1986

**Argentines protest the visit of American banker David Rockefeller.**

Thousands of Argentines demonstrated for two days against Rockefeller, whom they considered the symbol of the banking powers that controlled their foreign loans and demanded austerity measures that led to high unemployment, higher prices, and lower living standards. The police arrested 81 people, and many were injured, although the police refrained from gunfire.

### January 15, 1986

**U.S. budget expenditures for 1986 exceed Gramm-Rudman target; the Budget Office orders spending cuts on March 1, 1986.**

Under legislation to eliminate the federal deficit gradually, the Budget Office announced needed cuts and the General Accounting Office prepared the mandatory list of cuts across the board, except for Social Security benefits. The cuts came to $11.7 billion of previous appropriations. Since these were the first cuts in each department's budget, they had little effect on department expenditures during 1986 and 1987.

On July 7, the Supreme Court voided the bill's provision that allowed the Budget Office and the GAO to enact cuts. The Court ruled that Congress had to legislate Gramm-Rudman cuts, making members of Congress vote for the cuts required by the 1985 legislation. Accordingly, members of Congress faced hard choices in approving the 1987 budget in October.

See October 18, 1986.

## January 19, 1986

### Group of Five finance ministers agrees to lower interest rates.

At the first meeting under the Plaza Accord, which committed the five major industrialized nations to cooperate in stabilizing the currency of their countries, the Group of Five could not agree on lowering their interest rates. Eventually, the United States, France, West Germany, and Japan lowered their interest rates, but the United Kingdom refused to do so during 1986.

For the United States, Secretary of the Treasury James Baker advocated lower interest rates, but Paul Volcker, the Federal Reserve Board chairman, was cautious about this commitment. Beginning on March 7, 1986, the Federal Reserve lowered rates by reducing the Reserve's discount rate to banks from 7.5% to 7%. Later in 1986, the Federal Reserve again lowered rates, to 5.5% on August 20.

See September 22, 1985.

## January 20, 1986

### *Britain and France plan a 30-mile rail tunnel under the English Channel.*

British Prime Minister Margaret Thatcher and French President François Mitterrand indicated the project should be completed by 1993. There would be twin 30-mile rail tunnels between Folkestone, England, and Calais, France. Passenger and shuttle trains would operate in 30-minute crossings, the shuttles able to carry 4,000 cars per hour. At a cost of $3 billion to $7 billion, the project would provide 40,000 to 70,000 jobs in each country.

## January 28, 1986

### The U.S. space shuttle *Challenger* explodes, killing seven crew members.

The twenty-fifth shuttle mission exploded 74 seconds into liftoff, killing Francis R. Scobee, Michael J. Smith, Judith A. Resnik, Ellison S. Onizuka, Ronald E. McNair, Gregory B. Jarvis, and Sharon Christa McAuliffe. This flight had been widely publicized because McAuliffe was a schoolteacher, selected in a nationwide search to provide an educator with experiences of space flight.

The shock of the disaster caused President Reagan to postpone his scheduled State of the Union speech and the National Aeronautics and Space Administration to ground the three remaining shuttles. An interim panel was appointed to review the accident pending the establishment of a formal investigation board by President Reagan on February 3.

## February 1, 1986

### A Defense Department review panel recommends development of a mobile, single-warhead Midgetman missile.

Although the Pentagon's research director, Donald Hicks, wanted a larger missile capable of carrying three nuclear warheads, the commission of scientists and weapons experts recommended the small, single-warhead missile capable of mobility enabling it to survive an enemy's first nuclear strike.

See Scowcroft Report, April 11, 1983.

## February 2, 1986

### *El Salvador convicts two national guardsmen who murdered land reform agents; higher officials are not arrested.*

The killing of three agricultural workers in 1981 had been investigated reluctantly by El Salvadoran police because high-level politicians associated with the ARENA Party led by Roberto d'Aubuisson were involved in the murders (see January 3, 1981). On February 2, 1986, the two National Guardsmen who confessed to the murders were convicted and sentenced to 30 years in prison. Nevertheless, the Salvadoran government had not prosecuted two army officers associated with the ARENA Party and wealthy landowner Ricardo Sol Meza, who were said to have ordered the three assassinations.

See January 3, 1981.

## February 4, 1986

### *Israeli pilots mistakenly intercept a Libyan jet; PLO leaders are not on board.*

Because Israeli intelligence thought George Habash and other Palestinian leaders were on the Libyan plane flying from Tripoli, Libya, to Damascus, Israeli air force planes forced the jet to land in Israel. Because the jet carried only seven Syrian politicians and two low-level pro-Syrian Lebanese militants, Israel released it after a five-hour search.

On February 6, Syria sponsored a U.N. Security Council resolution to condemn Israel, for intercepting an airplane that was not flying over Israeli airspace, but the United States vetoed it. The Reagan administration said it deplored the action, but the resolution did not recognize the right of a state to intercept aircraft under "exceptional circumstances."

### February 7, 1986

*Haitian dictator Jean-Claude Duvalier is overthrown.*

Protests and incidents of violence by Haitians opposing the regime of President for Life Jean Claude Duvalier (Baby Doc) began in 1982 (see January 10, 1982) and steadily increased by 1986. To protect himself, Duvalier declared a state of siege on January 31, 1986, but opposition protests continued, with army factions that opposed Duvalier now joining the demonstrations.

In early February, there were reports that Duvalier fled the country, even though the Port-au-Prince embassies of Greece, Switzerland, and Italy rejected his request for asylum. On February 7, Duvalier persuaded Spain to grant him asylum. After Baby Doc left, Lieutenant General Henri Namphy attempted to restore order in Haiti. Namphy's job was difficult not only because Duvalier's dreaded security force, the Tonton Macoutes, terrorized citizens, but also because Haiti's army factions were involved in transporting cocaine between Columbian drug dealers and the United States.

Furthermore, in 1996 investigations by *The Nation* magazine's Alan Narin revealed that agents of the U.S. Central Intelligence Agency (CIA) and the U.S. Defense Intelligence Agency (DIA) had secretly funded two political groups: the Securite Intelligence Nationale (SIN) and the Front for the Advancement and Progress of Haiti (FRAPH), both of whom terrorized the population to keep people from voting for members of Haiti's liberal reform parties who wanted to end the rule of Haiti's wealthy elite, Haiti's army, and the Tonton Macoutes. Both the CIA and DIA wanted a strong central government such as Duvalier's to maintain order in Haiti and enable American investors such as General Motors and National City Bank of New York to profit after having built factories in Haiti during the 1970s.

On February 25, Namphy appointed the Haitian National Council to draft a new constitution, hold elections, and improve education for all Haitian children. When an election was held on October 19, 1986, only 21% of the Haitian eligible population voted because the SIN, FRAPH, and Tonton Macoutes terrorized the population and warned them not to vote. The election had 16 different parties on the ballot, and foreign journalists who observed reported chaos at most of the polling stations.

See March 4, 1986, and November 29, 1987.

### February 7, 1986

*Philippine President Ferdinand Marcos claims to win reelection, but the opposition charges fraud and calls for nonviolent protests.*

Marcos called for an early election in November 1985, hoping his opponents would remain divided and easy to defeat. The opposition had rallied around Corazon C. Aquino, the widow of the assassinated leader of the Philippine opposition. Early returns favored Aquino, but amid widespread complaints of fraud, Marcos claimed victory, and on February 15, the National Assembly declared him president with 53.8% of the vote.

By that time, however, international election observers reported there was fraud and violence committed by Marcos's supporters, and President Reagan changed his earlier endorsement of Marcos. The next day Aquino called for nonviolent protests to remove Marcos from office.

See February 25, 1986.

### February 11, 1986

*A prominent Soviet dissident Anatoly B. Shcharansky is freed in an exchange of nine prisoners in Berlin.*

An East-West prisoner exchange at the Berlin Wall included Shcharansky, whom the Soviets had convicted of spying for the West in 1978. Shcharansky was an outspoken critic of the Soviet Union's anti-Jewish policies. After his release, he went to Israel, where his wife, Avital, lived. He visited the United States in May 1986 to describe his ideas of and his treatment by the Soviet Union.

"Checkpoint Charlie" on the West Berlin side of the Berlin Wall, looking into East Berlin. Lester Brune

## February 12, 1986

### The United States extradites an ex-Nazi to Yugoslavia, where he is found guilty of murder.

Since 1953, the United States and Yugoslavia had argued about the extradition of Andrya Artukovic, a leader of the pro-Nazi Utashe in Croatia who, Yugoslavia said, had ordered the deaths of 231,000 people during World War II. Artukovic was returned to Belgrade, tried, and found guilty, and on May 14 was sentenced to death. Although an appeal and a request for a pardon were denied on July 25 and December 23, respectively, a stay of execution was accepted in April 1987. Artukovic died in a Zagreb prison on January 16, 1988.

## February 13, 1986

### Japan continues voluntary curbs on automobile exports to the United States.

This was the sixth year of voluntary curbs. Although in 1985, President Reagan no longer requested export limits, Japan maintained them for 1986 at the level set in 1985—2.3 million units. In 1985, the Japanese did not reach their expected U.S. market ceiling of 24.3%, having only 20.1%. The Japanese auto trade surplus was at $3 billion. Nevertheless, observers indicated that U.S. automakers had raised prices steadily since

1981 because Japan brought in higher-priced cars. The observers estimated that this cost the U.S. consumer about $2 billion more for car purchases.

On January 8, Japanese Foreign Minister Shintaro Abe agreed with U.S. Secretary of State George Shultz to continue talks to improve trade on specific items where they had achieved success in 1985.

See July 31, 1986.

## February 15, 1986

### Nine members of Congress visit Vietnam; they return with the remains of possible MIAs.

A congressional delegation headed by Gerald Solomon (R-N.Y.) arrived in Hanoi (January 6–7) one month after Assistant Secretary of Defense Richard L. Armitage had met with Vietnamese officials in Hanoi to discuss the MIAs. During those sessions Hanoi agreed to investigate 95 reports of live American servicemen in Vietnam.

Congressman Solomon's group received a similar response in Hanoi where they learned that bones of American servicemen would be turned over. On April 10, the remains of 21 soldiers were turned over to U.S. officials, but Foreign Minister Hoang Bich Son denied that any MIAs were still alive in Vietnam. These talks ended when Hanoi suspended them following the U.S air attack on Libya on April 15, 1986.

**February 18, 1986**

**The Senate Foreign Relations Committee is told that President Reagan wants $15 million for Angolan rebels.**

The Angolan government had combated rebels since the early 1970s after it obtained independence from Portugal. In August 1985, Congress had, at President Reagan's urging, repealed the Clark Amendment, which since 1976 had made secret aid to the rebels illegal (see July 10, 1985). Congress also allocated $30 million for aid to the National Union for the Total Independence of Angola (UNITA).

From January 28 to February 8, Jonas Savimbi, the leader of UNITA visited Washington. Savimbi hired a lobbying agent for $600,000 to gain favor with the U.S. public, and Reagan gave him a red carpet reception. Reagan did not promise him aid, deciding not to ask Congress for funds until later. Savimbi had many critics. All black African nations supported the existing Angolan government. South Africa was his one ally, supplying UNITA with weapons and often staging raids against Angola's army. Cuban volunteers served in Angola and their presence was a major reason the Reagan administration disliked Angola's government. Under the "Reagan Doctrine," Savimbi was hailed as a freedom fighter despite his ill repute in Africa.

See September 9, 1986.

**February 19, 1986**

**After delaying for 37 years, the U.S. Senate approves the U.N. Convention on the Prevention and Punishment of the Crime of Genocide.**

Proposed by the United Nations National Assembly in 1948 in the wake of the Nazi genocide against the Jews and other Peoples, this treaty was signed by the United States but the Senate had not approved it. Ninety nations including the Soviet Union had approved it, but certain senators prevented approval because it supposedly compromised U.S. sovereignty.

In 1986, a bipartisan group led by Senators Robert Dole, William Proxmire, and Rudy Boschwitz offered the treaty for Senate approval and President Reagan's ratification. It passed by a vote of 83 to 11. To prevent a filibuster, the Senate added an amendment that the treaty could not interfere with the U.S. Constitution, and that the International World Court at the Hague had no automatic jurisdiction over the United States.

**February 20, 1986**

**President Reagan admits to representatives of various Caribbean nations that two years of the CBI achieved little.**

At a conference of Caribbean nations in Grenada, President Reagan stated that his Caribbean Basin Initiative (CBI) had not worked well. The program to encourage a free-market economy with U.S. investments had actually damaged their economies. The U.S. Commerce Department reported that the CBI exports to the United States declined 23% in two years, while U.S. imports from the rest of the world increased 36%. Moreover, there had been no progress in gaining U.S investments, raising unemployment to 25%. Finally, the U.S. farm bill for 1985 reduced sugar imports from the islands, damaging Caribbean sugar producers. The president told the conference that the United States would try to improve the CBI by offering more favorable quotas for Caribbean sugar and other products.

**February 25, 1986**

**"People power" claims victory in the Philippines; President Marcos is exiled, and Corazon Aquino becomes president.**

Marcos's decision to fly to exile in Hawaii via Guam came after nine days of popular protest, the defection of key Philippine army officers, and a final nudge from Senator Paul Laxalt (R-Nev.), who represented President Reagan's views to Marcos.

The demonstrations by Aquino's followers in Manila and other cities had grown ever larger until on February 22 the Philippines defense minister, Juan Ponce Enrile, and the armed forces chief of staff, General Fidel V. Ramos, occupied the Defense Ministry at Camp Aquinaldo, resigned, and asked Marcos to resign. When Marcos ordered troops to attack the ministry, navy soldiers defected and the attack failed. Initially, Marcos told Laxalt that he might share power with Aquino, but after calling Washington, the senator advised Marcos to resign. Marcos left the Philippines with an entourage of 54 people who arrived in Hawaii on February 26. That same day, Aquino named a new cabinet with Enrile as minister of defense. She ordered the release of all political prisoners including two leading communists whose rebel groups the new president hoped to silence by changes she would make in the Philippines.

On March 25, President Aquino abolished the National Assembly and the constitution. She announced an interim constitution until a new document could be drawn up.

On April 24, President Reagan approved Aquino's government, agreeing to seek $150 million in additional economic and military aid for the Philippines.

On U.S. aid, see September 29, 1986; on a rebellion attempt, see July 8, 1986.

### February 25, 1986

*The 27th Congress of the Communist Party of the Soviet Union opens. Soviet leader Gorbachev seeks economic reforms.*

The congress met from February 25 to March 6. Its principal agenda was the approval of a five-year economic plan that First Secretary Mikhail Gorbachev had unveiled in October 1985. In addition, major changes in the party's Central Committee membership were announced.

After Gorbachev blamed economic stagnation on the 18-year rule of Leonid Brezhnev and offered his policy of economic reforms, called "PERESTROIKA" the Congress passed a resolution calling for "truly revolutionary changes." One major change began on November 19, 1986, when the Supreme Soviet approved the use of private enterprise to manufacture some consumer goods and to provide services such as women's hairdressing.

### February 25, 1986

*Iran launches attacks on northern Iraq, extending the front lines in the conflict.*

These Iranian attacks on the Kurdistan region of Iraq were part of a series of offensive movements in the five-year-old war. On February 11, Iran captured the Iraqi port of Fao. In May, Iraq took offensive measures, bombing a Tehran oil refinery on May 7 and overrunning the town of Mehran on May 17 before Iran counterattacked to retake its territory.

### February 28, 1986

*Swedish Prime Minister Olof Palme is assassinated in Stockholm.*

Palme was killed while he and his wife were walking home from a movie theater at 11:30 P.M. He was replaced as prime minister by Ingvar Carlsson. Following extensive investigation, Swedish police arrested Christer Pettersson, a local alcoholic. Pettersson was tried and convicted of murder on July 27, 1989, but a Swedish appeals court voided the conviction. In Swedish courts, two judges and six citizens are the jury, and while the majority convicted Pettersson, both professional trial judges voted against the conviction.

### March 2, 1986

*A Palestinian kills the Palestinian mayor of Nablus on West Bank territory.*

As a method of promoting peace in the West Bank, Israeli Prime Minister Shimon Peres appointed Palestinians as mayors of certain West Bank towns to give them limited autonomy. In 1985, Zafir al-Masri became mayor of Nablus, a decision strongly criticized by radical Palestinians who advocated independence. Although Masri did not take office until Jordan's King Hussein and PLO leader Yasser Arafat approved, the anti-Arafat Palestinians disliked such a compromise with Israel. Masri's assassin took orders from the Syrian-supported Palestinian Front for the Liberation of Palestine.

### March 4, 1986

*Former U.N. Secretary-General Kurt Waldheim is accused of collaborating with Nazis in helping deport Jews.*

A *New York Times* article claimed Waldheim had worked with the Nazis. Although Waldheim, who was a candidate for president of Austria, denied the allegation, on April 4 the United Nations made its secret 1948 war crimes file available to Israeli, Austrian, and American authorities. After investigating the U.N. file, the U.S. Justice Department recommended that Waldheim be barred from entering the United States. This began an inquiry into Waldheim's service with a German army unit connected with Nazi atrocities in the Balkans during World War II, a situation described in full by Robert Herzstein in his 1988 book, *Waldheim: The Missing Years*. Waldheim did not withdraw as an Austrian presidential candidate and won a runoff election on June 8 with 53.9% of the vote.

See February 9, 1988.

### March 8, 1986

*Two Frenchmen are executed by two pro-Iranian terrorist groups.*

Because France had sent military equipment to aid Iraq in its war against Iran, members of the pro-Iranian terrorist groups Islamic Jihad and the Revolutionary Justice Organization (RJO) executed two Frenchmen who had been taken hostage. On March 5, Islamic Jihad murdered Michel Serviat, whom they had captured in May 1985.

On March 8, 1986, the RJO seized four French television crewmen as hostages. On June 20, the RJO released Philippe Pochot and George Hansen, two members of the television crew. The RJO stated they were released because France had given them evidence of changing its policies toward Iran. On December 24, the RJO released television crewman Aurel Cornea, allegedly because ransom was paid, a claim the French government denied.

Jean-Louis Normandin, the fourth television crew member, was also murdered by the RJO in early 1987. An RJO spokesman said Normandin was executed because France refused to exchange Iranian Anis Naccache, whom French courts had sentenced to life in prison after he was found guilty of the attempted murder of Iran's former premier, Dr Shahpur Bakhtiar.

On Bakhtiar's role in the 1979 revolution that overthrew Iran's shah see February 1, 1979.

### March 14, 1986

*A U.N. report says Iraq used chemical weapons against Iran.*

This report by U.N. Secretary-General Javier Pérez de Cuellar was based on the findings of international experts who visited Iran but were refused permission to visit Iraq. This was the first report to specifically blame Iraq for using such weapons, especially mustard gas and nerve gas. The report said more extensive use of chemical weapons had been made by Iraq since 1984.

Secretary-General Pérez de Cuellar condemned Iraq for violating the 1925 Geneva Protocol ban on chemical weapons.

### March 14, 1986

**President Reagan offers a major policy change: he will oppose dictatorships on the right as well as on the left.**

In a foreign policy message to a joint session of Congress, Reagan urged democratic reforms of right-wing as well as left-wing governments. This decision moved him away from the so-called Kirkpatrick doctrine. Reagan's former U.N. representatives, Jeane Kirkpatrick, stressed that right-wing "authoritarian" regimes differed significantly from left-wing "totalitarian" regimes. Reagan now discarded this distinction, indicating that Haiti, the Philippines, and South Africa were examples of governments where democracy could replace right-wing rule. Nevertheless, Reagan emphasized the need to combat communist governments and rebels, especially in Central America. He ended the speech to Congress by asking Congress to provide $100 million for the Contra rebels fighting Nicaragua's Sandinista government.

See January 29, 1984.

### March 18, 1986

**The Soviet Union protests the incursion of two U.S. navy ships into its territorial waters near the Crimea.**

The U.S. vessels were the *Yorktown*, a guided-missile cruiser, and the *Caron*, a destroyer, which entered the Black Sea on March 10, traveling within six nautical miles of the Soviet coastline near the Crimean peninsula. The Soviet Union claimed territorial rights of 12 nautical miles. The White House said the U.S. ships simply tested the right of innocent passage. A Pentagon spokesman said the ships gathered intelligence data as Soviet ships did off the U.S. coastline.

### March 19, 1986

**President Reagan and Canadian Prime Minister Brian Mulroney endorse an acid-rain report and defense agreements.**

Meeting in Washington, D.C., the two leaders discussed acid-rain pollution in the northeastern

United States and Canada and renewed the long-lived North American Aerospace Defense Command System (NORAD).

The dispute over toxic sulfur dioxide being generated from coal-burning manufacturers and electric power plants in the United States and blowing into New England and Canada to pollute streams and lakes had become a major issue. In 1985, two experts, Drew Lewis of the United States and William Davis of Canada, were asked to investigate and report on acid rain. Their report was released on January 7, 1986, acknowledging that man-made pollution in the United States carried into Canada to damage the environment. It recommended $5 billion for a five-year program to develop technology to burn coal slowly and lower the amount of sulfur dioxide released into the air. Reagan and Mulroney endorsed the Lewis-Davis report, but environmental advocates pointed out that no action was taken to implement the study.

### March 24, 1986

**OPEC fails to agree on cuts in petroleum production. Soon after, U.S. crude oil prices drop below $10 per barrel.**

The ability of the members of the Organization of Petroleum Exporting Countries to regulate prices and production continued to deteriorate in 1986. On January 28, the United Kingdom refused OPEC's request to cut its North Sea oil production. Now, at a nine-day Geneva session, OPEC members could not agree on cutting oil output to 19 million barrels a day in order to raise prices.

The oil price decline also hurt investors and banks, especially in Texas where spending on new oil wells increased in the 1970s and early 1980s because of high oil prices. By April 1, the failure of OPEC to sustain unity caused the crude prices of West Texas intermediate grade to fall to $11 per barrel, and by April, below $10. Because of production expenses, Texas oil became unprofitable below $15, and Alaska oil could not be profitable below $10.

On April 6, Vice President George Bush visited King Fahd of Saudi Arabia and expressed concern for maintaining stable oil prices. The disruption of OPEC by a "free market" on oil caused confusion for the Reagan administration. Low oil prices cut U.S. inflation after 1981, but now the "free market," which Reagan lauded, caused difficulties for U.S. oil

producers. One benefit of lower prices was that, after the U.S. air raid against Libya on April 15, Libya's request that OPEC levy an oil embargo against the United States was rejected. OPEC members condemned the U.S. attack but also protected their own income.

See December 20, 1986.

### March 27, 1986

**West Germany agrees to participate in SDI research; Britain, Italy, Israel and Japan also join SDI research.**

At first, West Germany's Bundestag (Parliament) opposed any government role in America's SDI program because Chancellor Helmut Kohl's coalition partner, the Free Democrat Party, would not consent to have the German government fund missile defense research. To obtain a majority of Bundestag votes favoring a German role in SDI, Kohl and U.S. Defense Secretary Caspar Weinberger reached a compromise satisfactory to the Free Democrat Party. The agreement permitted West Germany's private companies and private research institutes to obtain U.S. contracts for SDI research, but no federal government funds could be used for such research.

When the full text of the U.S.-German agreement became public on April 8, 1986, members of Germany's Social Democratic Party and Green Party (environmental) criticized the agreement because West German companies having SDI contracts would be restricted on the sale of technological products to Eastern European countries.

West Germany was the second U.S. ally to join SDI research. On December 8, 1985, the United Kingdom's Defense Minister Michael Heseltine signed an agreement with Weinberger whereby British companies and research institutes could obtain contracts for SDI research, although the British Labour Party, a minority in Parliament, opposed the agreement. On May 6, 1986, Israel and the United States signed an agreement for Israeli companies to participate in SDI research. On September 9, Japan and the United States signed an agreement for Japanese institutes and companies to perform SDI research, and on September 19, Italy signed an agreement by which Italy became the fifth U.S. ally to participate in SDI research.

France was the principal European nation rejecting an American offer to cooperate in SDI research.

France established an anti-missile defense program called EUREKA, hoping members of the Western European Union (WEU) would help fund EUREKA. France was not successful in its quest for WEU funds because West Germany, Italy, and the United Kingdom rejected the French plans.

### March 29, 1986

*Italian courts acquit three Bulgarians and three Turks accused of the attempt on the life of Pope John Paul II in 1981; one Turk is found guilty.*

Six of the seven accused men were freed because the court found the evidence against them ambiguous. One Turk was found guilty of storing and delivering weapons used in the shooting. Earlier, Turkish citizen Mehmet Ali Agca had received a life sentence for shooting the pope.

See May 13, 1981.

### April 2, 1986

*A TWA plane explodes in the air, killing 4 Americans; 110 passengers survive.*

En route from Rome to Athens, a bomb exploded in the plane's cabin as it began to descend. The explosion ripped a hole in the fuselage, and four passengers were immediately flung out and killed. The pilot made a safe emergency landing, which saved the other passengers and crew.

An anonymous telephone caller said the bomb was in retaliation for U.S naval activity in Libya's Gulf of Sidra and was planted by the Arab Revolutionary Cells. Investigators believed the bomb had been planted by May Elian Mansour, a known terrorist, who flew from Cairo to Rome, where she disembarked before the flight continued to Athens.

see April 14, 1986.

### April 2, 1986

**President Reagan reorganizes the U.S. military.**

The president's changes were based on the February 28, 1986, report of the Blue Ribbon Commission on Defense Management chaired by former Deputy Secretary of Defense David Packard. The president enacted some reforms by executive order, such as overhauling the military procurement process, which took too long and cost too much.

In other cases, Congress enacted legislative measures, such as making the chairman of the Joint Chiefs of Staff an independent adviser of the president, speaking for all the armed services.

### April 5, 1986

**A terrorist's bomb explodes in West Berlin, killing one American; President Reagan blames Libya for the incident.**

At a West Berlin discotheque frequented by U.S. soldiers, a bomb exploded, killing 2 people and wounding 230 others, including 50 Americans. Immediately, the Reagan administration blamed Mu'ammar al-Gadhafi of Libya as the master controller of terrorists, later citing proof from intercepted messages to Berlin from Libya. On January 7, the president cut most economic ties with Libya and sent the U.S. ambassador Vernon A. Walters to the United Nations, to seek European support for sanctions and other measures against Libya. Reagan first sought sanctions against Libya after the Rome and Vienna airport attacks of December 27, 1985, but the Europeans responded only with rhetoric. European leaders, including British Prime Minister Margaret Thatcher, disagreed with U.S. action against Libya, believing diplomacy, not economic sanctions, would solve the problem. Although France and West Germany expelled two Libyan intelligence operatives, they did not break diplomatic relations with Libya or impose economic sanctions.

Reagan had mobilized Americans against Gadhafi by his television speeches, but Europeans did not subscribe to these messages. Even though there were three terror bombings in Paris between February 3 and 5, 1986, and a terror bombing of a German-Arab Friendship Society building in West Berlin on March 29, Europeans viewed these as domestic incidents not requiring a major international response. This is why many Europeans opposed the U.S. bombing of Libya.

See April 14 and May 6, 1986.

### April 6, 1986

*EEC members revalue their currencies.*

At a meeting of the European Economic Community (EEC) finance ministers, an agreement was made to revalue members' currencies. France devalued the franc by 3% against other currencies; West Germany and the Netherlands increased the value of the mark and the guilder by 3%; Belgium, Luxembourg, and Denmark increased the value of their currency by 1%. This was a step toward establishing a European monetary system in 1992.

## April 7, 1986

### John Gavin resigns as U.S. ambassador to Mexico.

President Reagan's 1981 appointment of movie actor John Gavin as ambassador to Mexico had been controversial from the start. While Reagan's California friends such as Edward Meese hoped the actor could improve relations with Mexico, the very right-wing, outspoken Gavin had tried to redirect Mexican politics. Gavin's constant complaints about Mexican policy caused feuds with the Mexican news media.

On two occasions the democratic journalists union voted to denounce Gavin as *persona non grata*. After Gavin's resignation was formally announced on May 15, the *El Universal* newspaper said his resignation was one of the best news stories Mexico ever received.

See August 14, 1986.

## April 8, 1986

### President Reagan issues a national security directive permitting the armed forces to combat drug trafficking.

The question about using regular U.S. armed forces in the war on drugs had been raised several times. The Pentagon was reluctant to divert its forces, and civil libertarians voiced concern about involving military personnel in law enforcement. U.S. law prohibited the use of the armed forces as a *posse comitatus*, or in the execution of the legal prosecution of citizens.

Nevertheless, President Reagan made the international drug trade a national security matter, justifying the use of U.S. armed forces to interdict or attack drug traffickers. This directive was implemented on July 14, 1986, when Reagan dispatched U.S. army forces to help Bolivia.

See July 14, 1986.

## April 8, 1986

### Soviet Ambassador Anatoly F. Dobrynin meets for the last time with President Reagan.

Dobrynin, who was Soviet ambassador to the United States for 24 years, resigned on March 6 and had his last official visits with the president and Secretary of State George Shultz. On May 20, Yuri V. Dubinin was appointed as the new ambassador. Although a former Soviet ambassador to the United Nations, Dubinin was neither trained in U.S.-Soviet relations nor fluent in English as Dobrynin had been.

## April 14, 1986

### U.S. aircraft bomb five Libyan targets in retaliation for Libyan leader Mu'ammar al-Gadhafi's support for terrorists.

Early in the morning of April 15 (April 14 at 7:00 P.M. Eastern Standard Time), American planes from aircraft carriers and bases in Great Britain attacked five targets in Libya: a military base and installation, the port at Sidi Bilat in Tripoli, and a military barracks and an air base near Benghazi. Bombs also struck the French embassy and buildings in the Bin Ashur district of Tripoli. Bombs hit near a residence of Gadhafi, killing his infant adopted daughter and seriously injuring two of his sons. Gadhafi was absent at the time of the bombing. The Americans lost one F-111 fighter bomber and its crew of two.

After the December 1985 attacks at airports in Rome and Vienna, President Reagan launched a campaign of vilification against Gadhafi, whom Reagan blamed for these and other terrorist raids. On January 9, Reagan levied economic sanctions on Libya; on March 24, U.S. navy planes attacked Libyan patrol boats in the Gulf of Sidra; and on April 5, the White House cited evidence that Libya had planned the terrorist attack on a West Berlin discotheque (see April 5, 1986). On April 9, Reagan called Gadhafi a "mad dog," saying the United States is "certainly going to take action in the face of specific terrorist threats."

After consulting with leaders of the U.S. Congress, Britain, France, West Germany, Spain, and Italy, President Reagan decided to attack Libya on the night of April 14–15. Secretary of State George Shultz's 1995 memoir *Turmoil and Triumph* explains that the Reagan administration wanted to get people close to Gadhafi by taking action against a state that

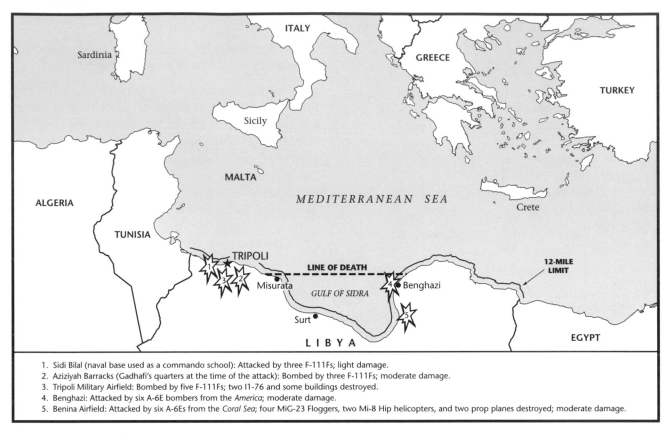

1. Sidi Bilal (naval base used as a commando school): Attacked by three F-111Fs; light damage.
2. Aziziyah Barracks (Gadhafi's quarters at the time of the attack): Bombed by three F-111Fs; moderate damage.
3. Tripoli Military Airfield: Bombed by five F-111Fs; two Il-76 and some buildings destroyed.
4. Benghazi: Attacked by six A-6E bombers from the *America*; moderate damage.
5. Benina Airfield: Attacked by six A-6Es from the *Coral Sea*; four MiG-23 Floggers, two Mi-8 Hip helicopters, and two prop planes destroyed; moderate damage.

U.S. air raid on Libya, 1986.

perpetuated terrorism. Shultz also wanted to alert Europeans to the dangers posed by Libya and inspire Libyan dissidents to overthrow Gadhafi, a hope that proved fruitless.

After the U.S. attack, a *New York Times*/CBS poll found that 77% of those polled backed the president, but European opinion was mixed regarding the bombing and its results. While British Prime Minister Margaret Thatcher approved the attacks and granted permission for the U.S. use of air bases in England to make the attack, a British opinion poll showed two-thirds opposed the raid. The London *Observer's* pundit Patrick Scale wrote that the attack would make Gadhafi an "Arab hero and put more American lives at risk." West Germany's Foreign Minister Hans-Dietrich Genscher told Shultz the U.S. should not have taken such drastic action and Europeans lauded French President François Mitterrand for resisting U.S. pressure to permit U.S. planes to fly over France on route to attack Libya. Furthermore, Gadhafi was not silenced by the attack (see August 25, 1986).

See April 5, 1986 and
August 25, 1986.

**April 16, 1986**

### *Soviet Foreign Minister Shevardnadze cannot normalize Soviet relations with China.*

Under Mikhail Gorbachev's leadership, the Soviet Union tried to revive good relations with China but with only slight success. Although China and the USSR agreed on March 21 to exchange engineers and technicians, on January 15 China rejected a Soviet proposal for a nonaggression pact. Soviet Foreign Minister Eduard Shevardnadze proposed on April 16 that China and the Soviets have a summit conference to normalize relations.

In response, China's Vice Foreign Minister Qian Qichen, who was visiting Moscow, replied that a summit was unrealistic until Soviet policy removed the "three obstacles"—lessening tension on the Chinese border by reducing the number of Soviet troops, withdrawing Soviet troops from Afghanistan, and ending support for Vietnam's occupation of Cambodia. In a speech on July 28, Gorbachev took steps to eliminate these three obstacles.

## April 18, 1986

### A Titan 34-D rocket carrying a secret military payload explodes after liftoff in California.

This accident was a setback to the military launching of such payloads (the Titan 34-D was believed to be carrying a reconnaissance satellite), adding to the problems of the U.S. space program since the *Challenger* exploded on January 28, 1986. Less than a month later, on May 3, 1986, a third space mission failed when a U.S. Delta rocket exploded after liftoff. The Delta carried a weather satellite, and after the rocket's power failed, ground control destroyed it.

## April 26, 1986

### The worst nuclear accident in history occurs at the Chernobyl nuclear power facility in Soviet Ukraine.

Located near Kiev, the CHERNOBYL power plant experienced a graphite fire that caused an explosion at the no. 4 reactor. The accident sent high levels of radioactive material into the atmosphere, reaching into central Europe and Scandinavia, where the Swedes reported abnormal levels of radioactive debris. When Sweden reported this on April 28, the USSR finally disclosed that the accident had occurred 48 hours earlier.

The Soviets rejected foreign assistance in fighting the reactor fires, but on May 4, First Secretary Mikhail Gorbachev proposed a four-point agenda to cooperate with the International Atomic Energy Agency. On August 25 and 26, Soviet scientists and engineers met with 500 delegates from 50 countries to discuss the accident which, the Soviets blamed on an unauthorized test that was further exacerbated by the faulty design of the reactor plant. On June 15, *Pravda*, the Communist Party newspaper, reported that several high officials had been dismissed, including the head of the Soviet nuclear power industry and the head of the State Committee for Atomic Safety.

## April 28, 1986

### Turkey arrests two Libyans for planning to bomb the U.S. Officers' Club in Ankara.

This plot was uncovered on April 8 when five Libyans were detained. By April 28, three of the Libyans were released under diplomatic immunity; the other two were arrested and convicted on May 13 of possession of explosives and sentenced to five years in prison. They were, however, acquitted of conspiracy "to kill a group of people."

## May 4, 1986

### Najibullah replaces Karmal as general secretary of the People's Democratic Party of Afghanistan.

Babrak Karmal resigned as party head because of his health. Najibullah had been head of the secret police in Afghanistan.

## May 5–6, 1986

### Jordan's King Hussein visits Syrian President Assad and indicates his dissatisfaction with Yasser Arafat.

Although Hussein and Palestine Liberation Organization leader Arafat seemed to have reached agreement in 1985, Hussein on February 19, 1986, ended peace efforts with the PLO. Hussein said he found Arafat to be untrustworthy and disagreed with the PLO's refusal to accept U.N. resolutions 242 and 338 as the basis for Middle East peace.

Hussein's visit with Assad launched a new Jordanian peace effort. Syria and Arafat had broken relations during Israel's 1982 invasion of Lebanon, when Syria supported anti-Arafat Palestinian groups. On July 7, 1986, Hussein closed down 25 offices where Arafat's Al-Fatah group conducted business in Jordan.

See February 11, 1985.

## May 6, 1986

### Tokyo economic summit of seven industrialized nations shows "good will."

President Reagan attended the summit as part of an extended visit to Asia. As in past meetings, the summit reflected the "good will" of the participants but resulted in no significant economic agreements. Most notable was the tough antiterrorist resolution that Reagan and British Prime Minister Margaret Thatcher persuaded the other five nations to accept. They did not impose economic sanctions on Libya, however, as Reagan desired.

During the 13-day Asian trip Reagan's other noteworthy meeting was with the foreign ministers of the Association of South East Asian Nations at Bali, Indonesia. The Asians complained that U.S. agricultural subsidies hindered their exports of rice and other commodities.

## May 6, 1986

### West German and Italian police implicate Syria, not Libya, in the Rome-Vienna airport attacks of December 1985.

Evidence collected in Germany and Italy indicated that President Reagan and other U.S. leaders had been too hasty in implicating Libya in the December airport bombings. Italian police told the Central Intelligence Agency in December 1985 that the surviving Rome terrorist, Muhammad Sarhan, had been trained in Syria and brought by Syrians through Eastern Europe to Rome before the incident. The Italian spokesman claimed not to know why the United States never followed up on the Syrian connection.

Similarly, on March 29, West Germans arrested Ahmed Nawaf Mansour Hazi for the bombing of a German-Arab office. Hazi was trained in Syria and obtained explosives from the Syrian embassy in East Berlin. Hazi, however, denied bombing the Berlin discotheque where Americans among others had been killed.

British authorities also believed that Syria, not Libya, was the central base of terrorist operations. They could not, however, persuade U.S. officials to act on this premise.

See April 5, 1986, and October 24 and November 26, 1986.

## May 6, 1986

### Thirteen nations meeting in Ecuador call on the United States to fund the war on drug traffic.

This meeting of 13 Latin American nations was one of several in 1986 indicating their willingness to help fight the drug traffic. The delegates said that because Americans were the largest drug consumers, the United States should provide funds to combat the drug traffickers.

From April 23 to 25, the Organization of American States created an Inter-American Drug Control Commission to cooperate in breaking up the drug trade. A week later, in the Andean Pact, the nations with the largest drug trade—Colombia, Ecuador, Peru, and Venezuela—agreed to cooperate as a regional bloc against trafficking in narcotics.

## May 13, 1986

### U.S.-Mexican relations are troubled when U.S. customs services describes corruption in Mexican law enforcement.

Tensions with Mexico arose because the U.S. customs commissioner told the Senate Subcommittee on Western Hemisphere Affairs that there was "ingrained corruption" in Mexico's police establishment and that the governor of the State of Sonora owned four ranches that grew opium poppies and marijuana.

Although Mexico protested and U.S. Ambassador John Gavin and Attorney General Edwin Meese apologized to Mexico, William von Raab, the customs commissioner, reaffirmed his charges on May 24. And, on October 30, 1986, Mexican authorities arrested the brother of the former governor of Sonora, Gilberto Ocana García, on charges of drug trafficking after discovering the marijuana fields on his plantation.

See also August 14, 1986.

## May 16, 1986

### As the Contra rebels move to unify their opposition to Nicaragua's government, Eden Pastora Gómez retires from the struggle.

Early in 1986 as the Reagan administration struggled to improve the public image of the Contra leaders and to bring unity to the movement, the United Nicaraguan Opposition (UNO) was formed under Alfonso Robelo Callejas, Arturo José Cruz, and Adolfo Calero Portocarrero. They received President Reagan's blessing at a March 3 meeting in Washington but needed the support of the southern group of anti-Sandinistas, which had been set up by Pastora Gómez. Pastora refused to work with the former Somoza National Guard's military leaders who dominated the northern, Contra group.

Pastora gradually lost influence after the U.S. cut his economic aid in 1984, but in 1986, the southerners were enticed by Washington's promise to renew aid if they joined the UNO. Pastora refused, but on May 9 his top officers accepted U.S. aid. As a result, on May 16, Pastora gave up the struggle and sought exile in

Costa Rica, where he formed a political party. Costa Rica granted him asylum on June 3.

See April 15, 1983.

## May 22, 1986

### President Reagan imposes a 35% import duty on Canadian cedar wood products.

Because the U.S. lumber industry claimed Canada encouraged exports of wood products at low prices, Reagan levied an import duty even though it contradicted his frequently modified "free trade" policy. In retaliation, Canada's Prime Minister Brian Mulroney threatened import duties on U.S. products. Following further trade negotiations, Canada and the United States reached a compromise on lumber products.

See December 30, 1986.

## May 22, 1986

### NATO defense ministers approve the U.S. production of chemical weapons, but congressional opponents say the full NATO council must do so.

The Reagan administration had pushed for the renewed production of chemical weapons but found Congress reluctant to fund the project. In the defense bill approved on December 19, 1985, Congress inserted a clause requiring the approval of the North Atlantic Treaty Organization before binary nerve gas weapons were produced. Subsequently, the Defense Department found it difficult to get NATO approval, finally convinced NATO defense ministers to do so despite the reluctance of NATO political leaders. No NATO nation permitted U.S. chemical weapons to be stored or used from its territory with the exception of West Germany, which allowed the United States to store some of its 30,000 tons of chemical weapons on its soil. West Germany also supported the U.S. binary nerve gas production provided that the United States would withdraw its existing stock from West German soil when the new weapons production began.

On May 22, NATO defense ministers approved U.S. production of chemical weapons provided they were not deployed in Europe. In Washington, members of Congress who opposed chemical weapons argued that the full NATO Council, not the defense ministers, must approve. The U.S. State Department disagreed, contending that the intent of the congressional legislation had been fulfilled. Congressional opponents still sought to delay production of the nerve gas. Although Congress approved $35 million for the nerve gas bombs and artillery shells, the omnibus spending bill that passed on October 3, 1986, stated that chemical weapon production could not begin before October 1, 1987.

See September 9, 1986.

## May 25, 1986

### Nearly 6 million Americans link "hands across America" to raise food for the hungry and homeless.

One result of President Reagan's huge defense budgets and decreased social spending was the increase in poverty and homelessness since 1981. For 1986, Congress approved more housing funds ($53.6 billion) than Reagan had requested ($46.6 billion), but the Reagan administration also cut welfare for two-parent homes, ruling that the Aid to Dependent Children program was for one-parent homes. In 1989, Congress also learned that Reagan's director of housing, Samuel Pierce, was implicated in widespread fraud in misusing the housing funds appropriated by Congress.

To call attention to the problems of the hungry and homeless, concerned Americans held hands across 4,150 miles from Long Beach, California, to Battery Park in New York City. Another 1.5 million people symbolically formed links where the transcontinental route did not reach. They raised over $100 million to help the needy.

Although President Reagan had, on May 21, said that individuals, not government policy, were to blame for poverty, a Harvard University study group reported that government directives caused homelessness by taking people off welfare rolls and evicting them from their homes. Reagan did not want to join the link, but his daughter, Maureen Reagan, finally persuaded her father and Mrs. Reagan to join the "hands" ceremony.

## June 5, 1986

### Saudi Arabia receives U.S. military equipment after the Senate fails to override President Reagan's veto.

President Reagan originally proposed to sell Saudi Arabia $354 million of defensive military missiles.

Both the Senate and the House had rejected the sale, and on May 20, the president compromised by withdrawing the request to sell 800 Stinger surface-to-air missiles. Many members of Congress claimed the Stingers would get into terrorist hands, even though the United States already supplied them to rebels in Afghanistan and Angola.

After Congress voted against the compromise measure, Reagan vetoed the bill and lobbied the Senate to prevent the veto from being overridden. After eight senators changed their vote, the Senate's two-thirds majority was lacking by one vote. Consequently, Sidewinder air-to-air missiles and Harpoon antiship missiles were sold to the Saudis, who, Reagan claimed, worked behind the scenes to combat terrorism.

### June 9, 1986

**The presidential commission on the space shuttle accident reports that a history of production mistakes made the accident more likely because of a faulty rocket seal.**

The commission investigating the January 28, 1986, explosion of the space shuttle *Challenger* blamed the management system of the National Aeronautics and Space Administration (NASA). A faulty seal on a booster rocket was the specific cause of the disaster; however, middle managers of NASA and the seal's manufacturer, Morton Thiokol, had warned higher-ups that the seal would not function in cold weather. The company's management at first refused to recognize the problem and, later, classified it as an acceptable risk. While Morton Thiokol personnel knew this, there was the possibility that NASA managers in Huntsville, Alabama, did not inform NASA's Washington officials.

### June 25, 1986

**Congress approves aid to the Contra rebels after previously refusing aid in 1986.**

Although the Iran-Contra hearings of 1987 indicated that the National Security Council had agreed on May 16, 1986, to solicit Contra funds from other friendly countries, President Reagan simultaneously urged Congress to approve $100 million of assistance.

On March 20, the House of Representatives rejected Reagan's $100 million request by a vote of 222 to 210. By June, however, six swing Democrats in the House, who wanted some type of Contra aid, proposed $300 million in aid to other Central American countries, thereby delaying the delivery of weapons until September 1 and requiring reports on Contra reform and peace talks. With these additions, the House gave $100 million for the Contras on June 25, the first time the House approved both military and economic aid. The vote was 221 to 209. The $300 million for the other Central American countries was never released by President Reagan.

*See also October 18, 1986.*

### June 25, 1986

**Israelis who killed two PLO prisoners are not punished.**

In 1984, many news reports expressed concern that two Palestinians had been killed while being questioned by Israel's domestic intelligence agency, Shin Beth. On June 25, Avraham Shalom, the head of Shin Beth, resigned in exchange for immunity from prosecution. On August 6, the Israeli supreme court approved a presidential pardon of four Shin Beth agents implicated in the affair. Soon after, on August 24, Israeli President Chaim Herzog pardoned seven more Shin Beth agents.

*See April 12, 1984.*

### June 27, 1986

**The International Court of Justice rules that the United States violated international law and Nicaragua's sovereignty; the United States rejects the ruling.**

Although the United States had previously rejected the World Court's jurisdiction over the Nicaraguan complaint, the court conducted 26 months of hearings before ruling against the United States. By a vote of 12 to 3, the jurists said the United States should pay reparations to Nicaragua and cease all violations of international law in coercing Nicaragua.

On October 8, 1986, the United States vetoed a U.N. Security Council resolution urging it to comply with the World Court ruling.

*See April 17, 1984.*

## July 4, 1986

*Syrian soldiers patrol Beirut, seeking to restore order in Lebanon.*

Throughout 1986, Lebanon experienced further civil war owing to arguments among Christians regarding Syria's role in Lebanon and differences among Muslim factions about political tactics. On January 13, rival Christian groups fought over a Syrian proposal before Lebanese President Amin Gemayel defeated the forces led by Eli Hobeika. These problems led Muslim Prime Minister Karami to call for an end to Christian dominance of Lebanon's government, a proposal that increased tensions.

After reviewing its efforts to obtain Christian-Muslim accords on July 4, Syria sent more troops to Beirut to stop the fighting but had no success. Gemayel's Christian forces failed to control opposing Christian armies in East Beirut, even though 552 persons died by September 2. Later on December 5, moderate Muslim Shiite leader Nabih Berri failed to get a cease-fire in southern Lebanon between Muslims and Palestinians loyal to Yasser Arafat.

## July 6, 1986

*Japanese Prime Minister Yasuhiro Nakasone wins a third term—a landslide victory.*

Nakasone's Liberal Democratic Party won both chambers of the Diet, with an unprecedented 304 of 512 seats in the lower house. Nakasone's party had changed its rules to permit him a third term as party chief and prime minister.

## July 8, 1986

*Philippine forces of former President Marcos fail to overthrow the Aquino government.*

On July 6, Marcos vice presidential candidate Arturo M. Tolentino occupied the Manila Hotel, rallying Philippine soldiers to overthrow President Aquino. Although a former supreme court judge swore Tolentino in as "president" and 3,000 soldiers supported him, the occupation ended when Defense Minister Enrile and army officers surrounded the hotel to force his surrender. The affair ended on July 8 when Aquino promised amnesty to those backing the rebellion.

For another rebellion, see November 27, 1986.

## July 9, 1986

*The U.S. ambassador to Chile attends the funeral of a U.S. citizen killed by Chile's police force and indicates dissatisfaction with the government's human rights record.*

Following President Reagan's decision to oppose both right-wing and left-wing dictators, U.S. policy toward Chile became a symbol of the new policy. The first evidence of Reagan's change came on March 12, when the U.S. ambassador to the United Nations offered a resolution criticizing President Pinochet's violations of human rights. The funeral attended by U.S. Ambassador Harry G. Barnes on July 19 was for an American resident born in Chile, Rodrigo Rojas de Negri. Rojas was one of six persons killed by Chilean security forces during a general workers strike against Pinochet on July 3, 1986. Allegedly, he had been killed when police poured gasoline on him and a girl and set them on fire. Rojas died because of his burns; the girl survived with burns on 65% of her body. The funeral of the six victims became a large-scale anti-Pinochet demonstration, and Ambassador Barnes's attendance protested Chile's methods. The funeral was also attacked by Chile's security officials, who broke up the mob of protestors with tear gas and water cannons.

On July 13, Senator Jesse Helms (R-N.C.) criticized Ambassador Barnes for attending the funeral. While visiting Chile, Helms praised his friend, General Pinochet, as a strong defender of freedom over communism. The State Department issued a statement on July 14 that supported Barnes's attendance as a humanitarian gesture. Secretary of State Shultz had appointed Barnes to implement Reagan's policy of opposing all dictators.

See March 14, 1986.

## July 14, 1986

*President Reagan sends army forces to help Bolivia combat cocaine processors.*

Known as Operation Blast Furnace, 6 Black Hawk helicopters, 170 U.S. army pilots, and supporting soldiers were sent to Bolivia, where since January 7 the government of Victor Paz Estenssoro had undertaken a campaign against his nation's cocaine establishment. Although U.S. troops were scheduled to remain in Bolivia for 60 days, they stayed, at the government's request, until November 15. The Reagan administration had been pressuring Bolivia and other drug-producing nations to fight drug traffickers. At an April International Drug Enforcement Conference, Bolivia, Peru, and Belize asked for U.S help in attacking isolated drug-processing places. After Bolivia's President Estenssoro made a specific request in July, Reagan agreed because Bolivia exported about half of the world's coca paste.

During the Bolivian activity, U.S. Drug Enforcement Agency officials assisted the U.S. army so that a drug agent with arresting authority was on all flights. When U.S. forces withdrew on November 15, they had dismantled 21 drug labs and destroyed 24 transshipment centers. No arrests of significant drug lords were made, because by the time the U.S.-Bolivian forces arrived, the camps were deserted, and most drugs had been taken away.

Bolivia took critical measures to cut back its drug centers. This caused economic problems because the drug trade brought in about $600 million a year and employed 400,000 people. In addition, Bolivia's tin mines were in poor shape because world tin prices had fallen by 50% since 1980. Because mining decreased, managers laid off 8,000 workers in 1986. Thus, U.S. military attacks did not solve the problem.

See September 21, 1987.

### July 15, 1986

*Great Britain and the Soviet Union settle a 69-year dispute over the debt of Czar Nicolas II.*

This agreement was completed between Soviet Foreign Minister Eduard A. SHEVARDNADZE and British Foreign Secretary Sir Geoffrey Howe. Essentially, each side dropped its claims against the other. With interest accumulated since 1917, the British claims totaled £82 billion; the Soviets' claim for British damage inflicted during its civil war was over £2 billion.

### July 21, 1986

*After Israeli Prime Minister Shimon Peres conducts peace talks with Moroccan King Hassan II, both are criticized by their followers.*

Although the peace talks bore no fruit, Peres's action was condemned by the opposing Likud Party in Israel, while Hassan was forced to resign as chairman of the Arab League Conference. Hassan had invited Peres to visit him for two days of discussions because the Israeli leader said he would explore any avenue to peace. The meeting was not successful. Although Peres claimed that good suggestions were made, King Hassan indicated that the Israeli leader rejected the basic Arab conditions for peace.

### July 24, 1986

**Jerry Whitworth of the Walker spy ring is convicted of espionage.**

Whitworth was the former U.S. navy radioman who worked for spymaster John Walker from 1975 to 1985. Affidavits released by the court indicated that the KGB (Soviet secret police) thought the Walker-Whitworth operation was the most important in KGB history. The director of U.S. Naval Intelligence, Rear Admiral William Studeman, said the secrets had "potential ... war-winning implications for the Soviet side," because they dealt with navy codes and communications. Whitworth had collected the most crucial secrets sold to the Soviets.

Whitworth was sentenced to 365 years in jail and fined $410,000. John Walker and his son received a better deal by plea bargaining: on November 6, John was sentenced to life in prison (parole possible in about ten years); his son Michael received a 25-year sentence (parole possible in about eight years). John Walker's brother, Arthur, had previously been sentenced to three life terms (parole possible in ten years).

See May 20, 1985.

### July 24, 1986

*Poland begins an amnesty program to release political dissidents.*

During the Congress of the United Workers (Communist) Party on July 24, First Secretary Wojciech Jaruzelski approved an amnesty to solve Poland's political and economic problems.

He released 369 criminal and political prisoners on July 24 and another 225 on September 13. The group included Solidarity leaders such as Bogdan Lis, Adam Michnik, and Zbigneiw Bujak. Nevertheless, when Bujak formed a seven-member Provisional Council of Solidarity on September 30, the government declared it illegal, a sign that Polish political activity continued to be forbidden.

See November 29, 1987.

## July 28, 1986

*At Vladivostok, Soviet First Secretary Gorbachev promises Soviet troop withdrawals from Mongolia and Afghanistan.*

Visiting eastern Asia, Gorbachev sought better relations between the Soviet Union and the People's Republic of China. China often cited the need to remove Soviet troops on the northern Chinese border, in Afghanistan, and in Cambodia. To eliminate these obstacles, Gorbachev agreed to withdraw about 60,000 of the 450,000 Soviet troops on China's border; to take six regiments from Afghanistan (i.e., about 6,000 of 120,000 troops); and to obtain peace in Cambodia where the Soviet ally, Vietnam, controlled the anti–Pol Pot regime.

Neither China nor the United States believed these steps were significant. The Chinese reacted cooly, saying the acts were insufficient. The Reagan administration said Gorbachev should give a timetable for total withdrawal, especially from Afghanistan. By December 1986, the Soviets had withdrawn the six regiments.

## July 31, 1986

### The United States and Japan end a trade dispute over semiconductor chips.

Amcrican computer chip manufacturers claimed that Japan dumped chips on the U.S. market at low prices, especially 64k and 256k chips. The July 31 agreement gave the United States a 20% share of Japan's chip market—up from 8% the previous year. Japan also agreed to police the "predatory" practices of its manufacturers to prevent them from dumping chips at prices too low for U.S. competition. This agreement represented the continuation of U.S.-Japanese tactics of negotiations on one item, a method called MOSS (market oriented, sector-specific).

See February 13, 1986, and March 27, 1987.

## August 1, 1986

### Prodded by Congress, President Reagan subsidizes wheat sales to the Soviet Union.

Reagan's subsidy covered up to $4.4 million of wheat (about 3.85 million metric tons). He increased the farm subsidy from $12 to $15 per metric ton to boost Soviet purchases of U.S. grain at a lower price.

The U.S. Senate passed an Export Enhancement Program on July 22 to subsidize grain sales to the USSR and China, but Reagan opposed this action as contrary to free trade. Although the senators accepted the August 1 compromise, the desired result was not achieved. Even with the subsidy of $15 per ton, U.S. wheat prices remained above world market prices.

## August 6, 1986

### The House of Representatives fails to override Reagan's veto of a bill limiting textile imports.

This law would limit textile imports from 12 countries, especially Hong Kong, Taiwan, and South Korea, replacing the Multi-Fiber International Textile agreement, which 54 nations, including the United States, had extended for five years on August 1, 1986. American labor and textile industry groups denounced the textile agreement as taking away U.S. jobs; North Carolina textile mills had lost 17,000 jobs in recent years. Under the August 1 extension agreement, the United States obtained the right to impose quotas to combat fraud in foreign exports, but U.S textile lobbyists said the agreement had too many loopholes to protect American textile mills.

In vetoing the bill, President Reagan said it unilaterally violated the August 1 agreement and cost American consumers $44 billion because of high U.S. textile prices. His veto was sustained in the House by a vote of 276 to 149, 8 votes short of the necessary two-thirds majority.

## August 14, 1986

### Mexican President de la Madrid visits the United States but cannot ease tensions.

A variety of causes led to poor relations between Mexico and the United States during the Reagan era—the U.S. ambassador to Mexico, John Gavin, was very unpopular; Mexico's economy weakened because oil prices fell; the Mexican immigration problem festered; and U.S. drug officials complained that corrupt Mexican politicians and law officers prevented the capture and prosecution of drug merchants. On August 13, while de la Madrid was in Washington, a U.S. drug agent, Victor Cortez Jr., was arrested, beaten, and tortured with electric shock by Mexican police before being released.

Consequently, while the two presidents agreed to cooperate more fully in drug enforcement and in solving Mexico's foreign debt problem, tensions between the two nations continued. To improve future relations with Mexico, President Reagan, on August 14, had nominated Charles J. Pilliod, Jr. to replace Gavin as ambassador to Mexico. With Washington's help, Mexico received a $12 billion aid package from the International Monetary Fund on September 30.

See April 7 and May 13, 1986.

### August 22, 1986

**Although Cuba began releasing political prisoners in June, President Reagan tightens trade restrictions on Cuba.**

There had been increasing evidence that Cuba circumvented the 26-year-old U.S. embargo by obtaining U.S. goods through Panama. One report said over 118 U.S. companies and individuals transshipped goods to Cuba through Panama. The Reagan administration wanted to stop this trade. Despite this trade problem, Reagan overruled a State Department decision on June 8, 1986, to prevent Cuba from releasing 67 political prisoners to the United States. Most of these had been officials in the government of Fulgencio Batista, whom Castro overthrew in 1959.

During 1986, the Castro regime also released the last two Cubans who fought under U.S. support at the Bay of Pigs in 1961. On June 8, Richard Montero Duque was released, and on October 18, Ramón Conte Hernández was freed. Both were aided in their release by Senator Edward Kennedy (D-Mass.).

See April 17, 1961.

### August 25, 1986

**The Reagan administration begins a disinformation campaign against Libyan leader Gadhafi.**

Based on a White House leak, the *Wall Street Journal* reported that U.S. intelligence believed Mu'ammar al-Gadhafi was "off his rocker" and had sponsored additional international terrorist attacks since April 15 (see entry for April 15, 1986), a policy placing Libya and the United States on another collision course. To destabilize Libya, the U.S. navy began naval maneuvers with Egypt off the coast of Libya. The CIA alleged that its operatives had prevented a Libyan plot for

Lebanese to blow up a West Berlin home on August 21 and to blow up the U.S. embassy in Cyprus on August 3. On August 25, President Reagan said he would respond militarily to any Libyan provocation.

The August disclosures were labeled disinformation by *Washington Post* reporter Bob Woodward on October 2, 1986. Woodward said the National Security Council had, on August 15, approved plans to generate internal opposition to Gadhafi by "foreign media placements" of the Central Intelligence Agency, but these disinformation reports fooled mainly the U.S. media.

On October 3, White House spokesman Larry Speakes said the administration did not lie but only "shaped the content" of stories about Libya. President Reagan later admitted approving a plan "to make Gadhafi go to bed every night wondering what we might do." On October 8, Bernard Kalb, the assistant secretary of state for public affairs, resigned because he refused to support American disinformation policy. According to Kalb, this practice damaged American credibility in world opinion more than it damaged Gadhafi.

See April 14, 1986.

### August 30, 1986

**Nicholas S. Daniloff is arrested in Moscow.**

Daniloff, the Moscow correspondent for *U.S. News and World Report*, was arrested after giving a Soviet acquaintance a package containing two maps marked "top secret." The Reagan administration claimed Daniloff had been framed in retaliation for the August 23 arrest in New York City of Soviet physicist Gennadi F. Zakharov, who the Federal Bureau of Investigation charged with purchasing classified documents. Because an exchange of letters between President Reagan and Soviet leader Gorbachev did not resolve the situation, the United States expelled 25 members of the USSR mission to the United Nations.

A deal was now worked out. On September 29, the Soviet Union dropped its charges against Daniloff and released him. On September 31, Zakharov was permitted to leave for home. Following the Icelandic summit on October 19, the Soviets expelled five U.S. diplomats; Washington expelled 55 Soviets.

## September 5, 1986

### A Pan Am airplane is hijacked in Pakistan; 21 die after a 16-hour ordeal.

The Pan Am 747 jumbo jet had arrived at Karachi from Bombay, India, and was to fly via Frankfurt, Germany, to New York. Before its doors closed, four Pakistani dissidents dressed as airport security guards jumped from a security van, stormed aboard the plane, and demanded to be taken to Cyprus. Because the cockpit crew managed to slip through an escape hatch, Pakistani authorities said the plane could not leave until another crew arrived.

Violence began almost as soon as the gunmen boarded the plane. They shot and killed Rajesh Kunn, an Indian who had recently become a naturalized American, but refrained from other killings for 16 hours. By then, the aircraft's generators had weakened, and when the plane's inside lights flickered, the gunmen fired at the passengers, apparently believing rescue commandos were shutting lights off. Pakistani commandos had assembled but were not ready when the shooting began. In the chaos of shooting and growing darkness, passengers opened doors and either jumped out or slid down safety chutes. The commandos finally boarded and arrested the hijackers, only one hijacker being wounded.

The passengers were not as lucky. Twenty-one were killed, including two Americans, and over 100 were wounded. Miraculously, nearly 300 had escaped. In retrospect, two factors seemed clear: first, the Pakistani authorities bungled the affair; second, the U.S. Delta Force, a quick strike commando force that flew from Fort Bragg, North Carolina, arrived too late. Some U.S. leaders wanted to scatter Delta Force bases around the world.

## September 6, 1986

### Arab terrorists attack a synagogue in Istanbul, killing 21.

The two armed gunmen entered the synagogue during worship services disguised as photographers. They blocked the door with an iron bar then opened fire on the congregation, killing 21 and wounding 4 others critically, then poured gasoline on several bodies and set them ablaze. As the terrorists left, Turkish police arrived, chasing the two men back inside. The gunmen committed suicide by detonating a grenade with a short fuse.

This was the first attack on Jews in Turkey that anyone could remember. Since the sixteenth century, Turkey had tolerated Jews and not molested them.

## September 9, 1986

### After a trip to Angola, Senator Orrin Hatch praises rebel leader Jonas Savimbi.

During Savimbi's January 28, 1986, visit to the United States, Senator Hatch (R-Utah) was one of Savimbi's principal supporters. Thus, it was no surprise that Hatch reported favorably on visits to rebel camps in Angola. The surprise was his video tapes of Savimbi's troops using Stinger missiles to shoot down Soviet planes used by Angola's army.

There had been controversy over giving Stinger missiles to Afghan rebels while refusing them to Saudi Arabia. Now, Stingers had been given to the National Union for Total Independence of Angola (UNITA), although the chances of their being captured by Cuban forces helping Angola's government were great. This gave Stinger technology to other nations. The United States later discovered Stingers in Iran.

See June 5, 1986, and October 19, 1987.

## September 9, 1986

### The United States again charges that the Soviets promote chemical warfare; U.S. evidence is unconvincing.

Since 1981, when Secretary of State Alexander Haig charged the Soviets with using chemical weapons in Southeast Asia and Afghanistan, the United States had repeated these charges even though the available scientific data disproved them.

In a 1987 article for *International Security*, Elisa D. Harris reviewed the charges, evidence, and studies made about "yellow rain." She concluded: "the errors and inconsistencies in the Reagan administration's case for Soviet-sponsored toxin warfare are beginning to be recognized by more than just its critics." Some U.S. Defense Department studies concluded that the charges were unfounded. Most scientists believed that yellow-colored bee feces found in Southeast Asian jungles caused illness that Haig and others called the "yellow rain" of chemicals.

Harris indicated that these charges were designed by the Reagan administration to justify the renewed production of chemical weapons by the United States.

She urged an international agreement on verification methods for the future.

See September 13, 1981; March 8, 1982;
August 11, 1987.

### September 12, 1986

*Egyptian and Israeli negotiators conclude four days of talks on the Middle East.*

Most notably, these were the first discussions between leaders of Egypt and Israel since 1981. Initially, on September 9 and 10, U.S. Assistant Secretary of State Richard W. Murphy assisted Egyptian and Israeli officials in international arbitration of a dispute over Taba, a beach resort in the Sinai peninsula that Egypt claimed but Israel did not vacate in 1980.

Next, on September 11 and 12, Prime Minister Shimon Peres came to Alexandria for talks with Egyptian President Hosni Mubarak. Although they disagreed on the Palestine Liberation Organization's role in peace talks, Egypt agreed to appoint an ambassador to Israel, a position vacant since Israel had invaded Lebanon in 1982.

### September 13, 1986

**Brazilian President Sarney visits Washington in an effort to ease tensions with the United States.**

Between September 9 and 13, President Jose Sarney addressed a joint session of Congress and met with President Reagan. A variety of disputes hampered U.S.-Brazilian relations including Brazil's diplomatic recognition of Cuba, Brazil's opposition to U.S. support of the Nicaraguan Contras, and the concern for Brazil's limits on U.S. imports.

Reagan praised Sarney as the first democratically elected Brazilian civilian leader in 30 years but urged him to adopt free trade. Sarney claimed most of Brazil's industries were "infants" and noted that 80% of the nation's trade surplus repaid its foreign debts.

### September 14, 1986

*Peace talks between rebels and Salvadoran President Duarte are canceled for security reasons.*

From April 26 to August 23, contacts among leaders of El Salvador's left wing rebels, the Farabund Marti

National Liberation Front (FMLN), and President José Napoleon Duarte resulted in a scheduled meeting for September 19 in the town of Sesori. On September 14, however, the FMLN indicated that the talks could not be held unless the government removed an army battalion that had recently moved to Sesori. Duarte refused, condemning the guerrillas for avoiding a chance for peace. The rebels distrusted the Salvadoran army and believed the troop presence in Sesori endangered the safe-conduct they had been promised.

### September 15, 1986

**GATT members agree on an agenda for trade talks in 1987.**

To be known as the Uruguay Round because the agenda was set at a conference at Punta del Este, Uruguay, the eighth round of talks since 1947 focused on the U.S. desire to protect trade in services, investments, and intellectual property, areas into which the U.S. economy had substantially moved since 1969. Agriculture subsidies would also be discussed, although there seemed little hope of reconciling other countries to the large commodity subsidies the U.S. gave its farmers.

### September 29, 1986

**The Senate refuses $200 million in aid to the Philippines but later approves it.**

Although Congress had provided an additional $150 million for the Philippines in the supplemental appropriation Bill of July 2, 1986, senators proved stubborn about adding $200 million to legislation for fiscal 1987. Their concerns were about whether President Corazon Aquino could handle the communist threat and her willingness to renew the U.S. leases at Clark Air Force Base and Subic Bay.

From August 15 to 24, Aquino visited the United States, making a stirring speech to Congress. Several senators remained unsatisfied, particularly because other foreign aid funds had been cut to meet the budget deficit guidelines of the Gramm-Rudman bill. Nevertheless, for a vote on the 1987 omnibus spending bill on October 3, the Senate Republicans rallied their votes, approving $200 million for the Philippines.

On Aquino's problems, see July 8 and
November 27, 1986.

## October 1, 1986

### President Reagan signs the defense reorganization bill.

This law resulted from congressional studies in 1985 and from the studies of the Commission on Defense Management chaired by Deputy Secretary of Defense David Packard, which reported on February 28, 1986. The changes would centralize the president's military advice given by the chairman of the joint Chiefs of Staff an independent status as his adviser and by consolidating the staffs of the three service secretaries (army, navy, air force).

The purpose was to cut down interservice rivalries and improve the Defense Department established in 1947, but its success seemed doubtful because Secretary of Defense Caspar Weinberger and the Joint Chiefs opposed the reform.

## October 2, 1986

### Congress overrides President Reagan's veto of sanctions against South Africa.

During 1986, conflict escalated between South Africa's white government and black Africans opposing the apartheid program. As in the past, South Africa used violence to suppress the black African majority. By the summer of 1986, many Western European and American protestors favored economic sanctions to pressure South Africa to end its suppression.

President Reagan had diverted Congress from legislation against South Africa in 1985 by placing mild sanctions on Johannesburg. On June 18, 1986, however, the House of Representatives passed a highly restrictive measure requiring all U.S. corporations to disinvest their holdings in South Africa and limiting U.S. imports from that country to items of essential strategic value. The Senate passed a less restrictive bill on August 15 before a House-Senate committee approved a compromise law.

Reagan vetoed the compromise act on September 26, having failed to head off Congress by extending his limited sanctions of 1985 for another year on September 4. On July 22, Reagan had argued that economic sanctions would not work, even though he used them against Nicaragua and Libya. Reagan declared his opposition to apartheid and asked South Africa to set a timetable for its gradual elimina-

tion, something Johannesburg had no intention of doing.

By October, Reagan's pro-South African policy was widely unpopular in the United States including in Congress. On September 29 and October 2, each house of Congress overrode the president's veto. The congressional act banned new U.S. investment in South Africa, prohibited the importation of certain products including coal and steel, and canceled landing rights of South Africa's airline.

## October 4, 1986

### Nicaragua shoots down a U.S. plane over Nicaraguan airspace near Costa Rica, capturing the American survivor, Eugene Hausenfus.

The downed plane had a crew of four men and military supplies for the Contra rebels. Although U.S. officials denied that the Central Intelligence Agency (CIA) had organized air shipments, Hausenfus told a press conference on October 9 that the flights and other rebel supplies were supervised by the CIA operating from El Salvador. In particular, he named Félix Rodríguez, alias Max Gómez, and Ramón Medina as CIA agents.

Hausenfus was tried in Managua by Nicaragua's Popular Anti-Somocista Tribunal and found guilty of terrorism and other crimes. He was sentenced to 30 years in prison but was pardoned by Nicaragua and set free on December 17, 1986.

See also October 11, 1986.

## October 5, 1986

### A London *Times* report that Israel possesses a nuclear weapons arsenal results in the affair of Mordechai Vanunu.

An Israeli nuclear arms technician, Vanunu, was brought from Australia to London to be debriefed by a British physicist, who confirmed the *Times* photos and details of Israel's underground nuclear weapons plant. Vanunu said the secret plant in Israel's Negev desert had been started by French nuclear experts between 1957 and 1964, a fact confirmed by the "father" of the French atomic capability, Francis Perrin, who built the Dimona Nuclear Research facility in Israel. Vanunu revealed that Israel was the sixth nation with nuclear weapons capacity, although the Israeli government denied it.

The Vanunu mystery developed after Vanunu disappeared from London on September 30. On November 9, Israel revealed that Vanunu had been charged with espionage for "pretending" to disclose state secrets. Vanunu had been kidnapped by Mossad, the Israeli intelligence agency, in Rome on September 30, having been lured there by a female Mossad agent. After a secret trial in Israel, which ended on March 24, 1988, Vanunu was found guilty of treason and espionage. Being remorseful and cooperative, he received a lenient sentence of 18 years in prison. Israel's handling of Vanunu gave every indication that it indeed had a nuclear arsenal.

### October 10, 1986

**Britain's Conservative Party resolves to maintain the nation's nuclear deterrent; the Liberal and Labour Parties offer qualified support for the deterrent.**

During the early 1980s, antinuclear advocates in Britain created a large following, causing political parties to divide on proposals for national security measures. The ruling Conservative Party under Prime Minister Margaret Thatcher favored Britain's independent nuclear force and cooperation with U.S. nuclear forces based in the British Isles to deter the Soviets.

On September 23, the Liberal Party Conference overrode its leadership in the Liberal-Social Democratic Alliance by opposing a British nuclear force, including all U.S. forces. The Labour Party conference on October 2 took a middle position. It called for ending nuclear forces in Britain but maintaining nonnuclear U.S. forces and intelligence assistance for Great Britain. Soon after the Labour Party conference, however, its leaders realized that its policy needed to change before the next general election, or Labour could not win.

### October 10, 1986

**Israeli Prime Minister Shimon Peres resigns; his office goes to Yitzhak Shamir, following agreements on sharing power.**

In 1984, when neither major Israeli party, Likud or Labor, could form a majority government, they agreed to share power with each other. Peres had been prime minister, a position now yielded to the Likud Party's SHAMIR, and Peres became foreign minister, a post previously held by Shamir. Despite predictions that power sharing could not work, it did, though Peres's peace efforts were handicapped.

### October 11, 1986

**Vice President Bush and his adviser deny connections with the downing of a U.S. plane in Nicaragua.**

On October 10, the *San Francisco Examiner* published a story on Eugene Hausenfus, claiming that George Bush and his aide, Donald Gregg, were associated with Félix Rodríguez as the CIA agent who directed operations from El Salvador. Because on October 1, Congress had extended the previous ban on a CIA secret fund for the Contra rebels, CIA assistance to Hausenfus would be illegal. An ex-marine from Wisconsin, Hausenfus said he flew at least ten flights in the C-123K cargo plane out of Ilopang Air Force Base in El Salvador. The two crew members who died in the crash had worked for the CIA, as Hausenfus confirmed. Rodríguez was the CIA field agent who directed the activity.

Bush claimed he had met Rodríguez, but they talked generally about El Salvador, not about private arms for the Contra rebels. There was extensive private U.S. assistance to the Contras as well as aid from Lt. Colonel Oliver North, a fact disclosed during the Iran-Contra hearings after November 1986. While Bush's role seemed marginal at best, following a briefing by CIA director William Casey in October 1986, Senator David Durenburg (R-Minn.) said he believed Ronald Reagan "sponsored all of this private action in aiding the Contras."

See October 4, 1986.

### October 11–12, 1986

**The Reagan-Gorbachev Iceland summit achieves no agreement.**

The summit meeting at Reykjavík, Iceland, was preceded by a variety of U.S. disagreements between the State Department and the National Security Council regarding arms control since the Geneva meetings (see November 21, 1985). On January 11, 1986, the Soviets extended the moratorium on nuclear tests, urging Reagan to stop U.S. testing. Despite appeals from international leaders and 60 members of Congress, Reagan approved a series of underground tests on March 22 that totaled 13 by the end of 1986.

President Reagan with
Soviet Chairman Mikhail
Gorbachev. Ronald Reagan
Library

The president argued that underground tests could not be verified. Hoping to prove Reagan wrong, the New York National Defense Council agreed with the Moscow Academy of Science to jointly monitor Soviet tests and on July 13 arrived in the Soviet Union to prepare to monitor future tests. Yet when the October 11 Iceland meetings began, the monitor testing had not begun, and the testing issue was not yet resolved.

Regarding intermediate and intercontinental missile reductions, talks were underway after January 16 but each side differed on how to achieve reductions. The Soviets proposed to ban all nuclear weapons by 2000 in three stages. The U.S. delegates offered a modified version of Reagan's zero option, first to reduce medium-range missiles over a three-year period. These sessions adjourned without compromises on March 3. After renewing the Geneva talks on May 8, the second round also failed to reach agreement, adjourning on June 26.

The Geneva talks failed principally because U.S. delegates feared Gorbachev would link the nuclear

reduction talks to limits on the Strategic Defense Initiative program. Eventually, the linking of nuclear reduction to SDI became a key issue at the Iceland talks. Although the Soviets saw the SDI as a first-strike strategy, Reagan insisted it was only a defensive program, even though the logical conclusion would make the SDI illegal under the 1972 ABM treaty. Although the U.S. Congress began limiting the funds for SDI, Reagan wanted to spend as much as possible even though after four years SDI laboratories had achieved no significant technological breakthroughs. As a result, neither the United States nor the Soviet Union was prepared to finalize any of these prior issues during the Iceland meetings.

Without a prepared agenda, Gorbachev offered a package of concessions at the first Iceland session on October 11. These included concessions on underground testing, long- and medium-range missiles, the 1979 SALT II, and the relationship of SDI to the 1972 ABM treaty. To counter Gorbachev's concessions and prevent Reagan from having to say no, the president's hard-line staff which opposed any arms control, devised more "sweeping proposals" that "they thought" Gorbachev would have to reject. These provided for a 50 percent reduction of strategic nuclear arsenals by 1991 during which period ABM research and development was permitted. In addition, during the years from 1991 to 1996, the remaining 50 percent of nuclear missiles would be eliminated, after which either side would be free to deploy defensive missiles.

Thus, at the final Iceland session, Reagan put forward these sweeping proposals, but when Gorbachev accepted them, Reagan had to reject his own proposals and walk out of the last session, returning immediately to Washington. Apparently, Reagan did not want to wait until 1996 to deploy the SDI.

Because reporters in Iceland believed Reagan's "sweeping proposals" were genuine and not merely deceptive, America's NATO allies became concerned about losing a deterrent to the Soviet's superiority in conventional weapons. After the Iceland meetings, the Reagan administration began a blitz campaign to emphasize that the administration stood firm on SDI, while Gorbachev argued that Reagan had backed down on his "sweeping proposals to abolish all nuclear weapons by 1996."

Although the SDI, test ban, and missile issues perplexed both sides, an INF missile treaty was accepted the next year.

See November 21, 1985, and December 18, 1986; February 28, November 17, and December 8, 1987.

## October 15, 1986

### The Senate approves Edward J. Perkins as ambassador to South Africa.

Perkins was an African American Foreign Service career officer, nominated as ambassador by President Reagan on September 30. Perkins was selected after the senior-ranking African American career officer, Terence A. Todman, refused, saying that no ambassador should go to South Africa until that government undertook a credible program to end apartheid. He remained as ambassador to Denmark. On November 27, when he presented his credentials to South African President P. W. Botha, the audience

Edward J. Perkins, U.S. ambassador to South Africa, with President Reagan. Ronald Reagan Library

was reported by journalists to have been "correct, quick, and cordial."

## October 15, 1986

**Senator Jesse Helms ends a dispute over diplomatic appointments after his candidate withdraws his nomination.**

Senator Helms (R-N.C.) disliked congressional opposition to his right-wing candidate—the 1986 nominee being James L. Malone as ambassador to Belize. President Reagan nominated Malone, but on April 10, 1986, the Senate Foreign Relations Committee rejected Malone's candidacy by a vote of 9 to 7, the first time in history that the Senate committee had blocked a nominee. Usually, the full Senate opposed a nominee or forced a withdrawal before a vote. The committee opposed Malone because he had broken a promise to them. In 1981, after Reagan appointed him to a State Department post, Malone promised the committee not to deal in any matters involving Japan, West Germany, or Taiwan, three nations for which he had lobbied. Because of his broken promise, the committee members would not accept him.

By October, 18 State Department appointments were pending because Helms had stalled to guarantee Malone's appointment, while Senator Ed Zorinsky (D-Neb.) mounted a filibuster against Malone. Finally, on October 14, Malone asked that his nomination be "temporarily laid aside," and Helms allowed the other appointments to be voted on by the Senate. One concession to Helms was an agreement by Democratic senators to let Helen Marie Taylor be appointed a representative to the U.N. General Assembly. They had formerly opposed her because she was a prominent member of the right-wing Moral Majority and the Eagle Forum.

## October 18, 1986

**President Reagan signs the 1987 omnibus spending bill including $291.8 billion for the military and $100 million for the Nicaraguan Contra rebels.**

The congressional compromises on the defense budget were linked to the Gramm-Rudman deficit limitations; those on Contra aid, to the reluctance of the House of Representatives to vote for assistance to the rebels. The fiscal 1987 defense authorization was 11% below 1986 and $28.5 billion less than

President Reagan requested in February. The $100 million for the Contras was divided into $27 million for nonlethal aid and $3 million for human rights enforcement officers to monitor the behavior of the rebels. Reagan certified that the Contras would try to end human rights abuses and agreed to the enforcement oversight.

The Gramm-Rudman limits were reached by accounting procedures. For example, the defense budget was reduced more than 11% because $3.8 million was taken out by assuming a lower inflation cost for 1987 than Reagan's original budget request assumed in February 1986.

See June 25, 1986.

## October 20, 1986

**The United States extradites an Irish terrorist to Great Britain for the first time.**

Previously, U.S. courts had refused to extradite Irish Republican Army (IRA) terrorists to Great Britain because the U.S. courts called IRA attacks "political." This led Britain and the United States to approve an extradition treaty on June 25, 1986. Meanwhile, a San Francisco court of appeals ruled on February 18, 1986, that William Quinn was eligible for extradition if all other terms were met. Quinn was extradited on October 20 because British officials had evidence that he had killed a London policeman in 1975.

See December 13, 1984.

## October 21, 1986

**The third American in six weeks is kidnapped in Lebanon.**

On October 21, Edward Austin Terry, a freelance journalist, was taken hostage by the Syrian-backed Revolutionary Justice Organization. On September 9, the same group had kidnapped Joseph James Cicippio, chief accountant at Beirut's American University. On September 9, the Iraqi-backed Arab Revolutionary Cells captured Frank H. Reed, director of a private Muslim school. Because these groups were backed by Syria and Iraq, they differed from the pro-Iranian Islamic Jihad, which released hostages in the Reagan administration's arms-for-hostages deal.

See November 2 and 3, 1986, and January 24, 1987.

## October 24, 1986

*Great Britain breaks diplomatic relations with Syria for aiding terrorists.*

Britain condemned Syria for assisting in a terror bombing against the Israeli El Al Airlines at London's Heathrow Airport on April 17, 1986. The British arrested Anne-Marie Murphy, whose luggage carried a bomb timed to explode while the plane flew to Tel Aviv. Murphy's fiancé, the Syrian-born Nezar Nawaf Mansour Hindawi, and his brother were arrested for planting the bomb. Nezar Hindawi was convicted of attempted bombing and sentenced to 45 years in prison on October 24.

The same day, Britain said the evidence implicated Syria in the bomb attempt and broke diplomatic relations. The United States and Canada did not sever relations but withdrew their ambassadors.

See May 6 and November 26, 1986.

## October 27, 1986

*London financial markets undergo a "historic" change in regulations.*

Known as the Big Bang to identify the change as if creating a new universe, deregulation of the centuries-old London stock exchange practices had been planned during a three-year period. In addition to around-the-clock trading, foreign brokerages could now own 100% of the firm (not 29.2% foreign as before), and trade was shifted from the exchange floor to the brokerage trading rooms, where computers and other electronic devices carried on trading. Among the new foreign brokerage firms were Merrill Lynch of the United States and Nomura International of Japan.

## October 27, 1986

*Religious leaders of many faiths observe one day of global peace.*

A day of prayers and peace around the world had been called for by Pope John Paul II during a speech in Lyon, France, on October 4. The day's centerpiece was an ecumenical prayer service at Assisi, Italy, where 150 religious leaders representing 120 religions joined in a day of prayer. The cease-fire was observed by many but not all groups. In Peru, for example, the Shining Path rebels refused to stop their attacks on Peru's government.

## November 2, 1986

*A U.S. hostage David P. Jacobsen, is released just before President Reagan's secret deal with Iran is revealed.*

Jacobsen was the third hostage held by the pro-Iranian Islamic Jihad in Lebanon. Benjamin Weir was released in 1985, and Lawrence Jenco was freed on July 26, 1986. When Jenco was released, his captors called it a "good will gesture"; when Jacobsen was released, his captors attributed it to "certain approaches that could lead, if continued, to a solution of the hostage crisis." Evidently, the "certain approaches" referred to Reagan's arms for hostages deal with Iran. As Lou Cannon's 2000 edition of *President Reagan: the Role of a Lifetime* explains, Reagan's diary entry for January 17, 1986 was "I agreed to sell TOWs to Iran." This entry refers to a secret finding Reagan signed that day permitting members of the National Security Council staff to use covert operations that continued until mid-November 1986. These covert ventures sent 2,004 TOW antitank missiles and 220 spare parts for ground-launched HAWK antiaircraft missiles to Iran in exchange for Iran's releasing American hostages held in Lebanon by pro-Iranian terrorist groups. Reagan's decision to send weapons to Iran violated Reagan's proclaimed policy of withholding weapons from nations sponsoring terrorist groups and a specific U.S. arms embargo on Iran.

See September 18, 1985; October 21, and November 3, 1986.

## November 3, 1986

*The Iran-Contra scandal begins with reports that the United States exchanged arms for hostages.*

An article published on November 3, 1986 in the Lebanese magazine *Al-Shiraa* provided information about the Reagan administration's arms-for-hostages deal with Iran. The magazine's editor received word from Iran's Ayatollah Hussein Ali Montezari, a political opponent of Iran's speaker of the Majlis (parliament) Hojatolislam Hashemi Rafsanjani. On November 4, Rafsanjani told Iran's parliament that Reagan's National Security Adviser Robert McFarlane and four other Americans visited Teheran in October 1985, although both Rafsanjani and *Al Shiraa* later corrected the date of McFarlane's visit to May 1985.

*Al-shiraa*'s report indicated the five Americans arrived in Tehran carrying Irish passports and were detained for five days, during which they offered to send Iran the TOW missiles requested by Rafsanjani if Iran released American hostages in Lebanon.

As Lou Cannon's 2000 edition of *President Reagan: The Role of a Lifetime* explains, on November 6, McFarlane called the magazine's report "fanciful," and on the same day Reagan denied there was a deal with Iran. Reagan told reporters the story from the Middle East "has no foundation" and such reports made it more "difficult for us in our efforts to get other hostages free."

On the release of Jacobsen, Lawrence Jenco, and Benjamin Weir, see November 2, 1986; see also November 25, 1986.

## November 4, 1986

### Democrats capture control of both houses of Congress in midterm elections.

President Reagan's personal popularity did not persuade the electorate to give the Republicans control of Congress. In the 1986 elections the Democrats gained five Senate seats, for a 55-to-45 margin. They also controlled the House of Representatives, having 258 to 177 seats.

## November 4, 1986

### The Northern Mariana Islands becomes a U.S. commonwealth state; other U.S. trusteeship islands gain independent status in 1986–1987.

After World War II, the United States assumed control of Micronesia as a trusteeship under the United Nations. By 1986, these islands evolved into four groups: the Marshall Islands and the Federated States of Micronesia, which became independent but "freely associated" with the United States on October 29, 1986; Palau, whose independent status as an "associated" state was delayed until August 4, 1987; and the northern Marianas, whose voters chose to become a U.S. commonwealth—the same as Puerto Rico in the Caribbean.

All these islands depended on economic aid from Washington and accepted a U.S. military presence; in the case of the Marshalls, Kwajalein Island was a missile testing range for U.S. weapons. The delay in the status of Palau resulted because its constitution forbade nuclear weapons unless 75% of the voters chose

otherwise. Because this conflicted with the U.S. policy of not identifying which U.S. naval vessels carried nuclear warheads, the voters had to change their constitution to permit nuclear weapons. Voters approved by 71% in a referendum on August 4, 1987.

## November 9, 1986

### Because Iceland violates the whaling moratorium, the Sea Shepherd Conservation Society destroys two Icelandic whaling ships.

Based in Canada, the Sea Shepherd's organization sank two Icelandic whaling ships in Reykjavík and destroyed the nation's only whale oil–processing plant in protest against violations of agreements with the International Whaling Commission (see July 23, 1982).

This sabotage was precipitated by Iceland's decision on August 6, 1986, to kill up to 120 whales each year, using 57% of the meat domestically. The United States had warned Iceland not to violate the 1984 Whaling Agreement or it would boycott the importation of fish from Iceland. After Iceland began killing whales, the Sea Shepherds attacked the Icelandic ships and processing plant. Paul Watson, the Sea Shepherd spokesman, said the attacks were planned to avoid human deaths or injuries.

## November 14, 1986

### Great Peace March ends as 1,000 walk from Los Angeles to Washington, D.C.

The peace advocates began the walk on March 1, 1985, with 1,400 participants. Lacking enough funds, the trek ended near Barstow, California. After being reorganized, however, the walk continued to November 14.

## November 22, 1986

### India seeks $3 billion in damages from Union Carbide for the 1984 Bhopal accident.

Although the Union Carbide Company offered families of the Bhopal victims $350 million on March 24, 1986, India rejected the offer, and lawyers for the victims sought relief by suit in U.S. courts. On May 12, 1986, the U.S. District Court in New York City ruled that the lawsuits should be filed in India, a verdict the U.S. Supreme Court refused to review on October 5, 1987.

Meanwhile, legal procedures began in India, and on November 22, the Indian government claimed $3 billion should be held in escrow by Union Carbide pending a settlement. Trial was to begin on November 27, 1987, but the Bhopal judge delayed it, urging the matter to be settled out of court. A settlement was reached on December 22, 1988, when India accepted $470 million for the Bhopal victims, who numbered 3,289, according to Indian authorities.

### November 25, 1986

**President Reagan discloses pertinent aspects of the Iran-Contra affair during a televised press conference.**

After denying the existence of an arms-for-hostage deal on November 4, American newspapers headlined the story of a deal based on Rafsanjani's admitting to Iran's parliament that the Americans visited Tehran (see November 3, 1986). Although on November 6, Reagan refused to comment on these news reports, congressional leaders became concerned that Reagan had rewarded Iranian terrorists. Before November 3, three U.S. hostages were released—Benjamin Weir, Lawrence Jenco, and David Jacobsen—but three other Americans were kidnapped in Lebanon during the fall of 1986 (see October 21, 1986) and four more Americans were kidnapped after November 3 (see January 4, 1987 and February 17, 1988).

On November 25, when Reagan met with reporters for a televised briefing, Reagan announced that National Security Adviser John Poindexter and Oliver North, a marine working for the National Security Council, would no longer work for the Reagan administration and that he would appoint a presidential panel to investigate the National Security Council's role in assuming duties usually associated with the CIA, the State Department, or the Defense Department. Both Secretary of State George Shultz and Defense Secretary Caspar Weinberger had opposed Reagan's agreement to exchange arms to Iran for the release of hostages. As for the CIA Director, William Casey became hospitalized in December with a cerebral seizure (see January 29, 1987).

Apparently between $10 and $30 million had been paid for arms sent to Iran, and there was a special account at Credit Suisse Bank used by North to assist Nicaragua's Contra rebels during a period when the Boland Amendment limited or stopped aid to the Contras. McFarland, Poindexter, and North had transshipped arms to Iran through Israel by using former Marine General Richard Secord's Enterprise Corporation. Secord worked with North to send arms to Iran, whose payments for the TOW missiles and other armaments were used to purchase arms that were sent by air transport to the Contras.

Despite these and other disclosures about the arms-for-hostages deal, President Reagan continued to argue that the arms deal with Iran had nothing to do with the release of hostages. Reagan told *Time* magazine columnist Hugh Sidney in an article published by *Time* on December 8, 1986, that North was a "national hero" and that this "whole thing boils down to a great responsibility on the part of the press" in preventing the release of more hostages.

On December 9, North and Poindexter invoked the Fifth Amendment during a hearing of the Senate Intelligence Committee, claiming their testimony might incriminate themselves. In contrast, McFarland told the Senate Committee that in August 1985, President Reagan had approved the transfer of Israel's TOW missiles to Iran and the replenishing of Israel's TOWs with U.S. stocks, testimony Reagan confirmed before the presidential commission (the Tower Commission for its Chairman former Senator John G. Tower) on January 26, 1987.

In addition to the Tower Commission, both the Senate and the House appointed separate Special Select Committees that conducted joint hearing in investigating the Iran-Contra affair. Also, on December 19, three judges of the Washington, D.C. Federal District Court appointed Lawrence E. Walsh as an independent counsel to investigate this affair.

See February 22, 1987 for Tower Commission Report and May 5, 1987 for the opening of the Joint Senate-House hearings. On Casey, see January 29, 1987.

### November 26, 1986

**West Berlin court convicts two men of bombing an Arab social club; West Germany expels Syrian diplomats.**

Because West Germany saw terrorist links to Syria and not Libya, on November 27 the West German government expelled three Syrian diplomats, reduced Syrian military attachés from three to two, and stopped development aid and low-interest loans to

Damascus. Syria retaliated by expelling three West German diplomats.

See May 6 and October 24, 1986.

## November 27, 1986

### Communist rebels in the Philippine Islands accept a cease-fire.

This cease-fire ended a third attempt to unseat President Corazon Aquino since she gained office in February 1986. An attempt from July 6 to 8 was easily put down, as had been a rally of Marcos forces from October 26 to 29. In November, Defense Minister Enrile challenged Aquino's leadership, but the threat subsided after the U.S. State Department announced continued support for and confidence in Aquino. The rebels then signed a cease-fire.

Enrile's threat materialized because thousands of protesters rallied following the November 13 slaying of Rolando Olahia, head of the major Philippines leftist group and its largest labor union, the May First Movement. Although Aquino formed a special task force to investigate the murder, left-wing demonstrations continued for nearly two weeks. On November 23, Aquino asked her cabinet to resign. She replaced Enrile with Deputy Defense Minister Rafael Ileto. She feared Enrile might try another coup d'état. Ileto and Aquino took special pains to get a cease-fire with the rebels, achieving this on November 27. Peace talks with the rebels began on December 23.

See February 2, 1987.

## December 7, 1986

### U.S. helicopters ferry Honduran troops to defend against Nicaragua.

U.S. helicopters answered a request from Honduran President José Azcona Hoyo, who said that since December 4, Nicaraguan troops had overrun a border post at Las Mietes and penetrated three miles into Honduras, near the area where 20,000 Contra rebels and their families lived. President Reagan ordered nine U.S. helicopters to carry 1,000 Honduran soldiers to the border, but it had become quiet by December 8. Nicaragua claimed it held war games in December but since this involved 6,500 troops, Azcona said they were "provocative."

In response, on December 29, 1986, the United States started Big Pine '87 in Honduras, a four-month U.S.-Honduran military exercise.

See May 13, 1987.

## December 12, 1986

### U.S. nuclear reactor in Richland, Washington, is closed for safety.

This reactor at the Hanford Nuclear Reservation had been ordered shut down by the Department of Energy on October 8, 1986. Opened in 1963 and producing most U.S. weapons-grade plutonium, it resembled the reactor that failed at Chernobyl in the Soviet Union. Although cited for 54 violations in two years, the plant did not close immediately because politicians feared the effect on Richland's economy and the future of nuclear reactors. Critics wished to close all plants designed like Chernobyl's.

See April 26, 1986.

## December 18, 1986

### President Reagan sends $15 million in military aid to Chad.

Libya's Mu'ammar Gadhafi had caused trouble in Chad since 1981. Every time Gadhafi agreed to remove Libyan forces from Chad, he broke his promises (see March 16 and October 30, 1981; June 23 and August 23, 1983; and November 19, 1984).

On February 10, 1986, Libya again intervened on behalf of Chad's rebels who were fighting Chad's government forces. After Libyan planes bombed the airport serving Chad's city of N'Djamena, France sent a squadron of aircraft and 500 French soldiers as a deterrent force on February 17, 1986. On December 18, 1986, President Reagan decided to assist Chad by sending military arms and ammunition to help supply Chad's army. Conflict in Chad continued until 1988 (see September 11, 1987).

See November 19, 1984, and May 25, 1988.

## December 18, 1986

### The Soviet Union proposes a nuclear test moratorium.

The Soviet Union's General Secretary Mikhail Gorbachev initially proposed a moratorium on nuclear testing in July 1985 (see July 29, 1985), but President Ronald Reagan refused to accept the moratorium because he claimed such tests could not be verified. The United States continued nuclear tests and conducted another nuclear test on December 13, 1986, just two months after Reagan's summit meeting with Gorbachev in Iceland (see October 11, 1986). On December 18, 1986, Gorbachev again urged Reagan to accept a nuclear test ban agreement. If not, the Soviet Union would renew its nuclear testing after the first 1987 nuclear test by Americans. On December 19, Soviet Ambassador to the United States Yuri V. Dubinin indicated that if both countries renewed nuclear testing, U.S. scientists from the Natural Resources Defense Council, an independent environmental group, could use the Soviet monitoring station in the Soviet Republic of Kazakhstan to monitor Soviet tests.

Disregarding Moscow's warning, the Reagan administration staged another nuclear test on February 3, 1987. Two days after the U.S. test, Soviet Deputy Foreign Minister Vladimir Petrovsky called the U.S. test "provocative," indicating the Soviet Union would renew its nuclear testing. On February 26, 1987, the Soviets conducted their first nuclear test since Gorbachev announced a unilateral moratorium on nuclear tests in July 1985.

See October 11–12, 1986.

### December 18, 1986

**The Contadora group criticizes the United States for preventing peace in Central America.**

Throughout 1986, the four Latin American nations of the Contadora group—Mexico, Venezuela, Colombia, and Panama—and five support members—Costa Rica, Nicaragua, El Salvador, Honduras, and Guatemala—were frustrated in peace attempts for Central America. As early as January 12, the nine nations urged Nicaragua and the United States to accept peace negotiations. After proclaiming a "last version" peace draft on June 7, the group obtained what seemed to be Nicaragua's approval, but because acceptance depended on the withdrawal of U.S aid to the Contras, no results followed. The U.S. State Department rejected Contadora plans unless Nicaragua agreed to negotiate with the Contras, who gained more aid from the U.S. Congress in 1986.

Thus, meeting at Rio de Janeiro, Brazil, on December 18, the nine nations particularly criticized the United States for sustaining a war. They called on the United States and Nicaragua to negotiate for peace.

See October 18, 1986.

### December 20, 1986

**OPEC members accept a production cut to raise oil prices.**

Since their March 24, 1986, meeting, OPEC members tried to decrease oil production to raise prices. The first breakthrough was on August 25, when OPEC agreed to cut oil production by 3 million barrels per day. A price rise resulted and West Texas Intermediate crude prices rose from below $10 to $15.30 per barrel. On October 24, OPEC extended its production-sharing controls and on December 20 accepted a recommendation from its pricing committee to cut production by 7% in 1987 to increase premium oil prices to $18 per barrel. Only Iraq rejected this limit.

### December 25, 1986

**Hijacking of an Iraqi Airways plane leads to 67 deaths.**

The Iraqi plane was hijacked either by Iranians or dissident Iraqis en route from Baghdad to Amman, Jordan. After taking over, the hijackers engaged in a gunfight with security guards, exploding two grenades in the cabin. The plane crash-landed in Saudi Arabia, killing 67 of the 107 passengers. Because Iraq and Saudi Arabia established a news blackout, reporters did not know whether Iranians or dissident Iraqis caused the crash.

### December 30, 1986

**The United States and Canada compromise on trade in softwood lumber products.**

The question about Canadian wood imports was raised initially in 1986, when President Reagan approved a tariff of 35% on Canada's wood products (see May 22, 1986). While negotiations were pending on October 16, 1986, the United States Commerce Department imposed an additional 15% tariff on Canadian construction imports. The Commerce Department's action led to negotiations that achieved a compromise agreement on December 30, 1986. Under terms of the compromise, the United States laid aside its recent tariffs on Canadian wood products and Canada agreed to levy a 15% Canadian export tax on softwood lumber exports to the United States, while also charging a "stumpage" fee when Canadian lumbermen cut trees on Canada's government land.

# 1987

### January 6, 1987

*Portugal agrees to return Macao to China by 1999.*

Portugal and the People's Republic of China agreed that Macao would become a special administrative zone of China with considerable autonomy. The arrangement resembled Britain's deal for Hong Kong (see September 25, 1984).

### January 8, 1987

**Secretary of State George Shultz begins an eight-day tour of six African nations.**

This journey covered six pro-Western black African countries—Senegal, Kenya, Nigeria, Ivory Coast, Cameroon, and Liberia. Generally, Shultz praised Africa's trend away from socialism but offered no new U.S. aid programs.

### January 10, 1987

**A U.S. investigation discloses Soviet electronic devices are in the new U.S. embassy in Moscow.**

The investigation of the U.S. embassy situation was precipitated on January 10, 1987 by the arrest of U.S. Marine Corps Sergeant Clayton Lonetree, a member of the Marines who guarded the embassy. Lonetree was charged with giving secret information to a female agent of the KGB (the Soviet Union's secret police) with whom he had sexual relations. Lonetree was courtmartialed, found guilty of espionage, and sentenced to 30 years in prison on August 24, 1987. After Lonetree cooperated by giving detailed information about his recruitment as a spy and disclosing Soviet secrets he knew about, a Marine Corps appeals court granted clemency to Lonetree and reduced his sentence by five years.

The information Lonetree gave to U.S. authorities provided essential data enabling U.S. investigators to find the electronic bugs placed inside the new U.S. embassy building being built in Moscow.

See June 8, 1987.

### January 15, 1987

**The United States lifts controls on exports of oil-drilling equipment to the Soviet Union.**

The Commerce Department ended the limitation that President Jimmy Carter began in July 1978 to punish the Soviets for the trial and imprisonment of two human rights dissenters—Aleksandr Ginzberg and Anatoly Shcharansky. U.S. business firms were hurt more than the Soviets, who found other suppliers for the oil-drilling equipment. In 1978, Carter's action cost U.S. manufacturers $2 billion in contracts. Some U.S. oil-drilling equipment was advanced in 1978, but by the mid-1980s such equipment was widely available from other countries.

### January 24, 1987

**Three Americans are abducted in Lebanon; the State Department tells Americans to leave Lebanon.**

Gunmen had taken four faculty members from the American University in Beirut. Their captors were the Islamic Jihad for the Liberation of Palestine. President Reagan blamed the professors for ignoring State Department suggestions that Americans leave Lebanon. On January 28, the State Department prohibited travel to Lebanon on American passports, giving the approximately 1,500 Americans there 30 days to leave.

On June 16, an ABC journalist in Beirut, Charles Glass, was kidnapped. On August 18, Glass escaped and, after encountering Syrian troops, was taken to Damascus and freed.

### January 25, 1987

*West German Chancellor Kohl is reelected.*

While Helmut Kohl's Christian Democratic Union and the Free Democrats maintained their coalition, both Kohl's party and the Social Democratic Party lost seats in the Bundestag (lower house of parliament) while the Free Democrats and the Green Party increased their votes. Kohl's party vote was down to 44.3% from 48.8% in 1983; the Free Democrats, up to 9.1% from 2.1%. The Social

Democrats' vote dropped to 34.8% from 37%; the Green Party's increased to 8.3% from 5.6%.

## January 27, 1987

*Soviet Union's Communist Party Central Committee meeting approves General Secretary Mikhail Gorbachev's proposed reforms.*

As described in Gorbachev's 1995 *Memoirs*, General Secretary Gorbachev began in December 1986 to change the Soviet Union's direction toward democratizing both the Communist Party of the Soviet Union (CPSU) and the structure of the Soviet government in order to implement his *perestroika* (reforms) and revitalize the country. Prior to the January 27 meeting of the Central Committee, Gorbachev's ideas about democratizing the country were discussed with CPSU Politburo members. Somewhat to Gorbachev's surprise, all the Politburo members, including Andrei Gromyko and Boris Yeltsin, supported his proposals. The Politburo was the policy making body of both the CPSU and the Soviet government. Its proposals could be questioned or revised by the Party's Central Committee, although this seldom occurred regarding major political and economic affairs.

When the Central Committee members met on January 27, 1987, the Central Committee approved Gorbachev's reform program with little debate. The reforms allowed more than one candidate to be on the ballot in secret elections for Party representatives and officials. Other significant reforms permitted Communist Party members to file grievances against Party officials and granted greater regional control in Party affairs.

Having gained approval from the CPSU Central Committee, Gorbachev was able to begin carrying out political reforms on June 21, 1987, when representatives of the Party's Council of Representative Delegations were elected in secret ballots. The June elections permitted multiple candidates on the ballots, but only 76 of the 3,912 Council seats were contested with two or more candidates. Nevertheless, Gorbachev believed the precedent was set for multiple candidates to be on future ballots.

When the Supreme Soviet of the USSR (a parliament) met to approve the legislation recommended by the Central Committee, the Supreme Soviet enacted the necessary legislation in two working days: June 29 and 30, 1987.

## January 28, 1987

### Secretary of State Shultz meets with Oliver Tambo of the African National Congress (ANC).

Tambo represented the leading black South African group fighting the apartheid policies of South Africa. He wanted the United States and other Western nations to apply economic sanctions against South Africa, something he had little chance of persuading Shultz to promote. On January 8, 1987, the State Department issued a report claiming the ANC was "deeply beholden" to the South African Communist Party, a charge Shultz asked Tambo to refute. The ANC, like other black African rebel groups, found Moscow ready to help when Western powers refused to do so.

Because of Tambo's communist connections, the State Department emphasized that his meeting with Shultz was only symbolic of the ANC role in any South African settlement. Shultz urged Tambo to cut Soviet ties and avoid the use of violence. Nevertheless, conservatives in the United States opposed the meeting. At an official gathering on February 20, Representative Jack Kemp (R-N.Y.) said Shultz should resign for entertaining Tambo and disrupting President Reagan's foreign policies.

## January 29, 1987

### A Senate Intelligence Committee report contradicts President Reagan's claim that sending arms to Iran sought better relations.

During December 1986, the Senate Intelligence Committee had briefings with Central Intelligence Agency Director William Casey and others to learn details of the Iran-Contra affair. The major issue was Reagan's purpose in selling arms to Iran, using the money to support the Contras, and negotiating the hostages' release.

Anticipating the Senate report, on January 9 the White House had released an intelligence finding of January 17, 1986, signed by Reagan and stating that the arms sale had the strategic goal of a more moderate Iranian government. At the bottom of the document National Security Adviser John Poindexter noted that Reagan signed but did not read it. During his January 27 State of the Union speech, Reagan argued that the Iranian effort was worthy, and his major regret was that it did not improve Iranian relations and get the release of all the hostages.

On January 29, the Senate Intelligence report was released. One of its principal findings was that the main purpose of the affair had *not* been to improve Iranian relations or to aid moderate Iranians. The Senate found no evidence that Reagan knew about Oliver North's diversion of funds to the Contras. Other new Senate information on the affair was that the Reagan administration had solicited aid for the Contras from at least six countries. One was the sultan of Brunei, who put $10 million in secret Swiss accounts for North to use in Central America.

The Senate Intelligence Committee was the only investigative group obtaining testimony from Casey. They heard Casey on December 10, five days before he was hospitalized for a cerebral seizure. After surgery to remove a malignant brain tumor on December 18, Casey died on May 5, 1987. Following the 1987 congressional hearings, Bob Woodward of the *Washington Post* claimed in his book *The Veil* to have visited Casey on his deathbed, where Casey said he knew about and approved the diversion of funds to the Contras.

Regarding news about soliciting aid for the Contras from other sources, the White House issued a statement on May 14, 1987, declaring that while Congress could limit the federal monies, nothing limited the "constitutional and historic power of the president" to decide foreign policy and raise private money for the Contras. On May 15, Reagan told journalists it was his idea to obtain private aid for the Contras because Congress had restricted it.

See November 3 and 25, 1986.

### February 2, 1987

#### *Six days after a failed coup, Filipino voters approve a new constitution.*

In February 1986, when "people power" ended the rule of Ferdinand Marcos, Corazon Aquino became President and announced an interim constitution pending the preparation of a new constitution (see February 25, 1986). On January 24, the eve of a referendum on the Philippine's new constitution, about 500 Filipino soldiers loyal to Marcos attacked military bases and took over several broadcasting stations and public utility buildings in an attempt to bring Marcos back from exile in Hawaii. The coup failed, and on January 29 rebel leader Colonel Oscar Canales surrendered.

Following the failed coup, Filipino voters approved the new constitution with an 87% majority of the votes favoring the constitution. When a new Congress was elected on May 11, 1987, Aquino's candidates won 22 of 24 Senate seats and 200 of the 250 seats in the House of Representatives.

### February 4, 1987

#### A Colombian drug dealer is captured by police in Bogotá and flown to Florida for trial.

A leading drug trafficker, Carlos Enrique Lehder Rivas, was arrested after a shootout in Bogotá, Colombia. He was accused of smuggling billions of dollars of cocaine into the United States. His trial in U.S. Federal Court in Miami, Florida began on November 16, 1987. After being found guilty on May 19, 1988, Lehder was sentenced on July 20 to life in prison without parole plus 135 years and fined $350,000. The judge rejected Lehder's claim to be an illegal political prisoner.

### February 9, 1987

#### The United States is alarmed by the Soviets naval buildup at a Vietnamese base; Australian authorities disagree.

During the Reagan era, the U.S. navy moved toward a "maritime strategy" to control narrow "choke points" of the world's sea lanes to gain naval superiority. In line with this, the United States argued that the USSR sought to dominate the Pacific Ocean through its Vietnamese base at Cam Ranh Bay. The Reagan administration indicated that the Soviets had quadrupled their base size in a major effort to dominate the region.

This U.S. belief was questioned by Australian Defense Minister Kim Beazly, as reported in the *Far East Economic Review* for June 18, 1987. Using American photographs as proof, Beazly argued that the Soviets had none of their "first line craft" at Cam Ranh Bay. Moreover, he claimed, the U.S. navy's recent expenditures had checkmated all Soviet efforts in the Pacific.

## February 18, 1987

### Returning from Iraq, Representative Robert G. Torricelli (D-N.J.) says Iran benefited greatly from the U.S. sale of arms.

The Iran-Contra impact on the Iran-Iraq war was overlooked by many U.S. commentators. Reports, however, suggested that there were benefits to Iran and costs to Iraq resulting from these sales. After a five-day visit to Baghdad, Torricelli learned from Iraqi Foreign Minister Tariq Aziz that because of the sale of U.S. Hawk antiaircraft missiles, Iraq lost 45 to 50 warplanes—10% of its air force. In addition, during a recent Iranian offensive, Iraq blamed its extremely high tank losses on the U.S. sale of TOW antitank missiles to Iran.

According to Reagan administration officials, two types of weapons were sent to Iran: parts for the Hawk antiaircraft missiles sold to the shah before 1979, and 2,008 TOW tube-launched, optically tracked, wire-guided antitank missiles. Although President Reagan said he had authorized only "small amounts of defensive weapons" that did not affect the Iran-Iraq military balance, military experts said these two weapons caused considerable damage to Iraq and could determine the war's course.

## February 19, 1987

### President Reagan lifts economic sanctions from Poland.

In 1984, Reagan had removed some of the sanctions levied in December 1981 because the Polish government instituted martial law to break the Solidarity trade union led by Lech Wałęsa. He now removed the last sanction by ending a ban on U.S. trade credits and granting Poland most-favored nation status, which lowered U.S. tariffs on Polish exports.

The United States took two other steps in 1987 to encourage Poland to grant greater political and economic reform. On September 22, diplomatic relations were restored when Ambassador John Davis went to Warsaw. Second, from September 26 to 28, Vice President George Bush visited Poland and indicated that Washington would help Poland reschedule its foreign debt to help rebuild its economy.

See July 21, 1984.

## February 22, 1987

### Leaders of Pakistan and India fail to end tensions regarding border disputes.

Pakistani President Muhammad Zia ul-Haq and Indian Prime Minister Rajiv Gandhi nearly engaged their nations in large-scale war between January 23 and 31 when each moved forces to the borders of the Indian provinces of Punjab and Kashmir, where Pakistan claimed territorial rights. War was averted on January 31 after each agreed to pull back troops from the border regions.

The February 21–22 meeting attempted but failed to resolve the Kashmir problem. On September 23, conflict began again when Pakistani forces attacked a glacier in a strategic location in Kashmir but failed to dislodge the Indian units.

## February 23, 1987

### The trial of a Lebanese terrorist begins in France during which the United States participates as a civil plaintiff.

The United States wanted a role in the trial of Georges Ibrahim Abdallah, who was charged with violent attacks on three foreign diplomats, including Lt. Colonel Charles Ray, an American military attaché in Paris killed in 1982. The United States feared that France would be too lenient, but the French judges proved otherwise, thwarting the prosecutor's request for a ten-year prison term by sentencing Abdallah to life in prison. The prosecutor had argued that a severe sentence would damage French diplomatic efforts in the Middle East.

## February 26, 1987

### The Tower Commission claims that President Reagan's management style caused the Iran-Contra débâcle.

Appointed by Reagan on November 26, this commission consisted of former Senator John G. Tower (R-Tex.) as chairman, former Secretary of State Edmund S. Muskie, and former National Security Adviser Brent Scowcroft. After reviewing the secret events of the Iran-Contra affair and the National Security Council's procedures, the report concluded that the president had not insisted on accountability for NSC activity. It believed no criminal activity was involved but recommended reviewing NSC procedures so that "loose cannons" such as Lt. Colonel North could not act independently, as he had done during these operations.

On March 4, President Reagan told a television audience that he accepted full responsibility for the affair, conceding that his honorable intentions deteriorated into an arms-for-hostages deal. This was the closest Reagan came to admitting a mistake or apologizing for action contrary to his public posturing about no deals with terrorists.

The Tower Commission report included a chronology of major events of the scandal, which historians may compare to publicized events at particular moments. The most important of these were the following:

Sept. 2, 1984:    Lt. Colonel North suggests private donors give the Contras a helicopter.

July 3, 1985:    David Kimche of the Israeli Foreign Ministry tells NSC Director McFarlane that Iran seeks "discourse" with the United States; soon after, Reagan approves "discourse."

Aug. 30, 1985:    NSC Director McFarlane believed Iran might release hostages if the United States sent weapons, 100 U.S. TOW antitank missiles are sent to Iran via Israel.

Sept. 14, 1985:    Israel delivers another 408 missiles to Iran; the Rev. Benjamin Weir is the first hostage released.

Dec. 7, 1985:    After the CIA wants explicit presidential authority before sending more weapons to Iran, a high-level meeting is held among Reagan, Vice President Bush, CIA director Casey, Secretary of State Shultz, Secretary of Defense Weinberger, and NSC advisers McFarlane and Poindexter. Shultz and Weinberger oppose the deal, but the NSC staff favors it. Immediately afterward, claiming Reagan approved the dealing of arms for hostages, McFarlane and Oliver North go to London (December 8) to meet with arms dealer Adnan M. Ghorbanifar.

Jan. 6, 1986:    Reagan authorizes covert action to ship Iran arms for hostages.

(Reagan could not recall signing it, but on January 17, he signed a second authorization less clearly worded on hostages but providing permission for the CIA's sending missiles to Iran.)

Apr. 4, 1986:    North memo to Poindexter seeks $12 million from Iran arms sale for Nicaraguan Contras.

(Reagan's role is uncertain, but North helped fund the Contras, and on October 7, a CIA officer told Casey that Iranian funds may have been diverted.)

May 25–28, 1986:    McFarlane and North fly to Tehran, on a plane carrying an arms shipment.

July 26, 1986:    Hostage the Rev. Lawrence Jenco is freed in Lebanon.

Oct. 29, 1986:    The CIA's last 500 TOW missiles were sent to Iran via Israel.

Other shipments were sent in August, September, and November 1985, and February, May, and August 1986.

Nov. 3, 1986:    The affair is made public by a Lebanese magazine.

As a note of historical interest, the president's wife, Nancy, had since December 1986 marshaled forces to blame the White House chief of staff, Donald T. Regan, for the affair and to seek his resignation. An expert in domestic matters, Regan seems to have had little direct role in the Iran-Contra deal, but he did not monitor NSC staff members Poindexter and North. On February 27, Regan resigned and was replaced by former Senator Howard Baker (R-Tenn.). On July 30, 1986, Regan told the House-Senate committee on the Iran-Contra affair that Mrs Reagan thought he "let Ronnie down."

## February 28, 1987

### Soviet First Secretary Mikhail Gorbachev offers a plan to eliminate Intermediate-Range Nuclear Forces (INF) in Europe: President Reagan reacts favorably.

Mikhail Gorbachev's February 28 proposal to eliminate Intermediate-Range Nuclear Forces (INF) was based on his decision to separate negotiations on INF from such arms control issues as President Reagan's Strategic Defense Initiative (SDI). Following Gorbachev's offer, subsequent negotiations resulted in the December 1987 INF Treaty (see December 8, 1987).

Before announcing his proposal, Gorbachev began a "peace offensive" to convince Americans and Europeans he wanted to end the Cold War. On February 4, he convened a meeting in Moscow that was co-sponsored by the Council on Foreign Relations, a private group located in New York City. The American delegation included former U.S.

Cabinet officials Harold Brown, Henry Kissinger, Peter Peterson, and Cyrus Vance.

From February 14 to 16, Gorbachev hosted an international meeting on peace and disarmament attended by 700 artists, scientists, business leaders, and politicians. The most important result of this international meeting was a speech by physicist Andrey Sakharov to a meeting of scientists. Sakharov called on Gorbachev to stop linking negotiations on INF and arms reduction treaties to Reagan's SDI program. Sakharov said no SDI system would be effective against a massive attack by Soviet intercontinental ballistic missiles (ICBMs). SDI, he argued, was only a "Maginot line in space," a reference to France's ineffective Maginot line in 1940 (see June 17, 1940). By February 28, Gorbachev decided Sakharov and other Soviet scientists who made similar comments about SDI were correct. Thus, the December INF Treaty could be finalized as the first of other strategic arms reduction treaties (START) made between the Soviet Union or Russia with the United States during the 1990s.

See June 3, 1990.

### March 3, 1987

**Secretary of State Shultz visits China and learns about the Chinese interest in Western-style free markets.**

When Shultz arrived in China on May 1, he met with the leader of the Chinese Communist Party Deng Xiaoping, who told Shultz that China's political difficulties had slowed down its economic modernization program. The party, Deng said, wanted Western help in economic affairs but not in China's political and cultural matters.

The political problems Deng referred to included the forced resignation of the Communist Party's General Secretary Hu Yaobang, who, in the Chinese tradition following the overthrow of the "gang of four" and the 1960s cultural revolution (see August 18, 1966 and December 15, 1978), had confessed to his mistakes in being too pro-Western and his failure to prevent the extensive student demonstrations from January 1 to 5, 1987. Hu's mistakes also led the Chinese Communist Party to expel Wang Ruowang, a university Marxian theorist, and Liu Binyan, a journalist for China's *People's Daily*. Hu was replaced by Premier Zhao Ziyang while the Communist Party's Politburo came under the influence of Deputy Premier Li Peng, who opposed political reforms in China.

### March 5–6, 1987

*An earthquake in Ecuador kills about 1,000 people and disrupts the nation's economy.*

The act of nature made 30,000 people homeless and prevented Ecuador from meeting payments of $8.3 billion of its foreign debts in 1987. The quake destroyed part of the main oil pipeline to the port of Balao, preventing Ecuador from exporting oil, a major source of its income.

### March 27, 1987

**President Reagan levies 100% tariffs on Japanese electronic products; he later partially removes them.**

The president imposed high tariffs because Japan had not, as promised, opened its markets to U.S. semiconductor chips nor stopped the sale of Japanese chips at below-cost prices. On June 8, Reagan lifted the tariff on a few electronic goods. On November 4, he dropped tariffs on all electronics imports except laptop and high-powered desktop computers. In accordance with previous agreements with the United States, Japan stopped dumping computer chips on the U.S. market at low price, but the United States wanted Japan to give American made chips a larger share of Japan's market.

See July 31, 1986; see also May 29, 1987.

### April 1, 1987

*British Prime Minister Thatcher visits Moscow; British-Soviet relations are improved.*

Prime Minister Margaret Thatcher spent five days in the USSR and had a lengthy visit with Soviet leader Mikhail Gorbachev. As when Gorbachev visited London in 1984, Thatcher and he got along splendidly. Minor agreements were made to upgrade the telephone hot line between London and Moscow and to exchange scientific and cultural personnel.

See December 18, 1984.

## April 13, 1987

**The U.S. ambassador to South Africa, Edward Perkins, attends a protest service against South African limits on political protests and detaining of children.**

After South Africa's national police commissioner forbade protests regarding political detainees, even with bumper stickers or petitions, Perkins showed U.S. dissatisfaction by going to a church protest service conducted by Anglican Archbishop Desmond Tutu on an interdenominational basis. Perkins said South Africa's latest restrictions put basic freedoms in "serious jeopardy."

## April 13, 1987

**Secretary of State George Shultz and Soviet Foreign Minister Eduard Shevardnadze discuss INF weapons and space probes.**

Meeting in Moscow for three days, the two diplomatic delegations discussed the Soviet proposal of February 28, 1988, to eliminate intermediate-range nuclear

Left to right: Soviet Foreign Minister Eduard Shevardnadze and Secretary of State George Shultz. Department of State

forces (INF). They also signed an accord to share data obtained from unmanned planetary space flights.

On April 27, the Soviet Union formally presented a draft treaty to eliminate INF in Europe.

For the final treaty, see December 8, 1987.

## April 20, 1987

***PLO meeting in Algiers brings more unity around a hard-line approach to Israel; Syria seeks aid from Moscow.***

Meeting in Algiers from April 20 to 26, the Palestine Liberation Organization's leader, Yasser Arafat, wanted dissident factions to unite against Israel. The PLO comprised competing groups from its start in the 1960s, but the 1982 Israeli attack on Lebanon had caused greater divisions.

Arafat was reelected chairman of the PLO with support from two principal splinter groups—the Popular Front for the Liberation of Palestine, headed by George Habash; and the Democratic Front for the Liberation of Palestine, under Nayef Hawatmeh. Other smaller factions did not come to Algiers, including pro-Syrian leaders such as Abu Musa and Abu Nidal. To obtain support, Arafat adopted a tougher approach toward Israel, which damaged his relations with Egypt and Jordan.

While Arafat sought to rebuild the PLO's strength, Syrian President Hafiz al-Assad visited Moscow on April 23 and 24 to request advanced armaments and to reschedule Syria's debt to the Soviet Union. Soviet leader Mikhail Gorbachev told Assad he would aid Syria if it ended its antagonism toward Arafat and helped pro-Syrian Palestinians reunite with the PLO. Gorbachev favored an Arab-Israeli peace conference to settle Middle Eastern problems.

See November 8, 1987.

## April 23, 1987

***East German leader Erich Honecker rejects the Soviet Union's economic and political reforms.***

East German Communist Party leader, Honecker, was one of the few Eastern European leaders who refused to adopt the reform practices of the Soviet Union under Mikhail Gorbachev. Honecker told a trade union congress that the East German economy worked well and needed no change. His desire to maintain the status quo was demonstrated on June 6–8, when East German security forces broke up a large group of young people at the Berlin Wall trying to listen to a rock concert on the West Berlin side. While East German police used weapons to restrain the students and arrested 30, many of the youths chanted, "Gorby, Gorby, we want freedom."

See September 7, 1987.

### May 5, 1987

**Joint hearings begin for the House-Senate investigation of the Iran-Contra affair.**

These hearings lasted until August 4, 1987. The following are highlights of the testimony other than those recorded in the Tower Commission report:

May 11, 1987:    Robert McFarlane testified that he frequently briefed President Reagan on Contra aid.

May 19, 1987:    Adolfo Calero, the principal Contra leader, gave North $90,000 in blank traveler's checks in 1985 to finance Drug Enforcement Agency attempts to contact hostages. He did not say where he obtained the $90,000.

May 28, 1987:    Lewis Tambs, former U.S. ambassador to Costa Rica, was asked by North in 1985 to develop a southern Contra front.

June 25, 1987:    Assistant Attorney General Charles Cooper explained at a meeting on November 20, 1986, that CIA Director Casey, Lt. Colonel North, and National Security Adviser Admiral John Poindexter planned false testimony to conceal sending Hawk missiles to Iran.

July 7–10, 1987    Lt. Colonel Oliver North shredded documents before President Reagan's television address about the Iran Contra affair on November 22–23, 1986; he recommended the diversion of Iranian funds to the Contras, leaving a small space on the bottom of the page for the president to initial but giving the memos to Poindexter; he stated that Iranian arms merchant Adnan M. Ghorbanifar proposed diverting funds to the Contras while Poindexter approved it and CIA Director Casey was "very enthusiastic."

July 15, 1987:    John Poindexter, national security adviser until November 25, 1986, testified that Reagan authorized the Iran arms sale but that it was Poindexter's decision to divert funds to the Contras.

On other matters, Poindexter had many memory lapses.

July 23, 1987    Secretary of State, George Shultz, described a "battle royal" with Casey, McFarlane, and Poindexter, who lied to him and withheld data from President Reagan. Shultz said he opposed the deal with Iran and disliked National Security Council (NSC) officers directing State Department officials to report to them, as were John H. Kelly, U.S. ambassador in Beirut, and Lewis Tambs in Costa Rica.

See February 26, 1987, and November 18, 1987.

### May 6, 1987

**Rival Nicaraguan Contra leaders form the National Resistance Army and a seven-member directorate.**

Since February 16, 1987, when Adolfo Calero resigned from the triumvirate governing the Contras in Miami, Florida, rival rebels quarreled over the proper methods to take over the government. On March 9, a liberal member, Arturo Cruz, resigned in a dispute with the third member, Alfonso Robelo.

Knowing that the Reagan administration disliked such factionalism, the rivals created a new group on May 6, separating army functions from the civilian and uniting the three rebel armies into one National Resistance Army. A dozen Nicaraguan exile groups had been meeting to form a 54-member assembly, which elected a seven-man directorate. Cruz was not selected but Calero, who headed the largest group, the Nicaraguan Democratic Force (FDN), and Robelo, of the Social Democratic Party, were on the directorate.

### May 13, 1987

**The United States stages combined air-sea exercises near Nicaragua's border.**

U.S. support for the Contra rebels fighting against the Nicaraguan government included extensive displays of U.S. forces in the Contra sanctuary territory located in Honduras. The Big Pine '87 U.S. military exercise begun in Honduras on December 29, 1986, lasted beyond the original plan of four months and became part of the larger military exercise called Operation Solid Shield.

Deploying 40,000 troops in a landing assault at Trujillo, Honduras, near the Nicaraguan border gave U.S. troops practice while at the same time threatening Nicaragua. One U.S. official said Operation Solid

Shield would "wave a big stick at Nicaragua" while defending Honduras and the Contra bases.

## May 15, 1987

### Japanese government bans Toshiba Machine Company from selling to the Soviet Union because it sold the Soviets sensitive technology.

Toshiba sold the Soviets a computer program for milling submarine propeller blades in June 1984 and tools for manufacturing these blades in December 1982. U.S. Secretary of Defense Caspar Weinberger stated that the security of both Japan and the United States was damaged because these sales permitted the Soviets to acquire quieter submarines, making their detection more difficult. On July 1, the chairman and president of Toshiba resigned because of the government ban.

## May 17, 1987

### Iraqi missiles hit a U.S. navy ship, killing 37 Americans; President Reagan accepts Iraq's apology.

While patrolling in the Persian Gulf, the U.S. navy guided missile frigate USS *Stark*, was hit by two missiles launched from an Iraqi plane. One missile exploded, and the unexploded missile was defused by the *Stark*'s crew. Thirty-seven of the *Stark*'s 220-man crew died in the explosion.

Although both the *Stark*'s radar and an AWACS reconnaissance plane operated jointly by the United States and Saudi Arabia had tracked the Iraqi jet, the Americans did not view Iraq as an enemy, and the *Stark*'s advanced electronic equipment failed to detect the firing of the French-made, sea-skimming Exocet missile. Later, the United States reported that the AWACS crew requested Saudi planes to force the Iraqi jet to land, but the Saudi ground controller lacked authority to order this action.

Ironically, although Iraq was responsible for over two-thirds of the attacks on 300 ships in the Persian Gulf during the Iran-Iraq war and the *Stark* attack killed 37 Americans, President Reagan blamed Iran for the incident. In a May 19 speech in Chattanooga, Tennessee, he said Iran was at fault because it refused to negotiate an end to the war. His reaction complied with recent U.S. policy to placate Iraq and moderate Arab states since the U.S. arms sale to Iran benefited Tehran. Iraqi President Saddam Hussein accepted the blame for the incident and informed Washington that Iraq would pay compensation for the American lives and damage to the ship. After an investigation, the U.S. navy on June 19, 1985, relieved the *Stark*'s captain Glenn R. Brindel, and two other officers from their posts because of negligence, but they were not court-martialed.

See February 18, 1987.

## May 19, 1987

### President Reagan agrees to fly U.S. flags on Kuwaiti oil tankers in the Persian Gulf escorted by the U.S. navy.

After discussions with Kuwait that began in early 1987, on March 23, the United States offered Kuwait naval protection, and on April 4, the U.S. navy added a naval battle group to the existing U.S. aircraft carrier *Kitty Hawk* in the Persian Gulf. The Gulf problem arose after Iraq started attacking commercial ships headed for Iranian ports while Iran retaliated against both Iraqi and Kuwaiti ships because Iran claimed that Kuwait had assisted Baghdad. Between March 22 and April 10, Iran began deploying Silkworm anti-ship missiles along its coastline. Because the Silkworm was made in China, the United States warned Beijing against continuing the sale of Silkworms because the missile endangered all ships in the gulf and the Indian Ocean.

On April 6, Kuwait proposed that its oil tankers be registered under the U.S. or the Soviet flag for protection. The Soviet Union agreed on April 14 to lease three of its tankers to Kuwait while Soviet naval ships escorted those tankers. This led the Reagan administration to reconsider the situation, but until the USS *Stark* was hit on May 17, the president had not decided to accept Kuwait's offer.

Congress now became involved. On May 21, the Senate voted 91 to 5 to request a detailed report on the reflagging plans, causing Reagan to delay the process.

See July 22, 1987.

## May 29, 1987

### Soviet air defenses fail when a West German lands a small plane in Red Square.

Mathias Rust, a young West German who said he was on a "peace mission," flew a Cessna 172 plane 500 miles from Finland into Moscow, where, after buzzing Red Square, he landed near the Kremlin Wall. He got out and talked with people in the square before being arrested. Coincidentally, he did this on the day the Soviets celebrated Border Guards Day. During his journey, only one Soviet plane passed Rust's plane but did not interfere with him.

The main consequence of this exploit was that Soviet leader Mikhail Gorbachev dismissed the defense minister and air defense commander. Gorbachev then appointed a personal political ally, Dimitry Yazov, as the new Soviet defense minister.

Rust was tried by a Soviet court and sentenced to four years in a Soviet labor camp. His plane was returned to the Hamburg, West Germany, flying club that owned it. On August 3, 1988, at the order of the Presidium of the Supreme Soviet (parliament), Rust was freed and returned to West Germany.

### May 29, 1987

### Japan approves a $43 billion program to stimulate its economy and ease trade friction with the United States.

To stimulate consumer demand, Japan reduced interest rates and spent funds for public works, education, and housing loans. The U.S. trade representative believed this was a serious Japanese effort to cut its $58 billion trade surplus with the United States.

See October 2, 1987.

### June 1, 1987

### Lebanese Prime Minister Rashid Karami is killed.

Karami was a Sunni Muslim who had served as prime minister in the coalition government of President Amin Gemayel, a Christian. Karami had resigned on May 4 because renewed Christian-Muslim fighting had broken out in February. Gemayel had rejected Karami's resignation because replacing him might have been impossible.

Karami was killed in a bomb blast aboard a helicopter carrying him from his Tripoli home to Beirut. He was replaced by another Sunni Muslim, Selim al-Hoss. Karami's assassins were never discovered, but Lebanese Shiites who opposed Karami's compromising with Christians were suspected of planting the bomb on the helicopter.

### June 2, 1987

### President Reagan renews most-favored-nation status for Romania, Hungary, and China.

Despite constant reports of human rights violations in Romania and student dissent in China, Reagan granted these countries the trade status they desired to compete favorably in exporting products to the United States. Notably excluded from Reagan's list was the Soviet Union, whose leader, Mikhail Gorbachev, had urged the United States to grant it status equal to that of other "friendly" U.S. trading partners. The United States used this as a bargaining chip to seek other Soviet concessions such as changing Soviet emigration policy.

### June 3, 1987

### The originator of South Africa's Sullivan Code, the Reverend Leon Sullivan, states that the plan fails to end apartheid.

The Sullivan antidiscrimination code of conduct for U.S. companies doing business in South Africa had, since 1977, given U.S. businesspeople an option for investing in South Africa despite its apartheid policies. Sullivan now claimed that the program for desegregating U.S. business operations in South Africa had wrought no significant changes for black Africans.

Therefore, Sullivan urged U.S. corporations to withdraw from South Africa and asked the Reagan administration to sever diplomatic relations with that country. The reaction of U.S. corporations varied. Mobile Oil's chief executive officer said it would stay; Citicorp, the largest U.S. bank, said it would pull out on July 1, 1987; and Ford Motor Company withdrew on June 14, 1987.

### June 8, 1987

### A special State Department panel recommends eliminating the three top floors of the U.S. embassy in Moscow.

Since the arrest of a U.S. embassy guard in Moscow (see January 10, 1987), not only were marine guard practices examined, but an investigation of embassy security disclosed that the U.S. embassy building under construction was implanted with electronic listening devices by the Soviets. After two members of Congress visited the embassy unannounced in April, they reported that the Soviet electronic devices "fully compromised" the integrity of the embassy building.

Headed by former Secretary of Defense James Schlesinger, a special panel of experts visited Moscow and reported its findings on June 8, with the final report released June 26. The panel recommended razing the top three floors, although congressional visitors to Moscow wanted the entire building torn down and rebuilt. On October 26, 1988, President Reagan ordered the entire building razed.

*See January 10, 1987.*

## June 11, 1987

### Economic summit of seven major industrialized nations meets in Venice.

The meeting in Venice was attended by the leaders of the industrial nations of the United States, Great Britain, France, West Germany, Japan, Italy, and Canada. When the first economic summit of the industrialized nations met in 1974, the summit's purpose was to improve economic relations between the nations (see February 11, 1974). In contrast to the earlier annual summits, the Venice summit spent more time on foreign policy issues concerning the Iran-Iraq war that continued into its seventh year (see September 4, 1980).

Despite the time spent on foreign policy affairs, the final communiqué issued by the seven summit leaders reported their need to cooperate on trade relations and the economic imbalances between wealthy and poor nations. They praised Soviet First Secretary Mikhail Gorbachev for his economic reforms and offered an ambiguous statement about keeping the sea lanes open in the Persian Gulf. Notably during the summit, President Ronald Reagan failed to persuade the other six leaders to support a United Nations resolution that would place an arms embargo on Iran or Iraq if either nation refused to negotiate peace with U.N. representatives. The seven leaders did approve the plan of United States Secretary of the Treasury James Baker to aid debtor nations, promising to provide $9 billion to fund loans for African states (see October 11, 1985).

Regarding the Venice Summit, the *Washington Post* reported on June 11, 1987 that President Reagan's stature had diminished among the other six leaders, owing to the Iran-Contra affair and the fact that the United States had become the world's largest debtor nation by 1986. Most of the American debts were held by the other six nations at the summit.

*See September 30, 1987.*

## June 11, 1987

### British Prime Minister Thatcher wins a third term.

Margaret Thatcher was the first British prime minister to win a third term in 160 years; her Conservative Party obtained 375 seats in the House of Commons, a reduction in the Conservative majority from 144 to 100. The Labour Party, under Neil Kinnock, won 229 seats. While the Conservatives' policies of more home and stock ownership, tax cuts, and legislation to stop labor strikes won votes from the prosperous, the Labour Party's call for unilateral nuclear disarmament damaged Kinnock's campaign.

## June 24, 1987

### West Germany and the United States agree that a suspect in the 1985 TWA hijacking will be tried in West German courts.

West German customs officers had arrested Muhammad Ali Hamadei on January 13 when he entered Germany at the Frankfurt airport. Hamadei was believed to be one of the three hijacking leaders in 1985. Although a U.S. court had indicted Hamadei, West Germany insisted it had primary jurisdiction and told the United States that he would be punished to the fullest extent if guilty.

Hamadei was turned over to juvenile court authorities because he was under 21, Germany's legal age of adulthood. During his trial, which began on July 5, 1988, Hamadei admitted being involved in the hijacking as a "foot soldier" taking orders from superiors. American witnesses could not agree on which of the Arabs shot and killed the U.S. navy officer on the TWA plane.

*See June 14, 1985, and September 12, 1988.*

## June 25, 1987

### Colombia's extradition treaty with the United States is declared unconstitutional by Colombia's supreme court.

Following the extradition to the United States of Colombia's top drug dealer, members of the Medellin Colombian drug cartel issued death threats against Colombian judges who extradited drug dealers to America (see February 4, 1987). In December 1986, after many judges were killed by drug traffickers, Colombia's Supreme Court ruled the extradition law was invalid because Colombia's individuals accused of crimes should be tried in Colombian courts. Nevertheless, in early 1987, Colombia's President Virgilio Barco Vargas offered parliament a new law to continue the extradition process, a law that the Supreme Court again declared invalid on June 25.

Colombia's Supreme Court decisions greatly impaired the United States' fight against drug dealers. Although sixteen drug traffickers had been extradited to the United States, the extradition of 40 other drug dealers was pending in 1987. On November 21, Colombian police arrested one of the top drug dealers, Jorge Thuis Ochoa Vasques. He was released, however, on December 30, despite U.S. attempts to extradite him on drug indictments made in U.S. courts in 1984 and 1986.

See February 4, 1987, and April 20, 1988.

### June 25, 1987

**At a Communist Party Central Committee plenum, party First Secretary Gorbachev calls for ending central economic controls and subsidized prices.**

At the plenum, Mikhail Gorbachev proposed detailed guidelines for restructuring the Soviet economy, the policy of perestroika. These included decentralizing the economy to allow more local responsibility and making state-owned enterprises self-sustaining and competitive. Previously, on May 1, 1987, Soviet laws were changed to allow citizens to be licensed to sell their skills privately in 40 business categories.

### June 25, 1987

**Hungary announces two leaders will retire.**

Both President Pál Losonczi and Prime Minister György Lazar retired from their posts. The Communist Party announced they would be replaced by Karoly Nemeth as president and Karoly Grosz as prime minister. These changes occurred because Hungary began economic austerity

programs to rectify its hard currency trade deficit with Western European nations. On July 20, 1987, the government raised prices of consumer goods, reduced subsidies to certain businesses, and levied a value-added tax.

### July 1, 1987

**South Korean president Chun Doo Hwan approves sweeping democratic political reforms.**

South Korea had experienced an increasing number of riots since January 14, after a student, Park Chong Chol, was killed by police. By June 9, Seoul's worst antigovernment riots in years began, and a state of emergency was decreed. Eventually, when President Reagan sent President Chun Doo Hwan a personal letter asking him to negotiate with leaders of the protest movement, a change of climate took place in Korea. After several meetings with opposition leader Kim Young Sam, Chun and his designated successor, Roh Tae Woo, instituted democratic changes. On July 1, Chun approved changes to provide direct presidential elections, guaranteed human rights, and offered greater autonomy for local governments.

As a result on August 31, governing and opposition political parties met to draft a new constitution, which included direct presidential elections, a presidency of five years, prohibitions on the president from dissolving the National Assembly, keeping the military neutral in politics, and granting such rights as habeas corpus. This constitution was approved by the National Assembly on October 12 and ratified in a public referendum on October 27, 1987.

See December 16, 1987.

### July 21, 1987

**Israel tests a new intermediate-range missile.**

Known as Jericho II, it replaced Jericho I, which Israel developed in the 1960s with French help. The new missile range was between 500 and 900 miles, capable of hitting most Middle Eastern targets and the Soviet Union. After the report was published, the Soviets warned Israeli leaders against deploying such weapons. Moscow radio said the Soviets might give Syria SS-23 surface-to-surface missiles if Israel threatened its neighbors.

## July 22, 1987

### Two reflagged Kuwaiti oil tankers are escorted into the Persian Gulf—one is hit by a mine.

Although Congress held up the U.S. flagging of Kuwaiti ships, which President Reagan had proposed on May 19, Reagan rejected further delays and ordered the navy to reflag and escort Kuwaiti ships. The lull in the Persian Gulf conflict after an Iraqi missile hit the USS *Stark* on May 17 had ended on June 20, when Iraq began a series of six attacks on Iran-bound ships, and Iranian sea mines damaged other ships.

On July 22, three U.S. ships began escorting two reflagged Kuwaiti ships through the Strait of Hormuz into the Persian Gulf, while U.S. navy planes patrolled the skies. On July 24, just before reaching Kuwait's port, the tanker *Bridgeton* hit a sea mine, but the 400,000-ton ship was not damaged enough to stop, and it soon reached port. The U.S. navy was embarrassed because on July 19 it had swept the area for mines and said it was clear. On July 29, Defense Secretary Caspar Weinberger ordered eight minesweepers to the gulf and asked West Germany, Britain, and other European nations to send minesweeping equipment.

Obtaining U.S. minesweepers was not simple because it was a weapon system the U.S. navy had allowed to deteriorate. The only active navy minesweepers were built in the 1950s. On July 31, however, the navy sent several small coastal sweepers that had been used in Vietnam. The best sweepers available were eight RH-53D Sea Stallion helicopter minesweepers, which were dispatched on July 29. Because Great Britain had the best minesweepers, Washington was pleased on August 11 when both Britain and France agreed to send some of their minesweepers.

## July 26, 1987

### India and Sri Lanka try to end the Tamilese uprising.

A perennial problem in the 1980s was the rebellion of the Tamil minority in Sri Lanka to gain independence. Because the Tamilese were a majority in a southern Indian province, the rebels obtained assistance from India. Now, however, Indian Prime Minister Rajiv Gandhi and Sri Lankan President Jayawardene met in Colombo, Sri Lanka, to end the rebellion. India sent armed forces to help put down the rebellion while Sri Lanka gave more local autonomy to the two northern provinces where Tamilese predominated. These efforts failed. Although India sent over 50,000 troops, guerrilla warfare continued. India withdrew some troops on July 7, 1988, but did not agree to withdraw completely until the Tamilese rebels signed a cease-fire on September 16, 1989.

## July 28, 1987

### Bulgaria's Todor Zhivkov joins the reform program advocated by Soviet First Secretary Mikhail Gorbachev.

First Secretary of Bulgaria's Communist Party Todor Zhivkov adopted Gorbachev's *perestroika* reform program. During a July 28 speech to Bulgaria's Communist Party's Central Committee, Zhivkov called for the Central Committee to restructure Bulgaria's State Assembly and the Communist Party's policy making Politburo. Zhivkov said Bulgaria should adopt a free market economy that would give Bulgaria's currency—the Lev—a value equal to the Soviet Union's rouble, and approve free trade relations for the nation's enterprises. Zhivkov's speech brought few immediate changes in Bulgaria but in 1988, the Central Committee allowed more than one candidate to run for each local office and on July 20, 1988 Zhivkov told a Communist Party Plenum to initiate specific economic reforms to implement those called for in 1987.

See December 27, 1989.

## July 31, 1987

### Muslim pilgrims to Mecca riot at the Grand Mosque: Saudi Arabia blames Iran for the tragedy.

During the annual holy pilgrimage to Mecca, Iranian pilgrims blocked the streets in Mecca and waved banners praising Iranian leader Ayatollah Ruholla Khomeini. Iran had sent 155,000 pilgrims to Mecca, and as they demonstrated, Saudi Arabian police used water cannons to disperse the rioters, who threw rocks, overturned cars, and, allegedly, used knives. As the Iranians retreated, 402 people died, many of whom were trampled to death, mostly women. Iran blamed the Saudis for using guns, but Saudi authorities claimed "not a single shot was fired."

### August 3, 1987

#### U.S. Representative John Vessey meets with Vietnamese Foreign Minister Thach. Vietnam agrees to release Amer-Asian children.

Vessey and Foreign Minister Nguyen Co Thach discussed Americans missing in action during the Vietnam War. One agreement was to revive the Orderly Departure Program, which returned Amer-Asian children to families or fathers in the United States. This program was started in 1979 but was disrupted because U.S. immigration rules were too strict in screening the children, who were considered misfits by Vietnamese society because their fathers were American soldiers. As a result of Vessey's agreement, 65 Amer-Asian children arrived in Bangkok on December 31 en route to the United States as part of a group of a total of 350 expected to come to the United States in the near future.

### August 4, 1987

#### The Reagan administration offers a peace plan for Nicaragua.

Anticipating the meeting of Central American presidents on August 7 to sign the Arias Peace Plan, President Reagan and U.S. Speaker of the House James Wright (D-Tex.) announced a proposal for peace in Nicaragua. The proposal called for an immediate cease-fire, the end of all foreign military support to either side, the restoration of Nicaraguan civil rights and open elections, talks between the Central American leaders and the United States, and amnesty for the Contra rebels. The proposal threatened the resumption of U.S. military aid to the Contras if no progress was made by September 30, 1988.

Reagan's plan provoked criticism both in the United States and abroad. Conservatives such as Senator Jesse Helms (R-N.C.) said the plan was a dream especially since the Contras were starting to win the war; liberals such as Senator Edward Kennedy (D-Mass.) said it was a show to justify renewal of U.S. military aid to the Contras on October 1, 1988, if the Sandinistas rejected the plan. The president wanted $150 million in aid for the Contras for the next 18 months. Reagan's plan never got off the ground because, as Cynthia Arnson's *Crossroads* explains, the Arias Peace Plan of 1986 gained support from Central America's Contadora, as well as peace groups in Latin America and Europe (see August 7, 1987).

### August 7, 1987

#### The Arias Peace plan is signed by five Central American governments.

President Oscar Arias Sánchez of Costa Rica drafted a peace plan for Central America early in 1987 and lobbied extensively to achieve agreement on August 7. Beginning on January 7, Costa Rica's Foreign Minister Rodrigo Madrigal Nieto met in Miami with Assistant Secretary of State Elliott Abrams and Special Presidential Envoy Philip Habib to describe the peace initiative for ending civil wars in Nicaragua, El Salvador, and Guatemala.

The Arias plan assumed greater significance after a January 19–20 meeting of the Contadora group failed to make progress on peace. President Arias and his colleagues quietly met with many groups throughout Latin America and Europe to promote the proposal and prepare for the August meeting in Guatemala City. Although the United States acted indifferently toward the plan, President Reagan's August 4 proposal for peace in Nicaragua did not conflict seriously with Arias's concepts except for the deadline of September 30 for Nicaragua to act.

As signed on August 7, the Arias Peace Plan included timetables for cease-fires in the three civil wars to be verified by an international commission, negotiations with unarmed guerrilla groups, freedom of the press and free elections, and ending the various states of emergency.

On August 13, El Salvador offered to meet with leftist rebels if they renounced violence; and on August 21, the Contras accepted the plan, provided the Nicaraguan government began direct negotiations with them. Guatemalan rebels of the National Resistance Union met with government delegates in Madrid, Spain, in October.

See October 4, October 7, and December 2, 1987.

### August 11, 1987

#### The United States and the Soviet Union accept "challenge inspections" of each other's chemical weapons facilities.

This agreement permitted chemical weapons experts to visit each nation's chemical production facilities on 48 hours' notice to determine what weapons if any were being made. The first Soviet delegation visited the U.S. chemical storage facilities at Tooele, Utah, on November 19, 1987.

In addition to this bilateral agreement, the Soviet Union permitted a U.N. delegation to visit its chemical weapons complex at Shikhany on October 3, 1987. The U.N. delegates watched the Soviets destroy a 550-pound chemical bomb containing nerve gas.

Final agreements on chemical weapons were still pending, however. On October 5, the Soviet U.N. delegate denounced the United States for undertaking new chemical weapons production. The U.S. delegate responded that the United States began new production only because the Soviet arsenal of chemical weapons was so much larger than the American. He claimed that in addition to Shikhany, the Soviets had 14 to 20 secret chemical production facilities.

See December 17, 1987.

### August 23, 1987

*The three Soviet Baltic republics stage protest marches for independence.*

Nationalist protest demonstrators in Estonia, Latvia, and Lithuania objected that the Nazi-Soviet Pact signed on August 23, 1939, gave the Soviet Union illegal control over their territory. Subsequently, in reaction to Soviet leader Mikhail Gorbachev's policies of glasnost and perestroika, the native inhabitants of these three Soviet republics demanded their independence from Soviet control. The August 1987 demonstrations were put down by local police but the national opposition did not disappear. In 1989, the Baltic states' nationalists adopted non violent methods and political measures to fulfill their desire for independence (see July 1, 1989), Gorbachev faced similar nationalist stirrings among its Warsaw Pact allies of eastern Europe (see January 15, 1989).

### August 28, 1987

*A right-wing attempt to overthrow Philippine President Aquino fails.*

In this second right-wing attempt to oust Aquino in 1987, Colonel Gregorio Honasan led 1,350 rebel soldiers in attacks on Manila and Cebu City. Although the rebels took over Cebu City, loyal army forces put down the revolt in a little over

24 hours. Twelve government soldiers, 19 rebels, and 22 civilians died in the fighting. Although Honasan escaped, he was later captured on December 9, 1981. Former Defense Minister Juan Ponce Enrile was implicated in the coup attempt, although he denied any involvement.

The right-wing groups believed Aquino had not dealt forcefully enough with left-wing rebel groups. She had held peace talks with rebel leaders for nearly a year. The talks were suspended on January 22, 1987, and on March 22, Aquino called for the military to combat both communist and right-wing rebels. To further counter left-wing groups, she announced plans for a land reform program on July 21, 1987.

See February 2, 1987, and October 17, 1988.

### September 4, 1987

**U.N. Security Council resolution 598 fails to end the Iran-Iraq war; the United States finds evidence of Iranian sea mines on September 21.**

Although the Security Council resolution for a cease-fire was approved, it had only a slight immediate effect. On September 8, Iraq struck at two oil tankers near the Iranian island of Kharq and bombed 13 Iranian cities. Libya offered, on September 10, to send Iran more sea mines.

On September 21, the United States obtained the first definite evidence that Iranian ships were laying sea mines, a charge Teheran had denied. After U.S. ships saw an Iranian vessel mining the sea near Bahrain, a U.S. helicopter fired on the ship, but it again began planting its mines. The U.S. helicopter again struck the vessel, stopping it dead in the water while its crew abandoned ship. The Americans rescued 26 Iranians, who later were returned to Iran. Although a U.S. navy videocamera filmed the ship as it was dropping mines, the film came out blank, and reporters could be shown only some captured mines.

Nevertheless, on September 22, Iranian President Sayyed Ali Khamenei addressed the U.N. General Assembly, claiming Iraq had refused to accept Iran's peace terms. He said Iran would not bow down to the superpowers' efforts to stop it from defending itself. Iraq, he correctly noted, started the war in 1980, he asserted that Iraq should be punished. U.S. policy now favored Iraq, however.

## September 7, 1987

*Pakistan and Afghanistan meet with a U.N. mediator to try and end the Afghanistan war.*

Generally, the rebel forces in Afghanistan were stalemated in their civil war against the government, which was backed by Soviet troops and equipment. The rebel forces benefited from Pakistani and U.S. aid. Particularly after the Reagan administration sent the rebels shoulder-fired Stinger antiaircraft missiles, the rebels operated effectively against Soviet helicopters and Afghan troop transports. On February 9, a Stinger downed a transport plane, killing 37 troops, and on June 11, another downed a troop plane, killing 53 of the 55 aboard.

The Soviet Union wanted to withdraw its troops, but agreements among the rebels, Pakistan, and the United States would be necessary to protect the Kabul government. At the September 7 meeting with U.N. mediator Diégo Cordovez, the principal issue concerned coordinating outside assistance to the rivals in Afghanistan with the pullout of Soviet troops. While the Afghan government wanted to stretch the Soviet withdrawal over a 16-month period, Pakistan wanted only 8 months. The two sides ended their meeting on this difference.

## September 7, 1987

*East German leader Erich Honecker visits West Germany for the first time.*

The general secretary of East Germany, Erich Honecker, made a four-day visit to West Germany to meet with Chancellor Helmut Kohl on September 7–8. Although a few agreements on trade, nuclear safety, and the environment were made, the visit was a first step toward more cooperation. Honecker had planned a visit in 1984, but incidents in East-West relations caused him to cancel it.

See September 4, 1984.

## September 11, 1987

*The Organization of African Unity (OAU) mediates a cease-fire between Chad and Libya.*

Kenneth Kaunda, president of Zambia and chairman of the OAU, used his office to obtain a cease-fire in a conflict waged since 1983 between Chad and Libya, with Libyan-backed rebels. The United States and France backed Chad, but French President Mitterrand's peace plans of 1984 had not worked. Following skirmishes in Chad during 1985, the war heated up on February 10, 1986, when France dispatched 5,000 troops to help Chad defend against a new Libyan incursion. President Reagan sent Chad $15 million in military aid in 1987, and soon after, French and Chadian forces started an offensive that captured the northern town of Fada on January 3. By March 25, Libyan troops had evacuated their last stronghold in Chad.

After Chad's troops crossed into Libya to attack the Matan as Sarra air base on September 9, Libyan leader Mu'ammar al-Gadhafi accepted President Kaunda's offer for a cease-fire. This was finalized two days later.

See June 23, 1983; November 19, 1984; May 25, 1988.

## September 18, 1987

*The FBI brings a hijacker to the United States for trial.*

Using a Middle Eastern CIA agent to lure Fawas Younis, a Syrian terrorist, onto a yacht sailing in international waters, Federal Bureau of Investigation agents captured Younis and brought him to the United States. In 1986, Congress had passed legislation giving the U.S. jurisdiction over terrorists who endangered U.S. nationals. The FBI claimed Younis was involved in the 1985 hijacking of a Jordanian airliner on which four Americans were aboard.

On February 23, 1988, a U.S. federal court judge dropped several charges against Younis, after ruling that the FBI had obtained his confession illegally. Younis had not been advised of his constitutional rights and had been detained too long before arraignment. Younis's wrists were broken and FBI agents had refused to treat him; Younis said that FBI agents broke his wrists in gaining his confession. Eventually, Younis was tried by a federal court and convicted on March 14, 1989. He was sentenced to 30 years in jail.

According to *Newsweek* magazine, a Pentagon source said that millions of dollars were spent to prosecute Younis, and a major CIA source in the Middle East was blown so President Reagan and the Justice Department, according to the Pentagon source who told *Newsweek*, could "look good at the height of Iran-Contra disclosures."

October 3, 1987　　1111

### September 21, 1987

**The Reagan administration warns that Bolivia may lose economic aid because it failed to reduce its coca crop.**

Although the State Department said Bolivia had improved its enforcement of narcotic laws, Washington warned Bolivia that if it did not eradicate 450 hectares (1,110 acres) of its coca crop by September 30, it would lose U.S. funds, as prescribed by Congress in 1986 legislation. Bolivia had eliminated only 25 hectares (62 acres) in six months of 1987. Many Bolivian growers opposed U.S. interference and refused to convert their crops to substitute programs.

See July 14, 1986.

### September 21–24, 1987

*French and West German forces hold joint military exercises in West Germany.*

Known as Bold Sparrow, these exercises involved 20,000 French and 55,000 West German troops in war games to counteract an attack by Warsaw Pact nations. According to reports from France and West Germany, these countries planned to form a Joint Defense Council by 1989 to supplement their defenses because France had refused since 1966 to coordinate its military with NATO.

### September 30, 1987

**Treasury Secretary Baker tries to revive interest in the Baker Plan of 1985.**

On September 29, Secretary of the Treasury James Baker met with board members of the World Bank and International Monetary Fund (IMF). Baker urged these board members to revive interest in the Baker Plan's approach to relieving the enormous debts of Third World nations (see October 11, 1985). Baker told the board members that since March 27, 1985, the Baker Plan created a pool of $3.1 billion plus another $9 billion added to loans for an African fund during the Venice economic summit (see June 11, 1987). These funds had not only relieved the debts of Argentina, Mexico, and several African nations, but also enabled these countries to achieve averaged annual growth rates of 3.7% for the last two years, their best growth rates in six years. In addition, the Baker Plan's successful growth rates in Argentina,

Mexico, and Africa, these countries moved toward a free market requiring less government control over the nation's economy.

Despite the Baker Plan's success in several Third World countries, the IMF / World Bank board members decided the Baker Plan would be only used as one option in the IMF / World Bank's case-by-case decisions about a particular nation's needs. Secretary Baker disapproved of the IMF / World Bank members' decision to continue working on a case-by-case system because it slowed down the transition of each Third World nation's movement from a regulated state-controlled economy to a free market economy.

On August 5, 1988, Baker resigned as Secretary of the Treasury and his successor Nicholas Brady continued to support the Baker Plan. After George Bush became president in 1989, Brady introduced the Brady Plan that attempted to help developing nation's reduce their debts (see March 10, 1989).

On the Baker Plan's origins, see October 11, 1985.

### October 2, 1987

**Japan ends plans to build a new fighter plane and agrees to buy the U.S. F-16 fighter modified as an "FSX."**

Japan's Defense Minister Yuko Kurehare announced this decision after meeting in Washington with U.S. Defense Secretary Caspar Weinberger. Although Japan considered purchasing the McDonnell-Douglas F-15 on November 29, 1988, it announced that the General Dynamics F-16 would be used as the basis for the advanced fighter FSX, with Japan's Mitsubishi Corporation as the main contractor in a joint U.S.-Japanese project. In part, the FSX would improve submarine detection, which had been impaired by the Toshiba scandal. But a separate antisubmarine project was also to be set up at the U.S. naval base in Yokosuka, Japan. The formal accord on the joint U.S.-Japanese production of a new jet fighter was signed on November 29, 1988.

See May 29, 1987.

### October 3, 1987

**The United States-Canadian bilateral treaty ends tariffs over a 10-year period.**

This historic agreement was settled after negotiators resolved a final problem on binding arbitration of trade disputes. On September 23, the Canadian dele-

Secretary of State James Baker looks on as Reagan signs the Free Trade Agreement with Canada. Ronald Reagan Library

gates walked out of talks on the issue, but Secretary of the Treasury James Baker saved the day by convening high-level discussions with Canada on September 28. Baker granted a significant concession in accepting a binding arbitration panel to decide disputes.

In addition to arbitration, the treaty was unique in setting guidelines for exchanges of services, the first such trade treaty clause although the United States pursued service relations in the current round of talks at the General Agreement on Tariffs and Trade. The United States-Canada treaty would take effect on January 2, 1989, with all tariffs eliminated by the year 2000.

Although opposition to the treaty existed in both countries, it was overcome. After a final draft of the treaty was prepared for President Reagan and Prime Minister Mulroney to sign on January 11, 1988, the measure and implementing legislation was sent to Canada's parliament and the U.S. Congress.

In the United States, some changes were drafted on May 26, 1988, but conflicts were resolved on July 14, and Congress passed the necessary measures—the House on August 9 by a vote of 366 to 40; the Senate on September 19, by voting 83 to 9.

The debate was more intensive in Canada, but the treaty passed the House of Commons with some amendments on August 30, 1988. In Canadian elections on November 21, Mulroney won, accepting the vote as a mandate favoring the trade law. The bill passed parliament on December 24 by a vote of 141 to 111, and the royal assent of Queen Elizabeth was given on December 30, 1988.

## October 4, 1987

### Salvadoran rebels begin peace talks with government representatives.

Following many preliminary proposals to act in accordance with the Arias Peace Plan, Salvadoran President José Napoleon Duarte and rebel delegates met from October 4 to 6 but disagreed regarding the withdrawal of foreign military advisers and left-wing participation in the government. They formed two commissions to negotiate peace but accomplished little in 1987, largely because of right-wing opposition. For example, Defense Minister, Hector Alejandro Gramajo rejected all talks with the rebels until they laid down their arms.

See August 7 and November 23, 1987.

## October 7, 1987

### Guatemalan rebels and the government hold unsuccessful peace talks.

Acting in accord with the Arias Peace Plan (see August 7, 1987), Guatemalan President Marco Cerezo Arevalo met in Madrid, Spain, with members of the left-wing National Resistance Union. The Guatemalan conflict received less attention in the United States than Nicaragua's warfare because Guatemala's President Arevalo's armed forces avoided atrocities in their combat with left-wing rebels. In 1985, Arevalo became the first civilian president in 15 years by replacing military generals. Subsequently, Arevalo undertook a few moderate economic, political and military reforms. Unfortunately, Arevalo's moderate reforms were not sufficient to end Guatemala's conflict with the rebels.

See December 8, 1985, and November 25, 1988.

### October 8, 1987

**President Reagan obtains congressional agreement on arms sales to Saudi Arabia by withdrawing Maverick antitank missiles.**

On May 29, President Reagan notified Congress of his intention to sell 1,600 Maverick missiles to the Saudis, but on June 11, he withdrew the offer because of congressional opposition. Events in the Persian Gulf and the Iranian violence at Mecca on July 31 made the U.S. Defense Department believe more than before that Saudi Arabia needed defensive weapons. Subsequently, the Reagan administration renewed overtures to Congress regarding the supply of advanced weapons to the Saudis.

The compromise, which Reagan and Congress reached on October 8, permitted the administration to sell 12 F-15 fighter planes to the Saudis plus $1 billion worth of other arms. However, Reagan withdrew the Maverick missile offer because Israeli lobbyists did not want antitank missiles to reach Arab armies. War in the Middle East usually involved tank battles.

See July 8, 1988.

### October 19, 1987

**U.S. stock market crash occurs: the Dow Jones Industrial Average falls 508.32 points.**

The market dropped 22.6% in one day, the largest single decline since 1914. The one-day drop on October 29, 1929, was 12.9%. Partly, the 1987 drop reflected a large-scale increase in stock values since 1982, the market price rising from 776.92 to 2722.42 in August 1987. One consequence of the fall was to make the U.S. Congress and President Reagan willing to work down the nation's annual budget deficit.

The London and Tokyo stock exchanges also suffered declines on October 19 and 20, with the Tokyo market losing 14.9% on October 20. To counteract this, other European banks cut their interest rates in December.

See November 20 and December 3, 1987.

### October 19, 1987

**Secretary of State Shultz visits the Middle East without results for peace process.**

U.S. policy sought an international conference on the Middle East that might move Israel and the Palestine Liberation Organization toward peace. Shultz had no success largely because Israeli Prime Minister Yitzhak Shamir opposed talks with the Palestinians. In Israel's joint cabinet of Labor and Likud members, Labor Party leader Shimon Peres, who was foreign minister, wanted an international peace conference, the Likud Party leader Shamir, who was prime minister, did not. On February 25, 1987, Peres visited Cairo to solicit the agreement of Egyptian President Hosni Mubarak for a conference. On returning home, however, Peres found that Shamir was enraged because he visited Mubarak. These two leaders symbolized the general Israeli disagreement about solving the Palestinian problem.

Shultz's visit in October clarified the divisions but offered no solution. The United States, as often, had little leverage on Israeli politics because U.S. political groups supported Israel.

### October 19, 1987

**U.S. destroyers bombard an Iranian oil rig after an Iranian missile strikes a U.S.-flagged tanker near Kuwait; President Reagan bans Iranian imports.**

The Kuwaiti tanker flying the U.S. flag as the *Sea Isle City* was hit by an Iranian Silkworm missile on October 16. Eighteen U.S. crewmen were injured and the ship's captain, John Hunt, was blinded by glass fragments.

President Reagan ordered a "measured response." On October 19, U.S. ships bombarded an offshore Iranian oil rig for 85 minutes. By the time fire had consumed a whole section of the rig, Navy SEALS went aboard to dynamite the rest of the structure, which had been used as a gunboat base. Few Iranians were injured because the bombardment began after the Americans warned everyone to abandon the rig.

In retaliation, Iran fired a Silkworm missile at an offshore Kuwaiti oil terminal on October 22, seriously damaging the structure. Although Iran said the U.S. bombardment on October 19 was an act of war, President Reagan responded that the United States was a peaceful nonbelligerent.

The oil rig attack was the second Persian Gulf action by the United States in October. On October 8, U.S. American helicopter gunships attacked four Iranian patrol boats that had allegedly fired on another U.S. helicopter. After capturing the gunboats, they found U.S. Stinger missiles in Iranian possession. The Stingers, which the United States supplied to rebels in Afghanistan and Angola, had reached the Iranians.

On October 26, President Reagan used an executive order to ban all Iranian imports. He added several militarily useful items to the list of banned exports to Iran.

On Stingers, see May 27, 1988.

### October 22, 1987

**Following lengthy debate, the U.S. Senate asks President Reagan to report on Persian Gulf policy in 30 days.**

Ever since President Reagan proposed to reflag Kuwaiti ships with U.S. flags on May 19, Congress had debated what action it should take to limit the president. At best, perhaps, Senate debate made the president cautious because he had begun reflagging on July 22, and neither house of Congress found a suitable way to restrict him.

Democratic members of Congress preferred to invoke the War Powers Act, debating with Republicans and each other about its applicability to escort vessels. In the Senate, all efforts to vote on results dealing with the War Powers Act of 1973 were filibustered by the Republicans.

Finally, after a U.S. attack on an Iranian oil rig on October 19, 1987, the Senate secured enough votes to stop the filibuster. It passed a compromise resolution regarding Reagan's unilateral decisions, asking the administration to clarify its intentions in the gulf region in 30 days.

### October 22, 1987

**The Reagan administration acts against China for selling Iran missiles but defends the presence of Chinese forces in Tibet.**

Because the Reagan administration alleged that China sold Silkworm missiles to Iran for use in the Persian Gulf, the United States prohibited the sale of high-technology products to China. Early in October, however, President Reagan had defended China for using force to suppress demonstrations in Tibet by Buddhist monks against the Chinese government.

The U.S. Senate differed with Reagan, voting 98 to 0 on October 10 to condemn China for its conduct in Tibet.

### November 5, 1987

**Defense Secretary Caspar Weinberger resigns and is replaced by Frank Carlucci; Colin Powell becomes national security adviser.**

Weinberger resigned because his wife had cancer. He pointed out that he did not object to the arms control treaty being finalized by the United States and the USSR.

To replace Carlucci, who had been Reagan's national security adviser, President Reagan selected a Jamaican-born, naturalized citizen, Lt. General Colin L. Powell, to be national security adviser. Carlucci assumed office after Senate approval on November 20, 1986. Although Weinberger was often involved in conflicts with Congress, Carlucci, a pragmatic career official, knew how to compromise.

### November 7, 1987

*The prime minister of Tunisia removes from office President Habib Bourguiba, who is senile.*

The president was removed by using Article 57 of Tunisia's constitution and by a health report showing that Bourguiba was mentally incompetent. His incapacity had been shown dramatically during September, when he ordered the trial of 90 radical Islamic followers who plotted to overthrow him, 37 of whom were tried in absentia.

Prime Minister Ben Ali determined it was necessary to remove Bourguiba peacefully to avoid a civil war. Bourguiba had been president since 1956, when Tunisia gained independence from France. Ben Ali's plans succeeded and were accepted by the United States and European countries.

### November 8, 1987

*An Arab League meeting makes a major realignment of Arab states in the Middle East.*

Arranged by King Hussein of Jordan, the Arab League met in Amman. The session of 16 Arab heads of state and 5 other Arab state delegates condemned Iran for refusing to negotiate peace and backed Iraq in the gulf war. The League declared that members could restore diplomatic relations with Egypt if they chose, thereby returning Egypt to the Arab League's good graces, which it lost by signing the 1979 peace treaty with Israel. Most notably, the sessions brought Iraqi

Secretary of Defense Frank Carlucci and National Secretary Adviser Lt. General Colin Powell in the Oval Office. Ronald Regan Library

Saddam Hussein and Syrian Hafiz al-Assad together after years of enmity.

Arab leaders who objected to the new unity brought about by the moderate Arab states were extremists Mu'ammar al-Gadhafi of Libya and Iran's Ayatollah Khomeini. The moderate leaders wanted an international conference on the Middle East as a means to bring Israel and the Palestine Liberation Organization to negotiate peace.

See March 26, 1979.

## November 16, 1987

### *Japanese Prime Minister Nakasone is replaced by Noboru Takeshita.*

Although Yasuhiro Nakasone had been elected to a historic third term as prime minister in 1986, he became less popular after proposing a new sales tax, which the Japanese Diet (parliament) defeated after a three-day filibuster forced the measure to be withdrawn on May 12, 1987. Subsequently, on October 20, Nakasone selected Takeshita, a former finance minister, to become his successor. The Diet confirmed this action on November 16.

## November 17, 1987

### President Reagan and congressional leaders compromise on interpretations of the 1972 ABM treaty in relation to the SDI.

As work proceeded on the Strategic Defense Initiative (SDI), the Reagan administration's proposal for a broad interpretation of the 1972 Anti-Ballistic Missile (ABM) treaty in order to test and partially deploy SDI was contested by congressional leaders as well as scholars of the 1972 treaty.

Beginning with a letter to President Reagan on February 7, 1986, Senator Sam Nunn (D-Ga.), the chairman of the Senate Armed Services Committee, warned the president against a unilateral broadening of the 1972 ABM treaty. House speaker James Wright (D-Tex.) and other House leaders sent a similar letter, which emphasized that a broad interpretation would erode House support for SDI funds.

On May 13, President Reagan sent Congress two new studies by Abraham Sofaer, legal counsel of the Department of Defense, of the 1972 treaty. Sofaer analyzed declassified records of the 1972 negotiations and of the U.S. Senate ratification hearings on the treaty. He concluded that the Soviets told negotiators that unknown devices on future technology should not be limited and that no Senate action or statement prevented the United States from testing future technology. This study was hotly contested by several arms control and international law specialists, including those in the Nixon administration who had negotiated the ban. John Rinelander, who had served as the legal adviser to the ABM treaty negotiations, complained that the reading of the treaty by the Regan administration was "absurd as a matter of policy, intent, and interpretation."

Neither Senator Nunn nor other congressional Democrats were convinced of the Sofaer interpretation. Nunn offered an amendment to the defense appropriations bill for 1988, which required the president to obtain congressional permission before conducting any SDI tests that might violate the strict interpretation of the 1972 treaty, a tactic that caused Senate Republican leaders to begin a four-month filibuster to prevent a vote on the Nunn Amendment. Because the 1988 fiscal year budget could not operate after October 1 without funding, Republican Senate minority leader Robert Dole (R-Kans.) stopped the filibuster, and on September 27, the Nunn Amendment passed by a 58-to-38 vote.

President Reagan argued that such congressional action hampered negotiations with the Soviet Union and vowed to veto the final 1988 spending bill if the Nunn Amendment was retained. This led to a November 7 meeting between the president and congressional leaders during which a compromise was approved. In the final appropriations bill, the 1972 treaty was not mentioned. The bill prohibited the administration from purchasing any equipment for testing SDI that required a broad interpretation of existing arms control measures. Thus, Congress obtained some control over future SDI tests.

On December 13, Secretary of State Shultz told reporters that the Reagan administration would no longer push for a broad interpretation of the ABM treaty. It would instead seek specific funds from Congress whenever individual tests were proposed.

See October 11–12, 1986, and August 31, 1988.

### November 18, 1987

**House and Senate committees on the Iran-Contra scandal release their final report.**

Drawing on evidence and public hearings, the committees said they could not determine President Reagan's precise role in the decisions, partly because of the documents shredded by Lt. Colonel Oliver North. They concluded, however, that "if the President did not know what his National Security Advisers were doing, he should have." The report criticized North, John Poindexter, and Robert McFarlane for subverting the nation's democratic process.

Regarding money involved in the Iran-Contra dealings, the report said profits from the Iran sale were $16 million, but only about $3.8 million reached the Contras. Of the rest, about $4.4 million went as commissions to retired Major General Richard V. Secord and to the Iranian-born arms dealer Albert Hakim, a partner in a company that arranged the arms sale.

The committees also found that under North's direction, Carl Channel set up a private funding network to help the Contras. This fund raised $10 million, but only $4.5 million was spent on the Contras, including $1 million for political advertising and lobbying. On April 29, 1986, Channel pleaded guilty to conspiring to defraud the government by raising tax-exempt funds for the Contras. He named North as a coconspirator. On July 7, 1989, Channel was sentenced to two years' probation.

Finally, the committee's report recommended that the president should give prior notice to designated members of Congress for all but the "most exceptional" of covert operations, in which cases a delay of 48 hours could be approved. It suggested that covert operations should not be conducted by the National Security Council.

The day before the report was issued, a press leak disclosed that a minority of two Republican senators and six Republican representatives charged that the majority report was politically biased. The Senate's 11-member committee had 5 Republicans; the House's 15-member committee had 6 Republicans.

See May 5, 1987.

### November 20, 1987

**President Reagan and congressional leaders agree on budget reduction tactics to cut the annual deficit.**

President Reagan accepted a meeting with Congress but commented on October 22 that Congress was to blame for the deficits because it authorized spending. Regarding a possible tax increase, Reagan, whose 1981 tax cuts stimulated the large deficits, said he would look at any proposal. However, Reagan's budget director, James C. Miller, told newsmen: "If you've got taxes on the table, the President is off."

The meeting between congressional leaders and the president on November 20 finally set the foundation for a deficit reduction bill, which was approved with the Omnibus Spending Bill on December 22, 1987. Under the compromise achieved, a reduction of $30 billion would be made in 1988 and $46 billion in 1989. For 1988, military expenditures were cut $5 billion, and domestic spending, $6.6 billion. There would be a tax increase of about $9 billion by charging user fees for federal facilities, increasing corporate and individual taxes on the wealthy, and charging for Medicare insurance.

See also December 22, 1987.

## November 20, 1987

### The United States and the Soviet Union agree to hold joint nuclear underground tests in 1988 to study test verification procedures.

This agreement resulted from talks between the two nations, that began in Geneva on November 9. If verification methods for such tests could be agreed upon, it was expected that a comprehensive test ban treaty could be negotiated.

See September 14, 1988.

## November 23, 1987

### The United States pays $90 million to help resolve the U.N. budget crisis.

The U.N.'s inability to meet its staff payroll in December 1987 had been reported to President Reagan in a private letter from the secretary-general on October 26. The United States had paid only $10 million of its 1987 assessment, and after having agreed to pay $90 million; it owed $112 million. The United States also owed $147 million from 1986 and $61 million for U.N. peacekeeping forces in the Middle East.

The United States and other nations had urged the United Nations to cut back its staff and other "exorbitant" expenditures but to no avail. Nations having small assessments benefited by voting to increase the budget. On December 21, 1987, the U.N. General Assembly approved a 1988–1989 budget of $1.77 billion. The United States, Japan, and Australia abstained from the vote to protest the high expenditures voted with insufficient revenues.

See September 13, 1988.

## November 23, 1987

### Two Salvadoran rebel leaders test peace possibilities.

Under previous plans, El Salvador's rebel leaders had hoped the ARIAS PEACE PLAN would work despite the opposition of right-wing groups. Following the October 4 negotiations, the rebels canceled scheduled talks because right-wing death squads assassinated human rights activist Herbert Anya Sanabria on October 26.

On October 27, the Salvadoran National Assembly granted amnesty not only to leftist guerrillas but also to soldiers accused of murder, except those who killed Archbishop Oscar Romero in 1980. As to the archbishop's death, President Duarte on November 22, 1987, accused his right-wing political rival, Roberto d'Aubuisson, of ordering Captain Alvaro Rafael Saravia to kill Romero. Police arrested Saravia on November 24, 1988, but most observers believed d'Aubuisson would never be successfully prosecuted.

Because of the amnesty, two leaders of the rebel Democratic Revolutionary Front returned to El Salvador. On November 21, the group's vice president, Rubén Zamora, returned. Two days later, its president, Guillermo Ungo, returned. They stayed only until December 2 because Duarte refused to negotiate with them.

See October 4, 1987; February 18 and March 20, 1988.

## November 25, 1987

### The U.N. Security Council condemns South Africa for intervening in Angola to aid rebel forces.

South Africa sent armed forces into Angola on November 2 to help Jonas Savimbi's UNITA rebels. Savimbi launched an offensive against Angolan government forces on October 22 using U.S.-supplied TOW antitank missiles and Stinger antiaircraft missiles to win a large battle early in November. South Africa aided UNITA by diverting Cuban and Soviet forces that assisted Angola.

The U.N. resolution condemning South Africa was significant because the United States did not veto the resolution. Nevertheless, South Africa ignored the resolution and refused to withdraw its troops from Angola on December 20, 1987.

See December 13, 1988.

### November 25, 1987

*Suriname elects a civilian government to replace the military rule of Desi Bouterse.*

This election followed a vote on September 30, 1987, that approved a new constitution setting up the role of the group with a majority in the National Assembly. As a result, Bouterse's Conservative Party gained only 9% of the assembly vote; the opposition United Front for Democracy and Development won 85% and controlled the government. At his inauguration as president on January 25, 1988, Ramsewak Shankar said he desired better relations with the United States and the Dutch, the former colonizer of Suriname.

### November 29, 1987

*The Reagan administration suspends all "nonhumanitarian" aid to Haiti after its efforts at democratic elections fail.*

Haiti had been in turmoil for some time. The approval of a new constitution on March 29, 1987, was designed to prevent future dictatorships, but the elimination of the existing regime of General Henri Namphy remained an obstacle. Namphy promised free elections, but these were called off on November 29 after a series of demonstrations and riots finally led the notorious former militia of the Duvalier family, the Tontons Macoutes, to attack polling places, where they killed at least 34 people and wounded over 70 others.

Consequently, Washington stopped most economic aid to Haiti, including $62 million in development aid.

See February 7, 1986, and September 17, 1988.

### November 29, 1987

*A national referendum in Poland on economic reforms disapproves the proposals.*

In addition to releasing almost all political prisoners in 1986–1987, Poland's leader, Wojchiec Jaruzelski, wanted popular backing to enact stringent economic measures to improve the nation's economic performance. He failed, however, to get the backing of the Solidarity trade union, which asked its members to boycott the referendum. Poland needed the union's backing to enact economic reforms.

See May 11, 1988.

### November 29, 1987

*Turgut Ozal is reelected prime minister after violent attacks by Kurdish tribes on Turkey's eastern border.*

Although Ozal, leader of Turkey's Motherland Party, tried to govern democratically by releasing political prisoners and lifting political bans on two former prime ministers, he had to contend with incidents by Kurds who sought independence not only from Turkey but also from Iran and Iraq, on whose borders Kurdish tribes had lived for centuries. On February 22, June 20, and July 8, Kurdish forces attacked Turkish villages in the eastern provinces, forcing Ozal to send Turkish warplanes to retaliate against Kurds in Iraq and along Syria's border. Their attacks did not end the Kurdish threat, which also affected Iran and Iraq.

See August 24, 1988.

### December 1, 1987

*U.S. and British officials criticize France for making a deal with Iran to free French hostages.*

Circumstantial evidence since November 27 seemed to indicate that France had made a deal with Iran. On November 27, two French hostages were freed by the pro-Iranian Revolutionary Justice Organization. On November 29, an Iranian terrorist, Wahid Gordji, was allowed to leave his haven at Iran's Paris embassy and fly to Tehran, where a French consul, Paul Torri, was released by Iran. Of course, after President Reagan's Iran-Contra disclosures, U.S criticism was difficult to justify.

### December 2, 1987

*Nicaraguan Contras begin peace talks with the Sandinistas without success.*

Following the signing of the Arias Peace Plan, Nicaragua took steps toward making peace with the Contra rebels, whom the United States backed. On

October 1, the opposition newspaper *La Prensa* resumed publication, and the next day the Roman Catholic Church's radio station resumed broadcasting. (Both had been shut down in 1980.) On October 7, an amnesty for the Contras began, with Sandinista troops leaving 1,500 square miles of territory to Contra control. The Contra response, however, was to attack five towns on October 15.

The December 2 talks in Santo Domingo, Dominican Republic, began only after the Sandinistas freed 985 political prisoners and 200 former members of former President Somoza's National Guard on November 22. Mediated by Nicaragua's Cardinal Miguel Obando y Bravo, the discussions lasted fewer than two days because the Sandinistas demanded that U.S. aid to the Contras stop before a cease-fire began.

Following reports that the Soviet Union agreed to supply Nicaragua with more armaments on December 13–14 and a brief Sandinista offensive and Contra counterattack on December 20–21, a two-day Christmas truce was accepted on December 22. Only gradually did the rebels and the government move toward a settlement.

See August 7, 1987, and April 1, 1988.

### December 3, 1987

**The West German Bundesbank cuts its prime lending rate to stimulate the West German economy after the October stock market decline.**

Throughout 1987 there had been a disagreement among the United States, West Germany, and Japan on how to stimulate their economies. Initially, the issue focused on stabilizing the U.S. dollar, whose fluctuation influenced other nations' economies. On January 21, Secretary of State James Baker and Japanese Foreign Minister Kiichi Miyazawa discussed the recent fall of the dollar but no suitable response was made. On February 22, finance ministers of the Group of Five (the United States, France, Great Britain, West Germany, and Japan), plus Canada met in Paris and in the Louvre Agreement tried to stabilize the dollar, but again, no specific targets were set for the dollar value.

Because of this failure, the economic tensions among the allies was one possible cause of the October 17 stock market decline. On October 15, Secretary Baker had publicly criticized West

Germany for not cutting interest rates to stimulate its economy. The West Germans and Japanese used tight-money policies to prevent inflation and maintain their prosperity. The United States, they argued, should reduce its debt and increase taxes. Individual taxes were higher in West Germany and Japan than in the United States, and Reagan's 1981 tax cut helped generate the American deficits.

In addition to criticizing West Germany, Baker hinted that the United States might let the dollar's value drift lower. This signaled a wave of selling on the U.S. stock exchange to allow sellers to take profits before the dollar fell. The United States rectified this policy on November 20, when President Reagan and Congress agreed on tax increases and budget reductions for 1988 and 1989. Now, on December 3, West Germany's central bank cut its commercial bank rate to 2.5%; Britain, France, Switzerland, Belgium, Austria, and the Netherlands made similar cuts in December 1987.

On the Group of Five and the 1985 Plaza Accord, see September 22, 1985.

### December 8, 1987

**President Reagan and Soviet leader Mikhail Gorbachev sign a treaty eliminating their nations' intermediate-range missiles: the 1987 INF treaty.**

During a three-day Washington, D.C., summit meeting, Reagan and Gorbachev met in the East Room of the White House to sign the INF treaty, which resulted from six years of bilateral negotiations, finalized on November 24 when Secretary of State George Shultz met with Soviet Foreign Minister Eduard Shevardnadze in Geneva.

By the terms of the treaty, the two superpowers would destroy 2,611 intermediate-range missiles with flight ranges from 300 to 3,400 miles (500 to 5,000 kilometers). Principally, these would include U.S. Pershing II and cruise missiles and Soviet SS-4s, SS-12s, SS-20s, and SS-23s. It excluded 72 West German–based short-range Pershing IA missiles.

A significant part of the treaty provided for detailed verification procedures by which each power could inspect the other's facilities. Over the next 13 years, both resident and short-notice on-sight inspections would be conducted at 140 INF-related facilities in the two countries. On December 8, it was reported that Soviet inspectors would be

Soviet Chairman Mikhail Gorbachev and President Reagan sign the INF treaty. Ronald Reagan Library

located outside a Hercules Aerospace plant in Magna, Utah, where Pershing II and the MX strategic missile were assembled. This was one of 9 sites in the United States and 12 sites in 5 NATO countries that the Soviets could inspect. U.S. inspection teams could visit 70 sites in the Soviet Union and 7 sites in East Germany and Czechoslovakia.

On December 9, American reporters disclosed that a secret appendix to the treaty revised the previously publicized numbers of INF weapons that each side possessed. The United States had 429 Pershing IIs and ground-launched cruise missiles in Western Europe, not the previously cited 364. The Soviets had 470 deployed SS-4 and SS-20 missiles and 105 SS-4 and SS-20s that were not deployed, plus 387 deployed SS-12s and SS-23s, with another 506 undeployed missiles of these categories.

President Reagan launched a campaign in favor of the INF treaty during a television speech on December 3. Referring to it as a historic treaty, he claimed that those who opposed it were either ignorant of advanced verification techniques or believed that a nuclear war was inevitable. Throughout his meetings with Gorbachev, Reagan would repeat the phrase "the wisdom in an old Russian proverb ... *doveryai no proveryai*. Trust but verify."

Gorbachev also promoted the treaty. In a November 30 television interview, he called the INF treaty a step to more vital strategic long-range missile reduction treaties. He also admitted that the Soviet Union engaged in secret space-based missile defense research to counteract the U.S. Strategic Defense Initiative program sometimes called by the press "Star Wars" program.

In order to meet with members of the U.S. Congress, Gorbachev entertained them at the Soviet embassy in Washington, D.C., on December 9 because right-wing Republicans had persuaded President Reagan not to schedule Gorbachev for an address to Congress, which would normally be the proper protocol. Democratic leaders wanted Gorbachev to speak in a joint session, but on November 19, 75 members, mostly Republicans, opposed this idea. Therefore, senators and representatives were invited to the Soviet embassy to talk with the Soviet leader about the INF and other matters.

On December 11, 1987, NATO foreign ministers met in Brussels to support the INF treaty and urged the U.S. Senate to ratify it. (For treaty ratification, see May 26 and June 1, 1988.)

Although Reagan and Gorbachev avoided comments about Soviet opposition to the SDI program, two post-summit announcements revealed the continued disagreement. On December 13, Secretary of State Shultz said the administration would not seek congressional approval for the "broad" interpretation of the 1972 ABM treaty but would seek funds for SDI tests on a case-by-case basis. On December 29, National Security Adviser Colin Powell said the Soviets had reserved the option of revoking strategic arms reduction proposals if the United States violated the 1972 ABM treaty by testing SDI in space.

### December 9, 1987

**The beginning of Palestinian protests known as the Intifada, begins in the West Bank and Gaza Strip, occupied by Israeli forces since 1967.**

Tensions had steadily built up in the occupied territories not only because Israeli authorities mistreated Arab Palestinians but also because Israel supported and financed the growth of Jewish settlements in the occupied territory. Some Israelis advocated displacing all the Palestinians so that the Jewish state could possess its historic biblical lands of Judah and Samaria.

The first protest by young Palestinians, who had spent their entire lives under the occupation authorities, soon grew and gained widespread world sympathy as Israeli forces tried to subdue them. As rioting spread into Jerusalem on December 21, Palestinians living in Israel staged a one-day sympathy strike in favor of the Palestinian cause. The Palestinians had no guns but used rocks, barricades, and whatever else they could to harass Israeli citizens in the occupied areas. On December 21, Israeli soldiers shot and killed three protestors who, they said, had thrown fire bombs.

On December 22, Israeli leaders cracked down on the demonstrations. They arrested over 1,000 Palestinians in three days, closed Arab schools and colleges, sealed off Arab refugee camps, and shut down Jerusalem's largest Palestinian newspaper, al-Fajr.

On December 22, the U.N. Security Council passed a resolution deploring the handling of the protests by Israeli troops and police. The council vote was 14 to 0; the United States abstained rather than cast its usual veto on Israel's behalf. The State Department said the United States deplored the "excessive use of live ammunition" against innocent people who had

no guns. The INTIFADA demonstrations had just begun, however.

See January 26, 1976.

### December 12, 1987

**OPEC fails to agree on oil production limit.**

Between 1984 and 1987, the Organization of Petroleum Exporting Countries was no longer able to restrict production and raise oil prices, as they had done from 1973 to 1980. First, at a meeting in June, now at a second Vienna session, the member nations disagreed about methods to increase prices. Petroleum analysts said that current production was about 2.5 million barrels per day above market demand, meaning that the OPEC-preferred price of $18 per barrel was ignored, with most sales between $15 and $17 per barrel.

See November 28, 1988.

### December 14, 1987

**The United States accepts Israel as a major "non-NATO" ally.**

U.S. Defense Secretary Frank Carlucci and Israeli Defense Minister Yitzhak Rabin signed a 10-year agreement giving Israel this special position—an agreement held previously only by Australia and Sweden. Under this arrangement, Israel could purchase certain U.S. advanced weapons systems and compete with American firms for U.S. defense contracts. President Reagan suggested this idea on February 18, 1987, when Israeli Prime Minister Yitzhak Shamir visited him at the White House. Shamir accepted because it added a new format for U.S. aid to Israel.

### December 14, 1987

**Summit meeting of the Association of Southeast Asian Nations declares its region a nuclear-free zone and seeks peace in Cambodia.**

This was only the third meeting of the leaders of ASEAN nations since 1967. The two main concerns on which the leaders agreed was to make Southeast Asia a nuclear-free zone of peace and neutrality and, second, to urge a settlement of the Cambodian conflict by having Vietnam withdraw its forces in favor of a negotiated peace.

Because there were three competing groups in Cambodia, peace was difficult to obtain. On December 2, 1987, Prince Sihanouk, the former ruler and leader of one faction, met with Hun Sen, whom the Vietnamese had made prime minister of Cambodia. This meeting achieved no results because Sihanouk wanted Hun Sen to allow the third political group to be represented in negotiations. Hun Sen refused to talk with delegates from Pol Pot's Khmer Rouge because they had killed millions of Cambodians before Vietnam attacked in 1978.

See December 3, 1978; July 25, 1988.

## December 16, 1987

### Roh Tae Woo wins election as president of South Korea.

Opposition groups in South Korea had failed to compromise on a single candidate to oppose Roh. The two opposition leaders, KIM DAE JUNG and KIM YOUNG SAM, had formed a United Party of Reunification and Democracy on April 8, 1987, selecting Kim Young Sam as its leader on May 1. By October 28, however, the two Kims had a falling out, and Kim Dae Jung formed the Party for Peace and Democracy, becoming its presidential nominee.

Following the December 16 election, Roh's opponents claimed ballot-box corruption, but most observers disagreed, and President Reagan sent congratulations to President Roh on December 17. Roh said that if he lost a vote of confidence following the 1988 Seoul Olympic Games, he would resign and hold new elections.

See April 26, 1988.

## December 17, 1987

### The U.S. Defense Department announces it has begun production of chemical weapons.

President Reagan decided that the United States should renew its chemical weapons production despite much opposition at home and abroad. The House of Representatives had delayed action on production of such weapons until October 1, 1987, when the president could renew production if he declared it to be in the interest of national security.

On October 16, Reagan certified the need for the United States to begin producing binary gas weapons because no chemical weapons had been produced since 1969, and the Soviets held large quantities of

lethal gas weapons. In line with this, the Defense Department prepared to spend the $35 million authorized by Congress in producing binary artillery shells at a plant in Pine Bluff, Arkansas. The shells would hold only alcohol while in storage but could be used in battle after adding the organic chemical known as DF. When combined, these substances gave off lethal nerve gas. The Defense Department said it would begin production of Bigeye bombs and rockets early in 1990 as two other binary weapons.

See May 22, 1986; September 23, 1988.

## December 18, 1987

### President Reagan and Congress compromise on aid to the Nicaraguan Contra rebels.

The perennial issue of U.S. aid for the Contras arose again in 1987, lasting until a compromise was reached after Reagan threatened to veto the omnibus spending legislation if no Contra assistance was included. The Reagan administration wanted at least $9 million of military and nonlethal aid, while Speaker of the House James WRIGHT (D-Tex.) argued that a cease-fire was near under the plan of Costa Rica's President Arias. On October 13, Arias won the Nobel Peace Prize for his efforts to settle the dispute, leading Wright to assert that a vote for aid would damage the process.

On September 30, 1987, Reagan signed a stop-gap appropriation of $3.5 million in nonlethal aid to the Contras that maintained U.S. aid until a final bill for fiscal 1988 was approved. Subsequently, on December 18, Congress compromised with Reagan's demands, providing $8.1 million of nonlethal aid to operate until February 29, 1988, when the peace agreement was expected to be completed.

See April 1, 1988.

## December 22, 1987

### Congress passes the 1988 spending bill and a deficit-reduction bill.

The deficit-reduction bill had been worked out during a November 20 conference between President Reagan and congressional leaders. This bill and the spending bill were both approved by Congress on December 22 and later signed by the president.

The 1988 spending authorization was for $603.9 billion and included $270.5 billion for the military, $12.2 billion for foreign aid, and $7.7 billion for military construction. According to the budget reduction calculations the budget deficit would be $33.4 billion less than previously approved. By 1987, however, the Gramm-Rudman plans to end the budget deficit between 1985 and 1991 did not appear to be succeeding.

### December 26, 1987

*Arab leaders in the gulf region meet to discuss the Iran-Iraq war and attacks on ships in the Persian Gulf.*

The six-member nations of the Gulf Cooperative Council met in Riyadh, Saudi Arabia, whose King Fahd wanted to take strong action against Iran. However, because the United Arab Emirates and Oman feared antagonizing Iran, the only result was a weak statement by the council that urged the U.N. Security Council to levy sanctions against Iran for refusing to accept a cease-fire in the Iran-Iraq war.

# 1988

### January 12, 1988

*A Honduran official who had testified about compliance with the Arias Peace Plan is murdered.*

Miguel Ángel Pavon of the Honduran Human Rights Commission had testified against the disappearance of four people in 1982 and, just before his murder, testified to the International Verification Commission about the Honduran military's abuse of human rights. Pavon was the second witness to be killed. On January 5, Sergeant José Isaias Vilario was killed by four gunmen before he could testify to the commission. On November 1, the *Washington Post* reported that a Honduran army defector, Sergeant Fausto Reyes Caballero, disclosed that the Honduran military had murdered Pavon.

The International Commission had been part of the Arias Peace Plan agreed to by Central American nations on August 7, 1987. When it reported to a Central American summit on January 16, its report harshly criticized U.S.-backed regimes in Honduras and El Salvador, as well as the Nicaraguan rebels. Because the Reagan administration thought the com-

mission was pro-Sandinista, it was dismissed in Washington and its report ignored.

See April 1, 1988.

### January 13, 1988

*Israel deports four Palestinians from the West Bank although the United States voted for a U.N. Security Council resolution urging Israel not to.*

Attempting to stop the Palestinian uprisings that began in December 1987, Israeli authorities arrested nine activists whom it claimed were the chief instigators. On January 3, after Israel announced it would expel the men, world opinion rallied against such action. On January 5, the U.N. Security Council voted unanimously to urge Israel not to deport any Palestinian citizens. The United States did not cast its veto against the resolution, as it usually did to favor Israel. Nevertheless, on January 13, Israel deported 4 of the accused to southern Lebanon. Later, on April 11, Israel deported 8 more Palestinians and indicated that 12 others would soon follow them.

Neither the deportations nor the Israeli policy of "force, might and beatings" begun on January 19 silenced the INTIFADA protests. The Palestinians began a campaign of civil disobedience and a boycott of Israeli-made cigarettes. In response, the Israeli army arrested dozens of protestors, jailing them without trial for six months or more. Israeli soldiers grew more violent. In one notorious incident two Israeli soldiers buried four protestors alive. The two Israelis were arrested on February 16.

Although Israeli Defense Minister Yitzhak Rabin said the "beatings" policy substituted for the use of live ammunition, excessive brutality by the soldiers grew, causing protests not only by the United States but also by Israeli citizens in Tel Aviv. On January 24, Rabin ended the beatings policy, but the INTIFADA uprisings continued.

See June 13, 1988.

### January 13, 1988

*Taiwanese President Chiang Ching-Kuo dies and is succeeded by Vice President Lee Teng-hui.*

As president since 1978, Chiang saw Taiwan prosper economically but was unsuccessful in finding a means to reunite Taiwan with the Chinese mainland. After taking office, President Lee was soon confirmed as chairman of the Kuomintang Party, which had ruled the island since 1949.

## January 15, 1988

**Complying with a congressional restriction on aid to Pakistan, President Reagan exempts Pakistan from the Nuclear Non-Proliferation Treaty.**

President Reagan issued this exemption because he said that ending aid to Pakistan would jeopardize U.S. national security.

## January 29, 1988

**The United States cancels special trade privileges for Hong Kong, Singapore, South Korea, and Taiwan.**

These four countries had previously been able to send many products duty-free to the United States, helping their trade surplus of $37.3 billion in 1987 compared with $30.7 billion in 1986. Beginning on January 1, 1989, they would be removed from the Generalized System of Preferences by which developing countries exported products duty-free to the United States.

## February 4, 1988

**A U.S. court indicts Panamanian General Manuel Noriega for racketeering and drug trafficking.**

Although NORIEGA's indictments by federal United States courts in Miami and Tampa were not announced until February 5, the Panamanian leader had been implicated in the drug trade by a former political adviser, José Blandon, who testified to the U.S. grand jury. Because of this indictment, Panamanian's President Eric Arturo Delvalle tried to force Noriega's resignation as head of Panama's armed forces but was ousted by Noriega and his cohorts in the National Assembly, which voted on February 26 to remove the president. Both President Reagan and Congress backed Delvalle by withholding $7 million in payments due to the Panama Canal Commission. Subsequently, Noriega closed all of Panama's banks and on March 18 declared a "state of urgency" because, he said, the United States engaged in an "undeclared war" with Panama.

The irony was that President Reagan's domestic war on drugs implicated a Panamanian whom Vice President George Bush had encouraged into clandestine activity in 1975 when Bush headed the Central Intelligence Agency. Noriega had close ties with both the U.S. Defense Department and the Central Intelligence Agency. Allegedly, he had provided these groups with intelligence on Cuba and Nicaragua and helped to arrange several major drug seizures. There was no public evidence that Noriega was in the drug trafficking business until 1983, when Admiral Daniel Murphy told a Senate subcommittee that Noriega laundered drug money. Although Murphy was Vice President Bush's chief of staff at the time, Bush denied knowing about Noriega's drug connections until 1987.

Efforts to bring Noriega to court on these drug charges were unsuccessful until U.S. troops invaded Panama on December 20, 1989, to overthrow Noriega and install Guillermo Endara as president. Endara claimed to have won Panama's election during May 1989.

See May 25, 1988.

## February 9, 1988

***An international panel of historians finds that Austrian President Kurt Waldheim misrepresented his war record but committed no war crimes.***

This group followed up prior accusations against former U.N. Secretary-General Waldheim at the request of the Austrian government. Its report said Waldheim had been connected with war crimes committed by German army units in Yugoslavia, but he failed to admit this after the war. In response, Waldheim declared on February 15 that the report indicated nothing to require his resignation as Austria's president, a position to which he was elected after the charges were levied against him.

See March 4, 1986.

## February 11, 1988

***Armenians in the Soviet Republic of Azerbaijan demonstrate to join the Armenian Republic.***

Various nationalities in the Soviet Union began to demand autonomy after Soviet leader Mikhail Gorbachev broadened political participation.

Armenians in the autonomous region of Nagorno-Karabakh in Soviet Azerbaijan became one of the first groups to seek changes, by demonstrating to become part of the Soviet Armenian Republic. Subsequently, both the Armenian and the Azerbaijani Republics agitated for greater autonomy.

On February 27, Gorbachev persuaded the Armenians to suspend their demonstrations, but on February 28, members of the two ethnic groups rioted in the Caspian Sea town of Sumgait in Azerbaijan, leaving 32 Armenians dead. On March 26, Gorbachev sent troops to Armenia's capital, Yerevan, to prevent mass demonstrations of support for Armenians living in Nagorno-Karabakh.

See July 4, 1988.

### February 17, 1988

**An American army officer serving the United Nations in Lebanon is kidnapped by a pro-Iranian Shiite group.**

Lt. Colonel William Richard Higgins was kidnapped in southern Lebanon, and two days later the Organization of the Oppressed on Earth, a group linked to the pro-Iranian Hezbollah (Party of God), claimed responsibility. Higgins was a commander for a U.N. peacekeeping group, and despite a U.N. search, he was not found in 1988. On March 22, the kidnappers released a videotape that listed their demands for him to be freed; it included the release of all Lebanese and Palestinians in Israeli jails, withdrawal of all Israeli forces from Lebanon, and a halt to U.S. intervention in Lebanon.

On July 31, 1989, the pro-Iranian Hezbollah released a videotape showing they had hanged Higgins. On December 12, 1988, the terrorists said Higgins had confessed to being a CIA agent and an Israeli spy, charges that the United States and Israel denied.

### February 18, 1988

**A Salvadoran recants testimony that a left-wing rebel killed a Salvadoran official to prevent peace talks.**

Jorge Alberto Miranda, who had confessed on U.S. television on January 4, 1988, that the guerrillas killed an official as a pretext to end peace talks in 1987, now claimed the confession was false because it was made when he was drugged and abused in a Salvadoran prison in December 1987. Miranda had confessed to killing Herbert Ernesto Anaya Sanabria, who was president of El Salvador's Human Rights Commission.

Whether or not Miranda lied, Salvadoran President José Napoleon Duarte became seriously ill during 1987–88, and the government again came under the influence of the right wing. This halted El Salvador's efforts to carry out the Arias Peace Plan in Central America.

See November 23, 1987, and March 20, 1988.

### February 22, 1988

**France and West Germany establish joint councils on defense and economics.**

A step in Franco-German cooperation resulted from this agreement signed by French President François Mitterrand and West Germany Chancellor Helmut Kohl. Their agreement included a 2,000-man joint brigade to be stationed in Boblingen, West Germany. This was important to European defenses because France had terminated integration of its forces with NATO during the 1960s (see February 6, 1966).

### February 23, 1988

**Balkan nations agree to foster better relations, but Turkey opposes making the region a nuclear-free zone.**

An unusual meeting took place when the foreign ministers of Albania, Bulgaria, Greece, Romania, Turkey, and Yugoslavia met in Belgrade, Yugoslavia to discuss ways to establish better relations. Bulgaria, in particular, promised to end mistreatment of its ethnic Turkish minority. Greece proposed an agreement to declare the Balkans a nuclear-free zone. Although Greece, like Turkey, was a member of NATO, Turkey's leaders opposed it because NATO and the United States objected to creating such zones without superpower agreements making them effective through nuclear arms control.

### February 26, 1988

**Romania relinquishes its most-favored-nation trade status with the United States because the United States criticizes its human rights record.**

Romania announced it did not need U.S. special trade rights after Deputy Secretary of State John Whitehead visited Bucharest to explain to Romanian leader Nicolae Ceauşescu why Romania should improve treatment of its ethnic Germans and Jews who wanted to emigrate. Ceauşescu, Whitehead said, told him not to meddle in Romania's internal affairs. If Romania had not ended its special trade status, the United States might have taken such action because many members of the U.S. Congress opposed President Reagan's granting Romania special trade status.

See June 2, 1987.

### March 2, 1988

#### A congressional attempt to close PLO offices in New York is opposed by U.N. groups.

On March 2, the U.S. Justice Department announced that the Palestine Liberation Organization had to leave its offices in New York by March 21, 1988, because of a congressional amendment to the 1988 budget bill passed on December 22, 1987. American Jewish groups had pressured legislators to close PLO offices in Washington and New York, and the congressional amendment required the U.S. Justice Department to do so despite State Department opposition.

Closing the Washington office in December 1987 met with little resistance, but orders against the New York PLO office were contested because this served as the headquarters of official PLO observers to the United Nations. Therefore, the U.N. General Assembly voted its opposition on March 2 by a vote of 143 to 1; and the International Court of Justice gave an advisory opinion against the United States action on April 26, 1988.

The issue reached a federal district court in New York City. On June 29, the court ruled that the Justice Department had no legal authority to close the PLO mission because the 1987 amendment violated the 1947 Headquarters Agreement ratified by the United States when U.N. headquarters were established in New York.

### March 9, 1988

#### The United States lifts sanctions on high-technology goods to China.

On the final day of talks among China's Foreign Minister Wu Xuequian, President Reagan, and Secretary of State Shultz, the United States announced the lifting of sanctions on high-tech goods to China, which were imposed in October 1987 because the Chinese had sold Silkworm anti-ship missiles to Iran. The sanctions were lifted because China agreed to support a U.N. arms embargo against Iran if the U.N. Security Council approved it. The Chinese still sent some arms to Iran but claimed these fulfilled old contracts. China did not keep its agreement. On April 22, it vetoed a U.N. arms embargo resolution, claiming to do so because of U.S. clashes with Iran after a U.S. frigate was sunk.

See April 18, 1988.

### March 14, 1988

#### Senate approves treaty to curb depletion of ozone layer by CFCs.

Drafted by an international conference in Montreal during September 1987, this treaty sought to reduce by 50% the chlorofluorocarbons (CFCs) entering the earth's atmospheric ozone layer by 1999. To become effective, 11 industrial nations out of the 31 signatories would have to approve it because their production of CFC represented two-thirds of the world total. The United States was one of the 11 because it produced one-third of the world's CFC pollution. On December 16, 1988, after 20 nations ratified this treaty, it became effective.

### March 16, 1988

#### *Two incidents disrupt the funeral of three Irish Republican Army (IRA) terrorists.*

Three IRA terrorists accused of planning a bombing attack in Gibraltar on March 6, 1988, were killed by British security forces. At the subsequent funeral of the IRA members on March 16, a Protestant gunman killed 3 mourners and injured 50 others before being arrested. Finally, on March 19, at the funeral of one of those killed on March 16, two British soldiers were beaten to death by IRA mourners.

IRA terror continued, however. On May 1, IRA terrorists killed three British soldiers stationed in the Netherlands. On June 15 and August 20, a total of 14 British soldiers died when the IRA bombed army units in Northern Ireland. Later, on August 30, three IRA members were ambushed and killed by a British army group.

## March 16, 1988

**After visiting Soviet Defense Minister Dmitry Yazov, U.S. Defense Secretary Frank Carlucci claims the Soviets have not changed defense force structures.**

An important issue for U.S. national security policies relative to Soviet leader Mikhail Gorbachev's policy of perestroika (restructuring) was whether the Soviet armed forces had significantly shifted from offensive to defensive strategies in case of future war. Some U.S. military analysts had described the shift in Soviet policy between 1977 and 1986. Led by writings of Soviet Marshall Ogarkov, whose works Gorbachev preferred to the ideas of other Soviet military officials, the Soviet armed forces doctrine had concluded that a nuclear war could not be won and that high-technological conventional weapons were so destructive that the best doctrine would be defending the homeland rather than pursuing an offensive action if war began. Not unexpectedly, the U.S. Defense Department wanted definite proof of the Soviet changes before decreasing the U.S. defense budget. Thus, following talks with Yazov in Bern, Switzerland, Carlucci concluded that there was no evident change in Soviet policy.

Yazov and Carlucci met again from August 1 to 4, 1988, when Carlucci visited the USSR to inspect the Soviet's Blackjack bomber and other aircraft at the Kubinka Air Base near Moscow. This August meeting was preceded on July 6 to 11 by the visit to the United States of the Soviet Union's chief of staff, Sergey Akhromeyev. He met with President Reagan and also inspected the B-1 bomber and a U.S. aircraft carrier. These exchanges of high-level U.S.-USSR defense officials set a new precedent, allowing each side to inspect the other's advanced weapons.

## March 20, 1988

*Salvadoran elections enable the right-wing Arena party to control the legislature.*

Since being elected in 1984, President José Napoleon Duarte failed to fulfill American expectations that he would provide land reform, make peace with the guerrillas, and give moderates power over the right wing. Peace talks never got off the ground, right-wing death squads continued their terror tactics with few arrests being pursued by Duarte, and the status of Roberto d'Aubuisson's ARENA (National Republican Alliance) Party steadily grew.

In the March 20 election results reported on April 2, ARENA obtained 30 legislative seats while Duarte's moderate Christian Democrats (PDC) received 23, and the National Conciliation Party (PCN) earned 7. The defection of a PCN candidate to ARENA on May 19 gave the right wing a majority in the assembly. On June 7, Duarte underwent surgery for stomach cancer in New York and was found to be terminally ill. He decided to return to El Salvador, however, and remain in office until his death or his term expired in 1989.

See November 23, 1987.

## March 23, 1988

*Nicaragua and the Contra rebels sign the Sapoa truce.*

Meeting at Sapoa, Nicaragua, representatives of the Sandinista government and the Contra rebel leader Adolfo Calero Portocarreo signed a cease-fire and provisions for a return to normal civilian life. Under a 60-day truce, Contra forces would move to special zones, and the Sandinistas would grant amnesty to former army officers of the former dictator Anastasio Somoza Debayle. A national dialogue on reconciliation would begin with "unrestricted freedom of expression," humanitarian aid to the Contras, and the release of political prisoners.

See April 1, 1988.

## March 23, 1988

**On the SDI's fifth birthday, ground is broken for its National Test Facility (NTF).**

The NTF would be the coordinating point for regional facilities doing research on the Strategic Defense Initiative (SDI). On March 14, President Reagan told a conference on SDI that the United States was moving toward its goal to make SDI a "truly comprehensive defense." He said, "as it becomes ready, we will deploy it." To achieve this, technology required a major breakthrough to make a space defense viable.

During their 1987 meeting, President Reagan and Soviet leader Mikhail Gorbachev agreed to observe the 1972 ABM treaty while continuing research on anti-ballistic missile defenses. Despite Reagan's vision of a comprehensive defense, most advocates of SDI believed it would be primarily a defense for U.S. ICBM missiles not the entire nation.

See December 8, 1987.

## April 1, 1988

### President Reagan signs legislation for $47.9 million of "humanitarian" aid to the Nicaraguan Contras.

Congress had been divided about continuing aid to the Contra rebels because Nicaragua's Sandinista government made serious efforts to fulfill the terms of the Arias Peace Plan of August 7, 1987. During a meeting on January 16, 1988, the Central American presidents persuaded Nicaraguan President Daniel Ortega Saavedra of Nicaragua to end the state of siege, free some political prisoners, and negotiate directly with the rebels. Although the January 28–29 negotiations between Ortega and the Contras did not lead to a cease-fire, Ortega had abolished Nicaragua's radical leftist Anti-Somocista Tribunals, who opposed talks with the rebels. Subsequently, some headway for peace was made on Contra-Sandinista talks on February 18–19.

Because of these negotiations, the U.S. House of Representatives twice rejected proposals for aid to the Contras. On February 3, it opposed President Reagan's request for $3.6 million in military aid and $32.6 million in nonlethal aid. Later on March 3, it voted down Democratic Majority Leader James Wright's proposal for "humanitarian" aid to the Contras.

President Reagan did not accept the House actions. After U.S. aid to the Contras ran dry on February 29, the president revived U.S. military intervention in Central America by sending 3,200 U.S. troops to Honduras on March 16, claiming that 2,000 Nicaraguan forces had invaded Honduras. Although the Sandinistas argued that they had used only artillery to bomb Contra bases in Honduras, the Honduran air force bombed the border area on March 17, just as the first Americans arrived at Palmerola Air Base in central Honduras. Reagan said U.S forces would help defend Honduras.

Despite the border incident, the Contra rebel leader, Adolfo Calero, reached agreement with the Sandinistas. As a result of these agreements, Reagan began to withdraw U.S. troops from Honduras on March 28. In addition, the House of Representatives approved the "humanitarian aid" to the Contras on March 30 by a vote of 345 to 70. The Senate agreed, and on April 1, Reagan signed the legislation. Nevertheless, Nicaraguan peace efforts had not been fully resolved.

See March 23 and July 11, 1988.

## April 13, 1988

### China's National People's Congress concludes a three-week session during which more economic reforms are passed.

Although the sessions were notable for reelecting Deng Xiaoping to his office of chairman of the Central Military Commission and confirming Li Peng as premier, the Communist Party's call for continued economic reforms was the highlight of the congress. During the remainder of 1988, the government undertook several significant reforms. On May 15, it moved toward a market economy by ending price controls on eggs, pork, vegetables, and sugar in Beijing and Shanghai. Price controls were removed from cigarettes and alcohol on July 25. On August 17, the Communist Party's Politburo approved a five-year plan to liberalize price controls on many other products.

Because of the inflation resulting from the end of price controls, the government retreated a bit on September 26. Party General Secretary Zhao Ziyang gave orders to freeze prices on some consumer goods and to reduce investments in fixed assets. He said these steps were essential because inflation was running as high as 50%.

One other notable economic change in China took place on March 22, 1988, when the government began receiving foreign bids for long-term land-use leases in Shanghai, the first time the Communist Chinese had permitted foreigners to lease Chinese land.

## April 14, 1988

### Geneva accords are signed for Soviet troop withdrawal from Afghanistan.

Following lengthy negotiations, the United States, the Soviet Union, Pakistan, and Afghanistan signed agreements providing for Soviet forces to leave Afghanistan between May 15, 1988, and February 15, 1989. Two other separate agreements were signed. First, Pakistan and Afghanistan agreed not to interfere in each other's affairs and to repatriate Afghan refugees from the conflict. Second, the United States and the USSR agreed not to interfere in the signatories' internal affairs and to act as guarantors of the agreements.

The crucial decision making the Geneva accords possible was announced on February 8, 1988, when Soviet leader Mikhail Gorbachev said that Soviet troops would follow the withdrawal of the May 15–

February 15 timetable if the Geneva settlement were reached. Gorbachev also accepted terms on which the United States had insisted, that a major pullout should be at the beginning and that the withdrawal should not depend on keeping a pro-Soviet regime in power in Kabul.

See August 14, 1988.

## April 18, 1988

### The United States retaliates against Iran for damaging a U.S. ship in the Persian Gulf.

While the Iran-Iraq War had quieted from its intensity of 1987, the war had not stopped because Iran and Iraq regularly attacked each other. The United States became involved again on April 14 when an Iranian sea mine struck a U.S. frigate, the *Samuel B. Roberts*, causing damage and injuring 10 American sailors.

After the U.S. navy found and destroyed two other nearby mines, six U.S. warships attacked two oil rigs used as radar stations by Iran. When six Iranian naval vessels attacked the U.S. ships, the Americans also sank or disabled those ships in a series of naval attacks.

## April 20, 1988

### Amnesty International reports that Colombia is in a state of emergency owing to politically motivated killings.

Colombian President Virgilio Barco Vargas's determination to eliminate the drug traffickers dominating the Colombian countryside led to widespread disorder after the Colombian supreme court allowed threats by drug leaders to persuade it to invalidate the extradition treaty with the United States on June 25, 1987. In addition to the drug wars, Colombia's right- and left-wing guerrillas began to rebel against the government in 1987, even though they opposed the drug traffickers as well. On April 14, Barco declared a state of emergency in Uraba after 40 peasants were massacred by a neo-Nazi group. Amnesty International reported that one person was killed every six hours in Colombia by the drug lords or the rebels. The killings extended to law enforcement officers and judges as well as peasants and political candidates.

Colombia's difficulties continued, and in August 1989, U.S. President George Bush sent arms, ammunition, and military advisers to help Barco fight the drug lords. Barco reinstated the extradition treaty on August 19 and made peace with the left-wing rebel group M-19 on September 26, 1989.

## April 26, 1988

### South Korea's ruling party fails to win a majority of seats in assembly elections.

Although President Roh Tae Woo was inaugurated for a five-year term on February 25, 1988, his Democratic Justice Party won only 125 seats in South Korea's 299 seat assembly during elections on April 26. Other parties were divided, however, as they had been when Roh was elected president on December 16, 1987. A major issue arising in 1988 was the desire of many students to negotiate unification with North Korea.

See August 19, 1988.

## May 8, 1988

### French president François Mitterrand wins reelection.

Gaining 54% of the national votes, the Socialist Party's Mitterrand defeated Jacques CHIRAC, who had been French Premier after his center-right coalition parties gained control of parliament in 1986. Later, in parliamentary elections on June 5 and 12, 1988, Mitterrand's center-left coalition regained control of parliament, making Socialist Michael ROCARD premier. In the French parliament's total of 574 members, Rocard's left-center coalition had 274 seats; Chirac's right-center coalition had 271 seats; the Communist Party had 27 seats but usually voted in favor of Rocard's coalition.

## May 11, 1988

### Polish parliament gives the government emergency power to resolve strikes.

About two months after the government of Poland undertook austerity measures to raise prices and devalue the currency to promote a Western-style market economy, demonstrations and strikes disrupted many Polish cities. When transportation workers in Bydgoszcz struck on April 25, the government quickly raised their salaries by 63%. But when steelworkers at Nowa Huta began a strike for better pay on April 26 and shipyard workers at Gdansk went on strike, the government could not fulfill their demands.

By May 13, police and demonstrators had fought in 15 cities. Riot police ended the strikes by May 11, and the next day parliament gave Communist Party First Secretary Wojchiec Jaruzelski more authority to solve the economic problems if he could.

See August 31, 1988.

## May 12, 1988

### Vietnam appeals for aid because of a food shortage leaving 3 million near starvation.

Vietnam's appeal for help was correlated with its efforts to improve international relations by beginning to withdraw its armed forces from Cambodia and releasing data on more Americans missing in action during the Vietnam War. Nevertheless, Vietnam had acute food shortages since 1987 because drought, typhoons, and insect infestations had reduced the rice crop by over 1 million tons. On June 25, the United Nations announced it would send Vietnam $9.1 million of food to offset its shortages.

See July 25, 1988, and July 13, 1988.

## May 23, 1988

### Japan's five-year plan will increase domestic demand and reduce its trade surplus.

As in several previous springs, Japan announced measures to reduce its trade surplus. This year a five-year plan was proposed to stimulate economic growth by 3.75% and increase demand by 4.25%. This decision followed the annual meeting of January 12–16 of Japan's prime minister with the U.S. president and other Americans, and its March 29 decision to allowing U.S construction firms to bid on public works projects in Japan. Later, on June 14, the Japanese cabinet approved a $50 billion foreign aid expenditure, double that spent since 1983, and on June 20, it dropped import quotas on U.S. beef and oranges but imposed tariffs on both products.

See May 29, 1987.

## May 25, 1988

### Libyan leader Mu'ammar Al-Gadhafi recognizes the government of Chad peace results.

Having agreed to a cease-fire between Chad's rebels and Chad's government, Gadhafi avoided further conflict in Chad by dropping his support of the rebels and recognizing the government of Habré, which French forces and the United States had supported. Gadhafi said all problems had ended with Chad, but negotiations should begin regarding the disputed territory of Aozou, near the southern border of Libya. Habré agreed, and on October 3, 1988, the two nations reestablished formal diplomatic relations.

See September 11, 1987.

## May 25, 1988

### Panamanian General Noriega refuses a U.S. proposal to dismiss drug charges if he will give up power in Panama.

Since Manuel Noriega's overthrow of President Delvalle on February 26, Noriega met with two U.S. State Department officials, William Walker and Michael Kozak, on March 18–19, but no agreements were concluded. Rather, Noriega controlled his opponents in Panama by arresting about 50 protestors and journalists on March 28. As a result, U.S. President Ronald Reagan sent 1,300 more U.S. troops to Panama to reinforce the U.S. bases there. These troops arrived between April 5 and 8, 1988. By May 25, Noriega indicated he would hold fast to power in Panama despite U.S. threats.

See February 4, 1988.

## May 26, 1988

### The Senate places a binding condition on its approval of the 1987 INF treaty.

During Senate hearings on the Intermediate Nuclear Forces Treaty (see December 8, 1987), several Democratic senators raised questions about future interpretations of the treaty because the Reagan administration had altered accepted interpretations of the 1972 ABM treaty to justify experiments with the SDI program (see November 17, 1987).

Initially in February 1988, Senators Sam Nunn (D-Ga.) and Robert C. Byrd (D-W. Va.) asked Secretary of State Shultz to make all administration testimony to the Senate on the treaty legally binding for future interpretations. On February 9, Shultz gave the Senate qualified support for their concerns about testimony. Some senators were satisfied, but Senator Joseph Biden (D-Del.) proposed that a "binding condition" should be passed to assert the Senate's constitutional power in treaty interpretations.

Although Biden became ill in April and was absent from Senate discussions, Senator Robert C. Byrd proposed a modified form of Biden's amendment, which the Senate passed on May 26. Byrd's amendment stated that the "binding condition" referred only to the INF treaty of 1987 and that if questions arose about which the Senate and the president had not reached agreement in Senate hearings, the president could make interpretations. This Byrd amendment qualified the final Senate approval of the treaty's ratification when it passed on May 29.

### May 27, 1988

**Stinger antiaircraft missiles that President Reagan gave Afghan's rebels reach many countries.**

While various sources reported that Stingers had been sold by U.S.-supplied rebels, a *London Times* article gave details about Afghan guerrillas (mujahideen) selling them at $300,000 each. These shoulder-fired antiaircraft weapons provided by the United States to rebels in Angola and Afghanistan were much desired. Their sale to U.S. enemies was first confirmed when the U.S. navy discovered some on Iranian gunboats on October 19, 1987.

Subsequently, on December 3, 1987, the U.S. Senate sought to ban Stinger sales to Persian Gulf nations, but President Reagan insisted on selling 70 to Bahrain as a defense against Iranian aircraft. On March 31, 1988, the *Los Angeles Times* reported that Qatar had purchased Stingers from Iran. These stories were confirmed by the *Times* report, which said the Afghan rebels had sold at least 33 to Iran and 10 more to drug smugglers in Central America. Stingers in the hands of drug lords meant President Reagan's clandestine aid had come full circle to damage his "war on drugs" program at home.

### June 1, 1988

**President Reagan and Soviet leader Mikhail Gorbachev sign the 1987 Intermediate Range Nuclear Forces Treaty.**

Gorbachev showed his eagerness to fulfill the terms of the INF treaty of 1987 on February 27, 1988, when he began dismantling 30 SS-12 medium-range missile bases in Waren and Bischofswerda, East Germany. NATO leaders met in Brussels on March 2–3 and approved the INF treaty, and discussed the timing

for upgrading American-made Lance tactical missiles in West Germany. There was no agreement on the Lance because some NATO members believed these weapons were obsolete. The U.S. Senate approved the treaty on May 29 by a vote of 93 to 5, acting two days before President Reagan met in Moscow with Gorbachev.

Reagan visited Moscow from May 29 to June 2, signing the INF documents of ratification on June 1. While the president spoke out against Soviet human rights violations, most of his visit was pleasant. He strolled with Gorbachev in Red Square, addressed students at Moscow University, and signed nine other agreements on arms control, student exchanges, nuclear power research, maritime rescues, fisheries, transportation, and radio navigation.

See May 26, 1988.

### June 2, 1988

**Thirty-three nations agree to regulate commercial mining in Antarctica to protect the environment.**

Delegates met in Auckland, New Zealand, to finalize the Antarctic treaty, an agreement they had negotiated for six years. Although some conservationist groups such as Greenpeace opposed any commercial activity in the Antarctic, others accepted the strict regulations that would govern such activity and protect the environment.

### June 7, 1988

**Secretary of State George Shultz makes no progress on a Middle East peace plan despite four months of effort.**

Beginning on February 25, 1988, Shultz visited Jerusalem to revive peace efforts among Israel, its Arab neighbors, and the Palestinians. The essence of Shultz's proposal was to hold elections to give autonomy to Palestinians in the occupied territories. This would be followed by peace talks between Israel and its Arab neighbors to decide territorial matters.

In Jerusalem, the Labor-Likud coalition government was split on most peace proposals. For Shultz's suggestion, Labor's Shimon Peres was willing to try; Likud's Prime Minister Yitzhak Shamir opposed giving up any territory or Israel's control over the occupied territories. Nevertheless, Shultz visited Syria, Jordan, and Egypt to seek backing for his plan. On

June 7, after his last stop in Cairo to see Egyptian President Hosni Mubarak, Shultz gave up. He said that everyone liked what he was trying to do but that no one would clearly back his plan or any other. This outcome may have been one reason that Shultz and Reagan decided in December to try opening a dialogue with the Palestine Liberation Organization.

See December 14, 1988.

### June 13, 1988

#### U.S. State Department strongly objects to Israel's expulsion of a Palestinian American.

Mubarak Awad, who, since January 7, had become a leader of civil disobedience groups in the West Bank occupied territories, was arrested by Israeli forces who ordered his expulsion on May 6. After Awad began a hunger strike, the United States indicated he should not be forced to leave Israel without due process of law. Israeli courts delayed his deportation, but on June 5, its supreme court upheld the expulsion, and Awad was put on a flight to New York on June 13, an action the State Department opposed but could not stop.

Awad was born in Jerusalem but came to the United States in 1969 and was naturalized as an American citizen. Since 1983, he had been in Jerusalem at the Palestine Center for the Study of Non-violence, advocating tactics such as Dr. Martin Luther King used during the U.S. civil rights movement. Israeli authorities first tried but failed to deport him in November 1987, for his activities, before the *intifada* protests began.

### June 14, 1988

#### *Canada expels eight Soviet diplomats for spying to obtain advanced technology.*

Canada claimed the Soviets tried to steal secrets from a Montreal defense contractor, Paramax Electronics, a subsidiary of the U.S. UNISYS corporation. The USSR denied the charges and retaliated by expelling two Canadian diplomats and denying reentry to three others.

### June 21, 1988

#### Annual "Group of Seven" economic summit concludes in Toronto, reaffirms existing policies.

These annual meetings enabled the leaders of the United States, Britain, France, West Germany, Japan, Canada, and Italy to demonstrate their cooperation even though few policy changes resulted. At the end of this summit, the leaders reaffirmed the need for a stable U.S. dollar, for expanded East-West trade, and for continued reductions in the nuclear arsenals of the two superpowers.

Heads of state meet for their annual economic summit at Toronto. Ronald Reagan Library

### June 28, 1988

**Terrorist bomb kills a U.S. naval officer in Greece; in Italy on April 14.**

These two terrorist attacks against U.S. navy personnel showed the randomness of such exploits. The April bombing was at a United Service Organization (USO) club in Naples, where three Italian nationals also died. At the second, in Athens, a U.S. military attaché died when a car bomb exploded near his home.

### July 3, 1988

**U.S. navy ship in Persian Gulf shoots down an Iranian passenger liner, killing 209 persons.**

Iran Airlines Flight 655 had just left the coastal city of Bandar Abbas to fly across the Strait of Hormuz to Dubai in the United Arab Emirates, when the cruiser USS *Vincennes* destroyed it with a heat-seeking surface-to-air missile. There were no survivors; the victims included 66 children, 16 crew members, and citizens of several different nations.

Admiral William J. Crowe Jr., chairman of the Joint Chiefs of Staff, described to newsmen how the *Vincennes* had been in a skirmish with three Iranian gunboats (two destroyed, one damaged) just before Flight 655 appeared on its radar screen and was mistaken to be a F-14 fighter plane. Believing the plane was descending to attack, Captain William Rogers ordered the missile to be fired. Admiral Crowe blamed Iran for the accident because it had rejected a U.N.-sponsored cease-fire in the Iran-Iraqi war. (Iraq had also objected to the U.N. terms for peace.)

Investigations soon proved that many of Crowe's details were incorrect, even though the skirmish with gunboats and mistaken identification were not. A U.S. navy board of inquiry reported on August 19 that the *Vincennes* crew was nervous and lacked experience, which caused its radar operators to give Captain Rogers wrong information. Of significance was that other U.S. navy ships in the area did not mistake the airliner for an F-14. Two inexplicable errors were why Rogers fired on an F-14 that naval officers knew to be a fighter aircraft incapable of attacking a ship, and why the electronics officer said the airliner was *descending* when tapes of the radar screen clearly showed it was *ascending*. The navy board claimed that the ship's Aegis electronic gear worked perfectly. It was noteworthy that Rogers and other *Vincennes* officers

were not punished for shooting and killing 209 passengers, whereas three officers of the USS *Stark* were punished for not shooting at an Iraqi plane on May 17, 1987.

On December 2, 1988, the International Civil Aviation Organization's team of experts blamed the U.S. navy for poor planning. Not only was the crew unprepared for battle, but the navy's ships, unlike the ships of other nations, did not bother to monitor civil aviation flights. Moreover, Flight 655 was in the center of the known commercial airway and was ascending.

When a Pan Am airliner exploded later on December 21, 1988, pro-Iranian terrorists said it was revenge for Flight 655. And after Iran sought compensation by suit filed against the United States at the World Court on May 17, 1989, the U.S. State Department offered to pay families of the victims. Five nations of the victims accepted, but Iran did not drop its suit.

### July 4, 1988

**A general strike in Soviet Armenia requires Soviet troops to intervene.**

Since February, Armenians in the Armenian Soviet republic and in the Nagorno-Karabakh region of the neighboring Soviet republic of Azerbaijan had developed more antagonism toward the Azerbaijanis and the Soviet government (see February 11, 1988). On June 15, the Supreme Soviet of the Armenian republic passed a resolution urging the reunification of Nagorno-Karabakh with Armenia. After the strike began on July 4, some 400 protesters clashed with Soviet troops at the Yerevan airport, and the legislature of Nagarno-Karabakh voted to secede from Azerbaijan. Sporadic violence continued while Soviet soldiers attempted to keep order. On December 7, 1988, an earthquake diverted attention in Armenia to other difficulties because it leveled two Armenian towns and killed an estimated 25,000 people.

### July 8, 1988

**Great Britain sells Saudi Arabia $12 billion to $30 billion of modern armaments.**

In 1987 (see October 8) and again in April 1988, the U.S. Congress opposed President Reagan's request to sell arms to Saudi Arabia because of pressure from pro-Israeli lobbyists. Thus in 1988, the Saudis purchased missiles from China (March 18) and France

(June 7), but the largest Middle East arms purchase to date was the British sale announced by the Saudis on July 8. One Saudi official said his country preferred U.S. armaments but was "not going to pay billions of dollars to be insulted." President Reagan called the deal a blow to U.S. political and economic interests.

The Saudis had decided to make Great Britain their main arms supplier for the next decade. The sale included 50 Tornado jet fighters, 50 Hawk jet trainers, over 80 helicopters, 6 mine-hunting ships, and the construction of 2 new air bases. This deal saved thousands of British jobs. The purchase from China was for intermediate-range (1 to 2,000 miles) missiles using conventional warheads; the French sold the Saudis helicopters armed with Exocet missiles as well as fast patrol boats. Regarding the Chinese sale, after Israel threatened a preemptive strike against the Saudis, both the United States and Egypt warned Israel against such a move.

On July 7, the U.S. Senate blocked Reagan's request to sell Kuwait $1.9 billion of arms because it included Maverick air-to-ground missiles. Kuwait purchased $300 million of armored carriers from the Soviet Union on July 9 and said it would ask Britain for other weapons it wished to purchase.

### July 11, 1988

**Nicaragua expels the U.S. ambassador, claiming he incited rebellion.**

The Sandinistas' decision to expel U.S Ambassador Richard Melton and seven other U.S. diplomats came after a protest march of 3,000 people in Nicaragua became violent. Opposition parties had been allowed to operate in Nicaragua following peace talks between the government and rebel leaders. These talks ended in disagreement on April 30, but Nicaraguan President Ortega released political prisoners and allowed freedom for the opposition to organize. Further talks from May 26 to June 9 also failed, but the two states' military forces maintained the cease-fire without setting a date for further talks.

Subsequently, on July 10, protest marchers organized by the Democratic Coordinator coalition became violent when demonstrators threw rocks and bottles at the police, who arrested 42 protesters. The government asserted that Ambassador Melton and his colleagues incited the violence, hoping it would renew the Contra rebellion against President Ortega. The United States denied the accusations and retaliated by expelling Ambassador Carlos Tunnermann Bernheim and seven other Nicaraguans. Nevertheless, a senior administration official said on July 13 that Melton, who became ambassador in May 1988, wanted opposition groups to gain greater freedom under the terms of the cease-fire and the Arias Peace Plan of 1987

See April 1, and July 19, 1988.

### July 13, 1988

**For the third time in 1988, Vietnam returns remains of Americans missing in action (MIA) from the Vietnam War.**

The return to U.S. officials of the remains of 25 MIA service personnel on July 13 had been replicated on March 2, when the remains of 17 were returned, and on April 6, when 27 were returned. The remains of 23 MIA were returned on November 3, and those of 38 MIA on December 15. As usual, American officials came to Noi Boi airport in Hanoi to receive the remains.

### July 19, 1988

**As Nicaraguan Contras come under right-wing control, seven commanders resign and others form new organizations.**

While the Sandinista government of Nicaragua moved toward political changes to extend the cease-fire and resolve the conflict with Contra rebels (see April 1, 1988), Contra leaders directing rebel operations from Miami, Florida had internal disputes. Two of the seven directors of the Contra's National Resistance, Adolfo Calero and Pedro Chamorro opposed the growing influence of Contra Commander Enrique Bermudez, an Army colonel who served Nicaragua's National Guard under President Anastasio Somoza who was overthrown in 1979 (see July 17, 1979). Calero and Chamorro wanted to replace Bermudez as the Contra's military commander but the other five members of the Miami directorate agreed with Bermudez's hard-line opposition to the Sandinistas and preferred to end the cease-fire.

Because the Central Intelligence Agency backed Bermudez, the directors did not oust him but allowed him to attend the peace talks in Managua on May 26–28 and June 7–9. At both meetings, Bermudez's hard-line attitude caused tension and prevented a peaceful settlement. Subsequently, Bermudez promoted his candidacy for the directorate, and on July 18, a meeting of the Contras' National Resistance Assembly elected him and voted Chamorro out of office.

A wider split now developed in the Contra organization. On July 19, seven Contra field commanders on the "southern front" near Costa Rica resigned from the National Resistance because of Bermudez's election. Later, on October 14, Alfredo César, another opponent of Bermudez, formed the Democratic Center Coalition. Made up of three Nicaraguan political factions, César's group advocated political, not military, confrontation with the Sandinistas. César said the right-wing tactics of the National Resistance failed to bring peace, and on November 8 he sought new peace talks with the Sandinistas.

See May 6, 1987, and April 1, 1988.

### July 25, 1988

*Cambodian opposition groups meet in Indonesia since Vietnam had begun troop withdrawals from Cambodia.*

Because Vietnam began withdrawing its troops from his country early in 1988, Cambodian Premier Hun Sen agreed to meet with leaders of three rebel groups to decide on a future government. China proposed this meeting on July 1, indicating it would act as a guarantor of a Cambodian peace settlement made by the four factions represented: Hun Sen for the Vietnamese-backed government; Khieu Samphan of the communist Khmer Rouge; Son Sann of the noncommunist Khmer People's National Liberation Front; and Prince Norodom Ranariddh, who represented his father, Prince Sihanouk. Representatives from Indonesia, Vietnam, and the Association of Southeast Asian Nations (ASEAN) also attended.

Although the four factions agreed to a four-party "national reconciliation council" to arrange free elections, the three rebel groups disagreed with Hun's demand that his regime be allowed to rule until elections. The second problem involved the timetable for all Vietnamese troops to leave. This was discussed between Soviet and Chinese representatives from August 28 to September 2 in Beijing, but they could not agree.

Despite disagreement on Cambodia's final form of government, Vietnam began to withdraw its forces as early as February 1988. On February 23, a Japanese news agency reported that Vietnam pledged to withdraw all of its 125,000 troops from Cambodia by 1990. Other sources said Vietnam had withdrawn another 40,000 of its troops from Laos by early 1988.

See December 14, 1987.

### July 31, 1988

*Jordan relinquishes claims to the West Bank in favor of the Palestine Liberation Organization.*

Before Israeli troops occupied the West Bank of the Jordan River and Jerusalem in 1967, Jordan made claims to that area. Consequently, many peace talks on the Israeli–West Bank issue focused on a role for Jordan's King Hussein in a political settlement for that region (see September 1, 1982).

King Hussein now surrendered all Jordanian claims, announcing that he would end Jordan's legal and administrative ties to the Israeli-occupied lands. On August 4, when Jordan stopped paying salaries to 21,000 Palestinian civil servants on the West Bank, the PLO said it would maintain its responsibility as sole legitimate representatives of the Palestinians. PLO chairman Yasser Arafat did criticize Hussein, however, for not consulting him first.

### August 8, 1988

**While Secretary of State Shultz is visiting Bolivia, a bomb explodes near his car.**

While on a tour of several South American nations, Shultz was traveling in a car from the La Paz airport to town when a bomb, set off by remote control, exploded alongside his limousine. His special security car suffered no real damage but there was slight damage to other cars in the caravan. No one was hurt. The State Department believed the small bomb was meant to intimidate Shultz, whose August 4, 1988 speech to Bolivia's National Assembly encouraged the nation's war on drug traffic. Although Bolivia had difficulty shutting down its coca farms, the United States helped fund its efforts to combat the cocaine industry.

See July 14, 1986.

### August 14, 1988

*Soviet troop withdrawals from Afghanistan meet interim goals.*

As required by the Geneva accords, the Soviet Union withdrew 100,000 of its troops by August. The U.N.

Good Offices Mission monitoring the withdrawal reported that one-half of the Soviets' "limited contingent" was withdrawn on schedule.

Despite the Soviet withdrawal, leaders of Afghanistan's mujahideen rebels said they would continue fighting because they were not represented at Geneva and the Kabul government of the Communist-backed President Mohammad Najibullah remained in control. Almost immediately, the rebels captured two provincial capitals, Qalat and Mohammad Agha. The rebels' early success did not last because disputes ensued between rival guerrilla factions. In addition, the Soviet Union attempted to make the rebels accept peace terms. (See December 3, 1988.)

In Kabul, President Najibullah tried to broaden his power base by naming Muhammad Hapsan Sharq as prime minister. He also convened the first Afghan parliament since 1973, but no rebel leaders attended. Najibullah's difficulties with the mujahideen rebels multiplied. (See January 15, 1989.)

See April 14, 1988; for efforts to bring rebels into the government, see December 3, 1988.

### August 17, 1988

**Pakistani President Zia ul-Haq and the U.S. ambassador to Pakistan are killed when their plane crashes.**

Exploding just minutes after leaving Bahawalpur airport for Rawalpindi, the transport plane carrying President Zia ul-Haq, U.S. Ambassador Arnold Raphel, and 28 other U.S. and Pakistani officials crashed, killing everyone aboard. The chairman of the Pakistani Senate, Ghulam Ishaq Khan, became acting president and promised to carry out the mandate of the November elections. On October 16, a Pakistani military board reported that the crash was a "criminal act of sabotage" but did not accuse anyone or explain how it happened.

See December 1, 1988.

### August 19, 1988

*North and South Korean delegates begin unification talks.*

These talks between the two Koreas were inspired by student demonstrations in both regions. The demonstrations in the south had been especially large since May 15, when a South Korean student jumped to his death from a Seoul building to dramatize his desire for unification while blaming the United States for blocking that goal. Subsequently, persistent student protest marches, ranging in size from 25,000 to 100,000 demonstrators, on 78 university campuses in South Korea caused thousands of injuries and arrests, that the government wanted to avoid because of the forthcoming Olympic Games in September. As late as August 14, students had to be prevented from marching north to the 38th parallel to meet North Korean students who advocated unity.

In this atmosphere, the unity talks took place from August 19 to August 26 at Panmunjom, a village on the border between North and South. Although North Korea's delegates withdrew their demand that U.S. forces leave South Korea before meaningful talks could begin, the two sides soon became stalemated regarding the process and goal of unification talks, and their sessions ended on August 26. On December 28, prime ministers of the two Koreas agreed on talks, but they were canceled on March 2, 1989.

South Korea conducted the 24th Summer Olympic games in Seoul from September 17 to October 2 without serious incident.

### August 20, 1988

*Iran and Iraq officially begin a cease-fire, but peace talks face problems.*

A cease-fire ending the eight-year Iran-Iraq war had been negotiated by U.N. Secretary-General Pérez de Cuellar. Even though the fighting had been intensive since February 1988, Pérez de Cuellar persuaded Iran's Ayatollah Khomeini to reverse earlier demands that Iraqi President Saddam Hussein resign. On July 19 Khomeini said the decision to stop fighting was "more deadly than taking poison," but he accepted U.N. resolution 598. Iraq now grew reluctant, saying that it wanted peace talks as well as a cease-fire. This was agreed upon, and on August 8, Pérez de Cuellar announced the August 20 cease-fire agreement, with peace talks to start on August 25. The peace talks became stymied over the future possession of the river Shatt al Arab, which Iraq wanted to control when it first invaded Iran in 1980. The cease-fire returned the Shatt al Arab to its status under the 1975 Algiers convention, which divided the waterway between the two nations.

Iran and France had restored diplomatic relations on June 16, 1988. Britain resumed diplomatic relations on September 30.

### August 23, 1988

## President Reagan signs a revised trade bill that he previously vetoed.

The persisting U.S. trade deficit had stirred sufficient protectionist sentiment by 1988 that Congress passed a tough trade restriction bill on April 27, but after President Reagan vetoed it, the Senate lacked the two-thirds vote needed to override the veto. By August a compromise trade bill was approved and signed by Reagan after Congress dropped a section restricting the export of Alaskan oil and passed a separate bill that required manufacturers to give 60-day notice to their workers before closing a plant or laying off personnel. Reagan had objected to these sections in May, but he signed into law both the revised trade bill and the 60-day notice. The trade bill depended on the administration's using the new authority that Congress gave the president to negotiate trade treaties and to respond to unfair trade practices by other nations.

### August 24, 1988

## Turkey admits Kurdish refugees who allege Iraq used chemical weapons.

As the Iran-Iraq war moved to a cease-fire on August 20, Iraq attacked Kurdish tribes on its northern border because Iran had incited them to rebel during the war. Iraqi President Saddam Hussein wanted to punish the Kurds, and as early as March 15, Kurds claimed that up to 4,000 people had died from poison gas when Iraq's army destroyed the village of Halabja. Iran flew 30 Kurd victims to several hospitals in Europe and a New York hospital for treatment as evidence of Iraq's use of chemical weapons.

After Iraq began an offensive against the Kurds on July 30, a U.N. team visited Turkey and Iran to examine victims; Iraq would not admit the investigators. On August 23, the U.N. team reported that Iraq had used mustard gas principally but also cyanide and Tabun nerve gas. The next day, Turkey said 100,000 Kurdish refugees had flocked across its border, but later reports said only one-half that number had fled.

From September 16 to 18, Iraq flew Western reporters by helicopter to view the ravaged villages of Kurdistan. While no signs of poison gas were found, the journalists were shocked by the devastation committed by Iraq. Whether or not chemicals were used, after Iraq declared an amnesty for refugees, few Kurds returned. On March 29, 1989, the *New York Times* reported that while several hundred returned, and some went to Iran, 36,000 Kurds remained in Turkey, living in tents.

Since 1983, the Reagan administration had played down Iraq's use of chemical weapons. Congress, however, proposed sanctions against Iraq. On September 9, 1988, the Senate voted unanimously to levy economic penalties on Iraq, and on September 27, the House of Representatives passed a similar but weaker resolution. President Reagan approved these measures and strong White House lobbying prevented final passage before Congress adjourned on October 22.

Reagan continued to believe Saddam Hussein could be a moderating influence whom the United States could manipulate. Reagan's successor, George Bush, followed a similar policy until Iraq invaded Kuwait on August 1, 1990.

See November 26, 1984.

### August 28, 1988

## Three Italian jet planes crash during an air show in West Germany, killing 70 spectators and raising questions about NATO air exercises over West German territory.

During an air show at the U.S. Air Force base in Ramstein, West Germany, an Italian precision flying team made an error in a stunt, causing one plane to hit two others before it flew toward and crashed into a crowd of spectators. The other two planes crashed beyond the crowds.

The accident caused West Germany to question the frequent maneuvers and accidents by NATO planes flying over its territory. Some West Germans wanted NATO to reduce or end the number of such training missions. For example, on December 8, 1988, when a U.S. fighter plane in Remscheid crashed into an apartment building and killed six people including the pilot, it was the twenty-second crash of a NATO jet plane in West Germany during 1988.

## August 31, 1988

### ABM review talks end in disagreement.

The success of future arms control agreements between the Soviet Union and the United States seemed to depend on the settlement of disputes about the U.S. Strategic Defense Initiative (SDI) program and its connection with the 1972 ABM treaty. The Soviet Union wanted to limit the SDI and objected to the Reagan administration's broad interpretation of the 1972 treaty. On August 8, 1988, President Reagan agreed to abide by the narrow interpretation of the treaty while new reviews of the agreement took place.

From August 24 to August 31, 1988, negotiations between United States and Soviet delegates failed to produce agreement on the proper interpretation of the 1972 ABM Treaty. Following President Ronald Reagan's announcement of Strategic Defense Initiative (SDI) in 1983 (see March 23, 1983), the Reagan administration reviewed the status of the ABM Treaty and decided a broad interpretation of the treaty would permit the development and deployment of an "exotic" space-based missile defense system. Reagan's broad interpretation contrasted significantly with previous interpretations by the administrations of Presidents Richard Nixon, Gerald Ford, and Jimmy Carter. Even congressional leaders such as Senator Sam Nunn questioned the validity of Reagan's broad interpretation of the ABM Treaty, as did General Secretary of the Soviet Union Mikhail Gorbachev (see November 17, 1987).

In 1987, Gorbachev agreed to separate the issue of the ABM Treaty's interpretation from negotiations on the Intermediate Nuclear Forces (INF) Treaty that was signed in 1987 (see December 8, 1987) and the strategic arms reduction talks (START). Nevertheless, during the August 31 ABM review conference, United States delegates continued to insist that the broad interpretation of the ABM treaty was valid and that the SDI program could develop and deploy an effective anti-missile system that could be used to destroy Soviet ICBMs in space. Yet, five years after Reagan's 1983 speech, the SDI program had not developed any effective missile defense system.

In addition to reaffirming their differences on the 1972 ABM treaty's interpretation, the 1988 conference delegates discussed the Reagan administration's claim that the Soviet Union's Krasnoyarsk radar station violated the 1972 ABM Treaty. The Soviet delegates denied the radar station violated the treaty but offered to dismantle the radar station if the United States accepted the narrow interpretation of the 1972 ABM Treaty. The American delegates not only refused this offer because it would prevent tests and deployment of any SDI system under development but also stated that neither the START negotiations nor other arms control agreements would be signed until the Soviets dismantled the Krasnoyarsk radar station. Subsequently, the ABM interpretation issue stalled START negotiations until September 1989, when the Soviets agreed to dismantle their radar station.

On the two interpretations, see November 17, 1987.

## August 31, 1988

### Polish Solidarity leader Lech Wałęsa ends strikes, bringing changes in the government.

In April, May, and August, Poland suffered waves of demonstrations and strikes by coal miners, dock workers, and Gdansk shipyard workers seeking better wages and the legalization of Solidarity as the workers' union. Finally, on August 31, after Wałęsa met with Interior Minister Czesław Kiszizak, they agreed to negotiate. Solidarity called an end to strikes, and by September 19 a parliamentary investigation criticized the government's economic policy. A new premier, Mieczysław Rakowski, was appointed on September 27, but he proved to be disappointing. Rakowski shut down the Gdansk shipyard because it lost $3.5 million in 1987. Another nationwide strike was averted only when new talks began between the government and Solidarity delegates on November 17, 1988.

## September 12, 1988

### Lebanese Shiite terrorists release a West German hostage who influenced German prosecution of a hijacker.

On January 17 and 21, 1987, Shiite terrorists calling themselves members of Strugglers for Freedom kidnapped two West German businessmen, Alfred Schmidt and Rudolf Cordes. Schmidt had been released on September 7, 1987; Cordes was released on September 12, 1988. Each time, West Germany declared there was no deal, but West German Foreign Minister Hans Dietrich Genscher said "quiet diplomacy" with Iran gained the release of the men.

Not until January 26, 1989, did a West German official admit that the release of the two men "influenced" their prosecution of Muhammad Hamadei, whom West Germany refused to extradite to the United States for prosecution as a TWA hijacker. The Germans did, however, convict Hamadei and sentenced him to life in prison on May 17, 1989.

See June 14, 1985, and June 24, 1987.

## September 13, 1988

### A major policy change for the Reagan administration: U.S. dues to the United Nations to be fully paid.

The right-wing influences that dominated President Reagan's first term dissipated considerably during his last three years in office. One area regarded Reagan's growing appreciation of the U.N.'s role that conservatives generally disdained. Thus, when the White House announced that it would make full payments on upcoming U.N. budgets as well as make up the $467 million the United States already owed, it was a significant policy change.

A White House spokesman said there were two reasons for the shift. First, the United Nations had undertaken reforms to decrease its often extravagant budgets. It had cut its staff by 12% with a goal of 15%, and the 1989–1990 budget being prepared was lower than prior budgets.

Second, Secretary of State Shultz persuaded Reagan that the United Nations played a vital role in U.S. global diplomacy. In particular, U.N. officials cooperated with Washington in solving problems in the cease-fire between Iran and Iraq, the Afghanistan cease-fire, and the Namibia-Angola problems. There were still U.S. areas of disagreement with UNESCO and other agencies, but generally the Reagan advisers saw its salutary role as worthy of support and agreed to help it finance operations.

See November 23, 1987, and December 21, 1988.

## September 14, 1988

### American and Soviet scientists monitor underground nuclear tests in Kazakhstan.

In accordance with a November 20, 1987, agreement, U.S. and Soviet experts monitored two underground nuclear explosions, one on August 17 in Nevada, the other on September 14 in Kazakhstan. Intended to permit the calibration of instruments for verification purposes, both the Soviet seismic method and the American Corrtex measuring system were used. In both 1988 experiments, the seismic system proved superior.

The U.S. experts were especially embarrassed after their Corrtex system measured 163 kilotons at the Nevada tests, making the test exceed the 150-kiloton limit, which was the agreed upon testing limit. The Soviets' seismic system measured it more accurately at 140 kilotons. According to Western analysts, the less effective Corrtex system was one reason that the United States previously complained about Soviet violations, which Moscow denied.

## September 17, 1988

### After Haiti's second coup d'état in three months the United States warns it against a drug trafficker in the army command.

Although Haiti adopted a new constitution in 1987, its first election on January 17, 1988, had only a 5% voter turnout because leading candidates charged fraud and boycotted the ballot. Leslie Manigot, a university professor, was declared the winner and became president on February 7. Within about four months, Manigot was overthrown on June 19 when General Henri Namphy seized power. Three months later, on September 17, Namphy was overthrown by Brigadier General Prosper Avril, a former aide to Haiti's longtime dictators François and Jean-Claude Duvalier.

The United States became concerned because at Avril's side in the new regime was Colonel Jean Claude Paul, who had been indicted by a U.S. federal court on March 9, 1988, for drug trafficking. Although Paul headed the army's powerful Dessolines Battalion, the United States warned Avril to get rid of Paul or lose the $70 million in aid that Congress had allocated to Haiti. On September 30, Avril removed Paul from office. On November 6, Paul died in his home after being poisoned. The person responsible for the poison was never disclosed.

## September 18, 1988

### *Months of disorder end in Burma with a right-wing coup by Burma's Defense Minister General Saw Maung.*

General Maung promised to restore law and order in a nation where violent protests had occurred from

March 13 to 20 and August 8 to 23, with 200 students killed in March and up to 1,500 perishing in August. Following more demonstrations, the country's ruling Burma Socialist Program Party (BSPP) agreed on September 10 to hold multiparty elections in six or twelve weeks.

After leading dissidents objected to elections before the existing government had resigned, General Maung overthrew President Maung Maung. The dissidents objected, and in clashes with the army from September 18 to 21, at least 400 more were killed. The military government abolished the BSPP and renamed the ruling party the National Unity Party. Elections did not take place, but following battles with guerrillas along the Chinese border, General Maung declared on October 3 that all worker's strikes had ended, and he lifted restrictions on foreign trade on October 31.

Through this turmoil, General Ne Win, who had ruled Burma since 1948 before resigning as president in 1988, remained in control of the National Unity Party.

### September 23, 1988

**Secretary of State Shultz and Soviet Foreign Minister Shevardnadze fail to break strategic arms talks deadlock but express concerns on chemical weapons.**

In December 1987, when the intermediate-range missiles reduction treaty (INF) was signed, Moscow and Washington hoped to conclude a strategic arms reduction treaty (START). By September, however, talks became stymied over divergent proposals by each side. Although Shultz and Shevardnadze did not resolve the issues, they said they had made some progress. Later, Shultz told reporters that START was unlikely to be completed before the November 1988 elections.

Shultz and Shevardnadze did take another step toward abolishing chemical weapons. The United States had previously listed the sites where it produced chemical weapons, and the Soviets said they would prepare a list of their own sites. Shultz also agreed to disclose the current size of the U.S. chemical arsenal.

See January 7, 1989.

### September 28, 1988

**Spain and the United States sign an eight-year bases agreement after the United States moves 72 aircraft to Italy.**

During more than two years of negotiations for U.S. military basing rights in Spain to replace an agreement due to expire May 14, 1988, the two key issues were Spain's desire to close the base at Torrejon, near Madrid, and whether U.S. naval ships should be allowed to visit Spanish ports if they carried nuclear missiles. The first question was resolved on January 15, when the United States agreed to remove 72 F-16 fighter-bombers from Torrejon. Italy agreed to base the planes in its southern city of Crotone to protect NATO's southern flank. The Italian parliament approved this move on June 30, 1988. Regarding the visits of U.S. ships, Spain agreed not to inspect them when they made calls at their ports, even though antinuclear advocates in Spain wished to prevent visits by nuclear missile–carrying ships.

One additional change in the new agreement required no U.S. economic or military aid to be paid to Spain. The usual practice had been to require compensation, but as a member of NATO, Spain waived such payments.

### September 29, 1988

**The space shuttle *Discovery* is launched—the first U.S. shuttle since the *Challenger* exploded.**

The *Discovery* carried a crew of five on a one-week mission, returning to California on October 3, 1988.

See January 28, 1986.

### September 29, 1988

**President Reagan signs a $299.5 billion defense authorization bill that Defense Secretary Carlucci planned with Congress.**

Although on August 3, the president vetoed a defense bill authorizing $299.5 billion, Defense Secretary Frank CARLUCCI and Congress adjusted the funding to increase allowances for the MX missile and the Strategic Defense Initiative as desired by Reagan. The MX received $600 million and the "Star Wars" program $4.1 billion. Although Congress and the president were aware of the need to cut the budget deficit, they did not meet the 1985 Gramm-Rudman targets to balance the budget by the early 1990s. On October 28, 1988, the Treasury Department reported that the target had been exceeded by about $9 billion in fiscal year 1988.

The Reagan administration's defense expenditures escalated during the period 1981–1988 while its outlays for other international programs decreased until the Republicans lost control of Congress in 1983; but defense expenditures were cut again from 1985 to 1989.

### October 5, 1988

#### *Chileans oust President Pinochet.*

Augusto Pinochet had ruled Chile since the overthrow of President Allende Gossens in 1973. As Pinochet's military junta came under increased criticism at home and abroad, he agreed to a presidential plebiscite, and on August 31, 1988, 16 opposition parties agreed to maintain order if the election turned against him. The October 5 plebiscite went against Pinochet by a vote of 54.7% to 43%. On November 20, Chile's junta announced that Pinochet would not run in a new presidential election on December 14, 1989. In that election, Pinochet's designated candidate lost to the nominee of the Coalition for Democracy, Patricio Aylwin.

See October 24, 1970, and September 11, 1973.

### October 14, 1988

#### President Reagan ends an attempt to get $16.3 million of military funds for the Nicaraguan Contras.

Although Congress had approved $27 million in non-lethal aid for the Contras on September 30, Reagan's desire for military aid had been voted down by the Senate on August 10 by a vote of 49 to 47. The Senate's Democratic Party leaders offered a compromise plan to vote on stockpiled military support later in 1988 if Reagan certified that there was an "emergency situation," but the White House rejected this idea. The Democrats also wanted a package of trade incentives to encourage the Sandinistas to carry out the Arias Peace Plan of 1987, but Reagan opposed that.

The Contras had received no military aid from the United States since 1985, and most observers, including pro-Contra Assistant Secretary of State Elliott Abrams, believed the Contra military effort had ended. On November 8, Abrams said a "post-Contra era" had begun. In December, President-elect George Bush indicated that he would emphasize diplomatic methods to end the Nicaraguan civil war.

### October 17, 1988

#### The Philippines extend U.S. military base rights through 1991.

Since the overthrow of Philippines President Ferdinand Marcos on February 25, 1986, the outcome of the U.S. bases issue had been uncertain because some Philippine nationalists wanted the Americans to leave. On October 17, an interim agreement to extend U.S. use of the base at Subic Bay and Clark Air Base for three years was signed in Washington by Secretary of State George Shultz and Philippine Foreign Minister Raul Manglapus. In this agreement, the United States gave the Philippines $500 million in export credits through 1991, as well as $481 million in military and economic aid in 1990 and 1991.

On December 22, 1988, following a meeting in Manila with Soviet Foreign Minister Eduard Shevardnadze, Foreign Minister Manglapus told reporters that the Soviet Union was considering closing its naval base at Cam Ranh Bay in Vietnam. U.S. authorities cited this Soviet base as proof that the Soviets were increasing their Pacific Ocean naval power, an act justifying the U.S. bases in the Philippines.

Philippine President Corazon Aquino needed U.S. support because her government faced threats from the left and the right. To satisfy the left, Aquino signed a land reform bill on June 10, providing for land redistribution over a 10-year period. It had already encountered criticism, however, because the law had loopholes for wealthy landowners to avoid giving up control of their land. On the right, Aquino's Vice President Salvador Laurel abandoned her coalition on August 27 to form a right-wing coalition of his own, the Union for National Action. Former Defense Minister Juan Ponce Enrile became vice chairman of the group.

### November 8, 1988

**George Bush is elected president, winning 53.4% of the vote over Massachusetts Governor Michael Dukakis.**

Bush and his running mate, Senator Dan Quayle (R-Ind.), defeated Dukakis and Senator Lloyd Bentson (D-Tex.). Although the Republicans continued to occupy the White House, the Democratic majority controlled the Senate and House of Representatives. During the 1988 campaign, the candidates paid little attention to foreign policy, with issues of crime and race relations dominating both the presidential and the congressional contests.

### November 8, 1988

*Protests in Kosovo oppose the policies of the Serb Republic's President Slobodan Milošević.*

The United States had given financial aid to Yugoslavia after General Secretary of the Yugoslav Communist Party Marshall Tito (Josip Broz) broke with General Secretary of the Soviet Union Joseph V. Stalin (see November 14, 1951). In 1982, the Reagan administration cut off all financial aid to Yugoslavia after Yugoslav leaders declared martial law in the Serb Republic's autonomous province of Kosovo following student demonstrations during which Serb police killed many (Kosovars claim 1,000) students. Yet, as Susan Woodward's *Balkan Tragedy* explains, the International Monetary Fund, an organization using some U.S. money (see July 22, 1944), gave financial aid to Yugoslavia until 1987.

Most historians attribute Yugoslavia's demise to Serbian President Slobodan Milošević, who gained control of the Republic of Serbia in 1987 by raising the banner of Serbian nationalism. Using nationalistic myths about the 1389 battle at Kosovo-Polje that Serbs lost to the Ottoman Empire, Milošević proposed that Serbs establish a Greater Serbia by uniting all Serbs, including Serb minorities living in other Yugoslav republics of Croatia, Bosnia, and Macedonia. By the end of 1987, Milošević gained control of Serbia's Communist Party and the government of the Serb Republic. Milošević's next step was to strengthen his power in federal Yugoslavia by controlling four of the eight votes on Yugoslavia's presidency (see May 4, 1980). Milošević experienced no problems gaining votes in the province of Vojvodina, where many Serbs lived, but he had serious troubles in

Kosovo, whose population was 90% ethnic Albanian (Kosovars). Having been frequently persecuted by Serbs (see October 16, 1913), the Kosovars organized demonstrations against the Serbs but were unable to prevent the Serb Republic's takeover of Kosovo.

See November 14, 1951, and March 23, 1989.

### November 21, 1988

**In Canadian elections, where the trade treaty dominated, Prime Minister Mulroney's party wins. The U.S.-Canadian trade bill is approved.**

Mulroney, who was working closely with President Reagan on acid rain issues (see March 19, 1986) as well as the ratification of the U.S.-Canada trade bill signed on January 2, 1988, experienced a tough debate from his political opponents. Nevertheless, Mulroney kept control of parliament, and on December 24, the House of Commons gave final approval by a vote of 141 to 111. The free-trade bill would become effective on January 1, 1989, because both houses of the U.S. Congress approved it and because President Reagan had signed enabling legislation on September 28, 1988.

### November 22, 1988

**Australia and the United States agree on maintaining U.S. intelligence bases in Australia for the next 10 years.**

This pact renewed existing agreements but gave Australian personnel a greater role in base operations and full knowledge of the facilities related to the nation's interests and sovereignty. One base, at Pine Gap in the north, helped monitor arms control agreements; the other, at Nurrungar in the south, was a ground station for U.S. satellites in the defense support program.

### November 25, 1988

**America's Watch gives Guatemala and El Salvador low marks for violation of human rights.**

The activities of El Salvador's right-wing death squads received more publicity in the United States than did the more subtle tactics used by Guatemala's President Marco Cerezo and his military leaders in punishing political dissenters. Nevertheless, America's Watch reported that these two countries had the worst record in the Western Hemisphere for political murders. In Guatemala 621 people had been killed in the first nine months of 1988; in El Salvador, military death squads killed 91 civilians, up 44% from 1987. Unlike El Salvador, Guatemala required little military assistance from the United States, although it had received $5 million in 1987.

## November 28, 1988

### OPEC agrees to production limits to raise oil prices by $6 per barrel.

Oil prices had fallen during 1988 to $12 per barrel, causing members of the Organization of Petroleum Exporting Countries, meeting in Vienna, to try once again to hold down production to raise the price of oil. Their disagreements focused on Iraq's demand for a production quota equal to Iran's. Iraq had been exempted from the production control for two years, and in order to bring it back, Iraq was given a quota equal to Iran's after 11 other producers each gave Iraq part of their quotas.

See December 12, 1987.

## December 1, 1988

### Benazir Bhutto becomes Pakistan's first woman prime minister after her Pakistani People's Party (PPP) forms a coalition.

Although Bhutto needed a coalition with other parties to form a government, the PPP had the largest bloc with 92 seats, the next largest being the 55 members of the Islamic Democratic Alliance. On November 30, when the National Assembly elected 20 delegates for seats reserved to women, the PPP received 12 more. General elections had been held on November 16, but the assembly did not meet and elect Bhutto until December 1. On December 12, the honorific role of president was again awarded to Ishaq Khan by the Pakistan electoral college.

## December 2, 1988

### President Reagan reports to Congress that Moscow has complied with the 1987 INF treaty, except for a few technicalities.

In his annual report to Congress on Soviet compliance with arms control treaties, Reagan cited five minor violations of the intermediate-range nuclear missile treaty of 1987. Overall, the Soviets complied, having

destroyed 80 of their 654 SS-20s and removed all their shorter-range missiles and launchers to sites for their destruction.

See December 8, 1987.

## December 3, 1988

### Soviet delegates meet with Afghan rebels in Saudi Arabia to seek peace in Afghanistan.

To secure a more broadly based Afghan government following Soviet troop withdrawals, Soviet Deputy Foreign Minister Yuli Vorontsov headed a delegation to Taif, Saudi Arabia to meet with Afghan rebels. The Soviets urged the rebels to participate in a new Afghan government but also wanted to guarantee safe passage for the withdrawing Soviet forces. The rebels promised not to attack major cities until the Soviets had departed.

See April 14, and August 14, 1988.

## December 5, 1988

### Guidelines for the Uruguay round of GATT are negotiated; the dispute over agricultural subsidies is not resolved.

Meeting in Montreal, members of the General Agreement on Tariffs and Trade (GATT) set guidelines for an expected two years of multilateral negotiations. Although the United States and the European Economic Community (EEC) agreed to cut tariffs on many Third World exports, a lengthy debate on the status of agricultural subsidies achieved no results. The United States wanted to phase out all subsidies gradually, while the Europeans wanted to cut but not eliminate subsidies.

On December 10, the EEC announced that on January 1, 1989, it would impose a ban on all U.S. meat from cattle treated with growth hormones. This action indicated one of the trade problems between the United States and Western Europe.

## December 6, 1988

### A military uprising in Argentina ends after President Alfonsin compromises with rebel leaders.

A mutiny led by Lt. Colonel Mohamed Ali Seineldin took over a military school near Buenos Aires, demanding the appointment of a new chief of army staff and the end of prosecution of officers who

Soviet President Mikhail Gorbachev, President Reagan, and President-elect Bush tour New York City. Ronald Reagan Library

violated human rights during the "dirty war" of the last decade. After various army units joined Seineldin's group in sympathy strikes, Argentine President Raul Alfonsin agreed to appoint a new chief of staff and to cut back on future prosecutions.

Alfonsin admitted that while prior military abuses could not be forgiven, they could be understood in the context of national problems. There had been other protests against the trials in April 1987 and January 1988, and the president hoped these would end. Argentine's problems continued, however, and a new president, Carlos Saul Menem, was elected on May 14, 1989.

### December 6, 1988

**_During a U.N. address Mikhail Gorbachev indicates that he will reduce Soviet forces by 500,000 men._**

Soviet leader Gorbachev said Soviet forces in the USSR and Eastern Europe would be cut by 10,000 tanks, 8,500 artillery pieces, and 800 combat planes by 1991. He claimed that the USSR's military doctrine followed a strictly defensive stance. Gorbachev's U.N.

address was the first by a Soviet leader since Premier Nikita Khrushchev spoke in 1960. He stated: "Today, we face a different world" from that in 1917 (the era of the Russian Revolution) and there must be a "consensus as we move forward into a new world order."

Western analysts estimated that the troop cutback for Eastern Europe represented about 10% of the Soviet total of 600,000 troops and 30,000 tanks. Gorbachev also said he would withdraw 4 of the 57 divisions on the Soviet-Chinese border and pledged a broadening of human rights in the Soviet Union.

Gorbachev visited New York City from December 6 to 8, meeting with President Ronald Reagan and President-elect George Bush. The State Department said this was not a summit but a symbolic "passing of the torch" from Reagan to Bush. Gorbachev planned to visit Cuba and Great Britain on his way home, but a massive earthquake in Soviet Armenia on December 8 caused him to fly directly back to Moscow.

See March 16, 1988.

### December 13, 1988

**_Angola, Cuba, and South Africa agree on Namibian independence and Cuba's withdrawal from Angola._**

At a meeting in Brazzaville, Congo, the three previous competitors signed the prologue to a protocol that allowed for Namibia's transition to independence from South Africa and for Cuba to withdraw its 50,000 troops gradually from Angola. Half of the 50,000 would leave by November 1, 1989; another 25,000 would move north from Namibia's border. The final 25,000 would leave by July 1991, although Angola had to resolve its civil strife with Jonas Savimbi's rebel group, UNITA.

South Africa agreed to reduce its forces in Namibia from 60,000 to 1,500 by July 1989. The United Nations would supervise elections in Namibia on November 1, 1989, after which all South African forces would leave. The one problem in Namibia was to persuade the rebel group SWAPO (South-West African People's Organization) to accept these terms.

Namibia's plans succeeded in 1989, while Angola had to contend with the rebel forces of UNITA, led by Jonas Savimbi, to whom the United States continued to give military aid. Namibia held elections from November 7 to 11, 1989, and SWAPO, led by Sam

Nujoma, won 41 of 72 seats for the constituent assembly. Savimbi agreed to a truce with Angolan President Jose Eduardo dos Santos, effective June 23, 1989. However, fighting broke out again on August 23, and dos Santos blamed the United States for urging Savimbi to fight. The Bush administration had decided to continue arming Savimbi until peace was finalized. After meeting with President Bush on October 5, 1989, Savimbi agreed to another cease-fire.

See November 25, 1987.

### December 14, 1988

**PLO leader Arafat recognizes Israel's right to exist; the United States begins discussions with the PLO.**

The Reagan administration's decision to begin a dialogue with the Palestine Liberation Organization (PLO) followed an intricate series of maneuvers leading Arafat to accept U.N. resolutions 242 and 338, which recognized Israel's right to exist as a state.

Events leading to Arafat's decision began on November 3, 1988, when the Palestine National Council met in Algiers and voted 253 to 46 to accept explicitly the two U.N. Security Council resolutions on Israel and the Middle East. These resolutions stated that Palestinians had the right to autonomy in the region but did not define those rights specifically. The Algiers vote suffered a setback on November 15 when Arafat declared that there should be an independent state on "our Palestinian territory, with holy Jerusalem as its capital." The United States denounced this statement on November 26 and denied Arafat a visa to come to New York to address the U.N. General Assembly. U.N. members objected to this U.S. action and voted to convene in Geneva to hear Arafat speak.

Before going to Geneva for his December 13 address to the United Nations, Arafat met on December 6 in Stockholm, Sweden, with a group of American Jews headed by Rita Hauser, chairman of the U.S. branch of Tel Aviv's International Center for Peace in the Middle East. On December 7, Arafat and the American Jewish group stated that the Palestine National Council had established an independent state in Palestine, recognized Israel as a "state in the region," and rejected terrorism "in all its forms."

During his address to the General Assembly, Arafat asked Israel to open peace talks with the PLO but did not explicitly recognize Israel's right to exist.

Knowing the U.S. State Department wanted a clear statement on what he considered to be Israel's rights, Arafat held a news conference on December 14 in which he accepted rights of "Palestine, Israel and other neighbors" to exist. In addition, he denounced terrorism and accepted U.N. resolutions 242 and 338.

Within hours, the State Department agreed to "diplomatic dialogue" with the PLO and on December 16 designated U.S. Ambassador to Tunisia Roberto Pelletreau as its liaison. Talks began but reached no quick resolution of the problem because Israel refused to talk with the PLO.

### December 21, 1988

**Terrorist bomb explodes on a Pan American Boeing 747 flying over Scotland, killing 259 people on board and 11 people on the ground.**

Following this explosion, a pro-Iranian terrorist group called news media and disclosed that it had planted the bomb to avenge the Iranian passenger plane shot down by a U.S. warship on July 3. An extensive investigation of the crash began with preliminary evidence showing that the bomb may have been placed aboard the plane at its originating point in Frankfurt, West Germany. A sophisticated bombing device, probably made by a terrorist in Syria and smuggled to West Germany, triggered the explosion by a timing device that relied on barometric pressure to set it off as the plane rose to a higher altitude following its stop in London. The plane was en route across the Atlantic to New York.

### December 21, 1988

**The U.N. General Assembly revises its 1988 and 1989 budgets to streamline them after the United States takes steps to pay its back dues.**

For several years, the United States led other nations in calling for the United Nations to tighten its budget by cutting waste and enhancing administrative efficiency. During the General Assembly sessions that began on September 20, the organization drew up a budget that cut excess staff and reduced expenses. Previous budgets for 1988 and 1989 were revised to meet the U.N. goal of cutting waste in the budget.

In conjunction with this U.N. action, President Reagan ordered the release of the U.S. dues of $44 million owed to the United Nations. They had been held in escrow. He also ordered the State Department to draw up a schedule to pay the organization $520 million of past dues owed by the United States.

See September 13, 1988.

### December 21, 1988

**President Reagan reveals that the United States is investigating a possible chemical arms plant in Libya.**

As early as September 14, 1988, the United States Department of State found evidence that Libya was on the verge of producing poison weapons at a chemical plant being constructed near Rabat, Libya by West Germany's Imhausen-Chemil's chemical firm. When West German Chancellor Helmut Kohl visited Washington on November 15, 1988, Secretary of State George Shultz and National Security Adviser General Colin Powell briefed Kohl on the evidence involving Imhausen-Chemil. Kohl refused to make any promises about what could be done but agreed that a United States technical team could visit Germany to discuss the situation with West German intelligence officers. After the U.S. technical team returned home in early December, they reported that West German intelligence had evidence about the Libyan plant and had passed it along to high-level West German officials, who never acted on their reports.

On December 21, President Ronald Reagan used the information obtained by the State Department and the technical team to tell a television interviewer about Libya's chemical plant. Without disclosing details of the U.S. evidence, Reagan also told the interviewer the United States was consulting with America's NATO allies about possible action against Libya. These consultations succeeded because early in 1989 West Germany's Imhausen-Chemical firm stopped its construction of Libya's chemical plant and withdrew its personnel from Libya.

### December 22, 1988

*Israel's two main political parties again form a national coalition government.*

As in 1984, the Likud and Labor Parties held a close balance of power in the 120-member Knesset. Likud and its allies won 46 seats in the November 1 elections; Labor and its allies won 48 seats. Other parties held the remaining 18 seats. Likud's Prime Minister Yitzhak Shamir tried for nearly seven weeks to form a right-wing coalition, but his failure meant a Likud-Labor coalition was best with Shamir as prime minister and Labor's Shimon Peres as finance minister.